African-Americans
in Worcester County, Maryland Court Records
1742-1800

African-Americans
in Worcester County, Maryland Court Records
1742-1800

Kimberly A. Chase

ANCESTORYBOOK PUBLISHING
Fort Washington
2022

Copyright © 2022 Kimberly A. Chase.

All rights reserved.

Cover design by Kimberly A. Chase

First published in 2022 by ANCESTORYBOOK Publishing
Typeset in Times New Roman
Printed in the United States of America

Publisher's Cataloging-in-Publication Data

Names: Chase, Kimberly A.
Title: African-Americans in Worcester County, Maryland court records 1742-1800 / Kimberly A. Chase.
Description: Fort Washington, MD : Ancestorybook Publishing, 2022. | Includes index. | Summary: A compilation of Worcester County, MD court records which pertain to transactions including African-Americans.
Identifiers: LCCN 2022943262 | ISBN 9780977282241 (pbk.)|
Subjects: LCSH: Worcester County (Md.) -- Genealogy. | United States, Maryland, Worcester -- Court records. | African Americans -- Genealogy. | African Americans - History -- 18th century. | Court records -- Maryland – Worcester County. | BISAC: HISTORY / African American & Black. | HISTORY / United States / State & Local / Middle Atlantic (DC, DE, MD, NJ, NY, PA). | LAW / Court Records.
Classification: LCC KFM1716.W67 2022 | DDC 975.2 C43--dc23
LC record available at https://lccn.gov/2022943262

Introduction

Genealogy and family history has fascinated me since the early 1990s. Before census records became accessible online, I would spend much of my free time at the National Archives. Because I was young, I was often assumed by my fellow researchers to be an Archives employee. I am fortunate that many of my ancestors were freeborn or emancipated decades prior to the U.S. Civil War. However, some ancestors remained elusive because records documenting their pre-1865 existence were indexed by the names of grantors and grantees, if they were indexed at all. Enslaved persons who were being bought, sold, bequeathed, gifted, or imported were not indexed by their names. This is what genealogists call an enormous "brick wall" for researching enslaved African-Americans.

While carrying out postgraduate research for a house étude, I stumbled upon the online access point for Maryland land records. I soon realized that the collection which had been categorized as county court "Land Records" was not limited to real property transactions. A cursory perusal of any pre-1865 volume revealed personal/moveable conveyances of enslaved persons, livestock, household furnishings, etc. By the time the colonies declared independence, deeds of manumission were being entered. Before the end of the 18th century, lists of Negroes being imported into or removed from Maryland appeared. Apprenticeship indentures came after the turn of the century.

My goal was to skim every page of every Liber of the Worcester County (Maryland) Court Land Records from 1742 to 1864 for every mention of named African-Americans. When I say African-American, I include those referred to as Negro, mulatto, black, colored, or any other terminology used at that particular time period regardless of his or her birthplace. I wanted this compilation and transcription to provide a multivolume, readily accessible, and easier to use resource for myself and other genealogists and historians researching the African-Americans of Worcester County, Maryland. This volume covers the original Liber A through Liber T from 1742 to 1800. This project was not solicited or commissioned by any public or private entity. I work for the ancestors in spirit.

In this volume, you will find the following firsts in Worcester County:

- Sale of a Negro on 2/26/1743 (Liber A, 20-21)
- Gifting of Negroes on 5/27/1743 (Liber A, 76)
- Sale of land to a free Negro on 6/6/1744 (Liber A, 193-194)
- Use of Negroes as collateral on 3/19/1754 (Liber C, 125-126)
- Sale of land by a free Negro on 3/15/1762 (Liber E, 294-296)
- Deed of manumission on 1/6/1776 (Liber I, 640)
- Sale of a Negro who left with the British Army on 7/11/1778 (Liber K, 90)
- Self-indenture of a Negro on 7/2/1779 (Liber K, 187-188)
- Deposition regarding the ownership of a Negro on 3/9/1787 (Liber M, 129-130)
- Manumission of a Negro by a Negro on 4/26/1787 (Liber M, 173)
- Lease of land to a free Negro on 1/31/1789 (Liber M, 473-474)
- Deed of manumission which included dates of birth on 1/4/1790 (Liber N, 168)
- Bastardy bond by a free Negro on 6/15/1784 (Liber O, 326)
- Certificate of importation of Negroes in Maryland on 10/30/1792 (Liber O, 595)
- Purchase of a Negro by a free Negro on 2/7/1795 (Liber P, 83-84)
- Maintenance bond by a free Negro for an "imported" Negro on 5/2/1794 (Liber R, 105-106)
- Sale of a runaway Negro on 8/27/1796 (Liber R, 319-320)
- Sale of a Negro jailed in another state on 7/5/1797 (Liber R, 605-606)
- Articles of agreement to educate a slave 12/31/1798 (Liber T, 96-97)

Please remember that genealogy and local history research in Worcester County, Maryland will likely require records from four areas: the counties of Somerset, Wicomico, and Worcester in Maryland and Sussex County, Delaware. Worcester County was created from a portion of

Somerset County, Maryland in 1742. Wicomico County, Maryland was created from a portion of Worcester County in 1867. Some of the early "Worcester County" land records clearly make reference to areas as far north as Indian River that are now considered within the bounds of Sussex County, Delaware.

Some advice on the transcription format:

1) This is not a full-diplomatic or semi-diplomatic transcription; therefore, the original layout and lineation are not maintained; However, the original spellings and superscript are maintained.
2) Contracted words, if decipherable, are expanded with brackets. Words or part of words that cannot be deciphered are replaced with curly brackets and question marks.
3) Most improperly used apostrophes were omitted for the ease of reading.
4) The folio/page number of the liber/book and the date of the record entry are bolded and underlined.
5) The record entry follows the folio/page number and date.
6) The names of known African-Americans are in bold print.
7) All surnames are fully capitalized. This is a personal preference that carries over from genealogical research. Also, there is a prevalence of the region's earliest surnames being used as first and middle names later. The capitalization helps makes the distinction obvious.
8) A few lengthy, more repetitively worded land transactions are more likely to be abbreviated.
9) The index does not include the names of justices of the peace or court clerks who were involved in the final recordation of the conveyance entries.
10) The page numbers in the index may shift slightly during the publishing process. Check the previous and following page if a record cannot be located where initially indicated.

Kimberly A. Chase

Table of Contents

Worcester County Court (Land Records) 1742-1800	Page
Liber A (1742 - 1747)	1
Liber B (1747 - 1753)	11
Liber C (1753 - 1755)	30
Liber D (1756 - 1760)	40
Liber E (1760 - 1763)	48
Liber F (1763 - 1766)	59
Liber G (1766 - 1769)	75
Liber H (1769 - 1771)	85
Liber I (1772 - 1776)	113
Liber K (1776 - 1784)	144
Liber L (1784 - 1786)	177
Liber M (1786 - 1789)	208
Liber N (1789 - 1791)	250
Liber O (1791 - 1793)	273
Liber P (1793 - 1794)	302
Liber Q (1794 - 1795)	328
Liber R (1795 - 1797)	348
Liber S (1797 - 1798)	387
Liber T (1798 - 1800)	416

Liber A, Folios 20-21; 26 February 1742/43

"…Know all men by these Presents that I Sarah TAYLOR the wife of Peter TAYLOR of Worcester County Planter by Virtue of a power to me given by my said Husband bearing date the Twenty fourth of this Instant February Written and by him Signed Have Bargained sold and delivered and by these Presents {?} bargain sell and Deliver unto William TURPIN Son of John TURPIN for and in Consideration of the Sum of +forty Six pounds Nineteen Shillings Current Money of Maryland to me in hand paid by the said William TURPIN Before the Ensealing and delivery thereof the receipt whereof I do hereby acknowledge and thereof do acquit and Discharge the said William TURPIN his Executors Administrators and Assigns by these presents at the Severall rates and prices following vizt. One Negroe Boy named **Bobb** att the price of twenty pounds, One High Ch[e]ss of Drawers at the price of three pounds, One large new Desk at the price of three pounds, One Wallnutt Table at fifteen shillings, six high back flagg Chairs, at twelve shillings Two Feather beds two Closters and four pillows. W^{tt}. ninety pounds, at four pounds Ten shillings, four pillow Cases, four pairs of Sheets. two Blanketts, two Quilts One White Coverlett {id} two Suits Callico Curtains att the price of five pounds, two pewter Dishes and One Dozen of new pewter plates at the price of Seventeen Shillings, Six Case Knifes and forks at Six Shillings, One Large Iron Pott, One middling D[itt]o. One Iron Spitt at Thirty Shillings, One pair And Irons at ten Shillings, One middling Looking Glass without a frame, at Six Shillings, One Tea Kettle at Six Shillings, five Cups and Saucers of China, at five Shillings, One box Iron and Heaters, at Eight Shillings, One Gray Horse Called Pompey at five pounds, two Brass Candle Sticks, at four Shillings, and one Damask table Cloth, at Ten Shillings, amounting in the whole To the aforesaid Sum of forty Six pounds nineteen Shillings, To Have and to hold all and Singular the Negro Boy and Goods… aforesaid unto the said William TURPIN his heirs and assigns for Ever, In Witness Whereof I have here unto set my hand and seal This Twenty Sixth day of February Anno Dom[ini] One thousand seven hundred and forty two three.
Sealed and Delivered   Sarah TAYLOR (seal)
In P[re]sence of us..
Ara ALLEN
Mary ALLEN"

*followed by acknowledgment of Justice of the Peace John SCOTT and recordation by court clerk Robert KING Jr. on folios 20 and 21.[1]

Liber A, Folio 76; 27 May 1743

"To all Christian People to whom these present Shall Come I Jesse JENKINSON of Worcester County in the Province aforesaid, Send Greetings Know Yee That I Jesse JENKINSON for and in Consideration of the Paternal Love, good will and affection which I have and do bear unto my Loving Son John JENKINSON of the County and Province aforesaid Have given and Granted and by these presents, do fully freely, clearly and absolutely, Give Grant unto the said John JENKINSON and his Heirs for Ever, my Negroe Boy Called **Abner**, and my Negroe Woman Called **Pleasant** with her Increase to be Possest and Enjoy[e]d by the said John JENKINSON at my Decease Together w[i]th all the right title In trust Claim and demand whatsoever, which I now have, or which any or Either of my Heirs Executors or Administrators may hereafter have of to or {?} said Granted the premisses To Have and to Hold the said Negro's, to Wit, **Abner** and **Pleasant** - with her Increase as aforesaid unto him the said John JENKINSON and his Heirs for Ever, absolutely without any manner of Condition as I the said Jesse JENKINSON have fully freely and absolutely and of my Own Account Sett and Putt, In further Testimony In Witness Whereof I have here unto Sett my hand and Seal this Twenty Seventh Day of May Anno Domini One Thousand Seven hundred forty and Three.
Jno SCOTT . .   Jesse JENKINSON (seal)
Jno SCARBOROUGH"

---

[1] Worcester County Court (Land Records). Deed from TAYLOR, Sarah to TURPIN, William. 26 February 1742/43. A, pp. 20-21, MSA CE 30-1. www.mdlandrec.net : accessed 17 September 2021.

*followed by acknowledgment by Justice of the Peace John SCOTT and recordation by court clerk Robert KING Jr. on 27 May 1743, also on folio 76.[2]

Liber A, Folios 142-143; 11 February 1743

"Know all men by these Presents that I Rebecca JENKINS of the County of Worcester for and in consideration of forty pounds paper money of this Province to me in hand paid by Littleton TOWNSEND of the aforesaid County at and before the Ensealing and Delivery of these presents where with I confess my Self to be fully satisfyed contented and paid Have Bargained and Sold and by these presents do fully Clearly and absolutely bargain and Sell unto the said Littleton TOWNSEND one Negro Wench named **Juda** to Have and to Hold the said Negro Wench to the said Littleton TOWNSEND His Executors, Administrators, and assigns to his and their own Proper use and Behoofs for Ever and I the said Rebecca JENKINS, my Executors and Administrators and Every of us the said Negroe Wench unto the said Littleton TOWNSEND his Executors and Adm[inistrator]^s against all people shall and with warrant acquit and for Ever defend by these presents In Testimony whereof I have hereunto set my hand and affixed my seal this Eleventh Day of February Anno Domini One thousand Seven Hundred and forty three

                                                                                  her
Rebeka O JENKINS (seal)

Witn[es]s. Arthur MACKALLAN   mark
Witness. W[illia]^m KITCHEN"

*followed on folio 143 with the recordation on 27 May 1743 by court clerk Robert KING Jr.[3]

Liber A, Folios 185-186; 19 May 1744

"To all Christian People To whom these Presents Shall Come I Jonathan CLIFTON of Sussex County Upon Dellaware. Send Greeting. Know Yee that I Jonathan CLIFTON for and in Consideration of the Sum of forty five Pounds Curr[en]^t money of Maryland To me in hand well and truly paid and before the Sealing and Delivery of these Presents the receipt whereof accordingly I the said Jonathan CLIFTON do hereby acknowledge and for divers other Good Causes and Valluable Considerations me there unto moving. Have Given Granted Bargained sold and Delivered and by these Presents In Plain and open market Do give, grant, Bargain Sell and Deliver unto Andrew COLLINS of Worcester County in the Province of Maryland Planter A Certain Negro Wench named **Rebeckah** Aged about Sixteen years, To Have and To Hold the said Negro wench for Ever, freely Quietly and Peaceably and Intirely without any Contradiction Claim disturbance or hindrance of any person or persons whatsoever and without any account to me or any other person whatsoever to be made or answered or How after to be Rend[e]red so that Neither I the Said Jonathan CLIFTON nor any for me or in my name to Claim any right, Title, Property or Interest, of or in the said Negro **Rebeckah** but from all Actions Records Claim or Demands Shall be Wholly barred and Excluded by force of these Presents and I the Said Jonathan CLIFTON my heirs Exec[utor]^s, Adm[inistrator]^s or Assigns the Said **Rebeckah** afores[ai]^d to the said Andrew COLLINS his Exec[utor]^s, and Adm[inistrator]^s against all People shall and will warr[an]^t and for Ever defend by these Presents of which said Negro **Rebeckah** I the said Jonathan CLIFTON have put the said Andrew COLLINS In full and Peaceable possession by the delivery of the Said **Rebeckah** at the time of the Sealing and delivery of these Presents In Witness whereof I the said Jonathan CLIFTON have here unto Set my hand and Seal This 19th Day of May Anno Dom[ini] 1744.

                                                                                  his
Signed Sealed and delivered In the presence of us.   Jonathan IC CLIFTON (seal)
Tho[ma]s COLLINS. John COLLINS.   mark
William COLLINS. William DART{?}"

---

[2] Worcester County Court (Land Records). Deed from JENKINSON, Jesse to JENKINSON, John. 27 May 1743. A, p. 76, MSA CE 30-1. www.mdlandrec.net : accessed 17 September 2021.

[3] Worcester County Court (Land Records). Deed from JENKINS, Rebecca to TOWNSEND, Littleton. 11 February 1743/44. A, pp. 142-143, MSA CE 30-1. www.mdlandrec.net : accessed 18 September 2021.

*followed by recordation by court clerk Robert KING Jr. on 21 May 1744 on folio 186.[4]

Liber A, Folios 192-193; 01 June 1744

"Know all men by these Presents that I Peter TAYLOR of Worcester County In The Province of Maryland planter for and in Consideration of the Sum of forty two pounds Current mon[e]y of Maryland to him in hand paid and for Divers good Causes and Valuable Considerations me thereto Especially moveing Have Bargain[e]d and Sold and by these presents do bargain and Sell unto William TURPIN of Somersett In the Province of Maryland One Negroe boy Called **Bob**. and I hereby warrent the said Negroe boy to the said William TURPIN and his assigns against the Claims and Demand of any person Whatsoever In Witness whereof I Have here unto Sett my Hand and fixt my Seal the first day of June Seventeen Hundred forty four

Sealed and Delivered In the Presents of Georg[e] JONES   P[ete]r. TAYLOR (seal)
                                                 {?}. S. SCOTT"

*followed on folio 193 by an acknowledgment by John SCOTTS on 01 June 1744 and recordation by court clerk Robert KING Jr. on 05 May 1744.[5]

Liber A, Folios 193-194; 06 June 1744

"This Indenture made this Sixth day of June Anno Domini One thousand Seven Hundred forty and four Between Abraham OUTTEN of Worcester County In the Province of Maryland and Rhoda his wife on the one Part, and **Samuel COLLECT** of the Same Place of the other part Witnesseth That whereas the Right Honourable the Lord Proprietor of the Province of Maryland by his deed of Grant under the great Seal used In the said Province for Granting of Lands, did grant unto John MURRAY all that tract or Parcel of Land Called the Red Oak Ridge lying and being in Worcester County in the Indian Town on the North side of Pocomoke River, back in the woods, Bounded as Followeth Begining at a Marked white Oak, Standing on a Ridge, Between Two Swamps" ... "Containing and Laid out for forty Nine Acres of Land more or less. Now This Indenture Witnesseth That the said John MURRAY did Sell alienate and make Over the Said forty nine Acres of Land to Abraham OUTTEN Now This Indenture Witnesseth that the said Abraham OUTTEN and Rhoda his Wife for and in Consideration of Eleven Pounds Current money of Maryland to them in hand paid by the above said **Samuel COLLECT** the receipt whereof doth make it appear, and they doe Acknowledge themselves to be fully Satisfied Contented and Paid and doth Exonerate acquit and discharge the said **Samuel COLLECT**, his Heirs and assigns for Ever Hath Given Granted Bargaind Sold alienated Enfolded Conveyed and Confirmed unto the said **Samuel COLLECT** his heirs and assigns for Ever, the said forty nine Acres of Land Called the Red Oak Ridge, together with all and Singular the Profitts, Priviledges, Improvements and appurtenances to the Same Belonging To Have and To Hold the Said Forty Nine Acres of Land free and Clear from all manner of Incumbrances whatsoever (the Quit Rents to become due to the Land of the fee thereof only Excepted) and the said Abraham OUTTEN and Rhoda his Wife doth for themselves their Heirs Executors and Administrators Covenant and Agree, with the Said **Samuel COLLECT** his heirs and assigns to warrant and Defend the said forty Nine Acres of Land from all Persons Claiming any Right title or Intrust to any Part or Parcel thereof from in by or under them In Witness whereof we doe hereunto Sett our hands and fix our Seals the Day and Year above written ~

Sign[e]d Sealed and delivered   Abraham OUTTEN   (Seal)
In the Presence of . .
John CALDWELL . . . .   Rhoda + OUTTEN   (Seal)
Jno. SCARBROUGH . . ."

---

[4] Worcester County Court (Land Records). Bill of sale from CLIFTON, Jonathan to COLLINS, Andrew. 19 May 1744. A, pp. 185-186, MSA CE 30-1. www.mdlandrec.net : accessed 18 September 2021.

[5] Worcester County Court (Land Records). Deed from TAYLOR, Peter to TURPIN, William. 01 June 1744. A, pp. 192-193, MSA CE 30-1. www.mdlandrec.net : accessed 18 September 2021.

*followed on folio 194 with the acknowledgment by Justices of the Peace John CALDWELL and John SCARBROUGH, the receipt of the alienation fee by Thomas GILLIS, and the recordation by court clerk Robert KING Jr.[6]

*The grantee's race/ethnicity is revealed in later records. The surname is later spelled COLLICK.

*This transcription has been abbreviated due to its length. The original may be viewed at the citation provided.

Liber A, Folios 220-221; 16 July 1744

"To all Christian people to whom these Presents Shall Come I Sarah HENDERSON of Worcester County In Maryland Send Greeting. Know Yee that I Sarah HENDERSON for and in Consideration of the Love, Good will and affection, which I have and do bear towards my Loving Daughter Sarah of the Same County Have Given and Granted And by these Presents, do fully freely Clearly and absolutely Give and Grant unto the said Sarah her heirs and assigns One Negroe boy named **Adam** Together with all the Right Title Intrust Claim and Demand Whatsoever which I now have or Which any or Either of my Heirs Executors Administrators or Assigns may here after have of to or in the said Granted Premises in any Part thereof To Have and To Hold the Said Negro **Adam** unto her the said Sarah her heirs or Assigns for Ever, Absolutely without any manner of Condition as I the said Sarah HENDERSON have fully freely and absolutely and of my own Account Set and Put In further Testimony In Witness Whereof I Have here unto set my Hand and Seal this 16th of July Anno{?} Dom[ini] 1743/4

Sealed and Delivered　　　　　　　　　　　　　　　　　　　　her
In the Presents of us　　　　　　　　　　　　　Sarah X HENDERSON (seal)
　　　　　　　　　　　　　　　　　　　　　　　　　　　Mark"

*followed on folio 221 by acknowledgment by Justice of the Peace William LANE on 16 July 1744 and recordation by court clerk Robert KING Jr. on 17 July 1744.[7]

Liber A, Folio 223; 17 July 1744

"Know all men by these presents that I John HOUSTON of Worcester County in the Province of Maryland Planter, as {?}ell for the natural Love and affection which I bear to my Son Joseph HOUSTON of Sussex County upon Delaware in the Territorys of Pensilvania, as for the Consideration of Five Shillings Current money of Maryland to me paid by the said Joseph at and before the Sealing and delivery here of the Receipt whereof I hereby doe acknowledge have given Granted bargained and Sold and doe hereby Give Grant bargain and Sell to the said Joseph his Executors Administrators and Assigns for Ever these Slaves following to Wit. **Harry** a man Slave, **Betty** a woman Slave, **Dick** a boy, **Pleasant** a Girl, **Rose** a Girl, and **Jeffrey** a Boy all Issue of the said **Betty**, and also all of the Said Six Slaves in the actual Possession of the said Joseph now being To Have and To Hold the Said Six Slaves and Every their future Issue to the said Joseph HOUSTON his Executors administrators and assigns for Ever, To the only proper use of the said Joseph his Executors administ[rator]s and Assigns for Ever and no other use or uses whatsoever In Testimony whereof I have hereto affixed my hand and Seal this Seventeenth day of July Anno D[omi]ni Seventeen hundred forty and four

Sealed and delivered in Presence of　　　　　　　　　　　his
Geo[rge] DOUGLAS….　　　　　　　　　　John + HOUSTON (seal)
W[illia]m BEAVENS….　　　　　　　　　　　　　Mark
Joseph FEDDEMAN…
Joseph FEDDEMAN Jun[io]r…."

---

[6] Worcester County Court (Land Records). Deed of Sale from OUTTEN, Abraham and Rhoda to **COLLECT, Samuel**. 06 June 1744. A, pp. 193-194, MSA CE 30-1. www.mdlandrec.net : accessed 16 June 2022.
[7] Worcester County Court (Land Records). Deed from HENDERSON, Sarah to HENDERSON, Sarah. 16 July 1744. A, pp. 220-221, MSA CE 30-1. www.mdlandrec.net : accessed 18 September 2021.

*followed by acknowledgment by Justices of the Peace John MILLER and John KILBEE and recordation by court clerk Robert KING Jr. on 07 August 1744.[8]

Liber A, Folios 238-239; 08 September 1744

"To all People to whom these Presence Shall Come I John HOUSTON do Send Greeting. Know ye that I the Said John HOUSTON of the County of Worcester in the Province of Maryland Planter, for and In Consideration of the Love Good Will and Affection which I have and doe bare towards my Son in Law William BRITTINGHAM, and my Daughter Rachell BRITTINGHAM Wife to the Said William Have Given and Granted by these Presents doe freely Clearly and absolutely Give and Grant unto the Said William BRITTINGHAM and Rachell his Wife and To their Heirs and Assignes for Ever My Negro Called **Rose** and **Nimrod** and **Harry**. To Have and To Hold the Said Negro's. In this Deed mentioned To the af[oresai]d William BRITTINGHAM and Rachell his Wife and their Heirs and Assignes for Ever, freely Clearly and Absolutely without any manner of Condition In Witness Whereof I Have hereunto Sett my hand and Seal this Eighth Day of September Anno Dom[ini] One thousand Seven hundred forty Four

Sealed and Delivered
In Presence of
W[illia]m LANE.
Jesse JENKINSON

John X HOUSTON (seal)
his Mark

Be it Rememb[e]red that Before Signing the above named, John HOUSTON would Have the Negroes abovementioned after the decease of the afor[e]s[ai]d William and Rachell to be disposed of as followeth, that is **Nimrod** to Rebecca and **Rose** to Lavina and **Harry** to Suffiah daughters of the afores[ai]d William and Rachell and to their Heirs and Assignes for Ever."

*followed by acknowledgment of William LANE on 08 September 1744 and recordation by court clerk Robert KING Jr. on 15 September 1744[9]

Liber A, Folio 287; 22 January 1745

"To all Persons to whom these present Writing Shall Come I Isaac BRITTINGHAM of the County and Province abovesaid Gentleman, Send Greeting. {?} Know Ye that I the said Isaac BRITTINGHAM for and in Consideration of the Natural Affection, and Love which I have and bear unto my well beloved Daughter Rhodia HENDERSON wife of John HENDERSON of the Same County and Province abovesaid, as Also for divers good Causes and Valuable Considerations me at this present Especially moving have given and Granted, and by these, do give grant and Confirm unto the Said Rhodia HENDERSON her Heirs of her Body and no further a Certain Negro Girl Called **Betty** which is now in the Possession of the said Rhodia HENDERSON from the day of the date hereof To have and To Hold the said Negro **Betty** as their own use and Behoofs, and to Dispose at her or their Will and Pleasure without any manner of Challenge Claim or demand of me the said Isaac BRITTINGHAM or of any other person, or persons for me In my name by my means or Procurement And further Know Ye that I the said Isaac BRITTINGHAM for the like Causes as abovesaid do give grant and Confirm unto the abovesaid Rhodia HENDERSON on her heirs or Assignes one Chest of Drawers, and the one fifth of a Styll holding forty four Gallons or thereabouts after the decease[e] of the said Isaac BRITTINGHAM, and then to have and to hold the Same, as her or their own proper goods and Chattles without any manner of Challenge Claim or demand of me the said Isaac BRITTINGHAM or of any other person or persons for me in my name by my means or Procurement. And In confirmation of this present writing I the said Isaac have by the Delivery unto her at the Ensealing hereof One Coined peice of Silver Commonly Called two pence fixed on the Seal of these Presents. In Witness whereof I have hereunto set my hand and fixed my Seal this Twenty Second day of January Seventeen hundred forty four five –

---

[8] Worcester County Court (Land Records). Deed from HOUSTON, John to HOUSTON, Joseph. 17 July 1744. A, p. 223, MSA CE 30-1. www.mdlandrec.net : accessed 18 September 2021.

[9] Worcester County Court (Land Records). Deed from HOUSTON, John to HOUSTON, Joseph. 08 September 1744. A, pp. 238-239, MSA CE 30-1. www.mdlandrec.net : accessed 18 September 2021.

Signed Sealed and Delivered   Isaac BRITTINGHAM (seal)
In Presence of
Jnº SCOTT
Elisabeth SCOTT"

*followed by acknowledgment by John SCOTT on 22 January 1744/45 and recordation by court clerk Robert KING Jr. on 05 February 1744/45.[10]

Liber A, Folios 349-350; 18 November 1745

"Worcester Ss/ Know all men by these Present that I John RIGGS of the County aforesaid & Province of Maryland for and in Consideration of Thirty pounds cur[rent] money of the Province aforesaid to me in hand paid by James MARTIN of the County aforesaid the Receipt whereof I do hereby Acknowledge and myself hereof fully Satisfyed and Contented have Bargained Sold set over and Delivered and by these Presents in plain & open Market have Bargained sold set over and Delivered unto the said James MARTIN his heirs and Assigns one Negro Girl Named **Moll** To have, and To hold the said Bargained Premisses to him the said James MARTIN his heirs, and Assigns for Ever which Said Negro **Moll** Do hereby Acknowledge to be the Right and Property of the said MARTIN his heirs and Assigns to his and there Proper use & Behoof which said Negro I will warr[ant] Defend to the said MARTIN and his Assigns against all manner of Persons laying any Right Title or Claim thereto In Wittness whereof I have hereunto set my hand and seal this Eighteenth day of November Anno Dom[ini] 1745.
Sealed and Delivered   John RIGGS (seal)
In Presents of
John HENRY"

*followed on folio 350 by an acknowledgment by John HENRY and recordation by court clerk Robert KING Jr. on 18 November 1745.[11]

Liber A, Folios 369-370; 01 February 1745/46?

"Worcester, to wit, This Indenture made the first day of February in the year of our Lord God One thousand Seven Hundred Forty and Five, Between Thomas LAMBDEN of Worcester County in the Province of Maryland Merchant of the one Part and Robert KING of Somerset County in the Province af[oresai]d Esquire of the other Part; Wittnesseth that the said Thomas LAMBDEN for and in Consideration of the Sum of Fifty Pounds Sterling money of Great Brittain to him by the said Robert KING in hand Paid at and before the Sealing and delivery of these Presents, the Receipt whereof the said Thomas LAMBDEN doth hereby acknowledge and Confess, and thereof doth acquit, release and Discharge the said, Robert KING his heirs Exec[utor]s and Adm[inistrator]s He the said Thomas LAMBDEN, Hath bargained, & sold, assigned and transferred and by these Presents, doth bargain, Sell, assign and transfer unto the said Robert KING his Ex[ecutor]s Adm[inistrator]s and Assigns, one Negro man Slave named **Jamey**, and also One Negro woman Slave named **Pleasent**, both which said Negroes are now in the Possession of the af[oresai]d Thomas LAMBDEN To have and to hold the af[oresai]d Two Negro Slaves unto the only Proper use and Benefitt of the said Robert KING his Exe[cutor]s Admi[inistrator]s or Assigns forever, and to no other use, Intent or Purpose whatsoever, And the af[oresai]d Thomas LAMBDEN, for himself his heirs Ex[ecutor]s and Admi[inistrator]s doth Covenant Promise and agree, to and with the said Robert KING his Ex[ecutor]s Adm[inistrator]s and Assigns, That the the said Thomas LAMBDEN his Ex[ecutor]s & Adm[inistrator]s the af[oresai]d Two Negroes, **Jamey & Pleasent**, unto the said Robert KING his Ex[ecutor]s Adm[inistrator]s or Assigns against the Legal Claim of all other Persons whatsoever shall, & will forever Warrant and defend, by these Presents. Provided always and

---

[10] Worcester County Court (Land Records). Bill of sale from BRITTINGHAM, Isaac to Rhodia and HENDERSON, John. 22 January 1744/45. A, p. 287, MSA CE 30-1. www.mdlandrec.net : accessed 18 September 2021.
[11] Worcester County Court (Land Records). Bill of sale from RIGGS, John to MARTIN, James. 18 November 1745. A, pp. 349-350, MSA CE 30-1. www.mdlandrec.net : accessed 18 September 2021.

it is the true Intent and meaning of these Presents, that if the above named Thomas LAMBDEN his Ex[ecutor]s or Admi[inistrator]s shall well and truely Pay or Cause to be Paid unto the said Robert KING his Ex[ecutor]s Adm[inistrator]s or Assigns the full and Just Sum of Fifty Pounds Sterling money of Great Brittain with Legal Interest for the Same on or before the first day February which will be in the year of our Lord God One thousand Seven Hundred Forty and Six, and also Pay the Costs and Expenses of the makeing and Recording this Present writeing, Then the Deed and Every matter and thing in the same Contained to be Null, Void, and of no Effect any thing herein before to the contrary, notwithstanding and the af[oresai]d Thomas LAMBDEN doth further Covenant, that he the said Thomas LAMBDEN, his heirs Ex[ecutor]s or Adm[inistrator]s shall and will well and truely Pay or Cause to be Paid unto the af[oresai]d Robert KING his Ex[ecutor]s Adm[inistrator]s or Assignes the af[oresai]d Sum of Fifty Pounds Sterling with Legal Interest for the Same together with the Costs and Expenses above mentioned on or before the first day of February in the Proviso af[oresai]d Specified, according to the true intent and meaning thereof In Testimony whereof the Party's af[oresai]d to these presents Interchangeably their hands have set and Seal's affixed the day and year first above written.
Sealed & Delivered   Thomas LAMBDEN (seal)
In Presence of
Robert Jenkins HENRY
R. KING Jun[io]r"

*followed on folio 370 by acknowledgment of Justice of the Peace John SCARBOROUGH, receipt of payment, and recordation by court clerk Robert KING Jr. on 07 February 1745.[12]

Liber A, Folios 380-381; 11 March 1745/46

"Know all men by these Presents that I William KITCHEN of Worcester County in the Province of Maryland Marriner for and in Consideration of the sum of Twenty five Pounds Sterling money of Great Brittain to me in hand by Thomas LAMBDEN of the County and Province af[oresai]d well and Truly paid before the Ensealing and Delivery hereof the Receipt Whereof I do hereby Acknowledge and my Self therewith fully Satisfied and Contented have gained bargained and Sold and by these Presents for my heirs Ex[ecutor]s and Adm[inistrator]s do grant Bargain and Sell fully Clearly and Absolutely unto the said Thomas LAMBDEN and to his heirs and Assigns forever the following goods & Chattles Vitz. One Negro Woman Called **Betty** Two Horses Three Cows Two Feather beds and Furniture with all and Singular Every other moveable whatsoever now being In the Possession of me the said William KITCHEN To have & To hold the same Negro Women Called **Betty**, Two Horses Three Cows Two Feather Beds and Furniture, with all and Singular every other moveable whatsoever unto him the said Thomas LAMBDEN his heirs and Assigns forever To his and Their only proper use Benefitt and Behoof forever and I the said William KITCHEN My Ex[ecutor]s & Adm[inistrator]s and every of us the Negro Called **Betty** Two Horses Three Cows Two Feather beds and Furniture with all and Singular every other moveable whatsoever unto the said Tho[mas] LAMBDEN his heirs or Assigns against all manner of Persons whatsoever shall and will forever hereafter Warr[an]t Secure and Defend by these Presents provided all ways and it is the True Intent and meaning of these Presents that if the said William KITCHEN his Exe[cutor]s or Adm[inistrator]s or any of them do well and Truly pay or Cause to be paid unto the said Thomas LAMBDEN his heirs or Assigns the full sum of Twenty five pounds Ster[ling] on or before the first day of August which shall be in the year of our Lord one Thousand Seven Hundred & Forty Eight without fraud or Covin then this bill of Sale and everything therein Contained to be Utterly void and of no Effect or Elce to stand and Remain in full force and Virtue in Law, Wittness my hand and seal this 11th Day of March one Thousand seven Hundred and forty five
Sealed & Delivered   W[illia]m KITCHEN (seal)
together with one Featherbed and furniture
part of the goods afore Mentioned
In Presents of

---

[12] Worcester County Court (Land Records). Deed from LAMBDEN, Thomas to KING, Robert. 01 February 1745/46. A, pp. 369-370, MSA CE 30-1. www.mdlandrec.net : accessed 18 September 2021.

John BENNETT
Jnº SHELDON   Jnº SCOTT"

*followed on folio 381 by the acknowledgment of Justice of the Peace John SCOTT on 11 March 1745 and recordation by court clerk Robert KING Jr. on 14 March 1745.[13]

Liber A, Folios 395-396; 07 April 1746

"To all Persons to whome this Present writing shall Come I Isaac BRITTINGHAM of the County and Province above said Gent[leman] send Greeting & Know ye that I the said Isaac BRITTINGHAM for and in Consideration of the Natrul Affection, and Love which I have and bear unto my well beloved Daughter Rhodia HENDERSON wife of John HENDERSON of the Same County and Province abovesaid as also for Divers good Causes and Valuable Considerations to me at the Present especially moveing have given and granted and by these Presents do give grant and Confirm unto the Said Rhodia HENDERSON and to her heirs a Certain Negro Garle Called **Betty** which is now in the Possession of the said Rhodia HENDERSON from from the day of the date hereof To have and To hold the said Negro **Betty** as their own Use and behoofs, and to Dispose of at her or their will and Pleasure without any manner of Challinge Clame or Demand of me the said Isaac BRITTINGHAM or of any other person or persons for me in my Name by my means or procurement and further Know Ye that I the said Isaac BRITTINGHAM for the Like Causes as above said do give grant and confirm unto the above said Rhodia HENDERSON her heirs or Assigns one Chest of Drawers, and one fifth part of a Still holding forty four Gallons or their abouts after the Decease of the said Isaac BRITTINGHAM and then To have and To hold the same as her or their own proper Goods or Chattles without any manner of Challenge Claim or Demand of me the said Isaac BRITTINGHAM or of any other person or persons for me in my name, by my means or procurement and in Confirmation of this present Writing I the said Isaac have by the Delivery unto her at the ensealing hereof one Coined peace of Silver Commonly Called Two pence fixed on the Seal of these Presents In Witness whereof I have hereunto set my hand and fixed my seale this 7th day of April 1746

Sined Sealed & Delivered   Isaac BRITTINGHAM (seal)
In the Presents of us
John SCARBOROUGH
Shadrick CLAYWELL"

*followed on folio 396 by acknowledgment by Justice of the Peace John SCARBOROUGH on 07 April 1746, confirming the previous bill of sale dated 22 January 1744, and recordation by the court clerk Robert KING Jr. on 11 April 1746.[14]

Liber A, Folios 396-397; 07 April 1746

"To all Persons to whome this Present Writing shall Come I Sarah HENDERSON of the County & Province above said Gentlewoman send Greeting & Know ye that I the said Sarah HENDERSON for and in Consideration of the Natrul Affection and Love which I have and bare unto my well beloved son John HENDERSON of the same County and Province above said as also for Divers good Causes and Valuable Considerations to me at this Present Especially moveing have given and Granted and by these Presents do give grant and Confirm unto the said John HENDERSON his heirs and Assigns all the Increase of a Certain Negro Garle Called **Dinah** if any she ever has which said Negro is now in the Possession of the said Sarah HENDERSON To have and To Hold the said Negro **Diner** Children or his one use and Behoofs and to Dispose of them at his own will and pleasure without any manner of Challenge Claim or Demand of me the said Sarah HENDERSON or of any other person or persons for me in my Name by my means or procurement and Further Know ye that I the said Sarah

---

[13] Worcester County Court (Land Records). Deed from KITCHEN, William to LAMBDEN, Thomas. 11 March 1745. A, pp. 380-381, MSA CE 30-1. www.mdlandrec.net : accessed 18 September 2021.
[14] Worcester County Court (Land Records). Bill of sale from BRITTINGHAM, Isaac to HENDERSON, Rhodia. 07 April 1746. A, pp. 395-396, MSA CE 30-1. www.mdlandrec.net : accessed 18 September 2021.

HENDERSON for the like Cause as above said do give grant and Confirm unto the above said John HENDERSON his heirs or Assigns one Buckanneow gun one Large Iron pot one Loom Stays and Gears one hand mill frame and a pair of Culling Stones after the Decease of the said Sarah HENDERSON and then To have and To hold the same as his own proper goods and Chattles without any manner of Challings Claim or Demand of me the said Sarah HENDERSON or of any person or persons for me in my Name by my means or procurement and in Confirmation of this Present Writing I the said Sarah have by the Delivery unto him at the Ensealing hereof one Coined peace of Silvr Commonly Called Two pence fixed on the seal of these Presents In Wittness whereof I have hereunto set my hand and fixt my Seal this 7th day of April

Sined Sealed & Delivered
In The Presents of us
Jnº SCARBOROUGH
Shadrick CLAYWELL"

              her
Sarah X HENDERSON (seal)
              mark

*followed on folio 397 by acknowledgment by Justice of the Peace John SCARBOROUGH on 07 April 1746 and recordation by the court clerk Robert KING Jr. on 13 April 1746.[15]

Liber A, folios 400-401; 24 April 1746

"To all Christian People to whomb the Presents shall Come I Nehemiah HOLLAND of Worcester County in Maryland send Greeting Know ye that I Nehemiah HOLLAND for and in Consideration of the Love and Goodwill and Affection I bare and have towards my Loveing Children of the same County and Province Namely for {?} Nehemiah HOLLAND my Eldest son have given granted and by these Presents do fully freely and Clearly and Absolutely give grant unto the said Nehemiah his heirs and Assigns all the Land with my Plantation whereon I Now Dwell with the Priveledges thereunto Belonging to the southwest of Mattoponey Land where itt now stands together with all the Right Title and Intent which I now Claim or shall Claim and Demand whatsoever which I now have Together with my Still and hand mill$_{XX}$ I also give in the same manner and for me all the Remainder of my Lands being to the north East of the Same Road abovementioned to my son Thomas HOLLAND together with my Negro Called **Ned** to him his heirs and Assigns ~ In Like manner I give to my Daughter Sarah HOLLAND my Desk and best bed and furniture and {?} ~ ~ I Doe in the same manner give to my Daughte Tabitha HOLLAND my Chattles {?} together with a good Bed and furniture to her forever In the Like form give to my Daughter Bridgett HOLLAND five Likely young Cattle together with the Next best bed and furniture. ~. /. ~ In the forme above give to my Daughter Betty HOLLAND three Likely Cows and year olds together with a good bed and Furniture ~ ~ Lastly I give to my son William HOLLAND T{?} Head of Likely Cattle with as many Likely Sheep and a Good horse and Saddle at the Price of Twelve Pounds Cash His horse and Sadle, to be Levied out of my Estate to him his heirs ~ In Wittness whereof I have hereunto set my hand and Seal ~./.~

Test. John SCARBOROUGH   Neh[emiah] HOLLAND (seal)
E.P. WAGGAMAN

*followed on folio 401 by acknowledgment by Justices of the Peace John SCARBOROUGH and E.P. WAGGAMAN on 24 April 1746 and recordation by court clerk Robert KING Jr. on 25 April 1746.[16]

Liber A, folios 440-441; 18 August 1746

"To All Christian People to whome these Presents Shall come I Mary ALLEN of Worcester County in the province of Maryland Widow and I Jacob HINDMAN of Talbot County and Province Af[oresai]^d Gent[leman] Send Greeting know ye that I Mary ALLEN for and in

---

[15] Worcester County Court (Land Records). Bill of sale from HENDERSON, Sarah to HENDERSON, John. 07 April 1746. A, pp. 396-397, MSA CE 30-1. www.mdlandrec.net : accessed 18 September 2021.
[16] Worcester County Court (Land Records). Deeds from HOLLAND, Nehemiah to HOLLAND, Nehemiah etal. 24 April 1746. A, pp. 400-401, MSA CE 30-1. www.mdlandrec.net : accessed 18 September 2021.

Consideration of the Love good will and Affection that I have and do bear unto my Loving Children as Follows Vitz. William ALLEN Joseph ALLEN Elianor ALLEN Mary ALLEN Moses ALLEN & Eliz[abe]th ALLEN of Worcester County and Province Af[oresai]^d and know ye that I Jacob HINDMAN for and in Consideration of the Love good will and Affection that I have and do bear unto my Loving Brothers and Sisters as follows To William ALLEN Joseph ALLEN Elianor ALLEN Mary ALLEN Moses ALLEN & Eliza[be]th ALLEN as well for and in Consideration of the sum of five Shillings Current money in hand p[ai]d to Mary ALLEN and Jacob HINDMAN Af[ore]s[ai]^d by ye Af[ore]s[ai]d William Joseph Elianor Mary Moses & Eliz[abe]th ALLEN the Receipt Whereof I the s[ai]d Mary ALLEN and Jacob HINDMAN do hereby acknowledge from the Af[ore]s[ai]d William Joseph Elianor Mary Moses & Eliz[abe]th ALLEN and have Given granted and by these presents do Give and fully freely and Absolutely Grant unto William ALLEN a negro fellow named **Mingo** And a negro Girl named **Judy** to Joseph ALLEN A negro boy named **Benn** and a negro Girl named **Bess** to Elianor ALLEN A negro Boy named **Daniel** & a negro Girl named **Rachel** to Mary ALLEN A Negro Boy named **Will** a Girl named **Hannah** & one Named **Jenny** to Moses ALLEN A Boy Named **Tom** & A Girl named **Rose** & to Elizab[e]th ALLEN two girls Named **Alic** & **Jioe** to them their Heirs and Assigns In Testimony whereof we have hereunto Sett our hands and Seals this Eighteenth Day of Aug[us]t Anno Domini Seventeen hundred and forty Six ~

Signed Sealed & Delivered   Mary ALLEN (seal)
In the Presents of ~   Ja^c[ob] HINDMAN (seal)
Jn° SCOTT
{?} ALLEN   Will[ia]^m HOPKINS"

*followed on folio 441 by acknowledgment of Justice of the Peace John SCOTT on 18 August 1746 and recordation by the court clerk Robert KING Jr. on 19 August 1746.[17]

Liber A, folios 446-447; 28 August 1746

"Know all men by these presents that I Mary ROBINSON of Worcester County and province of Maryland for and in consideration of the sum of Thirty five pounds Current money of maryland have bargained and sould unto Thomas ROBINSON one Negro man Called & known by the Name of **Jack** and by these presents do fully clearly & absolutely bargain and sell unto the said Thomas ROBINSON the said Negro to have & to hold the same to the said Thomas ROBINSON his heirs Exec[utor]^s Adm[inistrator]^s and Assigns to his and their own proper use and behoof for ever and I the said Mary ROBINSON my heirs Exec[utor]^s Adm[inistrator]^s and Every of us the said Negro Will warrant and forever Defend by these presents in Testimony whereof I have here unto sett my hand and fixed my seale this 23 Day of August Anno Domini 1746 ~

Signed Sealed & Delivered   her
In presents of us ~   Mary m ROBINSON (seal)
William RICKARDS   mark
Sam[ue]^l WALLER"

*followed on folio 447 by the recordation by Robert KING Jr. on 03 September 1746.[18]

Liber A, folios 465-466; 06 November 1746

"To all Christian People to whome these Presents Shall Come I Elisha PURNELL of Worcester County in the Province of Maryland Send Greeting in our Lord God Everlasting Know ye that I the said Elisha PURNELL for the Love and affection that I the said Elisha PURNELL do bare unto my Children Viz: Lamuel PURNELL Luranah PURNELL Chesed PURNELL William PURNELL and Sarah PURNELL I the said Elisha PURNELL being in Perfect memory have Given Granted and Confirmed and by this Present Writing do fully freely and absolutely give

---

[17] Worcester County Court (Land Records). Bill of sale from ALLEN, Mary and HINDMAN, Jacob to ALLEN, William etal. 18 August 1746. A, pp. 440-441, MSA CE 30-1. www.mdlandrec.net : accessed 19 September 2021.
[18] Worcester County Court (Land Records). Bill of sale from ROBINSON, Mary to ROBINSON, Thomas. 23 August 1746. A, pp. 446-447, MSA CE 30-1. www.mdlandrec.net : accessed 19 September 2021.

grant and Confirme unto my Children (viz) Lemuel Luranah Chesed William and Sarah PURNELL as above said the following Negroes (viz) **Ned, Dinah, Ann, Young Betty, Ruth, Comfort, Esler,** and **Dorkus,** they and their Increse unto the Lemuel PURNELL Lurana PURNELL Chesed PURNELL William PURNELL and Sarah PURNELL and to their heirs for Ever Equily in joynt Stock they the said Negroes and their Increse to be Equily Devided amongst the said Children (after my Decease) and In Case any of my Above named Children Should Die before me or without Issue then the said Negroes and their Increase to be Equily Devided amongst the Surviveing Children and their heirs and I the said Elisha Purnell all and Singular the said Negroes unto the said Lemuel PURNELL, Lurana PURNELL Chesed PURNELL, William PURNELL and Sarah PURNELL to them and their heirs forever will warrant and Defend by these Presents from all Person or Persons whatsoever and I the said Elisha PURNELL have put the said Lemuel PURNELL, Lurana PURNELL Chesed PURNELL William PURNELL and Sarah PURNELL in full and Peaceable Possession by the Gift and Delivery of one Silver Spoon which to the said Lemuel PURNELL Lurana PURNELL Chesed PURNELL William PURNELL and Sarah PURNELL the day and Date of these Presents I have given and Delivered in the Name of Possession and Seisen of all and Singular the said Negroes in Witness hereunto I Have set my hand and fixed my Seal this Sixth Day of November anno Domini one thousand Seven hundred and forty six ~

Sealed & Delivered & Quiet Possesion and   Elisha PURNELL (seal)
Seisin given and Delivered by ye S[ai]d Silver Spoon
According to the Effect of this Present Writing in the
Presence of
Jnº SCOTT
Jos. MILLER"

*followed on folio 466 by the acknowledgment of William LANE and recordation by court clerk Robert KING Jr. on 10 November 1746.[19]

Liber A, folio 487; 27 March 1747

"Know all men by these Presents that I John KILBIE for and in Consideration of forty one Pound Current money in hand paid to the said John KILBEE by Jerrard WILLEY of Worcester County whereof I do hereby acknowledge the receipt and therewith fully satisfyed haveing bargained sold and set over one Negroe Woman Called **Silvia** unto the said Jarrard WILEY his heirs Exec[utor]s Adm[inistrator]s and Assigns to his one Proper use and behoof of the said Jerrard WILEY his Exec[utor]s adm[inistrator]s and assigns forever and I the said John KILBEE for my self my heirs Exe[cutor]s adm[inistrator]s or Assigns shall and will warrant and for ever defend by these Presents Whereof I have hereunto sett my hand and Seal March the 27th : 1747
John BROWN   Jnº KILBEE (seal)
John FITZ"

*followed by the recordation by court clerk Robert KING Jr. on 04 April 1747.[20]

Liber B, folios 18-19; 07 November 1747

"This Indenture made the Seventh day of November Anno Dom[ini] one Thousand Seven Hundred and forty seven, Between Saul TOWNSEND of Worcester County Planter of the one part, and Arthur MACKALLAN and William Bartholomew TOWNSEND of the said County of the other part, Witnesseth that the said Saul TOWNSEND for and in Consideration of Thirty four pounds Current money of the Province af[ore]s[ai]d to him the said Saul TOWNSEND by the said Arthur MACKALLAN and William Bartholomew TOWNSEND in hand paid before the Ensealing and delivery hereof the Receipt whereof the said Saul TOWNSEND hereby doth acknowledge, hath granted, bargained and sold, and doth hereby grant, bargain and sell to the

---

[19] Worcester County Court (Land Records). Bill of sale from PURNELL, Elisha to PURNELL, Lemuel etal. 10 November 1746. A, pp. 465-466, MSA CE 30-1. www.mdlandrec.net : accessed 19 September 2021.
[20] Worcester County Court (Land Records). Bill of sale from KILBEE, John to WILLEY, Jerrard. 04 April 1747. A, p. 487, MSA CE 30-1. www.mdlandrec.net : accessed 19 September 2021.

said Arthur MACKALLAN and William Bartholomew TOWNSEND one Negroe fellow named **Adam** now the property of the said Saul TOWNSEND and in his possession, to have & to hold the af[ore]s[ai]^d bargained Premises to the said Arthur MACKALLAN and William Bartholomew TOWNSEND their Exec[utor]^s Adm[inistrator]^s and assigns and to the only use and behoof of the said Arthur MACKALLAN and William Bartholomew TOWNSEND their Exec[utor]^s or assigns and to no other uses or uses whatsoever and the said Saul TOWNSEND hereby Covenants for himself his Heirs Exec[utor]^s and Adm[inistrator]^s that the above Bargained Premises at and before the Ensealing and delivery hereof is the property of the said Saul TOWNSEND and that he hath good Right to bargain grant and sell the same in manner and form af[ore]s[ai]^d: and that the af[ore]s[ai]^d bargained Premises are free and Clear and discharged of every prior Incumbrances whatsoever Provided allways that if the af[ore]s[ai]^d Saul TOWNSEND his Heirs or Exec[utor]^s shall pay to the said Arthur MACKALLAN and William Bartholomew TOWNSEND their Heirs Exe[cutor]^s Adm[inistrator]^s or assigns the sum of thirty four pounds Current money of Maryland together with all the Costs that has accrued in a suit brought by Christopher GLASS against the said Saul TOWNSEND in Worcester County Court, on or before the tenth day of February next ensuing the date whereof and all the other Costs that shall accrue thereon then the af[[oresai]^d bargain and sale to be void and of none Effect, Else to be & remain in full force and virtue in Law.
Sealed & Delivered
In presence of   Saul TOWNSEND (seal)
Robert ALLAN"

*followed on folio 19 by acknowledgment by Justice of the Peace John HENRY and recordation by court clerk Robert KING Jr. on 07 November 1747[21]

Liber B, folios 38-39; 23 December 1747

"To all people to whom these presents shall Come I Elizabeth HENDERSON do send greeting Know ye that I Elizabeth HENDERSON of the County af[oresai]^d Widow for and In Consideration of Love good will and attention which I have and do bare towards my Loving Grand Daughter Betty Barnaby HENDERSON daughter of Benjamin HENDERSON of the County af[oresai]^d have given and granted and by these presents do freely Clearly and absolutely give and grant unto the said Betty Barnaby HENDERSON a Negro Garle Called **Mary** to have and to Hold the said Negro Garle **Mary** from henceforth as her Proper wright absolutely without any manner of Condition In Witness whereof I hereunto set my hand and seal this twenty Third day of December 1747.
Signed Sealed & Delivered   her
In the Presence of   Elizabeth + HENDERSON (seal)
John WILLIAMS   Stephen STOY   mark"

*followed on folios 38-39 by the acknowledgment of Justice of the Peace William LANE on 03 February 1747 and recordation by court clerk Robert KING Jr. on 10 February 1747.[22]

Liber B, folios 39-40; 23 December 1747

"To all people to whom these presents shall Come I Elizabeth HENDERSON do send greeting know ye that I the said Elizabeth HENDERSON of the County af[oresai]^d Widow for and in Consideration of Love good will and affection which I have and do bear towards my Loving Grandson William HENDERSON Son of Charles HENDERSON of the County af[oresai]^d have given and granted and by these presents do freely Clearly and absolutely give and grant unto the said William HENDERSON a Negro boy Called **Adam** to have and to hold the said Negro boy _ _ _ _ **Adam** from henceforth as his proper wright absolutely without any manner

---

[21] Worcester County Court (Land Records). Deed of mortgage from TOWNSEND, Saul to MACKALLAN, Arthur and TOWNSEND, William Bartholomew. 07 November 1747. B, pp. 18-19, MSA CE 30-2. www.mdlandrec.net : accessed 22 September 2021.

[22] Worcester County Court (Land Records). Deed from HENDERSON, Elizabeth to HENDERSON, Betty Barnaby. 23 December 1747. B, pp. 38-39, MSA CE 30-2. www.mdlandrec.net : accessed 22 September 2021.

of condition in Witness whereof I _ _ hereunto set my hand and Seal this twenty third day of December 1747.

Signed Sealed and Delivered
In the presence of
John WILLIAMS   Stephen STOY

Elizabeth + HENDERSON (seal)
(her mark)

*followed by acknowledgment of Justice of the Peace William LANE on 03 February 1747 and recordation by court clerk Robert KING Jr. on 20 February 1747.[23]

Liber B, folios 40-41; 23 December 1747

"To all people to whom these presents shall Come I Elizabeth HENDERSON do send greeting know ye that I the said Elizabeth HENDERSON of the County af[oresai]^d Widow for and in Consideration of Love good will and affection what I have and do bear towards my Loving daughter Alice HENDERSON the wife of my son James HENDERSON of the County af[oresai]^d have given and granted and by these presents do freely Clearly and absolutely give and grant unto the said Alice HENDERSON my Negro Woman Called **Sarah** dureing the said Alice HENDERSON's Life and at hir death to my Grand Son James HENDERSON Son of the af[oresai]^d James And Alice HENDERSON To Have and To hold the said Negro Woman **Sarah** from hence forth as her and his proper Wright absolutely without any manner of condition In Witness Whereof I hereunto set my Hand and Seal this Twenty third day of December 1747. /
~

Signed Sealed & delivered
In the presence of
John WILLIAMS; Stephen STOY

Elizabeth + HENDERSON (seal)
(her mark)

* followed on folio 41 by the acknowledgment by Justice of the Peace William LANE on 03 February 1747 and the recordation by court clerk Robert KING Jr. on 26 February 1747.[24]

Liber B, folios 45-46; 04 March 1747

"Be itt Known unto all men by these presents that I Saul TOWNSEND of Worcester County in the province of Maryland for and in Consideration of thirty five pounds Current money of Maryland to me in hand paid by John HALL of the same place at the Ensealing and delivery of these presents have bargained and sold and according to Costom have delivered unto the said John HALL one Negro Girl Named **Esther** being about Seven years of age To have and To hold the said Negro Girl unto the said John HALL his Heirs Exe[cutor]^s Adm[inistrator]^s or assigns for Ever, Provided always that if the said Saul TOWNSEND my Exec[utor]^s or Adm[inistrator]^s do well and Truley Pay or Cause to be paid unto the said John HALL his heirs Exec[utor]^s Admi[nistrator]^s or Assigns the full and just sum of thirty five pounds Current money of Maryland with Legall Intrest for the same on or before the first day of March next Insueing the date of this present that then the above Bill of Sale shall be Void and of none Effect Else to stand and Remain in force power and Virtue and I the said Saul TOWNSEND for my self my heirs Exec[utor]^s and Adm[inistrator]^s do Covenant and agree with the said John HALL his heirs or assigns by these presents that if default be made in Payment of the said sum of thirty five Pounds with the Legal Intrest that then I the Saul TOWNSEND my heirs Exec[utor]^s and Adm[inistrator]^s and Every of us shall and will for ever Warrant and defend the said Negro Girl unto the said John HALL his heirs and assigns for Ever against all persons by these presents In Witness whereof I the said Saul TOWNSEND do hereunto set my hand and fix my seal this fourth day of March Anno Domini one thousand and seven hundred and Forty seven

Signed Sealed and Delivered
In the presence of / -
William NILSON,   his

Saul TOWNSEND (seal)

---

[23] Worcester County Court (Land Records). Deed from HENDERSON, Elizabeth to HENDERSON, William. 23 December 1747. B, pp. 39-40, MSA CE 30-2. www.mdlandrec.net : accessed 22 September 2021.

[24] Worcester County Court (Land Records). Deed from HENDERSON, Elizabeth to HENDERSON, Alice. 23 December 1747. B, pp. 40-41, MSA CE 30-2. www.mdlandrec.net : accessed 22 September 2021.

Daniel D DONOHO
mark"

*followed on folio 46 by acknowledgment of Justice of the Peace John SCARBROUGH and recordation by court clerk Robert KING Jr. on March 1747.[25]

Liber B, folios 60-61; 24 March 1747

"Be it Known unto all men by these presents that I Saul TOWNSEND of Worcester County in the province of Maryland for and in Consideration of the sum of twenty five Pound Current money of Maryland to me in hand paid at the Ensealing and delivery of these presents by William COTTINGHAM of the County af[oresai]d in the province af[oresai]d have bargained and sold and according to Costom have delivered unto the said William COTTINGHAM his heirs and assigns for ever a Negro boy Called **Ben** aged about Six years, To have and to Hold the said Negro unto him the said William COTTINGHAM his heirs and assigns for ever Provided always that if I the said Saul TOWNSEND my heirs Exec[utor]s or Adm[inistrator]s do well and Truly pay or Cause to be paid unto the said William COTTINGHAM his heirs Exec[utor]s Adm[inistrator]s or Assigns the full and just sum of twenty five Pound Current money of Maryland with Legall Intrest for the same at or before the twenty fourth day of September comes 12 month next Insuing the date of this present that then the above Bill of Sale shall be void and of none affect Else to stand and Remain in full force power and Virtue and I the said Saul TOWNSEND for my self my heirs Exec[utor]s and Adm[inistrator]s do Covenant and agree to and with the said William COTTINGHAM his heirs and Assigns by these presents that if default be made in payment of the said sum of twenty five pound Current money with the Legall Interest for the same that then I the said Saul TOWNSEND my heirs Exec[utor]s and Adm[inistrator]s shall and will forever warrant and defend the said Negro boy unto the said William COTTINGHAM his heirs and Assigns against all persons by these presents in Witness whereof I do hereunto set my hand and fix my Seal this twenty fourth day of March Anno Dom[ini] One Thousand Seven hundred and forty seven

Signed Sealed and Delivered   Saul TOWNSEND (seal)
In the presence of
John COTTINGHAM; Daniel COTTINGHAM"

*followed on folio 61 by recordation by court clerk Robert KING Jr. on 31 March 1748.[26]

Liber B, folio 83; 06 June 1748

"To All people to whom these presents shall Come I Elizabeth HENDERSON do send Greeting Know ye that I the said Elizabeth HENDERSON of the County af[oresai]d Widow for and in Consideration of Love good will and Affection which I have and do bear towards my Loving Daughter Alice HENDERSON the wife of my son James HENDERSON of the County af[oresai]d have given and Granted and by these presents do freely Clearly and Absolutely give and grant unto the said Alice HENDERSON my Negro Woman Called **Sarah** dureing the said Alice HENDERSONs Life and at her death to my Grandson James HENDERSON Son of the af[oresai]d James and Alice HENDERSON to have and to hold the said Negro Woman **Sarah** from henceforth as her and his proper Wright absolutely without any manner of Condition In Witness whereof I have unto set my hand and Seal this Sixth day of June Anno Dom[ini] 1748.
Testes Wm LANE;   her
                                                    Elizabeth H HENDERSON (seal)
                                                            seal"

*followed by acknowledgment by Justice of the Peace William LANE on 13 June 1748 and recordation by court clerk Robert KING Jr. on 18 June 1748.[27]

---

[25] Worcester County Court (Land Records). Bill of sale from TOWNSEND, Saul to HALL, John. 04 March 1747. B, pp. 45-46, MSA CE 30-2. www.mdlandrec.net : accessed 22 September 2021.

[26] Worcester County Court (Land Records). Bill of sale from TOWNSEND, Saul to COTTINGHAM, William. 24 March 1747. B, pp. 60-61, MSA CE 30-2. www.mdlandrec.net : accessed 22 September 2021.

[27] Worcester County Court (Land Records). Deed of gift from HENDERSON, Elizabeth to HENDERSON, Alice. 06 June 1748. B, p. 83, MSA CE 30-2. www.mdlandrec.net : accessed 22 September 2021.

Liber B, folios 159-160; 01 May 1749

"This Indenture made this first day of May in the year of our Lord God One thousand Seven hundred forty and Nine Between Robert KING Esq. of Somerset County in the Province of Maryland of the one Part and Thomas LAMBDEN of the County of Worcester and Province af[oresai]^d Gentleman of the other Part Witnesseth Whereas the af[oresai]^d Thomas LAMBDEN heretofore towit on the first day of February in the year of our Lord God One thousand Seven hundred forty and five by his Certain Deed in writing Legally Executed Acknowledged and Inrolled amongst the Records of Worcester County for the Consideration therein mentioned did bargain Sell Assign and Transfer unto the said Robert KING his heirs Exe[cutor]^s Adm[inistrator]^s and Assigns one Negro man Slave Named **Jamey** and also one Negro Slave Woman named **Pleasant** both which said Negro's then were and now are in the Possession of the said Thomas LAMBDEN To have and to hold the af[oresai]^d two Negro Slaves unto the said Robert KING his Exe[cutor]s Adm[inistrator]s and Assigns under such Conditions Covenants & Agreements as in the said Deed is Expressed and Set for the Recourse thereto being had may more fully and at Large Appear Now this Indenture Witnesseth that the said Robert KING for and in Consideration of the Sum of one Shilling Sterling money of Great Brittain to him by the said Thomas LAMBDEN in hand Paid before the Ensealing and delivery of these Presents the Receipt whereof the said Robert KING doth hereby Acknowledge and thereof doth Acquit Release and discharge the said Thomas LAMBDEN his heirs Executors and Adm[inistrator]^s forever have Remised Released and Quit Claim and by these Presents doth Remise Quit Claim and release unto the said Thomas LAMBDEN his Exe[cutor]^s Adm[inistrator]s and Assigns forever all his the said Robert KINGs right Title Intrest & Claim Property and demand of in and unto the said two Negro Slaves to wit, **Jamey** and **Pleasant** af[oresai]^d which he the said Robert KING his heirs Exe[cutor]^s Adm[inistrator]^s or Assigns hath or ought to have by force and vertue of the above Recited deed To have and to hold the said Two Negro Slaves to the said Thomas LAMBDEN his heirs and Assigns for Ever free and Clear from all Claims and demands of him the said Robert KING his heirs Exe[cutor]^s Adm[inistrator]^s and Assigns which he or they or Either of them hath or ought to have by vertue of the said Recited deed bearing date the first day of February Seventeen hundred forty and five as af[oresai]^d the Intent of these Presents being to Sett the said Thomas LAMBDEN his heirs or Assigns in the same State and Condition in Regard to his or their Title to the said two Negro Slaves above mentioned as if the said Recited deed had never been made or Executed In Testimony whereof the said Robert KING hath to these Presents sett his hand and fixed his seal the day and year first above written

Sealed and Delivered.   John WATERS . / . ~   R. KING (seal)
In Presence of …..   W[illia]^m McCLEMMEY . / . ~"

*followed on folio 160 by acknowledgment by Justice of Peace Robert Jenkins HENRY and recordation by court clerk Robert KING Jr. on 01 May 1749.[28]

Liber B, folios 176-177; 08 June 1749

"Know all men by these Presents that I Thomas PEEL of Worcester County in the Province of Maryland for and in Consideration of twenty Pounds and Eight Shillings Current money of Maryland to me in hand Paid by Wheetley DENNIS of the same Place at and before the Sealing and Delivery of this Present wherewith I Confess my Self to be Satisfied Contented and Paid have bargained and Sold and by these Presents do fully Clearly and Absolutely Sell unto the said Wheetly DENNIS one Large Ovell Table and One Negrow man Called **Sampson** and five head of Cattle and one bay horse To have and to hold the said Table and Negrow Cattle and horse to the said Wheetley DENNIS his heirs and assigns for Ever and I the said Thomas PEEL heirs Ex[ecutor]^s and Ad[ministrator]^s and Every of us the said Table Negrow Cattle and Horse unto the said Wheetley DENNIS his heirs and Assigns shall and will forever warrant and defend Provided always that If the said Thomas PEEL shall well and truely Pay or Cause to be Paid

---

[28] Worcester County Court (Land Records). Deed of release from KING, Robert to LAMBDEN, Thomas. 01 May 1749. B, pp. 159-160, MSA CE 30-2. www.mdlandrec.net : accessed 23 September 2021.

unto the said Wheetly DENNIS his heirs or Assigns the full and Just Sum twenty Pounds & Eight Shillings Current money of Maryland at or before the first day of February Next Insuing the date of this Present with Legall Intrest for the same that then this Present bill of Sale shall be void and of none Effect Else to Stand & Remain in full force Power & vertue in Law
Signed Sealed and Delivered In the Presence of us this 8th day of June 1749
William NILSON
Joshua STURGIS Sen[ior]   Thomas PEAL (seal)"

*followed on folio 177 by acknowledgment of Justice of the Peace Ephraim WAGGAMAN on 08 June 1749 and recordation by court clerk Robert KING Jr. on 09 June 1749.[29]

Liber B, folio 215; 13 February 1749

"Know all men by these Presents that I John POPE of Worcester County in the Province of Maryland for and in Consideration of thirty Six Pounds Current money of Maryland to me in hand Paid by John HALL Jun[io][r] of the Same Place before the Sealing and Delivery here wherewith I Confess my Self to be fully Satisfied Contented and Paid have bargained & Sold and by these Presents So fully Clearly and Absolutely bargained and Sell unto the said John HALL one Negrow boy Called **Andrew** about the Age of thirteen Years To have and To hold the said Negrow boy to the said John HALL his heirs Ex[ecutor][s] and Adm[inistrator][s] and Every of us the said Negrow unto the said John HALL his heirs or Assigns against all People Shall and will forever warrant and Defend by these Presents Provided Always that If I the said John POPE my heirs Ex[ecutor][s] or Adm[inistrator][s] or any of us do well and truely Pay or Cause to be Paid unto the said John HALL his heirs Ex[ecutor][s] Adm[inistrator][s] or Assigns the full and Just Sum of thirty Six Pounds Current money of Maryland at or before the tenth day of February next Insuing the date of this Present that then this Present bill of Sale of the said Negrow shall be utterly Void and of none Effect Else to Stand and remain in full force Power and Vertue in Law February 13th 1749. ~ / . ~
Signed Sealed & Delivered   William NILSON   John POPE Jun[io][r]. (seal)
In the Presence of ….   Henry AYRES.."

*followed by acknowledgment by Justice of the Peace John SCARBOROUGH and recordation by court clerk Robert KING Jr. on 13 February 1749.[30]

Liber B, folios 216-220; 12 February 1749

"This Indenture made the twelfth day of February in the Year of our Lord God one thousand Seven hundred forty and Nine Between Thomas LAMBDEN of Worcester County in the Province of Maryland Merchant and Sarah LAMBDEN Attorney in fact, of the said Thomas LAMBDEN of the one Part & Robert Jenkins HENRY of Somerset County in the Province aforesaid Esquire and John HENRY of Worcester County in the Province af[oresai][d] Esquire of the other Part Whereas the said Thomas LAMBDEN by a Certain Writing or Letter of Attorney under his hand and Seal duly Executed dated the Eleventh day of December in the Year of our Lord One thousand Seven hundred forty and Nine af[oresai][d] amongst Other things therein Contained did Constitute and Appoint the said Sarah LAMBDEN his well beloved wife his Lawfull Attorney for him and in his Name to Aske sue for Levie require recover and receive of all and Every Person & Persons whatsoever all and Every Such debts & Sums of money and Tobacco as were then due unto him"…"Now This Indenture Witnesseth that for and in Consideration of the Sum of five Shillings Current money of Maryland and towards the Raising Securing & Paying such Publick Debts wherewith the said Robert Jenkins HENRY and John HENRY are or may be in any manner chargeable as being Securitys af[oresai][d] and towards keeping them their and Each of their heirs Ex[ecutor][s] and Adm[inistrator][s] Saved harmless & Indemnified from all Costs Charges damages disbursements & Expences Whatsoever which

---

[29] Worcester County Court (Land Records). Deed of sale from PEEL, Thomas to DENNIS, Wheetley. 08 June 1749. B, pp. 176-177, MSA CE 30-2. www.mdlandrec.net : accessed 23 September 2021.
[30] Worcester County Court (Land Records). Deed of mortgage from POPE, John to HALL, John Jr. 13 February 1749. B, p. 215, MSA CE 30-2. www.mdlandrec.net : accessed 23 September 2021.

hath been or may be Occasioned by means of the said Robert Jenkins HENRY & John HENRY become bound for the said Thomas LAMBDEN as af[oresai]^d he the said Thomas LAMBDEN by his said Attorney Hath bargained and Sold Assigned and Transfered and by these Presents doth bargain and Sell Assign and Transfer unto the said Robert Jenkins HENRY and John HENRY their heirs and Assigns One Negro man Slave Named **Jemmey** and one Negro Woman Slave Named **Joan** Also the following bonds and Notes due unto the said Thomas LAMBDEN from the Sundry Persons"…"and the said Thomas LAMBDEN by his Attorney af[oresai]^d doth hereby Constitute Authorise and Appoint the said Robert Jenkins HENRY & John HENRY and Each of them or their Representatives to Aske demand recover and receive in the name of the said Thomas LAMBDEN all and Singular the money and Tobacco Debts Abovementioned and the af[oresai]^d Negroes to Sell an[d] the whole amount when Received to Apply to the Purposes af[oresai]^d And Also giveing and Granting unto the said Robert Jenkins HENRY & John HENRY and Each of them as full and Ample Power in the Premises to all Intents Constructions and Purposes Whatsoever as the said Sarah LAMDEN is by the above Recited Power Invested with In Witness whereof the Partys af[oresai]^d to these Presents Interchangeably their hands have Set and Seals have fixed the day and year first above written.

Signed Sealed and Delivered   Thomas LAMBDEN by Sarah LAMBDEN (seal)
In Presence of us……   has attorney………
Nath[anie]^{ll} WHITAKER
W[illia]^m HAYWARD..
Ep[hraim] WAGGAMAN."

*followed on folios 219 and 220 by acknowledgment by Justice of the Peace Ephraim WAGGAMAN and recordation by court clerk Robert KING Jr. on 16 February 1749.[31]

*Due to its true length, this transcription has been shortened to its most relevant portions. The full original deed can be viewed at the citation provided.

Liber B, folio 222; 08 March 1749

"Know all men by these Presents that I Saul TOWNSEND of Worcester County in the Province of Maryland for and in Consideration of thirty five Pounds Current money of Maryland to me in hand Paid by Samuel ATKINSON of the same Place before the Sealing and Delivery of these Presents wherewith I Confess myself to be fully Satisfied Contented and Paid have bargained and Sold and by these Presents do fully Clearly and Absolutely bargain and Sell unto the said Samuel ATKINSON one Negrow man Called **Adam** To have And To hold the said Negrow man to the said Samuel ATKINSON his heirs Executors Adm[inistator]^s or Assigns to his and their own Proper use and behoofs for Ever and I the said Saul TOWNSEND my heirs Ex[ecutor]^s and Adm[inistrator]^s and Every of us the said Negrow man unto the said Samuel ATKINSON his heirs and Assigns against all People shall and will for Ever warrant and defend by these Presents Provided always that If I the said Saul TOWNSEND my heirs Ex[ecutor]^s or Adm[inistrator]^s or any of us do well and truely Pay or Cause to be Paid unto the said Samuel ATKINSON his heirs Ex[ecutor]^s Adm[inistrat]ors or Assigns the full and Just Sum of thirty five Pounds Current money of Maryland at or before the fifteenth day of february next that then this Present Bill of Sale of the said Negrow man shall be Void and of none Effect Else to Stand and remain in full force Power and Vertue in Law March the Eight Ann[o] Dom[ini] One thousand Seven hundred & forty Nine

Signed Sealed and Delivered   William NILSON.
In the presence of…..   Philip GUTTERY.   Saul TOWNSEND. (seal)"

---

[31] Worcester County Court (Land Records). Deed from LAMBDEN, Thomas and Sarah to HENRY, Robert Jenkins and HENRY, John. 12 February 1749. B, p. 216-220, MSA CE 30-2. www.mdlandrec.net : accessed 23 September 2021.

*followed by the acknowledgment by Justice of the Peace Joseph MILLER and recordation by court clerk Robert KING Jr. on 08 March 1749.[32]

Liber B, folios 226-229; 19 March 1749

"This Indenture made this Nineteenth day of March in the year of our Lord God One thousand Seven hundred forty and Nine Between Benjamin HENDERSON of Worcester County in the Province of Maryland Planter of the one Part and Robert KING Esquire of the County of Somerset and Province aforesaid of the Other Part Witnesseth that the said Benjamin HENDERSON for and in Consideration of the Sum of Eighty two Pounds ten Shillings Curr[en]^t whole Gold of the Province of Maryland to him in hand Paid by the said Robert KING at or before the Sealing and Delivery of these Presents the receipt whereof he doth hereby Acknowledge and Confess and thereof doth Acquit release and discharge the said Robert KING his heirs Executors and Administrators forever by these Presents Hath granted Bargained and Sold Aliened released and Confirmed and by these Presents doth Grant Bargain and Sell Alien release and Confirm unto the said Robert KING his heirs and Assigns forever all that tract or Parcel of Land Called Hap Hazzard Scituate lying and being formerly in Somerset County but now in the County of Worcester and on the South Side of Pocomoke River"… "And the said Benjamin HENDERSON for and in Consideration of the Sum of money abovementioned doth hereby bargain and Sell and by these Presents, hath granted Bargained and Sold Assigned and transferred unto the af[oresai]^d Robert KING his Executors Administrators and Assigns forever five Negro Slaves, to wit, one Negro man named **Harry** about the age of Sixteen years two Negro women the one Named **Eve** about the age of forty years the Other named **Abbow** about the age of thirty Six years, two Negro Girls the one Named **Barsheba** about the age of one and a half years, the other named **Pleasant** about the age of one years, one black Coloured Gelding abought the age of Eight Years, one dark bay Coloured Gelding about the age of thirteen Years, two Stears one about three, the other about four years old one a dark brown the other a black one, and three Cows all which Cattle are marked with a Crop in both Years and under bitt in both now in the Possession of the said Benjamin HENDERSON also To have and To hold the af[oresai]^d five Negroes Named **Harry**, **Eve**, **Abbow**, **Barsheba**, and **Pleasant** and the said two horses, two Stear's and three Cows unto the only Proper use and Benefit of the said Robert KING his Executors Administrators or Assigns and to no other use or Purpose whatsoever, And the said Benjamin HENDERSON for himself his heirs Executors and Administrators, doth Covenant Promise Grant and agree to and with the said Robert KING his heirs Executors Administrators & Assigns that he the said Benjamin HENDERSON at the time of Executing these Presents hath good right full Power and Lawfully Authority to Sell and dispose the aforesaid Land Called Haphazzard with Every the Appurtenances thereto belonging and that he hath the Sole and Absolute Property of and in the af[oresai]^d five Negro Slaves named **Harry**, **Eve**, **Abbow, Barsheba** and **Pleasant** as aforesaid and Every other the goods and Chattles abovementioned and that the same Slaves with Every the goods and Chattles af[oresai]^d and the Land Called Haphazzard as aforesaid with Every the appurtenances are free and Clear from all former Incumbrances whatsoever, And further that he the said Benjamin HENDERSON his Executors and Administrators the af[oresai]^d Land and Premisses with Every it's Appurtenances Called Haphazzard and the said five Slaves Called **Harry, Eve, Abbow, Barsheba & Pleasant** as af[oresai]^d with the goods and Chattles and Every of them abovementioned"…

"Sealed and Delivered   W[illia]^m LANE.
In Presence of us…   Ep[hraim] Waggaman   Benjamin B HENDERSON (seal)
                                                                                 his
                                                                                 mark"

*followed on folio 229 by acknowledgment by Justices of the Peace William LANE and Ephraim WAGGAMAN on 19 March 1749, receipt of alienation fee by Thomas GILLISS on 24 March 1749, and recordation by the court clerk Robert KING Jr. on 25 March 1749.[33]

---

[32] Worcester County Court (Land Records). Bill of sale from TOWNSEND, Saul to ATKINSON, Samuel. 08 March 1749. B, p. 222, MSA CE 30-2. www.mdlandrec.net : accessed 23 September 2021.

[33] Worcester County Court (Land Records). Deed of mortgage from HENDERSON, Benjamin to KING, Robert. 19 March 1749. B, pp. 226-229, MSA CE 30-2. www.mdlandrec.net : accessed 23 September 2021.

*Due to its true length, this transcription has been shortened to its most relevant portions. The full original deed can be viewed at the citation provided.

Liber B, folios 229-232; 19 March 1749

"This Indenture made this Nineteenth day of March in the year of our Lord God one thousand seven hundred Forty and Nine Between William GILLET of Worcester County in the Province of Maryland Planter of the one Part and Robert KING Esquire of the County of Somerset and Province af[oresai]^d of the Other Part Witnesseth that the said William GILLET for and in Consideration of the Sum of Sixty Pounds ten Shillings Current whole Gold of the Province of Maryland to him in hand Paid by the said Robert KING at or before the Sealing and Delivery of these Presents the Receipt Whereof he doth hereby Acknowledge and Confess and thereof doth Acquit Release and discharge the said Robert KING his heirs Executors and Administrators forever by these Presents Hath Granted Bargained and Sold Aliened Released and Confirmed and by these Presents doth Grant Bargain and Sell Alien Release & Confirm unto the said Robert KING his heirs and Assigns forever all them two Tracts or Parcels of Land one Called Kings Land the Other Hogquarter Scituate lying and being in the County of Worcester and on the South or Southeast Side of Pocomoke River"… "and the said William GILLET for and in Consideration of the Sum of money above mentioned hath Granted, Bargained and Sold, Assigned and transferred and by these Presents doth hereby Grant Bargain and Sell Assign and transfer unto the af[oresai]^d Robert KING his Executors Administrators and Assigns forever one Negro boy Named **Adam** about the age of Eleven Year's, one black Coloured Gelding about the age of five year's, one barren Cow of a brindle Colour, one Cow and Yearling of a Red Colour, and one four year old Heiffer big with Calf all marked with a Slitt and under bitt in the right ear and a Crop in the left Ear the said Gelding was at Joshua CHAPMAN's the other Chattles abovementioned now in the Possession of the said William GILLET also To have and To hold the aforesaid Negro boy **Adam** the Gelding afores[aid] and the Cow's Heiffer and Yearling aforesaid unto the only Proper use and Benefit of the said Robert KING his Executors Administrators or Assigns and to no Other use or Purpose Whatsoever"… "for the Consideration above Acknowledged to have Received shall at any time hereafter whom required by the said Robert KING his heirs, Executor's, Administrator's or Assign's Execute and in due form of Law Acknowledge any Other deed or writing whatsoever that may by the said Robert KING his heir's, Executor's, Administrator's or Assign's or his or their Council Learned in the Law be thought Necessary to Confirm the Right of the Lands & Premisse's with Every the Appurtenance's and the Negro Slave and Other Chattles abovementioned unto the said Robert KING his heir's and Assigns forever and that the Slave and Other Chattles and Every of them be at the Resque of the said William GILLET his heir's, Executor's and Administrator's so long as they or any of them remain in his or their Possession, In Testimony whereof the Parties aforesaid to these Presents Interchangeably their hands have Set and Seal's Affixed the day and year first above written

Sealed and Delivered   W[illia]^m LANE.   William GILLETT (seal)
In Presence of us…   Ep[hraim]. WAGGAMAN"

*followed on folio 232 by acknowledgment of Justices of the Peace William LANE and Ephraim WAGGAMAN on 19 March 1749, receipt for the alienation fine by Thomas GILLISS on 24 March 1749, and recordation by court clerk Robert KING Jr. on 25 March 1749.[34]

*Due to its true length, this transcription has been shortened to its most relevant portions. The full original deed can be viewed at the citation provided.

Liber B, folios 318-319; 08 March 1750

"Know all men by these Presents that I Thomas PEAL of Worcester County Planter for and in Consideration of the Sum of forty One Pounds fifteen Shillings and Six Pence Current money

---

[34] Worcester County Court (Land Records). Deed of mortgage from GILLETT, William to KING, Robert. 19 March 1749. B, pp. 229-232, MSA CE 30-2. www.mdlandrec.net : accessed 23 September 2021.

of Maryland to him in hand Paid by Thomas JONES of Somerset County Merchant whereof the said Thomas PEAL hereby doth Acknowledge the Receipt thereof hath bargained Sold set over & Delivered and by these Presents do bargain Sell set over and Deliver unto the said Thomas JONES one Negro man Called **Sampson** one Hand Mill Cullen Stones three Cows and one Yearling Seven Ewes & Lambs Seven Chairs one Ovell Table one other Large Black Walnut Table To have & To Hold the said Bargained Premises unto the said Thomas JONES his Executors Adm[inistrator]^s and Assigns forever and the said Thomas JONES his Exe[cutor]^s Adm[inistrator]^s and Assigns against all Persons shall and will warrant and forever defend by these Presents Provided always and it is the True Intrest and meaning of these Presents that if the said Thomas PEAL his Exec[utor]^s or Adm[inistrator]^s do and shall save herself and keep Indemnify'd the abovesaid Thomas PEAL his heirs Exec[utor]^s or Adm[inistrator]^s from all Cost Charge or Damage which he the said Thomas JONES his heirs Exec[utor]^s or Adm[inistrator]^s or any of them should be Put to by means of the Said Thomas JONES's Executing a bond of Indemnification unto William FLEMING Conditioned to Save harmless and keep Indemnify'd the said William FLEMING by means of his becoming Security to Henry WAGGAMAN for the said Thomas PEAL by Bond for the Payment of the Sum of forty Pounds Six Shillings Current money of Maryland with Intrest while Paid and also the said Thomas PEAL Pay all Costs and Expences of makeing and Recording these Presents then this writing and Every matter and thing therein Contained to be null and Void and of no Effect anything herein before Comprised to the Contrary Notwithstanding but it is further the True Intent and meaning of these Presents that if any of the above bargained Premises should dye or be any way distroyed before the same are Received in the Possession of the said Thomas JONES that the same shall be the Loss of the said Thomas PEAL his Ex[ecutor]^s or Adm[inistrator]^s In Testimony whereof the Partys afores[ai]^d to these Presents their hands have sett and Seals affixed this Eighth day of March Ann[o] Dom[ini] 1750

Sealed and Delivered   J. SCARBOROUGH   Thomas PEALE (seal)
In Presence of . .   L. DENNIS."

*followed by acknowledgment by Justice of the Peace John SCARBOROUGH and recordation by county clerk Robert KING Jr. on folio 319 on 08 March 1750.[35]

Liber B, folios 327-328; 22 March 1750

"Know all men by these Presents that I Samuel SMOCK of Worcester County in the Province of Maryland for and in Consideration of thirty Pounds Current money of Maryland to me in hand Paid by John HALL Jun[io]^r of the same Place at or before the Sealing or Delivery of these Presents wherewith, I confess myself to be fully Satisfyed Contented and Paid have bargained and Sold and by these Presents do fully Clearly and Absolutely bargain and Sell unto the said John HALL one Negrow Woman Called **Yeany** about Twenty three Years old To have and To hold the said Negrow Woman to the said John HALL his heirs Executors Adm[inistrator]^s or Assigns to his and their own Propper uses and behoofs forever and I the said Samuel SMOCK my heirs Execu[tor]^s and Adm[inistrator]^s and Every of us the said Negrow Woman unto the said John HALL his heirs Execut[or]^s Adm[inistrator]^s and Assigns against all People shall and will warrant and defend forever by these Presents Provided always that if I the said Samuel SMOCK my heirs Exec[utor]^s or Adm[inistrator]^s or any of us do well and truly Pay or Cause to be Paid to the said John HALL his heirs Ex[ecutor]^s or Assigns the full and Just Sum of thirty Pounds Current money of Maryland with Legall Interest for the same at or before the Twenty first day of March next Ensuing the date of these presents that then this Present Bill of Sale of the said Negrow shall be Void and of none Effect of Else to Stand and remain in full force Power and Vertue In Witness whereof I the said Samuel SMOCK do hereunto set my hand and fix my seal this Twenty Second day of March Anno Domini one thousand Seven hundred and fifty. ~

---

[35] Worcester County Court (Land Records). Deed of mortgage from PEALE, Thomas to JONES, Thomas. 08 March 1750. B, pp. 318-319, MSA CE 30-2. www.mdlandrec.net : accessed 23 September 2021.

Signed Sealed and Delivered   William NILSON   Samuel SMOCK (seal)
In the Presence of….
                                    his
                                John V POINTER
                                    mark"

*followed on folios 327-328 by the acknowledgment of Justice of the Peace John SCARBOROUGH and recordation by county clerk Robert KING Jr. on 22 March 1750.[36]

Liber B, folio 331; 29 March 1751

"Maryland Worcester Co[un]ty, to wit, Know all men by these Presents that I the within Mortgagee John HALL for and in Consideration of the Sum of Eighteen Curr[en]^t money of Maryland to me in hand Paid by Comfort POPE the Widow and Administratrix of the within Mortgagor John POPE Jun[io]^r do by these Presents for myself my heirs Exec[utor]^s Adm[inistrator]^s and Assigns release and hereby quit all Claim Right Title Intrest Property or demand which I the said John HALL my heirs Ex[ecutor]^s Adm[inistrator]^s or Assigns have ought to have or may have of in or to the within Negro boy Called **Andrew** by Vertue of the within Deed of Mortgage unto the afores[ai]^d Comfort POPE Widow and Adm[inistratri]^x of the John POPE Jun[io]^r To have and To hold the said Negro boy **Andrew** unto the said Comfort POPE Widow and Adm[inistratri]^x as afores[ai]^d or the Legal representatives of the said John POPE Jun[io]^r as the Law {?} in Such Cases direct to her or their Proper use and behoofs forever in as full and Ample a manner to all intents and Purposes as the within Mortgage deed of the said Negro **Andrew** to me had never been made In Testimony whereof I have hereunto Affixed my hand and seal this Twenty Ninth day of March Ann[o] Dom[ini] Seventeen hundred Fifty one

Signed Sealed and Delivered   J. SCARBOROUGH   John HALL (seal)
In Presence of…..   PURNELL"

*followed by acknowledgment of Justice of the Peace John SCARBOROUGH on 29 March 1751 and recordation by court clerk Robert KING Jr. on 12 April 1751.[37]

Liber B, folios 351-352; 31 July 1751

"To all Christian People to whome this Present writing shall Come I Thomas LAMBDEN of Worcester County in the Province of Maryland send Greeting: Know Ye that I the said Thomas LAMBDEN as well for the Indemnity discharge and Saving harmless of Joshua ATKINSON (of Worcester County in the Province of Maryland) his heirs Ex[ecutor]^s and Adm[inistrator]^s and Every of them of and from all manner of Bonds and writings Obligatory whatsoever wherein the said Joshua ATKINSON is and Standeth bound for me the said Thomas LAMBDEN in any Sum or Sums of money and Tobacco or any other Specie whatsoever together with what_ever sum or Sums of money I may at this time be Indebted unto him as also for Divers other Good Causes and Considerations me hereunto moving have given Granted Bargained, Sold and Confirmed and by these Presents do give grant Bargain Sell and Confirm unto the said Joshua ATKINSON all and Singular the Goods and Chattles hereafter mentioned to wit one Negro man named **Hector** one Negro woman named **Pleasant** and a Negro child named **Violet** also Six feather Beds & furniture three Cows and Two Calves one Yoak of Oxen one Sorrell Horse Seven Sheep also the Reversion of what money and Tobacco shall remain in the hands of Col[onel] Rob[ert] Jenkins HENRY Col[onel] John HENRY Mr Alexander BUNCLE and Col[onel] Samuel HOPKINS as & Assignment to them made of my late Sheriffs Books and what might be due thereon together with the Legal Intrest on Such Reversion Ariseing due to me the said Thomas LAMBDEN To Have and to Hold all and Singular the afores[ai]^d Granted Premisses to him the said Joshua ATKINSON his heirs Ex[ecutor]^s Adm[inistrator]^s and Assigns to his and their own Proper use and behoof for Ever and I the said Thomas LAMBDEN and my heirs all and Singular the said Goods and Chattles and other the

---

[36] Worcester County Court (Land Records). Bill of sale from SMOCK, Samuel to HALL, John Jr. 22 March 1750. B, pp. 327-328, MSA CE 30-2. www.mdlandrec.net : accessed 23 September 2021.
[37] Worcester County Court (Land Records). Release of mortgage from HALL, John to POPE, Comfort. 29 March 1751. B, p. 331, MSA CE 30-2. www.mdlandrec.net : accessed 23 September 2021.

Premises unto the said Joshua ATKINSON his Exec[utor]s Adm[inistrator]s and Assigns to his and their own Proper use as afores[ai]d shall and will warrant and for Ever defend by these Presents Provided always and it is the true Intent and meaning of these Presents that if I the said Thomas LAMBDEN my Executors and Adm[inistrator]s or Assigns or any of us do or shall from time to time and at all times hereafter Clearly Acquit and discharge or Otherwise Sufficiently save and keep harmless the said Joshua ATKINSON his Executors Administrators and Assignes and all his and their Goods Chattles Lands Tenements and the said Hereditaments and Every of them of and from all and Singular Bonds and Writings Obligatory whatsoever wherein or whereby the said Joshua ATKINSON at the Request and for the Debt of use the said Thomas LAMBDEN is and Standeth Bound to any Person or Persons whatsoever (and of and for the Proper Amount of the said Joshua ATKINSON against me) for any sum or Sums of money Tobacco or Other Specie of any Nature or kind whatsoever and of and from all manner of Actions Suits Charges Troubles Expences and demands whatsoever which shall or may in any wise hereafter happen Come grow or be to or against the said Joshua ATKINSON his Executors or Adm[inistrator]s or any of them for or by reason or means of the same obligations or writings Obligatory or any of them or any thing in them or any of them mentioned or Contained that then this Present Deed or Grant and Everything herein Contained shall be utterly Void and of none Effect anything herein Contained or before Specified to the Contrary thereof in any wise Notwithstanding In Witness whereof I have hereunto sett my hand and Affixed my seal this thirty first day of July Anno Dom[ini] 1751

Signed Sealed and Delivered   Will[ia]m ALLEN   Tho[ma]s LAMBDEN (seal)
In the Presence of us..   Jno SHELDON"

*followed on folio 352 by the acknowledgment of Justice of the Peace John SCOTT and recordation by court clerk Robert KING Jr. on 06 August 1751.[38]

Liber B, folios 354-355; 07 August 1751

"This Indenture made this Seventh day of August Anno Dom[ini] MDCCLI Between Daniel WELLS of Worcester County in the Province of Maryland Planter of the one Part and Thomas ROBINS and Elisha PURNELL of the County aforesaid of the Other Part Witnesseth that whereas Margaret DAVIS now the wife of the said Daniel while she was Sole and some small time before her Intermarriage with the said Davis was Possessed of these slaves following to wit **Betty May ju{??} Sarah, Abel, Caleb & Patience** and had an Estate in them dureing her life and Intending to Secure her said Intrest in the said Slaves to her own use without being subject to the disposal of the said David with whom she then Intended to Intermarry did with the Privity and Consent of the said Daniel before her Intermarriage with him by her Deed Poll only Executed dated the tenth day of February Anno Dom[ini] MDCCXLII for the Consideration therein mentioned Bargain and Sell the said Slaves to Thomas ROBINS and Elisha PURNELL for and during her Natural life under this trust then Promised that the said Thomas and Elisha should Permit the said Slaves to remain in her Possession and to be for her Sole and Separate use during her Natural life without being at the disposal or liable to the Creditors of the said Daniel with whom she So {?} afterwards Intended and Actually did Intermarry and whereas in order Effectually to Secure the said Slaves for the uses and Purposes afores[ai]d the said Deed ought to have been Acknowledged before a Justice of the Peace for the County where the said Margaret resided and where the said Slaves then Lived and to have been Recorded or Inrolled among the Records of the said County Court in Order to have made the said Deed Effectually have Operated for the Purposes afores[ai]d Now This Indenture Witnesseth that in order to fulfill the Intent of the said Margaret the said Daniel for the Consideration of five Shillings Current money of Maryland to him Paid by the said Thomas and Elisha before the Sealing and Delivery hereof the receipt whereof the said Daniel hereby doth Acknowledge Hath Bargained & Sold and doth hereby Bargain and Sell to the said Thomas and Elisha their Ex[ecutor]s and Adm[inistrator]s and Assigns the Slaves above named and also **Shadrack** and **Dick** born Since of the body of the abovenamed **Sarah** To have and To hold the

---

[38] Worcester County Court (Land Records). Deed of mortgage from LAMBDEN, Thomas to ATKINSON, Joshua. 31 July 1751. B, pp. 351-352, MSA CE 30-2. www.mdlandrec.net : accessed 23 September 2021.

said before named Slaves to the said Thomas and Elisha their Ex[ecutor]ˢ Adm[inistrator]ˢ and Assigns during the life of the said Margaret to the only use of the said Thomas and Elisha their Ex[ecutor]ˢ Adm[inistrator]ˢ and Assigns shall Permit the said Margaret to have the use and disposal of the Slaves af[oresai]ᵈ dureing the whole time afores[ai]ᵈ without the Controul of the said Daniel or any Person Claiming under him and Bargain Sell Assign and Set over the said Slaves or any of them from time and to Such Person or Persons as the said Margaret by her request in writing Signed by her in the Presence of Two Witnesses shall direct In Testimony whereof the Partys af[oresai]ᵈ hereto Affixed their hands and Seals Interchangeably the day and Year first above written ~

Sealed and Delivered   Daniel WELLS (seal)
In Presence of ...."

*followed on folio 355 by the acknowledgment of Justices of the Peace John SCOTT and William DRAPER, and recordation by court clerk Robert KING Jr. on 07 August 1751.[39]

Liber B, folio 356; 07 August 1751

"This Indenture made the Seventh day of August in the Year of our Lord One thousand Seven hundred Fifty and one Between Thomas PEELE of Worcester County in the Province of Maryland Planter of the one Part and Thomas JONES Merchant of the same Place of the Other Part Witnesseth that the said Thomas PEELE for and in Consideration of the Sum of Twenty Pounds Current money of Maryland to him by the said Thomas JONES in hand Paid at or before the Sealing and Delivery hereof the receipt whereof he doth hereby Confess and Acknowledge and thereof doth Acquit Release and discharge the said Thomas JONES his heirs Ex[ecutor]ˢ and Adm[inistrator]ˢ forever by these Presents Hath Granted, Bargained, Sold, Assigned, Setover and Transferred and by these Presents doth Grant Bargain Sell Assign Setover and Transferr unto the said Thomas JONES his heirs and Assigns forever one Negro man Named **Sampson** and one handmill frame with a Pair of Cullen Stones there unto belonging To Have and To hold the said Negro man **Sampson** and the afores[ai]ᵈ Handmill frame and Stones unto the said Thomas JONES his heirs and Assigns forever and to no other use Intent Purpose or Construction whatsoever and the said Thomas PEALE for himself his heirs Ex[ecutor]ˢ and Adm[inistrator]ˢ doth Covenant, Promise, Grant, and Agree to and with the said Thomas JONES his heirs and Assigns that he the said Thomas PEELE the afores[aid] Negro man Named **Sampson** and the afores[ai]ᵈ Hand Mill frame and Cullen Stones unto the said Thomas JONES and his heirs against himself and his heirs and all other Persons Lawfully Claiming the same shall and will Warrant and forever defend by these presents In Witness whereof the Partys af[oresai]ᵈ to these Presents Interchangeably their hands have Set and Seals have fixed the day and year first above written

Sealed and Delivered   Rob[er]ᵗ GEDDES.   Thomas PEELE (seal)
In Presence of ....   W[illia]ᵐ HAYWARD."

*followed by the acknowledgment of Justice of the Peace John SCOTT on 07 August 1751 and recordation by court clerk Robert KING Jr. on 08 August 1751.[40]

Liber B, folio 363; 02 September 1751

"This Indenture made this Second day of September Anno Dom[ini] MDCCLI Between Nicholas FOUNTAIN of Worcester County of the one Part and William STEVENS of the same Place of the Other Part Witnesseth that the said Nicholas for and in Consideration of the Sum of Sixty Pounds Current money of Maryland to him in hand by the said William STEVENS at and before the Sealing and Delivery hereof the receipt whereof the said Nicholas hereby doth Acknowledge hath bargained Sold Set over & Delivered and by these Presents doth bargain Sell Set over and Deliver unto the said William STEVENS and his Assigns one Negro man

---

[39] Worcester County Court (Land Records). Deed of trust from WELLS, Daniel to ROBINS, Thomas and PURNELL, Elisha. 07 August 1751. B, pp. 354-355, MSA CE 30-2. www.mdlandrec.net : accessed 23 September 2021.
[40] Worcester County Court (Land Records). Deed of sale from PEELE, Thomas to JONES, Thomas. 07 August 1751. B, p. 356, MSA CE 30-2. www.mdlandrec.net : accessed 23 September 2021.

slave Named **James** now in the Possession of the afores[ai]^d Nicholas To have and To hold the said Bargained Premises to the said William STEVENS and his Assigns to the only Proper use and Benefit of the said William STEVENS and his Assigns and to no Other use or uses whatsoever and the said Nicholas FOUNTAIN for himself his heirs Ex[ecutor]^s and Adm[inistrator]^s doth hereby Covenant to and with the said William STEVENS and his Assigns that at and before the Bargain and Sale hereof the said Nicholas had Good right & full Authority to bargain and Sell the same in manner and form afores[ai]^d and that he will warrant & defend the same from all Persons Claims and Titles whatsoever by these Presents Provided always and it is the true Intent and meaning of these presents that if the afores[ai]^d Nicholas FOUNTAIN his Ex[ecutor]^s Adm[inistrator]^s do and shall Pay or Cause to be Paid unto the afores[ai]^d William STEVENS his Ex[ecutor]^s Adm[inistrator]^s or Assigns the Sum of Sixty Pounds Current money of Maryland with Legal Intrest for the same on or before the first day of April Anno Dom[ini] one thousand Seven hundred fifty and Two without fraud or delay then this Indenture to be Void Otherwise to be and remain in full force Power and Vertue In Testimony whereof I have hereunto set my hand and Seal the day & year first above written. ~

Sealed & Delivered   John HAMILTON   Nich[olas] FOUNTAIN (seal)
In Presence of …   {?} DENNIS…"

*followed by the acknowledgment of Justice of the Peace Robert Jenkins HENRY, receipt of consideration by Nicholas FOUNTAIN, and recordation by court clerk Robert KING Jr. on 02 September 1751.[41]

Liber B, folios 364-365; 05 September 1751

"This Indenture made the fifth day of September in the Year of our Lord God one thousand Seven hundred Fifty and one Between William NEWLAND of Worcester County in the Province of Maryland Chirurgion of the one Part and Clement DASHIEL of Somerset in the Province afores[ai]^d Gentleman of the Other Part Witnesseth that the afores[ai]^d William NEWLAND for and in Consideration of the Sum of Twenty Pounds Nineteen Shillings and Nine Pence Current money of Maryland to him in hand Paid by the said Clement DASHIEL at or before the Sealing and Delivery of these Presents the receipt whereof the said William doth hereby Confess and Acknowledge and thereof doth Acquit release and discharge the said Clement his heirs Executors and Administrators forever by these Presents hath bargained and Sold and by these Presents Doth Bargain and Sel unto the said Clement DASHIEL and his Assigns one Negro man Slave named **Daniel** now in the Possession of the said William NEWLAND To have and To hold the afores[ai]^d man Slave unto the said Clement DASHIEL his Executors Adm[inistrator]^s or Assigns To the only Proper use Profitt Benefitt and Behooff of the said Clement DASHIEL his Executors Adm[inistrator]^s or Assigns forever and to on Other Purpose whatsoever And the said William NEWLAND for himself his heirs Executors and Adm[inistrator]s doth Covenant Promise and agree to and with the said Clement DASHIEL his Ex[ecutor]^s Adm[inistrator]^s and Assigns That he the said William NEWLAND his heirs Executors and Adm[inistrator]^s the afores[ai]d Negro Slave named **Daniel** unto the said Clement DASHIEL his Executors Adm[inistrator]^s or Assigns shall and will warrant and forever Defend by these Presents Provided always that if the said William NEWLAND his heirs Executors or Adm[inistrator]^s shall well and truly Pay or Cause to be Paid unto the said Clement DASHIEL his Exe[cutor]^s Adm[inistrator]^s or Assigns the full and Just Sum of Twenty Pounds Nineteen Shillings and Nine Pence Current money of Maryland with Legal Intrest for the same and also the Costs and Charges of makeing and recording this Deed on or before the fifth day of December next ensuing the date hereof with[ou]^t fraud or further delay then this Deed and Every matter and thing therein Contained to be Null and Void anything herein before Contained to the Contrary in any ways Notwithstanding In Witness whereof the Parties afores[ai]^d to this Indenture Interchangeably their hands of Set and Seals Affixed the day and Year first above written

---

[41] Worcester County Court (Land Records). Deed of mortgage from FOUNTAIN, Nicholas to STEVENS, William. 02 September 1751. B, p. 363, MSA CE 30-2. www.mdlandrec.net : accessed 23 September 2021.

Sealed and Delivered	Joshua HELLAM	W[illia]^m NEWLAND Surgeon (seal)
In Presence of ….	Hannah HOUR."	

*followed by acknowledgment of Justice of the Peace Robert Jenkins HENRY, receipt of consideration by Clement DASHIEL, and recordation by court clerk Robert KING Jr. on 05 September 1751 on folio 365.[42]

Liber B, folios 400-401; 27 December 1751

"This Indenture made this twenty Seventh day of December in the year of our Lord God 1751~Between William NEWLAND of Worcester County in the Province of Maryland Chirurgeon of the one Part and John SCARBOROUGH Jun[io]^r of Worcester County in the Province af[oresai]^d Gent[leman] of the other Part Witnesseth that the af[oresai]^d William NEWLAND for and in Consideration of the sum of Thirty Pounds Eight Shillings and Six Pence Current money of Maryland to him in hand Paid by the said John SCARBOROUGH at or before the Sealing and delivery of these Presents the receipt whereof the said William doth hereby confess and Acknowledge and thereof doth Acquit release and discharge the said John his heirs Execu[tor]^s and Adm[inistrator]^s forever by these Presents, hath bargained and Sold and by these Presents doth Bargain and Sell unto the said John SCARBOROUGH and his Assigns One negro woman Slave named **Rachel** now in the Possession of the said William NEWLAND To have and to hold the afores[ai]^d woman Slave unto the afores[ai]^d John SCARBOROUGH his Exec[utor]^s Adm[inistrator]^s or Assigns to the only Proper use Profitt benefit and behoof of the said John SCARBOROUGH his Execu[tor]^s Adm[inistrator]^s or Assigns forever and to no other Purpose whatsoever. And the said William NEWLAND for himself his heirs Exec[utor]^s and Adm[inistrator]^s doth Covenant Promise and agree to and with the said John SCARBOROUGH his Exec[utor]^s and Adm[inistrator]^s and Assigns that he the said William NEWLAND his heirs Execu[tor]^s and Adm[inistrator]^s the af[oresai]^d negro Slave named **Rachel** unto the said John SCARBOROUGH his Execu[tor]^s and Adm[inistrator]^s or Assigns shall and will Warrant and forever defend by these Presents, Provided always that if the said William NEWLAND his heirs Execu[tor]^s or Adm[inistrator]^s shall well and truely Pay or cause to be Paid unto the said John SCARBOROUGH his Execu[tor]^s Adm[inistrator]^s or Assigns, the full and Just sum of thirty Pounds Eight Shillings and Six Pence Current money of Maryland with Legal Intrest for the same and also the Cost and Charges of making and Recording this deed on or before the tenth day of April next Ensueing the date thereof without fraud or further delay then this Deed and Every matter and thing therein contained to be Null and Void, any thing herein before Contained to the Contrary in any ways Notwithstanding, In Witness whereof the Parties af[oresai]^d this Indenture interchangeably their have sett and. Seals Affixed the day and year first above Written

Sealed and Deliver[e]^d	Jos[hu]^a MITCHELL	W[illia]^m NEWLAND (seal)
In Presence off …	B. HARRIS..	surgeon"

*followed on folio 401 by the acknowledgment by Justice of the Peace John SCARBOROUGH, the receipt of consideration by William NEWLAND on 10 January 1752, and the recordation by court clerk Robert KING Jr. 15 January 1752.[43]

Liber B, folios 446-447; 28 March 1752

"This Indenture made the 28th day of March Annoq[ue] Dom[ini] 1752~ Between William NEWLAND of Worcester County in the Province of Maryland Chirurgeon of the one Part and Daniel WELLS of the County and Province aforesaid reedmaker of the other Part Witnesseth that the said William NEWLAND for and in Consideration that the said Daniel WELLS at the Instance and request of the said William NEWLAND on the fifteenth day of November 1750 did Indorse a Certain sett of Bills of Each. {?} by the said William NEWLAND drawn on William NEWLAND Sen[io]^r Merch[an]^t in London, in favour of the rever[en]^d Nathaniel

---

[42] Worcester County Court (Land Records). Deed of mortgage from NEWLAND, William to DASHIEL, Clement. 05 September 1751. B, pp. 364-365, MSA CE 30-2. www.mdlandrec.net : accessed 23 September 2021.

[43] Worcester County Court (Land Records). Deed of mortgage from NEWLAND, William to SCARBOROUGH, John. 27 December 1751. B, pp. 400-401, MSA CE 30-2. www.mdlandrec.net : accessed 23 September 2021.

WHITAKER for the Sum of Seventeen Pounds Ten Shillings Ster[ling] hath Given Granted Bargained and Sold and by these Presents for himself his heirs Executors and Adm[inistrator]ˢ doth give Grant bargain and Sell unto the said Daniel WELLS his heirs and Assigns forever two Negros to wit one Negro Boy Called **Southy** of about four years old and another Negro boy Called **Standbridge** of about a year old or upwards To have and to hold the said two Negroes to him the said Daniel WELLS his heirs and Assigns forever which said two Negros now being in the Possession of the said William NEWLAND he doth by these Presents for himself his heirs Exe[cutor]ˢ Adm[inistrator]ˢ further Covenant Promise and Engage that he will warrant Secure and defend them from the Lawfull Claim of any Person or Persons whatsoever unto him the said Daniel WELLS his heirs and Assigns forever by these Presents Provided Nevertheless that if the said William NEWLAND do and shall well and truly from time to time and at all times forever hereafter Save Indemnify'd and keep Harmless the said Daniel WELLS his heirs Executors and Adm[inistrator]ˢ from any Cost damage Suits Trouble or other hurt that Possibly may arise for or by means or Occasion of his Indorsing the Bills aforesaid Then the above Deed and Every thing therein Contained shall be Void and of no Effects or Else shall remain in full force Strength and Vertue in Law In Witness whereof the said William NEWLAND hath to this Present Indenture Sett his hand and Affixed his Seal the day and Year in the first Line above written.

Signed Sealed & Delivered   Jn.º SCOTT   W NEWLAND Surgeon (seal)
In the presence of us   Jnº SHELDON"

*followed on folio 447 by acknowledgment of Justice of the Peace John SCOTT, receipt of consideration by Daniel WELLS on 28 March 1752, and recordation by court clerk Henry JOHNSON on 16 April 1752.[44]

Liber B, folios 453-454; 03 April 1752

"Know all men by these presents that I Samuel HOPKINS of Worcester County in the Province of Maryland Marchant doe hereby Acknowledge to have received of William BRITTINGHAM of said County the full and Just Sum of thirty two Pounds ten Shillings Current money of Virginia for and in Consideration of one Negro Woman Named **Silva** Bought of me the said Samuel by the said William and I the said Samuel doe hereby Warrant and defend the said Negro Woman from all Person or Persons whatsoever Claiming any right to her and att all times hereafter shall at the Cost and Charge of the said William BRITTINGHAM his heirs or assigns Grant any further assurance or assurance that the said William shall any time hereafter shall Require In Witness whereof I have hereunto Sett my hand this third day of April 1752~

Test. Alex[ander] BUNCLE   Sam[uel] HOPKINS
    Henry TURNER"

*followed on folio 454 with the recordation by court clerk Henry JOHNSON on 21 April 1752.[45]

Liber B, folios 454-455; 05 May 1752

"Know all men by these Presents that I Robert PITTS of Worcester County in the Province of Maryland for and in Consideration of the Sum of thirty Pounds Current money of Maryland to me in hand Paid by Samuel ATKINSON of the same Place before the Sealing and delivery hereof have Sold and delivered unto the said Samuel ATKINSON one Negro boy named **Peter** about Eleven Years Old To have And To hold the said Negro Boy unto the said Samuel ATKINSON his heirs and Assigns and I the said Robert PITTS my heirs Executors and Adm[inistrator]ˢ the said Negro Boy to the said Samuel ATKINSON his heirs or Assigns against all People shall and will for ever warrant and by these Presents defend Provided always and is Nevertheless Agreed by the abovesaid Parties that if the said Robert PITTS his heirs

---

[44] Worcester County Court (Land Records). Deed of mortgage from NEWLAND, William to WELLS, David. 28 March 1752. B, pp. 446-447, MSA CE 30-2. www.mdlandrec.net : accessed 23 September 2021.
[45] Worcester County Court (Land Records). Bill of sale from HOPKINS, Samuel to BRITTINGHAM, William. 03 April 1752. B, pp. 453-454, MSA CE 30-2. www.mdlandrec.net : accessed 23 September 2021.

Exe[cutor]ˢ or Adm[inistrator]ˢ shall well and truely Pay or Cause to be Paid unto the said Samuel ATKINSON his heirs or Assigns the full and Just Sum of thirty Pounds Current money of Maryland at or before the first day of May next Ensueing the date of this Presents that then the above Bill of Sale for the said Negro Boy shall be Void and of none Effect Else to Stand and remain in full force Power and Vertue In Witness whereof I the said Robert PITTS do hereunto set my hand and fix my Seal this fifth day of May Anno Dom[ini] One thousand Seven hundred and fifty two

Signed Sealed and Delivered	William NILSON	Robert PITTS (seal)
In the Presence of	Samuel NILSON"	

*followed on folio 455 by the acknowledgment by Justice of the Peace John SCARBOROUGH on 08 May 1752 and the recordation by court clerk Henry JOHNSON on 12 May 1752.[46]

Liber B, folios 469-471; 06 June 1752

"Know all men by these Presents that I Joshua MORSS of Worcester County in the Province of Maryland Shipwright for and in Consideration that Edward FRANKLYN and John POPE both of the County af[oresai]ᵈ Gent[leman] hath this day at the Especial instance and Request of me the said Joshua MORSS Superseaded a Certain Judgment Recovered against me for twenty Seven Pounds Twelve Shillings and two Pence Current money of Maryland & five hundred four and a half Pounds of Tobacco Payable to Colo[nel] Sam[uel] HOPKINS of the County af[oresai]ᵈ the Performance of which I do Acknowledge and myself therewith fully Satisfied and Contented by these Presents for myself my heirs Ex[ecutor]ˢ and Adm[inistrator]ˢ have Bargained Sold Sett over and delivered unto them the said Edward FRANKLYN and John POPE and their Heirs and assigns forever one Negro Woman Called **Dinah** and negro man child of about Seven Weeks old Named **will** now in the Possession of me the said Joshua MORSS and so to remain at the risque of me the said Joshua MORSS my heirs Executors and Adm[inistrator]ˢ untill the Tenth day of February next To have and to Hold the said two negroes aforementioned to them the said Edward FRANKLYN and John POPE their heirs and Assigns forever to the only Proper use benefit and behoofs of them the said Edward FRANKLYN and John POPE their heirs and Assigns forever and I the said Joshua MORSS for myself my heirs Ex[ecutor]ˢ and Adm[inistrator]ˢ do further Covenant to with the said Edward FRANKLYN and John POPE their heirs and Assigns the said two Negroes forever hereafter to Warrant Secure and Defend from all manner of Persons whatsoever Provided Nevertheless that it is the true Intent and meaning of these Present that if I the said Joshua MORSS my heirs Executors and Administrators do and shall well and truly Pay or Cause to be Paid unto them the said Edward FRANKLYN and John POPE their heirs Ex[ecutor]ˢ & Adm[inistrator]ˢ or to Colo[nel] Samuel HOPKINS the af[oresai]ᵈ Sum of Twenty Seven Pounds Twelve Shillings and two Pence Current money of Maryland and five hundred four and a half Pounds of Tobacco together with all the cost that may Accrew by means of the said Superseading or Otherwise from time to time and at all times forever hereafter save and keep Harmless the said Edward FRANKLYN and John POPE their heirs Exec[utor]ˢ and Adm[inistrator]ˢ from all Cost damage Trouble or Charge of any Nature or kind whatsoever that may happen be grow or arise to upon and Against them or any of them their heirs Execu[tor]ˢ Adm[inistrator]ˢ or Either of them by means or Reason of the Superseading as af[oresai]ᵈ then this Present Deed or Instrument of writing shall be Void and of none Effect or Else shall Stand be and Remain in full force Strength and Vertue in Law In Witness whereof I have hereto Sett my hand and Affixed my Seal this 6ᵗʰ day of June Anno Dom[ini] 1752

Signed Sealed & Delivered	John HENRY.	Joshua MORSS (seal)
In Presence off	Benj[amin] HANDY"	

---

[46] Worcester County Court (Land Records). Bill of sale from PITTS, Robert to ATKINSON, Samuel. 05 May 1752. B, pp. 454-455, MSA CE 30-2. www.mdlandrec.net : accessed 23 September 2021.

*followed with the acknowledgment by Justice of the Peace John HENRY on folio 470 and recordation by court clerk Henry JOHNSON on folio 471.[47]

Liber B, folios 489-490; 13 August 1752

"Know all men by these Presents that I William NEWLAND of Worcester County in the Province of Maryland Chirurgeon do give Grant Bargain Sell make Over and Convey and hath by these Presents for myself my heirs Executors and Administrators Given Granted Bargained Sold made Over and Conveyed unto Thomas JONES of Worcester County in the Province aforesaid his heirs and Assigns forever Two Negroes to wit One Negro Boy Called **Southy** of about four years old and Another Negro Boy Called **Standbridge** of about Two years old To have and To hold the said Two Negroes to him the said Thomas JONES his heirs and Assigns forever which said Two Negroes (being now in the Possession of the said William NEWLAND I do for my Self my heirs Executors and Administrators further Covenant Promise and Engage that I will warrant Secure and Defend them from the Lawfull Claim of any Person or Persons whatsoever unto him the said Thomas JONES his heirs and Assigns forever by these Presents The Consideration of the above Bill of Sale being the Sum of thirty Pounds Sterling money of Great Brittain to me already Paid by the said Thomas JONES the Receipt whereof I do hereby for myself my heirs Executors and Administrators Acknowledge Acquitt and discharge the said Thomas JONES his heirs and Assigns for ever from In Confirmation hereof the said William NEWLAND to this Present Bill of Sale have Sett my hand and Affixed my Seal this thirteenth day of August Anno Dom[ini] 1752.
Signed Sealed & Delivered   W[illia]m SCOTT   W[illia]m NEWLAND (seal)
In Presence of us ….   Cha. BALLARD Jr."

*followed on folio 490 by acknowledgment of Justice of the Peace John SCOTT on 13 August 1752 and recordation by court clerk Henry JOHNSON on 19 August 1752.[48]

Liber B, folios 503-505; 18 September 1752

"This Indenture made the Eighteenth day of September in the year of our Lord God one thousand Seven hundred fifty and two Between Benjamin HENDERSON of Worcester County in the Province of Maryland Planter of the one Part and Robert KING of Somersett County in the Province af[oresai]d Esq[uire] of the Other Part Whereas the said Benjamin HENDERSON by his Deed Indented bearing date the Nineteenth day of March in the Year of our Lord God Seventeen hundred and forty Nine for the Consideration of Eighty two Pounds and Ten Shillings Current whole Gold of the said Province of Maryland to him Paid By the Said Robert KING did Grant Bargain and Sell Alien Release & Confirm unto the said Robert KING his heirs and Assigns forever all that tract or Parcel of Land Called Hap Hazzard Scituate Lying and Being formerly in Somerset County but now in the County of Worcester about on the South side of Pocomoke River about two miles from the Same Containing and Laid out for Seventy Acres of Land more or less" … "and the said Benjamin HENDERSON for the Consideration af[oresai]d by the Same Deed above mentioned did Grant Bargain and Sell Assign & Transferr unto the aforesaid Robert KING his Executors Adm[inistrator]s and Assigns forever five Negro Slaves to wit one Negro man names **Harry** then about the Age of Sixteen years two Negro Women the one named **Eve** then about the Age of forty Years the Other Named **Abbow** then about the Age of thirty Six years two Negro Girls the one named **Barsheba** then about the Age of one and a half years the Other named **Pleasant** then about the Age of one year one Black Coloured Gelding then about the age of thirteen years two Stears One then about three the other about four years Old one a dark Brown the other a Black one and three Cows all which Cattle are Marked with a Crop in Both Ears and under Bit in Both then in the Possession of the said Benjamin HENDERSON" … "And Whereas the af[oresai]d time of Payment is Long since Elapsed and no part of the Principal money Interest or Costs and Expences af[oresai]d Paid and

---

[47] Worcester County Court (Land Records). Deed from MORSS, Joshua to FRANKLIN, Edward and POPE, John. 06 June 1752. B, pp. 469-471, MSA CE 30-2. www.mdlandrec.net : accessed 23 September 2021.

[48] Worcester County Court (Land Records). Bill of sale from NEWLAND, William to JONES, Thomas. 13 August 1752. B, pp. 489-490, MSA CE 30-2. www.mdlandrec.net : accessed 23 September 2021.

there being now due unto the said Robert KING from the said Benjamin HENDERSON the sum of Eighteen Ounces in Current whole Gold of the Value on Ninty Nine Pounds Current whole Gold of the Province af[oresai]^d upon the said Mortgage and to the End that the said Benjamin HENDERSON may be Excluded from his Equity of Redemption of and in the said Lands and Chattles and the said Deed become Absolute Now this Indenture Witnesseth that the said Benjamin HENDERSON for and Consideration of the af[oresai]^d Eighteen Ounces in Current whole Gold of the Value af[oresai]^d from him the said Benjamin HENDERSON due Owing and unpaid unto the said Robert KING he the said Benjamin HENDERSON Hath Granted Remised Released and forever Quit Claimed and by these Presents doth Remiss Release and forever Quit Claim unto the said Robert KING his heirs and Assigns forever all the above mentioned Lands with their and Every of their Appurtenances and unto the said Robert KING his Executors Adm[inistrator]^s and Assigns all and Singular the Personall Chattles above mentioned" … "and to the same Premises shall and will forever hereafter be Excluded and Debarred by these Presents. In Witness whereof the Partys af[oresai]^d to this Indenture Interchangeably their hand have Set and Seals Affixed the day and year first above written.

Signed Sealed & Delivered　　Levin WILSON
In Presence of us　　　　　　　　　　　　　　　　Benjamin B HENDERSON (seal)
　　　　　　　　　　　　　Archibald A WHITE
　　　　　　　　　　　　　　　　mark"

*followed on folio 505 with the acknowledgment of Justice of the Peace Robert Jenckins HENRY on 18 September 1752 and recordation by court clerk Henry JOHNSON on 29 September 1752.[49]

*Due to its true length, this transcription has been shortened to its most relevant portions. The full original deed can be viewed at the citation provided.

Liber B, folios 506-508; 18 September 1752

"This Indenture made the Eighteenth day of September in the year of our Lord God One thousand Seven hundred fifty and two Between William GILLET of Worcester County in the Province of Maryland Planter of the One Part and Robert KING of Somerset County in the Province af[oresai]^d Esquire of the Other Part Whereas the said William GILLET by his Deed Indented bearing date the Nineteenth day of March in the year of our Lord God Seventeen hundred forty and nine for the Consideration of Sixty Pounds & Ten Shillings Current whole Gold of the said Province of Maryland to him Paid by the said Robert KING did Grant Bargain and Sell Alien Release and Confirm unto the said Robert KING and his heirs and Assigns forever two Tracts or Parcels of Land Scituate Lying and Being on the South or South:East Side of Pocomoke River in the said County or Worcester the one called Hogquarter Containing one hundred Acres of Land more or Less the Other Called Kings Land that is to Say so much of the said Last mentioned tract as was Devised to the af[oresai]^d William GILLET by his Late father Samuel GILLET deceased Containing by Estimation one hundred and forty five Acres of Land" … "And the same William GILLET for the Consideration aforesaid by the Same Deed abovementioned did Grant Bargain and Sell Assign and Transferr unto the af[oresai]^d Robert KING his Executors Adm[inistrator]^s and Assigns forever one Negro Boy named **Adam** about the Age of Eleven Years, Black Coloured Gelding then about the age of five years one Baron Cow of a Brindle Colour one Cow and yearling of a Red Colour and one then four years old Heiffer big with Calf all the said Cattle marked with a Slitt and underbitt in the Right Ear and a Crop in the left the said Gelding then at one Joshua CHAPMANs and the other Chattles then in the Possession of the said William GILLET To hold the af[oresai]^d Negro Gelding and Cattle unto the only Proper use and Benefit of the af[oresai]^d Robert KING" … "And Whereas the aforesaid time of Payment is Long Since Elapsed and no part of the Principal money Interest or Costs and Expences af[oresai]^d paid and there being now due unto the said Robert KING from the said William GILLET the Sum of thirteen Ounces five pennyweights two grains in Current

---

[49] Worcester County Court (Land Records). Deed from HENDERSON, Benjamin to KING, Robert. 18 September 1752. B, pp. 503-505, MSA CE 30-2. www.mdlandrec.net : accessed 24 September 2021.

whole Gold of the Value of Seventy two pounds Seventeen Shillings and Eleven Pence half Penny Current whole Gold of the Province af[oresai]^d upon the said Mortgage and to the End that the said William GILLET may be Excluded from his Equity of Redemption of and in the said Lands and Chattles and the said Deed become Absolute Now this Indenture Witnesseth that the said William GILLET for and in Consideration of the af[oresai]^d thirteen ounces five pennyweights and two Grains in Current whole Gold af[oresai]^d of the Value af[oresai]^d from him to said William GILLET due Owing and unpaid unto the Robert KING he the said William GILLET Hath Granted Remised Released and for Ever Quit Claimed and by these Presents doth remise release and forever Quit Claim unto the said Robert KING his heirs and Assigns forever All the above mentioned Lands with their and Every of their Appurtenances and unto the said Robert KING his Executors Adm[inistrator]^s and Assigns all and Singular the Personall Chattles abovementioned" … "and to the same Premisses shall and will forever hereafter be Excluded and Debarred by these Presents, In Witness whereof the Partys af[oresai]^d to this Indenture Interchangeably their hands have Set and Seals Affixed the day and year first above written.

Signed Sealed & Delivered   Levin WILSON.

In Presence of   his   William GILLETT (Seal)

Archibald A WHITE
mark"

*followed on folio 508 with the acknowledgment of Justice of the Peace Robert Jenckins HENRY on 18 September 1752 and recordation by court clerk Henry JOHNSON on 29 September 1752.[50]

*Due to its true length, this transcription has been shortened to its most relevant portions. The full original deed can be viewed at the citation provided.

Liber B, folios 573-574; 13 February 1753

"This Indenture written this thirteenth day of February One thousand Seven hundred and three Between Joseph HOUSTON Sen[io]^r of the one Part and Comfort CHAILLE of the Other Part Witnesseth that whereas the af[oresai]^d Joseph haith Covenanted and Agreed with his said Daughter Comfort CHAILLE to give unto her and the heirs of her Body two Negros and Sundry other Good Vizt. The Negros **Daul** and **Amey** one Strung Dusk that I bought of M^r. Thomas HANDY one Bed and furniture one Small Painted Trunk one young Gray Mare named Janey of five years old all which Goods I the said Joseph HOUSTON Sen[io]^r do by these Presents Give unto my said Daughter Comfort CHAILLE and her heirs upon the Consideration of five Shillings To me paid but more Especially for the Love and Respect that I the said Joseph Beareth unto my said Daughter Comfort CHAILLE. In Witness whereof I have hereunto Sett my hand and fixed my Seal this day and year above written ~

Signed Sealed & Delivered   Benj^a[min] HANDY   his

In Precence off   John HANDY   Joseph ɟ HOUSTON (Seal)

m   mark"

*followed on folio 574 with acknowledgment of Justice of the Peace Benjamin HANDY and recordation by court clerk Henry JOHNSON.[51]

Liber C, folios 64-65; 21 September 1753

"To all Christian people to whom these presents shall Come I Sarah MAXFIELD of Worcester County in the Province aforesaid Send Greeting Know Yee that I Sarah MAXFIELD for and in Consideration of the of the Paternal Love goodwill and Affection which I have and do bear unto my Loving Children Vizt. Stephen MAXFIELD of Susannah MAXFIELD of the County and Province aforesaid have given and Granted and by presents do fuly freely Clearly and Absolutely Give & Grant unto the said Steven and Susanah MAXFIELD and their heirs forever

---

[50] Worcester County Court (Land Records). Deed from GILLETT, William to KING, Robert. 18 September 1752. B, pp. 506-508, MSA CE 30-2. www.mdlandrec.net : accessed 24 September 2021.

[51] Worcester County Court (Land Records). Deed from HOUSTON, Joseph Sr. to CHAILLE, Comfort. 13 February 1753. B, pp. 573-574, MSA CE 30-2. www.mdlandrec.net : accessed 24 September 2021.

the Negros following Vizt. **Nan & Leah** with their Increase & all my Right of my of my deceast Daghter Easten's Estate Exclusive of one feather Bed to be Possest and Enjoyed by the said Steven and Susanah at my decease together with all the Right Title Interest Clame & demand whatsoever which I now have or which any or Either of my heirs Executors or Adm[inistrator]s may hereafter have of to or in the said Granted Premises with their Increase To have and To hold the said Negroes to wit **Nan and Leah** with all my Right of my af[oresai]d deceast Daghter Estate with their Increase as afores[ai]d unto them the said Stephen and Susannah MAXFIELD and their heirs to be Equally devided when they shall Come to full Age to Receive the same by Law forever absolutely without any manner of Conditions I the said Sarah MAXFIELD have fully freely and Absolutely and of my Own Accord have given and Granted the afores[ai]d Premisses In Witness whereof I have hereunto Sett my hand and seal this 21st day of Septemb[e]r Anno Dom[ini] 1753
J SCARBOROUGH   Ep[hraim] Waggaman   Sarah MAXFIELD (Seal)"

*followed on folio 65 with acknowledgment by Justice of the Peace J. SCARBOROUGH on 21 September 1753 and recordation by court clerk Henry JOHNSON on 28 September 1753.[52]

Liber C, folios 71-72; 07 November 1753

"This Indenture made this Seventh day of November in the year of our Lord one thousand Seven hundred and fifty Three, Between Robert PITTS of the County of Worcester of the one part Cooper, and Nathaniel WHITAKER of Somerset County Cl[er]k Witnesseth that the same Robert PITTS for and in Consideration of the Sum of one hundred and fifty Pounds Currant Money of Maryland to him in hand paid by the said Nathaniel WHITAKER the Receipt whereof is hereby Acknowledged Hath Granted Released and for Ever quit Claimed and by these Presents doth for himself his heirs Ex[ecutor]s and Adm[inistrator]s Release Grant and Convey unto the same Nathaniel WHITAKER his heirs and assigns the Equity and Right of Redemption of in and to a certain Tract of Land Called Adventure Scituate on the south side of Pocomoke River Containing one hundred Acres, it being Part of a Tract Granted to a certain Thomas DAVIS which said one hundred Acres by sundry Conveyances and Disents Came to the af[oresai]d Robert PITTS also the right and Equity of Redemption of in & to a Certain Negro male Slave Called **Boatswain** To have and to Hold the af[oresai]d one hundred Acres of Land and Negro with all and Singular the profits and Appurtenances to the same Land Belonging or in any wise appertaining free and Clear of and from the Claim of him the same Robert PITTS or any person Claiming or to Claim by from or under him the same Robert or his heirs, unto the same Nathaniel WHITAKER his heirs and assigns for Ever And the Said Robert PITTS Doth Covenant for himself his heirs & to and with the said Nathaniel his heirs & Assigns that he the said Nathaniel his heirs & Assigns shall and may hold Occupy Possess and Enjoy the Land af[ore]s[ai]d and the Negro afo[resai]d freely and Clearly against the Claim of him the Same Robert his heirs & and all Persons Claiming under him. In Testimony whereof the said Robert PITTS hath hereunto Set his hand & Seal the Day and Year above mentioned
Sealed & Delivered   Robert PITTS (Seal)
In presence of
Joshua MORSS.   W[illia]m GRAY~"

*followed on folio 72 with acknowledgment by Justices of the Peace John SCOTT and William DRAPER on 08 November 1753, receipt of alienation fine by Thomas GILLISS on 09 November 1753, and recordation by court clerk on 09 November 1753.[53]

---

[52] Worcester County Court (Land Records). Deed of gift from MAXFIELD, Sarah to MAXFIELD, Stephen and Susannah. 21 September 1753. C, pp. 64-65, MSA CE 30-3. www.mdlandrec.net : accessed 01 October 2021.

[53] Worcester County Court (Land Records). Deed from PITTS, Robert to WHITAKER, Nathaniel. 07 November 1753. C, pp. 71-72, MSA CE 30-3. www.mdlandrec.net : accessed 01 October 2021.

Liber C, folios 125-126; 19 March 1754

"This Indenture Made the Nineteenth day of March in the year of our Lord One thousand Seven hundred fifty and four Between John DAGWORTHY of Worcester County in the Province of Maryland Gent[lema]n of the one Part and William McILVAINE and David McILVAINE of the City of Philadelphia Merchants of the other part Witnesseth that the said John DAGWORTHY for and in Consideration of the Sum of Sixty four Pounds two Shillings and one Penny half penny Current money of Maryland to him in hand Paid by the said William McILVAINE and David McILVAINE the Receipt whereof he doth hereby Confess and Acknowledge and thereof doth Acquit and Discharge the said William McILVAINE and David McILVAINE and their and Each of their heirs Ex[ecutor]s and Adm[inistrator]s for Ever by these Presents Hath Bargained Sold Assigned set over Transfered and Delivered and by these Presents doth Bargain sell Assign set over Transfer and Deliver unto the said William McILVAINE and David McILVAINE and to their Heirs Ex[ecutor]s Adm[inistrator]s & Assigns for Ever One Negro man Slave named **Tony** and one Negro Girl Slave Named **Sarah** To have and to hold the Said Negroes unto the said William McILVAINE and David McILVAINE and to their heirs Ex[ecutor]s Adm[inistrator]s and Assigns for Ever And the said John DAGWORTHY for himself his heirs Ex[ecutor]s and Adm[inistrator]s doth hereby Covenant to and with the said William McILVAINE and David McILVAINE and their Heirs Ex[ecutor]s Adm[inistrator]s and Assigns That he the said John DAGWORTHY and his heirs Ex[ecutor]s & Adm[inistrator]s the af[oresai]d Slaves against him and them and all other Persons Claiming the same unto the said William McILVAINE and David McILVAINE shall and will Warrant and for Ever Defend by these Presents Provided always and it is the true Intent and Meaning of these Presents that if the said John DAGWORTHY and his heirs Ex[ecutor]s and Adm[inistrator]s do and shall well and truely pay unto the said William McILVAINE and David McILVAINE the sum of Sixty four Pounds two Shillings and one Penny half penny Current money of Maryland with the Legal Interest thereon and all the Costs and Expence of Makeing and recording these Presents on or before the Nineteenth day of August Next Ensuing the date thereof then this present Instrument of writing to be null and Void any thing herein the Contrary Notwithstanding, And the af[ore]s[ai]d John DAGWORTHY for himself his heirs Ex[ecutor]s and Adm[inistrator]s doth hereby Covenant to and with the said David McILVAINE and William McILVAINE and their heirs Ex[ecutor]s Adm[inistrator]s and Assigns that he the af[oresai]d John DAGWORTHY will well and truely pay unto the said William and David McILVAINE the af[ore]s[ai]d sum of Sixty four Pounds two Shillings and one penny half penny Current money af[oresai]d with the Legal Interest thereon and all the Costs and Expence of Makeing and recording these Presents on or before the af[oresai]d Nineteenth day of August next Ensueing the Date hereof without fraud or further delay In Witness the Parties to these Presents Interchangeably their hands have Set & Seals have fixed the day and Year first above written./

Signed Sealed & Delivered
In Presence of   John DAGWORTHY (Seal)
Thomas SLOSS, W[illia]m HAYWARD"

*followed on folio 126 with the acknowledgment by Justice of the Peace Robert Jenckins HENRY on 19 March 1755 and recordation by court clerk Henry JOHNSON on 20 March 1755.[54]

Liber C, folios 145-147; 17 May 1754

"Worcester to wit Know all Men by these Presents that I Joshua MORSS of Worcester County in the Province of Maryland Shipwright for diverse good Causes and valuable Considerations me hereunto moveing but more especially for and in Consideration that Nathaniel RAMSEY of Worcester County and Province afores[ai]d Merchant of his being bound for me in Sundry Sums of money to Sundry Persons before the Ensealing & Delivery hereof truely and firmly

---

[54] Worcester County Court (Land Records). Deed of mortgage from DAGWORTHY, John to MCILVAINE, William and David. 19 March 1754. C, pp. 125-126, MSA CE 30-3. www.mdlandrec.net : accessed 02 October 2021.

bound in and for the said Sums of money whereof I do acknowledge myself therewith fully Satisfyed and Contented have granted bargained Sold and Delivered, and by these Presents for myself my heirs Executors & Administrators, do fully freely and absolutely grant bargain Sell and deliver unto the said Nathaniel RAMSEY his heirs and Assigns for ever one Negro Wench named **Dinah**, one Negro Boy named **Mingo** and one other Negro Boy named **Will** which said Negroes is now in my Possession in the County af[ore]s[ai]^d To have and to hold the said Negroes to him the said Nathaniel RAMSEY his Heirs and Assigns forever, to his and their only proper Use forever; and I the said Joshua MORSS for myself my heirs Executors and Administrators do Covenant and Agree to Warrant & Defend the said Negroes unto him the said Nathaniel RAMSEY his heirs Assigns forever against the lawfully Claim or Demand of any or all Persons whatsoever, Provided Nevertheless that if the said Joshua MORSS do well and truly and faithfully save harmless and keep Indemnifyed the said Nathaniel RAMSEY him his heirs Ex[ecutor]^s and Adm[inistrator]^s from the af[ore]s[ai]^d Sums of money which the Nathaniel RAMSEY is bound for him the said Joshua MORSS, then this Present Instrument of writing is to be Void & of no Effect otherwise to Remain in full power strength and Virtue in Law, In Witness whereof I have here to sett my hand & Seal this 17th day of May anno Dom[ini] 1754~

Sealed & Delivered
In Presence of ....   Joshua MORSS ./~ (Seal)
Adam SPENCE   W[illia]^m GRAY~"

*followed on folio 147 with the acknowledgment by Justice of the Peace Adam SPENCE and recordation by court clerk Henry JOHNSON on 17 May 1754.[55]

Liber C, folios 170-171; 22 June 1754

"Know all Men by these Presents that I Wheaty DENNIS of Worcester County in the Province of Maryland Planter for and in Consideration of the Sum of One hundred and fifty pounds current money of Maryland by Matthew OUTTEN of the County and Province af[ore]s[ai]^d well and truly paid unto M^r. Nathaniel HOUGH for my redemption out of Goal as Security on my releasment, I have bargained sold assigned, set over and delivered any by these Presents for the Consideration af[ore]s[ai]d do bargain sell assign, set over and deliver unto the said Matthew OUTTEN and to his Heirs and Assigns, One Negro Woman called **Flowra** and one desk, ten head of Cattle and one Mare and thirty Head of Hoggs, and two Beds and furniture, To have and to hold the aforesaid several things abovementioned unto the said Matthew OUTTEN and his Heirs and Assigns forever, and I the said Wheatly DENNIS do hereby Engage to Warrant Secure and Defend the same from the Claim of any Person whatsoever unto the said Matthew OUTTEN his Heirs and Assigns forever, provided Nevertheless and it is the true Intent and meaning of this Present Bill of Sale that if the said Matthew OUTTEN be intirely saved and kept harmless from all Cost and Charge or other Trouble that hath may or shall become chargeable to the said Matthew OUTTEN by means of his Suretyship or Releasment of me from the Goal af[ore]s[ai]^d then the above Bill of Sale shall be Void and of no Effect or else shall be and Remain in full force strength and Virtue in Law, In Witness whereof I have hereunto set my hand and Seal this twenty second Day of June Anno Dom[ini] One thousand seven hundred fifty and four.~

Sealed & Delivered   Wheatly DENNIS (Seal)
In Presence of us ...
Sam[ue]^l TAYLOR./~   Ebenezer EVANS./~"

*followed on folio 171 with the acknowledgment by Justice of the Peace John EVANS on 22 June 1754 and recordation by court clerk Henry JOHNSON on 03 July 1754.[56]
* "Goal" is a misspelling of Gaol, meaning jail.

---

[55] Worcester County Court (Land Records). Bill of sale from MORSS, Joshua to RAMSEY, Nathaniel. 17 May 1754. C, pp. 145-147, MSA CE 30-3. www.mdlandrec.net : accessed 02 October 2021.

[56] Worcester County Court (Land Records). Bill of sale from DENNIS, Wheatly to OUTTEN, Matthew. 22 June 1754. C, pp. 170-171, MSA CE 30-3. www.mdlandrec.net : accessed 02 October 2021.

Liber C, folios 232-234; 31 January 1748/49

"Maryland Ss Know all men by these presents that I Mary SELBY Widow of Capt Parker SELBY late of Worcester County in the Province aforesaid am held and firmly bound unto my Son John SELBY in the same place Planter in the full and Just Sum of three hundred pounds Sterline money of Great Brittain to the which payment well and Truly to be made and done unto the said John SELBY his Certain Attorney heirs Executors Administrators or Assigns I doe hereby bind and Oblige my self my heirs Ex[ecutor]^s or any Claiming from or under me In Witness whereof I have hereunto Sett my hand and Seal the thirty one day of January 1748~ The Condition of the above Obligation is such that if the above Bound Mary SELBY or any Claiming from or under her shall give up relinquish and forever Quit Claim all her Right Title and Interest of Right of Dower that she hath or may Lawfully Clame by her Intermarriage with the above Capt. Parker SELBY her late husband deceased in and unto the Lands whereon the said John SELBY now Lives Called Bantry Containing by Estimation seven hundred and fifty acres be the same more or less Bequeathed to him the said John SELBY by his fathers Last will and Testament dated the Eight day of November One thousand Seven hundred forty and Six Recourse thereunto being had may more fully Appear To have and To hold the above Right of Dower to him the af[oresai]^d John SELBY his heirs and Assigns forever and to no other use or uses whatsoever and shall at all times hereafter and the Cost and Charge of the above John Give and further writting or deed as his Councill Learned in the Law shall Advise for the more Sure making of the above Relinquishment of my Right of Dower which when Performed according to the true intent and meaning thereof then this obligation to be void and of none Effect otherways to be and remain in full force and vertue in Law

Signed Sealed & Delivered
In the Presence of
George DRUMMOND, Parker SELBY, Job WALTON.~

Mary M SELBY (Seal)
her mark

Maryland Ss Be it Remembred that it is mutually Agrees the within Mary SELBY and John SELBY that in Case the said Mary shall Continue a Widow and not Mary again of if she should become a Widow by the death of any person whom she shall Mary, that the said John Binds and obliges himself that he shall build her a house at the Quarter twenty five feet Long and Eighteen feet wide with one Brick Chimney and Plank floor and until such house be built she shall Live in the Mantion house as she now doth And it is further Mutualy Agreed that dureing her Natural Life shall Quietly & Peaceably Enjoy two thirds of the Clear Ground that is now under fence at the Quarter and theat a Divisional fence shall be run by Consent of both Partys to devid the said Clear Ground Right across the head of said Land with use of the Houses thereon and also what Ground to the Wesward of said Divisional fence as Negro **Abraham** a slave of the said Mary's Can Tend or Clear and to no Other use or uses whatsoever and also to have Liberty of Pastarage for twenty head of Cattle and twenty head of Sheep in any of the Paster Grounds belonging to said Plantation Called Bantry for the true performance of all and Singular the above Resitted Premisses I the above John SELBY do hereby bind and oblige myself my heirs Executors or Administrators firmly by these Presents as witness my hand and Seal the 31st day of January 1748 or 9.~

Signed Sealed & Delivered
In the presence of.
Geo[rge] DRUMMOND, Parker SELBY, Job WALTON.~"

John SELBY (Seal)

*followed on folio 234 with the recordation by court clerk Henry JOHNSON on 09 November 1754.[57]

---

[57] Worcester County Court (Land Records). Deed from SELBY, Mary to SELBY, John. 31 January 1748. C, pp. 232-234, MSA CE 30-3. www.mdlandrec.net : accessed 02 October 2021.

Liber C, folios 260-261; 12 February 1755

"Worcester Ss {?} in the Province of Maryland Know all men by these Presents that I Isaac DECKESON of Worcester County Carpenter for and in Consideration of the Sum of twenty two Pounds ten Shillings and Six Pence Current money to me in hand Paid by Levin DECKESON Miler the Receipt whereof I do hereby Acknowledge and Accquit discharge the said Levin from every Part and Parcell thereof Have Bargained Sold and delivered and by these Presents do Bargain Sell and deliver unto the said Levin a Certain Negro Boy called **Harry** Aged about Sixteen Years old to him and his heirs and Assigns forever And the said Isaac for himself his heirs Executors Administrators doth Covenant to and with the said Levin DECKESON that he hath full Power and Lawfull Authority{?} and dispose of the said Negro Boy and doth by these Presents Warrant and defend the said Boy from any Person or Persons whatsoever Claiming any Right Title or interest from by or under him or from any other Person or Persons whatsoever in Testimony whereof the said Isaac DECKESON hath hereunto Sett his hand and Seal this 12th February 1755~

Test. Caleb MILBOURN   Isaac DICKESON (Seal)
      Thomas MILBOURN"

*followed on folio 261 with the recordation by court clerk Henry JOHNSON on 13 February 1755.[58]

Liber C, folios 301-302; 26 March 1755

"This Indenture made this twenty Sixth day of March in the year of our Lord One thousand Seven hundred Fifty and five Between Charles PARKER of Worcester County in the Province of Maryland Planter of the one Part and Poynter BRITTINGHAM of the Same Place Planter of the other Part Witnesseth that the said Charles PARKER for and in Consideration of the Sum of Forty Six Pounds Ten Shillings Current money of Maryland to him by the said Poynter BRITTINGHAM in hand paid at or before the Sealing and delivery hereof the Receipt whereof the said Charles PARKER doth hereby Confess and Acknowledge and thereof doth Acquit Release and discharge the said Poynter BRITTINGHAM his heirs Executors Adm[inistrator]s and Assigns forever by these Presents Hath Granted Bargained Sold Assigns Setover and transferred and by these Presents Doth Grant Bargain Sell Assign Setover and Transfer unto the said Poynter BRITTINGHAM his heirs and Assigns forever one Negro woman named **Rose** To have and To hold the said Negro woman **Rose** unto the said Poynter BRITTINGHAM his heirs and Assigns forever and to no Other use Intent purpose or Construction whatsoever and the said Charles PARKER for himself his heirs Executors and Admi[inistrator]s doth Covenant Promise Grant and Agree to and with the said Poynter BRITTINGHAM his heirs and Assigns that he the said Charles PARKER the af[oresai]d Negro woman Named **Rose** unto the said Poynter BRITTINGHAM and his heirs against himself the said Charles and his heirs and all other Persons Lawfully Claiming the same shall and will Warrant and forever Defend by these Presents In Testimony whereof the Partys af[oresai]d to these Presents Interchangeably their hands have Set and Seals Affixed the day and year above written~

Sealed & Delivered   Jn:o SCARBOROUGH
In presence of   John EVANS   Charles C PARKER (Seal)
                                                              his mark"

*followed on folio 302 with the acknowledgment by Justices of the Peace John SCARBOROUGH and John EVANS and recordation by court clerk Henry JOHNSON on 26 March 1755.[59]

---

[58] Worcester County Court (Land Records). Bill of sale from DICKESON, Isaac to DICKESON, Levin. 12 February 1755. C, pp. 260-261, MSA CE 30-3. www.mdlandrec.net : accessed 02 October 2021.

[59] Worcester County Court (Land Records). Deed from PARKER, Charles to BRITTINGHAM, Poynter. 26 March 1755. C, pp. 301-302, MSA CE 30-3. www.mdlandrec.net : accessed 03 October 2021.

Liber C, folios 305-307; 01 April 1755

"This Indenture made the first day of April in the year of our Lord God thousand Seven hundred fifty and five Between Sarah HENDERSON or Worcester County in the Province of Maryland of the one part and John HENDERSON son of the aforesaid Sarah of the Same Place of the other Part Witnesseth that the said Sarah HENDERSON for and in Consideration of the Natural Love and Affection which she hath and doth bear to her said Son John HENDERSON and also for and in Consideration of the Sum of five Shillings Current money of Maryland to her in hand paid by the said John HENDERSON before the Sealing and delivery hereof the Receipt whereof she doth hereby Confess and Acknowledge and thereof doth Acquit Exonerate and discharge the said John HENDERSON his Executors Adm[inistrator]s and Assigns forever Hath Given Granted Bargained Sold Assigned Set over and transferred and by these Presents doth give Grant Bargain Sell Assign settover and transferr unto said John HENDERSON his Executors Admi[nistrator]s Assigns forever One Negro Boy named **Adam** One Good feather Bed, Sheet, Blankett and Rugg, one Yoke of Steers, one plough and one Iron Plough Chain To have and To hold the said Negro Boy named **Adam** together with the feather Bed Sheet Blankett and Rugg Yoke of Steers plough and Plough Chain before mentioned unto the said John HENDERSON his heirs and Assigns forever and to no other use Intent Purpose or Construction whatsoever after the death of her the said Sarah she reserving to her self dureing her Natural Life the use of the said Negro named **Adam** and the Bed Sheet Blankett Rugg Yoke of Steers Plough and Ploug Chain before mentioned and the said Sarah HENDERSON doth Covenant Promise Grant and Agree to and with the said John HENDERSON his heirs and assigns that she the Said Negro Boy named **Adam** together with the feather Bed Sheet, Blankett, Rugg, Yoke of Steers Plough and Plough Chain abovementioned against her heirs and all other Persons Lawfully Claiming the Same Shall and will Warrant and forever Defend by the presents. In Testimony whereof the Partys aforesaid to This Indenture Interchangeably their hands have Sett and Seals Affixed the day and year first abovewritten.

Sealed & Delivered   Adam SPENCE.
In Presence off.   Mag:t SPENCE.   Sarah   her X   HENDERSON (Seal)
                                                                 mark"

*followed on folio 307 with the acknowledgment of Adam SPENCE and recordation by court clerk Henry JOHNSON on 01 April 1755.[60]

Liber C, folios 307-308; 01 April 1755

"This Indenture made this first day of April in the year of our Lord God One thousand Seven hundred fifty and five Between Isaac BRITTINGHAM of Worcester County in the province of Maryland of the One Part and Sarah HENDERSON and Mary HENDERSON Grandchildren of the aforesaid Isaac BRITTINGHAM of the Same place of the other Part Witnesseth that the said Isaac BRITTINGHAM for and in Consideration of the Natural Love and Affection which he hath and doth bear to his Grandchildren aforesaid and also for and in Consideration of the Sum of five Shillings Sterling money of Great Brittain to him in hand paid by his said Grandchildren the receipt whereof he doth hereby Confess and Acknowledge and thereof doth Acquit Exonerate and discharge his said Grandchildren and Each of them and Each of their Executors and Adm[inistrator]s Hath Given Granted Bargained Sold Assigned Setover and Transferred and by these Presents doth Give, Grant, Bargain, Sell, Assign, Setover and Transferr unto his said Grandchildren and to their husband Assigns forever one Negro **Florrow**, the said Isaac BRITTINGHAM reserving the use of the said Negro Girl called **Florrow** to himself and wife dureing their Natural Lives or in Case the wife of the said Isaac should Survive him then the use of the said Negro Girl to her dureing her Widowhood and at her death or Intermarriage the use of the said Negro to John HENDERSON and wife dureing their Natural Lives or during the Life time of Either of them and at the death of the said John HENDERSON and Wife the said Negro Girl named **Florrow** and her Increase to be Equally divided between the said Sarah HENDERSON and Mary HENDERSON their heirs and Assigns forever To have

---

[60] Worcester County Court (Land Records). Deed from HENDERSON, Sarah to HENDERSON, John. 01 April 1755. C, pp. 305-307, MSA CE 30-3. www.mdlandrec.net : accessed 03 October 2021.

and To hold the said Negro Girl **Florrow** and her Increase after the deaths before mentioned to the said Sarah HENDERSON and Mary HENDERSON their heirs and Assigns as before mentioned and no other use or uses whatsoever then what is in this Indenture before {?}ed In Witness whereof the Partys af[oresai]^d have hereunto Set their hands and Seals Affixed the day and year first above written~.

Sealed and Delivered   Adam SPENCE   Isaac BRITTINGHAM (Seal)
In presence off   Magt SPENCE"

*followed on folio 308 with the acknowledgment by Justice of the Peace Adam SPENCE on 01 April 1755 and recordation by court clerk Henry JOHNSON on 04 April 1755.[61]

Liber C, folios 365-368; 15 July 1755

"This Indenture made the fifteenth day of July in the year of our Lord God One thousand Seven hundred fifty and five. Between John DENNIS of Worcester County in the Province of Maryland Gentleman of the one part; And the Honourable William NELSON of York Town in the Colony of Virginia Esquire of the other part; Witnesseth that the said John DENNIS for and in Consideration of the Sum of Four hundred and fifteen Pounds and fifteen Shillings Current money of the said Colony of Virginia to him in hand paid by the said William NELSON at or before the Sealing and delivery of these Presents the Receipt whereof the said John DENNIS doth hereby Confess and Acknowledge and thereof doth Acquit Release and discharge the said William NELSON his heirs Executors and Adm[inistrator]^s Hath Bargained and Sold and by these Presents Doth Bargain and Sell unto the said William NELSON his heirs and Assigns forever all that part or Parcel of a Certain Tract of Land Assureance otherwise called Security Originally Granted unto one Robert HOUSTON Scituated Lying and being formerly in Somerset County in the Province of Maryland and now in the County of Worcester on the Eastermost Side of Pocomoke River which lyeth Adjacent and Contiguous to the Present Dwelling Plantation of the said John DENNIS" ... "And the said John DENNIS for and in Consideration of the Sum abovementioned Hath also bargained and sold Assigned and Transferred And by these Presents Doth Bargain and Sell Assign and Transferr unto the said William NELSON his heirs Executors Administrators and Assigns the Severall Negro Slaves following now in the Possession of the said John DENNIS to wit one man Named **Oaford**, three Women Named **Appleby**, **Lucey**, and **Let**, And **Bett**, **Terrey**, **Milley**, **Nan** and **Rachel**, and four Boys Named **Sam**, **Dick**, **Harry**, and **Arnold** any every of them and the Increase / which from any of the said Slaves hereafter may arise To have and To hold the aforesaid Two hundred and fifty Acres of Land by these Presents bargained and Sold or so intended to be with the Rights members and Appurtenances unto the said William NELSON his heirs and Assigns to the only Proper use and Behoof of the said William NELSON and of his heirs and Assigns forever And also To have and To hold the abovementioned Slaves and every of them and the Increase from any of them may Arise unto the Proper use Benefit and Behoof of the said William NELSON his Executors Administrators or Assigns forever" ... "And the said John DENNIS for himself his heirs Executors and Adm[inistrator]^s Doth Covenant Promise Grant and Agree to and with the said William NELSON his heirs & Assigns that he the said John DENNIS and his heirs the aforesaid Two hundred and fifty Acres of Land with the Appurtenances unto the said William NELSON his heirs & Assigns And that he the said John DENNIS his heirs Executors and Administrators the aforesaid Slaves and every of them unto the said William NELSON his Executors Adm[inistrator]^s or Assigns against the Legal Claim of all other Persons whatsoever shall and will Warrant and forever Defend by these Presents" ... "In Witness whereof the Parties af[oresai]^d to this Indenture interchangeably their hands have Sett and Seals Affixed the day and year first above written

Sealed & Delivered   W[illia]^m L MASSEY   J[ohn] DENNIS (Seal)
In Presence of   Augustine MOORE."

---

[61] Worcester County Court (Land Records). Deed from BRITTINGHAM, Isaac to HENDERSON, Sarah and HENDERSON, Mary. 01 April 1755. C, pp. 307-308, MSA CE 30-3. www.mdlandrec.net : accessed 03 October 2021.

*followed on folio 368 with the acknowledgment by Justice of Peace Robert Jenckins HENRY on 15 July 1755, receipt of consideration by John DENNIS Jr. on 15 July 1755, receipt of alienation fine by Thomas GILLISS on 28 July 1755, and recordation by the court clerk Henry JOHNSON on 28 July 1755.[62]

*Due to its true length, this transcription has been shortened to its more relevant portions. The full original deed can be viewed at the citation provided.

Liber C, folios 383-384; 06 August 1755

"This Indenture made this Sixth day of August Anno Dom[ini] One thousand Seven hundred and fifty five Between Paris CHIPMAN and Sarah his wife of the one Part and Sarah CHIPMAN of the other Part Witnesseth that the said Paris for and in Consideration of the Love and Affection which he hath to his af[oresai]d Daughter Sarah as also for and in Consideration of the Sum of Ten Shillings Current money to him in hand Paid by the aforesaid Sarah Daughter of said Paris the receipt whereof the said Paris hereby doth Acknowledge hath given Granted Bargained and Sold and by these Presents doth give Grant Bargain and Sell unto the af[oresai]d Sarah CHIPMAN his Daughter her heirs and Assigns forever one tract of Land called Homstead Containing one hundred Acres being the Land whereon his Mills now Stand fifty Acres called Chancery Adjoyning unto the af[oresai]d tract and fifty Acres called Homstead which said tracts are Bounded and described as in and by the Several Grants thereof is Expressed and mentioned Re{?}rse to the same being had more at Large will Appear and also two Yoke of Oxen and a Cart two feather Beds and furniture and half the Pewter now in my Possession as also one Negro man named **Ben** and one Woman **Phillis** and Six Cows, To have and to hold the af[oresai]d bargained and Granted Premises with the Appurtenances unto the same belonging unto her the said Sarah his Daughter for the uses and purposes hereafter mentioned that is to Say for the use of him the said Paris Chipman during his Natural Life and after his decease to and for the use of the af[oresai]d Sarah wife of the said Paris for and dureing her Life of Widowhood which shall first happen, and then to and for the use of the aforesaid Sarah Daughter of said Paris her heirs and Assigns forever, and for no other use or uses whatsoever In Testimony whereof the Partys afores[ai]d to these Presents their hands have Set and Seals affixed the day and year af[oresai]d

Signed Sealed & Delivered   Jos[hu]a MITCHELL   Peris CHIPMAN (Seal)
In Presence of -   Jos[eph] DIRICKSON"

*followed on folio 384 with acknowledgment by Justices of the Peace Joshua MITCHELL and Joseph DIRICKSON on 06 August 1755 and recordation by court clerk Henry JOHNSON on 07 August 1755.[63]

Liber C, folios 384-385; 23 January 1748/49

"To all Christian People to whom these Presents shall come I Benjamin HANDY of Worcester County and Province of Maryland Gent[lema]n Send Greeting in our Lord God everlasting Know Ye that I the said Benjamin HANDY as well for the Love and Affection that I the said Benjamin HANDY have and doe bear unto my well beloved son John HANDY as also for divers good causes and Considerations me thereunto moving have given granted and Confirmed and by this my Present writing do fully freely and absolutely give Grant and Confirm unto the said John HANDY Two of my Negros to wit the one called **Phillis** with all her Increase the other called **George** a Boy with the remaining Part of my Portion by my first Wife that is to Say that Part that is now in the hands of my mother in Law To have and To hold all and Singular the aforesaid Negros and the Remaining Part of my Portion by my first wife unto the said John HANDY his heirs Executors Administrators and Assigns to his and their own Proper use and Behoofe forever without any manner of Challenge Claim or Demand from me the said

---

[62] Worcester County Court (Land Records). Deed from DENNIS, John to NELSON, William. 15 July 1755. C, pp. 365-368, MSA CE 30-3. www.mdlandrec.net : accessed 03 October 2021.
[63] Worcester County Court (Land Records). Deed from CHIPMAN, Peris and Sarah to CHIPMAN, Sarah. 06 August 1755. C, pp. 383-384, MSA CE 30-3. www.mdlandrec.net : accessed 03 October 2021.

Benjamin HANDY or from any other Person or Persons whatsoever for me or Authorized or Powered by me without any money or other thing to be Yielded therefore unto me the said Benjamin HANDY my heirs Executors or Administrators and I the said Benjamin all and Singular the Negros and the remaining Part of my portion by my first wife unto the said John HANDY his heirs Executors Adm[inistrator]s and Assigns against all People shall and will Warrant and for ever defend by these Presents And further Know Ye that I the said Benjamin HANDY have put the said John HANDY in Possession of all and Singular the Negros and the remaining part of my portion by my first wife aforesaid by the delivery of the Sum of five Shillings Current money unto the said Benjamin HANDY In Witness whereof I have hereunto put my hand and Affixed my seale This twenty third day of January Anno Dom[ini] 1748/49.

Signed Sealed & Delivered   Walter RENCH.   Benj[a][min] HANDY (Seal)
In Presence of   John HANDY."

*followed on folio 385 with the recordation by court clerk Henry JOHNSON on 20 August 1755.[64]

Liber C, folios 416-418; 12 August 1755

"This Indenture made the Twelfth day of August in the year of our Lord God One thousand Seven hundred fifty and five Between Robert NAIRNE of Worcester County in the Province of Maryland Planter of the one Part, And John NAIRNE of Somerset County Eldest son of the said Robert of the other part Witnesseth that the said Robert NAIRNE for and in Consideration of the Natural love and Affection which the said Robert hath and doth bear unto the said John his son and also for and in Consideration of the Sum of one Shilling current money of the said Province of Maryland by the said John unto the said Robert in hand paid at or before the Sealing and delivery of these presents the receipt whereof the said Robert doth hereby confess and Acknowledge Hath Given bargained and Sold Assigned and Transferred and Set over and by these Presents Doth give Bargain and Sell Assign Transferr and Set over unto the said John NAIRNE and his Assigns Three Negro man Slaves now in the Possession of the said Robert and John or one of them, one named **Glasgow** one other named **Jacob** and one other named **Harry** To have and To hold the aforesaid Slaves and every of them with all Benefits Profitts and Advantages to the Same belonging or in any manner Appertaining unto the said John NAIRNE his Executors Adm[inistrator]s and Assigns to his and their proper use only and the said Robert NAIRNE for himself his Executors and Adm[inistrator]s doth Covenant Promise and Agree to and with the said John NAIRNE his Executors Adm[inistrator]s and Assigns that he and they the three Negros above named against him and themselves and all other persons legally Claiming or who hereafter Lawfully may claim the same Negroes or any of them unto the said John NAIRNE his Ex[ecutor]s Adm[inistrator]s or Assigns shall and will Warrant and forever Defend by these Presents And the Said John NAIRNE for himself his heirs Executors Adm[inistrator]s and Assigns doth Covenant Promise and Agree that the said Robert NAIRNE his father may Possess and Enjoy the Occupation Direction use and labour of the aforesaid three Negroes and every of them unto the proper Benefitt and Advantage of him the said Robert for and dureing the Term of his Natural Life without any Let hindrance interruption molestation disturbance or denyal of him the said John his Executors Adm[inistrator]s or Assigns or of any other Person by his Consent permission or procurement whatsoever In Witness whereof the Partys aforesaid to this Indenture Interchangeably their hands have set and Seals Affixed the day and year first above written.

Sealed & Delivered   James GUNBY   Rob[er]t NAIRNE (Seal)
In Presence of   Benj[amin] LANKFORD.   John NAIRNE (Seal)"

---

[64] Worcester County Court (Land Records). Deed from HANDY, Benjamin to HANDY, John. 23 January 1748/49. C, pp. 384-385, MSA CE 30-3. www.mdlandrec.net : accessed 03 October 2021.

*followed on folio 418 with acknowledgment of Justice of the Peace Robert Jenckins HENRY on 12 August 1755 and recordation by court clerk Henry JOHNSON on 05 September 1755.[65]

Liber D, folio 46; 17 May 1756

"To all People to whom these presents shall come, I Elizabeth TRUIT of Worcester County in the Province of Maryland do Send Greeting, Know ye that I the said Elizabeth TRUIT for and in Consideration of the Love and good Will and Affection which I have and do bear towards my two daughters, Viz, Mary SELBY Wife of Micajah SELBY and Tabitha TRUIT both of Worcester County in the Province aforesaid have given, and granted and by these Presents do freely give & grant unto the said Mary SELBY and Tabitha TRUIT their Heirs, Ex[ecutor]^s Adm[inistrator]^s or Assigns all my whole Right Title and Interest that I have to my Negro Woman called **Lidia** and all her Increase, To have and to hold the said Negroes to them the said Mary SELBY and Tabitha TRUIT their Heirs, Ex[ecutor]^s, Adm[inistrator]^s or Assigns as their proper Right without any Manner of Condition In Witness whereof I have hereunto Set my Hand and Seal this Seventh Day of May Anno Domini One thousand Seven hundred fifty and six.~

Signed, Sealed and delivered   J. SCARBOROUGH   her
In the Presence of …   John EVANS .. ~   Elizabeth E ✝ TRUIT. (Seal)
                                                                                                                 mark"

*followed with the acknowledgment by Justices of the Peace John SCARBOROUGH and John EVANS and recordation by court clerk Henry JOHNSON[66]

Liber D, folio 77; 04 August 1756

"Know all Men by these Presents that I Henry SATCHELL of Worcester County in the Province of Maryland, for and in Consideration of Ten pounds sixteen shillings Current money of Maryland to me in hand Paid by James NOBLE of the same Place, before the Sealing & Delivery hereof wherewith I Confess myself to be fully satisfied Contented & Paid, Have Bargained & Sold and by these Presents do fully clearly and absolutely Bargain and Sell to the said James NOBLE, one Negro Boy named **Joshua** about one year and Nine Months old. To have & to hold the said Negro Boy to the said James NOBLE his Heirs & Assigns forever to his and their own proper Use and Behoof forever, And I the said Henry SATCHELL my Heirs Ex[ecutor]^s & Adm[inistrator]^s and every of Us, the said Negro Boy unto the said James NOBLE his Heirs & Assigns against all People shall & will Warrant and forever Defend by these Presents. Provided always that if I the said Henry SATCHELL my Heirs Ex[ecutor]^s or Adm[inistrator]^s or any of Us do well & truly pay or cause to be paid unto the said James NOBLE his Heirs or Assigns the full and just Sum of ten pounds & Sixteen Shillings Current money of Maryland at or before the tenth day of February next ensuing the Date of this Present, with legal Interest for the same that then this Present Bill of Sale of the said Negro Boy shall be utterly Void and of none Effect else to stand and Remain in full force and Virtue in Law. In Witness whereof I the said Henry SATCHELL do hereunto set my hand & Seal this fourth day of August Anno Dom[ini] 1756.~

Sealed & Delivered ~   Samuel NILSON ~   Henry SATCHELL (Seal)
In the presence of ~   William NILSON ~"

*followed with acknowledgment by Justice of the Peace John EVANS and recordation by court clerk Henry JOHNSON[67]

---

[65] Worcester County Court (Land Records). Deed from NAIRNE, Robert to NAIRNE, John. 12 August 1755. C, pp. 416-418, MSA CE 30-3. www.mdlandrec.net : accessed 03 October 2021.

[66] Worcester County Court (Land Records). Bill of sale from TRUIT, Elizabeth to SELBY, Mary and TRUIT, Tabitha. 17 May 1756. D, p. 46, MSA CE 30-4. www.mdlandrec.net : accessed 07 October 2021.

[67] Worcester County Court (Land Records). Bill of sale from SATCHELL, Henry to NOBLE, James. 04 August 1756. D, p. 77, MSA CE 30-4. www.mdlandrec.net : accessed 07 October 2021.

Liber D, folios 82-83; 13 August 1756

"This Indenture made this thirteenth Day of August Anno Dom[ini] one thousand seven hundred and fifty Six Between Bartholomew PETTIT of New Town in Kent County in the Province of Maryland of the one part and Isaac ATKINSON of the County of Worcester of the other part. Witnesseth that the said Bartholomew for and in Consideration of the Sum of twenty five pounds Current money of Maryland to the said Bartholomew in hand paid before the Sealing and delivery hereof the Receipt whereof is hereby Acknowledged hath Bargained and Sold, and by these doth Bargain and Sell to the said Isaac Atkinson his Executors Administrators and Assigns a Negro Wench or Girl called **Marina**, and one Silver Watch, and one small bright Bay Gelding or horse ~ To have & to hold the said Wench or Negro Girl, the said Silver Watch and small bright Bay Gelding to the said Isaac his Ex[ecutor]^s Adm[inistrator]^s and Assigns forever to the only proper Use and Behoof of the said Isaac his Ex[ecutor]^s Adm[inistrator]^s & Assigns forever and no other Use or Uses whatsoever Provided always and it is the true intent and meaning of these Presents that if the said Bartholomew PETTIT his Ex[ecutor]^s & Adm[inistrator]^s shall and do well and truly save harmless and keep indemnifyed the said Isaac his Ex[ecutor]s Adm[inistrator]s & Assigns at all times hereafter from all Cost Trouble Suits or Expences whatsoever which may happen to him the said Isaac for and by means of the said Isaac ATKINSONs undertaking to be forthcoming for the said Bartholomews Appearance at Snowhill Town at the Court house of Worcester County af[ore]s[ai]^d to Answer the Suit of a certain Custis WHARTON at November next and also pay all the Costs accruing for and by means of drawing and Recording this Indenture of Mortgage, that then this Indenture to be Void as if the same had never been made Provided also and it is further Agreed between the Parties af[ore]s[ai]^d that the said Isaac immediately after the Execution hereof shall have and take Possession of the said Slave & other Premises above Bargained and Sold without any Lett or hindrance from the said Bartholomew or any other person claiming under him. In Testimony whereof the said Parties have hereunto set their Hands and Seals the day and Year above written ~

| Sealed & Delivered | Jn.º SCARBOROUGH ~ | Bartholomew PETTIT (Seal) |
| In Presence of | Ad[a]^m SPENCE ~" | |

*followed on folio 83 with the acknowledgment by Justices of the Peace John SCARBOROUGH and Adam SPENCE on 05 August 1756 and recordation by court clerk Henry JOHNSON on 13 August 1756[68]

Liber D, folios 140-141; 17 February 1757

"Know all men by these Presents that whereas KENNET dece[ase]d by his Last Will in writing duly Published, in his lifetime, Bequeathed to his two Sons Pasgrave KENNETT and Turville KENNETT a Negro Girl called **Esther** and if it Should happen that Either of his said Sons should die without Issue in the Life of the other then the said Negro was to descend to the Surviving Brother by the said will Now know ye that are the said Turville & Pasgrave KENNETT for & on Consideration of forty five pounds Current money of Maryland to us in hand paid by William DUNLAP before the Sealing and delivery hereof the Receipt whereof is hereby Acknowledged, have bargained and Sold and by these Presents we and Each of us do Bargain and Sell to the said William DUNLAP his Executors Adm[inistrator]^s & Assigns the said Negro Girl called **Esther** and all the Right Title Interest Claim or Demand which we or Either of us can or may Claim by means of any Contingency of dying without Issue of Either of us or any other Right that doth or hereafter may Appertain to us or Either of us by the said Will for the said Negro Girl Called **Esther** To have and to hold the said Negro Girl to the said William DUNLAP his Executors Adm[inistrator]^s & Assigns to the only Proper Use of the said William DUNLAP and his Assigns and no other use or Uses whatsoever In Testimony whereof we have hereunto Set our hands and Seals this Seventeenth day of February Anno Dom[ini]

---

[68] Worcester County Court (Land Records). Deed of mortgage from PETTIT, Bartholomew to ATKINSON, Isaac. 13 August 1756. D, pp. 82-83, MSA CE 30-4. www.mdlandrec.net : accessed 07 October 2021.

one thousand Seven hundred and fifty Seven.~   Turvile KENNETT~ (Seal)
Sealed & Delivered in Presence of John EVANS.~   Presgrave KENNETT (Seal)"

*followed on folio 141 with the acknowledgment by Justice of the Peace John EVANS on 17 February 1757 and recordation by court clerk Henry JOHNSON on 22 February 1757[69]

Liber D, folio 167; 06 November 1756

"This Indenture made this Sixth day of November in the year of our Lord One thousand Seven hundred fifty and Six Between Mary MARTIN of Worcester County of the one part and Benjamin HANDY and Elizabeth his wife of the other part Witnesseth that the said Mary MARTIN for and in Consideration of the Sum of Sixty pounds current money of Maryland to her in hand paid by the said Benjamin and Elizabeth his wife the Receipt whereof she doth hereby Confess and Acknowledge and thereof doth Acquit Exonerate and discharge the said Benjamin and Elizabeth their heirs Executors and Adm[inistrator]s firmly by these presents Hath Bargained Sold Assigned Setover Transferred and Delivered and by these Presents Doth Bargain Sell Assign Setover Transfer and deliver unto the said Benjamin HANDY and Elizabeth his wife and to their heirs Executors Administrators and Assigns forever and Negro Woman Slave Named **Moll**, one Negro Girl Slave Named **Rose**, one Negro Girl Slave Named **Rhoda**, and one Negro Boy Slave Named **Bristor**. To Have and To hold the aforesaid Slaves unto the aforesaid Benjamin and Elizabeth and to his heirs Executors Adm[inistrator]s and Assigns forever And the said Mary doth hereby Covenant Promise and Agree to and with the said Benjamin and Elizabeth their heirs Executors Adm[inistrator]s and Assigns that she the aforesaid Mary the aforesaid Slaves against herself and all other Persons Legally Claiming the same by from and or or in Trust for her, her heirs Ex[ecutor]s and Assigns unto the said Benjamin and Elizabeth and to their heirs Executors Adm[inistrator]s and Assigns shall and will warrant and forever Defend by these Presents In Witness whereof the Partys af[oresai]d have hereto Set their hands and fixed their Seals the day and year above written.~
Sealed & Delivered   Jn.º SCARBOROUGH   Mary MARTIN (Seal)
In Presence of ~   Jos[eph] DIRICKSON."

*followed with the acknowledgment by Justices of the Peace John SCARBOROUGH and Joseph DIRICKSON and receipt of consideration on November 1756, and recordation by court clerk Henry JOHNSON on 15 March 1757.[70]

Liber D, folios 173-174; 31 March 1757

"Know all men by these Presents that we Jonathan HAZARD of Rhoad Island and Zadock PURNELL of the Province of Maryland in the County or Worcester for and in consideration of four hundred and Seventy five Bushells of Indian Corn to us in hand paid by John CAMPBELL of the aforesaid Province of Maryland and County of Worcester at and before the Sealing and delivery hereof the receipt whereof we do hereby Acknowledge have Bargained and sold and by these Presents do Bargain and Sell unto the said John CAMPBELL one Negro Girl called **Cloe** To have and to hold the said Negro Girl called **Cloe** to him the said John CAMPBELL his heirs and Assigns and for no other use or uses whatsoever and they the said Jonathan and Zadock and Each of them for themselves their and Each of their heirs Ex[ecutor]s & Administrators do and Each of them doth Covenant to and with the said John CAMPBELL his heirs and Assigns that before the Sealing and delivery hereof they have and Each of them hath good Right and full Power to Bargain & Sell the said Negro in manner and form aforesaid and that they the said Jonathan and Zadock and Each of them from time to time and at all times hereafter shall and will warrant and forever defend the said Negro and her Increase from all Persons whatsoer Claiming any Right or Title to the Same In Witness as hereof we have hereunto Set our hands and Seals this 31st day of March 1757.

---

[69] Worcester County Court (Land Records). Bill of sale from KENNETT, Presgrave and Turvile to DUNLAP, William. 17 February 1757. D, pp. 140-141, MSA CE 30-4. www.mdlandrec.net : accessed 07 October 2021.
[70] Worcester County Court (Land Records). Bill of sale from MARTIN, Mary to HANDY, Benjamin and Elizabeth. 06 November 1756. D, p. 167, MSA CE 30-4. www.mdlandrec.net : accessed 07 October 2021.

Sealed & Delivered Jonathan HAZARD (Seal)
In Presence of ~ Zadok PURNELL (Seal)
Jn:º SCARBOROUGH
Bowd:ⁿ ROBBINS"

*followed on folio 174 with the acknowledgment by Justice of the Peace John SCARBOROUGH and recordation by court clerk Henry JOHNSON.[71]

Liber D, folios 181-182; 26 April 1757

"Know all men by these Presents that I Thomas JONES for and in Consideration of the Sum of Forty five Pounds Current money of Maryland to me in hand paid by Samuel DAVIS the Receipt whereof I do hereby Acknowledge and forever discharge the said Samuel DAVIS his heirs Executors Administrators and Assigns from have Sold Conveyed and Confirmed and do by these Presents Sell Convey and Confirm unto the said Samuel DAVIS one Negro Boy called **George** unto him to said Samuel DAVIS his heirs and Assigns forever To have and To hold the said Negro Boy **George** unto him the said Samuel DAVIS his heirs and Assigns forever hereby for myself my heirs Executors and Administrators disclaiming any Right Title or Interest in and to the said Negro Boy **George** and warranting and defending the said Samuel DAVIS in a Just Right to the said Negro Boy called **George** against any and all Persons Claiming any Right Title or Interest to the said Negro by from or under me and {?} use against all Persons whatsoever claiming In further Testimony hereof I have hereunto Set my hand and Affixed my seal this 26ᵗʰ day of April Anno Dom[ini] Seventeen hundred fifty & Seven
Sealed & Delivered   Ad[a]ᵐ SPENCE   Thomas JONES L (Seal)
In presence of us.   John SELBY."

*followed on folio 182 with the acknowledgment by Justice of the Peace Adam SPENCE and recordation by court clerk Henry JOHNSON[72]

Liber D, folio 184; 02 May 1757

"Worcester County to wit To all People to whom these Presents shall come I Alice HENDERSON do send Greeting Know ye that I the said Alice HENDERSON of the County aforesaid for and in consideration of the Love goodwill and Affection which I have and do bear towards my Loving Son in Law John MERRILL and Comfort his wife of the County aforesaid Have given and Granted and by these Presents do freely Clearly and Absolutely give and Grant unto the said John MERRILL and Comfort his wife my Negro Boy called **George** to them and Each of them during their and Each of their Natural Lives and after their decease to such of all Children of the said John and Comfort as the aforesaid John and Comfort proper Right Absolutely without any manner of Consideration In Witness whereof I have hereunto Set my hand and Seal this 2.ᵈ day of May anno Dom[ini] 1757
Sealed & Delivered   Thomas HANDY   her
In Presence of   John SELBY   Ailce 1 HENDERSON (Seal)
                                                        mark"

*followed with acknowledgment by Justices of the Peace Thomas HANDY and John SELBY on 02 May 1757 and recordation by court clerk Henry JOHNSON on 04 May 1757[73]

Liber D, folios 215-216; 29 August 1757

"This Indenture made this Twenty Ninth day of August in the year of our Lord One thousand Seven hundred and fifty and Seven Between John MARTIN of Worcester County of the one

---

[71] Worcester County Court (Land Records). Bill of sale from HAZARD, Jonathan and PURNELL, Zadok to CAMPBELL, John. 31 March 1757. D, pp. 173-174, MSA CE 30-4. www.mdlandrec.net : accessed 07 October 2021.
[72] Worcester County Court (Land Records). Bill of sale from JONES, Thomas to DAVIS, Samuel. 26 April 1757. D, pp. 181-182, MSA CE 30-4. www.mdlandrec.net : accessed 07 October 2021.
[73] Worcester County Court (Land Records). Bill of sale from HENDERSON, Alice to MERRILL, John. 02 May 1757. D, p. 84, MSA CE 30-4. www.mdlandrec.net : accessed 07 October 2021.

part and Thomas MARTIN and Henry AYRES of the other part Witnesseth that the said John MARTIN for and in Consideration of the Sum of five Shillings Current money to him paid by the aforesaid Thomas MARTIN and Henry AYRES at and before the Sealing and delivery hereof the Receipt whereof he hereby doth Acknowledge as also for the saving harmless and keeping Indemnified the aforesaid Thomas MARTIN and Henry AYRES from all Costs Charge Damage and Expence that they or Either of them hath shall or may Sustain for or by means of their becoming Security for the said John in a bond for the proper debt of the said John MARTIN unto a Certain David JAMERSON of York Town in Virginia on which Bond they are already Said Hath given granted Bargained and Sold and by these presents doth give grant Bargain and Sell unto the said Thomas MARTIN and Henry AYRES their heirs and Assigns forever all his Right and Title both in Law & Equity of and into part of all that Tract or Parcell of Land Scituate in Worcester County Near Snowhill Town called Snow : Hill containing and laid out for four hundred Acres more or Less being all the Lands of that Tract Except such part as was laid of for Snowhill Town that part being one hundred Acres together with the Appurtenances unto the same belonging or in any Sort Appertaining which Tract is Cutted Bounded and discribed as in and by the Pattent thereof is Expressed and mentioned Recorse to the same being had more fully and at Large will Appear as also the Sundry Goods and Chattles following to wit one Negro man called **Hope** one other called **Paul** one Negro Woman called **Rose** one Girl called **Martha** and one Small Girl called **Bridget** To have and To hold the aforesaid Lands and Tenements Goods and Chattles together with their Appurtinances unto the same belonging or in any sort Appurtaining to the only proper Use Benefit and Behoof of them the said Thomas MARTIN and Henry AYRES their heirs and Assigns forever and for no other Use or Purpose whatsoever and the said John MARTIN for himself his heirs Executors and Adm[inistrator]s doth Covenant Grant and Agree to and with the said Thomas MARTIN and Henry AYRES and their heirs and Assigns forever that the aforesaid Granted and Bargained Premisses unto the said Thomas MARTIN and Henry AYRES their heirs and Assigns forever he will against the Claim Right and Title of every Person whatsoever Warrant and Defend In Testimony whereof the said John MARTIN to these presents his hand hath Set and Seal Affixed the day and year first above written./.~

Signed Sealed & Delivered   Benj[a][min] HANDY.
In Presence of us   Ad[a]m SPENCE   Jn:º MARTIN   (Seal)"

*followed on folio 216 with acknowledgment of Justices of the Peace Benjamin HANDY and Adam SPENCE, the receipt of the alienation fine by John DENNIS, and recordation by court clerk Henry JOHNSON on 10 September 1757[74]

Liber D, folio 247; 15 February 1758

"Know all men by these Presents that I Ebenezer EVANS of Worcester County in the Province of Maryland have Bargained and Sold unto Thomas MIDZLEY for the consideration of Fifty Pounds Good and Lawfull money aforesaid One Negro Boy called **Will** for which I do hereby Set over and confirm the Right Use and Property of the said Negro to him the said MIDZLEY his heirs Ex[ecutor]s Adm[inistrator]s or Assigns and their Use And do hereby these Presents bind me myself my heirs Ex[ecutor]s or Adm[inistrator]s to Warrant and Defend the said Negro to the said MIDZLEY from all Persons and against all Persons whatsoever or farther at any time Required to make a better Property to the said Negro as he his heirs or Certain Attorney at any time shall Require In Witness whereof I have hereunto Sett my hand and Seal in the Presence of us the Subscribers this 15th day of February in the Year MDCCLViii.~
John EVANS, Brickus TOWNSEND.~   Ebenezer EVANS   (seal)"

*followed with the acknowledgment by Justice of the Peace John EVANS on 15 February 1758 and recordation by court clerk Henry JOHNSON on 17 February 1758[75]

---

[74] Worcester County Court (Land Records). Deed from MARTIN, John to MARTIN, Thomas and AYRES, Henry. 29 August 1757. D, pp. 215-216, MSA CE 30-4. www.mdlandrec.net : accessed 07 October 2021.
[75] Worcester County Court (Land Records). Bill of sale from EVANS, Ebenezer to MIDZLEY, Thomas. 15 February 1758. D, p. 247, MSA CE 30-4. www.mdlandrec.net : accessed 07 October 2021.

Liber D, folios 250-251; 31 March 1758

"Know all men by these Presents that we Thomas MARTIN & Henry AYRES for and in consideration of the Sum of Two hundred and fifty Pounds Current money of Maryland to us paid by John MARTIN at and before the Sealing and delivery hereof the Receipt whereof we hereby do Acknowledge hath Released and forever Quit Claimed and by these Presents doth Release and forever Quit Claim unto the aforesaid John MARTIN and his Assigns forever all our Right and Title both in Law and equity of and unto the following Slaves to wit one Man called **Hope** one other called **Paul** one Woman called **Rose** one called **Martha** and one Girl called **Bridget** To have and To hold the af[oresai]^d Negroes unto the said John MARTIN his heirs and Assigns to and for the only Use Benefit and Behoof of the said John MARTIN his heirs and Assigns forever and for no other use or purpose whatsoever In Testimony whereof we have hereunto set our hands & Seals this 31st day of March Anno Dom[ini] 1758.~

Sealed & Delivered	John SCARBOROUGH	Thomas MARTIN (Seal)
In Presence of	Thomas HANDY ~	Henry AYRES (Seal)"

*followed with the acknowledgment of Justices of the Peace John SCARBOROUGH and Thomas HANDY and the recordation by court clerk Henry JOHNSON[76]

Liber D, folios 251-252; 31 March 1758

"This Indenture made this thirty first day of March in the year of our Lord one thousand Seven hundred and fifty Eight Between John MARTIN of Worcester County of the one Part and John DONE of Somerset County of the other part Witnesseth that the said John MARTIN for and in consideration of the Sum of Three hundred and Nine Pounds Twelve Shillings Current money of Maryland to him paid by the aforesaid John DONE at and before the Sealing and delivery hereof the Receipt whereof he hereby doth Acknowledge Hath Bargained and Sold and delivered and by these Presents doth Bargain Sell and deliver unto the aforesaid John DONE his heirs and Assigns forever the following Slaves to wit one Man named **Hope** and one named **Paul** one Woman called **Rose** one called **Martha** and one Girl called **Bridget** and also one Lott Number   Scituate in Snowhill Town it being whereon the House of the said John MARTIN newly Repaired Stands together with all the Appurtinances thereunto belonging To have and To hold the aforesaid Slaves and Lott and Appurtinances unto the said John DONE and his Assigns forever to and for the only Use and Benefit of the said John DONE his heirs and Assigns forever and for no other purpose whatsoever Provided always and it is the true intent and meaning hereof that if the said John MARTIN his Executors Adm[inistrator]^s or Assigns do and shall well and truly pay unto the aforesaid John DONE his Executors Administrators or Assigns the Sum of Three hundred and Nine pounds and Twelve Shillings Current money of Maryland to be paid in Spanish Gold or Pieces of Eight together with the Legal Interest thereon on or before the last day of August next ensuing the date hereof And the said John MARTIN for himself doth covenant grant and Agree to and with the said John DONE his Executors Adm[inistrator]^s or Assigns that in case the said John MARTIN do not the said money in the sp{??}es aforesaid at the time above Expressed with the Legal Interest that then it shall and may be Lawfull for the said John DONE his Ex[ecutor]^s Adm[inistrator]^s or Assigns Immediately thereon to Possess himself with the said Slaves and Lott with its Appurtinances and to make Sale of the said Slaves and Lott and Houses thereon towards the raising all or any part of the said money And the said John MARTIN for the well and faithfull payment and discharge of the said money by the time af[oresai]^d with the Interest he hereby obliges himself his heirs Ex[ecutor]^s and Adm[inistrator]^s for and in the Penal Sum of five hundred pounds Current money aforesaid firmly by these Presents In Testimony whereof the said John MARTIN to these presents his hand hath set and Seal Affixed the day and year first above written.~

Signed Sealed & Delivered	John SCARBOROUGH	Jn:^{o} MARTIN (Seal)
In Presence of us ~	Thomas HANDY ~."	

---

[76] Worcester County Court (Land Records). Bill of sale from MARTIN, Thomas and AYRES, Henry to MARTIN, John. 31 March 1758. D, pp. 250-251, MSA CE 30-4. www.mdlandrec.net : accessed 07 October 2021.

*followed on folio 252 with the acknowledgment by Justices of the Peace Thomas HANDY and John SCARBOROUGH and recordation by court clerk Henry JOHNSON[77]

Liber D, folios 261-262; 07 April 1758

"Know all men by these presents that I William MARTIN of Worcester County in the province of Maryland for and in consideration of the Sum of One hundred and Twenty five pounds Current money of Maryland to me paid at and before the Sealing and delivery hereof by John MARTIN of the County and Province aforesaid the Receipt whereof I do hereby Acknowledge Have Bargained Sold Assigned Transferred and delivered and by these presents do Bargain Sell Assign Transferr and deliver unto the said John MARTIN his heirs Executors Adm[inistrator]^s or Assigns One Negro Boy slave named **Jethro** now Remaining and being in the Possession of my Mother Mary MARTIN To have and To hold the said Negro Boy by these Presents Intended to be Bargained and Sold unto the said John MARTIN his heirs Executors Adm[inistrator]^s or Assigns forever And I the said William MARTIN for myself my heirs Ex[ecutor]^s and Adm[inistrator]^s the Negro Boy aforesaid unto the said John MARTIN his Executors and Adm[inistrator]^s and against all and every other person or persons whatsoever shall and will Warrant and forever Defend by these presents Provided always and it is the true intent and meaning of these presents that if I the said William MARTIN (who now intends with Gods permission to make a voiage to Sea) should Return and well and truly pay and Satisfie the said John MARTIN his heirs Executors or Administrators the Consideration herein before mentioned then this present Instrument of writing to be totally Null and Void anything herein to the Contrary Notwithstanding In Witness whereof I the said William MARTIN have hereunto set my hand and Affixed my Seal this Seventh day of April in the year of our Lord one thousand Seven hundred fifty and Eight ~

Sealed & Delivered   Jn.º SCARBOROUGH   W[illiam] MARTIN   (Seal)
In the presence of.   H JOHNSON ~"

*followed on folio 262 with the acknowledgment by Justice of the Peace John SCARBOROUGH and recordation by court clerk Henry JOHNSON on 08 April 1758[78]

Liber D, folio 262; 14 April 1758

"Know all men by these Presents that I Mary MARTIN of Worcester County and Province of Maryland for and in consideration of the Sum of thirty pounds Current money of the Province of Maryland unto me well and truly paid by John DONE of Somerset County and province aforesaid Surgeon the Receipt whereof I doe hereby Acknowledge have granted Bargained and Sold and by these presents do Grant Bargain Sell unto the said John DONE a Certain Negro Boy called **Moses** Aged Nine Years or thereabouts To have and To hold the said Negro **Moses** unto the said John DONE his Executors Adm[inistrator]^s and Assigns to the only proper Use benefit and behoof of him the said John DONE his Ex[ecutor]^s Adm[inistrator]^s and Assigns forever And I the said Mary MARTIN my Executors and Adm[inistrator]^s the said Negro **Moses** unto the said John DONE his Executors Adm[inistrator]^s and Assigns against all Persons whatsoever shall and will Warrant and forever defend by these Presents In Witness whereof I the said Mary MARTIN have hereunto set my hand and seal this fourteenth day of April Anno Dom[ini] 1758.

Sealed & Delivered   W[illiam] MARTIN   Mary u MARTIN (Seal)
In Presence of ~   James MARTIN.   her Mark"

---

[77] Worcester County Court (Land Records). Deed of mortgage from MARTIN, John to DONE, John. 31 March 1758. D, pp. 251-252, MSA CE 30-4. www.mdlandrec.net : accessed 07 October 2021.
[78] Worcester County Court (Land Records). Bill of sale from MARTIN, William to MARTIN, John. 07 April 1758. D, pp. 261-262, MSA CE 30-4. www.mdlandrec.net : accessed 07 October 2021.

*followed with acknowledgment by Justices of the Peace John SCARBOROUGH and recordation by court clerk Henry JOHNSON on 14 April 1758[79]

Liber D, folios 297-298; 08 June 1758

"Maryland Worcester {?} Know all men by these presents that we John ROSS of Worcester County William ALLEN Tubman LOWES and Thomas DASHIELD of Somerset County for and in Consideration of the Sum of One hundred and Twenty Nine pounds Tens Shillings Current money of the Province aforesaid to us in hand paid by Joshua MITCHELL of Worcester County the Receipt whereof we do hereby Acknowledge and ourselves therewith fully Satisfied have Granted Bargained and Sold and by these presents do plainly and Openly Sell and deliver unto the said Joshua MITCHELL One Negro Man Named **Hope** and One Negro Woman named **Martha** To have and To hold the said Negros unto the said Joshua MITCHELL his heirs Executors Adm[inistrator]s and Assigns forever and we the said John ROSS William ALLEN Tubman LOWES and Thomas DASHIELD for ourselves our heirs Ex[ecutor]s and Adm[inistrator]s the said Negros unto the said Joshua MITCHELL his heirs Executors Adm[inistrator]s and Assigns against all and all manner of persons shall and will Warrant and forever defend by these Presents In Witness whereof we do hereunto Set our hands and Seals this Eighth day of June 1758

Signed Sealed & Delivered	Benj[amin] HANDY ~	John ROSSE (Seal)
In Presence of us ~	Thomas JONES.	W[illia]m ALLEN (Seal)
		Tubman LOWES (Seal)
		Tho[ma]s DASHIELD (Seal)"

*followed on folio 298 with the acknowledgment by Justice of the Peace Benjamin HANDY on 08 June 1758 and recordation by court clerk Henry JOHNSON on 09 June 1758[80]

Liber D, folios 415-416; 21 July 1759

"This Indenture made this twenty first day of July in the Year of our Lord one thousand Seven hundred and fifty nine Between Mary HUDSON of Worcester County in the Province of Maryland of the one Part and Isaac BRITTINGHAM of the same Place of the other Part Witnesseth that the said Mary HUDSON for and in Consideration of the Natural Love and Affection which she hath and doth bare unto her brother in law Isaac BRITTINGHAM as also for the better Support and mantainance of her the said Mary during her Natural Life and also for and in Consideration of the sum of five Shillings Current money of Maryland to her the said Mary in hand Paid by the aforesaid Isaac BRITTINGHAM at and before the Sealing and Delivery of these Presents the Receipt whereof the said Mary HUDSON hereby doth Acknowledge she Hath given granted bargained and sold and by these Presents doth give grant bargain and sell unto the aforesaid Isaac BRITTINGHAM all her right and title of and into in a Certain Tract or Parcell of Land called None Such as one of the Coheirs of Robert HUDSON Deceased unto the said Isaac BRITTINGHAM his Heirs and Assigns forever and the said Mary HUDSON for and in Consideration of the Natural Love and Affection which she hath and doth bare unto her brother in Law Isaac BRITTINGHAM and for and in Consideration of the Sum of five other Shillings Current money af[oresai]d to her the said Mary HUDSON in hand paid by the said Isaac BRITTINGHAM at and before the sealing and Delivery of these Presents the Receipt whereof the said Mary HUDSON hereby doth Acknowledge she hath Given Granted Bargained and Sold and by these Presents doth give Grant bargain and sell unto the said Isaac BRITTINGHAM his Heirs and Assigns forever one Negro man Slave called **Caleb** one negro boy called **Shadrick** one Negro Woman called **Betty** one other Negro Woman called **Sarah** as also a debt of twenty Pounds Current money of Maryland which hath Arrisen due in Consequence of a Sail of Part of a Tract of Land divised to her the said Mary by the last will

---

[79] Worcester County Court (Land Records). Bill of sale from MARTIN, Mary to DONE, John. 14 April 1758. D, p. 262, MSA CE 30-4. www.mdlandrec.net : accessed 07 October 2021.
[80] Worcester County Court (Land Records). Bill of sale from ROSS, John, ALLEN, William, LOWES, Tubman, and DASHIELD, Thomas to MITCHELL, Joshua. 08 June 1758. D, p. 297-298, MSA CE 30-4. www.mdlandrec.net : accessed 08 October 2021.

and Testament of Robert HUDSON Deceased and also Eighteen Pounds of Like money being her Part of the Residue of her Fathers Estate and half a Silver Spoon divised to the said Mary by the Last will and Testament of her Father Robert HUDSON unto the said Isaac BRITTINGHAM his Heirs and Assigns forever and also Eight Pounds of Like money which hath become due unto the said Mary in Consequence of the hire of a Negro man slave to the said Isaac BRITTINGHAM his Heirs and Assigns forever. To have and To hold the said Several things above mentioned unto him the said Isaac in Trust to and for the uses and Purposes hereafter mentioned and for no other use whatsoever / that is to say/ to him the said Isaac in Trust that out of the Profits thereof he shall maintain and Support the said Mary during the Life of the said Mary and after the Death of the said Mary to and for the use of the Issue of the said Mary forever in Case she should have any but in Case the said Mary should dye without Issue then to the Issue of the said Isaac _____ Begotten or to be begotten on the Body of the now Wife of the said Isaac to Such of them as the said Isaac by his Deed in his Life shall give the same unto or Such of them as the said Isaac by his last Will and Testament shall Bequeath or devise the same unto but in Case the said Isaac should die in the Life of the said Mary and the said Mary should die after without Issue then the said Premises shall be to the use of the Children of the said Isaac as aforesaid to be Equally divided among them after the death of the said Mary. In Testimony whereof the said Mary to these Presents her hand hath set and Seal Affixed the day and year first above Written. ~

Sealed & Delivered Jnº SCARBOROUGH
In Presence of us Ad[a]ᵐ SPENCE   her
                                                        Mary 0 HUDSON ./. (Seal)
                                                           Mark

*followed on folio 416 with the acknowledgment by Justices of the Peace John SCARBOROUGH and Adam SPENCE, the receipt of the alienation fine by Benjamin HANDY, and the recordation by court clerk Henry JOHNSON[81]

Liber E, folios 43-44; 25 July 1760

"This Indenture made this twenty fifth day of July Anno Dom[ini] one thousand seven hundred and Sixty, Between John LONG of the one part and John JARMAN of the other part Witnesseth that the said John LONG for the Consideration of the Sum of five pounds Current money to him in hand paid by the afores[ai]ᵈ John JARMAN at and before the Sealing and Delivery hereof the Receipt whereof the said John LONG hereby doth Acknowledge hath given granted bargained and sold and by these Presents doth give grant bargain and sell unto the afores[ai]ᵈ John JARMAN his Heirs and Assigns forever a Tract of Land called Borsworth which is Situate in Worcester County and is bounded and Discribed, as in and by a Deed for the same to the said John LONG from a certain Thomas DUNKIN is bounded and Described the same containing one hundred and fifty four Acres more or Less as also the sundry Goods and Chattles following, one Negro named **Sarah** one named **Leah** one Negro Man named **Watt** one named **Jesper** and one named **George**, as also all his Household Goods and Furniture, and all his Horses Cattle Hoggs and Sheep and all other his Estate whatsoever except a Negro Woman called **Patience**, To have and To hold the afores[ai]ᵈ Lands so as afores[ai]ᵈ Described as also the afores[ai]ᵈ Goods and Chattles unto the afores[ai]ᵈ John JARMAN his Heirs and Assigns forever to and for the only use and behoof of the said John JARMAN his Heirs and Assigns forever and for no other use or purpose whatsoever and the said John LONG for himself his Heirs Ex[ecutor]ˢ and Adm[inistrator]ˢ doth Covenant Grant and Agree to and with the said John JARMAN his Heirs and Assigns forever that he will warrant and forever defend the aforesaid Lands and Premises and other the Goods and Chattles aforesaid unto the aforesaid John JARMAN his Heirs and Assigns forever against the Right and Title of him the said John LONG his Heirs and Assigns forever and of every other Person claiming by from or under him or any of them. In Testimony whereof the said John LONG to these Presents his hand hath set and Seal affixed the day and year first above written. ~

---

[81] Worcester County Court (Land Records). Deed from HUDSON, Mary to BRITTINGHAM, Isaac. 21 July 1759. D, pp. 415-416, MSA CE 30-4. www.mdlandrec.net : accessed 08 October 2021.

Signed Sealed & Delivered   Ad[a]m SPENCE   John LONG   (Seal)
In Presence off us ~   John SELBY"

*followed on folio 43 with the acknowledgment by Justices of the Peace Adam SPENCE and John SELBY on 25 July 1760, receipt of the alienation fine by Benjamin HANDY on 07 August 1760, and recordation by court clerk Henry JOHNSON on folio 44 on 08 August 1760[82]

Liber E, folios 61-62; 05 November 1760

"Know all men by these Presents that I David MURRAY of Worcester County for and in Consideration of fifty pounds Current money to me paid by Isaac MURRAY at and before the Sealing and Delivery hereof the Receipt whereof the said David hereby doth Acknowledge hath bargained sold and Delivered and by these Presents doth bargain sell and deliver unto the afores[ai]d Isaac MURRAY his Heirs and Assigns, one Negroe Man named **London**, two Beds & furniture, The Said Negroe and Beds and Furniture now being in the Possession of the said Isaac, To Have and To hold the afores[ai]d Negroe Beds and Furniture unto the Isaac MURRAY his Heirs and Assigns forever to and for the only use of the said Isaac his Heirs and Assigns and for no other use or Purpose whatsoever and the said David by these Presents doth hereby Warrant and Defend the afores[ai]d Negroe Beds and Furniture unto the said Isaac his Heirs and Assigns against the Claim right and Title of all and every Person whatever. In Testimony whereof the said David to these Presents his hand hath set and Seal affixed this fifth day of November Anno Dom[ini] 1760. ~
Sealed and Delivered   David MURRAY   (Seal)
In Presence of ~"

*followed with the acknowledgment by Justice of the Peace William ELLAGOOD and recordation on 06 November 1760 by court clerk Henry JOHNSON.[83]

Liber E, folios 251-252; 09 November 1761

"Know all Men by these Presents that I William SELBY of Worcester County in the Province of Maryland for and in Consideration of the Love and Affection that I have and do bear unto my loving Daughter Sarah MARTIN (Wife of Thomas MARTIN) and for the further Consideration of the Sum of Five shillings Current money of Maryland to me in hand paid by the said Sarah MARTIN at and before the Sealing and Delivery of these Presents the Receipt whereof I do hereby Confess and Acknowledge and my self these with fully satisy'd contented and paid and do by these Presents acquit and discharge the said Sarah MARTIN her Heirs Ex[ecutor]s and Adm[inistrator]s forever he the said William SELBY Hath given granted bargained and sold set over and delivered and Doth by these Presents give grant bargain and sell sett over and deliver unto the said Sarah MARTIN her Heirs Ex[ecutor]s Adm[inistrato]rs and Assigns forever the following Negroes (to wit) **Ceaser, Robin, Jacob, Jer, Zadock** Males, and also **Phebe, Tab, Patience & Hannah** Females and their and Each of their future Increase. To have and to hold the several Negroes abovementioned to be given granted bargained and sold set over and delivered and Each of them with their and Each of their future Increase to Her the said Sarah MARTIN her Heirs Ex[ecuto]rs Adm[inistrato]rs and Assigns to the only proper use benefit and behoof of Her the said Sarah MARTIN her Heirs Ex[ecuto]rs Administrato]rs and Assigns forever. In Witness whereof I have hereunto set my Hand and Seal this ninth Day of November in the Year of our Lord God one thousand seven hundred seven sixty and one. ~
Sealed and Delivered
In Presence of ~~~~~   W[illia]m SELBY. ~ (Seal)

                              her
Ad[a]m SPENCE ~   Mary + PORTER ~
                              Mark"

---

[82] Worcester County Court (Land Records). Deed from LONG, John to HARMAN, John. 25 July 1760. E, pp. 43-44, MSA CE 30-5. www.mdlandrec.net : accessed 13 October 2021.
[83] Worcester County Court (Land Records). Bill of sale from MURRAY, David to MURRAY, Isaac. 05 November 1760. E, pp. 61-62, MSA CE 30-5. www.mdlandrec.net : accessed 13 October 2021.

*followed with the acknowledgment by Justice of the Peace Adam SPENCE and recordation on 14 November 1760 by court clerk Henry JOHNSON.[84]

Liber E, folios 267-268; 22 December 1761

"Know all men by these Presents that I Mary MARTIN of Worcester County for the Consideration of the Sum of Forty five pounds Current money to me paid by Thomas MARTIN at and before the Sealing and Delivery hereof the Receipt whereof the said Mary hereby doth Acknowledge. Hath Bargained Sold and Delivered and by these Presents Doth bargain sell and Deliver unto the aforesaid Thomas MARTIN his Heirs and Assigns forever one Negro Boy called **Jethro** now in possession of the said Mary. To have and to hold the aforesaid Negro Boy called **Jethro** to the said Thomas MARTIN his Heirs and Assigns forever for the Uses and Purposes following to wit the Use of the said Mary during Her natural Life and after Her decease to the only Use and Benefit of the said Thomas MARTIN his Heirs and Assigns forever and for no other Use or Purpose whatsoever. And the said Mary for herself her Heirs Ex[ecutor]s and Adm[inistrator]s doth Covenant to and with the said Thomas MARTIN his Heirs and Assigns forever that She had good wright and full power to bargain and sell the said Negro as aforesaid and that She will Warrant and Defend the said Negro unto the said Thomas and his Assigns forever against the Claim Right and Title of all and every Person whatsoever ~ In Witness whereof the said Mary to these Presents her Hand hath set and Seal affixed this Twenty second Day of December Anno Dom[ini] 1761. ~

Sealed & Delivered
In Presence of ~
John SELBY ~ George MARTIN.

Mary M MARTIN. (Seal)
her Mark"

*followed on folio 268 with acknowledgment by Justice of the Peace John SELBY and recordation by court clerk Henry JOHNSON[85]

Liber E, folios 268-269; 12 December 1761

"Know all men by these Presents that I Samuel HOPKINS for the Consideration of the Sum of Fifty pounds Current money to me paid by James ROUND at and before the Sealing and Delivery hereof the Receipt whereof the said Samuel HOPKINS hereby doth Acknowledge Hath bargained sold and Delivered and by these Presents Doth bargain sell and Deliver unto the said James ROUND his Heirs and Assigns forever one Negro Man slave named **Orson**. To have and to hold the aforesaid Man slave unto him the said James ROUND his Heirs and Assigns forever to and for the only use benefit and behoof of the said James ROUND his Heirs and Assigns forever and for no other use or purpose whatsoever. In Witness whereof the said Samuel Hopkins to these Presents his Hand hath set and Seal affixed this twelfth Day of December Anno Dom[ini] 1761.

Sealed & Delivered ~
In Presence of ~
John EVANS. ~ Math[e]w HOPKINS Jun[ior]./~"

Sam[ue]l HOPKINS (Seal)

*followed with the acknowledgment by Justice of the Peace John EVANS and recordation on 25 December 1761 by court clerk Henry JOHNSON[86]

Liber E, folios 294-296; 15 March 1762

"This Indenture made this fifteenth Day of March Anno Domini one thousand seven hundred and sixty two. Between **George BLAKE** of Worcester County in the Province of Maryland of the one part, and Elizabeth HANCOCK Wife of William HANCOCK of the other part.

---

[84] Worcester County Court (Land Records). Bill of sale from SELBY, William to MARTIN, Sarah. 09 November 1761. E, pp. 251-252, MSA CE 30-5. www.mdlandrec.net : accessed 13 October 2021.
[85] Worcester County Court (Land Records). Bill of sale from MARTIN, Mary to MARTIN, Thomas. 22 December 1761. E, pp. 267-268, MSA CE 30-5. www.mdlandrec.net : accessed 13 October 2021.
[86] Worcester County Court (Land Records). Bill of sale from HOPKINS, Samuel to ROUND, James. 12 December 1761. E, pp. 268-269, MSA CE 30-5. www.mdlandrec.net : accessed 14 October 2021.

Witnesseth the said **George BLAKE** Malatto for and in Consideration of Ten pounds Current money of Maryland unto him in Hand paid by the aforesaid Elizabeth HANCOCK before the Sealing and Delivery hereof the Receipt whereof the said **George BLAKE** doth hereby Acknowledge, and Hath granted bargained and sold, and Doth hereby grant bargain and sell by these Presents to the said Elizabeth HANCOCK her Heirs and Assigns forever fifty Acres of Land part of a Tract of Land called Pardnership taken up and had Surveyed by the aforesaid **George BLAKE** bareing Date the twenty ninth Day of September Anno Domini one thousand seven hundred and fifty nine containing 1357 Acres the aforesaid Quantity of fifty Acres bounded as followeth. Begining at a marked Pine standing in a Gulley that issueth into Littleton Creek where Solomon CARYs Road intersect Bowdoin ROBINS new Road that Leadeth to Gibbs Ferrey from thence North twenty seven Degrees West eighty six Poles from thence North thirty eight Degrees West eighty Poles, from thence North sixty one Degrees West twenty Poles from thence South thirty one Degrees West thirty two Poles, from thence North eighty Poles from thence East fifty four Poles from thence South eighteen Degrees East two hundred and fourteen Poles to Bowd[oi]ⁿ ROBINSON new Road from thence with a right Line to the first begining lay out and containing fifty Acres of Land more or less. To have and to hold the said fifty Acres of Land be the same more or less. To her the said Elizabeth HANCOCK her Heirs and Assigns forever, with all the Appurtenances to the same belonging free and clear from all manner of Incumbrances (the Quit Rents to become Due to the Lord of the fee thereof only Excepted) and the said **George BLAKE** for himself his Heirs Ex[ecuto]ʳˢ and Adm[inistrato]ʳˢ doth hereby Covenant with said Elizabeth HANDCOCK her Heirs and Assigns forever that at the time of Sealing and Delivery hereof he is seized of and in the said fifty Acres of Land in Fee simple and that he hath a good Right to sell to the said Elizabeth HANCOCK her Heirs and Assigns forever the said granted Premisses from all Persons whatsoever claiming by from or under him will Warrant and forever Defend by these Presents, and the said **George BLAKE** for himself his Heirs Executors doth further Covenant with the said Elizabeth HANCOCK her Heirs and Assigns to Grant unto Her or Them such further Assurances to the said fifty Acres of Land as Her or their Council learned in the Law shall at any time require. In Witness whereof the said **George BLAKE** hath hereunto set his Hand and affixed his Seal the Day and Year above written. ~

Sealed and Delivered.   Ad[a]ᵐ SPENCE
In the Presence of ~ ~   John SELBY ~   **George** X **BLAKE** (Seal)
                                                                        his Mark"

*followed on folio 295 with the acknowledgment by Justices of the Peace Adam SPENCE and John SELBY, the receipt of the alienation fine on 19 March 1762 by Joseph ALLEN, and the recordation on folio 296 by court clerk Henry JOHNSON[87]

*The acknowledgment includes the name of the grantor's wife Esther.

Liber E, folios 302-303; 15 March 1762

"This Indenture made this fifteenth Day of March Anno Domini one thousand seven hundred and sixty two. Between **George BLEAK** of Worcester County and Province of Maryland of the one part, Robert LAMBERSON of the other part Witnesseth that whereas the Right Honourable Frederick Lord Baron of Baltimore by his Deed of Grant under the Great Seal used in Maryland for Granting of Lands and Grant unto the aforesaid **George BLEAK** all that Tract of Land called Partnership containing Thirteen hundred and fifty seven Acres bareing Date the Twenty ninth Day of September one thousand seven hundred and fifty nine lying and being in Worcester County between Pocomoke River and the Sea side. Now this Indenture further Witnesseth that the aforesaid **George BLEAK** for and in Consideration of the Sum of Twenty pounds Current money of Maryland to the said **George** by the said Robert LAMBERSON paid before the Sealing and Delivery of these Presents the Receipt whereof the said **George** hereby doth Acknowledge Hath granted bargained and sold by these Presents Doth give grant bargain

---

[87] Worcester County Court (Land Records). Deed from **BLAKE, George** to HANCOCK, Elizabeth. 15 March 1762. E, pp. 294-296, MSA CE 30-5. www.mdlandrec.net : accessed 17 June 2022.

and sell to the said LAMBERSON his Heirs and Assigns forever all that part of a Tract of Land called Partnership bounded as followeth Begining at a marked red Oak standing on the West side of the great Holly Swamp, thence running North sixty six Degrees West through a pon Ninety poles, thence South thirty one Degrees West ninety Poles, thence South sixty six Degrees East ninety one Poles, and from thence with a right Line drawn to the beginning containing and now laid out for Fifty one Acres of Land more or less. To have and to hold he Granted and bargained Premises with the Appurtenances to the said Robert LAMBERSON for his Heirs and Assigns forever to the only Proper use and Behoof of the said Robert LAMBERSON his Heirs and Assigns forever, and the said **George BLEAK** for himself his Heirs Executors and Administrators doth Covenant with the said Robert LAMBERSON his Heirs and Assigns that he is Seized of the said granted Premises the Appurtenances at and before the Sealing and Delivery hereof in Fee and that the same is free and clear from any Incumbrance whatsoever, to the said Robert LAMBERSON his Heirs and Assigns forever, the said Granted and bargained Premises from all Persons whatsoever claiming by from or under him will Warrant and forever Defend by these Presents, and the said **George BLEAK** for himself his Ex[ecuto]rs and Administrators doth further Covenant with the said LAMBERSON his Heirs and Assigns forever, that he the said **George** and his Heirs forever will at any times when thereto required by the said LAMBERSON his Heirs or Assigns make and Execute and suffer any further Act Deed or Device in the Law such as by the said above granted Premises with the Appurtenances to the said Robert LAMBERSON his Heirs and Assigns forever, and that the same be made at the proper cost and charges of the LAMBERSON his Heirs and Assigns requireing the same. In Testimony whereof the Party aforesaid have to these Presents affixed his Hand and Seal the Day and Year above written. ~

Sealed and Delivered ~   Ad[a]m SPENCE   his
In Presence of ~   John SELBY   **George** + **BLAICK**. ~ (Seal)
                                                                                       Mark"

*followed on folio 303 with the acknowledgment by Justices of the Peace Adam SPENCE and John SELBY, the receipt of the alienation fine on 09 April 1762 by Joseph ALLEN, and the recordation by court clerk Henry JOHNSON[88]

*The acknowledgment includes the name of the grantor's wife Esther.

Liber E, folios 312-313; 24 March 1762

"Maryland Worcester {?}s:t Know all Men by these Presents that We William DUNLAP & George COCHRAN both of this County, for and in Consideration of the Sum of Sixty five pounds Current money of the Province of Maryland to us in Hand paid by Thomas GRAY of the same County, the Receipt whereof We do hereby Acknowledge and Ourselves therewith fully satisfied. Have granted bargained and sold, and by these Presents Do plainly and openly sell and deliver unto the said Thomas GRAY one Negro Woman named **Esther**, To have and to hold the said Negro Woman named **Esther** and her Increase unto the said Thomas GRAY his Heirs Ex[ecutor]s Adm[inistrator]s and Assigns forever, and We the said William DUNLAP and George COCHRAN for Ourselves joyntly and severally our Heirs Ex[ecutor]s Adm[inistrator]s and Assigns against all & all manner of Persons shall and will Warrant and forever Defend by these Presents. In Witness whereof We the said William DUNLAP and George COCHRAN have hereunto set our Hands and fixed our Seals this 24th Day of May 1762.
Signed Sealed & Delivered
In the Presence of us ~~~~   W[illia]m DUNLAP   (Seal)
Jos[hu]a MITCHELL.~   Abel M:cCAY ~   George COCHRAN   (Seal)"

---

[88] Worcester County Court (Land Records). Deed from **BLAKE**, George to LAMBERSON, Robert. 15 March 1762. E, pp. 302-302, MSA CE 30-5. www.mdlandrec.net : accessed 17 June 2022.

*followed on folio 313 with the acknowledgment of Justice of the Peace Joshua MITCHELL and recordation by court clerk Henry JOHNSON on 02 June 1762[89]

Liber E, folios 329-330; 21 July 1762

"This Indenture made this Twenty first Day of July in the Year of our Lord one thousand seven hundred and sixty two. Between William WHARTON of the one part, and John WHARTON one of the Sons of the said William WHARTON of the other part. Witnesseth that the said William for and in Consideration of the natural Love and Affection which he hath and doth bare unto his aforesaid son John as also for the Consideration of the Sum of Five shillings Current money by the said John to the said William paid at and before the Sealing and Delivery hereof the receipt whereof the said William hereby doth Acknowledge, Hath bargained and sold, and by these Presents Doth bargain and sell unto the aforesaid John his Heirs and Assigns forever, one Negro Man called **Adam** one Bed and Furniture and one Iron Pitt. To have and to hold the aforesaid bargained Premisses with the Appurtenances unto the said John his Heirs and Assigns forever for the Uses and under the Limitations hereafter Expressed that is to say all the above bargained Premisses to remain in the use and quiet and peaceable possession of the said William dureing the natural life of the aforesaid William. And that on the Death of the said William all and every the Articles first mentioned and intended to be hereby Conveyed to remain to the Sole use benefit and behoof of the said John his Heirs and Assigns forever and for no other use or purpose whatsoever. In Witness whereof the said William to these Presents his Hand hath set and Seal affixed the Day and Year first above written.~
Signed Sealed & Delivered
In Presence of us ~~~~~~   Will[ia]m WHARTON.~ (Seal)
William EVENS.~ Ephraim EVENS."

*followed with the acknowledgment of Justice of the Peace Robert Jenckins HENRY and the recordation on 23 July 1762 by court clerk Henry JOHNSON[90]

Liber E, folios 331-333; 21 July 1762

"This Indenture made this Twenty first Day of July in the Year of our Lord one thousand seven hundred and sixty two. Between William WHARTON of Worcester County of the one part. And Charles WHARTON one of the Sons of the said William of the other part. Witnesseth that the said William for the Consideration of the natural Love and Affection which he hath and doth bear unto his aforesaid Son Charles as also for the Consideration of the Sum of Five Shillings Current money by the said Charles to the said William paid at and before the Sealing and Delivery hereof the Receipt whereof the said William hereby doth Acknowledge and for further Considerations hereafter expressed to be performed by the said Charles Hath bargained and sold, and by these Presents Doth bargain and sell unto the aforesaid Charles his Heirs and Assigns forever a Parcell of Land situate in Worcester County aforesaid being a part of a Tract of Land called Cowley containing One hundred Acres of Land more or less, it being the Lands which the said William purchased of Samuel BRITTINGHAM as also One feather Bed and Furniture which is now in the possession of the said Charles as also one Negro Boy called **Hope**, One looking Glass, One sett of Smiths Tools, One pair of Stillards and all the Cattle which is now called the said Charles's. To have and to hold the aforesaid bargained Premisses with the Appurtenances unto the said Charles his Heirs and Assigns forever for the uses and under the Limitations hereafter expressed that is to say all the Lands which lyeth to the Eastward of the main Road that leads from Stephens's Ferry to Snowhill and all the Personal Estate to remain in the Quiet and Peaceable possession of the said William during his natural Life" …
"as also all other Articles before mentioned and also one Negro Man named **Adam** / commonly called **Bob** / as also all the work Creatures and Utensils which the said William hath now in possession & the same to continue in the Service aforesaid for the purpose aforesaid during the

---

[89] Worcester County Court (Land Records). Bill of sale from DUNLAP, William and COCHRAN, George to GRAY, Thomas. 24 May 1762. E, pp. 312-313, MSA CE 30-5. www.mdlandrec.net : accessed 14 October 2021.
[90] Worcester County Court (Land Records). Bill of sale from WHARTON, William to WHARTON, John. 21 July 1762. E, pp. 329-330, MSA CE 30-5. www.mdlandrec.net : accessed 14 October 2021.

natural Life of the said William, And that on the death of the said William all and every the Articles first mentioned and intended hereby to be Conveyed to remain to the Sole use benefit and behoof the said Charles his Heirs and Assigns forever and for no other use or purpose whatsoever. In Witness whereof Each of the said Parties to these Presents their Hands have set and Seals affixed the Day and Year first above written. ~ ~

Signed Sealed & Delivered. Will[ia]m WHARTON. ~ (Seal)
In Presence of ~~~~~~~~ Charles WHARTON. (Seal)
William EVENS. ~   Ephraim EVENS."

*followed on folio 332 with the acknowledgment by Justice of the Peace Robert Jenckins HENRY, receipt of the alienation fine by Joseph ALLEN on 27 July 1762, and recordation on folio 333 by court clerk Henry JOHNSON[91]

Liber E, folios 338-340; 16 June 1762

"This Indenture made this sixteenth Day of June in the Year of our Lord one thousand seven hundred and sixty two. Between John ALEXANDER of the one part. And James MURRAY of the other part. Witnesseth that the said John ALEXANDER for and in Consideration of the Sum of Fifty pounds Current money to the said John ALEXANDER paid by the aforesaid James MURRAY at and before the Sealing and Delivery hereof the Receipt whereof the said John ALEXANDER hereby doth Acknowledge. Hath given granted bargained & sold and by these Presents Doth give grant bargain and sell unto the aforesaid James MURRAY his Heirs and Assigns forever, One lott of Ground situate in Snowhill Town in Worcester County known by Number Six together with all the Houses and other Improvements and Appurtenances thereto belonging, as also one Negro Girl named **Bridget**. To have and to hold the aforesaid Lott together with the said Houses and Appurtenances unto the said Lott belonging and the Negro Girl aforesaid unto the said James MURRAY his Heirs and Assigns forever, to and for the uses and purposes hereafter mentioned that is to say that the said James MURRAY and his Heirs shall stand seized of the said Lott and Houses and Negro aforesaid for the Sole use benefit and behoof of Mary ALEXANDER Wife of the aforesaid John ALEXANDER for and during her natural Life and after her Death then to and for the Sole use benefit and behoof of John Sheldon ALEXANDER the Son of the aforesaid John ALEXANDER and his Heirs and Assigns forever, and for no other use or purpose whatsoever And the said John ALEXANDER for the more effectual execution of these Presents and for the better Acknowledgeing the Lands and Premisses herein contained as also the Negro aforesaid and hereby doth ordain constitute and appoint his trusty Friends William ALLEN & Littleton DENNIS my Attorneys and Jointly and severally to Acknowledge the Lands and Premisses herein mentioned as also the said Negro unto the aforesaid James MURRAY and his Heirs forever for the uses and purposes herein expressed according the Laws and Customs of the Province of Maryland herein Acting and Doing in the same manner as if I was personally present hereby ratifying whatever my said Attorney or Attorneys may do in and concerning the same. In Witness whereof I have hereto set my Hand and Seal the Day and Year first above written. ~ ~

Signed Sealed & Delivered ~ ~
In Presence of us ~ ~ ~ ~ ~ ~ ~ John ALEXANDER. ~ (Seal)
John RIGGEN. ~ Peter CORBIN. ~"

*followed on folio 340 with the receipt of the alienation fine by Joseph ALLEN on 05 August 1762 and recordation by court clerk Henry JOHNSON on 06 August 1762[92]

Liber E, folios 454-455; 14 February 1763

"Maryland {?} Know all men by these Presents that I Rencher ROBERTS of Worcester County in the Consideration of the Sum of One hundred and twenty two pound to me in hand paid by

---

[91] Worcester County Court (Land Records). Deed from WHARTON, William to WHARTON, Charles. 21 July 1762. E, pp. 331-333, MSA CE 30-5. www.mdlandrec.net : accessed 14 October 2021.
[92] Worcester County Court (Land Records). Deed from ALEXANDER, John to MURRAY, James. 16 June 1762. E, pp. 338-340, MSA CE 30-5. www.mdlandrec.net : accessed 14 October 2021.

William TOADVINE, Have Bargained sold Released and Confirmed, and by these Presents do Bargain sell Release and Confirm unto the said William TOADVINE two Negroes Viz.^{t} one Negro Woman named **Bess** about nineteen years of Age, and Negro Boy named **Sam** Aged about thirteen years. To have and to hold the aforesaid Negro Woman and Boy and every of them have by these Presents Bargained Sold Released Granted and Confirmed unto the only proper use and behoof of the said William TOADVINE his Executors and Administrators and Assigns forever freely quietly peaceably and intirely without any Contradiction Claim or disturbance or hindrance of any person whatsoever and without any Account to me or to any other whatsoever to be made answered or hereafter to be Rendered so that neither I the said Rencher ROBERTS nor any other for me or in my name hath any Right title interest or demand of in to and for the said Negroes or any part Parcell or increase of the said Negroes ought to Challange Exact Claim or Demand at any time or times hereafter but from all time or times from all Actions Rights and Estates, Claim Demand Possession and Interest shall be wholy barred and Excluded by force and Vertue of these Presents, and I the said Rencher ROBERTS for myself my Executors and Adm[inistrator]^s all and singular the above named Negroes unto the said William TOADVINE his Heirs Ex[ecutor]^s or Adm[inistrator]^s and Assigns and against all of every Person or Persons whatsoever shall and will Warrant and forever Defend by these Presents of which Negroes I have put the said W[illia]^m TOADVINE in full possession before the Signing and delivery of these Presents this 14th Day of Feb[ruar]^y 1763.
Signed Sealed & Deliver[e]d
In Presence of us ....   Ransher ROBARDS   (Seal)
Benj[amin] HANDY. James HANDY~"

*followed on folio with the acknowledgment by Justice of the Peace Benjamin HANDY on 10 March 1763 and recordation by court clerk Henry JOHNSON on 14 March 1763[93]

Liber E, folios 457-460; 02 May 1763

"This Indenture made this second Day of March Anno Domini one thousand seven hundred & sixty three Between **George BLAKE** Negro or Malato of Worcester County in the Province of Maryland of the one part, and Bowdoin ROBINS of the same place of the other part. Witnesseth that the Right Honorable Frederick Lord Baron of Baltimore and by his Deed of Grant under the Great Seal used in Maryland for Granting of Lands did Grant unto the aforesaid **George BLAKE** Negro on a Resurvey on the twenty nine Day of September Anno Domini one thousand seven hundred and fifty nine, on two Tracts of Land one call[e]d Elbow Ridge the other called Blakes Lott containing fifty Acres of Land Each and was Included in one intire Tract containing thirteen hundred and fifty seven Acres of Land now Call[e]d Pardnership bareing Date the twelfth Day of September Anno Domini one thousand seven hundred and sixty. Now this Indenture farther Witnesseth that the aforesaid **George BLAKE** for & in Consideration of the Sum of One hundred & forty pounds Current money of Maryland to the said **George BLAKE** by the said Bowdoin ROBINS paid at or before the Sealing & Delivery hereof the Receipt whereof the said **George BLAKE** hereby do Acknowledge have Granted Bargained and Sold, and do hereby Give Grant Bargain and Sell to the said Bowdoin ROBINS his Heirs and Assigns forever part of the abovesaid Tract of Land called Pardnership to contain Eight hundred & Eighty four Acres of Land Limitted and Discribed as followeth." ... "And the said **George BLAKE** his Heirs forever will Warrant and Defend the same Bargained Premisses with Appurtenances unto the said Bowdoin ROBINS his Heirs and Assigns forever against all Persons Claiming titles whatsoever And the **George BLAKE** for himself his Executors Adm[inistrato]^{rs} do further Covenant to and with the said Bowdoin his Heirs and Assigns will at all times when thereunto Required by the said Bowdoin his Heirs or Assigns at the Cost and Expence of in the Law of the said Bowdoin his Heirs and Assigns requireing make do suffer and Execute every other such further Act Deed or Devise in the Law for the further Assuring the said bargained Premisses with the Appurtenances to the said Bowdoin ROBINS his Heirs and Assigns forever and the said Bowdoin ROBINS his Heirs and Assigns his or their Councill

---

[93] Worcester County Court (Land Records). Bill of sale from ROBARDS, Ransher to TOADVINE, William. 14 February 1763. E, pp. 454-455, MSA CE 30-5. www.mdlandrec.net : accessed 14 October 2021.

in the Law learned shall be advised devised or required. In testimony thereof he have affixed his Hand and Seal the Date first within written.

Signed Sealed and Delivered
In Presence of us …………..
John SELBY ~ W[illia]m ELLEGOOD. ~

George + BLAKE. ~ (Seal)
_{his Mark}

Easter X BLAKE. ~ (Seal)
_{her Mark"}

*followed on folios 459 and 460 with the acknowledgment of the Justices of the Peace John SELBY and William ELLEGOOD of Easter's release of Right of Dower on 02 March 1763, receipt of alienation fine by Joseph ALLEN on 12 March 1763, and recordation by court clerk Henry JOHNSON on 25 March 1763[94]

Liber E, folios 461-462; 18 March 1763

"Know all men by these Presents that I Jemima HENDERSON of Worcester County for the Natural Love & Affection which I bear unto my Sister Comfort MERRILL Wife of John MERRILL as also unto her Son John MERRILL and for the Consideration of the sum of five Shillings Current money to me paid by the af[oresai]d John MERRILL the Younger at and before the Sealing & delivery hereof the Receipt whereof I hereby do Acknowledge hath given bargained and sold and by these Presents doth give bargain and sell unto the af[oresai]d Comfort MERRILL and John MERRILL the Younger a Negro Girl named **Amey** now in my Possession To have & to hold the said Negro Girl called **Amey** to the said Comfort dureing her Natural Life and after her decease to and for the only Use of the af[oresai]d John MERRILL the Younger & for no other Use or Purpose whatsoever. And the said Jemima for herself doth Covenant and Agree to and with the said Comfort and John the Younger that She will forever Warrant and defend the said Negro Girl named **Amey** unto them the said Comfort and John against the Claim Right and Title of her the said Jemima and of every other Person whatsoever Claiming or that shall hereafter Claim any Right or Title to the said Girl from by or under her by these Presents Sealed with my Seal and dated this Eighteenth day of March Anno Dom[ini] 1763.

Sealed & Deliver[e]d
In Presence off
Benj[amin] HANDY. ~

Jemimah + HENDERSON (Seal)
_{her Mark"}

*followed on folio 462 with the acknowledgment of Justice of the Peace Benjamin Handy and recordation by court clerk Henry JOHNSON on 25 March 1763[95]

Liber E, folios 463-465; 02 March 1763

"This Indenture made this second Day of March Anno Domini one thousand seven hundred and sixty three. Between **George BLAKE** of Worcester County in the Province of Maryland of the one part, and **Samuel BLAKE** of the same place of the other part. Witnesseth that the said **George BLAKE** for and in Consideration of Ten pounds Current money of Maryland to him in hand paid by the said **Samuel BLAKE** before the Sealing and Delivery hereof the Receipt whereof the said **George BLAKE** doth hereby Acknowledge and hath Granted Bargained and Sold and Doth hereby Grant Bargain and Sell to the said **Samuel BLAKE** his Heirs and Assigns forever part of a Tract of Land called Partnership to Contain fifty four Acres of Land where now he the said Samuel Dwelleth Begining at a small Swamp red Oak standing on the South side of a small Branch or Drean that Issueth out of the great Holley Swamp and near the Edge of Cleared Ground Northerly from the said **Samuel** House where he now Lives from thence South East eighty five poles from thence South West eighty seven poles, from thence North

---

[94] Worcester County Court (Land Records). Deed from **BLAKE, George** and Easter to ROBINS, Bowdoin. 02 May 1763. E, pp. 457-460, MSA CE 30-5. www.mdlandrec.net : accessed 14 October 2021.

[95] Worcester County Court (Land Records). Bill of sale from HENDERSON, Jemimah to MERRILL, Comfort and John the Younger. 18 March 1763. E, pp. 461-462, MSA CE 30-5. www.mdlandrec.net : accessed 14 October 2021.

sixty four Degrees West forty five poles from thence North twenty three Degrees West sixty five poles from thence with right Line to the first Begining small Swamp red Oak containing fifty four Acres of Land be the same more or less. To have and to hold the said fifty four Acres of Land to him the said **Samuel BLAKE** his Heirs and Assigns forever, with all the Profitts Priviledges Improvements and Appurtenances to the same belonging free and clear from all manner of Incumbrances (the Quit Rents to become Due to the Lord of the fee thereof only excepted) and that the said **George BLAKE** for himself his Heirs Executors or Administrators doth hereby Covenant with the said **Samuel BLAKE** his Heirs and Assigns that at the time of the Sealing and Delivery hereof he is Seized of and in the said fifty four Acres of Land in fee Simple and that he hath a good Right to Sell and Convey the same to the said **Samuel BLAKE** in the manner and form aforesaid, and the said **George BLAKE** for himself his Heirs Executors or Administrators doth further Covenant with the said **Samuel BLAKE** his Heirs and Assigns to Grant unto him or them such further Assurances to the said fifty four Acres of Land as his or their Councill Learned in the Law shall any time require. In Witness whereof the said **George BLAKE** hath hereunto sett his Hand and affixed his Seal the Day and Year above written. ~

Signed Sealed and Delivered
In the Presence of ~ ~
John SELBY ~   W[illia]^m ELLEGOOD. ~

George + BLAKE ~ (Seal)
(his mark)

Ester & BLAKE ~ (Seal)
(her mark)"

*followed on folio 464 with the acknowledgment by Justices of the Peace John SELBY and William ELLEGOOD, the receipt of the alienation fine on 29 March 1763 by Joseph ALLEN, and the recordation by court clerk Henry JOHNSON on folio 465[96]

*Samuel's race/ethnicity is not noted in any land records in this series. The assumption is based on his surname and residence on George's land prior to purchase.

Liber E, folios 471-472; 02 March 1763

"This Indenture made the 2.^d Day of March Anno Dom[ini] one thousand seven hundred Sixty and three By & Between **George BLAKE** of Worcester County Negro or Molatter & Ester his Wife of the one Part and Ezekiel LANE of the other Part. Witnesseth that the afores[ai]^d **George BLAKE** and Ester his Wife for & in Consideration of Fifty pounds Current money of Maryland to them in hand Paid by the afores[ai]^d LANE before the Ensealing and Delivery hereof Do Bargain & Sell, and by these Presents have Bargained and Sold unto the afores[ai]^d Ezekiel LANE Two hundred & Eighteen Acres of Land lying and being Worcester County being Part of a Tract of 1357 Acres Surveyed for the afores[ai]^d **BLAKE** the 29th of September Anno Dom[ini] 1759 called Partnership the 218 a[cres] afores[ai]^d is Bounded as followeth to begin at the second Bounder of the afores[ai]d Tract it also being the first Bounder of a Tract of Land called Hogg Quarter now in the Possession of W[illia]^m HANCOCK and Bowden ROBBINS" … "thence with a straight Line drawn to the first Bounder Containing and now Layd of for Two hundred and eighteen Acres be the same more or less for which the afores[ai]^d **George BLAKE** and Easter his Wife doth Acknowledge themselves fully satisfied and payd and for every Part & Parcel thereof doth fully and clearly Acquit and Discharge the afores[ai]^d Ezekiel LANE his Heirs Ex[ecutor]^s and Adm[inistrator]^s & Assigns forever & by these Presents hath Bargained Sold Aliened and Confirmed unto the afores[ai]^d Ezekiel LANE his Heirs and Assigns forever all and singular the afores[ai]^d Two hundred and Eighteen Acres according to the Meets and Bounds afores[ai]^d together with all the Rights Profits & Priviledges thereunto Belonging free and clear from all Incumbrances the Quit Rents Insuing only excepted and the afores[ai]^d **George BLAKE** do hereby oblige Myself my Heirs Ex[ecutor]^s and Adm[inistrator]^s to forever Warrant and Defend all and singular of the hereby Demised Premisses from all manner of

---

[96] Worcester County Court (Land Records). Deed from **BLAKE, George** to **BLAKE, Samuel**. 02 March 1763. E, pp. 463-465, MSA CE 30-5. www.mdlandrec.net : accessed 16 June 2022.

Person or Persons whatsoever unto him the afores[ai]d Ezekiel LANE his Heirs and Assigns forever, In Witness whereof we have hereunto Set our Hands and fixed our Seals the Day and Year first above written. ~

Signed Sealed & Delivered
In Presence of us ~~~~~~
John SELBY. W[illia]m ELLEGOOD~

George + BLAKE (Seal)
his Mark

Easter 0 BLAKE (Seal)
her Mark"

*followed on folio 472 with the acknowledgment of Justices of the Peace John SELBY and William ELLEGOOD, receipt of the alienation fine by Joseph ALLEN on 03 March 1763, and recordation by court clerk Henry JOHNSON on 08 April 1763[97]

Liber E, folio 511; 13 April 1763

"This Indenture made this 13th Day of Aprill in the Year of our Lord one thousand seven hundred sixty and three. Between Edward WOODEN of the one part, and John WOOTEN of the other party. Witnesseth that the said Edward WOOTTEN for and in Consideration of the Sum of ten pounds Current money of Maryland to him in Hand paid by the said John WOOTEN the Receipt whereof the said Edward WOOTTEN doth hereby Confess and Acknowledge and thereof doth Acquit Exonerate and Discharge the said John WOOTTEN and his Heirs Executors & Adm[inistrator]s firmly by these presents Hath Bargained Sold Assigned Sett Over Transfer[e]d and Deliver[e]d, and these Presents Doth Bargain Sell Assign Sett over Transfer and Deliver unto the said John WOODEN and his Heirs and Assigns one Negro man Slave named **Pompy** one of my best Beds and furniture my Riding Saddle and Bridle my Squirrill gun my Chist that is at his House and everything that is Contained within the Chist my Curring Knife my part of a Still and Crosscut saw with the Use of my Smiths and Coopers tools. To have and to hold the aforementioned Negro Slave and a good aforesaid unto the said John WOODEN his Heirs and Assigns forever, and the said Edward WOODEN doth hereby Covenant and Agree to and with the said John his Heirs Ex[ecutor]s Adm[inistrator]s or Assigns that he the said Edward WOODEN the afores[ai]d Man Slave and goods as aforesaid against Himself and all Persons legally Claiming the same by from or under Him or in trust for Him his Heirs Ex[ecutor]s or Adm[inistrator]s unto the said John WOODEN his Heirs Ex[ecutor]s Adm[inistrator]s or Assigns will Warrant and forever Defend by these Presents. In Witness whereof the Partyes aforesaid have hereunto Set their Hand and fixed their Seals the Day and Year first above written.

Sealed and Deliver[e]d In the Presence
Benj[amin] HANDY. ~~~~~~~~~~

Edward X WOODEN (Seal)
his Mark"

*followed with the acknowledgment by Justice of the Peace Benjamin HANDY, the receipt of full consideration by Edward WOODEN, and recordation by court clerk Henry JOHNSON on 12 May 1763[98]

Liber E, folios 527-528; 10 June 1763

"This Indenture made this tenth day of June Anno Dom[ini] Seventeen hundred Sixty and three, Between Levin LARRAMORE of Worcester County in the Province of Maryland of the one part, and Joseph COLLINGS of the County and Province af[ore]s[ai]d of the other part. Witnesseth that the said Levin LARRAMORE for and in Consideration of five Shillings Current money of Maryland to him in hand paid by the af[ore]s[ai]d Joseph COLLINGS at and before the Sealing and Delivery hereof the Receipt whereof the af[ore]s[ai]d Levin LARRAMORE doth hereby Confess and Acknowledge and thereof doth Acquit Exonerate and Discharge him the said Joseph COLLINGS his Heirs and Assigns forever by these presents,

---

[97] Worcester County Court (Land Records). Deed from **BLAKE, George** and Easter to LANE, Ezekiel. 02 March 1763. E, pp. 471-472, MSA CE 30-5. www.mdlandrec.net : accessed 14 October 2021.
[98] Worcester County Court (Land Records). Deed from WOODEN, Edward to WOOTEN, Ezekiel. 13 April 1763. E, p. 511, MSA CE 30-5. www.mdlandrec.net : accessed 14 October 2021.

Hath Given Granted bargained Conveyed Confirmed and Assigned over, and by these presents doth Give Grant Bargain Convey Confirm and Assign over unto the said Joseph COLLINGS his Heirs and Assigns forever the five Negro Slaves Named and Called as following to wit. **Sambo, Bess, Coffe, Sampson, and Watt** together with all his Moveable Goods and Chattels, Including the whole of his personal Estate. To have and to hold the af[ore]s[ai]^d Bargained Negroes together with the whole of his Personal Estate unto him the said Joseph COLLINGS his Heirs and Assigns forever, and to and for no other Use purpose or Intent whatsoever. And the aforesaid Levin LARRAMORE for himself his Heirs Executors and Administrators doth further Covenant Promise and Agree to and with the aforesaid Joseph COLLINGS his Heirs Executors Administrators and Assigns, that he the said Levin LARRAMORE his Heirs Executors and Administrators the aforesaid Bargained premisses unto him the said Joseph COLLINGS his Heirs and Assigns forever from all Persons whatsoever shall and will Warrant and forever Defend by these presents. In Witness whereof the Parties hereto have Interchangeably set their hands and affixed their Seals the day and Year first above written.
Sealed and Delivered   Littleton DENNIS.   Levin LARRAMUR. ~ ~ (Seal)
In Presence of ~   Josiah POLK"

*followed on folio 528 with the acknowledgment by Justices of the Peace John EVANS and William ELLEGOOD and recordation by court clerk Henry JOHNSON[99]

Liber F, folios 16-17; 09 September 1763

"This Indenture made this Ninth day of September in the Year of our Lord one thousand Seven hundred and Sixty three Between Avery MORGAN the Elder of Worcester County of the One part And John MORGAN, Avery MORGAN the Younger, Mary MORGAN & Sarah MORGAN all Children of the af[oresai]^d Avery the Elder of the other part. Witnesseth that the said Avery MORGAN the Elder for and in Consideration of the Natural love & Affection which he hath and doth bear unto the af[oresai]^d Children, as also for the Consideration of the Sum of fifty pounds Current money to him by each of them respectively paid at and before the Sealing and delivery hereof the receipt whereof the said Avery MORGAN the Elder hereby doth Acknowledge hath given Bargained Sold and Delivered and by these presents doth give Bargain Sell and deliver unto his af[oresai]^d Children to wit John, Avery the Younger, Mary & Sarah the Slaves in manner following to wit unto his af[oresai]^d Son John one Negro called **Young Caesar**, and one called **Cupit** to the said John & his Heirs and Assigns forever, unto his Son Avery MORGAN Jun[ior] his Heirs and Assigns forever one Negro called **Old Caesar** one called old **Hanah**, and one called **Solomon**, unto his Daughter Mary MORGAN her Heirs and Assigns forever one Negro called **Susanah** one called Young **Hanah**, and unto his af[oresai]^d Daughter called Sarah to her & her Heirs forever one Negro called **Capel** and one called **Esther**. To have and to hold the af[oresai]^d Negroes unto the af[oresai]^d Children & their Heirs and Assigns respectively as herein particularly nominated & directed to their sole proper use benefit and behoof and for no other use or purpose whatever And the said Avery MORGAN for himself his Heirs Exe[cuto]^{rs} and Adm[inistrator]^s doth Covenant Grant and Agree with the af[oresai]^d John Avery the Younger Mary & Sarah respectively and with their respective Heirs and Assigns that he will Warrant and defend the af[oresai]^d Slaves to Each of them as herein particularly Sold & Conveyed unto them, against the claim right title possession and demand of him the said Avery MORGAN the Elder and against all and every other Person whatsoever In Witness whereof the said Avery the Elder to these presents his hand hath set & Seal affixed the day and Year first above written
Signed Sealed & Deliver[e]d In Presence of us   A[ver]y MORGAN. ~ (Seal)
John SELBY. ~   W[illia]^m ALLEN. ~"

---

[99] Worcester County Court (Land Records). Deed from LARRAMUR, Levin to COLLINGS, Joseph. 10 June 1763. E, pp. 527-528, MSA CE 30-5. www.mdlandrec.net : accessed 14 October 2021.

*followed on folio 17 with the acknowledgment by Justice of the Peace John SELBY and recordation by court clerk Henry JOHNSON[100]

Liber F, folio 91; 10 March 1764

"Worcester {?} Know all Men by these Presents that I Elias TOWNSEND of Worcester County in the Province af[oresai]^d Maryland Marriner for and in Consideration of the Sum of Twenty four Pounds fifteen Shillings and eleven Pence Current money of Maryland to me in Hand paid by William BEAVENS Jun[io]^r (Son of Thomas) of said County and Province Planter, the Receipt whereof I do hereby Acknowledge and my self therewith Contented and Satisfied, and forever do Acquit and Discharge the said William BEAVENS his Heirs and Assigns. have given delivered bargained and sold, and do by these Presents give grant bargain and sell unto the said William BEAVENS his Executors Administrators and Assigns one Negro Girl called **Leah** aged three Years or thereabouts. To have and to hold the said Bargained Premisses unto the said William BEAVENS Jun[io]^r his Heirs Executors Administrators and Assigns, and further against all Persons claiming by from or under me, that I will Warrant and the same forever Defend. In Witness whereof I the said Elias TOWNSEND my Hand have set and Seal affixed this tenth day of March Anno Domini Seventeen hundred sixty and four.

Sealed and Deliver[e]d   John TENESSY   Elias TOWNSEND. (Seal)
In Presence of us.   Joshua HALL"

*followed with the acknowledgment of Justice of the Peace Thomas HANDY and recordation on 17 March 1764 by court clerk Henry JOHNSON[101]

Liber F, folios 100-101; 24 March 1764

"This Indenture made the Twenty fourth day of March in the Year of our Lord God one thousand seven hundred sixty and four. Between Robert STEVENSON of Worcester County in the Province of Maryland Planter (Eldest Son and Heir at Law of Robert STEVENSON late of the County and Province af[ore]s[ai]^d deceased) of the one part, and Samuel STEVENSON of the said County of Worcester in the Province af[ore]s[ai]^d Planter (one other Son of the said Robert STEVENSON deceased) of the other part. Witnesseth that the said Robert STEVENSON for and in Consideration of the natural Love and Affection which he hath and doth bear unto his said Brother Samuel STEVENSON and also for and in Consideration of the Sum of Five Shillings Current money of Maryland to him the said Robert STEVENSON by the said Samuel STEVENSON in Hand paid at or before the Sealing and Delivery of these Presents the Receipt whereof he doth hereby Confess and Acknowledge and thereof Acquit release and Discharge the said Samuel STEVENSON his Heirs Executors Administr[ato]^{rs} and Assigns forever. Hath given granted bargained and sold aliened released and confirmed, and by these Presents doth give grant bargain and sell alien release and confirm unto the said Samuel STEVENSON his Heirs and Assigns forever, all the Estate Right Title Interest Possession Claim Property and Demand whatsoever which he the said Robert STEVENSON hath or of Right ought to have of in and unto all that Parcel of Land formerly Purchased by John MILLS Grand Father of the said Robert STEVENSON party to these Presents of a certain Henry BAYLY and Elizabeth his Wife and one Whittington BAYLY and Lisha his Wife being Part of a Tract of Land called Kings'-Land containing five hundred Acres" … "And also the said Robert STEVENSON for and in Consideration of the natural Love and Affection which he doth bear unto the said Samuel STEVENSON his Brother, and in Consideration of the further Sum of Five Shillings Current money of Maryland he the said Robert STEVENSON hath given bargained sold assigned and transferred, by these Presents doth give bargain sell assign and transferr unto the said Samuel STEVENSON and to his Executors Administ[rato]^{rs} and Assigns forever one Negro Slave named **Peter** and all Profitts Benefitts and Advantages to the same

---

[100] Worcester County Court (Land Records). Bill of sale from MORGAN, Avery to MORGAN, John, Avery, Mary, and Sarah. 09 September 1763. F, pp. 16-17, MSA CE 30-6. www.mdlandrec.net : accessed 18 October 2021.
[101] Worcester County Court (Land Records). Bill of sale from TOWNSEND, Elias to BEAVANS, William Jr. 10 March 1764. F, p. 91, MSA CE 30-6. www.mdlandrec.net : accessed 18 October 2021.

Slave belonging or in any manner arising. To have and to hold the af[ore]s[ai]^d Two hundred Acres of Land with the Rights Members and Appurtenances unto the said Samuel STEVENSON his Heirs and Assigns forever, To the only proper Use and Behoof of the said Samuel STEVENSON and of his Heirs and Assigns forever And also To have and to hold the said Negro Man Slave **Peter** with all Profitts Benefitts and Advantages from the said Slave arising unto the only proper use and Behoof of him the said Samuel STEVENSON his Executors Administrators and Assigns forever, and to no other use or purpose whatsoever." …
"and also that he said Robert STEVENSON his Heirs Executors and Adm[inistrator]^s the af[oresai]^d Negro **Peter** against him and themselves and all other Persons whatsoever now Claiming or who hereafter Legally may claim the said Slave by from or under him them or any of them unto the said Samuel STEVENSON his Exe[cutor]^s Adm[inistrator]^s and Assigns shall and will Warrant and forever Defend by these Presents. In Witness whereof the Parties af[oresai]^d to this Indenture interchangeably their Hands have Set and Seals affixed the Day and Year first above written.

Sign[e]d Seal[e]d & Deliver[e]d   Rob[er]^t STEVENSON. (Seal)
In Presence of ~
Benjamin SCOTT. ~ John JORDAN."

*followed on folio 101 with acknowledgment by Justice of the Peace Robert Jenckins HENRY and recordation on 30 March 1764 by court clerk Henry JOHNSON[102]

*Due to its true length, this transcription has been shortened to its most relevant portions. The full original deed can be viewed at the citation provided.

Liber F, folio 103; 20 March 1764

"This Indenture made this Twentieth day of March Anno Domini one thousand seven hundred and sixty four. Between Robert STEVENSON and Samuel STEVENSON both of Worcester County in the Province of Maryland Planters of the one part, and Benjamin SCOTT of the same County and Province af[oresai]^d of the other part. Witnesseth that the said Robert STEVENSON and Samuel STEVENSON for divers good Causes and Considerations them thereunto moveing and for the love and good will which they have and do bear unto him the said Benjamin SCOTT and more Especially for and in Consideration of the Sum of five Shillings Current money of Maryland to them in Hand paid by the af[oresai]^d Benjamin SCOTT at and before the Ensealing and Delivery of these Presents the Receipt whereof the said Robert STEVENSON and Samuel STEVENSON doth Acknowledge themselves therewith fully Satisfied Paid and Contented do by these presents give grant make over deliver and confirm unto him the said Benjamin SCOTT his Heirs and Assigns forever, all our Rights Title and Interest which we do Claim of and in three Negroes to wit. **Dinah, Nancy, and Pleasent** and their Increase. To have and to hold the af[oresai]^d Negros and their Increase to wit. **Dinah, Nancy, and Pleasent**, to him the said Benjamin SCOTT and his Heirs and Assigns forever to his and their proper use and behoof. And furthermore we the af[oresai]^d Robert STEVENSON and Samuel STEVENSON for us our Heirs Executors Administrators do Covenant to and with the said Benjamin SCOTT his Heirs Executors Administrators to Warrant and Defend the af[oresai]^d Negros as aforementioned and their Increase from all manner of Persons Claiming any Right or Title by from or under us or our Heirs. In Testimony whereof we have hereunto our Hands have Set and Seals affixt this Day and Year first above written. ~

Signed Sealed and Delivered.   Robert STEVENSON. (Seal)
In Presence of us. ~   Samuel STEVENSON. (Seal)
John JORDAN. / . ~"

---

[102] Worcester County Court (Land Records). Deed of Gift from STEVENSON, Robert to STEVENSON, Samuel. 24 March 1764. F, pp. 100-101, MSA CE 30-6. www.mdlandrec.net : accessed 18 October 2021.

*followed with the acknowledgment by Justice of the Peace Robert Jenckins HENRY and recordation on 30 March 1764 by court clerk Henry JOHNSON[103]

Liber F, folios 155-156; 10 June 1764

"Know all Men by these Presents that I Thomas POPE of Worcester County and in Consideration of John SELBY of the County af[oresai]^d having become bound as Bail for me the said Thomas in Worcester County in two Suits one Prosecuted against me by Daniel QUINTON on a Mortgage Deed for the Payment of fifteen Pounds and Interest, and one other Prosecuted by Isaac PAIN against me on a Bond for forty Pounds have Bargained and Sold and Delivered, and by these Presents doth Bargain Sell and Deliver unto the af[oresai]^d John SELBY his Executors Adm[inistrato]^{rs} or Assigns one Negro Man Slave named **Jesse**. To have and to hold the af[oresai]^d Negro Man Slave unto the af[oresai]^d John SELBY his Executors Adm[inistrato]^{rs} or Assigns to and for the only use benefit and behoof of the said John SELBY {his} Executors Adm[inistrato]^{rs} or Assigns and for no other use or purpose whatsoever, And I the said Thomas POPE for myself my Heirs Executors and Adm[inistrato]^{rs} doth Covenant and Agree to and with the said Selby his Ex[ecuto]^{rs} Adm[inistrato]^{rs} and Assigns that he hath good right to bargain and sell the said Negro {?} manner and form as af[oresai]^d and also shall and will permit and suffer the said John SELBY {?} into the Possession the af[oresai]^d Slave and him to detain and put to Service and hire at the proper risque of the said Thomas the profits arrising from his said Service to be applyed for the use of the said Thomas during the time and so long as the time and terms hereafter limit{?}Provided always and it is the true intent and meaning hereof that if the said Thomas {?} save harmless and keep indemnifyed the af[oresai]^d John SELBY his E[xecuto]^{rs} or Adm[inistrato]^{rs} from all Dama{ge?} Costs & Expence that the said John or his Ex[ecuto]^{rs} or Adm[inistrato]^{rs} shall Sustain by means of his beco{?} Bail as af[oresai]^d but if default be made therein then the said Thomas hereby agrees with the said John SELBY that it shall be Lawfull for the said John to Sell and Dispose of the said Negro and the Money arrising from such Sale to be applyed to the Discharg{e?} of the Debts af[oresai]^d In Witness whereof the said Thomas to these Presents his Hand hath Set & Seal affixed the 10 day of June Anno Dom[ini] 1764. ~

Sealed & Delivered   Thomas POPE   (Seal)
In Presence of ~
Jn.º SCARBOROUGH. ~   Jn.º SCARBOROUGH Jun[ior]"

*followed on folio 156 with the acknowledgment by Justice of the Peace John SCARBOROUGH and recordation on 09 June 1764 by Henry JOHNSON[104]

*The right edge of folio 155 was worn away affected the readability of any words along the edge.

Liber F, folios 236-238; 14 September 1764

"This Indenture made this fourteenth Day of September Anno Domini one thousand seven hundred and sixty four. Between **George BLAKE** (Negro) of Worcester County in the Province of Maryland of the one part, and Bowdoin ROBINS of the same place of the other part. Witnesseth that the right Honourable Frederick Baron of Baltimore and by his Deed of Grant under the great Seal used in Maryland for granting of Lands did grant unto the af[ore]said **George BLAKE** (Negro) on a Resurvey on the twenty fifth Day of September one thousand and seven hundred and fifty nine on two Tracts of Land one called Elbow Ridge and the other called Blakes Lott containing fifty Acres of Land each and was included in one intire Tract containing thirteen hundred and fifty seven Acres of Land now called Pardnership bearing Date the twelfth Day of September one thousand seven hundred and sixty, and the aforesaid **George**

---

[103] Worcester County Court (Land Records). Deed of Gift from STEVENSON, Robert and Samuel to SCOTT, Benjamin. 20 March 1764. F, p. 103, MSA CE 30-6. www.mdlandrec.net : accessed 18 October 2021.
[104] Worcester County Court (Land Records). Bill of sale from POPE, Thomas to SELBY, John. 10 June 1764. F, pp. 155-156, MSA CE 30-6. www.mdlandrec.net : accessed 19 October 2021.

BLAKE has by sundry Conveyances Alienated and Sold twelve hundred and fifty seven Acres of Land out of the aforesaid Tract of Land called Pardnership. Now this Indenture further Witnesseth that the af[ore]said **George BLAKE** for and in Consideration of the Sum of forty Pounds current Money of Maryland to the said **George BLAKE** by the said Bowdoin ROBINS paid at or before the Sealing and Delivery hereof the Receipt whereof the said **George BLAKE** hereby do Acknowledge have granted bargained and sold, and do hereby give grant bargain and sell to the said Bowdoin ROBINS his Heirs and Assigns forever, all the Remainder of the af[ore]said Tract of Land called Pardnership by Estimation one hundred Acres of Land be the same more or less. To have and to hold the aforesaid remainder with all the whole Right Title Claim and Interest of and to the af[ore]said Tract of Land called Parndnership with the Appurtenances unto the said Bowdoin ROBINS his Heirs and Assigns forever to the only use and behoof of the said Bowdoin ROBINS his Heirs and Assigns forever, and no other use or uses whatsoever, and for the better and further assurances of the Granted and bargained Premisses with the Appurtenances to the said Bowdoin ROBINS his Heirs and Assigns forever, the said **George BLAKE** for himself his Heirs Executors and Administrators do hereby Covenant and Agree to and with the said Bowdoin ROBINS his Heirs and Assigns forever, that the said **George BLAKE** before the Sealing and Delivery hereof is Seized thereof to his proper use in fee simple and have a good Right to Bargain and Sell the same to the said Bowdoin ROBINS his Heirs and Assigns forever in manner or form aforesaid, and that the same are free and clear of all Incumbrances whatsoever. And that the said **George BLAKE** his Heirs forever will Warrant and Defend the same bargained Premisses with the Appurtenances unto the said Bowdoin ROBINS his Heirs and Assigns forever against all Persons Claims Titles whatsoever: and the said **George BLAKE** for himself his Heirs Executors Administrators do further Covenant to and with the said Bowdoin ROBINS his Heirs and Assigns will at all times when thereunto required by the Bowdoin ROBINS his Heirs and Assigns at the Cost and Expence in the Law of the said Bowdoin his Heirs and Assigns Requiring make do suffer and execute every other such and further Act Deed or Devise in the Law for the further and better assuring the bargain[e]d Premisses with the Appurtenances to the said Bowdoin ROBINS his Heirs and Assigns forever as the said Bowdoin his Heirs and Assigns his or their Councill in the Law learned shall be advised or devised or required. In Testimony thereof he has Sett his Hand and affixed his Seal the Day and year first above written. / ~

Signed Sealed and Delivered	Jn.º SCARBOROUGH	his
In the Presence of …….	John SELBY	**George** + **BLAKE** (Seal)
		Mark"

*followed on folio 237 with the acknowledgment of Justices of the Peace John SELBY and John SCABOROUGH, the receipt of the alienation fine by Joseph ALLEN on 21 September 1764, and recordation on 12 November 1764 by court clerk Henry JOHNSON on folio 238[105]

Liber F, folios 300-301; 01 March 1765

"This Indenture made this first day of March in the Year of our Lord one thousand seven hundred & sixty five Between William WILLIAMS of Somerset County in the Province of Maryland Innholder of the one part, and John DONE of the same place Gent[lema]ⁿ of the other part. Witnesseth that he the said William WILLIAMS for & in Consideration of the sum of One hundred & fifty four Pounds eleven Shillings and ten Pence current Money of Maryland to him in hand paid by the said John DONE at and before the Sealing & Delivery of these presents the Receipt whereof the said William WILLIAMS doth hereby Confess & Acknowledge & thereof doth acquit exonerate & discharge the said John DONE his Heirs Exec[uto]ʳˢ Adm[inistrato]ʳˢ & Assigns forever, Hath Granted Bargained & Sold Assigned & set Over, and by these presents doth Bargain Grant & Sell Assign & set Over unto the said John DONE his Heirs & Assigns forever, one Lott of Ground lying and being in Snowhill Town in Worcester County & Province aforesaid it being the Lott whereon the said William WILLIAMS lately dwelt & whereon a

---

[105] Worcester County Court (Land Records). Deed from BLAKE, George to ROBINS, Bowdoin. 14 September 1764. F, pp. 236-238, MSA CE 30-6. www.mdlandrec.net : accessed 19 October 2021.

certain Jesse ENNIS now lives & is called and known by the name of Lott Number Twenty seven, as also one Negro Wench called **Rose**, as also six Beds & Furniture with one Bolster two Pillows, Blanketts Rug & c. appertaining to each Bed, being the Beds & Furniture now in use by the said William WILLIAMS in his House in Princess Ann Town in the County & Province aforesaid together with all Improvements Profitts Priviledges Hereditaments & Appurtenances unto the said Lott belonging or in any manner appertaining. To have & to hold the said Lott of Ground with the Appurtenances unto the same belonging or in any manner appertaining, as also the said Negro Wench called **Rose** & all the Beds Furniture & c. thereto belonging as before mentioned unto the said John DONE his Heirs & Assigns forever, to the only proper use & behoof of the said John DONE his Heirs & Assigns forever, & to no other use intent or purpose whatsoever. Provided always & it is the true intent & meaning hereof that if the said William WILLIAMS do & shall well & truly Pay or Cause to be Paid unto the said John DONE his Heirs Exe[cuto]^{rs} Administrators or Assigns the just & full Sum of One hundred & fifty four Pounds eleven Shillings and ten Pence current Money of Maryland with legal Interest thereon on or before the first Day of March which shall happen in the Year of our Lord one thousand seven hundred & seventy, Then this Instrument of Writing & every matter & thing herein Contained to be null & Void as if the same had never been made & the said William WILLIAMS doth hereby Covenant & Agree to & with the said John DONE that he the said William WILLIAMS hath in himself full power good Right true Title & lawfull & absolute Authority to Grant & Assign the said before mentioned bargained premises & c. unto the said John DONE his Heirs & Assigns forever, in manner & form afores[ai]^d & that it may & shall be lawfull to & for the said John DONE his Heirs Ex[ecuto]^{rs} Adm[inistrato]^{rs} or Assigns immediately from & after any breach or default that shall happen to be made of the Proviso or Condition afores[ai]^d by the said William WILLIAMS to take into his Custody & Sell & dispose of all or such part of the said bargained Premises & c as he the said John DONE his Ex[ecuto]^{rs} Adm[inistrato]^{rs} or Assigns shall think fit, at such Price or Prices as may be reasonably had or obtained for the same & thereout in the first place to deduct or retain to him or themselves for the Payment of the Sum of Money afores[ai]^d with the Interest thereon or such part thereof as shall be then due & unpaid to the said John DONE & the Overplus of such Money (if any) together with the remainder of he said bargained Premises (if any shall happen to be unsold or undisposed of] shall be & is hereby agreed to be rendered or delivered to the said William WILLIAMS his Heirs & Assigns forever, In Witness whereof the Parties aforesaid to this Indenture have hereto put their Hands & Seals affixed the Day & Year above written. ~
Sealed & D[elivere]D   Jo^s[eph] DIRICKSON   William WILLIAMS (Seal)
In Presence of ~   W[illia]^m ELLEGOOD"

*followed on folio 301 with the acknowledgment by Justices of the Peace Joseph DIRICKSON and William ELLEGOOD, the receipt of the alienation fine by Joseph ALLEN on 08 March 1765, and recordation by court clerk Henry JOHNSON[106]

Liber F, folios 306-307; 04 March 1765

"Know all Men by these that I William BENSON of Worcester County and Province of Maryland Brick layer for and in Consideration of Fifty Pounds to me in hand paid by Joseph FORMAN of the County of Somerset at and before the Sealing and Delivery of these presents wherewith I Confess myself fully satisfied and contented & paid have Bargained and Sold, and by these presents do Bargain and Sell in an absolute manner within the County aforesaid one Negro Wench named **Rose** To have and to hold the said Negro Wench to the said Joseph FORMAN his Heirs Ex[ecuto]^{rs} Adm[inistrato]^{rs} or Assigns to his and their own proper use benefit & behoof forever. And I the said W[illia]^m BENSON, my Executors Adm[inistrato]^{rs} and every of them the above mentioned Wench called **Rose** unto the said Joseph FORMAN his Ex[ecuto]^{rs} Adm[inistrato]^{rs} or Assigns against all People will forever Warrant and Defend by these presents. Provided allways that if the said W[illia]^m BENSON his Heirs & c or any of them do well and truly pay or cause to be paid to the said Joseph FORMAN whatever Debt the

---

[106] Worcester County Court (Land Records). Deed of mortgage from WILLIAMS, William to DONE, John. 01 March 1765. F, pp. 300-301, MSA CE 30-6. www.mdlandrec.net : accessed 19 October 2021.

said FORMAN can make appear against him the said BENSON with the Cost & Intrest thereon on or before the first Day of June next ensuing the Date. Then this present Bargain to be Void else to remain in full force & virtue witness my Hand & Seal March 4th 1765

Seal[e]d & D[elivere]d   Jos. HILCH   William BENSON. (Seal)
In Presence of ~   Ebene[ze]r WALLER"

*followed on folio 307 with the acknowledgment of Justice of the Peace William ELLEGOOD and recordation by court clerk Henry JOHNSON[107]

Liber F, folio 318; 28 February 1765

"To all People to whom these presents shall come I Thomas CLARKSON do send Greeting. Know ye that I the said Thomas CLARKSON of the County of Worcester and Province of Maryland Planter, for and in Consideration of the love and good will and for the good services that Obadiah OUTTEN and Thomas ONEAL have done me both of Worcester County and the af[ore]s[ai]d Province I do Grant and freely Give unto the afores[ai]d OUTTEN and the af[ore]s[ai]d ONEAL my two Negroes Vizt **Venis** and her Child **Dick**. that they may have them hold them She their Heirs Executors Administrators or Assigns, untill the time be that I pay or Cause to be paid all the Debts Dues and Demands that these af[ore]s[ai]d two Men have been my Securities to pay. And to the performance of this I do bind myself my Heirs Executors Admin[i]st[rators] and Assigns in the penal sum of three hundred and seventy Pounds currency of Maryland, and I do allso give grant unto the af[ore]s[ai]d two Men Vizt OUTTEN and ONEAL upon the af[ore]s[ai]d Condition that is say untill the paying of the af[ore]s[ai]d Debts be all well and truly paid, I say I give and freely grant One hundred Acres of Pattent Land lying upon Nanticoke River adjoining to Lewises Creek named Clarksons Lot, and allso a Still and two Feather Beds and two yoke of Oxen and one Horse, and ten good Sows and **George** a younger Negro, and I Thomas CLARKSON will Deliver the af[ore]s[ai]d Effects unto the af[ore]s[ai]d two Men OUTTEN & ONEAL when ever the Demand the same upon the af[ore]s[ai]d Conditions and to the whole performance of this Concerning my part I do hereby set my hand and Seal this Twenty eighth Day of Febr[uary] one thousand seven hundred and sixty five.
Witness present
James BAPTIST.
Bennah CLARKSON   Tho[ma]s CLARKSON. (Seal)
           her
Elizabeth + THOMAS.
         Mark"

*followed with the acknowledgment by Justice of the Peace William ELLEGOOD and recordation by court clerk Henry JOHNSON[108]

Liber F, folios 321-322; 21 March 1765

"This Indenture made this Twenty first Day of March in the Year of our Lord one thousand seven hundred sixty and five. Between George ADAMS of Worcester County of the one part and John ADAMS of the other part. Witnesseth that the said George ADAMS for and in Consideration of the Sum of Forty Pounds ten Shillings Sterling Money of Great Britain to him in hand paid by the said John ADAMS at and before the Sealing and Delivery of these presents the Receipt of which the said George ADAMS hereby Acknowledges, he hath bargained and sold, and by these doth bargain and sell unto the said John ADAMS his Heirs and Assigns three Negroes called **Sipeo Joabe & David** to the said John ADAMS his Heirs and Assigns forever, To have and to hold the three Negroes called **Sipeo, Joab & David** to the said John ADAMS his Heirs and Assigns forever, and for no other use or purpose whatsoever. Provided always

---

[107] Worcester County Court (Land Records). Bill of sale from BENSON, William to FORMAN, Joseph. 04 March 1765. F, pp. 306-307, MSA CE 30-6. www.mdlandrec.net : accessed 19 October 2021.
[108] Worcester County Court (Land Records). Deed of gift from CLARKSON, Thomas to OUTTEN, Obadiah and ONEAL, Thomas. 28 February 1765. F, p. 318, MSA CE 30-6. www.mdlandrec.net : accessed 19 October 2021.

that the said George ADAMS do well and truly pay or cause to be paid unto Mary WAGGAMAN the Sum of forty Pounds ten Shillings Sterling Money of Great Britain for which the said John ADAMS hath become Security in a Bond bearing date the Twenty first day of March 1765 that immediately after the Discharge of the said Bond and the aforesaid Sum of Money paid to the abovesaid Mary WAGGAMAN that then this present Indenture Shall become Void and of no Effect, as Witness my Hand and Seal the Say and Year above written.
/.~./.~./.~./.~./.~
Signed Sealed & Deliver[e]d
In Presence of us ~   George ADAMS   (Seal)
W[illia]m ADAMS. ~   La[?] ROBERTSON"

*followed on folio 322 with the acknowledgment by Justice of the Peace William ADAMS and recordation on 10 April 1765 by court clerk Henry JOHNSON[109]

Liber F, folio 330; 13 March 1765

"Maryland Worcester County Ss.t To all People & c I Lucrecia CLAYWELL of ye County and Province afores[ai]d send Greeting. Know ye, that I the said Lucrecia CLAYWELL for and in Consideration of the natural Love and Affection which I have and bear unto my Daughter Comfort SMITH and to Moses SMITH her Husband (both of the County & Province afores[ai]d) and also for other good Causes and Considerations me thereto moveing Have given and granted and by these presents do give grant and confirm unto the said Comfort SMITH and to Moses SMITH her Husband one young Negro Man **Abel**, and one Negro Woman Named **Leah** with two feather Beds & furniture one Writing Desk now in the Possession of John FENICY, one large Iron Pot and Hooks, one Bedstead that is in the possession of Solomon CLAYWELL, one four Gallon Iron Pot in the possession of Levin HILL and all my wearing Cloaths to my afores[ai]d Daughter Comfort SMITH and her Heirs by ye s[ai]d Moses SMITH and in what Place or Places foever the same shall be found as well in my own Custody or Posession as in the Posession or Custody of any other Person or Persons whatsoever (or all those Goods and Chattels above mentioned. To have and to hold all and singular the s[ai]d Goods and Chattels and all the other afores[ai]d Premises (after my Decease) yet Retaining my Entire Right and Property to Each of the afores[ai]d several Articles During my Life Excluding myself only from having a power to Devise the afores[ai]d Premises any way Contrary to these Presents to the afores[ai]d Comfort SMITH and Moses SMITH her Husband and to the s[ai]d Comfort SMITHs Heirs begotten by the afores[ai]d Moses SMITH after the afores[ai]d Comforts & Moses's Decease to their own proper use and uses forever. And I the said Lucrecia CLAYWELL all and singular the afores[ai]d Goods Chattels and Premises to the s[ai]d Comfort and Moses SMITH and their Heirs as afores[ai]d against all Persons do Warrant and do forever Defend by these Presents. In Witness whereof I have hereunto set my Hand and Seal this 13 Day of March in the Year of our Lord one Thousand seven hund[re]d and sixty five.
John DAVIS
George Smith   her
George SMITH Sen[io]r   Lucresy /\ CLAYWELL   (Seal)
                                                                                              mark"

*followed with the acknowledgment by Justice of the Peace William ELLEGOOD on 18 April 1765 and recordation by court clerk Henry JOHNSON on 19 April 1765[110]

Liber F, Folio 335; 02 March 1765

"Know all Men by these presents that I Henry WILLIAMS of Dorchester County and Province of Maryland Planter and in Consideration of the Sum of twenty five Pounds current Money of Pennsylvania to me in Hand paid by John MITCHELL of Worcester County & Province af[ore]s[ai]d Merchant whereof I do hereby Acknowledge the Receipt and myself therewith

---

[109] Worcester County Court (Land Records). Bill of sale from ADAMS, George to ADAMS, John. 21 March 1765. F, pp. 321-322, MSA CE 30-6. www.mdlandrec.net : accessed 19 October 2021.
[110] Worcester County Court (Land Records). Deed of gift from CLAYWELL, Lucresy to SMITH, Comfort and Moses. 13 March 1765. F, p. 330, MSA CE 30-6. www.mdlandrec.net : accessed 19 October 2021.

fully and entirely satisfied have bargained sold set over and Delivered, and by these presents in plain Market according to the Just and Due form of Law in that Case made and provided Do bargain set over and Deliver unto the said John MITCHELL one Ink Stand, and one Negro fellow called **Pomp**. To have and to hold the said bargained Premises unto the said John MITCHELL his Heirs Executors Administrators and Assigns to the only proper use and behoof of him the said John MITCHELL his Heirs Ex[ecuto]^{rs} Adm[inistrato]^{rs} and Assigns for and During the space of six Years from the aftermentioned Date And I the said Henry WILLIAMS for myself my Executors Administrators the said bargained Premises unto the said John Mitchell his Ex[ecuto]^{rs} Adm[inistrato]^{rs} and Assigns against all and all manner of Persons shall and will Warrant and Defend by these presents In Witness whereof together with the Delivery of the bargained Premises I have hereunto set my Hand and Seal the second Day of March and in the Year of our Lord one thousand seven hundred and sixty five. / . ~ . / . ~ . / . ~ . / . ~

Signed Sealed & Delivered   Joseph GRIFFITH   Henry WILLIAMS.   (Seal)
In Presence of us ~   Rob[er]^t MITCHELL"

*followed with the recordation by court clerk Henry JOHNSON on 24 April 1765[111]

Liber F, folios 356-357; 14 March 1765

"Island of Dominica By this Publick Instrument of Protest be it known and manifest unto all Persons whom it doth or may concern That on thursday the fourteenth day of March in the year of Our Lord one thousand seven hundred and sixty five, and in the fifth year of his Majesty's Reign, Before me John KINGSLOW Notary and Tabellion public by lawfull Authority duly Admitted and Sworn and dwelling in Charlotvill Personally appeared William JONES Mate of the Sloop called the Betsey (whereof the late Daniel NEWTON was Master) and John BANKS foremast Man on Board said Sloop, who being severally duly Sworn on the holy Evangelists of Almighty God depose and say that they these appearers in the said Sloop did on the Eighteenth day of November last past set Sail from the Port of Kingston in the Island of Jamaica in order to proceed to Maryland in America having on Board a Cargoe of Malasses and two Hogsheads and four Casks of Rum, that the latter end of the month of December last past, Captain NEWTON with three other Men belonging to said Sloop Viz:^{t} Samuel COLWELL Lemuel AMMON and Ellis WILMAN were taken Ill of the small pox and on or about the twelfth Day of January now last past they all Died of the Distemper af[oresai]^d that on the first Day of said Month of January being then in Latitude thirty six degrees and forty minutes North and Longitude Seventy Degrees West from London there Arose an hard Gale of Wind beginning at SW and hawling to NE which Continued fourteen Days in which time notwithstanding all possible care the main Sail of said Sloop was carried away and by the Violence of the af[ore]s[ai]^d Gale of Wind the other Sails of said Sloop were very much Damaged, that in that Condition they were Obliged to make what Sail they could to get to the Southward finding it Impracticable to make any Port to the Northward, as well from the small Number of Hands then on Board said Sloop, as from the Ruinous Condition of the said Sloop Sails These appearers further say that some time in the Month of February last past then in Latitude thirty six Degrees North, and Longitude sixty Eight degrees West from London afores[ai]^d there arose one other Gale of Wind at S: and howling W: which Continued three Days and Occasioned a very bad cross Sea, that said Sloop in that time Ship'd several heavy Seas one of which laid her on her beam ends, and shifted the Cargoe in her hold, in which situation said Sloop lay for the space of an Hour, when these appearers found it absolutely necessary, as well for the preservation of the said Sloop and the remaining part of her Cargoe as for the Lives of these appearers to cause five Hogsheads of Melasses and one of Rum to be Scutled and Stove, upon which said Sloop Righted, but these appearers have reason to believe (but cannot be positive) that there might be great leakage of the remaining part of said Sloop Cargoe by its shifting in manner af[oresai]^d these appearers say that by this time their provisions were almost Exhausted, still Continuing to make Sail to the Southward in hopes of Speaking with some Vessell and get supplies, That

---

[111] Worcester County Court (Land Records). Bill of sale from WILLIAMS, Henry to MITCHELL, John. 02 March 1765. F, p. 335, MSA CE 30-6. www.mdlandrec.net : accessed 19 October 2021.

on the morning of the Eighteenth day of said Month of February being then in Latitude thirty degrees and forty three minutes North Longitude 57$^{d[egrees]}$ 28$^{m[inutes]}$ they saw a Sail bearing NE distance about four Leagues it being then Calm, these appearers with the Assistance of Asher DONAMA passenger on bard said Sloop and a Negro Man hoisted out their Boat and went on Board said Sail, which proved to be the Sloop charming Sally Jonathan PARSONS Junior Master of and from Newbury in New England bound to the West indies, these appearers further say that the said PARSONS offered to supply these Appearers with every thing he could conveniently Spare, but the Supplies offered to these Appearers not being sufficient, these Appearer William JONES (being then in a very bad state of health occasioned by his having the small pox) and the Asher DONAM agreed to remain on board said Sloop charming Sally, and the Appearer John BANKS and the af[ore]s[ai]^d Negroe named **Dick** returned on board said Sloop Betsey with two of the Crew of the said Sloop charming Sally and remained on board untill her Arrival at this Island which was yesterday. Therefore I the said Notary at the Request of the said Appearers Do Solemnly protest against the Wind & Weather aforesaid for all Loses Costs Damages and Expences sustained or that may be hereafter be sustained by any Person or Persons interested or concerned in the said Sloop called the Betsey and her Cargoe by reason of the Circumstances before particularly specified. ~ This done and protested at my Office of Notary Public the Day & Year first within written.

William JONES ~   Jn° KINSLOW

     his
John + BANKS
    mark

Sworn to by Asher DONHAM"

*followed on folio 357 with the recordation on court clerk Henry JOHNSON on 24 May 1765[112]

Liber F, folios 391-392; 19 March 1765

"This Indenture made the nineteenth Day of June Anno Dom[ini] one thousand seven hundred and sixty five. Between William WAGGAMAN of Worcester County of the one part, and James GRAY of Virginia of the other part. Witnesseth that the said William for and in Consideration of the Sum of Two hundred and ninety six Pounds two Shillings and five Pence half Penny current Money of Maryland, and also the legal Interest thereon from the Eighth day of April last past, hath bargained sold and delivered, and by these Presents doth bargain sell and deliver unto the af[oresai]^d James GRAY his Heirs and Assigns forever, the following Negro Slaves to wit. one Negro Man named **John**, one Negro Man called **Conselo**, one Negro Man named **Monday**, one Negro Man named **Frank**, one Negro Man named **Daniel**, one Negro Woman named **Cloe**, one Negro Woman named **Jenny**, one Negro Girl called **Bett**, one Negro Woman named **Betty**. To have and to hold the af[oresai]^d Negroes unto the af[oresai]^d James GRAY his Heirs and Assigns forever, to and for the only use benefit and behoof of the said James GRAY his Heirs and Assigns forever, and for no other use or purpose whatsoever. Provided always and it is the true intent and meaning hereof that in Case the said William shall pay unto shall pay unto the af[oresai]^d James GRAY his Executors Adm[inistrato]^{rs} or Assigns the af[oresai]^d Sum of Money with the legal Interest thereon, then the above Writing to be Void and of none Effect. Otherwise to be & remain in full force and Virtue. And the said William for himself his Heirs Executors & Adm[inistrato]^{rs} doth Covenant and Agree to and with the said James his Executors Adm[inistrato]^{rs} or Assigns that in default of payment of the Money as af[oresai]^d that then in such Case it shall and may be Lawfull for the said James GRAY his Ex[ecuto]^{rs} Ad[ministrato]^{rs} or Assigns to take into his or their possession the Slaves af[oresai]^d and all or such part thereof to Sell and Expose to Sale as shall be sufficient to pay the Sum of Money af[oresai]^d and the same Money to Receive to his own proper use. And the said William for himself his Heirs Executors and Adm[inistrato]^{rs} doth Covenant & Agree to and with the said James GRAY his Executors Adm[inistrato]^{rs} or Assigns that he will pay unto the af[oresai]^d

---

[112] Worcester County Court (Land Records). Public instrument of protest from JONES, William. 14 March 1765. F, pp. 356-357, MSA CE 30-6. www.mdlandrec.net : accessed 19 October 2021.

James GRAY his Executors Adm[inistrato]rs or Assigns the af[oresai]d Sum of Money with the legal Interest thereon on demand In Witness whereof the said William to these presents his Hand hath set & Seal affixed the Day and Year first above written. / . ~ . / . ~
Signed Sealed & Deliver[e]d W[illia]m E WAGGAMAN (Seal)
In Presence of us ~ . / . ~
Litt[leton] DENNIS. Josiah POLK. Geo[rge] HAYWARD."

*followed on folio 392 with the acknowledgment of Justice of the Peace Benton HARRIS on 29 June 1765 and recordation by court clerk Henry JOHNSON on 01 July 1765[113]

Liber F, folios 393-395; 18 May 1765

"This Indenture made this Eighteenth day of May in the Year of our Lord one thousand seven hundred and sixty five. Between Matthew OUTTEN of Worcester County of the one part, and Peter CHAILLE of the same place of the other part. Witnesseth that Whereas the said Peter heretofore to wit the third day of December in the Year of our Lord one thousand seven hundred and sixty three, at the Instance of the said Matthew became bound with the said Matthew as his Security in a writing Obligatory unto a certain James GRAY, Conditioned for the payment of the Sum of fourteen hundred and seventy pounds five shillings and Eight pence half penny. Now this Indenture further Witnesseth that the said Matthew for the saving harmless and keeping indemnifyed the af[oresai]d Peter CHAILLE his Heirs Executors Adm[inistrato]rs from all damages costs troubles and expences which he or they may or shall sustain by means of his Securityship as af[oresai]d as also for the further Consideration of five shillings Current money af[oresai]d to the said Matthew by the said Peter paid at and before the Sealing and delivery hereof the receipt whereof the said Matthew hereby doth acknowledge hath bargained sold assigned set over and delivered, and by these presents doth bargain sell assign set over and deliver unto the af[oresai]d Peter CHAILLE his Heirs and Assigns forever, The following Lands and Tenements, Slaves, Goods, Chattels, Rights and Creditts which is to say one hundred and seventy four Acres of Lands part of a Tract of Land called Outtens Security also sixty four Acres of Land part of a Tract of Land called Nelsons Security unto the af[oresai]d Peter CHAILLE his Heirs and Assigns forever, also one Negro Boy called **Jack**, one called **Filer**, and one other called **Jim** one Negro Girl called **Lid**, one called **Nell**, one Negro Man called **Sampson**, and one Negro Woman called **Florow** five Cows and Calves, Twelve head of Young Cattle, two Yoke of Oxen, thirty head of Sheep, one hundred and Twenty one pounds nine Shillings and Seven pence three farthings Sterlings worth of Goods at first Cost now in Snowhill as by the Invoice thereof hereto Annexed doth more fully appear, also Eighty one pounds five Shillings and seven pence three farthings Sterlings worth of Goods at first Cost in the possession of Levin STUART in Accomack County as by the Invoice hereto Annexed doth appear, as also five hundred and ninety six pounds Eight shillings and seven pence half penny Current money of Maryland due the af[oresai]d Matthew OUTTEN on his Snowhill Books from sundry persons as by a List of Ballances thereof hereto Annexed doth appear as also Two hundred and Eighty two pounds fifteen Shillings Current Money of Virginia due the af[oresai]d Matthew OUTTEN in Accomack County on a Book kept by Slocomb BLAKE from sundry persons as by a List of Ballances thereof hereto Annexed doth appear, also Seventy five pounds Seventeen shillings and Eleven pence Virginia Money due the af[oresai]d Matthew in Accomack County in a Book kept by Levin STUART, as also six hundred Bushells of Corn lying in Snowhill in the possession of the af[oresai]d Matthew OUTTEN unto the af[oresai]d Peter CHAILLE his Heirs and Assigns forever." ... "that the said Peter CHAILLE shall and will account fearly and reasonably with the said Matthew OUTTEN his Executors Adm[inistrato]rs or Assigns when he the said Peter shall be thereto reasonably required for all and singular his transactions about every matter and thing that shall or be done or Committed either by himself or any Attorney or Attorneys that he shall nominate and appoint of in or concerning the above recited Premisses, and in Case on such accounting and Settlement the af[oresai]d Peter or his Attorney or Attorneys shall have received more then shall be sufficient to discharge the Sum for which he stands

---

[113] Worcester County Court (Land Records). Bill of sale from WAGGAMAN, William to GRAY, James. 19 March 1765. F, pp. 391-392, MSA CE 30-6. www.mdlandrec.net : accessed 19 October 2021.

Charged in the Securityship af[oresai]d after deducting all the Necessary and reasonable Expences and Troubles in the transacting the same, that then he the said Peter shall pay and discharge the same unto the af[oresai]d Matthew OUTTEN his Executors Adm[inistrator]s or Assigns. In witness whereof Each of the said parties to these presents these their Hands have Set and Seals affixed the day and Year first above written.
Signed Sealed & Deliver[e]d
In Presence of us. ~   Matthew OUTTEN (Seal)
Benton HARRIS. A^d[a]m SPENCE. /. ~"

*followed on folio 395 by the acknowledgment of Justices of the Peace Benton HARRIS and Adam SPENCE, the receipt of the alienation fine by Joseph ALLEN on 18 June 1765, and the recordation by court clerk Henry JOHNSON on 22 July 1765[114]

*Due to its true length, this transcription has been shortened to its most relevant portions. The full original deed can be viewed at the citation provided.

Liber F, folios 492-493; 19 May 1766

"Know all Men by these presents that I Samuel HOPKINS for and in Consideration of the sum of Forty five Pounds current Money of Maryland to me in hand paid by William WHITTINGTON at and before the Sealing and Delivery of these presents the Receipt whereof the said Samuel doth hereby confess and acknowledge and thereof doth acquit release and discharge the said William WHITTINGTON his Heirs Executors Adm[inistrato]rs and Assigns Hath bargained & sold and by these presents doth bargain and sell unto the said William WHITTINGTON his Heirs and Assigns forever one Negro named **Edith**. To have and to hold the said Negro Girl named **Edith** to the said William WHITTINGTON his Heirs and Assigns forever to the proper use and behoof of the said William WHITTINGTON his Heirs and Assigns forever, and to and for no other use intent or purpose whatsoever. In Witness whereof I have hereto set my Hand & Seal affixed this Nineteenth day of May Anno Dom[ini] 1766. ~
Sealed & Delivered   Jn.º SCARBOROUGH   Samuel HOPKINS (Seal)
In Presence ~   Smith BISHOP"

*followed on folio 493 by the acknowledgment of Justice of the Peace John SCARBOROUGH and the recordation by court clerk Henry JOHNSON on 06 June 1766[115]

Liber F, folio 493; 06 June 1766

"Know all men by these Presents that I Robert HOUSTON of Worcester County in the Province of Maryland for and in Consideration of the natural Love and Affection which I have and bear unto my Daughter Sally Minors HOUSTON for her further advancement in Life, and also for and in Consideration of the sum of five Shillings current Money of Maryland to me in hand paid by the said Sally Minors my said Daughter the Receipt whereof I do hereby acknowledgment Have granted bargained and sold assigned and delivered, and by these presents do give grant bargain & sell assign and deliver unto the said Sally Minors HOUSTON her Heirs Executors Administrators & Assigns forever, one Negro Girl or Wench named **Beck** about the Age of eleven or twelve Years which came to me by my Intermarriage with Sally Simmons MINORS my late Wife now dec[ease]d who was the said Sally Minors HOUSTONs' Mother. To have and to hold the said Negro Girl or Wench named **Beck**, with all her future Increase unto the said Sally Minors HOUSTON her Heirs Executors Administrators & Assigns, to the only proper use and behoof of the said Sally Minors HOUSTON her Heirs Executors Administrators & Assigns forever, and to or for no other use intent or purpose whatsoever, In Testimony whereof I have hereunto affixed my Hand and Seal the sixth day of June in the Year of our Lord seventeen hundred & sixty six. ~

---

[114] Worcester County Court (Land Records). Deed of assignment from OUTTEN, Matthew to CHAILLE, Peter. 18 May 1765. F, pp. 393-395, MSA CE 30-6. www.mdlandrec.net : accessed 20 October 2021.

[115] Worcester County Court (Land Records). Bill of sale from HOPKINS, Samuel to WHITTINGTON, William. 19 May 1766. F, pp. 492-493, MSA CE 30-6. www.mdlandrec.net : accessed 20 October 2021.

Sealed and Delivered.   John EVANS   Rob[er]ᵗ HOUSTON (Son {?}.ⁿ)   (Seal)
In Presence of …….   John DAVIS"

*followed by the acknowledgment of Justice of Peace John EVANS and recordation by court clerk Henry JOHNSON[116]

Liber F, folios 518-519; 09 August 1766

"This Indenture made this ninth Day of August Anno Dom[ini] one thousand seven hundred and sixty six. Between Thomas WINGATE of Worcester County in the Province of Maryland of the one part, & Joseph COLLINS & William TUNNELL of the said County and Province of the other part. Witnesseth that the said Thomas WINGATE for & in Consideration of four hundred pounds Current Money of Maryland to him in Hand paid by the said Joseph & William at or before the Ensealing & Delivery hereof the Receipt whereof the said Thomas hath hereby bargained sold released aliened conveyed & confirmed & by these presents doth bargain sell alien release convey & confirm unto the said Joseph COLLINS & William TUNNELL their Heirs and Assigns forever, all that tract or parcel of land called Waples's Luck lying and situated in the County af[oresai]ᵈ limited bounded & described as by the original Grant {?} Recourse thereto being had may more fully appear containing one hundred Acres of Land and also nine feather Beds and furniture thereto, one Negro Man called **Frank**, four Cows & Calves, one Yoke of Oxen forty Head of Hogs & five Head of Horses & five Head of young Cattle. together with his remaining Household furniture & the dry Goods now on Hand in his Shop. To have and to hold the af[ore]s[ai]ᵈ Tract and Parcell of Land with all its Appurtenances and Improvements together with the Goods & Chattels af[ore]s[ai]ᵈ mentioned to the said Joseph COLLINS & William TUNNELL their Heirs and Assigns forever to and for no other use purpose or intent whatsoever. And the said Thomas for himself his Heirs Executors & Administrators doth hereby covenant, promise and agree to and with the said Joseph & William their Heirs Executors Administrators & Assigns that he the said Thomas the Land af[ore]s[ai]ᵈ with the Goods & Chattels af[ore]s[ai]ᵈ mentioned to the said Joseph & William he will Warrant & forever Defend by these presents against all Persons claiming the same. In Testimony whereof of the said Thomas hath hereto set his Hand and affixed his Seal the Day and Year above written. / . ~
Signed sealed & Deliv[ere]ᵈ   Thomas WINGATE   (Seal)
In presence of ~
John SELBY.   Aᵈ[a]m SPENCE"

*followed on folio 519 with the acknowledgment of Justice of the Peace John SELBY, receipt of the alienation fine by Adam SPENCE, and recordation by court clerk Henry JOHNSON[117]

Liber F, folios 522-523; 18 July 1766

"This Indenture made this Eighteenth day of July in the Year of our Lord one thousand seven hundred sixty six Between John DENNIS Jun[io]ʳ of Worcester County of the one part and William ALLEN & George HAYWARD of the same place of the other part. Witnesseth that the said John for and in Consideration of the several trusts hereafter expressed, as also for and in Consideration of the sum of five Shillings current Money to him by them paid at and before the Sealing and Delivery hereof the Receipt whereof he hereby doth acknowledge hath bargained sold, remised & released, and by these presents doth give grant bargain sell remise & release unto the af[ore]s[ai]ᵈ William ALLEN & George HAYWARD their Heirs and Assigns forever all the following Tracts and parcells of Land situate in the County af[ore]s[ai]ᵈ to wit one hundred Acres of Land called part of Bradshaws Purchase near Stephens's Ferry, two hundred & fifty two Acres on Pokomoke in Nasswadox Neck called West Swamp, one

---
[116] Worcester County Court (Land Records). Bill of sale from HOUSTON, Robert to HOUSTON, Sally Minors. 06 June 1766. F, p. 493, MSA CE 30-6. www.mdlandrec.net : accessed 20 October 2021.
[117] Worcester County Court (Land Records). Deed from WINGATE, Thomas to COLLINS, Joseph and TUNNELL, William. 09 August 1766. F, pp. 518-519, MSA CE 30-6. www.mdlandrec.net : accessed 20 October 2021.

hundred & seventy five Acres by Nelsons Swamp called Nelsons Discovery Eight hundred & seventy Acres being three different parcells of Land one called Sawmill Lott one called Buck Ridge & the other called Smallwoods Security together with a Sawmill on the same Lands errected, also seven hundred & ninety seven Acres near St. Martins called Dennis's Discovery forty five Acres part of Showells Adition near adjoining the same, also one Grist Mill and the Lands Condemned whereon the same is errected all which said Tracts and parcells of Land are bounded described & limited as expressed and mentioned in and by the several original Grants thereof and mesne Conveyances thereof recorse thereto being had may more fully appear, as also the following Slaves to wit **Oxford**, **Aproba**, **young Oxford**, **Betty** and her three Children, **Prim** and her two Children, **Dick**, **little Dick**, and **Jack**. To have and to hold the af[oresai]^d Granted and bargained premisses with all and singular the Appurtenances unto the same belonging unto the af[oresai]^d William ALLEN & George HAYWARD their Heirs and Assigns forever to and for the only use benefit and behoof of the said William ALLEN & George HAYWARD their Heirs and assigns forever in Trust. Nevertheless that they or the survivor of them or their Heirs shall dispose of all & singular the above premisses in such manner as they or the survivor of them or their Heirs shall think best and that after such Sale of all or any part these of that they shall first pay & satisfy unto Littleton DENNIS his Heirs Executors Adm[inistrato]^{rs} or Assigns out of the Money arising from such Sale as much as shall be sufficient to indemnify the said Littleton DENNIS his Heirs Executors and Adm[inistrato]^{rs} for and by means of his being Security for a Debt for the said John DENNIS unto a certain Richard AMBLER Esq[ui]^r[e] of York in Virginia as also for one other Debt unto a certain Levin DASHIELL of Somerset County, as also one other Debt due unto a certain William HAYWARD of Talbot County which said Debts are due by Bonds recorse to the same Bonds will manifest such Debts & the sums thereof, as also for one other Debt due unto a certain Caleb BALDING by Note of hand for about nineteen pounds, and then the remainder of the Money arising to be paid Equally to and amongst all the just Credittors of the said John DENNIS in proportion to their several demands. provided such Credittors shall produce their Claim within six Months after such disposition, and the Overplus thereof if any arrising from such Sale to be delivered and paid to the said John DENNIS or his Order. And the said John DENNIS for himself his Heirs Exec[utor]^s and Adm[inistrato]^{rs} doth Covenant Grant and Agree to and with the said William ALLEN & George HAYWARD & the survivor of them their Heirs Exec[utor]^s and Adm[inistrato]^{rs} that it shall and may be Lawfull for them or either of them or their Heirs or Assigns at any time after the Execution hereof to enter into and to take possession of all and singular the af[oresai]^d premisses and disposition thereof to make for the purposes af[oresai]^d In Witness whereof the said John DENNIS to these presents his Hand hath set and Seal affixed the day and Year first above written.

Signed sealed & Delivered John SELBY   J DENNIS Jr (Seal)
In Presence of us ~   A^d[a]m SPENCE"

*followed on folio 523 with the acknowledgment of Justices of the Peace John SELBY and Adam SPENCE, receipt of the alienation fine by Esme BAYLY on 12 August 1766, and recordation by court clerk Henry JOHNSON on 15 August 1766[118]

Liber F, folios 532-533; 05 August 1766

"Know all Men by these presents that I George LIVINGSTON of Worcester County in Consideration of the sum of Eleven pounds six Shillings and one penny Current Money of Maryland in Dollars at seven Shillings & six pence each Dollar to me in hand paid by William GEDDES of Somerset County Merchant the Receipt whereof I hereby acknowledge have Bargained Sold Assign[e]d Transfer[re]d unto the said William GEDDES his Executors Administrators or Assigns one Negro Girl called **Amelia** about the Age of three Years being now in the possession of the said George. To have and to hold the said Negro **Amelia** to the said GEDDES his Executors or Assigns to his and their only use and behoof. provided that if

---

[118] Worcester County Court (Land Records). Deed of trust from DENNIS, John Jr. to ALLEN, William and HAYWARD, George. 18 July 1766. F, pp. 522-523, MSA CE 30-6. www.mdlandrec.net : accessed 20 October 2021.

the said George LIVINGSTON shall pay unto the said William GEDDES his Executors Administrators or Assigns the said sum of Eleven pounds six Shilling and one penny Money aforesaid with the legal Interest thereon, and the Expence attending this present Deed within twelve Months from the Date hereof then this present Deed & Sale to be void. And the said George for himself his Heirs Executors Administrators doth hereby Covenant with the said William GEDDES that he will within the said time pay to the said GEDDES the Money aforesaid & Interest and Expence in manner aforesaid. In Testimony whereof the said George LIVINGSTON hath hereto sett his Hand Seal this 5th Day August Anno Domini 1766.

Signed sealed & Deliver[e]d.   Peter WATERS.   George LIVINGSTON   (Seal)
In Presence of ~   Sam[ue]l WILSON"

*followed with the acknowledgment by Somerset County Justice of the Peace Samuel WILSON, recordation by Somerset County court clerk Thomas Hayward on 19 August 1766, and recordation on folio 533 by Worcester County court clerk Henry JOHNSON on 27 August 1766[119]

Liber F, folios 544-545; 24 September 1766

"Know all Men by these presents that I Samuel STEVENSON of Worcester County in Consideration of the Sum of fifteen Pounds to me in hand paid by John MILLS have bargained and sold Released and Granted and Confirmed, and by these presents doth bargain sell release grant and confirm unto said John MILLS one Negro Man called **Ceasor**. one Oxchain, two Hoes, one broad Ax one Frow. To have and hold all and singular the said Goods and Household Stuff above mentioned and Every of them by these presents bargained sold released granted and confirmed unto the only proper use and behoof of the said John MILLS his Heirs Ex[ecuto]rs Adm[inistrato]rs and Assigns forever freely quietly peaceably and intirely without any Contradiction Claim disturbance Hindrance of any Person whatsoever and without any account to me or to any other whatsoever to be made answered or hereafter to Rendered so that neither I the said Samuel STEVENSON nor any Other for me or in my name any Right Title Interest or Demand of in to or for the said Good and to or any part or parcel thereof ought to exact challenge Claim or demand at any time or times hereafter but from Action Right Estate Title Claim Demand Possession Interest though shall be wholy barred and Excluded by force and virtue of these presents, & I the said Samuel STEVENSON for myself my Ex[ecuto]rs & Adm[inistrato]rs all singular the said Good for and Household Stuff unto the said John MILLS his Ex[ecuto]rs Adm[inistrato]rs and Assigns and against all and every other Person or Persons whatsoever shall and will Warrant and forever Defend by these presents of which Goods &c. I said Samuel STEVENSON puts the said John MILLS in full possession by delivering him the said Negro fellow in the name of all the Goods and Chattels at the Signing and Delivery hereof. In Witness whereof I the said Samuel STEVENSON have unto set my Hand and fixed my Seal this twenty fourth Day of September in the Year of our Lord one thousand seven hundred sixty and six. / . ~ . / . ~ . / . ~

Seal[e]d and Delivered   Samuel MILLS   Samuel STEVENSON. (Seal)
In the Presence of   his
                   James + CARY
                          Mark"

*followed on folio 545 by the acknowledgment of Justice of the Peace George LAYFIELD on 25 September 1766 and recordation by court clerk Henry JOHNSON on 09 October 1766[120]

Liber F, folio 550; 06 November 1766

"This Indenture made this Sixth day of November in the Year our Lord one thousand seven hundred sixty and six. Between William Elliot WAGGAMAN of Worcester County of the one part, and John DAVIS of the same place of the other part. Whereas the said John DAVIS in and

---

[119] Worcester County Court (Land Records). Bill of sale from LIVINGSTON, George to GEDDES, William. 05 August 1766. F, pp. 532-533, MSA CE 30-6. www.mdlandrec.net : accessed 20 October 2021.
[120] Worcester County Court (Land Records). Bill of sale from STEVENSON, Samuel to MILLS, John. 24 September 1766. F, pp. 544-545, MSA CE 30-6. www.mdlandrec.net : accessed 20 October 2021.

by one Bond or Obligation bearing date the sixth day of June in the Year af[ore]s[ai]^d at the Request and for the only proper Debt of the said William Elliot WAGGAMAN became bound with him the said William Elliot WAGGAMAN unto Samuel S{???}ly of the County af[ore]s[ai]^d in the Penal Sum of One hundred and twenty four Pounds ten Shillings, Conditioned for the payment of sixty two pounds five Shillings and one half penny as by the said Bond and Condition thereof relation being thereunto had may more at large appear. Now this Indenture Witnesseth that for the saving harmless and keeping Indemnified the said John DAVIS his Heirs Executors and Administrators of and from the said Bond and all Actions, Suits, Charges Costs and Damages touching or concerning the same Hath Granted Bargained Sold Assigned and sett over, and by these presents doth fully freely and absolutely Grant Bargain and Sell Assign and sett over unto the said John DAVIS his Executors Administrators and Assigns forever, one Negro Man named **Monday**, and one Negro Man named **Frank**. To have and to hold the Negro Man named **Monday** and the said Negro Man named **Frank** hereby Assigned or mentioned or intended to be hereby Assigned unto the said John DAVIS his Executors Administrators and Assigns forever. Provided allways and it is the intent & meaning that if the said William Elliot WAGGAMAN do and shall well and truly save and keep harmless and indemnified the said John DAVIS his Ex[ecuto]^{rs} Adm[inistrato]^{rs} of from the above recited Bond and from all Actions Suits Charges Costs and Damages touching or concerning the same, then this Writing to be null and void and it is Agreed by and between the said William Elliot WAGGAMAN and the said John DAVIS that in case the said William Elliot WAGGAMAN do not save and keep harmless and indemnified the said John DAVIS as above that it shall and may be lawfull for the said John DAVIS his Executors and Adm[inistrato]^{rs} immediately after any default made by the said William Elliot WAGGAMAN of the Condition hereof to take into his or their Custody the above named Negroe Man named **Monday** and the said Negro named **Frank** and them to make Sale of and out of the Money ariseing from such Sale pay of the principle and Interest of the said Sum of Money and also retaining in his or their hands Sufficient to pay all Costs Charges and Damages that the said John Davis may or shall be put to by means of the Premisses and the Residue (if any) to be paid to the said William Elliot WAGGAMAN. In Testimony whereof the said William Elliot WAGGAMAN hath hereto set his Hand & Seal affixed the day & year first above written. / . ~

Sealed and Delivered   Geo[rge] HAYWARD   W[illia]^m E: WAGGAMAN. (Seal)
In Presence of   Jo^s[eph] DIRICKSON"

*followed with the acknowledgment of Justice of the Peace Joseph DIRICKSON and recordation by court clerk Henry JOHNSON[121]

Liber F, folios 552-553; 21 November 1766

"Know all Men by these presents that I William GILLET of Worcester County in the Province of Maryland Planter for and in Consideration of the sum of thirteen Pounds current Money of Maryland to me in hand paid at and before the Sealing and Delivering of these presents by Benjamin AYDELOTT of the County and Province aforesaid Bricklayer the Receipt whereof I do hereby acknowledge have bargained and Sold, and by these presents do bargain and Sell unto the said Benj[ami]^n AYDELOTT one Negro Man called **Harry** now in the possession of William GILLETT. To have and to hold the said Negro Man and by these presents bargained and Sold unto the said Benjamin AYDELOTT his Executors Administrators and Assigns forever, and I the said William GILLETT for myself my Executors and Administrators the said Negro Man unto the said Benjamin AYDELOTT his Executors and Assigns against me the said William GILLETT my Executors Administrators and Assigns and against all and every Person or Persons whatsoever shall and will Warrant and forever Defend by these presents of which Negro Man I the said William GILLETT have put the said Benjamin AYDELOTT in full possession of In Presence whereof the said William GILLETT hath hereunto Set his Hand & fixed his Seal this 21st day of November 1766.

---

[121] Worcester County Court (Land Records). Bill of sale from WAGGAMAN, William to DAVIS, John. 06 November 1766. F, p. 550, MSA CE 30-6. www.mdlandrec.net : accessed 20 October 2021.

Signed sealed and Delivered   John SELBY   William GILLETT. (Seal)
In the Presence of us ~   Thomas ROBINS Jun[io]^r"

*followed on folio 553 with the acknowledgment by Justice of the Peace John SELBY and recordation 04 December 1766 by court clerk Henry JOHNSON[122]

Liber F, folio 554; 12 December 1766

"Maryland Worcester County. Know all Men by these presents that I Moses GOOTRY of this County in Consideration of the sum of thirty five Pounds current Money of this Province to me in hand paid by George SPENCE of the same place have bargained and sold released granted and confirmed any by these presents do bargain sell release grant and confirm unto the said George SPENCE one Negro Girl known by the name of **Roday** now remaining and being in the said SPENCEs possession. To have and hold the said Negro Girl by these presents bargain[e]d sold and released granted and confirmed unto the only proper use and behoof of the said George SPENCE his Ex[ecuto]^{rs} Administ[rato]^{rs} and Assigns forever freely quietly peaceably and intirely without any contradiction claim disturbance or hindrance of any Person whatsoever, so that neither I the said Moses GOOTRY or any other for me or in my name any Right Title Interest or demand of in to or for the said Negro Girl called **Rhoda** but from all Action Right Title Claim demand and Interest thereof shall be wholly barred and Excluded by force and virtue of these presents. And I the said Moses GOOTRY for myself my Execut[o]^{rs} and Administr[ato]^{rs} the said Negro Girl before mention[e]d unto the said George SPENCE his Execut[o]^{rs} Administ[rato]^{rs} and Assigns and against all and ever other Person or Persons whatsoever shall and will Warrant and forever Defend by these presents. In Witness whereof I have set my Hand and fixed my Seal this twelfth day of December one thousand seven hundred sixty and six.
John BELL. ~ Betty SPENCE. ~   Moses GOTHERY. / . ~   (Seal)"

*followed with the acknowledgment of Justice of the Peace A^d[a]m SPENCE and recordation on 29 December 1766 by court clerk Henry JOHNSON[123]

Liber G, folio 9; 13 February 1767

"Worcester {?} Know all Men by these presents that I Isaac HARDY of the County af[ore]s[ai]^d have by these presents Sold unto Peter CALLOWAY of ye same place one Negro Man Slave named **Jack** for and in Consideration of the sum of twenty Pounds in hand paid & the further sum of Twenty Pounds to be paid at or upon the first day of July next, which Negro Man I have a good Right to dispose of and will Warrant & defend forever the said Negro **Jack** unto the said Peter CALLOWAY his Heirs and Assigns forever against all Persons whatever. In Witness whereof I have hereunto set my Hand and affixed my Seal this 13th day of Feb[ruar]y 1767. / ~
                                                            Isaac HARDY. (Seal)"

*followed with the acknowledgment by Justice of the Peace J. DENNIS Jr. and recordation on 18 February 1767 by court clerk Henry JOHNSON[124]

Liber G, folio 21; 16 February 1767

"To all People to whom these presents shall come I Sarah WINGATE do send Greeting. Know ye that I the said Sarah WINGATE of Worcester County and Province of Maryland for and in Consideration & the Love good will and Effection which I have and do bear towards my Daughter Luranah WINGATE of the same County and Province af[ore]s[ai]^d have given granted and by these presents do freely give and grant unto the said Luranah WINGATE her

---

[122] Worcester County Court (Land Records). Bill of sale from GILLETT, William to AYDELOTT, Benjamin. 21 November 1766. F, pp. 552-553, MSA CE 30-6. www.mdlandrec.net : accessed 20 October 2021.
[123] Worcester County Court (Land Records). Bill of sale from GOTHERY, Moses to SPENCE, George. 12 December 1766. F, p. 554, MSA CE 30-6. www.mdlandrec.net : accessed 20 October 2021.
[124] Worcester County Court (Land Records). Bill of sale from HARDY, Isaac to CALLOWAY, Peter. 13 February 1767. G, p. 9, MSA CE 30-7. www.mdlandrec.net : accessed 01 November 2021.

Heirs Ex[ecuto]rs Ad[ministrato]rs a certain Negro Girl called **Sabary** which is now in my Possession of which before the Signing of these presents have Delivered her the said Luranah WINGATE the aforesaid Negro called **Sabary**. To have and to hold the said Negro her Heirs Ex[ecuto]rs Adm[inistrato]rs from thenceforth as her and their proper Right without any manner of Condition. In Witness whereof I have hereunto set my Hand and Seal this sixteenth day of February one thousand seven hundred sixty and seven. / . ~ . / . ~

Signed Sealed and Deliver[e]d   Cha[rle]s MINORS   Sarah WINGATE. (Seal)
In Presence of us ~   Levin DIRICKSON"

*followed with the acknowledgment of Justice of the Peace Joseph DIRICKSON on 18 February 1767 and the recordation by court clerk Henry JOHNSON on 05 March 1767[125]

Liber G, folios 21-22; 16 February 1767

"To all People to whom these presents shall come, I Sarah WINGATE do send Greeting Know ye that I the said Sarah WINGATE of Worcester County and Province of Maryland for and in Consideration of the Love good will and Affection which I have and do bear towards my Daughter Love WINGATE of the same County and Province af[ore]s[ai]d have given granted and by these presents do freely give and grant unto the said Love WINGATE her Heirs Execu[to]rs Adm[inistrato]rs a certain Negro Girl called **Nan** which is now in my Possession of which before the Signing of these presents I have Delivered her the said Love WINGATE the aforesaid Negro called **Nan**. To have and to hold the said Negro her Heirs Ex[ecuto]rs Adm[inistrato]rs from henceforth as her and their proper Right without any manner of Condition. In Witness whereof I have hereunto set my Hand and Seal this sixteenth Day of February one thousand seven hundred sixty and seven. / . ~

Signed Sealed & Delivered   Cha[rle]s MINORS   Sarah WINGATE. (Seal)
In Presence of us ~   Levin DIRICKSON"

*followed with the acknowledgment of Justice of the Peace Joseph DIRICKSON on 18 February 1767 and the recordation by court clerk Henry JOHNSON on 05 March 1767[126]

Liber G, folios 32-33; 06 March 1767

"Maryland {?}: Know all Men by these presents that I Josiah DICKESON of Worcester County for and in Consideration of the sum of Fifty five Pounds & Cost of Bill of Sale & Recording by Thomas JONES to me in Hand paid, the Receipt whereof I do hereby acknowledge and forever discharge and acquit the said Thomas JONES his Heirs and Assigns for ever from, have given granted bargained and sold, and do by these presents give grant bargain and sell unto the aforesaid Thomas JONES his Heirs and Assigns forever one Negro Man call[e]d **George**, one other called **Bartlett** both at this time in my Possession and one other Negro Girl called **Pleasant** now possest by the said JONES and to continue so To have and to hold the three Negroes aforesaid mentioned unto him the aforesaid Thomas JONES his Heirs and Assigns forever as his and their own proper Negroes, and to his and their own proper use, together with the Increase of the Negro Girl **Pleasant** above mention[e]d forever. And that it shall be lawful for the said Thomas JONES his Heirs Exec[utor]s Adm[inistrato]rs and Assigns from time to time and at all times after the 28th day of February next ensuing the date to possess have and hold the three Negroes above named, without any dispute and molestation from me Josiah DICKESON my Heirs and Assigns forever hereby Warranting and Defending the said Thomas JONES his Heirs and Assigns in his Title and Property of and to the three Negro's af[ore]s[ai]d from myself or from any Person claiming by from or under me or in any manner claiming whatever. In Witness whereof I have hereto put my Hand and affixed my Seal this sixth day of March Annoq Dom[ini] one thousand seven hundred sixty and seven. / . ~

---

[125] Worcester County Court (Land Records). Deed of gift from WINGATE, Sarah to WINGATE, Luranah. 16 February 1767. G, p. 21, MSA CE 30-7. www.mdlandrec.net : accessed 01 November 2021.

[126] Worcester County Court (Land Records). Deed of gift from WINGATE, Sarah to WINGATE, Love. 16 February 1767. G, pp. 21-22, MSA CE 30-7. www.mdlandrec.net : accessed 01 November 2021.

Sealed and Deliver[e]d   Jnº SCARBOROUGH   Josiah DICKESON (Seal)
In Presence of   Mathew SELBY"

*followed with the acknowledgment of Justice of the Peace John SCARBOROUGH and the recordation on 07 March 1767 by court clerk Henry JOHNSON[127]

Liber G, folio 37; 13 March 1767

"Know all Men by these presents that I Elizabeth TRUITT for and in Consideration of the sum of sixty five Pounds Current Money of Maryland to me in hand paid by Outten TRUITT at and before the Sealing and Delivery of these presents Have bargained and sold, and by these presents do bargain and sell unto the said Outten TRUITT his Heirs & Assigns forever, one Negroe Man Slave named **Jack**. To have and to hold the said Negro Man Slave named **Jack** unto the said Outten TRUITT his Heirs and Assigns forever to the only purpose of the said Outten TRUITT his Heirs and Assigns forever and to and for no other use intent or purpose whatsoever. In Witness whereof I have hereto sett my Hand & Seal affixed this 13th day of March 1767.

Sealed & Delivered   Jnº SCARBOROUGH   her
In Presence of   Benton HARRIS   Elizabeth E TRUITT. (Seal)
                                                         Mark"

*followed with acknowledgment by Justice of the Peace Benton HARRIS and the recordation on 27 March 1767 by court clerk Henry JOHNSON[128]

Liber G, folios 44-45; 28 March 1767

"Know all Men by these presents that I Elijah CANNON of Worcester County in the Province of Maryland for and in Consideration of one hundred and sixty pounds four Shillings and seven Pence one Farthing Current Money of Maryland to me in Hand paid by Peter CALLOWAY and Samuel HALL of said County and Province at or before the Sealing and Delivery hereof the Receipt whereof the said Elijah doth hereby confess and acknowledge & thereof doth acquit & discharge the said Peter & Samuel their Heirs Executors Administrators & Assigns forever have bargained sold assigned & transferred & by these presents doth bargain sell assign & transferr unto the said Peter CALLOWAY and Samuel HALL their Executors Administrators or Assigns the following Goods & Chattels to wit one Negro Man named **Will**, one Negro Woman named **Nell** one Negro Girl called **Tamer**, one Negro Boy named **Sampson**, one Negro Boy named **Dick**, one Negro Boy called **Caesar**; one Negro Boy called **George** & four Head of Horses. To have and to hold the af[ore]s[ai]^d bargained & assigned Negroes & Horses, to them the said Peter CALLOWAY & Samuel HALL their Executors Administrators & Assigns to the only proper use and behoof of the said Peter CALLOWAY & Samuel HALL their Executors Administrators & Assigns & to & for no other purpose or intent whatsoever. Provided always & it is the true intent & meaning hereof any thing herein to the contrary notwithstanding that if the said Elijah CANNON shall well and truly pay or cause to be paid unto a certain MITCHELL his Executors certain Attorney or Administrators the af[ore]s[ai]^d sum of Money with the Interest thereon on or before the fourth day of April next ensuing the date hereof that then this Writing & every Thing in the same contained shall be said & of no Effect. And I the said Elijah CANNON for my self my Heirs Executors & Administrators do hereby covenant promise & agree with the said Peter CALLOWAY & Samuel HALL their Executors Administrators & Assigns, that in Case I the said Elijah CANNON my Heirs Executors or Administrators or either of them should not pay unto the said John MITCHELL his certain Attorney Executors or Administrators the af[ore]s[ai]^d mentioned sum of Money with the Interest thereon on or before the said fourth day of April then it shall be lawfull for the said Peter CALLOWAY & Samuel HALL their Executors Administrators or Assigns to set up & expose to public Sale by way of Vendue the said assigned Negroes & Horses and if the said

---

[127] Worcester County Court (Land Records). Bill of sale from DICKESON, Josiah to JONES, Thomas. 06 March 1767. G, pp. 32-33, MSA CE 30-7. www.mdlandrec.net : accessed 01 November 2021.

[128] Worcester County Court (Land Records). Bill of sale from TRUITT, Elizabeth to TRUITT, Outten. 13 March 1767. G, p. 37, MSA CE 30-7. www.mdlandrec.net : accessed 01 November 2021.

Negroes & Horses should Sell for more than the said sum of Money, that then the Overplus of the said Money arising from the said sale shall be returned to the said Elijah CANNON his Heirs Executors and Administrators. In Testimony whereof I have hereto set my Hand & Seal this twenty eighth Day of March Anno Dom[ini] one thousand seven hundred & sixty seven
Signed Sealed and Deliver[e]^d Joseph DASHIELL   Elijah CANNON   (Seal)
In Presence of ~   John SOROGIN."

*followed on folio 45 with the acknowledgment by Justice of the Peace Joseph DASHIELL and recordation on 02 April 1767 by court clerk Henry JOHNSON[129]

Liber G, folios 70-71; 17 April 1767

"Maryland Worcester County {?} Know all Men by these Presents that I Outten TRUITT of the County & Province af[oresai]^d for and in Consideration of the sum of sixty five Pounds current Money of Maryland to me in hand paid by Walton PURNALL of the County af[oresai]^d Have bargained sold released granted and confirmed, and by these presents do bargain sell release grant and confirm unto the said Walton PURNALL one Negro Man called **Jack** the value of sixty five Pounds. To have and to hold the said bargained Negro **Jack** by these presents bargained sold released granted and confirmed unto the only proper use and behoof of the said Walton PURNAL his Executors Administrators and Assigns forever freely quietly peaceably and intirely without any contradiction, claim disturbance or hindrance of any Person whatsoever, and without any amount to me or to any other whatsoever to be made answered or hereafter to be rendered so that neither I the said Outten TRUITT nor any other form or in my name any Right Title Interest or demand of in or for the said Negro **Jack** or any part or parcel hereof ought to {?} challenge claim or demand at any time or times hereafter but from all action right title Estate claim demand possession and interest thereof shall be wholy bared and excluded by force and virtue of these Presents And I the said Outten TRUITT for my self my Executors & Adm[inistrato]^{rs} the said Negro **Jack** unto the said Walton PURNALL his Ex[ecuto]^{rs} Adm[inistrato]^{rs} and Assigns and against all and every other Person or Persons whatsoever, shall and will Warrant and forever defend by these presents which Negro **Jack** I the said Outten TRUITT have put the said Walton PURNAL in full possession by delivery at the Signing and Delivery hereof. In Witness whereof the said Outten TRUITT have hereunto set his Hand & Seal this 17th day of April Dom[ini] 1767. / . ~
Signed Sealed & Deliv[ere]d   Jno SCARBOROUGH   Outten TRUITT   (Seal)
In Presence of ~   John FEAGUS"

*followed with the acknowledgment by Justice of the Peace John SCARBOROUGH and recordation by court clerk Henry JOHNSON[130]

Liber G, folios 100-101; 29 May 1767

"This Indenture made this twenty ninth day of May in the Year of our Lord one thousand seven hundred sixty and seven. Between Martha SELBY of Worcester County and Province of Maryland Widow of the one part, and Hezekiah PURNELL of the County and Province af[ore]s[ai]^d Gentleman Son of the said Martha SELBY of the other part. Witnesseth that the said Martha SELBY as well for and in Consideration of the natural Love and Affection which She hath and beareth unto her beloved son Hezekiah PURNELL af[ore]s[ai]^d as also of the sum of five Shillings current Money of Maryland to her in hand paid by the said Hezekiah PURNELL She the Said Martha Selby Hath Given Granted and Confirmed and by these Presents doth Give Grant and Confirm unto her said Son Hezekiah PURNELL his Heirs and Assigns forever one Negroe Woman named **Charity**, one Negroe Boy called **Samuel** ___ & one Negroe Woman called **Pelinah**, one old Silver Tankerd, ten head of Cattle, ten head of Sheep, one feather Bed and furniture, one Case of Drawers, half a dozen of Silver Spoons, one

---

[129] Worcester County Court (Land Records). Bill of sale from CANNON, Elijah to CALLOWAY, Peter and HALL, Samuel. 28 March 1767. G, pp. 44-45, MSA CE 30-7. www.mdlandrec.net : accessed 01 November 2021.
[130] Worcester County Court (Land Records). Bill of sale from TRUITT, Outten to PURNALL, Walton. 17 April 1767. G, pp. 70-71, MSA CE 30-7. www.mdlandrec.net : accessed 01 November 2021.

Maar & one looking Glass. To have and to hold all and singular the said three Negroes Viz. **Charity, Samuel, and Pelinah,** one Silver Tankerd, ten head of Cattle, ten head of Sheep, one feather Bed and furniture, one Case of Drawers, half a dozen of Silver Spoons, one Maar & one Looking Glass, and all other the Premises af[ore]s[ai]^d unto the said Hezekiah PURNELL his Executors Administrators and Assigns to the only proper use and behoof of him the said Hezekiah PURNELL his Executors Administrators and Assigns forever. Provided always and upon Condition that he the said Hezekiah PURNELL his Executors Administrators and Assigns do and shall permit and suffer her the said Martha SELBY to have hold use occupy possess and enjoy the said three Negroes **Charity, Samuel & Pelinah**, one Silver Tankerd, ten head of Cattle, ten head of Sheep, one feather Bed & furniture, one Case of Drawers, half a dozen of Silver Spoons one Maar & Looking Glass, and all and singular the Premises above Granted for and during so long Time as She the said Martha SELBY shall happen to Live. And the said Martha SELBY for herself her Executors and Administrators doth Covenant Grant and Agree to and with the said Hezekiah PURNELL his Executors and Administrators that he the said Hezekiah PURNELL his Executors and Administrators and under the Conditions af[ore]s[ai]^d and not otherwise shall and may peaceably and quietly have hold and Enjoy all and singular the said three Negroes called **Charity, Samuel and Pelinah**, one Silver Tankard, ten head of Cattle, ten head of Sheep, one feather Bed and furniture, one Case of Drawers, half a dozen of Silver Spoons, one Maar & looking Glass, and Premises af[ore]s[ai]^d without any Molestation Hindrance or Interruption by any Person or Persons whatsoever Claiming under her or by her act means or procurement. In Witness whereof the said Martha SELBY hath hereto set her Hand & Seal affixed the day & Year first above written.

Sealed and Delivered   Mary TONE   her
In Presence of …   John SELBY   Martha + SELBY (Seal)
                                                                        Mark"

*followed on folio 101 with the acknowledgment of Justice of the Peace John SELBY and recordation by court clerk Henry JOHNSON[131]

*Maar is likely a misspelling of mirror.

Liber G, folios 114-115; 25 May 1767

"Maryland Worcester {?} Know all Men by these presents that I Elisha COLLINGS of the County af[ore]s[ai]^d for and in Consideration of the sum Twenty five Pounds 17 Shillings & 8 Pence current Money of the Province af[ore]s[ai]^d to me in hand Paid before the Sealing & Delivery hereof by Joseph SMITH of the same Place the Receipt whereof I do hereby acknowledge and myself therewith fully satisfied contented & paid have Granted Bargained and Sold, and by these Presents do Plainly & Openly Grant Bargain Sell & Deliver unto the said Joseph SMITH his Ex[ecuto]^rs Adm[inistrato]^rs & Assigns forever, one Negro Woman called **Dinah**, three Cows & one Year Old, one Horse and one feather Bed & furniture, together with all & singular the Residue of my Personal Estate of whatsoever kind it be of Goods & Chattels &c. To have and to hold the said bargained Premises unto the said Joseph SMITH his Ex[ecuto]^rs Adm[inistrato]rs & Assigns forever (Provided Nevertheless and it is the true intent & meaning of this present Writing that if I the said Elisha COLLINGS my Heirs Ex[ecuto]^rs Adm[inistrato]^rs or Assigns or any of us do well & truly Pay or cause to be Paid unto the said Joseph SMITH his Ex[ecuto]^rs Adm[inistrato]^rs or Assigns the Sum of Twenty five Pounds Seventeen Shillings & eight Pence current Money af[ore]s[ai]^d with legal Interest thereon. Together with whatsoever additional Costs may accrue to the Clerk By means of the Recording this Instrument or any Sum of Money that the said Joseph shall pay to any of the said Elisha's Creditors by his Order in Writing with Receipts for the same on or before the fifteenth day of August in the Year of our Lord one thousand seven hundred & sixty eight for the Redemption of the af[ore]s[ai]^d bargained Premises Goods or Chattels, then this present Writing or Bill of Sale to be void or Else to stand in full force power & virtue in Law) In Witness whereof I the said Elisha COLLINGS have hereunto set my hand & fixed my Seal this 25th Day of May 1767.

---

[131] Worcester County Court (Land Records). Deed of Gift from SELBY, Martha to PURNELL, Hezekiah. 29 May 1767. G, pp. 100-101, MSA CE 30-7. www.mdlandrec.net : accessed 01 November 2021.

Signed Sealed & Delivered Jos[hu]ᵃ MITCHELL   Elisha COLLINS (Seal)
In the Presence of us ~   Jn.º Pope MITCHELL"

*followed on folio 115 with the acknowledgment by Justice of the Peace Joshua MITCHELL and recordation on 03 June 1767 by court clerk Henry JOHNSON[132]

Liber G, folios 118-119; 04 June 1767

"Know all Men by these presents that I John WINGATE of Worcester County for and in consideration of the sum of sixty four Pounds eleven Shillings & six Pence current Money to me paid by Hezekiah ANDERSON the Receipt whereof I hereby do acknowledge hath bargained & sold and by these presents do bargain and sell unto the af[oresai]ᵈ Hezekiah ANDERSON his Heirs and Assigns forever the following Goods & Chattels to wit one Negro Man named **Fosida** & one Negro Boy named **Dorset**. To have and to hold the af[oresai]ᵈ bargained Premisses unto the said Hezekiah ANDERSON his Heirs and Assigns forever to and for the only use and behoof of the said Hezekiah ANDERSON his Heirs and Assigns forever and for no other use or purpose whatsoever. And I the said John WINGATE do for my self my Heirs Ex[ecuto]ʳˢ and Adm[inistrato]ʳˢ doth Covenant and agree to and with the said Hezekiah ANDERSON his Heirs and Assigns forever that I will Warrant and forever defend the af[oresai]ᵈ bargained & sold Premisses unto him against the Claim Right and Title of all and every Person whatever, and I do hereby agree that in case that I do not pay unto the af[oresai]ᵈ Hezekiah the Money af[oresai]ᵈ together with the legal Interest thereon, as also the Costs attending of this Writing at the time hereafter limitted, that there it shall be lawfull for the said Hezekiah to enter and take possession of the bargained Premisses af[oresai]ᵈ and them to sell and dispose of in order to raise and satisfy himself his debt and Claim af[oresai]ᵈ Provided always and it is the intent hereof that in Case the said John shall Pay and satisfy the debt and Costs & Interest af[oresai]ᵈ in or before the first day of November next ensuing. Then this Writing to be void else to be and remain in full force and virtue. In Witness whereof I have hereto set my Hand and Seal this fourth day of June Anno Dom[ini] 1767
Sealed and Deliv[ere]d   John WINGATE (Seal)
In Presence of us
W[illia]m HOLLAND . / . ~"

*followed on folio 119 with the acknowledgment by Justice of the Peace John DENNIS and recordation on 05 June 1767 by court clerk Henry JOHNSON[133]

Liber G, folio 125; 18 June 1767

"This Indenture made this 18ᵗʰ day of June Anno Domini one thousand seven hundred and sixty seven. Between John KENDALL of Accomack County in the Colony of Virginia of the one part, and Jonathan TILNEY of Worcester County in the Province of Maryland of the other part. Witnesseth that the said John KENDALL for and in Consideration of the sum of one hundred and twenty four Pounds current Money of Maryland to him in hand paid by the said Jonathan TILNEY at and before the Ensealing and Delivery of these Presents the Receipt whereof the said John KENDALL hereby doth acknowledge hath Given Granted Bargained and Sold, and by these Presents doth Give Grant Bargain and Sell unto him the said Jonathan TILNEY his Heirs Ex[ecuto]ʳˢ Adm[inistrato]ʳˢ and Assigns forever one Negroe Man Slave Called **Eben**, and also one other Negroe Boy slave called **Charles**. To have and to hold the af[oresai]ᵈ Negroes **Eben** and **Charles** unto him the said Jonathan TILNEY his Heirs and Assigns Forever and for no other use or purpose whatsoever. And the said John KENDALL for himself his Heirs Ex[ecuto]rs Adm[inistrato]ʳˢ doth Covenant and Agree to and with the said Jonathan TILNEY his Heirs and Assigns forever that he the said John KENDALL his Heirs Ex[ecuto]ʳˢ Administrators will Warrant and Defend the af[oresai]ᵈ Negroes **Eben** and **Charles** against the

---

[132] Worcester County Court (Land Records). Deed of Mortgage from COLLINS, Elisha to SMITH, Joseph. 25 May 1767. G, pp. 114-115, MSA CE 30-7. www.mdlandrec.net : accessed 01 November 2021.

[133] Worcester County Court (Land Records). Bill of sale from WINGATE, John to ANDERSON, Hezekiah. 04 June 1767. G, pp. 118-119, MSA CE 30-7. www.mdlandrec.net : accessed 01 November 2021.

Claim Right and Title of all manner of Persons whatsoever unto him the said Jonathan TILNEY his Heirs Ex[ecuto]rs Adm[inistrato]rs and Assigns forever. In Witness whereof the said John KENDALL to these presents his hand hath set and seal affixed the day and Year first above written. ~

Signed Sealed & Delivered   Esme BAYLY   John KENDALL. (Seal)
In Presence of ~   A^d[a]m SPENCE"

*followed with acknowledgment by Justice of the Peace Adam SPENCE and recordation on 22 June 1767 by court clerk Henry JOHNSON[134]

Liber G, folio 126; 05 June 1767

"Worcester {?} Know all Men by these presents that I Daniel TOWNSEND Jun[io]r of Worcester County & Province of Maryland for and in consideration of the sum of Fifteen Pounds lawful Money of Maryland to me in hand paid by James SMITH of the same place the Receipt whereof I do hereby acknowledge have bargained sold & delivered and by these presents do bargain sell and deliver unto the said James SMITH one Negro Woman named **Hannah**, two head of Horses, three Cows, twenty seven head of Hogs & two feather Beds & Furniture. To have and to hold the said bargained. Premises unto the said James SMITH his Executors Adm[inistrato]rs or Assigns forever. And I the said Daniel TOWNSEND for myself my Executors & Adm[inistrato]rs shall and will Warrant and forever Defend against all Persons by these presents the said bargained Premises unto the said James SMITH his Ex[ecuto]rs Adm[inistrato]rs & Assigns. Provided Nevertheless that if I the said Daniel TOWNSEND my Ex[ecuto]rs Adm[inistrato]rs and Assigns or any of us do and shall well & truly pay or cause to be paid unto the said James SMITH his Ex[ecuto]rs Adm[inistrato]rs or Assigns the sum of Fifteen Pounds on the xx:th day of this Instant June for the Redemption of the said bargained Premises. Then this present Bill of Sale to be void or else remain in full force. In Witness whereof I have hereunto set my hand & Seal this fifth day of June Anno Dom[ini] MDCCLXVII. / . ~ . / . ~

Signed sealed & Delivered   Jo^s[eph] DIRICKSON   Dan[ie]l TOWNSEND (Seal)
In Presence of ~   John SELBY"

*followed with the acknowledgment by Justices of the Peace Joseph DIRICKSON and John SELBY and recordation on 25 June 1767 by court clerk Henry JOHNSON[135]

Liber G, folios 205-206; 11 September 1767

"This Indenture made this 11th Day September in the Year of our Lord God one thousand seven hundred and sixty seven. Between Charles RICHARDSON Senior of Worcester County and Province of Maryland Planter of the one part, and Shadrack RICHARDSON and Isaac HILLOM of the same Place of the other part. Witnesseth that the said Charles RICHARDSON for divers good Causes and in Consideration of the sum of Five Shillings Current Money of Maryland to him in hand Paid by the af[oresai]d Shadrack RICHARDSON and Isaac HILLOM before the Sealing and Delivery hereof the Receipt whereof he doth hereby acknowledge and himself fully satisfied Hath Given Granted Bargained and Sold Assigned Transfered and Set over, and by these Presents doth Give Grant and Sel unto the af[oresai]d Shadrack RICHARDSON and Isaac HILLOM their Heirs Execu[tors] Admin[istrato]rs or Assigns forever four Negroes known by the following names **Stephen, Benjamin, Hanah** and **Leah**. To have and to hold the af[oresai]d Negroes called **Stephen, Benjamin, Hanah** and **Leah** before mentioned unto the af[oresai]d Shadrack RICHARDSON and Isaac HILLOM their Heirs and Assigns forever and to no other use intent or purpose or construction whatsoever. And the said Charles RICHARDSON doth Covenant Promise and Agree to and with the af[ore]s[ai]d Shadrack RICHARDSON and Isaac HILLOM their Heirs and Assigns, that he the said Charles the above named Negroes called **Stephen, Benjamin, Hanah** and **Leah** against his Heirs and

---

[134] Worcester County Court (Land Records). Bill of sale from KENDALL, John to TILNEY, Jonathan. 18 June 1767. G, p. 125, MSA CE 30-7. www.mdlandrec.net : accessed 01 November 2021.

[135] Worcester County Court (Land Records). Bill of sale from TOWNSEND, Daniel to SMITH, James. 05 June 1767. G, p. 126, MSA CE 30-7. www.mdlandrec.net : accessed 01 November 2021.

all other Persons Claiming the same shall and will Warrant and forever Defend by these presents. In Testimony whereof the Party af[ore]s[ai]d to this Indenture have set his Hand and fixt their Seal the Day and Year first above written.

Signed sealed and Delivered	A[d][a]m SPENCE	his
In Presence of ….	Pearce REED	Charles C R RICHARDSON (Seal)
		Mark"

*followed on folio 206 with the acknowledgment of Justice of the Peace Adam SPENCE and recordation 18 September 1767 by court clerk Henry JOHNSON[136]

Liber G, folios 264-265; 13 January 1768

"Know all Men by these presents that I Charles TENNENT Minister of the Gospel in the County of Worcester & Province of Maryland for the Consideration of five hundred Pounds Current Money to me in hand paid by William Macky TENNENT have bargained & sold & by these presents do bargain sell transfer makeover & convey all my right title & property of & into the sundry Goods & Chattels following to wit, one Negroe Wench named **Bess**, one Negroe Boy named **Sandy**, one Molattoe Boy named **Jack**, & one Negroe Boy named **Pompey**, one Eight Day Clock, one Walnut Desk, one Chest of Drawers, one Dressing Table, Tea Table, Oval Table Walnut, a dozen of leather bottomed Chairs, half a dozen rush bottomed D[itt]o Maple, two Windsor Chairs, one Close Stool D[itt]o & one arm Chair rush bottomed, a Couch, corner Cubbard, & a Book press with all the Books belonging to my Library, a Looking Glass, China ware & Del{?} D[itt]o of all sizes & Shapes, half a dozen large Silver Table Spoons, eight small Tea D[itt]o & one pair of Silver Tea Tonges, seven feather Beds, four blue & white Coverlets, one Rug one white Counter pane, one Stamped D[itt]o seven pair of Blankets w[i]th all the Bed Quilts, Sheets, Bolsters, pillows, pillow Cases, Curtains, Bedspreads & thereto belonging Pictures, Table Cloths, Napkins, Shovels, Tonges, hand-irons, flat-irons, Candle-sticks, iron Potts, Kettles, knives & forks, warming Pan, puter Dishes, plates, Steelyards, Griddle, Chests, Trunks &c all & every part of my household & kitchen Furniture, & moreover my Conicle & Harnish, two Horses, two Mares, & four colts a horse-Cart & all my farming Utensils, such as Ploughs, Harrows, Hoes, Mattocks, Spade, Axes & c. To have and to hold the afores[ai]d bargain[e]d Goods & Chattels, to him the said William Macky TENNENT his Heirs Exec[uto]rs Adm[inistrato]rs and Assigns to the only proper use & behoof of the said William Macky TENNENT his Heirs Exe[cuto]rs Adm[inistrato]rs and Assigns and to & for no other use purpose or intent whatsoever. In Testimony whereof I have hereunto set my Hand & Seal this thirteenth Day of Jan[ua]ry Anno Domini 1768. /. ~ . /. ~

Signed sealed & Delivered	Sam[ue]l SLOAN	Charles TENNENT (Seal)
In the Presence of ….	J DENNIS"	

*followed on folio 265 with the acknowledgment by Justice of the Peace John DENNIS and recordation 21 January 1768 by court clerk Henry JOHNSON[137]

Liber G, folios 350-351; 26 March 1768

"Maryland Worcester C[oun]ty Ss. Know all Men by these presents that I Moses GOTHERY of Worcester County & Province of Maryland Planter for and in consideration of the sum of ninety pounds Current money of Maryland to me in hand paid by Joshua EVANS of the County & Province af[ore]s[ai]d Have Given Granted Bargained & Sold and by these presents do Give Grant Bargain & Sell unto the said Joshua EVANS his Heirs and Assigns forever, one Negro Wench call[e]d **March**. To have and to hold the said Negro Wench called **March** unto the said Joshua EVANS his Heirs and Assigns forever, and to and for no other use intent or purpose

---

[136] Worcester County Court (Land Records). Bill of sale from RICHARDSON, Charles Sr. to RICHARDSON, Shadrack and HILLOM, Isaac. 11 September 1767. G, pp. 205-206, MSA CE 30-7. www.mdlandrec.net : accessed 01 November 2021.

[137] Worcester County Court (Land Records). Bill of sale from TENNENT, Charles to TENNENT, William Macky. 13 January 1768. G, pp. 264-265, MSA CE 30-7. www.mdlandrec.net : accessed 01 November 2021.

whatsoever. In Testimony whereof I have hereto set my Hand & Seal this Twenty sixth day of March Anno Dom[ini] 1768. ~

Sealed & Delivered   James POLK   Moses GOTHERY. (Seal)
In Presence of us   Math[e]^w HOPKINS"

*followed on folio 351 with acknowledgments of Justice of the Peace Benton HARRIS and recordation on 08 April 1768 by court clerk Henry JOHNSON[138]

Liber G, folios 378-379; 02 May 1768

"Maryland Worcester {?} Know all Men by these presents that I William ARBUCKLE of Accomack County in the Colony of Virginia Gent[leman] for and in Consideration of the sum of seventy seven Pounds three Shillings & nine Pence current Money to me in hand paid by Euphamia PURNELL of Worcester County in the Province of Maryland Gent[le]woman the Receipt whereof I do hereby acknowledge and my self there with fully satisfied have Granted Bargained & Sold and by these Presents do Grant Bargain & Sell unto the said Euphamia PURNELL three Negroes (Viz) one Negro boy called **Amos**, and two Negro Girls one called **Murrur** & the other called **Nany**. To have and to hold the said bargained Negroes unto the said Euphamia PURNELL her Heirs Ex[ecuto]^rs Adm[inistrato]^rs & Assigns forever And I the said William ARBUCKLE for my self my Heirs Ex[ecuto]^rs Adm[inistrato]^rs the said bargained Premisses unto the said Euphamia PURNELL her Heirs Ex[ecuto]^rs Adm[inistrato]^rs & Assigns against all and all manner of Persons shall & will Warrant and Defend by these Presents In Witness whereof I the said William ARBUCKLE have hereunto set my hand & fixed my Seal this 2^d Day of May 1768. ~

Signed sealed & Delivered   Ebenezer CAMPBELL   William ARBUCKLE (Seal)
In the Presence of us   Jos[hu]^a MITCHELL"

*followed with the acknowledgment by Justice of the Peace Joshua MITCHELL and recordation on 30 May 1768 by court clerk Henry JOHNSON[139]

Liber G, folio 384; 30 April 1768

"Worcester County {?} Know all Men by these presents that I Joseph WILLIAMS of said County in the Province of Maryland for and in Consideration of the sum of four pounds money of pensylvania to me in Hand paid by John MITCHELL of the County and province af[ore]s[ai]^d the Receipt whereof I do hereby acknowledge have Granted Bargained Sold and Conveyed, and by these presents do Give Grant Bargain and Sell unto the said John MITCHELL his Heirs and Assigns forever one third part of a Negro Man called **Pomp** which was Willed to said Joseph WILLIAMS by his father Thomas WILLIAMS. To have and to hold the above mentioned third of said Negro called **Pomp** unto the said John MITCHELL his Heirs and Assigns and to the proper use and behoof and to no other intent or purpose whatsoever, And the said Joseph WILLIAMS for himself his Heirs Executors Adm[inistrato]^rs doth Covenant promise and grant to and with him the said John MITCHELL his Heirs and Assigns that he the said Joseph WILLIAMS his Heirs Executors Administrators the Negro Man Slave af[ore]s[ai]^d unto the said John MITCHELL his Heirs and Assigns his or the said Joseph WILLIAMS his Heirs and all manner of Person or Persons whatsoever shall and will Warrant and forever Defend. In Witness whereof I have to these presents set my Hand Seal this thirtieth Day of April Anno Dom[ini] 1768

Signed sealed & Delivered   Joseph WILLIAMS (Seal)
In Presence of ~
Robert HOPKINS.   Rob[er]^t MITCHELL"

---

[138] Worcester County Court (Land Records). Bill of sale from GOTHERY, Moses to EVANS, Joshua. 26 March 1768. G, pp. 350-351, MSA CE 30-7. www.mdlandrec.net : accessed 02 November 2021.

[139] Worcester County Court (Land Records). Bill of sale from ARBUCKLE, William to PURNELL, Euphamia. 02 May 1768. G, pp. 378-379, MSA CE 30-7. www.mdlandrec.net : accessed 02 November 2021.

*followed with the recordation on 18 May 1768 by court clerk Henry JOHNSON[140]

Liber G, folios 484-485; 05 November 1768

"This Indenture made this fifth day of November in the Year seventeen hundred and sixty eight. Between George FARRINGTON of Worcester County of the one part, and Joseph DASHIELL and James MARTIN of the other part. Witnesseth that whereas the said George FARRINGTON for and in Consideration of the said Joseph DASHIELL and James MARTIN becomeing Security for the said George FARRINGTON in an Appeal by the said George FARRINGTON at the suit of a certain Ephraim KING as also for and in Consideration of the sum of five Shillings current Money of Maryland to the said George FARRINGTON in hand paid by the said Joseph DASHIELL and James MARTIN at and before the Sealing and Delivery hereof the Receipt whereof the said George hereby doth acknowledge, he hath Given Granted Bargained and Sold, and by these presents doth Give Grant Bargain and Sell unto the said Joseph DASHIELL and James MARTIN their Heirs and Assigns forever one Negro Man Slave called **Tylus** and one Negro Woman called **Thanah** to them the said Joseph DASHIELL and James MARTIN their Heirs and Assigns. To have and to hold the af[oresai]d two Negroes to the af[oresai]d Joseph DASHIELL and James MARTIN their Heirs and Assigns forever to and for the only proper use and behoof of the said Joseph DASHIELL and James MARTIN and to and for no other use or purpose whatsoever. Provided allways that if the af[oresai]d FARRINGTON do and shall save harmless and keep indemnified the af[oresai]d Joseph DASHIELL and James MARTIN their Heirs and Assigns for becomeing Security as af[oresai]d then the above Instrument of Writing shall be void and of no Effect. In Testimony whereof the said George FARRINGTON to these presents his Hand hath set and Seal affixed the Day and Year first above written.
Signed sealed & Delivered   G FARRINGTON   (Seal)
In presence of us ~
Jos[hu]a MITCHELL"

*followed on folio 485 with the acknowledgment by Justice of the Peace Joshua MITCHELL and recordation on 08 November 1768 by court clerk Henry JOHNSON[141]

Liber G, folios 509-510; 10 March 1769

"This Indenture made this Tenth day of March in the Year of our Lord one thousand seven hundred & sixty nine. Between James HOUSTON, Shipwright, of Worcester County in the Province of Maryland of the one part, and Samuel HANDY of the same Place of the other part. Witnesseth that the said James HOUSTON for and in Consideration of the Sum of fifty seven pounds fourteen Shillings & Eleven pence Current Money of Maryland to him in hand paid by the said Samuel HANDY at or before the Sealing and Delivery hereof the Receipt whereof the said James HOUSTON hereby doth acknowledge and thereof doth acquit and discharge the said Samuel HANDY his Heirs Execut[or]s and Administrators hath bargained and Sold, and by these present doth Bargain and Sell unto the said Samuel HANDY his Heirs and Assigns, one Negro Man Called **Lonnon**. To have and to hold the said Negro Man Called **Lonnon** to him the said Samuel HANDY his Heirs and Assigns to and for the only proper use of him the said Samuel HANDY his Heirs or Assigns, and for no other use or purpose whatsoever. And the said James HOUSTON doth Covenant and Agree by these presents that he the said James HOUSTON his heirs Executors or Administrators will Warrant and defend the af[oresai]d Negro Man Called **Lonnon** to him the said Samuel HANDY his Heirs or Assigns against the Right of Every person claiming or who shall hereafter Claim any Right or Title to the said Slave. Provided always and it is the true Intent and meaning hereof that if the af[oresai]d James HOUSTON do and shall pay unto the af[oresai]d Samuel HANDY his Executors or

---

[140] Worcester County Court (Land Records). Bill of sale from WILLIAMS, Joseph to MITCHELL, John. 30 April 1768. G, p. 384, MSA CE 30-7. www.mdlandrec.net : accessed 02 November 2021.

[141] Worcester County Court (Land Records). Bill of sale from FARRINGTON, George to DASHIELL, Joseph and MARTIN, James. 05 November 1768. G, pp. 484-485, MSA CE 30-7. www.mdlandrec.net : accessed 02 November 2021.

Adm[inistrato]rs the sum of fifty seven pounds fourteen Shillings & Eleven pence Current Money with the legal Interest thereon within six months from the date hereof then the Within writting to be void otherwise to stand in full force and virtue. In Witness whereof the said James hath hereto set his hand & Seal the day & year first within written. /. ~

Sealed & Deliver[e]d   James HOUSTON   (Seal)
In presence of
A[da]m SPENCE. /. ~"

*followed on folio 510 with the acknowledgment of Justice of the Peace Adam SPENCE and recordation on 15 March 1769 by court clerk Henry JOHNSON[142]

Liber G, folios 510-511; 31 January 1769

"Memorand[um] that this Day to witt the 31 Day of Janary 1769 Sold and Deliverd to William TOMSON of Kent County in Penselvano a Negro Woman named **Gone** for Vallen Recu{?}d which said Negro I Doe Warrant to him the said TOMSON and to his heirs or Asignes from my Selfe and all Maner of Persons that shall Lay Aney Clame to the af[oresai]d Negr[o] As Witness my hand the Day and year above Menssond ~

testus James CATHELL. ~   George DISHEROON.
       James BUCHANAN

Maryland {?} I do hearby assign over all my Right Title Clame or Intrest of the above bill of Sail to John HANDY Jun[io]r of Worcester County his Heirs and Assigns for Ever. As Witness my Hand this 1st Day of February Anno Dom[ini] 1769.

Test   James BUCHANAN.   Will[i]am TOMSON
       Peter GORDY. ~"

*followed on folio 151 with the recordation by court clerk Henry JOHNSON on 17 March 1769[143]

Liber H, folio 6; 17 April 1769

"Worcester {?} Know all Men by these Presents that I William JARMAN of the County af[ore]s[ai]d and Province of Maryland for and in consideration of the sum of Five Pounds Eight Shillings to me in Hand paid by John BALL of the same place before the ensealing and delivery hereof. Have bargained & sold, and by the Presents do bargain & sell unto the said John BALL a Negro Child Called **Sampson** about three months and a half old. To have and to hold all and singular the said Negro called **Sampson** by these presents bargained and sold unto the only proper use and behoof of the said John BALL his Ex[ecuto]rs Adm[inistrato]rs & Assigns forever, freely, quietly & intirely without any Contradiction Claim or hindrance of any Person whatsoever, & without any account to me, or to any other whatsoever to be made answered, or here after to be rendered, so that neither I the said William JARMAN nor any other for me, or in my name, any Right, Title, Interest or demand of in, to or for the said Negro ought to exact, challenge, claim or demand at any time or times hereafter, but from all Action, Right, or Title, Possession and Interest thereof shall be wholly barred and excluded by force & virtue of these presents. And I the said William JARMAN for myself my Ex[ecuto]rs & Adm[inistrato]rs the said Negro boy called **Sampson** unto the said John BALL his Ex[ecuto]rs Adm[inistrato]rs & Assigns will Warrant and forever defend against all and every other person or persons whatsoever by these presents. In Witness whereof the said William JARMAN hath hereunto set his hand and Seal affixed this Seventh Day of April anno Domini one thousand seven hundred and sixty nine.

Sealed and Delivered   William JARMAN. (Seal)
In the Presence of "

---

[142] Worcester County Court (Land Records). Bill of sale from HOUSTON, James to HANDY, Samuel. 10 March 1769. G, pp. 509-510, MSA CE 30-7. www.mdlandrec.net : accessed 02 November 2021.

[143] Worcester County Court (Land Records). Bill of sale from DISHEROON, George to TOMSON, William. 31 January 1769. G, pp. 510-511, MSA CE 30-7. www.mdlandrec.net : accessed 02 November 2021.

*followed with the acknowledgment by Justice of the Peace John SELBY and recordation by court clerk Henry JOHNSON[144]

Liber H, folios 11-12; 06 March 1769

"March the sixth Day Annoq Dom[ini] one thousand seven hundred & sixty nine. Then Received of John ATKINSON my Plantation and all the Lands and Improvements thereunto belonging, Also one Negro Man named **Fryday**, one Wench named **Fella**, and one Girl named **Rose**, and sundry other things to include all my Legacies also the amount of two hundred & seventy four Pounds two Shillings and two Pence my part of the Personal Estate also the amount of Two hundred and ninety one Pounds Six Shillings & ten Pence which is all my part of the Debts that he has as yet Receiv[e]d, the above is in full for my part of the Estate left me by my Deceas[e]d Father Angelo ATKINSON in his last Will, also in full of Every Demand that I have against the said John ATKINSON whatever. As Witness my Hand & Seal the Day and Year above mentioned. ~

Testes. Joshua ATKINSON. Angelo ATKINSON Ju[nio]r (Seal)
   Charles BEAVANS."

*followed with the recordation by court clerk Henry JOHNSON on 11 April 1769[145]

Liber H, folio 25; 03 April 1769

"Maryland {?} Know all Men by these presents that I Charles BROWN of Dorchester and said Province for and in Consideration & the sum of forty Pounds by Bond given to me in hand by Robert MITCHELL of Worcester County and said Province Yeoman the Receiving of which Bond I do hereby acknowledge, have Bargained and Sold and Delivered, and by these presents do Bargain and Sell and Deliver unto the said Robert MITCHELL one Negro Boy called **Benn**. To have and to hold the said bargained Premisses unto the said Robert MITCHELL his Heirs Executors Administrators and Assigns forever. And I the said Charles BROWN for my self my Heirs Executors and Administrators shall and will Warrant and forever Defend against all manner of Person or Persons whatsoever by these presents the said bargained Premisses unto the said Robert MITCHELL his Heirs and Assigns forever And in Witness whereof I have hereunto set my Hand and Seal the third Day of April one thousand seven hundred and sixty nine. ~

Signed sealed and Delivered Charles BROWN (of Charles) (Seal)
In Presence of ~   his
Robert HOPKINS. Morris X O CONNER:
              mark"

*followed with the recordation by court clerk Henry JOHNSON on 24 April 1769[146]

Liber H, folios 49-50; 08 June 1769

"Know all Men by these presents that I John SATCHELL of Worcester County in the Province of Maryland for and in Consideration of thirty four Pounds Current money of Maryland to me in hand paid by Esther RICHARDSON of the same place before the Sealing and Delivery hereof wherewith I confess myself to be fully Satisfied contented and paid, have bargained and sold, and by these presents do fully clearly and absolutely bargain and sell to the said Esther Richardson one Negro Boy called **Joshua** about fourteen years old. To have and to hold the said Negro Boy to the said Esther RICHARDSON her Heirs and Assigns forever to her and their own proper use forever. And I the said John SATCHELL my Heirs Ex[ecuto]rs Adm[inistrato]rs and Every of us the said Negro Boy unto the said Esther RICHARDSON her Heirs and Assigns against all People shall and will Warrant and forever Defend by these

---

[144] Worcester County Court (Land Records). Bill of sale from JARMAN, William to BALL, John. 17 April 1769. H, p. 6, MSA CE 30-8. www.mdlandrec.net : accessed 06 November 2021.

[145] Worcester County Court (Land Records). Receipt from ATKINSON, John to ATKINSON, Angelo Jr. 06 March 1769. H, pp. 11-12, MSA CE 30-8. www.mdlandrec.net : accessed 06 November 2021.

[146] Worcester County Court (Land Records). Bill of sale from BROWN, Charles to MITCHELL, Robert. 03 April 1769. H, p. 25, MSA CE 30-8. www.mdlandrec.net : accessed 06 November 2021.

presents. Provided allways that if I the said John SATCHELL my Heirs Ex[ecuto]rs or Adm[inistrato]rs or any of us do well and truly pay or cause to be paid unto the said Esther RICHARDSON her Heirs or Assigns the full and just sum of thirty four pounds Current Money of Maryland at or upon Demand after the Expiration of two years ensuing the date hereof with legal Interest for the same. That then the present Bill and Bargain of sale of the said Boy shall be utterly void and of none Effect, else to stand and remain in full force power and virtue in Law. In Witness whereof I the said John SATCHELL do hereunto set my hand and fix my Seal this Eighth day of June Anno Dom[ini] 1769. / . ~

Signed Sealed & Delivered   John SELBY   John SATCHELL   (Seal)
In the Presence of   Levi HOPKINS"

*followed on folio 50 with the acknowledgment by Justice of the Peace John SELBY and recordation by court clerk Henry JOHNSON[147]

Liber H, folios 50-51; 12 June 1769

"Maryland Worcester County Ss. Know all Men by these Presents that I James MURRAY of Worcester County Breeches Maker for and in Consideration of the sum of one hundred and fifty one Pounds Current money of Maryland to me in hand paid by Frederick SHINGLE of the City of Philadelphia and before the Sealing and Delivery hereof the Receipt whereof I the said James MURRAY do hereby confess and acknowledge, have Granted Bargained and Sold, and by these presents do Grant Bargain and Sell unto the said Frederick SHINGLE his Heirs and Assigns forever one old Negro Woman named **Flora**, one young Negro Woman named **Doll**, one Walnut Desk, three feather Beds and Bolsters two Ruggs one Blanket, one pair Sheets, one old Trunk, one dozen China Plates, one China Dish one Chest of Drawers, half dozen Chairs, three Tables, two Chests, two Saddles, one black Mare, four Bedsteads and four Iron Potts. To have and to hold the said Negro Woman named **Flora**, and the said Negro Woman named **Doll** & one Walnut Desk, three feather Beds and Bolsters, two Ruggs, one Blanket, one pair Sheets, one old Trunk, one dozen China Plates, one Dish, one Chest of Drawers, half dozen Chairs, three Tables, two Chests, two Saddles, one black Mare, four Bedsteads, and four Iron Potts af[ore]s[ai]d unto the said Frederick SHINGLE his Heirs and Assigns forever to the only proper use and behoof of the said Frederick SHINGLE his Heirs and Assigns forever and to and for no other use or purpose whatsoever. In Witness whereof I the said James MURRAY have hereunto set my hand & Seal this twelfth Day of June in the Year of our Lord one thousand seven hundred Sixty & nine.

Sealed & Delivered   Jam[e]s MURRAY.   (Seal)
In Presence of ......
Sam[ue]l HANDY.   Geo[rge] HAYWARD."

*followed on folio 51 with the acknowledgment by Justice of the Peace John SELBY on 13 June 1769 and recordation by court clerk Henry JOHNSON on 14 June 1769[148]

Liber H, folio 55; 30 June 1769

"Know all men by these Presents that I John PEPPER of Worcester County in the Province of Maryland farmer for and in Consideration of the sum of sixty Pounds Current money of Maryland to me in hand paid at and before the Sealing and Delivery of these Presents by Charles PARKER of the County and Province af[ore]s[ai]d the Receipt whereof I do hereby acknowledge, have Bargained and Sold, and by these Presents do Bargain and Sell unto the said Charles PARKER a Negro Man called **Leak**. To have and to hold the Negro **Leak** by these Presents Bargained and said unto the said Charles PARKER his Heirs Executors Administrators or Assigns forever. And I John PEPPER the said Negro **Leak** for myself my Heirs Executors and Administrators the said Negro **Leak** unto the said Charles PARKER his Heirs Ex[ecuto]rs

---

[147] Worcester County Court (Land Records). Bill of sale from SATCHELL, John to RICHARDSON, Esther. 08 June 1769. H, pp. 49-50, MSA CE 30-8. www.mdlandrec.net : accessed 06 November 2021.

[148] Worcester County Court (Land Records). Bill of sale from MURRAY, James to SHINGLE, Frederick. 12 June 1769. H, pp. 50-51, MSA CE 30-8. www.mdlandrec.net : accessed 06 November 2021.

Adm[inistrato]rs and Assigns and against all and every other Person and Persons whatsoever shall and will Warrant and forever Defend by these Presents the said Negro **Leak** unto the said Charles PARKER his Heirs and Assigns forever of which said Negro **Leak** I the said John PEPPER have put the said Charles PARKER in full Possession. In Witness my Hand & Seal this 30th Day of June Anno Domini Seventeen hundred and sixty nine. /. ~ ~ . / . ~

Signed Sealed and Delivered
In the Presence of ~
N. HOLLAND.   Henry TURNER.

John + PEPPER (Seal)
his Mark"

*followed with the recordation by court clerk Henry JOHNSON[149]

Liber H, folio 76; 03 August 1769

"Worcester Ss. Know all men by these presents that I Empson BIRD of New Castle County on Delaware for & in Consideration of the sum of Five Shillings Current Money & for divers other good Considerations me thereto moving, Have assigned transferred & set over, and by these Presents do assign transfer & set over unto Jacob GORDEY all my Right and Title of in & to a Negro Boy named **Jacob**. To have and to hold the said Negro Boy to Him the said Jacob GORDEY his Executors Administrators & Assigns to the only proper use and behoof of the said Jacob GORDEY his Executors Administrators & Assigns & to & for no other use or purpose whatever. In Testimony whereof I have set my Hand & affixed my Seal this third Day of August Anno Dom[ini] seventeen hundred & sixty nine.

Sealed and Delivered
In Presence of ~
Ebe[neze]^r CAMPBELL.   G. FARRINGTON."

Empson BIRD. (Seal)

*followed with recordation by court clerk Henry JOHNSON on 04 August 1769[150]

Liber H, folios 82-83; 11 August 1769

"Worcester Ss. Know all men by these presents that I Henry KELLY of Worcester County in the Province of Maryland for and in Consideration of the sum of fifty five Pounds Maryland Currency to me in hand paid by Charles GODFREY of the County and Province af[ore]s[ai]^d the receipt whereof I do hereby Acknowledge Have bargained and sold, set over & delivered and by these presents do bargain, sell set over and deliver unto the said Charles GODFREY his Ex[ecuto]rs Adm[inistrato]rs & Assigns a Negro Woman called **Lisha**. To have and to hold the aforesaid Negro Woman called **Lisha** to the af[ore]s[ai]^d Charles GODFREY his Heirs Ex[ecuto]rs Adm[inistrato]rs and Assigns and to his and their only proper use and behoof. And I the said Henry KELLY for myself my Heirs my Ex[ecuto]rs & Adm[inistrato]rs the said bargained premisses unto the said Charles GODFREY his Heirs Ex[ecuto]^{rs} Adm[inistrato]rs & Assigns against all and all manner of Persons whatsoever shall and will Warrant and forever defend by these presents. In Witness whereof I have hereunto Set my hand & Seal affixed this Eleventh day of August Anno Dom[ini] one thousand seven hundred sixty and nine.

Sealed and Delivered   W WHITTINGTON
In the Presence of   Samuel DAVIS

Henry + KELLY. (Seal)
his Mark"

*followed on folio 83 with the acknowledgment by Justice of the Peace N. HOLLAND and recordation by court clerk Henry JOHNSON[151]

---

[149] Worcester County Court (Land Records). Bill of sale from PEPPER, John to PARKER, Charles. 30 June 1769. H, p. 55, MSA CE 30-8. www.mdlandrec.net : accessed 06 November 2021.
[150] Worcester County Court (Land Records). Bill of sale from BIRD, Empson to GORDEY, Jacob. 03 August 1769. H, p. 76, MSA CE 30-8. www.mdlandrec.net : accessed 06 November 2021.
[151] Worcester County Court (Land Records). Bill of sale from KELLY, Henry to GODFREY, Charles. 11 August 1769. H, pp. 82-83, MSA CE 30-8. www.mdlandrec.net : accessed 06 November 2021.

Liber H, folio 83; 03 August 1769

"Worcester County In the Province of Maryland Know all men by these presents that I Thomas ROBINS farmer of the County & Province af[ore]s[ai]^d for and in Consideration of the sum of Thirty pounds Thirteen Shillings & Two Pence Current Money of the Province af[ore]s[ai]^d in hand paid by John Purnell ROBINS of the same place the Receipt whereof I do hereby Acknowledge, have bargained and sold, & by these presents do bargain & sell to him the said John Purnell ROBINS one Negro Girl called **Phillis**, which was Devis[e]d to me by my Father Thomas ROBINS, the said Negro for myself my Heirs Executors & Administrators & Assigns unto him the said John Purnell ROBINS him his Heirs Administrators & Assigns, I do hereby Warrant & Defend against any person or persons whatsoever. In Witness whereof I have hereunto set my hand and Seal affixed this third Day of August in the ninth Year of his Majestys Reign George the third King G[reat] Britain Anno Dom[ini] 1769. / . ~

Signed Sealed & Delivered   Thomas ROBINS. (Seal)
In Presence of us …..
Isaac CABELS.   Littleton ROBINS."

*followed with the acknowledgment by Justice of the Peace Adam SPENCE on 10 August 1769 and recordation by court clerk Henry JOHNSON on 18 August 1769[152]

Liber H, folios 164-165; 16 December 1769

"To all Christian People to whome these Presents shall come. We William ARBUCKLE & Milby ATKINSON of Worcester County in the Province of Maryland send Greeting. Know ye that we William ARBUCKLE & Milby ATKINSON for and in consideration of the love good will and affection which we have and do bare towards Ann PURNELL of the same Place, and for divers other good causes and Considerations us hereunto moveing have given and granted, and by these presents do give and grant unto the said Ann PURNELL her Heirs Ex[ecuto]^{rs} Adm[inistrato]^{rs} and Assigns one Negro Girl called **Murreah** To have and to hold the said Negro Girl called **Murreah** unto the said Ann PURNELL her Heirs Ex[ecuto]^{rs} Adm[inistrato]^{rs} and Assigns, to the only proper use and behoof of her the said Ann PURNELL her Heirs Ex[ecuto]^{rs} Adm[inistrato]^{rs} and Assigns forever. And we the said William ARBUCKLE & Milby ATKINSON the said Negro Girl called **Murreah** to the said Ann PURNELL her Heirs Ex[ecuto]^{rs} Adm[inistrato]^{rs} & Assigns against all Persons whatsoever, shall and will warrant and forever defend by these presents. In Witness whereof we have hereunto Set our hands & Seals this 16th Day of December Anno Dom[ini] 1769. / . ~

Signed Sealed & Delivered   William ARBUCKLE. (Seal)
In Presence of us   her   Milby ATKINSON. (Seal)
Jos[hu]^a MITCHELL   Betty X HOLLAND.
                             Mark"

*followed on folio 165 with the acknowledgment of Justice of the Peace Joshua MITCHELL and recordation on 05 January 1770 by court clerk Henry JOHNSON[153]

Liber H, folios 165-166; 03 January 1770

"This indenture made this third Day of January Anno Dom[ini] One thousand seven hundred and seventy. Between Lemuel JOHNSON of Worcester County in the Province of Maryland of the one part, and John TULL Ju[nio]^r of the County and Province aforesaid of the other part. Witnesseth that the said Lemuel JOHNSON for and in Consideration of the Sum of seventy pounds Current money of Maryland to him in hand or Secured to be paid by the said John TULL the Receipt whereof he doth hereby Acknowledge, hath Given Granted Bargained and Sold,

---

[152] Worcester County Court (Land Records). Bill of sale from ROBINS, Thomas to ROBINS, John Purnell. 03 August 1769. H, p. 83, MSA CE 30-8. www.mdlandrec.net : accessed 06 November 2021.

[153] Worcester County Court (Land Records). Deed of gift from ARBUCKLE, William and ATKINSON, Milby to PURNELL, Ann. 16 December 1769. H, pp. 164-165, MSA CE 30-8. www.mdlandrec.net : accessed 07 November 2021.

and by these Presents doth Give Grant Bargain Sell and Deliver unto the said John TULL Ju[nio]ʳ one Negro Man called **Daniel** aged about thirty Years. To have and to hold the aforesaid Bargained and Sold Negro unto the said John TULL his Heirs & Assigns forever and to the only use and behoof of the said John TULL Ju[nio]ʳ his Heirs and Assigns and for no other use or purpose whatsoever. And the said Lemuel JOHNSON for himself his Heirs Exe[cuto]ʳˢ Adm[inistrato]ʳˢ doth Covenant Grant and Agree to and with the said John TULL, that he will forever Warrant & Defend the aforesaid Negro **Daniel** unto the aforesaid John TULL Ju[nio]ʳ his Heirs Executors & c To and from all Persons claiming any Right or Interest thereunto In Witness whereof the said Lemuel his hand hath set and Seal affixed the Day and year aforesaid.
Signed Sealed & Deliver[ed]
In Presence of us ……   Lemuel JOHNSON   (Seal)
N: HOLLAND.   Outten STURGIS."

*followed on folio 166 with the acknowledgment by Justice of the Peace N. HOLLAND and recordation on 05 January 1770 by court clerk Henry JOHNSON[154]

Liber H, folio 193; 15 January 1770

"Somerset Ss. Know all men by these presents that I John FINCH of Worcester County in the Province of Maryland, for and in Consideration of sixty Pounds in Surcalating money of Maryland, to the said John FINCH in hand paid by George HANDY, have bargained sold conveyed & transferred, and by these presents do bargain sell convey and transferr unto the afores[ai]ᵈ Geo[rge] HANDY – his Heirs Executors Adm[inistrato]ʳˢ and Assigns all my Right, Title, Claim and Interest of in and to a young Negro Fellow ab[ou]ᵗ twenty five years of Age named **Pomp**. To have and to hold the af[ore]s[ai]ᵈ Negro **Pomp** to the said George HANDY his Heirs Ex[ecuto]ʳˢ Adm[inistrato]ʳˢ and Assigns forever, & to and for no other use or purpose whatever. And I the said John FINCH for myself my Heirs Ex[ecuto]ʳˢ & Adm[inistrato]ʳˢ do hereby covenant and agree to and with the said Geo[rge] HANDY his Heirs Ex[ecuto]rs Adm[inistrato]ʳˢ & Assigns. that I will the afores[ai]ᵈ bargained Negro Fellow to the said Geo[rge] HANDY his Heirs Ex[ecuto]ʳˢ Adm[inistrato]rs and Assigns Warrant & forever Defend. In Testimony whereof I have hereto set my Hand & Seal this fifteenth day of January Anno Dom[ini] one thousand seven hundred & seventy.
Signed Sealed & Delivered
In Presence of ……..   John FINCH.   (Seal)
Henry HANDY.   Joseph HANDY."

*followed with the acknowledgment by Somerset County Justice of the Peace William WINDER, recordation by Somerset County court clerk Thomas HAYWARD on 30 January 1770, and recordation by Worcester County court clerk Henry JOHNSON on 02 February 1770[155]

Liber H, folios 201-202; 05 February 1770

"Maryland Somerset Ss. Know all men by these Presents that I James CATHELL, of Worcester County and Province af[oresai]ᵈ for and in Consideration of the Sum of Eighty Pounds Current Money af[oresai]ᵈ to me in hand paid by William WINDER Jun[io]ʳ the Receipt whereof I do hereby Acknowledge, have Bargained and Sold, and by these presents do Bargain and Sell to said William a Negro Wench named **Unice** about twenty Years of Age, a Negro Girl call[e]d **Sylva**, about 2 Years of Age, also a Negro Child called **Phillis** about ten months old, a Copper Still of about 35 Gallons with the Appurtenances. To Have and to hold the said several Goods and Chattels aforesaid, to the said William his Executors Adminisᵗ[rators] and Assigns to his and their proper use Provided that if I the said James shall pay to the said William the said Sum of Eighty Pounds Current Money aforesaid with legal Interest at or upon the tenth Day of June

---

[154] Worcester County Court (Land Records). Bill of sale from JOHNSON, Lemuel to TULL, John Jr. 03 January 1770. H, pp. 165-166, MSA CE 30-8. www.mdlandrec.net : accessed 07 November 2021.
[155] Worcester County Court (Land Records). Bill of sale from FINCH, John to HANDY, George. 15 January 1770. H, p. 193, MSA CE 30-8. www.mdlandrec.net : accessed 07 November 2021.

next Ensuing the Date hereof, then this Deed to be void, which said Sum the said James for himself his Heirs Executors and Admins^t[rators] hereby Covenants with the said William to pay and it is further hereby Concluded by me that if I the said James do not pay to the said William the said Sum of Eighty Pounds Current Money aforesaid with legal Interest thereon on the said tenth Day of June, Then it shall and may be Lawfull for the said William to Sell and Dispose the Goods and Chattels af[oresai]^d to the best Price and out of the Purchase Money Satisfy and Retain the said Sum of Eighty Pounds and the Interest together with the Expence of this Deed and Recording, and Refund the Residue to me the said James. In Witness whereof I have hereunto Set my Hand and affixed my Seal this fifth Day of February Anno Domini 1770.
Seal[e]d and Delivered
In Presence of ……   James CATHELL Jr   (Seal)
W[illia]^m WINDER.   Leah DENWOOD."

*followed with the acknowledgment by Somerset County Justice of the Peace William WINDER, recordation by Somerset County court clerk Thomas Hayward on 13 February 1770, and recordation by Worcester County court clerk Henry JOHNSON on 15 February 1770[156]

Liber H, folios 206-208; 10 February 1770

"This Indenture made this Tenth day of February in the Year of our Lord one thousand seven hundred and seventy. Between Levin TOWNSEND of Worcester County of the one part, and George HAYWARD and Samuel HANDY of the same place of the other part. Witnesseth that the said Levin TOWNSEND for and in Consideration of the several Trusts hereafter Expressed, as also for and in Consideration of the sum of five Shillings Current Money of Maryland to him in hand paid at and before the Sealing and Delivery hereof the receipt whereof he doth hereby Acknowledge, hath Granted Bargained Sold remised and released unto the said George HAYWARD and Samuel HANDY their Heirs and Assigns forever five Feather Beds and Bedsteads, Cords and Matts, five pair Sheets, five Blankets, five Worsted Ruggs, one dozen and a half of Flagg Chairs, four Leather Chairs, two round Tables four Tables, three Iron Pot racks, five Iron Pots, all the Pewter Plates and Dishes, two pair of Hand Irons, all the Casks and Coopers Ware, one sorrel Mare, one Cart, one Negro Girl named **Rose**, which I got by my Wife and for which John TULL has Sued the said Townsend for, two pair of fire Tongs and Shovels, three Chests, and one Leather Trunk and also all the outstanding debts that are due and oweing to the said Levin TOWNSEND by any ways or means whatsoever. To have and to hold all and singular the Goods and Chattels, outstanding Debts above mentioned, unto the said George HAYWARD and Samuel HANDY their Heirs and Assigns forever, to the only use and benefit of the said George HAYWARD and Samuel HANDY their Heirs and Assigns forever in Trust Nevertheless that they the said George HAYWARD and Samuel HANDY or the Survivor of them or their Heirs shall dispose of all and singular the Goods and Chattels, and collect the outstanding Debts above mentioned in such manner as they or the Survivor of them or their Heirs shall think best, and that after such Sale of all or any part thereof, that they shall first pay and Satisfie unto Levin HOPKINS and Levin HILL their Heirs Ex[ecuto]^{rs} Adm[inistrato]^{rs} or Assigns out of the Money ariseing from such Sale the full and just Sum of one hundred and seventy three pounds four Shillings and Eleven Pence Current money of Maryland with legal Interest thereon, and then the remainder of the Money ariseing to be paid Equally to and amongst the just Creditors of the said Levin TOWNSEND for such debts as hath been by him Contracted since the Year of our Lord one thousand seven hundred and sixty in proportion to their several demands. Provided such Credittors shall produce their Claim within six Months after such Disposition, and the Overplus thereof if any ariseing from such Sale to be delivered and paid unto the said Levin TOWNSEND or his order. And the said Levin TOWNSEND for himself his Heirs Executors and Adm[inistrato]^{rs} doth Covenant Grant and Agree to and with the George HAYWARD and Samuel HANDY and the Survivor of them their Heirs Executors and Adm[inistrato]^{rs} that it shall and may be Lawfull for them or Either of them their Heirs or Assigns at any time after the Execution thereof to take Possession of all and singular the Goods

---

[156] Worcester County Court (Land Records). Bill of sale from CATHELL, James to WINDER, William Jr. 05 February 1770. H, pp. 201-202, MSA CE 30-8. www.mdlandrec.net : accessed 07 November 2021.

& Chattels, and Collect the outstanding Debts above mentioned, and Disposition thereof to make for the purpose af[ore]s[ai]^d. In Witness whereof the said Levin TOWNSEND hath hereto Set his Hand & Seal affixed the day & Year first above written.
Sealed & Delivered   Levin TOWNSEND   (Seal)
In Presence of ~ John SELBY."

*followed on folio 208 with the acknowledgment by Justice of the Peace John SELBY and recordation on 16 February 1770 by court clerk Henry JOHNSON[157]

Liber H, folios 208-209; 20 February 1770

"To all People to whom these Presents shall come Greeting. Whereas by Indenture bearing date the Nineteenth day of May in the Year of our Lord, one thousand seven hundred sixty and six, made between Samuel HOPKINS of Worcester County of the one part, and William WHITTINGTON of the same place Deceased, he the said Samuel HOPKINS in Consideration of the Sum of Money there in mentioned to be paid, did Grant Bargain and Sell unto the said William WHITTINGTON one Negroe Girl named **Edith**, To be had and Holden unto the said William WHITTINGTON his Executors Adm[inistrato]rs and Assigns. And Whereas the said William WHITTINGTON by his certain Writing Obligatory bearing date the day and year above mentioned did acknowledge himself to be held and firmly bound unto the said Samuel in the Sum of one hundred pounds Current Money of Maryland with Condition to be void in Case the said William WHITTINGTON should Release all his Right & Title of in and to the said Negro Girl named **Edith** unto the Said Samuel HOPKINS on his the said Samuels paying unto the said William WHITTINGTON the sum of Forty two pounds Seventeen Shillings and two pence with the legal Interest thereon due as also the Costs of a suit commenced by a certain Allen and Dennis against the said Samuel. And Whereas the said Samuel hath since paid and satisfied unto the said William WHITTINGTON in his Lifetime the af[ore]s[ai]^d Sum of Money & Costs of Suit af[ore]s[ai]^d Now Know ye therefore by these presents that I Mary King WHITTINGTON Widow and Executrix of the said William WHITTINGTON in Consideration thereof Have remised and released, and by these presents doth remise and release unto the said Samuel HOPKINS his Ex[ecuto]^{rs} Adm[inistrato]^{rs} and Assigns all the said Estate right Title Interest Claim and Demand whatsoever of her the said Mary King WHITTINGTON of in and to the said Negro Girl named **Edith**, for or by any ways or means whatsoever. To have and to hold the said Negro Girl named **Edith** unto the said Samuel HOPKINS his Executors Adm[inistrato]^{rs} or Assigns, to the only proper use and behoof of the said Samuel HOPKINS his Heirs or Assigns, and to and for no other use intent or purpose whatsoever. In Witness whereof I have hereto Sett my Hand & Seal this 20th day of February in the Year of our Lord, one thousand seven hundred and seventy. ~
Sealed & Delivered
In Presence of ....   Mary King WHITTINGTON   (Seal)
Hampton Hopkins WISE.   Thomas SELBY."

*followed on folio 209 with the recordation by court clerk Henry JOHNSON on 22 February 1770[158]

Liber H, folios 209-211; 23 February 1770

"This Indenture made this Twenty third Day of February in the Year of our Lord one thousand seven hundred and seventy. Between Thomas LAMBDEN Jun[io]^r of Worcester County of the one part, and Littleton DENNIS of the same place of the other part. Witnesseth that the said Thomas for and in Consideration of the sum of Thirty five Pounds Eleven Shillings Current Money to me paid by the af[ore]s[ai]^d Littleton DENNIS at and before the Sealing and Delivery

---

[157] Worcester County Court (Land Records). Deed of trust from TOWNSEND, Levin to HAYWARD, George and HANDY, Samuel. 10 February 1770. H, pp. 206-208, MSA CE 30-8. www.mdlandrec.net : accessed 07 November 2021.

[158] Worcester County Court (Land Records). Deed of release from WHITTINGTON, Mary King to HOPKINS, Samuel. 20 February 1770. H, pp. 208-209, MSA CE 30-8. www.mdlandrec.net : accessed 07 November 2021.

hereof the Receipt whereof the said Thomas hereby doth acknowledge, hath granted bargained sold and delivered, and by these presents doth give grant bargain sell and deliver unto the af[oresai]^d Littleton DENNIS his Heirs and Assigns forever all that Tract of Land or Swamp called Long Acre, Granted unto the said Thomas and is Bounded and Discribed as in and by the Pattent thereof is expressed recorse thereto being had more fully will appear, as also one Negro Girl called **Rach**, or **Rachell**, being the Negro which the said Thomas got by his Wife. To have and to hold the af[ore]s[ai]^d Granted and Bargained Premisses with the Appurtenances unto the said Littleton DENNIS his Heirs and Assigns forever, to and for the Only use benefit and behoof of the said Littleton DENNIS his Heirs and Assigns forever, and for no other use or purpose whatsoever. And the said Thomas LAMBDEN for himself his Heirs Ex[ecuto]^{rs} and Adm[inistrato]^{rs} doth covenant grant and agree to and with the said Littleton DENNIS his Heirs and Assigns forever" … "In Witness whereof the said Thomas to these presents his Hand hath set and Seal affixed the Day and Year first above written.
Signed Sealed & Deliver[e]d
In Presence of us ~   Tho[ma]^s LAMBDEN Jun[io]r   (Seal)
John SELBY.   A^d[a]m SPENCE."

*followed on folio 211 with the acknowledgment by Justices of the Peace John SELBY and Adam SPENCE and recordation on 24 February 1770 by court clerk Henry JOHNSON[159]

*Due to its true length, this transcription has been shortened to its most relevant portions. The full original deed can be viewed at the citation provided.

Liber H, folios 243-244; 19 February 1770

"Know all men by these presents that we Matthew SELBY, Mary WALTON and Parker SELBY all of Worcester County in the Province of Maryland for and in Consideration of the Sum of ten Pounds current Money of Maryland to us paid by Mary SELBY of the County af[oresai]^d at & before the Sealing and Delivery hereof, the Receipt whereof we hereby doth Acknowledge hath Bargained and Sold, and by these presents doth Bargained and Sell unto the af[oresai]^d Mary SELBY and her Heirs and Assigns forever the several Negroes hereafter named **Jacob, Dinah, Abraham, Isaac, Barshaba, Jeremiah and Solomon**. To have and to hold the af[oresai]^d Negroes **Jacob, Dinah, Abraham, Isaac, Barshaba, Jeremiah, and Solomon** to the only proper use benefit and behoof of the said Mary SELBY and her Heirs and Assigns forever. And the said Matthew SELBY, Mary WALTON and Parker SELBY doth Covenant for themselves their Heirs Ex[ecuto]^{rs} and Adm[inistrato]^{rs} with the said Mary SELBY and her Heirs Ex[ecuto]^{rs} and Adm[inistrato]^{rs} that at the time of the Bargain and Sale hereof they had full Power and Authority to Sell the af[oresai]^d Negroes **Jacob, Dinah, Abraham, Isaac, Barshaba, Jeremiah and Solomon**, and that they the said Matthew SELBY, Mary WALTON, and Parker SELBY will forever Warrant and Defend the said Negroes **Jacob, Dinah, Abraham, Isaac, Barshaba, Jeremiah and Solomon** unto the said Mary SELBY and her Heirs and Assigns forever against the Rights titles Claims and Demands of all and every Person or Persons whatsoever Claiming by from or under us or our Heirs or Assigns. In Testimoney whereof the said Matthew SELBY Mary WALTON & Parker SELBY hath hereunto set their Hands & fixed their Seals this 19 Day of February 1770. ~
Test. Bowd: ROBINS   Matthew SELBY.   (Seal)
       Parker SELBY.   Mary WALTON.   (Seal)
                                                                Parker SELBY. ~   (Seal)"

*followed on folio 244 with the acknowledgment by Justice of the Peace John SELBY and recordation on 09 March 1770 by court clerk Henry JOHNSON[160]

---

[159] Worcester County Court (Land Records). Deed of mortgage from LAMBDEN, Thomas Jr. to DENNIS, Littleton. 23 February 1770. H, pp. 209-211, MSA CE 30-8. www.mdlandrec.net : accessed 07 November 2021.

[160] Worcester County Court (Land Records). Bill of sale from SELBY, Matthew, WALTON, Mary, and SELBY, Parker to SELBY, Mary. 19 February 1770. H, pp. 243-244, MSA CE 30-8. www.mdlandrec.net : accessed 07 November 2021.

Liber H, folios 244-245; 10 March 1770

"This Indenture made this 10th day of March in the Year of our Lord one thousand seven hundred & seventy. Between Abraham OUTTEN of Accomack County in the Coloney of Virginia Silversmith of the one part, and Samuel HANDY of the County of Worcester in the Province of Maryland of the other part. Witnesseth that the said Abraham OUTTEN for and in Consideration of the sum of Twenty five pounds twelve Shillings and one penny farthing Current Money of Maryland to him in Hand paid by the said Samuel HANDY, at or before the Sealing & delivery hereof the Receipt whereof the said Abraham OUTTEN doth Acknowledge, and thereof doth Acquit and discharge the said Samuel HANDY his Executors & Administrators hath Bargained and Sold, and by these presents doth Bargain and Sell unto the said Samuel HANDY his Heirs and Assigns the Negroes following to wit **Rose, Esther, Sampson and Sarah** To have and to hold the said Negroes **Rose, Esther, Sampson and Sarah** to him the said Samuel HANDY his Heirs and Assigns to and for the only proper use of him the said Samuel HANDY his Heirs or Assigns and for no other use or purpose whatsoever. And the said Abraham OUTTEN doth Covenant and Agree by these presents that he the said Abraham OUTTEN his Heirs Executors or Administrators will Warrant and forever Defend the af[ore]s[ai]d Negroes to him the said Samuel HANDY his Heirs or Assigns against the Right of every Person claiming or who shall hereafter claim any Right or Title to the said Negroes. Provided always and it is true intent and meaning hereof that if the af[ore]s[ai]d Abraham OUTTEN do and shall pay unto the af[ore]s[ai]d Samuel HANDY his Executors or Administrators the Sum of Twenty five pounds twelve Shillings and one penny farthing Current Money with legal Interest for the same within Six Months from the date hereof. Then the within writing to be void, otherwise to stand in full force and virtue in Law. In Witness whereof the said Abraham hath hereto set his Hand & Seal the Day and Year first above written. ~
Sealed & Delivered
In Presence of ….. John SELBY.   Abraham OUTTEN. (Seal)"

*followed on folio 245 with the acknowledgment by the Justice of the Peace John SELBY and recordation on 12 March 1770 by court clerk Henry JOHNSON[161]

Liber H, folio 250; 16 March 1770

"Know all men by these presents that I John FINCH of Worcester County in the Province of Maryland for and in Consideration of sixty five Pounds common Currency to me in Hand paid or procured to be paid by W[illia]m ADAMS of Somerset County & Province af[oresai]d Have Granted Bargained and Sold, and by these Presents doth Grant Bargain and Sell to the said W[illia]m ADAMS a certain Negro fellow named **Pomp**. To have and to hold the said Negroe to him and his Heirs forever against any Person or Persons Lawfully Claiming or Demanding a Right thereto will Warrant and the same forever Defend. In Witness whereof I have sett my Hand and affixed my Seal this sixteenth Day of March one thousand seven hundred and seventy. Sealed and Delivered
In the Presence of ….
Geo[rge] HAYWARD. ~   L BISHOP   John FINCH. (Seal)"

*followed with the acknowledgment by Justice of the Peace John SELBY and recordation by court clerk Henry JOHNSON[162]

Liber H, folios 250-251; 15 March 1770

"Maryland Worcester County Ss. Know all Men by these presents that I Samuel HOPKINS of Worcester County in the Province of Maryland farmer, for and in Consideration of the Sum of fifty Pounds Current Money of Maryland to me in hand paid by John CHAMBERS of Somerset

---

[161] Worcester County Court (Land Records). Deed of mortgage from OUTTEN, Abraham to HANDY, Samuel. 10 March 1770. H, pp. 244-245, MSA CE 30-8. www.mdlandrec.net : accessed 07 November 2021.
[162] Worcester County Court (Land Records). Bill of sale from FINCH, John to ADAMS, William. 16 March 1770. H, p. 250, MSA CE 30-8. www.mdlandrec.net : accessed 07 November 2021.

County in the Province of Maryland, have granted bargained sold and delivered unto the af[ore]s[ai]^d John CHAMBERS his Executors, Administrators and Assigns a Negro Girl slave named **Edith** of the Age of Eighteen Years the Eighteenth day of February Anno Dom[ini] seventeen hundred & seventy. To have and to hold the af[ore]s[ai]^d Negro Girl named **Edith** of the Age af[ore]s[ai]^d together with her increase, unto the af[ore]s[ai]^d John CHAMBERS his Executors Adm[inistrato]^rs and Assigns, free and clear from any Incumbrance whatsoever. And the said Samuel HOPKINS doth for himself his Executors and Administrators covenant and agree to and with the said John CHAMBERS his Executors Administrators will Warrant and Defend the af[ore]s[ai]^d Negro Girl named **Edith** unto the af[ore]s[ai]^d John CHAMBERS his Executors Administrators and Assigns, free and clear from all manner of Persons whatsoever. In Witness whereof the said Samuel hath to these Presents sett his Hand & Seal this fifteenth Day of March Anno Dom[ini] seventeen hundred & seventy.
Signed Sealed & Delivered
In Presence of …….. Samuel HOPKINS. (Seal)
Benj^a[min] HANDY.   Hampton Hopkins WISE. ~"

*followed on folio 251 with the recordation by court clerk Henry JOHNSON on 16 March 1770[163]

Liber H, folios 251-252; 27 February 1770

"Know all men by these Presents that I Thomas ROBINS of Worcester County & Province of Maryland for and in Consideration of Sixty Pounds current Money to me in hand paid by Ebenezer CAMPBELL, the Receipt whereof I do hereby acknowledge, have Bargained and Sold, and by these presents do Bargain and Sell, make Over and Deliver unto the said Ebenezer CAMPBELL one Negro Boy called **Rodger** of the County af[ore]s[ai]^d and by these presents I do hereby for myself my Heirs Executors Administrators & Assigns, against all and every Person & Persons forever Warrant & Defend the said Negro unto Ebenezer CAMPBELL his Heirs Executors & Administrators & Assigns forever Claiming any Interest or Title thereunto in my behalf. In Witness whereof I have hereunto sett my Hand and affixed my Seal this 27th of February 1770. /. ~ . /. ~
Signed Sealed & Deliver[e]d
In Presence of …….. Thomas ROBINS. (Seal)
Isaac MURRAY.   Jehu HOUSTON."

*followed on folio 252 with the recordation by court clerk Henry JOHNSON on 20 March 1770[164]

Liber H, folios 264-265; 23 March 1770

"Know all men by these presents that we Charles RICHARDSON, Shadrack RICHARDSON & Isaac KILLAM all of Worcester County & Province of Maryland do for and in Consideration of the Sum of fifty Pounds current Money of the Province af[ore]s[ai]^d do Bargain & Sell & by these presents do Bargain & Sell three Negros Named, one **Hannah, Easther & Hannah jun[io]^r**, unto Adam Spence his Heirs & Assigns forever. To have & to hold the said Negros named **Hannah, Esther & Hannah jun[io]^r**, unto him the said Adam SPENCE his Heirs & Assigns forever & the said Charles RICHARDSON, Shadrack RICHARDSON & Isaac KILLAM doth further covenant that they will Warrant & Defend the said Negros call[e]^d **Hannah, Esther & Hannah jun[io]^r** unto him the s[ai]^d Adam SPENCE his Heirs & Assigns forever, against the Claim of all Persons whatever As Witness our Hand & Seals this twenty third Day of March Anno Dom[ini] 1770. ~

---

[163] Worcester County Court (Land Records). Bill of sale from HOPKINS, Samuel to CHAMBERS, John. 15 March 1770. H, pp. 250-251, MSA CE 30-8. www.mdlandrec.net : accessed 07 November 2021.
[164] Worcester County Court (Land Records). Bill of sale from ROBINS, Thomas to CAMPBELL, Ebenezer. 27 February 1770. H, pp. 251-252, MSA CE 30-8. www.mdlandrec.net : accessed 07 November 2021.

Signed Sealed and Delivered
In Presence of ……………..
John SELBY. ~   Michael TARR. ~

Charles CR RICHARDSON. (Seal)
(his Mark)

Shadrack RICHARDSON. (Seal)
Isaac KELLAM. ~ (Seal)"

*followed on folio 265 with the acknowledgment by Justice of the Peace John SELBY and recordation on 24 March 1770 by court clerk Henry JOHNSON[165]

Liber H, folios 265-266; 23 March 1770

"Know all men by these presents that we Charles RICHARDSON, Shadrack RICHARDSON & Isaac KILLAM all of Worcester County & Province of Maryland do for and in Consideration of the Sum of sixty Pounds Current Money of Maryland do Bargain & Sell, by these presents do Bargain & Sell a certain Negro Man Slave named **Stephen** unto John Purnell ROBINS his Heirs & Assigns forever. To have & to hold the said Negro Man Slave named **Stephen** unto him the said John Purnell ROBINS his Heirs& Assigns forever. & the said Charles RICHARDSON, Shadrack RICHARDSON & Isaac KILLAM doth further Covenant & Agree with the said John Purnell ROBINS his Heirs & Assigns, that they will Warrant & Defend the said Negro called **Stephen** against the Claim of all manner of Persons whatsoever, unto him the said John Purnell ROBINS his Heirs & Assigns forever. As Witness our Hands & Seals this twenty third Day of March Anno Dom[ini] 1770. /. ~

In Presence of ~
John SELBY. ~
Michael TARR. ~

Charles CR RCHARDSON (Seal)
(his Mark)

Shadrack RICHARDSON. (Seal)
Isaac KELLAM. ~ (Seal)"

*followed on folio 266 with the acknowledgment by Justice of the Peace John SELBY and recordation on 24 March 1770 by court clerk Henry JOHNSON[166]

Liber H, folios 303-304; 18 May 1770

"To all People to whome these Presents shall come Greeting Know ye that I Mary SELBY of Worcester County in the Province of Maryland this Eighteenth day of May in the Year of our Lord one thousand seven hundred and seventy, For and in Consideration of the natural Love and Affection which I owe and bear to my Son John SELBY and Zadock SELBY and my four Grand Children viz.ᵗ William SELBY (Son of William SELBY) Leah SELBY, and Levin SELBY, Daughter and Son of my Son called Micaijah SELBY, and Micaijah SELBY (Son of Zadock SELBY) and for the further Advancement of my said Sons and Grand Children, I Give them the following Sum of Money and several Negroes hereafter mentioned, to wit, to my Son John SELBY fifty Pounds current Money of Maryland Reserveing to myself the use of the said Money dureing my natural Life, to my Son Zadock SELBY the use of my Negroe Boy called **Isaac** dureing his natural Life, Reserveing to myself the use of Labour of the said Negro dureing my Life, and after my Son Zadock's Death to my Grand Son Micaijah SELBY (Son of Zadock SELBY), also I Give to my Grand Son William SELBY (Son of William SELBY) my Negroe Boy called **Jeremiah** only Reserveing to myself the use or Labour of the said Negroe called **Jeremiah** dureing my natural Life, also I Give to my Grand Daughter Leah SELBY my Negroe Girl called **Barshaba** as also I Give to my Grand Son Levin SELBY my Negro Boy called **Solomon** Daughter and Son of Micaijah SELBY Reserveing to myself the use of the said Negroe Girl called **Barshaba** and Negro Boy called **Solomon** for and Dureing my natural Life

---

[165] Worcester County Court (Land Records). Bill of sale from RICHARDSON, Charles, RICHARDSON, Shadrack, and KELLAM, Isaac to SPENCE, Adam. 23 March 1770. H, pp. 264-265, MSA CE 30-8. www.mdlandrec.net : accessed 07 November 2021.

[166] Worcester County Court (Land Records). Bill of sale from RICHARDSON, Charles, RICHARDSON, Shadrack, and KELLAM, Isaac to ROBINS, John Purnell. 23 March 1770. H, pp. 265-266, MSA CE 30-8. www.mdlandrec.net : accessed 07 November 2021.

Provided my said Grand Daughter Leah SELBY and Grand Son Levin SELBY as af[oresai]^d do Relinquish and forever quit their Claim Right & Title of and in the several Negroes hereafter mentioned to wit, **Rachel, Rhoda, Sarah, Jack** and **Bets**, unto William SELBY and his Heirs their Brother, but provided they the said Leah and Levin do refuse to give up their Right of the af[oresai]d Negroes, then I Give the said Negroes **Barshaba** and **Solomon** to be Equally divided between the said Leah SELBY Levin SELBY and William SELBY so as af[oresai]^d but provided that I should Die before the said Leah and Levin arive to Age of maturity or of Age to Receive their Estate, that then I Give the Use of the two Negroes called **Barshaba** and **Solomon** to my John SELBY and Zadock SELBY as Trustees for to be Delivered to my said Grand Children when at full Age to Receive them all which Sum of Money and said Negroes above mentioned I give and grant unto my Sons and Grand Children af[oresai]^d To have and to hold the said fifty Pounds unto my Son John SELBY and the said Negroes to my Son Zadock SELBY and my said Grand Children to them and to their Heirs forever in manner as af[oresai]^d all which said Negroes as af[oresai]^d I Warrant and Defend to my son Zadock SELBY and my four Grand Children, William, Leah, Levin and Micaijah as af[oresai]^d to them and their Heirs forever against the Claim Right & Title of all and Every Person or Persons whatsoever Claiming by from or under me or my Heirs. And the said Mary SELBY doth further Covenant with her said son John SELBY that if their should not be the quantity of fifty Pounds in Money in the Possession of the said Mary SELBY at the time of her Death that then She doth hereby Impower her said Son John SELBY to Receive so much of her the said Mary SELBY's Estate as shall make up or include the fifty Pounds current Money of Maryland so as af[oresai]^d And the said Mary SELBY doth hereby Warrant and Defend the said fifty Pounds to the said John SELBY his Heirs and Assigns forever against the Claim of all Persons whatsoever. In Witness whereof the said Mary SELBY to these Presents her Hand hath set and Seal affixed the Day and Year first above written. /.~./.~

Signed Sealed and Delivered
In the Presence of us
A^d[a]m SPENCE.   Elizabeth FERGUSON.

Mary m SELBY. (Seal)
her   Mark"

*followed on folio 304 with the acknowledgment by Justice of the Peace Adam SPENCE and recordation by court clerk Henry JOHNSON[167]

Liber H, folios 309-310; 01 June 1770

"Maryland County Ss. Know all men by these Presents that I Betty CORBIN of Worcester County in the Province of Maryland Widow for and in Consideration of the natural Love and Affection which I have and do bear unto my son Peter Spencer CORBIN but more Especially for and in Consideration of the Sum of five Shillings Current Money of Maryland to me in hand paid by the said Peter Spencer CORBIN at and before the Sealing and Delivery hereof the Receipt whereof I do hereby Confess and Acknowledge, have Given Granted Bargained and Sold, and by these presents doth Give Grant Bargain and Sell unto the said Peter Spencer CORBIN his Heirs and Assigns forever one Negro Woman named **Norah** & one Negroe Boy named **Aneas**. To have and to hold the said Negroe Woman named **Norah** and Negro Boy named **Aneas** to the said Peter Spencer CORBIN his Heirs and Assigns to the only proper use and behoof of the said Peter Spencer CORBIN his Heirs & Assigns forever, and to and for no other use intent construction or purpose whatsoever. In Witness whereof I have hereunto Sett my hand & Seal affixed this first day of June Anno Dom[ini] 1770. ~

Sealed & Delivered
In Presence off ......
John SELBY.   Geo[rge] HAYWARD."

Betty CORBIN. (Seal)

---

[167] Worcester County Court (Land Records). Deed of gift from SELBY, Mary to SELBY, John, SELBY, Zadock, SELBY, William, etal. 18 May 1770. H, pp. 303-304, MSA CE 30-8. www.mdlandrec.net : accessed 07 November 2021.

*followed on folio 310 with the acknowledgment by Justice of the Peace John SELBY and recordation on 02 June 1770 by court clerk Henry JOHNSON[168]

Liber H, folios 310-311; 01 June 1770

"Maryland Worcester County Ss. Know all men by these Presents that I Betty CORBIN of Worcester County in the Province of Maryland Widow for and in Consideration of the natural Love and Affection that I have & do bear unto my Son William CORBIN, but more Especially for and in Consideration of the Sum of five Shillings Current Money of Maryland to me in hand paid at and before the Sealing & Delivery hereof by my said Son William CORBIN, the Receipt whereof I do hereby Confess and Acknowledge, have Given Granted Bargained and Sold, and by these Presents do Give Grant Bargain and Sell unto the said William CORBIN his Heirs and Assigns forever one Negro Boy named **Abner**. To have and to hold the said Negroe Boy named **Abner** to the said William CORBIN his Heirs and Assigns to the only proper use and behoof of the said William CORBIN his Heirs forever & to and for no other use intent construction or purpose whatsoever. In Witness whereof I have hereto Sett my hand & Seal this first day of June Anno Dom[ini] 1770. ~
Sealed and Delivered
In Presence off …..   Betty CORBIN. (Seal)
John SELBY.   Geo[rge] HAYWARD."

*followed on folio 311 with the acknowledgement by Justice of the Peace John SELBY and recordation on 02 June 1770 by court clerk Henry JOHNSON[169]

Liber H, folios 323-324; 04 June 1770

"Know all men by these presents that I James CATHELL of Worcester County in the Province of Maryland for and in Consideration of the Sum of ninety Pounds current Money of Maryland to me in hand paid by William WINDER jun[io]^r before the Sealing and Delivery hereof the Receipt whereof is hereby confessed, have assigned transferred and set over, & by these Presents do assign transfer and set over unto the said William WINDER jun[io]^r all the Goods and Chattels following to wit one Negro Woman called **Eunice**, one Negro Girl called **Phillis**, and one Negro called **Sylby**, one thirty Gallon Still with Head & Worm, two yoke of Oxen, and two feather Beds with furniture, and also a young Horse (stoned) To have and to hold the af[oresai]^d assigned Premises unto the said William WINDER jun[io]^r his Executors Administrators and Assigns & to the only use of him the said William WINDER jun[io]^r & c. Provided that if the said James CATHELL shall pay unto the said William WINDER the aforesaid Sum of ninety Pounds with Interest thereon from the fifth Day of February last past, on or before the tenth Day of August next Ensuing the Date hereof, then this Bill of Sale to be void. And the said James CATHELL doth hereby agree to and with the said William WINDER that in Case the said Sum of ninety Pounds with Interest as af[ore]s[ai]^d be not paid to the said William WINDER on or before the said tenth Day of August, that it shall be lawfull for the said William to enter and take the said assigned premises and Expose the same to publick Sale for the paym[en]^t of the said Ninety Pounds with Interest as af[ore]s[ai]^d, and the Recording of two Bills of Sale of the said James to the said William. And the said James hereby binds himself and agrees to pay to the said William the said Sum of Money with Interest as af[ore]s[ai]^d with the Cost af[ore]s[ai]^d. In Witness whereof I have hereto set my Hand & Seal this 4th day of June 1770 ~
Sealed and Delivered   James CATHELL. (Seal)
In Presence of ~   A^d[a]m SPENCE."

---

[168] Worcester County Court (Land Records). Deed of gift from CORBIN, Betty to CORBIN, Peter Spencer. 01 June 1770. H, pp. 309-310, MSA CE 30-8. www.mdlandrec.net : accessed 07 November 2021.
[169] Worcester County Court (Land Records). Deed of gift from CORBIN, Betty to CORBIN, William. 01 June 1770. H, pp. 310-311, MSA CE 30-8. www.mdlandrec.net : accessed 07 November 2021.

*followed with acknowledgment by Justice of the Peace Adam SPENCE and recordation on folio 324 by Henry JOHNSON on 06 June 1770[170]

Liber H, folios 329-330; 07 June 1770

"Worcester County Ss.ᵗ Know all men by these Presents that I Solomon RUSSELL of Somerset County for and in Consideration of the Sum of sixty Pounds Current Money of Maryland to him in hand paid by Peter CALLAWAY before the Ensealing and Delivery of these presents, the receipt whereof the said Solomon RUSSELL doth hereby acknowledge, hath granted, bargained, sold & delivered, and by these presents doth grant bargain sell and deliver unto the af[ore]s[ai]ᵈ Peter CALLAWAY his Executors Administrators and Assigns a Negro Wench called **Patience** about nineteen Years of Age. To have and to hold the af[ore]s[ai]ᵈ Negro Wench named **Patience** unto the af[ore]s[ai]ᵈ Peter CALLAWAY his Executors Adm[inistrato]ʳˢ and Assigns free and clear from any incumbrance whatsoever. And the said Solomon RUSSELL doth for himself his Heirs Ex[ecuto]ʳˢ Adm[inistrato]ʳˢ covenant and agree to and with the said Peter CALLAWAY his Executors Adm[inistrato]ʳˢ and Assigns that he the said Solomon RUSSELL and his Heirs Executors & Adm[inistrato]ʳˢ the af[ore]s[ai]ᵈ Negro Wench named **Patience** will Warrant & Defend from him and his Ex[ecuto]ʳˢ Adm[inistrato]ʳˢ & Assigns and from all manner of persons whatsoever, unto the af[ore]s[ai]ᵈ Peter CALLAWAY his Executors Adm[inistrato]ʳˢ & Assigns. In Witness whereof I have hereto sett my Hand & Seal affixed this Seventh day of June Anno Dom[ini] 1770. ~
Signed Sealed & Delivered   Solomon RUSSELL. (Seal)
In Presence of ~
Joseph DASHIELL"

*followed on folio 330 with the acknowledgment by Justice of the Peace Joseph DASHIELL and recordation by court clerk Henry JOHNSON[171]

Liber H, folio 333; 11 June 1770

"Know all men by these presents that I John FINCH of Worcester County and Province of Maryland Planter for and in consideration of the sum of forty pounds Lawfull Money of Maryland to me in Hand paid by Edmund Northen NELMS the Receipt whereof I do hereby acknowledge, have Bargained Sold and Delivered, and by these Presents according to the due form of Law do Bargain Sell and Deliver unto the said Edmund Northen NELMS one Negro Woman named **Fillis** about Twenty Eight years of Age. To have & to hold the said Bargained Negro Woman unto the said Edmund Northen NELMS his Heirs Executors and Administrators forever. And I the said John FINCH for myself my Heirs Executors and Administrators the said Bargained Negro Woman unto the said Edmund Northen NELMS his Executors Administrators and Assigns against all Persons shall and will Warrant and forever Defend by these presents. In Witness whereof I have hereunto set my Hand and Seal this Eleventh day of June in the Year of our Lord one thousand seven hundred and seventy.
Sealed & Delivered   John FINCH. (Seal)
In Presence of ~

Thomas + LOWE.   Sarah + HOLTE.
    his mark   her mark"

*followed with the acknowledgment by Justice of the Peace Jon:ʰ CATHELL and recordation on 13 June 1770 by court clerk Henry JOHNSON[172]

---

[170] Worcester County Court (Land Records). Bill of sale from CATHELL, James to WINDER, William Jr. 04 June 1770. H, pp. 323-324, MSA CE 30-8. www.mdlandrec.net : accessed 07 November 2021.

[171] Worcester County Court (Land Records). Bill of sale from RUSSELL, Solomon to CALLAWAY, Peter. 07 June 1770. H, pp. 329-330, MSA CE 30-8. www.mdlandrec.net : accessed 07 November 2021.

[172] Worcester County Court (Land Records). Bill of sale from FINCH, John to NELMS, Edmund Northen. 11 June 1770. H, p. 333, MSA CE 30-8. www.mdlandrec.net : accessed 07 November 2021.

Liber H, folio 348; 29 June 1770

"To all People to whom these Presents shall come, I Martha SELBY of Worcester County in the Province of Maryland send Greeting. Know ye that I the said Martha SELBY for and in consideration of the natural Love and Affection which I have and bear unto my Grand Daughter Mary PURNELL the Daughter of John PURNELL Mattopanie in the County and Province aforesaid, and also for other good causes and considerations me hereunto moving. Have given and granted and by these Presents do give grant and confirm unto the said Mary PURNELL Daughter of John PURNELL Mattopanie, one Negro Girl called **Rhoda**, one Bed and furniture, one Silver Punch Bowl, one young Gray Mare, Six Heiffers, nine head of Sheep, two young Stears. To have, hold and enjoy all and singular the said Goods, Chattels, and Negro Girl called **Rhoda** af[ore]s[ai]^d, and all other the aforesaid Premises unto the said Mary PURNELL Daughter of John PURNELL aforesaid her Executors Administrators and Assigns, to the only proper use and behoof of her the said Mary PURNELL her Heirs Executors Administrators and Assigns forever, and to or for no other use intent or purpose whatsoever. And I the said Martha SELBY all and singular the aforesaid Goods Chattels and Premises to the said Mary Purnell her Executors Administrators and Assigns against all Persons whatsoever, shall and will Warrant and forever Defend by these Presents to be Enjoyed after my Decease and not before. In Witness whereof I the said Martha SELBY have hereunto set my Hand and Seal the Twenty ninth Day of June in the Year of our Lord one thousand seven hundred and seventy.

Signed Sealed & Delivered
In the Presence of …….. Martha X SELBY. (Seal)
Matthew OUTTEN. ~ .   A^d[a]m SPENCE. ~   her Mark"

*followed with the acknowledgment of Justice of the Peace Adam SPENCE and recordation by court clerk Henry JOHNSON[173]

Liber H, folios 355-356; 06 July 1770

"Know all persons whom it may concern that I Henry KELLY of Worcester County in the Province of Maryland Planter for and in Consideration of the Sum of Nineteen pounds Current Money of Maryland to me in hand paid by Turner DAVIS of the County aforesaid, the Receipt whereof I do hereby acknowledge, have Bargain[e]d and Sold, and by these presents according to the due form of Law do Bargain and Sell unto the said Turner DAVIS a Negro Boy called **Peter**. To have and hold the said Turner DAVIS his Heirs Executors Administrators and Assigns forever. And I the said Henry KELLY for myself my Heirs Ex[ecuto]^{rs} and Administrators the said Bargained Premisses unto the said Turner DAVIS his Heirs Executors and Administrators and Assigns against all Persons, and every Person whatsoever, shall and will Warrant and forever Defend by these presents the said Negro Boy called **Peter** clear from all manner of incumbrances whatsoever, of which said Negro Boy called Peter I the said Henry KELLY have put the said Turner DAVIS in full Possession. In Witness whereof I the said Henry KELLY have hereunto set my Hand and Seal this Sixth day of July in the Year of our Lord one thousand seven hundred and seventy.

Sealed and Delivered   Jno SCARBOROUGH   Henry KELLY. ~ (Seal)
In the Presence of   A^d[a]m SPENCE"

*followed on folio 356 by the acknowledgment of Justice of the Peace Adam SPENCE and recordation by court clerk Henry JOHNSON[174]

Liber H, folios 378-379; 20 August 1770

"Know all Men by these Presents that Peggy CLAYWELL of Worcester County in the Province of Maryland for and in Consideration of the Sum of twenty Pounds current Money of Maryland

---

[173] Worcester County Court (Land Records). Deed of gift from SELBY, Martha to PURNELL, Mary. 29 June 1770. H, p. 348, MSA CE 30-8. www.mdlandrec.net : accessed 07 November 2021.

[174] Worcester County Court (Land Records). Bill of sale from KELLY, Henry to DAVIS, Turner. 06 July 1770. H, pp. 355-356, MSA CE 30-8. www.mdlandrec.net : accessed 07 November 2021.

to me in hand paid by Mary SPENCE whereof I do hereby acknowledge the Receipt and myself therewith fully and entirely satisfied, have Bargained Sold Set over and Delivered and by these Presents in plain and open manner and in due form of Law in such cases made and provided do Bargain Set over and Deliver unto the said Mary SPENCE her Heirs and Assigns forever a Negro Girl called **Ame** the said Negro Girl called **Ame** To have and to hold to the proper use and behoof of her the said Mary SPENCE her Heirs and Assigns forever. And I the said Peggy CLAYWELL for myself my Heirs Ex[ecuto]rs and Adm[inistrato]rs the said Negro unto the said Mary SPENCE her Heirs and Assigns against all and all manner of Persons, shall and will forever Warrant and Defend by these Presents. In Witness whereof I have hereunto set my Hand and Seal affixed this twentieth Day of August seventeen hundred and seventy. / . ~ . / . ~

Signed Sealed and Delivered
In the Presence of ....   Peggy + CLAYWELL. (Seal)
Hannah STEVENSON.   Marg.t SPENCE.   (her mark)

*followed on folio 379 by the acknowledgment of Justice of the Peace Adam SPENCE and recordation on 01 September 1770 by court clerk Henry JOHNSON[175]

Liber H, folio 397; 07 September 1770

"Maryland Ss.t To all Christian People to whom these presents shall come I Elizabeth OWENS of Worcester County in the said Province send Greeting Know ye that I Elizabeth OWENS for and in Consideration of the Paternal Love good will and Affection which I have and do bear unto my loving Son Cyrus MITCHELL of the County and said Province have given and granted, and by these Presents do fully freely clearly and absolutely Grant unto the said Cyrus MITCHELL and his Heirs forever my Negro Boy called **Jacob** and my Negro Girl called **Loviey** with her Increase to be Possest and Enjoy[e]d by the said Cyrus MITCHELL as soon as said Negros are Capable of Working or of Supporting themselves by what Work they can Preform together with all the Right Title Interest Claim and Demand whatsoever which I now have or which any or Either of my Heirs Executors Administrators may hereafter have of to or in the said granted Premisses. To have and to hold the said Negros to wit **Jacob** and **Loviey** with her Increase as aforesaid unto him the said Cyrus MITCHELL and his Heirs forever absolutely without any manner of Condition as I the said Elizabeth OWENS have fully freely and absolutely and of my own accord sett and Putt in farther Testimony. In Witness whereof I have hereunto sett my hand and fixt my Seal this Seventh Day of Septem[ber] Anno Domini one thousand seven hundred and seventy 1770. ~

Signed Sealed & Delivered
In Presence of ....   Elisabeth OWENS   (Seal)
Rob[er]t MITCHELL.   Jon:a VAUGHAN."

*followed with the acknowledgment by the Justices of the Peace William ELLEGOOD and Jon:a VAUGHAN and recordation on 10 September 1770 by court clerk Henry JOHNSON[176]

Liber H, folio 406; 29 September 1770

" Worcester County Maryland. Know all Men by these presents that I Thomas ROBINS of the County af[ore]s[ai]d for and in Consideration of seventy Pounds to me in hand paid by Ebenezer CAMPBELL the Receipt whereof I do hereby acknowledge Have Bargained and Sold, and by these presents Do Bargain and Sell make Over & Deliver unto the said Ebenezer CAMPBELL, one Negro Ladd called **Rodger**, of the County af[ore]s[ai]d, and by these Presents I do hereby for myself my Heirs Ex[ecuto]rs Adm[inistrato]rs & Assigns against all & every Person & Persons forever Warrant and Defend the said Negro unto the said Ebenezer CAMPBELL his Heirs Ex[ecuto]rs & Adm[inistrato]rs forever in my behalf laying any Title Claim or Interest

---

[175] Worcester County Court (Land Records). Bill of sale from CLAYWELL, Peggy to SPENCE, Mary. 20 August 1770. H, pp. 378-379, MSA CE 30-8. www.mdlandrec.net : accessed 07 November 2021.
[176] Worcester County Court (Land Records). Bill of sale from OWENS, Elisabeth to MITCHELL, Cyrus. 07 August 1770. H, p. 397, MSA CE 30-8. www.mdlandrec.net : accessed 07 November 2021.

thereunto {?}oo. In Witness whereof I have hereunto set my hand & affixed my Seal this 29th Day of September 1770
Signed Sealed & Deliv[ere]d
In presence of ……………..   Thomas ROBINS. (Seal)

Rhoda | GAULTE. ~
(her mark)

*followed with the recordation by court clerk Henry JOHNSON on 05 October 1770[177]

Liber H, folios 406-407; 22 September 1770

"Know all Men by these presents that I Andrew SYMPLER Millright in the Province of Maryland hath bargained and sold unto Jordan HALL, Lining-wheelwright, of the same place for and in Consideration of the Sum of Fifty two pounds ten Shillings Current Money of the Province of Maryland to me in hand paid by the said Jordan HALL whereof I do hereby acknowledge the Receipt and myself therewith fully Satisfied, have bargained sold and delivered unto the said Jordan HALL two Negros, a Woman and her Child, the Woman is named **Nan**, and the Child is named **Bob**. To have and to hold the said Negros **Nan** and **Bob** unto the said Jordan HALL Executors Administrators and Assigns to the only proper use and behoof of the said Jordan HALL's Executors Administrators and Assigns forever. And I the said Andrew SYMPLER for myself Executors and Administrators the said bargained premises unto the said Jordan HALL's Executors Administrators and Assigns against all persons shall and will Warrant and forever Defend by these presents. In Witness whereof I have hereunto set my hand and Seal this 22 Day of September in the Year of our Lord one thousand seven hundred and seventy. ~
Signed Sealed and Delivered   Andrew SIMPLER. (Seal)
In the presence of ………….
Joshua HILL.   Ananias HUDSON."

*followed on folio 407 with the acknowledgment by Justice of the Peace Joshua HILL and the recordation on 08 October 1770 by court clerk Henry JOHNSON[178]

Liber H, folio 430; 07 November 1770

"Maryland Worcester Ss. Know all Men by these presents that I Josiah DICKERSON of the County & Province af[ore]s[ai]d for and in Consideration of the Sum of forty Pound current Money of the province aforesaid in hand paid by Benjamin WOODEN of the same place have Agreed Bargain[e]d & Sold a certain Negro Girl named **Pleasant** unto him the said Benj[a][min] WOODEN his Heirs & Assigns. To have & to hold the af[ore]s[ai]d Negro Girl named **Pleasant** to the only use & benefit of him the af[ore]s[ai]d Benj[a][min] WOODEN his Heirs & Assigns forever. & the said Josiah DICKERSON doth by these presents acknowledge him satisfied & Contented & doth Covenant for himself & his Heirs that he will forever Warrant & Defend the said Negro Girl unto the said Benj[a][min] WOODEN his Heirs & Assigns forever. As Witness my Hand & Seal this Seventh day of November Anno Dom[ini] 1770.
Sign[e]d Seal[e]d & Deliver[e]d   Josiah DICKESON (Seal)
In Presence of …..
Benton HARRIS.   Thomas BARNS."

*followed with the acknowledgment of Benton HARRIS and recordation on 07 November 1770 by court clerk Henry JOHNSON[179]

---

[177] Worcester County Court (Land Records). Bill of sale from ROBINS, Thomas to CAMPBELL, Ebenezer. 29 September 1770. H, p. 406, MSA CE 30-8. www.mdlandrec.net : accessed 07 November 2021.

[178] Worcester County Court (Land Records). Bill of sale from SIMPLEAR, Andrew to HALL, Jordan. 22 September 1770. H, pp. 406-407, MSA CE 30-8. www.mdlandrec.net : accessed 08 November 2021.

[179] Worcester County Court (Land Records). Bill of sale from DICKESON, Josiah to WOODEN, Benjamin. 07 November 1770. H, p. 430, MSA CE 30-8. www.mdlandrec.net : accessed 08 November 2021.

Liber H, folios 440-441; 09 November 1770

"Worcester County Ss. Know all Men by these presents that I Peter CALLAWAY of Worcester County in the Province of Maryland for and in Consideration of the Sum of thirty seven Pounds Current Money of Maryland to him in hand paid before the Ensealing and Delivery of these Presents the Receipt whereof the said Peter CALLAWAY doth hereby acknowledge hath bargained and sold, and by these Presents doth bargain and sell unto John READY of the County and Province of af[ore]s[ai]d a Negro Girl Slave named **Isabella** alias **Ibbey**. To have and to hold the af[ore]s[ai]d Negro Girl Slave unto him the said John READY his Executors Administrators and Assigns free from and disturbance or hindrance whatsoever. And the said Peter CALLAWAY doth for himself his Executors & Adm[inistrator]s covenant to and with the said John READY his Executors Adm[inistrator]s & Assigns that he will Warrant & Defend the af[ore]s[ai]d Negro Girl unto the af[ore]s[ai]d John READY his Executors Adm[inistrator]s & Assigns from all Persons whatsoever. In Witness whereof the said Peter CALLAWAY hath to these Presents his hand Sett & Seal affixed this 9th Day of November Anno Dom[ini] 1770.
Signed Sealed & Delivered   Peter CALLAWAY. (Seal)
In Presence of ....
Ad[a]m SPENCE.   Jonathan PARSONS."

*followed with the acknowledgment of Justice of the Peace Adam SPENCE and recordation on folio 441 by court clerk Henry JOHNSON[180]

Liber H, folio 454; 17 November 1770

"Somerset County Ss. Know all Men by these Presents that I Zachariah MADDUX of the County af[ore]s[ai]d for and in Consideration of the Sum of Sixty six Pounds Current Money of Maryland to me in hand paid by Peter CALLAWAY of Worcester County hath granted bargained sold and delivered, and by these Presents doth grant bargain sell and deliver unto the af[ore]s[ai]d Peter CALLAWAY his Executors Administrators and Assigns a Negro Man named **Bobb**. To have and to hold the af[ore]s[ai]d Negro Man named **Bobb** unto the af[ore]s[ai]d Peter CALLAWAY his Executors Administrators and Assigns free and clear from any manner of Incumbrance whatsoever. And the said Zachariah MADDUX doth for himself his Heirs Executors and Administrators covenant and agree to and with the af[ore]s[ai]d Peter CALLAWAY his Executors Adm[inistrator]s and Assigns that he said Zachariah his Heirs Executors Adm[inistrator]s and Assigns the af[ore]s[ai]d Negro Man named **Bobb** from himself his Executors Adm[inistrator]s & Assigns and from all manner of Persons whatsoever unto the af[ore]s[ai]d Peter CALLAWAY his Executors Adm[inistrato]rs & Assigns will forever Warrant and Defend. In Witness whereof ye s[ai]d Zachariah af[ore]s[ai]d have to these Presents set his Hand & Seal this Seventeenth day of November Anno Dom[ini] 1770.
Signed Sealed & Delivered   Zachariah MADDUX   (Seal)
In Presence of ....
Jonathan PARSONS.   Daniel DIKES."

*followed with acknowledgment by Jon.h CATHELL and recordation on 01 December 1770 by court clerk Henry JOHNSON[181]

Liber H, folios 463-464; 14 December 1770

"Maryland Worcester County Ss. Know all Men by these presents that I Edward HAMMOND Sen[io]r of Worcester County in the Province of Maryland Planter for and in Consideration of the natural Love and Affection which I have and bear unto my Grand Children Charles HAMMOND John HAMMOND, Martha HAMMOND and Mary HAMMOND Children of Edward HAMMOND Jun[io]r have by these presents Given Granted Bargained Sold and

---

[180] Worcester County Court (Land Records). Bill of sale from CALLAWAY, Peter to READY, John. 09 November 1770. H, pp. 440-441, MSA CE 30-8. www.mdlandrec.net : accessed 08 November 2021.
[181] Worcester County Court (Land Records). Bill of sale from MADDUX, Zachariah to CALLAWAY, Peter. 17 November 1770. H, p. 454, MSA CE 30-8. www.mdlandrec.net : accessed 08 November 2021.

Delivered, and by these presents doth Give Grant Bargain Sell and Deliver unto them the said Charles HAMMOND, John HAMMOND, Martha HAMMOND and Mary HAMMOND their Heirs Executors Adm[inistrato]^{rs} and Assigns one Negroe Girl named **Hannah** and one Negroe Girl named **Sall**. To have and to hold the said Negroe Girl named **Hannah** and Negroe Girl named **Sall** unto them the said Charles HAMMOND John HAMMOND, Martha HAMMOND & Mary HAMMOND, to the only proper use and behoof of the said Charles HAMMOND, John HAMMOND, Martha HAMMOND and Mary HAMMOND, and to and for no other use intent construction or purpose whatever. In Witness whereof I the said Edward HAMMOND Sen[io]^r hath hereto sett my Hand and Seal this fourteenth day of December in the year of our Lord one thousand seven hundred & seventy. /.~./.~./.~./.~./.~

Sealed and Delivered   Geo[rge] HAYWARD   his
In Presence of ……   Jos[hu]^a MITCHELL   Edward   H   HAMMOND   (Seal)
                                                                                      mark"

*followed with acknowledgment by Justice of the Peace Jos[hu]^a MITCHELL and recordation on 17 December 1770 by court clerk Henry JOHNSON[182]

Liber H, folios 464-465; 14 December 1770

"This Indenture made this fourteenth day of December in the year of our Lord one thousand seven hundred and seventy. Between Edward HAMMOND of Worcester County in the Province of Maryland Planter of the one part, and Edward HAMMOND Jun[io]^r (son of the said Edward of the County and Province af[ore]s[ai]^d of the other part. Witnesseth that the said Edward HAMMOND for and in Consideration of the said Edward HAMMOND Jun[io]^r his Maintaining and Supporting the said Edward HAMMOND and Esther the Wife of the said Edward for and during the Term of their and Each of their natural Life, and also for and in Consideration of the Sum of five Shillings Current money of Maryland to the said Edward HAMMOND in hand paid at and before the Sealing and Delivery of these Presents the Receipt whereof the said Edward HAMMOND doth hereby Confess and Acknowledge Hath Given Granted Bargained and Sold, and by these Presents doth Give Grant Bargain and Sell unto the said Edward HAMMOND Jun[io]^r his Heirs Executors Administrators and Assigns the several Goods and Chattels hereafter mentioned, to wit, one Negroe Man Slave named **Harry**, one Negroe Woman named **Dorcas**, four Cows, two Stears, three Yearlings, two Feather Beds and Furniture, twelve Grown Hoggs, fifteen Shoats, seven Head of Sheep, three Iron Potts, nine Pewter Plates, three Pewter Dishes, one Round Maple Table, one Copper Still, Head and Worm, and one Corn Hand Mill. To have and to hold all and Every the said Negroes, Cows, Stears, Yearlings, Feather Beds and Furniture, Hoggs, Shoats, Sheep, Iron Potts, Pewter Plates, Pewter Dishes, Table, Still, Head, and Worm, and Corn Hand Mill above mentioned unto the said Edward HAMMOND Jun[io]^r his Heirs Executors Adm[inistrato]^{rs} and Assigns forever to the only proper use and behoof of the said Edward HAMMOND Jun[io]^r his Heirs Executors Adm[inistrato]^{rs} and Assigns, and to and for no other use intent or purpose whatsoever. In Testimony whereof the said Edward HAMMOND hath hereto set his Hand and Seal affixed the day and Year first above written. /.~./.~./.~

Sealed and Delivered   Geo[rge] HAYWARD   his
In Presence of ……   Jos[hu]^a MITCHELL   Edward   H   HAMMOND   (Seal)
                                                                                      mark"

*followed on folio 465 with acknowledgment by Justice of the Peace Jos[hu]^a MITCHELL and recordation on 17 December 1770 by court clerk Henry JOHNSON[183]

Liber H, folios 466-467; 26 December 1770

"This Deed of Gift made this Twentieth day of December in the Year of our Lord seventeen hundred and seventy. Between Jacob BOUNDS of Broad Creek in Worcester County of the

---

[182] Worcester County Court (Land Records). Deed of gift from HAMMOND, Edward Sr. to HAMMOND, Charles, John, Martha, and Mary. 14 December 1770. H, pp. 463-464, MSA CE 30-8. www.mdlandrec.net : accessed 08 November 2021.

[183] Worcester County Court (Land Records). Deed of gift from HAMMOND, Edward to HAMMOND, Edward Jr. 14 December 1770. H, pp. 464-465, MSA CE 30-8. www.mdlandrec.net : accessed 08 November 2021.

one part, and Jesse BOUNDS, Jacob BOUNDS jun[io]^r and Ann GIBBINS of the other part. Witnesseth that for and in Consideration of the Love and Affection that the said Jacob bares to his said three Children Jesse, Jacob, & his Daughter Anne wife of Joshua GIBBINS, hath hereby freely given unto them the several Negroes as followeth. ~ ~ First I give unto my Son Jesse BOUNDS two Negroes, one a Man named **Plymoth** of about twenty five Years of age, the other a Boy named **Joe** of about ten years of age to him & his Heirs. 2$^{[nd]ly}$ I give unto my Son Jacob BOUNDS jun[io]^r two Negroes one a Boy named **Charles** about Eight Years of age, also a Negro Girl named **Jane** about four Years of Age and her Increase. 3$^{[r]dly}$ I also give unto my Daughter Anne GIBBINS a Negro Woman named **Amey** about twenty Years of age with her Child about one Year old named **Hanah** with all their Increase from this Day forward, reserving only my Lifetime and my Wife in the Service of all the abovemention[e]d Negroes. In Witness whereof I have hereunto set my Hand and affixed my Seal the day and year above written. ~
Signed Sealed & Delivered
In Presence of …………… Jacob BOUNDS. (Seal)
Simon KOLLOCK.   Elisha LONG."

*followed with the acknowledgment by Justice of the Peace Cor. KOLLOCK and recordation on folio 467 by court clerk Henry JOHNSON on 28 December 1770[184]

Liber H, folios 494-495; 11 January 1771

"This Indenture made this Eleventh day of January Anno Dom[ini] one thousand seven hundred and seventy one. Between Sarah MILBOURN Widow of Solomon MILBOURN of the one part, and Jacob ADDAMS of the other part. Witnesseth that the said Sarah for and in consideration of the natural Love and Affection which She hath and doth bear towards her Children as also for the advancement as well of the Children she hath now born and any hereafter to be born, as also for the consideration of the sum of Five shillings Current money to her paid by the af[ore]s[ai]^d Jacob ADDAMS at and before the Sealing and delivery hereof the Receipt whereof She hereby doth acknowledge hath bargained sold and delivered, and by these presents doth bargain sell and deliver unto the af[ore]s[ai]^d Jacob ADDAMS his Heirs and Assigns forever the following Slaves one Negro Woman called **Pleasant** and her child **Leveanah Jenkins**, and one Boy called **Isaac** one ditto called **Peter**. To have and to hold, the af[ore]s[ai]^d bargained premisses with their future increase unto the af[ore]s[ai]^d Jacob ADDAMS his Heirs and Assigns forever to and for the several uses and trusts hereafter declared. that is to say, to and for the use of the said Sarah for and during her natural Life, and on her death immediately after the same, to be divided among the two Children the said Sarah now hath, in case She shall have no issue born hereafter but in case of issue hereafter to be born then to such issue of the said Sarah that may hereafter be born of the Body of the said Sarah, or among the Survivor of such as shall be alive at her death and the legal Representatives of such of them as shall be dead, at that time and for no other uses or purposes whatsoever. Provided Nevertheless that it is the true intent and meaning hereof that in case the said Sarah shall have no issue born hereafter or not any living at her death that the af[ore]s[ai]^d Estate shall pass unto the af[ore]s[ai]^d two Children now born, that in such Case the said Estate & future increase thereof to be divided in manner following, that is to Say, William her youngest Son to have two thirds thereof, and the other Child one third. In Witness whereof the said Sarah to these presents her hand hath set & Seal affixed the day and year first above written. /.~./.~./.~
Sealed & Deliver[e]d   Dixon QUINTON   Sarah MILBOURN. (Seal)
In Presence of ……..   Littleton DENNIS"

*followed on folio 495 with the acknowledgment of Justice of the Peace Dixon QUINTON and recordation on 29 January 1771 by court clerk Henry JOHNSON[185]

---

[184] Worcester County Court (Land Records). Deed of gift from BOUNDS, Jacob to BOUNDS, Jesse, BOUNDS, Jacob Jr., and GIBBINS, Anne. 26 December 1770. H, pp. 466-467, MSA CE 30-8. www.mdlandrec.net : accessed 08 November 2021.

[185] Worcester County Court (Land Records). Deed from MILBOURN, Sarah to ADDAMS, Jacob. 01 January 1771. H, pp. 494-495, MSA CE 30-8. www.mdlandrec.net : accessed 08 November 2021.

Liber H, folio 506; 23 February 1771

"To all People to whom these Presents shall come, I Charles TENNENT of Worcester County in the Province of Maryland send Greeting; Know ye, that I the said Charles TENNENT for & in Consideration of Natural Affection, and for divers other good Causes & Considerations me hereunto moving, Have given & granted, & by these Presents do give and grant unto my two Daughters Ann TENNENT & Martha TENNENT equally between them, their Heirs and Assigns my four Negroes, **Phillis, Jack, Santy & Pomp**, also all my Horses, Cows, & Stock of every kind, with all my Household furniture and all and singular my Goods, Chattels, Plate, Bonds, Debts, & Personal Estate whatsoever, in whose Hands, Custody, or Possession they maybe (Except one hundred pounds my said two Daughters must pay to my son William TENNENT, and ten Shillings to my Daughter Katrine BELL & to Discharge all my just Debts) To have, hold and Enjoy, all and singular the said Negros, Stocks, Household furniture, Goods & Chattels, Plate, Bonds, Debts, and Personall Estate) whatsoever aforesaid, unto my said two Daughters Ann & Martha TENNENT their Executors Administrators and Assigns, to the only proper use and behoof of them the said Ann & Martha TENNENT their Executors Administrators and Assigns forever. And I the said Charles TENNENT all and singular the aforesaid Negroes, Stock, Goods, Chattels and premises to the said Ann TENNENT & Martha TENNENT their Executors Administrators and Assigns against all Persons whatsoever shall and will Warrant and forever Defend by these Presents. In Witness whereof I the said Charles TENNENT to these Presents my Hand have sett & Seal affix[e]d this twenty third Day of February Anno Domini 1771

Sealed & Delivered   Charles TENNENT. (Seal)
In the Presence of ...
John POSTLY.   Nath[anie]¹ RAMSAY."

*followed with the acknowledgment of Justices of the Peace J. DENNIS, John POSTLY, and Nathaniel RAMSAY and recordation on 25 February 1771 by court clerk Henry JOHNSON[186]

Liber H, folio 515; 07 March 1771

"Know all men by these presents that I Adam HALL of Worcester County & Province of Maryland for and in Consideration of the Sum of fifty Pounds current Money of the Province of Maryland, have Agreed Bargain[e]d & Sold, & by these Present do Agree Bargain & Sell unto W[illia]ᵐ PURNELL his Heirs & Assigns a certain Negro man Slave named **Peter**. To have and to hold the above named Negro Man Slave named **Peter** unto him the said William PURNELL his Heirs and Assigns forever & the said Adam HALL doth agree to & with the said William PURNELL his Heirs & Assigns that he will Warrant & Defend the Property thereof unto the said William PURNELL his Heirs & Assigns forever As Witness my Hand & Seal this Seventh day of March Anno Dom[ini] MDCCLXXI.

In Presence of ......   Adam HALL. (Seal)
John Purnell ROBINS.   James STEVENSON."

*followed with acknowledgment by Justice of the Peace Adam SPENCE and recordation by court clerk Henry JOHNSON[187]

Liber H, folios 515-516; 21 February 1771

"Worcester County Ss.ᵗ Know all Men by these presents that we Nahor GODWIN of Dorchester County & Elijah WEST of Worcester County both of Maryland for & in Consideration of the Sum of thirty four pounds Money of Pensylvania to us in hand paid by John MITCHELL of Worcester County & province afores[ai]ᵈ the Receipt whereof we do hereby acknowledge have Granted Bargained Sold & Conveyed, and by these presents do Give Grant Bargain and Sell

---

[186] Worcester County Court (Land Records). Deed of gift from TENNENT, Charles to TENNENT, Ann & Martha. 23 February 1771. H, p. 506, MSA CE 30-8. www.mdlandrec.net : accessed 08 November 2021.
[187] Worcester County Court (Land Records). Bill of sale from HALL, Adam to PURNELL, William. 07 March 1771. H, p. 515, MSA CE 30-8. www.mdlandrec.net : accessed 08 November 2021.

unto the said John MITCHELL his Heirs and Assigns forever two third parts of a Negro Man called **Pomp** which was Willed to said Nahor GODWIN & Elijah WEST by their Father in Law Thomas WILLIAMS. To have & to hold the above mentioned two thirds of said Negro called **Pomp** unto the said John MITCHELL his Heirs and Assigns forever and to the proper use and behoof and to no other intent or purpose whatsoever. And the said Nahor GODWIN and Elijah WEST for themselves their Heirs Executors Adm[inistrato]rs doth Covenant promise and Grant to and with the said John MITCHELL his Heirs and Assigns that they the said Nahor GODWIN & Elijah WEST their Heirs Executors Administrators the Negro Man Slave af[ore]s[ai]d unto the said John MITCHELL his Heirs and Assigns we the said Nahor GODWIN & Elijah WEST our and Each of our Heirs and all manner of Person or Persons whatsoever shall and will Warrant and forever Defend. In Witness whereof I have hereunto these presents Set my hand & Seal this Twenty first Day of February Anno Dom[ini] 1771 ~

Signed Sealed & Delivered
In Presence of ~   Nahor GODWIN   (Seal)
Test   Hughit CANNON. ~
W[illia]m STATON. / . ~ . / . ~"

*followed on folio 516 with the recordation on 07 March 1771 by court clerk Henry JOHNSON[188]

Liber H, folios 534-535; 12 March 1771

"Maryland Ss. To all Christian People to whom these Presents shall come, I Betty HEARN of Worcester County and Province afores[ai]d Widow send Greeting. Know ye that I Betty HEARN for and in Consideration of the Love and good will which I bear unto my Daughters Viz.t Betty HEARN and Prissa HEARN have Given Granted fully freely clearly and absolutely, and by these Presents do fully clearly freely and absolutely Give and Grant unto my afores[ai]d two Daughters Betty HEARN and Prissa HEARN their Heirs and Assigns one Negroe Wench nam[e]d **Dina** aged about Twenty six Years of age with only the Reversion of her Service to me during my natural Life, without any other Claim and Demand and whatsoever of all the Right Title or Interest which I now have, or which either my Heirs Ex[ecuto]rs Adm[inistrato]rs or Assigns may have hereafter, of to or in the said Negro Wench call[e]d **Dina** before Granted as is above mention[e]d unto the afores[ai]d Betty HEARN and Prissa HEARN their Heirs and Assigns forever absolutely without any other Condition than what is above Expresst. To have and to hold the s[ai]d Negro Wench called **Dina** unto the aboves[ai]d Betty HEARN and Prissa HEARN which I Give them of my own accord. In further Testimony and In Witness whereof I have hereunto set my Hand and Seal this twelfth Day of March one thousand seven hundred and seventy one.

Sign[e]d Seal[e]d and Deliver[e]d   John WILLIAMS ~
In Presence of ....   Mary WILLIAMS   Betty X HEARN. (Seal)
                                                                                                                    mark"

*followed on folio 535 with the acknowledgment of Justice of the Peace Jon:h CATHELL and on 14 March 1771 and recordation by court clerk Henry JOHNSON on 29 March 1771[189]

*the acknowledgment mentioned the name of Betty HEARN's late husband John HEARN and her subsequent marriage to Elijah SMITH

Liber H, folios 546-547; 05 April 1771

"Know all Men by these presents that we Moses GUTTERY & Joshua EVANS both of Worcester County Province of Maryland, have agreed bargain[e]d & sold two Negroes Viz.t a Negro Woman called **March** & her Child called **Stephen**, unto John SPENCE of the same place for and in Consideration of the Sum of Fifty five Pounds current Money of Maryland. To

---

[188] Worcester County Court (Land Records). Bill of sale from GODWIN, Nahor and WEST, Elijah to MITCHELL, John. 21 February 1771. H, pp. 515-516, MSA CE 30-8. www.mdlandrec.net : accessed 08 November 2021.
[189] Worcester County Court (Land Records). Deed of gift from HEARN, Betty to HEARN, Betty and Prissa. 12 March 1771. H, pp. 534-535, MSA CE 30-8. www.mdlandrec.net : accessed 08 November 2021.

have & to hold the af[ore]s[ai]^d Negro Woman **March** & her Child **Stephen** unto the af[ore]s[ai]^d John SPENCE his Heirs or Assigns forever. & the abovesaid Moses GUTTERY & Joshua EVANS doth oblige themselves & Each of their Heirs to Warrant & defend the property of the above mentioned Negroes unto him the af[ore]s[ai]^d John SPENCE his Heirs & Assigns forever, clear from any Claims or Expence whatever As Witness our hand & Seals this fifth day of April Anno Dom[ini] MDCCLXXI . / . ~ . / . ~ . / . ~

Sign[e]d Seal[e]d & Delivered   Moses GOTHERY. ~ (Seal)
In Presence of ~   Joshua EVANS (Seal)
John SELBY. ~   Geo[rge] SPENCE. ~"

*followed on folio 547 with the acknowledgment by John SELBY and recordation by court clerk Henry JOHNSON[190]

Liber H, folios 584-585; 02 August 1771

"To all People to whom these Presents shall come I Martha GLASGOW of Worcester County Widow send Greeting. Know ye that I the said Martha GLASGOW for and in Consideration of the natural Love and Affection which I have and do bear unto my beloved Daughter Betty GLASGOW of the County of Worcester and Province of Maryland and also for divers other Causes and Considerations me hereunto moving have Given and Granted and by these presents do Give Grant and Confirm unto the said Betty GLASGOW one Negro wench named **Deborah** and her Son **Job**, one Feather Bed and Furniture, one large Chest of Drawers, one large Walnut Table, four Walnut Chairs, one Arm Chair, one Bay Mare, a small Linnen Wheel, one Loom, two Table Cloaths, and one Riding Chaise, and also one fourth part of the Crop of Corn and Tobacco now Growing on the Plantation. To have and to hold the said Negro wench named **Deborah** and her Son **Job**, Feather Bed and Furniture, Chest of Drawers, Walnut Table, Walnut Chairs, Arm Chair, Bay Mare, Wheel, Loom, Table Cloaths, and Riding Chaise, unto the said Betty GLASGOW her Executors Administrators and Assigns to her and their own proper use and uses forever. And I the said Martha GLASGOW all and singular the af[ore]s[ai]^d Goods Chattels and Premisses to the said Betty GLASGOW her Executors Adm[inistrato]^{rs} and Assigns against all Persons do Warrant and forever Defend by these presents. In Witness whereof I the said Martha GLASGOW have hereto Sett my Hand and Seal affixed this Second Day of August in the year of our Lord one thousand seven hundred and seventy one. ~ ~

Sealed and Delivered   Benton HARRIS   her
In Presence off   A^d[a]m Spence   Martha m GLASGOW (Seal)
                                                          mark. ~"

*followed on folio 585 with the acknowledgment by Justice of the Peace Benton HARRIS and recordation by court clerk Henry JOHNSON[191]

Liber H, folios 585-586; 02 August 1771

"To all People to whom these Presents shall come I Martha GLASGOW of Worcester County in the Province of Maryland Widow send Greeting. Know ye that I the said Martha GLASGOW for and in Consideration of the natural Love and Affection which I have and do bear unto James WILSON of Somerset County and my Daughter Martha WILSON wife of the said James, and also for and in Consideration of the sum of five Shillings Current money of Maryland to me in hand paid by the said James WILSON and Martha his Wife, have Given Granted and Confirmed, and by these Presents do Give Grant and Confirm unto the said James WILSON and Martha his Wife one Negro Man named **Jesse**, one Negro Girl named **Abigail**, one Negro Boy named **Hope**, one China Dish, five China Plates, one large blue China Bowl, one pair of Silver Tea Tongs, one pair of Sheets and one large Table Cloath, and also the several Articles which I have before Given the said James WILSON and Martha his Wife to wit one bay Mare, one Walnut Desk one large Walnut Table, one Tea Table, one Bed and furniture, two Table

---

[190] Worcester County Court (Land Records). Bill of sale from GOTHERY, Moses and EVANS, Joshua to SPENCE, John. 05 April 1771. H, pp. 546-547, MSA CE 30-8. www.mdlandrec.net : accessed 08 November 2021.
[191] Worcester County Court (Land Records). Deed of gift from GLASGOW, Martha to GLASGOW, Betty. 02 August 1771. H, pp. 584-585, MSA CE 30-8. www.mdlandrec.net : accessed 08 November 2021.

Cloaths, one Tea Board, one pair of Stampt Cotton Curtains, and one large Cotton Counterpain. To have and to hold the said Negro Man named **Jesse**, Negro Girl named **Abigail**, Negro Boy named **Hope**, China Dish, China plates, China Bowl, Silver Tea Tongs, Sheets, Table Cloath, bay Mare, Walnut Desk, Walnut Table, Tea Table, Bed and Furniture, Table Cloaths, Tea Board, Cotton Curtains and Cotton Counterpain unto the said James WILSON and Martha his Wife their Executors Adm[inistrato]^{rs} and Assigns to them and their own proper uses and uses forever. And I the said Martha GLASGOW all and singular the Goods Chattels and Other Premisses to the said James WILSON and Martha his Wife their Executors Adm[inistrato]^{rs} and Assigns all Persons do Warrant and forever Defend by these Presents. In Witness whereof I the said Martha GLASGOW have hereto sett my hand and seal affixed this Second Day of August in the Year of our Lord one thousand seven hundred and seventy one. ~ ~ ~

Sealed and Delivered   Benton HARRIS   her
In Presence …..   A^d[a]m SPENCE ~   Martha m GLASGOW (Seal)
                                                                             mark"

*followed on folio 586 with the acknowledgment by Justice of the Peace Benton HARRIS and recordation by court clerk Henry JOHNSON[192]

Liber H, folios 586-587; 02 August 1771

"To all People to whom these presents shall come I Martha GLASGOW of Worcester County and Province of Maryland Widow send Greeting. Know ye that I the said Martha GLASGOW for and in Consideration of the natural Love and Affection which I have and do bear unto my Daughter Nancy GLASGOW and also for divers other Causes and Considerations me hereunto moveing, Have Given and Granted, and by these presents do Give Grant and Confirm unto the said Nancy GLASGOW one Negroe Man named **Stephen**, one Negroe Girl named **Fender**, one Negroe Boy **Frank**, one young Bay Mare and Colt, one Feather Bed and Furniture and Green Curtains one Tea Table one Pine Table, four Walnut Chairs, one small Blue and white China Bowl, half a dozen Pewter plates, and large Pewter Dish, two Table Cloaths, one small Looking Glass, and one Mohogony Stand, and also one fourth part of the Crop of Corn and Tobacco now growing on the Plantation. To have and to hold the said Negro Mand named **Stephen**, Negro Girl named **Fender**, Negro Boy named **Frank**, Mare and Colt, Feather Bed and Furniture, Green Curtains, Tea Table, Pine Table, Walnut Chairs, Cheney Bowl, Pewter Plates, Pewter Dish, Table Cloaths, Looking Glass & Mohogany Stand unto the said Nancy GLASGOW her Executors Adm[inistrato]^{rs} and Assigns to her and their own proper use and uses forever. And I the said Martha GLASGOW all and singular the Goods Chattels and Premisses to the said Nancy GLASGOW her Executors Adm[inistrato]^{rs} and Assigns against all Persons do Warrant and forever Defend by these Presents In Witness whereof I the said Martha GLASGOW have hereto sett my hand and Seal affixed this Second day of August in the year of our Lord one thousand seven hundred and seventy one. ~

Sealed and Delivered   Benton HARRIS   her
In Presence off …   A^d[a]m SPENCE   Martha m GLASGOW (Seal)
                                                                            mark"

*followed with acknowledgment by Justice of the Peace Benton HARRIS and recordation by court clerk Henry JOHNSON[193]

Liber H, folios 587-588; 03 August 1771

"This Indenture made this third Day of August in the year of our Lord one thousand seven hundred and seventy one. Between Martha GLASGOW of Worcester County in the Province of Maryland Widow of the one part, and Patrick GLASGOW Son of the said Martha GLASGOW of the County and Province af[ore]s[ai]^d of the other part. Witnesseth that the said Martha GLASGOW as well for and in Consideration of the natural Love and Affection which She hath and beareth unto the said Patrick GLASGOW, as also for and in Consideration of the

---

[192] Worcester County Court (Land Records). Deed of gift from GLASGOW, Martha to WILSON, James and Martha. 02 August 1771. H, pp. 585-586, MSA CE 30-8. www.mdlandrec.net : accessed 08 November 2021.
[193] Worcester County Court (Land Records). Deed of gift from GLASGOW, Martha to GLASGOW, Nancy. 02 August 1771. H, pp. 586-587, MSA CE 30-8. www.mdlandrec.net : accessed 08 November 2021.

sum of five Shillings Current money of Maryland to her in hand paid by the said Patrick GLASGOW, she the said Martha GLASGOW hath Given Granted Bargained Sold Aliened Released Conveyed and Confirmed, and by these presents doth Give Grant Bargain Sell Alien Release Convey and Confirm unto the said Patrick GLASGOW his Heirs and Assigns forever all those two Tracts or parcells of Land called Martha's Purchase the one containing one hundred Acres, and the other fifty Acres of Land more or less, which said two Tracts of Land is scituate lying and being in Worcester County af[ore]s[ai]d and is Bounded Limited and Discribed as in and by the original Grants thereof Recourse thereto being had may appear, also one Negro Boy named **Major**, one Negroe Man named **Lowhill** & all and singular her Cattle, Sheep, Hoggs, Plows Harrows, Hoes, Axes, and all other farming Utensils, one Hand mill, two Beds and furniture, all the Kitchen Furniture one large Walnut Table new, one Walnut Desk, one Sorrell Horse Colt, one Table Cloath, half a dozen Leather Chairs & one Bay Horse, and also two fourth parts of the Crop of Corn and Tobacco now Growing on the Plantation, and also all Trees Woods and Underwoods Proffitts Commodities Advantage Emoluments and Hereditaments whatsoever to the said Tracts of Land above mentioned belonging or any wise appertaining, or in or upon the same Tracts of Land Growing happening or arising, and also the Reversion and Reversions, Remainder and Remainders, of the said Lands and Premisses and of every part thereof, and allso all the Estate Right Title Interest claim and Demand whatsoever of her the said Martha GLASGOW of in and to the said two Tracts of Land and Premisses and every part thereof. To have and to hold the said two Tracts of Land and Premisses above mentioned with the Appurtenances unto the said Patrick GLASGOW his Heirs and Assigns forever to the only proper use and behoof of the said Patrick GLASGOW his Heirs and Assigns forever, and also all and singular the Goods Chattels and other Premisses abovementioned to the said Patrick GLASGOW his Heirs Executors Adm[inistrato]rs and Assigns to his and their own proper use and uses forever. And the said Martha GLASGOW for her and her Heirs the said two Tracts of Land and Goods Chattels and Premisses above mentioned, and every part thereof against her and her Heirs and against all and every other Person and Persons whatsoever to the said Patrick GLASGOW his Heirs and Assigns shall and will Warrant and forever Defend by these presents. In Witness whereof the said Martha GLASGOW hath hereto set her hand and Seal affixed the day & year first above written. ~

Sealed and Delivered   Benton HARRIS
In Presence off ~   A d[a]m SPENCE   Martha m GLASGOW (Seal)
                                                                                her   mark"

*followed on folio 588 with the acknowledgment by Justices of the Peace Benton HARRIS and A d[a]m SPENCE and recordation by court clerk Henry JOHNSON[194]

Liber H, folio 597; 08 August 1771

"Know all Men by these presents that I Jemima HENDERSON of Worcester County for the Consideration of the natural Love and Affection which I have and do bear unto my Brother in law John MERRILL, as also for the further Consideration of the sum of five Shillings to me paid by him at and before the Sealing and delivery hereof the receipt whereof I hereby do acknowledge, have given bargained and sold, and by these presents doth give bargain & sell unto the af[ore]s[ai]d John MERRILL his Heirs and Assigns forever two Negroe Boys to wit one named **Peter** & the other called **Harry**. To have and to hold the af[ore]s[ai]d two Negro Boys one named **Peter** and the other called **Harry** unto the af[ore]s[ai]d John MERRILL his Heirs and Assigns forever and for no other use or purpose whatsoever, And the said Jemima for herself her Heirs Executors and Adm[inistrato]rs doth Covenant and Agree to and with the said John MERRILL his Heirs and Assigns forever that She will Warrant and for defend the af[ore]s[ai]d Negroes unto the said John MERRILL his Heirs and Assigns forever against the Claim Right Title of her the said Jemima and her Heirs forever and all other Persons that shall or may Claim by from or under her or any of them. In Witness whereof the said Jemima to these presents her hand hath set and Seals affixed this 8th day of August Anno Domini 1771. / . ~ . / .

---

[194] Worcester County Court (Land Records). Deed of gift from GLASGOW, Martha to GLASGOW, Patrick. 03 August 1771. H, pp. 587-588, MSA CE 30-8. www.mdlandrec.net : accessed 08 November 2021.

		her	
Sealed and Delivered			
In Presence of ~ J DENNIS		Jemi[m]ᵃ + HENDERSON (Seal)	
		mark"	

*followed with the acknowledgment of Justice of the Peace J. DENNIS and recordation by court clerk Henry JOHNSON[195]

Liber H, folio 600; 03 August 1771

"Know all Men by these presents that I Thomas CANNON of Worcester County for and in Consideration of the sum of fifty seven Pounds lawfull Money of Maryland to me in hand paid by James NEVAN the Receipt whereof I do hereby acknowledge have bargained & Sold, by these presents do bargain & sell unto the said James NEVAN one Negro Girl called **Esther**. To have & to hold the said bargained Premisses unto the said James NEVAN his Executors Administrators and Assigns forever. And I the said Thomas CANNON for myself my Executors & Administrators shall & will Warrant and forever Defend against all Persons by these presents the said Bargained Premisses unto the said James NEVAN his Executors Administrators and Assigns. In Witness whereof I have hereunto set my hand & Seal this third Day of August one thousand Seven hundred & Seventy one

In Presence of
James HOUSTON.
J[o]shua CATHELL.
                              his
                        Thomas C CANNON. ~ (Seal)
                              Mark"

*followed with the acknowledgment by Justice of the Peace Jon.ⁿ CATHELL and recordation on 16 August 1771 by court clerk Henry JOHNSON[196]

Liber H, folio 611; 27 September 1771

"Maryland Worcester County Ss.ᵗ Know all men by these Presents that I Charles RICHARDSON Sen[io]ʳ of the Place af[ore]s[ai]ᵈ for and in Consideration of the sum of one hundred and twenty Pounds current Money of Maryland to me in hand Paid by Shadrack RICHARDSON of the same Place before the Insealling and Delivery hereof the Receipt whereof I doe hereby Acknowledge and myself fully satisfied, hath Granted Bargained and Sold, and by these Presents Doth Bargain and Sell unto the af[ore]s[ai]ᵈ Shadrack RICHARDSON and his Heirs and Assigns forever two Negro Slaves the one called **Nanne**, the other **Preseler**, together with six Cows, four Heifers, five small yearlings, one Yoak of Oxen, one Sorrel Horse, one black Mare and ten head of Sheep. To have and to possess the af[ore]s[ai]ᵈ Negroes the one called **Nanne**, the other called **Preseler**, together with six Cows, four Heifers, five small Yearlings, one Yoak of Oxen, one Sorrel Horse, one black Mare and ten Head of Sheep, to the only proper use of the s[ai]ᵈ Shadrack RICHARDSON his Heirs and Assigns forever. And the said Charles RICHARDSON doth Covenant to and with the af[ore]sai]ᵈ Shadrack RICHARDSON that at the time of bargain and Sale hereof he had full Power and Authority to Sell the af[ore]s[ai]ᵈ Negroes the one called **Nanne**, the other called **Preseler** together with six Cows, four Heifers, five small Yearlings, one Yoak of Oxen, one Sorrel Horse, one black Maire, and ten head of Sheep, And the af[ore]s[ai]ᵈ Charles RICHARDSON will forever Warrant and Defend the af[ore]s[ai]ᵈ Negroes, the one called **Nanne** the other called **Preseler**, as allso six Cows, four Heifers, five small yearlings, one Yoak of Oxen, one Sorrel Horse, One black Maire and ten head of Sheep unto the af[ore]s[ai]ᵈ Shadrack RICHARDSON his Heirs and Assigns against the Rights Claims and Demands of all and every Person whatsoever Claiming by with or under me. In Witness whereof I have hereunto Set my Hand and fixt my Seal this twenty seventh Day of September one thousand seven hundred and seventy one.

---

[195] Worcester County Court (Land Records). Bill of sale from HENDERSON, Jemima to MERRILL, John. 08 August 1771. H, p. 597, MSA CE 30-8. www.mdlandrec.net : accessed 08 November 2021.

[196] Worcester County Court (Land Records). Bill of sale from CANNON, Thomas to NEVAN, James. 03 August 1771. H, p. 600, MSA CE 30-8. www.mdlandrec.net : accessed 08 November 2021.

Signed Sealed and Delivered	John SPENCE		
In Presence of us ……	Sarah SPENCE	Charles C RICHARDSON (Seal)	
		his mark"	

*followed with the acknowledgment by Justice of the Peace Adam SPENCE and recordation by court clerk Henry JOHNSON[197]

Liber H, folio 623; 15 November 1771

"Know all Men by these Presents that I Macclama JONES of Worcester County and the Province of Maryland for and in Consideration of the sum of thirty pounds Current money of Maryland to me in hand paid at and before the Sealing and Delivery of these presents by Barkley TOWNSEND of the same place, the Receipt whereof I do hereby acknowledge, have Bargained and Sold, and by these presents do Bargain and Sell unto the said Barkley TOWNSEND one Negro Boy called **Jo**. To have and to hold the said Negro **Jo** by these Presents bargained and sold unto the said Barkley TOWNSEND his Executors Administrators and Assigns forever. And I the said Macclama JONES for myself my Executors and Administrators the said Negro **Jo** unto the said Barkley TOWNSEND his Executors Administrators and Assigns against me the said Macclama JONES my Executors Administrators and Assigns, and against all and every other Person and Persons whatsoever shall and will Warrant and forever Defend by these presents of which said Negro **Jo** I the said Macclama JONES have put the said Barkley TOWNSEND in full possession by Delivering him the said Negro Boy **Jo**. In Witness my hand and Seal this fifteenth Day of November 1771. / . ~

Signed Sealed & Delivered   A^d[a]m SPENCE   Macclemmy JONES. (Seal)
In the presence of ~   Charles BENNETT"

*followed with the acknowledgment of Justice of the Peace Adam SPENCE and recordation by court clerk Henry JOHNSON[198]

Liber H, folio 632; 02 February 1764

"1764   William ROBENSON Head of ye Sound   D[ebi]t & Contrac …..   C^r[edit]
Feb[ruar]ly ye 2[n]d To Negro Garl Name **Cobbo** @ £60   £60..0..0   Feb[ruar]ly By Cash   £30..0..0
              To Interest from Feb[ruar]ly ye 2[n]d 1764
              for the Negro   1..6..0   By Horse   10..0..0
                                                                                        £40..0..0
                                                                          Ballance due 21..6..0
                                                    £61..6..0   £61..6..0

                              Errors Excepted   Cornelius ROBINSON. ~
March 4th 1765   Came Cornelius ROBINSON & proved the above   Acc[oun]t in common
from agreeable to Law   Before me Jn.° DAGWORTHY
October 1765 the Contents of the within Acc[oun]t Rec[eive]d in full
Test. W[illia]m HOLLAND.   By Cornelius ROBINSON."

*followed with the recordation by court clerk Henry JOHNSON on 10 December 1771[199]

Liber H, folios 645-646; 11 December 1771

"Know all Men by these Presents that I John SCARBOROUGH Jun[ior] of Worcester County in the Province of Maryland for and in Consideration of the sum of Twenty five Pounds current Money of Maryland to me in hand paid at and before the Sealing and Delivery of these Presents by Macclammy JONES of the same County and Province aforesaid, the Receipt whereof I do

---

[197] Worcester County Court (Land Records). Bill of sale from RICHARDSON, Charles Sr. to RICHARDSON, Shadrack. 27 September 1771. H, p. 611, MSA CE 30-8. www.mdlandrec.net : accessed 08 November 2021.
[198] Worcester County Court (Land Records). Bill of sale from JONES, Macclemmy to TOWNSEND, Barkley. 15 November 1771. H, p. 623, MSA CE 30-8. www.mdlandrec.net : accessed 08 November 2021.
[199] Worcester County Court (Land Records). Account of ROBENSON, William. 02 February 1764. H, p. 632, MSA CE 30-8. www.mdlandrec.net : accessed 08 November 2021.

hereby acknowledge, have Bargained and Sold, and by these Presents do Bargain and Sell unto the said Macclammy JONES one Negro Boy called **Jo**. To have and to hold the said Negro Boy **Jo** by these presents Bargained and Sold unto the said Macclammy JONES his Heirs and Assigns forever. And I the said John SCARBOROUGH for myself my Heirs Executors and Adm[inistrato]^rs the said Negro Boy **Jo** unto the said Macclammy JONES his Heirs and Assigns forever against me the said John SCARBOROUGH my Heirs Executors Administrators and Assigns, and against all and every other Person and Persons whatsoever, shall and will Warrant and forever Defend by these Presents, of which said Negro **Jo** I the said John SCARBOROUGH have put the said Macclammy JONES in full possession by delivering the said Negro Boy. In Testimony whereof the said John SCARBOROUGH hath set his Hand and Seal this 11th Day of December Anno Domini one thousand seven hundred and seventy one. ~
Signed Sealed and Delivered
In the presence of ~   Jno SCARBOROUGH Jun[ior]   (Seal)
John SELBY. ~   Sam[ue]^l SCARBOROUGH. ~"

*followed on folio 646 with the acknowledgment by Justice of the Peace John SELBY and recordation on 14 December 1771 by court clerk Henry JOHNSON[200]

Liber H, folio 652; 28 December 1771

"Know all Men by these Presents that I John MORGAN of Worcester County in the Province of Maryland hath Bargin and Sold unto Peleg WALTER of the same place for & in Consideration of the sum of seventy two pounds ten Shillings Current Money of the province of Maryland to me in hand paid by the said Peleg WALTER where I do hereby acknowledge the Receipt and myself therewith fully satisfied have Bargined Sold and Delivered unto the said Peleg WALTER a Negro Man named **Cupet** To have and to hold the said Negro **Cupet** unto the said Peleg WALTER Executors Administrators and Assigns forever. And I the said John MORGAN for myself Executors and Administrators against all Persons shall Warrant and forever Defend by these presents. In Witness whereof I have hereunto set my hand and Seal this twenty eight Day of December in the year of our Lord one thousand seven hundred and seventy one.
Sealed and Delivered   Jn.º MORGAN.   (Seal)
In the presence of   Joshua HILL."

*followed with acknowledgment by Justice of the Peace Joshua HILL and recordation on 30 December 1771 by court clerk Henry JOHNSON[201]

Liber I, folios 7 - 8; 22 January 1772

"Worcester Ss.^t Know all men by these presents that I Tommison SMITH for and in consideration of the love and Affection that I bare unto Anna Gray SMITH my Daughter and my son Benjamin Dingley SMITH my Son have by these presents given and granted unto them my Daughter and & Son the several Mater and things herein Contained and Specified that is to Say, I first give and grant unto my daughter Anna one Negro Girl named **Siner** Reserving my lifetime in her and the increase from this time to be equalley devided between my said Daughter and my Son Benjamain of the said Negro I further give and grant unto my Son Benjamin Dingley SMITH a Negro boy named **Jesse** to him & his Assigns, reserving my life in the said Negro, and in case of both my childrens dearths before the arive at the Age appointed by Law to dispose of their Estates then the such part as is hereby given & I do hereby give to my four Sisters Jediah KING Anna GRAY Sarah ROACH & Mary GRAY & their heirs & Assigns. In Witness whereof I have hereunto set my hand & affixed my Seal this 22 Jan[uar]y 1772.

---

[200] Worcester County Court (Land Records). Bill of sale from SCARBOROUGH, John Jr. to JONES, Macclammy. 11 December 1771. H, pp. 645-645, MSA CE 30-8. www.mdlandrec.net : accessed 08 November 2021.
[201] Worcester County Court (Land Records). Bill of sale from MORGAN, John to WALTER, Peleg. 28 December 1771. H, p. 652, MSA CE 30-8. www.mdlandrec.net : accessed 08 November 2021.

Sealed & Deliv[ere]^d
In Presence of ~   Thompson SMITH.   (Seal)
Thomas GRAY Junior.   Robert DENNIS."

*followed on folio 8 with the acknowledgment by John DENNIS and recordation on 25 January 1772 by court clerk Henry JOHNSON[202]

Liber I, folio 17; 18 February 1772

"This Indenture made this Eighteenth day of February in the year of our Lord one thousand seven hundred and seventy two. Between George MARTIN of Worcester County in the Province of Maryland of the one part, and William JEATER jun[io]^r of the Colony of Virginia of the other part. Witnesseth that the said George MARTIN in consideration of the sum of Eighty pounds Current money of Virginia to him in hand paid by the said William JEATER the Receipt whereof he doth hereby acknowledge, hath bargained and sold, and by these presents doth bargain and sell unto the said William JEATER one Negro Man named **Frank**. To have and to hold the said Negro Man named **Frank** to him the said William JEATER his Heirs and Assigns to and for the only proper use and behoof of him the said William JEATER and his Heirs and Assigns and for no other use or purpose whatsoever against the claim right and title of him the said George MARTIN and his Heirs or any person claiming from by or under him them or any of them. In Testimony whereof the said George MARTIN to these presents his hand hath set and seal affixed the day and year above written.

Sealed and Delivered   Benton HARRIS   George MARTIN.   (Seal)
In Presence of ~   John DONE"

*followed with the acknowledgment by the Justice of the Peace Benton HARRIS and recordation on 19 February 1772 by court clerk Henry JOHNSON[203]

Liber I, folios 18-19; 18 February 1772

"This Indenture made this Eighteenth day of February in the year of our Lord one thousand seven hundred and seventy two. Between Elizabeth HANDY of Worcester County in the Province of Maryland of the one part, and John PARRET of Amelia County in the Colony of Virginia of the other part Witnesseth that the said Elizabeth HANDY in consideration of the sum of seventy pounds Current money of Virginia to her in hand paid by the said PARRET the receipt whereof she doth hereby acknowledge hath bargained and sold, and by these presents doth bargain and sell unto the said John PARRET one Negro Girl named **Rhoda**. To have and to hold the said Negro Girl named **Rhoda** to him the said John PARRET his Heirs and Assigns to and for the only proper use and behoof of him the said John PARRET his Heirs and Assigns and for no other use or purpose whatsoever against the Claim Right and title of her the said Elizabeth HANDY and her Heirs or any person or persons claiming from by or under her them or any of them. In Testimony whereof the said Elizabeth HANDY to these presents her hand hath set and seal affixed the day and year above written.

Sealed & Delivered   Benton HARRIS   Elizabeth HANDY   (Seal)
In Presence of ~   John DONE."

*followed with the acknowledgment by Justice of the Peace Benton HARRIS on 18 February 1772 and recordation on folio 19 by court clerk Henry JOHNSON on 19 February 1772[204]

---

[202] Worcester County Court (Land Records). Deed of gift from SMITH, Thompson to SMITH, Anna Gray and SMITH, Benjamin Dingley. 22 January 1772. I, pp. 7-8, MSA CE 30-9. www.mdlandrec.net : accessed 21 November 2021.

[203] Worcester County Court (Land Records). Bill of sale from MARTIN, George to JEATER, William Jr. 18 February 1772. I, p. 17, MSA CE 30-9. www.mdlandrec.net : accessed 21 November 2021.

[204] Worcester County Court (Land Records). Bill of sale from HANDY, Elizabeth to PARRET, John. 18 February 1772. I, pp. 18-19, MSA CE 30-9. www.mdlandrec.net : accessed 21 November 2021.

Liber I, folios 37-38; 04 March 1772

"Worcester Ss.^{t} Know all Men by these presents that I Nehemiah TILGHMAN of the County af[oresai]^d for and in Consideration of the Sum of thirty seven pounds Current money of Maryland to me in hand paid by Peter CALLAWAY of the County af[oresai]^d and before the Sealing and Delivery hereof the Receipt whereof I the said Nehemiah TILGHMAN do by these presents Acknowledge, I have bargained and Sold and by these presents do bargain and sell unto the af[oresai]^d Peter CALLAWAY, his Heirs and Assigns one Negro Girl called **Iby** unto the said Peter CALLAWAY his Heirs and Assigns forever. To have and to hold the af[oresai]^d Bargained and sold Negro Girl called **Iby** unto the af[oresai]d Peter CALLAWAY his Heirs and Assigns forever and to and for no other use or purpose whatsoever. And the said Nehemiah TILGHMAN for himself his Heirs Ex[ecutor]^s and Adm[inistrator]^s doth by these presents Covenant grant and agree to and with the af[oresai]^d Peter CALLAWAY his Heirs and Assigns forever that he the said Nehemiah TILGHMAN his Heirs Ex[ecutor]^s and Adm[inistrator]^s will warrant and forever Defend the af[oresai]^d Negro Girl called **Iby** unto the af[oresai]d Peter CALLAWAY his Heirs and Assigns forever against the Claim Right and title of all and every person Claiming or that shall hereafter claim the same Negro Girl af[oresai]^d. In Testimony whereof the said Nehemiah TILGHMAN to these presents his hand hath set and Seal affixed this 4th day of March Anno Dom[ini] 1772. ~

Sealed & Deliver[e]d	Parker SELBY	Nehemiah TILGHMAN.	(Seal)
In Presence of ~	James WILLIAMS."		

*followed on folio 38 with the recordation by court clerk Henry JOHNSON on 05 March 1772[205]

Liber I, folios 38-39; 05 March 1772

"Know all Men by these presents that we Samuel CAMPBELL & David FASSITT both of Worcester County and Province of Maryland for and in Consideration of the Sum of Fifty Pounds in hand paid and a Bond payable the Tenth of June next for fifty seven Pounds ten Shillings by Benjamin WOOTTEN of the Province af[ore]s[ai]^d have agreed bargained & sold two Negroes, the one a Boy named **Jacob** about Twelve years Old, the other a Negro Girl about nine Years of Age called **Hannah**. To have and to hold the above named Negroes called **Jacob & Hannah** unto him the said Benjamin WOOTTEN his Heirs and Assigns forever, Clear from any Claim or Demand whatsoever, & the above mentioned Samuel CAMPBELL & David FASSITT doth Covenant and Agree that they and each of them their Heirs and Executors shall from time to time and at all times forever hereafter Warrant and Defend the Title Property and Benefit of the above mentioned Negroes unto him the said Benjamin WOOTTEN his Heirs & Assigns forever As Witness our Hands and Seals this fifth day of March Anno Dom[ini] one thousand seven hundred and seventy two.~

Sign[e]d Seal[e]d & Delivered		Samuel CAMPBELL.	(Seal)
In Presence of ~		David FASSITT.	(Seal)
Tho[mas] PURNELL.	John Purnell ROBINS."		

*followed by acknowledgment by Justice of the Peace Adam SPENCE and recordation by court clerk Henry JOHNSON on folio 39[206]

Liber I, folios 90-91; 18 July 1770

"Maryland Ss^t. Know all Men by the Presents that I Mary WATTS Widdow of Charles WATTS Deceased of Worcester County in the Province af[ore]s[ai]^d am held and firmly bound unto

---

[205] Worcester County Court (Land Records). Bill of sale from TILGHMAN, Nehemiah to CALLAWAY, Peter. 04 March 1772. I, pp. 37-38, MSA CE 30-9. www.mdlandrec.net : accessed 21 November 2021.

[206] Worcester County Court (Land Records). Bill of sale from CAMPBELL, Samuel and FASSITT, David to WOOTTEN, Benjamin. 05 March 1772. I, pp. 38-39, MSA CE 30-9. www.mdlandrec.net : accessed 21 November 2021.

Charles WATTS son and Heir of the af[ore]s[ai]^d Charles WATTS Dec[eas]^ed and Rebeckah DICKENSON Daughter of the af[ore]s[ai]^d Mary WATTS in the full and Just Sum of Five Hundred Pounds Sterling Money of Great Brittain to the which payment well and truly to be made and done unto the af[ore]s[ai]^d Charles WATTS and Rebeckah DICKENSON to them there Heirs Execu[tor]^s Administrat[or]^s and any person or persons Claiming from and under me firmly by these Presents sealed with my Seal and Datted this 18th Day of July Anno Dommy 1770./.~

The Condition of the above Obligation is such that if the above bound Mary WATTS her Heirs Execu[tor]^s Administrat[or]^s or any Person or Persons whatsoever Claiming from or under her shall on the Day of her Marrage with any Person or Persons whatsoever Relinquish Renounce and Quit Clame during her Coverture all her Clame or Right of Dower She hath in and unto the Lands and Tennements of her Late Husband Charles WATTS Deceased unto his Son and Heir Charles WATTS as af[ore]s[ai]^d to him, his Assigns or Guardians forever as heir at Law of the af[ore]s[ai]^d Charles WATTS Deceased Be it likewise Remembered that I the af[ore]s[ai]^d Mary WATTS doe hereby make over Confirm and freely Give unto Charles WATTS and Rebeckah DICKENSON af[ore]s[ai]^d my Negro Wench **Judah** and Child called **Mellah** together until there Increas to them and there heirs forever and if in Case my Son Charles WATTS as af[ore]s[ai]^d Die without Ishue then the said Negros together with there increase I Give to my Daughter Rebeckah DICKENSON af[ore]s[ai]^d and to her heirs and Assigns forever Reserveing for my own Use Dureing my owne Natural life the said Negros **Judah & Mellea** and to no other use or uses whatsoever. I Doe also Give and bequeath unto Charles WATTS and Rebeckah DICKENSON af[ore]s[ai]^d thirty head of Cattle twenty head of Sheap five head of Horse Hind and twenty head of hogs to them and there Assignns or Guardians forever and if in Case my Son Charles Die without Isshue the whole to goe to my Daughter Rebeckah and to her heirs forever onely Reserveing the use of said Stock Dureing my Natural live as af[ore]s[ai]^d and for no other use or uses whatsoever I Doe also Give and bequeath unto Charles WATTS and Rebeckah DICKENSON af[ore]s[ai]d my Two beads and furniture One Safe, Two Chests, and my three best pots to them or there Assignes or Guardians forever and if in Case Charles should Die before he arrive to the Age of Twenty one Years I Give the whole to Rebeckah af[ore]s[ai]^d and her heirs forever onely Reserving the use of said Things Duering my own Natural live and for no other use or uses whatsoever. And for the true performance of all and singular the Recited Bequeathments I Doe hereby Bind and Oblige myself my heirs Execu[tor]^s Administra[tor]^s Assigns and any person or persons Claiming from and under me and I Doe further Bind and Oblige myself my heirs or any claimeing from or under me at all Times hereafter shall Give Grant and Confirm and make over unto Charles WATTS and Rebeckah DICKENSON any further Right or Conveyance as there Counsell Learned in the Law shall Advise or Devise for the {?}{?} making Good of the aforementioned Relinquishments of Right of Dower and Bequeathments which when Truelly and fully Comply'd with according to the true intent and meaning thereof. Then this Obligation to be void and of none Effect. Otherways to be and remain in full force and virtue in Law.

Signed Sealed & Delivered	Parker SELBY	Mary WATTS. (Seal)
In the Presence of us …	Parker SELBY Juner.	
	Jonathan HUTSON."	

*followed on folio 91 with the recordation by court clerk Henry JOHNSON on 12 May 1772[207]

Liber I, folios 93-94; 15 May 1772

"This Indenture made this 15th Day of May Ann° Seventeen hundred and seventy two Between **Samuel BLAKE** of Worcester County and Province of Maryland of the one part, and Daniel MIFFLIN of Accomack County and Coloney of Virginia of the other part. Witnesseth that the said **Samuel** for and in Consideration of the sum of twenty seven pounds Current Common money of Maryland to him in hand paid before the Sealing and Delivery hereof the Receipt

---

[207] Worcester County Court (Land Records). Bond from WATTS, Mary to WATTS, Charles and DICKENSON, Rebeckah. 18 July 1770. I, pp. 90-91, MSA CE 30-9. www.mdlandrec.net : accessed 21 November 2021.

whereof he hereby doth acknowledge and hath granted bargained and sold and hereby Doth grant bargain and sell to him the s[ai]^d Daniel MIFFLIN his Heirs and Assigns forever, all that Tract or parsel of Land he the s[ai]^d **Samuel** purchased of **George BLAKE** called Part of Partnership containing fifty four Acres the Alienation for which is Inroaled among the Records of Worcester County Recourse thereto being may more at Large appear. To have and to hold the s[ai]^d fifty four Acres of Land to him the said Daniel MIFFLIN his Heirs and Assigns forever with all the Appurtenances to the same belonging or in any wise appertaining free and Clear of all Incumberances the Quitrents to become due and payable to the Lord of the fee only Excepted And the s[ai]^d **Samuel BLAKE** for himself his Heirs Executors or Administrators doth hereby Covenant with the said Daniel MIFFLIN his Heirs and Assigns that at the Sealing and Delivery hereof he is Seized of and in s[ai]^d fifty four Acres of Land in fee Simple and that he hath a good Right to Sell and Convey the same in manner and form aforesaid And the s[ai]^d **Samuel** for himself his Heirs Executors or Administrators farther Covenants with the s[ai]^d Daniel his Heirs and Assigns to Grant unto him or them such farther Security to the s[ai]^d fifty four Acres of Land, as his or their Council in the Law learned shall at any time advise or require. In Witness whereof the said **Samuel** his Hand hath hereunto set and his Seal affixed the Day and Year afore written.

Signed Sealed and Delivered   John SELBY
In presence of . . . .   A$^{d[a]}$m SPENCE   **Samuel** >| **BLAKE** (Seal)
    (his mark)

*followed on folio 94 with the acknowledgment by Justices of the Peace John SELBY and Adam SPENCE, the receipt of Alienation fine by Parker SELBY on 15 May 1772, and the recordation by court clerk Henry JOHNSON[208]

*The acknowledgment includes the name of the Samuel's wife Mary.

Liber I, folio 97; 15 May 1772

"Know all Men by these Presents that I Sarah BRITTINGHAM for and in Consideration of the sum of Eighty pounds Current money of Virginia to me paid by Jonathan STEVENSON at and before the Sealing and Delivery hereof the Receipt whereof the said Sarah hereby doth acknowledge hath bargained and sold, and by these presents doth bargain and sell unto the said Jonathan STEVENSON his Heirs and Assigns forever one Negroe Man Slave named **Derrum** it being the Negroe which was delivered and paid to me by my Son Samuel BRITTINGHAM on his Administration of his Fathers Estate in satisfaction of my thirds together with some debts due from the said Estate to persons who gave me the benefit of their respective claims in order to Secure the title of the said Slave to me. To have and to hold the af[ore]s[ai]^d Negroe unto the said Jonathan STEVENSON his Heirs and Assigns forever to and for the Sole use benefit and behoof of the said Jonathan STEVENSON his Heirs and Assigns forever and for no other use or purpose whatsoever. And in order to enable the said Jonathan his Heirs Executors Adm[inistrator]^s or Assigns the better and more effectually to obtain the possession and use of the said Negroe I do hereby authorize deputize and put in my stead and place & also constitute and appoint the said Jonathan my true and lawful Attorney to ask demand Sue for and Implead any person that shall be found in possession of the said Negroe and any such So it so to be brought for the Recovery of the same Negroe to prosecute to final end and Judgment, and on delivery of the possession of such Negroe either before or after Suit brought Acquitances and Discharges in my stead name & place to give make & execute to any such person or persons as may have a Right to demand the same. And if it be needfull one or more Attorney or Attorneys to make constitute and appoint in my name and finally all and every other matter or thing needful and necessary in and about the premises to do execute and perform in all respects as fully as I myself might or could do hereby Confirming Irrevocable all that my said Attorney

---

[208] Worcester County Court (Land Records). Deed from **BLAKE, Samuel** to MIFFLIN, Daniel. 15 May 1772. I, pp. 93-94, MSA CE 30-9. www.mdlandrec.net : accessed 17 June 2022.

may or shall do of and upon the premisses af[ore]s[ai]^d In Witness whereof I have hereunto set my hand and Seal this fifteenth day of May Anno Dom[ini] 1772 ~

Sealed & Delivered	John SELBY		
In Presence off us	A^d[a]m SPENCE	Sarah +(her mark) BRITTINGHAM	(Seal)

*followed with the acknowledgment of Justices of the Peace John SELBY and Adam SPENCE and recordation on 02 June 1772 by court clerk Henry JOHNSON[209]

Liber I, folio 108; 30 May 1772

"I the Subscriber do acknowledge that I have Sold, unto Miss Sarah MILLER and received the full Value for one certain Negro Girl named **Beck**, And I do by these Presents promis to defend the said Negro from all other previous legal Claims Whatever, As Witness my Hand and Seal this 30th Day of May 1772. ~

Test. Edward ROWND.	Jacob BACON (Seal)
Ann ROWND."	

*followed by the recordation by court clerk Henry JOHNSON on 03 July 1722[210]

Liber I, folios 112-113; 20 July 1722

"Know all Men by these presents that I John HOUSTON of Worcester County (Pokomoke) for and in consideration of the sum of Forty pounds Current money to me paid by Littleton DENNIS at and before the Sealing and Delivery hereof the receipt whereof he the said John hereby doth acknowledge, hath bargained sold and delivered & by these presents doth bargain sell and deliver unto the said Littleton DENNIS his Heirs and Assigns forever one Negroe Man named **Jack** and all my Cattle and Household Goods of every Nature and kind whatever. To have and to hold the af[oresai]^d bargained premisses unto the said Littleton DENNIS his Heirs and Assigns forever to and for the use of the said Littleton DENNIS his Heirs and Assigns forever & for no other use or purpose whatever. Provided Nevertheless that in case the said John HOUSTON his Executors or Adm[inistrators] do and shall pay unto the said Littleton DENNIS his Heirs or Assigns the amount of a Judgment obtained by the said DENNIS against the said John in Worcester County Court with the Interest thereon due from the time the same become originally due, And also one other Judgment recovered by William Marshall RICHARDSON against the said John in the Court af[oresai]^d also with legal Interest by the twentieth day of July next ensuing, then the above writing to be void and in case, the said John shall fail in payment as above it is hereby Covenant and agreed by the said John with the said Littleton that it shall be lawfull for the said Littleton to take into his possession the af[oresai]^d Goods and Chattels, and the same to dispose of at Publick Sale or at least so much thereof as shall be sufficient to satisfie the Sum af[oresai]^d as also the Costs of the Execution of this Writing. In Witness whereof the said John to these presents his Hand hath set and Seal affixed this xxvth day of July Anno Dom[ini] 1772~

Sealed & Delivered	DENNIS	John HOUSTON (Seal)
In Presence off	Rob[er]^t DENNIS"	

*followed on folio 113 with the acknowledgment by Justice of the Peace ____ DENNIS, receipt by Littleton DENNIS, and recordation by court clerk Henry JOHNSON on 27 July 1772[211]

---

[209] Worcester County Court (Land Records). Bill of sale from BRITTINGHAM, Sarah to STEVENSON, Jonathan. 15 May 1772. I, p. 97, MSA CE 30-9. www.mdlandrec.net : accessed 21 November 2021.

[210] Worcester County Court (Land Records). Receipt from BACON, Jacob to MILLER, Sarah. 30 May 1772. I, p. 108, MSA CE 30-9. www.mdlandrec.net : accessed 21 November 2021.

[211] Worcester County Court (Land Records). Bill of sale from HOUSTON, John to DENNIS, Littleton. 20 July 1772. I, pp. 112-113, MSA CE 30-9. www.mdlandrec.net : accessed 21 November 2021.

Liber I, folios 135-136; 15 August 1772

"This Indenture made between John BRITTINGHAM of Worcester County of the one part & Littleton DENNIS of the other part Witnesseth that whereas the said John for and in Consideration of Leah BRITTINGHAM the Wife of the said John selling and disposing of her Lands and applying the money to the discharge of all the debts of the said John, Contracted before the date hereof, as also for the further Consideration of the sum of one Shilling current Money to the said John by the said Littleton DENNIS paid at and before the Sealing and Delivery hereof the receipt whereof the said John hereby doth acknowledge hath bargained sold and delivered, and by these presents doth bargain sell and deliver unto the af[oresai]^d Littleton DENNIS his Heirs and Assigns forever one Negroe Boy named **Harry** and all the Stock of Creatures and all other his personal Estate of every kind. To have and to hold the af[oresai]^d Negroe named **Harry** and other Estate as af[oresai]^d unto the af[oresai]d Littleton DENNIS to and for the use and purpose hereafter mentioned and for no other purpose whatsoever, that is to say that the said Littleton DENNIS shall stand possessed of the said Negroe & other Estate as af[oresai]^d for the use and benefit of the said Leah BRITTINGHAM for and during her natural life and at her death to and for such uses as the said Leah by Deed in her life or by any other Instrument in writing at her death She may appoint or direct, Provided Nevertheless that the Said Leah or some other person for her shall pay and discharge all the justs Contracts of the said John made before the date hereof and not yet complied with. In Witness whereof the said John BRITTINGHAM to this Instrument of writing his hand hath set and Seal affixed this 15th day of August in the year of our Lord one thousand seven hundred and seventy two.

Sealed & Delivered
In Presence off …
Dixon QUINTON. ~

John + BRITTINGHAM (Seal)
his mark"

*followed on folio 136 with the acknowledgment of Justice of the Peace Dixon QUINTON and recordation by court clerk Henry JOHNSON on 18 August 1772[212]

Liber I, folios 146-147; 25 September 1772

"Worcester Ss.^{t} Know all Men by these presents that I George DISHAROON of the County aforesaid for and in Consideration of the Sum of ten Shillings Current money to me in hand paid and also in Consideration of the Love and Affection I bear my three Children following, to wit, John, Stephen & Salley have bargained and sold assigned and transferred, and by these presents do bargain and sell assign and transfer unto my said Children these Negroes following, to wit, **Dick, Levin, Elisha** and **Hannah**. To have and to hold the said Negroes in manner following, to myself during my natural Life, and after my death the said Negro **Dick** to John DISHAROON for his proper use and behoof, the said Negro **Levin** and **Elisha** to Stephen DISHAROON for his proper use and behoof, and the said Negro **Hannah** to Salley DISHAROON to and for her proper use and behoof. In Witness whereof I have hereto set my Hand and Seal this 25th Day of September Anno Dom[ini] 1772./.~/~

Sealed & Delivered   Jno SCARBOROUGH   George DISHEROON (Seal)
In Presence of   Benton HARRIS"

*followed with the acknowledgment by Justices of the Peace John SCARBOROUGH and Benton HARRIS and recordation by court clerk Henry JOHNSON[213]

---

[212] Worcester County Court (Land Records). Deed of trust from BRITTINGHAM, John to DENNIS, Littleton. 15 August 1772. I, pp. 135-136, MSA CE 30-9. www.mdlandrec.net : accessed 21 November 2021.

[213] Worcester County Court (Land Records). Bill of sale from DISHEROON, George to DISHEROON, John, Salley, and Stephen. 25 September 1772. I, pp. 146-147, MSA CE 30-9. www.mdlandrec.net : accessed 21 November 2021.

Liber I, folios 194-195; 09 January 1773

"Know all Men by these presents that I Matthew SELBY of Worcester County in the province of Maryland Planter for and in Consideration of the Sum of seventy pounds Current money to me in hand paid at and before the Sealing & Delivery of these presents by Macclammy JONES of the same County and province aforesaid Planter, the Receipt whereof I do hereby acknowledge, have Bargained and Sold, and by these presents do Bargain and Sell unto the said Macclammy JONES his Heirs Executors Adm[inistrators] and Assigns one Negro Man called **Will**. To have and to hold the said Negro **Will** by these presents Bargained & Sold unto the said Macclammy JONES his Heirs and Assigns forever. And I the said Matthew SELBY for myself my Heirs Executors and Administrators, all and singular the said Negro **Will** (or **William**) unto the said Macclammy JONES his Heirs Executors Adm[inistrators] and Assigns and against all and Every other person or persons whatsoever shall and will Warrant and forever defend by these presents free and Clear of all manner of Incumbrance whatsoever, Of which Negro **Will** I the said Matthew SELBY have just the said Macclammy JONES in full possession. In Testimony whereof I have hereunto set my Hand and Seal this ninth Day of January Annoque Domini Seventeen hundred and seventy three.

Signed Sealed & Delivered   J. SCARBOROUGH   Matthew SELBY. (Seal)
In the presence of …   Sam[ue]ˡ SCARBOROUGH"

*followed with acknowledgment by Justice of the Peace John SCARBOROUGH and recordation on 15 January 1773 by court clerk Henry JOHNSON[214]

Liber I, folios 238-240; 26 March 1773

"This Indenture made this Twenty sixth day of March in the Year of our Lord one thousand seven hundred and seventy three Between Samuel TINDAL of Worcester County in the Province of Maryland of the one part, and Levinah TINDAL of County and Province af[ore]s[ai]ᵈ Daughter of the af[ore]s[ai]ᵈ Samuel TINDAL of the other part. Witnesseth that the said Samuel TINDAL for and in consideration of the natural Love and Affection which he hath and beareth unto the said Levinah TINDAL his Daughter as also for the better Maintenance and Preferment of the said Levinah TINDAL, have granted and by these presents do give and grant unto the said Levinah TINDAL the several Goods and Chattels, to wit, one Negroe Girl Slave called and known by the name of **Esther**, and ten Pounds in Spanish Milled Dollars at the rate of seven Shillings and six pence each dollar, To have and to hold and enjoy all and singular the Goods and Chattels aforesaid unto her the said Levinah TINDALL her Executors Administrators and Assigns to the only proper use benefit and behoof of her the said Levinah TINDAL her Executors Administrators and Assigns forever. And I the said Samuel TINDAL all and singular the Goods and Chattels aforesaid to the said Levinah TINDAL her Executors Administrators and Assigns forever against all persons whatsoever shall & will Warrant and forever defend by these presents. Now this Indenture further Witnesseth that the said Samuel TINDAL for and in consideration of the natural Love and Affection which I have and bear unto my Daughter Hannah TINDAL and for divers other good causes and considerations me hereunto moving, have given and granted, and by these presents do give & grant unto the said Hannah TINDAL, all and singular the Goods and Chattels following, to wit, one Negro Girl slave called and known by the name of **Venus**, and ten Pounds in Money to be paid in Spanish milled Dollars at the rate of Seven Shillings and six Pence each Dollar. To have and to hold and enjoy all singular the Goods and Chattels aforesaid to the said Hannah TINDAL her Executors Administrators and Assigns to the only proper use benefit and behoof of her the said Hannah TINDAL her Executors Administrators and Assigns forever. And I the said Samuel TINDAL all and singular the Goods & Chattels aforesaid to the said Hannah TINDAL her Executors Administrators and Assigns forever against all persons whatsoever will Warrant and forever Defend by these presents. Now this Indenture further Witnesseth that the said Samuel TINDAL for and in consideration of the natural Love and Affection which I have and bear unto my

---

[214] Worcester County Court (Land Records). Bill of sale from SELBY, Matthew to JONES, Macclammy. 09 January 1773. I, pp. 194-195, MSA CE 30-9. www.mdlandrec.net : accessed 21 November 2021.

Daughter Ann TINDAL and for divers other good causes and considerations me hereunto moving, have given and granted, and by these presents do give and grant unto the said Ann TINDAL all and singular the Goods and Chattels following, to wit, one Negroe Boy slave called and known by the name of **Missyrow**, and the sum of ten Pounds to paid in Spanish Milled Dollars at the rate of seven Shillings six pence each Dollar. To have and to hold and enjoy all singular the Goods and Chattels aforesaid to the said Ann TINDAL her Executors Administrators and Assigns to the only proper use benefit and behoof of her the said Ann TINDAL her Executors Administrators and Assigns forever. And I the said Samuel TINDAL all and singular the Goods and Chattels aforesaid to the said Ann TINDAL her Executors Administrators and Assigns forever against all Persons whatsoever will Warrant and forever Defend by these presents. Now this Indenture further Witnesseth that the said Samuel TINDAL for and in consideration of the natural Love and Affection which I have and bear unto my Daughter Sarah TINDAL and for divers other good causes and considerations me hereunto moving, have given and granted and by these presents do give and grant unto the said Sarah TINDAL all and singular the Goods & Chattels following, to wit, one Negroe Boy Slave called and known by the name of **Cuff**, and the sum of ten Pounds in Money to be paid in Spanish milled Dollars at the rate of seven Shillings & six pence each Dollar. To have and to hold and enjoy all and singular the Goods and Chattels aforesaid to the said Sarah TINDAL her Executors Administrators and Assigns, to the only proper use benefit and behoof of her the said Sarah TINDAL her Executors Administrators and Assigns forever. And I the said Samuel TINDAL all and singular the Goods and Chattels aforesaid to the said Sarah TINDAL her Executors Administrators and Assigns forever against all persons whatsoever will Warrant and forever Defend by these presents. Now this Indenture further Witnesseth that the said Samuel TINDAL for and in Consideration of the natural Love and Affection which I have and bear unto my Son Purnell TINDAL and for divers other good causes and considerations me hereunto moving have given and granted and by these presents do give and grant unto the said Purnell TINDAL all and singular the Goods and Chattels following, to wit, one Negroe Boy called and known by the name of **Moses**, and the sum of ten pounds in Money to be paid in Dollars at the rate of seven Shillings and six pence each Dollar. To have and to hold and enjoy all and singular the Goods and Chattels aforesaid to the said Purnel TINDAL his Executors Administrators and Assigns to the only proper use benefit and behoof of him the said Purnell TINDAL his Executors Administrators and Assigns forever. And I the said Samuel TINDAL all and singular the Goods & Chattels aforesaid to the said Purnel TINDAL his Executors Administrators and Assigns forever against all persons whatsoever will Warrant and forever Defend by these presents. Now this Indenture further Witnesseth that the said Samuel TINDAL for and in consideration of the natural Love and Affection which I have and bear unto my Daughter Holland TINDAL and for divers other good causes and considerations me hereunto moving have given and granted and by these presents do give and grant unto the said Holland TINDAL all and singular the Goods and Chattels following, to wit, one Negroe Boy Slave called and known by the name **Jacob** and the sum of ten Pounds in Money to be paid in Spanish milled Dollars at the rate of seven Shillings and six pence each Dollar. To have and to hold and enjoy all and singular the Goods and Chattels aforesaid to the said Holland TINDAL her Executors Administrators and Assigns to the only proper use benefit and behoof of her the said Holland TINDAL her Executors Administrators and Assigns forever. And I the said Samuel TINDAL all and singular the Goods and Chattels aforesaid to the said Holland TINDAL her Executors Administrators and Assigns forever against all Persons whatsoever will Warrant and forever Defend by these presents. In Witness whereof I have hereunto set my hand and seal affixed the day and year above written.

Signed Sealed and Delivered   Samuel TINDALL. (Seal)
In the presence of
Joseph DASHIELL.   Esme BAYLY."

*followed on folio 240 with the acknowledgment of Justice of the Peace Joseph DASHIELL and recordation by court clerk Henry JOHNSON[215]

Liber I, folio 245; 02 April 1773

"Maryland Worcester County Ss.ᵗ Know all men by these Presents that I Sacker MUMFORD of Worcester County in the Province of Maryland for and in consideration of the sum of one hundred Pounds Current money of Maryland to me in hand Paid by Joseph BRATTEN of the County and Province aforesaid at and before the Ensealing & Delivery of these Presents; wherewith I confess myself to be fully satisfied contented and paid, have Bargained and Sold and Delivered, and by these Presents do fully clearly and absolutely Bargain Sell and Deliver unto the said Joseph BRATTEN, one Negro Man named **Sam** about 22 years of age. To have & to hold the said Negro Man named **Sam**, unto the said Joseph BRATTEN his Heirs and Assigns forever and his and their proper uses and behoofs forever. And I the said Sacker MUMFORD my Heirs Executors and Administrators and every of us the said Negro to the said Joseph BRATTEN his Heirs Executors Administrators and Assigns against all Person or Persons whatsoever shall and will Warrant acquit and forever Defend by these presents. In Witness whereof the said Sacker MUMFORD to these Presents his Hand hath set & Seal affixed the second Day of April A[nno] Domini 1773.

Sealed and Delivered   Belitha GODFREY   Sacker MUMFORD   (Seal)
In the presence of
                        Robert + BURTON
                             his mark"

*followed with the recordation by court clerk Henry JOHNSON on 09 April 1773[216]

Liber I, folios 253-254; 01 May 1773

"To all Persons whom these Presents shall come or may concern I Rebecca ENNIS of Worcester County in the Province of Maryland send Greeting. Know ye that I the said Rebecca ENNIS as well for and in Consideration of the natural love & Affection which I bear unto my beloved Grandson Boaz ENNIS (Son to my beloved Son Nathaniel ENNIS) of the County & Province af[oresai]ᵈ as also for divers other good Causes and Considerations me hereunto moving have given and granted and confirmed, and by these presents do give grant and confirm unto the said Boaz ENNIS one Negro Man named **Isaac**, only saving Excepting & reserving unto my well beloved Son Nathaniel ENNIS the use service and labour of the af[oresai]ᵈ Negro Man **Isaac** dureing his natural Life, and at his decease the af[oresai]ᵈ given granted Negro Man **Isaac** unto the af[oresai]ᵈ Boaz ENNIS his Heirs & Assigns forever. To have and to hold the af[oresai]ᵈ given and granted and confirmed negro Man **Isaac** unto the af[oresai]ᵈ Boaz ENNIS (Excepting as is before excepted and reserved) to him his Heirs and Assigns forever and to the only proper use benefit and behoof of the said Boaz his Heirs and Assigns forever and to and for no other use or purpose whatever and without any manner of challenge claim or demand from me the said Rebecca unto the af[oresai]ᵈ given & granted Slave or from any other person or persons whatever for me or authorised and procured by me, & I the said Rebecca the af[oresai]ᵈ given & granted Negro Man **Isaac** unto the a[foresai]ᵈ Boaz his Heirs & Assigns and to the use af[oresai]ᵈ against all & every Person do & will Warrant & forever Defend. In Witness whereof I do hereby set my Hand & Seal affix this 1ˢᵗ day of May Anno Dom[ini] one thousand seven hundred & seventy three.

---

[215] Worcester County Court (Land Records). Deed of gift from TINDALL, Samuel to TINDALL, Levinah, Hannah, Ann, Sarah, Purnell, and Holland. 26 March 1773. I, pp. 238-240, MSA CE 30-9. www.mdlandrec.net : accessed 21 November 2021.
[216] Worcester County Court (Land Records). Bill of sale from MUMFORD, Sacker to BRATTEN, Joseph. 02 April 1773. I, p. 245, MSA CE 30-9. www.mdlandrec.net : accessed 22 November 2021.

Signed Sealed & Delivered		her
In Presence of ……		Rebecca R ENNIS. (Seal)
Sam[ue]ˡ. HANDY. John Purnell ROBINS.		Mark"

*followed on folio 254 with the acknowledgment by Justice of the Peace Adam SPENCE and recordation by court clerk Henry JOHNSON on 04 May 1773[217]

Liber I, folios 254-255; 07 May 1773

"This Indenture made this 7ᵗʰ day of May in the year of our Lord seventeen hundred and seventy three Between George ADAMS of Worcester County of the one part, and Stephen ADAMS of the other part. Witnesseth that the said George ADAMS for and in Consideration of the sum of fifty pounds Current money of Maryland to him in hand paid by the said Stephen ADAMS at and before the Sealing and Delivery of these presents the Receipt of which the said George ADAMS hereby acknowledge he hath bargained and sold, and by these presents Doth bargain and sell unto the said Stephen ADAMS his Heirs and Administrators two Negroes named **Nanny & Ben** to the said Stephen ADAMS his Heirs and Assigns forever. To have and to hold the two Negroes named or called **Nanny & Ben** to the said Stephen ADAMS his Heirs and Assigns forever and for no other use or purpose whatsoever provided always that the said George ADAMS do well and truly pay or cause to be paid unto the said Stephen ADAMS the sum of fifty pounds Current money of Maryland for which the said Stephen ADAMS has the George ADAMS bond for on lawfull Interest bearing Equal date with these presents that immediately after the discharging the said bond and Interest and the aforesaid Sum of Money paid to the said Stephen ADAMS with the Expence attending the Execution of this Bill of Sale, that then this present Indenture shall become Void and of no Effect, as Witness my hand and Seal the day and year above written./. ~./. ~./. ~

Signed Sealed and Delivered	And[re]ʷ ADAMS	Geo[rge] ADAMS. (Seal)
In the presence of …..	George JONES"	

*followed with the acknowledgment by Worcester County Justices of the Peace John ADAMS and William ADAMS, recordation by Somerset County clerk Thomas HAYWARD on 11 May 1773, and recordation on folio 255 by Worcester County court clerk Henry JOHNSON on 14 May 1773[218]

Liber I, folios 270-271; 03 July 1773

"Know all Men by these presents that I James CATHELL of Worcester County in the Province of Maryland for and in Consideration of the sum of Eighty pounds Current money to me in hand paid before the Sealing and Delivery of these presents, have bargained sold, released, granted and confirmed and by these presents do bargain, sell release grant and confirm unto John CATHELL a Negro Man called **Ned**. To have and to hold the said Negro Man called **Ned** unto the said John CATHELL and his Executors Administrators & Assigns forever freely quietly peaceably and entirely without any contradiction claim disturbance or hindrance of any Person whatsoever so that neither I the said James CATHELL nor any other for me or in my Name, any right, title, interest, or demand of in to or for the said Negro Man called **Ned** ought to exact, challenge, claim or demand at any time or times hereafter but from all Action right, Estate, Title, Claim, Demand, Possession, and Interest thereof shall be wholly barred and excluded by force and virtue of these presents And I the said James CATHELL my Heirs Executors and Administrators the afores[ai]ᵈ Negro Man called **Ned** to the said John CATHELL his Executors Administrators and Assigns against all manner of Persons will Warrant and forever defend by these presents, of which said Negro Man called **Ned** I the said James CATHELL have put the said John CATHELL in full and peaceable Possession. In Testimony

---

[217] Worcester County Court (Land Records). Deed of gift from ENNIS, Rebecca to ENNIS, Boaz. 01 May 1773. I, pp. 253-254, MSA CE 30-9. www.mdlandrec.net : accessed 22 November 2021.
[218] Worcester County Court (Land Records). Bill of sale from ADAMS, George to ADAMS, Stephen. 07 May 1773. I, pp. 254-255, MSA CE 30-9. www.mdlandrec.net : accessed 22 November 2021.

whereof the aforesaid James CATHELL hath to these Presents his hand set and Seal affixed this third Day of July in the Year of our Lord one thousand seven hundred and seventy three.

Signed Sealed & delivered   W[illia]m WINDER   James CATHELL. (Seal)
In presence of   Benjamin HANDY"

*followed on folio 271 with the acknowledgment by Justice of the Peace Adam SPENCE and recordation on 16 July 1773 by court clerk Henry JOHNSON[219]

Liber I, folios 271-272; 03 June 1773

"Know all Men by these presents that I James CATHELL of Worcester County for and in Consideration of the said John CATHELL's entring Security to Cap.t William WINDER for the sum of Eighty four pounds Eighteen Shillings & Eight pence and also for and in consideration of securing the said John CATHELL in the purchase of a Negro Man called **Ned** which I the said James CATHELL this day passed a Bill of Sale to the said John CATHELL for, have granted bargained sold and transferred, and by these presents do grant bargain sell and transfer unto the af[ore]s[ai]d John CATHELL the following Negroes, to wit, **Lear, Nice, Phillis**, and **Silbey** To have and to hold the said Negroes called **Lear, Nice, Phillis,** and **Silbey** unto the said John CATHELL his Executors Administrators and Assigns free and clear from any incumbrance whatsoever to the only proper use benefit and behoof of the said John CATHELL his Executors Administrators & Assigns And the said James CATHELL doth covenant to and with the said John CATHELL that he will Warrant and Defend the af[ore]s[ai]d Negroes from all manner of Persons whatsoever provided Nevertheless and it is always the true intent and meaning of these Presents that if the said James CATHELL does well and truly save harmless and keep indemnified the af[ore]s[ai]d John CATHELL his Executors & Administrators from all Damages Costs and Charges which he or they may sustain by means of the said John CATHELL's entring Security to the af[ore]s[ai]d William WINDER in a Bond bearing equal date with these presents, And also Warrant and Defend a Negro Man called **Ned** which the af[ore]s[ai]d James CATHELL passed his Bill of Sale for to the af[ore]s[ai]d John CATHELL, from the Claim and Claims of all manner of Persons whatsoever Claiming or that shall hereafter Claim any Right, Title, Interest, or property in or to the af[ore]s[ai]d Negro called **Ned**, then this present writing to be void, else to be in full force In Testimony whereof the af[ore]s[ai]d James CATHELL hath to these presents his hand set and Seal affixed this 3[r]d day of June Anno Domini 1773./. ~./. ~ ./. ~

Signed Sealed & delivered   Benjamin HANDY   James CATHELL. (Seal)
In Presence of …..   Jonathan PARSONS"

*followed with the acknowledgment by Justice of the Peace Adam SPENCE and recordation by court clerk Henry JOHNSON on 16 July 1773[220]

Liber I, folio 272; 03 August 1773

"This Indenture made this third Day of August Anno Dom[ini] one thousand seven hundred and seventy three. Between Edward PETTIT of Worcester County of the one part, and Littleton DENNIS of the same place of the other part Witnesseth that whereas the af[oresai]d Edward for and in consideration of the sum of one hundred pounds fifteen Shillings & five pence Current money to the said Edward by the said Littleton to the said Edward paid at and before the Execution hereof the Receipt whereof he hereby acknowledges, hath bargained sold & delivered, and by these presents doth bargain sell & deliver unto the af[oresai]d Littleton DENNIS his Heirs and Assigns forever all the following Goods, to wit, three Cows & Calves, one Heffer, two head of Horses, five Beds and furniture, twelve Hoggs, one case of Draws, one Desk, two Chests, one Trunk, one old Negro Wench called **Rose**, six Chairs, one Cart, twenty

---

[219] Worcester County Court (Land Records). Bill of sale from CATHELL, James to CATHELL, John. 03 July 1773. I, pp. 270-271, MSA CE 30-9. www.mdlandrec.net : accessed 22 November 2021.
[220] Worcester County Court (Land Records). Bill of sale from CATHELL, James to CATHELL, John. 03 June 1773. I, pp. 271-272, MSA CE 30-9. www.mdlandrec.net : accessed 22 November 2021.

pounds of pewter, three Spinning Wheels, one Case of Bottles, two pine Tables, one p[ai]r of flatt Irons, two Potts, two Kettles, and all other my Goods and Chattles whatever. To have and to hold the af[oresai]^d bargained premisses unto the af[oresai]^d Littleton DENNIS his Heirs and Assigns forever to and for the only proper use of the said Littleton DENNIS his Heirs and Assigns forever and for no other use or purpose whatsoever. In Witness whereof the said Edward to these presents his hand hath set and Seal affixed the day and year first above written.

Signed Sealed & Delivered   Edw[ar]d BETTIT. (Seal)
In Presence of   W[illia]m HOLLAND"

*followed with the acknowledgment of William HOLLAND and recordation by court clerk Henry JOHNSON[221]

Liber I, folios 282-283; 05 August 1773

"Know all Men by these Presents that I John McNEIL of Worcester County in the Province of Maryland for and in Consideration of Fifty seven pounds to me in hand paid at and before the Sealing and Delivery of these Presents by Thomas SELBY Jun[io]^r of the County and Province af[ore]s[ai]^d the Receipt whereof I do hereby acknowledge, have bargained and Sold and by these Presents do Bargain and Sell unto the said Thomas SELBY one Negro Wench called **Phillace** & Increase. To have and to hold the said Negro wench and increase by these Presents bargained and Sold unto the said Thomas SELBY his Heirs Executors Administrators Assigns forever. And I the said John McNEIL for myself my Heirs Executors and Administrators all and singular the said Negro Wench called **Phillace** and increase unto the said Thomas SELBY his Heirs Executors Administrators and Assigns and against all and every other Person or Persons whatsoever shall and will Warrant and forever Defend by these presents of which said Negro Wench called **Phillace** I the said John McNEIL have put the said Thomas SELBY in full Possession. In Witness my Hand this fifth Day of August Anno Domini one thousand seven hundred & seventy three./. ~

Signed and Delivered   J. DENNIS   John McNEALL (Seal)
in the Presence of   W[illia]^m SELBY Jun[ior]"

*followed on folio 283 with the acknowledgment of Adam SPENCE and recordation by court clerk Henry JOHNSON[222]

Liber I, folio 291; 09 August 1773

"Maryland Ss. Know all Men by these Presents that I James CATHELL of Worcester County for and in Consideration of the Sum of three hundred Pounds current Money of Maryland to me in hand paid by Joshua CATHELL of the same place and County af[oresai]^d at and before the Sealing and Delivery hereof the Receipt whereof, I hereby doth acknowledge, hath Bargained and Sold and by these Presents doth Bargain and Sell unto the af[oresai]^d Joshua CATHELL and his Heirs and Assigns one Negro Girl called **Silva**, one Desk, four feather Beds and furniture, one hand Mill, forty Hogs, two Cows, and two Yearlings, one Yoke of Oxen, two Chairs, two Carts, and all the Harness thereunto belonging, one Rone Mare and fifteen Sheep all my Crop with every Article of Household furniture that I now have in Possession. To have and to hold the af[oresai]^d sundry Articles of Household furniture as in and above Expressed and Described to the only proper use of the said Joshua CATHELL and his Heirs and Assigns. And the said James CATHELL doth Covenant to and with the said Joshua CATHELL that at the time of the Bargain and Sale hereof he had full Power and Authority to Sell and Dispose of the several Matters and things aforementioned, and that will forever Warrant and Defend the af[oresai]^d bargained Premisses unto the said Joshua CATHELL against the Rights Claims and

---

[221] Worcester County Court (Land Records). Bill of sale from BETTIT, Edward to DENNIS, Littleton. 03 August 1773. I, p. 272, MSA CE 30-9. www.mdlandrec.net : accessed 22 November 2021.
[222] Worcester County Court (Land Records). Bill of sale from McNEALL, John to SELBY, Thomas Jr. 05 August 1773. I, pp. 282-283, MSA CE 30-9. www.mdlandrec.net : accessed 22 November 2021.

Demands of all and Every person or person whatsoever. In Testimony whereof the said James CATHELL to these presents his Hand hath set and Seal this ninth Day of August 1773.

Signed Sealed and Deliver[e]d   James CATHELL (Seal)
In Presence of us…
Levin HOPKINS.   Moses GOTHERY.

*followed with the acknowledgment by Justice of the Peace Adam SPENCE and recordation by court clerk Henry JOHNSON[223]

Liber I, folio 320; 08 September 1773

"This Indenture made this Eighth day of September Anno Dom[ini] one thousand seven hundred and seventy three. Between James CATHELL of the one part and William LANE of the other part. Witnesseth that whereas the said James by his Deed bearing date the third Day of June Anno Dom[ini] one thousand seven hundred and seventy three for the consideration therein mentioned did Mortgage unto John CATHELL the following Slaves to wit **Sear, Nice, Phillis,** and **Silbey**, and the said James for the consideration of one Shilling by the af[oresai]^d William paid and also to Indemnify the said William for his being Security on the Administration for the said James for his Fathers Estate, hath Bargained Sold Remised and Released, and by these presents doth Bargain Sell Remise & Release unto the said William LANE and his Assigns all the Right and Equity of redemption of the Negroes af[oresai]^d so as af[oresai]^d Mortgaged unto the said John CATHELL To have and to hold the af[oresai]^d Negroes so as af[oresai]^d described unto the said William LANE his Heirs and Assigns forever to and for the only use and behoof of the said William LANE his Heirs and Assigns forever and for no other use or purpose whatsoever. In Witness whereof the said James to these presents his Hand hath set and Seal affixed the day and year first above written. ~

Seal[e]d & Deliver[e]d   Joseph ENNIS   James CATHELL (Seal)
In Presence of   Isaac KELLAM"

*followed with the acknowledgment of Justice of the Peace N. HOLLAND and recordation on 10 September 1773 by court clerk Henry JOHNSON[224]

Liber I, folio 321; 08 September 1773

"Know all Men by these presents that I John CATHELL of Worcester County in the province of Maryland of the one part, and William LANE of the same place of the other part. Witnesseth that the said John CATHELL for and Consideration of the sum of five Shillings Current money of Maryland to him in hand paid by the said William LANE at and before the Sealing and Delivery of these presents the receipt whereof the said John CATHELL hereby doth acknowledge, the said John CATHELL hath remised released and forever quit claim and by these presents doth remise release and forever quit claim unto the said William LANE his Heirs Executors Administrators and Assigns forever all the said John CATHELL's right title & interest of to and in the following Negroes to wit **Sear, Nice, Phillis** and **Silbey** unto him the said William LANE his Heirs and Assigns forever. To have and to hold the af[oresai]^d Negroes so as af[oresai]^d described unto the said William LANE his Heirs and Assigns forever to and for the only proper use benefit and behoof of him the said William LANE his Heirs and Assigns forever and for no other use or purpose whatsoever. In Witness whereof the said John CATHELL to these presents his Hand hath set and Seal affixed this Eighth day of September in the year of our Lord one thousand seven hundred and seventy three./. ~ ./. ~ ./. ~

Sealed and Delivered   Joseph ENNISS   John CATHELL. (Seal)
In the Presence off   Isaac KELLAM"

---

[223] Worcester County Court (Land Records). Bill of sale from CATHELL, James to CATHELL, Joshua. 09 August 1773. I, p. 291, MSA CE 30-9. www.mdlandrec.net : accessed 22 November 2021.
[224] Worcester County Court (Land Records). Deed of release from CATHELL, James to LANE, William. 08 September 1773. I, p. 320, MSA CE 30-9. www.mdlandrec.net : accessed 22 November 2021.

*followed with the acknowledgment of Justice of the Peace N. HOLLAND and recordation on 10 September 1773 by court clerk Henry JOHNSON[225]

Liber I, folio 330; 02 November 1773

"Know all Men by these presents that I William LANE of Worcester County in the Province of Maryland for and in Consideration of the sum of ninety Pounds current Money of Maryland to me in Hand paid at and before the Sealing and Delivery of these Presents by Henry JOHNSON of the County and Province af[oresai]^d the Receipt whereof I the said William LANE do hereby acknowledge, Have Bargained and Sold, and by these presents do Bargain and Sell unto the said Henry JOHNSON his Heirs Ex[ecutor]^s Adm[inistrator]^s or Assigns one Negro Man Slave called and known by the name of **Sear**, who is supposed to be about twenty Years of Age. To have and to hold the said Negro called **Sear** by these presents Bargained and Sold ad af[oresai]^d unto the said Henry JOHNSON his Heirs Ex[ecutor]^s Adm[inistrator]^s and Assigns forever And I the said William LANE for myself my Heirs Ex[ecutor]^s and Adm[inistrator]^s the Negro Man af[ore]s[ai]^d unto the said Henry JOHNSON his Heirs Ex[ecutor]^s Adm[inistrator]^s or Assigns against me the said William LANE my Heirs Ex[ecutor]^s or Adm[inistrator]^s and against all and every other Person or Persons whatsoever shall and will Warrant and forever Defend by these presents. In Witness whereof I the said William LANE to these presents my Hand have set and Seal affixed this 2$^{[n]d}$ Day of November Anno Dom[ini] 1773.

Sealed & Delivered   W[illia]m LANE   (Seal)
In Presence of   W[illia]m ALLEN."

*followed with the acknowledgment by Justice of the Peace William ALLEN and recordation by court clerk Henry JOHNSON[226]

Liber I, folio 342; 05 November 1773

"This Indenture made the fifth day of November Anno Domini Seventeen hundred seventy & three Between James ATKINSON of Worcester County in the Province of Maryland of the one part, and Christian JOHNSON of the County & Province af[oresai]^d of the other part. Witnesseth that the said James ATKINSON for and in Consideration of five Shillings Current money of Maryland to him in hand paid by the af[ore]s[ai]^d Christian JOHNSON at and before the Sealing and Delivering hereof the receipt whereof the af[ore]s[ai]^d James ATKINSON doth hereby confess and acknowledge and thereof doth acquit exonerate and discharge the said Christian JOHNSON her Heirs and Assigns forever by these Presents hath Given Granted Bargained Conveyed Confirmed and Assigned over, and by these presents doth Give Grant Bargain Convey Confirm and Assign over unto the said Christian JOHNSON her Heirs and Assigns forever one Negro Slave named and called **Nice**. To have and to hold the af[oresai]^d Bargained Negro unto her the said Christian JOHNSON her Heirs and Assigns forever and to and for no other use purpose or intent whatsoever. And the aforesaid James ATKINSON for himself his Heirs Executors and Administrators doth further Covenant promise and Agree to and with the aforesaid Christian JOHNSON her Heirs Executors Administrators and Assigns that he the said James ATKINSON his Heirs Executors and Adm[inistrator]^s the aforesaid Bargained Premisses unto her the said Christian JOHNSON her Heirs and Assigns forever from all Persons whatsoever shall and will Warrant and forever Defend by these presents. In Witness whereof Parties hereto have interchangeably set their Hands & affixed their Seal the day and year above written. ~

Sealed and Delivered   John SELBY   James ATKINSON. (Seal)
In Presence of   Thomas STURGIS"

---

[225] Worcester County Court (Land Records). Deed of release from CATHELL, John to LANE, William. 08 September 1773. I, p. 321, MSA CE 30-9. www.mdlandrec.net : accessed 22 November 2021.
[226] Worcester County Court (Land Records). Bill of sale from LANE, William to JOHNSON, Henry. 02 November 1773. I, p. 330, MSA CE 30-9. www.mdlandrec.net : accessed 22 November 2021.

*followed with the acknowledgment by Justice of the Peace John SELBY and recordation by court clerk Henry JOHNSON[227]

Liber I, folios 344-345; 02 September 1765

"Worcester County Ss.ᵗ Know all Men by these presents that we Moses SMITH and William CALDWELL both of the County af[oresai]ᵈ Planters, are and, each of us are held and firmly bound unto Solomon CLAYWELL of the same place in the full and just sum of two hundred and fifty Pounds Sterling Money of Great Britain, for the true payment whereof we bind ourselves over and each and every of our Heirs Executors and Adm[inistrator]s in and for the whole jointly and severally firmly by these presents, sealed with our Seals and Dated this second Day of September Anno Domini 1765.

The condition of the above Obligation is such that whereas the above bound Moses SMITH had sundry Matters and Things mentioned in a Deed of Gift by a certain Lucrecy CLAYWELL as followeth, one Bed and furniture, and one Negro Girl named **Leah**, and likewise all her Wearing-apparel, now the aforesaid Moses SMITH doth Relinquish and give up all the Matters herein mentioned for Consideration of the said Solomon CLAYWELL's keeping the said Lucresey CLAYWELL During her natural Life and in Consideration I the above bound Moses SMITH do Relinquish all the things mentioned in their Bond that was mentioned in the Deed af[oresai]ᵈ

Witness.
    Elizabeth + WRIGHT (her mark)
    Betty + SMITH (her Mark)"

Moses SMITH. (Seal)
William CALDWELL. (Seal)

*followed by the recordation by court clerk Henry JOHNSON on 12 December 1773[228]

Liber I, folio 345; 03 December 1773

"Know all men by these Presents that I Ezekiel PORTER of Worcester County in the province of Maryland Planter for and in Consideration of the sum of sixty five pounds current money of Maryland to me in hand paid at and before the Sealing and Delivery of these presents by William Barkley TOWNSEND of the same County and Province af[ore]s[ai]ᵈ the Receipt whereof I do hereby acknowledge, have Bargained and Sold, and by these presents do Bargain and Sell unto the said William Barkley TOWNSEND his Heirs and Assigns forever a Negro wench called **Leah** and Child called **Nan** To have and to hold the aforesaid Negro wench **Leah** and Child **Nan** by these presents Bargained and Sold unto the said William Barkley TOWNSEND his Heirs Executors Adm[inistrator]ˢ and Assigns forever. And I the said Ezekiel PORTER for myself my Heirs Executors and Administrators all and singular the said Negro wench **Leah** and Child **Nan** unto the said William Barkley TOWNSEND his Heirs Executors Administrators & Assigns and against all and every other person and persons whatsoever shall and will Warrant and forever Defend by these presents of which said Negro Wench called **Leah** and Child called **Nan** (or **Nancy**) I the said Ezekiel PORTER have put the said William Barkley TOWNSEND in full possession. In Testimony whereof I the said Ezekiel PORTER have hereunto set my hand and affixed my Seal this third Day of December Annoque Domini Seventeen hundred and seventy three. ~

Signed Sealed & Delivered   Jnᵒ SCARBOROUGH
In Presence of ~ ~   Thomas STURGIS   Ezekiel X PORTER. (Seal) (his Mark)

---

[227] Worcester County Court (Land Records). Bill of sale from ATKINSON, James to TOWNSEND, Christian. 05 November 1773. I, p. 342, MSA CE 30-9. www.mdlandrec.net : accessed 22 November 2021.

[228] Worcester County Court (Land Records). Bond from SMITH, Moses and CALDWELL, William to CLAYWELL, Solomon. 02 September 1765. I, pp. 344-345, MSA CE 30-9. www.mdlandrec.net : accessed 22 November 2021.

*followed by the acknowledgment of Justice of the Peace John SCARBOROUGH and recordation on 10 December 1773 by court clerk Henry JOHNSON[229]

Liber I, folios 345-346; 03 December 1773

"To all People to whom these presents shall come Greeting. Know ye that I Elizabeth TRUIT of Worcester County in the Province of Maryland this third Day of December in the Year of our Lord one thousand seven hundred and seventy three for and in Consideration of the natural Love and Affection which I owe and bear to my Grandchildren Elizabeth SELBY and William SELBY Children of my Son in Law called Micajah SELBY and my Daughter Mary SELBY Wife of the af[oresai]^d Micajah, and for the further Advancement of my said Grand Children, I Give them the following Man Slave called **Isaac** now in the possession of Lemuel JOHNSON only reserving to myself the use of said Negro **Isaac** for and dureing my natural Life which said Negro Man Slave called **Isaac** as abovementioned I give and grant unto my two Grand Children Elizabeth SELBY and William SELBY Children of Micajah SELBY and Mary SELBY as af[oresai]^d to them and to their heirs and Assigns forever to the only proper use benefit and behoof of them the said Elizabeth and W[illia]^m and the said and the said Elizabeth TRUIT doth further Covenant grant and agree to and with the said Elizabeth SELBY and W[illia]^m SELBY that She the said Elizabeth TRUIT and her heirs shall and will forever Warrant and Defend the said Negro Man Slave called **Isaac** as af[oresai]^d unto the af[oresai]^d Elizabeth SELBY and W[illia]^m SELBY & their heirs and Assigns forever against the lawfull Claim Right and Title of all and every Person or Persons whatsoever. In Witness whereof I have set my hand and Seal affixed this Day and Date above mentioned.

Signed Sealed and Delivered	John SELBY	
In the presence of us …..	Daniel FARSETT	Elizabeth ✝ TRUITT. (Seal) her mark"

*followed on folio 346 with the acknowledgment of Justice of the Peace John SELBY and recordation on 10 December 1773 by court clerk Henry JOHNSON[230]

Liber I, folios 354-355; 21 January 1774

"Know all Men by these Presents that I Thomas Givan SCHOOLFIELD of Worcester County in the Province of Maryland Wheal Wright for and in Consideration of the Sum of seventy pounds Current money of Maryland to me in hand paid at and before the Sealing and Delivery of the presents by Major TOWNSEND of the same County and Province afores[ai]^d the Receipt whereof I Thomas Givan SCHOOLFIELD do hereby acknowledge and myself sufficiently satisfied, have Bargained and Sold, and by these presents do Bargain and Sell unto the said Major TOWNSEND one Negro Wench Called **Esther** and her increase to him the said Major TOWNSEND and his Heirs and Assigns forever. To have and to hold the said Negro Wench **Esther** by these presents Bargained unto the said Major TOWNSEND his heirs Ex[ecutor]^s Administrators and Assigns forever. And I the said Thomas Givan SCHOOLFIELD for myself my heirs Ex[ecutor]^s Administrators all and singular the said Negro Wench **Esther** as above mentioned unto the said Major TOWNSEND his heirs and Assigns forever and against all and every other person or persons whatsoever, shall and will Warrant and forever defend against lawfull Claims by these presents of which said Negro Wench **Esther** I the said Thomas Givan SCHOOLFIELD have put the said Major TOWNSEND in full possession. In Testimony whereof I Thomas Givan SCHOOLFIELD have set my hand and Seal this twenty first Day of January Annoque Domini seventeen hundred and seventy four.

Signed Sealed & Delivered	Jesse ENNIS	Thomas Givan SCHOOLFIELD
In the Presence of	John BALL"	

---

[229] Worcester County Court (Land Records). Bill of sale from PORTER, Ezekiel to TOWNSEND, William Barkley. 03 December 1773. I, p. 345, MSA CE 30-9. www.mdlandrec.net : accessed 22 November 2021.
[230] Worcester County Court (Land Records). Deed of Gift from TRUITT, Elizabeth to SELBY, Elizabeth and William. 03 December 17735. I, pp. 345-346, MSA CE 30-9. www.mdlandrec.net : accessed 22 November 2021.

*followed on folio 355 with the acknowledgment by Justice of the Peace Benton HARRIS and recordation by court clerk Henry JOHNSON[231]

Liber I, folios 358-359; January 1774

"Know all Men by these presents that I Joseph GRAY of Worcester County in the Province of Maryland for and in consideration of the natural Love and affection which I bear to my Son Benjamin GRAY as also for and in consideration of the Sum of five pounds Current money of Maryland to me in hand paid by the said Benjamin the receipt whereof I do hereby Acknowledge, have given granted bargained and sold, and by these presents do absolutely give grant bargain and sell unto the said Benjamin GRAY his Heirs and Assigns forever one Negro Boy Slave called **Robin**. To have and to hold the af[oresai]ᵈ Given Granted and Sold Negro Slave called **Robin** as af[ore]s[ai]ᵈ unto the said Benjamin GRAY his heirs & Assigns forever to the only proper use benefit and behoof the said Joseph GRAY during the natural life and then after his decease to the only proper use benefit and behoof of the said Benjamin GRAY his heirs and assigns forever and to and for no other use intent or purpose whatever. And the said Joseph for himself his heirs doth hereby Covenant and agree to and with the said Benjamin and his heirs that the af[oresai]ᵈ Negro Slave **Robin** from any Right Title or Claim that may be derived from by or under him according to the true intent and meaning hereof will Warrant and forever Defend by these presents. In Witness whereof the said Joseph hath hereto set his hand & affixed his Seal this   day of January Anno Dom[ini] 1774./ ~

Signed Sealed & delivered	Rouse HARRISON	
In presence of	Jedidiah GRAY	Joseph T GRAY (Seal)
	John SCHOOLFIELD	his mark"

*followed on folio 359 with the recordation by court clerk Henry JOHNSON[232]

Liber I, folio 364; 11 February 1774

"Worcester Ss.ᵗ Know all Men by these presents that I Joseph GODFREY of the County af[ore]s[ai]ᵈ for and in Consideration of the Sum of sixty pounds curr[en]ᵗ money have Sold and Delivered unto Thomas GRAY Jun[io]ʳ one Negro Boy named **Abner**, which said Negro Boy I hereby do under{?} & promise to Warrant & defend against the Claim or Claims of any & every person whatever. In Witness whereof I have hereunto set my hand affixed my Seal 11ᵗʰ day of Febr[uar]y Anno Domini 1774./. ~ ./. ~

Sealed & Delivered   J. DENNIS   Joseph GODFREY (Seal)
in presence of"

*followed with the acknowledgment by Justice of the Peace J. DENNIS and recordation on 17 February 1774 by court clerk Henry JOHNSON[233]

Liber I, folios 416-417; 29 April 1774

"This Indenture made this twenty ninth Day of April in the Year of our Lord one thousand seven hundred & seventy four Between John SATCHELL of Worcester County in the Province of Maryland of the one part, & George STEWART & Major GUY of Accomack County in the Colony of Virginia of the other part. Witnesseth that the said John SATCHELL for and in Consideration of the sum of two hundred and fifteen pounds common Current money of the Province of Maryland in hand well and truly paid by the said George STEWART & Major GUY before the Execution hereof the Receipt whereof is hereby Acknowledged, hath Bargained and Sold, & by these presents doth Bargain and Sell unto them the said George

---

[231] Worcester County Court (Land Records). Bill of sale from SCHOOLFIELD, Thomas Givan to TOWNSEND, Major. 21 January 1774. I, pp. 354-355, MSA CE 30-9. www.mdlandrec.net : accessed 22 November 2021.
[232] Worcester County Court (Land Records). Bill of sale from GRAY, Joseph to GRAY, Benjamin. January 1774. I, pp. 358-359, MSA CE 30-9. www.mdlandrec.net : accessed 22 November 2021.
[233] Worcester County Court (Land Records). Bill of sale from GODFREY, Joseph to GRAY, Thomas Jr. 11 November 1774. I, p. 364, MSA CE 30-9. www.mdlandrec.net : accessed 22 November 2021.

STEWART and Major GUY their heirs Executors Administrators or Assigns the following Slaves Goods and Chattles that is to say, one Negro Lad Slave named **Joshua**, one Negro Boy named **Stephen**, and Negro Girl named **Levinah**, thirteen head of Horned Cattle fourteen head of Sheep, one Horse called Buck, one Ox Chain, one Sett of Carpenters Joiners & Turners Tools, twenty eight head of Hogs & one Yoke of Shears. To have and to hold the said Slaves Goods & Chattels unto them the said George STEWART & Major GUY their Executors Administrators or Assigns to the only proper use & behoof of them the said George STEWART & Major GUY their Executors Administrators or Assigns, and to or for no other use intent or purpose whatsoever. Provided always and it is the true intent & meaning of this Deed that the said John SATCHELL his Heirs Executors or Administrators shall well and truly pay or cause to be paid unto the said George STEWART & Major GUY or to either of them their Executors Administrators or Assigns the sum of two hundred and fifteen pounds Current money aforesaid on or before the first Day of January next ensuing the date hereof with legal Interest thereon, then this Deed and every Clause therein mentioned to be void, or Else to remain in full force and virtue in Law. In Testimony whereof I have hereto Set my hand & fixed my Seal the Day and Year abovementioned. ~ ./. ~ ./. ~

Sign[e]d Sealed & Delivered   Benton HARRIS   John SATCHELL. (Seal)
In Presence of ………   N. HOLLAND"

*followed with the acknowledgment of Justices of the Peace Benton HARRIS & N. HOLLAND and recordation on folio 417 by court clerk Henry JOHNSON[234]

Liber I, folios 444-445; 14 June 1774

"Maryland Ss. Know all Men by these presents that I David McGEE of Worcester County in the province af[ore]s[ai]^d have Sold & by these presents have Bargain[e]d and Sold unto Elijah SHOCKLEY & his Heirs & Assigns forever all the Right Title & Interest that I have in or to a Negro Woman named **Jane** for and in Consideration of the sum of twenty three pounds six Shillings & Eight pence Current money of af[ore]s[ai]^d to me in hand paid by the said Elijah SHOCKLEY. To have & to hold the af[ore]s[ai]d Negro Woman named **Jane** by the said Elijah SHOCKLEY & his Heirs & Assigns forever & the said David McGEE doth hereby Warrant & Defend the af[ore]s[ai]d Negro Woman named **Jane** against him the said David McGEE & against his Heirs Executors Adm[inistrator]^s or Assigns and against every person whatever Claiming the said Negro **Jane** from by or under him or his Heirs or Assigns forever. In Testimony whereof I hereunto my Hand set & Seal affixt this fourteenth day of June 1774./. ~

Signed Sealed & Delivered   his
In Presence of   David (| McGEE. (Seal)
Joseph DASHIELL   mark"

*followed on folio 445 with the acknowledgment of Justice of the Peace Joseph DASHIELL and recordation on 17 June 1774 by court clerk Henry JOHNSON[235]

Liber I, folio 461; 04 August 1774

"Maryland Worcester County Ss. Know all Men by these Presents that I Joseph GODFREY of Worcester County in the province of Maryland, for and in Consideration of the sum of Eighty pounds Current money of Maryland to me in hand paid by Henry BELL of the place afores[ai]^d at and before the Ensealing and Delivery of these presents wherewith I Confess myself to be fully sattisfied contented and paid, Have Bargained Sold and Delivered, & by these Presents do fully Clearly and absolutely Bargain Sell and Deliver unto the said Henry BELL one Negro Lad named **Abner** about fifteen years old. To have & to hold the said Henry BELL his Heirs

---

[234] Worcester County Court (Land Records). Deed of mortgage from SATCHELL, John to GUY, Major and STEWART, George. 29 April 1774. I, pp. 416-417, MSA CE 30-9. www.mdlandrec.net : accessed 26 November 2021.
[235] Worcester County Court (Land Records). Bill of sale from McGEE, David to SHOCKLEY, Elijah. 14 June 1774. I, pp. 444-445, MSA CE 30-9. www.mdlandrec.net : accessed 26 November 2021.

Executors Administrators and Assigns to his and their proper uses & behoofs forever. And I the said Joseph GODFREY my Heirs Executors & Administrators and every of us the said Negro to the said Henry BELL his Heirs Executors Administrators & Assigns against all Persons shall & will Warrant acquit & forever Defend by these Presents. In Witness whereof I have hereunto set my Hand and Seal the 4th Day of August Anno Domini 1774.

Seal[e]d & Delivered   J. DENNIS   Joseph GODFREY. (Seal)
In the Presence of   Isaac HOUSTON"

*followed with the acknowledgment of J. DENNIS and recordation by court clerk Henry JOHNSON[236]

Liber I, folios 472-473; 02 September 1774

"Know all men by these presents that I Sarah DOWNS of Worcester County in the Province of Maryland for and in Consideration of the sum of five Shillings Current money of the Province af[ore]s[ai]d in hand paid by George DOWNS of the same place the receipt whereof I do hereby acknowledge, do agree bargain and sell a certain Negro Child called **Levin** to him the said George DOWNS his heirs and assigns forever. To have and to hold the above Bargain[e]d and sold Negro Boy called **Levin** unto him the said George DOWNS his heirs and assigns & the said Sarah DOWNS doth agree to and with the said George DOWNS and his heirs that She will Warrant and Defend the above bargained and sold Negro against all and every claim of any person or persons whatsoever Claiming any Right Title or property by from or under her the said Sarah DOWNS heirs and assigns, as Witness my hand and Seal this second Day of September Anno Dom[ini] MDCCLXXIV

Levin HILL.   Benton HARRIS.   Sarah DOWNES. (Seal)"

*followed with the acknowledgment by Justice of the Peace Benton HARRIS and recordation by court clerk Henry JOHNSON[237]

Liber I, folios 475-476; 09 September 1774

"Maryl[an]d Worcest[e]r Co[un]ty Know all by these presents that I James WILLIAMS of the County and Province af[ore]s[ai]d for and in Consideration of the Sum of Eighty pounds Current money of Maryland to me in hand paid, by a certain Joseph RICHARDS at or before the Ensealing & delivery hereof the Receipt whereof I do hereby Acknowledge and of and from every part & parcell thereof doth hereby fully freely and absolutely acquit & discharge the said Joseph RICHARDS, & his heirs forever by these presents, have Given bargained & Sold, and by these presents do hereby Give bargain & sell unto the said Joseph RICHARDS his heirs and Assigns forever one Negro Man Slave named **Will**. To have and to hold the af[ore]s[ai]d bargain[e]d and sold Negro Man Slave named **Will** as af[ore]s[ai]d unto the said Joseph RICHARDS his heirs and Assigns forever, to the only proper use benefit and behalf of the said Joseph RICHARDS his heirs & Assigns forever and to and for no other use or purpose whatever. And the said James WILLIAMS for himself and his heirs doth Covenant & Agree to and with the Joseph RICHARDS and his heirs that the af[ore]s[ai]d Negro Man Slave **Will** as af[ore]s[ai]d against the Right title claim or demand of all and every person whatever unto the said Joseph RICHARDS & his Heirs will Warrant and forever defend. In Witness whereof I have hereto set my Hand and affixed my Seal this ninth day of September Anno Domini 1774.

Sign[e]d Seal[e]d & deliver[e]d   Benton HARRIS   James WILLIAMS. (Seal)
In Presence of   N. HOLLAND"

---

[236] Worcester County Court (Land Records). Bill of sale from GODFREY, Joseph to BELL, Henry. 04 August 1774. I, p. 461, MSA CE 30-9. www.mdlandrec.net : accessed 26 November 2021.
[237] Worcester County Court (Land Records). Bill of sale from DOWNES, Sarah to DOWNES, George. 02 September 1774. I, pp. 472-473, MSA CE 30-9. www.mdlandrec.net : accessed 26 November 2021.

*followed on folio 476 with the acknowledgment of Justices of the Peace Benton HARRIS and N. HOLLAND and the recordation by court clerk Henry JOHNSON[238]

Liber I, folio 481; 21 September 1774

"Worcester Ss. Know all Men by these presents that I John LINGO for and in Consideration of the sum of eighteen Pounds Current money of Maryland to me in hand paid by Mary FOOKS, the receipt whereof I doe by acknowledge, have bargained and sold, and by these presents doe bargain and sell one Negro Fellow call[e]d **Ben** about 34 years of Age. To have and to hold the said Negro **Ben** af[ore]s[ai]d to the said Mary FOOKS her Heirs Executors Administrators and Assigns to her and their proper use. Provided that if I the said John shall pay to the said Mary the said sum of eighteen pounds Current money aforesaid with legall Interest at or upon the first day of March next ensuing the date hereof, then this deed to be void, which said Sum the said John for him self his Heirs Executors and Administrators hereby Covenants with the said Mary to pay. And it is further hereby Concluded by me that if I the said John do not pay to the said Mary the said sum of Eighteen pounds Current money aforesaid with legal Interest thereon on the said first day of March next ensuing the date hereof, then it shall and may be lawfull for the said Mary to take the aforesaid Negro Fellow **Ben** to her own use and him retain as her own property if alive, if dead to recover the aforesaid Eighteen pounds with Interest as aforesaid. In Witness whereof I have hereunto set my Hand and affixed my Seal this 21st day of September one thousand seven hundred and seventy four. /. ~ ./. ~

Sign[e]d Seal[e]d and Delivered   Joseph DASHIELL.   John LINGOE   (Seal)"
In Presence of ……

*followed with the acknowledgment of Joseph DASHIELL and recordation on 28 September 1774 by court clerk Henry JOHNSON[239]

Liber I, folios 482-483; 03 September 1774

"Know all Men by these presents that I Alexander Thomas RUSSELL for an in Consideration of a certain Price RUSSELL's becoming bound for me for several considerable Sums of Money due and owing from me as my own proper debts, who in consequence of the said Securityship hath become chargeable & lyable to pay, as also in and for the further consideration of one hundred pounds current money of Maryland to me in hand paid by the said Price at or before the ensealing and delivery hereof the Receipt whereof I do hereby acknowledge and thereof and every part & parcel thereof doth acquit and discharge the said Price and his heirs forever by these presents and for divers other good Causes and Considerations me hereunto moveing, have given granted bargain[e]d & sold and by these presents doth absolutely give grant bargain & sell to the said Price and his heirs & assigns forever all and singular my Personal Estate of all and every kind whatsoever consisting of the following Negro Slaves, to wit, **Phillis, Robin, Patience, Phebe, Leah, Bella, Jacob, Thomas, Cynta, Cloe,** and **Green** with all my Horses, Cattle, Hogs, Sheep, Household Furniture, Plate & c with all and every of my Estate. To have and to hold all the af[ore]s[ai]d bargained and sold Premisses unto the said Price RUSSELL his heirs and assigns forever, and to the only proper use benefit & behoof of the said Price RUSSELL his heirs and assigns forever and to and for no other use or purpose whatever. In Witness whereof the said Alexander Thomas RUSSELL his hand hath set & Seal affixed this third Day of September anno Dom[ini] one thousand seven hundred and seventy four. ~

Sign[e]d Seal[e]d & delivered   Joseph DASHIELL   Alex tho RUSSELL.   (Seal)
In presence of ~   Ebenezer HANDY"

---

[238] Worcester County Court (Land Records). Bill of sale from WILLIAMS, James to RICHARDS, Joseph. 09 September 1774. I, pp. 475-476, MSA CE 30-9. www.mdlandrec.net : accessed 26 November 2021.
[239] Worcester County Court (Land Records). Deed of mortgage from LINGOE, John to FOOKS, Mary. 21 September 1774. I, p. 481, MSA CE 30-9. www.mdlandrec.net : accessed 26 November 2021.

*followed of folio 483 with the acknowledgment by Justices of the Peace Joseph DASHIELL and Ebenezer HANDY and recordation on 04 October 1774 by court clerk Henry JOHNSON[240]

Liber I, folio 505; 07 November 1774

"Maryland Worcester County. Know all men by these Presents that I Joseph DASHIELL of Worcester County and Province af[oresai]^d Gentleman for and in Consideration of the Sum of two hundred pounds Current money of Maryland to me the same Joseph in hand paid before the Signing and Ensealing of these presents the receipt whereof I do hereby acknowledge, have given granted bargained and sold, and by these presents do give grant bargain sell and confirm unto Josiah DASHIELL Esquire of Somerset County and the Province af[ore]s[ai]^d the following Negro Slaves, to wit, **James, Somerset, Steven, Pompy**. To have and to hold the several Negro Slaves before mentioned to him the s[ai]^d Josiah DASHIELL his Executors Administrators and Assigns forever, & to and for no other use intent or purpose whatsoever. And the same Joseph DASHIELL for himself his heirs Executors & Administrators doth further Covenant & agree to and with the same Josiah DASHIELL his Executors & Administrators that he the same Josiah DASHIELL his heirs Executors & Administrators will forever Warrant & Defend the several before mentioned Negro Slaves to him the said Josiah DASHIELL his Executors Administrators & Assigns from the Claim or Claims of him the said Joseph DASHIELL his heirs Executors Administrators & Assigns or any Person or Persons claiming the same from by or under him the said Joseph DASHIELL his heirs Executors Administrators or Assigns And he said Joseph DASHIELL further covenants to and with the said Josiah DASHIELL that he shall and will hereafter at the reasonable request & at the proper Cost and Expence of the said Josiah make any such further Conveyance or Assurance of the several before mentioned Negro Slaves to him the said Josiah DASHIELL his Executors Administrators or Assigns as by his or their Counsel learned in the Law may be judged necessary. In Testimony whereof the same Joseph hath hereunto set his hand and affixed his Seal this Seventh day of November Anno Domini one thousand seven hundred & seventy four.

Signed Sealed & delivered   Ebenezer HANDY.   Joseph DASHIELL. (Seal)"
In Presence of ....

*followed with the acknowledgment of Justice of the Peace Ebenezer HANDY and recordation on 21 November 1774 by court clerk Henry JOHNSON[241]

Liber I, folio 513; 06 December 1774

"Know all Men by these presents that I James HOUSTON of Worcester County in Maryland for and in Consideration of a Bond by me Executed unto Susanna DENNIS of the County af[ore]s[ai]^d bearing date the sixth day of December Anno Dom[ini] 1774 the Condition whereof is one hundred and twenty two pounds five Shillings with Interest from the date thereof, have given granted & delivered, and by these presents do give grant & deliver unto the af[ore]s[ai]^d Susanna DENNIS her heirs and Assigns forever, the Negroes by name vizt a Negro Man named **David**, a Negro Woman named **Racel**, a Negro Boy named **George**, a Negro Girl named **Hannah** & a small boy called **Abel**. To have & to hold the abovesaid & named Negroes unto the above Susanna DENNIS her heirs and Assigns forever, to the only proper use benefit and behoof of the said Susanna her heirs & assigns forever and to no other purpose or behoof whatever for the Satisfaction & Security of the above Recited Bond & do hereby agree that it shall and may be lawfull for the said Susanna at any time to Sell and Dispose of the said Negroes in and at any fair publick vendue and that the Sale after discharging the said Bond & her necessary Expence about & Concerning the Sale of the premisses & recording of these presents I the said James do Covenant to content myself with. In Testimony whereof I have hereunto Set

---

[240] Worcester County Court (Land Records). Bill of sale from RUSSELL, Alexander Thomas to RUSSELL, Price. 03 September 1774. I, pp. 482-483, MSA CE 30-9. www.mdlandrec.net : accessed 26 November 2021.
[241] Worcester County Court (Land Records). Bill of sale from DASHIELL, Joseph to DASHIELL, Josiah. 07 November 1774. I, p. 505, MSA CE 30-9. www.mdlandrec.net : accessed 26 November 2021.

my Hand and Seal this Sixth day of December in the year of our Lord one thousand Seven hundred and seventy four. ~

Sign[e]d Seal[e]d Acknowledged and Deliver[e]d In presence of	Mary POLIT John TEACKLE"	James HOUSTON (Seal)

*followed on 16 December 1774 with the acknowledgment of Justice of the Peace Benton HARRIS and the recordation by court clerk Henry JOHNSON[242]

Liber I, folio 523; 17 December 1774

"Know all Men by these presents that I William MASON of Worcester County in the Province of Maryland Labourer for & in the Consideration of seventy five pounds Pensilvania Currency to me in hand paid before the Sealing & delivery of these presents by Edward DINGLE the receipt whereof I do hereby acknowledge, have bargained & sold by these presents do bargain & Sell unto Edward DINGLE a Negro Boy named **Jabe** with all his Wearing Apparel. To have & to hold the afores[ai]^d Negro **Jabe** with his Wearing Apparel unto Edward DINGLE & his Heirs forever & I do hereby give S[ai]^d Edward DINGLE by these presents a Quit Claim to said Negro from myself & my Heirs forever & I the said W[illia]m MASON will Warrant & Defend S[ai]^d Negro **Jabe** to Edward DINGLE & his Heirs forever from all Persons, which said Negro I the said Mason have the s[ai]^d Edward DINGLE full Possession of by delivering the s[ai]^d Negro to Edward DINGLE in the presents of the Subscribing Witnesses this 17th day of December 1774./. ~

Signed Sealed & Delivered in the Presence of us	James MITCHELL Benjamin MILLS"	W[illia]^m MASON. (Seal)

*followed by the acknowledgment of Jos[hu]^a MITCHELL and recordation on 30 December 1774 by court clerk Henry JOHNSON[243]

Liber I, folio 524; 30 December 1774

"Know all Men by these presents that I Mary WATSON of Worcester County in the Province of Maryland for and in Consideration of the sum of sixty three Pounds fifteen Shillings Current Money to me in hand paid by James WILLIAMS of the County and Province af[ore]s[ai]^d whereof I do hereby acknowledge the Receipt, and my self therewith fully satisfied, and have Bargained Sold Setover and Delivered unto the said James WILLIAMS one Negro woman called **Tamer** and her Child **Esther**. To have and to hold the bargained Negro woman **Tamer** and her Child **Esther** unto the said James WILLIAMS his Heirs Executors Administrators and Assigns forever freely quietly peaceably and entirely without any Contradiction Claims disturbance or hindrance of any Person whatsoever, so that neither I the said Mary WATSON or any other for me in my name have any Right Title interest or Demand of in to or for the said Negro woman **Tamer** and her Child **Esther** or any part or parcel thereof ought to Exact Challenge Claim or Demand at any time or times hereafter But from all Action Right title Claims or demand thereof shall be wholy barred and excluded by force and virtue of these presents. And I the said Mary WATSON for myself my heirs Executors and Administrators the said Bargained Negro **Tamer** and her Child unto the said James WILLIAMS his Heirs Executors Administrators and Assigns and against all and every other Person or Persons whatsoever shall and will Warrant and forever defend by these presents. In Witness whereof I have hereunto Set my hand and Seal affixed this thirtieth day of December in the Year of our Lord one thousand seven hundred and seventy four. ~

---

[242] Worcester County Court (Land Records). Bill of sale from HOUSTON, James to DENNIS, Susanna. 06 December 1774. I, p. 513, MSA CE 30-9. www.mdlandrec.net : accessed 26 November 2021.
[243] Worcester County Court (Land Records). Bill of sale from MASON, William to DINGLE, Edward. 17 December 1774. I, p. 523, MSA CE 30-9. www.mdlandrec.net : accessed 26 November 2021.

		her	
Signed Sealed & delivered	Benton HARRIS		
In presence of ………	N. HOLLAND	Mary + WATSON (Seal)	
		mark"	

*followed by the acknowledgment of Justices of the Peace Benton HARRIS and N. HOLLAND and recordation by the court clerk Henry JOHNSON[244]

Liber I, folio 539; 31 January 1775

"Maryland Worcester County Ss. To all Christian People to whom these presents may come in our Lord God everlasting. Know ye that I Mary King WHITTINGTON of the County & Province af[ore]s[ai]^d for and in Consideration of the natural Love Affection & good will I have for & bare unto my Son William WHITTINGTON and Infant born after the Death of his father William WHITTINGTON and not provided for by his said father last Will & Testament, I do freely willingly and of my own accord out of my Dower or thirds Give Grant & Confirm unto him the said William WHITTINGTON (my Son) and by these present Deed of Gift do Give Grant & Confirm unto him the said William WHITTINGTON & his Heirs & Assigns forever, one Negro Woman called **Nan** and her Child **Esther** and their Increase to him my said Son William WHITTINGTON & to his heirs Executors & Adm[inistrator]^s & Assigns forever without any lett Molestation or hindrance whatever from me or Heirs or Assigns or any other Person whatever Claiming from by or under me my Heirs or Assigns. In Testimony whereof I have hereunto my Hand set & Seal affixt this thirty first Day of January anno Domini 1775.

Signed Sealed & delivered	Joseph DASHIELL	Mary King WHITTINGTON (Seal)
In Presence of us …..	Benton HARRIS"	

*followed by the acknowledgment Justice of the Peace Joseph DASHIELL and the recordation on 03 February 1775 by court clerk Henry JOHNSON[245]

Liber I, folios 540-541; 04 February 1775

"Know all Men by these Presents that I John DENNIS of Worcester County in the Province of Maryland for and in Consideration of the sum of seventy one pounds ten Shillings common money to me in hand paid by a certain William MORRIS at or before the Ensealing & delivery hereof the Receipt whereof hereby acknowledge and the said William MORRIS his heirs Executors and Adm[inistrator]^s and every of them do hereby fully & absolutely acquit & forever discharge by these presents, have bargain[e]d sold & deliver[e]d, and by these presents do absolutely bargain sell & deliver unto the said William MORRIS his heirs and assigns forever one Negro Man Slave named **Harry**. To have and to hold the af[ore]s[ai]d Negro Man Slave called **Harry** as af[ore]s[ai]^d bargain[e]d & sold unto the said William MORRIS his heirs & Assigns forever, and to the only proper use benefit and behoof of the said William MORRIS his heirs & assigns forever, and to and for no other use intent & purpose whatever. And the said John DENNIS doth for himself his heirs Ex[ecutor]^s & Adm[inistrator]^s covenant and agree to and with the said William MORRIS his heirs Ex[ecutor]^s & Adm[inistrator]^s that the af[ore]s[ai]^d bargain[e]d & sold Negro Slave call[e]d **Harry** from all and every person or persons claiming any Right Title Interest or Property in the said Negro Slave, unto the said William MORRIS his heirs Ex[ecutor]^s Adm[inistrator]^s or Assigns will Warrant & forever Defend by these presents. In Witness whereof I the said John DENNIS do set my Hand and affix my Seal this 4th day of February anno Dom[ini] 1775.

Sign[e]d Seal[e]d & deliver[e]d	W[illia]m BACON	J. DENNIS. (Seal)
In Presence of …..	Rob[er]^t DONE"	

---

[244] Worcester County Court (Land Records). Bill of sale from WATSON, Mary to WILLIAMS, James. 30 December 1774. I, p. 524, MSA CE 30-9. www.mdlandrec.net : accessed 26 November 2021.
[245] Worcester County Court (Land Records). Deed of gift from WHITTINGTON, Mary King to WHITTINGTON, William. 31 January 1775. I, p. 539, MSA CE 30-9. www.mdlandrec.net : accessed 26 November 2021.

*followed on folio 541 with the acknowledgment of Justice of the Peace William BACON and the recordation by court clerk Henry JOHNSON[246]

Liber I, folios 545-546; 06 February 1775

"I Comfort WATSON of Worcester County in the Province of Maryland for and in Consideration of the Sum of fifty pounds to her in hand paid by Darby RIGGEN hath Granted Bargained and Sold unto the said Darby RIGGEN two Negro Girls the one Called **Dinah** the other called **Hannah**, which said two Negro Girls I the said Comfort WATSON do Warrant and forever Defend from myself my heirs and all other Persons whatsoever, unto the said Darby RIGGEN his heirs and assigns forever As Witness my hand and seal this sixth day of Febr[uar]y anno Dom[ini] 1775.

Test. J.B. SCHOOLFIELD
Joshua DICKERSON

Comfort + WATSON (Seal)
(her mark)"

*followed on folio 546 with the recordation by court clerk Henry JOHNSON on 21 February 1775[247]

Liber I, folios 559-560; 04 March 1775

"To all Persons to whome this present writing shall come, I Mary COX of Worcester County in the Province of Maryland send Greeting. Know ye that I the said Mary COX for and in Consideration of the sum of six Shillings Current money to me in hand paid by Sarah FLEMING of the County and Province aforesaid, but more especially for the Love and Good will that I the said Mary COX have for my Loving Daughter Sarah FLEMING the now Wife of John FLEMING and in a further Consideration of the Maintainance of the said Mary COX dureing her natural Life that She the said Mary COX hath Given Granted and Sold, and by these presents do fully clearly & absolutely Give Grant Bargain and Sell unto the said Sarah FLEMING all and singular my Negros to wit One Negro Woman called **Eby**, also one Negro Girl called **Leah**, Also one Negro Girl named **Jenny**, Also one Negro Boy called **Adam**, all which Negros I Give unto my loving Daughter Sarah Fleming the now wife of John FLEMING during her natural Life, and after the Decease of the said Sarah FLEMING I Give the aforesaid Negros to be Equally devided between the now Children of the said Sarah FLEMING to them and their heirs and assigns forever, And also I Give unto my loving Daughter all and singular such of my Goods and Chattles as the afores[ai]d John FLEMING has now in his possession, also two thirds of my Stock Cattle Hoggs and Corn that the said Mary COX has in Somerset County. To have and to hold all and singular the Goods, Chattles, Implements of Household and Commodities whatsoever as aforesaid, to the aforesaid Sarah FLEMING her heirs Executors Administrators and Assigns to her and their only proper uses and behoofs forever hereof and therewith to do, use, and Dispose at her will and pleasure as of her and their own proper Goods and Chattels without any manner of Challenge Claim or Demand of me the said Mary COX or of any other Person or Persons from me in my name by my Cause, means Consent Procurement, and further know ye that I the said Mary COX have put the said Sarah FLEMING in full possession of all and singular the aforesaid Premises by the Delivery unto her as the Ensealing hereof As Witness my hand and Seal this fourth day of March anno Dom[ini] 1775.

Signed Sealed & Delivered
in Presence of

W[illia]m ALLEN
Edward HINDMAN

Mary X Cox. (Seal)
(her mark)"

---

[246] Worcester County Court (Land Records). Bill of sale from DENNIS, John to MORRIS, William. 04 February 1775. I, pp. 540-541, MSA CE 30-9. www.mdlandrec.net : accessed 26 November 2021.

[247] Worcester County Court (Land Records). Bill of sale from WATSON, Comfort to RIGGEN, Darby. 06 February 1775. I, pp. 545-546, MSA CE 30-9. www.mdlandrec.net : accessed 26 November 2021.

*followed on folio 560 with the acknowledgment by Justice of the Peace William ALLEN and the recordation on 08 March 1775 by court clerk Henry JOHNSON[248]

Liber I, folios 560-561; 04 March 1775

"To all Persons to whom this writing shall come, I Mary COX of Worcester County in the Province of Maryland Greeting. Know ye that I the said Mary COX for and in Consideration of the sum of Six Shillings current money to me in hand by Elizabeth HENDERSON of the County and Province afores[ai]^d but more Especially for the love and good will that that the said Mary COX hath for her loving Daughter Elizabeth HENDERSON the now Wife of William HENDERSON, and a further Consideration of the maintainance of said Mary COX during her natural Life, that She the said Mary COX hath given granted and sold, and by these presents do fully clearly and absolutely give grant bargain and sell unto the said Elizabeth HENDERSON the use of the two following Negroes, to wit, my Negro Wench called **Beck** & my Negro Girl called **Priss** during her natural Life & after her decease I give the aforesaid Negro Girl called **Priss** to my Grand Daughter Sarah Cox HENDERSON, if she survive her said Mother, and also I give the aforesaid Negro Wench called **Beck** to my Grand Daughter Rachel Handy COULBOURN if She survive her said Mother, and the future Increase of the said Negro Wench called **Beck** to be equally divided between them but if either of them should die before their said Mother then the aforesaid two Negroes to go to the Survivor, but if both my said Grand Daughters should die before their said Mother then I give the aforesaid two Negroes and their future Increase to be equally divided between such of my daughter Elizabeth HENDERSON's Children as shall be then living, I also Give unto my daughter Elizabeth HENDERSON all & singular Goods & Chattels that the aforesaid W[illia]m HENDERSON has in Possession also one third of my Cattle & Hoggs, and one third of my Corn that I the said Mary COX hath in Somerset County. To have and to hold the aforesaid Negroes Goods Chattels as before directed to the only proper use & behoof of the said Elizabeth HENDERSON as before directed, And further know ye that I he said Mary COX hath put the said Elizabeth HENDERSON in full Possession of the aforesaid Negroes Goods & Chattels be delivering the same unto her before the Ensealing and Delivery hereof As Witness my Hand & Seal this fourth day of March in the year of our Lord seventeen hundred and seventy five. ~

Signed and Delivered	W[illia]m ALLEN	
In the presence of	Edward HINDMAN	Mary + COX. (Seal) her mark"

*followed on folio 561 with the acknowledgment by Justice of the Peace William ALLEN and the recordation on 08 March 1775 by court clerk Henry JOHNSON[249]

Liber I, folios 577-578; 04 March 1775

"This Indenture made this fourth day of March in the year of our Lord seventeen hundred and seventy five. Between Peter CALLAWAY of Worcester County of the one part, and William McBRYDE of Somerset County of the other part. Witnesseth that the said Peter CALLAWAY for and in Consideration of the sum of one hundred and twenty nine pounds twelve Shillings & nine pence Current money due and owing by the said Peter CALLAWAY to the said William McBRYDE, as also for and in Consideration of the further sum of thirty one pounds Current money of Maryland, to him in hand paid by the said William McBRYDE at and before the Sealing & delivery hereof the Receipt whereof the said Peter hereby doth acknowledge that he hath bargained and Sold, and by these presents doth bargain and sell unto the said William McBRYDE his heirs Executors Adm[inistrator]^s and Assigns the following Negro Slaves, to wit, one Fellow named **Will**, one Fellow named **Bob**, one Wench named **Pleasant**, one Boy named **Abner**, and one Child named **Name**, unto the said William McBRYDE his heirs

---

[248] Worcester County Court (Land Records). Deed of gift from COX, Mary to FLEMING, Sarah. 04 March 1775. I, pp. 559-560, MSA CE 30-9. www.mdlandrec.net : accessed 26 November 2021.
[249] Worcester County Court (Land Records). Deed of gift from COX, Mary to HENDERSON, Elizabeth. 04 March 1775. I, pp. 560-561, MSA CE 30-9. www.mdlandrec.net : accessed 26 November 2021.

Executors Adm[inistrator]^s and Assigns forever. To have and to hold the af[oresai]^d Negro Slaves unto the af[oresai]^d William McBRYDE his heirs and Assigns forever to and for the only proper use and behoof of the said William McBRYDE his heirs and assigns forever, and to and for no other use or purpose whatsoever. And the said Peter CALLAWAY doth by these presents for himself his heirs Executors and Adm[inistrator]^s covenant grant and agree to and with the said William McBRYDE his heirs and Assigns forever that he the said Peter CALLAWAY his heirs Executors and Adm[inistrator]^s will at all times hereafter Warrant and Defend all and singular the af[oresai]^d Bargain and Sold Negro Slaves against the Claim right and title of all and every person or persons Claiming or that shall hereafter Claim the same or any of them, unto the said William McBRYDE his heirs and assigns forever. Provided allways and it is the true intent and meaning hereof that if the af[oresai]^d Peter CALLAWAY his heirs Ex[ecutor]^s or Adm[inistrator]^s do and shall on or before the first day of August in the year of our Lord seventeen hundred and seventy six pay or cause to be paid unto the said William McBRYDE his heirs Ex[ecutor]^s Adm[inistrator]^s or Assigns the af[oresai]^d sum of one hundred and twenty nine pounds twelve Shillings & nine pence Current money af[oresai]^d now due and owing by the said Peter CALLAWAY to the said William McBRYDE with the legal Interest thereon, as also the other sum of thirty one pounds Current money af[oresai]^d mentioned to be now paid by the said McBRYDE unto the said CALLAWAY before the Sealing and Delivery hereof with the legal Interest thereon together with the making and Recording this deed, then the above Indenture and all things therein contained to be void and of no effect as if the same had never been made. And the af[oresai]^d Peter CALLAWAY doth by these presents for himself his heirs Ex[ecutor]s and Adm[inistrator]s further covenant grant and agree to and with the said William McBRYDE his heirs and assigns that he the said Peter CALLAWAY his heirs Ex[ecutor]^s and Adm[inistrator]^s will well and truly on or before the day and year last af[oresai]^d pay or cause to be paid unto the said William McBRYDE his heirs or assigns the two several Sums of Money af[oresai]^d with legal Interest thereon together with the Cost of Executing and Recording this present writing and further that in case the several Sums of Money af[oresai]^d should be unpaid on the day and year af[oresai]^d for the payment thereof mentioned or any part thereof that than it shall be lawfull for the said William McBRYDE to take into his possession the Negroes af[oresai]^d and expose the same to publick Sale and retain and apply the Money arising from such Sale to the discharge of his the said McBRYDE several debts af[oresai]^d with the Interest thereon due and if any overplus to return the same to the said CALLAWAY his heirs Executors Adm[inistrator]^s or Assigns. And further that he the said Peter CALLAWAY his heirs Ex[ecutor]^s or Administrators will on the Request of the said William McBRYDE his heirs or Assigns upon such Sale of the Negroes af[oresai]^d Release his the said Peter CALLAWAY's Equity of Redemption of in and unto all or any of the Negroes af[oresai]^d so as af[oresai]^d to be sold unto the said William McBRYDE his heirs or assigns. In Witness whereof the said Peter CALLAWAY to these presents his hand hath set and Seal affixed the day & year first above written.

Signed Sealed & Delivered   Peter CALLAWAY. (Seal)
In Presence of ~
W[illia]m ELLEGOOD.   George GRUMBLE."

*followed on folio 578 with the acknowledgment by Justice of the Peace William ELLEGOOD and the recordation on 17 March 1775 by court clerk Henry JOHNSON[250]

Liber I, folios 583-584; 29 March 1775

"This Indenture made this 29th day of March in the year of our Lord God one thousand seven hundred & seventy five. Between Wilson BROWN & Nehemiah TOWNSEND of Worcester County in the Province of Maryland of the one part & Thomas BENSON of Somerset County of the other part. Witnesseth that the abovesaid Wilson BROWN & Nehemiah TOWNSEND for & in Consideration of the sum of twenty pounds lawfull Money of Maryland to them in

---

[250] Worcester County Court (Land Records). Deed of mortgage from CALLAWAY, Peter to McBRYDE, William. 04 March 1775. I, pp. 577-578, MSA CE 30-9. www.mdlandrec.net : accessed 26 November 2021.

hand paid by the said Thomas BENSON at or before the Ensealing and Delivery hereof the receipt whereof they the said Wilson BROWN & Nehemiah doth hereby confess and acknowledge, hath Granted Bargained and Sold, and by these presents doth Grant Bargain and Sell unto the said Thomas BENSON his heirs and assigns forever, all that part of a Tract of Land called Turners Choice situate lying and being in Worcester County aforesaid and **where one William JOHNSON (Molato) now Liveth**, and near the Plantation or Parcel of Land that the said Thomas BENSON bought of James ATKINSON Bounded as followeth. Begining at a marked Red Oak being the second Bounder of the original Tract of Land called Turners Choice, thence Runing South South East thirty six perches thence south eighty one degrees East one hundred and thirty one perches, thence North eleven degrees West ninety four perches, and from thence with a Line drawn to the begining containing fifty Acres of Land more or Less, and the Reversion and Reversions Remainder and Remainders Rents Issues & Profits thereof and every part and parsel thereof with the Appurtenances to the same belonging unto him the said Thomas BENSON his heirs and assigns forever. To have and to hold the af[oresai]^d part of a Tract of Land called Turners Choice as is above Described with the Appurtenances to the same belonging unto the said Thomas BENSON his heirs and assigns, to the only proper use and behoof of the said Thomas BENSON his heirs and assigns forever. And they the said Wilson BROWN & Nehemiah TOWNSEND for themselves their heirs Executors and Administrators doth Covenant Grant and Agree to & with the said Thomas BROWN his heirs and Assigns that they the said Wilson BROWN and Nehemiah TOWNSEND their heirs Executors Administrators the Lands and Premisses hereby before Granted Bargained and Sold unto him the said Thomas BENSON hie heirs and assigns against the lawful Claim Right and Title of them the said Wilson BROWN & Nehemiah TOWNSEND their heirs and assigns and every other person now Claiming or hereafter to Claim, unto him the said Thomas BENSON his heirs and assigns forever, they the said Wilson BROWN & Nehemiah TOWNSEND shall and will Warrant and forever Defend by these presents. In Witness whereof the Parties aforesaid to this present Indenture their hands have set and Seals affixed the day and year above written./.~

Signed Sealed & Delivered   Jn° SCARBOROUGH   Wilson BROWN (Seal)
in Presence off   John SELBY   Nehemiah TOWNSEND (Seal)"

*followed on folio 584 with the acknowledgment of Justices of the Peace John SELBY and John SCARBOROUGH, the receipt of the alienation fine by Parker SELBY, and the recordation by court clerk Henry JOHNSON[251]

Liber I, folio 599; 13 May 1775

"Maryland Worcester Ss. To all Persons Greeting. Know that I Elizabeth LANE of Worcester County and Province af[oresai]^d have for and in consideration of the sum of one Shilling Current money of Maryland this thirteenth day of May in the year of our Lord one thousand seven hundred & seventy five, in hand paid by Jedediah GRAY of the County afores[ai]^d have Bargained Sold and Delivered, and by these presents do bargain sell & deliver unto Eleanor GRAY Wife of Jedediah GRAY & unto the children of the afores[ai]^d Eleanor one Negro Girl called **Hanah** & her Increase. To have and hold unto the said Eleanor GRAY and her Children to them their heirs Executors Administrators or Assigns forever to their own proper use and behoof. And I the said Elizabeth LANE do by these presents Exonerate and Discharge the above mentioned Negro Girl called **Hanah** to the above mentioned Eleanor GRAY & her Children, and the aforesaid Elizabeth LANE do Warrant & defend from all Persons whatsoever to them the said Negro to them their heirs & assigns forever As Witness my Hand and Seal the Day and year above written ~
In presence of W[illia]m LANE

            her   her
          Rachel + MILLS   Elizabeth (| | LANE (Seal)
           mark   mark"

---

[251] Worcester County Court (Land Records). Deed from BROWN, Wilson and TOWNSEND, Nehemiah to BENSON, Thomas. 29 March 1775. I, pp. 583-584, MSA CE 30-9. www.mdlandrec.net : accessed 26 November 2021.

*followed with the recordation by court clerk Henry JOHNSON on 15 May 1775[252]

Liber I, folio 609; 16 June 1775

"To all Persons to whom these presents shall come Greeting. Know ye that we Jabez FISHER, James DAUGHERTY, and Zadock WRIGHT for and in consideration of the sum of five Shillings currency to us paid by Purnell WRIGHT at and before the Sealing and Delivery hereof the receipt whereof the said Jabez, James, and Zadock do hereby acknowledge do Bargain and Sell unto the said Purnell WRIGHT all our Right, Title, Interest, Claim and Demand of in and unto a Negro Boy named **Will**, formerly the property of Hezekiah WRIGHT late of Worcester County deceased (which said Negro we James DAUGHERTY and Zadock WRIGHT claim part of as Representatives of the said Hezekiah) and the said Jabez as Guardian to his Children who are likewise Representatives of the said Hezekiah. To have and to hold the said Negro Boy unto the said Purnell his Heirs and Assigns forever, to the only proper use of the said Purnell his Heirs and Assigns and for no other use whatever. In Testimony whereof we have hereto set our Hands and Seals the 16th of June 1775.

Sealed & delivered　　　　　　　　　　　　　　　　　　　　Jabez FISHER.　(Seal)
in presence of　　　　　　　　　　　　　　　　　　　　　James DAUGHERTY.　(Seal)
John SELBY.　Abraham Outten STURGIS.　　　　　　Zadock WRIGHT　(Seal)"

*followed with the acknowledgment by Justice of the Peace John SELBY and the recordation by court clerk Henry JOHNSON[253]

Liber I, folio 628; 23 August 1775

"To all Christian People to whom these Presents shall come, Greeting. Know ye that I John POLLITT of Somerset County and Province of Maryland, for and in Consideration of the sum of one hundred & twenty five Pounds common Money of Maryland to me in hand paid by Isaac HOUSTON of Worcester County and Province afores[ai]d at or before the Sealing and Delivering of the presents, the Receipt whereof the said John POLLITT doth hereby acknowledge, have bargained and sold, and by these presents do bargain and sell unto the said Isaac HOUSTON one Negro Slave called **Rose**, one Negroe Slave called **Hagar**, one Negroe Slave called **Athallah**, and one Negroe Slave called **Zepheniah**. To have and to hold the said Negroe Slaves unto the said Isaac HOUSTON his heirs & assigns forever to the only proper use and behoof of the said Isaac HOUSTON his heirs and assigns forever and for no other use of purpose whatsoever. And the said John POLLITT for himself and his heirs doth Covenant and Agree to and with the said Isaac HOUSTON and his heirs that he the said John POLLITT and his heirs the Negroe Slaves aforesaid, unto the said Isaac HOUSTON and his heirs shall and will Warrant and forever Defend And the said John POLLITT doth Covenant to and with the said Isaac HOUSTON that he the said John POLLITT hath a good title to sell and dispose of the said Negroes so as to Convey unto the said Isaac HOUSTON a good sure and firm title to the same, And that no person but the said John POLLITT hath any Right or Title to the same. In Testimony whereof the John POLLITT to these presents his hand hath put and seal affixed the twenty third Day of August anno Dom[ini] one thousand seven hundred & seventy five.

Sealed & Delivered　　N. HOLLAND　　　　　　　　　　　John POLLITT　(Seal)
in presence of …　　　Thomas STURGIS."

*followed with the acknowledgment by Justice of the Peace N. HOLLAND and the recordation on 12 September 1775 by court clerk Henry JOHNSON[254]

---

[252] Worcester County Court (Land Records). Bill of sale from LANE, Elizabeth to GRAY, Eleanor. 13 May 1775. I, p. 599, MSA CE 30-9. www.mdlandrec.net : accessed 26 November 2021.

[253] Worcester County Court (Land Records). Deed from FISHER, Jabez, DAUGHERTY, James, and WRIGHT, Zadock to WRIGHT, Purnell. 16 June 1775. I, p. 609, MSA CE 30-9. www.mdlandrec.net : accessed 27 November 2021.

[254] Worcester County Court (Land Records). Bill of sale from POLLITT, John to HOUSTON, Isaac. 23 August 1775. I, p. 628, MSA CE 30-9. www.mdlandrec.net : accessed 27 November 2021.

Liber I, folio 640; 06 January 1776

"This Indenture made this Sixteenth day of January anno Domini one thousand seven hundred and seventy six. Between Daniel MIFFLIN Sen[io]^r and Daniel MIFFLIN jun[io]^r of Worcester County of the one part, and Negroes **Frank (alias Frank ALLEN), James (called Kent JAMES)** and **Sophia** his wife with their Children to wit **Hanah Ben Rhoda Betty Fisher Ned Peggy** and **Betty BLAKE** with her Children to witt **Susey BLAKE Comfort BLAKE John BLAKE Mary BLAKE Hannah BLAKE** they and every of them being under the age of fifty years of the other part. Witnesseth that the said Daniel MIFFLIN Sen[io]^r & Daniel MIFFLIN jun[io]^r for and in Consideration of the Justice due them from us and the faithful Service of the abovementioned Negroes and their good {? ? ? ? ? ?} the said Negroes should be Manumited and forever set free from slavery. Reserving to ourselves the Guardianship & possession of the youth until the Male young ones arrive to the age of twenty one & the female young ones until the arrive to the age of Eighteen years after which we have Manumited set free and forever Discharged, and by these presents doth Manumit set free and forever discharge the said Negroes and their Issue from the said Daniel MIFFLIN Sen[io]^r & Daniel MIFFLIN jun[io]^r their Heirs and assigns And the said Daniel MIFFLIN Sen[io]^r & Daniel MIFFLIN jun[io]^r doth Covenant and agree to and with the said Negroes and their Heirs that they are by these presents forever Manumited and set free and that the said Daniel MIFFLIN Sen[io]^r & Daniel MIFFLIN jun[io]^r Our Heirs Executors or Administrators hath not nor shall have any Right title Interest Claim or Demand of in or unto the said Negroes more than above Reserved or either of them their or either of their Heirs. In Testimony whereof the said Daniel MIFFLIN Sen[io]^r and Daniel MIFFLIN jun[io]^r to these presents their hands hath put and Seals affixed the day and year abovementioned. ~ ./. ~ .

Sealed & Delivered	N. HOLLAND	Daniel MIFFLIN Sen[io]^r	(Seal)
In the presence of	John ALLEN	Daniel MIFFLIN Jun[io]^r	(Seal)"

*followed with the acknowledgment by Justice of the Peace N. HOLLAND and the recordation on 19 January 1776 by court clerk Henry JOHNSON[255]

Liber I, folio 641-642; 07 February 1776

"Maryland Worcester County Ss. Know all Men by these presents that I Sarah HAZZARD of Worcester County in the Province of Maryland for and consideration of the sum of twenty Pounds current money of Maryland to me in hand paid by Elihu HAZZARD of the County and Province aforesaid before the Sealing and Delivery of these presents & for the natural Affection which I have for him & for his { ? ? ? ? } to me in my Old Age wherewith I confess my self to be fully Sattisfied contented and paid Have Bargained Sold & Delivered, & by these presents do fully clearly & absolutely Bargain Sell & Deliver unto the said Elihu HAZZARD One Negro Woman called **Siss** & one Negro Girl called **Libb**. To have & to hold the said Negro Woman **Siss** & Negro Girl **Libb** unto the said Elihu HAZZARD his Heirs Executors Administrators & Assigns, to his & their own proper uses & behoofs forever. And I the said Sarah HAZZARD for myself my Heirs Executors & Administrators & every of us the said Negroes to the said Elihu his Heirs & Assigns against all People shall & will Warrant Acquit & Defend by these presents. In Testimony whereof the said Sarah HAZZARD to these Presents her hand hath set & Seal affixed this seventh Day of February A.D. 1776./. ~ ./. ~

Signed Sealed & Delivered	Jos[hu]^a MITCHELL	
In the Presence of us	Benjamin GRAY	Sarah + HAZZARD Seal (her mark)"

---

[255] Worcester County Court (Land Records). Deed of manumission from MIFFLIN, Daniel Sr. and MIFFLIN, Daniel Jr. to **ALLEN, Frank, JAMES, Kent, and BLAKE, Betty**, etal. 06 January 1776. I, p. 640, MSA CE 30-9. www.mdlandrec.net : accessed 27 November 2021.

*followed on folio 642 with the acknowledgment by Justice of the Peace Joshua MITCHELL and the recordation on 08 February 1776 by court clerk Henry JOHNSON[256]

Liber I, folios 642-643; 09 February 1776

"Know all Persons whom it may concern, That I Thomas POINTER of Worcester County in the Province of Maryland for and in Consideration of the Sum of seventy nine pounds ten Shillings, Lawfull money of this Province, to me in hand paid by Michael PURKINS & Benjamin PURNELL Jun[io]r the receipt whereof I do hereby acknowledge, have bargained sold & delivered, and by these presents, according to the due form of Law, do bargain sell & deliver unto the said Michael PURKINS & Benjamin PURNELL Jun[io]r the Negro Wench called **Jone** & her Child She has called **Leah** & an Assinement of Acc[oun]t against Duncan MURRAY of Eight pounds ten Shillings. To have & to hold the said bargained premisses unto the said Michael PURKINS & Benjamin PURNELL Jun[io]r their Executors Administrators & Assigns forever. And I the said Thomas POINTER for my self my Executors and Administrators, the said bargained Premisses unto the said Michael PURKINS & Benjamin PURNELL jun[io]r their Executors Administrators and Assigns against all persons shall and will Warrant and forever Defend by these presents. Provided nevertheless that if I the said Thomas POINTER my Executors Administrators or Assigns, or any of us, do & shall well & truly pay or cause to be paid unto the said Michael PURKINS & Benjamin PURNELL Jun[io]r their Executors Administrators or Assigns the sum of seventy nine pounds ten Shillings as Principal and Interest lawfull money of this Province for Redemption of the Bargained Premisses, then this present Bill of Sale shall be void and of none effect, But if default be made in the payment of the said seventy nine pounds ten Shillings in part or in the whole contrary to the manner & form before said that then it shall remain and in full force and virtue In Witness whereof I have hereunto Set my Hand & Seal, the ninth day of February anno Dom[ini] one thousand seven hundred and seventy six"

*The bottom of the page which included the witnesses, signatures, and seals is cut off.

*followed on folio 643 with the acknowledgment by Justice of the Peace William BACON and the recordation by court clerk Henry JOHNSON[257]

Liber I, folio 643; 14 February 1776

"Maryland Worcester County Ss. Know all Men by these presents that I John DENNIS of the County & Province aforesaid for and in consideration of a debt to Mr. William BALL of Philadelphia together with the Interest thereon to the Eleventh day of April next amounting to fifty six pounds three Shillings Pensylvania Currency have by these presents Sold & made over unto the s[ai]d W[illia]m BALL all three Negroes Viz one young Negro woman named **Roday** fifteen years old, one other named **Priss** fourteen years old, one other named **Leah** eight years old, all which s[ai]d Negroes I do hereby Engage to warrant & defend against all persons whatever to the s[ai]d W[illia]m BALL his heirs & assigns which said Negroes or as many as will discharge the above debt of fifty six pounds three Shillings with legal Interest, the said BALL his heirs or assigns shall be at liberty to Expose to public Vendue provided the s[ai]d J. DENNIS or his heirs shall not discharge the above debt & interest before the first day of May anno Domini one thousand seven hundred & seventy seven. In Witness whereof I have hereunto set my hand & affixed my Seal this 14th day of February A.D. 1776./. ~

Signed Sealed & Delivered	John BOWIE	J. DENNIS. (Seal)
In the presence of ~~	Henry SNEAD"	

---

[256] Worcester County Court (Land Records). Bill of sale from HAZZARD, Sarah to HAZZARD, Elihu. 07 February 1776. I, pp. 641-642, MSA CE 30-9. www.mdlandrec.net : accessed 27 November 2021.

[257] Worcester County Court (Land Records). Bill of sale from POINTER, Thomas to PURKINS, Michael and PURNELL, Benjamin Jr. 09 February 1776. I, pp. 642-643, MSA CE 30-9. www.mdlandrec.net : accessed 27 November 2021.

*followed with the acknowledgment by Justice of the Peace Jos[hu]ª MITCHELL and the recordation on 15 February 1776 by court clerk Henry JOHNSON[258]

Liber K, folio 22; 06 November 1776

"Know all Men by these Presents that I Elijah SHOCKLEY of Worcester County in the Province of Maryland for and in Consideration of the Sum of thirty pounds Current money of Maryland to me paid at and before the Sealing and Delivery of these presents by Henry JOHNSON of the County and Province afores[ai]ᵈ the receipt whereof I the said Elijah SHOCKLEY do hereby acknowledge Have Bargained Sold and Delivered and by these presents do bargain Sell and Deliver unto the said Henry JOHNSON his Heirs Ex[ecutor]ˢ Adm[inistrator]ˢ or Assigns one Negro Boy Slave called and known by the name of **Eli** who is supposed to be about Six years of Age. To have & to hold the said Negro Boy called **Eli** by these presents Bargained and Sold as aforesaid unto the said Henry JOHNSON his Heirs Ex[ecutor]ˢ and Adm[inistrator]ˢ or Assigns forever. And I the said Elijah SHOCKLEY for myself my Heirs Ex[ecutor]s the Negro Boy aforesaid unto the said Henry JOHNSON his Heirs Ex[ecutor]ˢ Adm[inistrator]ˢ or Assigns against me the said Elijah SHOCKLEY my Heirs Ex[ecutor]ˢ or Adm[inistrator]ˢ and against all and every other person or persons whatsoever shall and will Warrant and forever Defend by these presents. In Witness whereof I the said Elijah SHOCKLEY to these presents my Hand have set and Seal affixed this Sixth Day of November Anno Dom[ini] 1776./. ~ ./. ~

Sealed & Delivered   J. DENNIS   Elijah SHOCKLEY. (Seal)
In presence of ~~   N. HOLLAND"

*followed with the acknowledgment by Justices of the Peace J. DENNIS and N. HOLLAND and the recordation by court clerk Henry JOHNSON[259]

Liber K, folios 22-23; 06 November 1776

"Know all Men by these Presents that I Henry JOHNSON of Worcester County in the Province of Maryland for and in Consideration of the Sum of fifty pounds Current money of Maryland to me in hand paid at and before the Sealing and Delivery of these presents by Elijah SHOCKLEY of the County and province aforesaid the receipt whereof I the said Henry JOHNSON do hereby acknowledge have Bargained Sold and Delivered, and by these presents do Bargain Sell and Deliver unto the said Elijah SHOCKLEY his Heirs Ex[ecutor]ˢ Adm[inistrator]ˢ or Assigns, one Negro Woman Slave called and known by the name of **Pleasant**. To have and to hold the said Negro woman called Pleasant by these presents Bargained and Sold as aforesaid unto the said Elijah SHOCKLEY his Heirs Ex[ecutor]ˢ Ad[ministrator]ˢ or Assigns forever. And I the said Henry JOHNSON for myself my Heirs Ex[ecutor]ˢ Adm[inistrator]ˢ the Negro Woman aforesaid unto the said Elijah SHOCKLEY his Heirs Ex[ecutor]ˢ Adm[inistrator]ˢ or Assigns against me the said Henry JOHNSON my Heirs Ex[ecutor]ˢ or Adm[inistrator]ˢ and against all and every other Person or Persons whatsoever shall and will Warrant and forever Defend by these presents. In Witness whereof I the said Henry JOHNSON to these presents my Hand have set and Seal affixed this Sixth day of November Anno Dom[ini] 1776./. ~

Sealed & Delivered   J. DENNIS   H[enr]y JOHNSON (Seal)
In presence of ~   N. HOLLAND"

*followed with the acknowledgment by Justices of the Peace J. DENNIS and N. HOLLAND and the recordation by court clerk Henry JOHNSON[260]

---

[258] Worcester County Court (Land Records). Bill of sale from DENNIS, John to BALL, William. 14 February 1776. I, p. 643, MSA CE 30-9. www.mdlandrec.net : accessed 27 November 2021.
[259] Worcester County Court (Land Records). Bill of sale from SHOCKLEY, Elijah to JOHNSON, Henry. 06 November 1776. K, p. 22, MSA CE 30-10. www.mdlandrec.net : accessed 28 January 2022.
[260] Worcester County Court (Land Records). Bill of sale from JOHNSON, Henry to SHOCKLEY, Elijah. 06 November 1776. K, pp. 22-23, MSA CE 30-10. www.mdlandrec.net : accessed 28 January 2022.

Liber K, folio 29; 07 April 1777

"Know all Men by these Presents that I William ATKINSON of Worcester County for and in Consideration of the Sum of Seventy Six pounds five Shillings to me in hand paid by Robert DONE of the County af[ore]s[ai]^d Have Bargained and sold unto the said Robert DONE and by these Presents do bargain and sell unto the said Robert DONE his Heirs and Assigns one negro Wench named **Sylvia** and negro Girl named **Betty** to have and to hold the said negro Woman and Girl unto the said Robert DONE his Heirs and Assigns forever to the only proper use of the said Robert DONE his Heirs and Assigns forever and for no other use or purpose whatsoever. And the said William ATKINSON for himself and his Heirs doth covenant with the said Robert DONE and his Heirs to warrant and defend the said negro Wench and Girl to the said Robert DONE his Heirs & Assigns forever. In Testimony whereof the said William ATKINSON to these Presents his Hand hath put and Seal affixed the 7th of April, Anno Domini 1777./. ~ ./. ~

Sealed & delivered   N. HOLLAND.   William ATKINSON   (Seal)
in presence of ~"

*followed by the acknowledgment of N. HOLLAND and the recordation on 08 April 1777 by court clerk R. DENNIS[261]

Liber K, folios 30-31; March 1777

"Know all Men by these Presents that I Nathaniel WAPLES of Worcester County in the Province of Maryland (Sadler) for and in Consideration of the sum of Seventy pounds current money of Maryland to me in hand paid at and before the Sealing and delivery of these Presents by Luke ENNIS of the same County and Province af[oresai]^d (Taylor) the Receipt whereof I do hereby acknowledge, have bargained and sold and and by these Presents do bargain and Sell unto the said Luke ENNIS one negro Woman called **Sarah**. To have and to hold the said negro **Sarah** by these Presents bargained and sold unto the said Luke ENNIS his Heirs, Ex[ecuto]^{rs}, Administrators and Assigns forever, and I the said Nathaniel WAPLES for my self my Heirs, Executors and Administrators all and singular the said Negro **Sarah** unto the said Luke ENNIS his Heirs and Assigns, and against all and every other person or persons whatsoever shall and will forever warrant and defend by these Presents, of which said Negro **Sarah**, I the said Nathaniel WAPLES have put the said Luke ENNIS in full Possession. In Witness my Hand and Seal this   day of March anno Domini, Seventeen hundred and Seventy Seven. ~ ./ ~ ./. ~

Sign[e]d, Sealed & deliver[e]d   N. HOLLAND   Nathaniel WAPLES   (Seal)
in the presence of ~"

*followed with the acknowledgment of N. HOLLAND and the recordation on 26 April 1777 by court clerk R. DENNIS[262]

Liber K, folio 31; 26 April 1777

"Know all Men by these Presents that I William FRANKLIN of Worcester County in the State of Maryland Planter, for and in consideration of Seventy five Pounds lawfull Money of the State of Maryland to me in hand paid by Azarariah PURNELL of the State af[oresai]^d Planter at and before the sealing and delivery of these Presents, the Receipt whereof I do hereby acknowledge and myself therewith fully contented, satisfied and paid have bargained and Sold and by these presents do bargain sell and deliver unto the said Azariah PURNELL a certain Negro Wench named **Sue**, of the Age of twenty one years. To have and to hold the said Negro Wench to the said Azariah PURNELL his Heirs, Executors, Administrators and Assigns, to his and their own proper use and behoof forever. And I the said William FRANKLIN against myself my Heirs, Executors and Administrators and against all every person or persons

---

[261] Worcester County Court (Land Records). Bill of sale from ATKINSON, William to DONE, Robert. 07 April 1777. K, p. 29, MSA CE 30-10. www.mdlandrec.net : accessed 28 January 2022.
[262] Worcester County Court (Land Records). Bill of sale from WAPLES, Nathaniel to ENNIS, Luke. March 1777. K, pp. 30-31, MSA CE 30-10. www.mdlandrec.net : accessed 28 January 2022.

claiming by or under me to the said Azariah PURNELL his Heirs, Executors and Assigns will warrant and forever defend by these Presents. In Witness whereof I have hereunto set my Hand and affixed my my Seal this twenty sixth day of April and in the year of our Lord one thousand Seven hundred and Seventy seven. ~ . / ~ . / ~

Sealed and deliver[e]d   Thomas SELBY.   William FRANKLIN. ~ (Seal)
in presence of ~   James FALCONER."

*followed with the recordation on 13 May 1777 by court clerk R. DENNIS[263]

Liber K, folios 38-39; 05 July 1777

"This Indenture made this fifth day of July in the year of our Lord one thousand Seven Hundred and Seventy Seven Between Lemuel TOWNSEND and Zadock TOWNSEND Both of Worcester County this Indenture witnesseth that the Said Lemuel TOWNSEND for and in consideration of the Sum of Sixty Pounds Current money of maryland to him paid by the af[oresai]^d Zadock TOWNSEND at and before the sealing and Delivery hereof the Receipt whereof he hereby doth acknowledge hath Given Granted Bargained and sold by these presents doth Give Grant Bargain and Sell unto the af[ore]s[ai]^d Zadock TOWNSEND his heirs and assigns forever, one Negro girl Called **Phillis** and one still and one stalling Horse and one feather Bed the same belonging unto the Said Zadock TOWNSEND his Heirs and assigns forever to and for the only use benefit and behoof of the Said Zadock TOWNSEND his Heirs and assigns forever and for no other use or purpose whatsoever in witness whereof the Said Lemuel TOWNSEND to these Presents his hand hath set and seal affixed the day and year first above written

Signed Sealed and Delivered   Joshua TOWNSEND   Lemuel TOWNSEND (Seal)
In Presents of me ~"

*followed on folio 39 with the acknowledgment of Justice of the Peace Joshua TOWNSEND and the recordation on 06 August 1777 by court clerk John DONE[264]

Liber K, folio 65; 17 March 1778

"Worcester County Ss^t. To all people to whom these presents shall come. I Sarah HOUSTON of the County aforesaid do send Greeting Know ye that the said Sarah HOUSTON of the County aforesaid Widow for and in Consideration of the love good Will & affection which I have & do bear towards my loving Daughter Betsey Wise HOUSTON of the County aforesaid have given & granted & by these presents do freely and clearly & absolutely give & unto the said Betsey Wise HOUSTON her heirs Executors & Administrators four Negroes {?} Negro boys called **George Abel Hannah** and **Isaac** a Case of Draws and Desk Two Beds and furniture half a Dozen Silver Spoons. The Negroes to be given her at the day of her Marriage the other Goods not till my death from hence forth as her & there proper Goods absolutely without any manner of Condition whatsoever In Witness whereof I have hereunto set my hand & Seal this 17th day of March Anno 1778.

Signed Sealed & delivered   Sarah HOUSTON (Seal)
In the presence of us
Joshua TOWNSEND.   Nancy TOWNSEND."

*followed with the acknowledgment by Justice of the Peace Joshua TOWNSEND and the recordation by court clerk James R. MORRIS[265]

---

[263] Worcester County Court (Land Records). Bill of sale from FRANKLIN, William to PURNELL, Azariah. 26 April 1777. K, p. 31, MSA CE 30-10. www.mdlandrec.net : accessed 28 January 2022.
[264] Worcester County Court (Land Records). Bill of sale from TOWNSEND, Lemuel to TOWNSEND, Zadock. 05 July 1777. K, pp. 38-39, MSA CE 30-10. www.mdlandrec.net : accessed 28 January 2022.
[265] Worcester County Court (Land Records). Deed of gift from HOUSTON, Sarah to HOUSTON, Betsey Wise. 17 March 1778. K, p. 65, MSA CE 30-10. www.mdlandrec.net : accessed 28 January 2022.

Liber K, folio 90; 11 July 1778

"Maryland Worcester County} to wit Know all men by these presents that I Joshua DONOHOE now of the State and County af[ore]s[ai]^d for and in consideration of the sum of one hundred Pounds current circulating money of Maryland have Bargained and sold and by these presents do Bargain sell and convey to William POLLARD of the City of Philadelphia and State of Pennsylvania and his Heirs and Assigns a Negro Woman named **Poll** now supposed to be in the City of Philadelphia af[ore]s[ai]^d being a Wench that went off with the British Army from the head of Elk. To have and to hold the said Negro Woman named **Poll** to him the said William POLLARD his Heirs and Assigns to and for the only proper use of the said William POLLARD his Heirs and Assigns and for no other use or purpose whatsoever. In Witness whereof the said Joshua DONOHOE to these presents his hand hath set and Seal affixed this eleventh day of July one thousand seven hundred and seventy eight.

Sealed and delivered in presence of Jno. DONE. Rob[er]^t DONE.   Joshua DONOHO (Seal)"

*followed with the acknowledgment by Justice of the Peace Joshua TOWNSEND and the recordation by court clerk James R. MORRIS[266]

Liber K, folios 106-107; 18 September 1778

"This Indenture made this 18th day of Sept[embe]^r Anno Dom[ini] 1778. Between George STEWART and Major GUY both of the Commonwealth of Virginia of the one part and John SATCHELL of Worcester County in the State of Maryland of the other part Witnesseth that whereas the said John SATCHELL for and in consideration of the sum of two hundred and fifteen pounds Current money of Maryland to him in hand paid by the said George STEWART & Major GUY did by Deed of Mortgage bearing date the twenty ninth day of Apriel Anno Dom[ini] 1774 convey unto them the following Slaves, Goods & Chattles, to wit, one Negro Lad Slave named **Joshua**, one Negro boy named **Stephen**, one Negro Girl named **Levinah**, thirteen head of horned Cattle, fourteen head of Sheep, one Horse called Buck, one Ox Chain, one Set of Carpentures & Turners Tools, twenty eight head of Hogs, & one Yoak of Stears, upon Condition that in Case the said John SATCHELL should pay unto the said George STEWART & Major GUY the af[ore]s[ai]d sum of two hundred & fifteen Pounds current money af[ore]s[ai]^d by the first day of Janu[ar]^y ensuing the date of the af[ore]s[ai]^d Deed of Mortgage with the Interest thereon due that then the af[ore]s[ai]^d Deed of Mortgage shou[l]d be void and of no effects by recourse to the Deed af[ore]s[ai]^d being had more fully will appear. Now this Indenture further Witnesseth that the said George STEUART & Major GUY for and in consideration of the said John SATCHELLs haveing fully complied with the Defeasance contained in the said Deed as also for the further Consideration of five shillings current money of Maryland to them in hand paid by the said John SATCHELL at or before the Execution hereof have Given, Granted Bargained, Sold, released, and forever Quit Claim unto the said John SATCHELL his Heirs & Assigns forever all and every of the af[ore]s[ai]^d Mortgaged Premises with each & every Article & thing therein contained To have and to hold all the af[ore]s[ai]^d Articles & things in the Deed of Mortgage as af[ore]s[ai]^d expressed unto the said John SATCHELL his Heirs & Assigns forever, and to the only proper use benefit & behoof of the said John SATCHELL his Heirs & Assigns forever and to and for no other use intent or purpose whatever. In Witness whereof we have hereunto set our hands and affixed our Seals the Day and Year above written ~

Signed Sealed & delivered	N. HOLLAND &	George STEWART (Seal)
In presence of ~	Joshua TOWNSEND	Major GUY (Seal)"

---

[266] Worcester County Court (Land Records). Bill of sale from DONOHO, Joshua to POLLARD, William. 11 July 1778. K, p. 90, MSA CE 30-10. www.mdlandrec.net : accessed 28 January 2022.

*followed with the acknowledgment by Justices of the Peace N. HOLLAND and Joshua TOWNSEND and the recordation on 26 September 1778 by court clerk James R. MORRIS[267]

Liber K, folios 108-109; 14 September 1778

"Maryland Ss^t. Know all Men by these present that I John RIEN of the State of Maryland, for and in consideration of the sum of forty Pounds common Money to me in hand paid at and before the sealing and delivery of these presents by Jonathan CORDRAY of the State aforesaid the Receipt whereof I do hereby acknowledge have bargained and sold and by these presents do Bargain and Sell unto the said Jonathan CORDRAY all my Right and Title at present or ever shall have hereafter to a Negroe Woman called **Nancy** now in my Possession. To have and to hold all my right and Title to the said Negro Woman and her Issue by these presents bargaind and sold unto the said Jonathan CORDRAY his Executors and Adminestrators and Assigns forever. And I the said John RIEN for myself my Executors and Adminestrators all my said right and Title to the Negroe Woman and her Issue as afforesaid unto the said Jonathan CORDRAY his Executors, Administrators, and Assigns against me the said John RIEN my Executors Adminestrators, and Assigns will warrant and forever defend by these presents of which Negroe I the said John RIEN have put the s[ai]^d Jonathan CORDRAY in full possession of. In Witness Hand and Seal this 14th Day of September seventeen hundred and seventy eight

William CORDRAY – Abraham CORDRAY   John RINE   (Seal)"

*followed on folio 109 with the acknowledgment by Justice of the Peace Joshua TOWNSEND and the recordation on 07 October 1778 by court clerk James R. MORRIS[268]

Liber K, folio 109; 14 September 1778

"Maryland Ss^t. Know all men by these presents that I Abraham CORDRAY of the State of Maryland for and in consideration of the sum of sixty five Pounds common money to me in hand paid at and before the sealing and delivery of these presents by Jonathan CORDRAY of the State aforesaid the receipt whereof I do hereby acknowledge have Bargained and sold and by these presents do Bargain and Sell unto the said Jonathan CORDRAY all my right and Title at present or ever shall have hereafter to a Negro Woman called **Nancy** now in my possession. To have and to hold all my right and Title to the said Negro Woman and her Issue by these presents Bargain[e]d and Sold unto the said Jonathan CORDRAY his Executors Administrators and Assigns forever and I the said Abraham CORDRAY for myself my Executors and Administrators all my said Right and Title to the Negro Woman and her Issue as aforesaid unto the said Jonathan CORDRAY his Executors Administrators and Assigns against me the said Abraham CORDRAY my Executors Administrators and Assigns will warrent and forever defend by these presents of which Negro I the said Abraham CORDRAY have put the said Jonathan CORDRAY in full possession of. In Witness my hand and Seal this 14th Day of September seventeen Hundred and seventy eight ~

William CORDRAY.   John RINE.   Abraham CORDRAY   (Seal)"

*followed with the acknowledgment by Justice of the Peace Joshua TOWNSEND and the recordation on 07 October 1778 by court clerk James R. MORRIS[269]

Liber K, folio 119; 05 November 1778

"The State of Maryland. Know all men by these presents that I Robert SCHOOLFEILD of Worcester County & in the State af[ore]s[ai]^d for and in consideration of the sum of ninety five

---

[267] Worcester County Court (Land Records). Deed of release from STEWART, George and GUY, Major to SATCHELL, John. 18 September 1778. K, pp. 106-107, MSA CE 30-10. www.mdlandrec.net : accessed 28 January 2022.

[268] Worcester County Court (Land Records). Bill of sale from RINE, John to CORDRAY, Jonathan. 14 September 1778. K, pp. 108-109, MSA CE 30-10. www.mdlandrec.net : accessed 28 January 2022.

[269] Worcester County Court (Land Records). Bill of sale from CORDRAY, Abraham to CORDRAY, Jonathan. 14 September 1778. K, p. 109, MSA CE 30-10. www.mdlandrec.net : accessed 28 January 2022.

pounds Continental Currency in hand paid by George TRUITT Sen[io]r of the same place do sell unto him the said George TRUITT a certain Negro woman Slave named **Rachal** to him the said Geo[rge] TRUITT his Heirs and Assigns for ever To have and to hold the above Negro Woman called **Rachal** to him the said George TRUITT his Heirs and Assigns. And the said Robert SCHOOLFEILD doth agree and oblige himself & his Heirs, Ex[e]cut[ors] & Administraters to warrent and defend the above mentioned Negro Woman called **Rachal** with her increase unto the said George TRUITT his Heirs and Assigns forever as Witness my hand & Seal this fifth day of November Anno Dom[ini] one thousand seven hundred & seventy eight

Sign[e]d Seal[e]d & acknowledged   Rob[er]t SCHOOLFIELD (Seal)
In presence off John SELBY. John Purnell ROBINS"

*followed with the acknowledgment by Justice of the Peace John Purnell ROBINS and the recordation on 06 November 1778 by court clerk James R. MORRIS[270]

Liber K, folio 119; 13 October 1778

"Sussex County Oct[o]ber 13th 1778. Rec[eive]d of John COLBOARN the sum of two hundred Pounds & one shilling being in full for a Negro Woman called **Sarah** which Negro Woman was sold by the Subscriber at a vendue of William HOVENTONs on the 8th day of this instant which Estate was forfited to the Delaware State by the said William HOVENTON and sold by veirtue of an Act of General Assembly of this State impowering Levin DIRICKSON as Commissioner to sell all the forfifted Estats in said County and on the above said Day the said Negro woman was sold unto the above said John COLBARN and I do herby acknowledge the said Negro Woman to be the right, Title and property of the above named John COLBORNs and do promise to keep the s[ai]d John COLBORN safe, free and cleair from all persons claiming any right, Title or property unto the said Negro Woman as witness my hand the day and Year above writen ~   Levin DIRICKSON   Commissione

Testes W[illia]m Jordan HALL. Testes Jos[eph] DIRICKSON

*followed with the recordation by court clerk James R. MORRIS on 10 November 1778[271]

Liber K, folios 126-127; 27 August 1778

"This Indenture made this twenty seventh day of August Annoq Dom[ini] one thousand seven hundred & seventy eight. Between Levin BELL of Worcester County Maryland of the one part & Negroes **Sabra** & her Children **Jude, Bett, & Leah** as also all his half part of a Negro Man called **George** (left by his father to s[ai]d Levin & brother John they & every of them being under the age of fifty years of the other part. Witneseth that the said Levin BELL for & in consideration of the faithfull service of the above said Negroes and the Justice by him to them believed to be due as well as their good behavior in General and being desirous that the s[ai]d Negroes should be manumitted & forever set free from Slavery hath manumitted set free & forever discharged & by these presents doth manumit, set free & forever discharge the said Negroes & their Issue from him the s[ai]d Levin BELL his Heirs & Assigns. And the s[ai]d Levin BELL doth covenant & agree to & with the s[ai]d Negroes **Sabra, Jude, Bett, Leah & George** & their Heirs & Assigns. And the s[ai]d Levin BELL doth covenant & agree to & with the s[ai]d Negroes **Sabra, Jude, Bett, Leah & George** & their Heirs that they the s[ai]d Negroes **Sabra, Jude, Bett & Leah** & their Issue are by these presents forever manumitted & set free, also the s[ai]d Negroes **George** & his Issue as far as his perogative in point of Law can or may be deemed to that end & purpose effectual. And that the s[ai]d Levin BELL, his Heirs, Executors or Administrators hath not nor ever shall have any right, Title, Interest, claim or demand in or unto them or either of them the s[ai]d **Sabra, Jude, Bett, Leah & George**, or unto either of their Heirs, reserving only to himself the Guardianship & Tuition of ye above s[ai]d Children

---

[270] Worcester County Court (Land Records). Bill of sale from SCHOOLFIELD, Robert to TRUITT, George Sr. 05 November 1778. K, p. 119, MSA CE 30-10. www.mdlandrec.net : accessed 28 January 2022.

[271] Worcester County Court (Land Records). Bill of sale from HOVENTON, William to COLBORN, John. 13 October 1778. K, p. 119, MSA CE 30-10. www.mdlandrec.net : accessed 28 January 2022.

Jude, Bett & Leah till & only until they arive to the age of eighteen Years. In Testimony wereof the s[ai]^d Levin BELL to these presents his hand hath put & seal affixed the day & Year above written ~ Septem[ber] th day 1778.

Signed sealed and delivered James SELBY	Levin BELL (Seal)
In the presence of Sarah SELBY"	

*followed on folio 127 with the acknowledgment by Justice of the Peace James SELBY and the recordation on 29 December 1778 by court clerk James R. MORRIS[272]

Liber K, folio 128; 07 January 1779

"Know all men by these presents that I Hillary GREEN of Worcester County in the State of Maryland for and in consideration of three hundred pounds current money of Maryland to me in hand paid by Hillary PITT of the place afforsaid at and before the ensealing & delivery of these presents wherewith I confess myself to be fully satisfied contented and paid Have Bargained, Sold & delivered, & by these do fully clearly & absolutely Bargain, Sell & deliver unto the said Hillary PITT one Negro Man named **Luke** about twenty Years of Age. To have & to hold the said Negro man to the said Hillary PITT his Heirs, Executors, Administrators & Assigns to {? ? ? ? ?} & {?} And I the said Hillary GREEN my Heirs, Executors & Administrators & every of us the said Negro to the said Hillary PITT his Heirs, Executors & Administrators & Assigns against all people shall & will warrant, acquit & forever defend by these presents. Provided always that if the said Hillary GREEN his Heirs, Executors or Administrators or any of them shall & will well & truly pay or cause to be paid unto the said Hillary PITT his Heirs Executors Administrators or Assigns the afforsaid sum of three hundred pounds current money of Maryland with the lawfull interset thereon at or within the Term of five years from the date hereof without frad or Cozin that then this present Bill & the Bargain & Sale of the said Negro Man shall be utterly void and of none effect otherwise stand and abide in full force & virtue in Law. Witness my hand & Seal this Seventh day of January Anno Domini 1779 ~

Signed sealed & delivered William PITTS	Hillary GREEN. (Seal)
In the presence of Joseph GREEN ~"	

*followed with the acknowledgment by Justice of the Peace John POSTLY and the recordation on 15 January 1779 by court clerk James R. MORRIS[273]

Liber K, folios 129-130; 18 November 1778

"To all people to whome these presents shall come greeting know ye that I Sarah PURNIEL of Worcester County in the State of Maryland for and in consideration of the sum of three hundred and twenty pounds Current money of Maryland to me in hand paid by John TOWNSEND of the County & State aforesaid the receipt whearof I do hereby acknowledge am fully paid and satisfyed Have Granted, Bargained and Sold and by these presents I the said Sarah PURNIEL do Grant, Bargain and Sell unto the said John TOWNSEND one Negro Man named **Will** unto the said John TOWNSEND his Heirs and Assigns forever. And I the said Sarah PURNIEL do for myself my Heirs, Executors & Administrators covenant and Grant to and with the said John TOWNSEND his Heirs and Assigns forever by these presents that I the said Sarah PURNIEL and my Heirs, Executors and Administrators will forever warrant and defend the above mentioned bargained Negro **Will** against the lawfull Claim of any person or persons whatsoever unto the said John TOWNSEND his Heirs, Executors and Administrators without lett, trouble, denial, Mollestation hendrance or disturbance whatsoever. In Witness I my hand and Seal have sett this 18th Day of November seventeen hundred and seventy eight ~

---

[272] Worcester County Court (Land Records). Deed of manumission from BELL, Levin to **Sabra, Jude, Bett, Leah**, and **George**. 27 August 1778. K, pp. 126-127, MSA CE 30-10. www.mdlandrec.net : accessed 28 January 2022.
[273] Worcester County Court (Land Records). Bill of sale from GREEN, Hillary to PITT, Hillary. 07 January 1779. K, p. 128, MSA CE 30-10. www.mdlandrec.net : accessed 28 January 2022.

Signed sealed & delivered In presents off	Joshua TOWNSEND Methias P Mumford ^(his … Mark")		Sarah S PURNIEL (seal) ^(her … Mark)

*followed on folio 130 with the acknowledgment of Justice of the Peace Joshua TOWNSEND and the recordation on 25 January 1779 by court clerk James R. MORRIS[274]

Liber K, folios 130-131; 18 November 1778

"To all people to whome these presents shall come greeting know ye that we Sarah PURNIEL & Lucresla LONG of Worcester County in the State of Maryland for and in consideration of the sum of three hundred and twenty pounds Current money of Maryland to us in hand paid by John TOWNSEND of the County & State aforesaid the receipt whearof we do hereby acknowledge, am fully paid and satisfy Have Granted, Bargained and Sold and by these presents we the said Sarah PURNIEL and Lucresta LONG Grant, Bargain and Sell unto the said John TOWNSEND one Negro Man named **Will**. And we the said Sarah PURNIEL and Lucresta LONG do for ourselves and each of our Heirs, Executors and Administrator covenant and Grant to and with the said John TOWNSEND his Heirs and Assigns by these presents that we the said Sarah PURNIEL and Lucresta LONG our and each of our Heirs, Executors & Administrat[o]^{rs} will forever warrant and defend the above mentioned bargained Negro **Will** against the lawfull claim of any person or persons whatsoever to the said John TOWNSEND his Heirs and Assigns forever without Lett, trouble, denial, mollestation, hendrance or disturbance whatsoever. In Witness our hands and Seals this 18th Day of November seventeen hundred and seventy eight

Signed sealed & delivered Joshua TOWNSEND   Sarah S PURNIEL (Seal)
In presence off   Methias P MUMFORD (his Mark)   (her mark)
                                                 Lucresta + LONG (Seal)
                                                      (her Mark")

*followed with the acknowledgment by Justice of the Peace Joshua TOWNSEND and the recordation on folio 131 by court clerk James R. MORRIS on 25 January 1779[275]

Liber K, folios 136-137; 26 February 1779

"To all peopple to whome these presents shall come greeting know ye that I Moses CHAILLE of Worcester County in the State of Maryland and in Consideration of the sum of forty pounds current money of Maryland to me in hand paid by John TOWNSEND of County & State aforesaid the receipt whereof I do hereby acknowledge am fully paid and sattisfyed, Have Granted, Bargained and Sold and by these presents I the said Moses CHAILLE do Grand, Bargain and Sell unto the said John TOWNSEND one Negro Man named **Will** unto the said John TOWNSEND his Heirs and Assigns forever. And I the said Moses CHAILLE do for myself, my Heirs, Executors and Administrators covenant and Grant to and with the said John TOWNSEND his Heirs and Assigns by these presents that I the said Moses CHAILLE and my Heirs, Executors and Administrators will forever warrant and defend the above mentioned bargained Negro **Will** against the lawfull claim of any person or persons whatsoever claiming from by or under him or his Heirs unto the said John TOWNSEND his Heirs and Assigns forever without Lett, trouble, denial, mollestation, hendrance or disturbance whatsoever. In Witness my hand and Seal this 26th Day of February seventeen hundred and seventy nine ~

---

[274] Worcester County Court (Land Records). Bill of sale from PURNIEL, Sarah to TOWNSEND, John. 18 November 1778. K, pp. 129-130, MSA CE 30-10. www.mdlandrec.net : accessed 28 January 2022.

[275] Worcester County Court (Land Records). Bill of sale from PURNIEL, Sarah and LONG, Lucresta to TOWNSEND, John. 18 November 1778. K, pp. 130-131, MSA CE 30-10. www.mdlandrec.net : accessed 28 January 2022.

Signed sealed and delivered   Charles BENNETT   Moses CHAILLE   (Seal)
In presents off   Joshua TOWNSEND"

*followed with the acknowledgment by Justice of the Peace Joshua TOWNSEND and the recordation on folio 137 by court clerk James R. MORRIS[276]

Liber K, folios 153-154; 13 April 1779

"To all people to whome these presents shall come greeting know ye that I John WISE of Worcester County in the State of Maryland for and in consideration of the sum of five hundred pounds Current money of the state of Maryland to me in hand paid by William SELBY of the County and State aforesaid the Receipt whereof I do hereby acknowledge am fully paid and satisfied Have Granted, Bargained and Sold, and by these presents I the said John WISE do Grant, Bargain and Sell unto the said William SELBY one Negro Boy named **Jacob** unto the said William SELBY his Heirs and Assigns forever. And I the said John WISE do for myself my Heirs, Executors and Administrators, covenant and grant to and with the said William SELBY his Heirs and Assigns by these presents that I the said John WISE, and my Heirs, Executors and Administrators, will forever Warrant and defend the above mentioned, bargained Negro **Jacob** against the lawfull Claim or Claims of any person or persons whatsoever unto the said William SELBY his Heirs and Assigns forever, without Lett, Trouble, Denial, Mollestation, Hendrance or disturbance whatsoever. In Witness my hand and Seal have sett this 13th day of April Anno 1779 ~

Signed sealed and delivered   John WISE   (Seal)
In presents off   Edward HAMMOND"

*followed on folio 154 with the acknowledgment by Justice of the Peace Joshua TOWNSEND and the recordation on 17 April 1779 by court clerk James R. MORRIS[277]

Liber K, folios 163-164; 17 May 1779

"Know all men by these presents that I Daniel SELBY of Worcester County in the State of Maryland for an in consideration of the sum of one thousand pounds Current money of Maryland to me the said Daniel in hand paid at and before the sealing and delivery of these presents, the receipt whereof I hereby doth acknowledge, Hath Given, Granted, Bargained and Sold, and by these presents do give, Grant, Bargain and Sell unto Mary WALLIS and her Heirs and Assigns forever, the following Negrows hereafter mentioned one Negrow Man Slave called **Isaac**, one Negrow Woman called **Pleasent**, one Negrow Girl called **Sarah**, one called **Amy**, one called **Gib**, one called **Betts**, and one boy called **Adam**. To have and to hold the several Negrows above named unto the said Mary WALLIS her Heirs and Assigns forever, to the only use, bennifit and behoof of her the said Mary WALLIS and her Heirs and Assigns forever, and to and for no other use or purpose whatsoever. And the said Daniel doth covenant with the said Mary that he the said Daniel and his Heirs, Executors and Administrators will Warrant and forever defend the Negrows above mentioned namely **Isaac, Pleasant, Sarrah, Leah, Amy, Gib, Betts** and **Adam** unto the said Mary WALLIS and her heirs and Assigns forever, against the lawfull Claim of all and every person or persons whatsoever. In Testimoney whereof the said Daniel hath hereunto sett his Hand and fixed his Seal this seventeen day of May in the year of our Lord one thousand seven hundred and seventy nine ~

Signed, sealed and delivered   Parker SELBY   Daniel SELBY   (Seal)
In the presence of us   John SELBY"

---

[276] Worcester County Court (Land Records). Bill of sale from CHAILLE, Moses to TOWNSEND, John. 26 February 1779. K, pp. 136-137, MSA CE 30-10. www.mdlandrec.net : accessed 28 January 2022.

[277] Worcester County Court (Land Records). Bill of sale from WISE, John to SELBY, William. 13 April 1779. K, pp. 153-154, MSA CE 30-10. www.mdlandrec.net : accessed 28 January 2022.

*followed on folio 164 with the acknowledgment of Justice of the Peace John SELBY and the recordation on 21 May 1779 by court clerk James R. MORRIS[278]

Liber K, folio 164; 19 May 1779

"To all persons to whom these presents shall come Know ye that I William ALLEN of Worcester County in the State of Maryland being desirous to see free and Manumit after my decease the several and Respective negroe Slaves to wit ~ **Anas, Rose** and **Phillis** in consideration of their and each of their faithfull Services done and performed the said William ALLEN doth by these presents hereby give and grant set free and Manumit severally the aforesaid Negroes **Anas, Rose** and **Phillis** and that their freedom Shall commence and take effect immediately after the death of the said William ALLEN To have hold and freely enjoy to them the said **Anas Rose** and **Phillis** forever immediately after the death of the said William ALLEN their and each of their liberty and freedom in full and ample manner without any Let hindrance or authority of any person or persons whatsoever In Testimony whereof the said William ALLEN to these presents his Hand hath set and Seal affixed this ninteenth day of May Anno Domini one thousand seven hundred and seventy Nine.

Signed Sealed and delivered   John SELBY   W[illia]^m ALLEN (Seal)
In the presence of   Joshua TOWNSEND"

*followed with the acknowledgment of Justice of the Peace John SELBY and the recordation by court clerk James R. MORRIS[279]

Liber K, folios 187-188; 02 July 1779

"This Indenture made this second Day of July Anno Dom[ini] 1779. ~ Witnesseth that **Jacob** a free Negrow hath of his own free and voluntary Will placed & bound himself as a Servant or Slave unto Benjamin PURNELL Jun[io]^r his Heirs, Executors, Administrator or Assigns, and that he the said **Jacob** will continue and serve from the Day of the Date hereof until the full end of seven years, from thence next ensueing & fully to be compleat and ended; during all which time the said **Jacob** his s[ai]^d master well & faithfully serve, his lawfull command fully obay, the Goods of his s[ai]^d Masters he shall not Embezel or wast nor shall permit himself to be absent without his Master leave and that the s[ai]^d PURNELL is to find him wareing Cloths after the first Year from the Date hereof, and the s[ai]^d PURNELL is to find the said **Jacob** sufficient meat, drink, and Lodging & Working Cloths for the residue of the above term of time, as Witness our Hands & Seals the Day & year first above written ~

Signed, sealed & Delivered   **Jacob** | Negrow (Seal)
In presence   Joshua TOWNSEND"   mark | his

*followed on folio 188 with the recordation by court clerk James R. MORRIS on 03 May 1779[280]

Liber K, folios 195-196; 30 July 1779

"Know all men by these presents that I Nehemiah DORMAN of Worcester County in the State of Maryland for and in consideration of the Sum of seven hundred pounds Current money of Maryland to me in hand paid at and before the sealing and delivery of these presents by Elsey SPICER of Sussex County in the Delawair State the Receipt whereof I do hereby acknowledge Have Bargained and Sold and by these presents do Bargain and Sell unto the said Elsey SPICER one Negro Woman named **Leviner**. To have and to hold the said Negro **Leviner** by these presents Bargained and Sold unto the said Elsey SPICER his Heirs and Assigns forever. And I

---

[278] Worcester County Court (Land Records). Bill of sale from SELBY, Daniel to WALLIS, Mary. 17 May 1779. K, pp. 163-164, MSA CE 30-10. www.mdlandrec.net : accessed 28 January 2022.
[279] Worcester County Court (Land Records). Deed of manumission from ALLEN, William to **Anas, Rose**, and **Phillis**. 19 May 1779. K, p. 164, MSA CE 30-10. www.mdlandrec.net : accessed 28 January 2022.
[280] Worcester County Court (Land Records). Indenture from Jacob to PURNELL, Benjamin Jr. 02 July 1779. K, pp. 187-188, MSA CE 30-10. www.mdlandrec.net : accessed 28 January 2022.

the said Nehemiah DORMAN for my Self and my Heirs the said Negro **Leviner** unto the said Elsey SPICER his Heirs and Assigns against me the said Nehemiah DORMAN my Heirs, Executors & Administrators and against the lawfull Claim of any other person or persons whatsoever shall and will warrant and forever defend the said Negro **Leviner** by these presents of which Negro **Leviner** I the said Nehemiah DORMAN have put the said Elsey SPICER in full possession of by delivering him the said Negro **Leviner** at the sealing hereof. In Witness whereof I the said Nehemiah DORMAN have his hand sett and Seal affixed this 30th Day of July Anno Domini seventeen hundred and seventy nine ~

Signed & Sealed   Nehemiah DORMAN   (Seal)
In presents off   Henry AYRES. Belitha BRITTINGHAM ~"

*followed on folio 196 with the acknowledgment by Justice of the Peace Joshua TOWNSEND and the recordation by court clerk James R. MORRIS[281]

Liber K, folio 232; 28 December 1779

"To all People to whome these presents shall come I Mary ATKINSON of Worcester County in the State of Maryland send greeting Know ye that I the said Mary ATKINSON for and in consideration of Natural Affection me hereunto moving. Have Given and Granted and by these presents do Give and Grant unto the following persons Vizt. Laurence HOWARTH, Sarah HOWARTH, Ann SCOTT and Mary SCOTT the following Negroes (after my decease provided that I have no Children) that is to say I Give and Grant to the said Laurence HOWARTH one Negro Man named **Limas**, I also Give and Grant unto the said Sarah HOWARTH One Negro Boy named **George**, I also Give and Grant unto the said Ann SCOTT one Negro Girl named **Chloe**, And I also Give and Grant unto the af[oresai]d Mary SCOTT one Negro Girl named **Rose** all the above Negroes I give and Grant unto the af[oresai]d persons as they are mentioned, But that this Instrument of writing maybe more fairly and clearly understood be it known that if the said Mary ATKINSON should leave any Child or Children at her Death that this Gift shall be void and of none effect but if the said Mary ATKINSON should die without living Issue then the above Gift to be good in Law and it is further to be understood that neither of the above Negroes is to be given into the possession of either of the above named persons during the life of the said Mary ATKINSON. In Testimony of the above Gift I have hereunto set my hand and Seal this 28th Day of December Anno Dom[ini] one thousand seven hundred and seventy nine ~

Signed sealed and delivered   Mary ATKINSON   (Seal)
In presence off   Benjamin SCHOOLFIELD"

*followed with the acknowledgment by Justice of the Peace Joshua TOWNSEND and the recordation on 07 January 1780 by court clerk James R. MORRIS[282]

Liber K, folio 253; 12 February 1780

"The State of Maryland Worcester County Ss. Know all men by these presents that I Jesse GRAY of the County af[ore]s[ai]d for and in consideration of the sum of twelve hundred pounds of lawfull Money of the State & County af[ore]s[ai]d to me in hand paid by John Pope MITCHELL wherefore I do hereby acknowledge the Receipt and myself therewith fully and entirely satisfied. Have Bargained & Sold and by these presents in plain and Open Sale do Bargain and Sell unto the af[ore]s[ai]d John Pope MITCHELL a Negro Man named **Harrah** raisd by Joseph GRAY Se[nio]r the af[ore]s[ai]d Negro now is near about twenty eight Years of Age. To have and to hold all the Rite and Title of the af[ore]s[ai]d Negro **Harrah** unto the said John Pope MITCHELL his Heirs Exe[cutor]s Adm[inistrator]s and Assigns. And I the said Jesse

---

[281] Worcester County Court (Land Records). Bill of sale from DORMAN, Nehemiah to SPICER, Elsey. 30 July 1779. K, pp. 195-196, MSA CE 30-10. www.mdlandrec.net : accessed 28 January 2022.
[282] Worcester County Court (Land Records). Deed of gift from ATKINSON, Mary to HOWARTH, Laurence, HOWARTH, Sarah, SCOTT, Ann, and SCOTT, Mary. 28 December 1779. K, p. 232, MSA CE 30-10. www.mdlandrec.net : accessed 28 January 2022.

GRAY for myself my Heirs Ex[ecutor]ˢ Adm[inistrator]ˢ or any other person or persons claiming any Right from any Bargain or Sale from me heretofore the said Bargained Negro unto the said John Pope MITCHELL his Heirs Ex[ecutor]ˢ Adm[inistrator]ˢ and Assigns against all and manner of persons shall and will Warrat and forever defend by these presents In Witness whereof I have hereunto sett my hand and Seal this 12 Day of February Anno Domini 1780

Signed sealed and delivered   Henry SNEAD   Jesse GRAY   (Seal)
In presents of …..   Jesse POWELL"

*followed with the recordation by court clerk James R. MORRIS[283]

Liber K, folios 337-338; 15 August 1780

"Know all men by these Presents that I Isaac EVANS of Worcester County & State of Maryland for and in Consideration of the sum of one Thousand pounds Current money of the State af[ore]s[ai]ᵈ to me in hand paid by Joseph IRONSHIRE of the county & State af[ore]s[ai]ᵈ at or before the sealing & delivery of these presents, the receipt whereof I the said Isaac EVANS do hereby acknowledge, have granted bargained and sold & by these presents do grant bargain and sell unto the said Joseph IRONSHIRE his Exec[uto]ʳˢ Adm[inistrato]ʳˢ & assigns all the stock goods Household Stuff, Implements & furniture Particularly mentioned expressed & contained in the Schedule hereunto annexed to have & to hold all and singular the said Stock, goods Household Stuff & furniture above bargained & sold, or mentioned or intended so to be to the said Joseph IRONSHIRE his Exe[cuto]ʳˢ Adm[inistrato]ʳˢ or assigns forever. And I the said Isaac EVANS for myself my heirs Exe[cuto]ʳˢ & Adm[inistrato]ʳˢ all and singular the said Goods under mentioned unto the said Joseph IRONSHIRE his Exe[cuto]ʳˢ Adm[inistrato]ʳˢ & assigns against me the said Isaac EVANS my Ex[ecuto]ʳˢ & Adm[inistrato]ʳˢ & against all & every other person & persons whatsoever shall and will warrant and forever defend by these presents of all and singular which said stock & goods, Household Stuff, Implements & Furniture, I the said Isaac EVANS have put the said Joseph IRONSHIRE in full possession, by delivering to him the said Joseph IRONSHIRE one Silver Spoon at the sealing & delivery of these presents in the name of the holy premises hereby bargained & sold, or mentioned or intended so to be, unto him the said Joseph IRONSHIRE as aforesaid as Witness my hand and seal this 15ᵗʰ day of August Ann Domini 1780 ~

Signed sealed & Delivered   Jnº. POSTLY   Isaac EVANS   (Seal)
in the presence of ~   Anne POSTLY"

The afforesaid Schedule as followeth (To wit) 1 Negro man **George** 1 D[itt]º boy **Jesse** 1 D[itt]º woman **Jane** 1 D[itt]o **Sarah** one D[itt]o Girl **Hulda** 3 head of Horses 24 head of sheep 38 head of Hogs 5 Cows & Calves 1 yoke of oxen 1 barren Cow 5 yearlings 5 beds & furniture 1 still & appurtenances 3 pine chests 1 D[itt]º Cupboard 1 writing desk 11 Chairs 1 Duch fan 15 cyder Casks 30 bushells of Corn 11 oat stacks 2 large Silver Spoons 2 small ditto 3 Iron pots 1 duch oven 1 ½ Doz[en] Pewter Plats 150 lbs flax ~

*followed on folio 338 with the acknowledgment by Justice of the Peace John POSTLY and the recordation on 27 August 1780 by court clerk James R. MORRIS[284]

Liber K, folio 339; 25 August 1780

"Know all men by these presents that We Severn JOHNSON and Frederick CONNER of Worcester County in the State of Maryland for and in consideration of the sum of Thirty Pounds hard money to us in hand paid at and before the Sealing and delivery of these presents by Samuel JOHNSON of the county and State af[ore]s[ai]ᵈ the receipt whereof we do hereby acknowledge have bargained and sold and by these presents do bargain and sell unto the said

---

[283] Worcester County Court (Land Records). Bill of sale from GRAY, Jesse to MITCHELL, John Pope. 12 February 1780. K, p. 253, MSA CE 30-10. www.mdlandrec.net : accessed 29 January 2022.
[284] Worcester County Court (Land Records). Bill of sale from EVANS, Isaac to IRONSHIRE, Joseph. 15 August 1780. K, pp. 337-338, MSA CE 30-10. www.mdlandrec.net : accessed 29 January 2022.

Samuel JOHNSON one Negro fellow Named **Will**, To have and to hold the said Negro **Will**, by these presents bargained and sold unto the said Samuel JOHNSON his executors administrators and assigns forever And we the said Severn JOHNSON and Frederick CONNER for ourselves and our heirs will warrant and forever defend the said Negro fellow **Will** agains the lawfull claims of us and our heirs and all and every other person or persons whatsoever by these presents in Testimony whereof we the said Severn JOHNSON & Frederick CONNER have hereunto our hands Set and Seals affixed this twenty fifth day of August Anno Domini Seventeen hundred and Eighty ~

Signed sealed & Delivered   Joshua TOWNSEND   Severn JOHNSON   (Seal)
in presents off   Zebulon JOHNSON   Frederic CONNER (Seal)"

*followed with the acknowledgment by Justice of the Peace Joshua TOWNSEND and the recordation on 27 August 1780 by court clerk James R. MORRIS[285]

Liber K, folio 349; 15 September 1780

"Know all men by these presents that I Zadock SELBY of Worcester County in the State of Maryland for and in Consideration of the sum of forty Pounds (Gold and Silver) current money of Maryland to me in hand paid at and before the sealing and delivery of these presents by William SELBY (son of Thom of the same place, the receipt whereof I do hereby Acknowledge, have bargained and sold and by these presents do bargain and sell Unto the said William SELBY one Negro Girl called **Pegg** (alias **Margarit**) To have and to Hold the said Negro girl called **Pegg** with all and Singular the said bargained premisses, by these presents Unto the said William SELBY his heirs and Assigns forever, for and for no other use intent purpose or Construction whatsoever And I the said Zadock SELBY for my Self my heirs Executors and administrators and every of them all and singular the said Negro aforesaid bargained and Sold as aforesaid Unto the said William SELBY his heirs and assigns forever against me the said Zadock SELBY my heirs Executors Administrators and assigns and against all and every other person and persons whatsoever, shall and will warrant and for ever defend by these presents, of which said Negro Girl above mentioned I the said Zadock SELBY have put the said William SELBY in full possession, by delivering the said Negro at and before the Sealing hereof In Testimony whereof the said Zadock SELBY have hereunto his hand hath set and seal affixed this fifteenth day of September Anno Dom[ini] one thousand seven hundred and Eighty

Signed sealed & Delivered   Joshua TOWNSEND   Zadock SELBY   (Seal)
in the presence of ~   John BALL"

*followed with the acknowledgment by Justice of the Peace Joshua TOWNSEND and the recordation on 18 October 1780 by court clerk James R. MORRIS[286]

Liber K, folio 352; 06 November 1780

"Know all men by these presence that I Thomas CARREY of Worcester County and State of Maryland for and in consideration of the sum of five Shillings Lawfull money aforesaid to me in hand paid by Levin CARREY of the county and State Aforesaid have Transfered Sold Assigned and and by these presents doth Trasfer sell and assign unto the said Levin CARREY his heirs Executors Administrators and asines forever one negro boy Named **David** one Still two head of Cattle To have and to hold the said asined one negro boy one still Two head of Cattle to the said Levin CARREY his heirs Executors administrators and asines forever and to and for the only properties of the said Levin CARREY his heirs and asines. In Witness whereof

---

[285] Worcester County Court (Land Records). Bill of sale from JOHNSON, Severn and CONNER, Frederick to JOHNSON, Samuel. 25 August 1780. K, p. 339, MSA CE 30-10. www.mdlandrec.net : accessed 29 January 2022.

[286] Worcester County Court (Land Records). Bill of sale from SELBY, Zadock to SELBY, William. 15 September 1780. K, p. 349, MSA CE 30-10. www.mdlandrec.net : accessed 29 January 2022.

have hereunto set my hand and seal this six day of November one thousand seven hundred and Eighty ~ .. ~ .. ~ ..

Sined Sealed and Delivered   Benjamin JOHNSON
in the Presence of ~   Daniel DIKS ~   Thomas J CAIREY (Seal)
                                                                                      mark"

*followed with the acknowledgment by Justice of the Peace William HOPEWELL and the recordation on 10 November 1780 by court clerk James R. MORRIS[287]

Liber K, folio 352; 06 November 1780

"Know all men by these presence That I Thomas CAREY of Worcester County and State of Maryland for and in Consideration of the sum of five Shillings Lawfull money aforesaid to me in hand paid by John REDDISH of sumerset county and the State aforesaid have Trasfered Sold and assigned and by these presencs doth trasfer sell and assign unto the said John REDDISH his heirs Executors administrators and assigns forever one negro girl named **Sall** and her Child named **Epheram** and a horse To have and to Hold the said Assigned One negro and child and one horse to the said John REDDISH his heirs Executors administratoors and assigns forever and to and for the only properties of the said John REDDISH his heirs and assines In Witness whereof I have hereunto Set my hand and Seal this Sixth day of November one thousand Seven hundred and Eightty ~

Signed Sealed and Delivered   Benjamin JOHNSON
in the presence of ~   Daniel DIKS ~ .   Thomas J CAIREY (Seal)
                                                                                        mark"

*followed with the acknowledgment by Justice of the Peace William HOPEWELL and the recordation on 10 November 1780 by court clerk James R. MORRIS[288]

Liber K, folios 352-353; 03 November 1780

"Know all men by these presents that I Thomas CAREY of Worcester County and the State of Maryland for and I consideration of the sum of five Shillings Lawfull money Aforesaid to me in hand paid By Outerbridge DIXON of the county and State aforesaid Have Transfered sold and assigned and by these presence doth transfers sell and Assigns unto the said Outerbridge DIXON his heirs Executors administrators and Assign for ever, One Negro girl Named **Nell**. Also one negro girl Named **Genny** and one yoak of Oxen To have and to Hold the said assigned Two negro Girls & yoak of Oxen to the said Outerbridge DIXON his heirs Executors administr[ator]ˢ and assigns for ever and to and for the only proper use of the said Outerbridge DIXON his heirs and assigns In Witness whereof I have hereunto set my hand and Seal this third day of November one thousand seven Hundred and Eightty ~ . ~ . ~

Signed sealed and delivered   W[illia]ᵐ HORSEY ~
In the presence of ~ ~   Stephen HORSEY   Thomas } CAREY (Seal)
                                                                                          mark"

*followed on folio 353 with the acknowledgment by Justice of the Peace William HOPEWELL on 06 November 1780 and the recordation by court clerk James R. MORRIS on 10 November 1780[289]

---

[287] Worcester County Court (Land Records). Bill of sale from CAIREY, Thomas to CARREY, Levin. 06 November 1780. K, p. 352, MSA CE 30-10. www.mdlandrec.net : accessed 29 January 2022.
[288] Worcester County Court (Land Records). Bill of sale from CAIREY, Thomas to REDDISH, John. 06 November 1780. K, p. 352, MSA CE 30-10. www.mdlandrec.net : accessed 29 January 2022.
[289] Worcester County Court (Land Records). Bill of sale from CAREY, Thomas to DIXON, Outerbridge. 03 November 1780. K, pp. 352-353, MSA CE 30-10. www.mdlandrec.net : accessed 29 January 2022.

Liber K, folio 361; 14 December 1780

"Know all men by these presents That I Margaret SELBY of Worcester County in the State of Maryland for and in consideration of the sum of Five pounds current money of Maryland to me in hand paid at and before the Sealing and delivery of these presents by Charles PARKER of the same county and State aforesaid the receipt whereof I do hereby acknowledge Have bargained and sold and by these presents do bargain and Sell unto the said Charles PARKER his heirs and assigns forever one Negro boy called **Jim** (or **James**) a child of a Negro woman called **Rhoda**, Now remaining in my possession To have and to Hold all and Singular the aforesaid Negro **Jim** (or **James**) by these presents bargained and Sold unto the said Charles PARKER his heirs Executors Administrators and assigns forever And I the said Margarett SELBY for myself Executors and administrators all the singular the said Negro boy **Jim** aforesaid unto the said Charles PARKER his heirs Executors Administrators and assigns against me the said Margaret SELBY my executors and administrators and against all and every other person or persons whatsoever shall and will warrant and forever defend by these presents of which said Negro Boy called **Jim** (or **James**) aforesaid I the said Margaret SELBY have put the said Charles PARKER in full possession by a delivery of said Negro boy aforesaid this day at the Sealing hereof In Witness whereof I the said Margarett SELBY have set her hand and seal affixed this fourteenth day of December Anno Dom[ini] one thousand seven hundred and Eighty ~

Signed Sealed & delivered   William SELBY Jun[io]^r her
in the presents of …..   William SELBY ~ …..   Margaret \ SELBY (Seal)
                                                                                           mark"

*followed with the acknowledgment by Justice of the Peace Peter CHAILLE and the recordation on 23 December 1780 by court clerk James R. MORRIS[290]

Liber K, folios 383-384; 03 May 1781

"Worcester Ss^t. To all persons to whome these presents Come I Elizabeth GIBBS do send Greeting Know ye that I the said Elizabeth GIBBS of the Parish of Coventry and County of Worcester for and in Consideration of the love and good will and Effection which I have and do Bear towards my Loving Son & Daughters John GIBBS Polley GIBBS & Hannah GIBBS to them and all of them of the same parrish and County af[ore]s[ai]^d have given and granted and by these presents do freely Give and grant unto the said John GIBBS Polley GIBBS & Hannah GIBBS one Negro Whench called **Dinniah** to the said Polley GIBBS one Negro Girl called **Margo** Likewis to said Hannah GIBBS on Negro Girl Called **Hannah** and their Increase forever absolutely without any manner of Consideration from either of the said John GIBBS Polley GIBBS or Hannah GIBBS in Witness whereof I have hereunto set and my hand and afficted my Seal this 3 Day of May in the year of our Lord one thousand Seven hundred and Eighty one

Sign[e]d Seal[e]d and Delivered   Levin BLAKE ~ ~ ~   Elizabeth GIBBS   (Seal)
in presents of ~ ~ ~ ~ ~   George LAYFIELD ~
                                         John Ennals SCOTT"

*followed on folio 384 with the recordation by court clerk James R. MORRIS on 05 May 1781[291]

Liber K, folio 388; 06 June 1781

"Know all Persons whom it may concern that I William WALTON of Worcester County for and in consideration of sund[r]y valueable effects to me in hand paid and delivered by James

---

[290] Worcester County Court (Land Records). Bill of sale from SELBY, Margaret to PARKER, Charles. 14 December 1780. K, p. 361, MSA CE 30-10. www.mdlandrec.net : accessed 29 January 2022.
[291] Worcester County Court (Land Records). Deed of gift from GIBBS, Elizabeth to GIBBS, John, GIBBS, Polley, and GIBBS, Hannah. 03 May 1781. K, pp. 383-384, MSA CE 30-10. www.mdlandrec.net : accessed 29 January 2022.

TOWNSEND (of Littleton) of the said County the receipt whereof I do hereby acknowledge, have bargained Sold & delivered and by these presents do Bargain sell and deliver unto the said James TOWNSEND one Negro Woman of the age of about Twenty two years called **Sall** and also one Negro girl of the age of about two years called **Charity** & Daughter of the aforesaid Negro Woman To have and to Hold the said bargained premisses, unto the said James TOWNSEND his Executors Administrators and assigns forever and I the said William WALTON for myself myself my Executors and Administrators the said bargained premisses unto the said James TOWNSEND his Executors administrators and assigns, against all person shall and will Warrant and forever defend, by these presents: In Witness whereof I have hereunto set my Hand and seal this Sixth day of June one thousand seven Hundred and Eighty one ....

Sealed & Delivered   E VANDOME   W[illia]^m WALTON   (Seal)
In presence of ....
                     Her
                Luya   X   BALL
                     mark"

*followed with the recordation on 06 July 1781 by court clerk James R. MORRIS[292]

Liber K, folio 393; 10 August 1781

"Know all men by these presents that I Fisher WALTON of Worcester County in the State of Maryland for and in consideration of sum of one hundred pounds Specie to me in hand paid at the Sealing and delivery of these presents by Joshua TOWNSEND of Worcester County in the State of Maryland the receipt whereof I do hereby acknowledge have bargained and sold and by these presents do bargain and sell unto the said Joshua TOWNSEND one Negro woman called **Rhoda** one Negro girl called **laney** and one Negro boy called **george**. To have and to hold the said Negros **Rhoda laney**, and **George** and every of them by these presents bargained and sold unto the said Joshua TOWNSEND his Heirs Executors administrators and assigns forever and I the said Fisher WALTON for my self my Executors and administrators the said three Negroes unto the said Joshua TOWNSEND his Heirs and assigns and against all and every other and persons whatsoever shall and will warrant and forever defend by these presents of which negroes I the said Fisher WALTON have put the said Joshua TOWNSEND in full possession by delivering the said Negroes to him at the Sealing hereof in Witness my hand and seal the 10th day of August Anno Domini Seventeen hundred and Eighty one ~

Signed Sealed Delivered in Presents of   John BALL ~   Fisher WALTON   (Seal)"

*followed with the acknowledgment by Justice of the Peace John SELBY and the recordation by court clerk James R. MORRIS[293]

Liber K, folio 398; 15 September 1781

"Know all men by these presents that I Mary WALLIS of Worcester County in the State of Maryland for and in Consideration of the sum of five Pounds current money of Maryland af[ore]s[ai]^d to me in hand paid by Mary JOHNSON wife of Lemuel JOHNSON at and before the Sealing and delivery hereof the receipt whereof the said Mary WALLIS doth hereby acknowledge have given granted bargained and sold and by these presents do give grant bargain and sell unto the said Mary JOHNSON and her Heirs and Assigns forever one Negrow Woman called **Hannah**. To have and to Hold the said Negrow Woman called **Hannah** to her the said Mary JOHNSON and her Heirs and Assigns forever and the said Maty WALLIS and her Heirs do hereby further covenant to and with the said Mary JOHNSON and her Heirs that she Mary WALLIS and Heirs Ex[ecuto]^rs and Adm[inistrato]^rs will forever hereafter warrant and defend the af[ore]s[ai]^d Negrow called **Hannah** unto the said Mary JOHNSON and her heirs forever

---

[292] Worcester County Court (Land Records). Bill of sale from WALTON, William to TOWNSEND, James. 06 June 1781. K, p. 388, MSA CE 30-10. www.mdlandrec.net : accessed 29 January 2022.
[293] Worcester County Court (Land Records). Bill of sale from WALTON, Fisher to TOWNSEND, Joshua. 10 August 1781. K, p. 393, MSA CE 30-10. www.mdlandrec.net : accessed 29 January 2022.

against the Lawfull Claim of all and every person or persons whatsoever. In Testimony whereof the said Mary WALLIS have hereunto sett her Hand and seal affixed this fifteenth day of Septemb[e]ʳ Anno Dom[ini] 1781 . . . . .

Signed Sealed and delivered   John TARR
In the presence of us . . . . .   John SELBY   Mary O WALLIS (Seal)
                                                                                         her   mark"

*followed with the acknowledgment by Justice of the Peace John SELBY and the recordation on 10 October 1781 by court clerk James R. MORRIS[294]

Liber K, folio 398; 10 October 1781

"Know all men by these presents that I Samuel SCARBOROUGH of Worcester County in the State of Maryland for and in consideration of the sum of forty seven pounds Specie to me in hand paid at and before the sealing and delivery of these presents by Major TOWNSEND of the County and State aforesaid the receipt whereof I do hereby acknowledge have bargained and sold and by these presents do bargain and sell unto the said Major TOWNSEND one negro feller Named **Nabb** To have and to hold the said Negro feller called **Nabb** by these presents bargained and sold unto the said Major TOWNSEND his Heirs Executors Administrators and Assigns forever and I the said Samuel SCARBOROUGH for myself my Executors and Administrators the said Negro feller Named **Nabb**, unto the said Major TOWNSEND his Executors Administrators and Assigns against me the said Samuel SCARBOROUGH my Executors Administrators and Assigns and against all and every person & persons whatsoever shall and will warrent and forever defend by these presents which Negro **Nabb**, I the said Samuel have put the said Major TOWNSEND in full possession by delivering the said Negro **Nabb** to the said Major TOWNSEND before the Sealing of these presents In Witness my hand and seal the Tenth day of October Anno Domini Seventeen hundred and Eighty one

Signed Sealed and delivered   Joshua TOWNSEND   Sam[ue]ˡ SCARBOROUGH (Seal)"
In presents off . . . . .

*followed with the acknowledgment by Justice of the Peace Joshua TOWNSEND and the recordation on 12 October 1781 by court clerk James R. MORRIS[295]

Liber K, folios 399-400; 20 December 1781

"To all People whom these presents may concern Know ye that I Daniel SELBY of Worcester County in the State of Maryland Send Greeting for and in Consideration of the Natural love and Affection which I have and bear unto Alexander TAYLOR of the County and State aforesaid And also for other good causes and considerations me thereunto moving have given and granted, and by these presents do give grant and confirm unto the said Alexander TAYLOR his Heirs and Assigns forever, my Negroes by Name **Isaac, Ben, Adam, Pleasant, Amy, Sall** and **Leah** as well all other my Goods Chattels, Leases, Debts, Plate Household Furniture Creatures and Stock of what kind so ever and all my other Substance whatsoever, moveable and immovable of what kind, Nature and quality soever the same are in what place, or places soever the same shall be found as well in my Custody or possession as in the possession hands power Custody of any other person or persons whatsoever To have and to Hold all and Singular the said Negroes, and goods, Chattels, Leases Debts and all other the aforesaid above mentioned primisses unto the said Alexander TAYLOR his Heirs Executors Administrators and Assigns to his and their proper use and uses forever, And I the said Daniel SELBY all and Singular the aforesaid mentioned Negroes by name and goods Chattels and primisses to the said Alexander TAYLOR his Heirs Executors Administrators and Assigns forever against all person or persons, do Warrant and do ingage to defend by these presents In Witness whereof the said Daniel

---

[294] Worcester County Court (Land Records). Bill of sale from WALLIS, Mary to JOHNSON, Mary. 15 September 1781. K, p. 398, MSA CE 30-10. www.mdlandrec.net : accessed 29 January 2022.

[295] Worcester County Court (Land Records). Bill of sale from SCARBOROUGH, Samuel to TOWNSEND, Major. 10 October 1781. K, p. 398, MSA CE 30-10. www.mdlandrec.net : accessed 29 January 2022.

SELBY hath here unto his Hand set and seal affixed this Twentieth day of December Anno Dom[ini] one thousand seven hundred and Eighty one.

Signed Sealed & delivered   N. HOLLAND ~ ~
In the presence of . . . . .   John PARRAMORE   Dan[ie]¹ X SELBY (Seal)
                                                                                                           mark"

*followed on folio 400 with the acknowledgment by Justices of the Peace N. HOLLAND and John PARRAMORE and the recordation on 21 December 1781 by court clerk James R. MORRIS[296]

Liber K, folio 405; 21 January 1782

"This indenture made this twenty first Day January or first month Anno Seventeen Hundred and Eighty two Between Daniel MIFFLIN of Worcester Count in Maryland of the one part, And Negroes **Nead, Perrey, Joshua, John Sam, Liddia Sal** and her two Children (viz) **Rhoda** and **Thamer, Bette** and her daughter **Susey Leah** and her two Children **Isaac and George, Rachel** and her three Children (viz) **Nanney Charity** and **Gilbert** and **Ben,** they and every of them being under the age of fifty years of the other part Witnesseth that the s[ai]ᵈ Daniel for and in consideration of the faithfull service of the above s[ai]ᵈ Negroes and their good behaviour in General and being Desirous that the s[ai]ᵈ Negroes should be manumitted and forever with their issue) Set free from Slavery hath Manumitted sett free and forever discharged and by these presents doth Manumit set free and forever discharge the said Negroes and their issue from him the s[ai]ᵈ Daniel MIFFLIN his Heirs and Assigns Reserving only to himself and his Heirs and Assigns the Guardianship of the young ones till and only untill the Male arive to the age of twenty one years and the female till and only untill they arive to the age of Eighteen years and the said Daniel MIFFLIN doth covenant and argue to and with the said Negroes all and every of them and their Heirs that they are by these presents forever Manumitted and set free, and that he the said Daniel MIFFLIN his Heirs Executors or Administrators hath not nor shall have any Right Title, Intrest claim or demand of in or unto the said Negroes or either of them save only the young ones as above mentioned or either of their Heirs In Testimony whereof the s[ai]ᵈ Daniel MIFFLIN to these presents his hand hath put and Seal Affixed the day and year above written ……..

Signed Sealed and Delivered   John SELBY   Daniel MIFFLIN (Seal)
in presence of ~ ~ ~ ~   Daniel SELBY

In the foregoing Deed there appeared the following Interlineation { ? } the Wittnesses before whom the S[ai]ᵈ deed was Acknowledged, Certified that, that Interlineation was made before the Sealing & Delivery in the following words (to wit) the four Negroes Interlined (viz) **Rachel** & her three Children **Nanney Charity** and **Gilbert** and **Ben** Interlined before the Sealing & delivery hereof"

*followed with acknowledgment by Justice of the Peace John SELBY and the recordation on 26 January 1782 by court clerk James R. MORRIS[297]

Liber K, folio 407; 24 January 1782

"Know all men by these presents That I William BALLARD of Sommerset County in the State of Maryland for and in consideration of the sum of Sixty five pounds current money of Maryland to me in hand paid at and before the Sealing and delivery of these presents by William SELBY of Worcester County and State aforesaid the Receipt whereof I do hereby acknowledge have bargained and Sold and by these presents do Bargain and Sell unto the said William SELBY a Negro girl by the name of **Lydda** about fifteen years old To Have and to Hold the

---

[296] Worcester County Court (Land Records). Deed of Gift from SELBY, Daniel to TAYLOR, Alexander. 20 December 1781. K, pp. 399-400, MSA CE 30-10. www.mdlandrec.net : accessed 29 January 2022.

[297] Worcester County Court (Land Records). Deed of Manumission from MIFFLIN, Daniel to **Nead, Perrey, Joshua**, etal. 21 January 1782. K, p. 405, MSA CE 30-10. www.mdlandrec.net : accessed 29 January 2022.

said Negro girl called **Lydda** and her hereafter increase and every of them by these presents bargained and Sold unto the said William SELBY his Executors administrators and assigns forever and I the said William BALLARD for myself my Executors and adm[inistrato]^{rs} all and Singular the said Negro girl and increase unto the said William his Heirs Executors Administrators and Assigns against me the Said William BALLARD my Heirs Executors and Administrators and Assigns and against all and every other person or persons whatsoever, Shall and will warrant and for ever defend by these presents of Which said Negro Girl I the said put the said William SELBY in full possession by the delivery of these presents In Witness whereof I the said William BALLARD have hereunto Set my Hand and Seal this Twenty fourth day of January Anno Dom[ini] Seventeen hundred and Eighty two . . . . .

Signed Sealed & Delivered   William BALLARD (Seal)
in the presence of ~   Joshua TOWNSEND"

*followed with the acknowledgment by Justice of the Peace Joshua TOWNSEND and the recordation on 12 February 1782 by court clerk James R. MORRIS[298]

Liber K, folio 413; 23 February 1782

"Know all men by these presents that I John Ennals SCOTT of Worcester County in the State of Maryland for and in consideration of the Sum of Sixty five pounds current money of Maryland to me in hand paid at and before the sealing and delivery of these presents by James KELLAM of the same place the receipt Whereof I do hereby Acknowledge and myself fully Satisfied Contented and paid, Have Bargained and Sold and by these presents do Bargain and sell unto the said James KELLAM a Negro boy called **Handy**, about fourteen years old, now remaining and being in the possession of the said John Ennal SCOTT To have and to Hold the said Negro Boy called **Handy** as above mentioned by these presents bargained and sold unto the said James KELLAM his Heirs and Assigns forever, And I the said John Ennals SCOTT for myself my Heirs Executors and Administrators, all and Singular the said Negro Boy called **Handy** aforesaid unto the said James KELLAM his Heirs Executors Administrators and Assigns, against me the said John Ennals SCOTT my Heirs Executors Administrators and Assigns, and against all and every other person and persons whatsoever shall and will Warrant an forever defend by these presents of which said Negro Boy Called **Handy** af[ore]s[ai]^d I the said John Ennals SCOTT have put the said James KELLAM in full possession & by the delivery of the said Negro af[ore]s[ai]^d at the sealing hearof In Witness whereof I the said John Ennals SCOTT have hereunto set my hand and Seal affixed this twenty third day of February Anno Dom[ini] one thousand seven hundred and Eighty two. ~

Signed Sealed & Delivered   John Ennals SCOTT. (Seal)
in the presence of ~ ~   William SELBY Jun[io]^r"

*followed with the acknowledgment by Justice of the Peace Joshua TOWNSEND and the recordation on 06 March 1782 by court clerk James R. MORRIS[299]

Liber K, folio 418; 26 February 1782

"Know all men by these presents that I Henry WILLITT of Worcester County in the State of Maryland for and in Consideration of of the Sum of fifty pounds Specie to me in hand paid at and before the Sealing and delivery of these presents by McKinny PORTER of the County and State aforesaid the Receipt whereof I do hereby Acknowledge myself Sattisfied and paid have bargained and Sold and by these presents do bargain and Sell unto the said McKinny PORTER one Negro Girl called **Sue** about Ten years of age now in the possession of the said Henry WILLITT To have and to hold the said Negro girl called Sue by these presents bargained and Sold unto the said McKinny PORTER his Heirs and Assigns forever And I the said Henry

---

[298] Worcester County Court (Land Records). Bill of sale from BALLARD, William to SELBY, William. 24 January 1782. K, p. 407, MSA CE 30-10. www.mdlandrec.net : accessed 29 January 2022.
[299] Worcester County Court (Land Records). Bill of sale from SCOTT, John Ennals to KELLAM, James. 23 February 1782. K, p. 413, MSA CE 30-10. www.mdlandrec.net : accessed 29 January 2022.

WILLETT for my Self my heirs Executors and Administrators the said Negro girl called **Sue** will Warrant and forever defend unto the said McKinny PORTER his Heirs and Assigns forever against the lawful Claim of all manner Persons Whatsoever In Witness whereof I the said Henry WILLITT have hereunto set my hand and Seal affixed the 26th day of February Anno Domini Seventeen hundred and Eighty two.

Signed sealed and delivered   Henry WILLITT   (Seal)
in the presents of ~ ~ ~"

*followed with the acknowledgment by Justice of the Peace Joshua TOWNSEND and the recordation on 12 March 1782 by court clerk James R. MORRIS[300]

Liber K, folios 440-441; 04 June 1782

"Maryland Worcester County Know all men by these presents that we Thomas RICHARDSON and Charles SAWYER for and in Consideration of the Sum of Seventy pounds Specets in hand paid at and before the sealing and delivery of these presents by the said John BISHOP the receipt whereof we do hearby Acknowledge Have bargained and Sold and by these presents do bargain and Sell unto the said John BISHOP One Negro wench called **Leviner** late the property of Mr. John RICHARDSON (deceased) now in the possession of Thomas RICHARDSON and Charles SAWYER To have and to Hold the said Negro by these presents bargained and Sold unto the Said John BISHOP his Heirs Executors Admin[istrato]rs & Assigns forever and we the Said Thomas RICHARDSON and Charles SAWYER for ourselves our Executors Administrators the said Negro called **Leviner** unto the said John BISHOP his Executors administrators and Assigns against we the said Thomas RICHARDSON and Charles SAWYER our Executors Administrators and assigns and against all and every other person and persons Whatsoever Shall and will Warrant and forever defend by these presents of which Negro we the Said Thomas RICHARDSON and Charles SAWYER have put the said John BISHOP in full possession by delivering the said Negro Wench called **Leviner** at the sealing Hearof In Witness Whereof our Hands and Seals the 4th day of June 1783 ~ ~

Signed Sealed & Delivered   Joshua TOWNSEND   Thomas RICHARDSON (Seal)
in the presence of ~ ~   Charles SAWYER (Seal)"

*followed with the acknowledgment by Justice of the Peace Joshua TOWNSEND and the recordation on 04 June 1782 by court clerk James R. MORRIS[301]

Liber K, folio 471; 01 October 1782

"Maryland Worcester County to witt Know all men by these Presents that I Daniel SELBY of the County and State af[ore]s[ai]d am held and firmly bound unto Thomas TAYLOR of the same place in the full and just sum of two hundred pounds current money of the State Af[ore]s[ai]d Specia either Gold or Silver to the which payment well and truly to be made and done I bind myself my heirs Executors or Administrators and every of them firmly by these presents I bind myself unto the said Thomas TAYLOR his Heirs Executors or Administrators or Assigns firmly by these presence Sealed with my Seal and dated this first day of October Anno Domini Seventeen and Eighty two

The Condition of the above Obligation is Such that if the above bound Daniel SELBY his Heirs Executors Administrators or Assigns do make a good indefesable Wright and Title to a Negro Garle called **Jibb** and hur ever defend to be the wright Title and Intrust of Thomas TAYLOR his Heirs Executors administrators or Assigns then the above Obligation to be void otherwise of full force and virtue in Law.

---

[300] Worcester County Court (Land Records). Bill of sale from WILLITT, Henry to PORTER, McKinny. 26 February 1782. K, p. 418, MSA CE 30-10. www.mdlandrec.net : accessed 29 January 2022.
[301] Worcester County Court (Land Records). Bill of sale from RICHARDSON, Thomas and SAWYER, Charles to BISHOP, John. 04 June 1782. K, pp. 440-441, MSA CE 30-10. www.mdlandrec.net : accessed 29 January 2022.

Signed Sealed and Delivered	Geo[rge] TRUITT Jun[io]^r		
In presence of ~ ~	Levin BLAKE	Daniel X SELBY (Seal)	
		his mark"	

*followed with the recordation on 27 December 1782 by court clerk James R. MORRIS[302]

Liber K, folio 478; 01 October 1782

"Maryland Ss^t. All men by these presents that I Henry WILLETT of Worcester County in the State aforesaid have in consideration of the sum of twenty pounds Specie sold unto Francis RANDALL of the same place a certain Negro Girl named **Esther**, to him his Heirs and Assigns which said Negro Girl, the said Henry WILLETT doth hereby sell unto the said Francis RANDAL aforesaid & doth warran and defend the same against all and every person & persons claiming the same from, by or under him. In Testimony whereof I have hereto set my Hand and affixed my seal this first day of October Anno Domini 1782 . . . .

Signed, Sealed & Deliver[e]d in presence of   Peter CHAILLE   Henry WILLITT   (Seal)"

*followed with the recordation by court clerk James R. MORRIS[303]

Liber K, folios 478-479; 02 October 1782

"Know all men by these Presents that I Philip SELBY of Worcester County in the State of Maryland for and in consideration of the sum of Eighty Pounds current money od the State af[oresai]^d to me in hand paid by John SELBY of the same place at and before the sealing and delivery of these presents the Receipt whereof I do hereby acknowledge, and have given granted bargained and Sold and by these presents for give grant bargain and Sell unto the said John SELBY and his Heirs and Assigns forever one Negro man slave called **Jacob**. To have and to Hold the said Negro man Slave called **Jacob** unto the said John SELBY and his and Assigns forever only reserving the use of said Negro man Slave called **Jacob** unto the said Philip untill the first day of January next at which time the said Phillip SELBY doth bind and Oblidge him the said Phillip SELBY and his Heirs to Deliver the said Negrow man Slave called **Jacob** unto the John SELBY and his Heirs or Assigns, and the said Philip SELBY his Heirs or Assigns, and the said Philip SELBY doth covenant with the said John SELBY that he the said Philip his Heirs Ex[ecutor]^s and Administrators shall and will forever Warrant and Defend the said Negro man Slave called **Jacob** unto the said John SELBY and his Heirs and Assigns forever against the lawfull claim of all and every person or persons whatsoever with only the above Exception In Witness whereof the said Phillip SELBY to these Presents his Hand hath Sett and seal have affixed this second day of October Anno Dom[ini] 1782.

Signed Sealed and Delivered	Joshua TOWNSEND	Philip SELBY (Seal)
in the presence of us ~ ~	Parker SELBY"	

*followed on folio 479 with the acknowledgment by Justice of the Peace Joshua TOWNSEND and recordation by court clerk James R. MORRIS[304]

Liber K, folio 495; 18 February 1783

"Know all men by these presents that I James ATKINSON of Worcester County for and in consideration of Charles BENNETT and Henry ATKINSON their becoming my Securities to a certain John LEEDS of Talbot for the sum of Eighty three pounds Seven Shillings and nine pence by Bond bearing date the same day of these presents Have bargained and sold and by these presents do bargain and sell unto the said Charles BENNETT and Henry ATKINSON the

---

[302] Worcester County Court (Land Records). Bond from SELBY, Daniel to TAYLOR, Thomas. 01 October 1782. K, p. 417, MSA CE 30-10. www.mdlandrec.net : accessed 30 January 2022.
[303] Worcester County Court (Land Records). Bill of sale from WILLETT, Henry to RANDALL, Francis. 01 October 1782. K, p. 478, MSA CE 30-10. www.mdlandrec.net : accessed 30 January 2022.
[304] Worcester County Court (Land Records). Bill of sale from SELBY, Philip to SELBY, John. 02 October 1782. K, pp. 478-479, MSA CE 30-10. www.mdlandrec.net : accessed 30 January 2022.

following Negroes to with, **Jack, Shadrach,** and **Isaac** to have and to hold the said Negroes unto the said Charles BENNETT and Henry ATKINSON their Heirs, Executors and Administrators Provided Nevertheless and it is the true intent and meaning of these presents that the said James ATKINSON shall retain the use and possession of the said Negroes unless the said Charles BENNETT and Henry ATKINSON are Damnified by means of the Suretiship af[ore]s[ai]^d and it is hereby declared to be the full intent and meaning hereof that this Deed of Bargain and Sale is only and merely in Trust to save Harmless and keep indemnified the said Charles BENNETT and Henry ATKINSON their Executors and Adm[inistrator]^s from the said Suretiship and that if they or either of them shoud hereafter be damnified by means of the premisses may Take the possession of sell so many or the whole of the Said Negroes as make them whole, In Testimony whereof the said James ATKINSON hath hereto set his Hand and seal the 18 Feb[rua]^{ry} 1783 ~

Sealed & Delivered   James ATKINSON   (Seal)
in Presence of   Joshua TOWNSEND."

*followed with the acknowledgment of Justice of the Peace Joshua TOWNSEND and recordation by court clerk James R. MORRIS[305]

Liber K, folio 501; 06 March 1783

"Know all men by these presents that I Philip SELBY of Worcester County in the State of Maryland for and in consideration of the Sum of Sixty five pounds current money of Maryland to me in hand paid at and before the Sealing and delivery of these presents by William BRITTINGHAM Sener of the County and State aforesaid the receipt whereof I do hereby Acknowledge have bargained and Sold and by these presents do bargain and Sell unto the said William BRITTINGHAM one Negro Women called **Leah** to have and to hold the said Negro Women called **Leah** by these presents bargained and Sold unto the said William BRITTINGHAM his Heirs and Assigns forever and I the said Philip SELBY for myself my Heirs Executors and Administrators the said Negro Women called **Leah** unto the Said William BRITTINGHAM his Heirs Executors Administrators and Assigns against me the Said Philip SELBY my Heirs Executors and Administrators and against all and every other person or persons Whatsoever Shall and Will Warrant and forever Defend the said Negro women called **Leah** unto the Said William BRITTINGHAM his Heirs and Assigns forever in Witness Whereof I the Said Philip SELBY have hereunto my Hand Set and Seal Affixed the 6th day of March Anno Domini Seventeen hundred and eighty three ~

Signed Sealed and delivered   Littleton ROBINS   Philip SELBY   (Seal)
in the presents of   Joshua TOWNSEND"

*followed with the acknowledgment by Justice of the Peace Joshua TOWNSEND and recordation by court clerk James R. MORRIS[306]

Liber K, folio 501; 07 March 1783

"Know all men by these Presents that I William ATKINSON of Worcester County in the State of Maryland (Planter for and in consideration of the Sum of Sixty pounds Specia to me in hand paid at and before the Sealing and delivery of these presents, by Ezekiel COSTON of the Same place, the receipt whereof I do hereby Acknowledge and myself fully satisfied Contented and paid have bargained and Sold and by these presents do Bargain and Sell unto the said Ezekiel COSTON his Heirs and Assigns forever one Negro Wench called **Agur** and one Negro Child called **Sophia** To have and to Hold all and Singular the above mentioned Negroes Woman and Child, and every of them by these presents bargained and Sold unto the said Ezekiel COSTON

---

[305] Worcester County Court (Land Records). Bill of sale from ATKINSON, James to BENNETT, Charles and ATKINSON, Henry. 18 February 1783. K, p. 495, MSA CE 30-10. www.mdlandrec.net : accessed 30 January 2022.
[306] Worcester County Court (Land Records). Bill of sale from SELBY, Philip to BRITTINGHAM, William. 06 March 1783. K, p. 501, MSA CE 30-10. www.mdlandrec.net : accessed 30 January 2022.

his Heirs and Assigns forever And I the Said William ATKINSON for myself and my Heirs Executors and Administrators or any of them, or any other person or persons whatsoever, the Said Woman **Agur** & Child called **Sophia** Shall and Will Warrant and forever Defend by these presents unto the Said Ezekiel COSTON his Heirs and Assigns forever of which said Negro Woman & Child I the Said William ATKINSON have put the said Ezekiel COSTON in full possession by the of the Same In Testimony whereof the Said William ATKINSON have his Hand and Seal Affixed this Seventh day of March Anno Dom[ini] One thousand seven hundred and Eighty three.

Signed Sealed & Delivered in the Presence of.

    Joshua TOWNSEND.   William ATKINSON (Seal)"

*followed with the acknowledgment of Justice of the Peace Joshua TOWNSEND and recordation by court clerk James R. MORRIS[307]

Liber K, folio 521; 26 April 1783

"Maryland Sc^t. Know all men by these presents that I James AYRES of Worcester County for and in Consideration of the sum of fifty pounds Specie to me in hand paid by William S. HILL have Sold and these presents do sell unto the said William Steven HILL a certain Young Negro Girl Named **Betty** which said Girl the said James AYRES for myself my Heirs Executors and Administrators unto the said William Steven HILL his Heirs Executors administrators and Assigns will Warrant and Defend. In Testimony Whereof I have hereto set my Han and affixed my seal this twenty sixth day of April 1783   James AYRES (Seal)

Signed Sealed & Delivered in the presence of John SELBY"

*followed with the acknowledgment by Justice of the Peace John SELBY and recordation by court clerk James R. MORRIS[308]

Liber K, folios 523-524; 28 April 1783

"Know all men by these presents that we Margaret, Sarah & Rachel McALLEN of Worcester County in the state of Maryland for and in Consideration of the sum of thirty five pounds current money of Maryland to us in hand paid at and before the Sealing and delivery of these presents by Alexander McALLEN the receipt Whereof we do hereby Acknowledge have bargained and sold and by these presents doth bargain and sell unto the said Alexander McALLEN his heirs and Assigns one Negro woman called **Rose** & one negro Girl called **Rose** to have and to hold the said two Negroes by these presents bargained and sold unto the said Alexander McALLEN his heirs and Assigns forever and we the said Margaret Sarah and Rachel McALLEN for ourselves our Executors and Administrators the said two Negroes unto the said Alexander McALLEN his heirs Executors Administrators and Assigns against us the said Margaret Sarah and Rachell McALLEN ourselves our heirs Executors and Administrators and Against all and every person and persons Whatsoever shall and will Warrant and forever defend by these presents of Which Negroes we the said Margaret, Sarah and Rachel McALLEN have put the said Alexander McALLEN in full possession by delivering the said Negroes unto the said Allexander McALLEN at the sealing hereof In Witness whereof we the said Margaret Sarah and Rachel McALLEN our hands have set and seals affixed the 28th day of April Anno Domini Seventeen hundred and Eighty three ~

Signed Sealed and delivered Joshua TOWNSEND   her
in presents of ~ ~ ~   Margaret + McALLEN (Seal)
                   mark

                   her

---

[307] Worcester County Court (Land Records). Bill of sale from ATKINSON, William to COSTON, Ezekiel. 07 March 1783. K, p. 501, MSA CE 30-10. www.mdlandrec.net : accessed 30 January 2022.

[308] Worcester County Court (Land Records). Bill of sale from AYRES, James to HILL, William Steven. 26 April 1783. K, p. 521, MSA CE 30-10. www.mdlandrec.net : accessed 30 January 2022.

                                                  Sarah X McALLEN (Seal)
                                                     mark

                                                     her
                                                Rachel ⁺ McALLEN (Seal)
                                                      mark"

*followed on folio 524 with acknowledgment by Justice of the Peace Joshua TOWNSEND and the recordation on 29 April 1783 by court clerk James R. MORRIS[309]

Liber K, folio 537; 20 March 1783

"Know all men by these presents that I John BENSON for & in Consideration of the Sum of two hundred pounds current money of Maryland to me in hand paid by John STEWART of Worcester County in the State of Maryland at & before the Sealing & delivery here of the receipt whereof he doth hereby Acknowledge, Hath given granted bargained sold & delivered & by these presents doth for himself & his heirs freely clearly & Absolutely Grant bargain & sell unto the said John STEWART his heirs & Assigns forever One Negro Wench named **Hannah** twenty five years old & her Child named **Candis** three years old One Negro Girl named **Esther** Seven years Old One Negro boy named **Able** fourteen years old & one Negro boy **George** Sixteen year old To have & to hold all & every of the aforesaid Negros unto the said John STEWART his heirs & Assigns forever & to or for no other use Whatsoever. And the said John BENSON for himself his heirs Executors & Administrators all and every the aforesaid Negroes as above mentioned & described, unto the said John STEWART his heirs & Assigns forever, against all & every Person or Persons whatsoever now claiming or hereafter to Claim to all or either of them, Shall and will Warrant & by these presents forever defend In Testimony whereof the said John BENSON to these his hand hath Set and Seal Affixed the twentieth day of March A.D. 1783.

Signed Sealed & delivered   John POSTLY ~ ~   John BENSON (Seal)
In the presence of ~ ~ ~ ~   Joshua TOWNSEND"

*followed with the acknowledgment by Justice of the Peace John POSTLY and the recordation on 19 September 1783 by court clerk James R. MORRIS[310]

Liber K, folios 537-538; 11 August 1783

"The State of Maryland Worcester County Ss[t]. To all people to whom these presents shall come I John FRANKLIN of the County af[oresai]d send greeting. Know ye that I the said John FRANKLIN for and in Consideration of the sum of Ninety Pounds in Specia to me in hand paid by Henry FRANKLIN of the County af[oresai]d The receipt whereof I do hereby acknowledge have granted bargained and sold and by these presents do grant bargain and sell unto the said Henry FRANKLIN one Negro Woman called **Leah** and also one Negro Garle about three months old called **Sarah**. To have and to hold the aforesaid Negro Woman called **Leah** and the af[ore]s[ai]d Negro Garle called **Sarah** hereby granted bargained and Sold unto the said Henry FRANKLIN his Heirs Executors Administrators and Assignes as his and their own proper use and to his and their own proper use and uses forever and I the said John FRANKLIN do for myself my Heirs Executors and Administrators Covenant and grant to and with the said Henry FRANKLIN his Exec[uto]rs and Adm[inistrato]rs and Assigns that I the said John FRANKLIN at the Time of the sealing and delivery of these presents am the true and lawfull owner and proprietor of the said Negro Woman called **Leah** & Negro Garle called **Sarah** hereby granted and Sold, and have full power and lawfull Authority to grant and Convey the said Negro Woman & Negro Garle hereby mentioned unto the said Henrey FRANKLIN his Exec[uto]rs Adm[inistrato]rs or Assignes in manner and form af[oresai]d and that it shall and may be lawfull

---

[309] Worcester County Court (Land Records). Bill of sale from McALLEN, Margaret, McALLEN, Sarah, and McALLEN, Rachel to McALLEN, Alexander. 28 April 1783. K, pp. 523-524, MSA CE 30-10. www.mdlandrec.net : accessed 30 January 2022.

[310] Worcester County Court (Land Records). Bill of sale from BENSON, John to STEWART, John. 20 March 1783. K, p. 537, MSA CE 30-10. www.mdlandrec.net : accessed 30 January 2022.

to and for the said Henry FRANKLIN his Heirs Executors Administrators or Assigns from and after the twenty fifth day of December next peaceably and Quietly to have hold and enjoy the said Negro Woman called **Leah** & Garle called **Sarah** without any disturbance Molestation or Interruption of me the said John FRANKLIN my Exec[uto]^{rs} Adm[inistrato]^{rs} or Assignes or of any other person or persons Whatsoever lawfully claiming or to claim from by or under me them or any of them In Witness whereof I have hereunto set my Hand and Seal Affixed this 11th day of August Ano Domini one thousand seven hundred & eighty three

Seal[e]d & Delive[re]d In presents of   Josiah MITCHELL   John FRANKLIN (Seal)

her
Nancy X BETTS
mark"

*followed on folio 538 with the acknowledgment by Josiah MITCHELL and the recordation on 12 August 1783 by court clerk James R. MORRIS[311]

Liber K, folios 538-539; 06 June 1783

"This Indenture made the 6th day of June Seventeen hundred & eighty three Between Levin BLAKE of Worcester County in the State of Maryland of the one part and William BISHOP (Sener) of the same place of the other part Witnesseth that the said Levin BLAKE for and in Consideration of the sum of fifteen pounds Current Money of Maryland to him in hand paid by the said William BISHOP at and before the Sealing and delivery of these presents the Receipt whereof the said Levin BLAKE doth hereby Acknowledge he the said Levin BLAKE hath bargained and sold and by these Presents doth bargain and sell unto the said William BISHOP his Heirs and Assigns, one Negro Man called and named **Doary** to have and to hold the said Negro **Doary** above by these presents bargained and Sold unto the said William BISHOP his Heirs and Assigns forever provided always and upon Condition that if the said Levin BLAKE his Executors or Administrators do and shall well and truly pay or Cause to be paid unto the said William BISHOP his Heirs or Assigns the full and just sum of fifteen pounds paid Money on or before the first day of September next ensuing with legal Intrust theiron that then these presents and every thing theirin contained shall cease determine and be void any thing herein contained to the contrary in any wise notwithstanding and the said Levin BLAKE for himself his Heirs and Executors doth covenant and grant to and with the said William BISHOP his Heirs and Assigns that he the said Levin BLAKE his Executors and Administrators shall and will well and truly pay or cause to be paid unto the said William BISHOP his Heirs Executors Administrators and Assigns the said sum of fifteen pounds at the day and Time and in Manner and form aforesaid according to the true intent and meaning of these presents in Witness whereof the said Levin BLAKE his Hand hath set and seal affixed the day and year first above written ~

Signed Sealed and delivered   Levin BLAKE ~ ~ (Seal)
In presents off   Joshua TOWNSEND."

*followed on folio 539 with the recordation by court clerk James R. MORRIS on 13 August 1783[312]

Liber K, folios 540-541; 15 August 1783

"This Indenture made the fifteenth day of August Anno Domini seventeen hundred and eighty three Between Philip SELBY of Worcester County and State of Maryland of the one part and John GUN of the same place of the other part Witnesseth that the said Philip SELBY for and in Consideration of the sum of forty pounds current Money of Maryland to him in hand paid by the said John GUN at and before the Sealing and delivery of these presents the receipt whereof

---

[311] Worcester County Court (Land Records). Bill of sale from FRANKLIN, John to FRANKLIN, Henry. 11 August 1783. K, pp. 537-538, MSA CE 30-10. www.mdlandrec.net : accessed 30 January 2022.

[312] Worcester County Court (Land Records). Deed of mortgage from BLAKE, Levin to BISHOP, William. 06 June 1783. K, pp. 538-539, MSA CE 30-10. www.mdlandrec.net : accessed 30 January 2022.

the said Philip SELBY doth hereby confess and acknowledge, Hath granted, bargained and Sold and by these presents doth grant, bargain & Sell unto the said John GUN his Heirs and Assigns forever one Negro Girl named **Lyd** with her increase to have and to hold the said Negro Girl with her increase unto the said John GUN his Heirs and Assigns forever and to and for no other use intent or purpose whatsoever, And the said Philip doth hereby covenant and agree to and with the said John GUN his Heirs and Assigns forever that the said Philip SELBY and his Heirs the Negro Girl af[oresai]^d and her increase to the said John GUN and his Heirs and Assigns shall and Will Warrant and forever Defend ~ In Testimony whereof the said Philip to these presents his hand hath put and seal affixed the day and year above written.

Sealed & delivered	John SELBY	Philip SELBY (Seal)
in presence of	Ezekiel KNOX"	

*followed on folio 541 with the acknowledgment by Justice of the Peace John SELBY and the recordation on 16 August 1783 by court clerk James R. MORRIS[313]

Liber K, folio 541; 11 August 1783

"Know all men by these presents that we Margaret, Sarah & Rachel McALLEN of Worcester County in the State of Maryland for and in consideration of the sum of forty pounds current Money of Maryland to us in hand paid at and before the sealing and delivery of these presents by Alexander McALLEN of the County and State of aforesaid The receipt whereof we do hereby Acknowledge have bargained and Sold and by these presents do bargain and Sell unto the said Allexander McALLEN his Heirs and Assigns one Negro Boy named **Peter** and one Negro Girl called **Hatter** and each of them the said two Negroes {?} to the said Allexander McALLEN his Heirs Executors Administrators and Assigns forever, And we the said Margaret Sarah & Rachell McALLEN for Ourselves our and each of our Heirs the said two Negroes Unto the said Allexander McALLEN his Heirs and Assigns will warrant and forever defend, and against all and all Manner of Persons whatsoever ever hereafter claiming the said Negro **Peter** and Negro **Hatter** which Negroes we the said Margaret Sarah & Rachel McALLEN have put the said Allexander McALLEN in full possession by delivering him the same at the Sealing hereof In Witness whereof we the said Margaret Sarah and Rachel McALLEN have hereunto our hands set and Seals affixed the 11th day of August Anno Domini Seventeen hundred and eighty three ~

Signed Sealed and ~	Joshua TOWNSEND	Margaret X McALLEN (Seal) her Mark
delivered in presents off		
		Sarah X McALLEN (Seal) her Mark
		Rachel X McALLEN (Seal) her Mark"

*followed with the acknowledgment by Justice of the Peace Joshua TOWNSEND and the recordation on 19 August 1783 by court clerk James R. MORRIS[314]

Liber K, folios 541-542; 22 August 1783

"Know all men by these presents that I Benjamin HAYWARD of Worcester County in the State of Maryland for and in Consideration of the Sum of one hundred pounds current Money of Maryland to me in hand paid all and before the sealing and delivery of these presents by Joshua

---

[313] Worcester County Court (Land Records). Deed from SELBY, Philip to GUN, John. 15 August 1783. K, pp. 540-541, MSA CE 30-10. www.mdlandrec.net : accessed 30 January 2022.

[314] Worcester County Court (Land Records). Bill of sale from McALLEN, Margaret, McALLEN, Sarah, and McALLEN, Rachel to McALLEN, Alexander. 11 August 1783. K, p. 541, MSA CE 30-10. www.mdlandrec.net : accessed 30 January 2022.

TOWNSEND of the County and State aforesaid the receipt whereof I do hereby acknowledge have bargained and sold and by these presents do bargain and sell unto the said Joshua TOWNSEND his Heirs and Assigns forever one Negro Woman named **Dider** and one Negro Girl named **Mary** (Child of the said **Dider** to have and to hold the said two Negroes by these presents bargained and sold unto the said Joshua TOWNSEND his Heirs and Assigns forever And I the said Benjamin HAYWARD for myself my Executors and Administrators the said Two Negroes unto the said Joshua TOWNSEND his Heirs and Assigns against me the said Benjamin HAYWARD my Heirs Executors and Administrators and against all and all manner of persons whatsoever shall and will warrant and forever defend by these presents the said two Negroes unto the said Joshua TOWNSEND his Heirs and Assigns forever In Testimony whereof the said Benjamin HAYWARD, hereunto his Hand hath set and seal affixed the 22th day of August Anno Domini seventeen hundred and eighty three

Signed Sealed and   John SELBY   Benj^a[min] HAYWARD (Seal)
delivered in presents off   Philip QUINTON"

*followed on folio 542 with the acknowledgment John SELBY and the recordation by court clerk James R. MORRIS[315]

Liber K, folio 545; 22 August 1783

"Know all men by these presents that I Benjamin HAYWARD of Worcester County in the State of Maryland for and in Consideration of sum of fifty pounds to me in hand paid at and before the sealing and delivery of these presents by Philip QUINTON of the County and State aforesaid the Receipt whereof I do hereby acknowledge have bargained and Sold and by these presents do bargain and sell unto the said Philip QUINTON one Negro lad named **Sam**, to have and to hold the said Negro **Sam** by these presents bargained and Sold unto the said Philip QUINTON, and I the said Benjamin HAYWARD for myself my Heirs Executors and Administrators the said Negro **Sam** unto the said Philip QUINTON his Heirs and Assigns forever will warrant forever defend against all and every person or persons whatsoever. In Testimony whereof the said Benjamin HAYWARD to these presents his hand hath set and affixed 22th day of August Anno Domini Seventeen hundred and eighty three

Signed Sealed and delivered   John SELBY   Benj^a[min] HAYWARD (Seal)
in presents off   Joshua TOWNSEND"

*followed with the acknowledgment by John SELBY and the recordation by court clerk James R. MORRIS[316]

Liber K, folios 545-546; 20 August 1783

"Worcester County Ss^t. To all people to whom these presents shall come I Sarah HENDERSON do send greeting Know then that I the s[ai]^d Sarah HENDERSON of the County af[ore]s[ai]^d for and in Consideration of the Love good Will and Affection which I have and do bear towards my loving Son Levi HENDERSON of the County af[oresai]^d have given and granted and by these presents do freely clearly and absolutely give and grant unto the s[ai]^d Levi HENDERSON at my decease and not before, all my right and Title to my part of the Negro Woman called **Jenny**, she and her issue if any, to him and his Heirs to have and to hold the s[ai]^d Negro Woman called **Jenny** and her issue after my decease from that time henceforth as the s[ai]^d Levi's proper right absolutely without any manner of Consideration. In Witness whereof I have hereunto set my Hand and Seal affixed this 20 day of August Anno Domini 1783.

Signed sealed and delivered   James SELBY   Sarah HENDERSON (Seal)
in the presence of   James HENDERSON"

---

[315] Worcester County Court (Land Records). Bill of sale from HAYWARD, Benjamin to TOWNSEND, Joshua. 22 August 1783. K, pp. 541-542, MSA CE 30-10. www.mdlandrec.net : accessed 30 January 2022.
[316] Worcester County Court (Land Records). Bill of sale from HAYWARD, Benjamin to QUINTON, Philip. 22 August 1783. K, p. 545, MSA CE 30-10. www.mdlandrec.net : accessed 30 January 2022.

*followed on folio 546 with the recordation on 26 August 1783 by court clerk James R. MORRIS[317]

Liber K, folios 557-558; 20 October 1783

"Know all men by these presents that I James SELBY (son of Micajah) of Worcester County in the State of Maryland for and in consideration of the sum of Twelve Pounds Specia Current Money of Maryland to me in hand paid at and before the sealing and delivery of these presents by Selby PARKER of the same County and State aforesaid the receipt whereof I do hereby Acknowledge have bargained and Sold and by these presents do bargain and sell unto the said Selby PARKER his Heirs and Assigns forever a Negro Man called **Isaac** about thirty five Years old and now in the Possession of a certain Lemuel JOHNSON in the County aforesaid and all right and Title my personal Estate in his hands To have and to hold the said Negro called **Isaac** all and Singular by these presents bargained and sold unto the said Selby PARKER his Heirs Executors Administrators and Assigns forever and I the said James SELBY for myself my Heirs Executors or Adm[inistrato]rs or any of them all and Singular the said Negro above mentioned unto the said Selby PARKER his Heirs and Assigns, against me the said James SELBY or my Heirs Executors or Administrators and against all and every other person or persons whatsoever claiming any right Title or Interest by or under me the said James SELBY or my Heirs Executors or Administrators shall and will Warrant and forever defend by these presents unto the aforesaid Selby PARKER his Heirs and Assigns forever In Testimony whom of the Said James SELBY have interchangeably set his hand and Seal affixed this Twentyeth day of October Anno Dom[ini] Seventeen hundred and eighty three ~

Signed sealed & Delivered   W[illia]m SELBY (S.H   James SELBY   (Seal)
in the presence of ~"

*followed on folio 558 with the acknowledgment by Justice of the Peace Joshua TOWNSEND and the recordation on 28 October 1783 by court clerk James R. MORRIS[318]

Liber K, folio 558; 08 September 1783

"This Indenture made this Eighth day of September in the year of our Lord one thousand seven hundred and eighty three Between Leah AYRES of Worcester County in the State of Maryland of the one part and Selby PARKER of same place of the other part witnesseth that the said Leah AYRES for and in Consideration of the sum of sixteen pounds Current money of Maryland to her in hand paid by the said Selby PARKER before the Sealing and delivery of these presents the receipt whereof is hereby Acknowledge hath bargained and Sold and by these presents doth bargain and Sell assign and Transfer unto him the s[ai]d Selby PARKER his Heirs and Assigns all my Right and Title and Interest which I have or ought to have in Law or Equity in and unto a Negro Man called **Isaac** formerly belonging to my Father Micajah SELBY and also all my right & Title to the other personal Estate of my said Father To have and to hold the same unto him the said Selby PARKER his Heirs and Assigns forever and the said Leah AYRES doth hereby Warrant and Defend all her right and Title to the said Negro and other Personal Estate of her said Father unto the said Selby PARKER his Heirs and Assigns against all and every person who may claim by from or under her in Witness whereof the said Leah AYRES to these presents her hand has set and Seal Affixed the Day and year above Written

Signed Sealed & Deliver[e]d   N. HOLLAND   her
in presence of   John HOLLAND   Leah X AYRES (Seal)
                                                      mark"

---

[317] Worcester County Court (Land Records). Deed of Gift from HENDERSON, Sarah to HENDERSON, Levi. 20 August 1783. K, pp. 545-546, MSA CE 30-10. www.mdlandrec.net : accessed 30 January 2022.
[318] Worcester County Court (Land Records). Bill of sale from SELBY, James to PARKER, Selby. 20 October 1783. K, pp. 557-558, MSA CE 30-10. www.mdlandrec.net : accessed 30 January 2022.

*followed with the acknowledgment by Justice of the Peace N. HOLLAND and the recordation on 28 October 1783 by court clerk James R. MORRIS[319]

Liber K, folio 561; 02 August 1784

"Maryland Ss^t. Know all men by these presents that we Michael RILEY and Patrick JORDON for and in Consideration of the Sum of one hundred pounds Current money of Maryland to them in hand paid by Richard WELSH the Receipt whereof we do hereby Acknowledge, have bargained and Sold and by these presents do bargain and Sell unto the Said Richard WELSH his Heirs and Assigns forever one Negro Wench called **Mary** and one Negro Child Called **Sarah**, To have and to hold the Said Negro Woman called **Mary** and Negro Child Called **Sarah** unto the Said Richard WELSH his Heirs and Assigns forever, and for no other use or purpose whatsoever and the Said Michael RILEY and Patrick JORDON for themselves and their Heirs doth Covenant with the Said Richard WELSH and his Heirs to Warrant and defend the Negros above mentioned to the Said Richard WELSH his Heirs and Assigns for ever. In Testimony whereof we have hereunto Set our hands and affixed Our Seals this Second day of August Anno Dom[ini] Seventeen hundred & Eighty four ~ ~

Signed Sealed and Delivered	Joshua TOWNSEND	Michael RILEY (Seal)
in presence of		Patrick JORDAN (Seal)"

*followed with the acknowledgment by Joshua TOWNSEND and the recordation by court clerk James R. MORRIS[320]

Liber K, folios 562-563; 18 October 1783

"Maryland ~ Worcester County Ss^t. Know all men by these Presents that I Philip SELBY of the County and State af[ore]s[ai]^d for and in consideration of the sum of Sixty four pounds current money of Maryland to me in Hand Paid by Selby NEWTON of the Same Place the receipt whereof I do hereby acknowledge have bargained and Sold and by these presents do bargain and Sell unto the Said Selby NEWTON his Heirs and assigns a certain Negro man Named **George** which said negro man named **George** I the said Philip SELBY for myself my heirs Executors and administrators unto the Said Selby NEWTON his Heirs Executors Administrators and Assigns will Warrant and for ever defend Never the less it is the true intent and meaning of these presents and it is agreed by and between the parties af[ore]s[ai]^d that if the said negro man **George** Shall live and Serve the said Selby NEWTON his heirs or assigns faithfully the full Term of Six years {?} his labour and service at Eleven pounds five Shillings & year untill he shall by his service discharge the Same said sum of Sixty four pounds then the Said Selby NEWTON is to give up and return the said negro to the Said Philip SELBY and it is further agreed by and between the parties af[ore]s[ai]^d that if the said negro **George** should die before he hath Discharged the af[ore]s[ai]^d sum of sixty four pounds that the said Philip SELBY is to bear the loss of the said negro and to pay unto the said Selby NEWTON the ballance that Shall remain due of the af[ore]s[ai]^d Sum In Testimony Whereof I the Said Philip SELBY have hreto set my Hand and affixed my Seal this Eighteenth day of October Anno Dom[ini] 1783

Signed Sealed & delivered		Philip SELBY (Seal)
In presence of ~	John PARRAMORE."	

*followed with the acknowledgment of Justice of the Peace John PARRAMORE and the recordation on 07 November 1783 by court clerk James R. MORRIS[321]

---

[319] Worcester County Court (Land Records). Bill of sale from AYRES, Leah to PARKER, Selby. 08 September 1783. K, p. 558, MSA CE 30-10. www.mdlandrec.net : accessed 30 January 2022.
[320] Worcester County Court (Land Records). Bill of sale from RILEY, Michael and JORDAN, Patrick to WELSH, Richard. 02 August 1784. K, p. 561, MSA CE 30-10. www.mdlandrec.net : accessed 30 January 2022.
[321] Worcester County Court (Land Records). Bill of sale from SELBY, Philip to NEWTON, Selby. 18 October 1783. K, p. 561, MSA CE 30-10. www.mdlandrec.net : accessed 30 January 2022.

Liber K, folio 566; 24 July 1783

"This Indenture made this made this 24th Day of July in the year of our Lord one thousand Seven Hundred and Eighty three Between John CHAILLE of Worcester County in the State of maryland of the one part and Robert MILLS of the Same place Witnesseth that the Said John CHAILLE for and in the Consideration of the Sum of fifty five pounds current money of maryland to him in hand paid & Secured to be paid by the Said Robert MILLS Hath Bargained and Sold and by these presents do Bargain and sell unto him the Said Robert MILLS his heirs and assigns Two Negroes the one Called **Leah** the Other Called **Abner** To have and to hold The Said Two Negroes to him the Said Robert MILLS his heirs and Assigns to the only proper use Benefit and Behoof of him the Said Robert his heirs and Assigns and the Said John CHAILLE Doth by these presents Warrant and forever Defend The Said two Negroes unto him the Said Robert MILLS Against the Claim Right or Title of the Said John or his heirs and Every other person Whatsoever in Witness whereof the Said John CHAILLE to these presents his hand has Sett and Seal affixed the Day & Year above written ~

Signed Sealed & Delivered in presence of us	N. HOLLAND Stephen HALL"	John CHAILLE (Seal)

*followed with the acknowledgment of Justice of the Peace N. HOLLAND and the recordation on 09 December 1783[322]

Liber K, folio 577; 17 January 1784

"State of Maryland Worcester County. Know all men by these presents that Anne BRATTEN of the County and State aforesaid for and in consideration of the Sum one hundred and thirty nine 19/ Current Money of Maryland to me in hand paid by Hillary PITTS of the place aforesaid at and before the Sealing and delivery of these presents the Receipt whereof I the Said Anne BRATTEN do hereby Acknowledge Have Granted Bargained Sold & delivered and by these presents do Grant Bargain, Sell & deliver unto the Said Hillary PITTS his Executors, Administrators & Assigns all the Articles & things whatsoever herein after particularly mentioned that is to Say one Negro Wench named **Grace** about twenty Six years Old, one Negro Boy Named **Leven** about Six years old & one Negro Boy named **Isaac** about eighteen Months old & one bay horse about thirteen Years old one Yoke of oxen one desk & book Case and three feather Beds all which Negros & every of the aforesaid particulars above mentioned before the executing these presents are the property and in the possession & occupation of the Said Anne BRATTEN. To Have and to hold all & every of the aforesaid Negroes & every of the aforesaid particulars abovementioned or intended so to be the said Hillary PITTS his Executors, Administrators & Assigns forever and I the said Anne BRATTEN for myself my heirs, Executors and administrators all & Singular the Said Negroes & every the aforesaid Particulars above mentioned unto the Said Hillary PITTS his Executors Administrators & Assigns against me the said Anne BRATTEN my Executors and Administrators & against all & every other person & persons whatsoever Shall and will Warrant & forever defend by these presents of all & singular which said Negros & every the aforesaid particulars above named I the said Anne BRATTEN have put the Said Hillary PITT in full possession by delivering to him the said Hillary PITTS, the three aforesaid Negroes at the Sealing and delivery of these presents in the name of the whole premises hereby bargained and Sold or mentioned or intended So to be unto him the said Hillary PITT ad aforesaid. In Witness whereof the Said Anne BRATTEN to these presents her hand hath set and Seal affixed the Seventeenth day of January Anno D[omini] 1784

Signed Sealed and delivered in presence of John POSTLY
Thomas DALE   Anne + BRATTEN (Seal)
                      her mark"

---

[322] Worcester County Court (Land Records). Bill of sale from CHAILLE, John to MILLS, Robert. 24 July 1783. K, p. 566, MSA CE 30-10. www.mdlandrec.net : accessed 30 January 2022.

*followed with the acknowledgment by Justice of the Peace John POSTLY and the recordation on 05 February 1784 by court clerk James R. MORRIS[323]

Liber K, folio 578; 23 January 1784

"Know all men by these presents that I Benjamin HAYWARD of Worcester County in the State of Maryland (Mariner) for and in consideration of the Sum of forty five pounds Current Money of Maryland to me in hand paid at and before the ensealing and delivery of these presents by Samuel GUM of the same place the receipt whereof I the said Benjamin HAYWARD doth hereby Acknowledge Have bargained and Sold and by these presents do bargain and Sell unto the Said Samuel GUM one Negro Boy Called and known by the name of **Zadock**. To have and to hold the Said Negro Boy by these presents bargained and Sold unto the said Samuel GUM his Heirs, Executors, Administrators and Assigns forever and I the Said Benjamin HAYWARD for myself my heirs, Executors and Administrators the said Negro boy called **Zadock** unto the Said Samuel GUM his Heirs and Assigns against me the said Benjamin HAYWARD my Heirs, Executors and Administrators and against all and every other person or persons whatsoever shall and will Warrant and forever defend firmly by these presents of which said negro boy called **Zadock** I the said Benjamin HAYWARD have put the said Samuel GUM in full possession by the delivery of the said Negro boy at and before the Sealing and delivery of these presents. In Testimony whereof I the Said Benjamin HAYWARD have hereunto set my hand and Seal affixed this Twenty third day of January Anno Dom[ini] one thousand Seven hundred and eighty four ~

Signed Sealed and delivered   Jonathan HUTCHERSON   Benj[amin] HAYWARD   (Seal)
in presence of   John SELBY ~"

*followed with the acknowledgment by Justice of the Peace John SELBY and the recordation by court clerk James R. MORRIS[324]

Liber K, folios 581-582; 23 January 1784

"Know all men by these presents that I Benjamin HAYWARD of Worcester County in the State of Maryland (Mariner) for and in Consideration of the Sum of thirty pounds Current money of Maryland to me in hand paid at and before the ensealing and delivery of these presents by McKinney PORTER of the same place, the receipt whereof I the said Benjamin HAYWARD doth hereby Acknowledge have Bargained and Sold and by these presents do bargain and Sell unto the said McKinney PORTER one Negro boy Called **Nathan**. To Have and To hold the Said Negro Boy by these presents Bargained and Sold unto the said McKinney PORTER his Heirs, Executors, Administrators and Assigns forever. And I the said Benjamin HAYWARD for myself my Heirs Executors and Administrators the said Negro Boy called and known by the Name of **Nathan** unto the said McKinncy PORTER his Heirs and Assigns against me the Said Benjamin HAYWARD my heirs, Executors and Administrators and against all and every other Person or Persons whatsoever shall and will Warrant and forever defend firmly by these presents of which said Negro Boy called **Nathan** of the said Benjamin HAYWARD have put the said McKinney PORTER in full possession by the delivery of the said Negro Boy at and before the sealing and delivery of these presents In Witness Whereof the said Benjamin HAYWARD have here unto his hand and Seal affixed this 23[r]d day of January Anno Dom[ini] Seventeen hundred and eighty four.

Signed Sealed and delivered   Thomas COTTINGHAM   Benj[ami]n HAYWARD   (Seal)
in presence of   John SELBY"

---

[323] Worcester County Court (Land Records). Bill of sale from BRATTEN, Anne to PITTS, Hillary. 17 January 1784. K, p. 577, MSA CE 30-10. www.mdlandrec.net : accessed 30 January 2022.

[324] Worcester County Court (Land Records). Bill of sale from HAYWARD, Benjamin to GUM, Samuel. 23 January 1784. K, p. 578, MSA CE 30-10. www.mdlandrec.net : accessed 30 January 2022.

*followed on folio 582 with the acknowledgment by Justice of the Peace John SELBY and the recordation by court clerk James R. MORRIS[325]

Liber K, folio 583; 17 February 1784

"Know all men by these presents that I Lemuel JOHNSON of Worcester County in the State of Maryland for and in Consideration of the sum of ninety five pounds to me in hand paid by Zadok WRIGHT the receipt whereof I the said Lemuel JOHNSON do hereby Acknowledge have Bargained and Sold and by these presents do bargain and Sell unto the said Zadok WRIGHT his Heirs and Assigns one Negro Man named **Ben**. To have and to hold the said Negro man called **Ben** unto the said Zadok WRIGHT his Heirs and Assigns forever and I the said Lemuel JOHNSON for myself my heirs, Executors and Administrators will Warrant and for ever defend the said Negro man called **Ben** unto the Said Zadok WRIGHT his Heirs, Executors, Administrators and Assigns for ever against the Lawfull claim Right or Title of all person or persons Whatsoever In Testimony Whereof I the said Lemuel JOHNSON to these presents my heirs have set and Seal affixed the 17th day of February Anno Dom[ini] 1784.

Signed, Sealed and delivered in presence of Selby PARKER   Lem[uel] JOHNSON   (Seal)"

*followed with the acknowledgment by Justice of the Peace Joshua TOWNSEND and the recordation on 20 February 1784 by court clerk James R. MORRIS[326]

Liber K, folios 618-619; 27 March 1784

"Know all men by these presents that I Benjamin HAYWARD of Worcester County in the State of Maryland for and in Consideration of the sum of sixty pounds Current money of Maryland to me in hand paid by Levin LONG of the County and State aforesaid have bargained and sold and by these presents doth bargain and Sell unto the said Levin LONG his heirs and assigns forever one negro Woman named **Rose** the receipt whereof the said Benjamin HAYWARD do hereby acknowledge myself fully satisfied and paid the said negro named **Rose** being now in possession of the said Levin LONG to have and to hold the said negro **Rose** unto the said Levin LONG his heirs Executors administrators and assigns forever and I the said Benjamin HAYWARD do hereby warrant and forever defend the said negro **Rose** against the claim right or title of all person or persons whatsoever that ever hereafter shall Clame the said negro **Rose** unto the said Levin LONG his heirs Executors administrators & assigns forever which said Negro **Rose** I the said Benjamin HAYWARD have delivered to the said Levin LONG. in Witness whereof I the said Benjamin HAYWARD to these presents my hand have sett and seal affixed the 27th day of March Anno Dom[ini] Seventeen hundred and eighty four ~

Signed sealed and delivered   Benj[a][min] HAYWARD   (Seal)
in presence of
Joshua TOWNSEND"

*followed with the acknowledgment of Justice of the Peace Joshua TOWNSEND and the recordation on 01 April 1784 by court clerk James R. MORRIS[327]

Liber K, folio 622; 08 April 1784

"Know all men by these presents that I Philip SELBY of Worcester County and State of Maryland, for and in Consideration of the Sume of forty pounds of good and Lawfull money of the County af[ore]s[ai]d to me in hand paid by Darby RIGGEN of the County af[ore]s[ai]d at and before the sealing and delivery of these presence the receipt whereof I do hereby acknowledge and have hereby bargained and sold to him the said Darby RIGGON one negro

---

[325] Worcester County Court (Land Records). Bill of sale from HAYWARD, Benjamin to PORTER, McKinney. 23 January 1784. K, pp. 581-582, MSA CE 30-10. www.mdlandrec.net : accessed 30 January 2022.
[326] Worcester County Court (Land Records). Bill of sale from JOHNSON, Lemuel to WRIGHT, Zadok. 17 February 1784. K, p. 583, MSA CE 30-10. www.mdlandrec.net : accessed 30 January 2022.
[327] Worcester County Court (Land Records). Bill of sale from HAYWARD, Benjamin to LONG, Levin. 27 March 1784. K, pp. 618-619, MSA CE 30-10. www.mdlandrec.net : accessed 30 January 2022.

boy called **Levin** now in possession of the said RIGGON to have and to hold the said negro unto him the said Darby RIGGON his heirs and assigns forever and I the said Philip SELBY for myself my heirs Executors and administrators and assigns Do bargain and sell the said negro boy **Levin** to him the said RIGGON and against all and every other person and persons whatsoever claiming any right or title or property will forever hereafter defend in witness and full assurance whereof I the said Philip SELBY have hereunto my hand set and Seal Effixed this eighth day of April Anno Dom[ini] One thousand seven hundred and eighty four ~

Signed sealed & Delivered   Thomas COTTINGHAM   Philip SELBY (Seal)
in presence of us ~

                                his
                          Selby X NEWTON
                              mark"

*followed with the acknowledgment by Justice of the Peace John SELBY and the recordation on 09 April 1784 by court clerk James R. MORRIS[328]

Liber K, folio 626; 21 May 1784

"Know all men by these presents that I Benjamin HAYWARD of Worcester County for and in consideration of the natural affection that I have for my daughter Harriot HAYWARD and also for and in consideration of five Shillings current money of Maryland to me in hand paid by the said Harriot HAYWARD before the sealing and delivery of these presents have given, granted, Bargained and sold and by these presents do give, Grant, Bargain and sell unto the said given, granted, Bargained and sold and by these presents do give, Grant, Bargain and sell unto the said Harriot HAYWARD her heirs and assigns forever one negro Girl called **Patience** and her increase To have and to hold the said negro Girl called **Patience** and her increase to the said Harriot HAYWARD her heirs and assigns forever to the only proper use benefit and behoof of the said Harriot HAYWARD her heirs and assigns forever and to and for no other use intent or purpose whatsoever unless the use hereafter limitted and expressed, that is to say that it is the true intent and meaning hereof that the said Harriot HAYWARD shall permit and suffer her mother Leah HAYWARD to have hold occupy possess and enjoy the said negro Girl to her own use separately for and during the natural life of the said Leah HAYWARD In Testimony whereof I have hereto set my hand and seal the twenty first day of May anno Dom[ini] seventeen hundred and eighty four.

Sealed and delivered   Peter CHAILLE   Benj[a][min] HAYWARD (Seal)
in presence of"

*followed with the acknowledgment by Justice of the Peace Peter CHAILLE and the recordation by court clerk James R. MORRIS[329]

Liber K, folio 627; 19 May 1784

"To all Christian people unto whom these presents writing shall come, I Benjamin HAYWARD of Worcester County in the State of Maryland (Mariner) send Greeting Know ye that I Benjamin HAYWARD for divers good causes and Valuable considerations me hereunto moving, Have given and Granted and by these presents, do give, grant and Confirm unto Leah HAYWARD daughter of Coll. ENNELLS (deceased) my negro Girl, known by the name of **Patience**, now in the hands and possession of a certain John NEILLE Doct[o]r of the County & State af[ore]s[ai]d To have and to hold the said negro Girl called **Patience** unto the Leah HAYWARD her heirs and assigns forever, to her and their own proper use and uses, thereof and therewith, to do, order and dispose at her and their Wills and pleasures, as of their own proper Goods & Chattels freely and peaceably and quietly without any manner of Lett, trouble or denial of me the said Benjamin HAYWARD, or any other person or persons whatsoever, of which premisses

---

[328] Worcester County Court (Land Records). Bill of sale from SELBY, Philip to RIGGEN, Darby. 08 April 1784. K, p. 622, MSA CE 30-10. www.mdlandrec.net : accessed 30 January 2022.

[329] Worcester County Court (Land Records). Bill of sale from HAYWARD, Benjamin to HAYWARD, Harriot. 21 May 1784. K, p. 626, MSA CE 30-10. www.mdlandrec.net : accessed 30 January 2022.

I the said Benjamin HAYWARD have the said Leah HAYWARD above mentioned in full possession {?} {?} negro Girl called **Patience** by virtue hereof In Witness whereof I the said Benjamin HAYWARD have hereunto set my hand and seal affixed this nineteenth day of May Anno Dom[ini] One thousand seven Hundred and eighty four ~ ~

Signed Sealed & delivered   Joshua TOWNSEND.   Benj^a[min] HAYWARD   (Seal)
in the presence of "

*followed with the acknowledgment by Justice of the Peace Joshua TOWNSEND and the recordation by court clerk James R. MORRIS[330]

Liber K, folio 627; 14 May 1784

"To all whome it may concern: Know ye that we Charles PARKER & Thomas PARKER (Son of the s[ai]^d Charles PARKER) for and in Consideration of the sum of forty five pounds current money of Maryland to them in hand paid the receipt whereof we do hereby acknowledge by Levi OUTTEN hath bargained sold and delivered and by these presents doth bargain sell and deliver one negro boy called **James** as his own right and property and do forever warrant and defend the same to him the af[ore]s[ai]^d Levi OUTTEN his heirs and assigns as Witness our hands and Seals this fourteenth day of May Seventeen Hundred and Eighty four ~ . ~

Signed, sealed & Delivered   Edward HAMMOND
in presence of us . . . .   Major TOWNSEND. .   Charles X PARKER   (Seal)
                                                         mark"

*followed with the acknowledgment by Justice of the Peace Peter CHAILLE and the recordation by court clerk James R. MORRIS[331]

Liber L, folios 10-11; 18 June 1784

"Know all men by these presents that I Richard SHOCKLEY of Worcester County in the State of Maryland for and in Consideration of the sum of Five Shillings current money of Maryland to me in hand paid at and before the sealing and delivery of these presents by Solomon SHOCKLEY of the same place the receipt whereof I do hereby acknowledge, Have Bargained and Sold and by these presents do bargain and sell unto the said Solomon SHOCKLEY his heirs and assigns forever a Negro Boy called **George**, about Sixteen years of age and now in the possession of the said Solomon SHOCKLEY to have and to hold the said negro boy called **George** by these presents bargained and sold unto the Said Solomon SHOCKLEY his Heirs Executors Administrators and Assigns forever, and I the said Richard SHOCKLEY for myself and my heirs Executors, or Administrators or any of them, all and Singular the said negro Boy Called **George** unto the said Solomon SHOCKLEY his heirs and assigns, against me the said Richard SHOCKLEY my heirs Executors and administrators and against all and every other person or persons whatsoever, shall and will warrant and forever defend by these presents of which said negro boy called **George** I the said Richard SHOCKLEY have put the said Solomon SHOCKLEY in full possession by the delivering of these presents In Testimony whereof the said Richard SHOCKLEY have hereunto set his hand and Seal affixed the eighteenth day of June Anno Dom[ini] Seventeen hundred and eighty four ~

Signed sealed & delivered   James NAIRNE
in the presence of   John TOWNSEND   Richard R SHOCKLEY   (Seal)
                                                             mark"

---

[330] Worcester County Court (Land Records). Bill of sale from HAYWARD, Benjamin to HAYWARD, Leah. 19 May 1784. K, p. 627, MSA CE 30-10. www.mdlandrec.net : accessed 30 January 2022.

[331] Worcester County Court (Land Records). Bill of sale from PARKER, Charles and PARKER, Thomas to OUTTEN, Levi. 14 May 1784. K, p. 627, MSA CE 30-10. www.mdlandrec.net : accessed 30 January 2022.

*followed on folio 11 with the acknowledgment by Justice of the Peace Joshua TOWNSEND and the recordation on 19 June 1784 by court clerk James R. MORRIS[332]

Liber L, folios 11-12; 18 May 1784

"To all Christian People unto Whom this present writting shall come I Benjamin HAYWARD of Worcester County in the State of Maryland (Mariner) send Greeting Know ye that I Benjamin HAYWARD for divers good Causes and valuable considerations me hereunto moving, have Given and Granted and by these presents do give Grant and Confirm unto my Daughter Sally HAYWARD my negro Woman called **Rachell,** in whose hands or possession Custody or keeping so ever the same negro is or can or may be found, and the Child that the said Wench now has being my property and the increase that the said negro shall have hereafter for divers good Causes and valuable Considerations me hereunto moving Have given and granted and by these presents, do give grant and Confirm the same Child and increase af[ore]s[ai]ᵈ unto my daughter Polly HAYWARD my son Henry HAYWARD and my Daughter Harriet HAYWARD to be equally divided between them to have and to hold the said negro Woman called **Rachel** unto my said daughter Sally HAYWARD her heirs and assigns forever to her and their own proper use and uses thereof and therewith to do order or dispose at her and their Wills and pleasure as of their own proper Goods and Chattles, freely and peaceably and quietly, without and manner of Lett, Trouble or denial of me the said Benjamin HAYWARD or any other person or persons whatsoever excepting the increase of the said negro Woman called **Rachell** above mentioned and described as above given granted and Confirmed, unto my Daughter Polly Son Henry and daughter Harriet HAYWARD to have and to hold the said negro Child and increase as above mentioned unto my Daughter Polly HAYWARD my son Henry and Harriet HAYWARD and their heirs and assigns forever to their own purpose use and uses to do and dispose at their Wills and pleasures as of their own proper Goods and Chattels freely and peaceably and quietly without any manner of Lett trouble or denial of me the said Benjamin HAYWARD or any other persons whatsoever of all which premisses I the said Benjamin HAYWARD have my said Children as above given granted and Confirmed put in full possession by virtue hereof. In Witness whereof the said Benjamin HAYWARD have hereunto set my hand and Seal affixed this 18ᵗʰ day of May Anno Dom[ini] Seventeen hundred and Eighty four ~

Signed sealed and delivered   Peter CHAILLE   Benjᵃ[min] HAYWARD   (Seal)
in presence of"

*followed on folio 12 with the acknowledgment of Justice of the Peace Peter CHAILLE and the recordation on 19 May 1784 by court clerk James R. MORRIS[333]

Liber L, folio 13; 28 June 1784

"Know all men by these presents that I Margaret SELBY of Worcester County in the State of Maryland for and in Consideration of the Sum of five Shillings to me in hand paid at and before the sealing and delivery of these presents by Daniel SELBY the receipt whereof I do hereby acknowledge have bargained and sold and by these presents do give, grant bargain and Sell unto the said Daniel SELBY one negro boy called **Jacob** to have and to hold the said negro boy called **Jacob**, by these presents given, granted, bargained and Sold unto me the said Daniel SELBY his Executors administrators and assigns against me the said Margaret SELBY and all other persons whatsoever Claiming the same will warrant and forever Defend the said negro **Jacob** by these presents in Witness whereof I the said Margaret SELBY to these presents my hand have Sett and seal affixed the 28ᵗʰ day of June in the year of our Lord Anno Domini Seventeen hundred and eighty four. ~ ~ ~

---

[332] Worcester County Court (Land Records). Bill of sale from SHOCKLEY, Richard to SHOCKLEY, Solomon. 18 June 1784. L, pp. 10-11, MSA CE 30-11. www.mdlandrec.net : accessed 11 February 2022.
[333] Worcester County Court (Land Records). Bill of sale from HAYWARD, Benjamin to HAYWARD, Sally, Polly, etal. 18 June 1784. L, pp. 10-11, MSA CE 30-11. www.mdlandrec.net : accessed 11 February 2022.

Signed sealed and delivered   Joshua TOWNSEND
in presents off

Margaret ^{her} X _{mark} SELBY (Seal)

*followed with the acknowledgment by Justice of the Peace Joshua TOWNSEND and the recordation on 29 June 1784 by court clerk James R. MORRIS[334]

Liber L, folios 13-14; 01 July 1784

"The State of Maryland Worcester County (to wit). Know all men by these presents that I Jeremiah TOWNSEND of the County af[ore]s[ai]^d for and in consideration of the sum of twenty eight pounds one Shilling and ten pence Specie to me in hand paid by Benjamin PURNELL (of Walton) of the County af[ore]s[ai]^d Have Bargained, Sold released granted and Confirmed and by these presents do bargain sell release, grant and Confirm unto the said Benjamin PURNELL (of Walton) one negro man Called **Sam** Provided the said Je[remia]^h TOWNSEND does not pay back unto the af[ore]s[ai]^d B. PURNELL the af[ore]s[ai]^d consideration money at or before the last day of August next ensuing the date hereof & the value of Twenty eight pounds one Shilling and ten pence Specie to have and to hold the said bargained Negro **Sam** by these presents have bargained sold released granted and Confirmed unto the only proper use and behoof of the said Benjamin PURNELL (of Walton) his Executors administrators & assigns forever freely quietly peaceably and intirely without any consideration, Claim, disturbance or hendrance of any person or persons whatsoever and without my account to me or to any other whatsoever to be made answered or hereafter to be rendered so that neither I the said Jeremiah TOWNSEND nor any other for me or in my name any right Title Interest or demand of in to or for the said Negro **Sam** or any part or parcel thereof ought to exact Challenge claim or demand at any time or times hereafter, but from all action right Estate Title, claim demand, possession and Intrust thereof shall be wholly barred and excluded by force and virtue of these presents, and I the said Jeremiah TOWNSEND for myself my Executors & administrators the said negro **Sam** unto the said Benjamin PURNELL (of Walton) his Executors administrators and assigns and against all and every other person or persons whatsoever Shall and will warrant and forever Defend by these presents which negro **Sam** the said Jeremiah TOWNSEND have put the said Benjamin PURNELL in full possession by delivery at the signing and delivery hereof in Witness whereof I the said Jeremiah TOWNSEND have hereunto set my hand & seal this first day of July Anno Dom[ini] seventeen hundred & Eighty four ~~~

Signed sealed & deliver[e]d   W[illia]^m TOWNSEND   Jeremiah TOWNSEND
in the presence of ~   John POSTLY"

*followed on folio 14 with the acknowledgment by Justices of the Peace John POSTLY and William STEVENSON and the recordation by court clerk James R. MORRIS[335]

Liber L, folio 17; 07 July 1784

"Maryland Worcester County Sct. Know all men by these presents that I Robert SCHOOLFIELD of the State and County af[ore]s[ai]d for and in Consideration of one hundred pounds current money of Maryland to me in hand paid by John MARTIN and Mitchell DOWNES at and before the Sealing and Delivery hereof the receipt whereof I do Confess and acknowledge and thereof do acquit exonerate and discharge the said John MARTIN and Mitchell DOWNES their Heirs Executors & Administrators Have Granted Bargained and Sold & by these presents do grant, Bargain and Sell unto the said John MARTIN and Mitchell DOWNES their Heirs and assigns forever one negro man Slave named **Adam** To have and to hold the said negro man Slave named **Adam** to the said John MARTIN and Mitchell DOWNES & their Heirs and Assigns to the only proper use benefit and behoof of the said John MARTIN and Mitchell DOWNES their Heirs and Assigns forever and to and for no other use intent or

---

[334] Worcester County Court (Land Records). Bill of sale from SELBY, Margaret to SELBY, Daniel. 28 June 1784. L, p. 13, MSA CE 30-11. www.mdlandrec.net : accessed 11 February 2022.
[335] Worcester County Court (Land Records). Bill of sale from TOWNSEND, Jeremiah to PURNELL, Benjamin. 01 July 1784. L, pp. 13-14, MSA CE 30-11. www.mdlandrec.net : accessed 11 February 2022.

purpose whatsoever. And I do hereby Covenant for me my Heirs Ex[ecutor]s and Adm[inistrato]rs to and with the said John MARTIN & Mitchell DOWNES their Heirs Ex[ecuto]rs Adm[inistrato]rs and assigns that I the said Robert SCHOOLFIELD my Heirs Ex[ecuto]rs and Adm[inistrato]rs the af[ore]s[ai]d negro man Slave named **Adam** to the said John MARTIN and Mitchell DOWNES their Heirs and Assigns shall and will warrant and forever defend In Testimony whereof I the said Robert SCHOOLFIELD to these presents my hand have put and Seal affixed the seventh day of July Anno Dom[ini] Seventeen Hundred and Eighty four. ~

Sealed and delivered   Joseph KILLIM   Robert SCHOOLFIELD . . . (Seal)
in Presence of"

*followed with the acknowledgment by Justice of the Peace Joshua TOWNSEND and the recordation on 08 July 1784 by court clerk James R. MORRIS[336]

Liber L, folio 19; 02 July 1784

"Know all men by these presents That I William SELBY (son of John) of Worcester County in the State of Maryland for and in Consideration of the sum of Thirty one pounds, four Shillings and two pence Specie to me in hand paid at and before the Sealing and delivery hereof by Zadok SELBY of the same place, Have bargained and Sold and by these presents do bargain and sell unto the aforesaid Zadock his heirs and assigns forever a negro man called **Peter** now in the possession of the said William SELBY, and I the said William SELBY for myself my Heirs Executors and administrators do Covenant Grant and agree to and with the said Zadock SELBY his Heirs and assigns, that the said William SELBY and his Heirs will and shall warrant and defend forever, the said negro Man called **Peter**, against the Claim and demand of all and every person or persons Whatsoever, unto the af[ore]s[ai]d Zadock his Heirs and Assigns forever, of which said negro called **Peter** I the said William SELBY have put the said Zadock SELBY in full possession by the delivery of these presents. In Testimony whereof I the said William SELBY have hereunto set my hand and affixed my seal that 2[n]d day of July Anno Dom[ini] Seventeen Hundred and Eighty four ~ ~ ~

Signed Sealed & delivered   Josiah MITCHELL   William SELBY (Seal)
in the presence of"

*followed with the acknowledgment by Justice of the Peace Josiah MITCHELL, the recordation by court clerk James R. MORRIS on 22 July 1784, and the receipt of payment by Benjamin PURNELL[337]

Liber L, folio 31; 23 August 1784

"This Indenture made the twenty Third day of August, one thousand seven Hundred Eighty four Between Philip SELBY of Worcester County in the State of Maryland of the one part and William HOLLAND of the County and State af[ore]s[ai]d of the other part witnesseth that the said Philip SELBY for and in Consideration of the sum of two hundred & forty pounds Current money of Maryland to him in hand paid by the said William HOLLAND before the sealing and delivery of these presents Hath Bargained and sold assigned and Transfered & by these presents doth sell assign and Transfer unto the said William HOLLAND his heirs and assigns the following Negroes (to wit.) **Pleasant Tamar Argill Caprell, Abraham, Sarah** and **George** To have and to hold the aforesaid Slaves and Every of them and all their Increase and profits of every nature whatsoever and the said Philip SELBY for himself and his heirs doth Covenant hereby with the said William HOLLAND & his heirs and assigns that he and they the Slaves aforesaid will warrant & forever defend by these presents against the Claim right and Title of

---

[336] Worcester County Court (Land Records). Bill of sale from SCHOOLFIELD, Robert to MARTIN, John and DOWNES, Mitchell. 07 July 1784. L, p. 17, MSA CE 30-11. www.mdlandrec.net : accessed 11 February 2022.
[337] Worcester County Court (Land Records). Bill of sale from SELBY, William to SELBY, Zadock. 02 July 1784. L, p. 19, MSA CE 30-11. www.mdlandrec.net : accessed 11 February 2022.

all persons whatsoever. In Witness whereof the said Philip SELBY to these presents his hand hath set & seal affixed the day and year above written… ~ .. ~.. ~

Signed sealed & delivered   Nehemiah HOLLAND   Philip SELBY.. (Seal)
in presence of us …..   John PARRAMORE…"

*followed with the acknowledgment by Justices of the Peace Nehemiah HOLLAND and John PARRAMORE and the recordation on 23 September 1784 by court clerk James R. MORRIS[338]

Liber L, folios 32-33; 24 September 1784

"Know all men by these presents that I William Atkinson SELBY of Worcester County in the State of Maryland, (Planter) for and in Consideration of the sum of one hundred pounds current money of Maryland to me in hand paid at and before the sealing and delivery of these presents by Barkley WHITE of the same Place the Receipt whereof I the said William Atkinson SELBY doth hereby acknowledge have bargained and sold and by these presents do bargain and Sell unto the said Barkley WHITE his Heirs and assigns forever three Negroes (to wit) a negro Woman called **Milla** about twenty two years old, a negro Boy called **Ben**, about three years old and the other called **Lige** about six months old To have and to hold thee said three Negroes above mentioned by these presents, Bargained and Sold, and every of them unto the said Barkly WHITE his heirs and assigns forever, and I the said William Atkinson SELBY for myself my Heirs Executors and administrators and every of them all and Singular the said Negroes unto the said Barkly WHITE his Heirs and assigns forever against me the said William Atkinson SELBY my Heirs Executors, and Administrators and every of them, and against every other person or persons whatsoever shall and will warrant and forever defend by these presents, of which said Negroes I the said William Atkinson SELBY have put the said Barkley WHITE in full Possession by the delivery of the said Negroes above mentioned. In Testimony whereof I the said Barkly WHITE have hereunto set my hand seal affixed this 24th day of September Anno Dom[ini] One thousand seven Hundred and eighty four

Signed sealed and delivered   Nehemiah HOLLAND   William A. SELBY (Seal)
in the presence of ……."

*followed on folio 33 with the acknowledgment by Justice of the Peace Nehemiah HOLLAND and the recordation on 25 September 1784 by court clerk James R. MORRIS[339]

Liber L, folios 33-34; 24 September 1784

"Know all men by these presents that I Barkley WHITE of Worcester County in the State of Maryland, for and in Consideration of the of the sum of Sixty pounds Current money of Maryland to me in hand paid at and before the sealing and Delivery of these presents, by William SELBY (S.H.) of the same County and State aforesaid the receipt whereof I the said Barkley WHITE do hereby acknowledge have Bargained and Sold and by these presents do bargain and Sell unto the said William SELBY his Heirs and assigns forever, a Negro Woman called **Comfort** about twenty years old and negro Child called **Peter** and now in the possession of the aforesaid William SELBY To have and to hold the said Negro woman called **Comfort** & Child called **Peter**, all and Singular the Said Negroes by these presents, Bargained and sold, unto the said William SELBY his Heirs and assigns forever and I the said Barkley WHITE for myself my Heirs Executors, Administrators, or any of them all and Singular the said Negroes above mentioned, unto the said William SELBY his Heirs and assigns forever against me the said Barkley WHITE my Heirs Executors and administrators and against all and every other person or persons whatsoever shall and will Warrant and forever defend by these presents of which said negroes I the said Barkley WHITE have put the said William SELBY in full possession, by the delivery of the said Negroes, In Witness whereof I the said Barkley WHITE

---

[338] Worcester County Court (Land Records). Bill of sale from SELBY, Philip to HOLLAND, William. 23 August 1784. L, p. 31, MSA CE 30-11. www.mdlandrec.net : accessed 11 February 2022.
[339] Worcester County Court (Land Records). Bill of sale from SELBY, William Atkinson to WHITE, Barkley. 24 September 1784. L, pp. 32-33, MSA CE 30-11. www.mdlandrec.net : accessed 11 February 2022.

have Set my Hand and Seal affixed this 24th day of September Anno Dom[ini] one thousand Seven hundred and Eighty four ~

Signed Sealed and delivered Joshua TOWNSEND   Barkley WHITE… (Seal)
in the presence of"

*followed on folio 34 with the acknowledgment by Justice of the Peace Joshua TOWNSEND and the recordation 01 October 1784 by court clerk James R. MORRIS[340]

Liber L, folios 48-49; 05 June 1784

"This Indenture made the fifth day of June Anno Dom[ini] seventeen hundred and Eighty four Between Levin BLAKE of the one part and George STEWART of the other Witnesseth that the said Levin BLAKE for and in consideration of the sum of one hundred and Seventy pounds Current money of Maryland to him paid by the said George STEWART the receipt whereof he doth hereby acknowledge Hath Granted Bargained and sold assigned, transferred and set over and by these presents doth grant Bargain and sell, assign transfer and set over unto the said George STEWART his Ex[ecuto]rs Adm[inistrato]rs and assigns all the Lands and premisses mentioned in the annexed Lease with the appurtenances and all the Estate right and title and Term of years yet to come and unexpired. To have and to hold the said Land and premisses and term yet to Come and unexpired unto the said George STEWART his Executors, adm[inistrato]rs and assigns, provided always and it is the true intent and meaning hereof that if the said Levin BLAKE his Ex[ecuto]rs or Adm[inistrato]rs shall pay and satisfy unto the said George STEWART the sum of one hundred and Seventy pounds af[ore]s[ai]d on or before the Sixth day of July next then these premisses to be void and of none effect and it is further Covenanted and agreed between the said Levin BLAKE and George STEWART that if the said Levin BLAKE and Mary his wife shall makeover and Convey unto the said George STEWART his heirs Exe[cuto]rs or adm[inistrato]rs the full Estate that they have in the premisses or pay unto him the said one hundred and seventy pounds on or before the the af[ore]s[ai]d Sixth day of July ensuing that then these presents to be void and the said Levin BLAKE to have Credit the said sum of one hundred and Seventy pounds on an Execution now issued and depending by the said George STEWART against the said Levin BLAKE otherwise the said BLAKE by virtue Set their hands and seals the day and year first above written ~

Sealed & delivered Samuel SMYLY   Levin BLAKE. (Seal)
in presence of Robert DONE ..   George STEWART … (Seal)

N.B. It is agreed by James TOWNSEND & Levin BLAKE that the two following Negroes **Friday** & **Tillan** shall remain on the plantation whereon BLAKE now lives and the said TOWNSEND to have the labour and profits of said Negroes if any and in Case said old **Friday** should prove troublesome and Expenceve the said BLAKE doth agree to be at the Expence of maintance of said negro **Friday** & said negro to live on said if life should last.

Testes.   Levin BLAKE (Seal)
Jabez WILLISS.   James TOWNSEND … (Seal)"

*followed on folio 49 with the receipt for Sarah TOWNSEND on 23 December 1783, the acknowledgment by Justices of the Peace John SELBY and Nehemiah TOWNSEND, and the recordation on 01 November 1784 by court clerk James R. MORRIS[341]

Liber L, folios 61-62; 25 June 1785

"Know all men by these presents that I George DASHIELL of Somerset County in the State of Maryland for and in consideration of the sum of ninety Pounds current Money af[ore]s[ai]d to me in hand Paid by George SLOCUM of Dorchester County, the receipt whereof I do hereby

---

[340] Worcester County Court (Land Records). Bill of sale from WHITE, Barkley to SELBY, William. 24 September 1784. L, pp. 33-34, MSA CE 30-11. www.mdlandrec.net : accessed 11 February 2022.
[341] Worcester County Court (Land Records). Lease from BLAKE, Levin to STEWART, George. 05 June 1784. L, pp. 48-49, MSA CE 30-11. www.mdlandrec.net : accessed 11 February 2022.

acknowledge have bargained and sold and delivered and by these presents do bargain sell and deliver unto the said George SLOCUM af[ore]s[ai]^d one negro man Call[e]d **Joe**, to have and to hold the s[ai]^d Negro man af[ore]s[ai]^d unto the s[ai]^d George SLOCUM his Heirs Executors Adm[inistrato]^rs or Assigns forever, And I the s[ai]^d George DASHIELL for myself my Heirs Executors and Adm[inistrato]^rs shall and will warrant and forever defend against all persons the af[ore]s[ai]^d negro Man, in witness whereof I have hereto set my hand and affix[e]d my Seal the 25th June 1785

Sign[e]d Seal[e]d & delivered   Joseph DASHIELL   George DASHIELL (Seal)
in presence off   Ebenezer HANDY"

*followed on folio 62 with the recordation on 19 July 1785 by court clerk James R. MORRIS[342]

Liber L, folio 65; 28 January 1785

"Know all men by these presents That I William SPIERS of Worcester County in the State of Maryland, for and in Consideration of the Sum of Seventy Pounds current money of Maryland to him in hand paid at and before the Sealing and Delivery of these presents by Jonathan HUTCHESON of the Same place, The Receipt whereof the said William SPIERS doth hereby Acknowledge, Have bargained and Sold and by these presents do bargain and Sell unto the said Jonathan HUTCHESON his Heirs and Assigns forever, a Negro Woman called **Fan** and Child called **Pricilla**, now in the possession of the said HUTCHERSON To have and to Hold the above mentioned negro Woman and Child by these presents, bargained and Sold unto the aforesaid Jonathan HUTCHESON his Heirs Executors, Administrators and Assigns forever, And I the said William SPIERS for myself, and Heirs Executors, Adm[inistrato]^rs or any of them, all and Singular, the above mentioned Negro Woman and Child, unto the said Jonathan HUTCHESON his Heirs and Assigns, against me the said William SPIERS my Heirs Executors or Administrators and against all and every other person or persons whatsoever Shall and will warrant and forever defend by these presents, of which said negro Woman called **Fan** and Child the said William SPIERS have put the said Jonathan HUTCHESON in full possession by the Delivery hereof In Testimony whereof the said William SPIERS have herewith Set his Hand & Seal affixed This Twenty eight day of January Anno Dom[ini] One thousand seven hundred and Eighty Five. ~ . ~

Signed Sealed & Delivered   Joshua TOWNSEND   William SPIERS (Seal)
in the Presence of ~"

*followed with the acknowledgment by Justice of the Peace Joshua TOWNSEND and the recordation by court clerk James R. MORRIS[343]

Liber L, folio 65; 03 January 1785

"This Indenture of Manumition made the third day of January 1785 Between Rachel CORD of Worcester County in the State of Maryland and her Negro man **Tom** of the Same place Aged about thirty nine years Witnesseth That the said Rachel CORD for & in consideration that the said negro **Tom**, during the Time that he was her Slave hath behaved himself orderly & civilly & hath been a trusty Slave to her, Hath therefore Manumated & given the said Negro **Tom** his Freedom forever and by these presents for herself her Heirs Executors & Administrators doth give & Grant unto the said negro **Tom** a clear & Absolute Manumission & Freedom forever from her & them & every of them forever, Provided the present laws of the Land do allow of the Same, But if the present Laws of the Land do not allow of the Same, & any person not Claiming by with or under her, can Legally (inconsequence of the above Manumission or Freedom) take any Advantage of the said negro **Tom** so as to again Enslave him, Then the above Manumission or Freedom to be Void & the said Negro **Tom** again to be & remain the

---

[342] Worcester County Court (Land Records). Bill of sale from DASHIELL, George to SLOCUM, George. 25 June 1785. L, pp. 61-62, MSA CE 30-11. www.mdlandrec.net : accessed 11 February 2022.
[343] Worcester County Court (Land Records). Bill of sale from SPIERS, William to HUTCHESON, Jonathan. 28 January 1785. L, p. 65, MSA CE 30-11. www.mdlandrec.net : accessed 11 February 2022.

property of her & her Heirs as formerly, otherwise the above Manumission & freedom to be & remain in full force & virtue, In Testimony where of the said Rachel CORD to these presents her hand hath sett & Seal affixed the Day & year first above written ~

Signed Sealled & Delivered
in the presence of
John POSTLY
Anne POSTLY"

Rachell X CORD (Seal)
her / Mark

*followed with the acknowledgment by Justice of the Peace John POSTLY and the recordation on 04 January 1785 by court clerk James R. MORRIS[344]

Liber L, folios 67-68; 31 January 1785

"State of Maryland Worcester County Ss[t]. Know all men these presents That I Jemomy GODFREY for and in Consideration of the Sum of Ninety Seven pounds Ten Shillings lawfully money of the State af[ore]s[ai]^d to me hand paid by Elihu HAZZARD the receipt whereoff I do hereby acknowledge Have Bargained Sold and Delivered unto Elihu HAZZARD and by these presents according to due form of Law do Bargain Sell and Deliver unto the af[ore]s[ai]^d Elihu HAZZARD Two Negroes Viz. one Wench nam[e]^d **Rhody** and one boy Nam[e]^d **Luke** To have and to hold the said Bargained Negroes nam[e]^d **Rhody** and **Luke** unto the said Elihu HAZZARD his Heirs Ex[ecutor]^s administ[rator]^s and assigns forever and I the the af[ore]s[ai]^d Jemima GODFREY for myself my Heirs Ex[ecutor]^s Administ[rator]^s and assigns the said Bargained Negroes against all and every manner of person or persons whatsoever Shall and will forever warrant and Defend In Testmony whereoff I the said Jemima GODFREY have to this my plans and open Sale sett my Hand and affixed my Seal this Thirty first day of January Anno Dom[ini] 1785

Testes. John P. MITCHELL
        James KING

Jemima (/) GODFREY (Seal)
her / Mark"

*followed with the recordation on 08 February 1785 by court clerk James R. MORRIS[345]

Liber L, folio 68; 31 December 1784

"This Indenture this thirty first day of December Anno Do[mini] One thousand Seven hundred Eighty & four Between Martha MARCH of County of Worcester and State of Maryland of the one part and Ann BRATTEN widow of Joseph BRATTEN of the County and State af[ore]s[ai]^d of the other part Witnesseth that the said Martha MARCH for & in Consideration of the Sum on Ninty pounds to her in hand paid by the said Ann BRATTEN at and before the Sealing and delivery of these presents the receipt whereof the said Martha MARCH doth hereby acknowledge she the said Martha hath Bargained and Sold and by these presents doth bargain and sell unto the said Ann BRATTEN Six Negroes Namely **Coffee Comfort, Hannah, Amy Isaac** and **Rhoda** To have and to hold the said Negroes by these presents bargained and Sold unto the said Ann BRATTEN his Executors, Administrators forever, provided always and upon Condition that if the said Martha MARCH her Heirs Executors Administrators or Assigns do and Shall well and truly pay or cause to be paid unto the said Ann BRATTEN widow of Joseph BRATTEN her Heirs Executors, Administrators or Assigns the full Sum of Ninety pounds on and upon the thirty first day of August next coming, that then these presents and every thing therein contained shall Cease, determine and be Void, anything therein contained to the Contrary notwithstanding and the said Martha MARCH for herself her Executors and Admi[nistrator]^s doth Covenant and Grant to & with the said Ann BRATTEN (widow of Joseph BRATTEN) her heirs Executors Admi[nistrator]^s and Assigns that She the said Martha

---

[344] Worcester County Court (Land Records). Deed of manumission from CORD, Rachell to **Tom**. 03 January 1785. L, p. 65, MSA CE 30-11. www.mdlandrec.net : accessed 11 February 2022.

[345] Worcester County Court (Land Records). Bill of sale from GODFREY, Jemima to HAZZARD, Elihu. 31 January 1785. L, pp. 67-68, MSA CE 30-11. www.mdlandrec.net : accessed 11 February 2022.

MARCH his Execut[or]ˢ & shall and will well and truly pay or cause to be paid unto the said Ann BRATTEN widow of Joseph BRATTEN her Heirs Executors, Administrators or Assigns the said Sum of Ninety pounds of good and lawfull money as af[ore]s[ai]ᵈ at the day and time, & in manner and form af[ore]s[ai]ᵈ according to the true intent and meaning of these presents in Witness whereof the said Martha MARCH to these presents her hand hath set and Seal affixed the day and year first above written

Sealed and Delivered   Martha MARCH   (Seal)
in presents of us
Benjamin McCORMACK
Lemuel SHOWELL"

*followed with the acknowledgment by Justice of the Peace John POSTLY on 22 January 1785 and the recordation by court clerk James R. MORRIS on 08 February 1785[346]

Liber L, folio 74; 09 March 1773

"Worcester County to wit of. Know all men by these presents That I John CAMPBELL of the County of the aforesaid doth give unto John FASSETT the Negro Wench called **Sal** and all her Increas forever to him and assigns hereby I do own that I have no Right title Claim nor Intres unto the said **Sall** nor her increase but for her to be John FASSETT for ever hereby I do set my Hand & this Ninth day of March in the year of our Lord One thousand Seven hundred and Seventy Three ~.

Testes. Rouse FASSETT   John CAMPBELL   (Seal)
Releck HILL   mark +"

*followed with the recordation by court clerk James R. MORRIS on 02 March 1785[347]

Liber L, folios 96-97; 05 April 1785

"Know all men by these presents That I Jemima HENDERSON of Worcester County in the State of Maryland for and in Consideration for the kind Love and effection unto my Nephew Elijah MERRILL of the Same place, and Sundry Considerations me hereunto moving Have Given & Granted and by these presents do Give and Grant unto him the Said Elijah MERRILL his Heirs lawfully begotten of his body forever, One Negro Man Called **Moses** now in the possession of a certain Comfort MERRILL in the County af[ore]s[ai]d after my decease and the decease of my Sister Comfort MERRILL To have and to Hold the Said Negro man **Moses** unto the Said Elijah MERRILL and his heirs lawfully begotten to the only proper use benefit and behoof of him the Said Elijah MERRILL his heirs lawfully begotten of his body forever, after my and Sister Comfort MERRILL's Decease, and for and for no other use intent, purpose, or Construction whatsoever more than the above provisors excepted and the Said Jemima HENDERSON for herself and her heirs Executors and Administrators and every of them do quit all Claim, Right, Title, Interest, or Demand of and to the Same Negro above mentioned (excepting as above excepted) and will & Shall warrant and forever defend the Same against the lawful Right, Title and demand of all manner of person or persons whatsoever unto the Said Elijah MERRILL and his heirs lawfully begotten of his body forever In Testimony whereof the Said Jemima HENDERSON have hereunto Set her hand and Seal affixed this fifth day of April Anno Dom[ini] Seventeen hundred and Eighty five. ~

Signed Sealed & Delivered   John SELBY   her
in the presence of ~   W[illia]ᵐ SELBY (S.H)   Jemima X HENDERSON (Seal)
                                                              Mark"

---

[346] Worcester County Court (Land Records). Mortgage bond from MARCH, Martha to BRATTEN, Ann. 31 January 1784. L, p. 68, MSA CE 30-11. www.mdlandrec.net : accessed 11 February 2022.
[347] Worcester County Court (Land Records). Bill of sale from CAMPBELL, John to FASSETT, John. 09 March 1773. L, p. 74, MSA CE 30-11. www.mdlandrec.net : accessed 11 February 2022.

*followed on folio 97 with the acknowledgment of Justice of the Peace John SELBY and the recordation by court clerk James R. MORRIS[348]

Liber L, folios 97-98; 05 April 1785

"Know all men by these presents that I Comfort MERRILL of Worcester County in the State of Maryland, for and in Consideration of five Shillings current money of Maryland to me in hand paid by Hezekiah JOHNSON of the Same place, at and before the Ensealing and Delivery of these presents the receipt whereof I do hereby acknowledge and myself fully Satisfied contented and paid, Have Granted bargained and Sold and by these presents do Grant bargain and sell unto the said Hezekiah JOHNSON his heirs and Assigns forever, one Negro Boy called and known by the Name of **Peter** now in the possession of the said Hezekiah JOHNSON provided notwithstanding if the said Negro boy called **Peter** Should live longer then the Said Hezekiah JOHNSON and his wife Mary, Then in Such Case, for the above mentioned Consideration I Grant bargain and Sell the said Negro **Peter** unto Nancy JOHNSON daughter of the Said Hezekiah to her the Said Nancy JOHNSON her heirs Executors Admin[istrator]s and assigns forever To have and to hold the said Negro Boy **Peter** unto the Said Hezekiah JOHNSON and his wife Mary JOHNSON and after their decease to their daughter Nancy JOHNSON her heirs Executors Administrators and assigns forever and the Said Comfort MERRILL for herself heir heirs Executors, Administrators and every of them Shall and will warrant and forever defend the said Negro boy called **Peter** against the lawfull Right Title and Demand of all manner of Persons whatsoever unto the Said Hezekiah JOHNSON and his wife Mary JOHNSON and after their decease unto their daughter Nancy JOHNSON her heirs & assigns forever Of which said premisses I the said Comfort MERRILL have put the Said Hezekiah & his wife Mary and daughter Nancy in full possession by the delivery of these presents In Witness whereof I the said Comfort MERRILL have hereunto set my hand and Seal this fifth day of April Anno Dom[ini] Seventeen hundred & Eighty Five. ~

| Signed Sealed & Delivered in the presence of | John SELBY W[illia]m SELBY (? H) | Comfort | her X mark | MERRILL (Seal) |

*followed on folio 98 with the acknowledgment by Justice of the Peace John SELBY and the recordation by court clerk James R. MORRIS[349]

Liber L, folios 98-99; 05 April 1785

"Know all men by these presents That I Comfort MERRILL of Worcester County in in the State of Maryland for and in Consideration of the Sum of five Shillings current money of Maryland to me in hand paid by Arthur PRICE of the Same place the receipt whereof I the said Comfort MERRILL doth hereby acknowledge and myself fully Satisfied contented and paid Have Granted bargained and Sold and by these presents do Grant, bargain and Sell unto the aforesaid Arthur PRICE his heirs and assigns forever One Negro Girl called **Hannah** now in the possession of the said Arthur To have and to hold the said Negro Girl called **Hannah** and all and Singular the Said Negroes' increase unto the Said Arthur PRICE his heirs, Executors, Administrators and assigns to the only proper use benefit and behoof of him the said Arthur PRICE his heirs and assigns for ever from me the Said Comfort MERRILL my Heirs Executors, or Administrators or any of them all Rights, Titles, Interest, Claim or Demand, the Said Negro Girl and increase, will warrant and forever defend by these presents, against the lawful Right or Title of every other person or persons whatsoever unto the said Arthur PRICE his heirs and assigns forever, Of which said Negro Girl called and known by the Name of **Hannah**, I the Said the Said Comfort MERRILL have put the Said Arthur PRICE in full possession by the delivery of these presents In Witness whereof I the Said Comfort MERRILL have hereunto set

---

[348] Worcester County Court (Land Records). Deed of gift from HENDERSON, Jemima to MERRILL, Elijah. 05 April 1785. L, pp. 96-97, MSA CE 30-11. www.mdlandrec.net : accessed 11 February 2022.
[349] Worcester County Court (Land Records). Bill of sale from MERRILL, Comfort to JOHNSON, Hezekiah. 05 April 1785. L, pp. 97-98, MSA CE 30-11. www.mdlandrec.net : accessed 11 February 2022.

my Hand and affixed my Seal this fifth day of April anno Dom[ini] Seventeen hundred and eighty five ~

Signed Sealed & Delivered	Severn JOHNSON	
in the presence of ~	James BENNETT	Comfort + MERRILL (Seal)
		mark"

*followed with the acknowledgment by Justice of the Peace John SELBY and the recordation by court clerk James R. MORRIS[350]

Liber L, folios 102-103; 02 March 1785

"Maryland Somerset County C{?} Know all men by these presents that I Stephen MITCHELL of the State and County af[ore]s[ai]^d for and in Consideration of five Shillings in hand paid by Amela MORRIS of Worchester County in the State af[ore]s[ai]^d I dow ackolidge the Receipt and myself then with and myself fuly and Intirley Satesfied have Bargend Sold and delivard and by the presants do bargen set over and deliver Unto the s$^{a[i]d}$ Amela MORAS one Negro Woman Named **Rachel** and her Child named **Silva** them and thear Incras To have and to hold the said Negros as thare Incras and the Stephen MITCHELL for my self my Hears Excutors, Administrators do by these presants Warant and for ever Defend the Said Negro **Rachel** and **Silva** and them thare Incres Unto the s[ai]^d Amelay MORRIS her Hars Excutors Administrators or Assigns Against all and all maner of Persons In Witnes whareof together with the said Negros **Rachal** and **Silva** Sold sete over my Hand and Seal this 2$^{[nd]}$ day of March One thousand Seven hondred and eighty and five ~

Testas, Testast. ~ Stephen MITCHE[L]L (Seal)
Levin GURBY"

*followed with the recordation on 15 April 1785 by court clerk James R. MORRIS[351]

Liber L, folios 116-117; 12 May 1785

"This Indenture made this Twelfth day of May anno Domini one thousand Seven hundred and eighty five Between John WARRAN of Worcester County State of Maryland of the one part and McKemmy SMOCK of Kent County State of Delaware on the other part Witnesseth that I the Said John WARREN for divers good causes and Considerations me hereunto moving, Have given Granted bargained Sold, aliened Conveyed and Confirmed and by these presents do freely fully and Absolutely Give, grant, bargain, Sell alien Convey and Confirm of the Said McKimmey SMOCK his Heirs and Assigns forever, One Negro Woman called **Mirom** about 24 or 25 years of age and two of her Children the Eldest named **Stephen** about 4 years old the other about 2 years old called **Sal**, and also One Stone Horse called Bolton aged about Seven years old To have and to hold the said Granted and bargained premisses with all the appurtenances priviledges and Commodities to the Same belonging or in any wise appertaining to him the Said McKimmy SMOCK his Heirs and Assigns forever, to his and their own proper use, benefit and behoof forever, and I the said John WARREN for me my Heirs Executors Administrators, do Covenant, promise and Grant to and with the said McKimmy SMOCK his Heirs and assigns…Furthermore I the Said John WARREN for myself my Heirs Executors, Administrators do Covenant and promise at and upon the Reasonable Request (and at the proper Cost and Charge in the Law) of the Said McKimmy SMOCK his Heirs, to make do perform and execute any other further or other Lawful and Reasonable act or acts, thing or things Device or Devices in the Law needful or requisit{?} for the more perfect assurance Letting and the Sure making of the premisses as aforesaid, provided nevertheless and it is the true intent and meaning or Grantor and Grantee in these presents anything herein Contained to the contrary notwithstanding that if the above named John WARREN his Heirs, Executors, Administrators

---

[350] Worcester County Court (Land Records). Bill of sale from MERRILL, Comfort to PRICE, Arthur. 05 April 1785. L, pp. 98-99, MSA CE 30-11. www.mdlandrec.net : accessed 11 February 2022.

[351] Worcester County Court (Land Records). Bill of sale from MITCHELL, Stephen to MORRIS, Amela. 02 March 1785. L, pp. 102-103, MSA CE 30-11. www.mdlandrec.net : accessed 11 February 2022.

or Assigns do well and truly pay or cause to be paid unto the within named McKimmy SMOCK his Execu[to]rs adminis[trato]rs or assigns the Just and ful Sum for which he is now Sued in the Court of Kent in Delaware by Mark McCALL to wit the Principal one hundred and fifty pounds with all Interests Cost and Costs accruing on or before the 12th day of May in the year 1786, this above Written Deed or Obligation and every Clause and article therein contained Shall be Void and null and of none effect, or else Shall abide in full force and Virtue Sealed with my Seal and Dated in Dover in Kent County Delaware State, the day and year first above written ~

Sealed Sign[e]d & Delivered   John WARREN ~ (L/S)
In the presence of ..
N.B. The word causes in the Seventh Line and the second Word from the beginning of that line was interlined before the Ensealing and Delivery of this Mortgage ~
W[illia]m MOLLERTON
Tim. CALDWELL"

*followed on folio 117 with the recordation by court clerk James R. MORRIS[352]

*Due to its true length, this transcription has been narrowed to the most relevant portions. The full document can be viewed at the citation provided.

Liber L, folios 120-121; 13 May 1785

"Know all men by these presents That I Zadok SELBY of Worcester County in the State of Maryland planter for and in Consideration of the Sum of Fifty pounds current money of Maryland, to me in hand paid and before the Ensealing and Delivery of these presents by Jonathan ESHUN of the Same place, the receipt whereof I the Said Zadok SELBY doth hereby acknowledge, Hath Granted bargained and Sold and by these presents doth Grant, bargain and Sell unto the Said Jonathan ESHUN his heirs and Assigns for ever One Negro Boy called **Will** about Eleven years of age To have and to Hold the said Negro Boy called **Will** hereby Granted, bargained and Sold unto the aforesaid Jonathan ESHUN his Heirs and assigns forever And I the Said Zadok SELBY for myself and Heirs Executors and Administrators, all and Singular the Said Negro **Will** unto the Said Jonathan ESHUN his Heirs Executors, Administrators and Assigns against me the said Zadok SELBY my Heirs Executors and Administrators and every of them, and against every other person or persons whatsoever Shall and will forever warrant and defend, Of which Said Negro Boy called **Will** I the Said Zadok SELBY have put the Said Jonathan ESHUN in full possession by the delivery of these presents In Testimony whereof the Said Zadok SELBY have hereunto Set his hand and Seal affixed this thirteen day of May Anno Dom[ini] Seventeen hundred & Eighty five ~

Signed Sealed & Delivered   W[illia]m SELBY (S.H)   Zadok SELBY (Seal)
in the presence of ~"

*followed on folio 121 with the acknowledgment by Justice of the Peace Joshua TOWNSEND and the recordation court clerk James R. MORRIS[353]

Liber L, folio 125; 27 April 1785

"Know all men by these presents That I Hannah SELBY of Worcester County in the State of Maryland for the good will Love and affection which I owe and bare unto my Son Parker SELBY but more Especially for and in consideration of the Sum of five Shillings currant of the said State to me in hand paid by my said Son Parker SELBY before the Sealing and Delivery of these presents there receipt whereof the Said Hannah SELBY doth hereby acknowledge hath given granted bargained and Sold and by these presents to give grant bargain and Sell unto my Son Parker SELBY and his heirs and assigns forever One Negro man slave called **Able** : To

---

[352] Worcester County Court (Land Records). Deed of Mortgage from WARREN, John to SMOCK, McKemmey. 12 May 1785. L, pp. 116-117, MSA CE 30-11. www.mdlandrec.net : accessed 11 February 2022.
[353] Worcester County Court (Land Records). Bill of Sale from SELBY, Zadok to ESHUN, Jonathan. 13 May 1785. L, pp. 120-121, MSA CE 30-11. www.mdlandrec.net : accessed 11 February 2022.

Have and to hold the Said negro man Slave called **Able** unto him my Said Son Parker SELBY and his Heirs and assigns forever to the only use benefit and behoof of him the Said Parker SELBY and his Heirs forever and the Said Hannah SELBY doth Covenant with the Said Parker SELBY the She the Said Hannah SELBY and her Heirs Executors and Administrators the Said negro man Slave called **Able** will forever warrant and defend unto the Said Parker SELBY and his Heirs and assigns forever against the Lawfull Claim right and Tittle of all and every person or persons whatsoever, In Witness whereof the Said Hanah SELBY to these presents her hand hath Sett and Seal affixed this 27th day of April Anno Dom[ini] 1785 ~

Signed Sealed and Delivered   John SELBY
in presence of ~   Hanah X SELBY (Seal)
                                                                                              her   Mark"

*followed with the acknowledgment by Justice of the Peace Joshua TOWNSEND and the recordation on 13 May 1785 by court clerk James R. MORRIS[354]

Liber L, folios 138-139; 20 May 1785

"Know all men by these presents That I John Ennals SCOTT of Worcester County in the State of Maryland, for and in Consideration of the sum of Eighty Pounds current money of Maryland to me in hand paid by Barkley WHITE of the Same place the receipt whereof the Said John Ennals SCOTT doth hereby acknowledge, Hath bargained and Sold and by these presents do bargain & Sell unto the aforesaid Barkley WHITE his Heirs and assigns for ever, One Negro man called **Limus**, formerly the property of a certain Levin BLAKE, now in the possession of the Said Barkley WHITE To have and to hold the Said Negro man called **Lymus** hereby bargained and Sold unto the Said Barkley WHITE his Heirs and assigns to the only proper use benefit and behoof of him the Said Barkley WHITE his Heirs and assigns for ever and the Said John Ennals SCOTT for himself his Heirs, Executors and Administrators and every of them all and Singular the Said Negro man **Lymus**, unto the Said Barkley WHITE his Heirs and Assigns against me the Said John Ennals SCOTT, my Heirs, Executors and Administrators and against all and every other person and persons whatsoever, Shall and will warrant and for ever defend by these presents, Of which Said Negro, I the Said John Ennals SCOTT have put the Said Barkley WHITE in full possession by the delivery of these presents In Witness whereof I the Said John Ennals SCOTT have hereunto set my Hand and Seal affixed this Twentyeth day of May Anno Dom[ini] Seventeen hundred & Eighty five + +

Signed Sealed & Delivered   John Ennals SCOTT (Seal)
in the presence of ~   Tho[ma]s U VICTOR
                                                       Mark
                                   W[illia]m SELBY (S.H)"

*followed on folio 139 with the acknowledgment by Justice of the Peace N. HOLLAND and the recordation on 21 May 1785 by court clerk James R. MORRIS[355]

Liber L, folios 140-141; 27 May 1785

"know all men by these presents that I Samuel SCARBOROUGH of Worcester County the State of Maryland for and in Consideration of the Sum of fifty pounds current money of Maryland to me in hand paid at and before the Sealing and delivery of these presents by McKimmy PORTER of the County and State aforesaid the receipt whereof I do hereby acknowledge have bargained and Sold and by these presents do bargain and Sell unto the Said McKimmy PORTER One Negro woman Named **Ester**, to have and to hold the said Negro Woman by these presents bargained and Sold unto the Said McKimmy PORTER his Heirs Executors Administrators and assigns forever and I the said Samuel SCARBOROUGH for

---

[354] Worcester County Court (Land Records). Bill of Sale from SELBY, Hanah to SELBY, Parker. 27 April 1785. L, p. 125, MSA CE 30-11. www.mdlandrec.net : accessed 12 February 2022.
[355] Worcester County Court (Land Records). Bill of Sale from SCOTT, John Ennals to WHITE, Barkley. 20 May 1785. L, pp. 138-139, MSA CE 30-11. www.mdlandrec.net : accessed 12 February 2022.

myself my Heirs Executors and Administrators the Said Negro Woman unto the Said McKimmy PORTER his Heirs Executors, Administrators and assigns against me the Said Samuel SCARBOROUGH my Heirs Executors and Administrators and against all and every other person and persons whatsoever shall and will warrant and for ever defend firmly by these presents In Witness whereof I the Said Samuel SCARBOROUGH to these presents my Hand have Sett and Seal affixed the 27th day of May Anno Dom[ini] Seventeen hundred and Eighty five ~

Signed Sealed and Delivered   Peter CHAILLE   Sam[ue]l SCARBOROUGH (Seal)
in the presents off ~"

*followed on folio 141 with the acknowledgment by Justice of the Peace Peter CHAILLE and the recordation on 29 May 1785 by court clerk James R. MORRIS[356]

Liber L, folios 153-154; 07 June 1785

"Know all men by these presents that I Severn JOHNSON of Worcester County for and in consideration of the Sum of five Shillings current money of Maryland to me in hand paid before the Execution hereof by Patrick WATERS have Granted bargained and Sold and by these presents do Grant bargain and Sell unto the Said Patrick WATERS his Heirs Executors, and Administrators the Goods and Chattels following (to wit) One Negro man called **Ned**, One Lott of Land adjoining Mattapony Landing with all the Plank & Scanting on the Land, Three feather Beds and furniture, two Cows and Calves, Twelve head of Hogs, One Walnut Desk, One pine Safe, two painted Chests, One Small Gun of which Goods and Negro the said Severn JOHNSON hath at this time put the Said Patrick WATERS, in possession by delivering the Said Gun in the name of the whole, to have and to hold the Said Goods, and Negro unto the Said Patrick WATERS his Heirs Exec[uto]rs and Adm[inistrato]rs provided nevertheless that if the Said Severn JOHNSON Shall on or before the first day of June 1786 pay unto Joshua TOWNSEND and Peter CHAILLE the full Amount of Debts Due to the above named TOWNSEND & CHAILLE then these presents to be Void, Otherwise not, And the Said Severn JOHNSON doth hereby Covenant with the Said Patrick WATERS that if the Debt af[ore]s[ai]d is not Satisfied by the day aforesaid that the Said Patrick WATERS Shall have full power and Authority to Sell and dispose of the Goods and Negro af[ore]s[ai]d for Satisfaction for the Said Debt In Testamony whereof the Said Severn JOHNSON to these presents his Hand hath Set and his Seal affixed this Seventh day of June 1785.

Seal[e]d & Delivered   Peter CHAILLE   Severn JOHNSON (Seal)
in presents of"

*followed on folio 154 with the acknowledgment by Justice of the Peace Peter CHAILLE and the recordation by court clerk James R. MORRIS[357]

Liber L, folios 158-159; 15 March 1785

"This Indenture made this fifteenth day of March One thousand Seven hundred, Eighty and five between William HOLLAND of Worcester County in the State of Maryland of the one part and Philip SELBY of the Same place of the other part Witnesseth that the Said William HOLLAND for and in Consideration of the Sum of Two hundred and fifty pounds currency money of Maryland to him in hand paid before the Sealing and delivery of these presents Hath hearby Sett over Sol and Transferred unto him the Said Philip SELBY to his heirs and assigns for ever the following Slaves (to witt) One Negro woman called **Tamer** One Negro woman called **Pleasant**, one Negro boy called **Rafe**, one Negro boy called **Argile**, One Negro boy called **Abram** One Negro man called **George**, one Negro Girl called **Sarah** To have and to hold the Severall Negroes above mentioned any every of them unto him the Said Philip SELBY his

---

[356] Worcester County Court (Land Records). Bill of Sale from SCARBOROUGH, Samuel to PORTER, McKimmy. 27 May 1785. L, pp. 140-141, MSA CE 30-11. www.mdlandrec.net : accessed 12 February 2022.
[357] Worcester County Court (Land Records). Bill of Sale from JOHNSON, Severn to WATERS, Patrick. 07 June 1785. L, pp. 153-154, MSA CE 30-11. www.mdlandrec.net : accessed 12 February 2022.

Heirs and assigns for ever and the Said William HOLLAND by these presents doth warrant and for ever defend the Said Negroes unto him the Said Philip SELBY his Heirs and assigns against the Claim Right or Title of any person or persons Claiming by from or under him the Said William HOLLAND in Witnesseth whear of the Said William HOLLAND to these presents his Hand hath Sett and Seal affixed the day and year above written ~

Sign[e]d Sealed and Delivered   N. HOLLAND   W[illia]ᵐ HOLLAND (Seal)
in presents of   John PARRAMORE"

*followed on folio 159 with the acknowledgment by Justices of the Peace N. HOLLAND and John PARRAMORE and the recordation on 11 June 1785 by court clerk James R. MORRIS[358]

Liber L, folio 167; 15 November 1785

"Know all men by these presents That I Leah LANE (Wid[ow]) of Worcester County in the State of Maryland, for and in Consideration of the Sum of Thirty pounds current money of Maryland, to me in hand paid by Samuel GUNN of the Same place at and before the Signing whereof I the said Leah LANE, Have bargained and Sold and by these presents do bargain and Sell unto the af[ore]s[ai]ᵈ Samuel GUNN his heirs and Assigns forever, a Negro boy called **Sampson**, now in the possession of the said Leah LANE To have and to hold all and Singular the above mentioned Bargained and Sold Negro Boy called **Sampson** unto the said Samuel GUNN and his Heirs and assigns forever, and I the said Leah LANE for myself and my Heirs Executors and Administrators and against every of them, and against every other person whatsoever, will and Shall forever warrant and defend, the above mentioned Bargained and Sold Negro Boy **Sampson** I the said Leah LANE have put the Said Samuel GUNN in full possession by the delivery of these presents In Witness whereof I the said Leah LANE have here unto my Hand and Seal have set this fifteenth day of November Anno Dom[ini] One thousand seven hundred and Eighty five ~

Signed Sealed & Delivered   Philip QUINTON   Leah LANE (Seal)
In the presence of ~   John AYRES _"

*followed with the acknowledgment by Justice of the Peace Philip QUINTON and the recordation on December 1785 by court clerk James R. MORRIS[359]

Liber L, folios 185-186; 02 August 1785

"Know all men by these presents That I Levina JOHNSON of Worcester County in the State of Maryland for and in Consideration of the Sum of Fifty pounds current money of Maryland to me in hand paid by James BENNETT of the same place at & before the Ensealing hereof the receipt whereof I the said Levina JOHNSON doth hereby acknowledge, Have Granted, bargained & Sold and by these presents do Grant bargain and Sell unto the said James BENNETT his Heirs and assigns for ever, a Negro woman called and known by the name of **Rachell**, and a Child about Two months old called and named **Henny** To have and to hold all and Singular the said Negro wench and Child above Granted, bargained and Sold unto the said James BENNETT his Heirs and assigns for ever, and I the said Levina JOHNSON for myself my Heirs Executors and Administrators, and against every other person or persons whatsoever will warrant and forever defend the above mentioned bargained and Sold Negro woman and Child unto the Said James BENNETT his Heirs and assigns forever, Of which said Negro woman and Child have put the said James BENNETT in full possession by the delivery of these presents In Witness whereof I the said Levina JOHNSON have hereunto Set my Hand and Seal affixed this second day of August Anno Dom[ini] Seventeen hundred & Eighty five ~

---

[358] Worcester County Court (Land Records). Deed from HOLLAND, William to SELBY, Philip. 15 March 1785. L, pp. 158-159, MSA CE 30-11. www.mdlandrec.net : accessed 12 February 2022.
[359] Worcester County Court (Land Records). Bill of Sale from LANE, Leah to GUNN, Samuel. 15 November 1785. L, p. 167, MSA CE 30-11. www.mdlandrec.net : accessed 12 February 2022.

			her	
Signed Sealed & Delivered	Philip QUINTON			
in presence of ~	William SELBY (S.H)	Levina	X	JOHNSON (Seal)
			Mark"	

*followed with the acknowledgment by Justice of the Peace Philip QUINTON and the recordation on folio 186 by court clerk James R. MORRIS[360]

Liber L, folio 186; 09 August 1785

"State of Maryland Worcester County Know all men by these presents That I David COTTINGHAM of Somerset County and State of Maryland for divers good causes, but more Espechilly for and in Consideration of the sum of seventy five pounds current money of the State of Maryland to me in hand paid or Secured to be paid by Mary RICHARDSON the Receipt whereof I doe hereby acknowled and myself fully satisfied Have bargined Sold Coventented and agreed to and with my sister Mary RICHARDSON for a Negro man Slave called **Robert** and I doe by these presents Sell and Convey unto my sister Mary RICHARDSON her Heairs Ex[ecutor]ˢ Adm[inistrator]ˢ and assigns forever a good Right and tile of the said Negro man called **Robert**, Free and Clear of all Incumbrances whatsoever, and I doe Oblige myself my Hears Ex[ecutor]ˢ and Adm[inistrator]ˢ to warrant and defend the Title of the said **Robert** from all persons whatsoever, in Witness whearof I have hearto set my Hand and fixt my Seal this ninth day of Aug[u]sᵗ One thousand seven hundred and Eighty five ~

Signed Sealed and Acknowledged in presents of us ~   David COTTINGHAM (Seal)
Thomas COTTINGHAM
Pat[ric]ᵏ JORDAN ~"

*followed with the recordation by court clerk James R. MORRIS on 18 August 1785[361]

Liber L, folios 189-190; 08 September 1785

"Know all men by these presents That I William ALLEN of Worcester County in the State of Maryland for and in Consideration of the Sum of Sixty pounds current money of the State af[ore]s[ai]ᵈ to me in hand paid by William COTTMAN of Somerset County and State af[ore]s[ai]ᵈ whereof I do hereby acknowledge the Receipt and myself therewith fully Satisfied, have bargained Sold and delivered unto the Said William COTTMAN a Certain Negro man called **Mingo** To have and to hold the said Negro **Mingo** unto the said William COTTMAN his Executors administrators and assigns to the only proper use and behoof of the said William COTTMAN his Exe[cuto]ʳˢ Adm[inis]tr[ato]ʳˢ and assigns forever And I the said William ALLEN for myself, Executors administrators and Heirs against all persons Shall and will warrant and forever defend by these presents, In Witness whereof I have hereunto set my Hand and Seal this Eight day of September seventeen hundred and Eighty five ~

Sign[e]d Seal[e]d and Delivered   L WOOLFORD   W[illia]ᵐ ALLEN (Seal)
in presence of ~   Esme BAYLY"

*followed on folio 190 with the acknowledgment by Somerset County Justice of the Peace Levin WOOLFORD, the recordation by Somerset County court clerk Thomas HAYWARD, and the recordation by Worcester County court clerk James R. MORRIS[362]

Liber L, folio 192; 10 September 1785

"Know all men by these presents That I Elizabeth PORTER of Worcester County in the State of Maryland, for and in Consideration of the sum of Sixty pounds current money of Maryland

---

[360] Worcester County Court (Land Records). Bill of Sale from JOHNSON, Levina to BENNETT, James. 02 August 1785. L, pp. 185-186, MSA CE 30-11. www.mdlandrec.net : accessed 12 February 2022.
[361] Worcester County Court (Land Records). Bill of Sale from COTTINGHAM, David to RICHARDSON, Mary. 09 August 1785. L, p. 186, MSA CE 30-11. www.mdlandrec.net : accessed 12 February 2022.
[362] Worcester County Court (Land Records). Deed from ALLEN, William to COTTMAN, William. 08 September 1785. L, pp. 189-190, MSA CE 30-11. www.mdlandrec.net : accessed 12 February 2022.

to me in hand paid by John AYRES of the same place, at and before the Ensealing and Delivery hereof, I the said Elizabeth PORTER Have Bargained and Sold and by these presents, do bargain and Sell unto the said John AYRES his Heirs and assigns forever, a Negro woman called **Sarah**, and negro Child called **George** and Girl called **Comfort**, now in the possession of the said John AYRES To have and to hold all and Singular the said negro woman called **Sarah** and Children hereby bargained and Sold unto the said John AYRES his Heirs and assigns forever and for and to no other use intent purpose or Construction whatsoever, And I the said Elizabeth PORTER for myself my Heirs Executors and Administrators and every of them, and against every other person or persons whatsoever shall and will warrant and forever defend the above mentioned Negro woman called **Sarah** and Children hereby Bargained & Sold unto the Said John AYRES his Heirs and Assigns forever, Of which said Negro woman called **Sarah** and said Children I the said Elizabeth PORTER have put the said John AYRES in full possession by the delivery of these presents In Witness whereof I the said Elizabeth PORTER have hereunto Set my Hand and Seal this 10th day of September Anno Dom[ini] Seventeen hundred & Eighty five ~

Signed Sealed & delivered   Kendall SCARBOROUGH   her
in the presence of ~   Elizabeth B PORTER (Seal)
                                                                                    Mark"

*followed with the acknowledgment by Justice of the Peace Joshua TOWNSEND and the recordation on 14 September 1785 by court clerk James R. MORRIS[363]

Liber L, folios 194-195; 10 September 1785

"Know all men by these presents That I Samuel SCARBOROUGH of Worcester County in the State of Maryland for and in Consideration of the sum of Sixty pounds current money of Maryland to me in hand paid by Sally SCARBOROUGH, of the same at and before the Ensealing and Delivery Hereof Have bargained and Sold and by these presents do bargain and Sell unto the said Sally SCARBOROUGH her heirs and assigns forever a Negro Girl called **Comfort**, now in the possession of Sally SCARBOROUGH To have and to hold all and Singular the Said Negro Girl called **Comfort** hereby bargained and Sold unto the aforesaid Sally SCARBOROUGH and her Heirs and assigns forever, and the said Samuel SCARBOROUGH for himself his Heirs Executors and Administrators, and against every other person or persons whatsoever the said Negro called **Comfort** Shall and will warrant and forever defend the same bargained and Sold premisses unto the said Sally SCARBOROUGH and her Heirs and assigns forever of which the said Negro called **Comfort** I the said SCARBOROUGH have put the said Sally SCARBOROUGH in full possession by the delivery of these presents In Witness whereof I the said Samuel SCARBOROUGH have hereunto set my Hand and Seal this 10th day of September anno Dom[ini] One thousand seven hundred and Eighty five ~

Signed Sealed & Delivered   John AYRES   Sam[ue]^l SCARBOROUGH (Seal)
in the presence of ~"

*followed with the acknowledgment by Justice of the Peace Joshua TOWNSEND and the recordation on 14 September 1785 by court clerk James R. MORRIS[364]

Liber L, folios 195-196; 10 September 1785

"Know all men by these presents That I Sally SCARBOROUGH of Worcester County in the State of Maryland for and in Consideration of the sum of sixty Pounds current money of Maryland to her in Hand paid at and before the Ensealing hereof by Patrick WATERS of the same place she the said Sally SCARBOROUGH have bargained and Sold and by these presents do bargain and sell unto the aforesaid Patrick WATERS his Heirs and Assigns forever, a negro

---

[363] Worcester County Court (Land Records). Bill of Sale from PORTER, Elizabeth to AYRES, John. 10 September 1785. L, p. 192, MSA CE 30-11. www.mdlandrec.net : accessed 12 February 2022.

[364] Worcester County Court (Land Records). Bill of Sale from SCARBOROUGH, Samuel to SCARBOROUGH, Sally. 10 September 1785. L, pp. 194-195, MSA CE 30-11. www.mdlandrec.net : accessed 12 February 2022.

Woman called **Sinor**, now in the possession of the said Patrick WATERS To have and to Hold all and Singular the said Negro woman called **Sinor** and her increase from this day forward, hereby bargained and Sold unto the aforesaid Patrick WATERS his Heirs and assigns forever, and the said Sally SCARBOROUGH for herself her Heirs Executors and Administrators, and against every other person or persons whatsoever shall warrant and forever defend, unto the said Patrick WATERS his Heirs and assigns forever, Of which the said Negro woman called **Sinor** I the said Sally SCARBOROUGH have put the said Patrick WATERS in full possession by the delivery of these presents In Witness whereof I the said Sally SCARBOROUGH have hereunto Set my Hand & Seal this 10th day of September anno Dom[ini] Seventeen hundred and Eighty five ~

Signed Sealed & Delivered   John AYRES   her
in the presence of ~   Sally   X   SCARBOROUGH   (Seal)
                                                                           Mark"

*followed on folio 196 with the acknowledgment by Justice of the Peace Joshua TOWNSEND and the recordation on 14 September 1785 by court clerk James R. MORRIS[365]

Liber L, folios 196-197; 10 September 1785

"Know all men by these presents that I Elizabeth PORTER of Worcester County in the State of Maryland for and in Consideration of the sum of Five Shillings Current money of Maryland to her in hand paid at and before the Ensealing hereof by Kendall SCARBOROUGH of the same place she the said Elizabeth PORTER have bargained and Sold and by these presents do bargain and Sell unto the said Kendall SCARBOROUGH his Heirs and assigns forever, One Negro boy called **Levin** now in the Possession of the said Kendall SCARBOROUGH, To have and to hold the said Negro boy called **Levin** hereby bargained and Sold unto the said Kendall SCARBOROUGH his Heirs and assigns forever, and the said Elizabeth PORTER for herself and her Heirs shall and will warrant and forever defend the said Negro boy **Levin** unto the said Kendall SCARBOROUGH his Heirs and assigns forever Of which said Negro **Levin** the said Elizabeth PORTER have put the said Kendall SCARBOROUGH in full possession by the delivery of these presents In Witness whereof I the said Elizabeth PORTER have hereunto my Hand Set and Seal affixed the 10th day of September Seventeen and Eighty five ~

Signed Sealed and Delivered   John AYRES   her
in the Presents of ~   Elizabeth   B   PORTER   (Seal)
                                                                             Mark"

*followed with the acknowledgment by Justice of the Peace Joshua TOWNSEND and the recordation on 14 September 1785 by court clerk James R. MORRIS[366]

Liber L, folios 200-201; 03 August 1785

"State of Maryland Worcester County Ss. Know all men by these presents that we Jemima GODFREY and Nancy GODFREY of the County and State af[ore]s[ai]^d for and in consideration of the sum of Twelve pounds ten Shillings to us in hand paid by Elihu HAZZARD of the same place whereof we do hereby acknowledge the Receipt and ourselves there with fully and intirely Satisfied, have bargained Sold and delivered and by these presents in plain and open Market according to the Just and due form of Law in that Case made and provided, do bargain Set over and deliver unto the said Elihu HAZZARD One Negro Girl nam[e]^d **Leah**, to have and to hold the said bargained Negro unto the said HAZZARD his heirs Execu[to]^{rs} Admini[strato]^{rs} and assigns to the only proper use and behoof of him the said Elihu HAZZARD his Ex[ecuto]^{rs} Adm[inistrato]^{rs} and assigns for ever And we the said Jemima GODFREY & Nancy GODFREY our Selves our Heirs Executors, Admini[strator]^s the said bargained Negro

---

[365] Worcester County Court (Land Records). Bill of Sale from SCARBOROUGH, Sally to WATERS, Patrick. 10 September 1785. L, pp. 195-196, MSA CE 30-11. www.mdlandrec.net : accessed 12 February 2022.
[366] Worcester County Court (Land Records). Bill of Sale from PORTER, Elizabeth to SCARBOROUGH, Kendall. 10 September 1785. L, pp. 196-197, MSA CE 30-11. www.mdlandrec.net : accessed 12 February 2022.

unto the said Elihu HAZZARD his heirs Exe[cutor]ˢ Admi[nistrator]ˢ and assigns against, all and all manner of persons shall and will warrant and forever defend by these presents In Witness together with the delivery of the bargained Negro we have here unto Set our hands and Seals this third day of August anno Domini 1785

Sign[e]ᵈ Sealed and delivered In presents of ~	John WALTER Elizabeth GODFREY	Jemima X GODFREY (Seal) her Mark
		Nancy + GODFREY (Seal) her Mark"

*followed on folio 201 with the recordation on 04 October 1785 by court clerk James R. MORRIS[367]

Liber L, folios 201-202; 13 August 1785

"This Indenture made this thirteenth day of August in the year of our Lord one thousand seven hundred and eighty five between Leavin ROACH of Worcester County and State of Maryland of the one part and Sarah ROACH of the same place of the other part Witnesseth That for and in Consideration of taken care of in a christian like manner and provided for, with sufficient clothing, death, Washing, lodging and fi{?}ng during his natural life by the said Sarah ROACH or her heirs hath by these presents Sold, allienated conveyed and Confirmed unto the said Sarah ROACH during her natural life, all that Tract or part of a Tract of Land, lying and being in Somersett County called Mullingsfield and after her decease to be equally divided between the Children of the said Sarah ROACH, which she the said Sarah had by James ROACH (Vizt.) Anne, Matty, Mary Bozman, Betsey & Nelly ROACH, to them their Heirs and assigns forever, and the said Levin ROACH for and in Consideration as aforesaid doth further sell and by these presents made over unto the said Sarah ROACH, one Negro man named **Harry**, and all other the personal he hath, in law, equity or in any wise ought to have by the last Will and Testament of his father William ROACH and his mother Elizabeth's Will during her natural life and after her decease to her Children aforesaid to be equally divided Nevertheless the true intent and meaning of this deed is that if the said Sarah ROACH or Children herein mentioned shall at any time neglect or refuse to perform the duties herein before mentioned to me the said Levin ROACH, that on my complaint or on the complaint of any of my friends, or any other person for me to the Orphan Court in my behalf shall be heard and their order and Judgment in the premisses to be decisive binding and final to all Intents and purposes whatsoever, In Witness whereof I the said Levin ROACH to these presents my hand have set and Seal affixt the day and year above written ~

Signed Sealed Acknowledged and delivered in presence of us ~	Gilliss POLK Ja[me]ˢ BENNETT"	Leavin ROACH (Seal)

*followed on folio 202 with the acknowledgment by Somerset County Justices of the Peace Gilliss POLK and James BENNETT, the recordation by Somerset County court clerk Thomas HAYWARD on 16 August 1785, the acknowledgment by Worcester County Justices of the Peace Joseph DASHIELL and Ebenezer HANDY on 10 September 1785, and the recordation by Worcester County court clerk James R. MORRIS on 07 October 1785[368]

Liber L, folios 202-203; 03 October 1785

"Know all men by these presents That we Joseph BENSON, John CORDURY, Levin PAYNE and Thomas VICTOR Jun[io]ʳ all Worcester County in the State of Maryland, for and in consideration of the sum of Seven pounds Ten Shillings curr[en]ᵗ money of Maryland, to each

---

[367] Worcester County Court (Land Records). Bill of Sale from GODFREY, Jemima and Nancy to HAZZARD, Elihu. 03 August 1785. L, pp. 200-201, MSA CE 30-11. www.mdlandrec.net : accessed 12 February 2022.

[368] Worcester County Court (Land Records). Deed from ROACH, Leavin to ROACH, Sarah. 13 August 1785. L, pp. 201-202, MSA CE 30-11. www.mdlandrec.net : accessed 12 February 2022.

of us paid by Isaac KILLAM of the same place at and before the Ensealing hereof, Have Granted, bargained and Sold and by these presents do Grant, bargain and Sell unto the said Isaac KILLAM his Heirs and Assigns forever, One Negro man called **Benjamin** (or **Ben**) now in the possession of Jemima KILLAM To have and to hold all and Singular the above mentioned, bargained negro man called **Ben** (or **Benjamin** unto the above named Isaac KILLAM his Heirs and Assigns forever, and we the said Joseph BENSON, John CORDARY, Levin PAYNE & Thomas VICTOR Jun[io]r for ourselves and ea{?} of us, our and of our Heirs Executors and Adm[inistrato]rs and every of them, and against every other person or persons whatsoever Claiming by or under any of us our or any of our Heirs Executors, or Adm[istrato]rs will forever defend the said Bargained & Sold Negro above mentioned (excepting the lifetime of the above named Jemima KILLAM) unto the said Isaac KILLAM his Heirs and Assigns for ever Of which the said Negro called **Ben** we the Subscribers and each of us have Transferred our Rights and Title by the delivery of these presents unto the said Isaac KILLAM his Heirs and Assigns forever In Witness whereof we have hereunto set our Hands & Seals this third day of October Anno Dom[ini] Seventeen hundred & Eighty five ~

Signed Sealed & Delivered   N. HOLLAND   Joseph BENSON   (Seal)
in the Presents of ~   John CAUDRY   (Seal)
                                                                    Levin PAINE   (Seal)
                                                                   Thomas VICTOR   (Seal)"

*followed on folio 203 with the acknowledgment by Justice of the Peace N. HOLLAND and the recordation on 07 October 1785 by court clerk James R. MORRIS[369]

Liber L, folios 214-215; 04 October 1785

"To all to whom this present writing may concern ~ whereas I believe that it is unjust to hold people in Slavery ~ Do by these presents Manumitt and Sett free the following Slaves (to wit) **Capril** aged nineteen years, **Milby** aged ten years **Hornton** aged Six years ~ **Patience** aged four years, **George** aged Eight Months, that is to say, the said Negroes shall be free, the Males when they arive at the age of Twenty five, and the Females when they arive at the age of Twenty one years. And I do by these presents Relinquish all my Right, Title and Interest, and to the af[ore]s[ai]d Negroes when they come to the age above mentioned, For myself and my Heirs forever, have hereunto Set my Hand and affixt my Seal the 4th day of October 1785 ~

Sign[e]d Seal[e]d and Acknowledged   Jethro BOWIN ~   (Seal)
In presence of us ~
Isaac LAYFIELD. one of the Justices for Worcester County
Charles BISHOP
John BOWIN"

*followed on folio 205 with the recordation on 14 October 1785 by court clerk James R. MORRIS[370]

Liber L, folios 220-221; 28 October 1785

"Know all men by these presents That I Hannah BISHOP of Worcester County in the State of Maryland for and in Consideration of the sum of Seventy pounds current money of Maryland to her in hand paid by Joshua TOWNSEND Esq[uir]e at and before the Sealing and delivery hereof the Receipt whereof I the said Hannah BISHOP doth hereby acknowledge Have Bargained and Sold and by these presents do Bargain and Sell unto the said Joshua TOWNSEND his Heirs and Assigns forever, a Negro Man called **Jacob** and a Negro Boy called

---

[369] Worcester County Court (Land Records). Bill of sale from BENSON, Joseph, CAUDRY, John, PAINE, Levin, and VICTOR, Thomas to KILLAM, Isaac. 03 October 1785. L, pp. 202-203, MSA CE 30-11. www.mdlandrec.net : accessed 12 February 2022.

[370] Worcester County Court (Land Records). Deed of Manumission from BOWIN, Jethro to **Capril, Milby, Hornton, Patience,** and **George**. 04 October 1785. L, pp. 214-215, MSA CE 30-11. www.mdlandrec.net : accessed 12 February 2022.

Leeds, now in the possession of the said Hannah BISHOP in the County of Worcester To have and to hold all and Singular the abovementioned two Negroes, man and Boy hereby bargained & Sold unto them the said Joshua TOWNSEND his Heirs and assigns forever And the said Hannah BISHOP for herself and her Heirs and against every other person or persons whatsoever Claiming or Shall ever hereafter Claim any Right or Title to the above mentioned Sold Negroes unto the aforesaid Joshua TOWNSEND his Heirs and assigns forever Of which said Negroes above mentioned I the said Hannah BISHOP have put the said Joshua TOWNSEND in full possession by the delivery of these presents In Witness whereof I the said Hannah BISHOP have set my Hand and Seal affixed this 28th day of October Anno Dom[ini] Seventeen hundred & Eighty Five ~

Signed Sealed & Delivered   John SELBY   Hannah BISHOP (Seal)
in the presence of ~"

*followed on folio 221 with the acknowledgment by Justice of the Peace John SELBY and the recordation by court clerk James R. MORRIS[371]

Liber L, folio 228; 16 November 1785

"Know all men by these presents That I Philip SELBY of the County and State af[ore]s[ai]d in consideration of the sum of fifty five pounds current money of Maryland to me in hand paid by Selby NEWTON of the same place at and before the Sealing and delivery of these presents the Receipt whereof I the said Philip SELBY do hereby acknowledge have Granted bargained and Sold and by these presents do Grant bargain and Sell unto the said Selby NEWTON his Heirs Executors Administrators or assigns One Negro Woman Slave named **Tamer** about Twenty nine years of age and her Child called **James** about three or four months old To have and to hold the af[ore]s[ai]d Negroes as above bargained and Sold or mentioned or intended so to be unto the said Selby NEWTON his heirs Executors and administrators and assigns forever. And I the said Philip SELBY for my heirs Executors both the af[ore]s[ai]d Negroes named **Tamer** & **James** unto the said Selby NEWTON his Heirs Executors administrators and assigns against me the said Philip SELBY my Heirs Executors and administrators and against all and every other persons whatsoever Shall and will Warrant and forever defend by these presents In Testimony whereof I have hereunto set my Hand and Seal this Sixteenth day of November Anno Domini one thousand seven hundred and Eighty five ~

Signed Sealed and Delivered   John SELBY   Philip SELBY (Seal)
In presence of ~   John WISE"

*followed with the acknowledgment by Justice of the Peace and the recordation by court clerk James R. MORRIS[372]

Liber L, folios 254-255; 23 December 1785

"Maryland Wor[cester] County Sst. Know all men by these presents that I Zadok SELBY of the County af[ore]s[ai]d for & in Consideration the sum of Sixty pounds current money of Maryland to me in hand paid at and before the Sealing and delivery hereof by Benjamin PURNELL (of Walton) of the same place Have Bargained & Sold and by these presents do bargain and Sell unto the af[ore]s[ai]d Benjamin PURNELL (of Walton) his Heirs and assigns forever one Negro man called **Peter** and I the said Zadok SELBY for myself my Heirs Exe[cuto]rs & Adm[inistrato]rs do Covenant Grant & agree to and with the said Benja[min] PURNELL his Heirs Executors, Adm[inistrato]rs & assigns that he the said Zadok SELBY & his heirs will & Shall Warrant and defend forever the said negro man called **Peter**, against the Claim Emantipation and demand of all and every person or persons Whatsoever unto the af[ore]s[ai]d Benj[am]in PURNELL his Heirs and assigns forever Of which said Negro called **Peter** I the

---

[371] Worcester County Court (Land Records). Bill of sale from BISHOP, Hannah to TOWNSEND, Joshua. 28 October 1785. L, pp. 220-221, MSA CE 30-11. www.mdlandrec.net : accessed 12 February 2022.
[372] Worcester County Court (Land Records). Bill of sale from SELBY, Philip to NEWTON, Selby. 16 November 1785. L, p. 228, MSA CE 30-11. www.mdlandrec.net : accessed 12 February 2022.

said Zadok SELBY have put the said Benjamin PURNELL in full possession by the delivery of these presents In Testimony whereof I the said Zadok SELBY have hereunto set my hand and affixed my Seal this 23rd day of December Anno Dom[ini] Seventeen hundred & Eighty five ~

Signed Sealed & Delivered   John SELBY   Zadok SELBY   (Seal)
in the presence of ~"

*followed with the acknowledgment by Justice of the Peace John SELBY and the recordation on folio 255 by court clerk James R. MORRIS[373]

Liber L, folios 260-261; 24 December 1785

"Know all men by these presents That we Kendall SMOCK and Leah SMOCK booth of Worcester County in the State of Maryland for and in Consideration of the sum of seventy five pounds current money of Maryland to us in hand paid by Selby PARKER at and before the Sealing and delivery hereof the recept whereof wee hereby doth acknowledge and hath given granted bargained and sold and by these presents do give Grant bargain and Sell unto Selby PARKER and his Heirs and assigns forever one Negro Woman called **Margery** and one Negro Child called **Sarah** To have and to hold the said Negro woman called **Margery** and Negro Child **Sarah** to him the said Selby PARKER his Heirs and Assigns forever, to the only use benefit and behoof of him the said Selby PARKER and his Heirs and assigns for ever and to and no other use or purpose whatsoever and the said Kendall SMOCK and Leah SMOCK his wife doth Covenant to and with the said Silby and his Heirs, that he the said Kendall SMOCK and Leah SMOCK his wife will and shall forever warrant & defend the said Negro Woman called **Margery** and Negro Child called **Sarah** unto the said Selby PARKER and his Heirs and Assigns forever against the Claim right and title of all and every person or persons Whatsoever Claiming by, from under him the Said Kendall SMOCK and Leah SMOCK or their Heirs and all other persons whatsoever in Witness whereof we have hereunto Sett our Hands and Seals affixed this 24th day of December Anno Domini One thousand Seven hundred and Eighty five

Signed Sealed and Delivered   John SELBY.   Kendall SMOCK   (Seal)
in the presence of us ~   John SELBY   Leah SMOCK   (Seal)"

*followed on folio 261 with the acknowledgment by Justice of the Peace John SELBY and the recordation on 02 January 1786 by court clerk James R. MORRIS[374]

Liber L, folios 263-264; 31 December 1785

"This Indenture made the thirty first day of December in the year of our Lord one thousand seven hundred & Eighty five Between Martha MARCH of Worcester County in the state of Maryland of the one part and Lemuel SHOWELL of the same place of the other part Witnesseth that the said Martha MARCH for & in Consideration of the Sum of fifty pounds current money of Maryland due & owing from the said Martha unto Anne BRATTEN, which Sum with the Interest the said Lemuel became Security for the said Martha to the said Ann, which the said Martha doth acknowledge, and hath bargained & Sold assigned Transferred & delivered and by these presents doth bargain & Sell assign transfer & deliver unto the said Lemuel SHOWELL his Executors Administrators & Assigns one Negro Woman named **Comfort** about Twenty three years of age To have & to hold the said Negro woman unto the said Lemuel SHOWELL his Executors Administrators & Assigns, To the only proper use of the said Lemuel his Executors Administrators and Assigns & no other use & purpose whatsoever, Provided always & its is hereby declared to be the true intent & meaning of these presents that If the said Martha MARCH her Executors or Administrators shall well & truly pay the said Ann BRATTEN her Executors, Administrators or Assigns the afforesaid fifty pounds & Interest & the expence of

---

[373] Worcester County Court (Land Records). Bill of sale from SELBY, Zadok to PURNELL, Benjamin. 23 December 1785. L, pp. 254-255, MSA CE 30-11. www.mdlandrec.net : accessed 12 February 2022.
[374] Worcester County Court (Land Records). Bill of sale from SMOCK, Kendall and Leah to PARKER, Selby. 24 December 1785. L, pp. 260-261, MSA CE 30-11. www.mdlandrec.net : accessed 12 February 2022.

making & Recording this Deed on or before the first day of September next with all the necessary expence the said Lemuel his heirs, Executors or Administrators may be forced to an account of his being Security for the said Martha as afforesaid Then this Deed to be Void & of none Effect And the said Martha for herself her Executors & administrators doth hereby Covenant & agree with the said Lemuel SHOWELL that she will well & truly pay unto the said Ann or Lemuel the sums of money afforesaid with the Interest as afforesaid & the necessary Expences as afforesaid by the time afforesaid, And it is hereby further Covenanted & agreed between the parties aforesaid, That if the said Martha her Executors or Administrators do not pay the said Sums of Money with the Interest & necessary expences as afforesaid by the time afforesaid, That then it shall & may be Lawful for the said Lemuel SHOWELL his Executors or Administrators after giving tin days notice by Advertisements set up for that purpose, To sell the said Negro woman **Comfort** for Ready money, and from the money raised by such sale Sattisfy him or them the Debts afforesaid with the Interest & the necessary expences as afforesaid as far as it will do it and if there is any overplus pay it into the hands of the said Martha her Executors or Administrators In Testimony the said Martha MARCH hath hereunto Set her hand & Seal the day & year first within Written ~

Sealed & Delivered   John POSTLY   Martha MARCH   (Seal)
in the presence of   Thomas McNEAL"

*followed on folio 264 with the acknowledgment by Justice of the Peace John POSTLY and the recordation on 17 January 1786 by court clerk James R. MORRIS[375]

Liber L, folios 264-265; 24 January 1786

"Maryland Worcester County Ss^t. Know all men by these presents that I James GIVANS of the County and province af[ore]s[ai]^d for and in Consideration of the sum of seventy five pounds current money of Maryland to me in hand paid by Benjamin PURNELL (of Walton) of the County af[ore]s[ai]^d Have bargained Sold, released granted and Confirmed and by these presents do bargain Sell, release grant and Confirm unto the said Benjamin PURNELL one Negro man called **Will** the value of seventy five pounds to have and to hold the said Bargained Negro **Will** by these presents bargained Sold released, Granted and Confirmed unto the only proper use & behoof of the said Benjamin PURNELL his Heirs Executors, Administrators & assigns for ever freely quietly & entirely without any Contradiction Claim disturbance or hindrance of any person whatsoever and without any amount to me or to any other whatsoever to be made answered or hereafter to be rendered, so that I the said James GIVANS nor any other for me or in my Name, any Right title Interest or demand of in unto or for the said Negro **Will** or any part or parcel thereof ought to exact Challenge Claim or demand at any time or times hereafter, but from all Action right Estate title claim demand and possession Emancipation and Interest thereof shall be wholly barred and excluded by force and Virtue of these presents and I the said James GIVANS unto the said Benjamin PURNELL (of Walton) his Exe[cuto]^{rs} adm[inistrato]^{rs} and assigns and against all & every other person or persons whatsoever shall and will warrant and forever defend by these presents which Negro **Will** I the said James GIVANS hath put the said Benjamin PURNELL in full possession by delivery at the signing and delivery Hereof In Witness whereof the said James GIVANS have hereunto Set his Hand & Seal this Twenty fourth day of January Seventeen hundred & Eighty Six ~

Signed sealed & Delivered   Josiah MITCHELL   James GIVANS   (Seal)
I the presents of "

*followed on folio 265 with the acknowledgment by Justice of the Peace Josiah MITCHELL and the recordation by court clerk James R. MORRIS[376]

---

[375] Worcester County Court (Land Records). Deed from MARCH, Martha to SHOWELL, Lemuel. 31 December 1785. L, pp. 263-264, MSA CE 30-11. www.mdlandrec.net : accessed 12 February 2022.

[376] Worcester County Court (Land Records). Bill of sale from GIVANS, James to PURNELL, Benjamin. 24 January 1786. L, pp. 264-265, MSA CE 30-11. www.mdlandrec.net : accessed 12 February 2022.

Liber L, folio 271; 06 February 1784

"February the 6th 1784 then received of Thomas TAYLOR the full & Just sum of Twenty four pounds Specie in full for a Negro guirl called **Jebb**, which Negro Guirl I have sold to Said TAYLOR rec[eive]d
Testes   Philip QUINTON   Philip SELBY
Joshua TOWNSEND"

*followed with the recordation on 03 February 1786 by court clerk James R. MORRIS[377]

Liber L, folios 279-280; 02 March 1786

"This Indenture made the Second day of March Anno Domini One thousand Seven hundred and Eighty Six Between John WARRAN of the one part and Annanias HUDSON of the other part both of Worcester County and State of Maryland Witness that the said John WARRAN for and in Consideration of the sum of One hundred and Eighty five pounds, five Shillings current money of Maryland to him in hand paid by the said Annanias HUDSON at and before the Sealing and delivery of these presents, the receipt whereof he the said John WARRAN doth hereby acknowledge Doth bargain and Sell and by these presents do Seize Bargain and Sell unto the said Annanias HUDSON his Heirs Executors, Administrators and assigns on Stone Horse or Stallion called Bolton, a Negro woman called **mirom** a Negro boy called **Stephen** and a Negro Girl called **Sal** To have and to hold to the said Horse and Negroes above mentioned and every of them unto the said Annanias HUDSON his Heirs Executors Administrators and Assigns, provided and it is the intent of these presents and they are upon this Condition and it is the meaning of the said parties hereunto that if the said John WARRAN his Heirs Executors administrators or assigns do and shall well and truly pay or cause to be paid or Shall indemnify or discharge a Debt which the said Annanias HUDSON is answerable to William ROAN for that from thence forth every matter and thing herein contained Shall Cease and determine and be utterly null and void to all and every intent and purpose any thing herein contained to the contrary in any wise notwithstanding and lastly it is Covenanted and agreed upon by and between the said parties to these presents that untill the said Annanias HUDSON shall sustain damage on account of being Obliged to pay the af[ore]s[ai]d Sum of money to the said William ROAN or sustain any damage on account of being answerable for the same it shall and may be Lawfull to and for the said John WARRAN his Heirs Executors and Administrators to hold and keep possession of the af[ore]s[ai]d Horse and Negroes Bargained and Sold as af[ore]s[ai]d anything herein contained to the Contrary in anywise Notwithstanding and further the said John WARRAN Covenants for himself his Heirs Executors and Administrators to and with the said Annanias HUDSON his Heirs Executors, Administrators and Assigns if if the af[ore]s[ai]d Horse should die or any of the Negroes af[ore]s[ai]d Should die, that then the loss Shall fall upon him and that he will Mortgage or pledge some thing of equal value to the said Annanias HUDSON his Heirs Executors Administrators or assigns In Witness whereof the parties to these presents doth hereto interchanably set their Hands and Seals the day and year af[ore]s[ai]d ~

Testes.   Isaac PURNELL   John WARRAN   (Seal)
                                                                                                     Annanias HUDSON   (Seal)"

*followed on folio 280 with the acknowledgment by William STEVENSON on 04 March 1786 and the recordation by court clerk James R. MORRIS on 29 March 1786[378]

Liber L, folios 286-287; 09 February 1786

"Maryland Worcester Sst. February 9th 1786 ~ Know all men by these presents that I Charles PHILLIPSHILL of County and State af[ore]s[ai]d for and in Consideration of the sum of Eighty pounds Curr[en]t money of Maryland to me Paid by Joshua STURGIS the rece[i]pt whereof I

---

[377] Worcester County Court (Land Records). Receipt for payment from SELBY, Philip to TAYLOR, Thomas. 06 February 1784. L, p. 271, MSA CE 30-11. www.mdlandrec.net : accessed 12 February 2022.
[378] Worcester County Court (Land Records). Instrument of writing from WARRAN, John to HUDSON, Annanias. 02 March 1786. L, pp. 279-280, MSA CE 30-11. www.mdlandrec.net : accessed 13 February 2022.

do acknowledge have bargained and Sold and by these presents do bargain and sell unto the said Joshua STURGIS, a Negro named **Tom**, To have and to hold the said Negro Boy named **Tom** to the af[ore]s[ai]^d Joshua STURGIS his Heirs and Assigns forever ~

Test. Nehemiah DORMAN   Charles PHILLIPSHILL
     James SELBY ~"

*followed on folio 287 with the acknowledgment by Justice of the Peace Philip QUINTON and the recordation by court clerk James R. MORRIS[379]

Liber L, folios 288-289; 10 February 1786

"Know all men by these presents That I Henry PARKER of Worcester County in the State of Maryland for and in Consideration of the sum of fourty pounds current money of Maryland to me in hand paid by, at and before the ensealing and delivery of these presents by Zadekiah HAMMOND of the County and State afforesaid, the Receipt hereof I do hereby acknowledge have bargained and Sold and by these presents do bargain and Sell unto Zadekiah HAMMOND his Heirs and assigns for ever a Negro Boy known by the name of **Zadock** about Six years old and now in the Possession of the aff[ore]s[ai]^d Zadekiah HAMMOND, to have and to hold the said negro Boy called **Zadock** all and Singular he hear after in cause that he may have & every of them by these presents bargained and Sold unto the said Zedekiah HAMMOND his Heirs Executors Adm[inistrato]^rs and assigns forever I the said Henry PARKER Junior for myself my Heirs Executors or Administrators or any of them or any of their assigns all and Singular the said Negro Boy call **Zadock** unto the said Zedekiah HAMMOND his Heirs and assigns for ever against me the said Henry PARKER Jun[io]^r my Heirs Executors and Administrators and assigns, all and every other person or persons whatsoever Shall and will Warrant and forever defend by these, of which said Negro Boy called **Zadock** I the said Henry PARKER have put the said Zadekiah HAMMOND in full possession by the delivery of these presents In Testamoney Whereas the said Henry PARKER or have here unto Set his Hand and Seal affixed this 10th day of February Anno Dom[ini] Seventeen hundred & Eighty Six ~

Sign[e]^d Sealed & Delivered   John SELBY   Henry PARKER Jun[io]r (Seal)
In the presents of "

*followed on folio 289 with the acknowledgment by Justice of the Peace John SELBY and the recordation on 11 February 1786 by court clerk James R. MORRIS[380]

Liber L, folios 312-313; 10 March 1786

"Know all men by these presents That I William Atkinson SELBY of Worcester County in the State of Maryland for and in Consideration of the sum of Twenty five pounds current money of Maryland to me in hand paid by Thomas PARKER of the same place, the receipt whereof is hereby acknowledged Have Granted bargained and Sold and by these presents doth Grant, bargain, sell and deliver unto him the said Thomas PARKER his Heirs and assigns forever, one Negro Girl named **Nance**, now in the possession of the af[ore]s[ai]^d SELBY To have and to hold the above mentioned bargained and Sold Negro Girl unto him the said Thomas PARKER his Heirs or assigns forever, to the only proper use benefit and behoof of him the said Thomas PARKER his Heirs and assigns forever, And I the said William Atkinson SELBY for myself my Heirs Executors and Administrators, and against every other person or persons whatever will and Shall warrant and forever defend by these presents, Of which said Negro Girl **Nance** (or **Nancey**) I the said William Atkinson SELBY have put the said Thomas PARKER in full possession by the delivery of these presents In Witness whereof I the said William Atkinson

---

[379] Worcester County Court (Land Records). Bill of sale from PHILLIPSHILL, Charles to STURGIS, Joshua. 09 February 1786. L, pp. 286-287, MSA CE 30-11. www.mdlandrec.net : accessed 12 February 2022.

[380] Worcester County Court (Land Records). Bill of sale from PARKER, Henry Jr. to HAMMOND, Zadekiah. 10 February 1786. L, pp. 288-289, MSA CE 30-11. www.mdlandrec.net : accessed 13 February 2022.

SELBY have hereunto to Set my Hand and Seal affixed this 10th day of March anno Domini Seventeen hundred and Eighty Six ~

Signed Sealed & Delivered   John SELBY   W[illia]m A. SELBY (Seal)
in the presence of ~"

*followed on folio 313 with acknowledgment by Justice of the Peace John SELBY and the recordation on 11 March 1786 by court clerk James R. MORRIS[381]

Liber L, folios 313-314; 29 April 1785

"This Indenture made this Twenty ninth day of April Anno Dom[ini] Seventeen hundred and eighty five Between Free negro **Larry** of Worcester and State of Maryland of the one part and Thomas MARTIN (of James) of the County and State af[oresai]d of the other part Witnesseth that the said **Larry** hath of his own free and voluntary will bound himself by these presents as a servant unto Thomas MARTIN (of James) his Heirs Ex[ecuto]rs Adm[inistrator]s or assigns for a during the term of thirty years fully to be compleat and ended from the date of this said Indenture during all which time the said **Larry** his said MARTIN will well and faithfully serve his lawfull commands obey, and the Goods of his said master shall not Steal and waste, nor shall permit himself to be absent without the Consent of his master and the said Thomas covenants and agrees to and with the said **Larry** for and during the Term af[oresai]d he will find the said **Larry** sufficient Clothes, meat & lodging In Testimony whereof We have set our hands and seals affixed this 29th day of Ap[ri]l 1785 ~

Signed Sealed & Delivered   Sam[ue]l SMYLY   **Larry** (Seal)
In presence of   Matt. HANDY   Tho[ma]s MARTIN (Seal)"

*followed on folio 314 with the recordation by court clerk James R. MORRIS on 20 March 1786[382]

Liber L, folio 351; 26 April 1786

"Know all men by these presents that I Eleanor BLUETT of Worcester County and State of Maryland for and in Consideration of the natural Love and affection which I have and bear for my Grand Son Benjamin Frederick Augustus Ceesar DASHIELL and also for divers other good causes and Considerations me the said Eleanor BLUETT hereunto moving Have given granted and Confirmed, and by these presents do give grant and Confirm unto the said Benjamin Frederick Augustus Ceesar DASHIELL my Negro man **Isaac** To have hold and enjoy the said negro man **Isaac** aforesaid unto the said Benjamin Frederick Augustus Ceesar DASHIELL his Executors Administrators and assigns to the only use and behoof of the said Benjamin Frederick Augustus Ceesar DASHIELL his Executors administrators and assigns forever And I the said Eleanor BLUETT the negro man **Isaac** aforesaid to the said Benjamin Frederick Augustus Ceesar DASHIELL his Executors Administrators and assigns against me the said Eleanor BLUETT my Executors and Administrators and all and every other person and persons whatsoever shall and will warrant and forever defend by these presents In Witness whereof the parties have hereunto set their hands and Seals this Twenty sixth day of April in the year of our Lord one thousand seven hundred and eighty six ~

Signed Sealed and Delivered   Joseph DASHIELL   Elea[n]or BLUETT (Seal)
in presence of ~   Peter CHAILLE Jun[io]r"

---

[381] Worcester County Court (Land Records). Bill of sale from SELBY, William Atkinson to PARKER, Thomas. 10 March 1786. L, pp. 312-313, MSA CE 30-11. www.mdlandrec.net : accessed 13 February 2022.
[382] Worcester County Court (Land Records). Indenture from **Larry** "**free negro**" to MARTIN, Thomas. 29 April 1785. L, pp. 313-314, MSA CE 30-11. www.mdlandrec.net : accessed 13 February 2022.

*followed with the acknowledgment by Justice of the Peace Joseph DASHIELL and the recordation on 27 April 1786 by court clerk James R. MORRIS[383]

Liber L, folios 366-367; 05 July 1786

"Maryland Worchester County ~ Know all men by these presents that I Nathan CULVER of Worchester County planter for & in Consideration of the sum of one hundred pounds Specie to me in hand paid by Isaac HORSEY of Sussix County & Delaware state Merchant the receipt whereof I hereby acknowledge have bargained and Sold mad over & delivered unto him the said Isaac HORSEY five heads of Horses one Wagon & utensils belonging unto the said Wagon, one pair Timber Wheels & utensells belonging to said Wheals, also one Negro Wench & one Negro Child, and the aforesaid Nathan CULVER Covenant agree to and with the said Isaac HORSEY for himself heirs Executors & administrators that the said Nathan CULVER his Heirs Executors & administrators shall and will forever warrant and defend the said Bargained premisses against all persons whatsoever laying any Right tightle Claim or Interest to the same and that the said Isaac HORSEY his Heirs Executors administrators or assigns shall & may from time to time & from all times after have peacabble possession hold the said five head or Horses one Wagon & utensils belonging unto the said Wagon one pair Timber Wheals & Utencels belong to said Wheals, also one Negro Wench and one Negro Child that is now in possestion of said CULVER free and clear from all persons whatever & that the said Nathan CULVER shall and will forever warrant and defend the Right and property of the aforesaid to the said Isaac HORSEY his Heirs Executors, administrators and assigns forever In testymoney whereof I the said Nathan CULVER have hereunto set my Hand & Seal this fifth day of July one thousand seven hundred & Eighty six ~

Signed Sealed & Delivered   Ebenezer HANDY   Nathan CULVER (Seal)
In the presence of ~

Worcester County   Be it remembered that on the day and year within mentioned personally appeared the within named Nathan CULVER before me one of the united States Justices of the Peace for the County aforesaid and did acknowledge the within mentioned five head of Horses also one Wagon & utencels belonging unto said Wagon also one Timber Chart Whels and utencels belonging to said Wheals also one Negro Wench & one Negro Child, the Wench Name by the Name of **Heaster** & the Child belonging to the aforesaid Wench to be the Right and property of Isaac HORSEY his Heirs Executors, and Administrators & assigns forever and it being to the true Intent and meaning of the within Deed according to an act of Assembly in such case made & provided   Before Ebenezer HANDY"

*followed on folio 367 with the recordation by court clerk James R. MORRIS on 21 July 1786[384]

Liber L, folios 391-392; 27 May 1786

"This Indenture made this 27th day of May anno Dom[ini] one thousand Seven hundred and eighty six Between Charles BANESTER of Worcester County and State of Maryland of the one part and William BOWIN of the County and State aforesaid of the other part Mariner Witness that the said Charles BANESTER for and in Consideration of the sum of one hundred pounds current money of Maryland to him in hand paid by the said William BOWIN the receipt whereof he the said Charles BANESTER doth hereby acknowledge hath given Granted bargained and Sold & by these presents doth give grant bargain Sell and deliver unto the said William BOWIN one Negro woman named **Hannah** and her three Children one called **Jane** one **Comfort** and one **Milly** also one Negro woman called **Grace** and her child called **Mintay** and all of their Incress if there should be any also three Cows & Calves one Bed and furniture with the Sundry other goods and Chattels whaich the said William BOWIN has now in

---

[383] Worcester County Court (Land Records). Deed of gift from BLUETT, Eleanor to DASHIELL, Benjamin Frederick Augustus Ceesar. 26 April 1786. L, p. 351, MSA CE 30-11. www.mdlandrec.net : accessed 13 February 2022.
[384] Worcester County Court (Land Records). Bill of sale from CULVER, Nathan to HORSEY, Isaac. 05 July 1786. L, pp. 366-367, MSA CE 30-11. www.mdlandrec.net : accessed 13 February 2022.

possession To have and to hold the aforesaid Bargained and Sold negros together with the other aforesaid Goods and Chattels unto the aforesaid William BOWIN his Heirs Executors, administrators or assigns forever and to and for the only proper use benefit and behoof of the said William BOWIN his Heirs & and to and for no other use or purpose whatever and the said Charles BANISTER for himself his Heirs Executors or Adm[inistrato]rs doth covenant Grant and agree to and with said William BOWIN that he will forever warrant and defend the aforesaid Bargained and Sold negros or above mentioned together with the aforesaid Goods and Chattels unto the aforesaid William BOWIN his Heirs Executors adm[inistrato]rs or assigns To and from all persons Lawfully claiming any right title on Intrest thereunto In Witness whereof the said Charles BANISTER his hand hath set and Seal affixed the day and year first above written ~

Signed Sealed and Delivered   Josiah MITCHELL   Charles BANESTER   (Seal)
In presents of ~   James MARTIN"

*followed on folio 392 with the acknowledgment by Justice of the Peace Josiah MITCHELL and the recordation on 30 May 1786 by court clerk James R. MORRIS[385]

Liber L, folios 392-393; 02 June 1786

"To all Persons to whom these presents shall come Know ye that I Frederick CONNER of Worcester County in the State of Maryland being desirous to set free and manumit a certain negro man Slave called **Abner** in Consideration of his faithful Service done and performed the said Frederick CONNER doth by these presents give and Grant Set free and Manumit the aforesaid Negro man called **Abner** and that his freedom shall commence and take effect immediately from and after the date of these presents To have hold and freely enjoy to him the said **Abner** forever immediately after the date hereof his liberty and freedom in full and ample manner without any let hindrance or authority of any person or persons whatsoever In Testimony whereof the said Frederick CONNER to these presents his hand hath set and Seal affixed this Second day of June anno Domini One thousand Seven hundred and eighty Six ~

Signed Sealed and Delivered   W[illia]m PURNELL   Frederick CONNER   (Seal)
In the presence of ~   John WISE"

*followed on folio 393 with the acknowledgment by Justice of the Peace William PURNELL and the recordation by court clerk James R. MORRIS[386]

Liber L, folio 396; 15 April 1786

"Received april fifteeth day 1786 of Joshua TOWNSEND the Sum of Eight pounds, fifteen Shillings current money of Maryland in full for all my (and my wife's Right and Title of and to a certain negro women named **Phillis** and her two Children named **Will** and **Jacob** as Witness my Hand the day and year above written

Test. Mary ENNIS   Pr. W[illia]m A. PARKER"

*followed with the recordation by James R. MORRIS on 14 June 1786[387]

Liber L, folios 400-401; 14 July 1786

"Know all men by these presents that I **Amos CORNISH** (Molatto) of Worcester County in the State of Maryland for and in Consideration of the Sum of Eight pounds thirteen Shillings and six pence Current money of Maryland to me in hand paid at and before the Sealing & delivery hereof, Have bargained & Sold & by these presents doth bargain, Sell and deliver unto

---

[385] Worcester County Court (Land Records). Instrument of writing from BANESTER, Charles to BOWIN, William. 27 May 1786. L, pp. 391-392, MSA CE 30-11. www.mdlandrec.net : accessed 13 February 2022.
[386] Worcester County Court (Land Records). Deed of manumission from CONNER, Frederick to **Abner**. 02 June 1786. L, pp. 392-393, MSA CE 30-11. www.mdlandrec.net : accessed 13 February 2022.
[387] Worcester County Court (Land Records). Receipt from PARKER, William A. to TOWNSEND, Joshua. 15 April 1786. L, p. 396, MSA CE 30-11. www.mdlandrec.net : accessed 13 February 2022.

John TOWNSEND, Alexander McKALLEN and William SELBY (SH) and their Heirs & assigns forever, The one half of the Corn and Crop on the Ground on the plantation of Thomas BENSTON, being my past as per agreement with the said BENSTON (and now being in the County af[ore]s[ai]^d) To have and to hold all and Singular the said Crop, being the Right & Title of Said **CORNISH**, unto the said John TOWNSEND, Alexander McKALLEN and William SELBY (S.H.) and to their Heirs & assigns forever (provided the said **Amos CORNISH** do not pay & Satisfy the above mentioned Sum of money and Interest thereon and all legal C{?} that may be about the Settling their respective Debts &c. at or upon the first day of October next Otherwise notwithstanding the above to be and remain in full force and virtue to all intents & purposes whatsoever so far as to make each of them whole) Of which Crop & Corn above mentioned I the said **Amos CORNISH** have put the said John TOWNSEND, Alexander McKALLEN and William SELBY (S.H) in full possession by the delivery of these presents In Witness whereof I the said **Amos CORNISH** have hereunto set my Hand and Seal this 14th day of July Anno Dom[ini] 1786 ~

Signed Sealed & Delivered   William DRYDEN   his
In the presents of ~   **Amos** X **CORNISH** (Seal)
                                                                                      Mark"

*followed on 401 with the acknowledgment by Justice of the Peace William PURNELL and the recordation by court clerk James R. MORRIS[388]

Liber L, folios 429-430; 16 June 1786

"To all people to whome this present writing Shall send Greeting I Bartley TOWNSEND of Worcester County in the State of Maryland, Know ye that I the said Bartley TOWNSEND for and in consideration of the natural love and effection which I have and bear unto Isaac TOADVINE, and also for other good causes and Considerations me theirunto moving have given and Granted and by these presents doth give grant and confirm unto the said Isaac TOADVINE his Heirs and Assigns forever One Negro boy called **Ben**, but if the said Isaac dies without lawfull Issue of his body, then I grant and give the said Negro **Ben** to be equally divided between James TOADVINE & Nancy TOADVINE and their Heirs (excepting the use and service of the said Negro **Ben** dure the life time of my wife Mary, To have and to hold the said Negro boy **Ben** unto the said Isaac TOADVINE his Heirs and assigns forever agreable to the true intent and meaning hereof, to his and their own proper use and uses and I the said Bartly TOWNSEND will warrant and forever defend all my Right and title of the said Negro **Ben** unto the said Isaac In Witness whereof I the said Bartley TOWNSEND to these presents his hand hath Set and Seal affixed the 16th day of June Anno Domith 1786 ~

Signed Seal[e]d and   Joshua TOWNSEND   Barkley TOWNSEND   (Seal)
delivered in presents of "

*followed on folio 430 with the acknowledgment by Justice of the Peace John SELBY and the recordation by court clerk James R. MORRIS[389]

Liber L, folios 433-434; 17 June 1786

"Know all men by these presents that I Samuel TRUITT of Worcester County in the State of Maryland for and in consideration of the Sum of Sixty pounds current money of Maryland to me in hand paid at and before the Ensealing and delivery hereof by Joshua TOWNSEND Esq[uir]^e of the same place I the said Samuel TRUITT have bargained and Sold and by these presents do bargain and Sell unto the said Joshua TOWNSEND his Heirs and assigns forever the following Negro Slaves now in the possession of the af[ore]s[ai]^d TRUITT (to wit) One

---

[388] Worcester County Court (Land Records). Bill of sale from **CORNISH, Amos** to TOWNSEND, Joshua, SELBY, William, and McKALLEN, Alexander. 14 July 1786. L, pp. 400-401, MSA CE 30-11. www.mdlandrec.net : accessed 13 February 2022.
[389] Worcester County Court (Land Records). Deed of gift from TOWNSEND, Barkley to TOADVINE, Isaac. 16 June 1786. L, pp. 429-430, MSA CE 30-11. www.mdlandrec.net : accessed 13 February 2022.

negro Lad about Twelve years old called **Caleb**, One ditto about Six years old called **Levin** and a negro Woman Called **Su** about Twenty four years old To have and to hold all and Singular the above mentioned three Negroes hereby bargained & Sold unto him the said Joshua TOWNSEND his Heirs & Assigns forever, and the said Samuel TRUITT for himself his Heirs Execu[to]rs and Administrators and against every of them against every other person or persons whatsoever shall and will forever warrant and defend, Of which said Three Negroes I the said Samuel TRUITT have put the said Joshua TOWNSEND in full possession by the delivery of these presents In Witness whereof I the said Samuel TRUITT have hereunto put my Hand & affixed my Seal this seventeenth day of June Anno Dom[ini] One thousand seven hundred & Eighty six ~

Signed Sealed & Delivered   Peter CHAILLE   Samuel TRUITT (Seal)
In the presence of ~"

*followed with the acknowledgment by Justice of the Peace Peter CHAILLE and the recordation on 23 June 1786 by court clerk James R. MORRIS[390]

Liber L, folios 442-443; 18 March 1786

"Worcester County Ss[t]. Know all men by these presents, That I Henry BELL of Worcester County in the State of Maryland for and in consideration of the sum of Fifty five pounds current money of Maryland to me in hand paid by James KING of the County and State afforesaid, at or before the Ensealing and delivery of these presents wherewith I confess myself to be fully Sattisfied contented and paid Have bargained Sold and delivered & by these for myself my Heirs Executors and Administrators do fully clearly & absolutely bargain Sell & deliver unto the said James KING, one Negro boy named **Tom** about fourteen years of age To have & to hold the said Negro boy named **Tom** to the said James KING his Heirs Executors, Administrators or Assigns, to his & their own proper uses and behoofs forever, And I the said Henry BELL my Heirs Executors & Administrators and every of us, the said Negro to the said James KING his Heirs Executors Administrators & Assigns, against all people shall & will Warrant acquit & forever defend by these presents In Witness whereof I have hereunto set my hand & Seal this eighteenth day of March Anno Domini 1786 ~

Sign[e]d Seal[e]d & Deliver[e]d   John POSTLY   Henry BELL (Seal)
in the presence of ~   Josiah MITCHELL"

*followed with the acknowledgment by Justice of the Peace John POSTLY and the recordation on 30 June 1786 by court clerk James R. MORRIS[391]

Liber L, folio 446; 07 July 1786

"To all whom these presents may concern ~ Whereas I believe it is unjust to hold people in Slavery do by these presents manumit and set free the following negro Slaves to wit, **Charles**, **Rose** and **Sarah** aged about forty five years each Slave ~ And I do by these presents for myself and Heirs relinquish all my Right, title and Interest to the afores[ai]d Negroes forever agreeable to an act of Assembly in such Cases made and provided for the manumission of slaves, In Testimony whereof I have hereunto set my hand and affixed my Seal the Seventh day of July one thousand seven hundred & eighty six ~

Signed Sealed& Acknowledged   Outten STURGIS   Jethro BOWIN (Seal)
In presence of us ~   Philip QUINTON"

---

[390] Worcester County Court (Land Records). Bill of sale from TRUITT, Samuel to TOWNSEND, Joshua. 17 June 1786. L, pp. 433-434, MSA CE 30-11. www.mdlandrec.net : accessed 13 February 2022.

[391] Worcester County Court (Land Records). Bill of sale from BELL, Henry to KING, James. 18 March 1786. L, pp. 442-443, MSA CE 30-11. www.mdlandrec.net : accessed 13 February 2022.

*followed with the acknowledgment by Justice of the Peace Philip QUINTON and recordation by court clerk James R. MORRIS[392]

Liber L, folios 454-455; 08 July 1786

"Maryland Worcester County 8th July 1786 ~ Know all men by these presents that I John CULVER of Worcester County and State of Maryland planter for and in Consideration of the Sum of Thirty pounds Specie in hand paid by Robert SMYLY of Summerset County & State of Maryland Merch[an]t the receipt whereof I hereby acknowledge have bargained Sold and delivered & by these presents do bargin Sell & deliver unto the said Robert SMYLY One Negro Wench named **Rachell** thirty six years of age To have and to hold the said Bargained premisses unto the said Robert SMYLY his Heirs executors and assigns forever and I the said John CULVER for myself my executors & administrators shall and will Warrant & defend against all persons by these presents the said bargained premises unto the said Robert SMYLY his Heirs executors, administrators and assigns in Witness whereof I have hereunto Set my hand & Seal 8th day of July 1786

Signed Sealed & Delivered
in presence of ~
Joseph DASHIELL

John X CULVER (Seal)
his Mark"

*followed on folio 455 with the acknowledgment by Justice of the Peace Joseph DASHIELL and the recordation on 14 July 1786 by court clerk James R. MORRIS[393]

Liber L, folios 457-458; 22 July 1786

"Maryland Worcester County Know all men by these presents that I Hezekiah CAREY of the County af[ore]s[ai]d for and in consideration of the Sum of One hundred pounds, current money of Maryland him in hand p[ai]d by Stephen CHRISTOPHER hath Granted bargained & Sold & by these presents hath granted bargained & Sold unto the said Stephen CHRISTOPHER one negro woman called **Rose** & one Yoke of Oxen & two horses & all the Lumber lying at my Mill, and also two feather Beds & furniture, Provided nevertheless that if the above bound Hezekiah CAREY do & Shall well & truly pay to said Stephen the Sums of ninety pounds, & Twenty five pounds Six Shillings for James PERDUE, & to Moor TALBOTT the Am[oun]t of his ag[ain]st me on or before the first day of Jan[ua]ry next & for the true performance each of the above Articles I have hereunto Set my hand & Seal this 22[n]d July 1786 ~

Signed Sealed & delivered   Ebenezer HANDY
in presence off ~

Hezekiah X CAREY (Seal)
his Mark"

*followed with the acknowledgment of Ebenezer HANDY and the recordation on folio 458 by court clerk James R. MORRIS on 25 July 1786[394]

Liber L, folio 468; 10 August 1786

"Know all men by these presents That I William Atkinson SELBY of Worcester County in the State of Maryland for and in Consideration of Forty pounds current money of Maryland to me in hand paid at and before the Sealing and delivery hereof by John EVANS of the same County and State af[ore]s[ai]d, I the said William Atkinson SELBY Have bargained Sold and delivered and by these presents do bargain Sell and deliver unto him said John EVANS his Heirs and Assigns forever, a Negro Boy called **Eben** now in the possession of a certain John SELBY (of John) in the County af[ore]s[ai]d To have and to hold the said bargained and Sold negro boy

---

[392] Worcester County Court (Land Records). Deed of manumission from BOWIN, Jethro to **Charles, Rose**, and **Sarah**. 07 July 1786. L, p. 446, MSA CE 30-11. www.mdlandrec.net : accessed 13 February 2022.
[393] Worcester County Court (Land Records). Bill of sale from CULVER, John to SMYLY, Robert. 08 July 1786. L, pp. 454-455, MSA CE 30-11. www.mdlandrec.net : accessed 13 February 2022.
[394] Worcester County Court (Land Records). Bill of sale from CAREY, Hezekiah to CHRISTOPHER, Stephen. 22 July 1786. L, pp. 457-458, MSA CE 30-11. www.mdlandrec.net : accessed 13 February 2022.

called **Eben** above named unto him the said John EVANS his Heirs and Assigns forever, And I the said William Atkinson SELBY for myself my Heirs Executors & Administrators, and against every other person or persons whatever will and shall forever defend the abovesaid negro unto the said John EVANS his Heirs and Assigns forever Of which said negro boy above mentioned I the said William Atkinson SELBY have put the said John EVANS in full possession by the delivery of these presents In Witness whereof I the said William Atkinson SELBY have hereunto set my hand and Seal this 10th day of August Anno Dom[ini] Seventeen hundred and eighty six ~

Signed Sealed & Delivered   Peter CHAILLE   W[illia]m A. SELBY (Seal)
In the presence of ~"

*followed with the acknowledgment by Justice of the Peace Peter CHAILLE and the recordation on 18 August 1786 by court clerk James R. MORRIS[395]

Liber L, folio 469; 21 July 1786

"Maryland Sc[t]. Know all men by these presents that I Robert PURNELL of Worcester County and State af[ore]s[ai]d for and in consideration of the Sum of Sixty five pounds current money of Maryland to me in hand paid by Selby NEWTON of the same place at and before the Sealing and delivery of these presents the receipt whereof I the said Robert PURNELL do hereby acknowledge and myself fully Satisfied contended and paid, have granted bargained and sold and by these presents do Grant bargain and Sell unto the said Selby NEWTON his Heirs Executors, Administrators or Assigns, one negro man Slave called **Joshua** aged about twenty four years, To have and to hold the af[ore]s[ai]d negro man called **Joshua** or above bargained and sold unto the said Selby NEWTON his Heirs Executors Administrators and Assigns forever, And I the said Robert PURNELL for myself my Heirs Executors and Administrators the af[ore]s[ai]d Negro man Slave called **Joshua** unto the said Selby NEWTON his Heirs Executors Administrators and Assigns against me the said Robert, my Heirs Executors and Administrators and against all and every other person or persons whatsoever shall and will warrant and forever defend by these presents In Testimony whereof I have hereunto Sett my Hand and Seal this twenty first day of July Anno Domini One thousand Seven hundred and eighty Six ~ ,, ~ . ~ . ~ . ~ . ~

Signed Sealed and Delivered   Peter CHAILLE   Robert PURNELL (Seal)
In the presence of ~"

*followed with the acknowledgment by Justice of the Peace Peter CHAILLE and the recordation on 18 August 1786 by court clerk James R. MORRIS[396]

Liber M, folios 1-2; 20 October 1786

"Know all men by these presents that I Levin LONG of Worcester County in the State of Maryland for and in consideration of the sum of Seventy pounds current money of Maryland to me in hand paid at and before the Sealing and delivery of these presents by James BENNET of the County and State af[ore]s[ai]d the receipt whereof I do hereby acknowledge have bargained and Sold and by these presents do bargain and Sell unto the said James BENNETT one negro man named **Abner** To have and to hold the said negro man called **Abner** by these presents bargained and Sold unto the said James BENNETT his heirs Executors and Adm[inis]t[rato]rs and I the said Levin LONG for myself my Executors and Administrators the said negro man unto the said James BENNETT his heirs Executors, administrators and assigns against me the said Levin LONG my heirs Executors and Administrators and against all and every other person or persons whatsoever shall and will warrant and forever defend by these presents Of which said negro I the said Levin LONG have put the said James BENNETT in full possession of by

---

[395] Worcester County Court (Land Records). Bill of sale from SELBY, William Atkinson to EVANS, John. 10 August 1786. L, p. 468, MSA CE 30-11. www.mdlandrec.net : accessed 13 February 2022.
[396] Worcester County Court (Land Records). Bill of sale from PURNELL, Robert to NEWTON, Selby. 21 July 1786. L, p. 469, MSA CE 30-11. www.mdlandrec.net : accessed 13 February 2022.

delivering the said negro **Abner** at the Sealing hearof In Witness whereof I the said Levin LONG to these presents my hand have sett and Seal affixed the 20th day of October anno Domini 1786

Signed Sealed and Delivered   Jes.ª TOWNSEND   Levin LONG   (Seal)
in presents of ~"

*followed on folio 2 with the acknowledgment by Justice of the Peace Philip QUINTON and the recordation on 21 October 1786 by court clerk James R. MORRIS[397]

Liber M, folios 12-13; 01 September 1786

"Know all men by these presents That I James STEVENSON (Carpenter) of Worcester County in the State of Maryland for and in Consideration of the Sum of One hundred and thirty Seven pounds, ten Shillings current money of Maryland to me in hand paid by Angelo ATKINSON of the same place at and before the Sealing and delivery of these presents, I the said James STEVENSON Have bargained, Sold and delivered and by these presents doth bargain Sell and delivery unto him the said Angelo ATKINSON and to his Heirs and Assigns forever, the following negroes (to wit) one negro man called **Robin**, one negro woman called **Tab** with a Sucking Child and one negro Boy called **Peter**, now in the possession of the said James STEVENSON, in the County aforesaid, To have and to hold all and Singular the said Negroes hereby Bargained Sold and delivered unto him the said Angelo ATKINSON and to his Heirs and Assigns forever against me the said James STEVENSON, and my Heirs and against every other persons whatsoever shall and will warrant and forever defend the same unto him the said Angelo ATKINSON and to his Heirs and assigns forever, Of which said Bargained Sold and delivered Negroes I the said James STEVENSON have put the said Angelo ATKINSON in full possession by the delivery of these presents In Witness whereof I the said James STEVENSON have hereunto set my hand and affixed my Seal this 10th day of November Anno Dom[ini] one thousand Seven hundred and eighty Six. ~

Signed Sealed & Delivered   Levi OUTTEN   James STEVENSON   (Seal)
In the presence of ~   John POSTLY"

*followed on folio 13 with the acknowledgment by Justice of the Peace John POSTLY and the recordation 10 November 1786 by court clerk James R. MORRIS[398]

Liber M, folios 17-18; 01 September 1786

"Know all men by these presents That I William ATKINSON of Worcester County in the State of Maryland for and in Consideration of the Sum of Fifty pounds current money of Maryland to me in hand paid by Angelo ATKINSON of the same place, at and before the Sealing and delivery hereof I the said William ATKINSON have Bargained Sold and delivered and by these presents doth bargain Sell and deliver unto the said Angelo ATKINSON and his Heirs and Assigns forever, a negro man called **Adam**, now in the possession of of the said William in the County af[ore]s[ai]ᵈ the said negro man (or boy) being about Sixteen Years old, To have and to hold the said negro called **Adam** hereby bargained Sold and delivered unto him the said Angelo ATKINSON his Heirs and assigns forever against me the said William and my Heirs Executors and Administrators, and against every other person or persons whatever shall and will forever warrant and defend unto the said Angelo ATKINSON his Heirs and Assigns forever, Of which said negro man called **Adam** above mentioned I the said William ATKINSON have put the said Angelo ATKINSON in full possession by the delivery hereof In Witness I the said William ATKINSON have hereunto set my Hand & Seal affixed this 1st day of September Anno Dom[ini] Seventeen hundred and Eighty six ~

---

[397] Worcester County Court (Land Records). Bill of sale from LONG, Levin to BENNETT, James. 20 October 1786. M, pp. 1-2, MSA CE 30-12. www.mdlandrec.net : accessed 21 February 2022.
[398] Worcester County Court (Land Records). Bill of sale from STEVENSON, James to ATKINSON, Angelo. 10 November 1786. M, pp. 12-13, MSA CE 30-12. www.mdlandrec.net : accessed 21 February 2022.

Signed Sealed & Delivered   Peter CHAILLE   William ATKINSON (Seal)
In the presence of ~"

*followed on folio 18 with the acknowledgment by Justice of the Peace Peter CHAILLE and the recordation on 06 December 1786 by court clerk James R. MORRIS[399]

Liber M, folios 19-20; 30 November 1786

"Maryland Worcester County Know all men by these presents that Whereas Joshua STURGIS Sen[ior] of the County asc.[d] State of af[ore]s[ai][d] did enter into a Bond with Betsey RILEY then Betsey MIDDELTON for the due and faithfull administration of the Goods & Chattels of her late husbands Ignatious MIDDLETON and whereas the said Estate not yet being Settled and the Joshua STURGIS still his liable for it and the said Betsey & Benjamin RILEY her present Husband both being very desirious to save harmless & keep Indemnify'd the said Jo[s]. STURGIS & for no other porpose Hath given granted bargained & Sold & by these presents doth give grant bargain & Sell to the said Joshua STURGIS for the express purpose of Saving him from Injury, one Tract of Land called James Delight containing eighty acres More or less, one negro man **Bob**, one negro man **Jack**, one negro man **Ralph** one negro woman **Sall**, one negro Boy **Cato**, one negro boy **Levin** one negro **Lizey** one negro boy **Boatswan**, one Bay Horse 1 Gray Horse, thorty Barrels of Indian Corn, three Oxen one Chest of Draws & all my Household furniture (except one Desk & Table) and eight hundred pounds of Good Merch[an]t[able] Tobacco, all which Land & negroes & other things numerated in this Bill of Sale, the said Benja[min] & Betsey for themselves & their Heirs will warent and defend unto the said Joshua STURGIS & his Heirs for the express purpose af[ore]s[ai][d] and the said Joshua being released from the Bond & Securityship af[ore]s[ai][d] then the within mentioned Land & negroes and Other Goods mentioned, to return to the said Benja[min] & Betsey & their Heirs and assigns In testimony whereof the parties have hereunto their hands set & Seals affixed this 30 day of Nov[ember] Anno Dom[ini] 1786 ~

Sign[e]d Seal[e]d & Delivered Joshua DASHIELL   Benjamin RILEY (Seal)
in presence of   William Rit DASHIELL   Betsey RILEY (Seal)"

*followed on folio 20 with the acknowledgment by Justice of the Peace Joseph DASHIELL and the recordation on 16 December 1786 by court clerk James R. MORRIS[400]

Liber M, folios 35-36; 18 August 1786

"To all persons to whom these presents shall come Know ye that I Charles BISHOP of Worcester County in the State of Maryland being desirous to set free and Manumit the several and respective negro Slaves to wit, **Jacob**, **Comfort**, **Levin** and **Abner** (the said **Jacob** & **Comfort** now of full age, **Levin** aged three years & three months and **Abner** aged about nine months at this time) in Consideration of the faithful services of the said **Jacob** & **Comfort** done and performed, and for other good causes and considerations me thereunto moving, I the said Charles BISHOP do by these presents Give and Grant, set free and Manumit Severally the aforesaid negros **Jacob**, **Comfort**, **Levin** and **Abner** and that the freedom of the said **Jacob**, and **Comfort** shall commence and take effect immediately after the date of these presents and the freedom of the af[ore]s[ai][d] **Levin** and **Abner** shall commence and take effect immediately after they arive to the age of Twenty one years To have and to hold and freely enjoy to them the said **Jacob**, **Comfort**, **Levin** and **Abner** (**Jacob** and **Comfort** immediately after they arive to the age of twenty one years) their and each of their Liberty and freedom in full and ample manner without any Let hindrance or Authority of any person or persons whatsoever In Testimony whereof I the said Charles BISHOP have hereunto set my Hand and affixed my Seal this 18th day of August Anno Domini one thousand Seven hundred and eighty six~

---

[399] Worcester County Court (Land Records). Bill of sale from ATKINSON, William to ATKINSON, Angelo. 01 September 1786. M, pp. 17-18, MSA CE 30-12. www.mdlandrec.net : accessed 21 February 2022.
[400] Worcester County Court (Land Records). Bill of sale from RILEY, Benjamin & Betsey to STURGIS, Joshua Sr. 30 November 1786. M, pp. 19-20, MSA CE 30-12. www.mdlandrec.net : accessed 21 February 2022.

Signed Sealed and Delivered   Peter CHAILLE   Charles BISHOP (Seal)
I the presence of~"

*followed on folio 36 with the acknowledgment by Justice of the Peace Peter CHAILLE and the recordation on 05 January 1787 by court clerk James R. MORRIS[401]

Liber M, folio 41; 29 January 1787

"Know all men by these presents that I Duncan MURRAY of Worcester County and State of Maryland for and in consideration of Thirty six pounds Two Shillings and Six pence current money of Maryland to me in hand paid by William FRANKLIN (of William) at or before the Sealing and delivery of these presents, the receipt whereof I do hereby acknowledge Have bargained and Sold, set over and delivered and by these presents do bargain Sell, Set over and deliver unto the said William FRANKLIN (of William) a certain negro man named **Shederik**, To have and to hold the hereby bargained negro man unto unto the said William FRANKLIN his Heirs Executors, Administrator, and assigns forever I the said Duncan MURRAY for myself my Heirs Executors and Administrators the hereby bargained negro man unto the said William FRANKLIN his Heirs Executors Administrators and assigns against myself my Heirs and against all and every other person or persons whatsoever Lawfully claiming or to claim the same shall and will warrant and forever defend by these presents In Testimony whereof I have hereunto set my Hand and Seal this Twenty ninth day of January Anno Domini Seventeen hundred and eighty Seven ~

James QUINTON   Duncan MURRAY (Seal)
Lemuel FRANKLIN"

*followed with the acknowledgment by Justice of the Peace John POSTLY and the recordation on 30 January 1787 by court clerk James R. MORRIS[402]

Liber M, folios 62-63; 25 August 1786

"Know all men by presents That Bartlet WHITE of Worcester County in the State of Maryland for and in consideration of the Sum of Eighteen pounds current money of Maryland to me in hand paid by **Jacob ARMSTRONG** of the same place at and before the Signing and Sealing hereof the receipt whereof is hereby acknowledged, I the said Bartley WHITE Have bargained Sold and delivered and by these presents do bargain Sell & deliver unto the said **Jacob ARMSTRONG** and his Heirs and assigns forever, a certain Negro Girl named **Liza**, about four years old, now in the possession of the said WHITE To have & to hold the said negro Girl called **Liza** (or **Liz**) hereby bargained and Sold and delivered unto him the above named **Jacob ARMSTRONG** and his Heirs and Assigns forever against me the said Bartlet and my Heirs Executors and Adm[inistrato]rs and every of them and against every other person or persons whatever will and shall warrant and for ever defend the said negro Girl unto him the said **Jacob ARMSTRONG** and his Heirs and Assigns forever Of which said negro Girl named **Liza** I the said Bartlet WHITE have put the said **Jacob ARMSTRONG** in full possession by the delivery of these presents In Witness whereof I the said Bartlet WHITE have hereunto Set my hand & Seal this 25th day of August Anno Dom[ini] one thousand Seven hundred and eighty six ~

Signed Sealed & Delivered   Peter CHAILLE   Barkey WHITE (Seal)
In the presence of "

*followed on folio 63 with acknowledgment by Justice of the Peace Peter CHAILLE and the recordation by court clerk James R. MORRIS[403]

---

[401] Worcester County Court (Land Records). Deed of manumission from BISHOP, Charles to **Jacob**, **Comfort**, **Levin**, and **Abner**. 18 August 1786. M, pp. 35-36, MSA CE 30-12. www.mdlandrec.net : accessed 21 February 2022.
[402] Worcester County Court (Land Records). Bill of sale from MURRAY, Duncan to FRANKLIN, William. 29 January 1787. M, p. 41, MSA CE 30-12. www.mdlandrec.net : accessed 21 February 2022.
[403] Worcester County Court (Land Records). Bill of sale from WHITE, Barkley to **ARMSTRONG, Jacob**. 25 August 1786. M, pp. 62-63, MSA CE 30-12. www.mdlandrec.net : accessed 21 February 2022.

Liber M, folios 68-69; 28 August 1786

"To all, to whom these presents shall come, I Kendall SMOCK of Murderkill hundred in the County of Kent upon Delaware, do send Greeting, Know ye, that I the said Kendall SMOCK for and in Consideration of the Just and full Sum of Forty five pounds Good and lawfull money of the Delaware State to him in hand paid by David SELBY of Worcester County in the State of Maryland the Receipt whereof the said Kendall SMOCK doth hereby acknowledge and himself therewith fully Satisfied contented and paid, Have Granted bargained and Sold and by these presents I the said Kendall SMOCK, do Grant bargain and Sell, unto the said David SELBY, one Negro Man called (and known by the Name of **Derrah**) (now in the possession of a certain John AYRES) with all his Cloaths appertaining or belonging to him To have and to hold the said negro (named **Derrah**) hereby Granted unto the said David SELBY his Heirs Ex[ecuto]rs Administrators or assigns, as his or their own proper goods, and to his and there own proper use or uses forever, And I the said Kendall SMOCK do for myself my Heirs Executors & Administrators, covenant and Grant to and with the said David SELBY his Heirs Executors, Administrators & assigns by these presents That I the said Kendall SMOCK at the time of Sealing and delivery of these presents, am the true and lawfull owner and proprietor of the said negro (**Derrah**) and his Cloaths hereby Granted with the appurtenances and that I have full power and lawfull authority to Grant, bargain and Sell the said negro (**Derrah**) with the appurtenances hereby mentioned to be Granted unto the said David SELBY his Heirs Executors administrators and assigns, in manner afores[ai]d as also that it shall, and May be Lawfull to and for said David SELBY his Heirs and assigns, from time to time and at all times hereafter quietly and peaceably To have, hold, occupy, possess and enjoy the said negro **Derrah** and other the premises hereby Granted or intended to be Granted with the appurtenances, without the lett, Trouble, denial, molestation, hindrance or disturbance whatsoever of him the said Kendall SMOCK his Heirs, Executors, or Administrators or any other person or persons whatsoever, claiming or to Claim and that freed & discharged of and from all manner of incumbrances whatsoever made done or Committed by the said Kendall SMOCK In Witness whereof the said Kendall SMOCK hath hereunto Set his hand and affixed his Seal this Twenty eighth day of August Anno Domini Seventeen hundred and eighty six 1786 ~

Sealed & Delivered   Joseph OSBORN   Kendall SMOCK   (Seal)
In presence of us   John EMORY"

*followed on folio 69 with acknowledgment by Kent County, Delaware Justice of the Peace William MOLLESTON, the receipt by Kendall SMOCK, the recordation by Kent County court clerk James SYKES, and the recordation on 02 September 1786 by Worcester County court clerk James R. MORRIS[404]

Liber M, folios 78-79; 04 September 1786

"This Indenture made the fourth day of September in the year of our Lord, one thousand Seven hundred & eighty six Between Duncan MURREY of Worcester County in the State of Maryland Carpenter, of the one part & William COVENTON of the place afforesaid of the other part Witnesseth That the said Duncan MURREY for & in Consideration of the Sum of the one hundred & elven pounds, eleven & six pence current money of Maryland due & owing from the said Duncan to the said William & three hundred & ninety five pounds of Tobacco c{???} which the Duncan hereby doth acknowledge, Hath bargained & Sold assigned & Transfered, and by these presents doth bargain & Sell, assign & transfer unto the Said William COVENTON his Executors, Administrators or Assigns, one negro fellow **Sharp**, one negro boy named **Ned** & one Negro Girl **Nell** To have & to hold the said Negroes unto the said William COVENTON his Executors, administrators or assigns, to the only proper use of the said William COVINGTON his Executors Administrators or assigns and no other use or purpose whatever, provided always, & it is hereby declared to be the true intent & meaning of these presents, that if the said Duncan MURRAY his Heirs Executors or Administrators Shall

---

[404] Worcester County Court (Land Records). Bill of sale from SMOCK, Kendall to SELBY, David. 28 August 1786. M, pp. 68-69, MSA CE 30-12. www.mdlandrec.net : accessed 21 February 2022.

well & truly pay unto the said William COVENTON his Executors, Administrators, or assigns the Sum of one hundred & Eleven pounds, eleven Shillings & Six pence, & three hundred & ninty five pounds of Tobacco with the legal Interest for the same & the expence of making & recording this Deed, on or before the first day of September next Ensuing the Date Then this Deed to be void & of no effect, And the said Duncan MURRAY for himself his Executors & Administrators, doth hereby Covenant & agree with the said William COVINGTON that he or they will well & truly pay unto the said William his Executors Administrators or Assigns the Sums of money afforesaid & Tobacco afforesaid, with the Interest as afforesaid by the time afforesaid, And it is further hereby covenanted & agreed between the parties afforesaid, That if the said Duncan his Executors or Administrators do not pay to the said William his Executors, Administrators or Assigns the said Sums of money with Interests afforesaid by the time afforesaid, That then it shall & may be lawful for the said William COVENTON his Executors or Administrators, after giving two weeks notice by Advertisements Sett up for that purpose to Sell all, or as many of the said negroes, as he or they may think proper for ready money & from the money raised by Such sale, Sattisfy him or them, the debts afforesaid, with the Interest as afforesaid & the overplus of such money (if any) pay unto the Hands of the said Duncan MURRAY his Executors, or Administrators In Testimony whereof the said Duncan MURREY hath hereunto affixed his hand & Seal the day & year first above written ~

| Sign[e]d Seal[e]d & delivered in the presence of | John WISE John POSTLY | Duncan MURRAY (Seal) |

N.B. The above Sums to be reduced to the Bill of Cash (from the County Clerk) for the action brought by the said William against the said Duncan if the said Sums should be over the next balances of Debt & Cash due on the said action – The above minute made & agreed to by the parties before Executing

Testes John POSTLY"

*followed on folio 79 with the acknowledgment by Justice of the Peace John POSTLY and the recordation on 15 September 1786 by court clerk James R. MORRIS[405]

Liber M, folio 88; 03 October 1786

"Maryland Sc^t. Know all men by these presents that I William DYMOCK of Worcester County in the State of Maryland for and in Consideration of the Sum of one hundred pounds current money of Maryland to me in hand paid at and before the ensealing & delivery of these presents by Caleb TINGLE of the same place, I the said William DYMOCK have bargained and Sold, and by these presents do bargain & Sell unto the said Caleb TINGLE his Heirs and assigns forever the following negro Slaves & other personal property now in possession of the aforesaid William DYMOCK, to wit, one negro Woman named **Hanah** about thirty years old, one negro Boy named **Bob** about eleven years old, four Beds & furniture, Seven Tables, one Dozen Chairs, one large looking Glass, one small ditto, Two Mares, two Cows & Calves, one Chest of Drawers, eight head of Hogs & all other personal property the Estate of the said DYMOCK To have and to hold all and Singular the above mentioned negroes & other Estate hereby bargained & Sold unto him the said Caleb TINGLE his Heirs and assigns forever and the said William DYMOCK for himself his Heirs, Executors and Administrators and against every of them and every other person or persons whatsoever will forever warrant, defend, of which said negroes & other Estate I the said William DYMOCK have put the said Caleb TINGLE in full possession by these presents In Witness whereof I have hereunto set my Hand and Seal this third day of October Anno Domini 1786 ~

| Signed, Sealed & Delivered in presence of | Peter CHAILLE John P. MITCHELL" | William DYMOCK (Seal) |

---

[405] Worcester County Court (Land Records). Deed from MURRAY, Duncan to COVINGTON, William. 04 September 1786. M, pp. 78-79, MSA CE 30-12. www.mdlandrec.net : accessed 21 February 2022.

*followed with the acknowledgment by Justices of the Peace Peter CHAILLE and John P. MITCHELL and the recordation by court clerk James R. MORRIS[406]

Liber M, folios 88-89; 29 September 1786

"To all Christian people to whom these presents shall come Greeting Know ye that I Peter CHAILLE of Worcester County and State of Maryland, for and in Consideration of the Sum of Seventy pounds to me in hand paid by James HOUSTON of the County & State af[ore]s[ai]d at and before the Sealing and delivery of these presents the receipt whereof the said Peter CHAILLE doth hereby acknowledge, have bargained and Sold and by these presents do bargain and Sell unto the said James HOUSTON one Negro Slave called **Mereum** and one negro Slave called **Patience**, to have and to hold the said negro Slaves unto the said James HOUSTON his Heirs and assigns forever, to the only proper use and behoof of the said James HOUSTON his Heirs and assigns forever, and for no other use or purpose whatsoever, and the said Peter CHAILLE for himself and his Heirs doth Covenant and agree to and with the said James HOUSTON and his Heirs that the said Peter CHAILLE and his Heirs the negro Slaves af[ore]s[ai]d unto the said James HOUSTON and his Heirs, shall and will warrant and forever defend, and the said Peter CHAILLE doth Covenant to and with the said James HOUSTON, that he the said Peter CHAILLE hath a good Title to Sell and dispose of the said Negroes so as to convey unto the said James HOUSTON a good Sum and firm title to the Same, and that no person by the said Peter CHAILLE hath any right or title to the same In Testimony whereof the said Peter CHAILLE to these presents his hand set and Seal affixed the 29th day of Sept[embe]r Anno Dom[ini] 1786 ~

Sealed & Delivered   Isaac MARSHALL   Peter CHAILLE (Seal)
In presence of"

*followed on folio 89 with acknowledgment by Justice of the Peace Isaac MARSHALL and the recordation on 03 October 1786 by court clerk James R. MORRIS[407]

Liber M, folio 89; 04 October 1786

"Maryland Worcester County Viz^t. Know all men by these presents, that I Elizabeth BREINGTON of Worcester County for & in consideration of the Sum of Forty pounds current money of Maryland to me in hand paid by William BREWINGTON of the County af[ore]s[ai]d planter the receipt whereof I do hereby acknowledge, have bargained & Sold & delivered & by these presents do bargain, Sell & deliver unto the said William BREWINGTON one negro Man called **George**, To have and to hold the said Negroe called **George** unto him the said William BREWINGTON his Heirs, Executors, administrators and assigns forever, and I the said Elizabeth BREWINGTON, for myself my Executors and Administrators shall & will warrant & forever defend against all persons by these presents the said bargained negro man called **George** unto the said William his Executors, Administrators and assigns In Witness whereof I have hereunto set my hand and Seal the 4th day of October 1786 ~

Signed Sealed and delivered   Ebenezer HANDY   her
in presence of   Elizabeth U BREWINGTON (Seal)
                                                          Mark"

*followed with the recordation by court clerk James R. MORRIS[408]

---

[406] Worcester County Court (Land Records). Bill of sale from DYMOCK, William to TINGLE, Caleb. 03 October 1786. M, p. 88, MSA CE 30-12. www.mdlandrec.net : accessed 21 February 2022.

[407] Worcester County Court (Land Records). Bill of sale from CHAILLE, Peter to HOUSTON, James. 29 September 1786. M, pp. 88-89, MSA CE 30-12. www.mdlandrec.net : accessed 21 February 2022.

[408] Worcester County Court (Land Records). Bill of sale from BREWINGTON, Elizabeth to BREWINGTON, William. 04 October 1786. M, p. 89, MSA CE 30-12. www.mdlandrec.net : accessed 21 February 2022.

Liber M, folio 93; 14 February 1787

"Know all men by these presents that I Joshua BRITTINGHAM of Worcester County in the State of Maryland for and in Consideration of thirty five pounds in money in hand paid by me Anna ROBINS of the said County and State af[ore]s[ai]d do hereby bargain and Sell and convey and confirm unto her the af[ore]s[ai]d Anna ROBINS her Heirs or assigns forever, one negro man called **Daniel** To have and to hold the above named Negro **Daniel** to her the said Anna ROBINS and to her Heirs or assigns forever, to her own proper use benefit & behoof, and I the said Joshua BRITTINGHAM have a good right and title to the af[ore]s[ai]d negro **Daniel**, and do hereby bind myself my Heirs Executors and Administrators to warrant and will ever defend the af[ore]s[ai]d negro **Daniel** to her the af[ore]s[ai]d Anna ROBINS and to her Heirs and Assigns forever, against all Claims and demands whatsoever ~ I Witness whereof I have hereunto set my hand & Seal this fourteenth day February One thousand Seven hundred and eighty Seven

Signed Sealed & delivered	Littleton ROBINS	Joshua BRITTINGHAM (Seal)
In presence off	Sally SPENCE"	

*followed with the acknowledgment by court clerk William PURNELL and the recordation on 02 March 1787 by court clerk James R. MORRIS[409]

Liber M, folios 93-94; 03 March 1787

"Maryland Worcester Sst. Know all men by these presents That I Isaac EVANS EVANS of Worcester County in the State of Maryland for and in consideration of the sum of Twenty six pounds ten Shillings current money of Maryland to me in hand paid by William McGREGGOR of the same place at or before the Ensealing and delivery of these presents, the receipt whereof I do hereby acknowledge, I the said Isaac EVANS Have bargained Sold and delivered & by these presents do fully, clearly & absolutely bargain Sell & deliver unto the said William McGREGGOR one negro man **George** about thirty Seven years of age, To have & to hold the said negro man **George**, to the said William, his Executors, Administrators & Assigns to his & their own proper use & behoofs forever, And I the said Isaac EVANS my Heirs Executors & Administrators & every of us, the said negro man, to the said William McGREGGOR his Heirs & Assigns against all people whatsoever shall & will warrant acquit & by these presents forever defend, Witness my hand & Seal this third day March A.D. 1787 ~

Seal[e]d & Delivered	John POSTLY	Isaac EVANS (Seal)
in presence of	Josiah MITCHELL"	

*followed on folio 94 with the acknowledgment by Justice of the Peace John POSTLY and the recordation on 05 March 1787 by court clerk James R. MORRIS[410]

Liber M, folios 95-96; 02 February 1787

"Know all men by these presents That I William Anderson PARKER of Sussex County in the State of Delaware for and in consideration of the Sum of Five Shillings current money of Maryland to me in hand paid by my daughter Rebecca PARKER and for the further Consideration of my said daughter Rebecca quiting & forever never to claim any Right, Title or Interest in or to a certain negro boy called **George** now in my possession, The receipt whereof I the said William Anderson PARKER doth acknowledge have given granted bargained, and delivered unto my said daughter Rebecca PARKER and to Heirs and assigns forever, a Negro boy called **Charles** now in my possession, to be possessed and enjoyed by my said daughter Rebecca PARKER and her Heirs after my wife Rebecca and my own decease, or deaths, provided as above mentioned to wit, That my said daughter Rebecca and his Heirs, Executors,

---

[409] Worcester County Court (Land Records). Bill of sale from BRITTINGHAM, Joshua to ROBINS, Anna. 14 February 1787. M, p. 93, MSA CE 30-12. www.mdlandrec.net : accessed 21 February 2022.
[410] Worcester County Court (Land Records). Bill of sale from EVANS, Isaac to McGREGGOR, William. 03 March 1787. M, pp. 93-94, MSA CE 30-12. www.mdlandrec.net : accessed 21 February 2022.

Administrators or assigns never claims hereafter any Right, Title or property in or to the above named negro boy called **George** To have and to hold the af[ore]s[ai]^d Bargained, Sold and delivered negro the said negro Boy called **Charles** unto her the said Rebecca PARKER and to her Heirs and assigns forever, to the only proper use benefit and behoof of her the said Rebecca PARKER and to her Heirs and assigns forever (excepting only as above excepted) And I the said William Anderson PARKER against myself my Heirs Executors and Administrators and against every other person or persons whatever will and shall warrant and forever defend the said negro Boy called **Charles** unto her the said Rebecca PARKER and to her Heirs and assigns forever, on the above proviso and Conditions, Of which said negro Boy called **Charles** I the said William Anderson PARKER have put the said Rebecca PARKER, in full possession by the delivery of these presents to wit as to Title on the above Condition In Witness whereof I the said William Anderson PARKER have put my hand and affixed my Seal this second day of February Anno Dom[ini] Seventeen hundred and eighty Seven ~

Signed Sealed & Delivered   W[illia]^m MORRIS   W[illia]^m A. PARKER (Seal)
In the presence of. ~   Joshua TOWNSEND"

*followed on folio 96 with the acknowledgment by Justice of the Peace Philip QUINTON and the recordation by court clerk James R. MORRIS[411]

Liber M, folios 97-98; 05 March 1787

"Maryland Worcester Ss^t. Know all men by these presents that I Isaac EVANS of Worcester County in the State of Maryland for and in Consideration of the Sum of Sixty nine pounds five Shillings Current money of Maryland to me in hand paid by Ebenezer FRANKLIN of the same place at or before the ensealing and delivery of these presents the receipt whereof I do hereby acknowledge, I the said Isaac EVANS Have bargained Sold and delivered and by these presents do fully clearly and absolutely bargain Sell and deliver unto the said Ebenezer FRANKLIN the following Negros Viz^t. One Negro Woman named **Jenny** about thirty two years of age, and one Negro Girl named **Hulda** about ten years of age, also one Negro boy named **Jess** about Sixteen years of age, To have and to hold the said Negro's **Jenny**, **Hulda** & **Jess** to the said Ebenezer his Executors, Administrators & Assigns, to his & their proper uses & behoof forever And I the said Isaac EVANS my Heirs Executors & Administrators and every of us, the said Negros to the said Ebenezer FRANKLIN his Heirs & assigns, against all people whatsoever, shall & will warrant, acquit & by these presents forever defend Witness my Hand and Seal this fifth day of March Anno Domini 1787 ~

Sealed & delivered   John POSTLY   Isaac EVANS (Seal)
in presence of"

*followed on folio 98 with the acknowledgment by Justice of the Peace and the recordation by court clerk James R. MORRIS[412]

Liber M, folios 109-110; 08 March 1787

"This Indenture made this eight day of March anno Domini one thousand Seven hundred and eighty Seven Between Samuel TRUITT Sen[ior] of Worcester County State of Maryland of the one part and Ananias HUTSON of the same place on the other part Witnesseth that I the s[ai]^d Samuel TRUIT for divers good Causes & Considerations me hereunto moving Have given granted bargined and Sold Aliened Conveyed and Confirmed and by these presents do freely fully and absolutely give grant Bargin & Sell aliene Convey and Confirm to the said Annanias HUTSON his Heirs and Assigns forever, one negro wench called **Sue** about 25 years of age and one Bed and furniture and an hors called Ragor and a mare called Blase, and one Case of Draws To have and to hold the s[ai]^d granted and bargined premises with all the appertenances

---

[411] Worcester County Court (Land Records). Bill of sale from PARKER, William Anderson to PARKER, Rebecca. 02 February 1787. M, pp. 95-96, MSA CE 30-12. www.mdlandrec.net : accessed 21 February 2022.

[412] Worcester County Court (Land Records). Bill of sale from EVANS, Isaac to FRANKLIN, Ebenezer. 05 March 1787. M, pp. 97-98, MSA CE 30-12. www.mdlandrec.net : accessed 21 February 2022.

priviledges and Commodities to the same belonging or in any wise appertaining to him the s[ai]^d Annanias HUTSOND his Heirs and assigns for ever to his and their own proper use benefit and behoof forever" … "and it is the true intent and meaning of the Grantor, and Grantee in these presents anything herein Contained to the Contrary notwithstanding, that if the above named Samuel TRUIT his Heirs Executors Administrators and assigns dos agree to warrent and forever defend the afores[ai]^d premises aforesaid mentioned from any person or persons claiming now or that shall hereafter claim the same forever sealed with my Seal and Dated in Worcester County Maryland State the day and year written ~   Samel TRUITT (Seal)

Sealed Signed Deliver[e]d   N.B. be remember[e]d that the word own and th in 21 line
in the presents of   was subtraced before Si[g]ned Seal[e]d and deliver[e]d
Test   John RICHARDS ~ Stephen TAYLOR ~"

*followed on folio 110 with the recordation by court clerk James R. MORRIS[413]
*Due to its true length, this transcription has been narrowed to its most relevant portions.

Liber M, folio 118; 10 (month unknown) 1786

"Know all men by these presents That I Thomas BRITTINGHAM of Worcester County in the State of Maryland for and in consideration of the sum of Twelve pounds current Mone of Maryland to me in hand paid at the Sealing & delivery hereof by William PURNELL of the State & County af[ore]s[ai]^d Receipt thereof will sho I do herby acknowledge that I Have bargained & Sold & by these presents have bargained & Sold unto the aforesaid William PURNELL one negro Boy called **Melby** To have and to hold the af[ore]s[ai]^d negro boy and by these presents have bargained and Sold unto William PURNELL him his Heirs Executors, Administrators & assigns forever, and I the said Thomas BRITTINGHAM do for myself my Heirs Executors administrators have bargained & Sold the af[ore]s[ai]^d negro negro unto the af[ore]s[ai]^d William PURNELL him his Heirs Executors Administrators or Assigns, & against all & every other person or persons whatsoever shall and will warrant & for ever defend by these presents the af[ore]s[ai]^d negro boy I the said Thomas BRITTINGHAM have put the said William PURNELL in full possession by delivering him the af[ore]s[ai]^d negro Boy as Witness my Hand & Seail the day of tenth day one thousand Seven hundred & eighty six

Signed Sealled & Delivered   James SELBY   Thomas BRITTINGHAM (Seal)
In presence of"

*followed with the acknowledgment by Justice of the Peace James SELBY and the recordation on 10 March 1787 by court clerk James R. MORRIS[414]

Liber M, folios 118-119; 27 February 1787

"The State of Maryland Know all men by these presents, That I (Samuel HOSIER) in the County of Worcester, Planter, for and in consideration of the sum of Forty five pounds Current money of the State af[ore]s[ai]^d to me in hand paid by Isaac MARSHALL the receipt whereof I do hereby acknowledge, have bargained sold and delivered and by these presents according to the due form of Law, do Bargain, Sell and delivery unto the said Isaac MARSHALL a Negro Boy aged Fourteen years or thereabout nam[e]^d **Ruiksom** To have and to hold the said negro Boy unto the said Isaac MARSHALL his Heirs Executors, Administrators or Assigns forever, And I the said Samuel HOSIER, for myself my Heirs Executors & Administrators, the said Bargained premisses unto the said Isaac MARSHALL his Heirs, Executors, Administrators, and Assigns against all and every person or persons, shall and will warrant, and for ever defend by these presents In Witness I have hereunto set my Hand & my Seal affixed This twenty Seventh day of February, one thousand Seven hundred and eighty Seven ~

---

[413] Worcester County Court (Land Records). Instrument of writing from TRUITT, Samuel to HUTSON, Annanias. 08 March 1787. M, pp. 109-110, MSA CE 30-12. www.mdlandrec.net : accessed 21 February 2022.
[414] Worcester County Court (Land Records). Bill of sale from BRITTINGHAM, Thomas to PURNELL, William. 10 month unknown 1786. M, p. 118, MSA CE 30-12. www.mdlandrec.net : accessed 21 February 2022.

Signed Sealed & Delivered   W[illia]m PURNELL   Samuel HOSIERR (Seal)
In presents of ~"

*followed with the acknowledgment by Justice of the Peace William PURNELL and the recordation on 10 March 1787 by court clerk James R. MORRIS[415]

Liber M, folios 119-120; 06 March 1787

"Know all men by these presents that I Richard HALL of Worcester County in the State of Maryland for and in Consideration of the Sum of five Shillings current money of Maryland to me in hand paid by Schoolfield PARKER of the County and State af[ore]s[ai]d before the Ensealing and delivery of these presents, the receipt whereof I the said Richard do hereby confess and acknowledge, have granted, bargained Sold and aliened and by these presents do grant bargain Sell & alien unto the said Schoolfield PARKER his Heirs and assigns forever the following personal property Viz^t. a Negro man called **George** to be the absolute right and property of him the said Schoolfield PARKER his Heirs and assigns forever & for no other use or purpose whatsoever, and the said Richard for himself and his Heirs the above Bargained and Sold the said negro man called **George**, against himself and his Heirs, and against all other person or persons whatsoever claiming by from or under him, unto the said Schoolfield PARKER his Heirs and assigns forever defend, In Witness and Confirmation whereof the said Richard this present writing his Hand hath sett and Seal affixed this sixth day of March anno Dom[ini] 1787 ~

Signed Sealed and ~   W[illia]m PURNELL   Richard HALL (Seal)
Acknowledged before"

*followed with the acknowledgment by Justice of the Peace William PURNELL and the recordation on folio 120 by court clerk James R. MORRIS on 10 March 1787[416]

Liber M, folios 121-122; 12 March 1787

"Worcester Sc^t. Know all men by these presents that I Samuel TRUITT of the County af[oresai]d and State of Maryland for and in Consideration of the Sum of Ninety pounds four Shillings & six pence current money of Maryland to me in hand paid by James MARTIN of the County & State af[oresai]d the receipt whereof I do hereby acknowledge have given granted bargained, and Sold and by these do give, grant, bargain and Sell unto the said James MARTIN his Heirs & assigns forever Three negroes following to wit, one negro man called **Isaac**, one Handmill, one black Walnut Chest One negro boy called **Levin**, To have and to hold the said negros, Hand mill and Walnut Chest unto the said James MARTIN his Heirs and assigns forever, to the only proper use & behoof of the said James MARTIN his Heirs and assigns forever and to no other use intent or purpose whatever And the said Samuel TRUITT for himself & his Heirs hereby further covenants and agrees to & with the said James MARTIN his Heirs and assigns the af[oresai]d negroes and things against all and every person whatever to forever warrant & defend In Witness whereof he hath hereto set his hand & Seal affixed this Twelveth day of March Anno Domini 1787 ~

Signed Sealed & Deliv[ere]d   Josiah MITCHELL   Samuel TRUITT (Seal)
In presence of ~"

*followed on folio 122 with the acknowledgment by Justice of the Peace Josiah TRUITT and the recordation on 13 March 1787 by court clerk James R. MORRIS[417]

---

[415] Worcester County Court (Land Records). Bill of sale from HOSIERR, Samuel to MARSHALL, Isaac. 27 February 1787. M, pp. 118-119, MSA CE 30-12. www.mdlandrec.net : accessed 21 February 2022.
[416] Worcester County Court (Land Records). Bill of sale from HALL, Richard to PARKER, Schoolfield. 06 March 1787. M, pp. 119-120, MSA CE 30-12. www.mdlandrec.net : accessed 21 February 2022.
[417] Worcester County Court (Land Records). Bill of sale from TRUITT, Samuel to MARTIN, James. 12 March 1787. M, pp. 121-122, MSA CE 30-12. www.mdlandrec.net : accessed 21 February 2022.

Liber M, folios 124-125; 06 March 1787

"Know all men by these presents That I Joshua TOWNSEND of Worcester County in the State of Maryland for and in Consideration of the Sum of Ninety pounds, ten Shillings current money to me in hand paid at and before the ensealing and delivery of these presents, by Robert DENNIS, I the said Joshua TOWNSEND have bargained and Sold and by these presents do bargain and Sell unto the Robert DENNIS his Heirs and assigns forever, the following negro Slaves (lately in the possession of a Certain Samuel TRUITT) to wit, One negro Lad about Twelve years old named **Cable** One other boy named **Levin** about Seven years old & a negro Woman named **Sue** about Twenty four years old To have and to hold all and Singular the above mentioned Three negroes hereby bargained and Sold unto the said Robert DENNIS his Heirs and assigns forever & the said Joshua TOWNSEND for himself his Heirs, Executors and Administrators and every of them and against every other person and persons claiming under him or them shall and will forever warrant and defend, and of which said Three Negroes I the said Joshua TOWNSEND have and do put the said Robert DENNIS in full possession by the delivery of these presents, in Witness whereof I the said Joshua TOWNSEND have hereunto put my hand and affixed my Seal the Sixth day of March Anno Domini 1787 ~

Sign[e]^d Seal[e]^d, & Deliver[e]^d Josiah MITCHELL   Joshua TOWNSEND   (Seal)
in presence of ~"

*followed on folio 125 with the acknowledgment by Justice of the Peace Josiah MITCHELL and the recordation on 15 March 1787 by court clerk James R. MORRIS[418]

Liber M, folios 129-130; 09 March 1787

"The deposition of Edea ROBINSON of Worcester County being Sworn on the holy Evangels of Almighty God says Mr. Hezekiah CAREY of the County af[ore]s[ai]^d came frequently to to her to get her to write for him a Bill of Sale from an original Bill of Sale given by James DAVIS to Thomas CAREY father of the said Hezekiah & further told her & Frightened her this deponent into a Compliance by his passion & promises connected together, the She shou[l]d have ten pounds if she wou[l]d write it, or that She Shou[l]d have the biggest Child that **Jenny** has (now belonging to Outerbridge DIXON, And this deponant further Saith that the s[ai]^d Hezekiah Desired her to write the form of the said Bill of Sale by one he had got from Stephen CHRISTOPHER, only when she came to the names he would tell her what to write & told her to write, that James DAVIS Sold the said negro called **Jenny** to Thomas CAREY during of his life time & then to Hezekiah CAREY his Heirs & assigns forever, and some days after the s[ai]^d Hezekiah brought back the Bill of Sale which this Deponant wrote, & a new one with it, wrote in a smaller hand but to the best of her knowledge the same words & She asked Mr CAREY what made the one She wrote look so black, he said I have Smoaked it to make it to make it look more like the old one & further Saith not ~   Edea ROBINSON

Taken & Sworn before the Subscriber one of the Justices of the Peace of Worcester County this 9th day March 1787 ~   Ebenezer HANDY"

*followed on folio 130 with the recordation on 29 March 1787 by court clerk James R. MORRIS[419]

Liber M, folio 134; 23 March 1787

"Know all men by these presents That I Richard HALL of Worcester County and State of Maryland for and in Consideration of the Sum of Sixty three pounds current money of Maryland to me in hand paid by Peter CHAILLE of the County and State af[ore]s[ai]^d at and before the Sealing and delivery of these presents, the receipt whereof the said Richard HALL do hereby

---

[418] Worcester County Court (Land Records). Bill of sale from TOWNSEND, Joshua to DENNIS, Robert. 06 March 1787. M, pp. 124-125, MSA CE 30-12. www.mdlandrec.net : accessed 21 February 2022.
[419] Worcester County Court (Land Records). Deposition of ROBINSON, Edea. 09 March 1787. M, pp. 129-130, MSA CE 30-12. www.mdlandrec.net : accessed 21 February 2022.

acknowledge have bargained and Sold and by these presents do bargain and Sell unto the said Peter CHAILLE one negro Slave called **Liddy** one ditto Guirl cal[le]^d **Tamour** and one negro Slave ditto cal[le]^d **Sarah** & one D[itt]o cal[le]^d **Ginne** To have and to hold the said negro Slaves unto the said Peter CHAILLE his Heirs and assigns forever to the only proper use and behoof of the said Peter CHAILLE his Heirs and assigns forever and for no other use or purpose whatsoever, and the said Richard HALL for himself and his Heirs do covenant to and agree with the said Peter CHAILLE and his Heirs that the said Richard HALL & his Heirs the negro Slaves af[ore]s[ai]^d unto the said Peter CHAILLE and his Heirs, shall and will warrant and forever defend, and the said negroes, & the said Richard do covenant to and agree with the said Peter CHAILLE that he the said Richard have a good & Sufficient title to Sell and dispose of the said negro Slaves, so as to convey unto the said Peter CHAILLE a good sure and firm title to the same, and that no person but the said Peter CHAILLE have any Right or title to the same In Testimony whereof the said Richard HALL his hands have sett and Seal affixed this 23rd day of March Anno Dom[ini] 1787 ~

Signed Sealed & Delivered   Philip QUINTON   Richard HALL   (Seal)
in presence of ~"

*followed with the acknowledgment by Justice of the Peace Philip QUINTON and the recordation on 24 March 1787 by court clerk James R. MORRIS[420]

Liber M, folios 137-138; 07 March 1787

"State of Maryland Worcester County. ~ Know all men by these presents that I John WRIGHT of Worcester County in the State af[ore]s[ai]^d for and in Consideration of the Sum of five hundred pounds current money of Maryland to me in hand paid by William SCHOOLFIELD of the County and State af[ore]s[ai]^d before the Ensealing and delivery of these presents the receipt whereof I the said John WRIGHT by these presents do Confess and acknowledge have granted Bargined and Soald and by these presents do grant bargain and unto the s[ai]^d William SCHOOLFIELD his Heirs and assigns forever the following Negroes Viz. **Mary, Ben Belinda & Harry** To have and to hold the af[ore]s[ai]^d Several Negroes above mentioned unto him the s[ai]^d W[illia]^m SCHOOLFIELD his Heirs and assigns forever and for no other use or purpose whatsoever and the s[ai]^d John WRIGHT for himself and his Heirs the above bargained and Soald negroes unto the s[ai]^d William SCHOOLFIELD his Heirs and Assigns will warrant and forever defend, against all other person or persons whatsoever claiming by from or under him or any other person whatsoever In Witness whereof the s[ai]^d John WRIGHT to this presents heath Sett and affixed his Seal this 7th day of March 1787 ~

Sign[e]^d Seal[e]^d and   John SELBY   John WRIGHT   (Seal)
Delivered in before   Nehemiah DORMAN"

*followed on folio 138 with the acknowledgment by Justice of the Peace John SELBY and the recordation on 30 March 1787 by court clerk James R. MORRIS[421]

Liber M, folios 138-139; 07 March 1787

"Know all men by these presents that we James BUSSELLS and Sarah his wife of Worcester County in the State of Maryland for and in Consideration of the Sum of thirty five pounds current money of Maryland to them in hand paid by Elijah LAWS Jun[ior] of the same place at and before the Sealing and delivery hereof, the receipt whereof we the said James BUSSELLS and Sarah his wife doth hereby acknowledge, Have bargained Sold and delivered and by these presents, doth bargain Sell and deliver unto the said Elijah LAWS Jun[ior] and to his Heirs and assigns forever, a Negro woman called **Silvy** about twenty three years of age and one Negro Girl called **Minta** now in the possession of the said BUSSELLS & wife To have and to hold all

---

[420] Worcester County Court (Land Records). Bill of sale from HALL, Richard to CHAILLE, Peter. 23 March 1787. M, p. 134, MSA CE 30-12. www.mdlandrec.net : accessed 21 February 2022.
[421] Worcester County Court (Land Records). Bill of sale from WRIGHT, John to SCHOOLFIELD, William. 07 March 1787. M, pp. 137-138, MSA CE 30-12. www.mdlandrec.net : accessed 21 February 2022.

and singular the above mentioned two negroes hereby bargained and Sold unto him the said Elijah LAWS and his Heirs and assigns forever (provided notwithstanding that if the said James BUSSELLS, or his Heirs, Executors, or Administrators or any of them do well and truly pay or cause to be paid unto the abovenamed Elijah LAWS or his Heirs, the above mentioned Sum of Thirty five pounds, at or upon the Twenty fifth day of December next Then the above bargain and Sale to be Void, else to remain in full force and Virtue) And the said James BUSSELLS & Sarah his wife and against each of them and against each of their Heirs Executors and Adm[inistrato]rs and against every other person or persons whatsoever (provided as above said) Shall and will warrant and forever defend unto him the said Elijah LAWS Jun[ior] and to his Heirs and assigns forever Of which said negro woman and Child above bargained and Sold the Said James BUSSELLS and Sarah his wife have put the said Elijah LAWS in full possession by the delivery of these presents In Witness whereof we the said James & Sarah his wife have hereunto Set their Hands & Seals affixed this 7th day of March Anno Domini one thousand Seven hundred and eighty Seven

Signed Sealed & Delivered   Josiah MITCHELL   James BUSSELLS (Seal)
In the presence of . .   her
                                                 Sarah + BUSSELLS (Seal)
                                                 mark"

*followed on folio 139 acknowledgment by Justice of the Peace Josiah MITCHELL and the recordation on 27 March 1787 by court clerk James R. MORRIS[422]

Liber M, folios 144-145; 16 March 1787

"State of Maryland Worcester County …. Know all men by these presents that Angaler ADKINSON and James STEVENSON for an in consideration of the Sum thirty pounds in hand paid by Littleton ROBINS before the Sealing and delivery by these presents we Angaler ADKINSON and James STEVENSON do hereby bargain and Sell and Confirm unto him the af[ore]s[ai]d Littleton ROBINS his Heirs and assigns, a certain negro Lad called **Bob**. To have and to hold the above named Negro **Bob**, unto him the af[ore]s[ai]d Littleton ROBINS his Heirs or assigns for ever to his own proper use benefit and behoof and we the said Angaler ADKINSON and James STEVENSON do hereby Covenant with the said Littleton ROBINS, that we have a good right to Sell the above said negro **Bob**, and we do hereby bind Ourselves and each of our Heirs Executors Administrators to warrant and defend the said negro **Bob**, to him the said Littleton ROBINS his Heirs or Assigns against all claims and demands whatsoever In Witness whereof we have set our Hands and Seals this Sixteenth day of March 1787 ~

Sign[e]d Seal[e]d & Deliver[e]d   Joshua TOWNSEND   James STEVENSON   (Seal)
in presence off ~   Angello ADKINSON (Seal)"

*followed on folio 145 with the acknowledgment by Justice of the Peace William HANDY and the recordation on 30 March 1787 by court clerk James R. MORRIS[423]

Liber M, folios 150-151; 03 April 1787

"Know all men by these presents that I James STEVENSON of Worcester County (Carpenter) for and in Consideration of the Sum of Forty pounds current money of Maryland to me in hand paid by Moses CHAILLE of the County af[ore]s[ai]d at and before the Sealing and delivery of these presents, the receipt whereof the said James STEVENSON doth hereby acknowledge have bargained and Sold and by these presents do bargain and Sell unto the said Moses CHAILLE one negro woman called **Tab** and one negro Child called **Minta** To have and to hold the said negroes unto the said Moses CHAILLE his Heirs and Assigns forever to the only proper

---

[422] Worcester County Court (Land Records). Bill of sale from BUSSELLS, James and Sarah to LAWS, Elijah Jr. 07 March 1787. M, pp. 138-139, MSA CE 30-12. www.mdlandrec.net : accessed 21 February 2022.
[423] Worcester County Court (Land Records). Bill of sale from ADKINSON, Angello and STEVENSON, James to ROBINS, Littleton. 16 March 1787. M, pp. 144-145, MSA CE 30-12. www.mdlandrec.net : accessed 21 February 2022.

use and behoof of the said Moses CHAILLE his Heirs and Assigns forever, and for no other use or purpose whatsoever and the said James STEVENSON for himself and his Heirs doth Covenant and agree to and with the said Moses CHAILLE and his Heirs, that he the said James STEVENSON and his Heirs the negro Slaves af[ore]s[ai]^d unto the said Moses CHAILLE and his Heirs Shall and will forever warrant and defend, and the said James STEVENSON doth Covenant and agree to and with the said Moses CHAILLE that he the said James STEVENSON hath a good title to sell and dispose of the said negroes so as to convey unto the said Moses CHAILLE a good Sure and firm title to the same and that no person but the said James STEVENSON hath any right or title to the same In Testimony whereof the said James STEVENSON to these presents his Hand hath set and Seal affixed the 3[r]d day of April Anno Dom[ini] 1787 ~

Sealed & Delivered   W[illia]^m HANDY   James STEVENSON   (Seal)
in presence of ~"

*followed on folio 151 with the acknowledgment by Justice of the Peace William HANDY and the recordation by court clerk James R. MORRIS[424]

Liber M, folios 151-152; 03 April 1787

"Know all men by these presents that I Angelow ATKINSON of Worcester County for and in Consideration of the Sum of Fifty pounds current money of Maryland to me in hand paid by Moses CHAILLE of the County af[ore]s[ai]^d at and before the Sealing and delivery of these presents the receipt whareof the said Angelow ATKINSON doth hereby acknowledge have bargained and Sold and by these presents do bargain and Sell unto the said Moses CHAILLE one Negro woman called **Tab**, one negro child called **Minta** & one negro child called **Peter** To have and to hold the said negroes unto the said Moses CHAILLE his and Assigns forever to the only proper use and behoof of the said Moses CHAILLE his Heirs and Assigns forever, and for no other use or purpose whatsoever and the said Angelow ATKINSON for himself and his Heirs doth Covenant and agree to and with the said Moses CHAILLE and his Heirs, that he said Angelow ATKINSON and his Heirs the negroes Slaves af[ore]s[ai]^d unto the said Moses CHAILLE and his Heirs shall and will for ever warrant and defend and the said Angelow ATKINSON doth covenant and agree to and with said Moses CHAILLE that he the said Angelow ATKINSON hath a good title to Sell and dispose of the said negroes so as to convey unto the said Moses CHAILLE a good sure and firm title to the same and that no person, but the said Angelow ATKINSON haith any right or title to the same, In Testimony whareof of the said Angelow ATKINSON to these presents his Hand hath set and Seal affixed the 3[r]d day of April Anno Dom[ini] 1787 ~

Seal[e]d & delivered in the presents of W[illia]^m HANDY   Angello ATKINSON   (Seal)"

*followed on folio 152 with the acknowledgment by Justice of the Peace William HANDY and the recordation by court clerk James R. MORRIS[425]

Liber M, folios 16 March 1787

"State of Maryland Worcester County Ss^t. Know all men by these presents that I Samuel TRUIT Sen[ior] in Consideration of the Sum of One hundred pounds current money of Maryland to me in hand paid by Ananias HUDSON have, bargained and Sold, released Granted and Confirmed, and by these presents do bargain and Sell, release, grant and confirm unto the said Ananias HUDSON, one negro woman called **Sue**, one Bed and furniture one sorrel Horse called Roger, one mare called Blase, one Case of Draws To have and to hold all and Singular the Goods & articles aforesaid and every of them by these presents bargained and Sold, granted and Confirmed unto the only proper use and behoof of the said Ananias HUDSON his Heirs

---

[424] Worcester County Court (Land Records). Bill of sale from STEVENSON, James to CHAILLE, Moses. 03 March 1787. M, pp. 150-151, MSA CE 30-12. www.mdlandrec.net : accessed 21 February 2022.
[425] Worcester County Court (Land Records). Bill of sale from ATKINSON, Angello to CHAILLE, Moses. 03 March 1787. M, pp. 151-152, MSA CE 30-12. www.mdlandrec.net : accessed 21 February 2022.

Executors, Administrators and assigns forever and I the said Samuel TRUITT for myself my heirs Executors, and administrators all and Singular the said goods and articles unto the said Ananias HUDSON his executors, Administrators & Assigns, and against all and every other person or persons whatsoever Shall and will warrant and forever defend by these presents In Witness whereof I have hereunto Set my Hand and Seal affixed this Sixteenth Day of March A.D. 1787 ~

Sign[e]d Seal[e]d & Deliv[ere]d   Josiah MITCHELL   Samuel TRUITT (Seal)
in the presence of"

*followed with the acknowledgment by Justice of the Peace Josiah MITCHELL and the recordation on folio 156 by court clerk James R. MORRIS[426]

Liber M, folios 166-167; 14 April 1787

"Maryland Worcester County Ss^t. Know all men by these presents That I Isaac PHILLIPS of Somerset County for and in consideration of the sum of Twenty pounds two Shillings Current money of Maryland in hand paid by Alexander McKALLEN the receipt whereof he doth hereby acknowledge have granted, bargained & Sold & do by these presents, grant, bargain & Sell to the said Alexander McKALLEN one negro boy called **Saul** to him the said Alexander & his Heirs & the said Isaac doth hereby further covenant to & with the said Alexander McKALLEN that he the said Isaac PHILLIPS the aforesaid negro boy called **Saul** will for ever by these presents warrant & defend to the said Alexander McKALLEN In Testimony whereof I have hereto Sett my hand & Seal this 14th Ap[ri]l 1787 ~

Signed Sealed & delivered   Ebenezer HANDY   his
in presence off ~   Isaac + PHILLIPS (Seal)
                                                                  Mark"

*followed on folio 167 with the acknowledgment by Justice of the Peace Ebenezer HANDY and the recordation on 20 April 1787 by court clerk James R. MORRIS[427]

Liber M, folio 173; 26 April 1787

"To all Persons to whom these presents Shall come Greeting know ye that I **Jacob ARMSTRONG** of Worcester County in the State of Maryland, being desirious to set free and Manumit my daughter **Lycia ARMSTRONG** born of my wife **Comfort** Slave to a certain William SELBY (SH), for and in consideration of the natural love and effection that I do bear unto my said daughter **Lycia** do hereby set free and manumit my said daughter and that her Freedom shall commence and take effect immediately upon her my said daughter **Lycia** arrives to the full age of sixteen years after the date of these presents, To have and to hold and freely enjoy to her my said daughter forever immediately after her arrival of Sixteen years of age her liberty and freedom in full and ample manner without any let hindrance or authority of any person or persons whatever In Testimony whereof the said **Jacob ARMSTRONG** to the presents his hand hath set and Seal affixed this Twenty Sixth day of April anno Dom[ini] one thousand Seven hundred and Eighty Seven

Signed Sealed & Delivered   W[illia]m HANDY   his
In the presence of . .   **Jacob + ARMSTRONG** (Seal)
                                                                  mark"

*followed with the acknowledgment by Justice of the Peace William HANDY and the recordation by court clerk James R. MORRIS[428]

---

[426] Worcester County Court (Land Records). Bill of sale from TRUITT, Samuel to HUDSON, Ananias. 16 March 1787. M, pp. 155-156, MSA CE 30-12. www.mdlandrec.net : accessed 21 February 2022.

[427] Worcester County Court (Land Records). Bill of sale from PHILLIPS, Isaac to McKALLEN, Alexander. 14 April 1787. M, pp. 166-167, MSA CE 30-12. www.mdlandrec.net : accessed 21 February 2022.

[428] Worcester County Court (Land Records). Deed of manumission from **ARMSTRONG, Jacob** to **ARMSTRONG, Lycia**. 26 April 1787. M, p. 173, MSA CE 30-12. www.mdlandrec.net : accessed 21 February 2022.

Liber M, folio 176; 07 May 1787

"Know all men by these Presents I Henry KILLY of Worcester County in the State of Maryland for and in consideration of the Sum of Fourteen pound current money of Maryland to me in hand by at and befor the Ensealing and delivering of these presents by George TURNER of the County and State affor[e]s[ai]ᵈ the receipt whereof I do hereby acknowledge, Have bargained and Sold and by these presents do bargin and Sell unto the said George TURNER his Heirs and assigns for ever a negro Girl known by the name of **Leah** about Seven years old, now in the possession of the affo[resai]ᵈ George TURNER, To have and to hold the said negro Girl called **Leah** all and Singular hereafter in case that he may and every of them by these presents, bargained and Sold unto the said George TURNER his Heirs, Executors Administrators and Assigns for ever I the said Henry KILLY for my self my Heirs Executors or Administrators or any of them or any of their assigns all and Singular the said negro Girl called **Leah** unto the said George TURNER his Heirs and Assigns forever against me the said Henry KILLY my heirs Executors and administrators and assigns all and every other person or persons whatever Shall and will warrant and forever defend by these presents, of which said negro Girl called **Leah**, I the said Henry KILLY have put the said George TURNER in full possession by the delivery of these presents In Testamony whereof I the said Henry KILLY have hereunto set my hand and Seal affixed this Seventh Day of May Anno Dom[ini] Seventeen hundred and eighty Seven

Signed Sealed and Delivered   Josiah MITCHELL   his
In the presence off ~   Henry PARKER Jun[ior]   Henry X KILLY (Seal)
                                                                                                   Mark"

*followed with the acknowledgment by Justice of the Peace Josiah MITCHELL and the recordation by court clerk James R. MORRIS[429]

Liber M, folios 177-178; 01 May 1787

"Maryland Worssester County Know all men by these presents that I Philip SCROGIN of Worsister County in consideration of the sum of five Shillings to me in hand paid by Nathan CULVER and John SCROGIN and Robert SCROGIN all of Somerset County the receipt whareof I do hereby acknowledge and also in consideration of the said Nathan CULVER and John SCROGIN and Robert SCROGIN having heretofor become Security for Philip SCROGIN to Henary TRAYDER and others, have bargained Sold, released Granted and confirmed and by these presents do bargain, sell release grant and confirm unto the said Nathan CULVER, John SCROGIN, Robert SCROGIN all the Goods houshold stuff and Implements of houshold and all other Goods and Chattles whatsoever mentioned in the Schedule hereunto annexed now remaining"… "In Witness my hand and Seale this eleventh day of May Anno Domini 1787 ~ NB. The word Sixteen interlined between the fourth & fifth lines from the bottom was done before the executing this Bill of Sale

Sealed & Delivered   John POSTLY   Philip SCROGIN (Seal)
In presence of. ~

A Shedule of the above Goods as they ware delivered~

To One looking glass, To One Cubbard and all the furniture therein contained, To one {?}tary Desk   To three Beds and furniture Bedsteads Cords and Mats   To two horses & Saddle & B{?} **To one negro man named Levin B{?} Slave till 31 years**   To eleven chears flagd   To one large Trung   To one small d[itt]ᵒ   To one two gallon Judg   To 16 Silver Tea Spoons   To one pair of Bellasses   To one pare hand Irons   To Two Tables maple & pine   To two plows & one harrow   To one Wheale & pare of Cards   To one cord and Gears   To all my Book ac[coun]ts Bonds Note & Bills dated befor this date   To a pare of Tongs & Shovle   To one Tea Kettle copper   To one frying pan   To two Iron pots & dutch oven   To one pare Saddle Bags   To one

---

[429] Worcester County Court (Land Records). Bill of sale from KILLY, Henry to TURNER, George. 07 May 1787. M, p. 176, MSA CE 30-12. www.mdlandrec.net : accessed 21 February 2022.

Sord and Belt To one Gun & pair flat Irons To two wedding hoes To one grubbing hoe To three axes one Broad To one Tea Chest To one pare of S{?}yards To twelve peaces of wooden ware of different kinds To one hand saw To five Casks & 3 Cags To one hare Broom To one drawing knife To one pare Iron Wedges To one Bed stade To one old Sadle To two sets of harness for plowing"

*followed on folio 178 with the acknowledgment by Justice of the Peace John POSTLY and the recordation by court clerk James R. MORRIS on 11 May 1787[430]

*Due to its true length, this transcription has been narrowed to the most relevant portions.

Liber M, folios 179-180; 11 May 1787

"To all people to whome this present writeing shall send Greeting I Bartley TOWNSEND of Worcester County in the State of Maryland Know ye that I the said Bartley TOWNSEND for and in consideration of the natural love and efection which I bare and have to my daughter Martha TOWNSEND and also for other good causes and Considerations me hereunto moveing have given and granted and by these presents doth give grant and confirm unto the said Martha TOWNSEND her heirs and assigns forever one negro Girl named **Jenna**, To have and to hold the said negro Girl unto the said Martha TOWNSEND her Heirs and assigns forever, except and reserving the use and service of the said negro Girl to myself during my life, and I do hereby warrant and forever defend the said negro Girl unto the said Martha TOWNSEND her Heirs and assigns forever, excepted as before excepted, Intestimoney whereof I the said Bartley TOWNSEND to these presents my hand have set and Seal affixed the eleventh day of May Anno Domini 1787 ~

Sign[e]d Seal[e]d and Delivered   John SELBY   Bartley TOWNSEND (Seal)
in presents of ~"

*followed with the acknowledgment by John SELBY and the recordation on 12 May 1787 by court clerk James R. MORRIS[431]

Liber M, folio 181; 11 May 1787

"To all people to whome this present writing shall send Greeting I Bartley TOWNSEND of Worcester County in the State of Maryland Know ye that I the said Bartley TOWNSEND for and in Consideration of the natural love and effection which I have and bare to Outten TOADVINE and also for other good causes and consideration me hereunto moving have given and granted and by these presents doth give grant and confirm unto the said Outten TOADVINE his Heirs and assigns one negro boy named **Tom** (Six months old at this time) To have and to hold the said negro boy named **Tom** unto the said Outten TOADVINE his heirs and assigns forever to his proper use and uses and I the Bartley TOWNSEND doth hereby warrant and forever defend the said negro boy **Tom** against myself and my heirs and against the Lawfull claim right or title of anny other person or persons claiming the same from by or under me or my heirs, unto the said Outten TOADVINE his Heirs and assigns forever Intestimoney whereof the said Bartley TOWNSEND to these presents his hand hath set and seal affixed the eleventh day of May Anno Dom[ini] 1787 ~

Sign[e]d Seal[e]d and Delivered   John SELBY   Bartley TOWNSEND (Seal)
in presents of ~"

---

[430] Worcester County Court (Land Records). Bill of sale from SCROGIN, Philip to CULVER, Nathan, SCROGIN, John, and SCROGIN, Robert. 11 May 1787. M, pp. 177-178, MSA CE 30-12. www.mdlandrec.net : accessed 21 February 2022.

[431] Worcester County Court (Land Records). Deed from TOWNSEND, Bartley to TOWNSEND, Martha. 11 May 1787. M, pp. 179-180, MSA CE 30-12. www.mdlandrec.net : accessed 21 February 2022.

*followed with the acknowledgment by John SELBY and the recordation on 12 May 1787 by court clerk James R. MORRIS[432]

Liber M, folio 185; 25 May 1787

"Know all men by these presents That we James BUSSELLS and Richard SHOCKLEY Sen[ior] both of Worcester County in the State of Maryland for and in Consideration of the Sum of Thirty pounds current money of Maryland to us in hand paid by Solomon SHOCKLEY of the same place at and before the Ensealing and delivery hereof the receipt whereof is hereby acknowledged, we the said James BUSSELLS and Richard SHOCKLEY Sen[ior] Have bargained, Sold and delivered and by these presents doth bargain Sell and deliver unto him the said Solomon SHOCKLEY and his Heirs and assigns forever, a certain negro woman called **Silva** about Twenty three years and a negro Child called **Minta** now in the possession of the said James BUSSELLS To have and to hold the above bargained and Sold two negroes with their appurtenances unto him the said Solomon SHOCKLEY and to his Heirs and assigns forever and the said James BUSSELLS and Richard SHOCKLEY against each of them and against each of their Heirs and against every other person or persons whatever claiming any right or title in or to the same above said sold negroes will and shall forever defend unto him the said Solomon SHOCKLEY and his Heirs and assigns forever Of which said negroes we the said James BUSSELLS and Richard SHOCKLEY have put the said Solomon SHOCKLEY in full possession by the delivery of these presents In Testimony whereof we the said James BUSSELLS and Richard SHOCKLEY have hereunto set our Hands & Seals this 25th day of May Anno Dom[ini] 1787 ~

Signed Sealed & Delivered	John SELBY	James BUSSELLS (Seal)
In the presence of ~	W[illia]m MORRIS	Richard R SHOCKLEY (Seal) his Mark"

*followed with the acknowledgment by Justice of the Peace John SELBY and the recordation by court clerk James R. MORRIS[433]

Liber M, folios 185-186; 11 May 1787

"Know all men by these presents That I William Stephen HILL of Worcester County in the State of Maryland, of Mattapony Hundred, for and in Consideration of the Sum of Seventy pounds current money of Maryland to me in hand paid by Elizabeth HALL of the same place at or before the Sealing and delivery hereof the receipt whereof is hereby acknowledged Have Bargained Sold and delivered and by these presents doth bargain Sell and deliver unto unto her the said Elizabeth HALL and to her Heirs, Executors, administrators and assigns for ever a certain negro Man called and known by the name of **Jacob** now in my possession To have and to hold the said negro man hereby bargained Sold and delivered unto her the said Elizabeth HALL and to her Heirs and assigns forever against me the said William Stephen HILL my heirs Executors and Administrators, and against every other person or persons whatever will and shall warrant & for ever defend by these presents of which said negro man Slave called **Jacob** I the said William Stephen HILL have put the said Elizabeth in full possession by the delivery hereof In Testimony whereof I the said William Stephen HILL have Set my hand & Seal this eleventh day of May Anno Domini one thousand Seven hundred and eighty Seven ~

Signed Sealed & Delivered   John SELBY   W[illia]m Stephen HILL (Seal)
In the presence of ~"

---

[432] Worcester County Court (Land Records). Deed from TOWNSEND, Bartley to TOADVINE, Outten. 11 May 1787. M, p. 181, MSA CE 30-12. www.mdlandrec.net : accessed 21 February 2022.

[433] Worcester County Court (Land Records). Bill of sale from BUSSELLS, James and SHOCKLEY, Richard Sr. to SHOCKLEY, Solomon. 25 May 1787. M, p. 185, MSA CE 30-12. www.mdlandrec.net : accessed 21 February 2022.

*followed on folio 186 with the acknowledgment by Justice of the Peace John SELBY and the recordation on 19 May 1787 by court clerk James R. MORRIS[434]

Liber M, folios 189-190; 05 June 1787

"Know all men by these presents that I John AYRES of Worcester County in the State of Maryland for and in Consideration of the Sum of one hundred pounds current money of Maryland to me in hand paid at and before the Sealing and delivery hereof by Moses CHAILLE of the same place I the said John AYRES, Have bargained Sold and Delivered unto him the said Moses CHAILLE his Heirs, Executors, Adm[inistrato]rs and assigns forever, The following negro Slaves to wit, one negro man called **Ben**, and one negro man called **Abraham**, now in the County of Worcester aforesaid, and in my own possession To have and to hold the above mentioned two negro men hereby bargained Sold and delivered unto him the said Moses CHAILLE and to his Heirs and assigns forever to the only proper use benefit, and behoof of him the said Moses CHAILLE and his Heirs and assigns forever against me the said John AYRES and my Heirs Executors and Adm[inistrato]rs and against every other person or persons whatever will and shall forever warrant and defend, Of which above mentioned negroes hereby sold I the said John AYRES hath put the said Moses CHAILLE in full possession by these presents In Witness my Hand and Seal this fifth day of June Dom[ini] 1787 ~

Sealed and Delivered   Philip QUINTON   John AYRES   (Seal)
In presence of."

*followed on folio 190 with the certification by Philip QUINTON and the recordation by court clerk James R. MORRIS[435]

Liber M, folio 210; 22 June 1787

"Maryland Worcester Ss[t]. I the Subscriber Elijah LAWS Jun[io]r Do hereby assign and set over and Transfer all my right & property that I have or ought to have unto a certain negro woman named **Silva**, and Child named **Minta**, late the property of a certain James BUSSELLS, unto Solomon SHOCKLEY his Heirs and assigns forever, for the Consideration of Twelve pounds current money of Maryland, as Witness my hand and Seal this 22nd day of June Anno Dom[ini] 1787 ~

Test William SELBY. (SH)   Elijah LAWS Jun[io]r (Seal)"

*followed with the recordation by court clerk James R. MORRIS[436]

Liber M, folio 213; 07 July 1787

"1787 July 7[th] day rec[ei]v[e]d of Thomas TAYLOR a noat of hand sind over on Moses SHEALY for the amount of thirty pounds for Negro Garel cal[le]d **Sary** which is in full

Test   James SELBY   Henry J. WILLETT. ~
       Rob[er]t M RICHARDSON"

*followed with the recordation on 20 July 1787 by court clerk James R. MORRIS[437]

Liber M, folio 245; 06 October 1787

"Maryland Sst. Know all men by these presents That I Nancy NELMS of Somerset County for and in Consideration of the sum of one hundred pounds to me in hands paid by James

---

[434] Worcester County Court (Land Records). Bill of sale from HILL, William Stephen to HALL, Elizabeth. 11 May 1787. M, pp. 185-186, MSA CE 30-12. www.mdlandrec.net : accessed 21 February 2022.
[435] Worcester County Court (Land Records). Bill of sale from AYRES, John to CHAILLE, Moses. 05 June 1787. M, pp. 189-190, MSA CE 30-12. www.mdlandrec.net : accessed 21 February 2022.
[436] Worcester County Court (Land Records). Deed from LAWS, Elijah Jr. to SHOCKLEY, Solomon. 22 June 1787. M, p. 210, MSA CE 30-12. www.mdlandrec.net : accessed 22 February 2022.
[437] Worcester County Court (Land Records). Receipt from SHEALY, Moses to TAYLOR, Thomas. 07 July 1787. M, p. 213, MSA CE 30-12. www.mdlandrec.net : accessed 22 February 2022.

TOWNSEND of Worcester County before the Sealing and delivery of these presents the receipt whereof I do hereby acknowledge have bargained Sold and delivered and by these presents do bargain Sell and deliver unto the said James TOWNSEND one negro Girl Called **Nice** and one negro Girl **Bett** To have and to hold the said bargained premisses unto the said James TOWNSEND his Heirs Executors Administrators or Assigns forever And I the said Nancy NELMS for myself my Heirs Executors and Administrators Shall and will warrant and defend against all persons by these presents the said bargained premisses unto the said James TOWNSEND his Heirs Executors Administrators or Assigns forever As Witness whereof I have hereunto Sett my Hand and Seal this 6th day of October Anno Domini one thousand Seven hundred and eighty Seven ~

In presence of Ebenezer HANDY, John P. MITCHELL   Nancy NELMS   (Seal)"

*followed with the recordation on 09 October 1787 by court clerk James R. MORRIS[438]

Liber M, folio 249; 05 October 1787

"State of Maryland Worcester Ss^t. To all christian people to whome these presents shall come or may concern we Moses HOLLAWAY & Aaron HOLLAWAY Sen[io]^r of the State & County af[ore]s[ai]^d Send Greeting (Know ye, that we the said Moses & Aaron HOLLAWAY Sen[io]r in the Consideration of the Sum of forty five pounds current money of the State of Maryland to use in hand paid at and before the Ensealing and delivery of these presents by Joseph HOLLAWAY of the County and State af[ore]s[ai]^d the receipt whereof we do hereby confess and acknowledge & thereof have bargained and Sold and by these presents do bargain and Sell unto the said Joseph HOLLAWAY one negro boy called **Harry** and one negro Girl named **Cate** To have and to hold the said two negroes called **Harry** and **Cate** hereby bargained and Sold and all Our right title claim and Interest unto the said Joseph HOLLAWAY his Heirs Executors Administrators & assigns to him & their own proper use uses Benifit & behoof as his & their own proper goods forever, And we the said Moses & Aaron HOLLAWAY Sen[io]^r do hereby for ourselves our heirs Executors & Administrators Covenant promise Grant to & with the said Joseph HOLLAWAY his Heirs Executors & Administrators that the said two negroes called **Harry & Cate** now are and be and so shall forever at all times hereafter be remain & continue unto the said Joseph HOLLAWAY his Heirs Executors Administrators & assigns free and clear of and from all and all manner of other and former Grants Gifts Bargains Sales Assignments and Incumbrances whatever had made done or committed by us or any means previty or procurement   In Witness whereof we have hereunto set our Hands & have Seals this fifth day of October A.D. ~ 1787 ~

Signed Sealed & delivered   Benjamin W. CORMACK   his
In presents off   Thomas HOLLAWAY   Moses M HOLLAWAY (Seal)
                                                      Mark"

                                                 Aaron A HOLLAWAY (Seal)"

*followed with the recordation on 09 October 1787 by court clerk James R. MORRIS[439]

Liber M, folio 255; 29 October 1787

"Maryland Worcester Ss^t. Know all men by these presents That I Thomas GRAY Sen[io]^r of Worcester County in the State of Maryland for and in consideration of the Sum of fifty pounds current money of Maryland to me in hand paid by Johnson GRAY of the place afforesaid at and before the Ensealing and delivery of these presents wherewith I confess myself to be fully Satisfied contented and paid, Have bargained Sold and delivered and by these presents do fully clearly and absolutely Bargain Sell & delivery unto the said Johnson GRAY one negro Man called **Bobb** about twenty three years old, and one negro by called **Peter** above five years old

---

[438] Worcester County Court (Land Records). Bill of sale from NELMS, Nancy to TOWNSEND, James. 06 October 1787. M, p. 245, MSA CE 30-12. www.mdlandrec.net : accessed 22 February 2022.

[439] Worcester County Court (Land Records). Bill of sale from HOLLAWAY, Moses & Aaron Sr. to HOLLAWAY, Joseph. 05 October 1787. M, p. 249, MSA CE 30-12. www.mdlandrec.net : accessed 22 February 2022.

To have & to hold the said Negro man **Bobb** & the said negro boy **Peter** unto the said Johnson GRAY his Executors Administrators or Assigns his & their own proper uses and behoofs forever And I the said Thomas GRAY for myself my Heirs Executors & Administrators and every of us the afforesaid negro man & Negro boy unto the said Johnson GRAY his Heirs and Assigns against all people whatsoever shall & will warrant acquit and forever defend by these presents I Witness whereof I have hereunto Sett my hand & Seal affixed the 29th day of Octo[be]r Anno Domini One thousand Seven hundred & eighty Seven. ~ . ~

Sealed & delivered   John POSTLY
In the presence of   John Robins CORD   Thomas X GRAY (Seal)
                                                              his Mark"

*followed with the acknowledgment by Justice of the Peace John POSTLY and the recordation on 03 September 1787 by court clerk James R. MORRIS[440]

Liber M, folio 260; 05 November 1787

"State of Maryland Ss.t To all persons to whom these presents shall come Know ye that I Elizabeth PORTER of Worcester County and State af[ore]s[ai]d being desirous to set free and Manumit after my decease a certain Negro man Slave called **Levin** in Consideration of the Said **Levin**'s faithful service to me done and performed I do by these presents give and grant set free and Manumit the af[ore]s[ai]d negro man Slave called **Levin** and that his freedom Shall commence and take effect immediately after my death To have and to hold and freely enjoy to him the said negro man Slave called **Levin** forever immediately after the death of me the said Elizabeth his liberty and freedom in full and ample manner without any let hindrance Molestation or Authority of any person or persons whatsoever In Testimony whereof I the said Elizabeth PORTER to these presents my hand have set and Seal affixed this fifth day of November Anno Domini One thousand seven hundred and eighty seven ~

Signed Sealed and Delivered
In presence of ~   Elizabeth X PORTER (Seal)
                                                              her Mark"

*followed with the acknowledgment by Justice of the Peace James SELBY and the recordation by court clerk James R. MORRIS[441]

Liber M, folios 274-275; 24 November 1787

"Know all men by these presents That I James LECOUNT of Worcester County in the State of Maryland for and in Consideration of the sum of Five Shillings current money of Maryland (but more especially of Belitha BRITTINGHAM and a certain William Stephen HILL becoming Securities for the Balance of a certain Luke ENNIS'S Estate late of Worcester County aforesaid) to me in hand paid by the aforesaid Belitha BRITTINGHAM of the same place, the receipt whereof I do hereby acknowledge, Have bargained, Sold and delivered and by these presents doth absolutely bargain, Sell and deliver unto him the said Belitha BRITTINGHAM and his Heirs Executors, Adm[inistrato]rs or assigns forever the following negro Slaves to wit one negro woman called **Sarah** about twenty seven years old, one ditto Girl named **Esther**, ten years old, one Girl named **Leah** six years old, one Girl named **Hannah** about three years old, one ditto boy named **Caleb** above Six Months old, all in the possession of the said James LECOUNT (excepting the negro Girl named **Esther** and she being in the possession of a certain Joseph BISHOP in the County af[ore]s[ai]d To have and to hold all and Singular the above mentioned five negroes hereby bargained & delivered unto him the said Belitha BRITTINGHAM and his Heirs and assigns forever And I the said James LECOUNT for myself my Heirs Ex[ecuto]rs and Adm[inistrato]rs and every of them and against all other persons will

---

[440] Worcester County Court (Land Records). Bill of sale from GRAY, Thomas Sr. to GRAY, Johnson. 29 October 1787. M, p. 255, MSA CE 30-12. www.mdlandrec.net : accessed 22 February 2022.
[441] Worcester County Court (Land Records). Deed of manumission from PORTER, Elizabeth to **Levin**. 05 November 1787. M, p. 260, MSA CE 30-12. www.mdlandrec.net : accessed 22 February 2022.

and shall warrant and defend the above mentioned bargained negroes unto him the said Belitha BRITTINGHAM and his Heirs and assigns forever, Of which said negroes above mentioned I the said LECOUNT have put the said BRITTINGHAM in full possession by the delivery hereof In Testimony whereof I the said James LECOUNT have hereto Set my Hand and affixed my Seal this Twenty fourth day of November Anno Dom[ini] one thousand seven hundred & eighty Seven ~

Signed Sealed & Delivered   James LECOUNT (Seal)
In the presence of ~"

*followed with the acknowledgment by Justice of the Peace William HANDY and the recordation on folio 275 by court clerk James R. MORRIS on 23 November 1787[442]

Liber M, folios 283-284; 14 December 1787

"Worcester Ss^t. Know all men these presents That I Rachel MORRIS of Worcester County in the State of Maryland for and in Consideration of the Sum of forty pounds current money of Maryland to me in hand paid or secured to be paid by Joseph TILGHMAN of the same place at or before the Ensealing & delivery of these presents, which with I confess myself to be Satisfied Have bargained Sold & delivered and by these presents, do bargain Sell & deliver unto the said Joseph TILGHMAN one negro woman named **Hager** upwards of thirty years of age & her Child **Ben** about two years old To have & to hold the said negro woman **Hager** & her Child **Ben**, unto the said Joseph TILGHMAN his Executors, Administrators & assigns To his & their own proper uses & behoofs forever, & I the said Rachel MORRIS my Heirs Executors & Administrators & every of us, the said negro woman & Child unto the said Joseph TILGHMAN his Heirs & Assigns, against the Legal claim of all people shall & will warrant acquit & forever by these presents, Witness my hand & Seal the 14th day of December A.D. 1787 ~

Sealed & Delivered   Anne POSTLY   Rachel MORRIS (Seal)
in the presence of   John POSTLY"

*followed on folio 284 with the acknowledgment by Justice of the Peace John POSTLY and the recordation by court clerk James R. MORRIS[443]

Liber M, folios 284-285; 01 October 1787

"Rec[ei]ved October the 1st 1787 of Thomas TAYLOR the Sum of Thirty pounds in full for a Negro Boy called **Stephen** ~ rece[i]ved

Witness   Philip QUINTON   William B. HENDERSON"

*followed on folio 285 with the recordation by court clerk James R. MORRIS on 14 December 1787[444]

Liber M, folio 288; 04 January 1788

"Know all men by these presents that I John EVANS of Worcester County in the State of Maryland for and in consideration of Forty Pounds currant money of Maryland to me in hand paid at and before the Sealing and delivery hereof by John SELBY (of John) of the same County and State af[ore]s[ai]^d I the said John EVANS have, bargained Sold and delivered and by these presents do bargain, Sell and deliver unto him the said John SELBY his Heirs and assigns

---

[442] Worcester County Court (Land Records). Bill of sale from LECOUNT, James to BRITTINGHAM, Belitha. 24 November 1787. M, pp. 274-275, MSA CE 30-12. www.mdlandrec.net : accessed 22 February 2022.

[443] Worcester County Court (Land Records). Bill of sale from MORRIS, Rachel to TILGHMAN, Joseph. 14 December 1787. M, pp. 283-284, MSA CE 30-12. www.mdlandrec.net : accessed 22 February 2022.

[444] Worcester County Court (Land Records). Receipt from HENDERSON, William B. to TAYLOR, Thomas. 01 October 1787. M, pp. 284-285, MSA CE 30-12. www.mdlandrec.net : accessed 22 February 2022.

forever a negro Boy called **Eben** in the possession of the said John SELBY, To have and to hold the said bargained and Sold, negro boy called **Eben** abovenamed unto him the said John SELBY his Heirs and assigns forever, and I the said John EVANS for myself my Heirs Executors and Administrators and against every other person or persons whatever will and shall forever defend the above said negro unto the said John SELBY his Heirs and assigns forever, Of which said negro boy above mentioned I the said John EVANS have put the said John SELBY in full possession by the delivery of these presents In Witness whereof I the said John EVANS have hereunto Set my hand and Seal this fourth day of January Anno Domini Seventeen hundred and eighty eight

Signed Sealed & Delivered   Philip QUINTON   John EVANS (Seal)
In the presence of ~"

*followed with the acknowledgment by Justice of the Peace Philip QUINTON and the recordation on 07 January 1788 by court clerk James R. MORRIS[445]

Liber M, folio 296; 05 December 1787

"The State of Maryland Worcester Ss^t. To all persons to whom these presence may com know ye that I William Stephen HILL of the County af[ore]s[ai]^d for divers good causes & for & in Consideration of the Sum of forty pounds of good & Lawfull money of the County af[ore]s[ai]^d to me in hand paid by Elizabeth HALL at & before the Sealing & delivery of these presence, the receipt whereof he the said William Stephen HILL doth hereby agree, that he hath hereby Granted bargained and Sold unto the said Elizabeth HALL and to her heirs & assigns forever, one negro Girl called **Jenny** To hold and to have the said negro Girl called **Jenny** unto her the said Elizabeth HALL and to her heirs & assigns forever to her own proper use and property and to and for no other use or uses whatever In Witness whereof I the said William Stephen HILL have hereunto Set my hand & Seal Effixed this fifth day of December Anno Domini one thousand seven hundred and eighty Seven

Signed Sealed and Delivered   W[illia]^m HANDY   W[illia]^m Stephen HILL (Seal)
in the presence of ~"

*followed with the acknowledgment of Justice of the Peace William HANDY and the recordation on 25 January 1788[446]

Liber M, folio 297; 01 February 1788

"Know all men by these presents That I McKimmy PORTER of Worcester County in the State of Maryland for and in Consideration of the Sum of Thirty five pounds current money of Maryland to me in hand paid by Rhoda COSTON of the County and State aforesaid, have bargained and Sold and by these presents doth bargain and Sell unto the said Rhoda COSTON One Millotto man named **Abel**, To have and to hold the said millotto man named **Abel** by these presents bargained and Sold unto the said Rhoda COSTON her heirs and assigns, and I the said McKimmy PORTER for myself and my heirs the said Millotto man unto the said Rhoda COSTON and her heirs against me the said McKimmy PORTER and my heirs and against the lawfull claim right or title of any other person whatsoever shall and will warrant and forever defend by these presents Of which millotto man I have put the said Rhoda in full possession of at the Sealing hereof In Witness whereof I the said McKimmy PORTER have hereunto my hand set and seal affixed the first day of February Anno Domini 1788

Sign[e]^d & Seal[e]d   W[illia]^m HANDY   McKimmy PORTER (Seal)
In Presents of"

---

[445] Worcester County Court (Land Records). Bill of sale from EVANS, John to SELBY, John. 04 January 1788. M, p. 288, MSA CE 30-12. www.mdlandrec.net : accessed 22 February 2022.

[446] Worcester County Court (Land Records). Bill of sale from HILL, William Stephen to HALL, Elizabeth. 05 December 1787. M, p. 296, MSA CE 30-12. www.mdlandrec.net : accessed 22 February 2022.

*followed with the acknowledgment by Justice of the Peace William HANDY and the recordation by court clerk James R. MORRIS[447]

Liber M, folio 297; 07 February 1788

"Know all men by these presents That I Labin HILL of the State of Maryland and Resident of Worcester County in the province afforesaid hath for the Consideration of thirty Seven pounds ten Shillings cuarent money of Maryland to me in hand paid by Cornelius ENNISS Juner of the County and province afforesaid State and dow hearby Sell and deliver in plain and open Market unto the said Cornelius ENNISS a Neagro weoman called **Pashents** about forty five years was the said Labin HILLs, doth hereby deliver and will Warrant and defend her unto the Cornelius ENNISS his Heirs and assigns forever against all Lawfull Challing or demand of any person or persons whatever, in Witness whearof I have hereunto Sett my hand and Seal this Seven day of Febuary Ann[o] Dom[ini] One thousand seven hundred and eighty eighty ~

| Signed Sealed and Delivered | Joshua BRITTINGHAM | Labin HILL (Seal) |
| in the presents of | Joseph ENNISS" | |

*followed with the recordation by court clerk James R. MORRIS[448]

Liber M, folios 308-309; 21 January 1788

"Know all men by these presents that I Nathaniel DAVIS of Worcester County in the State of Maryland for and in Consideration of the Sum of fifty four pound Specie to me in hand paid by Anna ROBINS of Worcester County in the State af[ore]s[ai]d have bargain[e]d and Sold, release, Granted and Confirm and by these presents, do bargain Sell, release, Grant and Confirm unto the said Anna ROBINS her heirs assigns One negro Lad called **Sothy** eighteen years of age & one other Negro Boy called **George** eight years of age To have and to hold the af[ore]s[ai]d Negroes and every of them firmly by these presents have bargain[e]d Sold released, Granted and Confirmed unto the only proper use and behoof of the said Anna ROBINS her heirs & assigns forever freely quietly peaceably & intirely without any Contradiction claim disturbance or hindrance of any person or persons whatsoever so that neither of the said Nathaniel DAVIS nor any other person for me, or in my name, any right Title Interest or demand of, into or for the said Negroes mentioned as af[ore]s[ai]d sought Challinge claim or demand at any time or times hereafter, but from all actions right, Title claim demand possession & Interest hereof shall be wholly barred & excluded by force and virtue of these presents, and I the said Nathaniel DAVIS for myself my Executors and Administrators or Assigns to the two af[ore]s[ai]d Negroes unto the af[ore]s[ai]d Anna ROBINS heirs and assigns, and against all and every other person or persons whatsoever shall and will ever warrant and defend by these presents, the two af[ore]s[ai]d Negroes, as Witness my hand & Seal this Twenty first day of January 1788 ~

| Sign[e]d Seal[e]d & Deliver[e]d | W[illia]m PURNELL | Nathaniel DAVIS (Seal) |
| In presence of ~ ~" | | |

*followed on folio 309 with the acknowledgment by Justice of the Peace William PURNELL and the recordation by court clerk James R. MORRIS[449]

Liber M, folios 312-313; 03 March 1788

"Know all men by these presents that I Dennis HUDSON of Worcester County in the State of Maryland for the Consideration of the Sum of thirty five pounds Current money of Maryland to me in hand paid by John POWELL of the County af[ore]s[ai]d have bargained Sold released,

---

[447] Worcester County Court (Land Records). Bill of sale from PORTER, McKimmy to COSTON, Rhoda. 01 February 1788. M, p. 297, MSA CE 30-12. www.mdlandrec.net : accessed 22 February 2022.
[448] Worcester County Court (Land Records). Bill of sale from HILL, Labin to ENNISS, Cornelius Jr. 07 February 1788. M, p. 297, MSA CE 30-12. www.mdlandrec.net : accessed 22 February 2022.
[449] Worcester County Court (Land Records). Bill of sale from DAVIS, Nathaniel to ROBINS, Anna. 21 January 1788. M, pp. 308-309, MSA CE 30-12. www.mdlandrec.net : accessed 22 February 2022.

granted and Confirmed and by these presents do bargain Sell release Grant and Confirm unto the said John POWELL one Negro Garle called **Sal** about fourteen years of age now in the possession of the said John POWELL To have and to hold the said negro Garle called **Sal** by these presents bargained Sold released, Granted and confirmed unto the only proper use and behoof od the said John POWELL his heirs Executors administrators and assigns forever freely Quietly peacably and intirely without any Contradiction or claim of any person whatsoever so that nether I the said Dennis HUDSON nor any other for me or in my name any right, Title, Interest or Demand of in to or for the said Negro Garle called **Sall** or any part thereof but from all action, Right, Estate, Title claim and demand and Shall be wholly barred and excluded by by Virtue of these presents, And I the said Dennis HUDSON for myself my Executors and Administrators the said negro Girl **Sall** unto the said John POWELL his Executors, Administrators and assigns and against all and every other person or persons whatsoever shall and will warrant and forever defend by these presents In Witness whereof I have hereunto set my hand and Seal this third day of March Anno Dom[ini] 1788 ~

Signed Sealed & delivered	Josiah MITCHELL	
In the presence of ~ ~	Matthias DAVIS	Dennis X HUDSON (Seal) his Mark"

*followed on folio 313 with the acknowledgment by Justice of the Peace Josiah MITCHELL and the recordation on 05 March 1788 by court clerk James R. MORRIS[450]

Liber M, folios 333-334; 02 April 1788

"Know all men by these presents that we John DONE and Benjamin Frederick Augustus Ceazer DASHIELL of Worcester County in the State of Maryland, Administrators of all and Singular the Goods and Chattels of Joseph DASHIELL of the County and State af[ore]s[ai]^d deceased, for and in consideration of the Sum of Fifty pound current money of Maryland to us in hand paid by Hannah BACON of the County and State af[ore]s[ai]^d at and before the Sealing and delivery of these presents the receipt whereof the said Hannah BACON doth hereby acknowledge have, bargained and Sold and by these presents do bargain and Sell unto the said Hannah BACON one Negro man Slave called **Ishmael**, to have and to hold the said Negro Slave unto the said Hannah BACON to heirs and assigns forever to the only proper use and behoof of the said Hannah BACON her heirs and assigns forever, and for no other use or purpose whatsoever And the said John DONE and Benjamin F.A.C. DASHIELL for themselves and their Heirs do Covenant and agree to and with the said Hannah BACON and her heirs that they the said John DONE and Benjamin F.A.C. DASHIELL and their Heirs, the Negro Slave aforesaid unto the said Hannah BACON and her Heirs Shall and will warrant and forever defend, against the claim, right and title of all and every person or persons claiming from by or under the said Joseph DASHIELL or the said John DONE & Benjamin Frederick Augustus Cezar DASHIELL or their heirs Executors, Administrators or any of them In Testimony whereof the said John DONE and Benjamin F.A.C. DASHIELL to these presents their hands have Set and Seals affixed this Second day of April Anno Domini Seventeen hundred and eighty eight ~

Signed Sealed & delivered	John SELBY	John DONE (Seal)
in Presence of ~	John MARTIN	Benj[ami]^n F.A.C. DASHIELL (Seal)"

*followed on folio 334 with the acknowledgment by Justice of the Peace John SELBY and the recordation by court clerk James R. MORRIS[451]

---

[450] Worcester County Court (Land Records). Bill of sale from HUDSON, Dennis to POWELL, John. 03 March 1788. M, pp. 312-313, MSA CE 30-12. www.mdlandrec.net : accessed 22 February 2022.

[451] Worcester County Court (Land Records). Bill of sale from DONE, John and DASHIELL, Benjamin F.A.C. to BACON, Hannah. 02 April 1788. M, pp. 333-334, MSA CE 30-12. www.mdlandrec.net : accessed 22 February 2022.

Liber M, folios 347-348; 21 January 1788

"Know all men by these presents that I William UNDERHILL of Worcester County and State of Maryland in Consideration of the Sum of Seventy five pounds current money of Maryland to me to me in hand paid by Edward HENRY of Worcester County have bargained Sold released, Granted and confirmed and by these presents do bargain Sell release Grant and Confirm unto the said Edward HENRY a Negro man called **Peter** To have and to hold the said Negro by these presents bargained Sold released Granted and Confirmed unto the said Edward HENRY his Executors, Administrators & Assigns forever freely quietly peacably, and intirely without any Contradiction or disturbance of any person whatsoever or without any amount to me or any other person for me made or to be made, answered, or hereafter to be rendered, so that neither I the said William nor any other for me in my name any right title Interest or demand of in, to or for the said negro ought to exact claim or demand at any time or times hereafter, but from all action, right estate title or claim, demand possession & interest thereof shall be wholly barred & excluded by force of these presents, And I the said William for myself my Ex[ecuto]rs and Administrators the said negro **Peter** unto the said Edward his Executors & assigns, and against all and ever other person or persons whatsoever shall and will warrant and forever defend by these presents of which negro I the said William have put the said Edward in full possession by the delivery thereof at the Signing and delivery hereof In Witness said whereof I have hereunto my hand Set and Seal affixed this twenty first day of January Anno Domini 1788

Sealed & Delivered   Jnº. P. MARSHALL   William UNDRILL   (Seal)
in presence of ~"

*followed with the receipt by William UNDRILL, the acknowledgment by William PURNELL and Isaac MARSHALL on 02 February 1788, and the recordation by court clerk James R. MORRIS on 26 April 1788[452]

Liber M, folio 361; 23 May 1788

"Worcester Ss^t. Know all men by these presents that I Luke TOWNSEND of the County aforesaid in the State of Maryland for and in consideration of the sum of fifteen pounds current money of Maryland to me in hand paid at and before the ensealing and delivery of these presents by Mary BELL of the same place, the Receipt whereof I hereby acknowledge and have Bargained and Sold and by these presents do Bargain and Sell unto the said Mary BELL her heirs and assigns forever one negro Boy named **James** about nine or ten years old To have and to hold to the above named negro Boy **James** hereby bargained & Sold unto the said Mary BELL her heirs and assigns forever And the said Luke TOWNSEND for himself his heirs Executors and Administrators and every of them and against all and every other person or persons whatsoever shall and will forever Warrant and defend the said negro named **James** unto the said Mary BELL her heirs and assigns forever In Witness whereof I have hereto set my hand and Seal on the 23[rд] Day of May 1788~

Sealed Seal[e]^d & Delivered   Isaac MARSHALL   Luke TOWNSEND   (Seal)
in presence of ~"

*followed with the acknowledgment by Justice of the Peace Isaac MARSHALL and the recordation on 27 May 1788 by court clerk James R. MORRIS[453]

Liber M, folios 361-362; 27 May 1788

"Worcester Ss^t. Know all men by these presents that I Moses CHAILLE (of the County aforesaid in the State of Maryland) for an in consideration of the Sum of Two hundred pounds to me in hand paid by Joshua TOWNSEND, and the further Sum of Forty Six pounds current

---

[452] Worcester County Court (Land Records). Bill of sale from UNDRILL, William to HENRY, Edward. 21 January 1788. M, pp. 347-348, MSA CE 30-12. www.mdlandrec.net : accessed 22 February 2022.

[453] Worcester County Court (Land Records). Bill of sale from TOWNSEND, Luke to BELL, Mary. 23 May 1788. M, p. 361, MSA CE 30-12. www.mdlandrec.net : accessed 22 February 2022.

to me in hand paid by Robert DENNIS have bargained & Sold and by these presents do bargain & Sell unto the said Joshua TOWNSEND & Robert DENNIS their heirs and assigns forever the following Negroes to wit, one fellow called **Jack**, a woman called **Rachell** & her two Children **Esther** & **Caleb**, one other wench called **Candiss** & her two children, one other wench called **Lydia** & her two Children, and one other wench called **Tabb** & her two Children To have and to hold the aforesaid bargained & Sold Negroes unto the said Robert DENNIS and Joshua TOWNSEND their Heirs & assigns forever In Testimony whereof I have hereto set my hand & Seal this 27th Day of May 1788 ~

Signed, Seal[e]d & delivered   William HANDY   Moses CHAILLE (Seal)
in presence of ~"

*followed with the acknowledgment by the Justice of the Peace William HANDY and the recordation by the court clerk James R. MORRIS[454]

Liber M, folios 374-375; 10 July 1788

"Know all men by these presents that I Sarah DOWNES of Worcester County and State of Maryland for and in consideration of the Sum of one hundred pounds, to her in hand paid by George HANDY before the Sealing and delivery of these presents the receipt whereof I the said Sarah DOWNES do hereby acknowledge have bargained and Sold, and by these presents do bargain and Sell to the said George HANDY his heirs and assigns forever a Negro woman called **Lucy** and her two children, one called **Rose** about eight years old and the other called **Linda** about five years old, To have and to hold all and Singular the above mentioned negroes, **Lucy**, **Rose** and **Linda**, hereby bargained and Sold unto him the said George HANDY his Heirs and assigns forever And the said Sarah DOWNES for herself and her heirs and against every other person or persons whatsoever claiming or shall every hereafter claim any right or title to the above mentioned negroes unto the said George HANDY his heirs and assigns by these presents will warrant and forever defend In Witness whereof I the said Sarah DOWNES have Set my hand and affixed my Seal this tenth day of July Anno Dom[ini] Seventeen hundred and eighty eight. ~ . ~

Signed Sealed and Delivered   William HANDY   Sarah DOWNES (Seal)
in presence of ~   William PURNELL"

*followed with the acknowledgment by Justice of the Peace William HANDY and the recordation on 12 July 1788 by court clerk James R. MORRIS[455]

Liber M, folios 379-380; 22 May 1788

"Worcester County Sst. Know all men by these presents that I Elizabeth FARLOW of Worcester County in the State of Maryland for and in Consideration of the Sum of forty pounds current money of Maryland to me in hand paid by Levi CATHELL of County af[ore]s[ai]d whereof I do hareby acknowledge the receipt and myself fully and Intirely Satisfied therewith I have Bergained Sold set over and delivered and by these presents do bargain Sell Set over and deliver unto Levi CATHELL one negro Boy named **James** to have and to hold the said negro Boy unto the said Levi CATHEAL his heirs or assigns to the only propper use and behoof of him the said Levi CATHELL his heirs and assigns forever and I the said Elizabeth FARLOW for myself my heirs and assigns the aforesaid Bergained negro unto the said Levi CATHELL his heirs and assigns aganst all manner of persons shall and will forever defend and by these will forever warrent and defend in Witness whareof together with the deliver of the said negro Boy I have hareunto Set my hand and affixed my Seal this 22 day of May Anno dominy 1788 ~

---

[454] Worcester County Court (Land Records). Bill of sale from CHAILLE, Moses to TOWNSEND, Joshua. 27 May 1788. M, pp. 361-362, MSA CE 30-12. www.mdlandrec.net : accessed 22 February 2022.

[455] Worcester County Court (Land Records). Bill of sale from DOWNES, Sarah to HANDY, George. 10 July 1788. M, pp. 374-375, MSA CE 30-12. www.mdlandrec.net : accessed 22 February 2022.

Teste James X LEVENSTON   Elisabeth FARLOW (Seal)
Sarah LEVENSTON ~"

*followed on folio 380 with the recordation by court clerk James R. MORRIS on 09 June 1788[456]

Liber M, folio 387; 11 July 1788

"Know all men by these presents that I Henry Johnson WILLIT of Worcester County in the State of Maryland for and in Consideration of the Sum of twenty five pounds current money of Maryland to me in hand paid by at and before the Ensealing and delivering of these presents by Henry PARKER Jun[io]^r of the County & State aforesaid the receipt whereof I do hereby acknowledge have bargained and Sold and by these presents do bargain and Sell unto the said Henry PARKER Jun[io]^r his heirs and assigns forever a negro Girl called **Sarah** about eight years old and now in the possession of the said Henry PARKER Jun[io]^r To have and to hold the said negro Girl called **Sarah** all and Singular her hereafter in cause that he may have and every of them by these presents bargained and Sold unto the said Henry PARKER Jun[io]^r his heirs Executors Administrators and Assigns forever, I the said Henry Johnson WILLIT for my self my heirs Executors or Administrators or any of them or any of their assigns all and Singular the said negro Girl called **Sarah** unto the said Henry PARKER Jun[io]^r his heirs and assigns forever against me the said Henry Johnson WILLIT my heirs Executors and Administrators and assigns all and every person or persons whatsoever shall and will Warrant and forever defend by these presents of which said negro Girl called **Sarah** I the said Henry John WILLIT have put the said Henry PARKER Jun[io]^r in full possession by the delivery of these presents In Testimony whereof the said Henry Johnson WILLITT have hereunto Sett his hand and Seal affixed this 11th day of July Anno Domini 1788 ~

Signed Sealed & Delivered   Test W[illia]^m HANDY   Henry J WILLITT (Seal)
In the presence of …"

*followed with the acknowledgment by Justice of the Peace William HANDY and the recordation on 14 July 1788 by court clerk James R. MORRIS[457]

Liber M, folios 387-388; 13 June 1788

"Worcester County State of Maryland Know all men by these presents That I George RICHARDSON of the County of Worcester ~ and state of Maryland for and in consideration of the sum of Seventy five pounds lawful money of the said State to me in hand paid by Walter SMITH of the County and State aforesaid, The receipt whereof I do hereby acknowledge Have bargained, Sold, assigned and Set over, and by these presents, do bargain, Sell, assign and Set over unto the said Walter SMITH his heirs and assigns forever, all my Right, Title, Interest and property of in and to a certain Negro Man called or known by the name of **Robin**, To the only proper use and behoof of him the said Walter SMITH his heirs and assigns forever, And I the said George RICHARDSON do hereby for myself my heirs Executors and Administrators warrant and defend the aforesaid negro Man unto him the said Walter SMITH his heirs Executors, Administrators, and Assigns free and clear of and from any Incumbrance claim, title or demand of from or by me my heirs Executors and Administrators or of from or by any other person or persons whatsoever In Witness whereof I have hereunto set my hand and Seal this thirteenth day of June in the year of our Lord one thousand Seven hundred and eighty eight. ~

Signed Sealed and delivered   James SELBY   George RICHARDSON (Seal)
in the presence of ~"

---

[456] Worcester County Court (Land Records). Bill of sale from FARLOW, Elizabeth to CATHELL, Levi. 22 May 1788. M, pp. 379-380, MSA CE 30-12. www.mdlandrec.net : accessed 22 February 2022.
[457] Worcester County Court (Land Records). Bill of sale from WILLITT, Henry Johnson to PARKER, Henry Jr. 11 July 1788. M, p. 387, MSA CE 30-12. www.mdlandrec.net : accessed 22 February 2022.

*followed on folio 388 with the acknowledgment by Justice of the Peace James SELBY and the recordation on 14 June 1788 by court clerk James R. MORRIS[458]

Liber M, folios 392-393; 18 July 1788

"Know all men by these presents that I Henry Johnson WILLITT of Worcester County for and in concideration of forty thre pounds current money of Maryland to me paid at and before the ensealing and delivering of these presents by Charles BENNET of the County af[ore]s[ai]^d the receipt whereof I hereby acknowledge, have bargined and Sold and by these presents do bargin and Sell unto the said Charles BENNETT his heirs and assigns forever a Negro Boy known by the name of **Abram** about fourteen years old and now in the possession of the aforesaid Charles BENNETT, To have and to hold the said negro boy called **Abram** all and Singular he hereafter in case that he may have and every of them by these presents, bargined and Sold unto the said Charles BENNETT his heirs Executors, administrators and assigns forever, I the said Henry Johnson WILLETT for myself my heirs Executors or administrators or any of them or any of there heirs or assigns, the said negro Boy called **Abram** unto the said Charles BENNETT his heirs and assigns forever against me the said Henry Johnson WILLETT my heirs Executors and Administrators and assigns, all and every other person or persons whatsoever, shall and will Warrant and for ever defend by these presents of which said negro boy called **Abram** I the said Henry Johnson WILLETT have put the said Charles BENNETT in full possession off by the delivery of these presents in Testimoney whereof the said Henry Johnson WILLETT have hereunto Sett his hand and Seal affixed this eighteenth day of July Anno Dom[ini] one thousand Seven hundred and eighty eight. ~ /. ~

Signed Sealed and Delivered in the   John SELBY   Henry J. WILLETT   (Seal)
presents off ~"

*followed on folio 393 with the acknowledgment by Justice of the Peace John SELBY and the recordation on 25 July 1788 by court clerk James R. MORRIS[459]

Liber M, folio 401-402; 18 July 1788

"Know all men by these presents That I John VICTOR of Worcester County in the State of Maryland for and in Consideration of the Sum of Fifty pounds current money of Maryland to me in hand paid by Thomas VICTOR Sen[io]^r of the same place, the receipt whereof I do hereby {?} & acknowledge, Have bargained Sold and delivered and by these presents doth absolutely Bargain Sell and deliver him the aforesaid Thomas VICTOR and his heirs and assigns forever, a certain Negro Girl called and known by the name of **Rose** now in the possession of the aforesaid Thomas VICTOR To have and to hold the aforesaid bargained and Sold negro Girl unto him the said Thomas VICTOR and his heirs Executors, Administrators or assigns forever, against me the said John VICTOR , and my heirs, Executors and Adm[inistrato]^{rs} and against every other person or persons whatever, will and shall, forever Warrant and defend, Of which said negro Girl I the said John VICTOR have put the said Thomas VICTOR in full possession by the delivery of these presents In Testimony whereof I the said John VICTOR to these presents my hand hath set and Seal affixed this eighteenth day of July in the year of our Lord one thousand seven hundred and eighty eight. ~ / . ~

Signed Sealed & delivered   Philip QUINTON   John VICTOR   (Seal)
In the presence of ~"

*followed on folio 402 with the acknowledgment by Justice of the Peace Philip QUINTON and the recordation on 01 August 1788 by court clerk James R. MORRIS[460]

---

[458] Worcester County Court (Land Records). Bill of sale from RICHARDSON, George to SMITH, Walter. 13 July 1788. M, pp. 387-388, MSA CE 30-12. www.mdlandrec.net : accessed 23 February 2022.
[459] Worcester County Court (Land Records). Bill of sale from WILLETT, Henry Johnson to BENNETT, Charles. 18 July 1788. M, pp. 392-393, MSA CE 30-12. www.mdlandrec.net : accessed 23 February 2022.
[460] Worcester County Court (Land Records). Bill of sale from VICTOR, John to VICTOR, Thomas Sr. 18 July 1788. M, pp. 401-402, MSA CE 30-12. www.mdlandrec.net : accessed 23 February 2022.

Liber M, folio 404; 08 August 1788

"This Indenture made the 8 day of August Anno Dom[ini] one thousand Seven hundred and eighty eight between Samuel TARR Ju[nio]ʳ of Worcester County of the one part and negro **Peter GUY** being under the Age of fifty years of the other part Witnesseth that the said Samuel TARR for and in consideration of the faithful Servis of the above mentioned negro and his good behavior in genral and being desirous that the said negro should be manimitted and forever set free and forever discharge the said Negro **Guy** from the the said Samuel TARR his heirs, and the said Samuel TARR doth Covenant and agree to and with the said negro **Peter GUY** and his heirs that they are by these presents forever manumitted and set free, and that he the said Samuel his heirs Executors or Administrators hath not nor shall have any right title interest claim or demand of in or unto the said negro **Peter GUY** Intestimoney whereof the said Samuel TARR to these presents his hand hath put and Seal affixed the day and year above mentioned

Sealed and Delivered	Joshua DUER Sen[io]ʳ	Samuel TARR (Seal)
in the presents of us	Jesse JONES"	

*followed with the acknowledgment by Justice of the Peace John SELBY and the recordation on 08 August 1788 by court clerk James R. MORRIS[461]

Liber M, folios 404-405; 07 August 1788

"Know all men by these presents that I Elenar PURNELL of Worcester County and State of Maryland for good cause and considerations me hereunto moving Do hereby Immansipate and set absolutely free the following Negroe Slave (to wit, **Dolby Job** to be free at his own Liberty when he comes to the Age of twenty one years, And I do hereby Warrant and defend the freedom of said negro against myself my heirs Executors and Administrators claiming any right or title to the same by or from me under the Penal Sum of One hundred pounds current money of Maryland to be Recovered by said negro in case of any attempt to deprive him of his liberty by us as above Granted In Testimony whereof I have hereunto Set my hand and Seal this 7th Day of August A[nno] Domini 1788 ~

Signed and Sealed	Samuel TARR		her	
In presence of us	Esther STURGIS	Eleoner	+	PURNELL (Seal)
			mark"	

*followed on folio 405 with the acknowledgment by Justice of the Peace Outten STURGIS and the recordation on 08 August 1788 by court clerk James R. MORRIS[462]

Liber M, folio 405; 07 August 1788

"Know all men by these presents That I Nancy PURNELL of Worcester County and State of Maryland for good cause and consideration me hereunto moveing Do hereby Immansipate and set absolutely free the following negroe Slave **George Shadrach** to be free at his own Liberty when he comes to the Age of twenty one years, And I do hereby Warrant and defend the freedom of said negro against myself my heirs Executors & Administrators claiming any right to title to the same by or from me under the Penal Sum of one hundred pounds current money of Maryland to be Recovered by said negroe in case of any attempt to deprive him of his Liberty by us as above granted In Testimony whereof I have hereunto Set my hand and Seal this 7th Day of August Anno Domini 1788 ~

Signed and Sealed	Samuel TARR		her	
In presence of us	Esther STURGIS	Nancy	X	PURNELL (Seal)
			mark"	

---

[461] Worcester County Court (Land Records). Deed of manumission from TARR, Samuel Jr. to GUY, Peter. 08 August 1788. M, p. 404, MSA CE 30-12. www.mdlandrec.net : accessed 23 February 2022.

[462] Worcester County Court (Land Records). Deed of manumission from PURNELL, Eleoner to **Dolby Job**. 07 August 1788. M, pp. 404-405, MSA CE 30-12. www.mdlandrec.net : accessed 23 February 2022.

*followed with the acknowledgment by Justice of the Peace Outten STURGIS and the recordation on 08 August 1788 by court clerk James R. MORRIS[463]

Liber M, folios 412-413; 14 August 1788

"Know all men by these presence that I John KILLIOM of Worcester County in the State of Maryland for and in consideration of the Sum of Forty five pounds current money to me in hand paid by Rubin BROWNSON of the County of Summerset in the State of Maryland, the Recept whereof I hearby acknowledge and myself therewith fully and entirely Satisfyed have bargned Sold Set over and delivered and by these presents in plain and open market according to the Just and due fore of Law in that case maid and provided do bargin Set over and deliver unt the said Rubin BROWNSON one Negro fellow named **Handy** To have and to hold the said bargned premises unto the said Rubin BROWNSON his heirs Executors, Administrators, to the only proper use and behoof of him the said Reubin BROWNSON forever and I the said John KILLAM for myself my heirs Executors, Administrators or assigns the said Bargned premises unto the said Reubin BROWNSON, against all and all manner of persons Shall and will Warrant and for ever defend by the presents In Witness whereof together with the delivery of the said Bargned premises I have hearunto Set my hand and Seal this fourteen Day of August Anno Dominy 1788 ~

Signed Sealed and   John KILLEAM   (Seal)
delivered in the pr[e]sens of"

*followed on folio 413 with the acknowledgment by William HANDY and the recordation by court clerk James R. MORRIS[464]

Liber M, folio 416; 14 August 1788

"Know all men by these presents that I John JOHNSON (of Leonard) of Worcester County in the State of Maryland for and in consideration of the Sum of forty five pounds current money of Maryland to me in hand paid by John KILLAM of the same place at and before the Sealing and the delivery of these presents the receipt whereof I do hereby acknowledge have bargained and Sold and by these presents do bargain and Sell unto the said John KILLAM his heirs and assigns one negro man Slave called **Sampton** To have and to hold the said negro Slave unto the said John KILLAM his heirs and assigns forever to the only proper use benefit and behoof of the said John KILLAM his heirs and assigns forever and for no other use or purpose whatsoever and the said John JOHNSON for himself and his heirs doth Covenant and agree to and with the said John KILLAM that he the said John JOHNSON hath a good and Sufficient title to Sell and dispose of the said negro Slave so as to convey unto the said John KILLAM a good sure and firm title to the same and that no person but the said John JOHNSON hath any right or title to the same In Testimony whereof the said John JOHNSON his hand to these presents hath Set and Seal affixed this fourteenth day of August in the year of our Lord one thousand Seven hundred and eighty eight ~ / . ~

Signed Sealed & Delivered   W[illia]m HANDY   John JOHNSON (Seal)
in presence of. ~"

*followed with the acknowledgment by Justice of the Peace William HANDY and the recordation by court clerk James R. MORRIS[465]

---

[463] Worcester County Court (Land Records). Deed of manumission from PURNELL, Nancey to **George Shadrach**. 07 August 1788. M, p. 405, MSA CE 30-12. www.mdlandrec.net : accessed 23 February 2022.
[464] Worcester County Court (Land Records). Bill of sale from KILLEAM, John to BROWNSON, Reubin. 14 August 1788. M, pp. 412-413, MSA CE 30-12. www.mdlandrec.net : accessed 23 February 2022.
[465] Worcester County Court (Land Records). Bill of sale from JOHNSON, John to KILLAM, John. 14 August 1788. M, p. 416, MSA CE 30-12. www.mdlandrec.net : accessed 23 February 2022.

Liber M, folios 416-417; 13 August 1788

"Know all men by these presents That I Joseph TILGHMAN of Worcester in the State of Maryland for and in Consideration of the Sum of Forty pounds current money of Maryland to me in hand paid by Isaac COTTINGHAM of the same County and State aforesaid; The receipt whereof I the said Joseph TILGHMAN doth by these presents confess and acknowledge and hath bargained Sold and delivered and by these presents doth absolutely bargain Sell and deliver unto him the aforesaid Isaac COTTINGHAM his heirs, Executors, administrators and assigns forever, a certain negro Woman called **Edea** and Child called **Sal** about eight months old now in the possession of the said Isaac COTTINGHAM To have and to hold the above mentioned Two negroes hereby bargained Sold and delivered unto him the said Isaac COTTINGHAM and his heirs and assigns forever against me the said Joseph TILGHMAN my heirs Executors, and Adm[inistrato]rs and against all, and all and every other person or persons whatever claiming or hereafter to claim any right title or property in or to the above said bargained and delivered Negroes will and shall forever Warrant and defend Of which said two negroes I the said Joseph TILGHMAN have put the said Isaac COTTINGHAM in full possession by the delivery of these presents In Witness whereof I have hereunto Set my hand and affixed my Seal this 13th day of August Anno Domini one thousand Seven hundred and eighty eight ~ /. ~

Signed Sealed & delivered   Josiah MITCHELL   Joseph TILGHMAN   (Seal)
In the presence of"

*followed on folio 417 with the acknowledgment by Justice of the Peace Josiah MITCHELL and the recordation by court clerk James R. MORRIS[466]

Liber M, folio 439; 14 October 1788

"Maryland Ss. To all whom these presents shall come Greeting I John COLEBURN of worchester County in the State of maryland for Divers Good Causes and Considerations me thereunto moving do hereby declare Free Manumit, and Enfranchise the Negros following to wit, **Sarah Amy** and **Ezekiel, Sarah** and **amy** to be free on the first day of January Next and **Ezekiel** to be Free at the age of Twenty five which will be in the year one thousand Eight hundred and Eight I do hereby Acknowledge the said Negros discharged from all Claim of Service and right of Property whatever from me my heirs Executors or Administrators as witness my Hand and Seal this fourteenth day of October in the Year of Our Lord one thousand Seven Hundred and Eighty Eight ~

Sealed & Delivered   Peter CHAILLE   John COULEBURN   (Seal)
in presents off . .   John C. HANDY"

*followed with the acknowledgment by Justice of the Peace Philip QUINTON and the recordation by court clerk James R. MORRIS[467]

Liber M, folios 441-442; 07 August 1788

"Know all men by these presents that I Joseph CROPPER of the County of Worcester and State of Maryland for and in Consideration of the sum of Thirty five pounds Current money of Maryland to me in hand well and Truely paid by Zadok CROPPER of Sussex County in the State of Delaware, the Receipt whereof I do hereby acknowledge, have bargained and Sold, and by these presents do bargain & Sell unto the said Zadok CROPPER one Negro woman Named **Signer** and one Negro Girl Named **Leah** and one Negro girl Named **Mill**, To have and to hold all and Singular the above Named Negros and every of them, by these presents bargained and Sold unto the said Zadok CROPPER his Executors Administrators, and Assigns for Ever, and I the said Joseph CROPPER for myself my Executors and Administrators all and Singular the

---

[466] Worcester County Court (Land Records). Bill of sale from TILGHMAN, Joseph to COTTINGHAM, Isaac. 13 August 1788. M, pp. 416-417, MSA CE 30-12. www.mdlandrec.net : accessed 23 February 2022.

[467] Worcester County Court (Land Records). Deed of manumission from COULEBURN, John to **Sarah, Amy,** and **Ezekiel**. 14 October 1788. M, p. 439, MSA CE 30-12. www.mdlandrec.net : accessed 23 February 2022.

said Negros, unto the said Zadok CROPPER his Executors administrators and assigns, against me the said Joseph CROPPER my heirs Executors, Administrators and Assigns and against all and Every other person and persons whatsoever Shall and will Warrant and forever defend by these Presents of which Negros I the said Joseph CROPPER have put the said Zadok CROPPER in full possession by the delivery of the said Negros unto the said Zadok CROPPER, at the Sealing hereof In Witness whereof I the said Joseph have unto these presents set my hand Seal and affixt this Seventh day of Aug[us]ᵗ Anno D[omini] one thousand Seven hundred Eighty and Eight . . 1788 ~

Signed Sealed and Delivered   Benjamin McCORMACK   Joseph CROPPER (Seal)
in presents of . . . ."

*followed on folio 442 with the acknowledgment by Justice of the Peace John POSTLY and the recordation on 29 October 1788 by court clerk James R. MORRIS[468]

Liber M, folio 457; 14 October 1788

"State of Maryland Worcester County Ssᵗ. Know all men by these presents that I William Anderson PARKER of the County and State af[oresai]ᵈ am held for and in consideration of the sum of one hundred pounds in hand paid by Nancy PARKER of the same place the Receipt whereof I do hereby acknowledge I have Granted bargined and Sold unto Nancy PARKER a Negroe Boy named **Tom** except my life and and my wife Rebeccah in the af[oresai]ᵈ negro To have and to hold the af[oresai]ᵈ negroe unto Her the af[ore]s[ai]ᵈ Nancy PARKER her heirs and assigns forever and by these presents do Warrant and defend the af[ore]s[ai]ᵈ bargained and Sold negroe **Tom** unto her the af[oresai]ᵈ Nancy PARKER against all persons whatsoever claiming by or under me, as Witness my Hand and Seal this 14ᵗʰ day of Oct[obe]ʳ 1788 ~

Signed Sealed and delivered   John WRIGHT   W[illia]ᵐ A. PARKER (Seal)
in presents of ~"

*followed with the recordation by court clerk James R. MORRIS on 28 November 1788[469]

Liber M, folios 468-469; 01 January 1789

"Maryland & Worcester Ss. Know all men by these presents that we Joseph GREEN of the County and State afforesaid And Mary his wife, for and in consideration of the natural love & affection which we have and bear unto our Daughter Catty WHITE and because She is by Sickness become a Cripple not having the common use of one side of her body and limbs, and for Sundry good causes us hearunto moving, we have given granted and confirmed and by these presents do Give grant and confirm unto the said Catty WHITE one negro boy named **George** about four years old, to be the right and property of the said Catty WHITE at the decease of the said Mary wife of the said Joseph, but not before and to Continue the right and property of the Catty from that time during her natural life, and at her decease the said negro boy **George** to return to the said Joseph GREEN and his heirs To have and to hold the said Negro **George** to the said Catty WHITE in manner afforesaid during her natural life, then to return to the said Joseph GREEN and his heirs as afforesaid forever In Witness whearof we have hereunto Set our Hands and Seals affixed the first day of January 1789 one thousand Seven hundred & eighty Nine ~ / . ~

Sealed & delivered   John POSTLY   Joseph GREEN (Seal)
In presence of ~   Thomas DALE   Mary GREEN (Seal)"

---

[468] Worcester County Court (Land Records). Bill of sale from CROPPER, Joseph to CROPPER, Zadok. 07 August 1788. M, pp. 441-442, MSA CE 30-12. www.mdlandrec.net : accessed 23 February 2022.
[469] Worcester County Court (Land Records). Instrument of writing from PARKER, William Anderson to PARKER, Nancy. 14 October 1788. M, p. 457, MSA CE 30-12. www.mdlandrec.net : accessed 23 February 2022.

*followed on folio 469 with the acknowledgment by Justice of the Peace John POSTLY and the recordation by court clerk James R. MORRIS on 09 January 1789[470]

Liber M, folios 469-470; 08 January 1789

"Maryland Ss^t. Know all men by these presents That I Levin MARTIN of Worcester County and State af[ore]s[ai]^d for and in consideration of the Sum of Twenty five pounds current money of Maryland to me in hand paid by Walter SMITH of the County and State af[ore]s[ai]^d the receipt whereof I do hereby acknowledge, I the said Levin MARTIN with John WISE of the same place have granted bargained and Sold and by these presents do Grant bargain and Sell unto the said Walter SMITH his heirs and Assigns a certain Negro Girl called **Martha** about eight years of age (which said negro Girl was given by the said John WISE to the said Levin MARTIN and the said Wises' Right hath not been conveyed to the said MARTIN) which said negro Girl called **Martha** we the said Levin MARTIN and John WISE for ourselves and each of our heirs Executors and Administrators will warrant and defend the said negro Girl called **Martha** unto the said Walter SMITH his heirs Executors administrators and assigns from all and every person or persons claiming any right title or Interest in or to the said negro Girl from by or under the said Levin MARTIN or John WISE or their heirs or assigns or any person claiming by from or under them or any of them In Testimony whereof we the said Levin MARTIN and John WISE have hereto set our hands and Seals this eighth day of January Anno Domini 1789 ~

Signed Sealed & delivered   Levin MARTIN   (Seal)
In the presence of ~   John WISE   (Seal)"

*followed on folio 470 with the acknowledgment by Justice of the Peace Philip QUINTON and the recordation by court clerk James R. MORRIS on 10 January 1789[471]

Liber M, folio 472; 24 January 1789

"Know all men by these presents that I William WATTS for and in consideration of the Sum of Three hundred pounds current money of Maryland to me in hand paid Edward HARMONSON at or before the ensealing and delivery hereof the receipt whereof is hereby acknowledged and the said Edward his Executors, administrators and assigns acquitted exonerated and discharged hath bargained Sold and confirmed unto the said Edward, and by these presents do Grant bargain Sell and confirm unto the said Edward his Executors and assigns the following Negroes, horses & Stock of all kind whatsoever and farming Utensals and household and kitchen furniture Vizt. One Negro man called **Isaac** one Woman called **Hannah**, one Boy called **Amos** one Girl **Beck** one boy called **Robin**, Two horses, nineteen head of Cattle twenty one head of Hogs, one Cart three plows and harrows with all the rest of my farming tackel and furniture To have and to hold the aforesaid Negroes, horses, cattle, hogs and chattels unto the aforesaid Edward his Executors Administrators and Assigns forever, And to the only proper use and behoofs of him the said Edward his Executors Administrators and Assigns, and to no other use intent or purpose whatsoever, and the said William for himself his Executors, Administrators the aforesaid Negroes, horses cattle hogs and goods and Chattels unto the said Edward his Executors & assigns shall and will warrant and forever defend by these presents In Testimony whereof I have hereunto Set my hand and Seal affixed this twenty fourth day of January Anno Domini Seventeen hundred and eighty Nine ~

Signed Sealed and delivered   John POSTLY   William WATTS   (Seal)
in presence of ~   Isaac MARSHALL"

---

[470] Worcester County Court (Land Records). Deed of gift from GREEN, Joseph and Mary to WHITE, Catty. 01 January 1789. M, pp. 468-469, MSA CE 30-12. www.mdlandrec.net : accessed 23 February 2022.

[471] Worcester County Court (Land Records). Bill of sale from MARTIN, Levin and WISE, John to SMITH, Walter. 08 January 1789. M, pp. 469-470, MSA CE 30-12. www.mdlandrec.net : accessed 23 February 2022.

*followed with the acknowledgment by Justices of the Peace John POSTLY and Isaac MARSHALL, and the recordation on 28 January 1789 by court clerk James R. MORRIS[472]

Liber M, folios 472-473; 24 January 1789

"Know all men by these presents that I Samuel Hopkins ROWND of Worcester County in the State of Maryland Doct[o]ʳ for and in consideration of the Sum of one hundred pounds current money of Maryland to me in hand paid at and before the Sealing and delivery of these presents by Hampton ROWND of the same place af[ore]s[ai]ᵈ the receipt whereof I do hereby acknowledge, Give Grant, bargain & Sell and by these presents do bargain and Sell unto the said Hampton ROUND three negro Boys, one called **Elijah** ten years old, one called **Ned** five years old and another called **George**, three years old To have and to hold forever all and every of them by these presents bargained and Sold unto the said Hampton ROWND his heirs Executors administrators and assigns forever and I the said Samuel HOPKINS ROWND for myself my heirs Executors & Administr[ato]ʳˢ all and every of the said Negros unto the said Hampton ROWND his heirs Executors and administr[ato]ʳˢ and assigns, against me the said Samuel Hopkins ROWND my heirs Executors administr[ato]rs and assigns and against all and every other person and persons whatsoever shall & will warrant and forever defend by these presents, which negroes I the said Samuel Hopkins ROUND have put the said Hampton ROUND in full possession of at the Sealing of these presents hereof In Witness whereof I have hereunto Sett my hand and Seal this Twenty fourth day of January Anno Domini 1789 ~

Signed Sealed & delivered   Josiah MITCHELL   Sam. H. ROUND   (Seal)
In presence of us. ~"

*followed on folio 473 with the acknowledgment by Justice of the Peace Josiah MITCHELL and the recordation on 02 February 1789 by court clerk James R. MORRIS[473]

Liber M, folios 473-474; 31 January 1789

"This Indenture made this thirty first day of January Anno Domini One thousand Seven hundred and eighty nine Between John AYRES of Worcester County in the State of Maryland planter of the one part and Negro **Abner** (late a Slave of Frederick CONNER now manumitted and made free by the said Frederick CONNER) of the same place of the other part Witnesseth that the Said John AYRES for and in consideration of the Covenants and Rents herein after mentioned and {?e?i?ed}, on the part of the said **Abner**, to be paid done and performed, He the said John AYRES hath Granted, demised, leased, and to farm letten and by these presents doth Grant demise Lease and to farm let unto the said **Abner**, Thirty acres of Land Situate lying and being in the County af[ore]s[ai]ᵈ on the Eastside of the said John AYRES Plantation and adjoining the said AYRES' Plantation and on the Boquetenorton Road most convenient to the House the said **Abner** hath built on the said Land (which said demised premises is now in Possession of the said **Abner**) with the Houses already built thereon, and all the houses he shall hereafter build on the same with all improvements profits priviledges and appurtenances unto the said thirty acres of Land as af[ore]s[ai]ᵈ described belonging, or in any manner appertaining (Except and always Excepted out of this present demise or Lease that the said Land shall not be planted in Indian Corn two years together, nor any of the said Land Rented or let by the said **Abner** to any Person whatsoever, nor take in any horses or Cattle (from any person whatsoever, to pasture on the said demised premises during the Time he the said **Abner** shall hold the same) To have and to hold all and Singular the said Demised premises with all and every the appurtenances (Except as before Excepted) unto the said Negro **Abner** from the date hereof for and during and untill the full end and Term of six years and Eleven months Ensuing the date hereof to be fully compleat and ended, Yielding and paying therefore for and during the Term af[ore]s[ai]ᵈ unto the said John AYRES his heirs Executors administrators or assigns Yearly

---

[472] Worcester County Court (Land Records). Bill of sale from WATTS, William to HARMONSON, Edward. 24 January 1789. M, p. 472, MSA CE 30-12. www.mdlandrec.net : accessed 23 February 2022.
[473] Worcester County Court (Land Records). Bill of sale from ROUND, Samuel Hopkins to ROUND, Hampton. 24 January 1789. M, pp. 472-473, MSA CE 30-12. www.mdlandrec.net : accessed 23 February 2022.

and every year during the Term af[ore]s[ai]^d One days work for the use of the said Land" …
"And at the expiration of the said Term of six years and Eleven months that he the said **Abner** shall & will deliver up unto the said John AYRES his heirs Executors, Administrators or Assigns Quiet and peacable possession of all and Singular the aforesaid Demised premises with all improvements he shall put on the same and have the said premises in good Rentable order In Testimony of the above, the parties have bound themselves each to the other in the Penal Sum of Two hundred pounds current money of Maryland and have Interchangeably Set their hands and Seals the day and year first above written ~ / . ~

Signed Sealed and Delivered	Robert MARTIN	John AYRES (Seal)
In the presence of us ~	John WISE	
		Negro O/O **Abner** (Seal) his mark"

*followed on folio 474 with the recordation by court clerk James R. MORRIS on 06 February 1789[474]

Liber M, folio 477; 27 February 1789

"Know all men by these presents that I Zadok STURGIS (Sheriff of Worcester County) in the State of Maryland for and in Consideration of the Sum of Thirty six pound ten Shillings current money of Maryland to me in hand paid at and before the Ensealing and delivery of these presents by Henry PARKER of the County and State af[ore]s[ai]^d the receipt whereof I do hereby acknowledge, have bargained and Sold (by Virtue of a Writ of Vindishono – Exponoi to me directed by the Worshipful Court) and by these presents do bargain and Sell unto the said Henry PARKER his heirs and assigns forever a Negro Woman known by the Name of and called **Candis** is about Seventeen years of age and a Negro Girl known by the name and called **Sarah** about seven months old her and her Child **Sarah** hereafter in Case that he me have and every of them by these presents, bargained and Sold unto the said Henry PARKER his heirs Executors, Administrators and assigns forever I the said Zadok STURGIS for myself my Heirs Executors or Administrators or any of their heirs or assigns all and Singular the said negro woman called **Candis** and negro Girl called **Sarah** unto the said Henry PARKER his heirs and assigns forever against me the said Zadok STURGIS my heirs Executors, administrators and assigns by these presents of which said negro woman called **Candis** and negro Girl called **Sarah** which I the said Zadok STURGIS have put the said Henry PARKER in full possession of by the delivery of these presents, In Testimony whereof I the said Zadok STURGIS have hereunto Set my hand and Seal affixed this 27th of February Anno Dom[ini] Seventeen hundred and Eighty Nine ~

Signed Sealed & delivered	W[illia]^m HANDY	Zadok STURGIS (Seal)
In the presents of ~"		

*followed with the acknowledgment of the Justice of the Peace William HANDY and the recordation by court clerk James R. MORRIS[475]

* a "Writ of Vindishono – Exponoi" is a Writ of Venditioni Exponas.

Liber M, folio 471; 03 March 1789

"Know all men by these presents That I William HOLLAND of Worcester County in the State of Maryland for and in consideration of the Sum of thirty Six pound ten Shillings current money to me in hand paid at and before the Ensealing and delivering of these presents by Henry PARKER of the County and State af[ore]s[ai]^d the receipt whereof I do hereby acknowledge Have bargined and Sold and by these presents do bargin and Sell unto the said Henry PARKER

---

[474] Worcester County Court (Land Records). Deed of lease from AYRES, John to **Abner**. 31 January 1789. M, pp. 473-474, MSA CE 30-12. www.mdlandrec.net : accessed 23 February 2022.

[475] Worcester County Court (Land Records). Bill of sale from STURGIS, Zadok to PARKER, Henry. 27 February 1789. M, p. 477, MSA CE 30-12. www.mdlandrec.net : accessed 23 February 2022.

his Heirs and assigns forever a Negro Woman known by the name of and called **Candis** about Seventeen years of age, and a Negro Girl known by the Name and called **Sarah** about Seven months old her and her child **Sarah** hereafter in case that he may have and every of them by these presents bargined and Sold unto the said Henry PARKER his heirs, Executors, Administrators and Assigns forever I the said William HOLLAND for myself my heirs Executors or Administrators or any of them or any of their or Assigns all and Singular the said negro woman called **Candis** and negro Girl called **Sarah** unto the said Henry PARKER his heirs and assigns for ever against me the said William HOLLAND my heirs Executors Administrators and Assigns, all and every other person or persons whatsoever Shall and will warrant and defend forever by these presents, Of which said negro woman called **Candis** and negro Girl called **Sarah** I the said William HOLLAND have put the said Henry PARKER in full possession of by the delivery of these presents In Testamoney whereof I the said William HOLLAND have hereunto Sett my hand and Seal affixed this third of March Anno Dom[ini] Seventeen hundred and eighty Nine ~

Signed Sealed and delivered   W[illia]^m HANDY   W[illia]^m HOLLAND   (Seal)
In the presents off ~"

*followed with the acknowledgment by Justice of the Peace William HANDY and the recordation on 04 March 1789 by court clerk James R. MORRIS[476]

Liber M, folios 491-492; 14 March 1789

"To all whom these presents shall come know ye that I James Round MORRIS of Worcester County in the State of Maryland being desirous to set free and manumit Negro **Esther** now about two years old and Six months old daughter of negro **Isaac** Slave of William MORRIS and **Chloe** Slave of the said James R. MORRIS for divers and conditions me thereunto moving I the said James Round MORRIS do by these presents give and grant Set free and manumit the aforesaid Negro **Esther** immediately after she arrives at the age of Sixteen years, To have and to hold and freely enjoy to the said Negro **Esther** immediately after she arrives at the age of sixteen years af[ore]s[ai]^d her Liberty and freedom in full and ample manner without any let hindrance or authority of any person or persons whatsoever In Testimony whereof I have hereto Set my hand and affixed my Seal this 14th day of March Anno Dom[ini] 1789 ~ / . ~

Signed Sealed & Delivered   John SELBY   James R. MORRIS   (Seal)
In the presence of ~"

*followed with the acknowledgment by Justice of the Peace John SELBY and the recordation by court clerk James R. MORRIS[477]

Liber M, folio 495; 10 March 1789

"To all people to whom these presents shall come, Know ye that I Levin HOPKINS of Worcester County and State of Maryland as well for and in consideration of the natural effection which I do bear to my well beloved son William HOPKINS, as also for divers good causes and valuable considerations me at present moving have given and granted and by these presents do give grant and confirm unto the said William HOPKINS a Negro Boy called **Daniel** and a Feather Bed and furniture marked W H unto the said William HOPKINS his heirs Ex[ecuto]^rs Adm[inistrato]^rs or Assigns (excepting the said Levin HOPKINS' lifetime in the said negro boy before named) To have and to hold the said negro boy called **Daniel** and Feather bed and furniture to him the said William HOPKINS his heirs and assigns forever, to the only proper use and behoof of the said William HOPKINS his heirs and Assigns and no other freely and quietly without any matter of challenge claim or demand for me or in my name or by my procurement (except as before excepted) without any money or any other thing to be yielded

---

[476] Worcester County Court (Land Records). Bill of sale from HOLLAND, William to PARKER, Henry. 03 March 1789. M, p. 481, MSA CE 30-12. www.mdlandrec.net : accessed 23 February 2022.
[477] Worcester County Court (Land Records). Deed of manumission from MORRIS, James Round to **Esther**. 14 March 1789. M, pp. 491-492, MSA CE 30-12. www.mdlandrec.net : accessed 23 February 2022.

paid or done unto or for me the said Levin HOPKINS my heirs Ex[ecuto]rs Adm[inistrato]rs or Assigns And further know ye that I the said Levin HOPKINS have put the said William HOPKINS in quiet and peaceable possession of the said Negro boy called **Daniel** and the aforesaid Bed and furniture by delivering them to the said William HOPKINS before the sealing and delivery hereof and do covenant and agree with the said William HOPKINS his heirs and assigns to Warrant and forever defend the said Negro Boy called **Daniel** and feather Bed and furniture from all persons claiming any right Title or interest to any part or parcel of them from in or under him In Witness whereof the said Levin HOPKINS hath hereunto Set his hand and fixed his Seal this tenth day of March Anno Domini one thousand Seven hundred and eighty nine ~ / . ~

Signed Sealed and Delivered   John SELBY   Levin HOPKINS   (Seal)
In the presence of ~"

*followed with the acknowledgment by Justice of the Peace John SELBY and the recordation on 20 March 1789 by court clerk James R. MORRIS[478]

Liber M, folio 514; 14 March 1789

"Maryland Sst. Know all men by these presents that I George LIVINGSTON of Worcester County planter for & in consideration of the sum of five Shillings to me in hand paid by Ted LIVINGSTON of aforesaid County the receipt whereof I do hereby acknowledge have, bargained Sold and delivered and by these presents do bargain Sell & deliver unto the said Ted LIVINGSTON one negro boy called **Cesar** aged fourteen years, To have & to hold the said bargained premises unto the said Ted LIVINGSTON his Executors Administrators & assigns forever & I the said George LIVINGSTON for myself my Executors, administrators & assigns shall & will Warrant & forever defend against all persons by these presents the said Bargained premises unto the said Ted LIVINGSTON his Executors, administrators & assigns in Witness whereof I have hereunto Sett my hand & Seal this fourteenth Day of March one thousand Seven hundred & eighty nine ~ / . ~

Signed Sealed & Delivered   William FOOKS   George LIVINGSTON
In presence of ~   Benjamin LIVINGSTON"

*followed with the acknowledgment by Ebenezer HANDY and the recordation on 17 April 1789 by court clerk James R. MORRIS[479]

Liber M, folio 521; 02 March 1789

"To all persons to whom these presents shall come Know ye that I Joseph GILLETT of Worcester County in the State of Maryland being desirous to set Free and Manumit a Negro man **James** now of full age in consideration of the faithful Service of the said Negro done and performed, and for other good causes and considerations me thereunto moveing I the said Joseph GILLITT do by these presents, give and grant set free and, Manumit the said Negro **James**, and that the Freedom of the said Negro shall commence and take effect immediately after the Date of these presents To have and to hold and freely to enjoy to him forever immediately after the date of these presents, his Liberty and Freedom in a full and ample manner without any hindrance or authority of any person or persons whatsoever in Testimony whereof I the said Joseph GILLETT have hereunto the said Joseph GILLETT have hereunto Set my hand and affixed my Seal this 2nd day of March one thousand Seven hundred and eighty nine 1789 ~

                                                                Joseph GILLETT   (Seal)

---

[478] Worcester County Court (Land Records). Deed from HOPKINS, Levin to HOPKINS, William. 10 March 1789. M, p. 495, MSA CE 30-12. www.mdlandrec.net : accessed 23 February 2022.
[479] Worcester County Court (Land Records). Bill of sale from LIVINGSTON, George to LIVINGSTON, Ted. 14 March 1789. M, p. 514, MSA CE 30-12. www.mdlandrec.net : accessed 23 February 2022.

*followed with the acknowledgment by Justice of the Peace James SELBY and the recordation by court clerk James R. MORRIS[480]

Liber M, folio 523; 12 May 1789

"Know all men by these presents that I John NICHOLSON of the County of Worcester and State of Maryland for and in consideration of the sum of one hundred and Seventy five pounds current money of Maryland to me in hand paid by George WHITTINGTON of Accomack County and State of Virginia the receipt whereof I do hereby acknowledge have granted bargained Sold and delivered and by these presents according to the due form of Law do Grant bargain Sell and deliver unto the said George WHITTINGTON his heirs and assigns one Negro woman name **Moll** Three negro Girls Viz. **Hannah**, **Candis** and **Izabel**, three head of horses, Six head of Cattle, Sixteen head of hogs, one yoke of Oxen, wane and wheels, one cart 2 plows two harrows, all farming, utensils with all and every kind of Tools and working Implements, four Beds and all Bed furniture all Table Linen, one Desk, one Cupboard, two Looking Glasses all household and Kitchen furniture, one loome, four, wheels, all Meat Lard, Hides Tallow, all plate, pewter Chine Earthen & Glassware whatsoever, one Saddle & Bridle, and one old riding Carriage, to the only proper use of the said George WHITTINGTON his heirs and assigns and to no other uses whatsoever And I the said John NICHOLSON do Covenant with the said George WHITTINGTON that the property above mentioned is the property of me the Seller, and that I have Right to Sell and dispose of the same in manner afforesaid, and that I Will Warrant and defend the same from any person or persons claiming Right or Title whatsoever To the said George WHITTINGTON his heirs or assigns forever In Witness whereof I have hereunto Set my hand and Seal this 12th day of May 1789 ~ / . ~

W. PURNELL   John NICHOLSON (Seal)"

*followed with the acknowledgment of Justice of the Peace William PURNELL and the recordation by court clerk James R. MORRIS[481]

Liber M, folio 528; 09 May 1789

"Know all men by these presents That I Henry Johnson WILLETT of Worcester County in the State of Maryland, for and in consideration of the sum of forty five pounds current money of Maryland to me in hand paid at and before the Sealing and delivery hereof by John McLURE of Baltimore County and State aforesaid, I the said Henry Johnson WILLETT Have bargained Sold and delivered unto him the said John McLURE heirs, Executors, Administrators and Assigns forever one negro Girl called and known by the name of **Minta**, now in the County of Worcester aforesaid To have and to hold the above mentioned Negro Girl hereby bargained Sold and delivered unto him the said John McLURE and to his heirs and assigns forever to the only proper use benefit and behoof of him the said John McLURE and his heirs and assigns forever against me the said Henry Johnson WILLETT and my heirs Executors and Adm[inistrato]rs and against every other person and persons whatever will and shall forever Warrant and defend of which above mentioned Negro Girl I the said Henry Johnson WILLETT have put the said John McLURE in full possession by the delivery of these presents In Witness whereof I have hereto set my hand and Seal this 9th day of May Anno Domini 1789 ~ / . ~

Signed Sealed & delivered   W[illia]m HANDY   Henry J. WILLETT (Seal)
In presence of ~"

*followed with the acknowledgment of Justice of the Peace William HANDY, a memorandum by Henry J. WILLETT, and the recordation by court clerk James R. MORRIS[482]

---

[480] Worcester County Court (Land Records). Deed of manumission from GILLETT, Joseph to **James**. 02 March 1789. M, p. 521, MSA CE 30-12. www.mdlandrec.net : accessed 23 February 2022.
[481] Worcester County Court (Land Records). Bill of sale from NICHOLSON, John to WHITTINGTON, George. 12 May 1789. M, p. 523, MSA CE 30-12. www.mdlandrec.net : accessed 23 February 2022.
[482] Worcester County Court (Land Records). Bill of sale from WILLETT, Henry Johnson to McLURE, John. 09 May 1789. M, p. 528, MSA CE 30-12. www.mdlandrec.net : accessed 23 February 2022.

Liber M, folios 534-535; 25 April 1789

"To all christian people to whome these presents shall come or may concern I Joshua STEVENS of the State of Maryland in the County of Worcester Send Greeting Know ye that I the said Joshua STEVENS in the Consideration of the sum of Twenty two pounds current money of Maryland to me in hand well & truly paid at and before the Sealing and delivery of these presents by Samuel HOLLAND of the County and State af[ore]s[ai]^d the receipt whereof I do hereby acknowledge & confess & thereof have bargained and Sold & by these presents do bargain and Sell unto the said Samuel HOLLAND one negro Boy called **Ben** To have and to hold the said Negro Boy called **Ben** hereby bargained and sold & all my right title claim & Interest unto the said Sam[ue]^l HOLLAND his heirs Executors Administrators & Assigns, to him and their own proper use and uses benefit and behoof as his & their own proper Goods forever & I the said Joshua STEVENS do hereby for myself my heirs Executors & administrators Covenant promise and Grant & agree to and with the said Samuel HOLLAND his heirs Executors, administrators that the said Negro Boy called **Ben**, now are and be & and so shall at all times forever hereafter be remain & continue unto the said Samuel HOLLAND his heirs Executors Administrators and assigns free & Clear of and from all and all manner of former and other Gifts grants Bargains, Sales assignments & Incumbrances whatsoever had made done or committed by me my means, previty or procurement In Witness whereof I have hereunto set my hand and Seal this 25th day of April Anno Domini 1789 ~ / ~ / . ~

Signed Sealed & Delivered	Benjamin McCORMACK	Joshua STEVENS (Seal)
in presence of	Thomas HOLLAND	
	John P. MITCHELL"	

*followed on folio 535 with the acknowledgment by John P. MITCHELL and the recordation on 12 May 1789 by court clerk James R. MORRIS[483]

Liber M, folio 536; 15 May 1789

"Know all men by these presents That I Moses CHAILLE of Worcester County, for and in Consideration of the sum of one hundred pounds current money of Maryland to me in hand paid at and before the Sealing and delivery hereof by Patrick WATERS and John BISHOP of the same place, I do hereby bargain and Sell and by these presents have bargained and Sold unto the said Patrick WATERS and John BISHOP and their heirs and assigns forever the following negro Slaves to wit, one negro man called **Ben** and one negro man called **Abraham** now in the possession of John AYRES of the County af[ore]s[ai]^d To have and to hold the above mentioned bargained and Sold Slaves unto the said Patrick WATERS and John BISHOP and their heirs and assigns forever to the only proper use benefit and behoof of the said Patrick WATERS and John BISHOP and their heirs forever, And the said Moses CHAILLE for himself his heirs Executors and Administrators doth covenant and agree to and with the said Patrick WATERS and John BISHOP and their heirs forever, hereafter to defend the said negro Slaves against the claim right and title of the said Moses CHAILLE his heirs Executors and Administrators, and all other persons whatever claiming from by or under them or any of them Witness my hand and Seal this fifteenth day of May Anno Dom[ini] 1789

| Sealed & delivered | John SELBY | Moses CHAILLE (Seal) |
| In presence of ~" | | |

*followed with the acknowledgment by Justice of the Peace John SELBY and the recordation by court clerk James R. MORRIS[484]

---

[483] Worcester County Court (Land Records). Bill of sale from STEVENS, Joshua to HOLLAND, Samuel. 25 April 1789. M, pp. 534-535, MSA CE 30-12. www.mdlandrec.net : accessed 23 February 2022.
[484] Worcester County Court (Land Records). Bill of sale from CHAILLE, Moses to WATERS, Patrick and BISHOP, John. 15 May 1789. M, p. 536, MSA CE 30-12. www.mdlandrec.net : accessed 23 February 2022.

Liber M, folio 552; 09 June 1789

"I Levi TOWNSEND Son of William Barkley TOWNSEND deceased Do hereby Certify that I have this Nineth day of June 1789 taken & Rec[eive]^d, of & from my brother Barkley TOWNSEND a Deed of Conveyance of this Date for certain Lands as therein expressed, as also a negro Girl called **Hetty** togeather with other matters in full discharge to me my heirs Exe[cuto]^{rs} and Adm[inistrato]^{rs} of all my Right Title, claim & Interest of & to my part or Portion of the Real and personal Estate & every part thereof of the af[ore]s[ai]^d William Barkley TOWNSEND Deceased as Witness my hand & Seal the Day & Date above mentioned ~ / . ~

Witness present ~ W[illia]^m HANDY   Levi TOWNSEND"

*followed with the recordation by court clerk James R. MORRIS[485]

Liber M, folio 554; 09 June 1789

"Know all men by these presents that I Barkley TOWNSEND of Sussex County in the State of Delaware, for and in Consideration of the sum of Five Shillings current money of Maryland to me in hand paid by Levi TOWNSEND of Worcester County in the State of Maryland, I the said Barkley TOWNSEND Have granted, bargained Sold and delivered and by these presents doth Grant bargain, Sell and deliver unto him the said Levi TOWNSEND and to his heirs and assigns forever, a certain Negro Girl called **Hetty**, and one Feather Bed and furniture in Worcester County, late the property of a certain William BARKLEY TOWNSEND late of Worcester County aforesaid deceased To have and to hold all and Singular the said Negro Girl and feather Bed and furniture above mentioned and Sold and delivered unto him the aforesaid Levi TOWNSEND and to his heirs and assigns forever, against me the said Barkley TOWNSEND or my heirs, Executors and Administrators or any of them, doth and shall forever quit all Right Title or claim in, or to the above mentioned negro Girl and feather Bed, Of which I the said Barkley TOWNSEND have put and vested the said Levi TOWNSEND in full possession, of my Right and Title as possible by these presents In Witness whereof I the said Barkley TOWNSEND hath hereto set my hand and affixed my Seal this Ninth day of June Anno Dom[ini] one thousand Seven hundred and eighty Nine ~ / . ~

Signed Sealed & Delivered   John SELBY   Barkley TOWNSEND (Seal)
In the presence of ~   William HANDY"

*followed with the acknowledgment by Justice of the Peace William HANDY and the recordation on 12 June 1789 by court clerk James R. MORRIS[486]

Liber M, folios 557-558; 09 June 1789

"Know all men by these presents, that I Hampton ROWND of Worcester County in the State of Maryland (farmer) for and in consideration of the Sum of Two hundred and Seventy five pounds current money of the province af[ore]s[ai]^d to me in hand paid at and before the Sealing and delivery of these presents by James RACKLIFFE of the province af[ore]s[ai]^d (farmer) the receipt whereof I do hereby acknowledge have bargained and Sold and by these presents do bargain and Sell unto the said James RACKLIFFE all the Goods, chattels, Household stuff and implements of Household whatsoever now in Worcester in my possession Viz^t. One negro woman named **Sarah**, one negro Girle named **Rose**, four Negro Girls named **Amy**, **Rachel**, **Bett**, & **Hannah**, two Negro boys **Elijah** and **Ned**, one yoake Oxen, two Horses Bay, one old Mare, two horse Colts and one Mare Colt, three Cows and calves, two Cows & yearlings, two young Heifers, three two year old Steers and two yearlins Eight old sheep and three Lambs twenty Six head Shoats & one Sow, four feather Beds & furniture, one Walnut Square Table Six Winzor Chairs, one maple Dusk, one Walnutt chest of Draws one hair Trunk one Case and

---

[485] Worcester County Court (Land Records). Receipt from TOWNSEND, Levi to TOWNSEND, Barkley. 09 June 1789. M, p. 552, MSA CE 30-12. www.mdlandrec.net : accessed 23 February 2022.

[486] Worcester County Court (Land Records). Bill of sale from TOWNSEND, Barkley to TOWNSEND, Levi. 09 June 1789. M, p. 554, MSA CE 30-12. www.mdlandrec.net : accessed 23 February 2022.

Bottles, nine Raw hides, one wain, two plows & two harrows, one Iron Tea Kettle, two Iron potts two Iron Kettles one cracked, one Lume four pewter Basons, eighteen gun plates, one sett chania cups & sausers one Ink stand one small bowl, two Glass Tumblers and one Sugar dish, two flatt irons one warming pan, one frying pan, two narrow axes & two Broad axes one drawing knife, two augers, two narrow Chessels, one wife Chessels, one hand saw & one Cross Cut Saw one ox yoke and chain two spinning wheels, four Cyder Casks, one small Gun with a Silver Sights, one pair Stilyards, one pair Scales and weights, one mans Saddle & Bridle, Six knives & forks, four wieding hoes, one Grubing hoe, one looking Glass, three Tubbs four water Buckets two half Bushels, four Slays, one Dutch oven, One pair wool Cards, one pair Cotton Cards all the Crop of Corn & oats and flax & as it now stands To have and to hold all and Singular the said Goods and Chattels, Household stuff and implements of House hold and every thing firmly by these presents bargained and Sold unto the said James RACKLIFFE his heirs Exec[uto]^{rs} adm[inistrato]^{rs} and assigns forever" … "I the said Hampton ROWND have put the said James RACKLIFFE in full possession of by delivering him one negro Girle named **Amey**, one Bay horse & one feather Bed & at the Sealing and delivering hereof In Witness whereof I have hereunto sett my hand and Seal this Ninth day of June Anno Domini 1789 ~

Testes. Nehemiah DAVIS ~ Zeporah MASSEY Hampton ROWND (Seal)"

*followed on folio 558 with the acknowledgment by Justice of the Peace Isaac MARSHALL on 10 June 1789 and the recordation by court clerk James R. MORRIS on 13 June 1789[487]

Liber N, folio 3; 29 August 1789

"Know all men by these presents that I William CORBIN of Worcester County in the State of Maryland for divers good Causes but more Especially being convinced it is their Just Equitable right do by These presents Manumit Emancipate and for Ever set free from Slavery my negro man **Will** aged Thirty three years which negro I perchaised of a certain James BRODWATTE in Confirmation whereof I have Set my hand and affixed my seal this twenty Eighth day of August 1789 ~

Signed Seald & ~ Brittingham GIVANS William CORBIN (Seal)
Delivered in presents of
 Solomon X TOWNSEND (of Marshel)
  his mark"

*followed with the acknowledgment by Justice of the Peace John SELBY and the recordation by court clerk James R. MORRIS on 04 September 1789[488]

Liber N, folios 7-8; 16 June 1789

"Know all men by these presents That I William TRUITT Jun[io]^r of Worcester County in the State of Maryland for and Consideration of the Sum one hundred pounds current money of Maryland to me in hand paid by Samuel LONG of the County and State af[ore]s[ai]^d at and before the Sealing and delivery of these presents the receipt whereof the said William TRUITT doth hereby acknowledge, hath bargained and Sold and by these presents doth bargain and Sell unto the Said Samuel LONG one negro Boy Slave called **Ben**, one negro Girl Slave called **Charity** four feather Beds and furniture two Horses, two Cows two Heifers one yearling and one Calf one dish half a dozen Setting Chairs one Loome two ploughs three Harrows two Iron potts one Iron Kittle one Tea Kettle two Sows & fourteen Shoats eight head of Sheep Three hoes & two axes To have and to hold the said negro Boy called the negro Girl called **Charity** four feather Beds and furniture, two Horses two Cows two Heifers one Yearling one Calf, one Dish half a dozen Setting Chairs one Loom two ploughs three Harrows two Iron potts one Iron Kettle one Tea Kettle two Sows fourteen Shoats eight head of Sheep three hoes & two axes two

---

[487] Worcester County Court (Land Records). Bill of sale from ROWND, Hampton to RACKLIFFE, James. 09 June 1789. M, pp. 557-558, MSA CE 30-12. www.mdlandrec.net : accessed 23 February 2022.
[488] Worcester County Court (Land Records). Deed of manumission from CORBIN, William to **Will**. 29 August 1789. N, p. 3, MSA CE 30-13. www.mdlandrec.net : accessed 13 March 2022.

Black walnut Tables one Corner Cubbard my Crop of Corn Oats, Tobacco & flax now Growing unto the said Samuel LONG his heirs and assigns forever and for no other use or purpose whatsoever and the said William TRUITT for himself and his heirs doth Covenant and agree to and with the said Samuel LONG and his his heirs that the said William TRUITT and his heirs The Negroes Horses, Cattle Sheep, Hogs, plows, Harrows, potts Kettles, Hoes axes & loom af[ore]s[ai]^d unto the said Samuel LONG and his heirs shall and will Warrant and forever defend against the claim right and Title of all and every Person or Persons claiming from by or under the said William TRUITT his heirs Ex[ecuto]^{rs} Adm[inistrato]^{rs} or any of them In Testimony whereof the said William TRUITT to these presents his hand hath Sett and Seal affixed this Sixteenth day of June Anno Dom[ini] Seventeen hundred and eighty and Nine / . ~ / . ~

Signed Sealed & delivered   William TRUITT J[unio]^r (Seal)
In presence of ~
Morgan Jones"

*followed on folio 8 with the acknowledgment by Justice of the Peace John SELBY and the recordation by court clerk James R. MORRIS[489]

Liber N, folios 15-16; 21 February 1787

"Know all men by these presents that I Samuel Hopkins ROWND of Worcester County of the State of Maryland for an in an consideration of Recovering all Rights title, claim & Interest of Two Tracts of Land the one called Putnam the other Poplar Ridge, Give Grant bargain Sell & Transfer & deliver in these presents to Hampton ROWND his heirs executors, Administrators or assigns Three negroes Viz. **Elijah** aged eight years old & **George** age One year old, Sons of **Trip**, & **Ned** three years old Son of **Mertin** for which contract I bind myself my heirs Executors & Administrators, Value Receiv[e]^d as Witness my hand & Seal this Twenty first of February 1787 ~ / . ~

Test.   John + CROPPER   Sam[ue]^l H. ROUND (Seal)
              His mark"

*followed on folio 16 with the recordation by James R. MORRIS on 14 July 1789[490]

Liber N, folio 25; 04 July 1789

"Worcester Ss^t. Know all men these presents That I James ATKINSON of Worcester County and State of Maryland for and in consideration of the Sum of Forty pounds current money of Maryland to me in hand paid at and before the Sealing and delivery hereof by Joseph BOUSSEY of the County and State af[ore]s[ai]^d the receipt whereof I do hereby acknowledge, have bargained and sold and by these presents do bargain and Sell unto the said Joseph BOUSSEY his heirs Executors Administrators and Assigns forever one negro man Slave named **Hope** To have and to hold the af[ore]s[ai]^d negro man Slave to the Said Joseph BOUSSEY his heirs and assigns forever, to the only proper use and behoof of the said Joseph BOUSSEY his heirs and assigns, and to no other intent or purpose whatever, And the said James ATKINSON for himself his heirs Ex[ecuto]^{rs} and Administrators covenants and agrees to and with the said Joseph BOUSSEY his his heirs and Assigns, the af[ore]s[ai]^d negro man Slave named **Hope** against the Right title and claim of every person or persons forever to Warrant and defend In Witness whereof I have hereto Set my hand and affixed my Seal this Twenty fourth day of July Anno Dom[ini] 1789 ~

Seal[e]^d & Deliv[ere]^d John SELBY   James ATKINSON (Seal)
In presence of"

---

[489] Worcester County Court (Land Records). Bill of sale from TRUITT, William Jr. to LONG, Samuel. 16 June 1789. N, pp. 7-8, MSA CE 30-13. www.mdlandrec.net : accessed 13 March 2022.
[490] Worcester County Court (Land Records). Bill of sale from ROWND, Samuel Hopkins to ROWND, Hampton. 21 February 1787. N, pp. 15-16, MSA CE 30-13. www.mdlandrec.net : accessed 13 March 2022.

*followed with the acknowledgment by Justice of the Peace John SELBY and the recordation on 24 July 1789 by court clerk James R. MORRIS[491]

Liber N, folio 26; 24 July 1789

"Know all men by these presents that I Levin LONG of Worcester County in the State of Maryland for and in consideration of the Sum of thirty three pounds Current money of Maryland to him in hand paid by Joseph BOUSSEY of the same place at and before the Sealing of these presents, the receipt whereof the said Levin LONG doth hereby acknowledge, hath bargained and Sold and by these presents doth bargain and Sell unto the said Joseph BOUSSEY and his heirs and assigns forever one negro Girl called **Rachel** to have and to hold the said negro Girl called **Rachel** unto the said Joseph BOUSSEY his heirs and assigns forever to the only use benifet and behoof of the said Joseph BOUSSEY and his heirs and assigns forever and for no other use intent purpose or construction whatsoever, and the said Levin LONG for himself his heirs Executors and Administrators doth covenant and agree to and with the said Joseph BOUSSEY his heirs Executors and Administrators that he the said Levin LONG and his heirs will warrant and forever hereafter defend the above mentioned negro Girl called **Rachel** to him the said Joseph BOUSSEY his heirs and assigns forever against the claim, Right title of the said Levin LONG and his heirs, and all and every other person or persons claiming from by or under him, them or any of them In Testimony whereof I have hereunto Set my hand and Seal affixed this 24th day of July Anno Domini Seventeen hundred and eighty nine ~

Signed Sealed & Delivered   Leavin LONG   (Seal)
in presence of ~
John SELBY"

*followed with the acknowledgment by Justice of the Peace John SELBY and the recordation by court clerk James R. MORRIS[492]

Liber N, folios 26-27; 01 July 1789

"Know all men by these presents That I Levi BEACHBOARD of Worcester County in the State of Maryland for and in Consideration of the sum of five Shillings current money of Maryland, to me in hand paid at and before the Sealing and delivery hereof by Thomas MILBOURN of the same County and State aforesaid, The receipt whereof is hereby acknowledged I the said Levi BEACHBOARD Have bargained Sold and delivered, and by these presents doth absolutely bargain Sell and deliver unto him the said Thomas MILBOURN and to his heirs and assigns forever, The following negroes to wit, one negro called **Isaac** and one negro called **Jack**, lately in the possession of said BEACHBOARD, but now in the possession of a certain William MILBOURN in the County af[ore]s[ai]d also one Cow and Calf To have and to hold all and Singular the above mentioned two Negro men or Boys, and Cow and Calf hereby bargained and Sold unto him the said Thomas MILBOURN his heirs and assigns forever, to the only proper use benifet and behoof of him the said Thomas MILBOURN his heirs and assigns forever And the said Levi BEACHBOARD and his heirs doth hereby quit all Right Title or claim of in or to the above mentioned bargained Negroes and Cow and Calf unto him the said Thomas MILBOURN and his heirs, Of which said Negroes and Creatures I the said Levi have put the said Thomas MILBOURN in full possession by the delivery of these presents In Testimony whereof I the said Levi BEACHBOARD have hereunto Set his hand & Seal affixed this thirty first day of July in the year of our Lord one thousand Seven hundred and eighty nine

Signed Sealed & Delivered   Levin BEACHBOARD (Seal)
in the presence of ~
John SELBY   William HANDY"

---

[491] Worcester County Court (Land Records). Bill of sale from ATKINSON, James to BOUSSEY, Joseph. 04 July 1789. N, p. 25, MSA CE 30-13. www.mdlandrec.net : accessed 13 March 2022.
[492] Worcester County Court (Land Records). Bill of sale from LONG, Leavin to BOUSSEY, Joseph. 24 July 1789. N, p. 26, MSA CE 30-13. www.mdlandrec.net : accessed 13 March 2022.

*followed on folio 27 with the acknowledgment by Justices of the Peace John SELBY and William HANDY and the recordation on 31 July 1789 by court clerk James R. MORRIS[493]

Liber N, folios 35-36; 17 August 1789

"This Indenture made this Seventeenth day of August in the year of our Lord one thousand Seven hundred eighty Nine Between Daniel YOUNG of Worcester County in the State of Maryland of the one part and Bayley YOUNG Son of the said Daniel YOUNG of the other part Witnesseth that the said Daniel YOUNG for and in consideration of the Love and affection which he hath for, and doth bear toward Mary his wife and also for the further Consideration of five Shillings current money of Maryland to him in hand paid by the said Bayley YOUNG, before the Sealing and delivery of these presents the receipt whereof he doth hereby acknowledge and thereof doth forever acquit and discharge the said Bayley YOUNG his heirs executors Administrators and assigns, Hath given granted, bargained and Sold and by these presents doth give grant bargain and Sold unto the aforesaid Bayley YOUNG and his heirs and assigns forever part of two Tracts of Land, one called Recouting Choice the other called Adventure lying in Worcester County on Pocomoke River about two miles below Stevens's Ferry being the Lands whereon the said Daniel YOUNG now lives containing one hundred acres more of less being all the part of the aforesaid Two Tracts of Land which came to the said Daniel YOUNG by virtue of his Intermarriage with Mary PITTS his wife also all the Right, Title, and property which the said Daniel has in and to one negro Man called **Harry** to the aforesaid Bayley YOUNG and his heirs, for the uses and Trusts hereinafter expressed to wit, for the said Mary YOUNG wife of the said Daniel YOUNG for and during the Term of her natural Life and after her decease, then the said Bayley YOUNG is to convey the property of the said negro called **Harry** to my Daughter Nancy YOUNG and her heirs forever, To have and to hold to the aforesaid Bayley YOUNG and heirs the aforesaid Tracts of Land as above described, and the aforesaid negro man for the only uses and trusts above expressed, and for no other use intent or purpose whatsoever, And the said Daniel YOUNG for himself his heirs Executors and administrators doth covenant and agree to and with the aforesaid Bayley YOUNG and his heirs that he the said Daniel YOUNG his heirs executors & administrators will Warrant and forever defend all his Right Title and Estate in the two Tracts of Land above mentioned and the aforesaid negro **Harry** to the said Bayley YOUNG and his heirs, against the claim Right and Title of the said Daniel YOUNG and his heirs, and all and every person claiming by from or under him them or any of them In Testimony whereof the said Daniel YOUNG to these presents his hand hath Set and Seal affixed the day and year first above written…

Signed Sealed and Delivered	Outten STURGIS	Dannel YOUNG (Seal)
in presence of us ~	W[illia]^m STURGIS"	

*followed on folio 36 with the acknowledgment by Justices of the Peace Outten STURGIS and William PURNELL and the recordation by court clerk James R. MORRIS[494]

Liber N, folios 51-52; 10 September 1789

"Maryland Somerset County Ss^t. Know all men by these presents That I Thomas FURNIS of Worcester County planter for and in Consideration of the Sum of Forty five pounds current money of Maryland to me in hand paid by Pierce CHAPMAN of Somerset County planter the receipt whereof I do acknowledge hath bargained Sold and by these presents doth bargain & Sell unto the af[ore]s[ai]^d Peirce CHAPMAN one negro Woman named **Hager** and one negro child named **Nell**, to him the said Pierce CHAPMAN his heirs and assigns forever To have an to hold the said Negroe Woman and negro Child to and for the use of him the said Peirce CHAPMAN his heirs and assigns forever, and for no other use or uses whatsoever, and the said

---

[493] Worcester County Court (Land Records). Bill of sale from BEACHBOARD, Levi to MILBOURN, Thomas. 01 July 1789. N, pp. 26-27, MSA CE 30-13. www.mdlandrec.net : accessed 13 March 2022.

[494] Worcester County Court (Land Records). Deed from YOUNG, Dannel to YOUNG, Bayley. 17 August 1789. N, pp. 35-36, MSA CE 30-13. www.mdlandrec.net : accessed 13 March 2022.

Thomas FURNESS for himself his heirs Executors and Administrators doth covenant with the said Pierce CHAPMAN his heirs Executors and Administrators that at the time of the Sail of the af[ore]s[ai]^d Negroes he had good right and full power to bargain and Sell them the said negroes in manner as af[ore]s[ai]^d and that he will hereby warrant and defend the said negroes unto him the said Pierce CHAPMAN against the claim, Right, Title or property of all and every person whatsoever I Witness whereof I have hereunto Set my hand and Seal this tenth day of of September Anno Domini one thousand Seven hundred and eighty Nine /. ~ /. ~ /. ~

Signed Sealed & delivered   Thomas FURNISS ~   (Seal)
in the presence of ~
George LAYFIELD   Ismay BUNTING"

*followed with the acknowledgment by James SELBY on 17 September 1789 and the recordation by court clerk James R. MORRIS on 22 September 1789[495]

Liber N, folios 52-53; (day unknown) May 1789

"Know all men by these presents that I Solomon WEBB of Worcester County in the S^t[ate] of Maryland, have barganeid and Sold unto Joseph BOUSSY a negroe Garl named **Nancy** for the Sum of Twelve pounds cash in hand, which Negro I will warrant from me my heirs and Executors and Administrators and from any other person or persons that shall Challenge or lay any claim or claims to s[ai]^d negro garl and I the s[ai]^d Solomon WEBB will forever defend as Witness my hand and Seal this day of May Anno Domini 1789 /. ~ /. ~ /. ~

Signed and delivered   Elijah BRITTINGHAM   Solomon WEBB (Seal)
in the presents of ~   Ezekiel YOUNG."

*followed with the recordation by court clerk James R. MORRIS on 25 September 1789[496]

Liber N, folios 64-65; 22 September 1789

"Know all men by these presents that I Henry PARKER Junior of Worcester County in the State of Maryland for and in consideration of the Sum of Twenty Seven pound Ten Shillings current money of Maryland to me in hand paid at and befor the sealing and delivery of these presents by Joseph Gray TAYLOR {of the} same County & State af[ore]s[ai]^d the receipt whereof I do hereby ac{knowle}dge Have Bargined and Sold and by these presents do {bargin} and Sell unto the said Joseph Gray TAYLOR his heirs and {assig}ns forever a Negro Girl called and known by the nam of {**Sarah**} about eight years old and now in the possession of the said {Josep}h Gray TAYLOR To have and to hold the said negro Girl called **Sarah** and Singular her hereafter in case that She may have and every of them by these presents have bargined and Sold to the said Joseph Gray TAYLOR his heirs Executors Administrators and assigns forever I the said Henry PARKER for myself my heirs Executors and Administrators or any of them or any of their heirs or assigns all and Singler the said negro Girl called **Sarah** unto the said Joseph Gray TAYLOR heirs and assigns forever against me the said Henry PARKER all and every other person or persons whatsoever claiming any Right or title under me, and will Warrant and forever defend by these presents of which said negro Girl called **Sarah** I the said Henry PARKER have put the said Joseph Gray TAYLOR in full possession of by the delivery of these presents In Testamoney whereof I the said Henry PARKER have hereunto Sett my hand and Seal affixed this Twenty second day of Sept[emb]^{er} one thousand Seven hundred and eighty Nine ~

Signed Sealed and delivered   Henry PARKER (Seal)
in the presence of ~
W[illia]^m HANDY ~"

---

[495] Worcester County Court (Land Records). Bill of sale from FURNISS, Thomas to CHAPMAN, Pierce. 10 September 1789. N, pp. 51-52, MSA CE 30-13. www.mdlandrec.net : accessed 13 March 2022.
[496] Worcester County Court (Land Records). Bill of sale from WEBB, Solomon to BOUSSY, Joseph. May 1789. N, pp. 52-53, MSA CE 30-13. www.mdlandrec.net : accessed 13 March 2022.

*followed on folio 65 with the acknowledgment by Justice of the Peace William HANDY and the recordation on 09 October 1789 by court clerk James R. MORRIS[497]

Liber N, folios 67-68; 28 October 1789

"State of Maryland Worcester County Know all men by these Presents that William PITTS of the County Westmorland State of Pennsylvania for and in consideration of the sum of forty pounds Current money of Maryland to me in hand paid by Hillary PITTS of Worcester County State of Maryland, at or before the sealling & Delivery of these presents the receipt whereof I the said William PITTS do hereby acknowledge Have Granted Bargained sold and delivered, And by these Presents, Do Grant bargain sett and deliver unto the said Hillary PITTS his Executors administrators & assigns one Negro woman Named **minty** about twenty years old and her child **ned** about six years old which Negros before the Executing these, are the Property & in the Possession & occupation of the said William PITTS To have and to hold the afforesaid negroes to the said Hillary PITTS his Executors administrators & assigns forever. And I the said William PITTS for myself & my Heirs Executors & Administrators, unto the said Hillary PITTS his Executors & administrators aganst all & every other person and persons whatever, shall and will warrant and forever defend by these presents of all and singler of which said Negros I the said William PITTS have put the said Hillary PITTS in full possession by Delivering to him the said Hillary PITTS the said Negros at the sealling & Delivery of thes presents In Witness whareof the said William PITTS to these presents his hand hath set & Seal affixed the twenty Eighth day of October Anno D[omini] 1789 ~

Signed Sealed &   John POSTLY   William PITTS   (Seal)
Delivereer'd in the presence of"

*followed on folio 68 with the acknowledgment by Justice of the Peace John POSTLY and the recordation by court clerk James R. MORRIS[498]

Liber N, folio 105; 11 December 1789

"Know all men by these presents that I Moses CHAILLE of Worcester County for in consideration of the sum of Twenty pounds current money of Maryland to me in hand paid by William HANDY (Indian Town) of the County af[ore]s[ai]^d at and before the Sealing and delivery of these presents (the receipt whereof I do hereby acknowledge) Have bargained and Sold, released, granted and confirmed and by these presents do bargain and Sell, release, grant and confirm unto the said William HANDY his heirs and assigns forever one negro woman Slave called **Abel**. To have and to hold the said negro woman Slave by these presents bargained, Sold, released granted and confirmed unto the said William HANDY and his heirs and assigns forever to the only proper use benefit and behoof of the said William HANDY and his heirs and assigns forever, and for no other use purpose or construction whatsoever, And I the said Moses CHAILLE for myself my heirs Executors and Administrators the said negro Woman Slave unto the said William HANDY his heirs Executors, Administrators and assigns against me the said Moses CHAILLE my heirs Executors and Administrators and against all and every other person and persons Whatsoever Shall and warrant and forever defend by these presents In Witness whereof I have have hereunto Set my hand and affixed my Seal this 11th day of December Anno Dom[ini] Seventeen hundred and eighty Nine ~ / . ~

Sealed & delivered   Philip QUINTON   Moses CHAILLE   (Seal)
in presence of ~"

---

[497] Worcester County Court (Land Records). Bill of sale from PARKER, Henry Jr. to TAYLOR, Joseph Gray. 22 September 1789. N, pp. 64-65, MSA CE 30-13. www.mdlandrec.net : accessed 13 March 2022.
[498] Worcester County Court (Land Records). Bill of sale from PITTS, William to PITTS, Hillary. 28 October 1789. N, pp. 67-68, MSA CE 30-13. www.mdlandrec.net : accessed 13 March 2022.

*followed with the acknowledgment by Justice of the Peace Philip QUINTON and the recordation by court clerk James R. MORRIS[499]

Liber N, folio 142; 28 February 1790

"Know all men by these presents that I Nathaniel DAVIS of Worcester County in the state of Maryland for an in consideration of the sum of Sixty five pounds current money of Maryland to me in hand paid by Thomas PARKER of the same place I the said Nathaniel DAVIS Hath granted bargained sold and delivered and by these presents doth absolutely grant bargain Sell and deliver unto him the said Thomas PARKER his heirs and assigns forever, a Negro man slave called **Southy** now in the said Parker possession, To have and to hold the said negro man slave called **Southy** unto him the said Thomas PARKER and to his heirs and assigns forever to the only proper use benefit and behoof of him the said Thomas PARKER his heirs and assigns forever, and the said Nathaniel DAVIS for himself his heirs Executors and Administrators will and shall warrant and forever defend the said Negro man Slave called **Southy** against the Right and Title of all and all manner of person and persons whatever unto him the said Thomas PARKER his heirs and assigns forever, of which said Negro I the said Nathaniel have put the said Thomas in full possession by the delivery of these presents. In Witness my hand and seal Seal this 28th day of February Anno Dom[ini] one thousand seven hundred and ninety ~

Signed Sealed & delivered   Philip QUINTON   Nathaniel DAVIS (Seal)
In the presence of   Henry PARKER Jun[io]r"

*followed with the acknowledgment by Justice of the Peace Philip QUINTON and the recordation on 26 February 1790 by court clerk James R. MORRIS[500]

Liber N, folio 168; 04 January 1790

"I William LANE of Worcester County State of Maryland do give grant full and entire Liberty and freedom untill all the negroes I am entitled unto or hold as Slaves and do hereby Manumit and Set absolutely free these now particularly named who all are under fifty years of age and healthy and sound to witt Negroe **Joe** about thirty years of age **Richard** a man under thirty negroe man named **Elijah** **Betty** a negroe woman about fourty five years of age, negro man named **ben**, Negroe man named **Shadrack** both these under thirty years of age Negro woman named **Lydia** about Seventeen years of age **Esther** a woman about Sixteen years of age negro man named **Abner** about forty six years of age, negro woman named **Milla** about Twenty five, and **Middlesex** a young woman about Sixteen years of age, who all being of lawfull age to be free from the day and the younger ones who are underage to witt. The Children of Negro woman named **Joan** who is above fifty years of age. To wit boy **Peter** Born Septem[be]r 7 – 1772, her boy **Isaac** born Novemb[e]r 20 – 1777 her boy **George** born may 17 – 1781. The Children of woman **Betty** to wit boy **Lura** born febr[uar]y 3 – 1782 her girl **Tabitha** Born March 8 – 1778. The Children of Woman **Lydia** to witt her Boy **Kiah** born November 24 – 1781 her girl **Jenny** Born November 3[r]d – 1784 her girl **Betty** about Ten Months old when they shall arrive of Lawfull age to wit. The male at Twenty one and The female at sixteen years of age each and every of them then to be at there own disposal and at Liberty to {?}t for themselves as the first above named ones are this day without the Let Hindrance or Molestation of me or any person or persons claiming or to claim by from or under me forever, In Testimony whereof I have hereunto set my hand and affix my seal this fourth day of the first month in the year Seventeen hundred and ninety 1790   W[illia]m LANE (Seal)

N.B. before the Enseabng and delivery hereof it is noted that no words mentioned in the forepart of this emancipation shall be construed to take away the government of the young ones till they arrive of Lawfull age"

---

[499] Worcester County Court (Land Records). Bill of sale from CHAILLE, Moses to HANDY, William. 11 December 1789. N, p. 105, MSA CE 30-13. www.mdlandrec.net : accessed 13 March 2022.
[500] Worcester County Court (Land Records). Bill of sale from DAVIS, Nathaniel to PARKER, Thomas. 28 February 1790. N, p. 142, MSA CE 30-13. www.mdlandrec.net : accessed 13 March 2022.

*followed with the acknowledgment by Outten STURGIS on 25 February 1790 and the recordation by the court clerk James R. MORRIS on 04 March 1790[501]

Liber N, folios 173-174; 06 March 1790

"Know all men by these presents that I William PARKER of Worcester County in the State of Maryland for and in consideration of the sum of fifty pounds current money of Maryland to me in hand paid by Thomas SMITH Jun[io]^r of the same place the receipt whereof I do hereby confess and acknowledge, Have granted bargained sold and delivered and by these presents doth absolutely bargain and sell and deliver unto him the said Thomas SMITH his heirs and assigns forever, a negro man Slave called **George**, about Twenty one years old now in the possession of the said Thomas SMITH To have and to hold the said negro man slave called **George** unto him the said Thomas SMITH and to his heirs and assigns forever to the only proper use benefit and behoof of him the said Thomas SMITH his heirs and assigns forever, And the said William PARKER, against himself his heirs Executors and Adm[inistrato]^{rs} and against every other person and persons whatever will and shall warrant and forever defend the said Negro man unto the said Thomas SMITH his heirs and assigns forever, of which said Negro man slave called **George** I the said William PARKER have put the said Thomas SMITH in full possession by the delivery of these presents. In Testimony whereof I the said William PARKER to these presents my hand hath set and seal affixed the sixth day of March in the year of our Lord one thousand Seven hundred and Ninety ~

Signed Sealed & Delivered   Philip QUINTON   William PARKER   (Seal)
In Presence of ~"

*followed on folio 174 with the acknowledgment by Justice of the Peace Philip QUINTON and the recordation by court clerk James R. MORRIS[502]

Liber N, folios 175-176; 24 February 1790

"Know all men by these Presents that I Frederick HILL of Somerset County in the State of Maryland For and in Consideration of the sum of ninety Pounds Current money of Maryland to me in hand paid by Levin HILL of Worcester County the receipt whereof I do hereby acknowledge have bargained & Sold and delivered and by these Presents do bargain sell and deliver unto the said Levin HILL one Negro man named **Nathaniel** one Negro woman named **Pink** one Negro woman **Beck** one negro Girl Child named **Lue** and one negro Child called **Henney**. To have and to hold the said bargained negroes and Premisses unto him the said Levin HILL his heirs Executors admin[istrators] or assigns forever and I the said Frederick HILL for myself my Heirs Exe[cutors] or admin[istrators] shall and will warrant and forever defend the above Negroes from and against all Persons claiming the same unto him the said Levin HILL, his Heirs Executors Adm[inistrators] & Assigns in Witness whereof I have hereunto set my hand and Seal this 24th day of February Anno Dom[ini] Seventeen Hundred & Ninety ~

Signed Sealed & Delivered   Frederick HILL   (Seal)
in Presence of ~
John SELBY ~"

*followed on folio 176 with the acknowledgment by Justice of the Peace John SELBY and the recordation on 12 March 1790 by court clerk James R. MORRIS[503]

---

[501] Worcester County Court (Land Records). Deed of manumission from LANE, William to **Joe, Richard, Elijah, Betty, Ben, Shadrack, Lydia, Esther, Abner, Milla, Middlesex, Peter, Isaac, George, Lura, Tabitha, Kiah, Jenny,** and **Betty**. 04 January 1790. N, p. 168, MSA CE 30-13. www.mdlandrec.net : accessed 13 March 2022.
[502] Worcester County Court (Land Records). Bill of sale from PARKER, William to SMITH, Thomas Jr. 06 March 1790. N, pp. 173-174, MSA CE 30-13. www.mdlandrec.net : accessed 13 March 2022.
[503] Worcester County Court (Land Records). Bill of sale from HILL, Frederick to HILL, Levin. 24 February 1790. N, pp. 175-176, MSA CE 30-13. www.mdlandrec.net : accessed 13 March 2022.

Liber N, folios 186-187; 13 March 1790

"Worcester County & State of Maryland Know all men by these presents that I Leah HAMMOND of the County & State aforesaid for and in Consideration of the sum of Twenty pounds current money of Maryland in hand paid before the Sining Sealing and delivery hereof have bargained Sold and delivered and by these Presents do bargain sell and Deliver unto Rachel HAMMOND Daughter of Edward HAMMOND of the County and State aforesaid one Negro garl named **Sal** to her her heirs Exe[cuto]^{rs} adm[inistrato]^{rs} or assigns To have and to hold the Said bargained Premises and I the said Leah Do warr and defend the same from me my heirs Exe[cuto]^{rs} or adm[inistrato]^{rs} and from all other Parsons claiming any right title or interest in said Negro to her her heirs Exe[cuto]^{rs} adm[inistrato]^{rs} or assigns forever In Testamony whereof I have hereunto set my hand and Seal this Thirteenth day of March in the year of our Lord one thousand seven hundred and Ninety ~

Sined Sealed and
Delivered in presents of Test.   Leah X HAMMOND (Seal)
                                                          her
                                                          mark"

*followed on folio 187 with the acknowledgment by Justice of the Peace Purnell JOHNSON and the recordation on 17 March 1790 by court clerk James R. MORRIS[504]

Liber N, folio 199; 13 March 1790

"Maryland Worcester County. Know all men by these presents That I Avery MORGUN of Worcester County in the State of Maryland for and in consideration of the Sum of forty five pounds current money of Maryland, to me in hand paid by Joseph GREEN of the County & State afforesaid at or before the Ensealing & Delivery of these presents, the Receipt whereof, I the said Avery doth hereby acknowledge, & confess myself to be therewith fully satisfied, contented and Paid, Have Bargained, Sold and Delivered & by these presents do fully, clearly & absolutely, Bargain sell & Deliver, unto the said Joseph GREEN, one Negro woman named **Sall**, about twenty five years of age, with her child **Peet** about two years old. To have & to hold the said Negro woman **Sall** & her Child **Peet** about two years old. To have & to hold the said Negro Woman **Sall** & her Child **Peet** to the said Joseph GREEN his Executors Administrators or Assigns to his and their own proper uses & behoofs forever. And I the said Avery MORGAN my heirs Executors and Administrators & every of us the said Negro Woman & child to the said Joseph GREEN his heirs and Assigns against all people shall & will Warrant acquit & forever defend. As witness my hand & Seal the thirteenth day of March Anno Domini 1790.

Sealed & delivered   Avery MORGAN (Seal)
in presence of ~   John POSTLY"

*followed with the acknowledgment by Justice of the Peace John POSTLY and the recordation on 23 March 1790 by court clerk James R. MORRIS[505]

Liber N, folios 201-202; 02 April 1790

"Know all men by these presents that I Peter TOWNSEND of Worcester County in the State of Maryland for and in consideration of the sum of   Current money of Maryland to me in hand paid by Samuel BRADFORD of the Same place at and Before the Seallling and delivery of these presents their upon whereof I do hereby acknowledge have bargained and Sold and by these presents do bargain and Sell unto the said Samuel BRADFORD his heirs and assigns one negro Girl named **Taymor**. To have and to hold the said Gairl **Taymor** unto the said Samuel BRADFORD his heirs and assigns forever to the only proper use benefit and behoof of the said Samuel BRADFORD his heirs and assigns forever to the only proper use benefit and behoof of

---

[504] Worcester County Court (Land Records). Bill of sale from HAMMOND, Leah to HAMMOND, Rachel. 13 March 1790. N, pp. 186-187, MSA CE 30-13. www.mdlandrec.net : accessed 13 March 2022.

[505] Worcester County Court (Land Records). Bill of sale from MORGAN, Avery to GREEN, Joseph. 13 March 1790. N, p. 199, MSA CE 30-13. www.mdlandrec.net : accessed 13 March 2022.

the said Samuel BRADFORD his heirs and assigns forever and not the use or purpos whatsoever and the said Peter TOWNSEND for himself and his heirs doth covenant and agree to and with the said Samuel BRADFORD that he the said Peter TOWNSEND hath a good and Sofficient title to Sell and dispose of the said Nigro gairl **Taymor** so as to convey unto the said Samuel BRADFORD a good Shure and firm title to the same and no other person but the said Peter TOWNSEND hath any right or title to the same in Testimoney whereof the said Peter TOWNSEND his hand to this present hath Set and a Seale affixed this 2nd day of April in the year of our Lord one thousand seven hundred and Ninety ~

Signed Sealed Delivered   John SELBY.   Peter TOWNSEND (Seal)
in the presents of ~"

*followed on folio 202 with the acknowledgment by Justice of the Peace John SELBY and the recordation by court clerk James R. MORRIS[506]

Liber N, folios 214-215; 31 March 1790

"This Indenture made this Thirty first day of March in the year of our Lord one thousand seven hundred and ninety. Between Anna ROBINS of Worcester County in the State of Maryland of the one part and Thomas PARKER of the same place of the other part. Witnesseth that the af[ore]s[ai]^d Anna ROBINS for and in consideration of the sum of fifty pounds current money of the State aforesaid to her in hand paid by the said Thomas at and before the Sealing and delivery hereof the receipt whereof her the said Anna ROBINS doth hereby Acknowledge hath granted bargained and Sold and doth hereby give grant bargain & Sell to the said Thomas PARKER his heirs executors administrators or assigns one Negro Man called **Sothey** that formerly Belonging to Nathaniel DAVIS To have and to hold the abovementioned Negro called **Sothey** to the said Thomas PARKER his heirs or assigns forever to the only proper use and behoof of the said Thomas PARKER his heirs and assigns and no other use or uses Whatsoever In Testimony whereof the said Anna ROBINS hath hereunto Set her hand & Seal the day & year first above written ~

Signed Sealed & Delivered   W[illia]^m PURNELL   Anna ROBINS (Seal)
In presence of ~   John PURNELL"

*followed on folio 215 with the acknowledgment by Justice of the Peace William PURNELL and the recordation on 09 April 1790 by court clerk James R. MORRIS[507]

Liber N, folio 224; 31 March 1790

"This Indenture made this Thirty first day of March in the year of our Lord one Thousand seven hundred and ninety. Between Anna ROBINS of Worcester County in the state of Maryland of the one part and Nathaniel DAVIS of the same place of the other part. Witnesseth that the af[ore]s[ai]^d Anna ROBINS for and in consideration of the sum of Thirty pound specie current money of the state af[ore]s[ai]^d to her in hand paid by the said Nathaniel at and before the sealing and Delivery hereof the recept whereof her the said Anna ROBINS doth hereby acknowledge hath granted bargained and sold and doth hereby give grant bargain & Sell to the said Nathaniel DAVIS his heirs executors administrators or assigns one negro called **George**. To have and to hold the abovementioned negro **George** to the said Nathaniel DAVIS his heirs or assigns forever to the only proper use and behoof of the said Nathaniel DAVIS his heirs and Assigns and no other use or uses whatsoever. In Testimony whereof the said Anna ROBINS hath hereunto set her hand and seal the day & year first above written

---

[506] Worcester County Court (Land Records). Bill of sale from TOWNSEND, Peter to BRADFORD, Samuel. 02 April 1790. N, pp. 201-202, MSA CE 30-13. www.mdlandrec.net : accessed 14 March 2022.

[507] Worcester County Court (Land Records). Bill of sale from ROBINS, Anna to PARKER, Thomas. 31 March 1790. N, pp. 214-215, MSA CE 30-13. www.mdlandrec.net : accessed 14 March 2022.

Signed Sealed & Delivered	W[illia]m PURNELL	Anna ROBINS (Seal)
In Presence of ~	John PURNELL"	

*followed with the acknowledgment by Justice of the Peace William PURNELL and the recordation on 15 April 1790 by court clerk James R. MORRIS[508]

Liber N, folio 239; 27 April 1790

"Ton all whom this present writing shall send greeting I Bartley TOWNSEND of Worcester County in the State of Maryland Know ye that I the said Bartley TOWNSEND for and in Consideration of the natural love and affection which I have to my daughter Rhoda TOWNSEND and also for other good causes and considerations to me hereunto moveing have given granted and by these presents doth give grant and confirm unto the said Rhoda TOWNSEND her heirs and assigns one negro boy named **Ned**. To have and to hold the said Negro boy **Ned** unto the said Rhoda TOWNSEND her heirs and Assigns excepting and reserving to myself the use and Service of the said Negro boy dureing my life, and I do warrant the said Negro boy to my said daughter Rhoda her heirs and Assigns forever, excepting as before excepted In Testimony whereof I the said Bartley TOWNSEND to these presents my hand have set and Seal affixed the 27th day of April anno 1790. ~

Signed Sealed and delivered		Bartley TOWNSEND (Seal)
in presents of ~	Josiah MITCHELL."	

*followed with the acknowledgment by Josiah MITCHELL and the recordation by court clerk James R. MORRIS[509]

Liber N, folios 239-240; 04 April 1790

"Know all men by these presents that I Littleton ROBINS in consideration of the sum of three hundred and fifty pounds to me in hand paid by Edward VANDOME at or before the ensealing and Delivery of these presents the receipt and delivery whereof said Littleton ROBINS doth hereby acknowledge Have bargained Sold, released granted and Confirmed, and by these presents Do bargain, Sell, release, grant & Confirm unto the said Edward VANDOME all those Parcel of Negro Slaves, namely **Isaac Tamer** & her eight children Viz: **Levi, Adam, Sarah, Sue, Rachael, Will Flora & Leah** To have and to hold all and Singular the said Negroes and every of them by these presents bargained, sold, released granted & Confirmed unto the only proper use and behoof of the said Edward VANDOME his Executors administrators and assigns forever freely quietly peaceably & intirely without any contradictions, Claim disturbance or hindrance of any Person whatsoever and without any account to me or to any other whatsoever to be made, answered or hereafter to be rendered so that neither I the said Littleton ROBINS nor any other for me or in my name any Right Interest or demand of in to or for the said Negro Slaves or any part or parcel thereof ought to exact challenge Claim or demand at any time or times hereafter : but from all action Right Estate Title claim demand possession and Interest thereof shall be wholly barred and excluded by force & virtue of these presents and I the said Littleton ROBINS for myself my Executors and Administrators all and singular the said Negro Slaves unto the said Edward VANDOME his Executors administrators and assigns and against all and every other Person or Persons whatsoever shall and will warrant and forever defend these presents In Witness whereof I have hereunto set my hand & Seal this Fourth day of April One thousand seven hundred & ninety ~

Sealed & Delivered		Littleton ROBINS (Seal)
in the Presence of	W[illia]m PURNELL"	

---

[508] Worcester County Court (Land Records). Bill of sale from ROBINS, Anna to DAVIS, Nathaniel. 31 March 1790. N, p. 224, MSA CE 30-13. www.mdlandrec.net : accessed 14 March 2022.

[509] Worcester County Court (Land Records). Bill of sale from TOWNSEND, Bartley to TOWNSEND, Rhoda. 27 April 1790. N, p. 239, MSA CE 30-13. www.mdlandrec.net : accessed 14 March 2022.

*followed on folio 240 with the acknowledgment by Justice of the Peace William PURNELL on 10 April 1790 and the recordation by court clerk James R. MORRIS[510]

Liber N, folio 241; 28 April 1790

"To all whom these presents may Concern, Whereas I believe it is unjust to hold people in Slavery do by these presents manumit and sett free one negro girl called **Tinna** about the age of fourteen years her freedom to commence at the age of Sixteen and do by these presents for myself and heirs relinquish all my right title and interest to the af[ore]s[ai]d Negro (at the age af[ore]s[ai]d" for ever agreeable to an act of Assembly in such Cases made and provided for the manumission of Slaves In Testimony whereof I have here unto set my hand and affixed my seal the 28th day of April A[nno] Dom[ini] 1790.

Signed & Sealed In Presence of   John SELBY   John JOHNSON   (Seal)"

*followed with the acknowledgment and recordation by John SELBY & James R. MORRIS[511]

Liber N, folio 247; 22 April 1790

"Know all men by these presents that I Samuel PARKER of Samuel for and in consideration of the Sum of Five pounds current money of maryland to me in hand paid by John BALL before the sealing hereof have bargained and sold & by these presents doth bargain and sell unto the said John BALL one negro man named **Sampson** being the Same negro man as was formerly in the possession of John BALL father of the abovenamed John BALL, and I Samuel PARKER for myself and my heirs doth hereby warrant & forever defend the aforesaid Negro man called **Sampson** against the lawfull claim of all manner of person or persons that shall ever claim him the said Negro **Sampson** for by or under me or my heirs unto the said John BALL his heirs and assigns forever. In Testimoney whereof the said Samuel PARKER to these presents his hand hath set and seal affixed the 22nd day of April Anno Domini 1790

Signed & Seald in   Samuel PARKER   (Seal)
Present of   Philip QUINTON"

*followed with the acknowledgment by Philip QUINTON and the recordation on 04 May 1790 by court clerk James R. MORRIS[512]

Liber N, folios 249-249; 26 April 1790

"State of Maryland Worcester County. Know all men by these presents that I Henry Johnson WILLETT for and in Consideration of Twenty nine pounds ten Shillings to me in hand paid the receipt whereof I do hereby acknowledge have granted bargained and sold and by these presents do Bargain and Sell unto John McLURE of Baltimore Town one negro Boy by the name of **Davy** about seven years old, one red Cow and Earling about four years old one pide Bull to be delivered to the said John McLURE when call[e]d on or to this order the above negro boy to be delivered to the said John McLURE or his order on or before the first day of October next. To have and to hold the abovementioned articles to him his heirs and assigns forever, and I the said Henry Johnson WILLETT, will warrant and forever defend the said John McLURE the above articles, from me myself my Heirs Executors or administrators or any other person or persons Claiming any right or Title under me. In Testimoney whereof I have sett my hand and affixed my seal this Twenty six day of April one thousand seven hundred and ninety. ~

---

[510] Worcester County Court (Land Records). Bill of sale from ROBINS, Littleton to VANDOME, Edward. 04 April 1790. N, pp. 239-240, MSA CE 30-13. www.mdlandrec.net : accessed 14 March 2022.
[511] Worcester County Court (Land Records). Deed of manumission from JOHNSON, John to **Tinna**. 28 April 1790. N, p. 241, MSA CE 30-13. www.mdlandrec.net : accessed 14 March 2022.
[512] Worcester County Court (Land Records). Bill of sale from PARKER, Samuel to BALL, John. 22 April 1790. N, p. 247, MSA CE 30-13. www.mdlandrec.net : accessed 14 March 2022.

Sing[d] Sealed and delivered Henry J. WILLETT (Seal)
In the presence of "

*followed on folio 249 with the acknowledgment by Justice of the Peace Philip QUINTON and the recordation on 04 May 1790 by court clerk James R. MORRIS[513]

Liber N, folios 300-301; 15 October 1790

"Worcester Sc[t]. Know all men by these Presents that I Thomas MARTIN Senior of the County af[ore]s[ai]d and State of Maryland for and in consideration of the sum of five hundred Pounds to me in hand Paid by Thomas MARTIN my son the receipt whereof I do hereby acknowledge have bargained and sold and by these Presents do bargain and sell unto the said Thomas MARTIN his heirs and Assigns forever the following negroes Viz. **Easter, Hannah, Rhoda, Leah, Price, Dennis, Rohoda, Priscilla, Tabitha, John, Bersheba, Nancy, Grace, Betty, Isaac,** with all and singular their increase. To have and to hold the af[ore]s[ai]d negroes with their increase unto the said Thomas MARTIN his heirs and Assigns forever to the only Proper use & behoof of the said Thomas MARTIN his heirs and assigns forever & to no other intent or Purpose whatsoever. And I do hereby covenant to and with the af[ore]s[ai]d Thomas MARTIN the af[ore]s[ai]d Negroes with their increase against the right title and claim of every Person & Persons whatever forever to warrant & defend. In Testimony whereof I have hereto Set my hand & Seal affixed this fifteenth day of October 1790 ~

Isaac MARSHALL. Thomas MARTIN (Seal)"

*followed on folio 301 with the acknowledgment by Isaac MARSHALL and the recordation by court clerk James R. MORRIS[514]

Liber N, folios 304-305; 12 July 1790

"Know all men by these Presents that I Margraet FASSITT of Worcester County in the State of Maryland for and in consideration of the sum of one hundred and fifty Pounds current money to me in hand Paid by Joshua MITCHELL (surveyor) of the County af[ore]s[ai]d Have bargained sold, released, granted, and confirmed, and by these Presents do bargain sell release grant and confirm unto the said Joshua MITCHELL one Negro woman called **Leb** and her child called **Comfort** and one negro boy called **Edmond**, and one yoke of oxen, and three cowes and calves. To have and to hold all and singular the three aforesaid Negroes and Cattle and every of them by these Presents bargained sold released, granted and confirmed unto the only Proper use and behoof of him the said Joshua MITCHELL his heirs Executors administrators and Assigns forever freely quietly Peaceably and intirely without any contradiction claim Disturbance or hindrance of any Person whatsoever and without any account to me or to any other whatsoever to be made answered, or hereafter to be rendered, so that neither I the said Margaret FASSETT nor any other for me or in my name have any right Title Interest or demand of in to or for the said Cattle and negroes or any Part or Parcel thereof ought to exact challenge, claim or demand at any time or Times here afterwards but from all xctions rights estate Title claim Demand Possession and Interest thereof shall be wholy barred and excluded by force and virtue of these Presents And I the said Margraet FASSITT for myself my Executors and Administrators all and singular the said Negroes unto the said Joshua MITCHELL his Executors administrators and assigns and against all and every other Person or Persons whatsoever shall and will warrant and forever defend by these Presents In Witness whereof I have hereunto set my hand and seal affixed this 12[th] day of July Anno Dom[ini] 1790. ~

Sign[e]d Seal[e]d & Deliv[ere]d Josiah MITCHELL Margaret FASSITT (Seal)
In the Presence off ~ Mary MURRAY"

---

[513] Worcester County Court (Land Records). Bill of sale from WILLETT, Henry Johnson to McLURE, John. 26 April 1790. N, pp. 248-249, MSA CE 30-13. www.mdlandrec.net : accessed 14 March 2022.
[514] Worcester County Court (Land Records). Bill of sale from MARTIN, Thomas Sr. to MARTIN, Thomas. 15 October 1790. N, pp. 300-301, MSA CE 30-13. www.mdlandrec.net : accessed 14 March 2022.

*followed on folio 305 with the acknowledgment by Justice of the Peace Josiah MITCHELL and the recordation on 16 July 1790 by court clerk James R. MORRIS[515]

Liber N, folios 318-319; 28 July 1790

"Know all men by these Presents that I Stanton ADKINS of Worcester County in the State of Maryland for and in consideration of the sum of Sixty Pounds current money of maryland to me in hand Paid by Abijah DAVIS of the County and State af[ore]s[ai]^d Have bargained sold released granted and confirmed and by these Presents do bargain sell release Grant & Confirm unto the said Abijah DAVIS one Negro Man called **Shepard**. To have and to hold the said Negro Man called **Shepard** by these Presents bargained sold released granted and confirmed unto the only Proper use and behoof of him the said Abijah DAVIS his heirs Executors administrators and Assigns forever freely Quietly Peaceably and Intirely without any contradiction claim disturbance or hindrance of any Person Whatsoever so that neither I the said Stanton ADKINS nor any other for me or in my name have any right title claim Interest or demand of in to or for the said Negro Man **Shepard** {?} any Part or Parcel thereof ought to exact challenge Claime or Demand at any time or times hereafter, but from all actions right Estate Title Claim Demand Possession and Interest thereof shall be wholly barred and excluded by virtue and force of these Presents and I the said Stanton ADKINS for myself my Heirs Executors and Administrators the aforesaid negro man **Shepard** unto the said Abijah DAVIS his Executors Administrators and Assigns & against every other Person or Persons whatsoever shall & will Warrant and forever defend by these Presents In Witness whereof I have hereunto Set my hand and Seal affixed this Twenty eight day of July Anno Dom[ini] 1790 ~

Sign^{ed} Seal[e]^d & Deliv[ere]^d Josiah MITCHELL   Stanton ADKINS   (Seal)
In the Presence of   Isaac MITCHELL"

*followed on folio 319 with the acknowledgment by Justice of the Peace Josiah MITCHELL and the recordation on 11 August 1790 by court clerk James R. MORRIS[516]

Liber N, folios 245-346; 16 August 1790

"State of Maryland Worcester County Ss^t. Know all men by these Presents that I Stanton ADKINS of Worcester County for and in consideration of the Sum of forty five Pounds current money of Maryland to me in hand Paid by John ADKINS of the County af[ore]s[ai]^d Have bargained sold released granted and Confirmed by these presents do bargain sell release and confirm unto the said John ADKINS one Negro Woman called **Belender** and her two twin children about a fornet old. To have and to hold the three aforesaid Negroes and every of them by these Presents bargained, sold, released, granted, and confirmed unto the only Proper use and behoof of him the said John ADKINS his heirs Executors administrators and Assigns forever, freely, quietly Peaceably intirely, without any contradiction claim or Hindrance of any Person whatsoever so that neither I the said Stanton ADKINS nor any other Person for me, or in my name, any Right Title, Interest or demand of in, to or for the said Negro woman and her two children or any part thereof ought to claim or demand at any time or times hereafter, but from all action right, estate, Title, claim, Demand and Interest thereof shall be wholly barred and excluded by Vertue of those Presents, And I the said Stanton ADKINS for myself my heirs executors and Administrators the three aforesaid Negroes unto the said John ADKINS his heirs Executors, administrators and assigns and against all and every other Person or Persons whatsoever, shall and will warrant and forever defend by these Presents. In Witness whereof I have hereunto set my hand and seal this 16 day of August Anno Domini one thousand Seven hundred and ninety ~ ~

---

[515] Worcester County Court (Land Records). Bill of sale from FASSITT, Margaret to MITCHELL, Joshua. 12 July 1790. N, pp. 304-305, MSA CE 30-13. www.mdlandrec.net : accessed 14 March 2022.
[516] Worcester County Court (Land Records). Bill of sale from ADKINS, Stanton to DAVIS, Abijah. 28 July 1790. N, pp. 318-319, MSA CE 30-13. www.mdlandrec.net : accessed 14 March 2022.

Signed sealed & Delivered   Stanton ADKINS   (Seal)
In the Presence of.   Purnell JOHNSON. ~"

*followed on folio 346 with the acknowledgment by Justice of the Peace Purnell JOHNSON and the recordation on 28 September 1790 by court clerk James R. MORRIS[517]

* "fornet" likely means fortnight

Liber N, folio 347; 08 October 1790

"Maryland Ss. To all whome these Presents shall come greeting I Zadoc ENNIS in the State of Maryland for divers good causes and considerations me thereunto moving do hereby declare free Manumit and enfranchise the Negroe following to wit **Benjamin** aged forty and four to be free on the first day of November in the year of our Lord One thousand seven hundred and ninety **Sarah** aged twelve years to be free on the second day of March in the year of our lord one thousand seven hundred and ninety Six hereby acknowledging the said negroes discharged from all claim of Servis and right of Property Whatever from me my heirs executors or Administrators as Witness my hands and seal this eighth day of October in the year of our Lord one thousand seven hundred and Ninety.

Witness. Philip QUINTON.   Zadok ENNIS   (Seal)"

*followed with the acknowledgment by Justice of the Peace Philip QUINTON and the recordation by court clerk James R. MORRIS[518]

Liber N, folios 347-348; 08 October 1790

"Maryland Ss. To all whom these Presents shall come greeting I William FOOKS of the County of Worcester in the State of Maryland for divers good causes and considerations me thereunto moving do hereby declare free manumit and enfranchise the Negroes following to wit **Hager** aged Thirty five to be free on the first day of November in year of our Lord one thousand seven hundred and ninety **Eben** aged fourteen to be free on December the fifteenth day one thousand seven hundred and Ninety seven hereby acknowledging the said Negroes discharged from all Claim of Service and right of Property Whatever from me my heirs executors or Administrators as witness my hand and seal this eighth day of October in the year of our Lord One thousand seven hundred and ninety

Witness. Philip QUINTON.   William FOOKS   (Seal)"

*followed with the acknowledgment by Justice of the Peace Philip QUINTON and the recordation by court clerk James R. MORRIS[519]

Liber N, folio 358; 20 April 1788

"Received April the 20th day 1788 of Ellinor GUTHERY the sum of Seven Pounds ten Shillings being in full Satisfaction for one Negro Woman Sold her Called **Leah** in Testimony Whereof I have hereunto sett my hand this day and year above Written.   James SELBY"

*followed with the recordation 30 November 1790 by court clerk James R. MORRIS[520]

---

[517] Worcester County Court (Land Records). Bill of sale from ADKINS, Stanton to ADKINS, John. 16 July 1790. N, pp. 345-346, MSA CE 30-13. www.mdlandrec.net : accessed 15 March 2022.

[518] Worcester County Court (Land Records). Deed of manumission from ENNIS, Zadok to **Benjamin** and **Sarah**. 08 October 1790. N, p. 347, MSA CE 30-13. www.mdlandrec.net : accessed 15 March 2022.

[519] Worcester County Court (Land Records). Deed of manumission from FOOKS, William to **Hager** and **Eben**. 08 October 1790. N, pp. 347-348, MSA CE 30-13. www.mdlandrec.net : accessed 15 March 2022.

[520] Worcester County Court (Land Records). Receipt from SELBY, James to GUTHERY, Ellinor. 20 April 1788. N, p. 358, MSA CE 30-13. www.mdlandrec.net : accessed 15 March 2022.

Liber N, folio 365; 24 August 1790

"Maryland Ss. To all whome these presents shall come greeting I James MARTIN of Worcester County in the State of Maryland for divers good causes and considerations me thereunto moveing do hereby declare free Manumit and Enfranchise the negroes following to witt **Stephen** and **Sebb** to be free on this day. I do hereby acknowledge the said Negroes discharged from all claim of service and right of property whatever from me my heirs Executors or Administrators as witness my hand and Seal this 24th day of August in the year of our Lord one thousand one thousand seven hundred and ninety ~

Witness   Philip QUINTON   James MARTIN   (Seal)"

*followed with the acknowledgment by Justice of the Peace Philip QUINTON and the recordation by court clerk James R. MORRIS[521]

Liber N, folios 368-369; 16 October 1790

"Worcester Sst. Know all men by these presents that I William TURPIN of the County af[ore]s[ai]d in the State of Maryland for and in consideration of the Sum of thirty pounds to me in hand paid by Thomas MARTIN have bargained and Sold and by these presents Do bargain and Sell unto the said Thomas MARTIN his heirs and Assigns for Ever one Negro Girle called **Easter** to have and to hold the aforesaid bargened and Sold negro unto the said Thomas MARTIN his heirs and Assigns for ever in Testamoney whereof I have hereto Set and hand and Seal this 16th day of October 1790 ~

Sign[e]d Seal[e]d & delivered   William TURPIN   (Seal)
in presence off   Philip QUINTON"

*followed with the acknowledgment by Justice of the Peace Philip QUINTON and the recordation on 29 October 1790 by court clerk James R. MORRIS[522]

Liber N, folios 375-376; 29 October 1790

"State of Maryland Worcester Ss. Know all men by these presents that I Sarah MEARS of Worcester County in the State af[ore]s[ai]d for and in consideration of the sum of twenty pounds current money of Maryland to me in hand paid by Purnell JOHNSON of the County af[ore]s[ai]d have bargained sold released granted and confirmed and by these presents do bargain sell release and confirm unto the said Purnell JOHNSON one Negro Gairl called **Dinah** about Seven years old to have and to hold the afores[ai]d Negro by these presents bargained sold released granted and confirmed unto the Ondly proper use and behoof of him the s[ai]d Purnell JOHNSON his heirs Executors Administrators and Assigns for ever freely quietly intirely without any Contradiction claim of hindrance of any person whatsoever so that Neithe I the s[ai]d Sarah MEARS nor any other Person for me in my name any Right Title Intrust or deemed of in or to the said Negro Gairl or any part thereof ought to claim or demand at any time or times here after but from all the Action Right Estate title Claime demand intrust thereof shall be wholly barred and excluded by virtue of these presents and I the s[ai]d Sarah MEARE for myself my heirs Executor Administrators the afores[ai]d Negro unto the s[ai]d Purnell JOHNSON his heirs Executors Admin[istrators] and Assigns and against all and every other person or persons whatsoever shall & will warrant and forever defend by these presents In Witness whereof I have here unto Set my hand and Seal this 29th day of October Anno D[o]m[in]i One thousand Seven hundred & ninety. ~

---

[521] Worcester County Court (Land Records). Deed of manumission from MARTIN, James to **Stephen** and **Sebb**. 24 August 1790. N, p. 365, MSA CE 30-13. www.mdlandrec.net : accessed 15 March 2022.
[522] Worcester County Court (Land Records). Bill of sale from TURPIN, William to MARTIN, Thomas. 16 October 1790. N, pp. 368-369, MSA CE 30-13. www.mdlandrec.net : accessed 15 March 2022.

		her	
Sined Sealed & delivered		Sarah + MEARS	(Seal)
In Presents of ~		mark"	
John P. MITCHELL			

*followed with the acknowledgment by Justice of the Peace John P. MITCHELL and the recordation on 03 November 1790 by court clerk James R. MORRIS[523]

Liber N, folios 384-385; 09 November 1790

"To all persons To whom these presents shall come Know ye that I James TREHORN of Worcester County in the State of Maryland being desirous to Manumit and Set free in the manner and form following the several Negroes (Slaves) hereafter mentioned Viz^t. A negro woman Slave called **Rhoda** and her four Children named as follows Viz^t. **Soloman**, aged nine years, **Nathan** aged Six years, **Priscilla** aged three years and nine Months, and **Elijah** aged one year and three Months For and in consideration of the faithful Service of the said Negro Woman Slave called **Rhoda** by her done and performed I the said James TRAHERN do by these presents give grant, Manumit and Set free the said Nego's (Slaves) as above mentioned viz **Rhoda** and her four children **Solomon**, **Nathan**, **Priscilla**, and **Elijah** Severally And that the freedom of the said Negro Woman Slave called **Rhoda** shall commence and take effect immediately after the Execution of these presents and that the freedom of the said **Solomon**, **Nathan**, & **Elijah** the Male Children of the said Negro Woman Slave called **Rhoda** shall commence and take effect immediately after they Severally arrive to the age of twenty three years And that the said **Priscilla** the female child of the said Negro woman Slave called **Rhoda** shall commence and take effect immediately after she arrives at the age of Eighteen years To have and to hold and freely enjoy unto them the said Negroes Viz^t. **Rhoda**, **Solomon**, **Nathan**, **Priscilla** and **Elijah** negro Slaves Severally their and each of their freedom & Liberty for ever immediately after the several times above mentioned agreeable to the Tenor of this Instrument of writing as is above expressed in full and ample manner without any let hindrance Molestation control or authority of any Person or Persons whatever In Testimony whereof I the said James TREHERN have to these presents set my hand & affixed my Seal this Ninth day of November Anno Dom[ini] One thousand seven hundred & ninety.

Signed Sealed & delivered   James TRAHERN (Seal)
In presence of . . ~ Philip QUINTON"

*followed with the acknowledgment by Justice of the Peace Philip QUINTON and the recordation by court clerk James R. MORRIS[524]

Liber N, folios 393-394; 17 December 1790

"Worcester Sc^t. Know all men by these presents that I Thomas MARTIN Sen[ior] of the County aforesaid in the State of Maryland for and in consideration of the Sum of Seventy pounds to me in hand paid by George MARTIN have bargained Sold and by these presents do bargain and Sell unto the said George MARTIN his heirs and Assigns forever the following Negroes to wit **Belitha**, **Nathaniel** and **Dinah** to have and to hold the aforesaid bargened and Sold Negroes unto the said George MARTIN his heirs and Assigns forever in Testimony whereof I have hereto Set my hand Seal this 17th day of December 1790

Signed Sealed & delivered in presence of   Thomas MARTIN (Seal)
Isaac MARSHALL"

---

[523] Worcester County Court (Land Records). Bill of sale from MEARS, Sarah to JOHNSON, Purnell. 29 October 1790. N, pp. 375-376, MSA CE 30-13. www.mdlandrec.net : accessed 15 March 2022.

[524] Worcester County Court (Land Records). Deed of manumission from TRAHERN, James to **Rhoda**, **Solomon**, **Nathan**, **Priscilla**, and **Elijah**. 09 November 1790. N, pp. 384-385, MSA CE 30-13. www.mdlandrec.net : accessed 15 March 2022.

*followed on folio 394 with the acknowledgment by Justice of the Peace Isaac MARSHALL and the recordation on 24 December 1790 by court clerk James R. MORRIS[525]

Liber N, folios 394-395; 14 December 1790

"Worcester County State of Maryland, Know all men by the presents that I Marthew Purnell DAVIS of Worcester County in the State of Maryland for and in consideration of the Sum of Sixty pounds current money of Maryland to me in hand paid at or before the Sealing and delivering hereof by the aforesaid Anne ROBINS of the County and State af[ore]s[ai]^d the Receipt hereof will show I do hereby acknowledge that I have Sold and by these presents do bargain and Sell unto the aforesaid Anna ROBINS two Negroes one woman called **Mary** one Girl **Hannah** to have and to hold the said Negroes forever And I the said Matthew Purnell DAVIS do for myself my heirs Executors Administrators or Sassigns bargain and have Sold the af[ore]s[ai]^d Negros unto the said Anna ROBINS her heirs Executors Administrators or Assigns and do shall and will against all and every Person or Persons whatsoever forever warrant & Defend the said Bargained Negroes and I the said DAVIS have put the af[ore]s[ai]^d Anna ROBINS in full possession by delivering her the af[ore]s[ai]^d Negro Woman and Girl as Witness my hand Seal this the fourteenth day of December Anno Dom[ini] one thousand Seven hundred and ninety
Sign[e]d Seal[e]d & delivered in presence of us   Mathew Purnell DAVIS   (Seal)
W[illia]^m PURNELL"

*followed on folio 395 with the acknowledgment by Justice of the Peace William PURNELL and the recordation on 24 December 1790 by court clerk James R. MORRIS[526]

Liber N, folio 402; 24 November 1790

"Know all men by these presents that I Sarah SELBY of Worcester County in the State of Maryland for and in consideration of the Sum of Sixty pounds current money of Maryland to me in hand paid by William SELBY Junior and John SELBY both of the County and State aforesaid have granted bargained and Sold unto the s[ai]^d William & John all my Right, Title & Interest which I have in the following Negroes Viz One Negro Woman named **Leah** unto John his heirs & Assigns forever One Negro Boy named **Isaac** unto the said William his heirs and Assigns forever To have & to hold the s[ai]^d Negroes as above directed unto him the s[ai]^d William & John their heirs and Assigns for ever from her the s[ai]^d Sarah and from every other person claiming by from or under her unto them the s[ai]^d William and John their heirs and Assigns for ever provided nevertheless the s[ai]^d William and John is not to have the Labour or possession of the said Negroes af[ore]s[ai]^d untill after the death of the s[ai]^d Sarah and then to be at the disposal of the said William an John their Heirs and Assigns forever In Witness and Confirmation whereof the s[ai]^d Sarah to this present writing her hand and Seal hath Set this twenty fourth day of November Anno Dom[ini] Seventeen hundred ninety

Singned Sealed and delivered
in presence of ~ ~   Sarah H SELBY   (Seal)
Isaac MARSHALL   her mark"

*followed with the acknowledgment by Justice of the Peace Isaac MARSHALL and the recordation on 07 January 1790 by court clerk James R. MORRIS[527]

Liber N, folios 409-410; 13 January 1791

"Know all men by these presents that I Ezekiel COSTON of Worcester County in the State of Maryland for divers Causes and considerations me thereunto moving have by these presents

---

[525] Worcester County Court (Land Records). Bill of sale from MARTIN, Thomas Sr. to MARTIN, George. 17 December 1790. N, pp. 393-394, MSA CE 30-13. www.mdlandrec.net : accessed 15 March 2022.
[526] Worcester County Court (Land Records). Bill of sale from DAVIS, Mathew Purnell to ROBINS, Anna. 14 December 1790. N, pp. 394-395, MSA CE 30-13. www.mdlandrec.net : accessed 15 March 2022.
[527] Worcester County Court (Land Records). Bill of sale from SELBY, Sarah to SELBY, William Jr. and SELBY, John. 24 November 1790. N, p. 402, MSA CE 30-13. www.mdlandrec.net : accessed 15 March 2022.

Emancipate and Set free and by these presents do Emancipate and Set free the following named Negroes to be at perfect Liberty and freedom from me or my heirs at the Stated times and ages herein after mentioned Viz^t One negro woman named **Hagar** to be free immediately from the date hereof. One Negro Girl named **Sophia** ten years old to be free at Sixteen years old One Negro Boy named **Robert** three years old to be free at the age of twenty one years One negro boy named **Sam** one year old next March to be free at twenty one years of age And whereas I have a Riversion or Right in the following named Negroes after the death of my Mother Rebecca COSTON I do hereby Emancipate and Set free also in the following manner that is to Say one Negro Man named **Derry** twenty years old to be free at the age of twenty one years if my Mother should then be deceased but if she then lives to be free at her death one negro Boy named **Jacob** fourteen years old to be free at twenty years old or if my Mother then lives to be free at her death all which Negros I do hereby set free at the ages above expressed according to their present ages above expressed and they being able Bodied and of Sufficient understanding to get their own living by their Honest Labour In testimony whereof I have hereunto Set my hand and fixed my Seal this thirteenth day of January in the year of our Lord God Seventeen hundred and ninety one

Sealed and delivered   Ezekiel COSTON   (Seal)
in presents of" ...
"Philip QUINTON   Sam[ue]^l SMITH"

*followed on folio 410 with the acknowledgment by Justice of the Peace Philip QUINTON and the recordation on 17 January 1791 by court clerk James R. MORRIS[528]

Liber N, folio 413; 28 January 1791

"Worcester County Ss^t. State of Maryland Know all men by these presents that I Zadok STURGIS of the County aforesaid for and in consideration of the Sum of thirty pounds of good and Lawfull money of the County af[ore]s[ai]^d to me in hand paid by Thomas COTTINGHAM at and before the Sealing and delivery of these presents the Receipt whereof he doth agree and hath hereby bargained and Sold one Negro Boy called **Jack** unto the said Thomas COTTINGHAM and to his heirs and Assigns forever to have and to hold the aforesaid Negro Boy called **Jack** unto him the said Thomas COTTINGHAM and to his heirs and Assigns forever and the said Zadok STURGIS for himself and his heirs Executors and Administrators and every of them do Covenant promise and grant that he the said Thomas COTTINGHAM for himself and his heirs shall and may from time to time and at all times for ever hereafter have hold and possess the above bargained and Sold Negro Boy called **Jack** which said Negro was purchased by said STURGIS of said COTTINGHAM aforesaid and every part thereof without any let or hinder of him the said Zadok STURGIS or any other person or persons claiming any Right title or property of in or to the af[ore]s[ai]^d Negro Boy called **Jack** or any part thereof from by or under him In Witness whereof I the said Zadok STURGIS have hereunto my hand Sett and Seal Efixed this 28 day of January Anno Domini Seventeen hundred and Ninety one ~

Signed Sealed and delivered   Zadok STURGIS   (Seal)
In presence of ~
Philip QUINTON"

*followed with the acknowledgment by Justice of the Peace Philip QUINTON and the recordation by court clerk James R. MORRIS[529]

---

[528] Worcester County Court (Land Records). Deed of manumission from COSTON, Ezekiel to **Hagar**, **Sophia**, **Robert**, **Sam**, **Derry**, and **Jacob**. 13 January 1791. N, pp. 409-410, MSA CE 30-13. www.mdlandrec.net : accessed 15 March 2022.

[529] Worcester County Court (Land Records). Bill of sale from STURGIS, Zadok to COTTINGHAM, Thomas. 28 January 1791. N, p. 413, MSA CE 30-13. www.mdlandrec.net : accessed 15 March 2022.

Liber N, folios 415-416; 04 February 1791

"Maryland Ss. To all whom these presents shall come greeting I Valentine DENNIS of Worster County in the State of Maryland for divers good Causes and considerations me thereto moving do hereby declare free manumit and Enfranchise the Negros following to wit Negro woman **Ann** to be free from this day. Negro girl **Hannah** aged eleven years to be free at the age of twenty one years Negro Child **Priss** aged eight years to be free at the age of thirty one years Negro Child **Leah** aged five years to be free at the age of thirty one years those Negroes above named are to be and Shall be absolutely free at the ages above mentioned hereby acknowledgeing the said Negroes to be discharges from all claim of Service and right of property whatsoever from me my heirs Ex[ecuto]^{rs} or Adm[inistrator]^s as Witness my hand and Seal this fourth day of February in the year of our Lord One thousand Seven hundred and Ninety One

Valentine DENNIS   (Seal)"

*followed with the acknowledgment by Justice of the Peace Philip QUINTON and the recordation on folio 416 by court clerk James R. MORRIS[530]

Liber N, folio 416; 01 February 1791

"Know all men by these presents that I Ebenezer HANDY of Somerset County State of Maryland for and in consideration of the Sum of forty five pounds current money of Maryland to me in hand paid at and before the Sealing and delivery of these presents by McKimmey PORTER of the County af[ore]s[ai]^d the Receipt whereof I do hereby acknowledge have bargained and sold and by these presents do bargain and Sell unto the said McKimmey PORTER one Negro Boy named **George** To have and to hold the said Negro Boy by these presents bargained and Sold unto the said McKimmey PORTER his heirs Executors Administrators and Assigns forever and I the said Ebenezer HANDY for myself my Heirs Executors and Administrators the said Negro Boy unto the said McKimmey PORTER his Heirs Executors Administrators and Assigns against me the said Ebenezer HANDY my Heirs Executors and Administrators and against all and every other Person or Persons whatsoever shall and will warrant and forever defend firmly by these presents In Witness whereof I the said Ebenezer HANDY to these presents my hand have Set and Seal affixed the 1st day of February Anno Dom[ini] Seventeen hundred and Ninety One

Signed Sealed and delivered   Ebenezer HANDY   (Seal)
in the presents of
Will: STONE"

*followed with the acknowledgment by Justice of the Peace Will: STONE and the recordation on 05 February 1791 by court clerk James R. MORRIS[531]

Liber N, folio 425; 29 January 1791

"State of Maryland Worcester County Know all men by these Presents that I Nancy CORD of Worcester County in the State of Maryland for and in consideration of the sum of Thirty Pounds current money of Maryland to me in hand Paid by William CORD of the Place afforesaid at or upon the ensealing and delivery of these Presents, wherewith I confess myself fully sattisfied contented & Paid. Have bargained sold and delivered and by these presents do fully clearly & absolutely bargain sell and deliver unto the said William CORD one Negro boy about Sixteen years old, named **Jame**, To have and to hold Negro boy **Jame** to the said William CORD his Executors, administrators or Assigns, To his and their own Proper uses & behoofs forever, and I the said Nancy CORD my heirs Executors & administrators and every of us the said Negro boy **Jame** to the said William CORD his heirs and Assigns, against all People shall & will

---

[530] Worcester County Court (Land Records). Deed of manumission from DENNIS, Valentine to **Ann**, **Hannah**, **Priss**, and **Leah**. 04 February 1791. N, pp. 415-416, MSA CE 30-13. www.mdlandrec.net : accessed 15 March 2022.
[531] Worcester County Court (Land Records). Bill of sale from HANDY, Ebenezer to PORTER, McKimmey. 01 February 1791. N, p. 416, MSA CE 30-13. www.mdlandrec.net : accessed 15 March 2022.

warrant acquit and forever defend by these Presents In Witness whereof I have hereunto set my hand & Seal affixed the 29th day of January Anno Domini 1791.

Sealed and Delivered   John POSTLY   Ann CORD ~ (Seal)
in the Presence of."

*followed with the acknowledgment by magistrate John POSTLY on 29 January 1791 and the recordation by court clerk James R. MORRIS on 11 February 1791 [532]

Liber N, folios 432-433; 07 January 1791

"To all people to whom these presents shall come I Daniel MELSON Sen[io]r of Worcester County States of Maryland do send Greeting Know ye that I the said Daniel MELSON of the County and State aforesaid for and in consideration of the love, Good Will and affection which I have and bear towards my loving Grand Daughter Sarah ADKINS wife of Joseph ADKINS of the County and States af[oresai]d have given and granted and by these presents do freely give and grant unto the said Sarah ADKINS and to her heirs forever One Negro Girl named **Tempy**, about four years old : of which (before the signing of these presents) I have delivered her the said Sarah ADKINS with my own hand To have and to hold the said Negro Gairl from henceforth as her and her Heirs property absolutely without any manner of condition In Witness whereof I have hereunto put my hand Seal this Seventh day of January in the year of one thousand Seven hundred and ninety one & in the fifteenth year of Independance. ~

Signed Sealed and delivered
in the presence of. ~   Daniel his X MELSON (Seal)
Purnell JOHNSON ~   mark"

*followed on folio 433 with the acknowledgment by Justice of the Peace Purnell JOHNSON and the recordation on 15 February 1791 by court clerk James R. MORRIS [533]

Liber N, folios 433-434; 11 January 1791

"Know all men by these presents that I William BRUENTON of the County of Worcester in the State of Maryland for and in consideration of the Sum of fifty pounds current money of Maryland to me in hand paid by Gabriel SLOCUM of the County and State aforesaid at or before the Sealing and delivery of these presents the Receipt whereof I do hereby acknowledge I have bargained and Sold and by these presents do bargain and Sell unto him the said Gabriel SLOCUM his heirs Executors Administrators and Assigns one Negro Woman named **Casesa** aged about Seventeen years also one Negro Boy named **Thomas** aged about three years old also one Negro Garle named **Milley** aged about Six months and all their future Increase to have and to hold the said Negroes **Casesay** & **Thomas** & **Milley** and all their future increase unto him the said Gabriel SLOCUM his heirs Executors Administrators and and Assigns for ever and I the said William BRUENTON do for my Self my heirs Executors and Administrators Warrant the said Negroes **Casesay** & **Thomas** and **Milley** and all their future increase unto him the said Gabril SLOCUM his heirs Executors and Administrators and Assigns against their Claims and demand of me the said William BRUENTON my Heirs Executors and Administrators and all and every other Person or Persons whatsoever In Witness whereof I have hereunto Set my hand and affixed my Seal the Eleventh day of January 1791. ~

Sealed & Delivered in the presents of   William BRU[ENTO]N (Seal)
Edmond Northen NELMS
Frankey NELMS"

---

[532] Worcester County Court (Land Records). Bill of sale from CORD, Ann to CORD, William. 29 January 1791. N, p. 425, MSA CE 30-13. www.mdlandrec.net : accessed 15 March 2022.

[533] Worcester County Court (Land Records). Bill of sale from MELSON, Daniel Sr. to ADKINS, Sarah. 07 January 1791. N, pp. 432-433, MSA CE 30-13. www.mdlandrec.net : accessed 15 March 2022.

*followed on folio 434 with the recordation on 15 February 1791 by court clerk James R. MORRIS[534]

Liber N, folios 434-435; 07 February 1791

"This Indenture made this Seventh day of February in the year of our Lord one thousand Seven hundred and ninety one between William MILBURN of the one part and Jacob ADDAMS of the other part both of Worcester County Wittnesseth that the said William MILBURN for and in consideration of the Sum of five Shillings Current money of Maryland to me in hand paid at and before the Sealing and delivery of these presents by Jacob ADDAMS the Receipt whereof the said William doth hereby acknowledge hath bargained and Sould and delivered and by these presents do absolutely bargain Sell and deliver unto the said Jacob ADDAMS his heirs and Assigns forever the following Negroes to witt one negro man called **Isaac** and one negro called **Jack** lately in possession of a certain Thomas MILBURN To have and to hold all and Singular the above mentioned negroes hereby bargained and Sould unto him the said Jacob his heirs and assigns forever to the only use benefit and behoof of him the said Jacob and his heirs and Assigns forever and the said William MILBURN and his heirs doth hereby quit all claim right and title of in and to the above Negros and bargained premises and every part thereof unto the said Jacob ADDAMS his heirs and Assigns forever all which Negros the said William doth put the said Jacob ADDAMS and his heirs in full possession of excepting to Thomas MILBURN his right which he hath at Law by Virtue of Several Deeds of Sail recours thereunto being had may app{??} In Testimony whereof the said William hath to these presents Sett his hand and fixed his Seal the day and year first above written

Witness Philip QUINTON   William MILBOURN   (Seal)"

*followed on folio 435 with the acknowledgment by Justice of the Peace Philip QUINTON and the recordation on 18 February 1791 by court clerk James R. MORRIS[535]

Liber N, folios 446-447; 26 February 1791

"To all Christian people to whom these presents shall come or may concern I John MILLER of the State of Maryland in the County of Worcester Send Greeting Know ye that I the said John MILLER in the Consideration of thirty five pounds current money of Maryland to me in hand paid at and before the Ensealing & delivery of these presents by Joshua HUDSON of the County and State af[ore]s[ai]d the Receipt whereof I do hereby acknowledge & confess & thereof have bargained & Sold & by these presents do bargain & Sell unto the said Joshua HUDSON one Negro man named **George** To have and to hold the said Negro man called **George** hereby bargained & Sold & all my right title claim & Interest of & unto the said Negro Man {?} {?} said Joshua HUDSON his heirs Executors Administrators & Assigns to him and their own proper use uses benifit and behoof as his and their own proper Goods forever & I the Said John MILLER do hereby for my self my heirs Executors and Administrators Covenant promise grant & agree to & with the said Joshua HUDSON his heirs Executors & Administrators that the said Negro man now are and be & so Shall at all times forever hereafter be Remain and continue unto the said Joshua HUDSON his Heirs Executors Administrators & Assigns free & Clear of & from all and all manner of form or and other Gifts grants bargains Sales & incumbrances whatsoever had made done or committed by me my means privity or procurement In Witness whereof I have hereunto Set my hand & Seal this 26th day of February Anno Domini 1791

Signed Sealed and delivered in presence off   John MILLER   (Seal)
W[illia]m STEVENSON ~   Levin MILLER ~"

---

[534] Worcester County Court (Land Records). Bill of sale from BRUENTON, William to SLOCUM, Gabriel. 11 January 1791. N, pp. 433-434, MSA CE 30-13. www.mdlandrec.net : accessed 15 March 2022.
[535] Worcester County Court (Land Records). Bill of sale from MILBOURN, William to ADDAMS, Jacob. 07 February 1791. N, pp. 434-435, MSA CE 30-13. www.mdlandrec.net : accessed 15 March 2022.

*followed on folio 447 with the recordation on 28 February 1791 by court clerk James R. MORRIS[536]

Liber N, folio 447; 28 February 1791

"Know all men by these presents that I Bartley TOWNSEND of Worcester County in the State of Maryland for and in consideration of the Sum of forty three pounds Six Shillings & ten pence current money of Maryland to me in hand paid by Peter TOWNSEND of the Same place at and before the Sealing and delivery of these presents the Receipt whereof I do hereby acknowledge have bargained and Sold and by these presents do bargain and Sell unto the said Peter TOWNSEND his heirs and Assigns one Negro Boy called **David** To have and to hold the said Articles above mentioned unto the said Peter TOWNSEND his heirs and Assigns for ever to the only proper use benefit and behoof of the said Peter TOWNSEND his heirs and Assigns forever and for not their use or purpose whatsoever and the said Bartley TOWNSEND for himself and his heirs doth covenant and agree to and with the said Peter TOWNSEND that me the said Bartley TOWNSEND hath a good and Sefficiant title to Sell and dispose of the said Negro Boy **David** so as to convey unto the said Peter TOWNSEND a good Sure and firm title to the Same and that no person but the said Peter TOWNSEND hath any right & Title to the same In testimoney whereof the said Bartley TOWNSEND his hand to these presents hath Set and a Seal affixed this 28th day of February in the year of our Lord One thousand Seven hundred and Ninety One

Signed Sealed Delivered   Bartley TOWNSEND (Seal)
in presents of ~   Josiah MITCHELL"

*followed with the acknowledgment by Justice of the Peace Josiah MITCHELL and the recordation on 28 February 1791 by court clerk James R. MORRIS[537]

Liber N, folio 448; 24 February 1791

"State of Maryland Worcester County Ss[t]. Know all men by these presents that we William PURNELL and Margit FASSETT of the County af[ore]s[ai]d in consideration of the Sum of forty Seven pounds ten Shillings current money of Maryland to us in hand paid by Joseph GRAY of the County af[ore]s[ai]d have bargained sold released granted and confirmed and by these presents do bargain Sell release grant and confirm unto the said Joseph GRAY his heirs and Assigns forever a Negro man called **Sam** to have and to hold the said Negro man **Sam** by these presents bargained sold released granted and confirmed unto the only proper use and behoof of the said Joseph GRAY his heirs Executors Administrators and assigns forever freely quietly peaceably and intirely without aney contradiction clame disturbance or hindrance of of aney parson whatsoever and we the said William PURNELL and Margit FASSETT for ourselves our heirs Executors and Administrators the said Negro Man **Sam** unto Said Joseph GRAY his heirs Executors Administrators or Assigns and against all and every other Person or persons whatsoever Shall and will Warrant and forever defend by these presents In Witness whareof we the said William PURNELL and Marget FASSETT hath hereunto Set our hands and Seals this 14th day of February Anno Dom[ini] 1791. ~

Signed Seal[e]d & delivered   William PURNELL (Seal)
in presence of   Margaret FASSETT (Seal)
Josiah MITCHELL ~   John POSTLY. ~"

*followed with the acknowledgment by Justice of the Peace Josiah MITCHELL and the recordation on 28 February 1791 by court clerk James R. MORRIS[538]

---

[536] Worcester County Court (Land Records). Bill of sale from MILLER, John to HUDSON, Jacob. 26 February 1791. N, pp. 446-447, MSA CE 30-13. www.mdlandrec.net : accessed 15 March 2022.

[537] Worcester County Court (Land Records). Bill of sale from TOWNSEND, Bartley to TOWNSEND, Peter. 28 February 1791. N, p. 447, MSA CE 30-13. www.mdlandrec.net : accessed 15 March 2022.

[538] Worcester County Court (Land Records). Bill of sale from PURNELL, William and FASSETT, Margaret to GRAY, Joseph. 14 February 1791. N, p. 448, MSA CE 30-13. www.mdlandrec.net : accessed 15 March 2022.

Liber O, folios 54-55; 08 April 1791

"Know all men by these presents that I Henry TURNER of Henry of Worcester County in the State of Maryland for and in consideration of the Sum of ten pounds current money of Maryland to me in hand paid Before the Ensealing and delivery of these presents by Samuell TRUITT (of W[illia]^m) of the County and State aforesaid the Receipt whereof the said Henry TURNER doth hereby Acknowledge have bargained and Sold and by these presents do bargain & Sell unto the said Samuel TRUITT his heirs and Assigns forever a Negro Girl called **Esther** about nine years old in the possession of the said Samuel TRUITT To have and to hold the said Negro Girl called **Esther** all and Singular her hereafter increase that She may have and I the said Henry TURNER for myself and my heirs Executors or Administrators or any of them or their Assigns all and Singular the said Negro Girl called **Esther** unto the said Samuel TRUITT his heirs and Assigns forever against me the said Henry TURNER my heirs Ex[ecuto]^rs & Adm[inistrato]^rs and against all and every other Person or Persons whatsoever Shall and Will Warrant and forever Defend by these presents of which said Negro Girl called **Esther** I the Henry TURNER have put the said Samuel TRUITT in full possession by the Delivery of these presents In Testimony whereof the said Henry TURNER have hereunto set his hand and Seal affixed this Eighth day of April Anno Domini Seventeen hundred and Ninety One

Signed sealed & delivered   Henry TURNER   (Seal)
In the presence of ~
Philip QUINTON ~"

*followed on folio 55 with the acknowledgment by Justice of the Peace Philip QUINTON and the recordation by court clerk James R. MORRIS[539]

Liber O, folio 78; 26 April 1791

"Know All men by these presents that I Schoolfield PARKER of Worcester County in the State of Maryland for and in consideration of the sum of fifty pounds current money of Maryland to me in hand paid by Robert HUDSON and Thomas HALL of the same place at and before the sealing and delivery of these presents the Receipt whereof I do hereby Acknowledge have bargained and Sold and by these presents do bargain and sell unto the said Robert HUDSON and Thomas HALL their heirs and Assigns one Negro man name **George** To have and to hold the said Artickll above mentioned unto the said Robert HUDSON and Thomas HALL their heirs and Assigns forever to the only proper use benifit and behoof of the said Robert HUDSON and Thomas HALL thir hirs and Assigns for ever and for no other use or purpos whatsoever and the said Schoolfield PARKER for himself and his heirs doth Covenant and agree to and with the said Robert HUDSON and Thomas HALL that he the said Schoolfield PARKER hath a good and sofficient tittle to sell and dispose of the said Negro Man named **George** so as to convey unto the said Robert HUDSON and Thomas HALL a good sure and firm title to the same and that know person but the said Schoolfiel PARKER hath any Right or title to the same In testimony whereof the said Schoolfield PARKER his hand to these presents hath set and a seal affixed this twenty sixt day of Apriel in the yeare of our Lord One Thousand seven hundred and Ninety One ~

Signed sealed delivered   Schoolfield PARKER   (Seal)
in presents of ~
Philip QUINTON. ~"

*followed with the acknowledgment by Justice of the Peace Philip QUINTON and the recordation by court clerk James R. MORRIS[540]

---

[539] Worcester County Court (Land Records). Bill of sale from TURNER, Henry to TRUITT, Samuel. 08 April 1791. O, pp. 54-55, MSA CE 30-14. www.mdlandrec.net : accessed 21 March 2022.
[540] Worcester County Court (Land Records). Bill of sale from PARKER, Schoolfield to HUDSON, Robert and HALL, Thomas. 26 April 1791. O, p. 78, MSA CE 30-14. www.mdlandrec.net : accessed 21 March 2022.

Liber O, folios 89-90; 29 April 1791

"Worcester Ss^t. To all People to whom these presents shall or may come Know ye that I Peter CHAILLE of the County af[ore]s[ai]^d and State of Maryland for and in Consideration of the sum of seventy pounds Current money of Maryland to me in hand paid by Thomas HALL & Joshua BOWEN of the County & State af[ore]s[ai]^d have bargained and sold and by these presents do bargain and sell to the said Thomas HALL & Joshua BOWEN the following Negroes to wit **Lidde Tamar, Sarah** & **Rhoda** that is to say I Peter CHAILLE do grant bargain and sell to the af[ore]s[ai]^d Thomas HALL & Joshua BOWEN all my Right Title and claim to the af[ore]s[ai]^d Negroes provided Thomas PURNELL Sen[ior] shall or may accept and Order drawn on him in favour of Richard HALL by Charles RACKLIFFE ~

Witness my hand and seal this 29th day of April 1791

Sealed signed & Delivered   Peter CHAILLE   (Seal)
in presence of ~
Philip QUINTON"

*followed on folio 90 with the acknowledgment by Justice of the Peace Philip QUINTON and the recordation by court clerk James R. MORRIS[541]

Liber O, folios 90-91; 29 April 1791

"Know all men by these presents that I Matthias NICHOLSON of Worcester County and State of Maryland for and in consideration of the sum of eight pounds five shillings current money of Maryland to me in hand paid by James DUER at or before the sealing and delivery of these presents the Receipt whereof I do hereby Acknowledge and confess Have bargained sold and delivered unto him the said James DUER his heirs and Assigns forever the following two Negroes to wit One Negro Woman called **Mareor** and one Negro Boy called **Jacob** (already and at present to South Carolina by the aforesaid DUER) To have and to hold all and Singular the above bargained and sold Negroes unto him the said James DUER his heirs and Assigns forever to the only proper use benefit and behoof of him the said James DUER his heirs and Assigns for ever And I the said Matthias NICHOLSON for himself his heirs Executors and Adm[inistrato]^{rs} do hereby acquit all claim and Demand of in and the above mentioned bargained two Negroes and will and shall Warrant and forever defend the same unto the aforesaid James DUER his heirs and Assigns forever In Witness whereof I the said Matthias NICHOLSON to these presents my hand hath set and seal affixed this Twenty ninth day of April in the year of our Lord One Thousand seven hundred & Ninety One

Signed sealed & delivered In the presence of   Matthias NICHOLSON   (Seal)
Philip QUINTON"

*followed on folio 91 with the acknowledgment by Justice of the Peace Philip QUINTON and the recordation by court clerk James R. MORRIS[542]

Liber O, folio 100; 25 April 1791

"Maryland Ss^t. Worcester County Know all men by these presents that we John DISHAROON and Jacob RAMSON both of the State and County af[ore]s[ai]^d for and in consideration of the sum of twenty five pounds current money of the State of af[ore]s[ai]^d to them in hand paid by Johnson GRAY at and before the Sealing and delivery of these presents the Receipt whereof the said John DISHAROON and Jacob RAMSON doth hereby Acknowledge and thereof doth acquit Release and discharge the af[ore]s[ai]^d Johnson GRAY his heirs Executors

---

[541] Worcester County Court (Land Records). Bill of sale from CHAILLE, Peter to HALL, Thomas and BOWEN, Joshua. 29 April 1791. O, pp. 89-90, MSA CE 30-14. www.mdlandrec.net : accessed 22 March 2022.
[542] Worcester County Court (Land Records). Bill of sale from NICHOLSON, Matthias to DUER, James. 29 April 1791. O, pp. 90-91, MSA CE 30-14. www.mdlandrec.net : accessed 22 March 2022.

Adm[inistrato]^rs and Assigns forever hath bargained sold set over and delivered and by these presents do bargain sell set over and deliver unto the af[ore]s[ai]d Johnson GRAY his heirs and Assigns forever in plain and open Market One Negro Girl called **Amelia** To have and to hold the af[ore]s[ai]d bargin[e]d Primisses with all benifits priviledges and appurtenances thereunto belonging unto the said Johnson GRAY his heirs and Assigns forever and to and for no other use intent or purpose whatsoever and the said John DISHAROON and Jacob RAMSON doth hereby Jointly agree to and with the af[ore]s[ai]d Johnson GRAY that the said John DISHAROON and Jacob RAMSON the bargained primisses above mentioned with the priviledges and appurtenances thereunto belonging unto the above named Johnson GRAY his heirs and Assigns for ever against the just claim of all manner of Persons claiming the same by from or under them or their Heirs forever shall and will Warrant and forever defend In Witness whereof the said John DISHAROON and Jacob RAMSON hereunto their hands set and affixed their Seals this 25th day of April Anno Domini 1791 ~ // ~ // ~ // ~

Signed sealed and delivered   John DISHEROON   (Seal)
in the presence of ~   Jacob RAMSON   (Seal)
John P. MITCHELL"

*followed with acknowledgment by Justice of the Peace John P. MITCHELL and the recordation on 06 May 1791 by court clerk James R. MORRIS[543]

Liber O, folio 109; 25 July 1790

"Know all men by these presents that I Daniel MELSON of Worcester County & State of Maryland do of my own free will give unto my Granddaughter Hannah DORMAN one Negro woman called **Grace** both she and her increase to the said Hannah DORMAN of County and State aforesaid she her heirs Executors or Administrators or Assigns to the only proper use and behoof of the said Hannah DORMAN her heirs and Assigns forever and I the said Daniel MELSON for myself my heirs Executors or Administrators forever will Warrant and defend against the Lawfull Claims of all Persons In Witness whereof I hereto these presents set my hand and seal affix[e]d this twenty fifth day of July Anno Domini One thousand seven hundred and ninety. ~

Sign[e]d Seal[e]d and deliver[e]d   his
In presence of ~   his   Daniel ~ MELSON (Seal)
John WILLIAMS, William ~ MELSON   mark
                       mark

N.B John DORMAN & Hannah DORMAN his Wife is to take a Child that doth belong to this Negro Woman and keep it untill it is two years old and then or any time if the said Daniel MELSON should send for the s[ai]d Negro Child and Order in writing from under his own hand then the s[ai]d John DORMAN of his wife Hannah their heirs or Executors or Administrators is to deliver the said Child to him or his Order but if the said Daniel MELSON should not send for the Child in his lifetime it is to belong to the said John DORMAN his Wife Hannah they and their heirs and Assigns forever In testimony whereof we the said parties have hereunt interchangeably set our hands & Seals affix[e]d

In presence ~   his   his
John WILLIAMS, William ~ MELSON   Daniel ~ MELSON
                       mark   mark
                                              John DORMAN"

*followed with the recordation by court clerk James R. MORRIS on 20 May 1791[544]

---

[543] Worcester County Court (Land Records). Bill of sale from DISHEROON, John to RAMSON, Jacob. 25 April 1791. O, p. 100, MSA CE 30-14. www.mdlandrec.net : accessed 22 March 2022.
[544] Worcester County Court (Land Records). Bill of sale from MELSON, Daniel to DORMAN, Hannah. 25 July 1790. O, p. 109, MSA CE 30-14. www.mdlandrec.net : accessed 22 March 2022.

Liber O, folio 127; 09 June 1791

"Maryland Worcester C[ounty] Know all men by these presents that I Thomas GRAY Sen[ior] of Worcester County in the State of Maryland for and in consideration of the sum of fifty pounds current money of Maryland to me in hand paid by my son Johnson GRAY of the Place afforesaid at or before the Ensealing and delivery of these presents wherewith I confess myself to be fully satisfied contented and paid have bargained sold & delivered and by these presents do fully clearly and Absolutely bargain sell & deliver unto the said Johnson GRAY One Negro man called **Bobb** about twenty seven years old & one Negro boy called **Peter** about nine years old To have and to hold the said Negro man **Bobb** & the said Negro boy **Peter** unto the said Johnson GRAY his Executors Administrators or Assigns to his & their own proper uses and behooffs for ever And I the said Thomas GRAY for myself my heirs Executors and Administrators and every of us the aforesaid Negro man & Negro boy unto the said Johnson GRAY his Heirs and Assigns against all People whatsoever shall and will Warrant acquit and for ever defend by these presents In Witness whereof I have hereunto sett my hand and seal affixed the ninth day of June in the year of our Lord One thousand seven hundred and Ninety One

Sealed and delivered
in the presence of ~   Thomas W GRAY Sen[ior] (Seal)
John POSTLY, George BELL. ~   his mark"

*followed with the acknowledgment by Justice of the Peace John POSTLY and the recordation on 16 June 1791 by court clerk James R. MORRIS[545]

Liber O, folios 127-128; 15 June 1791

"This Indenture made this fifteenth day of June in the year of our Lord seventeen hundred and Ninety One Between William STEVENSON of Worcester County in the State of Maryland of the one part and George PURNELL of the same place of the other part Witnesseth that the said William STEVENSON for and in consideration of forty pounds current money of Maryland (to him in hand paid by the said George PURNELL before the Ensealing and delivery hereof the Receipt whereof the said William doth hereby Acknowledge and thereof the said George his Executors and Administrators doth for ever acquit and discharge) hath granted bargained and sold and by these presents doth grant bargain and sell unto the said George PURNELL his Executors Administrators and Assigns a certain Negro Boy called **Amos** To have and to hold the said Negro Boy called **Amos** to him the said George PURNELL his Executors Administrators and Assigns to the only proper use and behoof of him the said George his Executors Administrators and Assigns and the said William STEVENSON for himself his Heirs Executors and Administrators doth Covenant and agree to and with the said George that he the said William his Heirs Executors and Administrators and Assigns from the Claim or claims of all and every Person whatsoever will Warrant and forever defend In testimony whereof the said William hath hereunto set his hand and his seal affixed the day and year af[ore]s[ai]^d

Signed sealed and delivered   W[illia]^m STEVENSON (Seal)
in presence of ~
John DONE, Lam^l HYLAND"

*followed on folio 128 with the acknowledgment by Justice of the Peace John DONE and the recordation on 17 June 1791 by court clerk James R. MORRIS[546]

---

[545] Worcester County Court (Land Records). Bill of sale from GRAY, Thomas Sr. to GRAY, Johnson. 09 June 1791. O, p. 127, MSA CE 30-14. www.mdlandrec.net : accessed 22 March 2022.

[546] Worcester County Court (Land Records). Bill of sale from STEVENSON, William to PURNELL, George. 15 June 1791. O, pp. 127-128, MSA CE 30-14. www.mdlandrec.net : accessed 22 March 2022.

Liber O, folio 140; 21 June 1791

"Know all men by these presents that I Parker SELBY (Son of Matthew) of Worcester County and State of Maryland for and in consideration the sum of Forty pounds current money of Maryland to me in hand paid by Jonathan ESHUN of the same place at and before the sealing and delivery of these presents the Receipt whereof I do hereby Acknowledge and confess and have bargained sold and delivered and by these presents doth absolutely grant bargain sell and deliver unto him the said Jonathan ESHUN his Heirs and Assigns forever a certain Negro Woman called **Grace** now in the County aforesaid To have and to hold all and singular the said Negro Woman called **Grace**, unto him the said Jonathan ESHUN and to his Heirs and Assigns forever to the only proper use benefit and behoof of him the said Jonathan ESHUN & to his heirs and assigns forever And I the said Parker SELBY for myself my heirs Executors and Adm[inistrato]rs will and shall Warrant and forever defend the said bargained Negro Woman against the Right and Title of all manner of Person or Persons whatever In testimoney whereof I the said Parker SELBY to these presents my hand hath set and seal affixed this twenty first day of June in the year of our Lord One Thousand seven hundred and Ninety one ~ // ~ // ~ // ~

Signed sealed & delivered Parker SELBY of M (Seal)
In the presence of ~   Joshua TOWNSEND ~"

*followed with the acknowledgment by Justice of the Peace Joshua TOWNSEND and the recordation by court clerk James R. MORRIS[547]

Liber O, folios 169-170; 19 July 1791

"This Indenture made the 19th day of July Anno Domini seventeen hundred and Ninety one Between Parker SELBY (Son of Matthew) of Worcester County in the State of Maryland of the one part and Henry TOADVINE of the same place of the other part, Witnesseth that the said Parker SELBY for and in consideration of the sum of forty five Pounds to him in hand Paid by the said Henry TOADVINE the receipt whereof the said Parker SELBY doth hereby acknowledge hath bargained and sold unto the said Henry TOADVINE his heirs and Assigns forever, one negro man named **Shadrack** now being in the Possession of the said Henry TOADVINE, To have and to hold the aforesaid negro named **Shadrack** unto the said Henry TOADVINE his heirs and Assigns forever and I the said Parker SELBY for myself and my heirs will Warrant and forever defend the said Negro man named **Shadrack** against the lawful claim of all person or persons whatsoever unto the said Henry TOADVINE his heirs and Assigns forever. In Witness whereof I the said Parker SELBY to these presents my hand have set and seal affixed the day and year first above written

Signed sealed and Parker SELBY of M (Seal)
delivered in Presents of   Joshua TOWNSEND"

*followed on folio 170 with the acknowledgment by Justice of the Peace Joshua TOWNSEND and the recordation by court clerk James R. MORRIS[548]

Liber O, folios 172-173; 23 July 1791

"Maryland Sst. Know all men by these presents that I Ebenezer HANDY of Worcester County & State af[ore]s[ai]d for and in consideration of the Sum of the Value of fifty Pounds current money of this State to me in hand paid by John PARKER of the County and State af[ore]s[ai]d have bargained Sold set over & Delivered by these Presents in Plain & Open Market according to the Just and Due form of Law in that case made and Provided Do Bargin set over and deliver unto the said John PARKER one Negro Woman called **Silby** To have and to hold the said Bargained Premises unto the said John PARKER his heirs Executors admin[istrators] & assigns

---

[547] Worcester County Court (Land Records). Bill of sale from SELBY, Parker to ESHUN, Jonathan. 21 June 1791. O, p. 140, MSA CE 30-14. www.mdlandrec.net : accessed 22 March 2022.
[548] Worcester County Court (Land Records). Bill of sale from SELBY, Parker to TOADVINE, Henry. 19 July 1791. O, pp. 169-170, MSA CE 30-14. www.mdlandrec.net : accessed 22 March 2022.

forever and I the said Ebenezer HANDY for myself my heirs Executors and admin[istrators] the said bargained Premises unto the said John PARKER his heirs Executors admin[istrators] and assigns against all manner of Persons shall and will warrant & forever Defend by these Presents, In Witness whereof the said Bargained Premises I have hereunto set my hand and Seal this 23rd day of July 1791.

Signed Sealed & Delivered   Ebenezer HANDY (Seal)
in Presents of us . . .   Purnell JOHNSON"

*followed on folio 173 with the acknowledgment by Purnell JOHNSON and the recordation on 29 July 1791 by court clerk James R. MORRIS[549]

Liber O, folios 187-188; 11 August 1791

"Know all men by these Presents that I John DUNBARE of Worcester County in the State of Maryland for and in consideration of the affection and good will thereunto me moveing unto my only son James DUNBARE of the county aforesaid Have given Granted bargained, released, and confirmed, and by these Presents, do bargain, release and confirm unto him my said son James DUNBARE a negro woman called **Sino** and one negro boy called **Titus** & one Negro Garle called **Rodah** and als all her and their increase from the date of the Presents, To have and to hold all and singular the three aforesaid negroes and their increase and every of them by these Presents, bargained, released granted, and confirmed unto the only Proper use and behoof of him the said   DUNBARE his heirs Executors, administrators and Assigns forever freely quietly, Peacebly, and interely, without any contradiction claim disturbance or hindrance of any Person whatsoever so that neither I the said John DUNBAR, nor any other for me or in my name have any right title interest or demand of in to or for the af[ore]s[ai]d three Negroes or any Part or Parcel thereof ought to exact, challenge claim or demand at any time or times hereafter, but from all actions right Estate title claim, Demand, Possession and interest thereof shall be wholly barred and excluded by Vertue and force of these Presents, and I the said John DUNBAR for myself my heirs Executors & administrators all and singular the said Negroes unto the said James DUNBARE his Executors, administrators and assigns, and against every other Person or Persons whatsoever shall and will warrant and forever defend by these Presents, In Witness whereof I have hereunto set my hand and seal affixed this 11th day of August Anno Dom[ini] 1791 ~

Signed Sealed & Delivered   Josiah MITCHELL   John DUNBAR (Seal)
In Presence of . . ~   Caleb TINGLE Sen[ior]"

*followed on folio 188 with the acknowledgment by Justice of the Peace Josiah MITCHELL and the recordation on 12 August 1791 by court clerk James R. MORRIS[550]

Liber O, folios 197-198; 23 August 1791

"To all People to whome this Present writing may come that I John SMITH of Worcester County in the State of Maryland for and in consideration of the natural love and affection which I have and bear unto my son Purnell SMITH and also for other good causes and considerations me thereunto moveing haveing given and grant and by these Presents do give grant and confirm unto the said Purnell SMITH his heirs and Assigns forever the following goods and chattels Vizt. Two feather beds and furniture one large blew Cubbard one desk one large black walnut ovel table two Painted chests Six seting chairs three large Pewter Basons two large Pewter dishes ten Pewter Plates one Negro Man named **Jacob** one horse called Duncan and one colt named Jenney, Six head of young cows four young Stears Six head of sheep and all my Wareing apparel with a reserve of the use of all and every of the above articles to myself during my life, and I the said John SMITH all and Singular the aforesaid good and Chattels to the said Purnell

---

[549] Worcester County Court (Land Records). Bill of sale from HANDY, Ebenezer to PARKER, John. 23 July 1791. O, pp. 172-173, MSA CE 30-14. www.mdlandrec.net : accessed 22 March 2022.
[550] Worcester County Court (Land Records). Bill of sale from DUNBAR, John to DUNBAR, Isaac. 11 August 1791. O, pp. 187-188, MSA CE 30-14. www.mdlandrec.net : accessed 22 March 2022.

SMITH his heirs and Assigns against all Persons will warrant and defend by these Presents except as before excepted In Witness whereof I the said John SMITH to these Presents my hand have set and seal affixed the 23rd day of August Anno 1791 ~

Signed Sealed and delivered   John SMITH (Seal)
in Presents of . . . .   Joshua TOWNSEND"

*followed on folio 198 with the acknowledgment by Justice of the Peace Joshua TOWNSEND and the recordation by court clerk James R. MORRIS[551]

Liber O, folios 201-202; 17 June 1771

"Whereas it appears by affidavits that the title of the Slaves which Joseph STERLING dyed possessed of belonging unto the Children of John COX except the third part thereof which third amounts agreeable to Inventory of appraisement to forty one pounds six shillings and eight Pence and on the af[ore]s[ai]^d Affidavits the Commissary has taken the two thirds of the said Slaves out of Joseph STERLINGs Estate and it is now agreed that out of the Slaves **Jen** and **Lish** who are appraised to sixty pounds the said third part is to be made out of them and as a Consideration of the Natural love and Affection which we have and do bear unto our Mother do give unto her for and during her Natural life the overplus of the said two Negroes after deducting the thirds as af[ore]s[ai]^d and also do give her one Negro Girl called **Barsheba** & her future increase To have and to hold the said Negroes as af[ore]s[ai]^d for and during her Natural life and at her death to go and be disposed of by her to such of her Children as she shall think fit and for no other use or purpose whatsoever In Witness whereof have hereto set our hands & Seals this 17th day of June Anno Dom[ini] 1771

Signed sealed & Deliv[ere]^d   William COX (Seal)
In presence off ~   James JONES (Seal)
Litt[leton] DENNIS   Mary COX (Seal)"

*followed on folio 202 with the receipt by Mary COX, William COX, and James JONES on 17 June 1771, and the recordation by court clerk James R. MORRIS on 30 August 1791[552]

Liber O, folio 202; 01 September 1791

"Know all men by these presents that we Duncan MURRAY & William COVINGTON both of Worcester County & State of Maryland for and in consideration of the sum of fifty two pounds ten shillings current money of Maryland to us in hand paid at and before the sealing and delivery of these presents, by James KING of the County and State aforesaid wherewith we Acknowledge ourselves fully satisfied and paid and thereof and of every part thereof do hereby acquit exonerate and discharge the said James KING his Executors Administrators and Assigns: Have granted bargained and sold and by these presents, do fully clearly and absolutely grant bargain and sell unto the said James KING One Negro man named **Sharp** of the Age of about thirty eight years To have and to hold the aforesaid Negro Man name **Sharp** before by these presents bargained and sold unto the said James KING his Execut[or]^s Adm[inistrato]^rs and Assigns forever and we the said Duncan MURRAY and William COVINGTON for ourselves and each of our Heirs Ex[ecuto]^rs Adm[inistrato]^rs unto the af[ore]s[ai]^d James KING his Execut[o]^rs Adm[inistrator]^s and Assigns the af[ore]s[ai]d Negro Man called **Sharp** Will Warrant and forever defend by these presents As Witness our hands and seals this first day of September One thousand seven hundred and Ninety One

---

[551] Worcester County Court (Land Records). Deed of gift from SMITH, John to SMITH, Purnell. 23 August 1791. O, pp. 197-198, MSA CE 30-14. www.mdlandrec.net : accessed 22 March 2022.

[552] Worcester County Court (Land Records). Writing of agreement from COX, Mary & William, and JONES, James to the Executrix of Joseph STERLING. 17 June 1771. O, pp. 201-202, MSA CE 30-14. www.mdlandrec.net : accessed 22 March 2022.

Sealed & delivered   Duncan MURRAY   (Seal)
in presence of . .   W[illia]^m COVINGTON   (Seal)
John POSTLY, William STEVENSON."

*followed with the acknowledgment by Justice of the Peace John POSTLY and the recordation on 02 September 1791 by court clerk James R. MORRIS[553]

Liber O, folios 206-207; 07 September 1791

"Worcester County State of Maryland Know all men by these presents that I Dunkin MURRAY of the County or Worcester and State of Maryland and for and in Consideration of thirty five pounds Lawfull money of the said State to me in hand paid by Ebenezer FRANKLIN of the County and State af[ore]s[ai]^d the Receipt whereof I do hereby Acknowledge have bargained sold Assigned and set over unto the said Ebenezer FRANKLIN his Heirs and Assigns forever all my right, title and Interest and property of in and to a certain Negro woman called or known by the name of **Nell** to the only proper use and behoof of him the said Ebenezer FRANKLIN his Heirs and Assigns forever and I the said Dunkin MURRAY do hereby for myself my heirs Ex[ecuto]^rs Adm[inistrato]^rs and Assigns will Warrant and forever defend the af[ore]s[ai]^d Negro Woman unto him the said Ebenezer FRANKLIN his Heirs Ex[ecuto]^rs Adm[inistrato]^rs and Assigns free and Clear from any Clame by me the said Dunkin or his Heirs Executors and Adm[inistrator]^s or from or by any other persons claiming by or under him the same I have hereunto set my hand and seal this seventh day of September in the year of our Lord One Thousand seven hundred and Ninety one ~.

Signed sealed and delivered   Duncan MURRAY   (Seal)
in the presence of. ~
Isaac FRANKLIN,   Morg^n JONES"

*followed with the acknowledgment by Justice of the Peace Josiah MITCHELL and the recordation on folio 207 by court clerk James R. MORRIS on 08 September 1791[554]

Liber O, folios 208-209; 02 September 1791

"Know all men by these presents that I Moses CHAILLE of Worcester County for and in consideration of the Sum of Sixty four pounds two Shillings & four pence current money of Maryland to me in hand paid by Samuel HANDY of the County af[ore]s[ai]^d at and before the sealing and delivery of these presents the Receipt whereof I do hereby Acknowledge have bargained and Sold Released granted and Confirmed and by these presents do bargain and sell release grant and confirm unto the said Sam[ue]^l HANDY his Heirs and Assigns forever One Negro man Slave called **Abel** To have and to hold the said Negro man **Abel** by these presents bargained sold Released granted and confirmed unto the said Samuel HANDY and his Heirs and Assigns forever to the only proper use benefit and Behoof of the said Samuel HANDY and his Heirs and Assigns forever and for no other use purpose or construction whatsoever And I the said Moses CHAILLE for myself my heirs Executors and Administrators the said Negro Man **Abel** unto the said Samuel HANDY his Heirs Executors Adm[inistrato]^rs and Assigns against me the said Moses CHAILLE my heirs Executors and Adm[inistrato]^rs and against all and every other Person or Persons whatsoever shall and Will Warrant and forever defend by these presents In Witness whereof I have hereunto set my hand and affixed my Seal this Second day of September Anno Dom[ini] seventeen hundred and ninety one ~

Sealed & delivered   W[illia]^m BACON   Moses CHAILLE   (Seal)
In presence of ~   Philip QUINTON"

---

[553] Worcester County Court (Land Records). Bill of sale from MURRAY, Duncan and COVINGTON, William to KING, James. 01 September 1791. O, p. 202, MSA CE 30-14. www.mdlandrec.net : accessed 22 March 2022.

[554] Worcester County Court (Land Records). Bill of sale from MURRAY, Duncan to FRANKLIN, Ebenezer. 07 September 1791. O, pp. 206-207, MSA CE 30-14. www.mdlandrec.net : accessed 22 March 2022.

*followed on folio 209 with the acknowledgment by Justice of the Peace Philip QUINTON and the recordation on 16 September 1791 by court clerk James R. MORRIS[555]

Liber O, folio 229; 01 October 1791

"Know all men by these presents that I Daniel MELSON of Sussex County in the State of Delaware for an in consideration of the sum of five pounds Current money of Maryland to me in hand paid by William GORDY of Worcester County in the State of Maryland have bargained and sold and by these presents doth hereby bargain and sell unto the said William GORDY his Heirs and Assigns for ever One Negro Girl named **Kesiah** To have and to hold the aforesaid Negro Girl named **Kesiah** unto the said William GORDY his Heirs and Assigns forever And the said Daniel MELSON for himself and his Heirs doth hereby Warrant and forever hereafter defend the aforesaid Negro Girl named **Kesiah** against the Lawfull claim or claims of all manner of Person or Persons whatsoever that shall ever hereafter Claim her the said Negro Girl named **Kesiah** unto the said William GORDY His Heirs and Assigns forever In Testimony whereof the said Daniel MELSON to these presents his Hand hath sett and seal affixed the first day of October Anno Domini seventeen hundred and Ninety one

Signed sealed and delivered   Daniel MELSON (Seal)
in presents of ~   Purnell JOHNSON"

*followed with the acknowledgment by Justice of the Peace Purnell JOHNSON and the recordation on 03 October 1791 by court clerk James R. MORRIS[556]

Liber O, folios 229-230; 04 October 1791

"Know all men by these presents that I George SPENCE of the State of Maryland and County of Worcester for and in consideration of the sum of thirty five pounds Lawfull money of Maryland to me in hand paid by Adam SPENCE of the State and County aforesaid whereof I do hereby Acknowledge the Receipt and myself therewith fully and entirely satisfied have bargained and sold set over and delivered to the said Adam SPENCE a Negro Lad Named **Jacob** to the value af[ore]s[ai]^d To have and to hold the said bargained primises unto the said Adam SPENCE his Heirs and Assigns forever to the only purpose use and behoof of him the said Adam SPENCE his Heirs Executors Administrators or Assigns forever and I the said George SPENCE for myself my heirs Executors and Administrators the said bargained primises unto the said Adam SPENCE his Heirs Executors Administrators and Assigns against all and all manner of Person or Persons whatsoever shall & will Warrant and defend the same by these presents I Witness whereof I have hereunto set my hand and affixed my seal this fourth day of October one thousand seven hundred and Ninety one

Signed sealed and delivered   G^{eo}[rge] SPENCE (Seal)
in presents of us ~   W[illia]^m PURNELL"

*followed on folio 230 with the acknowledgment by Justice of the Peace William PURNELL and the recordation by court clerk James R. MORRIS[557]

Liber O, folios 231-232; 03 October 1791

"State of Maryland Worcester County ~ Know all men by these presents that I Samuel TAYLOR of the County and State aforesaid for and in Consideration of the sum of one hundred & fifty pounds Current money of the State af[ore]s[ai]^d to me in hand well & truly paid by Hampton HOPKINS of the County & State af[ore]s[ai]^d whereof I do hereby Acknowledge the Receipt and myself therewith fully and intirely satisfied have bargained sold set over &

---

[555] Worcester County Court (Land Records). Bill of sale from CHAILLE, Moses to HANDY, Samuel. 02 September 1791. O, pp. 208-209, MSA CE 30-14. www.mdlandrec.net : accessed 22 March 2022.
[556] Worcester County Court (Land Records). Bill of sale from MELSON, Daniel to GORDY, William. 01 October 1791. O, p. 229, MSA CE 30-14. www.mdlandrec.net : accessed 22 March 2022.
[557] Worcester County Court (Land Records). Bill of sale from SPENCE, George to SPENCE, Adam. 04 October 1791. O, pp. 229-230, MSA CE 30-14. www.mdlandrec.net : accessed 22 March 2022.

delivered & by these presents in plain and open market Accordingly to Law and in Just form in that Case made and provided do bargain set over One Horse five Cows & Calves five Heifer Yearling seven head & Sheep thirteen head of Young Hogs One sow & Pigs One Negro Girl **Nell** on Negro Boy **Robert** Farmers Utensels three feather Beds and furniture one Old Desk One Trunk one Chest one Case one Table One Spinning Wheel One Gunn One pair And Irons, two Potts & Hooks, Spid{?}& frying pan and Tea Kettle, Crop on Ground One Yoke Oxen one pair Cart wheels One Looking Glass & one Loom And all the Legacies which my wife or I have not Received of or from Executors of her Fathers Estate To have and to hold the said bargained premises unto the said Hampton HOPKINS his Executors Administrators & Assigns to the only proper use and behoof of him said Hampton HOPKINS heirs Executors Administrators & Assigns forever And I the said Samuel TAYLOR for myself my Heirs Executors Administrators the said Bargained primisses unto the said Hampton HOPKINS his Executors Administrators & Assigns against all manner of Persons shall and will Warrant & forever defend by these presents In Witness whereof together with the delivery of the bargained premises I have hereunto set my hand and seal this third day of October Anno Domini 1791

Signed Sealed and delivered   Benjamin McCORMACK   Samuel TAYLOR (Seal)
in presents of ~
                             Elizabeth X HARGRAVE
                                  her / mark"

*followed on folio 232 with the acknowledgment by Justice of the Peace Joshua TOWNSEND on 04 October 1791 and the recordation by court clerk James R. MORRIS[558]

Liber O, folio 252; 17 June 1771

"Whereas it appears by Affidavits that the title of the Slaves which Joseph STERLING dyed possessed of belonged unto the children of John COX except the third part thereof which third amounts agreeable to Inventory of Appraisement to forty one pounds six shillings and Eight pence and on the af[ore]s[ai]ᵈ Affidavits the Commissary has taken the two thirds of the said slaves out of Joseph STERLINGs Estate and it is now Agreed that out of Slaves **Jen** and **Lish** who are appraised to Sixty pounds the said third part is to be made out of them and as a Consideration of the Natural affection which we have and do bear unto our Mother do give unto her one Negroe Girl called **Bersheba** & her future increase To have and to hold the said Negroes af[ore]s[ai]ᵈ for and during her Natural life and at her death to go and be disposed of by her to such of her Children as she shall think fit and for no other use or purpose whatsoever In Witness whereof we have hereunto set our hands and seals this 17ᵗʰ day of June Anno Dom[ini] 1771

Signed sealed & deliv[ere]ᵈ   William COX ~ (Seal)
in presence off ~   James JONES ~ (Seal)
Litt[leton] DENNIS ~   Mary COX ~ (Seal)"

*followed with the acknowledgment by Justice of the Peace Philip QUINTON and the recordation on 17 February 1791 by court clerk James R. MORRIS[559]

Liber O, folios 257-258; 17 October 1791

"Maryland Worcester Ssᵗ. This Indenture Made the Seventeenth day of October in the year of Our Lord One thousand seven hundred and Ninety One Between Levi HOLLAND of the County and State afforesaid of the one part And Rachell MORRISS the same place of the other part Witnesseth that the said Levi HOLLAND for and in Consideration of the sum of fifty pounds One Shilling and Eleven pence Current money of Maryland due and Owing from the said Levi to the said Rachell which the said Levi doth hereby Acknowledge have bargained and

---

[558] Worcester County Court (Land Records). Bill of sale from TAYLOR, Samuel to HOPKINS, Hampton. 03 October 1791. O, pp. 231-232, MSA CE 30-14. www.mdlandrec.net : accessed 22 March 2022.
[559] Worcester County Court (Land Records). Writing of agreement from COX, William and Mary, and JONES, James to the Executrix of Joseph STERLING. 17 June 1771. O, p. 252, MSA CE 30-14. www.mdlandrec.net : accessed 22 March 2022.

sold Assigned and transfered Any by these presents doth Bargain & Sell & Assign and Transfer unto the said Rachell MORRIS her Heirs Executors Administrators & Assigns these Negroes following **Hager** & her Children **Ben** & **Ann** To have & to hold the said Negroe Woman **Hager** & her Children **Ben** & **Ann** to the said Rachell MORRISS her Executors Administrators and Assigns To the only proper use of the said Rachell MORRISS her Executors Administrators or Assigns and no other use or purpose whatever Provided always & it is hereby declared to be the true intent & meaning of these presents and of the parties hereunto That if the said Levi HOLLAND his Executors or Administrators, shall well & truly pay or cause to be paid unto the said Rachell MORRISS her Executors Administrators or Assigns the said sum of fifty pounds one shilling & eleven pence Current money of Maryland with Legal Interest for the same & the Expence of making and recording this Deed on or before the third Munday in June next Ensuing the date Then this Deed to be void & of none effect And the said Levi HOLLAND for himself his Executors & Administrators doth hereby covenant & agree with the said Rachel MORRISS her Executors Administrators & Assigns that he will well and truly unto the said Rachell the sums of Money aforesaid with the Interest as aforesaid by the time afforesaid And it is further hereby Covenanted & agreed by and between the parties afforesaid that if the said Levi HOLLAND his Executors or Administrators do not pay the said sums of money with the Interest as afforesaid by the time afforesaid That then it Shall and may be Lawfull for the said Rachel MORRISS her Executors or Administrators after giving ten days notice Publickly be Advertisement set up for that purpose To sell and or som any of the said Negroes as shee or they shall think proper for Ready money & from the money Raised by such sale satisfy her or themselves the Debts afforesaid with the Interest as afffforesaid & the Overpluss of such money pay into the hands of the said Levi HOLLAND his Executors or Administrators In testimoney whereof the said Levi HOLLAND hath hereunto affixed his Hand & Seal the day and year first above written ~

Sealed & delivered in presence of
John POSTLY ~ Mary HOLLAND

Levi X HOLLAND (Seal)
his mark"

*followed on folio 258 with the acknowledgment by Justice of the Peace John POSTLY and the recordation on 20 October 1791 by court clerk James R. MORRIS[560]

Liber O, folios 287-288; 29 November 1791

"Maryland Worcester S^s // Know all men by these presents that I Rives Rackliffe TOWNSEND of Worcester County in the State of Maryland for and in consideration of the sum of Sixty five current money of Maryland to me in hand paid by Annanias POWELL of the place afforesaid at and before the Ensealing and delivery of these presents the Receipt whereof is hereby Acknowledged Have given granted bargained and sold and by these presents do fully clearly & Absolutely give grant bargain and sell unto the said Annanies POWELL his Heirs and Assigns One Negro Man **George** about twenty six years of Age and to hold the said Negro man **George** unto the said Annanies POWELL his Heirs and Assigns forever & for no other use intent construction or purpose whatever And the said Rives Rackliffe TOWNSEND for himself his Heirs Executors & Administrators doth hereby Covenant & agree to & with said Annanies POWELL his Heirs & Assigns that he the said Rives Rackliffe TOWNSEND the said Negro man **George** unto the said Annanias POWELL his Heirs and Assigns against all persons whatever shall and will Warrant & by these presents forever defend In Witness whereof the said Rives Rackliffe TOWNSEND to these presents his hand hath set and seal affixed this twenty Ninth day of November Anno Domini One thousand seven hundred and Ninety One

Sealed and delivered   John POSTLY   Rives Rackliffe TOWNSEND (Seal)
in presence of ~   James GUTHERY"

---

[560] Worcester County Court (Land Records). Deed of Mortgage from HOLLAND, Levi to MORRISS, Rachel. 17 October 1791. O, pp. 257-258, MSA CE 30-14. www.mdlandrec.net : accessed 22 March 2022.

*followed on folio 288 with the acknowledgment by Justice of the Peace John POSTLY and the recordation by court clerk James R. MORRIS[561]

Liber O, folios 297-298; 26 November 1791

"Know all men by these presents that I Lemuel FRANKLIN of Worcester County in the State of Maryland for and in consideration of the sum of one hundred & fifty pounds current money of the State of Maryland to me in hand paid at and before the delivery and sealing of these presents by William FRANKLIN of Worcester County in the State of Maryland wherewith I acknowledge my self fully Satisfied and paid and thereof and every part thereof do hereby acquit exonerate and discharge the said William FRANKLIN his Heirs Executors and Administrators have granted bargained and sold by these presents do fully clearly & Absolutely grant bargin and sell unto the said William FRANKLIN one Negro man commonly called **Ben**, One Mare, two Cows & Erlings two Feather Beds & furniture one Dursk two Chests One Table three Chears, one Cart one Pot one Cittle six Hogs six Pigs and four Shotes one Spinning Wheel one Sheep and all the rest of goods and chattles whatever they may be To have and to hold the said Negro man and all the rest of my goods and chattels by these presents bargained and sold unto the said William FRANKLIN his heirs Executors and Assigns forever and the said Lemuel FRANKLIN for himself his Heirs Executors Administrators doth covenant promise and grant to and with the said William FRANKLIN his heirs Executors Administrators and Assigns by these and presents that he the said Lemuel FRANKLIN his Heirs Executors and Administrators and every of them the said Negro man and all the rest of my goods and chattles hereby bargined and sold unto the said William FRANKLIN his heirs Executors Administrators and Assigns against all Persons shall and will Warrant and forever Defend by these presents In Witness whereof I have hereunto Set my Hand & Seal this twenty sixth day of November 1791

Signed sealed and delivered   Josiah MITCHELL   Lemuel FRANKLIN (Seal)
in the presence of ~   James BRINGHAM"

*followed on folio 298 with the acknowledgment by Justice of the Peace Josiah MITCHELL and the recordation on 02 December 1791 by court clerk James R. MORRIS[562]

Liber O, folio 299; 02 December 1791

"This Indenture made this second day of December in the year of Our Lord one thousand seven hundred and ninety one Between Col°[nel] John DONE of Somerset county in the State of Maryland of the one part and **Moses DAVIS** of Worcester County in the State af[ore]s[ai]^d of the other part Witnesseth that the said Colonel John DONE for and in consideration of the sum of five shillings current money of Maryland to him in hand paid by the said **Moses DAVIS** before the sealing and delivery hereof the Receipt whereof the said Colonel John DONE does hereby Acknowledge & thereof doth forever acquit and discharge the said **Moses DAVIS** his heirs Executors Administrators and Assigns hath set free emancipated & forever discharged & by these presents doth set free emancipate and forever discharge the said **Moses DAVIS** from the Bonds of Slavery In testimony whereof the said Colonel John DONE to these presents his hand hath set & Seal affixed the day and year first above written

Signed sealed and delivered   John DONE (Seal)
In presence of ~   Isaac MARSHALL"

*followed with the acknowledgment by Justice of the Peace Isaac MARSHALL and the recordation on 03 December 1791 by court clerk James R. MORRIS[563]

---

[561] Worcester County Court (Land Records). Bill of sale from TOWNSEND, Rives Rackliffe to POWELL, Annanias. 29 November 1791. O, pp. 287-288, MSA CE 30-14. www.mdlandrec.net : accessed 22 March 2022.

[562] Worcester County Court (Land Records). Bill of sale from FRANKLIN, Lemuel to FRANKLIN, William. 26 November 1791. O, pp. 297-298, MSA CE 30-14. www.mdlandrec.net : accessed 22 March 2022.

[563] Worcester County Court (Land Records). Deed of manumission from DONE, Col. John to **DAVIS, Moses**. 02 December 1791. O, p. 299, MSA CE 30-14. www.mdlandrec.net : accessed 22 March 2022.

Liber O, folio 326; 15 June 1784

"Maryland Ss[t]. Know all men by these presents that we **Mary BLAKE** and John GUNN of Worcester County in the State of Maryland are held and firmly bound unto the State of Maryland in the full and just sum of thirty pounds Cur[ren]t money of Maryland to be paid unto the said State for which payment well and truly to be made and done we bind ourselves our and each of our heirs in and for the whole firmly by these presents sealed with our seals & dated the 15th day of June 1784 The Condition of the above Obligation is such that if the above bound **Mary BLAKE** do well & truely safe harmless keep the said State pertickler Worcester County from all costs & Charges that may arise on said Worcester County and Stait af[oresai]d by Reason of the said **Mary BLAKE** bareing a Bastard Child on the 10th day of Jan[uar]y 1783 called **Levin** then the above Obligation shall be void otherwise to stand and Remain in full force power and Virtue in Law. ~

Signed sealed and delivered
in presence off ~ ~ ~

   Joshua TOWNSEND. ~

            Mary \\ **BLAKE** (Seal)
            (her mark)

            John GUNN ~ (Seal)"

*followed with the recordation on 22 June 1791 by court clerk James R. MORRIS[564]

Liber O, folios 336-337; 20 January 1792

"A Scedule of the Goods & Chattels rights & Credits Lands & Tenements also the Debts of Israel TOWNSEND Sen[ior] Viz. 6 Setting Chairs 1 Logwood ax 1 p[air] oyster Tongues 1 Crocked Rake 1 p[ai]r pot hooks 8 Fish Hooks Debts viz. James MARTIN £16.0.0 James LAWS 2.0.0 Mary LAWRENCE 4.6 McKimmey HUDSON 2.3 Charles GODFREY 15.0 James BENNETT 1.15.0 Col. William MORRIS 9.17.6 John TULLY deceast 1.17.4 Peter TOWNSEND 1.5.0 Abisha DAVIS 3.5.0

            Isreal + TOWNSEND
            (his mark)

A Schedule of the goods & Chattels rights and credits Lands and Tenements as also the debts of Leven COFFEN viz[t]. 1 Jack plain. 1 Smooth plain 1 Iron Square 1 Plow and Grove {? ?} Cred[i]t[s] David MURRAY £1.8.0 **Negro Dick** 1.10.0 Benjamin CLERK 5.0 David LINCH 3.0 Abner COFFAN 5.0 John HESON 5.9 Debts Comfort COFFIN £6.0.6 Cornelius COFFIN 4.10.0 Abisha DAVIS 1.8.2 Isaac PURNELL Esq[uire] 5.0.0 Samuel TUBB 11.6 Molly LAWRENCE 18.0 John SCHOOLFEILD 2.5.0 Thomas WEBB 6.6 James DUER Joshua TOWNSEND 1.5.0 ~

            Levin X COFFEN
            (his mark)"

*followed on folio 337 with the acknowledgment by Justices of the Peace Philip QUINTON and Joshua TOWNSEND and the recordation by court clerk James R. MORRIS[565]

Liber O, folios 338-339; 15 February 1792

"Know all men by these presents that I William HANDY of Worcester County and State of Maryland am held & firmly bound unto Angelo ATKINSON, George ATKINSON, Benjamin ATKINSON Betsey ATKINSON & Ann ATKINSON (the Childern of Angelo & Comfort ATKINSON) of the County and State af[ore]s[ai]d in the full and Just Sum of One thousand

---

[564] Worcester County Court (Land Records). Bastardy bond from **BLAKE, Mary** and GUNN, John to the State of Maryland. 15 June 1784. O, p. 326, MSA CE 30-14. www.mdlandrec.net : accessed 17 June 2022.

[565] Worcester County Court (Land Records). Schedule of Goods, Chattels, Rights, Credits and Debts of TOWNSEND, Israel and COFFEN, Levin. 20 January 1792. O, pp. 336-337, MSA CE 30-14. www.mdlandrec.net : accessed 22 March 2022.

current money of Maryland to the which payment well & truly to be made & done. I bind myself my heirs Executors & Administrators firmly by these presents Sealed with my seal & dated this fifteenth day of February anno Dom[ini] one thousand Seven hundred and Ninety And Two. The Condition of the above obligation is such, that proved the said William HANDY and Comfort ATKINSON (Mother of the five children as af[ore]s[ai]^d) should Marry together, that them the said William HANDY shall and will freely and peaceably Covenant & agree the said Comfort ATKINSONs giving to her af[ore]s[ai]^d Children at any time she shall please and either by her last will and Testament, or by her Deed of Gift (Just as she shall think most proper) and that he shall & will ratify & Confirm the same the following Negroes and other property as herein expressed & now in said Comforts possession Viz^t. one Negro boy called **Harry** one Negro Girl called **Esther** (the daughter of **Hannah**) one Negro Girl called **Orris** one Negro Girl called **Esther** (the Daughter of **Dinah** one Negro Girl called **Rhody** and one Negro Girl called **Rachel** two feather beds and furniture (not exceeding the value of Eleven pounds five shillings both together) Six new Silver Spoons, twelve Silver Tea spoons one Copper {?} kettle the Comforts present riding Saddle one common pewter dish and one Copper Coffee pot provided which things, are now in the possession of the said Comfort ATKINSON, do live & are to be had, this bond to be renewed once in every Seven years if reasonably required, and the Contents of which bond to be Complyed with according to its true meaning and import then the same to be void & of no effect or otherwise to stand & remain in full force power & virtue in Law

Signed Sealed and delivered	John POSTLY	William HANDY (Seal)
in the presence of us ~	John L PURNELL	
	Levin RIGGON"	

*followed on folio 339 with the acknowledgment by Justice of the Peace John POSTLY on 17 February 1792 and the recordation by court clerk James R. MORRIS on 18 February 1792[566]

Liber O, folios 339-341; 08 February 1792

"This Indenture made this Eighteenth day of February anno Dom[ini] one thousand seven hundred Ninety & two between Comfort ATKINSON of Worcester County in the State of Maryland of the one part and Thomas Robins HANDY, Comfort HANDY, James HANDY & Joyce HANDY the Childern of William HANDY) all of Worcester County and State of Maryland of the other part Witnesseth that the said Comfort ATKINSON for the Sum of one thousand pounds current money of Maryland to her in hand paid by the said Thomas Robins HANDY Comfort HANDY, James HANDY & Joyce HANDY at & before the sealing & delivery of these presents, the Receipt whereof the said Comfort ATKINSON doth hereby confess & acknowledge, Hath given granted, Bargained and Sold & by these presents doth give grant bargain and Sell unto the said Thomas Robins HANDY, Comfort HANDY, James HANDY & Joyce HANDY their Heirs and Assigns forever all her the said Comfort ATKINSONs property as is herein after expressed, Vizt One Negro Man called **Jacob**, one Negro Woman called **Judah** one Negro Woman called **Hannah** One negro boy called **Harry** one Negro girl called **Rhody** one Negro girl called **Esther** (the daughter of **Dinah**), one Negro Girl called **Esther** (the Daughter of **Hannah**) one Negro Girl called **Leah** one Negro Girl called **Orris** one negro Girl called **Bridget** and one negro called **Rachel** and the half part of a Negro Man called **Pompey** (otherwise **Jacob**) together with all the increase of the said Negroes four head of Horses twenty head of Hogs Fourteen head of black cattle and fourteen head of Sheep for beds and furniture two Cases of Drawers one {?} old Riding Chair and all her remaining household property Kitchen furniture & plantation Implements & Utensels whatever together with her whole property of every kind & nature both real and personal To have & to hold the whole of the said property and every part & parcel thereof with the appurtenances thereunto belonging unto the said Thomas Robins HANDY Comfort HANDY, James HANDY & Joyce HANDY their heirs and Assigns forever {?} & to & for no other use or purpose Whatsoever

---

[566] Worcester County Court (Land Records). Bond from HANDY, William to ATKINSON, Angelo, George, Benjamin, Betsey, and Anne. 15 February 1792. O, pp. 338-339, MSA CE 30-14. www.mdlandrec.net : accessed 22 March 2022.

except as is hereinafter excepted Viz^t. Excepted and provided always and it is hereby positively and explicitly declared to be the only true intent and meaning of these presents, that if the said Comfort & William HANDY father of the four aforesaid Childern, should Marry together and the said Comfort ATKINSON should be left the widow of the said William HANDY the she do not nor shall not take receive claim nor demand any thirds dower part or parcel of the said William HANDYs Estate neither real nor personal nor receive any thing more then what the said William HANDY may give her by his last written will and Testament and that the said Comfort ATKINSON hath not nor shall by any act or Deeds of hers subject the said William HANDY his heirs Executors nor administrators to the payment of any secreat or under handed debt or debts, Bond or Bonds of any kind nor that she hath not nor shall not do any act or thing whereby to give or convey away her property in a secreat manner contrary to the knowledge & Consent of the said William HANDY all which Matters & things being truly & honestly adhered to & complied with by the said Comfort ATKINSON according to the true Meaning and import of these presents then this deed or Instrument of Writing to be void to all intents & purposes or of no effect whatsoever, otherwise to stand & remain in full force power & virtue in Law,

Signed Sealed and delivered in the presence of ~	John POSTLY John S. PURNELL"	Comfort ATKINSON (Seal)

*followed on folio 341 with the acknowledgment by Justices of the Peace John POSTLY and John S. PURNELL and the recordation on 24 February 1792 by court clerk James R. MORRIS[567]

Liber O, folios 346-347; 04 July 1792

"Know all men by these presents that I Solomon ESHUM of Worcester County in the State of Maryland for and in consideration of the Sum of two hundred Silver Dollars to me in hand paid by Barckley McGEE of the South West territory of the United States of America at and before the Sealing and delivery hereof Have bargained and Sold and by these do bargain Sell and deliver unto the said Barckley McGEE his heirs and Assigns forever a Negro Man called **Filer** now in the possession of the af[ore]s[ai]^d Barckley McGEE To have and to hold the af[ore]s[ai]^d Negro Man called **Filer** hereby bargained and Sold unto the said Barckley McGEE his heirs and assigns forever and the said Solomon ESHUM for himself his heirs Executors or administrators against every of them and against every other person or persons whatsoever Claiming forever hereafter to Claim any right or title to the abovementioned Negro shall and will Warrant and forever defend by these presents of which said Man called **Filer** I the said Solomon ESHUM have put the said Barkley McGEE in full possession by the delivery of these presents In Witness whereof I the said Solomon ESHUM have hereunto set my Hand and Seals this four Day of July Anno Dom[ini] Seventeen hundred and Ninety two. ~

Signed Sealed & Delivered in presents off ~	Philip QUINTON. ~"	Solomon ESHOM (Seal)

*followed on folio 347 with the acknowledgment by Justice of the Peace Philip QUINTON and the recordation by court clerk James R. MORRIS[568]

Liber O, folios 377-378; 06 March 1792

"This Indenture maid this sixth day of March in the year of our Lord one thousand seven hundred and Ninety two. Between Moses PAYNE Sen[ior] of Worcester County and State of Maryland of the one part and Jeptha PAYNE of the same place and County of the other part Witnesseth that said Moses PAYNE for and in consideration of five shillings lawfull money of

---

[567] Worcester County Court (Land Records). Deed of mortgage from ATKINSON, Comfort to HANDY, Thomas Robins, Comfort, James, and Joyce. 08 February 1792. O, pp. 339-341, MSA CE 30-14. www.mdlandrec.net : accessed 22 March 2022.
[568] Worcester County Court (Land Records). Bill of sale from ESHOM, Solomon to McGEE, Barkley. 04 July 1792. O, pp. 346-347, MSA CE 30-14. www.mdlandrec.net : accessed 22 March 2022.

Maryland to him in hand paid by the said Jeptha PAYNE before the sealing and Delivery hereof heath hereby Bargained and Sold unto the said Jepthah PAYNE him his Heirs and Assigns one Negro Man Named **Jerum** To have and to hold the said Negro Man **Jerum** to him the said Jepthah PAYNE his heirs and Assigns and the said Moses PAYNE Sen[ior] doth by these presents make over and sell all his right and title of the said Negro Man for himself and his heirs Exe[cutor]ˢ Adm[inistrator]ˢ or Assigns unto the said Jeptha PAYNE his heirs and assigns in Witness whereof the said Moses PAYNE to these presents his hand hath set and Seal affixed the day and year above written. ~

Signed sealed and Delivered
in the presents of us. ~   John S. PURNELL   Moses M PAYNE (Seal)
                                                    his Mark"

*followed on folio 378 with the acknowledgment Justice of the Peace John S. PURNELL and the recordation by court clerk James R. MORRIS[569]

Liber O, folios 396-397; 14 March 1792

"Know all men by these presents that we Robert HUDSON & Thomas HALL of Worcester County in the State of Maryland for and in consideration of the sum of five shillings current of Maryland to them in hand paid at and before the Sealing and delivery of these presents by Joshua BOWEN of the County and State af[ore]s[ai]ᵈ the receipt whereof the said Robert HUDSON and Thomas HALL doth hereby acknowledge have bargained and Sold and by these presents doth hereby bargain and Sell unto the said Joshua BOWEN his heirs & Assigns the one third part of One Negro man Named **George**, To have and to hold the af[ore]s[ai]ᵈ Negro Man named **George** by these presents bargained and Sold unto the said Joshua BOWEN his heirs and Assigns forever and we the said Robert HUDSON and Thomas HALL for ourselves and our heirs the said Negro **George** will Warrant and forever defend unto the said Joshua BOWEN his heirs and Assigns forever against the lawfull Claim or Claims of all manner of person or persons Whatsoever that shall ever hereafter claim the same from by or under us. In Witness whereof the said Robert HUDSON and Thomas HALL to these presents their hands have Set and Seals affixed the fourteenth day of March anno Domini Seventeen hundred & Ninety two ~

Signed Sealed and   John ENNIS   Robert HUDSON (Seal)
Delivered in presence of   Thomas HALL   (Seal)"

*followed on folio 397 with the acknowledgment by Justice of the Peace Joshua TOWNSEND and the recordation on 20 March 1792 by court clerk James R. MORRIS[570]

Liber O, folios 397-398; 14 March 1792

"Know all men by these presents that we Joshua BOWEN and Thomas HALL of Worcester County in the State of Maryland for and in consideration of the Sum of five shillings to us in hand paid at and before the Sealing and delivery of these presents by Robert HUDSON of the County and State af[ore]s[ai]ᵈ the receipt whereof the said Joshua BOWEN and Thomas HALL doth hereby acknowledge have bargained and Sold and by these presents doth hereby bargain and sell unto the said Robert HUDSON his heirs and Assigns, the one third part of Negro **Lydia** and her young child, the one third part of Negroes **Tamer**, **Sarah** and **Rhoda**, To have and to hold the one third part of the abovementioned Negroes by these presents bargained and Sold unto the said Robert HUDSON his heirs and Assigns forever, and we the said Joshua BOWEN and Thomas HALL for ourselves and our heirs the said one third part of the af[ore]s[ai]ᵈ Negroes will warrant and forever defend unto the said Robert HUDSON his heirs and Assigns forever against the claim right and title of us or our heirs or any other person or persons claiming

---

[569] Worcester County Court (Land Records). Bill of sale from PAYNE, Moses Sr. to PAYNE, Jeptha. 06 March 1792. O, pp. 377-378, MSA CE 30-14. www.mdlandrec.net : accessed 23 March 2022.

[570] Worcester County Court (Land Records). Bill of sale from HUDSON, Robert and HALL, Thomas to BOWEN, Thomas. 14 March 1792. O, pp. 396-397, MSA CE 30-14. www.mdlandrec.net : accessed 23 March 2022.

the same from by or under us or either of us. In Testimony whereof the said Joshua BOWEN and Thomas HALL to these presents our hands have set and Seals affixed the 14th day of March 1792

Signed Sealed and   John ENNIS.   Joshua BOWEN (Seal)
delivered in presents of   Thomas HALL (Seal)"

*followed on folio 398 with the acknowledgment by Justice of the Peace Joshua TOWNSEND and the recordation on 20 March 1792 by court clerk James R. MORRIS[571]

Liber O, folios 421-422; 07 April 1792

"Worcester County State of Maryland Know all men by these that I Eli SHOWELL of Worcester County in the State of Maryland for and in consideration of the sum of two hundred Pounds current money of Maryland to me In hand paid at and Before, the sealing and delivery of these presents by William MORRIS (of Thomas) of the County and State aforesaid the receipt whereof I do hereby acknowledged have bargained and Sold and by these presents do bargain and Sell unto the said William MORRIS his heirs and Assigns One Negro Woman by the Name of **Nell** two Negroes Boys one by the name of **Levin** the other by the name of **George** To have and to hold all and Singular the said Negroes known and called by their names **Nell Levin & George** and every of them by these presents Bargained and Sold unto the said William MORRIS his heirs and assigns forever, and I the said Eli SHOWELL for myself and my Heirs Will Warrant and forever defend the said three Negroes abovementioned by the Names of **Will** and **Levin** and **George** against me and My heirs and against all manner of person or persons whatsoever unto the said William MORRIS his heirs Executors adm[inistrato]rs or assigns forever In Witness Whereof I the said Eli SHOWELL to these presents my hand have Set and affixed the Seventh day of April 1792 ~

Burnett JOHNSON   Eli SHOWELL (Seal)"

*followed on folio 422 with the acknowledgment by Justice of the Peace Burnett JOHNSON and the recordation on 13 April 1792 by court clerk James R. MORRIS[572]

Liber O, folio 427; 15 April 1791

"Worcester County State of Maryland, April 15th day Anno 1791 Came Doctor Ezekiel HAYNIE and William TAYLOR before me the Subscriber one of the States Justices of the peace for Worcester County, and made Oath on the holy Evangils of Almighty God that they were in company together at the house of Elias TAYLOR on the 13th day of December last past (in the year 1790.) or there abouts and that the said Elias TAYLOR then gave a Negro Girl named **Leah** to his daughter Nancy TAYLOR in our presents taking the hand of the said **Leah** and puting it into the hand of his daughter af[ore]s[ai]d Reserving to himself the use and Service of the said Negro during his life, and this deponent further saith not

Sworn the 15th April Anno 1791   Ezek[ie]l HAYNIE
Before W. PURNELL   William TAYLOR"

*followed with the recordation by court clerk James R. MORRIS[573]

Liber O, folios 467-468; 01 June 1792

"Know all men by these presents that I Rives Rackliffe TOWNSEND of Worcester County and State of Maryland for and in consideration of the sum of forty pounds current money of the State af[ore]s[ai]d to me in hand paid by James GUTHERY of the County and State af[ore]s[ai]d

---

[571] Worcester County Court (Land Records). Bill of sale from BOWEN, Joshua and HALL, Thomas to HUDSON, Robert. 14 March 1792. O, pp. 397-398, MSA CE 30-14. www.mdlandrec.net : accessed 23 March 2022.
[572] Worcester County Court (Land Records). Bill of sale from SHOWELL, Eli to MORRIS, William. 07 April 1792. O, pp. 421-422, MSA CE 30-14. www.mdlandrec.net : accessed 23 March 2022.
[573] Worcester County Court (Land Records). Depositions of HAYNIE, Dr. Ezekiel and TAYLOR, William. 15 April 1791. O, p. 427, MSA CE 30-14. www.mdlandrec.net : accessed 23 March 2022.

the receipt whereof I do hereby acknowledge and of every part thereof do acquit and forever discharge the af[ore]s[ai]^d James GUTHERY his heirs executors and Administrators and by these presents do bargain and Sell the af[ore]s[ai]^d James GUTHERY his heirs and Assigns a certain Negro boy called **caleb** to the only use benefit & behoof of the af[ore]s[ai]^d James GUTHERY his heirs & Assigns & to no other Purpose Whatsoever and by Virtue of these Presents I the said Rives Rackliffe TOWNSEND for myself & my heirs do further covenant and agree to and with the af[ore]s[ai]^d James GUTHERY his heirs and assigns to Warrant & forever defend the aforesaid Negro Boy **caleb** from me and my heirs and from all and every Person or Persons Whatsoever Legally claiming the same in Witness whereof I have hereunto my hand Set & Seal affixed this day of June Anno Domini 1792 ~

Signed Sealed & delivered   Rives. R. TOWNSEND (Seal)
in presence of   W[illia]m PURNELL"

*followed with the acknowledgment by Justice of the Peace William PURNELL and the recordation on folio 468 by court clerk James R. MORRIS[574]

Liber O, folios 469-470; 02 June 1792

"Know all men by these presents that we **Nancy COLLECT** and **Samuel COLLECT Juner** of Worcester County in the State of Maryland am held and firmly bound to the State of Maryland in the full and Just sum of thirty pounds current money to be paid unto the said State of Maryland for which payment well and truely to be made and done we bind ourselves our and each of our heirs in and for the whole firmly by these presents sealed with Our Seals and dated the 2nd day of June 1792. The Condition of the above obligation is such that if the above bound **Nancy COLLECT** do well and truely save harmless keep Worcester County from all cost and charges as may or shall come against the said County by reason of the said **Nancy's** bareing a bastard child on or about the 10th day of January 1792 which child is named **Mary**. then the above obligation shall be void Otherwise to stand and remain in full force and Law ~

Signed & Sealed in   her
presents of ~   Joshua TOWNSEND. ~   **Nancy** (O) **COLLECT** (Seal)
                                                                          mark

                                                                          his
                                                                    Samuel + **COLLECT** (Seal)
                                                                          mark"

*followed on folio 470 with the recordation on 04 June 1792 by court clerk James R. MORRIS[575]

Liber O, folio 488: 29 May 1792

"Know all men by these presents that I Jacob RAMSON of Somerset County and State of Maryland for and in consideration of the Sum of five pounds Lawful money to me in hand paid by Polly DISHAROON Worcester County Before the sealling and delivering the receipt Whereof I the said Jacob RAMSON do hereby acknowledge I have granted Bargained and Sold and by these presents do grant Bargain and Sell unto the said Polly DISHAROON her heirs Executors administrators and Assigns one Negro Girl Named **Nancy** To have and to hold the said Negro **Nance** with all her increase to the said Polly DISHAROON her heirs Executors administrators or Assigns forever and I the said Jacob RAMSON for myself my heirs Executors administrators the said **Nance** will forever warrant and defend from all manner of persons whatsoever claiming any right title or claim unto the said Negro **Nance** unto the said Polly DISHAROON her heirs Executors administrators or Assigs forever in Witness whereof I have

---

[574] Worcester County Court (Land Records). Bill of sale from TOWNSEND, Rives Rackliffe to GUTHERY, James. 01 June 1792. O, pp. 467-468, MSA CE 30-14. www.mdlandrec.net : accessed 23 March 2022.

[575] Worcester County Court (Land Records). Bastardy bond from **COLLECT, Nancy** and **COLLECT Samuel Jr.** to the State of Maryland. 02 June 1792. O, pp. 469-470, MSA CE 30-14. www.mdlandrec.net : accessed 17 June 2022.

hereunto set my hand and seal this twenty Ninth day of May One thousand seven hundred and ninety two ~

Jacob RAMSON   (Seal)"

*followed with the acknowledgment by Justice of the Peace Purnell JOHNSON and the recordation on 14 June 1792 by court clerk James R. MORRIS[576]

Liber O, folio 489; 08 October 1791

"Know all men by these presents that I Jacob RAMSON of Sumerset County and State of Maryland for and in consideration of the Sum of Teen Pounds lawfull money to me in hand paid By Stephen DISHROON of Worcester County before the sealing and Delivery the receipt whereof I the said Jacob RAMSON Do harby acknowledge have granted Bargained and sold and By theas presents do grant bargain and sell unto the said Stephen DISHROON his hers Executors administrators and Assigns one Negro Woman named **Vilett** To have & to hold the said Negr **Vilett** with all her increes to the said Stephen DISHROON his heirs Executors administrators or Assigns forever & I the said Jacob RAMSON for myself my hirs Executors and administrators the said Negro Woman **Vilett** will forevery Warrant and defend from all manner of parsons whatsoever claiming any right title or claim unto the said Negro Woman named **Vilett** unto the said Stephen DISHROON his hers Executors administrators or Assigns forever In Witness whar of I have hareunto set my hand and seal this Eight day of October One thousand Seven hundred and ninety one ~

Before Purnell JOHNSON ~   Jacob RAMSON   (Seal)"

*followed with the acknowledgment by Justice of the Peace Purnell JOHNSON and the recordation on 14 June 1792 by court clerk James R. MORRIS[577]

Liber O, folios 498-499; 28 April 1792

"I the Subscriber now of Worster County and State of Maryland from mature deliberate considerations and a full pres{??}tion in my own mind that freedom is the natural right of all mankind and being in possession of the two Negroes following to wit **Zedegial** aged thirty five years **Betty** aged Seven years old I do for myself my heirs Executors and administrators hereby manumit and set them free they and Issue born in future to all intents constructions and purposes whatsoever at the time herein after Set down and Expressed to wit, **Zedegiel** on the first day of June next come twelve months **Betty** at the Expretion of Eleven years from the date hereof as witness my hand and Seal this 28th day of April A.D. 1792 ~

Sined Sealed & delivered   John POSTLY   William LISTER   (Seal)
In the presents of ~   Jesse STURGIS"

*followed on folio 499 with the acknowledgment by Justice of the Peace John POSTLY and the recordation on 15 June 1792 by court clerk James R. MORRIS[578]

Liber O, folios 523-524; 07 July 1792

"This Indenture made the seventh day of July in the year of our Lord one thousand Seven hundred & ninety two Between Rives R. TOWNSEND of Worcester County and State of Maryland of the one part and Zadok STURGIS of the same place on the other part. Witnesseth that for and in consideration of thirty pounds current money of the State af[ore]s[ai]ᵈ to me in

---

[576] Worcester County Court (Land Records). Bill of sale from RAMSON, Jacob to DISHAROON, Polly. 29 May 1792. O, p. 488, MSA CE 30-14. www.mdlandrec.net : accessed 23 March 2022.
[577] Worcester County Court (Land Records). Bill of sale from RAMSON, Jacob to DISHROON, Stephen. 08 October 1791. O, p. 489, MSA CE 30-14. www.mdlandrec.net : accessed 23 March 2022.
[578] Worcester County Court (Land Records). Deed of manumission from LISTER, William to **Zedegiel** and **Betty**. 28 April 1792. O, pp. 498-499, MSA CE 30-14. www.mdlandrec.net : accessed 23 March 2022.

hand paid by the af[ore]s[ai]^d Zadok STURGIS at and before the sealing and delivery of these presents the receipt whereof the said Rives Rackliffe TOWNSEND doth hereby acknowledge and himself satisfy[e]^d contented and paid and hath bargained and sold to the af[ore]s[ai]^d Zadok STURGIS a certain Negro man called **James** now in the possession of the af[ore]s[ai]^d Rives R. TOWNSEND to him the af[ore]s[ai]^d Zadok STURGIS his heirs and Assigns forever and to no other use or purpose whatsoever, and he the said Rives R. TOWNSEND doth covenant & agree for himself and his heirs do and with the af[ore]s[ai]^d Zadok STURGIS him his heirs Executors administrators or assigns that he the said Rives R. TOWNSEND & his heirs will Warrant and forever defend the af[ore]s[ai]^d negro man called **James** against the lawfull claim title or demand of all person or persons whatsoever, in Witness whereof the said Rives R. TOWNSEND hath hereunto his hand Set and Seal affixed the day and year above written ~

Signed Sealed & delivered   Rives R. TOWNSEND   (Seal)
in presence of   John POSTLY"

*followed on folio 524 with the acknowledgment by Justice of the Peace John POSTLY and the recordation on 10 July 1792 by court clerk James R. MORRIS[579]

Liber O, folios 545-546; 30? February 1792

"This Indenture maid this 30 day of February 1792 in the year of our lord one thousand seven hundred and Ninety two between Samuel TARR of Worcester County and State of Maryland of the one Pairt and Negro **Esther** of the other part Witnesseth that the said Samuel TARR for and in consideration of the Justice Dew the Negro and being desirous that the said Negro should be manumitted and forever set free from Slavery when she shall arrive to the age of twenty one years hath Manumitted set free and forever discharged and by these presents doth Manumit set free and forever discharge the said Negro from Slavery after the age of twenty one years and from him the said Samuel TARR his heirs or Assigns at the age of twenty one years and the said Samuel TARR doth covenant and agree to and with the said Negro **Ester** and her heirs that she the said **Esther** are by these presents manumitted and forever sett free at the age of twenty one years as far as his Perogative in Point of Law can or may be deemed to that end and purpose effectual and that the said Samuel TARR his heirs Executors or administrators hath not nor ever shall have any right title interest claim or demand in and unto her the said **Ester** after twenty one years old or unto her heirs in testimony Whereof said Samuel TARR to these presents his hand hath set and seal affixed the day and year above written ~

Signed Sealed and delivered   Outten STURGIS   Samuel TARR   (Seal)
In presents of us . . . .
                              Martha +̲ STURGIS
                                   mark"

*followed with the acknowledgment by Justice of the Peace Outten STURGIS and the recordation on 10 August 1792 by court clerk James R. MORRIS[580]

Liber O, folios 549-551; 13 August 1792

"Maryland Worcester Ss^t. Know all men by these presents that I William TOWNSEND of the County and State afforesaid for and in consideration of the sum of fifty five Pounds current money of Maryland to me in hand paid by Zadok POWELL of the same place at or before the Ensealing & delivery of these presents wherewith. I confess my self to be fully satisfied contented & paid, Have bargained sold and delivered, and by these presents do fully clearly and absolutely Bargain sell & deliver unto the said Zadok POWELL one Negro Man named **Joshua** about twenty five years old. To have and to hold the said Negro Man named **Joshua** unto the said Zadok POWELL his Executors Administrators or Assigns to him and their own proper

---

[579] Worcester County Court (Land Records). Bill of sale from TOWNSEND, Rives Rackliffe to STURGIS, Zadok. 07 July 1792. O, pp. 523-524, MSA CE 30-14. www.mdlandrec.net : accessed 23 March 2022.
[580] Worcester County Court (Land Records). Deed of manumission from TARR, Samuel to **Esther**. 30 February 1792. O, pp. 545-546, MSA CE 30-14. www.mdlandrec.net : accessed 23 March 2022.

uses and behoofs forever, And further it is hereby provided & agreed to by the said Willi TOWNSEND & his heirs that if the said Negro Man **Joshua** shall be legally claimed and recovered (by the legal claim of any other person whatever) from the said Zadok POWELL his heirs Executors or administrators, that then the said William TOWNSEND doth and shall bargain sell and deliver and by these presents doth bargain sell & deliver unto the said Zadok POWELL his heirs Executors Administrators or Assigns one other Negro man named **Kiah** about thirty years old (now in the possession and the property of the said William) in the room and stead of the said negro **Joshua** and in the same manner and form as the s[ai]^d Negro **Joshua** is hereby bargain & sold & also pay and satisfy to the said Zadok POWELL his heirs Executors or administrators all necessary legal expences he or they may sustain or be put to in defending their right in the said Negro **Joshua** And the said William TOWNSEND for himself his heirs Executors & Administrators hereby covenants and agrees to and with the said Zadok POWELL his heirs and Assigns that he the said William TOWNSEND and his heirs the said Negro Man **Joshua** unto the said Zadok POWELL his heirs and Assigns against all people shall and will Warrant & by these presents forever defend & also that if the said Negro **Joshua** shall by any person be legally claimed and recovered from the said Zadok or his heirs as afforesaid that then the said William and his heirs doth by these presents Warrant and defend the above named Negro **Kiah** in the room and place of the said Negro **Joshua** unto the said Zadok his heirs and Assigns against all persons whatever & also pay the necessary legal expence as afforesaid to the said Zadok POWELL his heirs or Assigns which he or they may sustain or be put to by defending their right in the said Negro **Joshua** against the legal claim of any person. In Witness whereof I have hereunto set my hand and seal this thirteenth day of August anno Domini 1792

Sealed & delivered 　　　　　　　　　　　　　　　　　　　　William TOWNSEND (Seal)
in presence of 　　　John POSTLY"

*followed on folio 550 with the acknowledgment Justice of the Peace John POSTLY and the recordation on 17 August 1792 by court clerk James R. MORRIS on folio 551[581]

Liber O, folio 551; 15 August 1792

"Maryland Worcester Ss^t. Know all men by these presents that I Samuel Hopkins ROUND of the County and State affores[ai]^d for and in consideration of fifty five pounds current money of Maryland to me in hand paid by Josiah DALE of the same place at and before the sealing and delivery of these Presents the receipt whereof he doth hereby acknowledge and confess himself to be fully satisfied contented and paid hath bargained sold and delivered by these presents doth bargain and sell and deliver, unto the said Josiah DALE his heirs and Assigns one Negro Man named **Armwell** about twenty two years of age. To have and to hold the said Negro Man **Armwell** unto the said Josiah DALE his heirs and Assigns to his and their own proper use benefit and behoof and no other use or purpose whatever, And the Samuel H. ROUND for himself and his heirs Executors and Administrators the said Negro Man **Armwell** unto the said Josiah DALE her heirs and Assigns, against the legal claim of all persons whatever shall and will warrant and by these Presents forever defend In Witness whereof I have hereunto set my hand and seal affixed this fifteenth day of August A.D. 1792 ~

Sealed & Delivered 　　　　　　　　　　　　　　　　　　　　Sam[uel] H. ROWND (Seal)
in presence of. 　　　John POSTLY"

*followed with the acknowledgment by Justice of the Peace John POSTLY and the recordation on 17 August 1792 by court clerk James R. MORRIS[582]

---

[581] Worcester County Court (Land Records). Bill of sale from TOWNSEND, William to POWELL, Zadok. 13 August 1792. O, pp. 549-551, MSA CE 30-14. www.mdlandrec.net : accessed 23 March 2022.
[582] Worcester County Court (Land Records). Bill of sale from ROWND, Samuel Hopkins to DALE, Josiah. 15 August 1792. O, p. 551, MSA CE 30-14. www.mdlandrec.net : accessed 23 March 2022.

Liber O, folios 559-560; 23 August 1792

"To all People to whom these presents shall or may come Know ye that we Margaret FASSITT, Robert MITCHELL Stephen WHITE and Mary MURAY for and in consideration of two thousand pounds to us in hand paid by John RICHARDS and Isaac AYRES at and before the delivery of these presents the receipt whereof we hereby acknowledge have granted bargained and Sold and by these presents do grant bargain and sell unto the af[ore]s[ai]d John RICHARDS & Isaac AYRES their heirs and Assigns forever the following Negroes to wit one Negro Woman called **Let** and her child **Ben** one Negro Woman called **Bradis** one Negro Woman called **Ciller** one Negro Woman called **Comfort**, one Negro Woman called **Bet** one Negro Woman called **Comfort** one Negro Girl Called **Sarah** one Negro Girl called **Pleasant** with her three children to wit. **Amos Leah** and **Abel** one Negro Boy called **John** one called **Sampson** one called **Glasgow** and one called **Joe** Negro Woman called **Hannah** and her two Children **Zebulon** and **Sarah** also the following articles to wit one Bed and furniture one old desk one Cupboard one Walnut Table, one Bed, the Picture of Matthew HALE ditto Frederick the third ditto Edward BARCOMEN To have and to hold the af[ore]s[ai]d Negroes and goods to the af[ore]s[ai]d John RICHARDS & Isaac AYRES their heirs and Assigns forever witness our hands & Seals this 23[r]d August A D. 1792 ~

Testes John P. MITCHELL	Margaret FASSETT (Seal)
William PURNELL	Robert MITCHELL (Seal)
Geo[rge] PURNELL	Stephen WHITE (Seal)
	Mary MURRY (Seal)"

*followed on folio 560 with the acknowledgment by Justice of the Peace John P. MITCHELL and the recordation on 29 August 1792 by court clerk James R. MORRIS[583]

Liber O, folio 560; 30 August 1792

"Worcester Ss^t. To all people to whom these presents shall or may come Know ye that I William TOWNSEND of the County af[ore]s[ai]d and State of Maryland for and in consideration of my having sold a negro Boy called **Hope** belonging to William BELL and converted the money arising from the sale of the said Negro to my own use do grant bargain and sell to the said William BELL his heirs and Assigns a Negro Boy called **Luke**, To have and to hold the Negro Boy for the Consideration af[ore]s[ai]d to him the said William BELL his heirs and Assigns forever. Witness my hand and Seal this 30th day of August A.D. 1792 ~

Josiah MITCHELL	William TOWNSEND (Seal)
Fra.^{s} Jen.^{s} HENRY"	

*followed with the acknowledgment by Justice of the Peace Josiah MITCHELL and the recordation on 31 August 1792 by court clerk James R. MORRIS[584]

Liber O, folio 562; 08 September 1792

"Know all men by these presents that I Esau WILLIAMS of Worcester County State Maryland farmer for and in consideration of the sum of fifty two pound ten shillings current money of the province af[ore]s[ai]d to me in hand paid by Ebenezer DALE of the same place af[ore]s[ai]d the receipt whereof I do hereby acknowledge in full give grant bargain and sell unto the said Ebenezer DALE all my right title claim & Interest of a certain Negro Man named **Sam** now in the possession of him the said Ebenezer DALE which said Negro, I warrant & defend against all persons whatsoever from me my heirs Executors administ[rators] unto the said DALE his

---

[583] Worcester County Court (Land Records). Bill of sale from FASSETT, Margaret, MITCHELL, Robert, WHITE, Stephen and MURRY, Mary to RICHARDS, John and AYRES, Isaac. 23 August 1792. O, pp. 559-560, MSA CE 30-14. www.mdlandrec.net : accessed 23 March 2022.
[584] Worcester County Court (Land Records). Bill of sale from TOWNSEND, William to BELL, William. 30 August 1792. O, p. 560, MSA CE 30-14. www.mdlandrec.net : accessed 23 March 2022.

heirs Executors & administ[rators] and Assigns forever in Witness whereof I have hereunto put my hand & Seal this 8th day of Sept[ember] Anno Domini 1792 ~

Testes. John P. MITCHELL Esau WILLIAMS (Seal)
Milby SMITH"

*followed with the acknowledgment by Justice of the Peace John P. MITCHELL and the recordation on 13 September 1792 by court clerk James R. MORRIS[585]

Liber O, folios 576-577; 21 July 1792

"This Indenture made and concluded this twenty first day of July One thousand Seven hundred and Ninety two Between Moses CHAILLE of Worcester County of the one part and Negro **Tab** female formerly the property of the said CHAILLE of the County af[ore]s[ai]d of the other part Witnesseth that whereas the said Moses CHAILLE for and in consideration of the Sum of fifteen pounds current money of the State of Maryland, to him in hand paid by the said Negro **Tabb** at or before the ensealing and delivering hereof the receipt whereof the said Moses CHAILLE doth hereby acknowledge, and the said **Tab** forever acquitted exonerated and discharged & the said Moses CHAILLE hath given granted released and discharged the said Negro **Tab** from Slavery, and by these presents doth give grant release and discharge the said Negro **Tab** from Slavery forever To have hold possess and enjoy the full clear and entire right use of her the said Negro **Tab**s Liberty fuly clearly and absolutely discharged from the said Moses CHAILLE his heirs Ex[ecuto]rs adm[inistrators] & Assigns forever and for no other use or purpose Whatsoever, And the said Moses CHAILLE for himself his heirs Ex[ecuto]rs adm[inistrators] & Assigns doth covenant and agree to and with the said **Tab** the full entire and perfect use and enjoyment of freedom, to the said **Tab** shall and will Warrant and forever defend by these presents. In Witness whereof the said Moses CHAILLE to these presents his hand hath set and seal affixed the day and year above Written ~

Signed seal[e]d & delivered Moses CHAILLE (Seal)
In presence of Isaac MARSHALL"

*followed on folio 577 with the acknowledgment by Justice of the Peace Isaac MARSHALL and the recordation on 01 October 1792 by court clerk James R. MORRIS[586]

Liber O, folio 595; 30 October 1792

"A bill of List of a Negro called **Hager** brought by the Subscriber from the State of Delaware to Worcester County in the State of Maryland to witt Negro **Hager** af[ore]s[ai]d was and is the daughter of Negro **Nance**, which Negro **Nance** and her child **Hager** now given to Jenny RICHARDS wife of the Subscriber by Bathsheba MILLERs last will and Testament which will beareth date the 23rd day of June 1790 which will is recorded among the records of Sussex County in the State of Delaware ~

October 30th 1792. Joseph RICHARDS (Seal)"

*followed with the recordation by court clerk James R. MORRIS[587]

Liber O, folios 631-632; 01 December 1792

"To all persons, To whom these presents shall come Know ye that I William MORRIS of Worcester County in the State of Maryland being desirous to Manumitt and sett free the several Negro Slaves following to wit **Sam**, **Jack**, **Sall**, **Nance**, and **Patience**. For and in consideration of the faithfull Services of the said Negroes I the said William MORRIS do by these presents,

---

[585] Worcester County Court (Land Records). Bill of sale from WILLIAMS, Esau to DALE, Ebenezer. 08 September 1792. O, p. 562, MSA CE 30-14. www.mdlandrec.net : accessed 23 March 2022.
[586] Worcester County Court (Land Records). Deed of manumission from CHAILLE, Moses to **Tab**. 21 July 1792. O, pp. 576-577, MSA CE 30-14. www.mdlandrec.net : accessed 23 March 2022.
[587] Worcester County Court (Land Records). Certificate of importation into Maryland from RICHARDS, Joseph for **Hager**. 30 October 1792. O, p. 595, MSA CE 30-14. www.mdlandrec.net : accessed 23 March 2022.

give, grant, Manumit set free and forever discharge, the said **Sam**, **Jack**, **Sall**, **Nance** and **Patience** the same to take effect upon the first day of January next ensuing the execution of these presents. To have and hold and freely to enjoy unto them the said Negroes **Sam**, **Jack Sall Nance** and **Patience** severally their and each of their Freedoms and Liberty forever after the first day of January next according to the tenor and effect of these presents in full and ample manner without any let Hindrance claim control or authority of any person or persons whatever. In Testimony whereof I the said William MORRIS hath to these presents my hand set and seal affixed this 1st day of December anno Dom[ini] 1792. ~

Signed Sealed and delivered   William MORRIS   (Seal)
In presence of ~   John DONE ~"

*followed on folio 632 with the acknowledgment by Justice of the Peace John DONE and the recordation by James R. MORRIS[588]

Liber O, folios 638-639; 17 October 1791

"State of Maryland Worcester County Ss^t. To all whome these presents may come or depend, Know ye, that I John TULL in a Weak and low condition and at this time have settled my worldly affairs as touching What I have been possesse[e]^d with in World only omitting as touching my promis and Engagements to Negro **Daniel** who I have held a slave a number of years past and on deliberate reflection I the said John TULL do by these presents Emancipate my said Negro **Daniel** aged about fifty years and set him the said **Daniel** to be free from the call, controul, command, or disposal of any heir or heirs of me my heirs or Executors. In Testimony whereof I the said John TULL to this my Emancipation of the above named Negro **Daniel**, declaring and pronouncing him to be forever hereafter a freeman have this seventeenth day of October A.D. 1791 Sett my hand and affixed my seal {?} presents off

John P. MITCHELL
Josiah MITCHELL   John J TULL (Seal)
                                                              his Mark"

*followed on folio 639 with the recordation on 28 December 1792 by court clerk James R. MORRIS[589]

Liber O, folio 639; 28 December 1792

"Maryland Worcester County. Know all men by these presents that I Robert SCHOOLFIELD of Worcester County and State of Maryland for and in consideration of the sum of Fifty pounds current money of Maryland to me in hand paid by Henry PARKER Junior of the same place and State af[ore]s[ai]^d at or before the Sealing and delivery of these presents, the receipt whereof I the said Robert SCHOOLFIELD do hereby acknowledge, Have granted, bargained and sold and by these presents do grant bargain and sell unto the said Henry PARKER his heirs Executors and administrators and Assigns a Negro Man named **Jack** and a Negro Woman named **Siller** Slaves To have and to hold the said Negro Man **Jack** and Negro Woman **Sillar** slaves above bargained and sold unto the said Henry PARKER his heirs Executors administrators and Assigns and I the said Robert SCHOOLFIELD for myself my heirs Executors and administrators all and singular the said Negro Slaves unto the said Henry PARKER his heirs Executors administrators and Assigns against me the said Robert SCHOOLFIELD my heirs Executors and administrators and against all {?} and every other person and persons whatsoever shall and will warrant and forever defend by these presents. In

---

[588] Worcester County Court (Land Records). Deed of manumission from MORRIS, William to **Sam, Jack, Sall, Nance, and Patience**. 01 December 1792. O, pp. 631-632, MSA CE 30-14. www.mdlandrec.net : accessed 24 March 2022.
[589] Worcester County Court (Land Records). Deed of manumission from TULL, John to **Daniel**. 17 October 1791. O, pp. 638-639, MSA CE 30-14. www.mdlandrec.net : accessed 24 March 2022.

Witness Whereof I have hereunto set my hand and Seal this 28th day of December anno Domini 1792 ~

Signed Sealed and   Robert SCHOOLFIELD (Seal)
delivered in presence of   Joshua TOWNSEND"

*followed with the acknowledgment by Justice of the Peace Joshua TOWNSEND and the recordation on 31 December 1792 by court clerk James R. MORRIS[590]

Liber O, folio 660; 05 January 1793

"Know all men by these presents that I John TULL of Worcester County for and in consideration of the sum of thirty three pounds ten shillings current money of Maryland to me in hand paid before the ensealing and delivery hereof by William VERNETSON of the County af[ore]s[ai]d the receipt whereof I do hereby acknowledge and therefrom do forever acquit and discharge the said William VERNETSON his executors administrators and assigns have given granted bargained and Sold and by these presents do give grant bargain and sell unto the said William VERNETSON One negro boy named **James**, To have and to hold the said negro boy **James** to the said to the said William VERNETSON and to his heirs and assigns forever and I the said John TULL for myself my heirs executors and administrators do hereby covenant and agree with the said William VERNETSON his Executors administrators and assigns that I will warrant and forever hereafter defend the aforesaid Negro boy **James** to the said William VERNETSON and his heirs executors administrators and assigns against the claim right and title of all persons whatever. Given under my hand and seal this fifth day of January in the year of our Lord one thousand Seven hundred and ninety three ~/ . ~ / . ~

Signed Sealed and   John TULL (Seal)
delivered in presence of   James SELBY"

*followed with the acknowledgment by Justice of the Peace James SELBY and the recordation on 18 January 1793 by court clerk James R. MORRIS[591]

Liber O, folio 661; 22 January 1793

"Know all men by these presents that I James SELBY of the County of Worcester Esq[uire] for and in consideration of the sum of fifty pounds current money to me in hand paid before the ensealing and delivery hereof by Levin MERRILL of the Co[unt]y afores[ai]d the receipt whereof I do hereby acknowledge and therefrom do forever acquit and discharge the s[ai]d Levin MERRILL his heirs Executors administrators and af[ore]s[ai]d have given granted bargained and sold and by these presents do give grant bargain and sell unto the s[ai]d Levin MERRILL one negro boy named **Robbin**. To have and to hold the s[ai]d negro boy **Robbin** to the s[ai]d Levin MERRILL and to his heirs and assigns forever and I the s[ai]d James SELBY for myself my heirs executors and administrators do hereby Covenant & agree with the s[ai]d Levin MERRILL his heirs Executors adm[inistrato]rs & ass[ign]s that I will warrant and forever defend the af[ore]s[ai]d negro boy **Robbin** to the s[ai]d Levin MERRILL and his heirs executors adm[inistrato]rs & ass[ign]s against the claim right and title of all persons whatever and also from all pretentions or claim of freedom that the said **Robbin** may pretend or claim under any colour or pretense whatever on acc[oun]t of this sale removal out of my service or any cause or act heretofore caused acted or done given under my hand and seal this 22nd day of January in the year of our Lord one thousand Seven hundred & ninety three

Signed sealed and   James SELBY (Seal)
delivered in presence of   Philip QUINTON ~"

---

[590] Worcester County Court (Land Records). Bill of sale from SCHOOLFIELD, Robert to PARKER, Henry Jr. 28 December 1792. O, p. 639, MSA CE 30-14. www.mdlandrec.net : accessed 24 March 2022.

[591] Worcester County Court (Land Records). Bill of sale from TULL, John to VERNETSON, William. 05 January 1793. O, p. 660, MSA CE 30-14. www.mdlandrec.net : accessed 24 March 2022.

*followed with the acknowledgment by Justice of the Peace Philip QUINTON and the recordation by court clerk James R. MORRIS[592]

Liber O, folio 664; 03 January 1793

"Know all men by these presents that I John SCOTT of Worcester County, in the State of Maryland for and in consideration of the sum of thirty seven pounds ten shillings circulating money to me paid by Daniell ARMWOOD of the same place at and before the sealing and delivery hereof the receipt whereof I hereby do acknowledge and hath bargained sold and delivered and by these presents doth bargain sell and deliver unto the Daniell ARMWOOD his heirs and assigns forever One negroe woman named **Gelica** To have and to hold the said negro woman unto the said Daniell ARMWOOD his heirs and assigns forever to and for the only use benefit and behoof of the said Daniell ARMWOOD his heirs and assigns forever and for no other use or purpose whatever and the said John SCOTT for himself his heirs executors and administrators doth covenant grant and agree to and with the said the said Daniell ARMWOOD his heirs executors administrators and assigns that he will warrant and forever defend the af[ore]s[ai]d Negroe woman called **Gelica** against the lawfull claim right and title of all and every person or persons that now claims or that shall ever hereafter claiming any right or title to the af[ore]s[ai]d negro woman. In Testimony whereof I the said John SCOTT my hand have set & seal affixed this third day of January in the year of our lord one thousand Seven hundred and ninety three ~

John SCOTT (Seal)

Sealed and Delivered in presence of us   Cornelius DICKESON, Joshua COTTINGHAM ~"

*followed with the recordation by court clerk James R. MORRIS on 25 January 1793[593]

Liber O, folio 665; 24 January 1793

"January ye 24th day 1793, these may certify whome it may concern that my negro Girl **Lidde** aged about fourteen years old is a garl that John JOHNSON gave to his daughter Fanna MARSHALL and Levin MARSHALL during each of their natural lives and after their decease to their heirs lawfully begotten for ever, as Witness my hand.

Test. Samuel TARR ~   his
                                                        Levin X MARSHALL
                                                            mark"

*followed with the recordation by court clerk James R. MORRIS on 25 January 1793[594]

Liber O, folios 668-669; 04 February 1793

"Know all men by these presents that I Thomas PURNELL of Worcester County in the State of Maryland for and in consideration of the sum of sixty pounds Current money of Maryland to him in hand paid by Levi MERRILL of said County have bargained and Sold and by these presents doth bargain and sell unto the said Levi MERRILL one negro man named **Caleb** and the said Thomas PURNELL doth hereby warrant and forever defend the af[oresai]d negro man called **Caleb** against {?} lawfull claim right and title of all manner of persons whatsoever unto the said Levi MERRILL his heirs and assigns forever In Witness whereof the said Thomas PURNELL to these presents his hand have set and seal affixed the fourth day of February 1793

---

[592] Worcester County Court (Land Records). Bill of sale from SELBY, James to MERRILL, Levin. 22 January 1793. O, p. 661, MSA CE 30-14. www.mdlandrec.net : accessed 24 March 2022.
[593] Worcester County Court (Land Records). Bill of sale from SCOTT, John to ARMWOOD, Daniell. 03 January 1793. O, p. 664, MSA CE 30-14. www.mdlandrec.net : accessed 24 March 2022.
[594] Worcester County Court (Land Records). Certificate of importation into Maryland from MARSHALL, Levin for **Lidde**. 24 January 1793. O, p. 665, MSA CE 30-14. www.mdlandrec.net : accessed 24 March 2022.

Signed sealed and   Tho[ma]^s PURNELL   (Seal)
delivered in presence of   Joshua TOWNSEND"

*followed on folio 669 with the acknowledgment by Justice of the Peace Joshua TOWNSEND and the recordation on 05 February 1793 by court clerk James R. MORRIS[595]

Liber O, folios 670-671; 22 January 1793

"Know all men by these presents that I James MARTIN Senior of Worcester County and State of Maryland for and in consideration of the sum of fifty pounds current money of the State af[oresai]^d to me in hand paid by William THARPE of the City of Philadelphia and State of Pennsylvania at and before the execution hereof, do bargain and sell and by these presents have bargained and sold unto the said William THARPE his heirs executors administrators or assigns for and during the term of twenty years from the date hereof fully to be completed and ended one negro boy named **Levi** and one negro girl named **Candis** and at the expiration of the af[ore]s[ai]d Term it is the will and intention of the said James MARTIN that the af[ore]s[ai]^d negro boy named **Levi** and negro girl named **Candis** should be discharged and acquitted from the Service controul and authority of the said William THARPE his heirs or assigns or any other person whatsoever. To have and to hold the af[ore]s[ai]d negro boy named **Levi** and negro girl named **Candis** unto the said William THARPE his heirs or assigns during the term af[ore]s[ai]^d and no longer and the said James MARTIN for himself and his heirs doth hereby warrant with the said William THARPE his heirs or assigns that he will warrant and defend the said Negroes unto the said William THARPE his heirs and assigns for during the term af[ore]s[ai]^d against the legal claim of any person whatsoever. In Testimony whereof he hath hereunto set his hand and affixed his seal the twenty second day of January Anno Dom[ini] 1793 ~

Signed sealed and   James MARTIN   (Seal)
delivered in presence of"

*followed on folio 671 with the acknowledgment by Justice of the Peace Philip QUINTON and the recordation on 11 February 1793 by court clerk James R. MORRIS[596]

Liber O, folios 671-672; 26 January 1793

"Know all men by these presents that I Francis Jnkens HENREY of Worcester County in State of Maryland for and in consideration of the sum of forty five pounds Current money of Maryland to me in hand paid by Annanias POWELL of the same place have bargained and sold released granted and confirmed unto the said Annanias POWELL one negro garle named **Alse**. To have and to holde the aforesaid Negro garle called **Alse** hereby bargained and sold granted and confirmed unto the only proper use and behoof of him the said Annanias POWELL his heirs executors administrators and assigns forever freely quietly peaceably and intirely without any claim disturbance or hindrance of any person whatsoever & without any account to me or to any other person whatsoever to be made answered or hereafter to be rendered, so that I the said Francis J HENRY nor any other person for me or in my name have any right title interest or demand of in to or for the aforesaid negro garle or any part or parcel thereof ought to exact challenge claim or demand at any time or times hereafter but from all actions right title claim demand possession and interest shall be wholly barred and excluded by virtue of these presents and I the said Francis J HENRY, for myself my Exec[uto]^{rs} and adm[inistrato]^{rs} the af[ore]s[ai]^d negro garle unto the aforesaid Annanias POWELL his Exe[cuto]^{rs} and administrators and assigns and against all and every other person or persons whatsoever shall and will warrant and forever defend by these presents. In Witness whereof I have hereunto set my hand and seal this twenty sixth day of January Anno Domini 1793 ~

---

[595] Worcester County Court (Land Records). Bill of sale from PURNELL, Thomas to MERRILL, Levi. 04 February 1793. O, pp. 668-669, MSA CE 30-14. www.mdlandrec.net : accessed 24 March 2022.
[596] Worcester County Court (Land Records). Bill of sale from MARTIN, James Sr. to THARPE, William. 22 January 1793. O, pp. 670-671, MSA CE 30-14. www.mdlandrec.net : accessed 24 March 2022.

Signed Sealed &   Fra[nci]s Jen[kin]s HENRY (Seal)
Delivered in presence of   Josiah MITCHELL"

*followed on folio 672 with the acknowledgment by Justice of the Peace Josiah MITCHELL and the recordation on 12 February 1793 by court clerk James R. MORRIS[597]

Liber O, folios 680-681; 16 February 1793

"State of Maryland A list and certificate of a negro boy brought in in to this State named **Abraham** given to the subscriber as here after mentioned Viz^t. negro boy named **Abraham** given to Mary PERKINS wife of the subscriber by Basheba MILLER as will appear by the last will and testament of the said Basheba MILLER dated the 23th day of June Anno Domini Seventeen hundred and ninety. I certify further that the will of Basheba MILLER above recited is recorded at George Town in Sussex County in the State of Delaware as witness my hand the 16th day of February 1793 ~ . /. ~ /. ~   John PERKINS"

*followed on folio 681 with the recordation by court clerk James R. MORRIS[598]

Liber O, folio 727; 19 April 1793

"A list of two negroes brought into the State of Maryland by Micajah SELBY to wit. 1 negro woman name **Lusey**. 1 negro girl named **mille** (child of the said **Lusey** the two above named negroes fell to a ceartain Zilpah LANE who intermarried with Micajah SELBY the subscriber by a distribution made agreeable to the last will and Testament of the said Zilpah^s father Israel LANE which will is dated the 24th day of April 1787 – and recorded at acomack Court house in common wealth of Virginia as Witness my hand the 19th day of april 1793 ~

                 Micajah SELBY"

*followed with the recordation on 19 April 1793 by court clerk James R. MORRIS[599]

Liber O, folios 727-728; 01 April 1793

"Maryland Know all men by these presents that I Henry ACKWORTH of Somerset County and State of Maryland for and in consideration of seventy pounds Current money of Maryland to me in hand paid by Jonathan HUTCHERSON of Worcester County & State af[ore]s[ai]^d at or before the sealing and delivery of these presents the receipt whereof the said Henry ACKWORTH doth hereby confess and acknowledge hath granted bargained and sold and by these presents doth grant bargain and sell to the said Jonathan HUTCHERSON his heirs and assigns forever all his the said Henry ACKWORTH's right and title to a negro man called **Handy** (Slave) unto the said Jonathan HUTCHERSON his heirs and assigns forever to the only proper use and behoof of the said Jonathan HUTCHERSON his heirs & assigns forever and for no other use intent or purpose whatsoever and the said Henry ACKWORTH doth hereby covenant and agree to and with the said Jonathan HUTCHERSON his heirs and assigns forever that the said Henry ACKWORTH and his heirs the negro man af[ore]s[ai]^d to the said Jonathan HUTCHERSON and his heirs and assigns shall and will warrant and forever defend from him and his heirs or any other person claiming by from or under him or any of them. In Testimony whereof the said Henry ACKWORTH hath hereunto set his hand and affixed his seal this first day of April Anno Domini 1793 ~

Signed sealed and delivered in presence of Esme BAYLY ~   Henry ACKWORTH (Seal)"

---

[597] Worcester County Court (Land Records). Bill of sale from HENRY, Francis Jenkins to POWELL, Annanias. 26 January 1793. O, pp. 671-672, MSA CE 30-14. www.mdlandrec.net : accessed 24 March 2022.

[598] Worcester County Court (Land Records). Certificate of importation into Maryland from PERKINS, John and Mary for **Abraham**. 16 February 1793. O, pp. 680-681, MSA CE 30-14. www.mdlandrec.net : accessed 24 March 2022.

[599] Worcester County Court (Land Records). Certificate of importation into Maryland from SELBY, Micajah and Zilpah for **Lusey** and **Mille**. 19 April 1793. O, p. 727, MSA CE 30-14. www.mdlandrec.net : accessed 24 March 2022.

*followed on folio 728 with the acknowledgment by Somerset County Justice of the Peace Esme BAYLY, the recordation by Somerset County court clerk William DONE on 16 April 1793, and the recordation by Worcester County court clerk James R. MORRIS on 18 April 1793[600]

Liber O, folios 734-735; 25 April 1793

"Know all men by these presents that I Zadok SELBY Senior of Worcester County & State of Maryland for and in Consideration of the sum of thirty pounds Current money of Maryland to me in hand paid by William SELBY Senior of the same place the receipt whereof I do hereby acknowledge and confess have bargained sold and delivered unto him the said William SELBY his heirs and assigns forever a certain negro girl Slave called **Phillis** about thirteen years old now in the possession of a certain James SELBY (son of Micajah) in Worcester County aforesaid. To have and to hold all and singular the said negro girl slave and her increase unto him the said William SELBY his heirs and assigns forever to the only proper use benefit and behoof of him the said William SELBY his heirs and assigns forever and I the said Zadok SELBY for myself my heirs executors and administrators will and shall warrant and forever defend the abovesaid negro girl slave and her increase unto him the said William SELBY his heirs and assigns forever of which said negro girl I the said Zadok SELBY have put the said William SELBY in full possession by the delivery of these presents In Witness whereof I the said Zadok SELBY to these presents my hand hath set and seal affixed this twenty fifth day of April in the year of our lord one thousand seven hundred and ninety three.

Zadok SELBY   (Seal)

Signed sealed and delivered in the presence of Joshua TOWNSEND"

*followed on folio 735 with the acknowledgment by Justice of the Peace Joshua TOWNSEND and the recordation on 26 April 1793 by court clerk James R. MORRIS[601]

Liber O, folios 742-743; 25 April 1793

"Know all men by these presents that I Joshua WHITE of worcester County in the State of Maryland for and in consideration of the sum of forty pounds current money of maryland to me in hand paid by James LECOUNT of the same place the receipt whereof I do hereby acknowledge and confess have bargained sold and delivered and by these presents doth absolutely bargain sell and deliver unto him the said James LECOUNT a negro girl slave called and known by the name of **Hinna** about fourteen years old now in the possession of the aforesaid James LECOUNT. To have and to hold the aforesaid negro unto the said James LECOUNT his heirs and assigns forever to the only proper use benefit and behoof of him the said James LECOUNT his heirs and assigns forever and the said Joshua WHITE for himself his heirs executors and administrators doth covenant grant and agree to warrant and defend the said bargained negro against the lawfull right title claim and demand of all manner of person or persons whatever unto him the said James LECOUNT his heirs and assigns forever of which said negro girl called **Henna** I have put the said LECOUNT in full possession by the delivery of these presents, In Witness whereof I the said Joshua WHITE to these present my hand hath set and seal affixed this twenty fifth day of April in the year of our Lord one thousand seven hundred and ninety three ~

his
Joshua + WHITE   (Seal)
mark

signed sealed and delivered In the presence of. Benjamin DENNIS ~"

---

[600] Worcester County Court (Land Records). Bill of sale from ACKWORTH, Henry to HUTCHERSON, Jonathan. 01 April 1793. O, pp. 727-728, MSA CE 30-14. www.mdlandrec.net : accessed 24 March 2022.

[601] Worcester County Court (Land Records). Bill of sale from SELBY, Zadok Sr. to SELBY, William Sr. 25 April 1793. O, pp. 734-735, MSA CE 30-14. www.mdlandrec.net : accessed 24 March 2022.

*followed on folio 743 with the acknowledgment by Justice of the Peace Benjamin DENNIS and the recordation on 26 April 1793 by court clerk James R. MORRIS[602]

Liber P, folios 6-7; 26 April 1793

"This Indenture made this 26th day of April Anno Domini one thousand seven hundred and ninety three Between Samuel GUNN of Worcester County and State of Maryland of the one part and Tabitha WISE of the same place of the other part. Witnesseth that the said Samuel GUNN for and in consideration of the sum of five shillings current money of Maryland to him in hand paid by the said Tabitha WISE at and before the sealing and delivery of these presents the receipt whereof the said Samuel GUNN doth hereby acknowledge and forever acquit the said Tabitha WISE and her heirs hath granted bargained and sold and by these presents doth grant bargain and sell unto the said Tabitha WISE her heirs and assigns forever all his the said Samuel GUNN right and title to a negro woman called **Sarah** and her child called **Ned** with her future increase unto the said Tabitha WISE her heirs and assigns forever and to and for no other use intent or purpose whatsoever and the said Samuel GUNN doth hereby covenant and agree to and with the said Tabitha WISE her heirs and assigns forever that he the said Samuel GUNN and his heirs the negro woman and her child af[ore]s[ai]d and her future increase to the said Tabitha WISE and her heirs and assigns shall and will warrant and forever defend from him and his heirs or any other person claiming by from or under him or them or any of them In Testimony whereof the said Samuel GUNN hath hereto set his hand affixed his seal the day and year above written ~ ~ ~ ~ ~ ~ ~ ~

Signed Sealed and   Benjamin DENNIS   Sam[ue]l GUNN   (Seal)
delivered in presence of "

*followed on folio 7 with the acknowledgment by Justice of the Peace Benjamin DENNIS and the recordation on 06 May 1793 by court clerk James R. MORRIS[603]

Liber P, folios 12-13; 17 May 1793

"Know all men by these presents that I William SELBY Senior of Worcester County and State of Maryland in consideration of the natural love and affection which I have and bear unto my beloved grand children to wit Micajah SELBY, Margaret SELBY and Mary SELBY children of my daughter Eleanor SELBY wife of James SELBY (son of Micajah) of Worcester County aforesaid and also for divers other causes and considerations me the said William SELBY hereunto moving, have given granted and confirmed and by these do give grant & confirm unto the said Micajah Margaret and Mary SELBY Minors and to the survivors of them their heirs and assigns forever (reserving and only excepting the natural life of my said daughter Eleanor) a certain negro girl called **Phillis** about fourteen years of age & negro boy called **Pompy** that I lately purchased of a certain Zadock SELBY. To have hold and enjoy all and singular the said negro girl af[ore]s[ai]d unto the said Micajah, Margaret and Mary SELBY my grand children above said their heirs and assigns forever (excepting as above excepted) to the only proper use benefit and behoof of the said Micajah, Margaret and Mary SELBY their heirs and assigns forever and I the said William SELBY all and Singular the said negro girl called **Phillis** her increase that she may hereafter happen to have and said negro boy called **Pompy** to the said Micajah, Margaret and Mary SELBY their heirs and assigns forever against me the said William SELBY, my executors administrators and all and every other person or persons whatsoever shall and will warrant and forever defend by these presents of which said negro girl I have put my above mentioned grand children in possession (to commence after the decease of my above said daughter Eleanor whom I give a lifer right in and no longer) by the delivery of these presents. In Witness my hand and seal this seventeenth day of May one thousand seven hundred and ninety three

---

[602] Worcester County Court (Land Records). Bill of sale from WHITE, Joshua to LECOUNT, James. 25 April 1793. O, pp. 742-743, MSA CE 30-14. www.mdlandrec.net : accessed 24 March 2022.
[603] Worcester County Court (Land Records). Bill of sale from GUNN, Samuel to WISE, Tabitha. 26 April 1793. P, pp. 6-7, MSA CE 30-15. www.mdlandrec.net : accessed 04 April 2022.

Signed sealed and	William SELBY sen[ior] (Seal)
delivered in the presence of Outten STURGIS"	

*followed on folio 13 with the acknowledgment by Justice of the Peace Outten STURGIS and the recordation by court clerk James R. MORRIS[604]

Liber P, folio 15; 31 May 1793

"I the subscriber of Worcester County and State of Maryland from mature deliberation considerations and a full persuasion in my own mind that freedom is the natural right of all mankind and been in possession of the fifteen following negroes to wit. **Philis** aged thirty years, **Pheby** aged twenty nine years, **Comfort** aged sixteen years, **Cate** aged twelve years, **Ary** aged ten years, **Joseph** aged four years, **Leven** aged two years, **Patience** aged fifteen years, **Jobe** aged twelve years, **Leven** aged ten years, **Littleton** aged nine years, **Luca** aged six years, **Jacob** freeborn aged four years, **Nancy** aged two years, **William** aged one year I do for myself my heirs executors and administrators hereby manumit and set them free they and their issue born in future to all intents constructions and purposes whatsoever at the time herein after severally set down and expressed to wit **Philis** from the date hereof, **Pheby** from the date hereof **Comfort** at the expiration of five years, **Cate** at the expiration of nine years, **Arcy** at the expiration of eleven years, **Joseph** at the expiration of eighteen years, **Leven** the younger at the expiration of twenty years, **Patience** at the expiration of seven years, **Jobe** at the expiration of ten years, **Leven the elder** at the expiration of twelve years, **Littleton** at the expiration of thirteen years, **Lucre** at the expiration of thirteen years, **Jacob Freeborn** at the expiration of eighteen years, **Nancy** at the expiration of nineteen years, **William** at the expiration of twenty one years, from the date hereof, as Witness my hand and seal this 31st day of May one thousand seven hundred and ninety three ~ ~

Signed sealed and	Nathaniel DIXON (Seal)
delivered in presence of Philip QUINTON"	

*followed with the acknowledgment by Justice of the Peace Philip QUINTON and the recordation on 01 June 1793 by court clerk James R. MORRIS[605]

Liber P, folio 16; 25 May 1793

"Worcester Ss[t]. Know all men by these presents that I Sarah ENNIS of the County & State af[ore]s[ai]d for the natural love and affection which I bare to my child Rachel ENNIS do give unto her my af[ore]s[ai]d daughter the sundry articles herein after expressed Viz. one negro woman known by the name of **Sabray** and **Easter** the child of the af[ore]s[ai]d **Sabray** two cows and calfs five sheep one bed and furniture one looking glass one large black walnut tabel. To have and To hold the af[ore]s[ai]d articles goods and chattels as above enumerated free from the claim of any person whatsoever and to the oly proper use and benefit of the af[ore]s[ai]d Rachel ENNIS her heirs and assigns forever. In Witness whereof I have hereunto set my hand and seal affix[e]d this 25 day of May Anno Dom[ini] 1793 ~ ~ ~

W[illia]m PURNELL	Sarah + ENNIS (Seal) her mark"

*followed with acknowledgment by Justice of the Peace William PURNELL and the recordation on 03 June 1793 by court clerk James R. MORRIS[606]

---

[604] Worcester County Court (Land Records). Deed of gift from SELBY, William to SELBY, Micajah, Margaret, and Mary. 17 May 1793. P, pp. 12-13, MSA CE 30-15. www.mdlandrec.net : accessed 04 April 2022.

[605] Worcester County Court (Land Records). Deed of manumission from DIXON, Nathaniel to **Philis, Pheby, Comfort, Cate, Joseph, etal.** 31 May 1793. P, p. 15, MSA CE 30-15. www.mdlandrec.net : accessed 04 April 2022.

[606] Worcester County Court (Land Records). Bill of sale from ENNIS, Sarah to ENNIS, Rachel. 25 May 1793. P, p. 16, MSA CE 30-15. www.mdlandrec.net : accessed 04 April 2022.

Liber P, folio 34; 12 June 1793

"Maryland, Worcester County Ss. To all to whom these presents shall come greeting I Levi MILLS of the County and State afforesaid for divers good causes and considerations me thereunto moving do hereby declare free manumit and enfranchise one negro named **Robin** to be free from this day and hence forward, and I do hereby acknowledge the said negro discharged from all claim of service and right of property whatever from me my heirs executors & administrators from henceforth and forever. As Witness my hand and seal this tweleth day of June in the year of lord one thousand seven hundred and ninety three ~

Witness present.   John POSTLY.   Sam[ue]¹ GUNN   Levi MILLS (Seal)"

*followed with the acknowledgment by Justice of the Peace John POSTLY and the recordation by court clerk James R. MORRIS[607]

Liber P, folios 34-35; 12 June 1793

"Worcester Ss. Know all men by these presents that I James TRACEY of Worcester County & State of Maryland for and in consideration of the value of thirty two pounds six shillings and eleven pence current money of the State of af[ore]s[ai]d in hand paid before the the ensealing and delivery of these presents Witnesseth that the James TRACEY for and in consideration of the above said sum do bargain sell transfer set over and deliver to the said Moses DREADEN his heirs and assigns forever the following articles and goods one bed and furnerture three head of Steers and timber cart two ploughs and harrows one cubbard and cradle one iron pot and hooks one looking glass one case of bottles and my crop as it now stands over negro woman called **Dinah** and two cows and one calf one bed and furnerture, To have and To hold the said bargained premisses unto the said Moses DREADEN his heirs Executors adm[inistrato]rs and assigns and the said James TRACEY for himself his heirs executors adm[inistrato]rs and assigns against all manner of persons shall & will warrant and forever defend the same by these presents, In Witness the James TRACEY have hereunto set his hand & seal affixed the 12th day of June 1793 ~

In presents off Philip QUINTON   James TRACEY ~ (Seal)"

*followed with the acknowledgment by Justice of the Peace Philip QUINTON and the recordation by court clerk James R. MORRIS[608]

Liber P, folio 35; 11 June 1793

"Know all men by these presents that I Sarah BEACHBORD of Worcester County in the State of Maryland for and in consideration of the sum of eighteen pounds current money of Maryland to me in hand paid before the sealing hearof by William MILBOURN have granted bargained and sold by these presents do grant bargain and sell unto the said William MILBOURN his heirs executors and administrators a negro man called **Jack** of which negro the Sarah BEACHBORD at this time put the said William MILBOURN in possession of by delivering the said negro in the name of the said MILBOURN. To have and To hold the said negro to him his heirs and assigns forever. In Testimony hearof I the said Sarah BEACHBORD hath set my hand and seal affixt this eleventh day of June Anno Domini one thousand seven hundred and ninety and three ~ ~ ~ ~

seal in the presend   James SELBY, Severn JOHNSON   Sarah BEACHBORD ~ (Seal)
of us the subscriber   John CHAILLE"

---

[607] Worcester County Court (Land Records). Deed of manumission from MILLS, Levi to **Robin**. 12 June 1793. P, p. 34, MSA CE 30-15. www.mdlandrec.net : accessed 04 April 2022.

[608] Worcester County Court (Land Records). Bill of sale from TRACEY, James to DREADEN, Moses. 12 June 1793. P, pp. 34-35, MSA CE 30-15. www.mdlandrec.net : accessed 04 April 2022.

*followed with the acknowledgment by Justice of the Peace Outten STURGIS and the recordation on 12 June 1793 by court clerk James R. MORRIS[609]

Liber P, folios 40-41; 13 June 1793

"State of Maryland Worcester County Ss^t. Know all men by these presents that I Thomas SELBY of the County and State af[ore]s[ai]^d for and in consideration of the sum of forty pounds Current passing money of the State of Maryland to me paid in hand by James FASSITT of the County and State af[ore]s[ai]^d whereof I do hereby acknowledge the recept and myself satisfied have bargained sold and unto the said James FASSITT one negro man named **Sam** about twenty four years of age, To have and To hold the said negro man, unto the said James FASSITT his heirs executors adm[inistra]t[o]^{rs} or assigns to the only proper use and behoof of the said James FASSITT his executors adm[inistra]t[o]^{rs}, and assigns forever and I the said Thomas SELBY for myself my executors and adm[inistra]t[o]^{rs}, the said bargained premisses unto the said James FASSITT his executor administrator and assigns against all persons shall and will warrant and forever defend by these presents. In Witness whereof I have hereunto set my hand and seal this thirteenth day of June Anno Dom[ini] 1793 ~ ~ ~ ~ ~

Sealed and delivered	Josiah MITCHELL	Thomas SELBY (Seal)
in the presents off.	Joshua MITCHELL"	

*followed on folio 41 with the acknowledgment by Justice of the Peace Josiah MITCHELL and the recordation on 14 June 1793 by court clerk James R. MORRIS[610]

Liber P, folios 48-49; 21 June 1793

"Know all men by these presents that we Comfort MERRILL and Hezekiah JOHNSON of Worcester County in the State of Maryland for and in consideration of the sum of five shillings to us in hand paid by Elijah MERRILL at and before the sealing and delivery of these presents do hereby acknowledge have bargained and sold and by these presents doth bargain and sell unto the said Elijah MERRILL his heirs and assigns forever all our right and title of one negro man named **Harry**. To have and to hold the said negro man named **Harry** unto the said Elijah MERRILL his heirs and assigns forever and the said Comfort MERRILL and Hezekiah JOHNSON doth hereby warrant and forever defend the said negro man unto the said Elijah MERRILL his heirs executors and adm[inistrators] against ourselves and against all person or persons claiming the said negro man from by or under us or either of us or our heirs. In Testimony whereof we the said Comfort MERRILL and Hezekiah JOHNSON to these presents our hands have sett and seals affixed the 21st day of June 1793 ~ ~ ~

Sign[e]d & Seal[e]d in presents of   Joshua TOWNSEND

                                                                                                                   her

                                                          Comfort X MERRILL (Seal)

                                                                         mark

                                                          Ezekiah JOHNSON (Seal)"

*followed on folio 49 with the acknowledgment by Justice of the Peace Joshua TOWNSEND and the recordation by court clerk James R. MORRIS[611]

Liber P, folio 50-51; 14 June 1793

"This Indenture made this fourteenth day of June in the year of our lord one thousand seven hundred and ninety three Between Capt. Thomas MARTIN of Worcester County in the State of Maryand of the one part and **Jacob ARMSTRONG** of the same place (free molatto) of the other part. Witnesseth that the aforesaid Thomas MARTIN for and in consideration of the sum

---

[609] Worcester County Court (Land Records). Bill of sale from BEACHBORD, Sarah to MILBOURN, William. 11 June 1793. P, p. 35, MSA CE 30-15. www.mdlandrec.net : accessed 04 April 2022.

[610] Worcester County Court (Land Records). Bill of sale from SELBY, Thomas to FASSITT, James. 13 June 1793. P, pp. 40-41, MSA CE 30-15. www.mdlandrec.net : accessed 04 April 2022.

[611] Worcester County Court (Land Records). Bill of sale from MERRILL, Comfort and JOHNSON, Hezekiah to MERRILL, Elijah. 21 June 1793. P, pp. 48-49, MSA CE 30-15. www.mdlandrec.net : accessed 04 April 2022.

of fifty pounds Current money of Maryland to him in hand paid at and before the sealing and delivery of these presents the receipt whereof is hereby acknowledged and confessed and the said **Jacob ARMSTRONG** his heirs Ex[ecuto]^{rs} administrators and assigns therefrom forever acquitted and discharged he the said Thomas MARTIN hath granted bargained sold conveyed and confirmed and by these presents doth absolutely grant bargain sell convey and confirm unto him the said **Jacob ARMSTRONG** his heirs and assigns forever all that part of a tract of land called Addition to Acquintico Savanah situate lying and being in Worcester County aforesaid in Acquango hundred and this part is bounded limitted and described as follows, to wit, Beginning at a marked small white gum standing on the west side of a savanah and near the said **Jacob's** fence thence with a line drawn north fifty three east eighty five poles to a small white oak thence north eight degrees west thirty four poles thence south eighty four degrees west one hundred and thirty four poles thence south twenty two degrees and forty minutes east seventy seven poles and from thence with a right line to the first bounder containing and now laid out for fifty acres of land be the same more or less together with all its rights members profits benefits priviledges and all other the appurtenances thereto belonging or in any manner appertaining. To have and To hold all and singular the above mentioned lands and premises with its appurtenances unto him the said **Jacob ARMSTRONG** his heirs and assigns forever to the only proper use benefit and behoof of him the said **Jacob ARMSTRONG** his heirs and forever and the said Thomas MARTIN for himself his heirs executors and administrators doth covenant and agree the lands and premises above set forth will and shall warrant and forever defend the same against the lawfull claim right title or demand of all manner or person or persons whatever unto him the said **Jacob ARMSTRONG** his heirs and assigns forever. In Testimony whereof the said Thomas MARTIN to these presents his hand hath set and seal affixed the day and year above written ~

Signed sealed and   Joshua TOWNSEND   Thomas MARTIN   (Seal)
delivered in the presence of   Benjamin DENNIS"

*followed on folio 51 with the acknowledgment by Justices of the Peace Joshua TOWNSEND and Benjamin DENNIS and the recordation on 25 June 1793 by court clerk James R. MORRIS[612]

Liber P, folio 53; 28 June 1793

"Worcester Ss^t. Know all men by these presents that I Elijah MERRILL of Worcester County and State of Maryland for and in consideration of the sum of fifty pounds of Maryland in hand paid at and before the sealing and delivery hereof the receipt I do hereby acknowledge have bargained and sold and by these presents do bargain and sell unto James LINDZEY his heirs and assigns forever one negro man named **Harry** about thirty years of age. To have and To hold the af[ore]s[ai]^d negro man **Harry** to the af[ore]s[ai]^d James LINDZEY his heirs and assigns to the only use of the af[ore]s[ai]^d the said James LINDZEY his heirs and assigns forever and to no other purpose whatever and the said Elijah MERRILL for himself and heirs agrees and convenants to and with the said James LINDSEY his heirs and assigns the af[ore]s[ai]^d negro man called **Harry** against the right title and claim of all manner of persons whatever to forever warrant and defend. In Witness whereof the said Elijah hereto set his hand and seal affixed this 28th day of June Anno Dom[ini] 1793 ~ ~ ~ ~ ~ ~ ~ ~

Seal[e]d & deliv[ere]d in presence of Benjamin DENNIS   Elijah MERRILL   (Seal)"

*followed with the acknowledgment by Benjamin DENNIS and the recordation on 12 July 1793 by court clerk James R. MORRIS[613]

---

[612] Worcester County Court (Land Records). Deed from MARTIN, Thomas to **ARMSTRONG, Jacob**. 14 June 1793. P, pp. 50-51, MSA CE 30-15. www.mdlandrec.net : accessed 04 April 2022.

[613] Worcester County Court (Land Records). Bill of sale from MERRILL, Elijah to LINDZEY, James. 28 June 1793. P, p. 53, MSA CE 30-15. www.mdlandrec.net : accessed 04 April 2022.

Liber P, folios 60-61; 02 July 1793

"This Indenture made this second day of July in the year of our Lord one thousand seven hundred and ninety three Between Elijah MERRILL of Worcester County & State of Maryland of the one part and William SLOCOMB of the same place of the other part Witnesseth that the said Elijah MERRILL for and in consideration of the sum of Sixty pounds Current money of Maryland to him in hand paid at & before the ensealing & delivery hereof the receipt whereof the said MERRILL doth hereby acknowledge and thencefrom doth acquit exonerate & discharge him the said William SLOCOMB his heirs and assigns forever hath given granted bargained and sold and by these presents doth give grant bargain and sell unto the af[ore]s[ai]d William SLOCOMB one negro man Slave named **Moses** given to said MERRILL by Jamina HENDERSON. To have and To hold the af[ore]s[ai]d negro to him the said William SLOCOMB him his heirs and assigns forever and the said Elijah MERRILL doth further covenant and agree to and with the said William SLOCOMB that he will at all times hereafter at the request of the said William SLOCOMB or his heirs execute any further act or deed for the more fully conveying the title of the af[ore]s[ai]d negro **Moses** to him the said William SLOCOMB or his heirs. In Testimony whereof the said Elijah MERRILL to these presents his hand hath set and seal affixed the day and date above written ~

Elijah MERRILL   (Seal)

Signed sealed and delivered in presence of John S. PURNELL"

*followed on folio 61 with the acknowledgment by Justice of the Peace John S. PURNELL and the recordation on 19 July 1793 by court clerk James R. MORRIS[614]

Liber P, folios 61-62; 19 July 1793

"Know all men by these presents that I Elizabeth SHOCKLEY of Worcester County in the State of Maryland for and in consideration of the sum of five hundred pounds to me in hand paid at and before the sealing of these presents by Joshua MORRIS of the County and State af[ore]s[ai]d the receipt whereof I the said Elizabeth SHOCKLEY do hereby acknowledge have bargained and sold and by these presents do bargain and sell unto the said Joshua MORRISS his heirs and assigns one negro boy called **Sampson** and all my right and title of the estate that is appraised in the Inventory of my husband Richard SHOCKLEY decease[e]d To have and To hold the said goods and chattels and every of them hereby bargained & sold unto the said Joshua MORRIS his heirs and assigns forever. In Testimony whereof I the said Elizabeth SHOCKLEY to these presents her hand have set and seal affixed the 19th day of July Anno Domini 1793. ~

Signed & sealed in presence of Joshua TOWNSEND

Elizabeth X SHOCKLEY (Seal)
her mark"

*followed on folio 62 with the acknowledgment by the Justice of the Peace Joshua TOWNSEND and the recordation by court clerk James R. MORRIS[615]

Liber P, folio 85; 08 October 1793

"To all whom these presents shall come Know ye that I William MORRIS of Worcester County in the State of Maryland being desirous to set free and Manumit Negro **Bess** for divers causes and conditions me thereunto moving I the said William MORRIS do by these presents give and grant set free and manumit the aforesaid Negro **Bess** immediately. To have and to hold and freely enjoy her freedom as aforesaid in full and ample manner without any let Authority or

---

[614] Worcester County Court (Land Records). Bill of sale from MERRILL, Elijah to SLOCOMB, William. 02 July 1793. P, pp. 60-61, MSA CE 30-15. www.mdlandrec.net : accessed 04 April 2022.
[615] Worcester County Court (Land Records). Bill of sale from SHOCKLEY, Elizabeth to MORRIS, Joshua. 19 July 1793. P, pp. 61-62, MSA CE 30-15. www.mdlandrec.net : accessed 04 April 2022.

hindrance of any person or persons Whatsoever. In Testimoney whereof I have hereto Set my hand and affixed my seal this 8th day of October Anno Domini 1793.

Signed Sealed & delivered   William MORRIS ~ (Seal) ~"
In presence of ~ ~ ~ ~"

*followed with the acknowledgment by Justice of the Peace John S. PURNELL and the recordation by court clerk James R. MORRIS[616]

Liber P, folios 94-95; 15 February 1794

"Maryland Worcester Sc^t. Know all men by these presents that I Nancey KERBY of Worcester County in the State of Maryland for and in consideration of the sum of forty five pounds current money of Maryland to me in hand paid by William BANUM of the place aforesaid at or before the Ensealing and delivery of these presents wherewith I confess myself to be fully Satisfied contented and paid, have bargained sold and delivered and by these presents do fully clearly and absolutely bargain sell and deliver unto the said William BANUM, one negro woman named **Bett** about twenty one years old and her child **Leah** about Eighteen months old, To have and to hold the said negro woman **Bett** and her Child **Leah** unto the said William BANUM his heirs Executors administrators and assigns, To his and their own proper uses and behoofs for ever And I the said Nancy KERBY my heirs Executors & administrators and every of us, the said Negro woman **Bett** & her Child **Leah** unto the said William BANUM his heirs and Assigns against all people what ever shall and will warrant and by these presents forever aquit and defend, Witness my hand and Seal this fifteenth day of February A.D. 1794 ~

Sealed and delivered   Anne POSTLY   Nancy KERBY ~ (Seal)
In the presence of   John POSTLY"

*followed on folio 95 with the acknowledgment by Justice of the Peace John POSTLY and the recordation on 04 March 1794 by court clerk James R. MORRIS[617]

Liber P, folios 101-102; 06 September 1793

"Know all men by these presents that Joshua TOWNSEND (Son of Major) of Worcester County in the State of Maryland for and in consideration of the Sum of Eighty pounds Current money to me in hand paid at and before the Sealing and delivery of these presents by Levi MERRILL of Worcester County in the State af[ore]s[ai]^d the Receipt whereof I doth hereby Acknowledge have bargained and Sold and by these presents doth hereby bargain and Sell unto the said Levi MERRILL his Heirs and Assigns forever the following four Negroes one Negro Woman named **Lydda** Boy **Georg** Girl **Easther** and Boy **Peter** and I the said Joshua TOWNSEND for myself and my heirs doth hereby Warrant and forever defend the above mentioned four negroes against the Lawfull claim Right and title of all manner of Persons Whatsoever as shall claim the Same or either of them from by or under me or my heirs In Testimoney whereof I the said Joshua TOWNSEND to these presents my hand have Sett and Seal affixed the sixth day of September Anno Domini Seventeen hundred and Ninety three ~

Signed Sealed and delivered   Joshua TOWNSEND (Seal)
in presents of ……   Joshua TOWNSEND."

*followed on folio 102 with the acknowledgment by Joshua TOWNSEND and the recordation on 07 September 1793 by court clerk James R. MORRIS[618]

---

[616] Worcester County Court (Land Records). Deed of manumission from MORRIS, William to **Bess**. 08 October 1793. P, p. 85, MSA CE 30-15. www.mdlandrec.net : accessed 04 April 2022.
[617] Worcester County Court (Land Records). Bill of sale from KERBY, Nancy to BANUM, William. 15 February 1794. P, pp. 94-95, MSA CE 30-15. www.mdlandrec.net : accessed 04 April 2022.
[618] Worcester County Court (Land Records). Bill of sale from TOWNSEND, Joshua to MERRILL, Levi. 06 September 1793. P, pp. 101-102, MSA CE 30-15. www.mdlandrec.net : accessed 04 April 2022.

Liber P, folios 111-112; 05 September 1793

"Worcester Ss^t. Know all men by these presents that I Schoolfield PARKER of Worcester County of the one part and George Anderson PARKER of the same place of the other part Witnesseth that the said Schoolfield PARKER for and in consideration of fifty pounds Current money of Maryland to him in hand paid by the said George A PARKER the Receipt whereof the said Schoolfield PARKER doth hereby Acknowledge and himself fully satisfied and contented he the said Schoolfield PARKER by these presents hath granted bargained and sold and by these presents doth grant bargain and Sell and deliver as hereafter set forth the following Negroes and other articles to witt Two Negroes called **Major** & **James** One Bed and furniture one small Iron Pott to be delivered to the said George A PARKER on the first day of January seventeen hundred and Ninety Six also two other Negroes called **Adam** & **Frederic** & one Case of Walnutt Drawers to be delivered at the said Schoolfield PARKER's decease free and clear of all Incumbrances unto the said George A PARKER his heirs and Assigns for ever the said Schoolfield PARKER doth Oblige him self his heirs and Executors under the Penalty of four hundred pounds Current money of Maryland to deliver the above named Negroes & other Articles death & fire Excepted at the above mentioned times and I the said Schoolfield PARKER by these presents doth hereby give full possession unto the said George Anderson PARKER at the above mentioned times In Witness whereof I the said Schoolfield PARKER have hereunto set my hand and Seal affixed this twenty fifth day of September Anno Domin[i] seventeen hundred and ninety three

| Signed sealed & Delivered | Joshua TOWNSEND | Schoolfield PARKER (Seal) |
| In the presence of ~ | William PARKER" | |

*followed with the acknowledgment by Justice of the Peace Joshua TOWNSEND and the recordation on folio 112 on 25 September 1794 by court clerk James R. MORRIS[619]

Liber P, folios 116-117; 23 October 1793

"Know all men by these presents that I Peter S CORBIN of Worcester County and State of Maryland for and in consideration of the Sum of thirty pounds Current money of Maryland to me in hand paid at and before the sealing and delivery hereof the Receipt Whereof I do hereby Acknowledge have bargained and sold and by these presents do bargain & Sell unto John JONES of the County and State aforesaid on Negro woman named **Hannah** about forty years of Age To have and to hold the af[ore]s[ai]^d Negro woman **Hannah** unto the said John JONES his Heirs and Assigns forever to the only use of the said John JONES and to no other intent or purpose whatever And the said Peter S CORBIN for himself & heirs Covenants and Agrees to and with the said John JONES his heirs and Assigns the said Negro woman **Hannah** against the Right title & claim of all manner of Persons whatsoever to forever warrant and defend In Witness whereof I have hereto set my hand & Seal affixed this twenty third day of October Anno Dom[ini] 1793

Peter S CORBIN (Seal)

Sealed and delivered in presence of"

*followed on folio 117 with the acknowledgment by Outten STURGIS and the recordation by court clerk James R. MORRIS[620]

Liber P, folios 125-127; 18 October 1793

"This Indenture made this 18th day of October One thousand seven hundred and Ninety three Witnesseth that I **Southy GEORGE** of Worcester County free Mulatto of his own free and Voluntary Will hath placed and bound himself a Servant unto Jenckins HENDERSON of the

---

[619] Worcester County Court (Land Records). Bill of sale from PARKER, Schoolfield to PARKER, George Anderson. 05 September 1793. P, pp. 111-112, MSA CE 30-15. www.mdlandrec.net : accessed 04 April 2022.
[620] Worcester County Court (Land Records). Bill of sale from CORBIN, Peter S. to JONES, John. 23 October 1793. P, pp. 116-117, MSA CE 30-15. www.mdlandrec.net : accessed 04 April 2022.

same place to Labour and Work at the trade or occupation of a farmer and with him the said Jenckins as a Servant to dwell continue and serve from the date hereof unto the full end and term of forty years from thence next ensueing and fully to be Compleat and ended during all which term of forty years af[ore]s[ai]^d the said Servant his said Master will and faithfully shall serve and his Lawfull commands gladly do and Obey and the said Jenckins HENDERSON in consideration thereof shall and will find and provide for his said Servant sufficient meat drink washing Lodging and all other necessaries fit and convenient for a Person in his Situation during his natural life Provided always that the said Jenckins shall not have a Right to sell or Assign over the time of Servitude of his said Servant as af[ore]s[ai]^d but if the said Jenckins shall Die before the time expires then the said Servant to go to Henry Jenckins HENDERSON (son of Jenckins) if the said Henry Henry should die before the expiration of the term af[ore]s[ai]^d then the said Servant to belong to Benj[ami]^n HENDERSON (son of Jenckins and if the s[ai]^d Benj[ami]^n shall die then the said Servant to go to Peter Holland HENDERSON (son of Jenckins af[ore]s[ai]^d) and if he should die before the Expiration of the term af[ore]s[ai]^d then to go to the Executors or Adm[inistrator]^s of the said Jenckins HENDERSON for the true performance of this Indenture the said parties by these presents do mutually bind themselves their Heirs Executors and Administrators Each to the other in the sum of One hundred pounds Current money of Maryland In Witness whereof the said **Southey GEORGE** and Jenckins HENDERSON have interchangeably Set their hands and seals affixed the day and year first above written

Signed sealed & delivered
in presence of ~ ~ ~ ~ ~   Isaac MARSHALL   **Southey** his ¥ **GEORGE** (Seal)
                                                         mark

                                              Jenckins HENDERSON (Seal)"

*followed on folio 127 with the acknowledgment by Justice of the Peace Isaac MARSHALL and the recordation by court clerk James R. MORRIS[621]

Liber P, folios 130-132; 05 October 1793

"State of Maryland Sc^t. This Indenture made this fifth day of October in the year of Our Lord One Thousand seven hundred and ninety three Between George DASHIELL of Worcester County in the State of Maryland of the one part and Tubman LOWES & James ADAMS of Somerset County of the other part Witnesseth that the said George DASHIELL for and in Consideration of the said Tubman LOWES & James ADAMS having entered into a Bond with the said George DASHIELL his Securities in the penalty of Seven hundred and fifty pounds Current money af[ore]s[ai]^d to Stay the proceedings of a Suit or Action at Law brought in the General Court of the State of Maryland against the said George DASHIELL by John GUNBY of Worcester County (Assignee of William McBRYDE) as also for and in consideration of the sum of five Shillings Cur[ren]^t money af[ore]s[ai]^d to the said George DASHIELL in hand paid before the Sealing and delivery hereof the Receipt whereof the said George DASHIELL doth hereby acknowledge and thereof doth acquit and discharge the said Tubman LOWES & James ADAMS their heirs Executors and Administrators each & every of them hath bargained and sold and Conveyed and by these presents doth bargain sell and Convey to the said Tubman LOWES and James ADAMS the following Negroes to wit **App, Sambo, Nebo, Jacob, David, Violett, Rachell, Sarah Nan**, To have and to hold the said Severall Goods and Chattels as af[ore]s[ai]^d Bargained Sold and Conveyed to the said Tubman LOWES and James ADAMS and their heirs and Assigns and for no other use intent or purpose whatsoever provided always and it is the true intent and meaning of these presents that if the said George DASHIELL his Heirs executors or Administrators do and shall from time to time and at all times hereafter well and truly save harmless and keep Indemnified the said Tubman LOWES & James ADAMS and their heirs Executors and Administrators from all Costs damages troubles and expence that shall or may Arise or Accrue from or by means of the said Tubman LOWES & James ADAMS

---

[621] Worcester County Court (Land Records). Indenture from **GEORGE, Southey** to HENDERSON, Jenckins. 18 October 1793. P, pp. 125-127, MSA CE 30-15. www.mdlandrec.net : accessed 04 April 2022.

Becoming Securities for the said George DASHIELL in a Bond entered into with the said George DASHIELL to stay the proceedings on a Suit of Action in Law brought by John GUNBY Assignee of W[illia]^m McBRYDE against the said George DASHIELL in the General Court of the State of Maryland. Then the above Instrument of writing and every matter clause and thing therein Contained to be Absolutely Void and of None effect In Testimony whereof the said George DASHIELL to these presents his Hand hath set and seal affixed the day and year above written ~

Signed sealed & delivered   George DASHIELL ~ (Seal)
In presence of ~ ~   Booz WALSTON"

*followed on folio 131 with the acknowledgment by Justice of the Peace Booz WALSTON and the recordation on folio 132 on 23 October 1793 by court clerk James R. MORRIS[622]

Liber P, folios 158-159; 26 August 1793

"Worcester County Know all men by these presents that I Alce JOHNSON for and in consideration of the sum of five pounds current money of Maryland to me in hand paid the receipt whereof I do hereby Acknowledge have bargained and sold and by these presents do bargain and sell unto Eleazar JOHNSON one negro boy slave called **David** To have and to hold the aforesaid Slave called **David** to the said Eleazar JOHNSON his heirs and assigns forever to the only proper use and behalf of the said Eleazar JOHNSON his heirs and Assigns and to no other intent or purpose whatsoever and it is further covenanted that the said Alce JOHNSON for herself and her heirs the aforesaid slave called **David** to the aforesaid Eleazar JOHNSON his heirs or Assigns will forever warrant and defend In Witness whereof I have hereunto set my hand and seal affixed this 26th day of August one thousand seven hundred ninety three ~

Signed and delivered in   Benjamin DENNIS   her
the presents of us   Wheetly DENNIS   Alce + JOHNSON (Seal)
                                                                              mark"

*followed on folio 159 with the acknowledgment by Justice of the Peace Benjamin DENNIS and the recordation on 19 November 1793 by court clerk James R. MORRIS[623]

Liber P, folios 183-184; 06 December 1793

"To all people to whom these presents shall come Greeting I Morgan BRADSHAW of worcester County in the State of Maryland planter, for and in consideration of the love goodwill and affection which I have and do bear towards my loving sister Sarah BRADSHAW of the same place, Have given and granted and by these presents do freely give and grant to the said Sarah BRADSHAW and to her lawfull issue forever a negro girl called and known by the name of **Lish** about eight years old with this proviso towit. that negro girl shall be my said Sister Sarah should die without issue as aforesaid. Then and in that case the said negro girl called **Lish** and all her increase should devolve & return to my estate to all intents and purposes as although this deed of gift had never taken place of which these presents I have delivered her the said Sarah BRADSHAW the said negro **Lish** To have and to hold all and singular the premises hereby given and granted to her the said Sarah BRADSHAW her lawfull issue henceforth forever, (with the above exception only excepted) In Witness whereof I have hereunto put my hand and seal this sixth day of December in the year one thousand seven hundred and ninety three ~

---

[622] Worcester County Court (Land Records). Instrument of Writing from DASHIELL, George to LOWES, Tubman and ADAMS, James. 05 October 1793. P, pp. 130-132, MSA CE 30-15. www.mdlandrec.net : accessed 04 April 2022.
[623] Worcester County Court (Land Records). Bill of sale from JOHNSON, Alce to JOHNSON, Eleazar. 26 August 1793. P, pp. 158-159, MSA CE 30-15. www.mdlandrec.net : accessed 04 April 2022.

Signed Sealed & delivered	Joshua TOWNSEND	Morgin BRADSHAW (Seal)
In the presence of	John COTTINGHAM"	

*followed on folio 184 with the acknowledgment by Justices of the Peace Joshua TOWNSEND and John COTTINGHAM and the recordation on 07 December 1793 by court clerk James R. MORRIS[624]

Liber P, folios 194-195; 09 December 1793

"Know all men by these presents that I Thomas HALL of worcester County State Maryland (Marin[e]^r) for and in consideration of the sum of one hundred pounds specie to me in hand paid at and before the sealing and delivery of these presents by Joshua BOWEN of the same County & State af[ore]s[ai]^d the receipt whereof I do hereby acknowledge have bargained and sold and by these presents do bargain & sell unto the said Joshua BOWEN all the goods and chattels house hold stuff and all other articles whatsoever hereafter mentioned which are as follows to wit one third part of a negro man named **George** one third of a negro woman named **Lydia** also one third of five negro children, children of the said negro **Lydia** two cows and calves three Beds and furniture, one corner cupboard two iron pots two Tables one dutch oven six chairs two pine chests one looking glass also every other Articles which I now possess not herein mentioned To have and to hold all and singular the af[ore]s[ai]^d goods and chattels & c & every of them by these presents bargained & sold unto the said Joshua BOWEN his heirs executors administrators & Assigns forever. And I the said Thomas HALL for myself my heirs Execut[o]^{rs} & administrators all and singular the said goods & Chattels household stuff & c unto the said Joshua BOWEN his executors administrators and Assigns against me the said Thomas HALL my Executors administrators and assigns and against all and every other person & persons whatsoever shall and will warrrent & forever defend by these presents, of which goods I have put the said Joshua BOWEN in full possession of by delivering him one negro man **George** at the sealing & delivery of these presents In Witness whereof I have hereunto sett my hand and seal affixed this 9th day of December Anno Domini 1793.

Thomas HALL (Seal)

Signed Sealed & delivered in presence of us   H ROUND"

*followed on folio 195 with the acknowledgment by Justice of the Peace Isaac MARSHALL and the recordation on 20 December 1793 by court clerk James R. MORRIS[625]

Liber P, folio 198; 28 December 1793

"This Indenture made the twenty eighth day of December in the year of our Lord one thousand seven hundred and ninety three Between Edward HORSEY of Worcester County and State of Maryland of the one part and negro **Jacob** now the property of the said Edward of the other part, Whereas the said Edward is desirous that the said Negro **Jacob** should become a free man in future and the Laws of the State will not allow masters to set their slaves free other wise then by Deed now This Indenture Witnesseth that the said Edward for and in consideration of the sum of twenty two pounds ten shillings current money of Maryland to him the said Edward in hand paid by the said negro **Jacob** the receipt whereof is hereby acknowledged hath granted released manumitted liberated and set free and discharged the said negro **Jacob** and by these presents doth grant release manumit liberate set free and discharge the said negro from all the claim right title interest property and demand which the said Edward his heirs executors administrators and assigns hath or may have to the said Negro To have use, and Enjoy his liberty and freedome at all times hereafter to the only use benifit and behoof of him the said negro

---

[624] Worcester County Court (Land Records). Deed of gift from BRADSHAW, Morgin to BRADSHAW, Sarah. 06 December 1793. P, pp. 183-184, MSA CE 30-15. www.mdlandrec.net : accessed 04 April 2022.

[625] Worcester County Court (Land Records). Bill of sale from HALL, Thomas to BOWEN, Joshua. 09 December 1793. P, pp. 194-195, MSA CE 30-15. www.mdlandrec.net : accessed 04 April 2022.

Jacob and to no other use intent or purpose whatsoever. In Witness whereof the said Edward hath hereunto his hand set & seal affixed the day and year within written

Sealed & delivered   John POSTLY   Edward HORSEY   (Seal)
In presence of   Josiah MITCHELL"

*followed with the acknowledgment by Justices of the Peace John POSTLY and Josiah MITCHELL and the recordation by court clerk James R. MORRIS[626]

Liber P, folios 211-212; 08 January 1794

"Know all men by these presents that I Hannah SELBY of worcester County in the State of Maryland for and in consideration of the sum of five shillings current money of Maryland to me in hand paid at and before the sealing and delivery of these presents by Joseph KELLAM of the County and State af[ore]s[ai]^d the receipt whereof I do hereby acknowledge have bargained and sold and by these presents doth bargain and sell unto the said Joseph KELLAM his heirs and assigns forever the following goods and chattels towitt Negro man named **Abel Abner** and **Jean** one hand mill one chest of draws one desk one iron pott 2 pair stillards two pott racks two pewter basons and one pewter dish and one hackle and also one looking glass To have and to hold all and singular the above mentioned goods and chattels and the said three negroes **Abel Abner & Jean** unto the said Joseph KELLAM his heirs and assigns forever and the said Hannah SELBY doth hereby warrant and forever defend the above mentioned goods and chattels against the lawfull claim of all persons whatsoever as shall claim the same or any part thereof from by or under me unto the said Joseph KELLAM his heirs and assigns forever of which goods and chattels I the said Hannah SELBY have put the said Joseph KELLAM in full possession by delivering him one chest of draws at the sealing hereof In Witness whereof I the said Hannah SELBY to these presents my hand have set and seal affixed the 8th day of February Anno Domini seventeen hundred and ninty four ~

Signed Sealed and delivered   her
In presents of   Philip QUINTON   Hannah + SELBY   (Seal)
                                                                                            mark"

*followed on folio 212 with the acknowledgment by Justice of the Peace Philip QUINTON and the recordation by court clerk James R. MORRIS[627]

Liber P, folios 215-216; 10 January 1794

"A true list of Negros that I moved into the State of Maryland from Accomack County State of Virginia the fourth day of January one thousand seven hundred and ninety four all of which were born in my family except **old Esther Ann** and **Priscilla** bequeathed to my wife by Thomas PARRAMORE Accomack County State of Virginia and I do assert that they were resadentors and the descendants from such Negros in the State of Virginia before the year one thousand seven hundred and eight three. Their names ages mail & feemail towit, **Cato** aged 42 years **Merica** 41 **Jacob** 33 **James** 15 **Daniel** 14 **George** 12 **John** 8 **Moses** 15 days old, **old Esther** aged 55 years **Ann** 30 **Leah** 29 **Prissella** 27 **Flora** 25 **Martha** 10 **Tabitha** 7 **Rachel** 6 **Rhoda** 5 **Comfort** 4 **Rebecca** 3 **Lisha** 2 **Mary** 3 **Esther** 6 months **Sabrough** 1 year As given under my hand this 10 day of January 1794

                                                                                                                Major GUY"

---

[626] Worcester County Court (Land Records). Deed of manumission from HORSEY, Edward to **Jacob**. 28 December 1793. P, p. 198, MSA CE 30-15. www.mdlandrec.net : accessed 04 April 2022.

[627] Worcester County Court (Land Records). Bill of sale from SELBY, Hannah to KELLAM, Joseph. 08 January 1794. P, pp. 211-212, MSA CE 30-15. www.mdlandrec.net : accessed 04 April 2022.

*followed with the oath made before Snow Hill Naval officer John GUNBY, the recordation on 11 January 1794 by Deputy Collector William SELBY of the Naval Office District of Snow Hill, and the recordation by Worcester County court clerk James R. MORRIS[628]

Liber P, folios 219-220; 11 January 1794

"Worcester County Ss^t. Know all men by these presents that I William HANDY of Somerset County in the State of Maryland for and in consideration of the sum of thirty pounds current money of Maryland to me in hand paid by Samuel HILMON of worcester County af[ore]s[ai]^d whereof I do hereby acknowledge the receipt and myself fully and intirely satisfied therewith have bargained sold set over and delivered and by these presents do bargain sell set over and deliver unto Samuel HILMON one negro man named **Pompy** and one negro woman named **Suffiah** To have and to hold the said negros unto the said Samu[e]l HILMON his heirs and assigns to the only proper use and behoof of him the said Samuel HILMON his heirs and assigns forever And I the said William HANDY for myself my heirs and assigns the aforesaid bargained negros unto the said Samuel HILMON his heirs and assigns against all manner of persons shall and will forever defend and by these presents will forever warrant and forever In Witness whereof together with the delivery of the said negros I have hereunto set my hand and affixed my seal this 11 laventh day of January Anno Dominy 1794

Sinned Sealled and   William HANDY (Seal)
Delivered befour me   Will STONE"

*followed on folio 220 with the Somerset County acknowledgment by Will STONE and the recordation on 17 January 1794 by Worcester County court clerk James R. MORRIS[629]

Liber P, folio 225; 21 January 1794

"Know all men by these presents that I John JONES of Worcester County and State of Maryland for and in consideration of the sum of Thirty pounds current money of Maryland to me in hand paid by Walter SMITH of the same place at and before the sealing and delivery of these presents the receipt whereof I do hereby acknowledge have bargained and sold and by these presents do bargain and sell unto the said Walter SMITH his heirs and assigns one negro woman named **Hannah** To have and to hold the said Negro woman unto the said Walter SMITH his heirs and assigns forever and for no other use or purpose whatsoever and the said John JONES for himself and his heirs doth covenant and agree to and with the said Walter SMITH that he the said John JONES hath a good and sufficient title to sell and dispose of the said Negro woman **Hannah** so as to convey unto the said Walter SMITH a good sure and firm title to the same and that no person but the said John JONES hath any right or title to the same In Testimony whereof the said John JONES his hand to these presents hath set and seal affixed this twenty first day of January in the year of our lord one thousand seven hundred and ninty four

Sign[e]d Sealed and delivered   John JONES (Seal)
In presence of   Joshua TOWNSEND"

*followed with the acknowledgment by Justice of the Peace Joshua TOWNSEND and the recordation by court clerk James R. MORRIS[630]

Liber P, folios 227-228; 26 August 1793

"Worcester County Know all men by these presents that I Alce JOHNSON for & in consideration of the sum of five pounds currant money of Maryland to me in hand paid the

---

[628] Worcester County Court (Land Records). Certificate of importation into Maryland from GUY, Major for **Cato, Merica, Jacob, James, Daniel, George, John, Moses, old Esther, Ann, Leah, Prissella, Flora, Martha, Tabitha**, etal. 10 January 1794. P, pp. 215-216, MSA CE 30-15. www.mdlandrec.net : accessed 04 April 2022.

[629] Worcester County Court (Land Records). Bill of sale from HANDY, William to HILMON, Samuel. 11 January 1794. P, pp. 219-220, MSA CE 30-15. www.mdlandrec.net : accessed 04 April 2022.

[630] Worcester County Court (Land Records). Bill of sale from JONES, John to SMITH, Walter. 21 January 1794. P, p. 225, MSA CE 30-15. www.mdlandrec.net : accessed 04 April 2022.

receipt whereof I do hereby acknowledge have bargained and sold and by these presents do bargain and sell unto John JOHNSON one negro boy slave called **Elijah** To have and to hold the af[ore]s[ai]^d slave called **Elijah** to the said John JOHNSON his heirs and assigns forever to the only proper use and behalf of the said John JOHNSON his heirs and assigns and to no other intent or purpose whatsoever, and it is further covenanted that the said Alce JOHNSON for herself and heirs the aforesaid slave called **Elijah** to the aforesaid John JOHNSON his heirs or assigns will forever warent and defend In Witness whereof I have hereunto set my hand and seal afixed this 26th day of August one Thousand seven hundred and ninety three

Signed and Delivered   Benjamin DENNIS   her
In the presents of us   Wheetly DENNIS   Alce + JOHNSON (Seal)
                                                                               mark"

*followed on folio 228 with the acknowledgment by Justice of the Peace Benjamin DENNIS and the recordation on 24 January 1794 by court clerk James R. MORRIS[631]

Liber P, folios 228-229; 24 January 1794

"January the 24th Anno Domini 1794 Then personally appeared before the subscriber a justice of the peace for worcester County Abisha DAVIS and made oath on the Holy Evangels of Almighty God that the following slaves towit **Eazer & Minna** male negroes have been inhabitants of some one of the United States for the space of three whole years preceeding the third day of January one Thousand seven hundred and ninety four and that he the said Abisha DAVIS being a Citizen of the State of Delaware did on the first day of January one thousand seven hundred and ninety three come unto the State of Maryland with a bonafide intention of settling therein, and have actaually resided in this State for one year at least since his first coming into the State and before the Importation of the said Negro slaves to wit **Eazer** and **Minna** which was on the third day of January one thousand seven hundred and ninety four

Sworn before Philip QUINTON"

*followed on folio 229 with the recordation by court clerk James R. MORRIS[632]

Liber P, folio 235; 29 January 1794

"Maryland Wor[cester] Co[un]ty. A List of Negroes that I William FASSITT moved in this State from the State of Delaware which were raised by John Simpson CAMPBELL of the said State and given to my wife (by her father) Marg^t Simpson FASSITT previous to her intermarriage with me Viz^t. Negroes **Sarah Luke** and **Comfort** ~

Given under my hand this twenty ninth day of January 1794   William FASSITT"

*followed with the oath made before Snow Hill Naval officer John GUNBY, the recordation by Deputy Collector William SELBY of the Naval Office district of Snow Hill, and the recordation by Worcester County court clerk James R. MORRIS[633]

Liber P, folio 244; 07 February 1794

"Know all men by these presents that I Elles JOHNSON of Worcester County and State of Maryland for and in consideration of the sum of twenty two pounds ten shillings current money of the State af[ore]s[ai]^d to me in hand paid by Belitha GRIFFEN the receipt whereof I do hereby acknowledge have granted bargained and sold assigned and delivered and by these presents do give grant bargain sell assign and deliver unto the said Belitha GRIFFEN his heirs

---

[631] Worcester County Court (Land Records). Bill of sale from JOHNSON, Alce to JOHNSON, John. 26 August 1793. P, pp. 227-228, MSA CE 30-15. www.mdlandrec.net : accessed 04 April 2022.

[632] Worcester County Court (Land Records). Certificate of importation into Maryland from DAVIS, Abisha for **Eazer** and **Minna**. 24 January 1794. P, pp. 228-229, MSA CE 30-15. www.mdlandrec.net : accessed 04 April 2022.

[633] Worcester County Court (Land Records). Certificate of importation into Maryland from FASSITT, William for **Sarah, Luke,** and **Comfort**. 29 January 1794. P, p. 235, MSA CE 30-15. www.mdlandrec.net : accessed 04 April 2022.

and assigns forever, one negro girl called **Chloe** To have and to hold the said negro girl called **Chloe** hereby bargained and sold unto the said Belitha GRIFFEN his heirs or assigns forever, and I the said Elles JOHNSON for myself my heirs executors and administrators the said negro girl **Chloe** unto the said Belitha GRIFFEN his heirs or assigns forever against me the said Elles JOHNSON my heirs Ex[ecuto]^rs or [a]dm[inistrato]^rs and against all and every other person or persons whatsoever shall and will warrant and forever defend by these presents. In Witness whereof I the said Elzey JOHNSON have hereto set my hand and seal affixed this seventh day of February Anno Dom[ini] 1794 ~

Sealed & delivered in presence of Isaac MARSHALL   Alce X JOHNSON (Seal)
                                                         her mark"

*followed with the acknowledgment by Justice of the Peace Isaac MARSHALL and the recordation by court clerk James R. MORRIS[634]

Liber P, folios 244-245; 16 August 1793

"Know all men by these presents that we **Elezebeth** (free negro) Thomas DIXON and Solomon TOWNSEND of Worcester County in the State of Maryland are held and firmly bond unto the State of Maryland in the full and just sum of thirty pounds current money of Maryland to be paid unto the said said State of Maryland, for which payment well and truly to be made & Done we bind ourselves our and each of our heirs executors and administrators in and for the whole firmly by these presents sealed with our seals and dated the 16 day of August Anno Domini 1793 ~ The Condition of the above obligation is such that if the above bounden, **Elizabeth**, Thomas DIXON and Solomon TOWNSEND their heirs executors and administrators do well and truly save harmless keep the State of Maryland more especially Worcester County from all Costs and charges as shall or may come against the said State and County by reason of **Elizebeth** (free negro) once the property of Doct[o]^r Thomas ROBERTSON Somerset County bearing a child called **Stephen** who is likely to become chargable to the said State, the said **Stephan** was born 03 July 1793. Then the above obligation to be void otherwise to stand and remain in full force power & virtue in the Law ~ ~

Signed sealed & delivered   **Elizebeth** + her mark (Seal)
in presence of   John COTTINGHAM   Tho[ma]^s DIXON (Seal)
                                                  Solomon TOWNSEND (Seal)"

*followed on folio 245 with the recordation on 07 February 1794 by court clerk James R. MORRIS[635]

Liber P, folios 257-259; 14 February 1794

"Know all men by these presents that I Matthias NICHOLSON of worcester County and State of Maryland for and in consideration of the sum of one hundred and five pounds current money of Maryland to me in hand paid by Lemuel SELBY of the same place at and before the sealing and delivery of these presents, have bargained sold and delivered and by these presents hath absolutely bargain sell and deliver unto him the said Lemuel SELBY his heirs and assigns forever the two following negro boys towit the one called **Fortune** about fourteen years old the other called **Jesper** about eleven years old now in the possession and delivered to the said SELBY To have and to hold all and singular the aforesaid two negroes hereby bargained and sold unto him the said Lemuel SELBY his heirs and assigns forever to the only proper use benifit and behoof him the said Lemuel SELBY his heirs and assigns forever And the said Matthias NICHOLSON the aforesaid negroes will and shall warrant and forever defend unto him the said Lemuel SELBY his heirs and assigns forever of which said negro boys I the said Matthias NICHOLSON have put the said Lemuel SELBY in full possession by the delivery of

---

[634] Worcester County Court (Land Records). Bill of sale from JOHNSON, Alce to GRIFFEN, Belitha. 07 February 1794. P, p. 244, MSA CE 30-15. www.mdlandrec.net : accessed 04 April 2022.

[635] Worcester County Court (Land Records). Bastardy bond from **Elizabeth** (free negro), DIXON, Thomas, and TOWNSEND, Solomon to the State of Maryland. 16 August 1793. P, pp. 244-245, MSA CE 30-15. www.mdlandrec.net : accessed 04 April 2022.

the same In Witness whereof I have hereto my hand hath set and seal affixed the fourteenth day of February in the year one thousand seven hundred and ninety four ~

Signed sealed & delivered　　John COTTINGHAM　　　　Matthias NICHOLSON　(Seal)
In presence of　　　　　　　　John BISHOP"

*followed on folio 258 with the acknowledgment by Justice of the Peace John COTTINGHAM and the recordation on folio 259 by court clerk James R. MORRIS[636]

Liber P, folios 259-260; 14 February 1794

"Worcester County St[ate] of Maryland Ss[t]. Know all men by these presents that I Levin MITCHELL of the County and State af[ore]s[ai]d for and in consideration of the sum of thirty seven pounds ten shillings lawfull money of the said State To me in hand paid by Walter SMITH of the County and State aforesaid the receipt whereof I do hereby acknowledge, have bargained sold and set over and by these presents do bargain sell assign and set over unto the said Walter SMITH his heirs and assigns forever all my right title intrust and property of in and to a certain negro girl named or known by the name of **Betty** or **Bet** to the only proper use and behoof of him the said Walter SMITH his heirs and assigns for ever and I the said Levin MITCHELL do hereby for myself my heirs executors and administrators warrant and defend the aforesaid negro girl unto him the said Walter SMITH his heirs executors administrators & assigns free and clear of and from any incumbrance claim title or demand of from or by me my heirs executors administrators or of from any other person or persons claiming or hereafter to claim by from or under me of them forever or by from or under any other person or persons whatsoever In Witness whereof I have hereunto set my hand and seal the fourteenth 14th day of February in the year of our Lord one thousand seven hundred and ninety four ~

Sign[e]d Seal[e]d and delivered　　　　　　　　　　　　　　　　Levin MITCHELL　(Seal)
In the presence of"

*followed on folio 260 with the acknowledgment by Justice of the Peace Outten STURGIS and the recordation by court clerk James R. MORRIS[637]

Liber P, folio 264; 15 February 1794

"To all whom these presents shall come Know ye that I James HANDY of worcester County in the State of Maryland being desirous to set free and manumit Negroe **Hope** about fifty years of age for divers causes and conditions me thereunto moving I the said James HANDY do by these presents give & grant set free and manumit the aforesaid negro **Hope** immediately To have and to hold and freely enjoy his freedom as aforesaid in full and ample manner without any let authority on hendrance of any person or persons whatsoever In Testimoney whereof I have hereto set my hand and affixed my seal this fifteenth day of February Anno Domini 1794 ~

Signed Sealed and delivered　　　　　　　　　　　　　　　　Jam[es] HANDY　(Seal)
In presence of　　　　　　　Benjamin DENNIS"

*followed with the acknowledgment by Justice of the Peace Benjamin DENNIS and the recordation on 20 February 1794 by court clerk James R. MORRIS[638]

Liber P, folios 265-266; 10 February 1794

"Know all men by these presents that I William FURNISS of Worcester County in the State of Maryland for and in consideration of three hundred pounds current money of Maryland to me in hand paid by Thomas FURNISS of the county af[ore]s[ai]d before the sealing and delivery

---

[636] Worcester County Court (Land Records). Bill of sale from NICHOLSON, Matthias to SELBY, Lemuel. 14 February 1794. P, pp. 257-259, MSA CE 30-15. www.mdlandrec.net : accessed 04 April 2022.
[637] Worcester County Court (Land Records). Bill of sale from MITCHELL, Levin to SMITH, Walter. 14 February 1794. P, pp. 259-260, MSA CE 30-15. www.mdlandrec.net : accessed 04 April 2022.
[638] Worcester County Court (Land Records). Deed of manumission from HANDY, James to **Hope**. 15 February 1794. P, p. 264, MSA CE 30-15. www.mdlandrec.net : accessed 04 April 2022.

these of the receipt whereof I do hereby acknowledge and therefrom do forever acquit and discharge the said Thomas FURNISS his executors and administrators have given granted bargained & Sold and by these presents do give grant bargain and sell unto the said Thomas FURNISS and to his Assigns forever all and singular the following goods and chattels towit five negroes **Grace Pat Hette Levin Charles** ten hade of Cattle ten hade of sheep five hade of hogs two hade of horses one riding Chair one Dusk three Walnut Tables two pine Tables two looking glasses fifteen chairs one chest and trunk one case and bottles one psalt kittle two pots one dutch oven one frying pan two pot Rack irons one {?} of Coopers ware eight casks and farming utentals one wain all the Chany and glasses four feather beds bedstets mats and furniture To have and to hold all and singular the aforesaid goods and chattels to the said Thomas FURNISS and to his assigns forever to and for the only proper use and behoof of the said Thomas FURNISS and his assigns forever ~ and for no other use intent or purpose whatever and I the said William FURNISS for myself my heirs executors and administrators do hereby covenant and agree to & with the said Thomas FURNISS and his heirs executors administrators and assigns that I the said William FURNISS and my heirs executors & administrators shall and will warrant and forever hereafter defend the aforesaid bargained and sold goods & Chattels to the aforesaid Thomas FURNISS and to his executors administrators and assigns against the claim right and title of all manner of persons whatever Given under my hand and seal this tenth day of February Anno Domini seventeen hundred and ninety four ~

Signed Sealed & delivered   George MARSHALL   William FURNISS   (Seal)
In presence of ~   Purnell BRITTINGHAM"

*followed on folio 266 with the acknowledgment by Justice of the Peace James SELBY and the recordation on 21 February 1794 by court clerk James R. MORRIS[639]

Liber P, folios 274-275; 14 March 1794

"State of Maryland Wor[cester] County Ss^ت. Know all men by these presents that I William HAMMON of the County af[ore]s[ai]^d for a consideration of the sum of sixty pounds specie to me in hand p[ai]^d by Benj[ami]^n PURNELL (of W) of the County af[ore]s[ai]^d have bargained sold released granted and confirmed and by these presents do bargain sell release grant and confirm unto the s[ai]^d Benj[ami]^n PURNELL (of W) one negro man called **David** the value of sixty pounds To have and to hold the said bargained negro **David** by these presents bargained sold released granted and confirmed unto the only proper use and behoof the said Benj[ami]^n PURNELL his executors administrators and assigns forever freely quietly peaceably and intirely without any contradiction claim disturbance or hindrance of any person whatsoever and without any account to me or to any other whatsoever to be made answered or hereafter to be rendered so that neither I the s[ai]^d William HAMMON nor any other for me or in my name any right title interest or demand of in to or for the s[ai]^d Negro **David** or any part or parcel thereof ought to exact challenge claim or demand at any time or times hereafter but from all actions rights estate title claim demand possession and Interest thereof shall be wholly barred and precluded by force and virtue of these presents and I the said William HAMMON for myself my executors and administrators the s[ai]^d negro **David** unto the s[ai]^d Benjamin PURNELL (of W) his executors adm[inistrato]^{rs} and assigns and against all and every other person or persons whatsoever shall and will warrant and forever defend & also against his Liberatio by these presents which negro **David** I the said William HAMMON have put the said Benjamin PURNELL (of W) in full possession by delivery at the signing and delivery hereof In Witness whereof the said William HAMMON have hereunto set his hand and seal this 14th day of March seventeen hundred and ninety four ~

Signed Sealed & delivered   W[illia]^m HAMMON   (Seal)
In presence of   Philip QUINTON"

---

[639] Worcester County Court (Land Records). Bill of sale from FURNISS, William to FURNISS, Thomas. 10 February 1794. P, pp. 265-266, MSA CE 30-15. www.mdlandrec.net : accessed 04 April 2022.

*followed on folio 275 with the acknowledgment by Justice of the Peace Philip QUINTON and the recordation by court clerk James R. MORRIS[640]

Liber P, folios 294-295; 14 February 1794

"Know all men by these presents that I Nathaniel ENNIS of worcester County in the State of Maryland for and in consideration of the sum of fifteen pounds current money of Maryland to me in hand paid by Milby PURNELL of the County & State af[ore]s[ai]d have bargained and sold unto the said Milby PURNELL his heirs and assigns forever the following personal property Viz one negro woman called { ?} one negro boy called **Amos** one negro girl called **Bett** one negro boy called **Will** one negro boy called **Isaac** one mare one horse ten head cattle twenty head hogs three beds and furniture with all other property that I am possessed To have and to hold the above mentioned property to him the said Milby PURNELL his heirs and Assigns forever all which property the said Nathaniel hath given the s[ai]d Milby possession of by an actual delivery at and before the ensealing & delivery of these presents as Witness my hand and seal this fourteenth day of February Anno Dom[ini] 1794

Signed Sealed & delivered   Nathaniel ENNIS   (Seal)
In presence of   Isaac MARSHALL"

*followed with the acknowledgment by Justice of the Peace Isaac MARSHALL and the recordation on 11 March 1794 by court clerk James R. MORRIS[641]

Liber P, folio 301; 25 March 1794

"Know all men by these presents that we **Levin CAMBRIDGE** (free molatter) & George CAMBRIDGE both of worcester County and State of Maryland are held and firmly bound unto the State of Maryland in the full and just sum of thirty pounds current money of the State af[ore]s[ai]d To which payment well and truly to be made and done we bind ourselves and each of us & each of our heirs In and for the whole firmly by these presents sealed with our seals and dated the 25th day of March 1794 ~ Whereas above bound **Levin CAMBRIDGE** hath been charged by the oath of **Mary BLAKE** of having begot a bastard child on the body of the said **Mary BLAKE** which said child was born November 1790 Called by the name of **Peggey**. Now the Condition of the above obligation is such that if the above bound **Levin CAMBRIDGE** or his heirs or executors do and shall at his or their Expence keep maintain and sufficiently support said bastard child so that County of Worcester aforesaid may not be burthin'd with the said bastard child then the above obligation to be void els to be and remain in full force in Law & c

Signed Sealed & delivered   Philip QUINTON   **Leavin CAMBRIDGE**   (Seal)
In presents off   William JONES   George CAMBRIDGE   (Seal)"

*followed with the recordation on 28 March 1794 by court clerk James R. MORRIS[642]

Liber P, folios 301-302; 14 March 1794

"A true List or an account of a Negro called **Sampson** that I Subscriber Henry GUNN moved unto the State of Maryland from New Castle County State of Delaware the fifteenth day of February one thousand seven hundred and ninety four and I do assert that the above named negro called **Sampson** was a residentor of the County and State aforesaid from the year one thousand seven hundred & ninety one untill the abovesaid date and that he was raised partly by my brother Samuel GUNN deceased of worcester County & State of Maryland (untill the above

---

[640] Worcester County Court (Land Records). Bill of sale from HAMMON, William to PURNELL, Benjamin. 14 March 1794. P, pp. 274-275, MSA CE 30-15. www.mdlandrec.net : accessed 04 April 2022.
[641] Worcester County Court (Land Records). Bill of sale from ENNIS, Nathaniel to PURNELL, Milby. 14 February 1794. P, pp. 294-295, MSA CE 30-15. www.mdlandrec.net : accessed 05 April 2022.
[642] Worcester County Court (Land Records). Bastardy bond from **CAMBRIDGE, Leavin** (free molatter) and CAMBRIDGE, George to the State of Maryland. 25 March 1794. P, p. 301, MSA CE 30-15. www.mdlandrec.net : accessed 05 April 2022.

mentioned year) where I and my family mean to reside and settle Given under my hand this fourteenth day of March one thousand seven hundred and ninety four ~

Henry GUNN ~"

*followed with the oath made before Deputy Naval Officer William SELBY of the Snow Hill district and the recordation on folio 302 on 15 March 1794 by court clerk James R. MORRIS[643]

Liber P, folios 302-303; 01 March 1794

"Know all men by these presents that I Levi MILLS of worcester County & State of Maryland for and in consideration of the Sum of Seventy pounds current money of the State af[ore]s[ai]^d to me in hand paid or Secured to be paid by Joshua PRIDEAUX of the County and State af[ore]s[ai]^d at or before the ensealing & delivery hereof have bargained sold and confirmed and by these presents do bargain sell and confirm unto the said Joshua PRIDEAUX his heirs Executors administrators and Assigns all my right title claim property or demand of and to a certain negro man named **Will** To have and to hold the aforesaid Negro man **Will** unto the af[ore]s[ai]^d Joshua PRIDEAUX his heirs Ex[ecuto]^{rs} adm[inistrato]^{rs} and assigns to the only proper use and behoof of him the said Joshua PRIDEAUX his heirs Exe[cutor]^s administr[ato]^{rs} and Assigns and I the said Levi MILLS for myself my heirs Executors and administrators the af[ore]s[ai]^d negro man **Will** unto the said Joshua PRIDEAUX his heirs Exe[cuto]^{rs} administr[ato]^{rs} and assigns shall and will warrant and defend by these presents Witness my hand and seal this first day of March one thousand seven hundred and ninety four ~

Signed Sealed & delivered   Levi MILLS ~ (Seal)
In presence of   Josiah MITCHELL ~"

*followed on folio 303 with the acknowledgment by Justice of the Peace Josiah MITCHELL and the recordation on 18 March 1794 by court clerk James R. MORRIS[644]

Liber P, folio 310; 17 March 1794

"Know all men by these presents that I Coulborn LONG of worcester County State of Maryland for and in consideration of the sum of twelve pounds ten shillings current money of the State af[ore]s[ai]^d to me in hand paid by Hampton ROUND the receipt whereof I do hereby acknowledge in full Give grant bargain and sell unto the said Hampton ROUND his heirs and Assigns one third part of a negro girl called **Lott** formerly the property of Cornelius ENNIS deceased and now in the possession of Samuel HOSIER To have and to hold unto the said Hampton ROUND the said negro girl **Lott** from my heirs Executors and adm[inistrato]^{rs} and from all and every person whatsoever will warrant and forever defend from all suits and damage of every kind unto him the said Hampton his heirs Executors administrators & Assigns forever as Witness my hand and seal this 17th day of March Anno Domini 1794

Signed Sealed & delivered Benjamin HENDERSON   Colevern LONG (Seal)
In presence of
        Jesse K STEEL
        (his mark)"

*followed with the acknowledgment by Justice of the Peace Isaac MARSHALL on 18 March 1794 and the recordation by court clerk James R. MORRIS on 21 March 1794[645]

---

[643] Worcester County Court (Land Records). Certificate of importation into Maryland from GUNN, Henry for **Sampson**. 14 March 1794. P, pp. 301-302, MSA CE 30-15. www.mdlandrec.net : accessed 05 April 2022.

[644] Worcester County Court (Land Records). Bill of sale from MILLS, Levi to PRIDEAUX, Joshua. 01 March 1794. P, pp. 302-303, MSA CE 30-15. www.mdlandrec.net : accessed 05 April 2022.

[645] Worcester County Court (Land Records). Bill of sale from LONG, Colevern to ROUND, Hampton. 17 March 1794. P, p. 310, MSA CE 30-15. www.mdlandrec.net : accessed 05 April 2022.

Liber P, folios 323-325; 18 March 1794

"This Indenture made this eighteenth day of March in the year one Thousand seven hundred and ninety four Between Zadok SELBY Senior of worcester County in the State of Maryland of the one part and Micajah SELBY of the same place of the other part Witnesseth that the aforesaid Zadok SELBY for and in consideration of a certain negro man called **Isaac** (as willed and bequeathed among other matters by Mary SELBY deceased after the decease of the aforesaid Zadok to his son Micajah SELBY party to these presents recourse being had to the said Will and Testament may more fully and at large appear) paid and delivered by the aforesaid Micajah SELBY at and before the sealing and delivery of these presents the receipt whereof is hereby acknowledged and confessed and the said Micajah SELBY his heirs Executors administrators and assigns forever therefrom Acquitted and discharged he the said Zadok SELBY hath granted bargained sold conveyed and by these presents doth absolutely grant bargain sell convey and confirm unto him the said Micajah SELBY his heirs and assigns forever" … "In Testimony whereof the said Zadok SELBY these presents his hand hath set and seal affixed the day & year above written ~

Signed Sealed & delivered   Philip QUINTON   Zadok SELBY (Seal)
In the presence of   Isaac MARSHALL"

*followed on folio 325 with the acknowledgment by Justices of the Peace Philip QUINTON and Isaac MARSHALL and the recordation on 04 April 1794 by court clerk James R. MORRIS[646]

* Due to its true length, this transcription has been shortened to its most relevant portions. The full original deed can be viewed at the citation provided.

Liber P, folios 325-326; 04 April 1794

"Know all men by these presents that I Joshua TOWNSEND of Snow Hill for and in consideration of the sum of thirty seven pounds ten shillings current money of Maryland to me in hand paid by Levin POLLITT the receipt whereof is hereby acknowledged have given granted bargained and sold and by these presents do give grant and sell unto the said Levin POLLITT his Executors adm[inistrato]^{rs} and assigns a negro boy called **Jacob** To have and to hold the said boy unto the said Levin POLLITT his Executors adm[inistrato]^{rs} and assigns and I the said Joshua TOWNSEND for myself my heirs Executors and adm[inistrato]^{rs} doth covenant and agree to and with the said Levin his Ex[ecuto]^{rs} adm[inistrato]^{rs} or assigns to warrant and forever defend a good legal and equitable right and title in the said boy to the said Levin his Ex[ecutor]^{s} adm[inistrato]^{rs} and assigns against the claim of all persons whatsoever Witness my hand and seal the 4th Ap[ri]^{l} 1794

Signed Sealed & delivered   Joshua TOWNSEND (Seal)
In presence of ~   Philip QUINTON."

*followed on folio 326 with the acknowledgment by Justice of the Peace Philip QUINTON and the recordation by court clerk James R. MORRIS[647]

Liber P, folios 330-331; 08 April 1794

"This Indenture made the eighth day of April Anno Domini one thousand seven hundred and ninety four Between John JONES of worcester County & State of Maryland of the one part and negroes **Southey Dinah Abraham Sabrough Isaac** and **Lucretia** all of worcester County and State of the other part Witnesseth that the said John JONES for and in consideration of the sum of five shillings current money of the State af[ore]s[ai]^{d} to him in hand paid by the several negroes above named before the sealing and delivery hereof the receipt whereof the said John

---

[646] Worcester County Court (Land Records). Deed of conveyance from SELBY, Zadok Sr. to SELBY, Micajah. 18 March 1794. P, pp. 323-325, MSA CE 30-15. www.mdlandrec.net : accessed 05 April 2022.

[647] Worcester County Court (Land Records). Bill of sale from TOWNSEND, Joshua to POLLITT, Levin. 04 April 1794. P, pp. 325-326, MSA CE 30-15. www.mdlandrec.net : accessed 05 April 2022.

JONES doth hereby acknowledge and thereof doth forever acquit and discharge the above mentioned slave negroes at the time anges, hereafter mentioned towit. Negro **Southy** and **Dinah** from and after the date hereof and **Abraham** eleven years of age last October when he shall attain the age of twenty four years **Isaac** Now about the age of seven years when he shall attain to the age of twenty four years and **Sabrough** now eight and **Lucretia** about the age of four years when they shall severally attain to the age of twenty years, hath set free and emancipated and forever discharge at the several ages af[ore]s[ai]^d In Testimony whereof I the said John JONES to these presents my hand hath set and seal affixed the day and year first above written.

Sign[e]^d Seal[e]d & del[ivere]d
In presence of
Philip QUINTON ~

John + JONES (Seal)
his mark"

*followed on folio 331 with the acknowledgment by Justice of the Peace Philip QUINTON and the recordation by court clerk James R. MORRIS[648]

Liber P, folios 337-338; 05 April 1794

"Maryland Worcester Ss^t Know all men by these presents that we Jemima GODFREY and Jonathan CAREY of the County and State afforesaid for and in consideration of the sum of forty pounds current money of Maryland to us in hand paid by Zadok POWELL of the same place at or before the ensealing and delivery the ensealing and delivery of these presents wherewith we confess ourselves to fully satisfied contented and paid, Have bargained sold and delivered and by these presents do fully clearly and absolutely bargain sell and deliver unto the said Zadok POWELL one negro woman **Comfort** about eighteen years old and her child **Sam** about thirteen months old To have and to hold the said negro wamon and her child to the said Zadok POWELL his executors administrators and assigns to his and their own proper uses and behoofs and no other use whatever and we the said Jemima GODFREY and Jonathan CAREY and each of us our heirs Executors and administrators the said negro woman and her said child to the Zadok POWELL his heirs and Assigns against the legal claim of all persons shall and will warrant and by these presents forever defend In Testimony whereof we have hereunto affixed our hands and seals this fifth day of Aprill A.D. 1794 ~

Sealed & delivered
In the presence of   John POSTLY ~

Jemima = GODFREY (Seal)
her mark

Jonathan CAREY (Seal)"

*followed on folio 338 with the acknowledgment by Justice of the Peace John POSTLY and the recordation on 11 April 1794 by court clerk James R. MORRIS[649]

Liber P, folios 338-339; 11 April 1794

"Know all men by these presents that I James SCOTT of worcester County in the State for and in consideration of the sum of ten pounds current money of Maryland to me in hand paid by James WEIR of the County and State afores[ai]^d the receipt whereof I do hereby acknowledge and by these presents do bargain & sell unto the said James WEIR his heirs and assigns all my right and title of and to a certain negro girl named **Hannah** now supposed to be in the possession of Honou{?} TAYLOR being the same negro girl that came of a woman named **Phillis** formerly the property of Elisha TAYLOR and the said James SCOTT for himself and his heirs doth hereby warrant and forever defend all his right and title of the said negro girl against the claim of all manner of persons that shall hereafter claim the said negro girl from by or under him the said James SCOTT to the said James WEIR his heirs and Assigns forever. In Testimony

---

[648] Worcester County Court (Land Records). Deed of manumission from JONES, John to **Southey, Dinah, Abraham, Sabrough, Isaac, and Lucretia**. 08 April 1794. P, pp. 330-331, MSA CE 30-15. www.mdlandrec.net : accessed 05 April 2022.

[649] Worcester County Court (Land Records). Bill of sale from GODFREY, Jemima and CAREY, Jonathan to POWELL, Zadok. 05 April 1794. P, pp. 337-338, MSA CE 30-15. www.mdlandrec.net : accessed 05 April 2022.

whereof the said James SCOTT to these presents his hand hath set and seal affixed this 11th day of April Anno Domini 1794 ~

Signed Sealed & delivered   John POSTLY ~
In presence of   Joshua + TAYLOR   James + SCOTT (Seal)
                                      (his mark)"

*followed on folio 339 with the acknowledgment by Justice of the Peace John POSTLY and the recordation by court clerk James R. MORRIS[650]

Liber P, folios 343-344; 07 April 1794

"Know all men by these presents that I Nathaniel ENNIS of worcester County in the State of Maryland for and in consideration of the sum of twenty pounds current money of Maryland to me in hand paid by Milby PURNELL of the County and State af[ore]s[ai]^d at and before the ensealing and delivery of these presents the receipt whereof the s[ai]^d Nathan[ie]^l doth confess and acknowledge himself to be fully content and satisfied Hath granted bargained sold and delivered and by these presents doth grant bargain sell and deliver unto the said Milby PURNELL his heirs & assigns forever the following articls towit one negro woman called **Pat** one negro boy called **Amos** one negro girl called **Bett** one negro boy called **Will** one negro boy called **Isaac** two Horses fourteen head cattle eighteen head hogs three feather beds and furniture also all the other property which I am in the world possessed of. To have and to hold the above mentioned articles from me the s[ai]^d Nathaniel ENNIS and my heirs unto him the said Milby PURNELL his heirs and assigns forever and from all other persons whatsoever In Witness whereof the s[ai]^d Nath[anie]^l to this present bill sale his hand set and seal affixed this seventh day of April Anno Dom[ini] 1794 ~

Signed Sealed & delivered   Nathaniel ENNIS (Seal)
In presence of   Isaac MARSHALL"

*followed on folio 344 with the acknowledgment by Justice of the Peace Isaac MARSHALL and the recordation on 18 April 1794 by court clerk James R. MORRIS[651]

Liber P, folios 362-363; 26 April 1794

"Know all men by these presents that I William JOHNSON of Accomack County in the State of Virginia for and in consideration of the sum of fifteen pounds current money of Maryland to me in hand paid at and before the sealing and delivery of these presents by James WIRE of worcester County in the State of Maryland the receipt whereof I do hereby acknowledge have bargained and sold and by these presents do bargain and sell unto the said James WIRE his heirs and Assigns forever one negro woman named **Hannah** the said Negro formerly being the property of Elisha TAYLOR or Patience TAYLOR late of worcester County deceased To have and to hold the said Negro woman named **Hannah** by these presents bargained and sold unto the said James WIRE his heirs Executors administrators and Assigns forever and I the said William JOHNSON for myself my heirs executors and administrators the said negro woman named **Hannah** unto the said James WIRE his heirs and Assigns forever against me my heirs Executors and administrators and against all or any other person or persons claiming from by or under me or my heirs will warrant and forever defend by these presents unto the said James WIRE his heirs and Assigns forever. In Witness whereof I the said William JOHNSON have hereunto my hand set and seal affixed the 26 day of Apriel Anno Domini 1794 ~

Signed Sealed & delivered   William JOHNSON (Seal)
In presents of   Outten STURGIS."

---

[650] Worcester County Court (Land Records). Bill of sale from SCOTT, James to WEIR, James. 11 April 1794. P, pp. 338-339, MSA CE 30-15. www.mdlandrec.net : accessed 05 April 2022.

[651] Worcester County Court (Land Records). Bill of sale from ENNIS, Nathaniel to PURNELL, Milby. 07 April 1794. P, pp. 343-344, MSA CE 30-15. www.mdlandrec.net : accessed 05 April 2022.

*followed on folio 363 with the acknowledgment by Justice of the Peace Outten STURGIS and the recordation on 30 April 1794 by court clerk James R. MORRIS[652]

Liber P, folios 405-406; 29 April 1794

"Worcester Sc^t. Know all men by these presents that we Mary PARRAMORE (widow of John PARRAMORE dece[ase]^d and Mary PARRAMORE daughter of the af[ore]s[ai]^d John PARRAMORE for and in consideration of the sum of sixty five pounds current money of Maryland to us in hand paid at and before the sealing and delivery hereof by Thomas MARTIN (of James) have bargained and sold and by these presents do bargain and sell unto the said Thomas MARTIN his heirs and Assigns forever one negro man named **James** aged about twenty years. To have and to hold the af[ore]s[ai]^d negro man **James** to the said Thomas MARTIN his heirs and Assigns forever to the only proper use and behoof of the said Thomas MARTIN his heirs and Assigns and for no other intent or purpose whatever, and it is further covenanted and agreed that we the said Mary PARRAMORE widow as af[ore]s[ai]^d and Mary PARRAMORE daughter as af[ore]s[ai]^d of the said John dec[ease]^d the said negro man **James** to the af[ore]s[ai]^d Thomas MARTIN his heirs and assigns, against the right title and claim of all manner of persons whatever will forever and defend. In Witness whereof we have hereto set our hands & seals affixed this 29th day of April Anno Dom[ini] 1794.

Sealed & deliv[ere]^d in presence of   Philip QUINTON   Mary PARRAMORE   (Seal)
                                                                       Mary PARRAMORE   (Seal)"

*followed on folio 406 with the acknowledgment by Justice of the Peace Philip QUINTON and the recordation on 10 June 1794 by court clerk James R. MORRIS[653]

Liber P, folios 409-410; 05 June 1794

"State of Maryland Worcester County Ss. Know all men by these presents that I Leonard JOHNSON of the County aforesaid for and in consideration of the sum of eighteen pounds to me in hand paid by Thomas WEBB of the same place the receipt whereof I the said Leonard JOHNSON do hereby acknowledge have granted bargained and Sold and by these presents do give grant bargain and sell unto the said Thomas WEBB one negro girl named **Leah** one cow and yearlin five sheep twelve head of hogs one bed and furniture, togather with all my houshold goods farming & utensils the whole estimated and sold for the said sum of Eighteen pounds To have and to hold the above bargained and sold goods and chattels unto the af[ore]s[ai]^d Thomas WEBB his heirs and Assigns and I the said Leonard JOHNSON do hereby for myself my heirs and executors warrant and forever defend the said bargained and sold goods and chattels unto the said Thomas WEBB his heirs and assigns from the legal claim or demand of any person whatsoever In Witness whereof togather with the delivery of the said goods and chattels I the said Leonard JOHNSON have to this my plain & open sale. Sett my hand and affixed my seal this fith day of June A.D. 1794

Signed Sealed & delivered
In presents of   John P. MITCHELL   Leonard + JOHNSON (Seal)
                                                                                    mark"

*followed on folio 410 with the acknowledgment by Justice of the Peace John P. MITCHELL and the recordation on 11 June 1794 by court clerk James R. MORRIS[654]

---

[652] Worcester County Court (Land Records). Bill of sale from JOHNSON, William to WIRE, James. 26 April 1794. P, pp. 362-363, MSA CE 30-15. www.mdlandrec.net : accessed 05 April 2022.

[653] Worcester County Court (Land Records). Bill of sale from PARRAMORE, Mary and PARRAMORE, Mary to MARTIN, Thomas. 29 April 1794. P, pp. 405-406, MSA CE 30-15. www.mdlandrec.net : accessed 05 April 2022.

[654] Worcester County Court (Land Records). Bill of sale from JOHNSON, Leonard to WEBB, Thomas. 05 June 1794. P, pp. 409-410, MSA CE 30-15. www.mdlandrec.net : accessed 05 April 2022.

Liber P, folios 412-413; 12 November 1793

"State of Maryland Worcester Ss. Know all men by these presents that we **Beck** & Matthew DALE am held am held and firmly bound unto worcester County Court in the penal Sum of eighty pounds to which payment well and truly to be made and done we bind ourselves and each of our heirs in and for the whole firmly by these presents sealed with our seals and dated this 12th day of Nov[ember] 1793 The Condition of the above obligation is such that if he the above bound Mathew DALE or his heirs do keep safe from any cost or charge in pursuance of the said negro **Beck** having a bastard child by the name of **Elijah** and about six weeks oald the County af[ore]s[ai]^d {?} any individual grieved thereby then the above obligation to be void else to stand be and remain in full force power & virtue in law ~

Signed & Seal[e]d in ~ presents of ~	John P. MITCHELL	her ~~Beck~~ .... (Seal) mark Matthew DALE (Seal)"

*followed on folio 413 with the recordation on 11 June 1794 by court clerk James R. MORRIS[655]

Liber P, folios 414-415; 12 June 1794

"Know all men by these presents that I Zadock PURNELL of worcester County for and in consideration of the sum of twenty pounds current money of Maryland to me in hand paid before the sealing and delivery hereof by William POLK the receipt whereof the said Zadock PURNELL doth hereby acknowledge and thereof and therefrom doth absolutely acquit and discharge the said William POLK his heirs Ex[ecuto]^{rs} and adm[inistrato]^{rs} from every part and parcel thereof Hath bargained and sold and by these presents doth bargain and sell unto the said William POLK his heirs Ex[ecuto]^{rs} adm[inistrato]^{rs} or assigns forever one negro man called **Milby** now in the possession of the said Zadock PURNELL. To have to hold the said Negro man **Milby** to the said William POLK his heirs and Assigns forever to the only proper use and behoof of the said William POLK his heirs and Assigns forever, and to no other use intent or purpose whatsoever, and the said Zadock doth hereby covenant and agree to & with the said William POLK his heirs Ex[ecuto]^{rs} and adm[inistrato]^{rs} or Assigns that he will warrant and defend the said bargained and sold negro man called **Milby** from all and all manner of person or persons whatever claiming or pretending any right or title to the said negro man provided Nevertheless that it is the true intent and meaning of these presents that if the af[ore]s[ai]^d Zadock PURNELL do and shall well and truly pay unto the said William POLK the sum of twenty pounds current money of Maryland with interest thereon from the date hereof on or before the first day of June next ensuing then this bill of sale to be void else to remain in full force, and the said Zadok doth further covenant and agree to & with the said William POLK thereto in case the said Zadok doth not pay the said William POLK the af[ore]s[ai]^d Sum of twenty pounds current money on or before the said first day of June next that then and in that case the said Zadok shall and will deliver the said Negro to the said POLK, and suffer and permit the said POLK to sell the said negro the said POLK returning the balance of the money arising from the sale of the said negro to the said PURNELL after deducting the said twenty pounds and interest together with the expences attending the sale In Witness whereof the said Zadok hath hereunto set his hand and seal this 12th day of June Anno Dom[ini] 1794 ~

Signed Sealed & delivered In presence of	Joshua TOWNSEND"	Z. PURNELL ~ (Seal)

---

[655] Worcester County Court (Land Records). Bastardy bond from **Beck** and DALE, Matthew to the State of Maryland. 12 November 1793. P, pp. 412-413, MSA CE 30-15. www.mdlandrec.net : accessed 05 April 2022.

*followed on folio 415 with the acknowledgment by Justice of the Peace Joshua TOWNSEND and the recordation by court clerk James R. MORRIS[656]

Liber P, folio 440; 19 July 1794

"This Indenture made this ninteenth day of July in the year one Thousand seven hundred and ninety four Between Isaac WARREN of the County of worcester and State of Maryland of the of the one part and negro **Santee** of the same place of the other ~~part~~ Witnesseth that the said Isaac for and in consideration fifty pounds current money of Maryland to him in hand paid by the said negro **Santee** and also from conscientious motives and principles Hath manumitted freed and forever discharged the said negro called **Santee** from the bonds of slavery and bondage & by these presents do forever discharge the said Negro called **Santee** Witness my hand and seal the day and year first above written ~

Testes   John P MITCHELL ~   Isaac WARREN   (Seal)"

*followed with the acknowledgment by Justice of the Peace John P MITCHELL and the recordation on 22 July 1794 by court clerk James R. MORRIS[657]

Liber P, folios 442-443; 01 August 1794

"Worcester {?}c^t. Know all men by these presents that we Mary PARRAMORE and William HOLLAND both of worcester County & State of Maryland for and in consideration of the sum of sixty pounds current money of Maryland to us in hand paid at & before the sealing and delivery hereof by John McIVER the receipt whereof we do hereby acknowledge have bargained and sold and by these presents do bargain & sell unto the said John McIVER his heirs and Assigns forever one negro woman called **Rhoda** also one negro boy called **Daniel** son of the said **Rhoda** To have and to hold the af[ore]s[ai]d **Rhoda** and **Daniel** to the said John McIVER his heirs and Assigns forever to the only use of the said John McIVER his heirs and Assigns and to no other intent or purpose whatever. And we the said Mary and William do covenant and agree for our selves and our heirs the af[ore]s[ai]^d negroes **Rhoda** and **Daniel** against the right title and claim of all manner of persons to forever warrant and defend to the said John McIVER his heirs & Assigns as Witness our hands and seals this first day of August Anno Dom[ini] 1794 ~

Seal[e]^d & deliv[ere]^d in   Tho[ma]^s MARTIN 2^d Mary PARRAMORE ~   (Seal)
presents of   & Philip QUINTON   W[illia]^m HOLLAND   (Seal)"

*followed on folio 443 with the acknowledgment by Justice of the Peace Philip QUINTON and the recordation by court clerk James R. MORRIS[658]

Liber P, folio 457; 13 August 1794

"To all whom these presents shall come Know ye that I David WILSON of worcester County in the State of Maryland being desirous to set free and manumit negro **Tom** for divers causes me thereunto moving. I the said David WILSON do by these presents give and grant set free and manumit the aforesaid negro **Tom** immediately To have and to hold and freely enjoy his freedom as aforesaid in full and ample manner without any let authority or henderance of any person or persons whatsoever In Testimony whereof I have hereto set my hand and affixed my seal this thirteenth day of August Anno Domini 1794

Test.   John S PURNELL   David WILSON   (Seal)"

---

[656] Worcester County Court (Land Records). Deed of mortgage from PURNELL, Zadock to POLK, William. 12 June 1794. P, pp. 414-415, MSA CE 30-15. www.mdlandrec.net : accessed 05 April 2022.
[657] Worcester County Court (Land Records). Deed of manumission from WARREN, Isaac to **Santee**. 19 July 1794. P, p. 440, MSA CE 30-15. www.mdlandrec.net : accessed 05 April 2022.
[658] Worcester County Court (Land Records). Bill of sale from PARRAMORE, Mary and HOLLAND, William to McIVER, John. 01 August 1794. P, pp. 442-443, MSA CE 30-15. www.mdlandrec.net : accessed 05 April 2022.

*followed with the acknowledgment Associate Justice John S. PURNELL and the recordation by court clerk James R. MORRIS[659]

Liber P, folio 464; 13 August 1794

"I the Subscriber do bargin an sell to Levi MERRILL one negro girl named **Peg** about ten years old for the sum of thirty pounds in hand paid and I acknowledge this as a receit for the same and will forever warrant and defend the same from any person or persons as Witness my hand and seal the 13 day of August 1794

Lemuel SELBY   Jesse HUDSON   (Seal)"

*followed with the acknowledgment by Justice Joshua TOWNSEND and the recordation on 14 August 1794 by court clerk James R. MORRIS[660]

Liber P, folios 464-465; 26 July 1794

"Know all men by these presents that I William MORRISS of Worcester County and State of Maryland for and in consideration of the sum of Seventy seven pounds ten shillings Specie to me in hand paid by James RITCHIE and Hugh GEMMILL surviving partners of William McBRYDE & Co[mpany] at and before the sealing and delivery of these presents the receipt whereof I do hereby acknowledge, have bargained sold and delivered and by these presents do bargain sell & deliver to them the af[ore]s[ai]^d James RITCHIE and Hugh GEMMILL their heirs Executors administrators and Assigns one Negro woman called **Nell** about twenty Six years of age with her child called **Levin** about six years of age To have and to hold the af[ore]s[ai]^d Negros unto them the s[ai]^d Ja[me]^s RITCHIE and Hugh GEMMILL their heirs & c. to them and their proper use and uses forever and to and for no other use whatsoever and I the s[ai]^d William MORRISS for myself and my heirs & c. do hereby covenant grant and agree to and with the said RITCHIE and GEMMILL their heirs & c. that the aforesaid Negroes unto them the s[ai]^d RITCHIE and GEMMILL their heirs & and Assigns against myself my heirs & c. & c. and against all and every person whatsoever I shall and will warrant and defend forever the aforesaid Negroes Wittness my hand & Seal this twenty Sixthd day of July 1794

Signed Sealed & delivered   W[illia]m MORRIS   (Seal)
In presence of us   Booz WALSTON"

*followed on folio 465 with the acknowledgment by Justice of the Peace Booz WALSTON and the recordation on 14 August 1794 by court clerk James R. MORRIS[661]

Liber P, folios 499-500; 03 September 1794

"Know all men by these presents that I Isaac WILLIAMS of the County of worcester and State of Maryland for and in consideration of the sum of twenty two pounds ten shillings current money of Maryland to me in hand paid at and before the sealing and delivery of these presents by Priselley ATKINS of the County and State af[ore]s[ai]^d the recet whereof I do hereby Acknowledge have bargained and sold and by these presents do grant bargain & sell unto the said Priscilly ATKINS all my right title and claim of and unto a certain Negro girl named **Bett** To have and to hold the said negro girl by these presents bargained and sold unto the said Priscelly ATKINS her Executors administrators & Assigns forever And I the said Isaac WILLIAMS for myself my executors and administrators the said Negro girl called **Bett** unto the said Priscilly ATKINS her heirs Executors & assigns against me the said Isaac WILLIAMS my Executors administrators Assigns and against all and every other person or persons

---

[659] Worcester County Court (Land Records). Deed of manumission from WILSON, David to **Tom**. 13 August 1794. P, p. 457, MSA CE 30-15. www.mdlandrec.net : accessed 05 April 2022.
[660] Worcester County Court (Land Records). Bill of sale from HUDSON, Jesse to MERRILL, Levi. 13 August 1794. P, p. 464, MSA CE 30-15. www.mdlandrec.net : accessed 05 April 2022.
[661] Worcester County Court (Land Records). Bill of sale from MORRIS, William to RITCHIE, James and GEMMILL, Hugh. 26 July 1794. P, pp. 464-465, MSA CE 30-15. www.mdlandrec.net : accessed 05 April 2022.

whatever shall and will warrant & forever defend by these presents of which Negro I the said Isaac WILLIAMS have put the said Priscielly ATKINS in full possession of by delivery of said Negro girl called **Bett** at the sealing hereof In Witness whereof I the said Isaac WILLIAMS have hereunto set my hand & seal this third day of September Anno Domini 1794 ~

Signed Sealed & delivered   Hannah (her + mark) ATKINS   Isaac WILLIAMS (Seal)
In presents of us ~   Hannah J (her + mark) ATKINS"

*followed with the acknowledgment by Justice of the Peace John POSTLY on 12 September 1794 and the recordation on folio 500 by court clerk James R. MORRIS[662]

Liber Q, folio 7; 01 November 1794

"Know all men by these presents that I Isaac SAVAGE of the County of Worcester and State of Maryland of the one part and Zadok STURGESS of the same place on the Other part Witnesseth that for and in consideration of the sum of thirty pounds current money of Maryland to me in hand paid by the said Zadok STURGESS before the sealing and delivery of these presents the receipt whereof the said Isaac SAVAGE doth hereby acknowledge and himself satisfied & contented & paid the bargained and sold unto the said Zadok STURGESS one negro boy called **Milby** in the possession of the af[ore]s[ai]ᵈ Isaac SAVAGE to him the af[oresai]ᵈ Isaack SAVAGE to him the af[oresai]ᵈ Zadok STURGESS his heirs and Assigns forever and to no other use or purpose whatever and the said Isaac SAVAGE doth further covenant and agree for himself and his heirs Executors administrators or assigns that he the said Isaac SAVAGE and his heirs will warrant and forever defend the af[oresai]ᵈ Negro boy called **Milby** against the lawful claims or demands of all persons whatever In Testimony whereof the said Isaac SAVAGE have hereunto set my hand and seal this first day of November A.D. 1794 ~

Signed Sealed & delivered   Benjamin McCORMACK   Isaac SAVAGE (Seal)
In presents of ~   Hampton BURBBAGE"

*followed with the acknowledgment by Justice Josiah MITCHELL and the recordation on 10 November 1794 by court clerk James R. MORRIS[663]

Liber Q, folios 44-45; 27 December 1794

"Maryland Ssᵗ. Worcester County Know all men by these presents that I Thomas ATKINSON of worcester County and State af[oresai]ᵈ have this day bargained sold and delivered unto John WILLIAMS of the same place three negrows by the names of **Nanny** and her two children by the names of **Rhody** and **Littleton** for and in consideration of the sum of sixty five pounds ten shillings current money of Maryland to me in hand paid the receipt whereof I do acknowledge the said **Nanncy** and **Rhody** and **Littleton** to be the right and title and Estate of him the said John WILLIAMS and his heirs and assigns forever and I do warrant and forever defend from all persons claiming any right thereunto and for the true performance I bind myself my heirs Executors and administrators or assigns as In Witness whereof I have set my hand and seal affixed this twentay seventh day of December in the year of our Lord one thousand seven hundred and ninety four ~

Signed Sealed and Delivered   John COTTINGHAM.   Tho[ma]s ATKINSON (Seal)
In presents of ~"

---

[662] Worcester County Court (Land Records). Bill of sale from WILLIAMS, Isaac to ATKINS, Priselley. 03 September 1794. P, pp. 499-500, MSA CE 30-15. www.mdlandrec.net : accessed 05 April 2022.

[663] Worcester County Court (Land Records). Bill of sale from SAVAGE, Isaac to STURGESS, Zadok. 01 November 1794. Q, p. 7, MSA CE 30-16. www.mdlandrec.net : accessed 26 April 2022.

*followed on folio 45 with the acknowledgment by John COTTINGHAM and the recordation on 29 December 1794 by court clerk James R. MORRIS[664]

Liber Q, folio 51; 18 December 1794

"This Indenture made this eighteenth day of December Anno Domini one Thousand Seven hundred and ninety four by and between Elihu HAZZARD of worcester County in the State of Maryland planter of the one part and Asher BURROUGHS (Taner) of the County and State aforesaid of the other part Witnesseth that the said Elihue HAZZARD for and in consideration of the sum of thirty eight pounds fifteen shillings current money of Maryland to him in hand paid by the said Asher BURROUGHS before the sealing and delivery of these presents the receipt whereof the said Elihue HAZZARD, doth, doth hereby acknowledge, doth hereby grant bargen sell and set over unto the said Asher BURROUGHS one neagro Garl named **Leah** To have and to hold the said negro as before mentioned to the only purpose and behooffe of the said Asher BURROUGHS his heirs and assigns forever, and This Indenture further Witnesseth that the said Elihu HAZZARD his heirs Executors administrators doth and shall warrant & forever defend the foresaid negro from all and every person or persons that doe hereafter claim any right or title to the same and that unto the said Asher BURROUGHS his heirs and assines forever In Testimony whereof the said Elihu HAZZARD hath to those presents Set his hand and seal this day and year first above written

Signed Sealed & Delivered   David GUY   Elihu HAZZARD   (Seal)
In the presents of us
                                                       her
                                            Rachel   +   HICKMAN
                                                      mark"

*followed with the recordation by court clerk James R. MORRIS on 07 January 1795[665]

Liber Q, folio 52; 12 January 1795

"A true list or account of a negro called **Cage** or **Micajah** that I the subscriber Philip WHITE of worcester County and State of Maryland planter do hereby assert that the above named Negro man called **Cage** was a residenture of Sussex County and State of Dellaware ever since his existance and formerly belonged to M^r. John AYDELOTT father of my wife Levinia until the third day of this instant January as given under my hand this 12th day of January 1795

Philip WHITE ~

January the 12th 1795 Then came Philip WHITE before me William SELBY Collector for Snowhill District in worcester County and State of Maryland and made Oath on the Holy Evangels of Almighty God that the above mentioned male negro called **Cage** had been ever as Inhabitant of the Dellaware State from his birth until the abovesaid third day of January instant and I do hereby declare that I have at this time moved the said negro into Worcester County and State of Maryland with a Bonafide intention and veiws only of keeping him in my service and not with any design of selling or disposing of him

Before William SELBY Coll[ecto]r."

*followed with the recordation by court clerk James R. MORRIS[666]

Liber Q, folios 65-66; 07 January 1795

"This deed of manumission dated this seventh day of January in the year of our Lord Seventeen hundred and Ninety five bears Testimony that I John PURNELL of worcester County in the State of Maryland have remised released manumitted and granted freedom unto and by these

---

[664] Worcester County Court (Land Records). Bill of sale from ATKINSON, Thomas to WILLIAMS, John. 27 December 1794. Q, pp. 44-45, MSA CE 30-16. www.mdlandrec.net : accessed 26 April 2022.
[665] Worcester County Court (Land Records). Bill of sale from HAZZARD, Elihu to BURROUGHS, Asher. 18 December 1794. Q, p. 51, MSA CE 30-16. www.mdlandrec.net : accessed 26 April 2022.
[666] Worcester County Court (Land Records). Certificate of importation into Maryland from WHITE, Philip for **Cage (or Micajah)**. 12 January 1795. Q, p. 52, MSA CE 30-16. www.mdlandrec.net : accessed 26 April 2022.

presents do remise release manumit and grant freedom unto the following negroes to witt. A certain Negro man called and known by the name of **Azariah** another called **Jacob** and a certain Negro Woman named **Rhodah** from this day hence forth and forever, And the said John doth hereby covenant and agree that the said Negroes shall be and are hereby declared to be free to all intents and purposes to contract and in law to bind themselves and each of them respectively and to be capable of using occupying and enjoying all and singular their rights both of person and property in a full and ample manner as any Citizen of this State Con[ditione]d by the Laws of the land or the laws of nature be entitled unto To have and to hold their said freedom free and clear of all manner of incumbrance of me the said the John or any person claiming by this or under me my executors administrators or assigns In Testimony whereof I have to these presents my hand set and my seal affixed the day and year aforesaid ~

Sealed and Delivered   W[illia]m PURNELL   John PURNELL   (Seal)
in the presence of   James B ROBINS"

*followed on folio 66 with the acknowledgment by Justice of the Peace William PURNELL and the recordation on 26 January 1795 by court clerk James R. MORRIS[667]

Liber Q, folio 68; 22 January 1795

"To all whom these presents shall come know ye that I William MORRIS of worcester County in the State of Maryland being desirous to set free and manumit Negro **Isaac** for divers causes and considerations me thereunto moving I the said William MORRIS do by these presents give grant set free and manumit the af[oresai]d Negro **Isaac** immediately. To have and to hold and freely enjoy his freedom as af[oresai]d in full and ample manner without any let authority or hindrance of any person or persons whatsoever. In Testimony whereof I have hereto set my hand and affixed my seal this 27th day of January Anno Domini 1795 ~

Signed Sealed and delivered   William MORRIS   (Seal)
In presence of ~   Philip QUINTON."

*followed with the acknowledgment by Justice of the Peace Philip QUINTON and the recordation on 27 January 1795 by court clerk James R. MORRIS[668]

Liber Q, folios 73-74; 02 February 1795

"A true list or account of a negro woman called **Phillis** that I the subscriber John PERKINS of worcester County and State of Maryland planter do hereby assert that the above named Negro woman called **Phillis** was a residenture of Sussex County and State of Dellaware ever since here existance till the 19th day of January last and formerly belonged to Mrs. Barsheba MILLER my wifes mother and that I removed the said negro called **Philis** into Worcester County and State of Maryland the said Nineteenth day of January in the year one Thousand seven hundred & ninety five as given under my hand this 2[n]d day of February 1795

John PERKINS

February the 2[n]d 1795 Then came John PERKINS before me William SELBY Collector for the District of Snow Hill (Maryland) and made Oath on the Holy Evangels of Almighty God that the above mentioned Negro woman called **Phillis** has been ever an inhabitant of Sussex County and State of Delaware from her birth until 19th day of January last. And I do hereby declare that I have moved the said negro into Worcester County and State of Maryland with a bona fide intention and view only of keeping her in my Service and not with any design of Selling or disposing of her ~

Sworn before William SELBY Coll[ecto]r"

---

[667] Worcester County Court (Land Records). Deed of manumission from PURNELL, John to **Azariah, Jacob,** and **Rhodah**. 07 January 1795. Q, pp. 65-66, MSA CE 30-16. www.mdlandrec.net : accessed 26 April 2022.
[668] Worcester County Court (Land Records). Deed of manumission from MORRIS, William to **Isaac**. 22 January 1795. Q, p. 68, MSA CE 30-16. www.mdlandrec.net : accessed 26 April 2022.

*followed on folio 74 with recordation by court clerk James R. MORRIS[669]

Liber Q, folio 74; 02 February 1795

"A true List or account of a negro girl called **Prissey** that I the subscriber Solomon PERKINS of worcester County & State of Maryland planter, do hereby assert that the above Negro girl called **Prissey** was a residenture of Dellaware State for about thirteen years past, but was born in worcester County aforesaid and was the property of a certain Annanias ROBINSON for the last thirteen years until the 14th day of January last and that I removed the said negro girl called **Prissey** as the property of my son James PERKINS given him by the aforesaid Annanias ROBINSON by his last will and Testament, into worcester County aforesaid the said 14th day of January in the year one Thousand seven hundred and ninety five

Solomon PERKINS

February the 2[n]d 1795 Then came Solomon PERKINS before me William SELBY Collector for the District of Snow Hill (Maryland) and made oath on the Holy Evangels of Almighty God that the above mentioned Negro girl called **Prissey** has for the last thirteen years past been an Inhabitant of Sussex County and State of Dellaware until the 14th day of January aforesaid and I do hereby declare that I have moved the said negro for the use of my said son James PERKINS a minor into worcester County aforesaid bonafide intention and views only for his use and service and not with any design of selling or disposing of her

Sworn before William SELBY Coll[ecto]^r"

*followed with the recordation by court clerk James R. MORRIS[670]

Liber Q, folios 83-84; 07 February 1795

"Know all men by these presents that I John JONES of worcester County Maryland for and in consideration of Seven shillings and six pence Specia to me paid by **Southy PITTS** free negro of the same place the receipt whereof I hereby acknowledged have bargined and sold and by these presents do bargain and sell unto the said **Southy PITTS** free negro, one Negro woman named **Rachel** To have and to hold the said **Rachel** unto the af[oresai]d **Southey PITTS** his heirs & c. forever and for no other use purpose whatsoever, and also do further covenant to and with the af[oresai]d **Southy** that I have a just right title and claim to the said **Rachel** and that I will by these presents warrant and defend forever from the claim of all persons whatsoever. In Testimoney whereof I have hereunto set my hand and seal this Seventh day of February 1795

Signed and Sealed	W[illia]m HOLLAND	
In the presents of	Nehemiah HOLLAND	John X JONES Sen[ior] (Seal)
		his / mark"

*followed on folio 84 with acknowledgment by Justice of the Peace John HOLLAND and the recordation on 12 February 1795 by court clerk James R. MORRIS[671]

Liber Q, folios 95-96; 10 February 1795

"Alexander McALLEN. John PERKINS. The Deposition of Nancy WILLIAMS of lawful age being Sworn on the Holy Evangelus of almighty God deponeth & Saith that she belives about the year of Anno Dom[ini] 1790 she this deponant being in company with John PURKINS in Snow Hill Town when she this deponant asked said PURKINS if he the said PURKINS had sent out to Carolina by John MARTIN for his money due there for a negro, said PURKINS replied he did not know that MARTIN had received his order but that he sent one down to him,

---

[669] Worcester County Court (Land Records). Certificate of importation into Maryland from PERKINS, John for **Phillis**. 02 February 1795. Q, pp. 73-74, MSA CE 30-16. www.mdlandrec.net : accessed 26 April 2022.
[670] Worcester County Court (Land Records). Certificate of importation into Maryland from PERKINS, Solomon for **Prissey**. 02 February 1795. Q, p. 74, MSA CE 30-16. www.mdlandrec.net : accessed 26 April 2022.
[671] Worcester County Court (Land Records). Bill of sale from JONES, John to **PITTS, Southy**. 07 February 1795. Q, pp. 83-84, MSA CE 30-16. www.mdlandrec.net : accessed 26 April 2022.

further saith not   Nancy WILLIAMS
Sworn the 10th day of February 1795 Before Philip QUINTON ~

The deposition of Jacob RICHARDS of lawfull age sworn on the Holy evangelus of God deponeth and saith that in the year of 1793 he this deponant being in company with Mrs. Mary PURKINS wife of John PURKINS at which time he this deponant heard the said Mrs PURKINS say that John MARTIN had orders from her, said Mrs PURKINS's husband and that he said MARTIN had recovered a negro belonging to her husband from some person in Carolina and had not {?}ed her husband well and that if ever John MARTIN come back Mr PURKINS would sue him ~ further saith not   Jacob RICHARDS
Sworn the 10th day of february 1795 Before Philip QUINTON ~"

*followed on folio 96 with the acknowledgment with the certification by Philip QUINTON and the recordation on 14 February by court clerk James R. MORRIS[672]

Liber Q, folios 108-109; 28 February 1795

"Know all men by these presents that I Jesse ENNIS of worcester County in the State of Maryland for and in consideration of the sum of forty pounds current money of Maryland to me in hand paid by Coventon REED of the County & State af[oresai]^d the receipt whereof the s[ai]^d Jesse doth confess and acknowledge at and before the ensealing and delivery of these presents the receipt whereof the s[ai]^d Jesse doth confess and acknowledge have granted bargained and sold and delivered and by these presents doth grant bargain sell and deliver unto the s[ai]^d Coventon his heirs and assigns forever a negro girl called **Lotte** to have and to hold the s[ai]^d negro from him the s[ai]^d Jesse and his heirs and from every other person claiming by from or under him or them to him the s[ai]^d Coventon his heirs and Assigns forever, And the s[ai]^d Jesse doth further covenant and agree to warrant and defend the said negro to the s[ai]^d Coventon his heirs and Assigns forever ag[ain]s^t the claim of every person whatsoever In Witness & Confirmation whereof the s[ai]^d Jesse to this present bill of sale his hand hath set and seal affixed this twenty eighth day of February Anno Dom[ini] 1795

Signed Sealed & Delivered
In presence of   Isaac MARSHALL   Jesse + ENNIS (Seal)
                                                       his mark"

*followed on folio 109 with the acknowledgment by Justice of the Peace Isaac MARSHALL and the recordation 02 March 1795 by court clerk James R. MORRIS[673]

Liber Q, folios 109-110; 03 March 1795

"A true List or account of the following negroes to wit one Negro woman called **Lott**, one Negro boy called **George** one Negro boy called **Sampson** one ditto called **Jacob** that I the subscriber Francis LANE moved into the State of Maryland Worcester County from Accomack County in the State of Virginia in the year one thousand seven hundred and ninety five and I do assert that the above mentioned negro woman called **Lott** was born in the State of Maryland and the other three negroes to wit **George Sampson** and **Jacob** were born in Accomack County and State of Virginia that they all became residentures of Accomack County aforesaid before the year above mentioned as given under my hand this third day of March in year seventeen hundred and ninety five   Francis LANE

March the 3^{[r]d} 1795 Then came before me William SELBY Naval Officer for the District of Snow Hill and Worcester County and made Oath on the Holy Evangels of Almighty God that the several Negroes enumerated in the above list were inhabitants and residentures of Accomack County in the State of Virginia above mentioned until the twentyeth day of February

---

[672] Worcester County Court (Land Records). Depositions of WILLIAMS, Nancy and RICHARDS, Jacob. 10 February 1795. Q, pp. 95-96, MSA CE 30-16. www.mdlandrec.net : accessed 26 April 2022.

[673] Worcester County Court (Land Records). Bill of sale from ENNIS, Jesse to REED, Coventon. 28 February 1795. Q, pp. 108-109, MSA CE 30-16. www.mdlandrec.net : accessed 26 April 2022.

last and I do hereby declare that I have and did then move the said Negroes and myself and family in Worcester County in the State of Maryland with a bonafide intention of settling in the same and that I have brought the said negroes with me with views of continuing them in my own Service and not with any design of selling or disposing of them

Sworn before W[illia]m SELBY Naval Officer"

*followed on folio 110 with the recordation by court clerk James R. MORRIS[674]

Liber Q, folios 127-128; 24 March 1795

"A true list or account of the Negro girl Slave called **Niomi** aged about thirteen years that I the subscriber Horsey SOMMERS of Somerset County and State of Maryland (shipwright) moved the aforesaid negro girl from Accomack County and State of Virginia the fourth day of March instant and I do assert that the said Negro girl was born in the State of Virginia and continued ever since until then the property of Abraham RICE who gave the said Negro his daughter, daughter Nancy now my present wife as given under my hand this twenty fourth day of March in the year one thousand seven hundred and ninety five   Horsey SUMMERS

March the twenty fourth 1795 Then came before me William SELBY Naval Officer for the District of Snowhill and Worcester County and made Oath on the holy Evangels of Almighty God that the above mentioned negro girl called **Neomi** was an inhabitant of Accomack County and State of Virginia from her birth until the fourth instant March, and I do hereby declare that I have and did then move the said negro (and my wife Nancy) in Somerset County and State of Maryland with bonafide intention of settling in the same with views of continuing her in my own service and not with any design of selling or disposing of her the said negro

Sworn before William SELBY (NO)"

*followed on folio 128 with the recordation by court clerk James R. MORRIS[675]

Liber Q, folios 128-130; 25 March 1795

"Know all men by these presents that I Francis CRIPPS of Buckingham in the County of worcester and State of Maryland for and in consideration of the sum of one hundred and thirty pounds current money of the state aforesaid to me in hand paid by James DUER and John COTTINGHAM the former of Snow Hill and the latter of Meswadix in said County at or before the sealing and delivery of these presents the receipt whereof I the said Francis CRIPPS do hereby acknowledge have granted bargained and Sold and by these presents do grant bargain and sell unto the said James DUER and John COTTINGHAM their executors administrators and Assigns the following Negroes to wit one Negro woman **Nance** one ditto boy **Stephen** one ditto girl **Rachel** and boy **Ben** with these beds and furniture two Tables six chairs three chests one Safe two pots one Dutch oven one skillet one frying pan two linen wheels and one wool one loom and one tea kettle with all and singular my household furniture of what kind soever with two horses two yearlings one sow and seven pigs one plow one harrow with all and singular my farming utensils and one horse cart all and Singular which said premises are now remaining standing and being in a certain messuage or tenement situate in Buckingham af[oresai]ᵈ and now in the occupation of me the s[ai]ᵈ Francis CRIPPS To have and to hold all and singular the negroes goods household stuff and furniture and other the premises above bargained and sold or mentioned or intended so to be unto the said James DUER and John COTTINGHAM their Execu[to]ʳˢ Admi[ni]st[rato]ʳˢ an assigns forever. And I the said Francis CRIPPS for myself my heirs Exe[cu]t[o]ʳˢ & admi[nis]tr[ato]ʳˢ all and singular the said negroes goods household stuff and furniture and other the said premises above bargained and Sold unto the said James DUER and John COTTINGHAM their Exe[cuto]ʳˢ adminis[trator]ˢ & assigns against me the said Francis CRIPPS my Execut[or]ˢ and adminis[trato]ʳˢ against all and every other person and persons whatsoever shall and will warrant and forever by these presents of all and singular the

---

[674] Worcester County Court (Land Records). Certificate of importation into MD from LANE, Francis for **Lott, George, Sampson, etal**. 03 March 1795. Q, pp. 109-110, MSA CE 30-16. www.mdlandrec.net : accessed 26 April 2022.

[675] Worcester County Court (Land Records). Certificate of importation into Maryland from SUMMERS, Horsey for **Niomi**. 24 March 1795. Q, pp. 127-128, MSA CE 30-16. www.mdlandrec.net : accessed 26 April 2022.

said negroes goods household stuff and furniture and other the said premises above bargained & sold and I the said Fran[ci]ˢ CRIPPS have put the said James DUER and John COTTINGHAM in full possession be delivering to them one horse at the Sealing and delivery of these presents in the name of the whole premises hereby barginid and sold or mentioned or intended so be unto them the said James DUER and John COTTINGHAM as af[oresai]ᵈ In Witness whereof I the said Francis CRIPPS have hereunto set my hand and seal affixed this twenty fith day of March Anno Domini one thousand seven hundred and ninety five 1795 ~

Signed Sealed & Delivered   Fran[ci]ˢ CRIPPS   (Seal)
In presents off   Philip QUINTON"

*followed with the acknowledgment by Justice of the Peace Philip QUINTON and the recordation on folio 130 by court clerk James R. MORRIS on 26 March 1795[676]

Liber Q, folios 144-146; 21 March 1795

"This Indenture made this twenty first day of March Anno Dom[ini] one thousand seven hundred ninety and five Between Jean RICHARDS of Worcester County in the State of Maryland of the One part and Mills BEVANS James BEVANS and William BEVANS (the children of Rowland BEVANS) all of Worcester County & State of Maryland of the Other part Witnesseth that the said Jean RICHARDS for the sum of six hundred pounds current money of Maryland to her in hand paid by the said Mills James and William BEVANS at and before the sealing and delivery of the presents the receipt whereof the said Jean RICHARDS doth hereby confess and Acknowledge hath given granted bargained and sold & by these presents doth give grant bargain and sell unto the said Mills BEVANS James BEVANS and William BEVANS their heirs and assigns forever all her the said Jean RICHARDS's property as is hereafter expressed Viz. One Negro woman called **Sall**, one Negro Boy called **Will**, two beds & furniture and one mahogany desk To have and to hold the whole of the said property together with the said Jeans whole property of what nature or kind soever it is or may be and which or division of my deceased husbands estate & c. may more fully appear and every part and parcel of her estate unto the said Mills BEVANS James BEVANS and William BEVANS their heirs and Assigns forever and to and for no Other use or purpose whatsoever Except as is herein after excepted Vizᵗ. excepted and provided always and it is hereby positively and explicitly declared to be the only true intent and meaning of these presents that if the said Jean RICHARDS and Rowland BEVANS father of the af[oresai]ᵈ Mills James & William BEVANS should many together and the said Jean RICHARDS should be left the widow of the said Rowland BEVANS that them she do not nor shall not take receive claim nor demand any thirds dower part or parcel of the said Rowland BEVANS's estate except what brought by her neither real nor personal nor receive anything more then what the said Rowland BEVANS may give her (if any thing) by his last written Will and Testament and that the said Jean RICHARDS hath not nor shall not by any act or deed of hers subject the said Rowland BEVANS his heirs Ex[ecuto]ʳˢ nor adm[inistrato]ʳˢ to the payment of any secret or under handed debt or debts bond or bonds of any kind by way of fraud not that she hath not nor Shall not do any flagrant act or thing whereby to convey her property befor marriage in a secreat manner contrary to the knowledge of the said Rowland BEVANS, all which matters and things being truly and honestly complied with by the said Jean RICHARDS according to the true intent and meaning of these presents. Then this deed or instrument of writing to be void to all intents and purposes and of no effect whatsoever Otherwise to stand & remain in full force power and virtue in Law ~

Signed Sealed & Delivered   Benjamin DENNIS   Jane RICHARDS (Seal)
In the presence of   John COTTINGHAM"

---

[676] Worcester County Court (Land Records). Bill of sale from CRIPPS, Francis to COTTINGHAM, John. 25 March 1795. Q, pp. 128-130, MSA CE 30-16. www.mdlandrec.net : accessed 26 April 2022.

*followed on folio 145 with the acknowledgment by Justices of the Peace Benjamin DENNIS and John COTTINGHAM and the recordation on folio 146 by court clerk James R. MORRIS on 03 April 1795[677]

Liber Q, folio 156; 04 April 1795

"This Indenter mad this forth day of April in one Thousand Seven hundred and Ninety five Between Zadok STURGIS of Worcester County & State of Maryland of the one part and Zadok SAVAG of the same Place of the other part witnesseth that for and in Consideration of Nine pounds Current Money of of the State af[oresai]^d to me in hand paid by the af[oresai]^d Zadok SAVEG before the Sealling and Delivering of these Presents the Receipt whereof the said Zadok STURGIS Doth hereby acknowledg himself Satisfied Contented and paid hath bargned and Sold to the af[oresai]^d Zadok SAVEG a Certain Negrow Boy Called **Milby** now in the Possession of the af[oresai]d Zadok SAVEG to the af[oresai]d Zadok SAVEG his Heirs and Assigns forever and the af[oresai]d Zadok STURGIS will warrant and Defend the Lawfull Clames Titles and Demands of all Persons Claiming by or under him in whatsoever in Witness whereof the said Zadok STURGIS hear unto his Hand and Seal Affixed the Day & Year above Written

Testes   Zadok STURGIS   (Seal)
John P. MITCHELL"

*followed with the acknowledgment by Justice of the Peace John P. MITCHELL and the recordation on 11 April 1795 by court clerk John C. HANDY[678]

Liber Q, folios 158-159; 21 March 1795

"Know all men by these presents that I Rowland BEVENS of Worcester County & State of Maryland am held and firmly Bound unto John PAYNTER of Sussex County in the State of Delaware Jacob RICHARDS Barshaba RICHARDS Joseph RICHARDS & Daniel MADDUX (Son of Marey) of Worcester County & State of Maryland in the full and Just Sum of Six hundred pounds Current Money of Maryland To which payment well & truly to be made and done I bind myself my Heirs, Exec[utor]^s & Adm[inistrator]^s firmly by the Presents Sealed with my Seals & dated this 21st day of March Anno Dom[ini] one thousand Seven hundred Ninety & five. ~
The Condition of the above Obligation is such that provided the said Rowland BEVANS & Jean RICHARDS should marry together That in that Case the said Rowland BEVANS shall and will fully freely & peaceably Consent to & agree in the said Jean RICHARDS Giving back to her Children or to any others who she may please & at any Time she may Choose and either by her Last Will & Testament or by her Deed of Gift & which is either way shall be Last as she may think most proper for the Giving disposing of any part of her present Estate as she now it & whether at or before her Death as also the Increase of any Child or Children that may be born of Negro **Sall** Together with her whole Dower (real & personal or Right to Thirds of her deceased Husbands Estate, as s[ai]^d Inventory may more fully appear, particularing the following Articles Viz^t Negro **Sall** (before mentioned) Negro **Will** and Negro **Phillis**, Two Beds & Furniture, one Mahogina Desk one Looking Glass one Horse Called Swaper Two Cows and four head of Sheep one hundred Bushels of Corn, Six hundred weight of Bacon one Barrel of Pork one Horse called Toping four Large & Six small Silver Spoons & Tea Tong{?} Togeather with sundry Articles too tedious to mention and the said BEVANS the same shall and will Ratify and Confirm according to the true Meaning & Intention hereof It is fully and poritionly provided Nevertheless that shou[l]d any of the aforesaid three Negroes Die or Runaway so as to Render it impossible (from any Act of Providence) that said Negro or Negroes Could be Returned & c. Then in that Case neither they nor the value of them the said BEVANS shall not

---

[677] Worcester County Court (Land Records). Deed from RICHARDS, Jane to BEVANS, Mills, James, and William. 21 March 1795. Q, pp. 144-146, MSA CE 30-16. www.mdlandrec.net : accessed 26 April 2022.
[678] Worcester County Court (Land Records). Bill of sale from STURGIS, Zadok to SAVAG, Zadok. 04 April 1795. Q, p. 156, MSA CE 30-16. www.mdlandrec.net : accessed 26 April 2022.

be Accountable for It is also further more provided & Agreed upon that if Negro **Philis** (before mentioned) should have any Child or Children born during the natural Life Time both of the said Jean RICHARDS & Rowland BEVANS together that such Increase of Negro **Philis** shall become the Right & property of said Rowland BEVANS and further more that the said Rowland BEVANS shall Receive in money or otherwise & to be settled every year by the said Jean RICHARDS, the Sum of Twelve pounds ten Shillings for keeping Schooling and Maintaining John RICHARDS (Son of Nathaniel) for and during the Time of said BEVANS so keeping said Child John RICHARDS ~ This Bond or Instrument of writing to be Recorded & the same Renewed & Recorded once between Seven & Twelve years by the said BEVANS when duly and Reasonably Required And the Contents of this obligation being Complyed with according to its True Meaning & Import Then the same to be void and of no Effect otherwise to Stand & Remain in full force power and virtue and virtue in Law. ~

Signed Sealed & Delivered   Rowland BEVANS (Seal)
In presence of us.
William HANDY
John COTTINGHAM"

*followed on folio 159 with the acknowledgment by Justice of the Peace Benjamin DENNIS and recordation on 13 April 1795 by court clerk John C. HANDY[679]

Liber Q, folio 161; 25 May 1795

"To all Persons to whom these writings shall Come Know ye that I John KIRBY of the State of Maryland and Worcester County for Divers Causes and Valuable Considerations thereunto moving but more Especially for fifty pounds in hand paid me By my Negro Man Named **Mingo** the Receipt whereof I hereby Acknowledg and for which I John KIRBY have manumated Released and forever Quit Claim and by these presents do for me my Heirs Executors administrators or any other person or persons freely and fully Relinquish all Right Title Claim or Pretensions to any Property or Interest in the affores[ai]^d Negro Man named **Mingo** whom I have Remised Released and forever Quit Claim to he is freely and fully at Liberty at all Times and in all Places wheresoever he may Go or Be from me or any Claiming under me forever in Testimony whereof I have hereunto set my hand and affixt my Seal this 25th day of May 1795 in the year of our Lord one thousand Seven hundred & Ninety five

Signed Sealed and Delivered   John KIRBY
in Presence of us.
Adam BRAVARD
William DALE"

*followed with the recordation on 10 June 1795 by court clerk John C. HANDY[680]

Liber Q, folios 161-162; 11 April 1795

"Know all Men by these Presents that I Coventon REED of Worcester County in the State of Maryland for and in Consideration of the Sum of Thirty Seven pounds Current Money Maryland to him in hand paid by Eli BOWEN of the County and State af[oresai]^d the Receipt whereof the said Coventon doth Confess and Acknowledge at and before the ensealing and Delivery of these presents hath Grant Bargained Sold and Delivered and by these presents doth Grant bargain Sell & deliver unto the said Eli BOWEN his Heirs & Assigns forever a Negro Girl Called **Lotte** To have and to hold the above Negro, to him the said Eli his Heirs and Assigns forever and the said Coventon doth further Covenant and agree for himself his Heirs Ex[ecuto]^{rs} and adm[inistrator]^s with the said Eli his Heirs Ex[ecuto]^{rs} Adm[inistrator]^s and Assigns to

---

[679] Worcester County Court (Land Records). Deed from BEVANS, Rowland to PAYNTER, John, RICHARDS, Jacob, RICHARDS, Barshaba, RICHARDS, Joseph, and MADDUE, Daniel. 21 March 1795. Q, pp. 158-159, MSA CE 30-16. www.mdlandrec.net : accessed 26 April 2022.

[680] Worcester County Court (Land Records). Deed of manumission from KIRBY, John to **Mingo**. 25 May 1795. Q, p. 161, MSA CE 30-16. www.mdlandrec.net : accessed 26 April 2022.

warrant and forever defend the said Negro to the said Eli his Heirs & Assigns forever against the claim of every Person whatsoever which said Negro the said Coventon hath Given the said Eli Possession of by an Actual Delivery In Witness whereof the said Coventon to this present Bill of Sale his hand hath set & Seal affixed this Eleventh day of April anno Dom[ini] 1795

Signed Sealed and   Coventon REED   (Seal)
Delivered in presence of   William PARKER."

*followed on folio 162 with the acknowledgment by Justice of the Peace William PARKER and the recordation on 14 April 1795 by court clerk John C. HANDY[681]

Liber Q, folios 172-173; 24 April 1795

"This Indenture made this Twenty fourth Day of April in the year one Thousand Seven hundred and ninety five Between **Levin CAMBRIDGE (alias Hunt)** of Worcester County and State of Maryland of the one part and Charles GODFREY of the same place of the other Part Witnesseth that the aforesaid **Levin CAMBRIDGE** for and in Consideration of the Sum of Eleven pounds one Shilling and ten pence Current Money of Maryland to him in hand paid by the aforesaid Charles GODFREY at and before the sealing and Delivery of these presents the Receipt whereof is hereby Acknowledged and Confessed He the said **Levin CAMBRIDGE** Hath Granted bargained Sold and Conveyed and by these presents doth absolutely Grant bargain Sell and Convey unto him the said Charles GODFREY his Heirs and Assigns forever all that part or Tract of Land Called Williams Choice Situate Lying and being in Worcester County aforesaid in Acquango Hundred being the same Tract or parcel of Land that a Certain William CAMBRIDGE late of the County aforesaid did by his Last Will and Testament among other Things did Give and bequeath unto his son **Levin CAMBRIDGE** partie to these presents Recourse being had to the said Will may more at Large appear Containing One hundred and Twenty Eight Acres of Land more or Less Together with all Rights Members Profits issues and Priviledges and all other the appurtenances thereunto belonging To have and to hold all and singular the above bargained and sold Lands and Premises unto him the said Charles GODFREY his Heirs and assigns forever to the only proper use Benefit and Behoof of him the said Charles GODFREY his Heirs and Assigns forever And the said **Levin CAMBRIDGE** for Himself his Heirs, Executors and Administrators doth Covenant and agree to quit all Right Title or Claim either in Law or Equity, to the above set forth mentioned Lands and premises and will and Shall forever Warrant and forever defend the same against the Right, Title or Claim of all Manner of Person or persons whatever Claiming by from or under him or his Heirs unto him the said Charles GODFREY his Heirs and Assigns forever In Testimony whereof the said **Levin CAMBRIDGE** to these presents his hand hath Set and Seal affixed the Day and Year above written.

Signed Sealed and Delivered   **Leavin CAMBRIDGE**   (Seal)
In the Presence of
Philip QUINTON
Benjamin DENNIS."

*followed on folio 173 with the acknowledgment by Justices of the Peace Philip QUINTON and Benjamin DENNIS and the recordation by court clerk John C. HANDY[682]

Liber Q, folios 187-188; 05 May 1795

"Wise FOUNTAIN being of Lawful age and Sworn on the holy Evangels of Almighty God deponeth and Saith that she this Deponant hath often heard her mother Hanah SELBY say that she hath Given a Negro Man Called **Able** to her Son Parker SELBY and that she had Given a Bill of Sale for the said negro to the said Parker that at the Time this Conversation passed M^rs

---

[681] Worcester County Court (Land Records). Bill of sale from REED, Coventon to BOWEN, Eli. 11 April 1795. Q, pp. 161-162, MSA CE 30-16. www.mdlandrec.net : accessed 26 April 2022.
[682] Worcester County Court (Land Records). Deed of Conveyance from **CAMBRIDGE, Leavin** to GODFREY, Charles. 24 April 1795. Q, pp. 172-173, MSA CE 30-16. www.mdlandrec.net : accessed 26 April 2022.

SELBY Lived with this Deponant and that the said Negro was in the Possession of the said Parker SELBY and as well as this Deponant Can Recollect the said Negro has been in the said Parkers Possession nine or Ten years and further this Deponant saith that her Mother Mrs SELBY told her that Capt[ain] John SELBY Came to her House and was present when the said Bill of Sale was Given & further this Deponant saith not.

Sworn Before Philip QUINTON a Justice of the Peace.

                                                      Wise + FOUNTAIN (her mark)

                                                      May 5th 1795.

Kendall SCARBOROUGH of Lawfull age being sworn on the Holy Evangels of Almighty God deponeth and saith that some Time after Parker SELBY had the Possession of a Negro Fellow Called **Able** this Deponant heard Mrs Hanah SELBY Mother of the s[ai]^d Parker say that she had Given the said Negro Called **Able** to the said Parker SELBY and that also she had Given a Bill of Sale for the said Negro to the said Parker SELBY that this Conversation pasted as well as this Deponant Recollects about Five or Six Years ago and before the said Mrs SELBY Gave a Bill of Sale to Mr Joseph KILLAM this Deponant further saith to the best of his knowledge the said Parker SELBY has had Possession of the said Negro Called **Able** for as much as Nine years and that the said Negro was in the said Parkers Possession at the Time the said Mrs SELBY Gave a Bill of Sale to Mr Joseph KELLAM last fall and further this Deponant saith not.

                                                      Kendall SCARBOUGH

Sworn before Philip QUINTON a Justice of the Peace. May the 5th 1795.

Samuel FOUNTAIN of full age being sworn on the Holy Evangels of Almighty God deponeth and Saith that he the Deponant hath often heard Mrs Hanah SELBY who Lived with this Deponant say that she had Given to Parker SELBY her Son a negro man named **Able** at the Time this Conversation passed the said Negro was in the said Parker SELBYs possession that as well as this Deponant remembers this Conversation passed about six years ago that at the Time this Conversation passed Mrs SELBY Lived with the Deponant and that the said Negro was in Possession of the said Parker and this Deponant says that the said Negro has been in the said Parker SELBY Possession ever since he Lived in the Neighborhood which has been about Eight years at the Time the above Conversation passed Mrs SELBY did not Set up any Right to the s[ai]^d Negro but whenever she Spoke of or about the s[ai]^d Negro she would mention him as being **Parker Able** & further this Deponant saith not. ~

Sworn Before   Sam[ue]^l FOUNTAIN.
Philip QUINTON a Justice of the Peace   May the 5th 1795."

*followed on folio 188 with the acknowledgment by Justice of the Peace Philip QUINTON and the recordation on 06 May 1795 by court clerk John C. HANDY[683]

Liber Q, folios 188-189; 18 April 1795

"To all whom these presents Shall Come Know Ye that I Benjamin FOOKS of Worcester County in the State of Maryland being desirous to set free and manumit Negro **Dover** Supposed to be about thirty years old at this Time for divers Causes and Considerations me thereunto moving I the said Benjamin FOOKS do by these presents give and Grant Set free and manumit the aforesaid Negro **Dover** immediately To have and to hold and freely Enjoy his freedom as aforesaid in full and Ample manner without any Let Authority or hinderance of any person or persons whatsoever. In Testimony whereof I have hereto set my hand and affixed my Seal this Eighteenth day of April Anno Dom[ini] 1795.

---

[683] Worcester County Court (Land Records). Depositions of FOUNTAIN, Wise, SCARBOUGH, Kendall, and FOUNTAIN, Samuel. 05 May 1795. Q, pp. 187-188, MSA CE 30-16. www.mdlandrec.net : accessed 26 April 2022.

Signed Sealed and Delivered   Benjamin FOOKES   (Seal)
in Presence of   Booz WALSTON."

*followed on folio 189 with the acknowledgment by Justice of the Peace Booz WALSTON and the recordation by court clerk John C. HANDY[684]

Liber Q, folio 195; 15 May 1795

"A true List of Negroes as follows to wit, one Negro Woman Called **Esther**, Negro **Phillis**, ditto **Nann**, **Moses**, **Comfort**, **Candis**, and **Sarah** & Girl **Flora** That I John WALLOP moved into the State of Maryland, Worcester County, from Accomack County State of Virginia in the year one Thousand Seven hundred and Ninety Five And I do assert that part of the above mentioned Negroes were born in Accomack County to wit Negroes, **Moses**, **Comfort** and **Sarah** the Remaining part were born in Worcester County aforesaid, that they all became Residenters of Accomack County aforesaid before the year aforesaid as Given under my hand this fifteenth day of May and Year 1795.   John WALLOP.

May the 15th 1795 Then Came before me William SELBY Naval Officer for the District of Snow Hill and Worcester County and made Oath on the holy Evangels of Almighty God that the Several Negroes enumerated in the above List were Inhabitants and Residenters of Accomack County in the State of Virginia as above mentioned untill the eighth of January last And I do hereby declare, that I have and did then move the said Negroes and myself and Family into Worcester County in the State of Maryland, with Bona Fide Intentions of Settleing in the same and that I have brought the said Negroes with me with views of Continuing them in my own service and not with any design of Selling or disposing of them.

                                                                                 Sworn before William SELBY
                                                                                                 Naval Officer."

*followed with the recordation by court clerk John C. HANDY[685]

Liber Q, folio 196; 04 May 1795

"Maryland Ss[t]. Know all men by these presents that I John MELSON of Worcester County and State af[oresai]d Planter for and in Consideration of the Sum of the value of Sixty five pounds Current Money of Maryland to me in hand paid by Elisha PARKER of the County and State af[oresai]d have bargained Sold Set over and Delivered by these presents in plain and open Market according to the Just and Due Form of Law in that Case Made and provided Do Bargin set over and Deliver unto the said Elisha PARKER one Negro Man Called **Magor** To have and to Hold the said Bargained Premises unto the said Elisha PARKER his Heirs Executors Administrators and Assigns forever and I the said John MELSON for myself my Heirs Executors and Adm[inistrato]rs and the said bargained premises unto the said Elisha PARKER his Heirs Executors Adm[inistrato]rs and assigns against all manner of Persons shall and will warrant and forever Defend by these presents in Witness whereof the bargained Premises unto the said I have hereunto set my hand and Seal this fourth Day of May Anno Domini one Thousand Seven hundred Ninety and Five ~

Signed Sealed and Delivered   Booz WALSTON   John MELSON   (Seal)
In the presence of us   Porter PARSONS"

---

[684] Worcester County Court (Land Records). Deed of manumission from FOOKES, Benjamin to **Dover**. 18 April 1795. Q, pp. 188-189, MSA CE 30-16. www.mdlandrec.net : accessed 26 April 2022.

[685] Worcester County Court (Land Records). Certificate of importation into Maryland from WALLOP, John for **Esther, Phillis, Nann, Moses, Comfort, Candis, Sarah,** and **Flora**. 15 May 1795. Q, p. 195, MSA CE 30-16. www.mdlandrec.net : accessed 26 April 2022.

*followed with the acknowledgment by Justice of the Peace Booz WALSTON and the recordation on 15 May 1795 by court clerk John C. HANDY[686]

Liber Q, folios 201-202; 25 May 1795

"This Indenture made this 25th of May in the year of our Lord one Thousand seven hundred and ninety five Between William FLOYD of Worcester County of the one part & free Negro Woman **Esther** of the same place Witnesseth that the af[oresai]d Negro **Esther** for and and in Consideration of the sum of five pounds to her in hand paid by the said William FLOYD before the Execution hereof and for many Good and Obliging favours done to and bestowed on me by the said William FLOYD heretofore I the said **Esther** do hereby of my own free will voluntarily & without Fear or Duress or Threats by the said Floyd Indent myself a Servant unto the abovenamed Floyd to serve him in all Respects as a Good and faithfull Servant seven whole Years from the second day of May one thousand seven hundred and Ninety Five and in all Reasonable & Lawfull Requests and Commands of the said FLOYD I the said **Esther** do bind & oblige myself to obey as a Good and faithfull Servant ought to do. I do hereby for Value Received Release and forever quit Claim the said William FLOYD his Ex[ecuto]rs or Adm[inistrato]rs of all Actions or Causes of Action & all other Demands whatever that have arisen or are now Subsisting between her the said **Esther** and the said William FLOYD from the Beginning of the World to the Date hereof, And in Consideration of the premisses the said William FLOYD agrees for himself his Heirs Ex[ecuto]rs & Adm[inistrato]rs to find and furnish the said **Esther** & her Children (if any) with Sufficient meat food Lodging and Cloathing suited to a Servant in her station and in all Respects will Demean himself as a master ought to do agreeable to Law. In Witness whereof the said Parties have interchangably set their Hands & Seals affixed to these presents the Day and year first above written. ~

Signed Sealed & Delivered   Philip QUINTON   William FLOYD (Seal)
In presence of

                                                                     her
                                                    Free woman **Esther** X (Seal)
                                                                                   mark."

*followed with the acknowledgment by Justice of the Peace Philip QUINTON and the recordation on folio 202 by court clerk John C. HANDY on 26 May 1795[687]

Liber Q, folios 205-206; 29 May 1795

"Know all Men by these presents that I Major WHITE of Worcester County for the natural Love & Affection which I Entertain for my Daughter Polly EVANS & Also for & Consideration of the Sum of five Shillings Current Money of Maryland to me in hand paid I do hereby Give Grant & Sell unto my said Daughter Polly EVANS during her natural Live & After her Death to her Children Sally EVANS Elisa EVANS & John EVANS & their Executors Administrators and Assigns Equally to be divided as tenants in Common the following Goods & Chattels to wit a Negro Boy Called **George**, a Negro Girl Called **Esther** and and the Negro Girl Called **Lanta** and their Children issue & Increase To have and to Hold the said three Negroes **George Esther** and **Lanta** and their Issue & Increase unto my said Daughter Polly EVANS for & during her natural Life and after her Death to have and hold the same and their Issue & Increase unto my said Daughters Children to wit Sally EVANS Elisa EVANS and John EVANS their Executors Adm[inistrato]rs & Assigns equally to be divided as tenants in Common; the said Negroes & their Issue to the only proper use of my said Daughter During her natural Life & after her Death the said Negroes & their Issue those Born in the Life Time of my Daughter Polly as well as those born after her Death unto the only proper use of the said Sally EVANS Elisa EVANS & John EVANS (Children of my said Daughter Polly EVANS, to them their

---

[686] Worcester County Court (Land Records). Bill of sale from MELSON, John to PARKER, Elisha. 04 May 1795. Q, p. 196, MSA CE 30-16. www.mdlandrec.net : accessed 26 April 2022.
[687] Worcester County Court (Land Records). Indenture of free Negro **Esther** to FLOYD, William. 25 May 1795. Q, pp. 201-202, MSA CE 30-16. www.mdlandrec.net : accessed 26 April 2022.

Ex[ecuto]^rs Adm[inistrato]^rs and Assigns Equally as Tenants in Common. In Witness whereof I have hereto set my hand & Seal affixed this 29th of May 1795.

Major WHITE   (Seal)

Signed Sealed & Delivered in presence of. ~   Philip QUINTON ~."

*followed on folio 206 with the acknowledgment by Justice of the Peace Philip QUINTON and the recordation by court clerk John C. HANDY[688]

Liber Q, folio 224; 09 June 1795

"Know all Men by these presents that I Moses PAYNE of Worcester County have Remised Released and Quit Clamed and by these presents do for me my Heirs Executors and Administrators and every of them Remise Release and forever quit Claim unto Negro **Majar** Aged Twenty years **Susannah** Aged Twenty five **Jemimah** Aged seven years **Feaby** Aged Two years of the County and State aforesaid there Heirs and every of them all and all Manner of Personal Actions and Demands Personal whatsoever from the Date hereof in Witness whereof I set my hand and Seal affixed this ninth Day of June Anno Domini Seventeen hundred and ninety five ~.

Signed Sealed & Delivered   Moses PAYNE   (Seal)
in the Presence of
William PARKER. ~"

*followed with the acknowledgment by Justice of the Peace William PARKER and the recordation by court clerk John C. HANDY[689]

Liber Q, folio 227; 24 July 1795

"Know all men by these presents that I Zebulon JOHNSON of Worcester County in the State of Maryland for and in Consideration of the Sum of Seven pounds ten shillings Current Money of the State af[oresai]^d to me in hand paid by **Charles BOWEN** (free Negro) of the same place at and before the Sealing & Delivery hereof the Receipt whereof I do hereby Acknowledge have granted bargained sold and delivered and by these presents do grant bargain sell and deliver unto the said **Charles BOWEN** his Heirs and Assigns forever a Negro Woman named **Sarah** now in the Possession and delivered to the said **Charles BOWEN** hereby bargained and Sold unto him the said **Charles BOWEN** his heirs & assigns forever. And I the said Zebulon JOHNSON will warrant and forever defend the said negro unto him the said **Charles BOWEN** his heirs & assigns for ever In Witness whereof I have hereto set my hand and affixed my Seal this 24th day of July Anno Domini 1795

Signed Sealed & Deliv[ere]^d   Zebulon JOHNSON   (Seal)
in presence of   Jn°. GUNBY"

*followed with the acknowledgment by Justice of the Peace John GUNBY and the recordation by court clerk John C. HANDY[690]

Liber Q, folio 234; 09 June 1795

"To all Persons to whom these Presents shall Come Know ye that I Warner MIFFLIN of Kent County in the State of Delaware being Desirous to manumit and Set free a Certain Negro Man named **Robert** left to me by a Certain William ALLEN dec[ease]^d late of Worcester County and State of Maryland for and in Consideration of the faithfull Service of the said Negroe Man

---

[688] Worcester County Court (Land Records). Bill of sale from WHITE, Major to EVANS, Polly, Sally, Elisa, and John. 29 May 1795. Q, pp. 205-206, MSA CE 30-16. www.mdlandrec.net : accessed 27 April 2022.
[689] Worcester County Court (Land Records). Deed of manumission from PAYNE, Moses to **Majar, Susannah, Jemimah,** and **Feaby**. 09 June 1795. Q, p. 224, MSA CE 30-16. www.mdlandrec.net : accessed 27 April 2022.
[690] Worcester County Court (Land Records). Bill of sale from JOHNSON, Zebulon to **BOWEN, Charles** (free negro). 24 July 1795. Q, p. 227, MSA CE 30-16. www.mdlandrec.net : accessed 27 April 2022.

Robert I the said Warner MIFFLIN do by these presents Give Grant Manumit set free and forever discharge the said Negro **Robert** the same to Take Effect immediately upon the Execution of these presents To have hold and freely Enjoy unto him the said Negro **Robert** his freedom and Liberty forever according to the Tenor and Effect of these presents in full and ample manner without any let hindrance Controul or Authority of any person or persons whatever Claiming or to Claim by from or under me In Testimony whereof I the said Warner MIFFLIN hath to these presents my hand hath set and Seal affixed this ninth Day of the 6th Month Anno Domini 1795.

Signed Sealed and delivered   Warner MIFFLIN   (Seal)
In presence of   John P. MITCHELL"

*followed with the acknowledgment by Justice of the Peace John P. MITCHELL and the recordation on 10 June 1795 by court clerk John C. HANDY[691]

Liber Q, folios 234-235; 10 June 1795

"Worcester County Know all Men by these presents that I Isaac CARPENTER now of Philadelphia in Pensylvania State do hereby Acknowledge & Confess that Some Time ago I executed a Deed of Manumission in favour of my Wife **Leah** and Children **Caleb** (or **Calop**) and **Hannah CARPENTER** and that I never did Consider them or either of them From the Time of my purchase of them in any other Light than as free serving the Authority of an Husband to the said **Leah** and of a Parent to the said **Caleb** or **Calop** & **Hannah** and whereas it is Represented to me by George ROSSE in whose Care the said Deed was that while he was Confined by Sickness after his Return from the Army, the said Deed of Manumission was lost or mislaid so as he has not yet been able to find the same and whereas I fully Remember to have duly Executed such a Deed in the presence of Elizabeth ROSSE and the said George and bring a written and Sealed Declaration of what I had from the Time of the Purchase and that it was Executed while I lived in this County and the Consideration of Natural Love & Affection a Sinn of Justice and Good faith as also of ten pounds Current Money of Maryland to me in hand paid the Receipt whereof is hereby Acknowledged & the said **Caleb** or **Calop** & **Hannah** thereof discharged hath and hereby manumit and Set free the said **Hannah CARPENTER Leah CARPENTER** and **Caleb** or **Calop CARPENTER** from their State of Bondage, Recognizing them as free Members & Citizens of the State of Maryland. In Evidence whereof I have hereunto set my hand & Affixed my seal this tenth day of June AD 1795.

Sign[e]d Seal[e]d & Delivered & Acknowledged   his
In presence of   Isaac + CARPENTER (Seal)
William PARKER.   Mark"

*followed on folio 235 with the acknowledgment by Justice of the Peace William PARKER and the recordation by court clerk John C. HANDY[692]

Liber Q, folios 260-261; 25 May 1778

"Know all Men by these Presents that I Robert SCHOOLFIELD of Worcester County in the State of Maryland am held and do Stand Bound unto Major MUMFORD of the same Place in the full and Just Sum of Two Thousand Pounds Continantal Currency to which payment well and truly to be made and done I bind myself my Heirs Ex[ecuto]rs & Adminis[trato]rs firmly by these presents Jointly and Severally unto him the said Major MUMFORD his Heirs Executors administ[rators] and Assigns as Witness my hand and Seal this Twenty fifth Day of March Anno Dom[ini] one Thousand Seven hundred and Seventy Eight ~.

---

[691] Worcester County Court (Land Records). Deed of manumission from MIFFLIN, Warner to **Robert**. 09 June 1795. Q, p. 234, MSA CE 30-16. www.mdlandrec.net : accessed 27 April 2022.
[692] Worcester County Court (Land Records). Deed of manumission from CARPENTER, Isaac to **Hannah, Leah,** and **Caleb**. 10 June 1795. Q, pp. 234-235, MSA CE 30-16. www.mdlandrec.net : accessed 27 April 2022.

The Condition of the above obligation is such that if the above bound Robert SCHOOLFIELD him his Heirs Execut[or]^s Adminis[trator]^s do Stand too and abide by the mutual agreement and Division of the said Major MUMFORD & Robert SCHOOLFIELD here mentioned of Several Negroes and by this obligation shall forever Quit all Claim Right Title Interest or property to those mentioned hereafter to the said Major his Heirs & and Assigns forever the Division to be as follows Viz^t **Tite Martha** and **Santa** to be the Part and Property of the above mentioned Major MUMFORD his Heirs and Assigns forever with the Increase And **Celar Adam Sinah Ben** and **Dol** to be the part and Property of the said Robert SCHOOLFIELD his Heirs and Assigns forever with their Increase and the said Robert SCHOOLFIELD doth oblige himself his Heirs Execut[or]^s administrat[or]^s and Assigns to give and further Surety Bill of Sale or Instrument of Writing for the more effectually Securing the above mentioned negroes with their Increase unto him the s[ai]^d Major MUMFORD his Heirs and Assigns at any Time hereafter when he shall or may Require or demand the same or by his Heirs or Assigns Then this present obligation void otherwise to Remain in full force Power and virtue in Law.

Sign[e]^d Seal[e]^d and Delivered in   Nicolas VALLANU   Rob[er]^t SCHOOLFIELD (Seal)
Presence off   J. P. ROBINS"

*followed on folio 261 with the oath of Littleton ROBINS, the acknowledgment by Justice of the Peace Philip QUINTON, and the recordation by court clerk John C. HANDY in 03 July 1795[693]

Liber Q, folios 265-266; 22 May 1795

"Know all Men by these presents that We William SELBY James SELBY Dan[ie]^l SELBY & Nancy GUNBY of Worcester County for and in Consideration of the Sum of Thirty five pounds to me in hand paid by John GUNBY of the same County at or before the Sealing and Delivery of these presents the Receipt whereof we the said William SELBY Jam[e]^s SELBY Dan[ie]^l SELBY Nancy GUNBY do thereby Acknowledge have Granted Bargained & Sold and by these presents do Grant bargain & Sell unto the said John GUNBY his Heirs Executors & Administrators one Negro Woman Called **Hannah** with her youngest Child Called **Barbary**, late in the Occupation of the af[oresai]^d William SELBY To Have and to Hold the af[oresai]^d Negroes towit **Hannah & Barbary** bargained and Sold to the said John GUNBY his Heirs and Assigns forever and We the said William SELBY James SELBY Dan[ie]^l SELBY & Nancy GUNBY for ourselves and our Heirs Executors and Administrators the af[oresai]^d Negroes **Hannah** and **Barbary** unto the said John GUNBY his Ex[ecuto]^{rs} Adm[inistrato]^{rs} or Assigns against us the said William SELBY James SELBY Daniel SELBY & Nancy GUNBY and all and every person or Persons shall and will warrant and forever Defend and by these presents the said Negroes **Hannah** & **Barbary** the said William SELBY James SELBY Daniel SELBY & Nancy GUNBY have put the said John GUNBY in full possession by delivering the said Negroes **Hannah** & **Barbary** to the said John GUNBY at the sealing and delivery of these presents in Witness our Hands & Seals this 22$^{[n]d}$ Day of May Anno Dom[ini] 1795.

	William SELBY (Seal)
Witness Geo[rge] PURNELL	James SELBY (Seal)
	Danie[l] SELBY (Seal)
	Ann GUNBY (Seal)"

*followed on folio 266 with the acknowledgment by Justice of the Peace Outten STURGIS and the recordation on 10 July 1795 by court clerk John C. HANDY[694]

---

[693] Worcester County Court (Land Records). Bond from SCHOOLFIELD, Robert to MUMFORD, Major. 25 May 1778. Q, pp. 260-261, MSA CE 30-16. www.mdlandrec.net : accessed 27 April 2022.

[694] Worcester County Court (Land Records). Bill of sale from SELBY, William, SELBY, James, SELBY, Daniel, and GUNBY, Ann to GUNBY, John. 22 May 1795. Q, pp. 265-266, MSA CE 30-16. www.mdlandrec.net : accessed 27 April 2022.

Liber Q, folios 266-267; 10 July 1795

"Worcester County to wit. Know all Men by these presence that I William SELBY of the County af[oresai]^d for the Consideration of the Sum of Twenty Two pounds ten Shillings Current Money of Maryl[an]^d to me in hand paid by Ann SELBY of the County af[oresai]^d have Given Granted Sold and Delivered possession of and by these presence do Give Grant and Sell and deliver possession of one Negro Slave Named **Rose** to the said Ann SELBY To Have and to Hold the said Slave **Rose** unto the said Ann SELBY her Executors Administrators and Assigns forever to her & her only proper use, Benefitt and Behoof In Witness whereof the said William SELBY hereto hath affixed his hand & Seal this 10th day of July in the year Seventeen hundred and ninety five ~.

Signed Sealed and Delivered   William SELBY (Seal)
in the Presence of   J[oh]n GUNBY."

*followed on folio 261 with the acknowledgment by Justice of the Peace John GUNBY and the recordation by court clerk John C. HANDY[695]

Liber Q, folios 267-268; 10 July 1795

"Worcester County to wit. Know all Men by these presents that I William SELBY of the County af[oresai]^d for the Consideration of the Sum of Twenty five pounds Current Money of Maryland to me in hand paid by Zadok SELBY of the County af[oresai]^d have Given Granted sold and delivered Possession of and by these presents do Give Grant Sell and deliver Possession of one Negro Slave Named **Comfort** To the said Zadok SELBY To Have and to Hold the said Slave **Comfort** unto the said Zadok SELBY his Executors Adm[inistrato]^{rs} and Assigns forever to Him & their only proper use Benefitt and Behoof In Witness whereof the said William SELBY hereto hath Affixed his hand and Seal this 10th day July in the year Seventeen hundred & Ninety five ~

Signed Sealed and Delivered   William SELBY (Seal)
in the presence of . . . .   J[oh]n GUNBY."

*followed on folio 268 with the acknowledgment by Justice of the Peace John GUNBY and the recordation by court clerk John C. HANDY[696]

Liber Q, folios 269-270; 04 July 1795

"Maryland Worcester Ss. Know all Men by these presents That I Isaac WARREN of the County afforesaid for & in Consideration of the Sum of Two hundred pounds Current Money of Maryland to me in hand paid by Thomas DALE of the same place afforesaid at or before the sealing and Delivery of these presents the Receipt whereof I the said Isaac WARREN do hereby acknowledge & have Granted bargained & Sold & Delivered by these presents do Grant bargan & Sell unto the said Thomas DALE his Heirs Executors Administrators & Assigns five Negroes to wit Named as follows **Rose Isaac Minta Jacob & Rhoda** also one mare & Colt one horse & one Mare without a Colt To Have and To Hold the said Negros & Creatures hereby Granted Bargained & Sold or mentioned or Intended so to be unto the said Thomas DALE his Heirs Executors Administrators & Assigns forever as his own proper Goods & to & for his own proper use & uses forever And the said Isaac WARREN for myself my Heirs Executors & Administrators the said Negros & Creatures hereby Granted Bargained & sold unto the said Thomas DALE his Heirs Executors Administrators & Assigns against me the said Isaac WARREN my Executors & Administrators & against all & every other person or persons whatsoever shall & Will Warrant & by the presents forever defend In Witness whereof I have hereunto Set my hand & Seal affixed this the fourth Day of July Anno Domini 1795.

---

[695] Worcester County Court (Land Records). Bill of sale from SELBY, William to SELBY, Ann. 10 July 1795. Q, pp. 266-267, MSA CE 30-16. www.mdlandrec.net : accessed 27 April 2022.

[696] Worcester County Court (Land Records). Bill of sale from SELBY, William to SELBY, Zadok. 10 July 1795. Q, pp. 267-268, MSA CE 30-16. www.mdlandrec.net : accessed 27 April 2022.

Signed Sealed & Delivered	Anne POSTLY	Isaac WARREN (Seal)
in the presents of.	John POSTLY"	

*followed on folio 270 with the acknowledgment by Justice of the Peace John POSTLY and the recordation on 13 July 1795 by court clerk John C. HANDY[697]

Liber Q, folios 270-271; 14 July 1795

"Know all Men by these presents that I Jacob ADDAMS of Worcester County and State of Maryland for and in Consideration of the Sum of Six pounds Current Money of Maryland to me in hand paid by William MILBOURN of the same place Have bargained Sold Released and Quit all Right Claim and Title of and to Two Certain Negro Men now in the Possession of the said William MILBOURN to wit Negro **Isaac** and Negro **Jack** being the same Negroes heretofore Sold and a Bargain of Sale for made by the said MILBOURN to the said ADDAMS To Have and to Hold all and singular the said Negroes **Isaac** and **Jack** above mentioned unto Him the said William MILBOURN unto him the said William MILBOURN his Heirs and Assigns forever and the said Jacob ADDAMS for Himself his Heirs Executors and Administrators doth hereby forever hereafter Quit all Right Title and Demand of and to the said Negroes above mentioned As Witness my Hand and Seal Affixed to these presents this fourteenth day of July in the Year one Thousand Seven hundred and Ninety Five ~

Signed Sealed & Delivered		Jacob ADDAMS (Seal)
In the presence of	Philip QUINTON"	

*followed on folio 271 with the acknowledgment by the Justice of the Peace Philip QUINTON and the recordation by court clerk John C. HANDY[698]

Liber Q, folio 277; 09 June 1795

"To all Persons to whom these Presents shall Come know ye that I Warner MIFFLIN of Kent County in the State of Delaware being desirous to manumit and set free a Certain Negro Man named **James** Left to me by William ALLEN Esq[ui]r[e] late of Worcester County and State of Maryland dec[ease]d for and in Consideration of the faithfull service of the said Negro man **James** I the said Warner MIFFLIN do by these presents Give Grant Manumitt Set free and forever discharge the same to Take Effect immediately upon the Execution of these presents To Have hold and freely enjoy his Freedom and Liberty, forever According to the Tenor and Effect of these presents in full and Ample Manner without any Let Hindrance Controul or Authority of any person or persons whatever Claiming or to Claim by from or under me In Testimony whereof I the said Warner MIFFLIN hath to these presents my hand hath set and Seal affixed this 9th day of 6 mo[nth] Anno Dom[ini] 1795.

Signed Sealed and Delivered		Warner MIFFLIN (Seal)
In presence of	John P. MITCHELL"	

*followed with the acknowledgment by Justice of the Peace John P. MITCHELL and the recordation 24 July 1795 by court clerk John C. HANDY[699]

Liber Q, folios 278-279; 16 July 1795

"State of Maryland Worcester County Know all Men by these presents that I John SMITH of Worcester County Late of Somerset and State of Maryland in Consideration that I owe and am Indebted unto William TAYLOR of the County and State aforesaid for a Sum of Money and being willing to Secure the said William TAYLOR the Payment of the same In Consideration

---

[697] Worcester County Court (Land Records). Bill of sale from WARREN, Isaac to DALE, Thomas. 04 July 1795. Q, pp. 269-270, MSA CE 30-16. www.mdlandrec.net : accessed 27 April 2022.
[698] Worcester County Court (Land Records). Bill of sale from ADDAMS, Jacob to MILBOURN, William. 14 July 1795. Q, pp. 270-271, MSA CE 30-16. www.mdlandrec.net : accessed 27 April 2022.
[699] Worcester County Court (Land Records). Deed of manumission from MIFFLIN, Warner to **James**. 09 June 1795. Q, p. 277, MSA CE 30-16. www.mdlandrec.net : accessed 27 April 2022.

thereof as also for and in Consideration of the Sum of One hundred and Sixty Pound Current money of Maryland to me in hand paid by the said TAYLOR at and before the Sealing and delivery hereof the Receipt whereof I the said John SMITH do hereby Acknowledge I have Given Granted bargained and Sold and by these presents do Give Grant Bargain and Sell unto him the said TAYLOR his Heirs and Assigns forever the following Articles to wit one Negro Fellow Named **Rielman** Twenty three Years of Age one Negro Wench Named **Cary** and two Negro Boys one named **Sandey** and one **Jacob** and one Girl Child named **Rose** one white Mare and two Horse Colts one three Years old and one a year old and one Yoake of Oxen Three milk Cows and Calves and one Hifer Three Feather Beds and Furniture one Case Draws and thirteen Heads of Hoggs Two Walnut Round Leaf Tables Two Chest and Cubart To Have and to Hold the said Several Articles above mentioned unto him the said TAYLOR his Heirs and Assigns forever and to and the proper use and Benefit Behoof of him the said TAYLOR his Heirs and Assigns forever and to and for no other use Intent or purpose whatsoever and I the said John SMITH do hereby Covenant and Agree to and with the said TAYLOR that I the said John SMITH will Warrant and forever defend unto him the said TAYLOR his Heirs and Assigns forever all, and every of the above Named Articles Against the Claim Rit or Title of any Person or Persons whatsoever Claiming or that may hereafter Claim the same In Testimony whereof I the said John SMITH have hereto Set my hand and Seal this sixteenth day of July one Thousand Seven hundred and ninety five.

Signed Sealed and Delivered   John SMITH   (Seal)
in the Presence of . . . . .   Isaac MARSHALL"

*followed with the acknowledgment by Justice of the Peace Isaac MARSHALL and the recordation by court clerk John C. HANDY[700]

Liber Q, folios 290-291; 31 July 1795

"Know all Men by these Presents that I Rives R. TOWNSEND of Worcester County in the State of Maryland for and in Consideration of the Sum of forty five pounds Currant Money of the State aforesaid to me in hand paid by Robert M. RICHARDSON of the County and State af[oresai]d before the sealing & Delivering of these presents the Receipt whereof I do hereby acknowledge have bargained and Sold and by these presents do bargain and Sell unto the said Robert M RICHARDSON his Heirs and Assigns forever one Negroe Woman Called **Comfort** to Have and to hold the above named Negroe Woman unto the said Robert M. RICHARDSON his Heirs and assigns forever and for no other use or purpose whatsoever and the said Rives R TOWNSEND for himself and his Heirs doth Covenant and agree to and with the said Rob[er]t M. RICHARDSON that he the said Rives R. TOWNSEND hath a good and Sufficient Title to sell and dispose of the said Negro Woman nam[e]d **Comfort** so so do to Convey unto the said Rob[er]t M. RICHARDSON a good Sure or firm Title to the same and that no person but the s[ai]d Rives R TOWNSEND hath any Right or Title to the same In Testimony whereof the said Rives R TOWNSEND his hand to these presents hath set and Seal affixed this 31st day of July in the Year of our Lord one thousand seven hundred and ninety five ~

Signed Seal[e]d Delivered   Rives R. TOWNSEND   (Seal)
in presents of.   Philip QUINTON"

*followed on folio 291 with the acknowledgment by Justice of the Peace Philip QUINTON and the recordation on 06 August 1795 by court clerk John C. HANDY[701]

Liber Q, folios 301-302; 08 August 1795

"State of Maryland Worcester County Ss Know all Men by these presents that I Thomas PURNELL of William of the County and State af[oresai]d for and in Consideration of the Sum

---

[700] Worcester County Court (Land Records). Bill of sale from SMITH, John to TAYLOR, William. 16 July 1795. Q, pp. 278-279, MSA CE 30-16. www.mdlandrec.net : accessed 27 April 2022.
[701] Worcester County Court (Land Records). Bill of sale from TOWNSEND, Rives R. to RICHARDSON, Robert M. 31 July 1795. Q, pp. 290-291, MSA CE 30-16. www.mdlandrec.net : accessed 27 April 2022.

of Thirty Seven pounds ten Shillings Current Money of Maryland to me in hand well and truly paid at and before the Sealing and Delivery of these presents by Zeno EVANS of the County & State af[oresai]^d the Receipt whereof I do hereby Acknowledge have bargained and Sold and by these presents do grant bargain and Sell unto the said Zeno EVANS one Negro Girl Named **Sue** by these presents bargained and Sold unto the said Zeno EVANS his Heirs Executors Administrators & assigns forever And I the said Thomas PURNELL of William for me my Heirs Executors & Administrators the said Negro Girl Called **Sue** unto the said Zeno EVANS his Heirs Executors Administrators & Assigns against me the said Thomas PURNELL of William my Executors Administrators and Assigns And against all and evry other Person & Persons whatever Shall and will warrant and by these presents forever defend of which Negro Girl Named **Sue** I the said Thomas PURNELL of W[illia]^m have put the said Zeno EVANS in full Possession by delivery of the said **Sue** to zeno EVANS at, the Sealing of these presents In witness whereof I the said Thomas PURNELL of William have hereunto Set my hand and Seal this Eight day of August Anno Domini 1795.

Signed Sealed and Delivered   Thomas PURNELL   (Seal)
In presents of . . . . . .   Joshua PREDEAUX."

*followed on folio 302 with the acknowledgment by Justice of the Peace Josiah MITCHELL and the recordation by court clerk John C. HANDY[702]

Liber Q, folios 362-363; 16 October 1795

"State of Maryland Worcester County Know all Men by these presents that I Hannah VICTOR for and in Consideration of the Sum of forty three pounds Currant money of Maryland to me in hand paid by James DENNIS the Receipt whereof I do hereby acknowledge have bargained and Sold and by these presents do bargain and Sell unto James DENNIS One Negro Woman Slave named **Peg** to have and to hold the aforesaid Slave Called **Peg** to the said James DENNIS his Heirs and Assigns forever to the only proper use and behalf of the said James DENNIS his Heirs and Assigns and for no other ~~use~~ Intent or purpose whatsoever and it is further Covenanted that the said Hanah VICTOR for herself and her Heirs the aforesaid Slave Called **Peg** to the aforesaid James DENNIS his Heirs or Assigns will forever warrent and Defend in Witness whereof I have Sett my hand and Seal affixed this Sixteenth Day of October one Thousand seven hundred and Ninety five

Signed Sealed and Delivered   Hannah VICTOR   (Seal)
in the Presents of . . . .   Benjamin DENNIS"

*followed with the acknowledgment by Justice of the Peace Benjamin DENNIS and the recordation on folio 363 on 23 October 1795 by court clerk John C. HANDY[703]

Liber Q, folios 365-366; 23 October 1795

"This Indenture made this 23$^{[r]d}$ day of October Anno Dom[ini] 1795. Between Hannah VICTOR of Worcester County & State of Maryland of the one part and Negro **Sarah** of the other part Witnesseth that the said Hannah VICTOR for and in Consideration of the Sum of three pounds to me in hand paid and for her former and faithful Service done here by her said Negro Woman do forever manumit & Sett free the said Negro Woman **Sarah** & her future Increase from all Trouble hindrance or Molestation of any person claiming the same or ever Claim hereafter to from by or under her said Hannah VICTOR or her Heirs forever In Testimony whereof I have hereunto set my Hand and Seal this 23$^{[r]d}$ day of October Anno Dom[ini] 1795.

---

[702] Worcester County Court (Land Records). Bill of sale from PURNELL, Thomas to SELBY, Zeno. 08 August 1795. Q, pp. 301-302, MSA CE 30-16. www.mdlandrec.net : accessed 27 April 2022.
[703] Worcester County Court (Land Records). Bill of sale from VICTOR, Hannah to DENNIS, James. 16 October 1795. Q, pp. 362-363, MSA CE 30-16. www.mdlandrec.net : accessed 27 April 2022.

Signed Sealed and delivered   Philip QUINTON   Hannah VICTOR   (Seal)
In presents of . . . . .   Elisha PURNELL"

*followed on folio 366 with the acknowledgment by Justice of the Peace Philip QUINTON and the recordation on 26 October 1795 by court clerk John C. HANDY[704]

Liber R, folio 9; 30 October 1795

"Know all Men by these presents that I William BREUTON of Worcester County and State of Maryland for and in Consideration of the Sum of one hundred pounds Specie money of the State of af[ore]s[ai]^d to me in hand paid by Francis BREUTON and Polly Adkins BREUTON my Infant Daughter and by there friend Nany BREUTON the Rec[eip]^t whereof I do hereby Acknowledge and my Self therwith fully Satisfyde have bargind Sold and delivered unto the said Frances BREUTON and Polley Adkins BREUTON Each one the Hereafter named negroes Viz^t. Negro **Nany** to Francs BREUTON and Negro **Charles** to Polly Adkins BREUTON To Have and To Hold the said Negros **Nancy** & **Charles** unto the said Francs & Polly A BREUTON their Executors Administrators or Assigns to the only proper use and Behoof of the said Frances & Polly BREUTON their Executors or Administrators forever and I the said William BREUTON for myself Executors or administrators the said bargind Primisses unto the said Frances & Polly BREUTON their Heirs or Assigns against all Persons shall and will warrent and forever defend by these presents In Witness whereof I have hereunto Set my Hand and Seal this Thirtieth Day of October Anodominy Seventeen hundred and Ninty five ~

Signed Seald and delivered   his   W[illia]^m BREUTON   (Seal)
In presents of us . . . . .   George   +   BREUTON
                                    mark

                             Philip SEROGIS"

*followed with the acknowledgment by Justice of the Peace Booz WALSTON and the recordation on 06 November 1795 by court clerk John C. HANDY[705]

Liber R, folios 9 – 10; 29 October 1795

"Whereas Controversies and Disputes have been and yet are depending between Joseph KILLAM and Samuel FOUNTAIN for the determination and final Ending of which the said Parties have Submitted themselves and become bound Each to the other by their several obligations in the Sum of one Thousand Pounds Current money of Maryland of for the performance of the award order Judgment and determination of us John Selby PURNELL and Littleton ROBINS Indifferently nominated Elected and Chosen as well on the Part of Joseph KILLAM or on the part and behalf of Samuel FOUNTAIN to award order adjudge and determine of the Right Title Claim of the aforesaid Samuel FOUNTAIN of and unto a Certain Negro Girl named **Jenny** in the Possession of the said Joseph KILLAM so as the said award be made by us the said Arbitrators and Ready to be delivered to the parties at or upon the first day of November in the year of one Thousand Seven hundred and ninety five as by the said obligations and Conditions doth appear. Now Know ye that us the said Arbitrators John Selby PURNELL and Littleton ROBINS taking upon ourselves the Burthen of the said Award and having heard the sayings allegations and Exhibits of both the said Parties Concerning the Premisses and being desirous to Settle Amity and Friendship between them do make our Award order and determination of and Concerning the premisses af[oresai]^d in manner and Form following that is to say First we Award Order and determine the aforesaid Negro Girl named **Jenny** to be the Right Title and Property of the said Joseph KILLAM and the Claim of the said Samuel FOUNTAIN forever hereafter to Cease and Lastly we award & order that the said Parties shall pass Sufficient Release Each to the other of and Concerning the Premisses

---

[704] Worcester County Court (Land Records). Deed of manumission from VICTOR, Hannah to **Sarah**. 23 October 1795. Q, pp. 365-366, MSA CE 30-16. www.mdlandrec.net : accessed 27 April 2022.

[705] Worcester County Court (Land Records). Bill of sale from BREUTON, William to BREUTON, Francis and BREUTON, Polly Adkins. 30 October 1795. R, p. 9, MSA CE 30-17. www.mdlandrec.net : accessed 04 May 2022.

af[oresai]^d in Witness whereof we the said Arbitrators to this our award our hands have set and Seals affixed this Twenty Ninth day of October in the year one thousand seven hundred Ninety five.

John Selby PURNELL (Seal)
Littleton ROBINS (Seal)"

*followed on folio 10 with the recordation on 06 November 1795 by court clerk John C. HANDY[706]

Liber R, folios 12 -13; 07 November 1795

"Maryland Ss. Know all men by these presents that I Robert McNEAL of Worcester County in State af[oresai]^d have for and in Consideration of the Sum of forty Six pounds three ~~Shillings~~ and four pence ½ d to me in hand by Joseph MILLER of the same place the Receipt whereof I do hereby acknowledge and am therewith fully Satisfied have bargained Sold and delivered unto the af[oresai]^d Joseph MILLER his Heirs and Ass[ig]^ns a Negro Woman named **Tib** and I do hereby and will warrant and defend unto the af[oresai]^d Joseph MILLER the af[oresai]^d Bargained Negro Woman **Tib** against the Right Title of and Claim all and every Person or Persons whatever Claiming In Witness whereof I have hereunto Set my hand and my Seal affixed this Seventh day of November Anno Dom[ini] 1795

Signed Sealed and delivered in   Robert McNEIL (Seal)
Presence of . . . . . .   John POSTLY."

*followed on folio 13 with the acknowledgment by Justice of the Peace John POSTLY and the recordation on 09 November 1795 by court clerk John C. HANDY[707]

Liber R, folio 13; 07 November 1795

"Know all Men by these presents that I Elizabeth COLLINS of Worcester County in the province of Maryland have bargained and Sold unto John WATSON of the same County and province aforesaid one Negro Man named **John** for the Sum of fifty pounds Maryland Money I the said Elizabeth COLLINS will warrant him from me my Heirs Executors and Administrators and from any other persons or person that shall Challang or Claim any Right Title or Intrest to the said Negro and will the same forever defend In Witness I have hereunto set my Hands and Seals this seventh day of November Anno Domini one Thousand seven hundred and ninety five

Testes   Elijah BRITTINGHAM   her
         Isaac BRITTINGHAM   Elizabeth + COLLINS (Seal)
                                                           mark"

*followed with the acknowledgment by James SELBY and the recordation on 10 November 1795 by court clerk John C. HANDY[708]

Liber R, folio 19; 18 December 1794

"State of Maryland Worcester County Know all Men by these presents that I Asher BURROUGHS doth not hold nor Claim a Negro Garl belonging to Elihu HAZZARD which is left in my Custide untill such Time as the said Elihu HAZZARD see proper to demand her or take her away as I renounce any Right Title Claim or any Bill Bond or Sail whatever as Witness

---

[706] Worcester County Court (Land Records). Award from PURNELL, John Selby and ROBINS, Littleton to KILLAM, Joseph. 29 October 1795. R, pp. 9-10, MSA CE 30-17. www.mdlandrec.net : accessed 04 May 2022.
[707] Worcester County Court (Land Records). Bill of sale from McNEIL, Robert to MILLER, Joseph. 07 November 1795. R, pp. 12-13, MSA CE 30-17. www.mdlandrec.net : accessed 04 May 2022.
[708] Worcester County Court (Land Records). Bill of sale from COLLINS, Elizabeth to WATSON, John. 07 November 1795. R, p. 13, MSA CE 30-17. www.mdlandrec.net : accessed 04 May 2022.

whereof I have set my hand and Seal this Eightteenth Day of December Anno Domini one Thousand Seven hundred and Ninetey four ~

Signed Sealed and Delivered David GRAY
in presents of us . . . .   Asher + BURROUGHS (Seal)
                                 Rachel + HICKMON   mark
                                           mark"

*followed with the recordation on 26 November 1795 by court clerk John C. HANDY[709]

Liber R, folios 19 - 20; 25 November 1795

"State of Maryland Worcester County Know all Men by these presents that I Moses PANKS and Betty PANK of Worcester County for and in Consideration of the sum of Twenty Pounds Currant money of Maryland to us in hand paid the Receipt whereof we do Acknowledge have Bargained and Sold and by these presents do bargain and Sell unto James LEVINGTON one Negro Woman Called **Casandra** to have and to hold the aforesaid Negro Called **Cassandra** to the said James LEVINGTON his Heirs and assigns forever and to no other Intent or purpose whatsoever and it is further Covenanted that the said Moses PANK and Bety PANK for themselves and their Heirs the aforesaid Negro Woman Called **Casandra** to the aforesaid James LEVINGTON his Heirs and Assigns will forever warrant and defend I witness we have hereunto Sett our Hands and Seals affixed this twenty fifth day of November one Thousand Seven hundred and Ninety five.

Signed Sealed and acknowledged   Moses PANK (Seal)
In the presents of . . . .   Benjamin DENNIS   her
                                                         Betty + PANKS (Seal)
                                                              mark"

*followed on folio 20 with the acknowledgment by Justice of the Peace Benjamin DENNIS and the recordation by court clerk John C. HANDY[710]

Liber R, folio 26; 28 November 1795

"Know all Men by these presents that I Zadok SELBY of Worcester County State of Maryland for and in Consideration of the Sum of Thirty one pounds ten Shillings Currant Money of Maryland to me in hand paid at or before the Sealing and Delivery of these presents by McKimmy PORTER of the County and State af[oresai]^d the Receipt whereof I do hereby Acknowledge have bargained and Sold and by these presents do bargain and Sell unto the said McKimmy PORTER one Negro Girl named **Comfort** To Have and to Hold the said Negro Girl by these presents bargained and Sold unto the said McKimmy PORTER his Heirs Executors Administrators and Assigns forever and I the said Zadok SELBY for myself my Heirs Executors and Administrators the said Negro Girl unto the said McKimmy PORTER his Heirs Executors Administrators and Assigns and against me the said Zadok SELBY my Heirs Executors and Administrators and against all and every other person and persons whatsoever shall and will Warrant and forever defend firmly by these presents In Witness whereof I the said Zadok SELBY to these presents my Hand have set and Seal affixed this 28st Day of November Seventeen hundred and Ninety five ~

Signed Sealed and   James SELBY   Zadok SELBY (Seal)
Delivered in presents off   William NILSON"

---

[709] Worcester County Court (Land Records). Bond from BURROUGHS, Asher to HAZZARD, Elihu. 18 December 1794. R, p. 19, MSA CE 30-17. www.mdlandrec.net : accessed 04 May 2022.
[710] Worcester County Court (Land Records). Bill of sale from PANK, Moses and PANKS, Betty to LEVINGTON, James. 25 November 1795. R, pp. 19-20, MSA CE 30-17. www.mdlandrec.net : accessed 04 May 2022.

*followed with the acknowledgment by Justice of the Peace John GUNBY and the recordation by court clerk John C. HANDY[711]

Liber R, folio 26; 27 July 1795

"This is to Certifie to all whome it may Concern that I Daniel SELBY of Worcester County do hereby Give Grant & Relinquish unto Zadok SELBY his Heirs and Assigns forever All my Right Interest & Property Claim to one Negro Girl Called **Comfort** aged about Eleven Years as Witness my Hand & Seal the 27t[h] July 1795

Test   John HOLLAND.   Daniel SELBY   (Seal)"

*followed with the recordation by court clerk John C. HANDY on 28 November 1795[712]

Liber R, folio 27; 08 August 1795

"This is to Certifie to all Persons to whome it may Conern that I James SELBY of Worcester County do hereby give Grant & Relinquish unto Zadok SELBY his Heirs forever all my right Title Claim & Interest to one negro Girl Called **Comfort** aged about Eleven years Witness my hand & Seal the Eight Day of August Anno Dom[ini] 1795.

Test   Joseph DELASTATIUS.   James SELBY   (Seal)"

*followed with the recordation by court clerk John C. HANDY on 28 November 1795[713]

Liber R, folio 27; 21 August 1795

"This is to Certifie to all Persons to whome it may Concern that I Nancy GUNBY of Worcester County do hereby give Grant & Relinquish unto Zadok SELBY his Heirs forever all my Right Title Claim & Interest to one Negro Girl Called **Comfort** about Eleven Years old Witness my Hand & Seal this 21st day of August Anno Dom[ini] 1795

Don in presence of.   J[oh]n GUNBY.   Ann GUNBY   (Seal)"

*followed with the recordation by court clerk John C. HANDY on 28 November 1795[714]

Liber R, folio 36; 07 November 1795

"Know all Men by these presents that I Elizabeth COLLINS of Worcester County have Remised Released and Quit Clamed and by these presents do for me my Heirs Executors and Administrators and every of them remis release and forever quit Clame unto a Negro Woman Named **Ufamey STEAVENS** aged twenty one year or there about also one Negro Boy Named **Auther** aged Six Months or there about and their Heirs forever and by these presents do grant unto them there Liberty from the Date hereof in Witness whereof I set my Hand and fix my Seal this sevent Day of November one thousand Seven hundred and Eighty Five.

Signed Sealed and Delivered James SELBY.   her
In the Presence of . . . . .   Del ? James COTTINGHAM   Elizabeth + COLINS (Seal)
                                                                                  mark."

---

[711] Worcester County Court (Land Records). Bill of sale from SELBY, Zadok to PORTER, McKimmy. 28 November 1795. R, p. 26, MSA CE 30-17. www.mdlandrec.net : accessed 04 May 2022.

[712] Worcester County Court (Land Records). Covenant from SELBY, Daniel to SELBY, Zadok. 27 July 1795. R, p. 26, MSA CE 30-17. www.mdlandrec.net : accessed 04 May 2022.

[713] Worcester County Court (Land Records). Covenant from SELBY, James to SELBY, Zadok. 08 August 1795. R, p. 27, MSA CE 30-17. www.mdlandrec.net : accessed 04 May 2022.

[714] Worcester County Court (Land Records). Covenant from GUNBY, Nancy to SELBY, Zadok. 21 August 1795. R, p. 27, MSA CE 30-17. www.mdlandrec.net : accessed 04 May 2022.

*followed with the acknowledgment by James SELBY and the recordation on 01 December 1795 by court clerk John C. HANDY[715]

Liber R, folio 56; 19 December 1795

"Know all Men by these Presents that I Jacob TEAGUE of Worcester County in State of Maryland for and in Consideration of the Sum of thirty Five Pounds Currant Money of Maryland to me in hand paid at and before the Sealing and Delivery of these Presents by McKimmy PORTER of the County and State aforesaid the Receipt whereof I do hereby acknowledge have bargained and Sold and by these Presents do bargain and Sell unto the said McKimmy PORTER one Negro Boy Named **Stephen** To Have and to hold the said Negro Boy by these Presents bargained and Sold unto the said Negro Boy by these Presents bargained and Sold unto the said McKimmy PORTER his Heirs Executors and administrators and Assigns forever and I the said Jacob TEAGUE for myself my Heirs Executors and Administrators the said Negro Boy unto the said McKimmy PORTER his Heirs Executors Administrators and Assigns against me the Jacob TEAGUE my Heirs Executors and Administrators and against all and every other Person and Persons whatsoever shall and will warrant and forever defend firmly by these Presents In Witness whereof I the said Jacob TEAGUE to these Presents my Hand have sett and Seal affixed the 19th Day of December Anno Domini Seventeen hundred and Ninety five.

Signed Sealed and Delivered   Jacob TEAGUE   (Seal)
in the Presents off . . . .   Philip QUINTON"

*followed with acknowledgment by Justice of the Peace Philip QUINTON and the recordation by court clerk John C. HANDY[716]

Liber R, folios 56-57; 25 December 1795

"This Indenture made this Twenty fifth Day of December in the year one Thousand Seven hundred and Ninety Five Between Charles GODFREY of Worcester County and State of Maryland of the one part and **Levin CAMBRIDGE (alias HUNT)** of the same place of the other part Witnesseth that the aforesaid Charles GODFREY for and in Consideration of the Sum of Eleven pounds Sixteen Shillings and one penny Current Money of Maryland to him in hand paid by the aforesaid **Levin CAMBRIDGE** at and before the Sealing and Delivery of these Presents whereof is hereby Acknowledged and Confessed he the said Charles GODFREY hath Granted bargained sold and Conveyed and by these presents doth absolutely Grant bargain Sell and Convey unto him the said **Levin CAMBRIDGE** his Heirs and Assigns forever all that Tract or parcel of Land Called Williams Choice being the same Tract of Land that the aforesaid **Levin** did by his Deed of Bargain and Sale bearing Date the Twenty fourth Day of April last Past duly Recorded among the Records of Worcester County aforesaid Conveyed unto the aforesaid Charles Recourse being had thereto will more fully and large Together with all its Rights Members Profits Benefits Priviledges and all other the appurtenances thereto belonging To Have and To Hold all and Singular the above bargained Lands and Premises with its Appurtenances unto him the said **Levin CAMBRIDGE** his Heirs and Assigns forever to the only Proper use Benefit and Behoof of him the said **Levin CAMBRIDGE** and to his Heirs and Assigns forever and the said Charles GODFREY for himself his Heirs Executors and Administrators doth hereby Covenant and agree to quit all Right and Title of and to the above mentioned Lands and Premises and Will and shall Warrant and forever defend the same against the Lawful Right or Title of all manner of Person or Persons whatever Claiming by from or under him or his Heirs In Testimony whereof the said Charles GODFREY to these presents his hand hath set and Seal affixed the Day and year above written

---

[715] Worcester County Court (Land Records). Deed of manumission from COLINS, Elizabeth to STEAVENS, Ufamey and **Arthur**. 07 November 1785. R, p. 36, MSA CE 30-17. www.mdlandrec.net : accessed 04 May 2022.

[716] Worcester County Court (Land Records). Bill of sale from TEAGUE, Jacob to PORTER, McKimmy. 19 December 1795. R, p. 56, MSA CE 30-17. www.mdlandrec.net : accessed 04 May 2022.

Signed Sealed and Delivered   Philip QUINTON
In the Presence   Benjamin DENNIS.   Charles X GODFREY (Seal)
his mark"

*followed on folio 57 with the acknowledgment by Justices of the Peace Philip QUINTON and Benjamin DENNIS and the recordation by court clerk John C. HANDY[717]

Liber R, folio 60; 21 December 1795

"Know ye That I Jacob DALE of Worcester County State of Maryland have bargained Sold and delivered and do hereby bargain Sel and deliver unto Thomas VICTERY Blacksmith of the same place one Sertain Negro Boy named **Jack** age fourteen years I do hearby these Presents bind myself my Heirs Ex[ecutor]^s to warrant the Property of the said Negro Boy **Jack** to be the said Thomas VICTERY his Heirs or Assigns forever and will defend him from the Clame or Clames of any Person or persons whomsoever as Witness my Hand and Seal this Twenty first Day of December Anno Domini one Thousand Seven hundred and Ninety five.

Testes   John P. MITCHELL   Jacob DALE (Seal)"

*followed with the acknowledgment by Justice of the Peace John P. MITCHELL and the recordation on 29 December 1795 by court clerk John C. HANDY[718]

*In the acknowledgment, the grantee is named as Thomas VICTOR.

Liber R, folios 67-68; 05 January 1796

"Know all Men by these Presents that We William MILBOURN and Sarah BEACHBOARD both of Worcester County and State of Maryland for and in Consideration of the Sum of one hundred Pounds Current money of Maryland to them in hand paid by James BENNETT of the same Place Receipt whereof they and each of them doth hereby acknowledge and Confess they the said William MILBOURN and Sarah BEACHBOARD hath bargained Sold and Delivered and by these Presents doth absolutely bargain Sell and deliver unto him the said James BENNETT his Heirs and Assigns forever a Certain Negro Man Called **Isaac** now in the County of Worcester late in the said William MELBOURNs To Have and to Hold the said Negro Man **Isaac** hereby bargained and delivered unto him the said James BENNETT his Heirs and Assigns forever to the only proper use Benefit and Behoof of him the said James BENNETT his Heirs and Assigns forever and the said William MILBOURN and Sarah BEACHBOARD for themselves & their Heirs doth hereby Covenant and agree that they will and Shall warrant and forever defend the said Negro Man hereby bargained and delivered against the Right Title and Claim of all manner of Person or Persons whatever unto him the said James BENNETT his Heirs and Assigns forever of which said Negro they the said MILBOURN and BEACHBOARD have put the said BENNETT in full Possession by the Delivery hereof In Testimony whereof the said William MILBOURN and Sarah BEACHBOARD to these presents their Hands have set and Seals affixed this fifth Day of January in the year one Thousand Seven hundred and Ninety Six

Signed Sealed and Delivered   Benjamin DENNIS   William MILBOURN (Seal)
In the Presence of.   Sarah BEACHBOARD (Seal)"

*followed on folio 68 with the acknowledgment by Justice of the Peace Benjamin DENNIS and the recordation by court clerk John C. HANDY[719]

---

[717] Worcester County Court (Land Records). Deed of Conveyance from GODFREY, Charles to **CAMBRIDGE (alias HUNT), Levin**. 25 December 1795. R, pp. 56-57, MSA CE 30-17. www.mdlandrec.net : accessed 04 May 2022.
[718] Worcester County Court (Land Records). Bill of sale from DALE, Jacob to VICTERY, Thomas. 21 December 1795. R, p. 60, MSA CE 30-17. www.mdlandrec.net : accessed 04 May 2022.
[719] Worcester County Court (Land Records). Bill of sale from MILBOURN, William to BEACHBOARD, Sarah. 05 January 1796. R, pp. 67-68, MSA CE 30-17. www.mdlandrec.net : accessed 04 May 2022.

Liber R, folios 70-71; 05 January 1796

"An Accurate Account of the following Negro Boy Called **Harry** about fifteen Years old That I the Subscriber Betsey DELASTATIUS moved unto the State of Maryland Worcester County from Accomack County and State of Virginia in the year one Thousand Seven hundred and ninety Six and I do assert that the above mentioned Negro Boy Called **Harry** was born in the County of Accomack aforesaid and became a Residenture of the said State of Virginia as given under my Hand this fifth day of January 1796.

her
Betsy + DELASTATIUS
mark

January the 5th 1796 Then Came before me William SELBY Naval officer for the District of Snow Hill and Worcester County and made Oath on the Holy Evangels of Almighty God that the above named Negro Boy in the above account set forth was Inhabitant and Residenture of Accomack County and State of Virginia as above mentioned untill the 4th of this Instant (January) and I do hereby declare that I have and then did Remove the said Negro and myself unto Worcester County and State of Maryland with Bona Fide Intention of Settling in the same and that I have brought the said Negro with me with Views of Continuing him in my own Service and not with any design of Selling or disposing of him.

Sworn before W[illia]m SELBY N.O."

*followed on folio 71 with the recordation by court clerk John C. HANDY[720]

Liber R, folio 73; 12 January 1796

"A true list of the following Negroes to wit Negro Woman Called **Comfort** one Negro Man Called **Adam** one Negro Man Called **Daniel** and one Called **Shadrack** that I the Subscriber Isaac BOSTON moved into the State of Maryland Worcester County from Accomack County in the State of Virginia in the year one Thousand Seven hundred and Ninety Six And I do Assert that the above mentioned Negroes to wit **Daniel** and **Shadrack** and **Adam** was born in the State of Maryland and Negro **Comfort** was born in Accomack County aforesaid that they all became Residenters of Accomack County aforesaid before the year above mentioned and has been upwards of three years Residenters and Inhabitants of the united States of America as given under my Hand this Twelfth day of January in the year one Thousand Seven hundred and ninety Six

Isaac BOSTON.

January the 12th 1796. Then Came before me William SELBY Naval Officer for the district of Snow Hill and Worcester County and made oath on the Holy Evangels of Almighty God that the several Negroes enumerated in the above list were Inhabitants and Residenters of Accomack County in the State of Virginia as above mentioned until the fifth Day instant (January) and I do hereby declare that I have and did then move the said Negroes and myself and Family in Worcester County in the State of Maryland with Bonfide Intention of Settling in the same and that I have brought the said Negroes with me with Views of Continuing them in my own Service and not with any design of Selling or disposing of them.

Sworn before W[illia]m SELBY N.O."

*followed with the recordation by court clerk John C. HANDY[721]

---

[720] Worcester County Court (Land Records). Certificate of importation into Maryland from DELASTATIUS, Betsy for **Harry**. 05 January 1796. R, pp. 70-71, MSA CE 30-17. www.mdlandrec.net : accessed 04 May 2022.

[721] Worcester County Court (Land Records). Certificate of importation into Maryland from BOSTON, Isaac for **Comfort, Adam, Daniel,** and **Shadrack**. 12 January 1796. R, p. 73, MSA CE 30-17. www.mdlandrec.net : accessed 04 May 2022.

Liber R, folio 83; 25 January 1796

"This Deed of Manumission dated this Twenty fifth Day of January in the year of our Lord Seventeen hundred and ninety Six Bears Testimony That I James B. ROBINS do hereby manumit Release and by these presents set free a Certain Negro Woman called **Lisha** and do hereby authorize and empower the said **Lisha** to act do and in all Things perform the part of a free woman as fully and amply to all Intents and Purposes as if the said **Lisha** had been born free any Law Statute or Act to the Contrary Notwithstanding To Have and To Hold her said Freedom for & during the Term of her natural Life without the Let Hindrance or Molestation of any person or Persons whatever In Testimony whereof I do to these presents Set my Hand & my Seal affixed the Day & year above written ~.

Sealed & Delivered   James WILSON   James B. ROBINS (Seal)
In presence of . . .   Zadok PURNELL."

*followed with the recordation by court clerk John C. HANDY on 30 January 1796[722]

Liber R, folios 90-91; 03 February 1796

"Know all Men by these presents That I Samuel SCARBOROUGH of Worcester County and State of Maryland for and in Consideration of the Sum of five pounds Current Money of Maryland to me in hand paid by **Abner** Free Negro late the Property of a Certain Frederick CONNER of the same Place the Receipt whereof I do hereby Confess and Acknowledge and myself fully Satisfyed Contented and paid have bargained Sold and delivered and by these presents doth absolutely bargain Sell and deliver unto him the said **Abner** and his Heirs and Assigns forever a Negro Woman Called **Sarah** now the Wife of the aforesaid **Abner** and in his Possession To Have and To Hold the aforesaid Negro Woman Called **Sarah** unto him the said **Abner** his Heirs and Assigns forever to the only Proper use benefit and Behoof of him the said **Abner** and his Heirs and Assigns forever And I the said Samuel SCARBOROUGH for myself my Heirs Executors and Administrators doth hereby Quit forever hereafter all Right Title or Claim of and to the said Negro Woman Called **Sarah** of which I the Subscriber have put the said **Abner** in full Possession of by the delivery hereof In Witness whereof I the said Samuel SCARBOROUGH to these presents my Hand hath Set and Seal affixed this third day of February in the year one Thousand Seven hundred and ninety Six

Signed Sealed and Delivered   Frederick CONNER   Sam[ue]l SCARBOROUGH (Seal)
In the Presence of . . . .   Jesse BENNITT"

*followed on folio 41 with the acknowledgment by Justice of the Peace Jesse BENNITT and the recordation on 05 February 1796 by court clerk John C. HANDY[723]

Liber R, folios 91-92; 30 January 1796

"Know all Men by these presents That I Betty PORTER Widow and Relic of McKimmy PORTER of Worcester County and State of Maryland for and in Consideration of the Sum of five pounds Current money of Maryland to me in hand paid by Samuel SCARBOROUGH of the same place the Receipt whereof I do hereby Acknowledge and Confess have bargained and Sold and delivered and by these presents doth absolutely bargain Sell and deliver unto him the said Samuel SCARBOROUGH his Heirs and Assigns forever the following Negroes to wit Negro Woman Called **Sarah** one ditto Boy **Jake** one ditto Boy **Abb** & one ditto Boy Called **Isaac** now in Worcester County aforesaid and in the Possession of the aforesaid Samuel SCARBOROUGH To Have and To Hold all and singular the above mentioned bargained and Sold four Negroes unto him the said Samuel SCARBOROUGH his Heirs and Assigns forever to the only proper use Benefit and Behoof of him the said Samuel SCARBOROUGH his Heirs

---

[722] Worcester County Court (Land Records). Deed of Manumission from ROBINS, James B. to **Lisha**. 25 January 1796. R, p. 83, MSA CE 30-17. www.mdlandrec.net : accessed 04 May 2022.
[723] Worcester County Court (Land Records). Bill of sale from SCARBOROUGH, Samuel to **Abner** (free negro). 03 February 1796. R, pp. 90-91, MSA CE 30-17. www.mdlandrec.net : accessed 04 May 2022.

and Assigns and the said Betty PORTER for herself and Heirs Executors and administrators the four above named Negroes will and Shall Quit all Right or Title of of which said Negroes have put the said Samuel SCARBOROUGH in full Possession of by the Delivery hereof In Testimony whereof I the said Betty PORTER to these presents my hand have set and Seal affixed this thirtieth day of January in the year one Thousand seven hundred and ninety Six. ~

Signed Sealed and Delivered	J[oh]n GUNBY	
In the Presence of	Jn°. SCARBOROUGH	Betty R PORTER (Seal) her mark"

*followed with the acknowledgment by Justice of the Peace John GUNBY and the recordation on 12 February 1796 by court clerk John C. HANDY[724]

Liber R, folio 92; 12 February 1796

"Maryland State Worcester County Ss^t. Know all Men by these presents that We Benjamin TRUITT & Samuel TRUITT of the County and State af[oresai]^d for and in Consideration of the Sum of three pounds Current money of the County & State af[oresai]^d to us in hand paid by John K. TRUITT of the County af[oresai]^d have bargained Sold Released Granted & Confirmed and by these presents do bargain Sell Release Grant & Confirm unto the said John K. TRUITT all our Right Title Interest & Claim of in & to a Negro Girl Called **Leah** the value of three pounds to have and To Hold the said Bargained Negro **Leah** by these Presents Bargained Sold Released granted and Confirmed unto the only proper use and Behoof of the said John K. TRUITT his Executors Adm[inistrato]^{rs} and Assigns forever freely quietly and entirely without any Contradiction Claim Disturbance or Hinderance from us or our Heirs Executors or Administrators and we the said Benjamin TRUITT & Samuel TRUITT for ourselves or our Heirs will warrant and forever defend the said Negro Girl Called **Leah** against Lawful Right Title or Claim of us or any person Claiming by from or under us In Testimony We have hereunto Set our Hands & Seals affixed this 12th day of February Anno Dom[ini] 1796.

Signed Sealed & Delivered	Philip QUINTON	Benj[ami]^n TRUITT (Seal)
in Presents of		Samuel TRUITT (Seal)"

*followed with the acknowledgment by Justice of the Peace Philip QUINTON and the recordation by court clerk John C. HANDY[725]

Liber R, folio 95; 03 February 1796

"A True List or Amount of the following Negroes to wit one Negro Woman Called **Judy** one Negro Girl Called **Grace** and one Negro Boy Called **Henry** the Boy aforesaid about three Months old that I the Subscriber Shadrack REDDEN of Worcester County and State of Maryland do hereby assert that the above named Negroes was born in Accomack County and State of Virginia and was late the Property of Michael ROBINS of the said State of Virginia fully three years last past (excepting the Boy Called **Henry** and him has been from his Birth only three months or thereabouts which said Three negroes he the said ROBINS has given unto his Daughter Susanna REDDEN my Spouse as given under my hand this third day of February in the year one Thousand Seven hundred and ninety Six

Shadrack REDDEN

February 12th 1796 Then Came before me William SELBY Naval Officer for the District of Snow Hill and Worcester County and made Oath on the Holy Evangels of Almighty God that the Several Negroes enumerated in the above list were Inhabitants and Residenters of Accomack County in the State of Virginia as above mentioned until the Eighteenth Day of January last past and I do hereby declare that I have and then did move the said Negroes into

---

[724] Worcester County Court (Land Records). Bill of sale from PORTER, Betty to SCARBOROUGH, Samuel. 30 February 1796. R, pp. 91-92, MSA CE 30-17. www.mdlandrec.net : accessed 04 May 2022.

[725] Worcester County Court (Land Records). Bill of Sale from TRUITT, Benjamin and TRUITT, Samuel to TRUITT, John K. 12 February 1796. R, p. 92, MSA CE 30-17. www.mdlandrec.net : accessed 04 May 2022.

Worcester County and State of Maryland with Bona Fide Intention of Remaining in the same and that I have brought the said Negroes with Views of Continuing them in my own Service and not with any Design of Selling or disposing of Them.

Sworn before W[illia]^m SELBY N.O."

*followed with the recordation by court clerk John C. HANDY[726]

Liber R, folios 105-106; 02 May 1794

"Know all by Men these presents that We **Nimrod JACOBS** free negro & Robert M. RICHARDSON Merchant both of Worcester County & State of Maryland are held and firmly ~~bound~~ unto the State af[oresai]^d in the Just Sum of Thirty pounds Current money of said State to be paid to said State or Certain Attorney to which payment will & truly to be made & done we & each of us bind ourselves & each of our Heirs Executors & Administrators for and in the whole firmly by these presents Sealed with our Seals & dated this 2 day of May Anno Dom[ini] one Thousand Seven hundred and ninety four. ~ . Whereas the above bound **Nimrod JACOBS** hath lately purchased and brought into Worcester County from Accomack County & State of Virginia a Negro Woman Slave by the named of **Prisciller** and Mother of him said **Nimrod** and whereas the said Negro Woman being aged & Infirm may become burthensome to the County af[oresai]^d after gaining her Freedom & Residence therefore The Condition of the above Obligation is such that if the above bound **Nimrod JACOBS** or RICHARDSON them there Heirs Executors or Administrators do & Shall at all Times during the Residence of the af[oresai]^d Negro Woman **Prisciller** imported as af[oresai]^d keep maintain & Support her the said Negro Woman so that she the said Negro Woman shall not at any Time hereafter become chargeable to the said County of Worcester Then above Obligation to be void else to be and Remain in full Force & Virtue in Law. ~ .

Signed Sealed & Delivered
In presents of . . . .   Philip QUINTON ~ .   **Nimrod** u **JACOBS** (Seal)
                                                              mark

                                                        Robert M RICHARDSON   (Seal)"

*followed on folio 106 with the recordation on 25 February 1796 by court clerk John C. HANDY[727]

Liber R, folios 108-109; 01 March 1796

"Worcester County Maryland viz. Know all Men by these presents that I Jonathan SHOCKLEY of the County and State aforesaid for and in Consideration of the Sum of Sixty five pounds Specie to me in hand paid by Sarah McBRYDE of Sommerset County at and before the Sealing & delivery hereof the Receipt whereof is hereby Acknowledged do hereby make over grant bargain and Sell unto her the s[ai]^d Sarah McBRYDE her Heirs and Assigns forever one Negroe Man named **Stephen** do Sell Ratify and Confirm and will forever warrant an defend the s[ai]^d Property from all person or Persons now Claiming or ever hereafter may Claim the s[ai]^d Negroe to be the proper Right Title Benefit and Interest of whereof her the said Sarah McBRYDE her Heirs and Assigns forever according to the true Intent purport and meaning hereof In Testimony I have hereunto Set my Hand and affixed my Seal this first day of March Seventeen hundred and Ninety Six

Signed Sealed and Delivered   Philip QUINTON   Jonathan SHOCKLEY   (Seal)
In presence of us . . .   James RITCHIE"

---

[726] Worcester County Court (Land Records). Certificate of importation into Maryland from REDDEN, Shadrack for **Judy, Grace,** and **Henry.** 03 February 1796. R, p. 95, MSA CE 30-17. www.mdlandrec.net : accessed 04 May 2022.

[727] Worcester County Court (Land Records). Bond of Maintenance from **JACOBS, Nimrod** and RICHARDSON, Robert M. for **Prisciller.** 02 May 1794. R, pp. 105-106, MSA CE 30-17. www.mdlandrec.net : accessed 04 May 2022.

*followed with the acknowledgment by Justice of the Peace Philip QUINTON and the recordation on 02 March 1796 by court clerk John C. HANDY on folio 109[728]

Liber R, folios 118-119; 10 March 1796

"Know all Men by these presents that I William AYDELOTT of Worcester County and State of Maryland doth by these presents absolutely mancipate Free and let at Liberty a Certain Negro Woman Called **Esther** about forty years of Age or thereabouts being an Inhabitant of the County aforesaid for more than three years last past and late my the said William AYDELOTTs Property now in the said County with full Power and Authority henceforth to act and do for herself to all Intents and Purposes as if she was born free To Have and to Hold unto the said Negro Woman **Esther** her above said Freedom and Liberty from myself my Heirs Executors and Administrators and from the Right Title Claim or demand of all other Person or Persons whatever Claiming by from or under me or my Heirs will and shall warrant and forever defend In Witness whereof I the said William AYDELOTT to these presents my Hand and affixed my Seal this tenth day of March in the year one Thousand seven hundred and ninety Six.

Signed Sealed and delivered   Benjamin DENNIS.   William AYDELOTT   (Seal)
In the presents of . . . ."

*followed on folio 119 with the acknowledgment by Justice of the Peace Benjamin DENNIS and the recordation on 11 March 1796 by court clerk John C. HANDY[729]

Liber R, folios 123-124; 11 March 1796

"This Indenture made this 11th day of March Anno Domini Seventeen Hundred and Ninety Six Between Robert GIVAN of Worcester County in the State of Maryland of the one part and **Caleb** Negro of the same County & State afforesaid of the other part Witnesseth that the said Robert for and in Consideration of the Sum of Five pounds Current money of Maryland to Him in hand paid at and before the Ensealing and delivery of these presents by the said **Caleb** the Receipt whereof the said Robert doth hereby acknowledge and himself fully Satisfied and Contented he the said Robert do by these presents Acquit and fully discharge the said **Caleb** forever by these presents from any Service or Labour to me or my Heirs and by these presents do declare him free and Clear from me and my Heirs and will warrant and defend the said **Caleb** free from every other person Claiming any Right Title Interest or Estate in or to him In Testimony whereof I the said Robert GIVAN hath to these presents Set his Hand and Seal affixed the day and year above written

Sighned Sealed and Delivered   Robert GIVAN   (Seal)
In the Presents of   William PARKER"

*followed with the acknowledgment by Justice of the Peace William PARKER and the recordation by court clerk John C. HANDY[730]

Liber R, folios 129-130; 29 February 1796

"Maryland Ss^t. Know all Men by these Presents that I William GORDY of Worcester County and State af[oresai]^d Planter for and in Consideration of the Sum of the Value of Seventy three Pounds Specie to me in hand paid by Samuel PARKER of the County and State af[oresai]^d have bargained Sold Set over and delivered by these presents in plain and open Market according to the Just and due Form of Law in that Case made and provided do bargain set over and deliver unto the said Samuel PARKER one Negro Man Called **Cuggo** To Have and To Hold the said Bargained Premises unto the said Samuel PARKER his Heirs Executors Administrators and

---

[728] Worcester County Court (Land Records). Bill of Sale from SHOCKLEY, Jonathan to McBRYDE, Sarah. 01 March 1796. R, pp. 108-109, MSA CE 30-17. www.mdlandrec.net : accessed 04 May 2022.

[729] Worcester County Court (Land Records). Deed of Manumission from AYDELOTT, William to **Esther.** 10 March 1796. R, pp. 118-119, MSA CE 30-17. www.mdlandrec.net : accessed 04 May 2022.

[730] Worcester County Court (Land Records). Deed of Manumission from GIVAN, Robert to **Caleb.** 11 March 1796. R, pp. 123-124, MSA CE 30-17. www.mdlandrec.net : accessed 04 May 2022.

Assigns forever and I the said William GORDY for myself my Heirs Executors and Administrators the said Bargained Premisses unto the said Samuel PARKER his Heirs Executors Administrators and Assigns against all manner of Persons shall and Will Warrant and forever defend the same by these presents In Witness I Whereof the said bargained Premises I have hereunto Set my Hand and Seal affixed this 29th day of February Anno Domini Seventeen hundred and ninety Six

Signed Sealed and Delivered   William GORDY   (Seal)
In the Presents off   Booz WALSTON"

*followed on folio 130 with the acknowledgment by Justice of the Peace Booz WALSTON and the recordation on 19 March 1796 by court clerk John C. HANDY[731]

Liber R, folio 130; 13 February 1796

"Maryland Ss^t. Know all Men by these Presents that I Peter PETERSON of Somerset County and State aforesaid for and in Consideration of the Sum of the value of Seventy Five Pounds Specie to me in hand paid by John PARKER of Worcester County and State af[oresai]^d have bargained Sold Set over and delivered by these presents in plain and open Market according to the Just and due form of Law in the Case made and provided do bargain Set over and deliver unto the said John PARKER one Negro Man Called **Daniel** To Have and To Hold the said Bargained Premisses unto the said John PARKER his Heirs Executors Administrators or Assigns forever and I the said Peter PETERSON for myself my Heirs Executors and Administrators the said bargained Premisses unto the said John PARKER his Heirs Executors Administrators or Assigns against the lawfull Claim Right and Title of all Persons Shall and will Warrant and forever defend the same by these Presents In Witness whereof the said bargained Premisses I have hereunto Set my Hand and Seal this Thirteenth Day of February 1796.

Signed Sealed and Delivered   Peter PETERSON   (Seal)
In Presents off . . . .   Booz WALSTON"

*followed with the acknowledgment by Justice of the Peace Booz WALSTON and the recordation on 19 March 1796 by court clerk John C. HANDY[732]

Liber R, folios 130-131; 09 December 1795

"Know all Men by these Presents that I John LAWS of Worcester County and State of Maryland for in the Consideration of the Sum of Forty Pounds Cash in hand paid by Ezekiel HALL of the County of Baltimore and State af[oresai]^d the Receipt for which payment the said John LAWS doth Confess and the said Ezekiel HALL his Heirs and Assigns acquitted and Released therefrom doth by these presents Sell make over and deliver in the Possession of the said Ezekiel HALL one Negro Boy named **Jesse** provided the said John LAWS doth not pay the said Ezekiel HALL the Sum above mentioned in Twelve months then the said John LAWS doth by these presents Coven[an]^t promise and agree with the said Ezekiel HALL that he will forever warrent and defend the above negro Boy **Jesse** against himself and all other Persons whatever hereafter Claiming him to the said Ezekiel HALL his Heirs and Assigns forever In Testimony whereof the said John LAWS hath hereto Sett his Hand and affixed his Seal this the ninth day of December Anno Domini Seventeen hundred and ninty five

Sealed and Delivered   Morgin BRADSHAW   John LAWS   (Seal)
in the Presents of . . .   Mark
                         Christian + HILL"

---

[731] Worcester County Court (Land Records). Bill of Sale from GORDY, William to PARKER, Samuel. 29 February 1796. R, pp. 129-130, MSA CE 30-17. www.mdlandrec.net : accessed 04 May 2022.
[732] Worcester County Court (Land Records). Bill of Sale from PETERSON, Peter to PARKER, John. 13 February 1796. R, p. 130, MSA CE 30-17. www.mdlandrec.net : accessed 04 May 2022.

*followed on folio 131 with the acknowledgment on 12 March 1796 by Justice of the Peace John GUNBY and the recordation on 21 March 1796 by court clerk John C. HANDY[733]

Liber R, folios 132-133; 07 March 1796

"To all Persons whom these Presents shall Come Know ye that whereas I William MORRIS of Worcester County in the State of Maryland am desirous to manumit the following negroes to wit **Isaac** (Commonly Called **Savannah Isaac**) **George** and **Charity** as well for and in Consideration of past Service as for sundry other good Causes and Considerations me hereunto moving I do hereby accordingly manumit set free and forever discharge from Slavery from myself and my Heirs the af[oresai]^d Negroes **Isaac George** and **Charity** To Have and To Hold to them the af[oresai]^d **Isaac George** and **Charity** free their Freedom af[oresai]^d from all Molestation Let or Interruption whatever from me my Heirs Ex[ecuto]^{rs} and Adm[inistrato]^{rs} forever. In Witness whereof I have hereto annexed my Hand and Seal this Seventh Day of March Anno Dom[ini] one Thousand Seven hundred and ninety Six ~

Signed Sealed and Delivered   William MORRIS   (Seal)
In Presence of   William PURNELL."

*followed on folio 153 with the acknowledgment by Justice of the Peace William PURNELL and the recordation on 25 March 1796 by court clerk John C. HANDY[734]

Liber R, folio 133; 07 March 1796

"To all Persons whom these presents shall Come greeting Know ye that I Mary ROWND of Worcester County in the State of Maryland for and in Consideration of Past Service of Negro **Stephen** as well for and in Consideration of the Sum of forty five Pounds Current money to me in hand paid or secured to be paid by the said **Stephen** at or before the Ensealing and delivery hereof the Receipt whereof I do hereby Acknowledge have manumitted set free and forever discharge from Slavery and by these presents do absolutely manumit Set free and forever discharge from Slavery the af[oresai]^d Negro **Stephen** To Have and To Hold to him the said **Stephen** his Freedom af[oresai]^d free from all Molestation Let or Interruption whatever In Witness whereof I have hereto Set my Hand and affixed my Set this Seventh day of March Anno Dom[ini] Seventeen hundred and Ninety Six.

Signed Sealed and Delivered   Mary ROWND   (Seal)
In Presence of William MORRIS"

*followed with the acknowledgment by Justice of the Peace William MORRIS and the recordation on 25 March 1796 by court clerk John C. HANDY[735]

Liber R, folio 134; 16 February 1796

"A true List of Negroes that I moved into the State of Maryland from Northumberland County and State of Virginia the Eighteenth Day of January in the year one Thousand Seven hundred and ninety Six and I do assert that they were Residenters and the Descendants from such Negroes in the said State of Virginia as were Residentures and Inhabitants before the year one thousand Seven hundred and ninety two their Names are as follows to wit. **Cato Margery Jesse Frank Fanny** and **Robin** which Negroes aforesaid I became possessed of by Marriage and Guardianship as Given under my hand this 16th day of February in the year one Thousand Seven hundred and ninety Six

David BALL (Clk)

---

[733] Worcester County Court (Land Records). Bill of Sale from LAWS, John to HALL, Ezekiel. 09 December 1795. R, pp. 130-131, MSA CE 30-17. www.mdlandrec.net : accessed 04 May 2022.
[734] Worcester County Court (Land Records). Deed of Manumission from MORRIS, William to **Isaac, George,** and **Charity.** 07 March 1796. R, pp. 132-133, MSA CE 30-17. www.mdlandrec.net : accessed 04 May 2022.
[735] Worcester County Court (Land Records). Deed of Manumission from ROWND, Mary to **Stephen.** 07 March 1796. R, p. 133, MSA CE 30-17. www.mdlandrec.net : accessed 04 May 2022.

1796. February the 16th Then Came before me William SELBY Naval Officer for Snow Hill District and Worcester County The above named The Rev[eren]d Mr. David BALL and made oath on the Holy Evangels of Almighty God that the Several Negroes enumerated in the above list were Inhabitants and Residenters of Northumberland County in the State of Virginia from their Birth until the 18th day of January last and that he hath moved the said Negroes into the County of Worcester aforesaid and State of Maryland with Bona fide Intention of Continuing them in the Same with him & with Views only of doing his Service and not with any Design of Selling or disposing of them

Sworn before W[illia]m SELBY Naval Officer"

*followed with the recordation on 20 February 1796 by court clerk John C. HANDY[736]

Liber R, folios 142-143; 25 March 1796

"Know all Men by these presents that Whereas I Littleton TOWNSEND have for some time past boarded with a certain Isaac NICHOLSON of Worcester County, and whereas the said NICHOLSON hath furnish[e]d me with many other Necessaries & Sold to me a Riding Creature of which I much needed, and was necessary from my Degree and occupation, and for which Creature and Board as af[ore]s[ai]d : I acknowledge and confess myself to be indebted to the said Isaac NICHOLSON in the Sum of Forty Nine pounds and seven pence and also for and in consideration of the Sum of One pound seven Shillings and Nine pence Current Money to me in hand paid by the said Isaac, the receipt whereof I do acknowledge and also many other meritorious acts of friendship and kindness extended to me by the said NICHOLSON I the said Littleton TOWNSEND have granted bargained and Sold conveyed and confirmed and by these presents do grant bargain and sell convey and confirm unto the said Isaac NICHOLSON his Executors Adm[inistrato]rs and Assigns a Negro Man called **Levin** together with all my right and title of in or to the said Negro, To have and to hold the said Negro unto the said Isaac NICHOLSON his Executors Adm[inistrato]rs or Assigns. To the only proper use and behoof of the said Isaac his Executors Adm[inistrato]rs and Assigns, and I the said Littleton doth Covenant and agree for myself my Heirs Executors and Administrators to and with the said Isaac NICHOLSON his Executors and Adm[inistrato]rs and Assigns that I have a good right and title to the Negro Man, and that I possess full power authority and Capacity to dispose of him and further that I will for ever warrent and defend a good right and title to the said Negro ag[ains]t myself and all persons claiming by through or from me or in my right or from my Executors & Administrators and all other Persons except those who claim from or in right of my deceas[e]d Father Joshua TOWNSEND – In Witness whereof I have hereto set my hand and seal affix[e]d this 25th day of March 1796

Sign[e]d seal[e]d & deliver[e]d   Littleton TOWNSEND   (Seal)
in presence of"

*followed on folio 143 with the acknowledgment by Justice of the Peace John GUNBY and the recordation on 29 March 1796 by court clerk John C. HANDY[737]

Liber R, folios 143-144; 01 April 1796

"This Indenture made this first day of April one thousand seven hundred and Ninety Six between William AYDELOTT of Worcester County State of Maryland on the one part and Esther KENDEL of the County and State aforesaid of the other part Witnesseth that the said William AYDELOTT for and in consideration of the Sum of Ten Pounds Current Money of Maryland to him the said William AYDELOTT in hand paid by the said Esther KENDEL at and before the ensealing and delivering hereof the receipt, Whereof I do hereby acknowledge hath bargained, sold, and deliver[e]d and by these presents do bargain sell and deliver unto the

---

[736] Worcester County Court (Land Records). Certificate of importation into Maryland from BALL, David for **Cato, Margery, Jesse, Frank, Fanny,** and **Robin**. 16 February 1796. R, p. 134, MSA CE 30-17. www.mdlandrec.net : accessed 04 May 2022.
[737] Worcester County Court (Land Records). Bill of Sale from TOWNSEND, Littleton to NICHOLSON, Isaac. 25 March 1796. R, pp. 142-143, MSA CE 30-17. www.mdlandrec.net : accessed 04 May 2022.

said Esther KENDEL a Negro Man called **Esaw**. To have and to hold the said Negro Man called **Esau** unto the said Esther KENDEL her Heirs and Assigns for ever to and for the only use benefit and behoof of the said Esther KENDEL her Heirs and assigns forever and for no other use or purpose whatsoever and the said William AYDELOTT do further covenant and agree to and with the said Esther KENDEL, that he will warrant and for ever defend the said Negro Man called **Esau** against the claim of all Names or Persons claiming any right title or interest to said Negro whatever, In witness whereof I the said William AYDELOTT hath herewith my hand set and seal affixt the day and year first above written ~ Signed sealed delivered and acknowledged before ~ William AYDELOTT (Seal)"

*followed on folio 144 with the acknowledgment by Justice of the Peace Jesse BENNETT and the recordation by court clerk John C. HANDY[738]

Liber R, folio 146; 18 March 1796

"To all Persons to whom these presents shall come Greeting – Whereas I Elizabeth PORTER of Worcester County in the State of Maryland did on the Fifth day of November Anno Dom[ini] One thousand seven hundred and Eighty seven by deed duly executed and Recorded for and in consideration of the faithful service done and performed by Negro Man Slave called **Levin**, grant set free and manumit the said Negro **Levin** only reserving to myself during my natural Life the service of the said Negro **Levin** and that his freedom should commence and take effect immediately after my Death. Now Know ye that I the said Elizabeth PORTER for divers causes and considerations me thereunto moving since the execution of the af[oresai]^d Deed do by these presents grant set free and manumit the af[oresai]^d Negro **Levin** immediately. To have and to hold and freely enjoy his freedom forever after the dates of these Presents in full and ample manner without any let authority or hinderance of me the said Elizabeth PORTER or any other Person or Persons whatsoever. In Testimony whereof I have here set my hand affix[e]d my Seal this Eighteenth day of March Anno Dom[ini] Seventeen hundred and Ninety Six ~

Signed Sealed and deliver[e]d	Sam[ue]^l SCARBOROUGH		Her	
in presence of ~ ~ ~ ~ ~ ~ ~ ~	Jesse BENNETT.	Elizabeth	X	PORTER (Seal)
			Mark"	

*followed with the acknowledgment by Justice of the Peace Jesse BENNETT and the recordation on 01 April 1796 by court clerk John C. HANDY[739]

Liber R, folio 156; 06 April 1796

"A Certificate of a Negro Man which I moved into Maryland from Northumberland County and State of Virginia on the twelfth day of March one thousand seven hundred and ninety six ~ And I do assert that he was a Resident and a descendent of such Negroes as were Residents in the State of Virginia and Inhabitants thereof before the year one thousand seven hundred and ninety two ~ his name is **Robin** of whom I became possessed by Marriage ~ Given under my hand this fifth day of April 1796 ~ ~ ~ ~ ~   David BALL (Clk)

April the 6th 1796 Then came before me William SELBY Navil Officer from Snow Hill District and Worcester County the above named the Rev[eren]^d M^r. David BALL, and made Oath on the holy Evangels of Almighty God, that the above said Negro Man, in the above List or Certificate were an Inhabitant residenture of Northumberland County in the State of Virginia from his Birth untill the Twelfth day of March last, and that he hath moved the said Negro into Worcester County and State of Maryland with Bona fide intention of continuing him in the same, with him and with views only of doing his Service, and not with any design of selling or disposing of him ~

---

[738] Worcester County Court (Land Records). Bill of Sale from AYDELOTT, William to KENDEL, Esther. 01 April 1796. R, pp. 143-144, MSA CE 30-17. www.mdlandrec.net : accessed 04 May 2022.

[739] Worcester County Court (Land Records). Deed of Manumission from PORTER, Elizabeth to **Levin**. 18 March 1796. R, p. 146, MSA CE 30-17. www.mdlandrec.net : accessed 04 May 2022.

Sworn Before ~ W[illia]^m SELBY N[aval] Officer"

*followed with the recordation by court clerk John C. HANDY[740]

Liber R, folio 156; 06 April 1796

"A True List of Negroes that I moved into the State of Maryland from Sussex County in the Delaware State the Eleventh day of March in the Year One thousand seven hundred and ninety Six, and I do assert they were Residentures and descendents from such Negroes in the State of Delaware aforesaid, as were Residentures and Inhabitants before the year One thousand seven hundred and ninety two, their Names are as follows to Wit, One Woman called **Patty**, and Boy called **Isaac**, which Negroes aforesaid I became possess[e]d of by a bequest of a certain John EVANS late of the County of Sussex aforesaid, as given under my hand this sixth day of April 1796

Thomas DALE

1796 April 6th Then came before me William SELBY Navil Officer for Snow Hill District and Worcester County the above named Thomas DALE, and made Oath on the holy Evangels of Almighty God that the several Negroes enumerated in the above List were Inhabitants and Risidentures of Sussex County and State of Delaware from their Birth, untill the Eleventh day of March last and that he hath mov[e]d the said Negroes into the County of Worcester and State of Maryland with Bona fide intention of continuing them in the same with him and with views only of doing his own service, and not with any design of selling or disposing of them ~

Sworn before ~ W[illia]^m SELBY N Officer"

*followed with the recordation by court clerk John C. HANDY[741]

Liber R, folio 161; 06 April 1796

"Know all Men by these presents that I Jacob TEAGUE of Worcester County and State of Maryland as Administrator to the Estate of a certain Belitha BRITTINGHAM for and in consideration of the Sum of Thirty Pounds current Money of Maryland to me in hand paid by James DUER of the same place Merchant at and before the Sealing and delivery of these presents the receipt whereof is hereby acknowledg[e]d and confess[e]d, hath Granted, sold and deliver[e]d and by these presents doth absolutely grant Sell and deliver unto him the said James DUER his Heirs and Assigns for ever, a certain Negro Boy called **Dolby** about Ten years old now in the possession of the said DUER To have and to hold the aforesaid bargained and deliver[e]d negro boy called **Dolby** unto him the said James DUER his Heirs and Assigns for ever to the only proper use benefit and behoof of him the said James DUER his Heirs and Assigns for ever, and I the said Jacob TEAGUE for myself my heirs Executors and Administrators, doth hereby Covenant and agree, that I and mine will and shall warrant and for ever defend the above mentioned negro, against the Lawful Right Title, claim or demand of all manner of person or persons whatever, unto him the said James DUER his heirs and assigns for ever, of which said Negro I have put him the said DUER in full possession by the delivery hereof In Witness whereof I the said Jacob TEAGE to these presents have set my hand and seal this Eighth day of April in the year One thousand seven hundred and ninety six

Signed Seal[e]d and ~   Jacob TEAGUE (Seal)
deliver[e]d in the presence of   J[oh]n GUNBY"

*followed with the acknowledgment by Justice of the Peace John GUNBY and the recordation on 08 April 1796 by court clerk John C. HANDY[742]

---

[740] Worcester County Court (Land Records). Certificate of importation into Maryland from BALL, David for **Robin**. 06 April 1796. R, p. 156, MSA CE 30-17. www.mdlandrec.net : accessed 04 May 2022.

[741] Worcester County Court (Land Records). Certificate of importation into Maryland from DALE, Thomas for **Patty** and **Isaac**. 06 April 1796. R, p. 156, MSA CE 30-17. www.mdlandrec.net : accessed 04 May 2022.

[742] Worcester County Court (Land Records). Bill of Sale from TEAGUE, Jacob (Administrator) to DUER, James. 06 April 1796. R, p. 161, MSA CE 30-17. www.mdlandrec.net : accessed 04 May 2022.

Liber R, folios 169-170; 05 April 1795

"This Indenture made this fifth day of April in the year of our Lord One Thousand Seven hundred and ninety Six between **Levin CAMBRIDGE** of Worcester of the one part and Samuel HANDY of the same County of the other part Witnesseth that the af[oresai]^d **Levin CAMBRIDGE** for and the consideration of the sum of thirteen twelve Shillings and Eight pence Current Money of Maryland to him in hand paid by the af[oresai]^d Samuel HANDY at and before the sealing and delivery hereof the Receipt whereof he doth hereby acknowledge hath bargained and sold remised released and forever quit Claim and by these presents doth for ever quit claim and by these presents doth bargain sell release remise and for ever quit claim unto the af[oresai]^d Samuel HANDY his Heirs and Assigns for ever Twenty Acres of Land it being part of a Tract of Land Called Williams Choice to be Wood Land and laid of in the following manner begining on the line of the af[oresai]^d HANDY at the Edge of the Cleared Land running towards the House of Esther CAMBREDG's by the side of the Clear[e]d Land so far as will include Twenty Acres of Land with a pariell line with the af[oresai]^d Samuel HANDY Line _ To have and to hold the af[oresai]^d Bargained Remised premises with all and every Appertinances thereunto belonging unto the af[oresai]^d Samuel HANDY to him and his Heirs and Assigns forever and to no other use or uses behoff or behoofs whatsoever and the af[oresai]^d **Levin CAMBRIDGE** for himself his heirs Executors & Administrators doth bargain covenant and agree to and with the af[oresai]^d Samuel HANDY that he the af[oresai]^d **Levin CAMBRIDGE** is Lawfully Seize of the premises above mentioned and the af[oresai]^d **Levin CAMBRIDGE** Covenanteth that he his Heirs Executors and Administrators will warrant and forever defend the af[oresai]^d parcel of Land unto the af[oresai]^d Samuel HANDY his Heirs and Assigns from all and every person claiming or pretending to claim the af[oresai]^d Land In Testimony whereof he the said **Levin CAMBRIDGE** hereunto his hand hath set and Seal affixed the day and year above written.

Signed Sealed and acknowledged John COTTINGHAM **Levin CAMBRIDGE** (Seal)
in the presence of ~ ~ ~ Jesse BENNITT ~ ~"

*followed on folio 170 with the acknowledgment by Justices of the Peace Jesse BENNETT and John COTTINGHAM and the recordation on 12 April 1796 by court clerk John C. HANDY[743]

Liber R, folios 199-200; 28 April 1796

"State of Maryland Know all Men by these presents that I Esther HUDSON of Worcester County in Consideration of the Sum of Eighty five pounds current Money to me in hand paid by Jesse POWELL, have bargained Sold released granted and confirmed, and by these presents, do bargain, sell, release, grant and confirm unto the said Jesse POWELL one Negro Man called **George** To have and to hold the said Negro Man **George** by these presents bargained and sold, granted and confirmed unto the only proper use and behoof of him the said Jesse POWELL his heirs, Executors, Administrators or Assigns for ever freely quietly peacably and intirely, without any Contradiction, claim disturbance or hinderance of any person whatsoever and without any account to me or to any other whatsoever to be made, answered, or hereafter to be rendered, so that neither I the said Esther HUDSON nor any other for me or in my Name any right, title, Interest or demand of, in or to or for the said Negro Man **George** or any part of him thereof ought to exact, challenge claim, or demand at any time or times hereafter, but from all Actions, right Estate, Title, Claim demand possession and Interest thereof shall be wholly barred and excluded by force and virtue of these presents, and I the said Esther HUDSON for myself my Executors and Administrators the said Negro Man **George** unto the said Jesse POWELL his Executors Administrators or Assigns and against all and every other person or persons whatsoever shall and will warrant and forever defend, by these presents In Witness whereof I have hereunto set my hand and seal affixed this twenty Eighth day of April Anno Domini 1796

---

[743] Worcester County Court (Land Records). Deed from **CAMBRIDGE, Levin** to HANDY, Samuel. 05 April 1796. R, pp. 169-170, MSA CE 30-17. www.mdlandrec.net : accessed 04 May 2022.

Signed Sealed & delivered	Josiah MITCHELL	Esther HUDSON (Seal)
in the presence of ~ ~ ~ ~	Joshua DALE ~ ~"	

*followed on folio 200 with the acknowledgment by Justice of the Peace Josiah MITCHELL and the recordation on 03 May 1796 by court clerk John C. HANDY[744]

Liber R, folios 210-211; 19 May 1796

"State of Maryland Worcester County Ss^t. Know all Men by these presents that we Esther HUDSON and Isaac HUDSON of the County and State aforesaid, in consideration of the Sum of Eighty pounds Current Money to us in hand paid by Belitha POWELL of the County aforesaid have bargained sold released and confirmed, and by these presents do bargain sell release and confirm unto the said Belitha POWELL one Negro Man named **Robin**, to have and to hold the said Negro **Robin** by these presents bargained and sold released, granted and confirmed unto the only proper use and behoof of the said Belitha POWELL his Executors Administrators and Assigns for ever, freely quietly, peaceably, and intirely, without any contradiction claim disturbance or hindrance of any person whatsoever, and without any account to us or to any other whatsoever to be made, answered, or hereafter or to be rendered, so that neither we the said Esther HUDSON & Isaac HUDSON nor any other for us or in our names any right title interest or demand of in to or for the said Negro man **Robin** or any part of him thereof ought to exact, challenge claim or demand at any time or times hereafter, but from all Actions right Estate title claim demand possession and Interest thereof shall be wholly barred and excluded by force and virtue of these presents and we the said Esther HUDSON and Isaac HUDSON for ourselves our Executors and Administrators the said Negro Man unto the said Belitha POWELL his Executors Administrators or Assigns and against all and every other person or persons whatsoever shall and will warrant and forever defend by these presents In Witness whereof we have hereunto set our hands and seals affixed this 19th day of May Anno Domini 1796

Signed Sealed & delivered		Esther HUDSON (Seal)
in the presence of	Josiah MITCHELL	Isaac HUDSON (Seal)"

*followed on folio 211 with the acknowledgment by Justice of the Peace Josiah MITCHELL and the recordation on 26 May 1796 by court clerk John C. HANDY[745]

Liber R, folio 219-220; 23 May 1796

"State of Maryland Know all Men by these presents that I John DENNIS of Worcester County in consideration of the sum of fifty pounds Current Money of Maryland to me in hand paid by James CORNFEET (Marchant) have bargain[e]d sold released Granted an Confirmed and by these presents do bargain sell release Grant and confirm to the said James CORNFEET one Negro Girl called **Gin**, to have and to hold the said Negro **Gin** by these presents, bargained sold, released granted and confirmed unto the only proper use and behoof of him the said James CORNFEET his Executors Administrators and Assigns for ever freely quietly peacably and intirely, without any contradiction claim disturbance or hindrance, of any person whatsoever and without any account to me or any other person whatsoever to be made, or rendred, so that neither I the said John DENNIS nor any other for me or in my name any right title Interest or demand of in to or for the said Negro Garle **Gin** or any part or parcel thereof ought to exact challenge claim or demand at any time or times hereafter, but from all Actions, Right Estate title claim, demand possession and Interest thereof shall be wholy barred and excluded by force and virtue of these presents, and I the said John DENNIS for myself my Executors and Administrators the said Negro **Gin** unto the said James CORNFEET his Executors Administrators and Assigns, and against all and every other person or persons whatsoever, shall

---

[744] Worcester County Court (Land Records). Bill of Sale from HUDSON, Esther to POWELL, Jesse. 28 April 1796. R, pp. 199-200, MSA CE 30-17. www.mdlandrec.net : accessed 05 May 2022.

[745] Worcester County Court (Land Records). Bill of Sale from HUDSON, Esther and Isaac to POWELL, Belitha. 19 May 1796. R, pp. 210-211, MSA CE 30-17. www.mdlandrec.net : accessed 05 May 2022.

and will warrant and for ever defend by these presents In Witness whereof I have hereunto set my hand and seal affixed this twenty third day of May Anno Domini 1796

Signed Sealed & delivered John DENNIS (Seal)
in the presence of ~ ~ Josiah MITCHELL"

*followed on folio 220 with the acknowledgment by Justice of the Peace Josiah MITCHELL and the recordation on 02 June 1796 by court clerk John C. HANDY[746]

Liber R, folios 220-221; 03 June 1796

"This Indenture made this third day of June in the year of our Lord seventeen hundred and ninety six between Samuel SCARBOROUGH of Worcester County in the State of Maryland of the one part and Molly SCARBOROUGH Daughter of the said Samuel of the same place of the other part Witnesseth, that whereas a certain part of a parcel of land known by the name of New Timber Quarter hath been sold unto a certain Arthur ROLEY by the said Samuel SCARBOROUGH and since the sale thereof their arisses a probiblity that the part of a Tract af[oresai]^d will become the Right and Title of said Molly SCARBOROUGH Now this Indenture further Witnesseth that for an inducement unto the said Molly SCARBOROUGH and as well for the natural Love and Efection which I have for the said Molly and also for the consideration of the sum of five shillings to me in hand paid before the sealing and delivery of these presents have Granted and by these presents Grant give and transfere unto my said Daughter Molly two Negros one by the name of **Jacob** and one by the name of **Isaac** to the only proper use and Bennefitt of her the said Molly and to her heirs and Assigns for ever and I the said Samuel for myself and my heirs will forever defend the af[oresai]^d Negroes as a sure Estate of Inheritance unto the said Molly SCARBOROUGH and to her heirs and Assigns for ever provided always Nevertheless and it is the true intent and meaning of these presents that in case the said Molly SCARBOROUGH shall Execute such Deed or other assurance unto the af[oresai]^d Arthur ROLEY when he shall reasonably request the same for all the right title claim or Interest of in and unto the part of a Tract of Land as af[oresai]^d described containing all her right title Claim or Intrest that she hath or ever shall unto the said Land as af[oresai]^d unto him the said Arthur and his heirs and assigns for ever that the two Negroes **Jacob** and **Isaac** to be the right title and property of her the said Molly SCARBOROUGH and her heirs and assigns forever, but in case the said Molly SCARBOROUGH shall refuse or neglect when reasonably requested to make such deed or other assurance of his right of the part of a parcel of Land as aforesaid unto said ROLEY as aforesaid, that then this present Deed of Gift to be nul and Void to all intents and purpose and it is the true intent and meaning hereof that in case she the said Molly shall Refuse or neglect as af[oresai]^d that she shall be for ever Bared of the Negroes as aforesaid In testimony I the said Samuel SCARBOROUGH have hereunto set my hand and seal affixed the day and year first above written

Signed Sealed & delivered Samuel SCARBOROUGH (Seal)
in presence of ~ ~ ~ ~ Jesse BENNITT"

*followed on folio 221 with the acknowledgment by Justice of the Peace Jesse BENNITT and the recordation by court clerk John C. HANDY[747]

Liber R, folios 240-241; 11 June 1796

"Know all Men by these presents that I John LAWES of Worcester County and State of Maryland, for and in consideration of the sum of Thirty One pounds four shillings to me in hand paid, at and before the sealing and delivery and delivery hereof by Joseph BOWSER of the County and State aforesaid the Receipt whereof I do hereby acknowledge, have bargained and sold and by these presents do bargain and sell unto the said Joseph BOSER Our Negro Girl

---

[746] Worcester County Court (Land Records). Bill of Sale from DENNIS, John to CORNFEET, James. 23 May 1796. R, pp. 219-220, MSA CE 30-17. www.mdlandrec.net : accessed 05 May 2022.
[747] Worcester County Court (Land Records). Deed of Gift from SCARBOROUGH, Samuel to SCARBOROUGH, Molly. 03 June 1796. R, pp. 220-221, MSA CE 30-17. www.mdlandrec.net : accessed 05 May 2022.

called **Milla**, to have and to hold the aforesaid Negro Girl by these presents bargained and sold unto the said Joseph BOWSER his E[xecuto]^{rs} Adm[inistrato]^{rs} and Assigns for ever and I the said John LAWES, for myself my Executors and Adm[inistrato]^{rs} all and singular the Negro Girl called **Milla** unto the said Joseph BOWSER his Executors Adm[inistrato]^{rs} and Assigns, against me the said John LAWES my Ex[ecuto]^{rs} Adm[inistrato]^{rs} and Assigns and against all and every other person and persons whatsoever, shall and will warrant and forever defend by these presents, of which Negro Girl I the said John LAWES, have put the said Joseph BOWSER in full possession of said Negro Girl called **Milla**, at the sealing hereof, In Witness whereof I have hereunto set my hand and affixed my seal this Eleventh day of June 1796 ~

Sealed & delivered in	William STEVENS	John LAWS (Seal)
the presence of us	John O. TWIFIRD"	

*followed on folio 241 with the acknowledgment by Somerset County Justice of the Peace William STEVENS and the recordation on 16 June 1796 by Worcester County court clerk John C. HANDY[748]

Liber R, folios 243-244; 22 June 1796

"Know all Men by these presents that I James MARTIN of Worcester County in the State of Maryland for and in consideration of the sum of fifty pounds Current Money of Maryland to me in hand paid before the Ensealing and delivery of these presents, the receipt whereof the said James MARTIN doth hereby acknowledge, hath bargained sold released granted and confirmed and by these presents have heretofore bargained solld released grant and confirm unto Mathias MILES his heirs Executors and Administrators and Assigns one Negro Man slave named **Sam** To have and to hold the said Negro Man slave named **Sam** unto the said Mathias MILES his heirs Executors Administrators and Assigns for ever freely quietly peaceably and entirely without any contradiction claim disturbance or hinderance of any person whatsoever, and I the said James MARTIN my heirs, Executors and Administrators the aforesaid negro Man slave named **Sam** to the said Mathias MILES his Executors Administrators and Assigns against all manner of persons will warrant and for ever defend by these presents of which said Negro Man slave named **Sam** I the said James MARTIN did put the said Mathias MILES in full and peaceable possession of In Testimony whereof I have hereunto set my hand and seal affixed this twenty second day of June Anno Domini 1796

Signed Sealed & delivercd		James MARTIN (Seal)
in the presence of	John COTTINGHAM"	

*followed with the acknowledgment by Justice of the Peace John COTTINGHAM and the recordation by court clerk John C. HANDY[749]

Liber R, folios 249-250; 04 July 1796

"Whereas I have purchased my daughter **Nelli STEVENS** and her Girl named **Anna** of John WATSON for the consideration in full he has given me a Receipt wherefore I do hereby manumit her my said Daughter and her Child and set them absolutely free to all intents and purposes further then the Girl **Anna** shall be under her Mother as the natural Guardian till she arrives of Lawfull age and then to Cetal her liberty as any free person of Colour under the Laws of Maryland, and according to an Act of Assembly in such case made and provided in Testimony whereof I have hereto set my hand and affixed my seal this fourth day of July in the year 1796 ~ my said Girl **Nelle** being about twenty one years of Age and healthy and Sound an able to provide a living, her Child aged about four years of age ~

---

[748] Worcester County Court (Land Records). Bill of Sale from LAWES, John to BOWSER, Joseph. 11 June 1796. R, pp. 240-241, MSA CE 30-17. www.mdlandrec.net : accessed 05 May 2022.
[749] Worcester County Court (Land Records). Bill of Sale from MARTIN, James to MILES, Mathias. 22 June 1796. R, pp. 243-244, MSA CE 30-17. www.mdlandrec.net : accessed 05 May 2022.

Signed Sealed & delivered   Philip QUINTON
in presence of ~   Littleton X STEVENS (Seal)
                                                                                      mark

Jun ye 15 day 1796 Rec[eive]^d of Littleton STEVENS in full for **Elinor STEVENS** and her Child, the Childs name **Anna** ~ Rec[eive]^d John WATSON ~ {?} {?}"

*followed on folio 250 with the acknowledgment by Justice of the Peace Philip QUINTON and the recordation by court clerk John C. HANDY[750]

Liber R, folios 268-269; 22 July 1796

"This Indenture made this twenty second day of July in the year of our Lord One thousand seven hundred and ninety six between Ameala JONES of Worcester County and State of Maryland of the one part and Zadok STURGIS of the same place on the other part Witnesseth that for and in consideration of twenty five pound Current Money of the State af[oresai]^d to me in hand paid before the sealing and delivery of these presents the receipt whereof the said Ameala JONES doth hereby acknowledg and her self contented and paid hath bargained and sold to the af[oresai]^d Zadok STURGIS a Certen Negro Boy called **James** now in the possession of the af[oresai]^d Ameala JONES to him the aforesaid Zadok STURGIS his hairs Executors Admenestrators or Assigns for ever and to no other purpose what so ever and the af[oresai]^d Ameala JONES her hairs will warrant and for ever defend the af[oresai]^d Negrow Boy called **James** against the lawfull Clames titles or demands of all persons what so ever in witness whereof the af[oresai]d Ameala JONES her hand and seal affixed the day and year above written ~

Signed Sealed & delivered   Aimla JONES (Seal)
in the presence of   Jesse BENNETT"

*followed on folio 269 with the acknowledgment by Justice of the Peace Jesse BENNETT and the recordation by court clerk John C. HANDY[751]

Liber R, folio 271; 18 July 1796

"Know all Men by these presents that I Thomas GRAY Sen[io]^r of Worcester County and State of Maryland, for and in Consideration of the Sum of Thirty pounds Current Money of Maryland to me in hand paid before the ensealing and delivery hereof have bargained Sold and delivered unto Johnson GRAY of the County and State af[oresai]^d a certain Negro woman called **Bett**, and a certain Negro Boy called **Ned** to him the said Johnson GRAY his heirs and Assigns forever, and the said Thomas GRAY Sen[io]^r for himself his heirs Executors and Administrators do warrant and defend the hereby bargained premises to the only proper use benefit and behoof of him the said Johnson GRAY his heirs and Assigns, against all and every other person or persons whatever claiming the same ~ In Testimony whereof I the said Thomas GRAY have hereunto set my hand and seal this Eighteenth day of July Anno Domini 1796 ~

Test. John P MITCHELL ~   Thomas X GRAY (Seal)
                                                                              mark"

*followed with the acknowledgment by Justice of the Peace John P. MITCHELL and the recordation on 26 July 1796 by court clerk John C. HANDY[752]

---

[750] Worcester County Court (Land Records). Deed of Manumission from STEVENS, Littleton to **STEVENS, Nelle** and **Anna**. 04 July 1796. R, pp. 249-250, MSA CE 30-17. www.mdlandrec.net : accessed 05 May 2022.

[751] Worcester County Court (Land Records). Bill of Sale from JONES, Ameala to STURGIS, Zadok. 22 July 1796. R, pp. 268-269, MSA CE 30-17. www.mdlandrec.net : accessed 05 May 2022.

[752] Worcester County Court (Land Records). Bill of Sale from GRAY, Thomas Sr. to GRAY, Johnson. 18 July 1796. R, p. 271, MSA CE 30-17. www.mdlandrec.net : accessed 05 May 2022.

Liber R, folio 302; 23 August 1796

"An Account of the following negro woman, to wit, Negro slave Woman called **Hannah** about twenty One years Old, that I the Subscriber William PORTER (Taylor) moved into the State of Maryland Worcester County from Accomack County in the State of Virginia in the year one thousand seven hundred and ninety six, and I do assert that the above mentioned Negro woman called **Hannah**, has been a Residenture more than three years last past, of the said County of Accomack, as given under my hand this twenty third day of August in the year One thousand seven hundred and ninety six ~ William PORTER

August the 23^d 1796 Then came before me William SELBY Naval Officer for the District of Snow Hill and Worcester County, the above named William PORTER and made Oath on the holy Evangels of Almighty God that the Negro Woman, above mentioned was an Inhabitant and Residenture of Accomack County and State of Virginia, untill the twentieth Instant (August) and I do hereby declare that I have and did then move the said negro, myself and family into Worcester County in the State of Maryland, with Bona fide intention of Settling in the same and that I have brought the said Negro with me, with views of continuing her in my own service, and not with any design of selling or disposing of her ~

Sworn before ~ W[illia]^m SELBY N.O."

*followed with the recordation on 24 August 1796 by court clerk John C. HANDY[753]

Liber R, folios 303-304; 26 August 1796

"Know all Men by these presents I Robert M. MERRILL of Worcester County in the State of Maryland for and in consideration of the sum of thirty four pounds ten shillings Current Money of Maryland to me in hand paid by Thomas IRONS of the same place at and before the sealing and delivery of these presents the Receipt whereof I do hereby acknowledge have bargained and sold and by these presents do bargain and sell unto the said Thomas IRONS his heirs and Assigns a Negro Wench named **Lucey** to have and to hold the said Wench above mentioned unto the said Thomas IRONS his heirs and assigns forever to the only proper benefit behoof of the said Thomas IRONS his heirs & assigns forever and for no other use or purpose whatsoever and the said Rob[er]^t M. MERRILL for himself and his heirs doth Covenant and agree to and with the said Thomas IRONS that he the said Rob[er]^t M. MERRILL hath a good and Sufficient title to sell and dispose of the said Negro Woman so as to Convey to the said Thomas IRONS a good Sure and firm title to the same, and that no person but the said Robert MERRILL hath any right or title to the same In Testimony whereof the said Robert MERRILL his hand to these presents hath set, and seal affixed this 26th day of August Anno Domini One thousand seven hundred and ninety six ~

Signed Sealed & delivered in the presence of	Joshua EVANS Philip QUINTON"	Rob[er]^t M. MERRILL (Seal)

*followed on folio 304 with the acknowledgment by Justice of the Peace Philip QUINTON and the recordation by court clerk John C. HANDY[754]

Liber R, folios 319-320; 27 August 1796

"Know all Men by these presents that I John JOHNSON of Worcester County in the State of Maryland for and in consideration of the sum of fifty pounds fifteen Shillings lawful Money of the State af[oresai]^d to me in hand paid by Edward SCARBOROUGH of the County and State at or before the Sealing and delivery of these presents the receipt whereof I the said John JOHNSON do hereby acknowledge have granted bargained and sold and by these presents do grant bargain and sell unto the said Edward SCARBOROUGH his Executors Adm[inistrato]^{rs}

---

[753] Worcester County Court (Land Records). Certificate of Importation into Maryland from PORTER, William for **Hannah**. 23 August 1796. R, p. 302, MSA CE 30-17. www.mdlandrec.net : accessed 05 May 2022.
[754] Worcester County Court (Land Records). Bill of Sale from MERRILL, Robert M. to IRONS, Thomas. 26 August 1796. R, pp. 303-304, MSA CE 30-17. www.mdlandrec.net : accessed 05 May 2022.

and Assigns one Negro Wench named **Lyda** aged about thirty One years now absconded ~ To have and to hold the said negro Wench named **Lyda** as she now runs with all and singular her Increase and profits to the said Edward SCARBOROUGH his heirs and Assigns forever, and I the said John JOHNSON for myself and my heirs and Assigns do Covenant and agree with s[ai]^d SCARBOROUGH that the said Negro Wench unto him the said Edward SCARBOROUGH and his heirs I the said John JOHNSON will warrant and for ever defend. In Testimony whereof I the said John JOHNSON has hereunto his hand set and seal affixed this the 27th day of Aug[us]^t 1796

Signed Sealed & delivered   William SELBY ~   J[oh]n JOHNSON   (Seal)
in the presence off ~   Jenkins HENDERSON"

*followed on folio 320 with the acknowledgment by Justice of the Peace John HOLLAND and the recordation on 09 September 1796 by court clerk John C. HANDY[755]

Liber R, folios 343-344; 07 October 1796

"Know all Men by these presents that we Esme MERRILL and Gertrude his wife of Somerset County and State of Maryland for and in consideration of the sum of five pounds Current Money of Maryland to them in hand paid by Thomas MILBOURN of Worcester County and State af[oresai]^d, the receipt whereof in hereby acknowledged and confessed, have bargained sold and delivered and by these presents doth bargain sell and deliver the following negro slaves, to Wit, negro man called **Will**, negro **Rachel**, negro **Jim** negro **Easter** and all now in the possession of the aforesaid Thomas MILBOURN & in Worcester County aforesaid, and were formerly the property of a certain Jacob ADAMS, late of the County aforesaid dece[ase]^d To have and to hold all and Singular the above mentioned negro Slaves unto him the said Tho[ma]^s MILBOURN his heirs and Assigns forever to the only proper use benefit & behoof of him the said Thomas MILBOURN his heirs and Assigns forever, and the said Esme MERRILL and Gertrude his Wife their heirs Executors and Administrators the said bargained and delivered Negro Slaves will and shall forever warrant and defend against themselves and their heirs and all persons claiming by from or under them or either of them of which above mentioned negroes, we the said Esme MERRILL & Gertrude his Wife have put the said Thomas MILBOURN in full possession by the delivery of these presents. ~ In Witness whereof we the said Esme MERRILL & Gertrude his wife to these presents their hands have set and seals affixed this seventh day of October in the year One thousand seven hundred and ninety six ~

Signed sealed & delivered   John COTTINGHAM   Esme MERRILL   (Seal)
in the presence of   Thomas DIXON   Gertrude MERRILL (Seal)"

*followed on folio 344 with the acknowledgment by Justices of the Peace Thomas DIXON and John COTTINGHAM and the recordation on 08 October 1796 by court clerk John C. HANDY[756]

Liber R, folio 374; 01 November 1796

"This Indenture made this first day of November Anno Domini seventeen hundred and ninety six between Colborn LONG and James B ROBINS both of Worcester County in the State of Maryland witnesseth that the said Colborn for and in consideration of the sum of One hundred and Eleven pounds to him in hand paid before the ensealing and delivery hereof the receipt whereof is hereby acknowledged hath granted bargained and sold and by these presents doth bargain and sell unto the said James his Executors Administrators and assigns the following Goods and Chattles, to wit, One Negro Woman named **Sabroe**, One Negro Boy called **James** three Negro Girls called **Grace Esther** and **Leah** also thirty head of horned Cattle twenty head of Sheep and four head of horse kind now in the said Coleburns possession to have and to hold

---

[755] Worcester County Court (Land Records). Bill of Sale from JOHNSON, John to SCARBOROUGH, Edward. 27 June 1796. R, pp. 319-320, MSA CE 30-17. www.mdlandrec.net : accessed 05 May 2022.
[756] Worcester County Court (Land Records). Bill of Sale from MERRILL, Esme to MILBOURN, Thomas. 07 October 1796. R, pp. 343-344, MSA CE 30-17. www.mdlandrec.net : accessed 06 May 2022.

all all and singular the said Goods & Chattles to him the said James his Executors and Assigns forever provided always and upon the Condition that if the said Coleborn shall not pay to the said James the sum of hundred and Eleven pounds Current Money of Maryland with legal Interest thereon from the date hereof on or before the first day of April next then the said James shall have full power to sell and dispose by public Vendue so much of the said property as shall pay the sum af[oresai]^d as witness the hand and seal of the said Coleborn the day and year af[oresai]^d

Sealed & delivered in the   Jesse BENNITT   Coleborn LONG   (Seal)
presence of ~"

*followed with the acknowledgment by Justice of the Peace Jesse BENNITT and the recordation by court clerk John C. HANDY[757]

Liber R, folios 374-375; 04 November 1796

"This Indenture made this fourth day of November in the year of our Lord seventeen hundred and ninety six between **Levin CAMBRIDGE** of Worcester County in the State of Maryland of the one part and James Bowdoin ROBINS of the same place of the other part Witnesseth that whereas a certain William Cambridge HUNT of Worcester County was seized in his demesne as of fee of a Tract of Land called Williams Choice situate in the County aforesaid near the head of Acquango Branch and being so seized did by his last Will duly Execute devise the said Tract of Land to his wife Esther during her natural life, with remainder in fee to his son the said **Levin HUNT (alias CAMBRIDGE)** now This Indenture further Witnesseth that the said **Levin** and in consideration of fifty pounds Current Money of Maryland to him in hand paid before the Ensealing and delivery thereof the Receipt whereof the said **Levin** doth hereby acknowledge and thereof the said James his heirs Executors Adm[inistrato]^{rs} and Assigns doth release exonerate and by these presents forever discharge hath granted bargained and Sold and by these presents doth grant bargain & Sell unto the said James his heirs and assigns all that tract or parcel of Land called Williams Choice with the appurtenances Rights and priveleges thereto belonging or in any manner appurtenances To have & to hold the said Tract of Land with the appurtenances unto the said James his heirs and assigns to the only proper use and behoof of him the said James his heirs and assigns forever provided always and upon this express Condition that if the said **Levin** shall pay and satisfy unto the said James his heirs Executors Administrators or assigns the sum of forty seven pounds ten shillings Current Money of Maryland on or before the first day of January Anno Domini One thousand Eight hundred then this present Instrument of writing to be void else to be and remain in full force and Virtue, and the said **Levin** doth for himself his heirs Executors Administrators and assigns Covenant and agree with the said James his heirs Executors Administrators or assigns the sum of Money aforesaid and will Execute whatever further assurance that the said James may think necessary for securing the same ~ In Testimony whereof the said **Levin** doth hereto set his hand and affixed his Seal the day & year af[oresai]^d

Sealed & delivered   Philip QUINTON   **Leaven CAMBRIDGE**   (Seal)
in the presence of us   Benjamin DENNIS"

*followed on folio 375 with the acknowledgment by Justices of the Peace Philip QUINTON and Benjamin DENNIS and the recordation by court clerk John C. HANDY[758]

Liber R, folios 389-391; 25 November 1796

"This Indenture made this twenty fifth day of November in the year One thousand seven hundred and ninety six, between Thomas MARTIN Senior of Worcester County and State of Maryland of the one part and Easter COLLICK of the same place wife of **Samuel COLLICK**

---

[757] Worcester County Court (Land Records). Bill of Sale from LONG, Coleborn to ROBINS, James B. 01 November 1796. R, p. 374, MSA CE 30-17. www.mdlandrec.net : accessed 06 May 2022.

[758] Worcester County Court (Land Records). Deed from **CAMBRIDGE, Leaven** to ROBINS, James Bowdoin. 04 November 1796. R, pp. 374-376, MSA CE 30-17. www.mdlandrec.net : accessed 06 May 2022.

(**Molatto**) Witnesseth that the af[oresai]^d Thomas MARTIN for and in consideration of the sum of five pounds Current Money of Maryland to him in hand paid by the aforesaid Easter COLLICK at and before the sealing and delivery of these presents the receipt whereof the said Thomas MARTIN doth hereby acknowledge and and himself fully satisfied contented and paid and the said Easter COLLICK her heirs Executors and Administrators therefrom forever acquitted and discharged hath granted bargained and sold and by these presents doth grant bargain sell Convey and confirm unto her heirs and Assigns forever all that part of a Tract of Land called Acquintico Savannah situate lying and being in Worcester County in Acquango hundred and is contained in the bounds and lines following to wit, Beginning at the first bounder of **Samuel COLLICK**s Land called Red Oak Ridge," … "containing and now laid Out for Eight and one half Acres of Land more or less, together with all its rights members profits benefits previledges and all other the appurtenances thereto belonging To have and to hold all and singular the above mentioned bargained and sold Lands and premises with its Appurtenances unto her the said Easter COLLICK her heirs Executors Administrators and assigns forever to the only proper use benefit and behoof of her the said Easter COLLICK her her heirs and assigns forever and the said Thomas MARTIN for himself her heirs Executors and Administrators doth hereby Covenant grant and agree to quit all right Title and claim of and to the aforesaid Lands and premises, and will and shall warrant and forever defend the same against lawful right Title claim or demand of all manner of person or persons whatever, now claiming or ever hereafter to claim by from or under him them or any of them unto her the said Easter COLLICK her heirs and assigns forever In Testimony whereof the said Thomas MARTIN to these presents his hand hath set and seal affixed the day and year above written ~

Signed sealed & delivered   William PARKER   Thomas MARTIN (Seal)
in the presence of ~   Jesse BENNITT"

*followed on folio 390 with the acknowledgment by Justices of the Peace William PARKER and Jesse BENNITT and the recordation on folio 391 by court clerk John C. HANDY[759]

Liber R, folio 408; 02 December 1796

"Know all Men by these presents that I Dan[ie]^l BALLARD of the County Somerset & state Maryland for the consideration of the sum of One hundred dollars to me in hand paid by Levin TOWNSEND of the County of Worcester and State af[oresai]^d the receipt thereof I do hereby acknowledge have bargained sold & delivered unto the said TOWNSEND a Negro Woman named **Sue** about forty years Old which Negro I the said Daniel BALLARD will warrant and defend in the quiet possession of the said Levin TOWNSEND his heirs and assigns forever ~ In Witness whereof I have set my hand and seal the 2^d day Dec[embe]^r 1796

Signed sealed & delivered   John AYRES   Dan[ie]^l BALLARD (Seal)
in presence of ~   Philip QUINTON"

*followed with the acknowledgment by Justice of the Peace Philip QUINTON and the recordation on 03 December 1796 by court clerk John C. HANDY[760]

Liber R, folio 410; 09 December 1796

"Know all Men by these presents that I James HOUSTON of Worcester County in the State of Maryland for and in consideration of the sum of sixty pounds Current Money of Maryland, to me in hand paid by John ROCK of the same place at and before the sealing and delivery of these presents the receipt whereof I do hereby acknowledge have bargained and sold and by these presents do bargain and sell unto the John ROCK his heirs and Assigns One Negro Boy called **Milby** to have & to hold said Negro Boy **Milby** unto the said John ROCK his heirs and assigns forever, to the only proper use benefit and behoof of the said John ROCK his heirs and

---

[759] Worcester County Court (Land Records). Deed of Conveyance from MARTIN, Thomas Sr. to COLLICK, Easter. 25 November 1796. R, pp. 389-391, MSA CE 30-17. www.mdlandrec.net : accessed 06 May 2022.

[760] Worcester County Court (Land Records). Bill of Sale from BALLARD, Daniel to TOWNSEND, Levin. 02 December 1796. R, p. 408, MSA CE 30-17. www.mdlandrec.net : accessed 06 May 2022.

Assigns forever, and for no other use or purpose whatsoever and the said James HOUSTON for himself and his heirs doth covenant and agree to and with the said John ROCK that he the said James HOUSTON hath a good & sufficient title to sell and dispose of the said Negro Boy **Milby** so as to convey to the said John ROCK a good sure and firm title to the same place and that no person but the said James HOUSTON hath any right or title to the said Boy called **Milby** ~ In Testimony whereof the said James HOUSTON his hand to these presents hath set and seal affixed this 9th day of December in the year of our Lord One thousand seven hundred and ninety six ~

Signed sealed & delivered   Tho[ma]s MARTIN   James HOUSTON   (Seal)
in the presence of ~   Philip QU"

*followed with the acknowledgment by Justice of the Peace Philip QUINTON and the recordation by court clerk John C. HANDY[761]

Liber R, folios 419-420; 16 December 1796

"I the Subscriber George MARSHALL do hereby Certify that I moved One Negro Woman called **Nancy** about sixteen years Old from Accomack County and State of Virginia into the County of Worcester and State of Maryland the 22nd day of November last, and the aforesaid Negro Woman belonged to Mrs. Rebecca WATTS, dec[ease]d of Accomack County af[oresai]d and being part of Rebecca MARSHALL, Daughter of the af[oresai]d Mrs. WATTS, my Spouses portion, as given under my hand this 16th day of December 1796

George MARSHALL

1796 December the 16th Then came before me the subscriber Naval Officer for the District of Snow Hill in Worcester County the above mentioned George MARSHALL and made Oath on the holy Evangels of Almighty God that the above named Negro Woman called **Nancy** was a Residenture of Accomack County and State of Virginia from her Birth untill the 22d day of November last, and I do hereby declare that I have at this time moved the said Negro, and past moved my Family into Worcester County and State of Maryland with Bonefide intention of settling in the same and that I have brought the said Negro with views of continuing her in my own service and not with any design of selling or disposing of her

Sworn before W[illia]m SELBY. Coll & N.O."

*followed on folio 420 with the recordation by court clerk John C. HANDY[762]

Liber R, folios 423-424; 23 December 1796

"This Indenture made this twenty third day of December in the year one thousand seven hundred and ninety six between Capt[ai]n Thomas MARTIN of Worcester County and State of Maryland of the One part and **Jacob ARMSTRONG** (Free Mollatto) of the same place of the other part Witnesseth that the aforesaid Thomas MARTIN for and in Consideration of the sum of twenty pounds Current Money of Maryland to him in hand paid by the aforesaid **Jacob ARMSTRONG** at and before the sealing and delivery of these presents, the Receipt whereof is hereby acknowledged and confessed and the said **Jacob ARMSTRONG** his heirs Executors Administrators and assigns therefrom forever acquitted and discharged he the said Thomas MARTIN hath granted bargained sold conveyed and confirmed, and by these presents doth absolutely Grant bargain sell convey and confirm unto him the said **Jacob ARMSTRONG** his heirs and Assigns forever Twenty Acres of land, being part of a Tract of Land called <u>Acquintico Savanah</u> situate lying and being in Worcester County aforesaid in Acquango Hundred which quantity of twenty Acres of land is bounded as follows Beginning at the third and beginning of the third line of the aforesaid **Jacob**'s former part of the aforesaid Tract of Land called

---

[761] Worcester County Court (Land Records). Bill of Sale from HOUSTON, James to ROCK, John. 09 December 1796. R, p. 410, MSA CE 30-17. www.mdlandrec.net : accessed 06 May 2022.
[762] Worcester County Court (Land Records). Certificate of Importation into Maryland from MARSHALL, George for **Nancy**. 16 December 1796. R, pp. 419-420, MSA CE 30-17. www.mdlandrec.net : accessed 06 May 2022.

Acquintico Savanah that he now lives on" … "containing and now laid Out for twenty Acres of land together with all its rights members profits, benefits privilidges, and all other the appurtenances thereto belonging or in any manner appertaining, To have & to hold all and singular the aforesaid bargained and sold Land with its appurtenances unto him the aforesaid **Jacob ARMSTRONG** his heirs and assigns forever to the only proper use benefit and behoof of him the said **Jacob ARMSTRONG** his heirs and assigns forever and the said Thomas MARTIN for himself his heirs Executors & Administrators the aforesaid bargained Lands and premises will and shall Warrant and forever defend the same against the lawful right, title or demand of all manner of person or persons whatever now claiming or ever to claim by from or under him or his heirs unto him the **Jacob ARMSTRONG** his heirs and assigns forever In Testimony whereof the said Thomas MARTIN his hand to these presents hath set and seal affixed the day and year first above written ~

Signed sealed & delivered   Philip QUINTON   Thomas MARTIN   (Seal)
in the presence of ~   Jesse BENNITT"

*followed on folio 424 with the acknowledgment by Justices of the Peace Philip QUINTON and Jesse BENNITT and the recordation on 29 December 1796 by court clerk John C. HANDY[763]

**Due to its true length, this transcription has been shortened to its most relevant portions. The full original deed can be viewed at the citation provided.

Liber R, folio 428; 06 January 1797

"A True list of Negro Slaves that I moved into the State of Maryland and Worcester County, from Accomack County and State of Virginia the twenty second day of December in the year One thousand seven hundred and ninety six, which said negro Slaves hereafter mentioned (the Negro Woman **Jenny**, have been an Inhabitant and residenture of Accomack County aforesaid more than three full years last past, to the said twenty second of December, and year aforesaid. Their Names and Ages, are to wit, One Negro Woman Aged about twenty three years, and called **Jenny**, and One Negro Girl called **Esther** about sixteen months old, as given under my hand this 6th day of January 1797

John MASSEY.

January the 6th 1797 Then came before me the subscriber, as Naval Officer of the District of Snow Hill, Worcester County, the above named John MASSEY and made Oath on the holy Evangels of Almighty God that the above named negro slaves, as enumerated in the above List, were Inhabitants & Residentures of Accomack County untill the aforesaid mentioned twenty second day of December, and said year therein mentioned, and I do hereby declare that I have moved the said Negroes, and myself and Family into Worcester County aforesaid with bonafide intention of settling in the same and that I have brought the said Negroes with me with views continuing them in my Own service and not with any design of selling or disposing of them contrary to Law

Sworn before W[illia]m SELBY. Coll. & Naval Officer"

*followed with the recordation by the court clerk John C. HANDY[764]

Liber R, folio 429; 06 January 1797

"A True list of Negroes that I moved into the State of Maryland from Accomack County State of Virginia the 29th day of December, One thousand seven hundred and ninety six, all which were Residentures and Inhabitants of Accomack County fully the space and time of three whole

---

[763] Worcester County Court (Land Records). Deed of Conveyance from MARTIN, Thomas to **Jacob ARMSTRONG (free mollatto)**. 23 December 1796. R, pp. 423-424, MSA CE 30-17. www.mdlandrec.net : accessed 06 May 2022.

[764] Worcester County Court (Land Records). Certificate of Importation into Maryland from MASSEY, John for **Jenny & Esther**. 06 January 1797. R, p. 428, MSA CE 30-17. www.mdlandrec.net : accessed 06 May 2022.

years before the above Date their names and Ages Males and Females, to wit, **Harry** aged Eighteen years, **saul** sixteen years **Patience** thirteen years and **Nancy** Eleven years Old, as given under my hand this sixth day of January 1797 ~   Thomas T. GORE.

1797 January the sixth, Then came before me the subscriber Naval Officer of Snow Hill in the County of Worcester County and State of Maryland the above named Thomas Teakle GORE and made Oath on the holy Evangels of Almighty God, that the several Negroes enumerated in the above List were Residentures and Inhabitants of Accomack County in the State of Virginia fully and more than three years last past, untill the 29th day of December in the year One thousand seven hundred and ninety Six, and I do declare that I have moved the said Negroes and myself into Worcester County in the State of Maryland with Bonafide intention of settling in the same and that I have brought the said Negroes with me with views of continuing them in my Own Service and not with any design of selling or disposing of them contrary to Law ~

         Sworn before W[illia]m SELBY, Coll & Naval Officer"

*followed with the recordation by court clerk John C. HANDY[765]

Liber R, folios 437-438; 06 January 1797

"Know all Men by these presents that I Tabitha BRUMBLY of Worcester County in the State of Maryland for and in consideration of the sum of Thirty seven pounds ten shillings lawful Money of the State aforesaid, to me in hand paid by John ALLEN of the County and State af[oresai]d at or before the sealing and delivery of these presents the Receipt whereof I the said Tabitha BRUMBLY do hereby acknowledge have granted Bargained and Sold and by these presents do grant bargain and sell unto the said John ALLEN his Executors Administrators and Assigns all my right and title to a Negro Boy called **Levin** and aged about Eight years. To have and to hold to possess and enjoy all and singular the said Negro Boy called **Levin** to the said John ALLEN his Ex[ecuto]rs Adm[inistrato]rs and assigns forever and I the said Tabitha BRUMBLY for myself and my Heirs Ex[ecuto]rs and Adm[inistrato]rs against all and every other person and persons whatsoever, shall and will warrant and forever defend unto the said John ALLEN his heirs and assigns, the above named Negro Boy ~ In Witness whereof I the said Tabitha BRUMBLY have hereto my hand set and seal affixed this the sixth day January 1797 ~

Signed Sealed & delivered   John HOLLAND   her
in the presence off ~   Tabitha + BRUMBLY (Seal)
                                                                       mark"

*followed on folio 438 with the acknowledgment by Justice of the Peace John HOLLAND and the recordation on 24 January 1797 by court clerk John C. HANDY[766]

Liber R, folios 451-452; 08 February? 1797

"Worcester County This Indenture made the Eighth day of   Anno Domini, Seventeen hundred and ninety seven, between John BONNEWELL of Accomack County in the State of Virginia of the one part, and Negro **Abel** of the County af[oresai]d and State of Maryland of the other part Witnesseth that he the said John BONNEWELL for and in Consideration of the sum twenty five pounds Current Money of Maryland to him paid, the receipt whereof is hereby acknowledged hath Manumitted released and for ever be liberated the af[oresai]d **Abel** from any further services as his slave, and he further warrants that the said **Abel**, shall not be called on as a slave by him, his heirs or assigns. In Witness whereof I have hereto set my hand and seal affixed the day and year above written ~

---

[765] Worcester County Court (Land Records). Certificate of Importation into Maryland from GORE, Thomas Teakle for **Harry, Saul, Patience,** and **Nancy**. 06 January 1797. R, p. 429, MSA CE 30-17. www.mdlandrec.net : accessed 06 May 2022.
[766] Worcester County Court (Land Records). Bill of Sale from BRUMBLY, Tabitha to ALLEN, John. 06 January 1797. R, pp. 437-438, MSA CE 30-17. www.mdlandrec.net : accessed 06 May 2022.

Sealed & delivered   Philip QUINTON   John BONNEWELL (Seal)
in presents of"

*followed with the recordation by court clerk Philip QUINTON and the recordation by court clerk John C. HANDY on folio 452 on 08 February 1797[767]

Liber R, folios 461-462; 04 February 1797

"Worcester Ss^t. Know all Men by these presents that I Solomon PEPPER of Worcester County in the State of Maryland for and in consideration of the sum of ten shillings to me in hand paid by Charles PRUITT before the Ensealing and delivery hereof the Right whereof do hereby acknowledge hath granted bargained and sold and by these presents do Grant bargain and sell unto the said Charles PRUITT his heirs and assigns forever One Negro Lad called **John**, and the said Solomon PEPPER doth for himself and heirs covenant and agree to and with the said Charles PRUITT, that he the said Solomon PEPPER the Negro **John** above mentioned will warrant and forever defend from all persons whatsoever claiming any right or title unto the said Negro ~

Signed sealed & delivered   John COTTINGHAM   Solomon + PEPPER (Seal)
in presents off   his mark"

*followed on folio 462 with the acknowledgment by Justice of the Peace John COTTINGHAM and the recordation by court clerk John C. HANDY[768]

Liber R, folio 469; 27 January 1797

"This Deed of Manumission dated this twenty seventh day of January in the year of our Lord Seventeen hundred and ninety seven Bears Testimony that George SPENCE of Worcester County in the State of Maryland moved by a spirit of Philanthropy as well as for Consideration of twenty pounds Current Money of Maryland to him in hand paid hath manumitted and set free and by these presents doth Grant release, manumit and set free a Negro Man called **George DULANY** from a State of Bondage and Slavery, to be and to Act in all respects as a free Man to all intents and purposes, to have and to hold his said liberty from hence forth to enjoy and conduct himself as a free Man to contract & to hold property and in fine to all and singular the Acts that any person (liberated under the existing Laws of this State) might or could do as well as to have remedy for any Injury he might sustain from any person whatever In Testimony whereof the said George SPENCE to these his hand hath set and seal the day and year first above written ~

signed sealed & delivered   Geo[rg]^e SPENCE (Seal)
in the presence of   Jesse BENNITT"

*followed with the acknowledgment by the Justice of the Peace Jesse BENNITT and the recordation by court clerk John C. HANDY[769]

Liber R, folio 473; ? March 1797

"Know all Men by these presents that I John SCARBOROUGH Sen[io]^r of Worcester County for and in Consideration of five shillings and the natural Love and Affection which I have for my daughter Bettey ROWLEY, have given granted bargained and sold and by these presents do give grant bargain and sell unto my said daughter Bettey ROWLEY her Executors Administrators and assigns the following Negroes to wit a Negroe Man called **Jacob** and a

---

[767] Worcester County Court (Land Records). Deed of Manumission from BONNEWELL, John to **Abel**. 08 February 1797. R, pp. 451-452, MSA CE 30-17. www.mdlandrec.net : accessed 07 May 2022.
[768] Worcester County Court (Land Records). Bill of Sale from PEPPER, Solomon to PRUITT, Charles. 04 February 1797. R, pp. 461-462, MSA CE 30-17. www.mdlandrec.net : accessed 07 May 2022.
[769] Worcester County Court (Land Records). Deed of Manumission from SPENCE, George to **DULANY, George**. 27 January 1797. R, p. 469, MSA CE 30-17. www.mdlandrec.net : accessed 07 May 2022.

Negro Boy called **Scott** to have and to hold the said two Negroes unto their only proper use and behoof of her the said Bettey ROWLEY her Executors Administrators and assigns, and which said Negroes I do hereby deliver possession of to the said Betty ROWLEY, as Witness my hand and Seal this   of March 1797 ~

Signed sealed & delivered   Jno. SCARBOROUGH   (Seal)
in presence of   Philip QUINTON"

*followed with the acknowledgment by Justice of the Peace Philip QUINTON and the recordation on 03 March 1797 by court clerk John C. HANDY[770]

Liber R, folios 473-474; 03 March 1797

"Know all Men by these presents that I John SCARBOROUGH Sen[io]^r For and in consideration of five shillings and the natural Love and affection which I have for my son McKimmy SCARBOROUGH I have given granted bargained and sold and by these presents do give grant bargain and sell unto my said son McKimmy SCARBOROUGH his Executors Administrators and assigns the following Negroes to wit a Negro fellow called **Bob**, a Negro Girl called **Hanah**, a Negro Girl called **Sarah** and a Negro Girl called **Judah** and their increase, to have and to hold the said Negroes unto the only proper use and behoof of my said son McKimmy SCARBOROUGH his Executors Administrators and assigns and I do hereby deliver possession of the said Negroes unto my said son McKimmy SCARBOROUGH, and Witness my hand and seal this third day of March 1797

Sealed signed & delivered   Jno. SCARBOROUGH   (Seal)
in presence of   Benjamin DENNIS"

*followed on folio 474 with the acknowledgment by Justice of the Peace Benjamin DENNIS and the recordation by court clerk John C. HANDY[771]

Liber R, folios 480-481; 10 March 1797

"This Indenture made this 10th day of March 1797 between George ROBERTSON of Somerset and Samuel HANDY of Worcester State of Maryland Witnesseth that that the said Samuel HANDY for and in Consideration of the sum of twenty pounds Current Money of Maryland to him in hand paid at and before the ensealing and delivery of the presents do bargain and sell and set over all his right title and property of any right or title that I have to one Negro Woman Called **Nell** together with her future Increase, to have hold occupy and enjoy the said Negro Woman called **Nell** unto him the said George ROBERTSON his heirs and assigns forever and to his only proper use & behoof of him the said George ROBERTSON and his heirs and assigns forever. In Testimony hereof I have hereto set my hand and affixed my seal the day and year above written

Signed sealed & delivered   Sam[ue]^l HANDY   (Seal)
in the presence of   Philip QUINTON"

*followed on folio 481 with the acknowledgment by Justice of the Peace Philip QUINTON and the recordation by court clerk John C. HANDY[772]

Liber R, folio 482; 28 February 1797

"Maryland Worcester County Sst Know all Men by these presents that I William CHAILLE of the County af[oresai]^d for and in consideration of the sum of thirty seven pounds ten shillings to me in hand paid by Elisha PARKER, have granted bargained and sold and do by these

---

[770] Worcester County Court (Land Records). Bill of Sale from SCARBOROUGH, John to ROWLEY, Bettey. March 1797. R, p. 473, MSA CE 30-17. www.mdlandrec.net : accessed 07 May 2022.
[771] Worcester County Court (Land Records). Bill of Sale from SCARBOROUGH, John to SCARBOROUGH, McKimmy. 03 March 1797. R, pp. 473-474, MSA CE 30-17. www.mdlandrec.net : accessed 07 May 2022.
[772] Worcester County Court (Land Records). Bill of Sale from HANDY, Samuel to ROBERTSON, George. 10 March 1797. R, pp. 480-481, MSA CE 30-17. www.mdlandrec.net : accessed 07 May 2022.

presents do Grant bargain and sell unto the said Elisha PARKER One Negro Boy called **Eben** Aged ab[ou]ᵗ five or six years and I do hereby engage to warrant and defend the said bargained premises to the said Elisha PARKER his heirs and assigns from myself my heirs and assigns from all and all Manner of persons claiming the same Given under my hand and seal this 28ᵗʰ February 1797 ~

Booz WALSTON   William CHAILLE (Seal)"

*followed with the acknowledgment by Justice of the Peace Booz WALSTON and the recordation on 15 March 1797 by court clerk John C. HANDY⁷⁷³

Liber R, folios 483-484; 11 March 1797

"Know all Men by these presents that I John BALL of Worcester County in the State of Maryland for and in consideration of the sum of forty five pounds current Money of Maryland to me in hand paid by John CUTLER of the County and State af[oresai]ᵈ at and before the sealing and delivery hereof, I the said John BALL have bargained sold and delivered and by these presents doth absolutely bargain sell and deliver unto him the said John CUTLER his heirs and Assigns forever One Negro Boy named **Bob** in Worcester County now in possession of the said John BALL. To have and to hold the above mentioned sold & delivered Negro **Bob** hereby intended to be sold unto him the said John CUTLER and to his heirs and assigns forever to the only proper use benefit and behoof of him the said John CUTLER and his heirs and assigns forever and the said John BALL for himself and his heirs Executors & Administrators and every of them and ag[ain]sᵗ every other person or persons whatever and shall forever warrant and defend the above mentioned bargained and sold Negro **Bob** unto him the said John CUTLER his heirs and assigns forever of which said Negro **Bob**, I the said John BALL have put the said John CUTLER in full possession of by the delivery of the above mentioned Negro **Bob**. In Testimony whereof I the said John BALL have hereto set my hand and affixed my seale the 11ᵗʰ day March Anno Dº[mini] 1797

Signed sealed & delivered   Philip QUINTON   John BALL   (Seal)
in the presence of ~   Rob[er]ᵗ SMITH"

*followed with the acknowledgment by Justice of the Peace Philip QUINTON and the recordation on 17 March 1797 by court clerk John C. HANDY⁷⁷⁴

Liber R, folios 509-510; 31 March 1797

"This Indenture made this thirty first day of March Anno Domini One thousand seven hundred and ninety seven between **Levin CAMBRIDGE** of Worcester County and State of Maryland of the One part and Valentine DENNIS of the County and State aforesaid of the other part Witnesseth that Whereas the said **Levin CAMBRIDGE** for and in consideration of the sum of Ten pounds Current Money of Maryland to him in hand paid by the said Valentine DENNIS the Receipt whereof the said **Levin CAMBRIDGE** doth hereby acknowledge and thereof and every part thereof the said Valentine DENNIS his heirs Executors Administrators and assigns doth release Exonerate and by these presents forever discharge, hath given Granted bargained and sold and by these presents doth give Grant bargain and sell unto the said Valentine DENNIS his heirs and assigns forever part of a Tract of Land known by the name of <u>Addition to Williams Choice</u>" … "containing & now laid out for Seventy four Acres be the same more or less, together with all and singular the rights previledges and Appurtenances thereunto belonging or in any manner appertaining To have and to hold the said parcel of land as above described with its appurtenances unto the said Valentine DENNIS and his heirs and assigns forever to the only proper use and behoof of him the said Valentine DENNIS his heirs and assigns forever and the said **Levin CAMBRIDGE** for himself and his heirs doth Covenant and agree to and with said

---

⁷⁷³ Worcester County Court (Land Records). Bill of Sale from CHAILLE, William to PARKER, Elisha. 28 February 1797. R, p. 482, MSA CE 30-17. www.mdlandrec.net : accessed 07 May 2022.
⁷⁷⁴ Worcester County Court (Land Records). Bill of Sale from BALL, John to CUTLER, John. 11 March 1797. R, pp. 483-484, MSA CE 30-17. www.mdlandrec.net : accessed 07 May 2022.

Valentine DENNIS and his heirs and assigns that he the said **Levin CAMBRIDGE** and his heirs will warrant and forever defend hereafter defend the above described lands and premises against the legal Claim of himself his heirs or any person whatever claiming under him or them unto the Valentine DENNIS his heirs and assigns forever. In Testimony whereof the said **Levin CAMBRIDGE** to these presents hath set and seal affixed the day and year first above written

Signed sealed & delivered   Benjamin DENNIS   **Leaven CAMBRIDGE**   (Seal)
in the presence of   Jesse BENNITT"

*followed with the acknowledgment by Justices of the Peace Benjamin DENNIS and Jesse BENNITT and the recordation by court clerk John C. HANDY[775]

the acknowledgment names the wife of **Leaven CAMBRIDGE as Elizabeth

***Due to its true length, this transcription has been shortened to its most relevant portions. The full original deed can be viewed at the citation provided.

Liber R, folios 524-524; 08 April 1797

"Know all Men by these presents that I Mary MARTIN of Worcester County and State of Maryland for and in consideration of the sum of sixty pounds Current Money of Maryland to me in hand paid by George MARTIN the receipt whereof is hereby acknowledged have given granted bargained and sold and by these presents do give grant bargain and sell unto the said George MARTIN his Executors Administrators and assigns a Negro Boy named **Tom** aged about Eleven years To have and to hold the said Negro Boy unto the said George MARTIN his Executors Administrators and Assigns and which Negro Boy named **Tom** I have this day delivered possession of unto the said George MARTIN and do affirm I have a good right and title to sell the same and the same will warrant and for defend unto the said George MARTIN against the right title & Claim of all persons whatsoever ~ In Testimony whereof I have hereunto set my hand and Seale affixed this Eight day of April Anno Domini 1797 ~

Signed sealed & delivered   Philip QUINTON   Mary MARTIN   (Seal)
in the presence off ~   Charles BENNITT"

*followed on folio 525 with the acknowledgment by Justice of the Peace Philip QUINTON and the recordation on 11 April 1797 by court clerk John C. HANDY[776]

Liber R, folios 525-526; 30 March 1797

"Know all Men by these presents that I Purnell SMITH of Worcester County in the State of Maryland for and in consideration of the sum of five pounds Current Money of Maryland to me in hand paid by Jesse JONES of County & State aforesaid have granted bargained sold and delivered the following personal property Viz. One Negro Woman Called **Anne** One Grey Mare ~ To have and to hold the above mentioned property to the only proper use and behoof of the said Jesse JONES his heirs and Assigns forever and the said Purnell SMITH doth further Covenant and agree to warrant and defend the above mentioned Articles from himself and his heirs and from the Claim and Claims of every other person whatsoever unto the said Jesse JONES his heirs and assigns forever all which property above mentioned the said Purnell SMITH hath given the said Jesse JONES possession of by an Actual delivery and further acknowledged himself fully content and satisfied by the said Jesse for the property above mentioned. In Witness and Confirmation the said Purnell to this present Bill of Sale his hand hath set and seal affixed this 30th day of March Anno Dom[ini] 1796 ~

---

[775] Worcester County Court (Land Records). Deed of Conveyance from **CAMBRIDGE, Leaven** to DENNIS, Valentine. 31 March 1797. R, pp. 509-510, MSA CE 30-17. www.mdlandrec.net : accessed 07 May 2022.
[776] Worcester County Court (Land Records). Bill of Sale from MARTIN, Mary to MARTIN, George. 08 April 1797. R, pp. 524-525, MSA CE 30-17. www.mdlandrec.net : accessed 07 May 2022.

Signed sealed & delivered					Purnell SMITH (Seal)
in presence of ~		William PURNELL"

*followed with a memorandum by Purnell SMITH and Jesse JONES, the acknowledgment by Justice of the Peace William PURNELL, and the recordation on 14 April 1797 by court clerk John C. HANDY[777]

Liber R, folios 533-534; 22 April 1797

"To all people to whom these presents may concern or Come I Laban HILL of Worcester County and State of Maryland send Greeting Know ye that I the said Labin HILL for and in consideration of the Natural Love and Affection which I have and bear unto my Daughter Sarah HILL and Elizabeth HILL and my Son Joshua HILL, and also for other good Causes and Considerations me thereunto moving have given & granted and by these presents do give grant and confirm unto the said Sarah HILL, Elizabeth HILL, and Joshua HILL One feather and furniture a piece and unto my said Daughters Sarah HILL & Elizabeth HILL, Six Silver Spoons, and then unto my five youngest Children by my first Wife all the remainder of my personal Estate (after my last Will & Testament is Complyed with of what kind or set soever the same are or may be to be equally divided between them be the same in what place soever the same may be found, as well in my own Custody & possession as in the possession or hands power & Custody of any other person or persons whatever as all those Goods & Chattles in the Schedule hereunto annexed mentioned To have and to hold all and singular the said Goods, Chattles, leases Debts and all other the said premises unto the said Sarah HILL, Elizabeth HILL, Joshua HILL Laban HILL and John HILL as above described their heirs Executors Administ[rato]^{rs} and assigns to their proper use and uses forever, and I the said Laban HILL the whole of the said Goods & Chattles unto the said Children as above described their heirs Executors Administrators and Assigns against all persons will warrant and defend forever by these presents ~ In Witness whereof I the said Labin HILL have hereunto set my hand and seal this 22^d day of April Anno Dom[ini] One thousand seven hundred ninety & seven ~ 1797 ~

							Labin HILL (Seal)

Memmerandum ~
The day and year first above written Livery & Seisen was delivered by the said Labin HILL Sen[io]^r unto the said Sarah HILL Elizabeth HILL, Joshua HILL, Labin HILL Jun[io]^r & John HILL, One Negro Man called **Ben**, One Negro Woman **Comfort** and thirty head of Cattle, One Waggon and Team, in the Name of all the Goods & Chattles within mentioned, hold to them the said Sarah HILL, Elizabeth HILL, Joshua HILL, Labin HILL Jun[io]^r and John HILL them their heirs Executors Administrators and assigns forever according to the true intent and meaning of the within written Deed ~"

*followed on folio 534 with the acknowledgment of Justice of the Peace Josiah MITCHELL and the recordation on 25 April 1797 by court clerk John C. HANDY[778]

Liber R, folios 574-575; 30 May 1797

"Know all Men by these presents that I Schoolfield PARKER of Worcester County and State of Maryland for and Consideration of the Sum of Seventy five pounds Current Money of Maryland to me in hand paid by Henry PARKER of the same place (Merchant) in behalf and for his Son Henry PARKER now a minor the Receipt whereof I the said Schoolfield PARKER doth hereby acknowledge and confess and hath bargained Sold and delivered and doth absolutely Bargain Sell and deliver unto my Grandson Henry PARKER and his heirs and Assigns forever, a certain Negro Man called **Major** (now on hire to a certain Richard

---

[777] Worcester County Court (Land Records). Bill of Sale from SMITH, Purnell to JONES, Jesse. 30 March 1797. R, pp. 525-526, MSA CE 30-17. www.mdlandrec.net : accessed 07 May 2022.

[778] Worcester County Court (Land Records). Deed of Gift from HILL, Labin to HILL, Sarah, HILL, Elizabeth, HILL, Joshua, HILL, Laban Jr., and HILL, John. 22 April 1797. R, pp. 533-534, MSA CE 30-17. www.mdlandrec.net : accessed 07 May 2022.

BETHARDS of the County af[oresai]ᵈ untill the first day of January next ensuing ~) To have and to hold the aforesaid Negro Man called **Major** (after his hier aforesaid expires) unto him my said Grandson Henry (Son of Son Henry PARKER) and heirs and assigns forever, to the only proper use benefit and behoof of him the said Henry PARKER (Minor) and his heirs and assigns forever and I the said Schoolfield PARKER for myself and heirs Executors and Administrators will and shall warrant and forever defend the said Negro Man called **Major**, of which said Negro I the said Schoolfield PARKER have put my said Grandson Son Henry, in full possession of (the hire above mentioned only excepted) by the delivery of these presents In Testimony whereof I the said Schoolfield to these presents my hand hath Set and Seal affixed this thirtieth day of May in the year One thousand seven hundred and ninety seven

Signed Sealed & delivered   John GUNBY   Schoolfield PARKER (Seal)
in the presence of   W[illia]ᵐ SELBY (SH)"

*followed with the acknowledgment by Justice of the Peace John GUNBY and the recordation on folio 575 on 31 May 1797 by court clerk John C. HANDY[779]

Liber R, folios 585-586; 31 May 1797

"Recved May 31ˢᵗ 1797 of Levin TOWNSEND of Jno. One hundred pounds in full payment for a Negro Sold him the said TOWNSEND by the name {?} **Patrick** the property which I forever Warrant and defend from all {?}ersons claiming or having any right too Witness my hand the day & {?} above written ~

{?} John CUTLER   Peter CHAILLE"

*followed on folio 586 with the recordation on 09 June 1797 by court clerk John C. HANDY[780]

Liber R, folio 591; 16 June 1797

"The following is a List of Negroes imported into the State of Maryland from the State of Virginia, by William WATTS Vizᵗ. One Negro Woman Named **Sarah** aged twenty three years One Negro Girl Named **Nanny** aged seven Months ~ I herby Certify the foregoing list of Negroes were Residentures of the State of Virginia previous to the year 1783 or descended from Residentures of that State previous to that time and which Negroes I devised my title to from the Death of my Mother Rebecca WATSON. Given under my hand the 16ᵗʰ day of June 1797

                                                                 William WATTS"

*followed with the recordation by court clerk John C. HANDY[781]

Liber R, folios 593-594; 21 June 1797

"Worcester Sct. Know all Men by these presents that I George WISE of Worcester County & State of Maryland for and in Consideration of the Sum of Seventy five pounds to me in hand the Receipt whereof I do hereby acknowledge have bargained and Sold and by these presents doth bargain and Sell unto Levin MARTIN his heirs and Assigns forever One Negro Man Named **Stephen** To have and to hold the af[oresai]ᵈ Negro Man **Stephen** to the said Levin MARTIN his heirs and assigns forever to the only proper use & behoof of the said Levin MARTIN his heirs and assigns and to no other intent or purpose whatever and the said Geo[rge] WISE Covenants further the af[oresai]ᵈ Negro Man Named **Stephen** against the title Claim & right of all and every person or persons whatever, to warrant and Defend and he further Covenants to make any further assurance or assurances for the af[oresai]ᵈ Negro **Stephen** (by Bill of Sale or otherwise) such as may be Devised or required by those learned in Law at any

---

[779] Worcester County Court (Land Records). Bill of Sale from PARKER, Schoolfield to PARKER, Henry Jr. 30 May 1797. R, pp. 574-575, MSA CE 30-17. www.mdlandrec.net : accessed 11 May 2022.

[780] Worcester County Court (Land Records). Receipt from CHAILLE, Peter to TOWNSEND, Levin. 31 May 1797. R, pp. 585-586, MSA CE 30-17. www.mdlandrec.net : accessed 11 May 2022.

[781] Worcester County Court (Land Records). Certificate of Importation into Maryland from WATTS, William for **Sarah** and **Nanny**. 16 June 1797. R, p. 591, MSA CE 30-17. www.mdlandrec.net : accessed 11 May 2022.

time when required by the said Levin MARTIN. In Testimony whereof I have hereto set my hand and Seal affixed this 21st day of June Anno Dom[ini] 1797

Sealed & delivered   Tho[ma]s DIXON   Geo[rge] K. WISE
in presence of"

*followed on folio 594 with the acknowledgment by Justice of the Peace Thomas DIXON and the recordation on 22 June 1797 by court clerk John C. HANDY[782]

Liber R, folios 605-606; 05 July 1797

"Worcester Sc[t]. Know all Men by these presents that I Walter SMITH of the County af[oresai]d and State of Maryland for and in consideration of the Sum of Ninety three pounds fifteen Shillings Current Money of Maryland to me in hand paid by William BANTEN of Lincoln County and State of Kentucke the Receipt whereof is hereby acknowled hath bargained and Sold and by these presents do bargain and Sell unto the said Will[ia]m BANTEN One Negro Man called **Bob** (who at present agreeable to advices Rec[eive]d is Confined in Washington Jail in Mason County in the State of Kentucke) To have and to hold the af[oresai]d Negro Man **Bob** unto the said William BANTEN his heirs and assigns forever to the only proper use and behoof of the said BANTEN his heirs and assigns and to no other intent or purpose whatever, and the said Walter SMITH for himself and heirs Covenants and agrees to and with William BANTEN his heirs and Executors the said Negro Man against the Right title and claim of every person and persons whatever, forever to warrant and defend and the said Walter further Covenants for himself theirs in case the af[oresai]d fellow **Bob** should escape from the Jail af[oresai]d before the said before the said BANTEN or some person for him and in his name takes possession of the said Negro that then and in succession he will repay the said BANTEN and above mentioned with Interest from the date hereof or Order the Sum of Money af[oresai]d. In Witness whereof I have hereto set my hand and Seal, affixed this 5th day of July Anno Dom[ini] 1797

Sign[e]d Se[ale]d & del[ivere]d in   Walter SMITH   (Seal)
presence of   Philip QUINTON"

*followed on folio 606 with the acknowledgment by Justice of the Peace Philip QUINTON and the recordation by court clerk John C. HANDY[783]

Liber R, folios 606-607; 05 July 1797

"Worcester County Maryland Sc[t]. Know all Men by these presents that I Walter SMITH of the County af[oresai]d and State of Maryland have Constituted made and appointed and by these presents do make Constitute and appoint my Good friend William BANTEN of Lincoln County of the State of Kentucke my true and lawful Attorney for me and in my name to ask demand and Receive all property of whatever kind that I may be entitled to as in any way have a Right to in the State of Kentucke but more especially my negro man **Bob** who agreeable to advices received is committed and Confined in Washington Jail in Mason County in the State of Kentucke hereby giving and granting unto my said Attorney by these presents my full and whole power strength and Authority in and about the premises to hand up and take all lawfull ways and means in my name for the Recovery thereof and upon the Receipt of the said Negro to give Acquittances or other Sufficient discharges for me and in my name and for me and in my name to do any and every Act or Acts device or devices in the law needfull and necessary to be done in or about the premisses and for me and in my name to do Execute and perform and fully and largely to all intents and purposes as I might or could do were I personally present or as if the matter required more especial authority than is hereby given Ratifying and Confirming

---

[782] Worcester County Court (Land Records). Bill of Sale from WISE, George K. to MARTIN, Levin. 21 June 1797. R, pp. 593-594, MSA CE 30-17. www.mdlandrec.net : accessed 11 May 2022.
[783] Worcester County Court (Land Records). Bill of Sale from SMITH, Walter to BANTEN, William. 05 July 1797. R, pp. 605-606, MSA CE 30-17. www.mdlandrec.net : accessed 11 May 2022.

all my said Attorney may do by virtue of the primisses by virtue hereof ~ In Witness whereof I have hereto set my hand and Seal affixed this 5th day of July Anno Dom[ini] 1797 ~

Seal[e]d & del[ivere]d   Thomas MARTIN   Walter SMITH   (Seal)
presence of   Philip QUINTON"

*followed on folio 607 with the acknowledgment by Justice of the Peace Philip QUINTON and the recordation by court clerk John C. HANDY[784]

Liber R, folios 615-616; 06 July 1797

"Know all Men by these presents that I McKimmy SCARBOROUGH of Worcester County and State of Maryland (Taylor) for and in Consideration of the Sum of fifty five pounds Current Money of Maryland to me in hand paid by John ATKINSON of the same place (planter) the Receipt whereof I the said SCARBOROUGH do hereby acknowledge and myself fully satisfied and deliver unto him the said John ATKINSON his heirs and assigns forever a certain negro Woman Slave called **Juda** about Seventeen years old now in the possession of the aforesaid ATKINSON ~ To have and to hold af[oresai]d Sold and delivered Negro Woman called **Juda** unto him the aforesaid John ATKINSON his heirs and Assigns forever and the said McKimmy SCARBOROUGH for himself his heirs Executors and Administrators doth hereby Covenant and agree that he and his his will and shall Warrant and forever defend the above bargained Negro Woman called **Juda** against the lawfull Right, title Claim or demand of all manner of person or persons whatsoever unto him the aforesaid John ATKINSON his heirs and assigns forever of which said Negro aforesaid I have put the said John ATKINSON in full possession by the delivery of these presents In Testimony whereof I the said McKimmy SCARBOROUGH to these presents my hand and Seal have set this Sixth day of July in the year One thousand Seven hundred and ninety Seven

Signed Sealed & delivered   McKimmy SCARBOROUGH   (Seal)
in the presence of   Philip QUINTON"

*followed on folio 616 with the acknowledgment by Justice of the Peace McKimmy SCARBOROUGH and the recordation by court clerk John C. HANDY[785]

Liber R, folios 621-622; 08 July 1797

"Worcester County to wit. Know all Men by these presents that I Edward SCARBOROUGH of the County af[oresai]d for the Consideration of the Sum of fifty pounds Current Money of Maryland to me in hand paid by John AYRES of the County af[oresai]d have given granted Sold and delivered possession of and by these presents do give grant Sell and deliver possession of One Negro Slave Named **Lidey** to the said John AYRES To have and to hold the said Slave **Lidey** unto the said John AYRES his Executors Adm[inistrato]rs and assigns forever to him and their only proper use benefit and behoof ~ In Witness whereof the said Edward SCARBOROUGH hereto hath affixed his hand and Seal this Eight day of July in the year Seventeen hundred and ninety Seven

Signed Sealed & delivered   John GUNBY   Edward SCARBOROUGH   (Seal)
in the presence of ~   George SELBY"

*followed on folio 622 with the acknowledgment by Justice of the Peace John GUNBY and the recordation on 14 July 1797 by court clerk John C. HANDY[786]

---

[784] Worcester County Court (Land Records). Power of Attorney from SMITH, Walter to BANTEN, William. 05 July 1797. R, pp. 606-607, MSA CE 30-17. www.mdlandrec.net : accessed 11 May 2022.
[785] Worcester County Court (Land Records). Bill of Sale from SCARBOROUGH, McKimmy to ATKINSON, John. 06 July 1797. R, pp. 615-616, MSA CE 30-17. www.mdlandrec.net : accessed 11 May 2022.
[786] Worcester County Court (Land Records). Bill of Sale from SCARBOROUGH, Edward to AYRES, John. 08 July 1797. R, pp. 621-622, MSA CE 30-17. www.mdlandrec.net : accessed 11 May 2022.

Liber R, folio 622; 08 July 1797

"Worcester County to wit Know all Men by these presents that I Edward SCARBOROUGH of Worcester County for the Consideration of the sum of Ten Shillings Current Money of Maryland to me in hand paid by Johnson HILL of County af[oresai]^d have given granted Sold and delivered possession of and by these presents do give grant and Sell and deliver possession of One Negro Slave Child Named **Harry** to the said Johnson HILL, To have and to hold the said Slave **Harry** unto the said Johnson HILL his Executors Adm[inistrato]^{rs} and assigns forever to him and their only proper use benefit and behoof ~ In Witness whereof the said Edward SCARBOROUGH hereto hath affixed his hand and Seal this Eight day of July in the year Seventeen hundred and Ninety Seven ~

Signed Sealed & delivered	J[oh]n GUNBY	Edward SCARBOROUGH (Seal)
in the presents of	John AYRES"	

*followed with the acknowledgment by Justice of the Peace John GUNBY and the recordation on 14 July 1797 by court clerk John C. HANDY[787]

Liber R, folios 623-624; 14 July 1797

"To all persons to whom these presents shall come Know ye that Whereas I William UNDRILL of Worcester County in the State of Maryland am desirous to Manumit Negro Woman Named **Flora** as well for and in Consideration of past Service as for sundry other good Causes and Considerations me hereunto moving I do hereby accordingly Manumit set free and forever discharge from Slavery from myself and my heirs the af[oresai]^d Negro Woman **Flora** ~ To have and to hold to her the af[oresai]^d **Flora** free her freedom af[oresai]^d from all Molestation Let or Interruption whatever from me my heirs Executors and Adm[inistrato]^{rs} forever ~ In Witness whereof I have hereto set my hand and affixed my Seal this 14th day of July Anno Dom[ini] Seventeen hundred and ninety Seven

Signed Sealed & delivered	John PURNELL	William UNDRILL (Seal)
in presence of	G.W. PURNELL"	

*followed on folio 624 with the acknowledgment by Justice of the Peace Elisha PURNELL and the recordation on 15 July 1797 by court clerk John C. HANDY[788]

Liber R, folios 624-625; 21 July 1797

"Know all Men by these presents that I Charles BENNETT of Worcester County and State of Maryland for and in Consideration of the Sum of Sixty One pounds fifteen Shillings Current Money of Maryland to me in hand paid by Lemuel SELBY of the same place at and before the Sealing and delivery hereof the receipt whereof I do hereby acknowledge & Confess have granted Sold and delivered and by these presents doth absolutely bargain sell and deliver unto him the said Lemuel SELBY his heirs and Assigns forever a certain Negro Boy called **Eben**, about the age of twelve years now in Worcester County af[oresai]^d BENNETTs ~ To have and to hold the aforesaid Negro boy called **Eben** hereby bargained Sold and delivered this day unto him the aforesaid Lemuel SELBY his heirs and Assigns forever, to the only proper use benefit and behoof of him the aforesaid Lemuel SELBY his heirs and assigns forever and the said Charles BENNETT for himself his heirs, Executors and Administrators will and Shall warrant and forever defend the aforesaid Bargained Negro Boy ag[ains]^t the lawfull Claim or Claims of all manner of person or persons whatever of which said Bargained and delivered Negro Boy called **Eben** I the said Charles BENNITT have put the said Lemuel SELBY in full possession by the delivery of these presents ~ In Testimony whereof I the said Charles BENNITT to these

---

[787] Worcester County Court (Land Records). Bill of Sale from SCARBOROUGH, Edward to HILL, Johnson. 08 July 1797. R, p. 622, MSA CE 30-17. www.mdlandrec.net : accessed 11 May 2022.

[788] Worcester County Court (Land Records). Deed of Manumission from UNDRILL, William to **Flora**. 14 July 1797. R, pp. 623-624, MSA CE 30-17. www.mdlandrec.net : accessed 11 May 2022.

presents my hand hath Set and Seal affixed this 21st of July in the year Seventeen hundred and Ninety Seven

Signed Sealed & delivered   John COTTINGHAM   Charles BENNITT   (Seal)
in the presence of   Jesse BENNITT"

*followed on folio 625 with the acknowledgment by Justices of the Peace Jesse BENNITT and John COTTINGHAM and the recordation on 21 July 1797 by court clerk John C. HANDY[789]

Liber R, folios 629-630; 20 July 1797

"State of Maryland Worcester County Know all Men by these presents that I John SCARBOROUGH Sen[io]^r of the County and State af[oresai]^d for an in Consideration of the Sum of twenty pounds Current money of Maryland to me in hand paid by Arthur ROWLEY of the same place at and before the Sealing and delivery of these presents have granted bargained and delivered unto the said Arthur ROWLEY and Bettey his Wife and their heirs and assigns forever One Negro Boy called **Levin** now in the possession of said Arthur ROLEY To have and to hold the said Negro **Levin** unto him the said Arthur ROWLEY and Bettey his Wife and to their heirs and assigns forever to the only proper use and benefit of him the said Arthur and Bettey his Wife and to their heirs and Assigns forever and the said John SCARBOROUGH for himself his heirs Executors & Administrators the said bargained sold and delivered Negro Boy called **Levin** af[oresai]^d will and shall forever Warrant and defend against the Right title claim of all manner of persons whatsoever of which said Negro Boy called **Levin** I the said John SCARBOROUGH have put the said Arthur ROLEY and Wife in full possession by the delivery hereof ~ In Testimony hereof I the said John SCARBOROUGH have hereunto set my hand and Seal this twenty day of July 1797 ~

Signed Sealed acknowledged & delivered   Jesse BENNITT   Jno. SCARBOROUGH   (Seal)
in the presents of ~   Nancy BENNITT"

*followed on folio 630 with the acknowledgment by Justice of the Peace Jesse BENNITT and the recordation on 28 July 1797 by court clerk John C. HANDY[790]

Liber R, folios 630-631; 22 July 1797

"State of Maryland Worcester County Know all Men by these presents that I John STURGIS of Worcester County in the State of Maryland for and in consideration of the Sum of twenty five pounds Current Money of the State af[oresai]^d to me in hand paid by John ALLEN of the State and County aforesaid at or before the Sealing and delivery of these presents the receipt whereof I the said John STURGIS do hereby acknowledge have granted bargained and sod and by these presents do grant bargain and Sell unto the said John ALLEN his heirs Ex[ecuto]^{rs} Adm[inistrato]^{rs} and Assigns One Negro Boy Aged about Seven years and called **Patrick** ~ To have and to hold to possess and enjoy the said bargained and Sold Negro Boy called **Patrick** and the said John ALLEN his heirs Ex[ecuto]^{rs} Adm[inistrato]^{rs} and assigns forever and the said John STURGIS for myself my heirs Executors & Administrators the said Negro Boy called **Patrick**, unto the said John ALLEN his Ex[ecuto]^{rs} Adm[inistrato]^{rs} and assigns against me the said John STURGIS my heirs Ex[ecuto]^{rs} Adm[inistrato]^{rs} and Assigns against all and every other person and persons whatever shall and will warrant and forever defend, In Witness whereof I the said John STURGIS have hereunto my hand set and Seal affixed this 22^d day of July 1797

Signed Sealed & delivered   John HOLLAND   John STURGIS   (Seal)
in the presence of ~"

---

[789] Worcester County Court (Land Records). Bill of Sale from BENNITT, Charles to SELBY, Lemuel. 21 July 1797. R, pp. 624-625, MSA CE 30-17. www.mdlandrec.net : accessed 11 May 2022.

[790] Worcester County Court (Land Records). Bill of Sale from SCARBOROUGH, John Sr. to ROWLEY, Arthur and Bettey. 20 July 1797. R, pp. 629-630, MSA CE 30-17. www.mdlandrec.net : accessed 11 May 2022.

*followed on folio 631 with the acknowledgment by Justice of the Peace John HOLLAND and the recordation on 28 July 1797 by court clerk John C. HANDY[791]

Liber R, folio 632; 01 August 1797

"The State of Maryland Worcester County Sc^t. Know all Men by these presents that I George ROSSE of Snow Hill Maryland hereby Certify that for a Valuable Sum of Money and in consideration of Affection to my Mother in law Elizabeth ROSSE I Sold to her a Negro Girl called **Alce** who was bequeathed to myself as a Legatee of my Uncle William ALLEN Esquire dec[ease]^d part of whose personal Estate the said Negro Girl was and that she was raised by him ~ In consequence whereof I have hereunto set my hand and Seal below, and also hereby know ye that I Elizabeth ROSSE af[oresai]^d for and in Consideration of the Son's af[oresai]^d assumption to me this day on behalf of James McFADDEN of Snow Hill af[oresai]^d I do hereby release to James McFADDEN af[oresai]^d the price of a Negro Girl called **Alce** agreeable to the Condition of a Bond by him possed to my Son George ROSSE for the amount and Assign and set over to him his heirs Executors Adm[inistrato]^{rs} and Assigns all my Right and title in and to **Alce** the Negro Girl af[oresai]^d now supposed to be about fourteen years old or thereabouts ~ In Evidence whereof we have hereunto set Our hands & affixed Our Seals this first day of August 1797 ~

*followed with the acknowledgment by Justice of the Peace Benjamin DENNIS and the recordation court clerk John C. HANDY[792]

Liber R, folios 654-655; 19 August 1797

"Know all Men by these presents that I Jackson TURNER of Worcester County in the State of Maryland for and in Consideration of the Sum of One hundred pounds Current Money of Maryland to me in hand paid by Levin TOWNSEND of the County and State af[oresai]^d at and before the sealing and delivery hereof I the said Jackson TURNER have bargained Sold and delivered and by these presents doth absolutely bargain Sell and deliver unto him the said Levin TOWNSEND his heirs and Assigns forever One Negro Man by the name of **Ben** formerly the property of George TURNER deceased and taken by Order of the Orphans Court of Worcester by the said Jackson TURNER as Surety for the said George TURNER in Worcester County now in possession of the said Jackson TURNER To have and to hold the above mentioned Sold and delivered Negro Man **Ben** hereby intended to be Sold unto him the said Levin TOWNSEND and to his heirs Executors and Administrators & Assigns forever to the only proper use benefit and behoof of him the said Levin TOWNSEND and his heirs and Assigns forever and the said Jackson TURNER for himself and his heirs Executors and Administrators and every of them and against every person or persons whatever and shall forever Warrant and defend the above mentioned bargained & Sold Negro **Ben** unto him the said Levin TOWNSEND his heirs and assigns forever of which said Negro **Ben** I the said Jackson TURNER have put the said Levin TOWNSEND in full possession of by the delivery of the above mentioned Negro **Ben** ~ In Testimony whereof I the said Jackson TURNER have hereto set my hand and affixed my Seal the Nineteenth day of August Anno Dom[ini] One thousand seven hundred and ninety seven

Signed Sealed & delivered   Jackson TURNER (Seal)
in the presence of   Philip QUINTON"

*followed with the acknowledgment by Justice of the Peace Philip QUINTON and the recordation by court clerk John C. HANDY[793]

---

[791] Worcester County Court (Land Records). Bill of Sale from STURGIS, John to ALLEN, John. 22 July 1797. R, pp. 630-631, MSA CE 30-17. www.mdlandrec.net : accessed 11 May 2022.

[792] Worcester County Court (Land Records). Bill of Sale from ROSSE, George to ROSSE, Elizabeth. 01 August 1797. R, p. 632, MSA CE 30-17. www.mdlandrec.net : accessed 11 May 2022.

[793] Worcester County Court (Land Records). Bill of Sale from TURNER, Jackson to TOWNSEND, Levin. 19 August 1797. R, pp. 654-655, MSA CE 30-17. www.mdlandrec.net : accessed 11 May 2022.

Liber S, folios 2-3; 11 August 1797

"Know all Men by these presents that I Francis CRIPPS of Worcester County and State of Maryland for and in consideration of the Sum of two hundred and forty Seven pounds ten Shillings Current Money of Maryland to him in hand paid by James DUER of the same place the receipt whereof is hereby acknowledged and confessed, I the said Francis CRIPPS have bargained Sold and delivered and by these presents doth absolutely bargain Sell and deliver unto him the said James DUER his heirs and Assigns forever the following Negroes Slaves to wit, One Negro called **Nell**, One Negro **Levi**, One Negro called **Nance**, One Negro called **Stephen**, One Negro called **Rachell**, One Negro called **Benn** & One Negro called **Bobb** all in the County afo[resai]^d, together with all their increase, hire and Services. To have and to hold all and singular the above named and mentioned Seven Negroes hereby Sold and delivered unto him the said James DUER his heirs and Assigns forever to the only proper use benefit and behoof of him the said James DUER his heirs and Assigns forever, And the said Francis CRIPPS for himself his heirs Executors and Administrators doth hereby Covenant Grant and agree, that he and his heirs will and shall warrant and forever defend the aforesaid Seven Negro Slaves against the lawful right title claim and demand of all manner of person or persons whatever unto him the said James DUER his heirs and Assigns forever, of which said Seven Negroes, by Name, have put the said James DUER in full possession by the delivery of these presents. In Witness whereof I the said Francis CRIPPS to these presents my hand hath set and Seal affixed this Eleventh day of August in the year One thousand Seven hundred and ninety Seven ~

Signed Sealed & delivered   Fran[ci]^s CRIPPS   (Seal)
in the presence of ~   Philip QUINTON"

*followed on folio 3 with the acknowledgment by Justice of the Peace Philip QUINTON and the recordation on 23 August 1797 by court clerk John C. HANDY[794]

Liber S, folios 14-15; 03 September 1797

"This Indenture Witnesseth that I **George BLAKE** (free Mulatto) for and in Consideration of the Sum of Twenty pounds to me in hand paid by Joseph DELASTATIUS, do hereby bind and put myself under the said Joseph DELASTATIUS as a Servant for the terms of Eighteen Months, to commence on the third day of September Instant and to end on the third day of March One thousand Seven hundred and ninety nine, and for and during the time af[oresai]^d as a Servant will well and faithfully serve the said Joseph DELASTATIUS his Ex[ecuto]^{rs} Adm[inistrato]^{rs} or Assigns his lawful Commands gladly Obey and the Goods of the said Joseph will not embezzle or waste nor absent myself without the leave of the said Joseph or his Ex[ecuto]^{rs} Adm[inistrato]^{rs} or Assigns and as a good faithful Servant will demean and behave himself towards my said Master and all his during the time af[oresai]^d and for the true and faithful performance whereof and every part of the said Articles In the said **George BLAKE** do bind myself my heirs Executors and Adm[inistrato]^{rs} unto the said Joseph in the penal Sum of five hundred pounds current Money provided that if I the said **George BLAKE** do well and truly pay unto the said Joseph the Am[oun]^t of all the fines fees and charges that the said Joseph have Assumed and became Security to pay for me on Acc[oun]^t of my conviction at last August Court & Commitment in consequence thereof or upon my indemnifying him from paying the same and all expences and Costs that ever may come ag[ains]^t him or Acc[oun]^t of becoming Security for me by giving him Bond and such Security as he shall approve then this Indenture to be void and of none effect ~ As Witness my hand and Seal this third day September Anno Dom[ini] 1797 ~

---

[794] Worcester County Court (Land Records). Bill of Sale from CRIPPS, Francis to DUER, James. 11 August 1797. S, pp. 2-3, MSA CE 30-18. www.mdlandrec.net : accessed 29 May 2022.

Signed Sealed & delivered in presence of ~	W[illia]^m WHITTINGTON	George + BLAKE (Seal) (his Mark)

*followed on folio 15 with the acknowledgment by Justice of the Peace Elisha PURNELL and the recordation on 08 September 1797 by court clerk John C. HANDY[795]

Liber S, folios 15-16; 09 September 1797

"Know all Men by these presents that we Nancy KILLIAM Widow of Isaac Josiah BRATTEN & Samuel BRATTEN all of Worcester County and State of Maryland for and in consideration of the Sum of Seventy five pounds Current Money of Maryland to them in hand paid by Thomas VICTOR of the County and State af[oresai]^d at and before the Sealing and delivery of these presents the Receipt whereof we do hereby acknowledge have given granted bargained and sold and by these presents do give grant bargain and Sell and deliver unto the said Thomas VICTOR his heirs Ex[ecuto]^rs Adm[inistrato]^rs One negro Man named **Ben** ~ To have & to hold the above bargained and Sold Negro called **Ben** to him the said Thomas VICTOR and to his heirs and Assigns forever to the only proper use benefit and behoof of him the said Thomas VICTOR his heirs and Assigns forever of which property we the said Nancy KILLAIM, Josiah BRATTEN & Samuel BRATTEN do put the af[oresai]^d Thomas VICTOR in full possession of and do hereby forever warrant and defend the af[oresai]^d bargained and Sold Negro W̶o̶man **Ben** unto the said Thomas VICTOR his heirs and assigns forever from all manner persons now claiming or hereafter to claim any right title or Interest therein to the said Negro **Ben** In Witness whereof the said parties do hereto sett their hands and Seals affixed the 9th day September 1797 ~

Signed Sealed & delivered in presence of ~ ~ ~	John CUTLER	Nancy X KILLAM (Seal) (her mark)
		Josiah BRATTEN (Seal)
		Samuel BRATTEN (Seal)"

*followed on folio 16 with the acknowledgment by Justice of the Peace Philip QUINTON and the recordation on 11 September 1797 by court clerk John C. HANDY[796]

Liber S, folios 18-19; 15 September 1797

"Know all Men by these presents that I William SELBY (Son of Zadok) of Worcester County and State of Maryland for and in Consideration of the Sum of thirty Seven pounds ten Shillings Current Money of Maryland to him in hand paid by Henry SMOCK of the same place at and before the Sealing & delivery of these presents the receipt whereof is hereby confessed and acknowledged, hath granted Sold and delivered and by these presents doth hereby bargain Sell and deliver unto him the said Henry SMOCK his heirs and Assigns forever, a certain Negro Boy called and known by the name of **Jack** about nine years old now in the possession of the aforesaid Henry SMOCK To have and to hold the aforesaid bargained and Sold Negro **Jack** unto him the said Henry SMOCK his heirs and Assigns forever to the only proper use benefit and behoof of him the said Henry SMOCK his heirs and assigns forever And the said William SELBY for himself his heirs Ex[ecuto]^rs and Adm[inistrato]^rs, The aforesaid bargained Sold and delivered Negro **Jack** will and shall forever Warrant and defend the same, against the lawful claimed right or demand of all manner of person or persons whatever unto him the said Henry SMOCK and his heirs and assigns forever, of which said Negro **Jack** I the said William SELBY have put the said Henry SMOCK in full possession by the delivery of these presents In Testimony whereof I the said William SELBY to these presents have set my hand and affixed

---

[795] Worcester County Court (Land Records). Deed of Indenture from **BLAKE, George** to DELASTATIUS, Joseph. 03 September 1797. S, pp. 14-15, MSA CE 30-18. www.mdlandrec.net : accessed 29 May 2022.

[796] Worcester County Court (Land Records). Bill of Sale from KILLAM, Nancy, BRATTEN, Josiah, and BRATTEN, Samuel to VICTOR, Thomas. 09 September 1797. S, pp. 15-16, MSA CE 30-18. www.mdlandrec.net : accessed 29 May 2022.

my Seal this fifteenth day of September in the year One thousand Seven hundred and ninety Seven ~

Signed Sealed & delivered   William SELBY (Seal)
in the presence of   Jesse BENNITT"

*followed with the acknowledgment by Justice of the Peace Jesse BENNITT and the recordation by court clerk John C. HANDY[797]

*The acknowledgment refers to "the Negro Boy called **John** or **Jack**…".

Liber S, folios 19-20; 15 September 1797

"Know all Men by these presents that I Joseph KILLAM of Worcester County and State of Maryland for and in consideration of Seventy five pounds ten Shillings of the State af[oresai]^d to me in hand paid by Samuel BISHOP of the same place at and before the Sealing and delivery of these presents have granted bargained Sold and delivered unto the af[oresai]^d Samuel BISHOP and his heirs and Assigns forever One Negro Man called **Bill** alias **Will** now in the possession of said Samuel BISHOP To have & to hold the said Negro called **Bill** unto the said Samuel BISHOP and his heirs and assigns forever to the only proper use and benefit and behoof of him the said Samuel and his heirs and assigns forever and the said Joseph KILLAM for himself and his heirs Ex[ecuto]^{rs} Adm[inistrato]^{rs} the af[oresai]^d bargained Sold and delivered Negro called **Bill** will and shall forever Warrant and defend against the Right title claim or Interest of all manner of persons whatsoever of which said Negro I the said Joseph KILLAM have put the said Samuel BISHOP in full possession by the delivery hereof ~ In Testimony hereof I the said Joseph KILLAM have hereunto set my hand and Seal this 15th day of September 1797

Signed Sealed & delivered   Jesse BENNITT   Joseph KILLAM (Seal)
in the presence of   Test.   [?] Nicl WISE"

*followed with the acknowledgment by Justice of the Peace Jesse BENNITT and the recordation by court clerk John C. HANDY[798]

Liber S, folios 31-32; 23 September 1797

"State of Maryland Worcester County Know all Men by these presents that I William BENNITT (Sea Side) of Worcester County and State af[oresai]^d for and in Consideration of the Sum of thirty seven pounds ten Shillings Current Money of Maryland to me in hand paid by Stephen ALLEN of the State & County af[oresai]^d at or before the Sealing and delivery of these presents the receipt whereof I the said William BENNITT do hereby acknowledge have granted bargained and Sold and by these presents do bargain and Sell unto the said Stephen ALLEN his heirs Executors Adm[inistrato]^{rs} and assigns the property herein mentioned that is to say ~ One Negro Girl named **Dianna** aged about sixteen years, and one Bay mare about two years Old. To have and to hold all & singular the said property above bargained and Sold or intended so to be the said Stephen ALLEN his heirs and Assigns forever ~ and I the said W[illia]^m BENNITT for myself my heirs Executors Adm[inistrato]^{rs} and Assigns all and singular the said property unto the said Stephen ALLEN his heirs Ex[ecuto]^{rs} & Adm[inistrato]^{rs} will Warrant and forever defend by these presents which said Goods or property I the said William BENNITT have put the said Stephen ALLEN in full possession by delivering to him s[ai]^d ALLEN the above named negro Girl in the name of the whole property hereby bargained & Sold ~ In Witness whereof I the said William BENNITT have hereunto my hand set and seal affixed the twenty third day of September 1797 ~

---

[797] Worcester County Court (Land Records). Bill of Sale from SELBY, William to SMOCK, Henry. 15 September 1797. S, pp. 18-19, MSA CE 30-18. www.mdlandrec.net : accessed 29 May 2022.

[798] Worcester County Court (Land Records). Bill of Sale from KILLAM, Joseph to BISHOP, Samuel. 15 September 1797. S, pp. 19-20, MSA CE 30-18. www.mdlandrec.net : accessed 29 May 2022.

Signed Sealed & delivered   William BENNITT (Seal)
in the presence of ~   John HOLLAND"

*followed with the acknowledgment by Justice of the Peace John HOLLAND and the recordation on 28 September 1797 by court clerk John C. HANDY[799]

Liber S, folios 58-59; 07 October 1797

"Know all Men by these presents that I Silvanus Uriah ROBERTS of Worcester County for and in consideration of the Sum of One hundred and Sixty Eight pounds Current Money of Maryland to me in hand paid before the Sealing & delivery hereof by John WHITTINGTON the Receipt whereof I hereby acknowledge have bargained and Sold and by these presents do bargain & Sell unto the said John WHITTINGTON and to his heirs Executors and Administrators the following Articles to wit, One Negro Man named **Benjamin**, twenty head of Hogs, one other negro Man called **Derry**, all my Crop of Corn now growing and One Feather Bed and furniture and the Crop of Tobacco now Growing. To have and to hold the af[oresai]^d Articles to the said John WHITTINGTON and to his heirs and Assigns forever and it is hereby Covenanted and agreed between the said Silvanus Uriah ROBERTS & the said John WHITTINGTON their Executors & Administrators that if the said Sylvanus shall not pay unto the said John WHITTINGTON on or before the first day of January the Sum of One hundred and Sixty Eight pounds and three pence Current Money with legal Interest thereon from this date then the said John shall have full power and authority to sell at public Vendue the whole or so much of the aforesaid property as shall raise the af[oresai]^d Sum of money for ready Cash and if the said Sylvanus shall either pay to the said John the af[oresai]^d Sum of money or give him Bond with such Security as he shall approve of on or before the first day of January next then in that case this Bill of Sale is to be Void and of no Effect ~ As Witness my hand and Seal this Seventh day of October 1797

Signed Sealed and   Silvanus U. ROBERTS (Seal)
delivered before   Tho[ma]^s DIXON"

*followed with the acknowledgment by Justice of the Peace Thomas DIXON and the recordation on 12 October 1797 by court clerk John C. HANDY[800]

Liber S, folio 60; 07 October 1797

"Worcester Ss^t. Know all Men by these presents that I Silvanus U. ROBERTS of Worcester County in the State of Maryland for & in consideration of the Sum of Seventy pounds to me in hand paid by David SMITH the Ensealing and delivering and hereof the receipt whereof I do hereby acknowledge hath granted bargained and Sold and by these presents do Grant bargain & Sell unto David SMITH his heirs and assigns forever One Negro Man called **Benjamin** and the said Silvanus U. ROBERTS doth forever for himself and his heirs Covenant to and with the said David SMITH that he the said Sylvanus u. ROBERTS the negro **Benjamin** above mentioned will warrant and forever defend from all persons whatever claiming any Right title unto the said Negro ~ In Witness whereof I do hereby set my hand and Seal this 7th day of October 1797

Sealed & delivered   Silvanus U. ROBERTS (Seal)
in the presents of   Tho[ma]^s DIXON"

*followed with the acknowledgment by Justice of the Peace Thomas DIXON and the recordation on 12 October 1797 by court clerk John C. HANDY[801]

---

[799] Worcester County Court (Land Records). Bill of Sale from BENNITT, William to ALLEN, Stephen. 23 September 1797. S, pp. 31-32, MSA CE 30-18. www.mdlandrec.net : accessed 29 May 2022.

[800] Worcester County Court (Land Records). Bill of Sale from ROBERTS, Silvanus Uriah to WHITTINGTON, John. 07 October 1797. S, pp. 58-59, MSA CE 30-18. www.mdlandrec.net : accessed 29 May 2022.

[801] Worcester County Court (Land Records). Bill of Sale from ROBERTS, Silvanus Uriah to SMITH, David. 07 October 1797. S, p. 60, MSA CE 30-18. www.mdlandrec.net : accessed 29 May 2022.

Liber S, folio 96; 22 November 1796

"Know all men by these presents that I Solomon PEPPER of Worcester County in the State of Maryland for and in Consideration of the sum of Thirty Pounds, of Lawfull money of Maryland to me in hand paid or secured to be paid by Saccar PEPPER of the County and State aforesaid Before the Sealing & Delivery of these presents the Receipt whereof I the said Solomon PEPPER Do hereby acknowledge have granted Bargained and sold and by these presents Do grant bargain & Sell unto the said Saccar PEPPER his Executors Adm[inistrato]rs & assigns ~ One Negro lad aged about Sixteen Years & called **Jack** To have and to hold to possess & Enjoy the s[ai]d Lad or Boy af[ore]s[ai]d after my death and not before & I the said Solomon PEPPER for myself my heirs Exe[cu]t[o]rs & Adm[inistrato]rs & assigns Do hereby Covenant and agree with the said Saccar PEPPER that I the said Solomon will against them Namely my heirs Ex[ecu]t[o]rs Adm[inistrato]rs & assigns & every other person Claiming any Right ~ or Title to the said Lad or Boy Called **Jack** Warrant & Defend him unto the said Saccar PEPPER his heirs & assigns forever In Testimony whereof I the said Solomon PEPPER hath hereunto my hand set & seal Affixed this 22d Day of November 1796 ~

Signed Sealed & Delivered
In the presence of ~
John HOLLAND

Solomon + PEPPER (Seal)
his mark"

*followed with the acknowledgment by Justice of the Peace John HOLLAND and the recordation on 08 February 1797 by court clerk John C. HANDY[802]

Liber S, folio 97; 10 November 1797

"Know all men by these presents that I Levin TOWNSEND of Worcester County and State of Maryland (Planter) for and in Consideration of the sum of Seventy five pounds Current money of Maryland to me in hand paid by Lemuel SELBY of the same place the receipt whereof I do hereby Acknowledge, Have bargained Sold and delivered and by these presents doth absolutely Bargain sell and deliver unto him the said Lemuel SELBY his heirs and Assigns forever, a Negro Man called **Adam** about the age of Eighteen years, old, late the Property taken by Fiera Facias, of the Sh[eri]ff of the County aforesaid and now in the possession of the aforesaid SELBY, To have and to hold the said Negro Man hereby sold and delivered unto him the said Lemuel SELBY his heirs and assigns forever, to the only proper use benefit and behoof of him the said Lemuel SELBY his heirs and assigns forever. And the said Levin TOWNSEND for himself his heirs Executors and administrators the aforesaid negro called **Adam**, will and shall warrant and forever defend against the Lawfull right Title claim and demand of all manner of person or persons whatever unto him the aforesaid Lemuel SELBY his heirs and assigns forever, Of which said negro I have put the said SELBY in full possession by the delivery of these presents, In Testimony whereof I the said Levin TOWNSEND to these presents my hand hath set and seal Affixed this tenth day of November in the year One thousand seven hundred and ninety seven ~ ~

Signed Sealed and Delivered
In the presents of ~ ~
Benjamin DENNIS

Levin + TOWNSEND (Seal)
his mark"

*followed with the acknowledgment by Justice of the Peace Benjamin DENNIS and the recordation on 24 November 1797 by court clerk John C. HANDY[803]

---

[802] Worcester County Court (Land Records). Bill of Sale from PEPPER, Solomon to PEPPER, Saccar. 22 November 1796. S, p. 96, MSA CE 30-18. www.mdlandrec.net : accessed 29 May 2022.

[803] Worcester County Court (Land Records). Bill of Sale from TOWNSEND, Levin to SELBY, Lemuel. 10 November 1797. S, p. 97, MSA CE 30-18. www.mdlandrec.net : accessed 29 May 2022.

Liber S, folio 107; 07 December 1797

"This Indenture made this 7th day of December One Thousand Seven hundred and Ninety seven Witnesseth that I **George BLAKE** Sen[io]r free Molatto for and in consideration of the sum of fifteen pounds to be paid by Mr John ROCK to me or for my use, I do hereby indent and put and bind myself as a servant unto the said John ROCK his Executors Administrators & assigns for the space of one year fully to be complete and ended to commence on the day of the date hereof; and I the said **George** do covenant and agree for myself my heirs Executors & administrators & to & with the said John ROCK his Executors Adm[inistrato]rs & assigns faithfully and dutifully to serve him the said John ROCK his Executors Adm[inistrato]rs or assigns as a Servants, his commands & orders will willingly & Obediently Observe, will not embezzle his property nor will I absent myself from his or their service without leave first had & obtained from him or them, And for the true & faithfull performance whereof and every part thereof I bind myself my heirs Ex[ecuto]rs Adm[inistrato]rs unto the said John ROCK his Executors Adm[inistrato]rs and assigns in the penal sum of fifty pounds current money. In Testimony whereof I have hereto set my hand & seal affixed the Day and year first above written ~

Sealed & delivered	The word Sen[io]r	
In presence of	interlined before	George + **BLAKE** Sen[ior] (Seal)
Philip QUINTON	Execution ~ ~	his mark"

*followed with the acknowledgment by Justice of the Peace Philip QUINTON and the recordation by court clerk John C. HANDY[804]

Liber S, folio 108; (day unknown) November 1797

"Worcester County Sst. Know all men by these presents that we Betsey WISE and George Ker WISE both of the County af[ore]s[ai]d and State of Maryland for and in consideration of the sum of Fifty pounds to us in hand paid the receipt whereof we do hereby acknowledge, have bargained and sold and by these presents doth bargain and sell unto Levin MARTIN his heirs and assigns forever One Negro boy named **Ephraim** To have and to hold the af[ore]s[ai]d Negro Boy **Ephraim** to the said Levin MARTIN his heirs and assigns forever to the only proper use and behoof of the said Levin MARTIN his heirs and assigns forever, to the only proper use and behoof of the said Levin MARTIN his heirs and assigns and to no other intent or purpose whatever and they the said Betsey WISE and George K WISE covenants further the af[ore]s[ai]d Negro Boy **Ephraim** against the title claim & right of all and every person or persons whatever to warrant and defend, And they further covenant to make any further assureance or assureances for the af[ore]s[ai]d Negro Boy **Ephraim** (by bill of Sale or otherwise) Such as may be devised or required by those learned in Law at anytime when required by the said Levin MARTIN ~ In Testimony whereof we have hereunto set our hands and Seals affixed this   day of   Anno Dom[ini] 1797

Signed Sealed & delivered	Betty M WISE (Seal)
In presence of ~	George K WISE (Seal)
J[oh]n GUNBY ~"	

*followed with the acknowledgment by Justice of the Peace John GUNBY on 27 November 1797 and the recordation by court clerk John C. HANDY on 08 December 1797[805]

*The acknowledgment refers to the grantors as "Elizabeth WISE and George WISE".

---

[804] Worcester County Court (Land Records). Indenture from **BLAKE, George Sr.** to ROCK, John. 07 December 1797. S, p. 107, MSA CE 30-18. www.mdlandrec.net : accessed 29 May 2022.

[805] Worcester County Court (Land Records). Bill of Sale from WISE, Betsey and WISE, George Ker to MARTIN, Levin. November 1797. S, p. 108, MSA CE 30-18. www.mdlandrec.net : accessed 29 May 2022.

Liber S, folios 121-122; 09 November 1793

"Know all men by these presents that we John HOLLAND William HOLLAND Nehemiah HOLLAND Thomas HOLLAND and Peter HOLLAND of Worcester County in the State of Maryland are held and firmly bound unto Scarboroug HOLLAND of the County and State aforesaid in the sum of one thousand pounds of Good and Lawful money of Maryland to be paid to the said Scarborough HOLLAND to which payment well and truly to be made we bind our Selves and every of us for and in the whole our heirs Executors and administrators and of every of us firmly by these presents Sealed with our Seals and Dated this the Ninth Day of November one thousand seven Hundred and ninety three ~ ~ The Condition of the above obligation is such that if the above Bound John HOLLAND William HOLLAND Nehemiah HOLLAND Thomas HOLLAND and Peter HOLLAND there heirs and assigns do well and Truly Give up and peaceably Deliver unto there mother Scarborough HOLLAND in Case she should be a widow the second Time from a Marriage intended between s[ai]^d scarbrough HOLLAND & Co^{lo}[nel] Peter CHAILLE all that Personal property given to her said sons by a Deed of gift bearing Date of our mother scarbrough HOLLAND to Deliver peaceably to Anne WALLOP one Negro woman Called **Dorcos** & two Boys called **sam** & **harry** & two feather Beds & Eight haed Cattle a Large Looking Glass & a Chest & Drawers & half a Dozen table spoons the above specified articles of property to be the right & Title of Anne WALLOP her heirs and assigns forever then the above obligation to be void otherwise of virtue of in Law

Outten STURGIS	signed sealed in	Jno. HOLLAND (Seal)
Benjamin DENNIS	presence of us	W[illia]^m HOLLAND (Seal)
		Nehemiah HOLLAND (Seal)
		Thomas HOLLAND (Seal)
		Peter HOLLAND (Seal)"

*followed on folio 122 with the acknowledgment by Justice of the Peace Philip QUINTON on 15 December 1797 and the recordation by court clerk John C. HANDY[806]

Liber S, folios 134-135; 22 December 1797

"State of Maryland Worcester County Know all men by these Presents that I John SCARBOROUGH Sen[io]^r of the County and State af[ore]s[ai]^d for an in consideration of the Sum of forty Pounds Current money of Maryland to me in hand paid by Arthur ROLEY of the same Place at and before the Sealing and delivery of these Presents have granted Bargained and delivered unto the af[ore]s[ai]d Arthur ROWLEY and his Heirs and Assigns for Ever one Negro woman called **Sarah** now in the possession of the said Arthur ROLEY. To have and to Hold the said Negro **Sarah** unto him the said Arthur ROWLEY his Heirs and Assigns for Ever to the only Proper use benefit and behoof of him the said Arthur ROWLEY his heis and Assigns for Ever and the said John SCARBOROUGH for Him Self his Heirs Executors and Adm[inistrato]^{rs} the af[ore]s[ai]^d bargained Sold and Delivered Negro Woman Called **Sarah** will and Shall Warrant and for Ever defend against the Right and Title of all manner of Persons what so Ever of which Said Nigro **Sarah** I the said John SCARBOROUGH sen[io]^r Have Put the said Arthur ROWLEY in full Possession by the delivery hereof ~ In Testimoney Hereof I the said John SCARBOROUGH to these Presence my hand have set and seeal affixed this 28th day of December 1797.

Signed Seeleled acknowledged	Jesse BENNETT	Jon SCARBOROUGH (Seal)
and delivered in Presence off	James HINNAN"	

---

[806] Worcester County Court (Land Records). Bond from HOLLAND, John, William, Nehemiah, Thomas, and Peter to HOLLAND, Scarborough. 09 November 1793. S, pp. 121-122, MSA CE 30-18. www.mdlandrec.net : accessed 29 May 2022.

*followed with the acknowledgment by Justice of the Peace Jesse BENNETT and the recordation on folio 135 by court clerk John C. HANDY on 29 December 1797[807]

Liber S, folio 136; 09 December 1797

"Worcester County to wit Know all men by these Presents that I Tabitha SELBY of the County af[ore]s[ai]^d for the consideration of the Sum of Thirty Seven Pounds ten Shillings current money of maryland to me in hand Paid by Henry SMOCK of the County af[ore]s[ai]^d have given Granted Sold and delivered Possession of and by these Presents do give Grant & Sell and deliver Possession of one negro Slave named **John** to the Said Henry SMACK To Have and to Hold the said Slave **John** unto the said Henry SMACK his his Executors administrators and assigns for ever to him & their only Proper use benefit and behoof In Witness whereof the said Tabitha SELBY here to hath affixed her hand and Seal this ninth day of December in the year Seventeen hundred & ninty Seven

Signed Sealed & Delivered　　　　　　　　　　　　　　　　　Tabitha SELBY　(Seal)
in the Presents of . ~ ~/ ~/.　　John GUNBY"

*followed with the acknowledgment by Justice of the Peace John GUNBY and the recordation 25 December 1797 by court clerk John C. HANDY[808]

Liber S, folios 137-138; 26 December 1797

"K　all men by these presents that I George C WISE of Worcester County and State of Maryland for And in Consideration of the Sum of Eighty Pounds Current money of Maryland to me in hand paid by Patrick WALTERS (Senior) of the Same place at and Before the Sealing and delivery of these presents the Rec[ei]p^t Whereof I do hereby acknowledge have bargained & Sold and by these presents do Bargain and Sell unto the Said Patrick WALTERS his heirs and Assigns One Negroe Man named **Stephen** formerly the property of Capt[ain] Samuel WISE To have and to hold the said Negroe man named **Stephen** unto the Said Patrick WALTERS his heirs and Assigns forever & for no other use or Purpose Whatsoever; and the said Ge^o[rge] C WISE for himself and his heirs doth Covenant and agree to and with the said Patrick WALTERS that the said George C WISE hath a good and Sufficient title to Sell and dispose of the Said man named **Stephen** was to Convey unto the said Patrick WALTERS a good Sure & Sufficient Title to the same and that no person but the said Ge^o[rge] C WISE hath any right or title to the said Negro named **Stephen** In Testimoney whereof the Said Ge^o[rge] C WISE his hand to these presents hath set and Seal affixed this 26th day December one thousand Seven hundred & Ninty seven

Signed Sealed & Dele[vere]^d　　　　　　　　　　　　　　　George K WISE　(Seal)
in the Presents of ~ ~　　Thomas DIXON"

*followed on folio 138 with the acknowledgment by Justice of the Peace Thomas DIXON and the recordation on 29 December 1797 by court clerk John C. HANDY[809]

Liber S, folio 154; 16 January 1798

"Maryland Worcester Know all men by these Presents that I Edward SCARBOROUGH of Worcester County and State of Maryland for an In Consideration of the sum of Sixty five Pounds Current money of Maryland to me in hand paid by Isaack RIGGAN of Summersitt County at and before the Sealing and delivery of these Presents have Granted bargained & delivred unto the af[ore]s[ai]^d Isaac RIGGAN and his Heirs and Assgns for Ever one Negro woman Called **Lishe** now in the Possession of the said Isaac RIGGAN To Have and to Hold

---

[807] Worcester County Court (Land Records). Bill of Sale from SCARBOROUGH, John Sr. to ROWLEY, Arthur. 22 December 1797. S, pp. 134-135, MSA CE 30-18. www.mdlandrec.net : accessed 29 May 2022.
[808] Worcester County Court (Land Records). Bill of Sale from SELBY, Tabitha to SMACK, Henry. 09 December 1797. S, p. 136, MSA CE 30-18. www.mdlandrec.net : accessed 29 May 2022.
[809] Worcester County Court (Land Records). Bill of Sale from WISE, George K. to WALTERS, Patrick. 26 December 1797. S, pp. 137-138, MSA CE 30-18. www.mdlandrec.net : accessed 30 May 2022.

the said Negro woman **Lishe** unto him the said Isaac RIGGAN and his Heirs and Assigns for ever to the only Proper use of him the said Isaac RIGGAN & his heirs and assigns for ever and the said Edward SCARBOROUGH for himself & his Heirs Executors Adm[inistrato]rs the af[ore]s[ai]d Bargained Sold and delived Negro woman called **Lishe** will and Shall warrent and for Ever defend against the Right and title of all maner of Persons whatsoever of which said Nigro I the said Edward SCARBOROUGH have put the said Isaac RIGGON in full Possision by the delivery heareoff In Testiomoney hereof I the said Edward SCARBOROUGH have Sett my hand and Seeal this 16th day of January 1798

Signed Seealed and delivered   Edward SCARBOROUGH   (Seeal)
In Presence ~ ~ ~ ~ ~ ~ ~ ~   ~ ~ ~ ~ ~ ~ ~ ~ ~ ~ ~ ~ ~ ~
Jno SCARBOROUGH Sen[ior]
Jesse BENNETT"

*followed with the acknowledgment by Justice of the Peace Jesse BENNETT and the recordation by court clerk John C. HANDY[810]

Liber S, folios 155-156; 12 January 1798

"Know all men by these Presents that I Elizabeth VICTOR Relict of the Late Thomas VICTOR of the County of Worcester and State of Maryland for and In consideration of the sum of one Hundred pounds good and Lawful money of the said State To me in hand paid and Before the Sealing and Delivery of these presents By James VICTOR son of the Late Thomas VICTOR of the County of Worcester the Receipt whereof I do hereby acknowledge have Bargaind and Sold and By these presents do Bargain and sell unto the said James VICTOR all my Right Tittle and Intrest in Three negros named **Ceaser Rose** and **George** togeather with all the Increase of the said Negros and all other with which I am now Possess or in any Part Possess & with all my Right of all Negro flesh that I m at this Time in Possession of or may By theire Increase Be Intitled unto Hereafter with this Provisor that I hold my Third part of the said Negros during the term of my Natural Life and after my Decease my part to Remain to the above Named James VICTOR His Heirs and assigns for ever and the same to have and to hold all and singular each and every of them or there Increase as By these Presents are Barganed and sold unto the said James VICTOR his Heirs Executors Administrators and Assigns for ever Provided always that She said Elizabeth VICTOR shall hold all her Right and Title to the same Negros during the Term of her natural Life and After her Decease to the above named James VICTOR His Heirs and Assigns for ever and I the said Elizabeth VICTOR for myself my Executors and Administrators all & the said Negros and their Increase unto the said James VICTOR his Executors admenstrators and assigns against her the said Elizabeth VICTOR my Executors administrators and assigns and against all and every other person or Persons whatsoever shall and will for ever warrant and defend By these presents In Witness whereof I have to these Presents set my Hand and affixed my seal twelveth day of January in the year of our Lord Seventeen Hundred and Ninety Eight

Signed Sealed and Delivered   her
In Presence of us ~ ~ ~ ~   Elizabeth + VICTOR (Seal)
Moses PANK   mark
Joshua STURGES   NB the Date was enterned Before
          Her   Before acknowledged
Elizabeth + PANK   Benjamin DENNIS
          mark"

*followed with the acknowledgment by Justice of the Peace Benjamin DENNIS and the recordation on folio 156 on 16 January 1798 by court clerk John C. HANDY[811]

---

[810] Worcester County Court (Land Records). Bill of Sale from SCARBOROUGH, Edward to RIGGAN, Isaac. 16 January 1798. S, p. 154, MSA CE 30-18. www.mdlandrec.net : accessed 30 May 2022.

[811] Worcester County Court (Land Records). Bill of Sale from VICTOR, Elizabeth to VICTOR, James. 12 January 1798. S, pp. 155-156, MSA CE 30-18. www.mdlandrec.net : accessed 30 May 2022.

Liber S, folio 159; 09 January 1798

"State of Maryland Worcester County Know all men by these Presents that I Elenor FLEMMING Executrix of John FLEMMING late of Worcester County deceased for and in consederation of the sum of sixty five Pounds Current money of maryland to me in hand Paid the receipt Whereof I do hereby acknowledge have Bargained and Sold & by these Presents do Bargain and Sell unto Wheatly DENNIS one negro man Slave Called **Addam** to hve & to hold the aforesaid Slave Called **Adam** to the said Wheatly DENNIS his heirs and assigns forever to the only use and behoof of the said Wheatly DENNIS his heirs and assigns forever to the only use and behoof of the said Wheatly DENNIS his heirs and assigns forever and to no other Intent or Purpose whatsoever and it is father covenanted that the said Elenor FLEMMING for her self & her heirs the af[ore]s[ai]d Slave Called **Adam** the aforesaid Wheatly DENNIS his heirs or Assigns will for ever warrant and Defend in Witness Whereof I have hereunto Set my hand and Seal affixed this Ninth day of January Anno Domini one thousand seven hundred ninety I have hereunto Set my hand and Seal affixed this Ninth day of January Anno Domini one thousand seven hundred ninety Eight

Singned Sealed & Delevered   Elennor FLEMMING (Seal)
in Presents off ~
William Quinton DIXON
Philip QUINTON"

*followed with the acknowledgment by Justice of the Peace Philip QUINTON and the recordation on 19 January 1798 by court clerk John C. HANDY[812]

Liber S, folios 162-163; 20 January 1798

"Know all persons whome it may Concern that I John LAWES of Worcester and state of Maryland & for and in consideration of the some of three hundred pounds Current money of Maryland to me in hand paid by Thomas LAWES of Somersit County in state afforesaid the Receit thereof I do hereby acknowledge as Well the Love and affection that I Bair to him have Bargained Sold and Delivered and By these presents according to the Due form of Law do bargain sell and deliver unto the said Thom[a]s LAWES one Negro woman Called **Luse** on Negro Woman Called **Merier** one Negro Boy Called **Danniel** one Negro Boy Called **Prince** one Negro girl Called **mary** and ten head of Cattel one White mair Two sowes and five pigs one Chest of Drawes three Walnut Tables one small Round Cedar Table three Beds and ferniture Eight chairs with flaged Bottoms one safe one Corner Cubbard one gun Two Lining Wheels twelve Cups and sassers twenty four Earthen plates twelve puter plates fore puter Dishes four puter Basons Eight glass Tumblers one Walnut Chest there pine Chest Two plowes and two harrows and four grubing hoes four Weeding hoes and Two hundred Bushells of Corn and five axxes To have and to hold the said Bargained premises unto the said Thomas LAWES his heirs or Assigns Executors or administrators for ever and I the said John LAWES for my self my heirs Executors and administrators the said Bargained premises unto the said Thomas LAWES his heirs Executors Administrators or assigns against all Persons shall and will Will Warrent and for ever Defend By these presents aginst all persons whatsoever claiming the same By or under me or any part thereof in Witness whereof I have Set to these presents my hand and seal affixt this 20 Day of January Anno Domini one thousand seven hundred and Ninety Eight

Signed sealed and acknowledged   John LAWES (Seal)
In the presence of ~ ~ ~ ~ ~ ~ ~   ~ ~ ~ ~ ~ ~ ~ ~ ~ ~
Booz WALSTON"

---

[812] Worcester County Court (Land Records). Bill of Sale from FLEMMING, Elennor to DENNIS, Wheatly. 09 January 1798. S, p. 159, MSA CE 30-18. www.mdlandrec.net : accessed 30 May 2022.

*followed with the acknowledgment by Justice of the Peace Booz WALSTON and the recordation on 22 January 1798 by court clerk John C. HANDY[813]

Liber S, folios 164-165; 26 January 1798

"Know all men by these presents that I William MILBOURN of Worcester County for and in consideration of the sum of Eighty Eight pounds fifteen Shillings current money to him in hand paid by Edward HAMMOND the Receipt Whereof is hereby acknowledged have granted bargained & Sold and by these Presents do Grant bargain and Sell unto the said Edward HAMMOND his Executors administrators & assigns a Negro man Slave called **Peter** To have and to hold the said Negro man Slave called **Peter** unto the only proper use and behoof of him the said Edward HAMMOND his Executors Adm[inistrator]ˢ & assigns and the said William MILBOURN doth covenant and agree for himself his heirs Executors & administrators and to & with the said Edward HAMMOND his Executors and Administrators & assigns to Warrant and forever defend the said negro man Slave called **Peter** unto the said Edward HAMMOND his Executors Adm[inistrator]ˢ and assigns against the Right title & claim of him the said William MILBOURN & all others whatever In Testimony whereof I have hereto set my hand & Seal affixed this 26ᵗʰ day of January 1798

Signed Sealed and delivered   W[illia]ᵐ MILBOURN   (Seal)
In Presence of ~ ~ ~ ~ ~ ~ ~
the said negro man Slave called
Peter " interlined before Execution thereof
Edward HAMMOND junier
John BALL
Philip QUINTON"

*followed on folio 165 with the acknowledgment by Justice of the Peace Philip QUINTON and the recordation by court clerk John C. HANDY[814]

Liber S, folios 176-177; 06 January 1798

"Maryland Worcester Ssᵗ. Know all men by these presents that I William MORRIS of the County & State af[ore]s[ai]ᵈ for and in consideration of the Services already done and performed by the Negro **Saul** aged about thirty years, do hereby manumit free and forever discharge the said negro **Saul** from all future services from me and my Heirs To Have and to hold the said negro **Saul** his full and absolute Freedom and liberty forever In Testimony whereof I have hereto set my hand and annexed my Seal this 6ᵗʰ day of January Anno Domini Seventeen hundred & Ninety Eight

Signed Sealed and delivered   William MORRIS   (Seal)
In Presence of ~ ~ ~ ~
Witness Esme PURNELL"

*followed with the acknowledgment by Justice of the Peace Esme PURNELL and the recordation on folio 177 on 29 January 1798 by court clerk John C. HANDY[815]

Liber S, folios 194-195; 17 December 1797

"This Indenture made this 17ᵗʰ ~ day of December in the year of our Lord Seventeen Hundred and ninety Seven Between **George DELANY** of Worcester County in the State of Maryland of the one part and George SPENCE of the same place of the other part Witnesseth that the said **George DELANEY** for and in Consideration of the Sum of thirty pounds Current money of

---

[813] Worcester County Court (Land Records). Bill of Sale from LAWES, John to LAWES, Thomas. 20 January 1798. S, pp. 162-163, MSA CE 30-18. www.mdlandrec.net : accessed 30 May 2022.
[814] Worcester County Court (Land Records). Bill of Sale from MILBOURN, William to HAMMOND, Edward. 26 January 1798. S, pp. 164-165, MSA CE 30-18. www.mdlandrec.net : accessed 30 May 2022.
[815] Worcester County Court (Land Records). Deed of Manumission from MORRIS, William to **Saul**. 06 January 1798. S, pp. 176-177, MSA CE 30-18. www.mdlandrec.net : accessed 30 May 2022.

maryland to him in hand paid before the Ensealing and Delivery hereof ye Receipt whereof the said **George DELANEY** doth hereby acknowledge and thereof and every part thereof the said **George DELANY** doth Release exonerate and by these Presents forever discharge hath granted bargained and Sold and by these presents do grant bargin sell unto him the said George SPENCE the following Goods and Chattels Viz: one Cow two Bulls of two years old two Heifers three years old and two Calves & one other Heifer two years old together with household Goods and Farmers Utensils To Have and To Hold the said Goods & Chattels unto him the said George SPENCE his Executors Administrators and Assigns to the only proper use and Benefit and behoof of him the said George SPENCE his heirs Executors Administrators and assigns to and for no other use whatever Provided always and upon this Express Condition that the said **George DELANEY** Shall by himself his Heirs executors or administrators will acquit himself the said George SPENCE & and will warrant and defend the aforesaid property from all and every person Claiming aney right title on intrust in the same ~ Then this present instrument of writing and every thing therein contained to be void In Testimoney whereof the said **George DELANY** hath hereto set his hand and seal the day & year aforesaid

Signed Sealed & delivered
in Presence off ~ . . .   Benjamin DENNIS   **George** + **DELANY** (Seal)
                                                                his mark"

*followed with the acknowledgment by Justice of the Peace Benjamin DENNIS and the recordation on folio 195 by court clerk John C. HANDY on 09 February 1798[816]

Liber S, folios 209-210; 10 February 1798

"Worcester County Maryland State Know all Men by these Presents that we Samuel PARKER and Isaac VINSON both of the County and State af[oresai]^d have bargained and Sold and delivered and by these Presents do bargain Sell and deliver unto Spencer DAVIS Sen[io]^r of the same Place and State af[oresai]^d one Negro Woman named **Fortune** for and in Consideration of the Sum of Twenty Pounds Current money of Maryland in Hand paid before the signing Sealing and delivery hereof which Negro Woman in the said Sam[ue]^l PARKER and Isaac VINSON do dowary and defend against ourselves our Heirs Ex[ecuto]^{rs} Adm[inistrato]^{rs} or assigns and all other Persons Claiming any Right Title or Interest in or to said Negro Woman Called **Fortune** unto him the said Spencer DAVIS his Heirs Ex[ecuto]^{rs} Adm[inistrato]^{rs} or Assigns forever In Witness whereof we have hereunto set our Hands and Effixed our Seals this Tenth day of Feb[ruar]^y in the year of our Lord 1798.

Signed Sealed and Delivered   Booz WALSTON.   Samuel PARKER (Seal)
In the Presence of us . . . .   his
                                                         Isaac y VINSON (Seal)
                                                              mark"

*followed on folio 210 with the acknowledgment by Justice of the Peace Booz WALSTON and the recordation on 14 February 1798 by court clerk John C. HANDY[817]

Liber S, folios 212-213; 10 February 1798

"Maryland Ss^t. Know all Men by these Presents that I William BREUSTON of Worcester County for and in Consideration of the Sum of fifty Pounds Current Money of Maryland to me in hand paid the the Receipt whereof I do hereby acknowledge have bargained Sold and Conveyed unto Margaret PARSONS of the said County a negro Man about seventeen or eighteen Ears of age Called **Samson** hearby warranting & defending unto the said Margrat PARSONS a full good & sufficient Title to the said Negro **Samson** against all manner of

---

[816] Worcester County Court (Land Records). Bill of Sale from **DELANY, George** to SPENCE, George. 17 December 1797. S, pp. 194-195, MSA CE 30-18. www.mdlandrec.net : accessed 17 June 2022.
[817] Worcester County Court (Land Records). Bill of Sale from PARKER, Samuel and VINSON, Isaac to DAVIS, Spencer Sr. 10 February 1798. S, pp. 209-210, MSA CE 30-18. www.mdlandrec.net : accessed 30 May 2022.

Persons whatsoever In Witness to which I have hereunto set my hand & Seal this Tenth Day of February Anno Dom[ini] one thousand Seven hundred and Ninety Eight ~

Signed Sealed & Delivered   William BREUSTON   (Seal)
In Presents of . . . .   Booz WALSTON"

*followed on folio 213 with the acknowledgment by Justice of the Peace Booz WALSTON and the recordation on 14 February 1798 by court clerk John C. HANDY[818]

Liber S, folio 213; 10 February 1798

"Maryland Ss^ت. Know all Men by these Presents that I William BREWERTON of Worcester County for and in Consideration of the Sum of Twenty five Pounds Current Money of Maryland to me in hand paid the Receipt whereof I do hearby Acknowledge have barganed and Sold and Conveyed unto Margar[e]^t PARSONS of the said County a Negro Girl Named **Leash** hearby warranting & defending unto the said Margar[e]^t PARSONS a full good & Sufficient Title to the said Negro against all Manner of Persons whatsoever In Witness to which I have heareunto set my Hand & Seal this Tenth Day of February Anno Dom[ini] one Thousand Seven hundred & Ninety Eight ~

Signed Sealed Delivered   William BRUSTON   (Seal)
In Present of . . .   Booz WALSTON."

*followed with the acknowledgment by Justice of the Peace Booz WALSTON and the recordation on 14 February 1798 by court clerk John C. HANDY[819]

Liber S, folios 216-217; 18 February 1798

"Know all Men by these Present that I Levin POLLITT Sheriff of Worcester County for and in Consideration of the Sum of one hundred and Sixty Eight Pounds six Shillings and Ten pence Current money and by Vertue of a fieri Facias at the Suit of Elijah James Nancy Polly and Joshua BELL against James SELBY have granted bargained and Sold and by these Presents do grant bargain and Sell unto George BELL the following Negroes Viz. a Negro Man Called **Abb**, **James TOWNSEND**, **James HANDY** a Negro Girl Called **Sussey**. To Have and To Hold the said Negroes unto the only proper use and Behoof of the said George BELL his Executors Adm[inistrato]^{rs} and Assigns The same being taken in Execution under the said Fieri Facias as the Property of said James SELBY and Sold on the second day of February Instant at public Vendue after legal Notice was duly given as well more fully appear by the Return of the said Fieri Facias and the Return and Schedule thereof thereto annexed remaining the Records of Worcester County Court he the said George BELL being the Highest Bidder for the same In Testimony whereof I have hereto set my Hand & Seal affixed this 15th day of February 1798

Signed Sealed & Delivered   Levin POLLITT late Sh[eri]ff   (Seal)
in Presence of . . . .   John POSTLY."

*followed with the acknowledgment by Justice of the Peace John POSTLY and the recordation on 16 February 1798 by court clerk John C. HANDY[820]

Liber S, folios 229-230; 21 February 1798

"Know all men by these presents that I McKimey SCARBOROUGH of Worcester County & State of Maryl[an]^d for & in Consideration of the sum of Ninty Pounds Current money of the State aforesaid to me in hand paid by Jno. ROCKE of the same place at and before the Sealing & delivery of these presents the Rece[i]p^t whereof I do hereby acknowledge do bargain and Sell

---

[818] Worcester County Court (Land Records). Bill of Sale from BREUSTON, William to PARSONS, Margaret. 10 February 1798. S, pp. 212-213, MSA CE 30-18. www.mdlandrec.net : accessed 30 May 2022.
[819] Worcester County Court (Land Records). Bill of Sale from BRUSTON, William to PARSONS, Margaret. 10 February 1798. S, p. 213, MSA CE 30-18. www.mdlandrec.net : accessed 30 May 2022.
[820] Worcester County Court (Land Records). Bill of Sale from POLLITT, Levin to BELL, George. 18 February 1798. S, pp. 216-217, MSA CE 30-18. www.mdlandrec.net : accessed 31 May 2022.

and by these presents do Bargain and Sell unto the said John ROCK his heirs and Assigns one Negro Boy named **Bob**, To have and to hold the said Negroe Boy named **Bob** unto the said John ROCK his heirs and Assigns forever to the only proper use Benefit and Behoof of the af[ore]s[ai]^d John ROCK his heirs and Assigns forever, and for no other use or purpose whatsoever; and the said McKimey SCARBOROUGH for himself and his heirs doth Covenant agree to and with the said John ROCK that he the said McKimey SCARBOROUGH hath a good and Sufficient title to Sell and dispose of the said negroe boy named **Bob** so as to Convey unto the said John ROCK, a good sure & firm title to the same, and that no person but the said McKimey SCARBOROUGH has any right or title to the same. In Testimony whereof the said McKimey SCARBOROUGH his hand to these Presents hath Set and Seal Affixed this 21st day of February in the year of our Lord one Thousand Seven hundred and Ninty Eight

Signed Sealed . . . .   McKimmy SCARBOROUG   (Seal)
and delivered in presence of
Thomas DIXON"

*followed on folio 230 with the acknowledgment by Justice of the Peace Thomas DIXON and the recordation by court clerk John C. HANDY[821]

Liber S, folios 230-233; 20 February 1798

"This Indenture made this 20th day of February Anno Domini seventeen hundred and Ninety Eight Between William CROPPER Sen[io]r of Worcester County and State of Maryland of the one part and Elizabeth SLAUTERY; Leah RIDLY and Soppiah CROPPER of the same place severally of the other part Witnesseth that the said William as well for and in consideration of the several sums of five Shillings Sterling money of Great Brittain in hand paid or secured to be paid by the aforesaid Elizabeth SLAUTERY Leah RIDLEY and Soppiah CROPPER severally unto the said William; as also for divers other good causes and valuable Considerations him the said William thereunto apprecably moving hath given granted bargained; sold and Confirmed and by these presents, doth absolutely give grant bargain sell and Confirm unto the aforesaid Elizabeth SLAUTERY from and after the decease of the said William all that part or parcel of a tract of Land called Hogquarter wheren the said William now lives in fee simple (except as herein after excepted) also one negroe Girl called **Rachel** & unto the aforesaid Leah RIDLEY her Executors and assigns one negroe girl call **Neomy** and one girl called **Sue** one cow with calf and one two year old heifer and one bead and furneture and unto the aforesaid Sophia CROPPER the priviledge of living on the aforesaid lands during her life as a home, and one negroe woman Called **Nancy** and one girl Called **amy** two Cows and two young stears one heifer one horse and two sowes and Shouts and two beads & furniture together with all the estate right title and entrust of him the said William in the aforesaid lands and other the said premesses or any of them To have and to hold the said mentioned granted messuage or Tenement and Premises with the appurtenances and every part thereof unto the said Elizabeth SLATERY Leah RIDLY and Sophia CROPPER severally and to their severall heirs Executors & Assigns severally according to the true intent and meaning of these presence To the only proper use and behoof the said Elizabeth Leah & Sophia severally and there several heirs and Assigns forever and to no other use intent or purpose whatsoever And the said William and his heirs and Assigns the said mentioned and granted premises with their appurtenances unto the said Elizabeth Leah & Sophia severally and these several heirs Executors & Assigns against the said William his heirs and Assigns shall and will warrant and forever defend by these presents. In Witness whereof the said William hath hereunto his hand set and seal Affixed the day and year first above written . . . .

Signed Sealed and delivered   William CROPPER   (Seal)
in presence of . . . . .

---

[821] Worcester County Court (Land Records). Bill of Sale from SCARBOROUGH, McKimmy to ROCK, John. 21 February 1798. S, pp. 229-230, MSA CE 30-18. www.mdlandrec.net : accessed 31 May 2022.

John POSTLY
Philip QUINTON"

*followed on folio 232 with the acknowledgment by Justices of the Peace John POSTLY and Philip QUINTON and the recordation on folio 233 by court clerk John C. HANDY[822]

Liber S, folios 235-237; 13 February 1798

"This Indenture made this thirteenth day of February one thousand seven Hundred ninety Eight Between Comfort BISHOP & Edward BISHOP her son of Worcester County in the State of Maryland of the one part and Solomon PURKINS of the same place of the other part Witnesseth that the said Comfort BISHOP and Edward BISHOP for and in Consideration of the sum of thirty pounds Current money of the State af[ore]s[ai]d to them in hand paid by the said Solomon at and before the sealing and delivery hereof the recept whereof she & her the said Comfort & Edward BISHOP doth hereby Acknowledge hath Granted bargained & sold and doth hereby Give Grant bargain and Sell to the said Solomon PURKINS his heirs Executors Administrators or Assigns one Negro Woman Called **Nice** formly Property of Mic{???} PURKINS Dece[a]s[e]d To have and to hold the said Negro Woman **Nice** above mentioned hereby bargaind & Sold and all our right tittle Claim & Intreast unto the said Solomon PURKINS his heirs executors Administrators and assigns To his and their own proper use and uses Benefit and Behoof as his and their own proper right for ever, and I the said Comfort & Edward do hereby for our selves our heirs executors & administrators covenant promise grant and agree to and with the said Solomon PURKINS his heirs Executors & administrators that the said negro woman are and be and so shall at all times forever hereafter be remain & continue unto the said Solomon PURKINS his heirs Executors Administrators and Assigns free & Clear off and from all and all manner of forms & and other Gifts Grants bargains & Sails assignments & Incumbrances Whatsoever, had made done or Commited by use or by our means Privately or Pr{???}ment as to our right Tittle or Claim in any manner, as to our Life time estate in us, unto the said negro Woman af[ore]s[ai]d In Testimony whereof the said Comfort BISHOP and Edward BISHOP hath hereunto Set our hands & Seals the day and year above written ~ ~.

Signed Sealed & Delivered
In the Presence of ~
Esme PURNELL

          mark
Comfort X BISHOP (Seal)
          her

Edward BISHOP (Seal)"

*followed on folio 236 with the acknowledgment by Justice of the Peace Esme PURNELL and the recordation on folio 237 by court clerk John C. HANDY on 26 February 1798[823]

Liber S, folios 237-238; 27 February 1798

"Know all men by these Presents that I Esther widow of Edward PETTIT In the County of Worcester and State of Maryland four and in Consideration of the Sum of one Hundred Pounds Current money of the State aforesaid to me in hand paid by John BISHOP Sen[i]or of the Same Place the Resit whereof I do hereby acknowledge have Bargained and Sold and Delivered and by these Presents, according the Due form of Law do bargain and Sell and Deliver unto the said John BISHOP one Negro Woman Named **Lish** one Negro boy Named **obed** one Negro girl Named **Nanny** & one negro Girl Named **Liza** them and there Increase to Have and to hold the said Bargained Premisses unto the said John BISHOP his Heirs and Assigns for Ever and I the said Esther for my self my Heirs the said bargined Premises unto the said John BISHOP his heirs and Assigns against all Persons Shall and will Warrant and fore Ever defend against the

---

[822] Worcester County Court (Land Records). Deed from CROPPER, William to SLATERY, Elizabeth, RIDLEY, Leah, and CROPPER, Sophia. 20 February 1798. S, pp. 230-233, MSA CE 30-18. www.mdlandrec.net : accessed 31 May 2022.
[823] Worcester County Court (Land Records). Deed from BISHOP, Comfort and Edward to PURKINS, Solomon. 13 February 1798. S, pp. 235-237, MSA CE 30-18. www.mdlandrec.net : accessed 31 May 2022.

Claims of all Persons what Ever as Witness my hand and Seal this 27 day of February Seventeen Hundred and Ninty Eight

Signed Sealed and delivered
in presence of . . . .   Easter +̇ PETTETT (Seal)
                                                                                                          (her mark)

Mary +̇ MUMFORD
(her mark)

Jesse BENNETT"

*followed on folio 238 with the acknowledgment by Justice of the Peace Jesse BENNETT and the recordation by court clerk John C. HANDY[824]

Liber S, folios 261-262; 05 March 1798

"Know all men by these Presents that I Negro **Jacob** Freeman of Worcester in the State of Maryland for and Inconsideration of the sum of Fifteen pounds Current money of Maryland to me in hand paid by Fredrick CONNER of the same Place at and before the sealing and delivery of these Presents have granted bargained Sold and delivered unto the said Fredrick CONNER and his heirs and Assigns for Ever one red Cow and Calf one Blue Sow and Seven pigs & one young hog one Iron kettle one Spider five earthen potts two Tubbs one half Bushel two Barrells one Cask one meat tubb one table one Horse Cart one Sifter one Can one piggin three Chaires one Spinning Wheal one Plow one Harrow two grubbing hoes two weading hoes one pair flat Irons one ax one bed and furniture two chests four Baskets one hammer one bucket one Saddle and one well bucket now in the Possission of the said Fredreck CONNER To Have and to hold the said property unto him the said Fredreck CONNER his heirs and Assigns for Ever to the only proper use bennefitt and behoof of him the said Fredrick CONNER and his heirs and Assigns for ever and the said Negro **Jacob** for himself his heirs Executors and Adm[inistrato]rs the af[ore]s[ai]d Bargarned Sold and delivered property as af[ore]s[ai]d will and shall warrent and fore ever defend against the right and Title of all manner of persons or persons what so ever of which s[ai]d negro **Jacob** have put the said Fredreck CONNER in full possession by the delivery hereof In Testimoney hereof I the said **Jacob** have hereunto to set my hand and seeal this fifth day of March 1798 ~ . . . . .

Signed Sealed and delivered
in the Presence off ~ . . . .   Negro +̇ **Jacob** (Seal)
Nancy BENNETT   (his mark)
Jesse BENNETT"

*followed on folio 262 with the acknowledgment by Justice of the Peace Jesse BENNETT and the recordation on 16 March 1798 by court clerk John C. HANDY[825]

Liber S, folios 273-274; 27 March 1798

"Know all men by these presents that Elenor FLEMMING of Worcester County in the State of Maryland for and in Concideration of the Sum of forty pounds to me in hand paid by John CUTLER of the same place at and before the sealing and delivery of hereof I the said Elenor FLEMMING have bargained and Sold and by these presents doth absolutely bargain Sell and deliver unto him the said John CUTLER his heirs and Assigns forever one nigro Girl named **Comfort** and her Increase forever in Worcester County now in Possession of the said Elenor FLEMMING. To have and to hold the above mentioned Sold and delivered negro Girl **Comfort** hereby intended to be sold unto him the said John CUTLER and his heirs Executors Administrators & Assigns forever to the only proper use benefit and behoof of him the said John CUTLER his heirs & Assigns for ever and the said Elenor FLEMMING for herself and

---

[824] Worcester County Court (Land Records). Bill of Sale from PETTETT, Easter to BISHOP, John Sr. 27 February 1798. S, pp. 237-238, MSA CE 30-18. www.mdlandrec.net : accessed 31 May 2022.

[825] Worcester County Court (Land Records). Bill of Sale from **Jacob (negro freeman)** to CONNER, Fredrick. 05 March 1798. S, pp. 261-262, MSA CE 30-18. www.mdlandrec.net : accessed 31 May 2022.

her heirs Executors and Administrators and every of them against every other person or persons whatever and shall forever warrent and defend the above mentioned bargained and sold negro girl known by the name of **Comfort** unto him the said John CUTLER his heirs and Assigns forever of which said negro Girl **Comfort** I the said Elenor FLEMMING have put the said John CUTLER in full possession of by the delivery of the above mentioned negro Girl Comfort In Testamoney whereof I the said Elenor FLEMMING have hereto set my hand and affixed my seale 27th Day of March Anno Domini One Thousand seven hundred and ninety Eight.

Signed Sealed & Delivered　　　　　　　　　　　　　　　　　Eleanor FLEMMING (Seal)
In presence of . . . ~ . . .　　Philip QUINTON"

*followed on folio 274 with the acknowledgment by Justice of the Peace Philip QUINTON and the recordation on 28 March 1798 by court clerk John C. HANDY[826]

Liber S, folios 274-275; 22 February 1798

"A List On the 22nd Day of February 1798 ~ . . . .
A List of a Slave removed & brough into this State by Joshua COTTINGHAM the owner thereof a Citizen & residentur of the Delaware State & who was posses{?} and Seized in Estate of Inheritance lying in his own Right in land Lying in this State Which Slave was resident of the State of Delaware an adjoining State before the twenty first day of April in the year one thousand seven hundred and Eighty three and is removed and brought into this state for the purpose of Employing or working on the land of the said COTTINGHAM within this State for the use and benefit of the said COTTINGHAM and his legal representative and not for Sale. Vise male one Negro man Slave named **Jacob** Thirty years of age devised to said Joshua COTTINGHAM by the Will of Elisha COTTINGHAM of Delaware dated Twenty eighth Day of January in the Year of our lord one thousand seven hundred and Ninety five and recorded in the Register office of Wills of Georgetown in the s[ai]d State of Delaware, As Witness my hand 29th Day of March one Thousand and Seven hundred and Ninety eight. To the Clerk of Worcester County Maryland { . . . .　　　　　　　　　　　Joshua COTTINGHAM"

*followed on folio 275 with the recordation on 30 March 1798 by court clerk John C. HANDY[827]

Liber S, folio 275; 30 March 1798

"A List of Slaves Brought into the State of Maryland by William LAW the owner thereof a Cetizen & Resident of the State of Maryland and who is seized and Possessed of land lying in the State af[ore]s[ai]d which Slaves were Residents & descended from Residents of the State of Delaware before the Twenty first Day of April in the year one Thousand seven hundred and Eighty three and are removed & brought into the State of maryland for the Purpose of being Employed & or working on the Land of the said William LAW within this State for the use of the said William LAW & his legal Representatives & not Sale viz one negro man named **Jid** aged twenty seven years one negro woman Called **Juda** aged forty seven years & one negro Girl Called **amy** aged three years the Title to which negroes I the s[ai]d W[illia]m LAW devised from my wife Catharin LAW under my hand this 30t[h] day of March Anno Domini 1798. ~ . . .
　　　　　　　　　　　　　　　　　　　　　　　　　William LAW"

*followed with the recordation by court clerk John C. HANDY[828]

---

[826] Worcester County Court (Land Records). Bill of Sale from FLEMMING, Eleanor to CUTLER, John. 27 March 1798. S, pp. 273-274, MSA CE 30-18. www.mdlandrec.net : accessed 31 May 2022.
[827] Worcester County Court (Land Records). Certificate of Importation into Maryland from COTTINGHAM, Joshua for **Jacob**. 22 February 1798. S, pp. 274-275, MSA CE 30-18. www.mdlandrec.net : accessed 31 May 2022.
[828] Worcester County Court (Land Records). Certificate of Importation into Maryland from LAW, William for **Jid, Juda,** and **Amy**. 30 March 1798. S, pp. 275, MSA CE 30-18. www.mdlandrec.net : accessed 31 May 2022.

Liber S, folio 276; 29 March 1798

"Maryland Worcester Know all Men by these presents that I George BELL of Worcester County in the State of Maryland for and in Consideration of the Sum of Seventy five pounds Current money of Maryland to me in hand paid by James SELBY of the County & State af[ore]s[ai]^d at and before the Ensealing and Delivery of these presents wherewith I Confess my self to be fully satisfied Contented and paid have Given Bargained Sold and Delivered and by these Presents do fully Clearly and Absolutely Bargain Sell and Deliver unto the said James SELBY one Negro man Called **James HANDY** about twenty years old. To have and to hold the said negro man Called **James HANDY** to the said James SELBY his heirs Executors and Administrators and Assigns to his and their proper use and behoof and I the said George BELL my heirs Executors and every of us the said negro to the said James SELBY his heirs Executors Administrators and Assigns against the Claim of all persons Claiming under him & his heirs Shall and will Warrant and forever Defend by these present In Testimony whereof I have hereunto Set my hand and Seal affixed this 29th Day of March A D 1798 . . . ~ . . .

Sealed and delivered	Stephn ANDRSON	George BELL (Seal)
in the presence of	Nancy BELL"	

*followed with the acknowledgment by Justice of the Peace John POSTLY and the recordation on 03 April 1798 by court clerk John C. HANDY[829]

Liber S, folios 277-278; 16 March 1798

"Maryland .. Worcester Ss^t. Know all men by these presents that I William MORRISS of the County afforesaid for and in Consideration of the sum of Sixty five pounds Current money of Maryland, to me in hand paid by Rouse GRAY of the same place at and before the Ensealing and Delivery of these presents, wherewith I confess my Self to be fully Sattisfied Contented and paid have bargained Sold and delivered & by these presents do fully Clearly & absolutely bargain Sell and deliver unto the said Rouse GRAY one Negro boy named **Milby** aged about ten years, To have and to hold the said Negro boy **Milby** unto the said Rouse GRAY his Executors Administrators and Assigns to his and their own proper uses and behoofs forever and I the said William MORRISS my heirs Executors and Administrators and every of us the said Negro boy **Milby** to the said Rouse GRAY his heirs Executors Administrators and Assigns against all persons Whatever Shall and will Warrant acquit & by these presents forever Defend In Testimony Whereof I have here unto set my hand and Seal affixed this Sixteenth Day of March one Thousand Seven hundred and Ninety Eight

Sealed and Delivered	Sterling JONES	W[illia]^m MORRIS (Seal)
in the Presence of . . .	John POSTLY"	

*followed on folio 278 with the acknowledgment by Justice of the Peace John POSTLY and the recordation on 03 April 1798 by court clerk John C. HANDY[830]

Liber S, folios 284-285; 06 April 1798

"This Indenture made this sixth day of April one Thousand Seven hundred and ninety Eight Between **Levin CAMBRIDGE** and James Bowdin ROBINS of Worcester in the State of Maryland of the one part and Samuel HANDY Sen[io]^r of the same place of the other part Witnesseth that they the said **Levin CAMBRIDGE** and James Bowdoin ROBINS for and in consideration of the sum of fifty five pounds Eight Shillings & seven pence half penny to the said James in hand paid and the sum of thirty five pounds to the said **Levin** in hand paid by the said Samuel HANDY before the execution hereof the receipt whereof is hereby acknowledged have granted bargained and Sold released conveyed and Confirmed and by these presents do

---

[829] Worcester County Court (Land Records). Bill of Sale from BELL, George to SELBY, James. 29 March 1798. S, p. 276, MSA CE 30-18. www.mdlandrec.net : accessed 31 May 2022.

[830] Worcester County Court (Land Records). Bill of Sale from MORRIS, William to GRAY, Rouse. 16 March 1798. S, pp. 277-278, MSA CE 30-18. www.mdlandrec.net : accessed 31 May 2022.

Grant bargain and sell convey and confirm unto the said Samuel HANDY his heirs and assigns forever, all their right title Interest and Estate of in or to a Certain Tract of land Called Addition to Williams Choice lying and being in Worcester County containing one hundred & Twenty eight acres of land more or less and all the rights privileges benefits and Appurtenances thereto belonging To have and to hold the same unto the only proper use and behoof of him the said Samuel HANDY his heirs and Assigns forever: & they the said **Levin** covenants for himself his heirs Executors and administrators and to and with the said Samuel HANDY his heirs and Assigns, to warrant and forever defend the said land and Appurtenances unto the said Samuel HANDY his heirs and Assigns against the right title and Claim of the said James and **Levin** and their heirs or Assigns or any person or persons Claiming by this or under them or any of them respectively : In Testimony whereof they have hereto set their hands and Seals affixed the Day & year first above written. ~

Signed Sealed & delivered	Philip QUINTON	**Levin CAMBRIDGE** (Seal)
in presence of . . ~.	Benjamin DENNIS	James B. ROBINS (Seal)"

*followed with the acknowledgment by Justices of the Peace Philip QUINTON and Benjamin DENNIS and the recordation by court clerk John C. HANDY[831]

Liber S, folios 285-286; 04 April 1798

"Know all men by these presents that I John SCARBOROUGH Sen[io]^r of Worcester County in the State of Maryland for and in Consideration of the Sum of one hundred pounds Current money of Maryland to me in hand paid by McKimmy SCARBOROUGH of the County & State af[ore]s[ai]^d at and before the sealing and delivery hereof I the said John SCARBOROUGH Sen[io]^r have Bargained and Sold and delivered and by these presents doth absolutely bargain sell and deliver unto him the said McKimmy SCARBOROUGH his heirs and Assigns forever one Negro Woman Named **Jean** and her daughter **Frank** and their Increase forever in Worcester County now in Possession of the said John SCARBOROUGH Sen[io]^r To have and to hold the above mentioned Sold and delivered negroes **Jean** and **Frank** and theire increase forever hereby intended to be sold unto him the said McKimmy SCARBOROUGH and his heirs Executors & Administrators and Assigns forever to the only proper use Benefitt and behoofe of him the said McKimmy SCARBOROUGH and his heirs and Assigns forever and the said John SCARBOROUGH sen[io]^r for himself and his heirs Executors & Administrators and every of them and against every other person or persons Whatever and Shall forever warrent and defend the above mentioned bargained and sold negroes **Jean** and **Frank** unto him the said McKimmy SCARBOROUGH his heirs and Assigns forever of which said negroes I the said John SCARBOROUGH Sen[io]^r have put the said McKimmy SCARBOROUG in full possession of by the delivery of the above mentioned negroes. In Testamoney whereof I the said John SCARBOROUGH Sen[io]^r have hereto sett my hand and affixed my seal the fourth Day of April one Thousand seven hundred and ninety Eight. ~

Signed Sealed & Delivered		Jn°. SCARBOROUGH Sen[io]^r (Seal)
In presence of ~ . . .	Philip QUINTON"	

*followed on folio 286 with the acknowledgment by Justice of the Peace Philip QUINTON and the recordation on 06 April 1798 by court clerk John C. HANDY[832]

Liber S, folios 286-287; 09 March 1798

"This Indenture made this ninth day of March in the year one thousand seven hundred & ninety eight Between Esther CAMBRIDGE Widow of William CAMBRIDGE deceased of Worcester County of the one part & Samuel HANDY sen[io]^r of the other part Witnesseth that She the said Esther CAMBRIDGE for and in Consideration of the sum of thirty pounds Current money

---

[831] Worcester County Court (Land Records). Deed from **CAMBRIDGE, Levin** and ROBINS, James Bowdoin to HANDY, Samuel. 06 April 1798. S, pp. 284-285, MSA CE 30-18. www.mdlandrec.net : accessed 31 May 2022.

[832] Worcester County Court (Land Records). Bill of Sale from SCARBOROUGH, John Sr. to SCARBOROUGH, McKimmy. 04 April 1798. S, pp. 285-286, MSA CE 30-18. www.mdlandrec.net : accessed 31 May 2022.

to her in hand paid by the said Samue HANDY the receipt whereof is now hereby Confessed have granted bargained & Sold released and Confirmed and by these presents doth grant bargain & Sell release & Confirm unto the said Samuel HANDY his heirs & assigns forever all her right title Interest & Estate whatever of in and to a tract of land Called Williams Choice and all the rights benefits and previledges thereunto belonging the same lying & being in Worcester County; the Bounds whereof will more fully appear by recourse being had to the Certificate and grant thereof To have and to hold the said land with all the Appurtenances af[ore]s[ai]^d thereto belonging unto the only proper use & behoof of the said Samuel HANDY his heirs & assigns forever & the said Esther CAMBRIDGE covenants for herself her heirs Executors and Administrators & to and with the said Samuel HANDY his heirs & assigns to Warrant & forever defend the said lands and appurtenances unto the said Samuel HANDY his heirs & assigns against the Right and title of her said Esther CAMBRIDGE & all persons claiming by from or under her and heirs or assigns, In Testimony whereof she the said Esther CAMBRIDGE have hereto set her hand & seal affixed the day & year first above written ~ . .

Signed Sealed & Deliv[ere]^d John COTTINGHAM
In the Presence of . . . .   Jesse BENNETT   Esther + CAMBRIDGE (Seal)
                                                her mark"

*followed on folio 287 with the acknowledgment by Justices of the Peace Jesse BENNETT and John COTTINGHAM and the recordation on 06 April 1798 with court clerk John C. HANDY[833]

*The names of Esther CAMBRIDGE and William CAMBRIDGE were not bolded in print because it is not known which was a person of color or if both were.

Liber S, folios 288-289; 24 March 1798

"Maryland Ss^s. Know all men by these presents that I John PORTER of Somerset County and State af[ore]s[ai]^d for and in Consideration of the sum of one hundred & fifteen Pounds Current money of the State af[ore]s[ai]^d to be paid unto the said John PORTER at or before the Delivery of a Negro man named **George** & a negro woman named **a Melia**; the Receipt whereof the said John PORTER doth hereby acknowledge, have bargained Sold and for ever quit claim to Zadock WHEELER of Worcester County and State af[ore]s[ai]^d to him his heirs and assigns forever the af[ore]s[ai]^d Negro man **George** & negro woman **a Melia**, to have and to hold the af[ore]s[ai]^d negroes for the Consideration af[ore]s[ai]^d to him his heirs & assigns forever, and for the proper use and behoof of the said Zadock WHEELER his heirs & assigns for ever and I the said John PORTER Shall and will Warrant and for ever Defend the said Negroes from all other persons Whatsoever by these presents In Witness whereof I have hereunto set my hand and Affixed my seal this 24 Day of March 1798. ~ . . .

Signed Sealed & Delivered   John PORTER   (Seal)
In presence of us ~ . . .   Tho[ma]^s DIXON"

*followed on folio 289 with the acknowledgment by Justice of the Peace Thomas DIXON and the recordation on 11 April 1798 by court clerk John C. HANDY[834]

Liber S, folios 290-291; 09 April 1798

"Know all men by these presents I Rebecca PARKER of Worcester County in the State of Maryland for and in Consideration of the Sum of Forty five pounds currant money of Maryland to me in hand paid at or before the Delivery of these presents by McKimmey PORTER of the County and State aforesaid the recept whereof I do hereby acknowledge have bargained and sold and by these presents do bargain and Sell unto the said McKimmey PORTER one Negro Girl named **Rhodey** about five years old to have and to hold the said Negro Girl by these

---

[833] Worcester County Court (Land Records). Deed from CAMBRIDGE, Esther to HANDY, Samuel. 09 March 1798. S, pp. 286-287, MSA CE 30-18. www.mdlandrec.net : accessed 31 May 2022.
[834] Worcester County Court (Land Records). Bill of Sale from PORTER, John to WHEELER, Zadock. 24 March 1798. S, pp. 288-289, MSA CE 30-18. www.mdlandrec.net : accessed 31 May 2022.

presents bargained and Sold unto the said McKimey PORTER his heirs or assigns for ever and I the said Rebecca PARKER for my self my heirs or assigns the said negro Girl unto the said McKemmey PORTER his heirs or assignes against me the said Rebecca PARKER my heirs Executors and administrators and against all and every other person and persons whatsoever shall and will warrant and for ever Defend firmly by these presents In Witness whereof I the said Rebecca PARKER to these presents my hand have sett and Seal affixed the 9th Day of April Anno Dom[ini] Seventeen hundred & ninety Eight

Signed Sealed and Delivered in the presents of   Philip QUINTON   Rebecca PARKER   (Seal)
John GUNBY"

*followed on folio 291 with the acknowledgment by Justices of the Peace John GUNBY and Philip QUINTON and the recordation on 13 April 1798 by court clerk John C. HANDY[835]

Liber S, folios 296-297; 07 April 1798

"Worcester Ss[t]. Know all men by these presents that I Rody BAUDES of Worcester County in the State of Maryland for and in the Consideration of the Sum of Fifty pounds to me in hand paid by John HENDERSON before the Ensealing & Delivery hereof the receipt Whereof I Do hereby acknowledge hath Given Granted bargained and Sold by these presents do give Grant bargin and Sell unto the s[ai]d John HENDERSON his hairs and Assigns for Ever one negro Woman Called **Venus** and one negro boy called **Peter** and the said Rody BANDS doth for her Self and her heirs Covnant and agree to and With the Said John HENDERSON that she the said Rody BAUDS the negroes above mentioned will warrent & forever Defend from all persons whatsoever Claiming any Right or Title unto the said negrosh In Witness whereof I have hereunto set my hand and Seal this the 7 Day of April Anno Dom[ini] 1798 ~ . . . .

Sealed and Deliv[ere]d   Thomas DIXON
In the Presents of   her
                                                       Rody + BANDS   (Seal)
                                                           mark"

*followed with the acknowledgment by Justice of the Peace Thomas DIXON and the recordation on 24 April 1798 by court clerk John C. HANDY[836]

Liber S, folios 301-302; 27 April 1798

"This Indenture made this Twenty seventh day of April Anno Domini one Thousand seven hundred and ninety Eight between Frances ROSSE of Worcester County in the State of Maryland of the one part and Samuel HANDY of the County & State af[ore]s[ai]d of the other part Witnesseth the said Francis ROSSE for and in Consideration of the sum of four hundred pounds Current money of Maryland to him in hand paid before the ensealing and delvery hereof the receipt Whereof is hereby acknowledged hath granted bargained and Sold and by these presents doth grant bargain & Sell unto the said Samuel HANDY his heirs Executors Administrators & Assigns forever the following Lotts of Ground lying and being in Snow Hill in Worcester County and known by and described by Lott Numbers Sixty one Sixty two and Sixty three and half a Lott number Sixty with their appurtenances and the following Goods & Chattles to wit one negro man Called **Matthias** one negro Woman Called **Sarah** one negro Boy Called **John** one negro Girl Called **Sib** and two Feather beds & Furneture & also all my right Title & Interest to the Proproperty I have in Scotland in Europe left me by my aunt ~ To have and hold the said Lotts of Ground with their appurtenances and all and Singular the Goods & Chattles abovementioned to him the said Samuel HANDY his heirs Executors administrators and assigns forever provided & always upon this Condition that if the said Francis ROSSE shall not pay unto William RICHARDSON Esq[ui]r[e] Inspector of Survey N°. 3 within six months from the date hereof the sum of Money which the said Francis ROSSE is Indebted to the said

---

[835] Worcester County Court (Land Records). Bill of Sale from PARKER, Rebecca to PORTER, McKimmy. 09 April 1798. S, pp. 290-291, MSA CE 30-18. www.mdlandrec.net : accessed 31 May 2022.
[836] Worcester County Court (Land Records). Bill of Sale from BANDS, Rody to HENDERSON, John. 07 April 1798. S, pp. 296-297, MSA CE 30-18. www.mdlandrec.net : accessed 31 May 2022.

William RICHARDSON as Revenue Money & for which payment the said Samuel HANDY Security to the said William RICHARDSON for that then the said Samuel HANDY shall have full power, and authority to Sell and dispose off at Public vendue so much of the said property as shall pay the sum that the said Sam[ue]l HANDY shall pay as security fo the said Francis ROSSE as Witness to hand & Seal of the said Frances ROSSE the day and year first above written ~ . . .

Signed Sealed & Delivered   John COTTINGHAM   Frances ROSSE   (Seal)
In the presence of ~ .   Jesse BENNETT"

*followed with the acknowledgment by Justices of the Peace John COTTINGHAM and Jesse BENNETT and the recordation on 27 April 1798 by court clerk John C. HANDY[837]

Liber S, folios 302-304; 26 April 1798

"This Indenture made this 26th day of April Anno Domini one Thousand Seven hundred and Ninety Eight Between Francis ROSSE of Worcester County in the State of Maryland of the other part and William WHITTINGTON of the same place of the other part Witnesseth that the said Francis ROSSE for and in consideration of the sum of one hundred and thirty pounds Current money of Maryland to him in hand paid before the execution hereof by the said William the receipt Whereof is hereby confessed hath Granted bargained and sold released Conveyed and Confirmed and by presents doth Grant bargain and Sell release convey and confirm unto the said William WHITTINGTON his heirs and Assigns forever the following Lotts of Ground in Snow Hill viz. The Lott and Dwelling house whereas and wherein the said ROSSE lives with the appurtenances and Lotts known and described as lotts number Sixty one Sixty two and Sixty three and half of a Lott number Sixty with the appurtenances and the following Goods and Chattels to wit one negro man Called **Matthias** one negro woman Called **Sarah** one negro Boy Called **John** one negro Girl Called **Sib** & two beds and furniture now in the said ROSSEs possession. To have and to hold the said lotts and appurtenances houses Goods and Chattels unto the only proper use and behoof of him the said William WHITTINGTON his heirs and Assigns forever provided always and upon Condition that whereas the said Francis ROSSE is indebted in the following Sums to wit, To John C HANDY William WHITTINGTON and Levin POLLITT in the sum of thirty seven pounds one Shilling and nine pence with Interest from the third day of September 1795 the day of the note and also in the further Sum of Eighty six pounds and ten pence to William WHITTINGTON with Interest from the 21st day of September 1797 ~ the date of the note now if the said Francis ROSSE his heirs Devisies Executors or administrators Shall will and Truly pay unto the said HANDY WHITTINGTON and POLLITT or to the Survivor of them the said sum of money due to them with Interest from the date of the note given to them by him on or before the first day of May one thousand and Seven hundred and ninety nine and Also shall well and Truly pay on or before said first day of may last above mentioned unto the said William WHITTINGTON his Executors Adm[inistrator]s or Assigns the af[oresai]d Sum of money due to him from the said ROSSE with Interest from the date of the note till paid then in that case this Deed to be void of none Effect otherwise to remain in full force & virtue in Law ~

                                                        Frances ROSSE   (Seal)"

*followed on folio 304 with the acknowledgment by Justices of the Peace Benjamin DENNIS and Jesse BENNETT and the recordation on 28 April 1798 by court clerk John C. HANDY[838]

Liber S, folios 314-315; 07 May 1798

"Know all men by these presents that I John WILLIAMS of the County of Worcester in the State of Maryland for and in Consideration of the Sum of Eighty pounds Current money of

---

[837] Worcester County Court (Land Records). Deed from ROSSE, Frances to HANDY, Samuel. 27 April 1798. S, pp. 301-302, MSA CE 30-18. www.mdlandrec.net : accessed 31 May 2022.
[838] Worcester County Court (Land Records). Deed from ROSSE, Frances to WHITTINGTON, William. 27 April 1798. S, pp. 302-304, MSA CE 30-18. www.mdlandrec.net : accessed 31 May 2022.

Maryland to me in hand paid by William McGREGOR of the Same place at or before the Sealing and delivery of these presents the receapt whereof I the said John WILLIAMS do hereby acknowledge have granted bargained and Sold and Delivered and by these presents do grant bargain sell and Deliver unto the said William McGREGOR his heirs Executors administrators or assigns one Negroman named **Tonney** aged twenty five years and now in the possession of said William McGREGOR To have and to hold the said Negro **Tonney** to the said William McGREGOR his heirs Executors administrators and Assigns for ever and I the said John WILLIAMS for my self my heirs Executors and administrators the said negro **Tonney** unto the said William McGREGOR his heirs Executors administrators and Assigns against me the said John WILLIAMS my heirs Executors and administrators and against all and every other person and persons whatsoever Claiming or to Claim Shall and will Warrant and for ever defend by these Presents the said Negro **Tonney** which I the said John WILLIAMS have put the said William McGREGOR in full possession of by Delivering the said Negro to him the said William McGREGOR at the Sealing and Delivery of these presents and hereby bargained and Sold to him the said William McGREGOR as aforesaid in Wittness whereof I have hereunto Set my hand and Seal Affixed this seventh day of May Anno Dommini one Thousand Seven hundred and Ninty Eight. 1798

Sinned Sealed & Delivered   John WILLIAMS   (Seal)
In Presence of ~ .   John POSTLY"

*followed with the acknowledgment by Justice of the Peace John POSTLY and the recordation on folio 315 by court clerk John C. HANDY on 11 May 1798[839]

Liber S, folio 323; 25 May 1798

"I Thomas DALE of Worcester County in the State of Maryland do hereby certifie that on the Twenty eight day of February last I brought a Negro Garle called **Elon** about ten years of age out of Sussex County in the State of Delaware which was the Property of John EVANS Senor of that County and by his last will and Testament bearing date the fifteenth day of February one Thousand seven hundred and Ninety one and being duly proven and Recorded at George Town in Sussex County the thirteenth day of October one Thousand seven hundred and Ninety five and among other things in his said Will he the said John EVANS did Give and bequeth the aforesaid Negro Garle **Elon** to my wife Elizabeth DALE all which I Certify under my hand this 25th day of May Anno Domini 1798 ~ . . . . . .

Thomas DALE"

*followed with the recordation by court clerk John C. HANDY[840]

Liber S, folios 359-360; 12 June 1798

"Know all men by these presents that I William UNDRILL of Worcester County in the State of Maryland for and in Consideration of the Sum of fifty five pounds current money of the State af[ore]s[ai]ᵈ to me in hand paid by John CUTLER of the County & State af[ore]s[ai]ᵈ at and before the sealing and delivery hereof I the said William UNDRILL have bargained Sold and delivered and by these presents doth absolutely bargain Sell and Deliver unto him the said John CUTLER his heirs and Assigns for Ever one Negro Womin named **Minty** and her increase forever, in Worcester County now in the Possession of the said William UNDRILL. To have and to hold the above mentioned Sold and Delivered Nigro Woman **Minty** and her increase forever hereby intended to be sold unto him the said John CUTLER and to his heirs Executors & administrators and Assigns forever to the only Proper use Benefitt & Behoof of him the said John CUTLER and his heirs and Assigns forever and the said William UNDRILL for himself his heirs Executors and administrators and every of them and against every other person or persons whatever and Shall forever warrant and defend the above mentioned bargained & Sold

---

[839] Worcester County Court (Land Records). Bill of Sale from WILLIAMS, John to McGREGOR, William. 07 May 1798. S, pp. 314-315, MSA CE 30-18. www.mdlandrec.net : accessed 31 May 2022.
[840] Worcester County Court (Land Records). Certificate of Importation into Maryland from DALE, Thomas for **Elon**. 25 May 1798. S, p. 323, MSA CE 30-18. www.mdlandrec.net : accessed 31 May 2022.

negro woman **Minty** unto him the said John CUTLER and his heirs and Assigns forever of which said Negro **Minty** I the said William UNDRILL have put the said John CUTLER in full Possession of By the delivery of the above mentioned Negro **Minty** In Testamoney whereof I the said William UNDRILL have hereto set my hand affixed my seale the Twelvth day of June in the year of our lord one Thousand seven hundred and Ninety Eight ~.

Signed Sealed & Delivered   William UNDRILL   (Seal)
In the Presence of ~   Jesse BENNETT"

*followed on folio 360 with the acknowledgment by Justice of the Peace Jesse BENNETT and the recordation on 13 June 1798 by court clerk John C. HANDY[841]

Liber S, folio 380; 02 June 1798

"Know all men by these Presents that I John WILLIAMS of the County of Worcester in the State of Mariland for and in Consideration of the Sum of thirty Seven Pound ten Shillings Current money of Maryland to me in hand paid by Selathal POAHEN of the Same Place at or before The Sealing and delivering of these Presents the recept whereof I the said John WILLIAMS do hereby acknowledg have granted bargaind and sold and Delivered and by these Presents do grant bargin Sell and deliver unto the said Selathal POAHER his heirs Executors administrators or a sins one nigrr woman Named **Ester** adged Sixteen years and was in Possession of the said Selathel BAKER to have and to hold the said Neger Called **Ester** to the said Selathel BAKER his heirs Executors administrators and assins for ever and I the said John WILLIAMS for my Self my heirs Executors and Administrators the said Negro **Ester** unto the said Selathil BAKER his heirs Executors administrators and asigns against me the said John WILLIAMS his ayrs Executors and administrators and against all and every other Person and Persons whatsoever Claiming on to Claim Shall and will warrant and forever defend by these Presents the said Negro **Estar** which I the said John WILLIAMS have put the said Selathel BAKER in full Possestion of by Delivering the said Negro to him the said Selathil BAKER at the Sealing and Deliveray of these Presents and hereby bargand and Sold to him the said Selathel BAKER as a foresaid in witness whereof I have hereunto Set my hand and Seal aforesaid this Second Day of June anno Domini one Thousand Seven hundred and Ninty Eight 1798. ~ ..

Signed Sealed and Delivered   Booz WALSTON   John WILLIAMS   (Seal)
In Presents of ~ . . . ."

*followed with the acknowledgment by Justice of the Peace Booz WALSTON and the recordation on 19 June 1798 by court clerk John C. HANDY[842]

Liber S, folios 390-391; 23 June 1798

"Maryland Worcester Ss^t. Know all men by these Presents that I James KING of Worcester County in the State of maryland for and in Consideration of the Sum of fifty Pounds Current money of Maryland to me in hand paid by Jesse POWELL of the County & State af[ore]s[ai]^d at and before the Ensealing and Delivery of these presents I the said James do fully Clearly and absolutely Bargain and sell unto the Said Jesse POWELL one negro Woman Called **Pleasent** about Sixteen years old and her Child **Rachell** about one month old To have and To Hold the af[ore]s[ai]d Negro Woman **Pleasent** & her Child unto him the said Jesse POWELL his heirs Executors and Administrators or Assigns to his and their own proper use and behoof forever and I the said James KING for my self and my heirs Executors and Administrators and every of us the af[ore]s[ai]^d Negro Woman **Pleasent** & Child unto the said Jesse POWELL his heirs and Assigns against all people whatever shall and will warrant and Defend Acquit and forever

---

[841] Worcester County Court (Land Records). Bill of Sale from UNDRILL, William to CUTLER, John. 12 June 1798. S, pp. 359-360, MSA CE 30-18. www.mdlandrec.net : accessed 31 May 2022.
[842] Worcester County Court (Land Records). Bill of Sale from WILLIAMS, John to BAKER, Selathal. 02 June 1798. S, p. 380, MSA CE 30-18. www.mdlandrec.net : accessed 31 May 2022.

Defend by these presents In Witness whereof I have hereunto Set my hand and seal Affixed this twenty third day of June Anno Dom[ini] one Thousand seven hundred & Ninety Eight.

Signed Sealed and   James KING (Seal)
Delivered in Presents of   John POSTLY"

*followed on folio 391 with the acknowledgment by Justice of the Peace John POSTLY and the recordation on 26 June 1798 by court clerk John C. HANDY[843]

Liber S, folios 406-407; 09 July 1798

"Know all men by these presents that I **Charles BOWEN** free negro of Worcester County in the State of Maryland for and in Consideration of the Sum of fifteen Pounds Current money of the State af[ore]s[ai]^d to me in hand paid by William Jarman HOUSTON of the Same place at and before the Sealing & Delivery hereof the recept whereof I do hereby acknowledge have granted bargained and Sold & delivered unto the said William HOUSTON his heirs and Assigns for Ever a negro Woman Called **Sarah** and two Childrn the oldest by the name **Huldy** the youngest is Called **Comfort** is about four or five months of age now in the possession and delivered to the said William J. HOUSTON to have and to hold the said negro Woman Called **Sarah** and Two Children hereby bargained and sold unto him the Said William J. HOUSTON his heirs and assigns for Ever, and I the said **Charles BOWEN** free negro will Warrant and for Ever defend the right and title of the said Negroes unto him the said William J HOUSTON his heirs and Assigns forever In Witness Whereof I have hereto set my Set my hand and affixed my seal this 9 Day of July Anno Domini seventeen hundred and Ninety Eight. ~

Signed Sealed & Deliverd   mark
In the Presence of . . .   Esme PURNELL   Charles + BOWEN (Seal)
                                                                                his"

*followed on folio 407 with the acknowledgment by Justice of the Peace Esme PURNELL and the recordation on 11 July 1798 by court clerk John C. HANDY[844]

*The acknowledgment names the eldest child as "Hulda".

Liber S, folio 418; 19 September 1794

"Notice is hereby certifyd that I set the bearer hereof **Will** free as Witness my hand this 19th September 1794. ~ ~ ~ .

                                                                                                    John HUDSON"

*followed with recordation on 21 January 1797 by court clerk John C. HANDY[845]

Liber S, folio 434; 03 August 1796

"Worcester County State of Maryland To all People To whom these presents Shall Come Greeting I Levi OUTTEN of the County & State afforesaid do for Divers good Causes and Consideration me thereunto moveing Do hereby Declair free Manumate and release forever the nigro following To wit negro **Nanny** is free Augost 4th 1796 Hereby Acknowledging the said Negro Discharged from all Claim or right of Property herafter Claimed by me and my Executors or Administrators as Witness my hand and seal this third Day of August one thous[an]d seven hundred and ninty Eight. ~ .

Jesse BENNETT   Levi OUTTEN (Seal)"

---

[843] Worcester County Court (Land Records). Bill of Sale from KING, James to POWELL, Jesse. 23 June 1798. S, pp. 390-391, MSA CE 30-18. www.mdlandrec.net : accessed 31 May 2022.

[844] Worcester County Court (Land Records). Bill of Sale from BOWEN, Charles to HOUSTON, William Jarman. 09 July 1798. S, pp. 406-407, MSA CE 30-18. www.mdlandrec.net : accessed 31 May 2022.

[845] Worcester County Court (Land Records). Certificate of Manumission from HUDSON, John to **Will**. 19 September 1794. S, p. 418, MSA CE 30-18. www.mdlandrec.net : accessed 31 May 2022.

*followed with the acknowledgment by Justice of the Peace Jesse BENNETT and recordation on 13 August 1798 by court clerk John C. HANDY[846]

Liber S, folios 436-437; 11 August 1798

"Worcester County State of Maryland Know all men by these presents that I William BREWINGTON of the County and State af[ore]s[ai]d being conscious the practice of holding human beings in perpetual Slavery is contrary to the law of God and the unalienable rights of man for these causes and other weighty Considerations me thereunto moving I the said William BREWINGTON do for my Self my heirs and Assigns forever discharge and Set free my Negros in manner and form following. To witt negro **George** to be at full liberty the first Day of January one thousand seven hundred ninety nine negro **Harry** to be at full liberty the first day of January one thousand Eighteen hundred and five I do hereby for my Self my heirs executors administrators and Assigns warrant and defend the freedom of the above negroes against the Claim or Claims of all and every person Whatever Claiming or that may hereafter claim the above mentioned negrors or any right or title to either of them after that date above Stated. In Witness hereof I set my hand and Seal this 11th Day of August one thousand seven hundred and ninety Eight. ~ . . . . .

Booz WALSTON   W[illia]m BRUTON   (Seal)
{?} CATHELL"

*followed on folio 437 with the acknowledgment by Justices of the Peace Booz WALSTON and John CATHELL and the recordation on 14 August 1798 by court clerk John C. HANDY[847]

Liber S, folios 440-441; 25 August 1798

"Know all men by these presents that for and in consideration of the sum of Eighty Dollars to me in hand paid the rec[eip]t whereof I hereby acknowledge and myself therewith fully Satisfied and content do by these presents make over bargain Sell and forever assign all my right title & interest in and unto a negro man named **Hector** to be the right & property of Ephraim FURNIS of Worcester County to him forever firmly by these presents Sealed with my seal and dated this 25 Day of August in the year 1798

Witness   John BRUFF   (Seal)
Littleton FURNIS"

*followed with the acknowledgment by Justice of the Peace Philip QUINTON and the recordation by court clerk John C. HANDY[848]

Liber S, folios 460-461; 01 March 1799

"Know all men by these presents that I Betty GUNN of Snow Hill Town in Worcester County & State of Maryland and Administratrix of all and Singular the Goods and Chattels, rights and credits of Samuel GUNN late of Said County deceased for & inconsideration of that a certain Thomas HARRISON hath paid unto Mr John EVANS of Philadelphia for my use the Sum of Two hundred Dollars and for divers other good Causes and Considerations me thereunto moving I have liberated discharged and Set free from Bondage and do by these presents liberate Discharge & set free from Bondage a certain negro man called **Zed** that belongs to my deceased husband Samuel GUNN's Estate and having Administered on the said Estate and being entitled to one third part thereof under the Statute of Distribution, I do hereby affirm that I have full power and Authority to dispose of any part thereof for the purpose of paying Debts due from the Said Estate, and whereas the Said Sum of money hath been Applied towards paying the

---

[846] Worcester County Court (Land Records). Deed of Manumission from OUTTEN, Levi to **Nanny**. 03 August 1796. S, pp. 434, MSA CE 30-18. www.mdlandrec.net : accessed 31 May 2022.
[847] Worcester County Court (Land Records). Deed of Manumission from BRUTON, William to **George** and **Harry**. 11 August 1798. S, pp. 436-437, MSA CE 30-18. www.mdlandrec.net : accessed 31 May 2022.
[848] Worcester County Court (Land Records). Bill of Sale from BRUFF, John to FURNIS, Ephraim. 25 August 1798. S, pp. 440-441, MSA CE 30-18. www.mdlandrec.net : accessed 31 May 2022.

Debts of Said deceased I have liberated and Set free the Said negro man Called **Zed** and I do hereby for my Self my Executors & administrators or other legal representative remise release & for ever quit Claim unto the Said {?} Called **Zed** all rights title and Claim Whatsoever to the Person of the Said **Zed** or to any Estate he shall or may Acquire hereby declaring the Said negro man **Zed** a freeman to all intents and purposes that the laws of the County will admit of. In Testimony whereof I have hereunto Set my hand & Seal affixed the first day of March Anno Domini one thousand Seven hundred and ninety nine

Signed Sealed & Delivered   Philip QUINTON   Betty GUNN   (Seal)
In Presence of ~ . .   John CUTLER . ."

*followed on folio 461 with the acknowledgment by Justice of the Peace Philip QUINTON and the recordation by court clerk John C. HANDY[849]

Liber S, folios 476-478; 17 August 1798

"This Indenture made this 17th day of August Anno Domini One thousand Seven hundred and Ninety and Eight between Betsy ATKINSON Daughter of Angello of Worcester County in the State of Maryland of the One part and William HANDY of the County and State af[ore]s[ai]d of the other part Witnesseth that the said Betsey ATKINSON for and in Consideration of the Sum of five Shillings Current money of Maryland to the said Betsy ATKINSON by the said William HANDY in hand paid at and before the Ensealing & delivery hereof the Receipt whereof the said Betsy ATKINSON doth hereby confessed and acknowledge, hath given Granted, bargained & Sold and by these presents doth give Grant, bargain & Sell alein Release Convey and Confirm unto the said William HANDY his heirs & assigns forever all that property matters & things as expressed in my mother Comfort HANDYs Deed of Gift to me. Bearing equal Date with these presents and which property matters & things are as follows viz. One negro Boy called **Harry** (provided he was in my mothers Right to give me) one negro Girl called **Esther** (the Daughter of **Hannah**) one negro girl called **Orris**, one negro Girl called **Esther**, the Daughter of **Dinah**, one negro Girl called **Rodah**, & one negro Girl called **Rachel** ~ Two Feather Beds & Furniture not exceeding, the value of Eleven pounds five Shillings, both put together ~ Six new Silver Spoons ~ Twelve Silver Tea Spoons ~ One Copper {?}ale Kettle the Riding Saddle of my mother & one Common pewter Dish (or so many or all of which things or are now in Being & that are now to be had as is contained in W[illia]m HANDYs Recorded Bond to my mothers children, Except one Copper Coffe pott ~ To have and to hold (except in Case of negro **Harry** he should be Deemed my property and not in my mothers Gift) all and Singular the negroes and other things above mentioned unto the said William HANDY his heirs & assigns forever and to & for no other use or purpose whatever ~ and the said Betsy ATKINSON for herself her heirs Ex[ecutor]s & Administrators doth hereby Covenant & Agree to & with the said William HANDY his heirs Executors Adm[inistrato]rs & assigns ~ That She the said Betsey ATKINSON will Warrant and forever defend the af[ore]s[ai]d negroes & other things as above expressed (with the above exception) unto the said William HANDY his heirs and assigns forever as the said William HANDY his heirs and assigns shall lawfully and Reasonably advise & require ~ In Testimony whereof the said Betsy ATKINSON hath hereunto set her hand & affixed her Seal the Day and Date first above written ~ ~ ~ ~

Signed Sealed & acknowledged   Betsy ATKINSON   (Seal)
In presence of ~ ~ ~
Jesse BENNITT"

*followed on folio 478 with the acknowledgment by Justice of the Peace Jesse BENNITT and the recordation on 04 September 1798 by court clerk John C. HANDY[850]

---

[849] Worcester County Court (Land Records). Deed of Manumission from GUNN, Betty to **Zed**. 01 March 1799. S, pp. 460-461, MSA CE 30-18. www.mdlandrec.net : accessed 31 May 2022.
[850] Worcester County Court (Land Records). Deed from ATKINSON, Betsy to HANDY, William. 17 August 1798. S, pp. 476-478, MSA CE 30-18. www.mdlandrec.net : accessed 31 May 2022.

Liber S, folios 479-482; 17 August 1798

"This Indenture made this 17th day of August Anno Domini one thousand seven hundred and Ninety Eight Comfort HANDY of Worcester County & State of Maryland of the one part and who claims the right & previledge of making this Deed by my written Marriage Contract, with my present husband William HANDY made in the month of February Anno Dom[ini] One thousand seven hundred and ninety and two may appear in the records of the County af[ore]s[ai]d thereby Entitling me to give certain property, as reserved to my own disposial either by may last will & Testament or by my Deed of Gift Just as I may choose to my children, Therefore in Virtue of which & Conformed by Thereto, I the said Comfort HANDY wife of William HANDY do by and with his Consent enter into & make this my Deed on my part to and with my Daughter Betsy ATKINSON & Anna ATKINSON on their part, and which Witnesseth that the said Comfort HANDY for and in Consideration of the Love and Good Will that she the said Comfort beareth unto her two af[ore]s[ai]d Daughters Betsy ATKINSON & Anna ATKINSON & likewise for the further Consideration of the Sum of five Shillings Current money of Maryland to the said Comfort HANDY by the said Betsy & Anna ATKINSON in hand paid at and before the Ensealing & Delivery hereof (the receipt whereof the said Comfort HANDY doth hereby confess & acknowledge) hath given Granted bargained & Sold and by these presents doth give, Grant, Bargain, & Sell alein Release & Convey unto the said Betsy ATKINSON her heirs & assigns forever, all that property the matters & things as was & is expressed in my af[ore]s[ai]d Husbands Bond to my five Children as is recorded in the County Clerks office and dated the fifteenth day of February Anno Dom[ini] One thousand Seven hundred ninety & two excepting from said property one Copper Coffee Pott which I give to my Daughter Anna & to her heirs and assigns forever, and all which remaining property as expressed in my said Husbands Bond unto my children so recorded as af[ore]s[ai]d & containing (besides which af[ore]s[ai]d Coffee pott) one negro Boy called **Harry** one negro Girl called **Esther** (the Daughter of **Hannah**) one negro Girl called **Orris**; one negro Girl called **Esther** (the Daughter of **Dinah**) one negro girl Called **Rodah** & one negro Girl called **Rachel** ~ Two Feather Beds & Furniture not exceeding the value of Eleven pounds five Shillings both put together Six new Silver Spoons twelve Silver Tea Spoons, one Copper Bale Kettle, the said Comforts Present Riding Saddle and one Common Pewter Dish, or so many or all of which things are now in being & that are to be had ~ To have and to hold all & Singular the negroes & other things as above mentioned unto the said Betsy ATKINSON her heirs & assigns forever & to and for no other use or purpose whatever) and the said Comfort HANDY for herself her heirs Executors & Adm[inistrator]s doth hereby Covenant, & agree to and with the said Betsy ATKINSON her heirs Ex[ecuto]rs & Adm[inistrato]rs & assigns that she the said Comfort HANDY by virtue of her af[ore]s[ai]d reserved Right will warrant & forever hereafter defend the af[oresai]d negroes & other things as above expressed unto the said Betsy ATKINSON her heirs and assigns for ever, as the said Betsy ATKINSON her heirs and assigns Shall Lawfully and Reasonably advise or require In Testimony whareof the said Comfort HANDY hath hereunto set her hand & affixed her Seal the Day & Date first above written ~

Signed Sealed & acknowledged   Comfort HANDY   (Seal)
In the Presence off
Jesse BENNITT ~"

*followed on folio 481 with the memorandum on 29 August 1798 by William HANDY, the acknowledgment by Justice of the Peace Jesse BENNETT, and the recordation on 04 September 1798 by court clerk John C. HANDY[851]

Liber S, folios 482-484; 01 September 1798

"Know all men by these presents that we William HANDY & Thomas Robins HANDY both of Worcester County & State of Maryland, am held & firmly bound unto Angello, George, Betsy, Benjamin & Anna ATKINSON (the children of my present wife) in the full and Just sum

---

[851] Worcester County Court (Land Records). Deed from HANDY, Comfort to ATKINSON, Betsy & Anna. 17 August 1798. S, pp. 479-482, MSA CE 30-18. www.mdlandrec.net : accessed 31 May 2022.

of one Thousand Pounds Current money of Maryland. To which payment well and truly to be made and done we bind ourselves, our heirs Executors & Adm[inistrato]^{rs} firmly by these presents sealed with our seals & dated this 1$^{s[t]}$ day of September Anno Dom[ini] One thousand seven hundred ninety and Eight ~ The Condition of the above obligation is such that whereas the above Bounden W[illia]^m HANDY did on the fifteenth day of February Seventeen hundred ninety & two enter into a Bond or written Marriage Contract, made with his present wife, by a sealed Instrument of writing from either to the others children as may appear in the records of the County clerks office and which was intended to bind each other unto the faithfull performance of our said Marriage Contract ~ and since which time, the legal and Executive right to my wife of said negroes, as expressed in my Bond or Marriage Contract (and which she had thought was abstracted from her deceased husband Estate, & free from any and every other claimant has since became disputed ~ and a law suit like to Ensue, my said Wife has therefore Engaged me, to defend & Support her Exclusive Just and legal Right (if any she had to said negroes: and also to try and bring into her former Husbands Estate certain negroes commonly called Germans negroes, as exclusively taken and claimed by Isaac WILLIAMS, Joshua ATKINSON & Isaac ATKINSON, & who is about to stir up a dispute about the negroes, that my wife Supposed to have been her own exclusive right and as mentioned in our said Marriage Contract ~ and which complicated disputes, with others likely to arise I will strive to settle either by Law arbitration or Compromise, as I may think best, & least expensive ~ and to defray which consequent Expence, and for other good causes & considerations my said wife through her Daughter, Betsy has vested or intended to vest me with the principal part of her af[ore]s[ai]^d reserved property ~ if their several Deeds for which purpose be valed & be recorded and out of which her reserved property, that I shall be Reimbursed for any Cost or expence in striving to settle all or any of the above Disputes and to give up for distribution, into my wifes former husbands Estate any which af[ore]s[ai]^d reserved negroes (to her disposial) as my wife had thought was her exclusive Right, On Proviso, which negroes, or any part of them should be taken and adjudged legally to belong to the Estate of her former Husband Now the Condition of this obligation further Witnesseth that if I bring Germans af[ore]s[ai]^d negroes into the Estate of my wifes former Husband or if that the negroes as willed to my said wife by her Father should be brought in, and adjudged to belong to the Estate of her former Husband ~ That then, and in that case, we bind ourselves, in the penalty of One thousand pounds as af[ore]s[ai]^d that I will forever disown & disclaim all manner of right or Title to my thirds of which {?} Except negro **Hannah** and her two young children that I have sold and I do absolutely & Intirely yield the rest unto my wifes own free disposal, Either by her last written will & Testament or by her written Deed of Gift, Just when she pleases, and as she may choose, my thirds of which af[ore]s[ai]^d negroes, together, with the Silver plate Beds and all other matters not being of negro Flesh, Just as Betsy ATKINSON has deeded them to me, after my af[ore]s[ai]^d Reimbursement are made and excepting in all cases as is excepted. ~ And nothing herein contained shall be understood to defeat or change the af[ore]s[ai]^d property, as by my wife in her af[ore]s[ai]^d Marriage Contract conditionally Deeded to my children the Several matters and things as above contained, being complied with according to their true intent and meaning, Then this obligation to be void and of no effect, or otherwise to stand and remain in full force power & virtue in Law, ~ ~ ~ ~

Signed Sealed & Delivered	William HANDY (Seal)
In the presence of us ~	Thomas R. HANDY (Seal)
Bowdoin ROBINS	
Frederick RANDALL"	

*followed on folio 484 with the recordation on 05 September 1798 by court clerk John C. HANDY[852]

---

[852] Worcester County Court (Land Records). Bond from HANDY, William and Thomas Robins to ATKINSON, Angello, George, Betsy, Anna, and Benjamin. 01 September 1798. S, pp. 482-484, MSA CE 30-18. www.mdlandrec.net : accessed 31 May 2022.

Liber S, folio 485; 02 July 1798

"We John Laws HENDERSON and Rhoday BOUD of Worcester County in the Stat of Maryland do acknowleg this day to have sold a negro woman named **venus** and child named **Peter** to William Bivens HENDERSON of Firaderck County in the Stat of Virginia for the Som of Fifty Pounds in hands pad this day by the said William Bivens HENDERSON to the said John Laws HENDERSON and Rhoday BOUDS we do word and defend the title of the said named **venus** and a child named **Peter** against any parson or parsons claming or to lay clame to any part thirof given under our hands and seals this 2^d day of July of July 1798 ~ ~

Hope TAYLOR   John Laws HENDERSON (Seal)
Levi HOUSTON   Rhoday X BOUD (Seal)
                                                                   her mark"

*followed with the recordation on 20 July 1798 by court clerk John C. HANDY[853]

Liber S, folios 496-497; 15 September 1798

"Maryland, Worcester County Sc^t. Know all men by these presents that I William BURTON of Worcester County, for & in consideration of one hundred & fifty pounds to me in hand paid by Margaret PARSONS the receipt, I do hereby acknowledge have granted bargained and Sold and do by these presents, grant bargain and Sell unto the said Margaret PARSONS her heirs or assigns all my personal property Viz. two negroes **Harry**, and **Nance**, two mares and one Colt twenty five of Hogs, ten head of Sheep Eleven head of Cattle, four Beds & furniture, household and Kitchen furniture and plantation Utensils &c. To have and to hold the aforesaid bargained & sold property to her the said Margaret PARSONS, her heirs and assigns, I do hereby, bind myself my heirs and assigns to warrant and defend against all and all manner of persons claiming, the same by from or under me or any other person or persons whatsoever, In Testimony I have hereto set my hand and fixed my seal this fifteenth day of September Anno Dom[ini] 1798 ~ ~ ~ ~

Signed Sealed & Deliv[ere]^d William BURETON (Seal)
in presence of.

Booz WALSTON"

*followed on folio 497 with acknowledgment by Justice of the Peace Booz WALSTON and the recordation on 17 September 1798 by court clerk John C. HANDY[854]

*The acknowledgment lists the grantor as "William BURINGTON".

Liber T, folios 1-2; 12 October 1798

"Worcester Sc^t. Know all men by these presents that I Comfort McCORMACK of Worcester County State of Maryland, for and in consideration of the sum of One hundred Dollars, to me in hand paid by Rouse GRAY of the same place at or before the Ensealing and Delivery of these presents wherewith I confess myself to be fully Satisfied contented paid Have bargained sold and delivered and by these presents do fully clearly and absolutely Bargain sell and deliver unto the said Rouse GRAY one Negro woman named **Juda**, about thirty five years of age, To have and to hold the said negro woman **Juda** to the said Rouse GRAY his Executors Administrators & assigns, to his and their own proper uses and behoofs forever & I the said Comfort McCORMACK my heirs Executors & Administrators, and every of us, the said negro woman **Juda**, to the said Rouse GRAY his heirs and assigns against all people {?} shall and

---

[853] Worcester County Court (Land Records). Bill of Sale from HENDERSON, John Laws and BOUD, Rhoday to HENDERSON, William Bivens. 02 July 1798. S, p. 485, MSA CE 30-18. www.mdlandrec.net : accessed 31 May 2022.

[854] Worcester County Court (Land Records). Bill of Sale from BURETON, William to PARSONS, Margaret. 15 September 1798. S, pp. 496-497, MSA CE 30-18. www.mdlandrec.net : accessed 31 May 2022.

will warrant, acquit, and forever defend by these presents, Witness my hand and Seal this 12th day of October ~~Anno Dom~~ 1798

Sealed & Deliv[ere]^d
in the presence of
John POSTLY

Comfort X McCORMACK (Seal)
her mark"

*followed with the acknowledgment by Justice of the Peace John POSTLY and the recordation on folio 2 by court clerk John C. HANDY on 15 October 1798[855]

Liber T, folios 34-35; 07 November 1798

"Know all men by these presents that I Levi TOWNSEND of Worcester County in the State of Maryland for and in Consideration of the Sum of Sixty pounds Current money of Maryland to him in hand paid at or before the sealing and delivery of these presents do bargain Sell & Convey four negroes as follows, viz. one negro woman called **Amelia**, one negro Girl called **Nancy** one negro Boy called **James**, and a negro Boy called **Ned**, unto Levin TOWNSEND his heirs Executors Administrators or assigns and the said Levi TOWNSEND doth for himself his heirs Executors Administrators forever Warrant and defend the said four above named negroes unto the said Levin TOWNSEND his heirs and assigns In Testimony whereof the said Levi TOWNSEND have hereunto set his hand and affixed his seal this Seventh day of November Anno Domini One thousand seven hundred and Ninety Eight ~

Sealed & Deliv[ere]^d
in presence of
John COTTINGHAM"

Levi TOWNSEND (Seal)

*followed on folio 35 with the acknowledgment by Justice of the Peace John COTTINGHAM and the recordation on 09 November 1798 by court clerk John C. HANDY[856]

Liber T, folios 35-37; 13 November 1798

"This Indenture made this thirteenth day of November in the year One thousand seven hundred and ninety Eight Between **Samuel COLLICK** of Worcester County and State of Maryland, Free Mollatto of the one part and Valentine DENNIS of the same place of the other part Witnesseth that the aforesaid **Samuel COLLICK** for and in Consideration of the sum of three Pounds fifteen Shillings Current money of Maryland to him in hand paid by the af[ore]s[ai]^d Valentine DENNIS at and before the Sealing and delivery of these presents the receipt whereof is hereby confessed & acknowledged hath Granted, bargained, sold Conveyed and confirmed & by these presents doth absolutely Grant, bargain, sell convey & Confirm, unto him the said Valentine DENNIS his heirs & assigns forever all his the aforesaid **Samuel COLLICK** right title, Claim or demand of or unto a tract of Land called Red Oak Ridge Situate lying and being in Worcester County aforesaid in Acquango Hundred, the aforesaid Right or title is estimated to be the quantity of Six acres of Land, together with all its rights members, profits Benefits priviledges and all other the appurtenances thereto belonging or in any manner appertaining To have and to hold the af[ore]s[ai]^d bargained Lands & premises unto him the aforesaid Valentine DENNIS his heirs and assigns forever, and the said **Samuel COLLICK** for himself his heirs executors and Administrators, doth hereby Covenant and Grant, to quit all right, title claim or demand that he now hath, or shall ever hereafter have unto the above mentioned Lands and premises, and will and shall forever Warrant and forever defend the same against the lawfull right or title of all manner of person or persons whatever claiming by from or under him, them or any of them, unto the aforesaid Valentine DENNIS his heirs or assigns forever In Testimony

---

[855] Worcester County Court (Land Records). Bill of Sale from McCORMACK, Comfort to GRAY, Rouse. 12 October 1798. T, pp. 1-2, MSA CE 30-19. www.mdlandrec.net : accessed 12 June 2022.

[856] Worcester County Court (Land Records). Bill of Sale from TOWNSEND, Levi to TOWNSEND, Levin. 07 November 1798. T, pp. 34-35, MSA CE 30-19. www.mdlandrec.net : accessed 12 June 2022.

whereof the aforesaid **Samuel COLLICK** to these presents his hand hath set and affixed the day & year above written ~

Signed Sealed & Deliv[ere]ᵈ **Samuel COLLICK** (Seal)
in presence of
Philip QUINTON   Elisha PURNELL"

*followed on folio 36 with the acknowledgment by Justices of the Peace Philip QUINTON and Elisha PURNELL and the recordation on folio 37 by court clerk John C. HANDY[857]

Liber T, folios 59-60; 28 November 1798

"Know all men by these presence that I James BRODWATTER of Worcester C[oun]ty St[ate] Mary[lan]ᵈ for an inconsideration of the sum of the sum of Eighty Two pounds & ten shillings Current Money of Maryland to me in hand paid by Boykins & Chalmers of the County of Southampton the receipt Whereof I the said James BRODWATTER do hereby acknowledge have granted bargained sold & Delivered unto the said Boykin & Chalmers & to their heirs & Assigns One Negro Man named **William** aged Eighteen years To have and to hold the said slave unto them the said Boykin & Chalmers & to their heirs & Assigns to the only proper use of them the said Boykin & Chalmers their heirs and Assigns forever And I do for myself my Heirs Exe[cutors] and Admin[istrato]rs covenant promise & grant to and with them the said Boykins & Chalmers their Heirs and Assigns that I will Warrant & forever defend the title of the said slave unto them the Said Boykin & Chalmers their heirs & assigns against the title Claim or demand of any person or persons whatsoever In Witness whereof I have hereunto set my hand & Seal this 28th Day of November 1798

Signed Sealed & Delivered   Jonathan HUDSON Jun[io]ʳ   James BRODWATTER (Seal)
In presence of . . .   Angelo ATKINSON . ."

*followed on folio 60 with the recordation on 07 December 1798 by court clerk John Custis HANDY[858]

Liber T, folio 62; 06 May 1799

"Worcester County Maryland State . . . .
Know all men by these presents that I Jacob POWELL rec[eive]ᵈ of Joshua AYDELOTT the full & Just sum of Eightty five pounds lawful paysing money of this plase for a Neagro Boy by the Name of **George** Aged about fourteen years which said Neagro I warrent and for Ever Defend from all persons unto the said Joshua AYDELOTT his heirs & ass[ig]ⁿˢ from me my heirs & Assigns for Ever as Witness I hereunto Set my hand & seal this the Sixth Day of May Anno Dom[in]i In the year of our lord one thousand seven hundred and ninety Nine 1799

Witness present. Test   Joseph SEALS & Mary AYDELOTT   Jacob POWELL (Seal)"

*followed with the recordation on 15 May 1799 by court clerk John Custis HANDY[859]

Liber T, folio 74; 18 January 1798

"Know all men by these presents that I Luke TOWNSEND of Worcester County and State of Maryland for divers Goods causes me thereunto moveing do this day Manumate and set at Liberty my negro woman named **Tabitha** about Forty years of age to be her own free woman forever from any claim or Demand of me or any of my heirs Executors Administrators or assigns for ever and from the claim or claims of all manner of person or persons whatsoever I do and will forever warrant and defend the freedom of the above said Neagro woman named

---

[857] Worcester County Court (Land Records). Bill of Sale from **COLLICK, Samuel** to DENNIS, Valentine. 13 November 1798. T, pp. 35-37, MSA CE 30-19. www.mdlandrec.net : accessed 12 June 2022.

[858] Worcester County Court (Land Records). Bill of Sale from BRODWATTER, James to Boykins & Chalmers. 28 November 1798. T, pp. 59-60, MSA CE 30-19. www.mdlandrec.net : accessed 12 June 2022.

[859] Worcester County Court (Land Records). Receipt from POWELL, Jacob to AYDELOTT, Joshua. 06 May 1799. T, p. 62, MSA CE 30-19. www.mdlandrec.net : accessed 12 June 2022.

Tabitha under the Penalty of Five Hundred Pounds current money of this State, In Testimony whereof I have hereunto set my hand affixed my seal this Eighteenth day of January Anno Domini Seventeen hundred and Ninety Eight

Signed sealed & Deliv[ere]^d   Luke TOWNSEND (Seal)
In the Presence of
Ezekiel WILLIAMS

Rachel X WEBBER
(her mark)

Nancy TOWNSEND"

*followed with the acknowledgment by Justice of the Peace Josiah MITCHELL on 26 May 1798 and the recordation on 30 December 1798 by court clerk John C. HANDY[860]

Liber T, folios 75-77; 19 December 1798

"This Indenture made this Nineteenth day of December in the year One thousand seven hundred & Ninety Eight Between Leah GUNN of Worcester County and State of Maryland of the one part and Nancy GUNN of the same place Minor, Witnesseth that the aforesaid Leah GUNN for and in consideration of the sum of five shillings current money of Maryland to her in hand paid but more especially for and in consideration of the love and effection that I the aforesaid Leah GUNN, have and doth bear unto my Daughter Nancy GUNN aforesaid Have Given Granted and delivered unto my said Daughter Nancy GUNN and her heirs and assigns forever after my decease excepting only my life time in said Goods & chattels herein mentioned & by these presents doth absolutely give Grant, Transfer, deliver & set over unto her the aforesaid Nancy GUNN her heirs & assigns forever The following personal Estate to be possessed & enjoyed by the aforesaid Nancy at the age of Sixteen years of age, to wit One negro woman called **Mary** one negro Boy called **Isaac** Three Gold Rings one pair silver shoe Buckles six silver Table spoons marked J.L.G. Twelve ditto Tea Spoons, one pair D[itt]° Tongs, One Mahogany Bowfat one walnut Bureau 1 Dining Walnut Table One Walnut Breakfast Ditto One D[itt]° Candle stand, one Large Looking Glass one Large Chinea Bowl six cups & Saucers D[itt]° one D[itt]° sugar Dish. Cream cup D[itt]° one doz[e]^n Blue & white plates two feather Beds & furniture including twelve sheets, three Blankets, one Blue & white Counterpin one stuff Bed Quilt three Summer Bed Quilts four Pillows & eight cases my own wearing apperral One large & one Small Trunk 1 Side Saddle 1 Large Bible & Watts Psalms. Together with all their Rights members profits Benefits previledges & appurtenances thereto belonging or in any manner Appurtaining To have and to hold all & singular the aforesaid Negroes, Household furniture Goods & Chattles aforesaid hereby intended to be given Transferred and set over unto her the aforesaid Nancy GUNN and to her heirs and assigns forever to the only proper use benefit & behoof of her the said Nancy GUNN her heirs and assigns forever and to and for no other use intent, purpose, or construction whatsoever, and I the said Leah GUNN for myself my heirs Executors & Administrators doth hereby covenant, Grant and agree that I will warrant & forever defend the several articles Goods & chattels as above mentioned and set forth provided the above mentioned Nancy GUNN shall arrive to the age of Sixteen years old, against the lawfull right Title claim or demand of all manner of person or persons whatever, unto her the aforesaid Nancy GUNN her heirs and assigns forever provided, as above provided and accepted. In Testimony whereof I the said Leah GUNN to these presents my hand hath set and seal affixed the day and year above written ~

Signed sealed & Deliv[ere]^d   Leah X GUNN (Seal)
In Presence of   (her mark)

N.B. the word after my decease excepted
only my life time in said Goods & Chattles

---

[860] Worcester County Court (Land Records). Deed of Manumission from TOWNSEND, Luke to **Tabitha**. 18 January 1798. T, p. 74, MSA CE 30-19. www.mdlandrec.net : accessed 12 June 2022.

herein mentioned at the sixth line were interlined
before the execution hereof ~
Esme PURNELL ~"

*followed on folio 76 with the acknowledgment by Justice of the Peace Esme PURNELL and the recordation on folio 77 on 31 December 1798 by court clerk John C. HANDY[861]

Liber T, folios 78-80; 09 February 1798

"State of Maryland Worcester County Sc^t. Know all men by these presents that I Solomon LONG of the County af[ore]s[ai]^d for and in consideration of the sum of Fifty Pounds specie to me in hand paid by Jesse GRAY of the same place the receipt whereof I do hereby acknowledge and myself therewith fully satisfied and paid have bargained & Sold unto the af[ore]s[ai]^d Jesse GRAY and his heirs and assigns and by these presents do Grant bargain Sell & Deliver unto him the Jesse GRAY his heirs & assigns in due form of Law the following articles (viz) One Negro man named **Jacob** Two Cows and Yearlings One Small Bull Three two year Old Heiffers two Sows and fourteen Shoats two Beds & furniture One Dish & two tables Six Old chairs Old hand Mill One pott & one kettle, one Chest, Cyder Cask and old Lumber also three hundred Bushels of Indian Corn and Looking Glass & Pewter amounting and estimated to Fifty Pounds Specie To have and to hold the af[ore]s[ai]^d bargained & Sold Goods and Chattles unto the af[ore]s[ai]^d Jesse GRAY his heirs and assigns forever and I the aforesaid Solomon LONG for my & my heirs and all and every the af[oresai]^d shall and will warrant & forever Defend the af[ore]s[ai]^d bargained & Sold Goods & Chattles unto the aforesaid Jesse GRAY and his heirs and assigns In Witness whereof I the af[ore]s[ai]^d Solomon LONG have to this my pen set my hand & affixed my seal this Eight day of February A.D. 1799 ~

Signed sealed & Deliv[ere]^d Solomon LONG   (Seal)
In the presence of
John P. MITCHELL"

*followed on folio 79 with the acknowledgment by Justice of the Peace John P. MITCHELL and the recordation on 22 February 1799 by court clerk John C. HANDY[862]

Liber T, folio 84; 31 December 1798

"List of Negroes Brought from the State of Virginia in the State of Maryland by me the subscriber the 31th of December 1798. Which Slaves has been a resident or is the Descendant of Slaves Resident of the State of Virginia before the Twenty first Day of April 1783 Viz 1 Negro Girl Called **Candis** aged about 8 or 9 years of age the Title to which Negro I Derive from my wife Tabitha MERRILL ~ ~

                        Thomas MERRILL ~ . ~ . ."

*followed with the recordation on 04 January 1799 by court clerk John C. HANDY[863]

Liber T, folio 96; 01 January 1799

"Know all men by these presents that I William MORRIS of Worcester County and State of Maryland for and consideration of the Services heretofore rendered me by negro **Capril** and **Dinah** as well as from a conviction of the impropriety of retaining in perpetual Bondage any of the human Species do hereby Manumit & forever discharge from Slavery the af[ore]s[ai]^d Negroes **Capril & Dinah** To have and to hold to the af[ore]s[ai]^d **Capril** and **Dinah** their respective freedoms forever against the right title or claim of the said William & his heirs and

---

[861] Worcester County Court (Land Records). Deed of Gift from GUNN, Leah to GUNN, Nancy. 19 December 1798. T, pp. 75-77, MSA CE 30-19. www.mdlandrec.net : accessed 12 June 2022.
[862] Worcester County Court (Land Records). Bill of Sale from LONG, Solomon to GRAY, Jesse. 09 February 1799. T, pp. 78-80, MSA CE 30-19. www.mdlandrec.net : accessed 12 June 2022.
[863] Worcester County Court (Land Records). Certificate of Importation into Maryland from MERRILL, Thomas for **Candis**. 31 December 1798. T, p. 84, MSA CE 30-19. www.mdlandrec.net : accessed 12 June 2022.

assigns forever. In Testimony whereof I have hereto set my hand & affixed my seal this 1ʰ day of January Anno Dom 1799 ~

Signed Sealed & Deliv[ere]ᵈ   William MORRIS (Seal)
In presence of
W[illia]ᵐ WHITTINGTON.   James MARTIN"

*followed with the acknowledgment by Justice of the Peace Jesse BENNETT on 22 January 1799 and the recordation by court clerk John Custis HANDY[864]

Liber T, folios 96-97; 31 December 1798

"Articles of Agreement made and Concluded on this 31ᵗʰ Day of December Anno Dom[ini] 1798 Between William MORRIS of the one part and Purnell PORTER of the other part Witnesseth that the said William for and inconsideration of the Covenant herein after mentioned hath bargained and sold to the said Purnell a negro Woman Slave Named **Hesse** aged some where about Twenty acres for and during the Terms of ten years freely to be Completed as also a young son She now has aged Somewhere about two years with whatever other Child or Children grand Child or grandchild that may be born of her or discend from her during the said Term the Child Children or grandchildren that may happen so to be born or descend from her to be retained by the said Purnell as servants to him and his heirs or assigns untill they shall respectevely attain their respective ages of Twenty Eight Years from the Day of their Births and the said Purnell on his part and behalf doth promise to pay unto the said William or order within one year from the date hereof the sum of Twenty pounds Current money of Maryland with legal Intrust thereon untill paid and he doth further Covenenant and agree for himself and his heirs that he and they will teach or cause to be taught all such Children and grandchildren that the af[oresai]ᵈ negro now has or may hereafter descend from her to learn to read In Testimony whereof the parties to these presents their hands have set and seals affixed the Day and year af[oresai]ᵈ . . . .

Signed sealed and . .   William MORRIS (Seal)
Delivered In presence of   Purnell PORTER (Seal)
Littleton R PURNELL
James DAVIS . . ."

*followed on folio 97 with the recordation on 22 January 1799 by court clerk John Custis HANDY[865]

* "acres" was mistakenly written instead of "years"

Liber T, folios 97-98; 31 December 1798

"Know all men by these presents that I William MORRIS of Worcester County in the State of Maryland for and in consideration of the Sundry Services hereto performed by negro Woman slave named **Hesse** as well as from a convection of the impropriety of retaining in perpetual Bondage any of the human species do hereby at the Expiration of ten years from this thirty first Day of December Anno Domini Seventeen hundred & ninety Eight manumit and forever discharge from bondage the said **Hesse** and a male child named **Isaac** aged two years with all other Children or grand Children or their issue that may discend from her or them when they shall respectively attain their ages of Twenty Eighty years and subject only to such servitude as is stipulated in an article of agreement entered into between me and a Certain Purnell PORTER of the date of these Presents To Have and to hold to the af[oresai]ᵈ **Hesse** and their issue af[oresai]ᵈ conformably the af[oresai]ᵈ articles of agreement at the Expiration of their Terms of Servitude af[oresai]ᵈ Their freedom forever against the right title or Claim of the said William

---

[864] Worcester County Court (Land Records). Deed of Manumission from MORRIS, William to **Capril** and **Dinah**. 01 January 1799. T, p. 96, MSA CE 30-19. www.mdlandrec.net : accessed 12 June 2022.
[865] Worcester County Court (Land Records). Articles of Agreement between MORRIS, William and PORTER, Purnell. 31 December 1798. T, pp. 96-97, MSA CE 30-19. www.mdlandrec.net : accessed 12 June 2022.

and his heirs and assigns forever In Testimoney whereof I have hereto set my name and affixed my Seal this 31ᵗʰ Day of December Anno Dom[ini] 1798. . ~ . . . . . .

Signed Sealed and Delivered		William MORRIS (Seal)
In presence of	NB That the words manumit and forever discharge from	
W[illia]ᵐ WHITTINGTON	Bondage the said **Hesse** between the 7ᵗʰ & 8ᵗʰ line from Top	
James MARTIN	was inserted previous to the Execution of the above Deed"	

*followed on folio 98 with the acknowledgment by Justice of the Peace Jesse BENNETT on 22 January 1799 and the recordation by court clerk John Custis HANDY[866]

Liber T, folio 98; 31 December 1798

"Articles of agreement made and Concluded on this 31ᵗʰ Day of December Anno Dom[ini] 1798 Between William MORRIS of the one part and Littleton R PURNELL of the other part witnesseth that the said William for and in consideration of the Covenant herein after mentioned and Expressed hath bargained and Sold unto the said Littleton a negro woman called **Minte** Aged about Twenty three years for and During the Term of three years from the date hereof and a negro child supposed about two named **Sal** with all other Children or grand children that may hereafter be born or descend from her during her Term untill the said Child Children or grandchildren shall respectively attain their ages of Twenty five years the said Child **Sal** with whatever descendants may be bear from her in his house to be retained by him the said Littleton and his heirs as servants untill their ages af[oresai]ᵈ Shall expire from the Day of their respective Berthes and the said Littleton on his part and behalf doth hereby promise to pay unto the said William or order the sum of Twelve pounds ten shillings Current money of Maryland and demand with legal Interest untill paid In Testimony Whereof the Said parties to these presents their hands have set and Seals affixed the Day and year af[oresai]d. . ~ . . . .

Signed sealed and Delivered	Samuel PORTER	William MORRIS (Seal)
In Presence of ~ ~	James DAVIS	Littleton P PURNELL (Seal)"

*followed with the recordation on 22 January 1799 by court clerk John Custis HANDY[867]

Liber T, folio 99; 31 December 1798

"To all Presents to whom this Presents may concern Know ye that I William MORRIS of Worcester County and State of Maryland for and in consideration of the Services heretofore rendered by a negro Woman Slave named **Minte** as well as from a conviction of the impropriety in perpetual Bondage any of the human species do hereby at the expiration of three years from this thirty first Day of December Anno Domini seventeen hundred and ninety Eight manumit and forever Discharge from bondage the Said **Minte** and also a male Child She now has aged two years named **Sub** with all other Children or grandchildren or their Issue that may descend from the said **Minte** or any of her Issue when they shall respectively arive to the age of Twenty five years & subject only to such servitude as is stipulated in articles of agreement entered into between me and a Certain Littleton R. PURNELL dated 31ᵗʰ December Anno Dom[ini] one thousand Seven hundred and ninety Eight To have and to hold unto the said **Minte Sub** and their issue af[oresai]ᵈ agreeably to the af[oresai]ᵈ articles of agreement at the experation of their respective Terms af[oresai]ᵈ their freedom forever against the right tittle or Claim of the said William and his heirs and Assigns forever In Testimony whereof I have hereto set my hand and affixed my Seal this 31ᵗʰ Day of December Anno Dom[ini] 1799.

Signed Sealed and Delivered	W[illia]ᵐ WHITTINGTON	William MORRIS (Seal)
In presence of	James MARTIN"	

---

[866] Worcester County Court (Land Records). Deed of Manumission from MORRIS, William to **Hesse** and **Isaac**. 31 December 1798. T, pp. 97-98, MSA CE 30-19. www.mdlandrec.net : accessed 12 June 2022.

[867] Worcester County Court (Land Records). Articles of Agreement between MORRIS, William and PURNELL, Littleton P. 31 December 1798. T, p. 98, MSA CE 30-19. www.mdlandrec.net : accessed 12 June 2022.

*followed with the acknowledgment by Justice of the Peace Jesse BENNETT on 22 January 1799 and the recordation by court clerk John Custis HANDY[868]

*The year written should be 1798 and the male child named **Sub** should probably be **Sal**.

Liber T, folio 100; 23 January 1799

"State of Maryland Worcester County Know all men by these presents that We John ARMSTRONG John AYRES and Bayham ARMSTRONG all of the County and State af[oresai]^d are held and firmlly bound unto the State of Maryland in the full and Just sum of thirty pounds Current money of the State af[oresai]^d to be paid unto the County of Worcester to which payment well and Truly to be made and done & we bind our selves and Each of our heirs Executors and administrators and Every of them for and in the whole firmly by these presents sealed with our Seals this 23^d Day of January 1799 And whereas **Molly BLAKE** on the 21th Day of December 1798 personally appeared Before Benjamin DENNIS Esq[ui]^r[e] one of the States Justices of the Peace for the County of Worcester and made oath on the holy Evangels of Allmighty god that John ARMSTRONG the princible in the above bond was the only and true Farther and no one Else of her female bastard Child born on or about the first Day of December 1798 Which Child is likely to become a Charge to the County of Worcester af[oresai]^d The Condition of the above obligation is such that if the above bound John ARMSTRONG princible John AYRES and Bayham ARMSTRONG securitys do and Shall at all times hereafter save harmless and undemnify the County of Worcester from all Costs Charge or damage that may doth or Shall arrise or in any manner or may become a Burthen or Charge to the County af[oresai]^d concerning or by means of the said Bastard Child in any manner or way what so Ever that then the above obligation to be void and of none Effect other May to be and remain in full force Power and virtue in the Law ~

Signed Sealed and Delivered Jesse BENNETT one of   John + ARMSTRONG (Seal)
In the presence of ~   the States Justices of the   mark
                              peace for the County of

                                                      John AYRES (Seal)

                                                      Bayham + ARMSTRONG (Seal)
                                                             mark"

*followed with the recordation on 25 January 1799 by court clerk John Custis HANDY[869]

***Molly BLAKE** is likely the same **Mary BLAKE** in previous records. John and Bayham ARMSTRONG may also be of African descent.

Liber T, folio 101; 22 January 1799

"Worcester County State of Maryland. Know all men by these presents that I Azariah PURNELL of the said County for the Consideration of the sum of Twenty Pounds to me in hand paid before the sealing and Delivering of these presents the receipt whereof I do acknowledge have bargained sold and Delivered unto **Stephen ROWND** fre negro of the said County one negro Women Called **Ruth** to have and to hold the said bargined negro Women **Ruth** to the said **Stephen ROWNDS** Free negro to him his heirs Executors or assigns for ever and I the said Azariah PURNELL for my self my heirs Executors or assigns do Warrent and forever Defend the said negro Woman **Ruth** to the said **Stephen ROWNDS** or his heirs or assigns the said women Called **Ruth** against all persons having any right Title Claim against

---

[868] Worcester County Court (Land Records). Deed of Manumission from MORRIS, William to **Minte** and **Sub**. 31 December 1798. T, pp. 97-98, MSA CE 30-19. www.mdlandrec.net : accessed 12 June 2022.
[869] Worcester County Court (Land Records). Bastardy Bond from ARMSTRONG, John, ARMSTRONG, Bayham, and AYRES, John to the State of Maryland. 23 January 1799. T, p. 100, MSA CE 30-19. www.mdlandrec.net : accessed 12 June 2022.

the said negro women Called **Ruth** given from {?}der my hand & Seal This 22 Day of January 1799 ~ . . . .

Signed Sealed & delivered   Esme PURNELL   Azariah PURNELL (Seal)
in the presence of ~ ~"

*followed with the acknowledgment by Justice of the Peace Esme PURNELL and the recordation on 01 February 1799 by court clerk John Custis HANDY[870]

Liber T, folios 115-116; 25 October 1798

"Sussex County State of Delaware To all to whom this writing shall come be it known that I John POSTLY late of Worcester County in the State of Maryland Esquire but at this time in the State of Delaware aforesaid for and in Consideration of the faithfull Services heretofore rendered unto me by my negro man slave **Job** who is at this time in the State of Delaware do by these presents manumit emancipate set at Liberty and from the Service of me my heirs Executors Administrators and Assigns forever discharge the aforesaid negro **Job** & do hereby Covenant and agree that he shall forever as far as regards any claim or title in me to him or his Services enjoy & have all the Priviledges of a free negro. In Witness whereof I have hereunto set my hand & seal in the Presence of two witnesses this twenty fifth day of October in the Year of our Lord one thousand seven hundred & ninety Eight ~

Sealed & Deliv[ere]d   John POSTLY (Seal)
In the presence of
James P. WILSON.   Caleb RODNEY."

*followed on folio 116 with an acknowledgment mentioning Samuel PAINTER (Security) by Sussex County Justice of the Peace Caleb RODNEY, the recordation by Sussex County recorder Philip KOLLOCK on 16 November 1798, and the recordation by Worcester County court clerk John C. HANDY on 12 February 1799[871]

Liber T, folios 127-128; 30 March 1799

"Know all Men by these Presents that I William WARWICK of Worcester County in the State of Maryland who intermarried with Eleanor FLEMMING of the same Place and late Executrix of John FLEMMING deceased for and in Consideration of the Sum of Seventy five Pounds Current Money of Maryland to him in hand paid at or before the Sealing delivery of these Presents do grant Bargain Sell and Convey a Certain Negro Boy named **Doctor** unto a Certain Thomas BYRD his Heirs Executors or Assigns and the said William WARWICK as Husband of the late Executrix (Eleanor FLEMMING) of John FLEMMING dece[ase]d for himself his Heirs Executors and Assigns forever warrant and defend the above said Negro Boy unto the said Thomas BYRD his Heirs and Assigns. In Testamoney whereof the said William WARWICK hath hereunto set his Hand and affixed his Seal this the thirtieth Day of March in the year of our Lord one Thousand seven hundred and ninety nine ~.

Sealed and Delivered   W[illia]m WARWICK (Seal)
in Presence of . . . .   Philip QUINTON"

*followed on folio 128 with the acknowledgment by Justice of the Peace Philip QUINTON and the recordation on 01 April 1799 by court clerk John C. HANDY[872]

---

[870] Worcester County Court (Land Records). Bill of Sale from PURNELL, Azariah to **ROWND, Stephen**. 22 January 1799. T, p. 101, MSA CE 30-19. www.mdlandrec.net : accessed 12 June 2022.
[871] Worcester County Court (Land Records). Deed of Manumission from POSTLY, John to **Job**. 25 October 1798. T, pp. 115-116, MSA CE 30-19. www.mdlandrec.net : accessed 12 June 2022.
[872] Worcester County Court (Land Records). Bill of Sale from WARWICK, William to BYRD, Thomas. 30 March 1799. T, pp. 127-128, MSA CE 30-19. www.mdlandrec.net : accessed 12 June 2022.

Liber T, folios 134-135; 05 February 1799

"Know all men by these Presents that I William SELBY of Accomack County in the Commonwealth of Virginia do hereby forever emanuate and set free from me and my heirs Executors and Administrators negro man **Robin**, as witness my hand & Seal this 5th day of February 1799 ~

Witness   William SELBY (Seal)
Littleton DENNIS. .   Dixon HALL"

*followed on folio 135 with the recordation on 24 June 1799 by court clerk John C. HANDY[873]

Liber T, folio 137; 15 February 1799

"The State of Maryland Worcester County Sc[t] Know all men by these Presents that I Jacob HANDY of Kent County Maryland ~ Nephew of William ALLEN Esq[ui][r][e] dec[ease][d] of Worcester County Md and of said ALLEN Legatee ~ as part of Distribution entitled to and made Sole and absolute owner & Proprietor of a certain negro woman Slave ~ called **Hannah** ~ for and in Consideration of five Pounds Current money of Maryland, the Receipt of which hereby is confessed, do assign ~ bargain, Sell, grant and give & hereby have assigned bargained, Sold Granted and given the said negro & all my Right & title to and interest in the said negro **Hannah** unto Levin LONG of Snow Hill Town, Worcester County Maryland his Executors & Administrators, In evidence whereof I have hereunto set my hand & Seal this fifteenth day of February A.D. 1799 ~

Witness   John HANDY (Seal)
Thomas DIXON"

*followed with the acknowledgment by Justice of the Peace Thomas DIXON and the recordation on 18 February 1799 by court clerk John C. HANDY[874]

Liber T, folios 137-138; 22 December 1798

"Worcester County State of Maryland To all whom these presents shall come know ye that I Jesse FOOKS of the County and State af[oresai][d] being Desirous to see free and manumit negro **Diannah** Supposed to be about forty years old and also Negro **Ann** which will be four years old the twenty Eight of May Seventeen hundred & Ninety Eight for divers causes and Considerations me thereunto moveing. I the said Jesse FOOKS do for myself my heirs Executors Administrators Give Grant set free and Manumit the af[oresai][d] **Diannah** Amediately and the af[oresai][d] **Ann** at the age of twenty One To have and to hold and freely enjoy their Freedom without any let hindrance or authority of any person or persons whatsoever, In Testimony whereof I the said Jesse FOOKS have hereunto set my hand and affixed my Seal This.

                                                                                 Jesse FOOKS (Seal)"

*followed on folio 138 with the acknowledgment by Justice of the Peace John CATHELL on 22 December 1798 and the recordation by court clerk John C. HANDY on 18 February 1799[875]

Liber T, folios 139-140; 16 February 1799

"Know all men by these Presents that I Moses CHAILLE of Worcester County for and in consideration of the Sum of Sixteen Pounds thirteen Shillings lawfull money of Maryland to me in hand paid by John PURNELL of the said County and State af[oresai][d] the receipt whereof I do hereby acknowledge have bargained Sold and Delivered and by these presents do bargain

---

[873] Worcester County Court (Land Records). Deed of Manumission from SELBY, William to **Robin**. 05 February 1799. T, pp. 134-135, MSA CE 30-19. www.mdlandrec.net : accessed 12 June 2022.
[874] Worcester County Court (Land Records). Bill of Sale from HANDY, Jacob to LONG, Levin. 15 February 1799. T, p. 137, MSA CE 30-19. www.mdlandrec.net : accessed 12 June 2022.
[875] Worcester County Court (Land Records). Deed of Manumission from FOOKS, Jesse to **Diannah** and **Ann**. 22 December 1798. T, pp. 137-138, MSA CE 30-19. www.mdlandrec.net : accessed 12 June 2022.

Sell and Deliver unto the Said John PURNELL one Negro Girl called **Leah** to have and to hold the said bargained **Leah** unto the said John PURNELL his heirs Executors or Administrators or assigns forever and I the said Moses CHAILLE for myself my heirs Executors or administrators shall warrant & forever defend against all persons by these presents the said bargained **Leah** unto the said John PURNELL his heirs and assigns forever provided Nevertheless that if I the said Moses CHAILLE my Executors or Administrators and assigns or any of us do and shall well and truly pay or cause to be paid unto the said John His heirs or Executors or assigns the Sum of Sixteen Pounds thirteen Shillings Principal & Interest thereon untill first day of August next for Redemption of the Said bargained **Leah** then this present Bill of Sale to be void or else to Remain in full force. In Witness whereof I have hereunto set my hand and Seal this 16 day of February 1799 ~

Testis.   Moses CHAILLE   (Seal)
Esme PURNELL"

*followed on folio 141 with the acknowledgment by Justice of the Peace Esme PURNELL and the recordation on 26 February 1799 by court clerk John C. HANDY[876]

Liber T, folios 140-141; 22 February 1799

"Maryland Worcester County Know all men by these Presents that we Abel HARMON Principle Edward SCARBOROUGH and John TARR (of M) all of the County and State af[ore]s[ai]d are held and firmly bound unto the State of Maryland and in the full and Just sum of thirty Pounds Current money of the State af[ore]s[ai]d to be paid unto the County of Worcester to the which Payment well and truly to be made and done the said County of Worcester we bind ourselves and each of our heirs Executors & Adm[inistrato]rs and every of them for and in the whole firmly by these presents Sealed with our Seals and dated the twenty Second day of February 1799. Whereas **Jenny HANDBY** Single free ~ woman appeared before John HOLLAND Esquire on the 7th day of January 1799 and made Oath on the holy Evangels of Almighty God that the male child she lately Delivered of was begotten on her body by a certain Abel HARMON the Principal in the above bond and being likely to become a burthen and charge to the county of Worcester, Now the Condition of the above Obligation is such that if the above bound Abel HARMON Edward SCARBOROUGH & John TARR (of Michael) do and shall at all times hereafter Save harmless and undemnifyed from all cost charge Expences or Damages that may can shall or in any manner arise or become due in any manner or way whatsoever by Reason or on Account of the above mentioned male Bastard child as af[ore]s[ai]d that then the above Obligation to be void and of none effect otherways to be and Remain in full force Power & virtue in the Law ~

Signed Sealed & Deliv[ere]d
In the Presence of . .   Abel X HARMON (Seal)
Jesse BENNITT ~   mark
                                                                           Edward SCARBOROUGH (Seal)
                                                                                    John TARR   (Seal)"

*followed on folio 141 with the recordation by court clerk John C. HANDY[877]

*Referring to Jenny as a "free woman" may or may not indicate her ethnicity.

Liber T, folios 143-144; 13 February 1799

"Maryland Worcester Sc.t Know all men by these presents that I William BELL of Worcester County in the State of Maryland for and in consideration of the Sum of Eighty Pounds Current

---

[876] Worcester County Court (Land Records). Bill of Sale from CHAILLE, Moses to PURNELL, John. 16 February 1799. T, pp. 139-140, MSA CE 30-19. www.mdlandrec.net : accessed 12 June 2022.
[877] Worcester County Court (Land Records). Bastardy Bond from HARMON, Abel, SCARBOROUGH, Edward, and TARR, John to the State of Maryland. 22 February 1799. T, pp. 140-141, MSA CE 30-19. www.mdlandrec.net : accessed 12 June 2022.

money of Maryland to me in hand paid by Henry BELL of the City of Philadelphia at and before the Ensealing & Delivery of these presents the receipt whereof is hereby acknowledged the said William have bargained Sold & Delivered and by these presents doth confess himself to be fully Satisfied Contented and paid and do fully clearly and absolutely bargain and Sell unto the said Henry BELL his heirs and assigns forever one negro Lad called **Luke** about Seventeen Years Old. To have and to hold the said negro Lad **Luke** unto the said Henry BELL his heirs Executors and Administrators and assigns forever to his & their own proper use and behoof forever and I the said William BELL for myself my heirs Ex[ecuto]^{rs} & Administrators and every of us the aforesaid negro Lad **Luke** unto the said Henry BELL his heirs and assigns against all people whatsoever shall and will warrant and defend acquit and forever defend by these presents In Witness whereof I have hereunto set my hand and seal affixed this thirteenth day of February Anno Domini One thousand seven hundred & ninety nine 1799

William BELL (Seal)

Sealed & Deliv[ere]^d In the Presence of John POSTLY."

*followed on folio 144 with the acknowledgment by Justice of the Peace John POSTLY and the recordation on 04 March 1799 by court clerk John C. HANDY[878]

Liber T, folio 171; 26 March 1799

"D[ea]^r Sir. I have Rec[eive]^d yours. I have give the Negroes you mention to my Daughter Amelia to wit. **Easter** & her Child **Stephen** & Lad **Harry** which you will please to have entered to your assessment.

I am with affection

General John GUNBY Peter CHAILLE"

*followed with the recordation by court clerk John C. HANDY on 27 March 1799[879]

Liber T, folios 183-184; 04 March 1799

"State of Maryland Worcester County Know all men by these presents that we Peter TOWNSEND and Thomas M PURNELL (of Wallops Neck) both of the County and State af[ore]s[ai]^d for and in Consideration of the sum of Eighty five Pounds current money of Maryland to them in hand paid by Henry BELL of the Same place at and before the ensealing & before the Ensealing and Delivery of these presents we the said Peter & Thomas doth hereby confess ourselves to be fully Satisfied contented and paid & have bargained Sold and delivered and by these presents do fully clearly and absolutely bargain & Sell unto the said Henry BELL one negro man called **Isaac** about thirty four years old, To have and to hold the said negro man called **Isaac** unto the said Henry BELL his heirs Executors Administrators, and assigns to his and their own proper use benefit & behoof forever and we the said Peter TOWNSEND & Thomas M PURNELL for ourselves and each of our heirs Executors and Administrators and every of us the af[ore]s[ai]^d negro man **Isaac** unto the af[ore]s[ai]^d Henry BELL his heirs and assigns against the claim of all persons whatsoever will and shall warrant and defend acquit and forever defend by these presents. In Witness whereof we have hereunto set our hand and Seal affixed this fourth day of March Anno Domini One thousand seven hundred and ninety nine ~

Sealed & Deliv[ere]^d	Peter TOWNSEND (Seal)
In the presence of	Thomas M PURNELL (Seal)
Josiah MITCHELL"	

---

[878] Worcester County Court (Land Records). Bill of Sale from BELL, William to BELL, Henry. 13 February 1799. T, pp. 143-144, MSA CE 30-19. www.mdlandrec.net : accessed 12 June 2022.

[879] Worcester County Court (Land Records). Letter from CHAILLE, Peter to unknown. 26 March 1799. T, p. 171, MSA CE 30-19. www.mdlandrec.net : accessed 12 June 2022.

*followed with the acknowledgment by Justice of the Peace Josiah MITCHELL and the recordation on folio 184 by court clerk John C. HANDY on 08 March 1799[880]

Liber T, folio 220; 22 January 1799

"I Griffin CALLAHAN of the County of Worcester in the State of Maryland do hereby set free from Bondage my Negro man **Harry** when he shall arrive to the age of twenty one years being now twenty years old last January hereby declaring him the said **Harry** absolutely free at that age from my Servis and the Servis of all those Claiming by from or under me an do by these Presents Relinquish him the said **Harry** all Prophits and Property that he may acquire by his Industry or Care after he arives to the said age of twenty years In testamony whereof I have hereunto set my Hand and Seal this 22^d day of January Anno Domon 1799

Sind Seald and Acknowledg[e]^d in   Esther LAYFIELD   Griffin CALLAHAN (Seal)
Presents of us . . . . . .   Caty LAYFIELD"

*followed with the acknowledgment by Justice of the Peace Isaac LAYFIELD and the recordation on 25 March 1799 by court clerk John C. HANDY[881]

Liber T, folios 237-238; 20 March 1799

"Know all Men by these Presents that I **Francis ALLEN** of Worcester County & State of Maryland for and in Consideration of the Sum of Twelve Pounds Eleven Shillings Current money of the s^t[ate] af[oresai]^d to me in hand paid by Peter Spencer CORBIN of the same Place the Receipt of which I do hereby acknowledge have given granted bargained & Sold and do by these Presents give grant bargain & Sell unto the af[ore]s[ai]^d Peter S CORBIN his Heirs or Assigns forever one yoke of oxen one Cow and yearly one Cart Two Beds & furniture one Iron Kettle Two Pots one frying Pan half a dusin Pewter Plates one dutch oven one Grind Stone three Barrells one Cubbard one Chest and all my other property debts dues and demand To Have and To Hold the af[oresai]^d Property unto him the af[oresai]^d Peter S CORBIN his Heirs and Assigns forever To the only Benefit and Behoof of them and I the s[ai]^d **Francis ALLEN** do covenant and agree to & with the s[ai]^d Peter S. CORBIN his Heirs and Assigns forever that I the s[ai]^d **Francis ALLEN** and my Heirs will forever warrant and defend to the af[oresai]^d Peter S. CORBIN his Heirs or assigns The af[oresai]^d Property against the Claim Rights & Title of all and every Person or Persons whatsoever in witness of which I have hereunto set my Hand & Seal affixed this 20th day of March 1799

Test.   Joseph DAVIS

                                                                his
                                                        Francis + ALLEN (Seal)
                                                                mark"

*followed on folio 238 with the acknowledgment by Justice of the Peace John HOLLAND and the recordation by court clerk John C. HANDY on 08 April 1799[882]

*The acknowledgment describes **Francis ALLEN** as a "free negro".

* "Yearly" is a misspelling of yearling, a young calf.

Liber T, folio 238; 13 March 1799

"State of Maryland Ss. Know all men by these Presents that I John BRADFORD of the County & State aforesaid for and in Consideration of the Sum of Seventy five Pounds Current Money of the State afforesaid to me in hand paid by Thomas DUNCAN of the County & State afforesaid whereof I do hereby acknowledge the Receipt & myself therewith fully Satisfied

---

[880] Worcester County Court (Land Records). Bill of Sale from TOWNSEND, Peter and PURNELL, Thomas M. to BELL, Henry. 04 March 1799. T, pp. 183-184, MSA CE 30-19. www.mdlandrec.net : accessed 12 June 2022.
[881] Worcester County Court (Land Records). Deed of Manumission from CALLAHAN, Griffin to **Harry**. 22 January 1799. T, p. 220, MSA CE 30-19. www.mdlandrec.net : accessed 12 June 2022.
[882] Worcester County Court (Land Records). Bill of Sale from **ALLEN, Francis** to CORBIN, Peter Spencer. 20 March 1799. T, pp. 237-238, MSA CE 30-19. www.mdlandrec.net : accessed 12 June 2022.

have bargained and Sold unto Thomas DUNCAN one Negro Man named **Jack** To Have and To Hold to the proper use & Behoof of the said Thomas DUNCAN his Heirs Executors Administrators & assigns forever and I the said John BRADFORD for myself my Heirs Executors & Administrators the said bargained & Sold Negro unto Thomas DUNCAN his Heirs and Assigns shall warrant & by these presents forever defend as Witness whereunto I set my Hand & Seal this thirteeth day of March one Thousand seven hundred and Ninety Nine.

Sign[e]d Seal[e]d & Deliver[e]d	John BRADFORD (Seal)
In the Presence off . . Test. Nixson DAVIS"	

*followed with the recordation by court clerk John C. HANDY on 08 April 1799[883]

Liber T, folios 238-239; 23 March 1799

"State of Maryland Worcester County Sc.̇ Know all Men by these Presents that I William ROUND of the County and State afforesaid for and in consideration of the Sum of Seventy five Pounds Current money of the County and State afforesaid to me in hand paid by Thomas DUNCAN of the County and State afforesaid whereof I do hereby acknowledge the Receipt & myself therewith satisfied Contented and paid have bargained & Sold unto Thomas DUNCAN a Certain Negro Woman named **Sarah** & her Child named **Rachel** To Have and To Hold to the proper use and behalf of the said Thomas DUNCAN his Heirs & Assigns forever and I the said William ROUND for myself my Heirs Executors & Administrators the said bargained & sold Negres unto Thomas DUNCAN his Heirs Executors & administrators & assigns shall Warrant & by these Presents forever defend. As witness Whereunto I set my Hand & Seal this twenty third Day of March one Thousand seven hundred & ninety nine.

Signed Sealed and delivered	Isaac GIVAN	William ROUND (Seal)
In Presence of	James READ"	

*followed on folio 239 with the recordation on 08 April 1799 by court clerk John C. HANDY[884]

Liber T, folios 239-240; 13 April 1799

"State of Maryland Worcester County Know all Men by these Presents that We William PURKINS, ann PURKINS John PURKINS Thomas WEBB of the County aforesaid in Consideration of the Sum of Twenty Pounds Current Money of Maryland to me in hand paid by Annanias POWELL of the County aforesaid; have bargained Sold granted and Confirmed and by these Presents do grant bargain and Sell and Confirm unto the said Ananias POWELL one Negro Woman Called **Mille** and her Child Called **Sal** to have and To Hold the two aforesaid Negroes and every of them by these presents, bargained and Sold granted and Confirmed unto the only proper use and behoof of him the said Ananias POWELL his Heirs Executors Administrators and Assigns forever, freely quietly peaceably and entirely without any contradiction, Claim Disturbance or Hindrance of any person whatsoever to be made or hereafter to be Rendered so that nither We the said William PURKINS Ann PURKINS, John PURKINS, Thomas WEBB nor any other Person of us in our Names any Right Title, Claim Interest or Demand of in to or for the two aforesaid Negros or any Part or parcel thereof ought to exact Challenge Claim or demand at any Time or Times hereafter, but from all actions, Right, Estate Title Claim Demand Possession and Interest thereof shall be wholy barred and excluded by Force and Virtue of these Presents and we the said William Ann & John PURKINS and Thomas WEBB for ourselves Executors Heirs & Administrators the two aforesaid Negroes Called **Mille** & **Sall** unto the said Ananias POWELL his Heirs Executors Adm[inistrato]rs or assigns and against all and every other Person or Persons whatsoever shall and will warrant and

---

[883] Worcester County Court (Land Records). Bill of Sale from BRADFORD, John to DUNCAN, Thomas. 13 March 1799. T, p. 238, MSA CE 30-19. www.mdlandrec.net : accessed 12 June 2022.

[884] Worcester County Court (Land Records). Bill of Sale from ROUND, William to DUNCAN, Thomas. 23 March 1799. T, pp. 238-239, MSA CE 30-19. www.mdlandrec.net : accessed 12 June 2022.

forever defend by these Presents. In Witness whereof we have hereunto set our Hands & Seals this 13th April 1799.

Signed Sealed and delivered	Josiah MITCHELL	William PURKINS (Seal)
In presence of . . .	W[illia]m DALE	Ann + PURKINS (Seal)
		(her / mark)
		John PURKINS (Seal)
		Thomas WEBB (Seal)"

*followed on folio 240 with the acknowledgment by Justice of the Peace Josiah MITCHELL and the recordation on 19 April 1799 by court clerk John C. HANDY[885]

Liber T, folios 242 -244; 26 April 1799

"This Indenture made this 26th day of April in the year one thousand seven hundred and ninety nine between Col°[nel] James MARTIN of Worcester County and State of Maryland of the One part and Negro **Jacob** Doct[or] John PURNELL's Freed-Man of the same place of the other part witnesseth that the af[ore]s[ai]d James MARTIN for and in Consideration of Seventeen pounds Seven Shillings and Six pence current money of Maryland to him in hand paid by the af[ore]s[ai]d negro **Jacob**, at and before the sealing and delivery of these presents the receipt whereof is acknowledged and confessed and the said Negro **Jacob**, (or (**Jacob PURNELL** his heirs Executors and Administrators therefrom forever acquitted and discharged, he the aforesaid James MARTIN hath granted bargained sold, conveyed and confirmed, and by these presents doth absolutely grant bargain sell convey and confirm unto him the af[ore]s[ai]d Negro **Jacob** (alias **Jacob PURNELL**) his heirs and Assigns forever Five Acres of Land, being part of two Tracts of Land to wit Allens Luck and part of a Tract of land called Dumfrize, situate lying and being in Worcester County aforesaid, about One Mile from Snow hill Town, bounded & limitted as follows to wit. Beginning at a marked red Oak small Saplin, marked with Eight notches, standing near the second line of a Tract called Mardike," ... "thence South West thirty Eight poles to a marked post standing near the Side of the aforesaid Col°[nel] MARTINs plantation and from thence with a right line to the first beginning containing and now laid Out for five Acres of land more or less, together with all rights members profits benefits previledges and all other the appurtenances thereunto belonging – To have and to hold all and Singular the aforesaid bargained lands and premises unto him the aforesaid Negro **Jacob** (alias **Jacob PURNELL**) his heirs & Assigns forever to the proper use benefit and behoof of him the af[ore]s[ai]d Negro **Jacob** his heirs and Assigns forever and the af[ore]s[ai]d James MARTIN for himself his heirs Executors and Administrators doth hereby covenant grant and agree to warrant and forever defend the above mentioned lands and premises against the lawful right title claim & demand of all and every person or persons whatsoever now claiming or ever hereafter to claim by or under him them or any of them as a sure Inheritance in Fee Simple unto him the af[ore]s[ai]d Negro **Jacob** (alias **Jacob PURNELL**) his heirs and Assigns forever In Testimony whereof the af[ore]s[ai]d James MARTIN to these presents his hand hath set and seal affixed the day and year above written ~

Signed Signed & delivered	Philip QUINTON	James MARTIN (Seal)
in presence of	James HOUSTON"	

*followed on folio 243 with the acknowledgment by Justices of the Peace Philip QUINTON and James HOUSTON and the recordation on folio 244 by court clerk John C. HANDY[886]

---

[885] Worcester County Court (Land Records). Bill of Sale from PURKINS, William, Ann, and John and WEBB, Thomas to POWELL, Annanias. 13 April 1799. T, pp. 239-240, MSA CE 30-19. www.mdlandrec.net : accessed 12 June 2022.

[886] Worcester County Court (Land Records). Deed of Conveyance from MARTIN, Col. James to **Jacob** (alias **PURNELL, Jacob**). 26 April 1799. T, pp. 242-244, MSA CE 30-19. www.mdlandrec.net : accessed 12 June 2022.

*The acknowledgment identified Mary MARTIN as the wife of James MARTIN.

Liber T, folio 258; 10 May 1799

"State of Maryland, Worcester County Ss^t. Know all Men by these presents that we the Subscribers, Thomas TIER of Worcester County and State of Maryland and Jacob TIER of Sussex County and State of Delaware for and in Consideration of the Sum of Seventy five pounds Current Money of the County and State aforesaid to me in hand paid by William ROWND of the County and State af[ore]s[ai]^d whereof we do hereby acknowledge Ourselves fully satisfied and paid have bargained and sold unto William ROWND a certain Negro Woman named **Patience** and her Child named **Peter** – To have and to hold to the proper use and, behoof of the said William ROWND his heirs and Assigns forever, and we the said Thomas TIER & Jacob TIER af[ore]s[ai]^d for Ourselves Our heirs Executors and Administrators the said bargained and Sold Negroes unto William ROWND his heirs Executors Administrators and Assigns shall warrant and by these presents forever defend as witness whereunto we the af[ore]s[ai]^d Thomas TIER and Jacob TIER Our hand have set and Seal affixed this tenth day of May One thousand seven hundred and ninety nine ~

Signed Sealed & delivered   John P MITCHELL   Thomas TIER (Seal)
in presence of   Isaac MITCHELL
                                                                       his
                                                           Jacob + TIER (Seal)
                                                                Mark"

*followed with the acknowledgment by Justice of the Peace John P. MITCHELL, the receipt by Jacob and Thomas TIER on 23 March 1799, and the recordation on 21 May 1799 by court clerk John C. HANDY[887]

Liber T, folios 263-264; 10 May 1799

"This Indenture made this tenth day of May in the year of Our lord one thousand seven hundred and ninety nine between, Between **Francis ALLEN** in Worcester County in the State of Maryland of the one part and Peter S. CORBIN of the af[ore]s[ai]^d County and State of the other part, Witnesseth that the said **Francis ALLEN** for and in Consideration of the Sum of fifteen pounds current money of Maryland in hand paid by the said Peter S. CORBIN, before the Sealing & delivery hereof the receipt whereof he the said **Francis ALLEN** doth hereby acknowledge hath Granted bargained and Sold and by these presents doth grant bargain and sell to the af[ore]s[ai]^d Peter S. CORBIN his heirs and assigns forever, a Lott of Land containing three Acres lying and in Worcester County in the State af[ore]s[ai]^d bound on the north by the lands of the heirs of Joshua STURGIS, and bound to the Eastward, Southward and Southwestward by the main post, and markett Roads, as also bound on the Northwestward by a small lott of Ground now in the possession of **Perry MIFFLIN** free negro – To have and to hold the above described lott of Ground with the appurtenances to the same belonging or in any wise appurtenancing, free and clear of all Incumbrances whatsoever unto him the said Peter S. CORBIN his heirs and Assigns forever – And the said **Francis ALLEN** by these presents doth Covenant and agree with the said Peter S. CORBIN and his heirs and Assigns, that he the said **Francis ALLEN** and his heirs and assigns will forever the above described land warrant and in the law defend free and clear of all titles claims or incumbrances whatsoever - In Testimony whereof the af[ore]s[ai]^d **Francis ALLEN** hath hereunto his hand set and Seal affixed the day & date above written

Signed Sealed & delivered   John HOLLAND   his
in the presence of   Elisha PURNELL   Francis + **ALLEN** (Seal)
                                                                                    Mark"

---

[887] Worcester County Court (Land Records). Bill of Sale from TIER, Thomas and TIER, Jacob to ROWND, William. 10 May 1799. T, p. 258, MSA CE 30-19. www.mdlandrec.net : accessed 14 June 2022.

*followed with the acknowledgment by Justices of the Peace John HOLLAND and Elisha PURNELL and the recordation by court clerk John C. HANDY on 04 June 1799[888]

*The acknowledgment identified **Francis ALLEN** as a "free negro".

Liber T, folio 264; 20 May 1799

"State of Maryland, Worcester County, Know all Men by these presents, that I Joshua BEACHBOARD of Worcester County, for and in Consideration of the Sum of Seventy Eight pounds fifteen Shillings Current Money of Maryland to me in hand paid by William SLOCOMB of the County af[ore]s[ai]^d at or before the Sealing and delivery of these presents the Receipt whereof I the said Joshua BEACHBOARD do hereby acknowledge, have Granted bargained and Sold, and by these presents, do Grant bargain and Sell unto the said William SLOCOMB his Executors Administrators and Assigns one negro fellow called **Jerom** and aged about thirty years. To have and to hold the above bargained and Sold negro above mentioned to the said William SLOCOMB his heirs & assigns forever, and I the said Joshua BEACHBOARD for myself my heirs Executors Adm[inistrato]^{rs} all and singular the said negro called **Jerom** unto the said William SLOCOMB his Executors Administrators and Assigns against me the said Joshua BEACHBOARD my Executors and Adm[inistrato]^{rs} and against all and every other person and persons whatever shall and will warrant and forever defend by these presents ~ In Witness whereof I the said Joshua BEACHBOARD have hereunto to my hand set and Seal affixed the 20th day of May 1799.

Signed Sealed & delivered   John HOLLAND   Joshua BEACHBOARD   (Seal)
in the presence of . ."

*followed with the acknowledgment by Justice of the Peace John HOLLAND and the recordation on 04 June 1799 by court clerk John C. HANDY[889]

Liber T, folios 882-883; 05 July 1799

"Worcester County Ss^t. To all to whom these presents shall come Greeting. Know ye that I Philip MARSH of the County aforesaid for and in consideration of the sum of Ten pounds to me in hand paid Current Money of Maryland, and for divers goods, causes and valuable Considerations, me thereunto especially moving have bargained, sold, released, granted and confirmed, and by these presents do bargin sell release grant, and confirm unto John SELBY all and singular the goods & Chattles household stuff and moveables as follows, to wit a chi[?}e two beds and Bedstead four pair of sheets four bed quilts and a counterpain two pillows and cases, one large iron pot two Walnut Tables a stand and case a cupboard and Looking glass a buckle and two pewter basins, with all and singular the personal property which I received by my present wife Polly at or since our intermarriage, together with the following Negroes To wit **Abel Isaac Solomon Leah James** and **William** which were hers also To have and to hold the said goods and chattles household stuff and moveables personal property and Negroes to the said John SELBY and his assigns forever freely quietly and peaceably without any claim, disturbance or hindrance whatever with the proviso only that the above specified property is to be liable for the payment of the debts of the late husband of my wife Parker SELBY of Matt[hew] dec[ease]d and the said John SELBY for good and sufficient causes him thereunto moving doth hereby covenant and agree with the said Philip MARSH that he shall enjoy the property aforesaid mentioned during the term of the natural life of him the said Philip and the said Philip for himself his Executors and administrators doth covenant and agree with the said John SELBY that he will keep the said property, goods, Chattles household stuff and moveable personal property and negroes safe and secure from all damage by him the said Philip In

---

[888] Worcester County Court (Land Records). Deed from **ALLEN, Francis** to CORBIN, Peter S. 10 May 1799. T, pp. 263-264, MSA CE 30-19. www.mdlandrec.net : accessed 14 June 2022.
[889] Worcester County Court (Land Records). Bill of Sale from BEACHBOARD, Joshua to SLOCOMB, William. 20 May 1799. T, p. 264, MSA CE 30-19. www.mdlandrec.net : accessed 14 June 2022.

Testimony whereof the parties aforesaid have interchangeably set their hands and affixed their Seals this fifth day of July anno Domini 1799.

The words since was interlined before execution   Philip MARSH   (Seal)
Signed sealed and Delivered in presence of   Philip QUINTON   John SELBY   (Seal)"

*followed on folio 283 with the acknowledgment by Justice of the Peace Philip QUINTON and the recordation by court clerk John C. HANDY[890]

Liber T, folios 297-298; 19 July 1799

"Worcester County State af[ore]s[ai]^d Know all men by these presents that I John PURNELL of the County af[ore]s[ai]^d for the consideration of the sum of seventeen Shillings and ten pence to me in hand paid before the sealing and Delivery of these presents the receipt whereof I do acknowledge have bargined & sold & delivered to the said Moses CHAILLEA of the same County one negro Girl called **Leah** to the said moses CHAILLA his Executors or Administrators or assigns and I the said John PURNELL for my self my heirs Executors or Assigns do warrant and for ever Defend the said negro Girl Called **Leah** to the said Moses CHAIELLEA or his heirs or assigns the said negro **Leah** against any person claiming any right tittle or claim under him to the said Negro **Leah** given from under my hand and seal this 19 Day of July 1799.

Esme PURNELL.   John PURNELL   (Seal)"

*followed with the acknowledgment by Justice of the Peace Esme PURNELL and the recordation by court clerk John C. HANDY on 04 August 1799[891]

Liber T, folios 299-300; 20 July 1799

"State of Maryland Worcester County. . Know all men by these presents that I molly BAKER of the County and State af[ore]s[ai]^d for and in consideration of the sum of forty pound to me in hand paid by Milby and Henry DUNCAN Jointly the receipt whereof I the said Molly BAKER do hereby acknowledge and my self thereunto satisfied have given granted bargained and sold unto the Said Milby and Henry DUNCAN one nigro Woman named **Tamer** to have and to hold the said bargained and sold nigro **Tamer** unto the af[ore]s[ai]^d Milby DUNCAN & Henry DUNCAN with all Increas hereafter If any to Equally Divided between the said Milby and Henry DUNCAN & their heirs which said Negro **Tamery** I the said Molly BAKER do by these presents reserver my life claim in and to and after my Deceas to be Equally divided agreeable Vallue between my Said Sons Milby and Henry DUNCAN and their heirs and Assigns and I the said Molly BAKER the said bargained and sold nigro **Tamer** shall and will warrant and Defend from and against all manner of persons agreeable to the true Intent of the Sale after my Deceas In Witness whereof I the said Molly BAKER hereunto this my Sale sett my hand and affixed my Seal this 20th Day of July AD 1799

Signed sealed and Delivered   John P MITCHELL   her
In Presence of . . . .   Molly + BAKER   (Seal)
                                                                              mark"

*followed on folio 300 with the acknowledgment by Justice of the Peace John P. MITCHELL and the recordation on 05 August 1799 by court clerk John Custis HANDY[892]

---

[890] Worcester County Court (Land Records). Bill of Sale from MARSH, Philip to SELBY, John. 05 July 1799. T, pp. 282-283, MSA CE 30-19. www.mdlandrec.net : accessed 14 June 2022.
[891] Worcester County Court (Land Records). Bill of Sale from PURNELL, John to CHAILLEA, Moses. 19 July 1799. T, pp. 297-298, MSA CE 30-19. www.mdlandrec.net : accessed 14 June 2022.
[892] Worcester County Court (Land Records). Bill of Sale from BAKER, Molly to DUNCAN, Milby and Henry. 20 July 1799. T, pp. 299-300, MSA CE 30-19. www.mdlandrec.net : accessed 14 June 2022.

Liber T, folios 300-301; 20 July 1799

"State of Maryland Worcester County, Know all men by these presents that I Molly BAKER of the County and State af[ore]s[ai]^d for and in consideration of the Sum of Twenty pounds to me in hand paid by Nancy DUNCAN of the same place the receipt whereof I the said Molly BAKER do hereby acknowledge and my self therewith satisfied and paid have granted bargained and sold and by these do give grant bargained sell and Deliver unto the af[ore]s[ai]^d Nancy DUNCAN One Negro girl named **Leah** to have and to hold the af[ore]s[ai]^d bargained and sold negro girl **leah** unto the af[ore]s[ai]^d Nancy DUNCAN her heirs and Assigns forever and I the said Molley BAKER do by these presents Warrant and forever defend the af[ore]s[ai]^d bargained and sold nigro **Leah** unto the af[ore]s[ai]^d Nancy DUNCAN and her heirs and Assigns forever In Witness whereof with the delivery I the said Molly BAKER have to this my plulain and open sale Sett my hand and affixed my seal this 20th Day of July AD 1799. ~ .

Signed Sealed and Delivered   John P. MITCHELL   her
In Presence of . . . .   Molly + BAKER (Seal)
                                                                                            mark"

*followed on folio 301 with the acknowledgment by Justice of the Peace John P. MITCHELL and the recordation on 05 August 1799 by court clerk John Custis HANDY[893]

*plulain should likely be *plain*.

Liber T, folios 301-302; 20 July 1799

"State of Maryland Worcester County Ss^t. Know all men by these presents that I Molly BAKER of the County and State af[ore]s[ai]^d for and in consideration of Thirty pounds to me in hand paid by Henry DUNCAN of the same place the rec[eip]^t whereof I the said Molly BAKER do hereby acknowledge and my self therewith fully satisfied and paid have bargained and sold and by these presents do bargain Sell and deliver unto the af[ore]s[ai]^d Henry DUN[CAN] one negro boy named **Isaac** one new bed and furneture and one Cow to have and to hold the af[ore]s[ai]^d bargained and sold nigro **Isaac** unto the af[ore]s[ai]^d Henry DUNCAN heirs and assigns and to the only use benefit and behoof of him the said Henry DUNCAN heirs and assigns forever and I the said Molly BAKER for my self my heirs and Executors the said bargained and sold negro shall and will warrant and defend unto the said Henry DUNCAN and his heirs & assigns In Witness whereof I the said Molly BAKER have hereunto sett my hand and affixed my Seal this 20th Day of July AD 1799.

Signed Sealed and . .   John P. MITCHELL,   her
Delivered In Presence of   Molly + BAKER (Seal)
                                                                                            mark"

*followed on folio 302 with the acknowledgment by Justice of the Peace John P. MITCHELL and the recordation on 05 August 1799 by court clerk John C. HANDY[894]

Liber T, folios 302-303; 20 July 1799

"State of Maryland Worcester County Ss^t. Know all men by these presents that I Molly BAKER of the County and State af[ore]s[ai]^d for and inconsideration of the sum of Twenty pounds to me in hand paid by Hannah GUNBY of the same place the receipt whereof I the said Molly BAKER do hereby acknowledge and my self therewith fully satisfied and paid have granted bargained and sold unto the af[ore]s[ai]d Hannah GUNBY One nigro boy named **Robbin** and by these presents do give grant bargain sell and Deliver unto the said Hannah GUNBY the af[ore]s[ai]^d bargained sold and Delivered negro **Robbin** unto her the said Hannah GUNBY and her heirs and Assigns forever and I the said Molly BAKER shall and will warrant and

---

[893] Worcester County Court (Land Records). Bill of Sale from BAKER, Molly to DUNCAN, Nancy. 20 July 1799. T, pp. 300-301, MSA CE 30-19. www.mdlandrec.net : accessed 14 June 2022.
[894] Worcester County Court (Land Records). Bill of Sale from BAKER, Molly to DUNCAN, Henry. 20 July 1799. T, pp. 301-302, MSA CE 30-19. www.mdlandrec.net : accessed 14 June 2022.

forever defend the af[ore]s[ai]^d bargained and sold negro **Robbin** unto the af[ore]s[ai]^d Hannah GUNBY and her heirs and assigns from the claim of all and every person whatsoever Claiming from by or under me the said Molly BAKER or my heirs In Testimony whereof I the said Molly BAKER have to this my Plain and open sale Sett my hand and affixed my Seal this 20th Day of July AD 1799

Signed Sealed and Delivered   John P. MITCHELL
In Presence of . . . .   his
                                                                       Molly + BAKER (Seal)
                                                                              mark"

*followed on folio 303 with the acknowledgment by Justice of the Peace John P. MITCHELL and the recordation on 05 August 1799 by court clerk John Custis HANDY[895]

Liber T, folios 311-312; 12 August 1799

"To all people to whom these presents shall come Know ye that I Elizabeth MITCHELL of Worcester County, State of Maryland, send Greeting, Know ye, that I the said Elizabeth MITCHELL for and in Consideration of the natural love and Affection which I have and bear unto James MUMFORT my Son and also for others good causes and consederations me thereunto moving, have given and Granted, and by these presents do give grant and confirm unto the said James MUMFORT, One Negro Girl, by the name of **Sarah**, and One Negro Boy by the name of **Sampson**, children of **Cloah**, and feather Bed and furniture, and One Cow and Calf, and One horse four years old these articles now mentioned to be delivered to the said James MUMFORD, when he is twenty One years of age, without any Expence for raising them of what kind nature and quality soever the same are and in what place or places soever, the same shall be found, as well in my own Custody or possession hands power and Custody of any other person or persons whatsoever (or all those Goods and Chattles in the Schedule hereunto annexed mention) to have and to hold all the Goods and Chattles above mentioned unto the said James MUMFORT to him and to his heirs lawfully begotten of his body, to his and their Own proper use and uses forever, and I the said Elizabeth MITCHELL and all singular the aforesaid Goods and Chattles to the said James MUMFORT to him and his heirs lawfully begotten of his Body against all persons, do Warrant and do forever defend by these presents, in witness this twelvth day of August Adomina 1799.

Witness present. Moses FREEMAN, John DUNBAR   her
                                                                    Elizabeth + MITCHELL (Seal)
                                                                              Mark"

*followed on folio 312 with the recordation by court clerk John C. HANDY[896]

Liber T, folios 312-313; 07 June 1799

"Baltimore Sc^t. Know all Men by these presents that I George Ker WISE of Baltimore Town and State of Maryland for and in Consideration of Thirty three pounds fifteen Shillings to me in hand paid at and before to sealing and delivery hereof the receipt whereof, I do hereby acknowledge have bargained and Sold and by these do bargain and Sell unto Thomas MARTIN of Worcester County and State af[ore]s[ai]^d all my right and title of in and to One negro Wench named **Priss** with all her increase born at present or which may hereafter be born, which said negro **Priss** was devised by Samuel WISE of Worcester County dec[ease]^d to my Sister Betsy WISE and myself as having recourse to the Will may appear ~ To have and to hold the one half part of the said negro Wench with her increase to the said Thomas MARTIN his heirs and Assigns forever, to the only use of the said Thomas MARTIN his heirs and assigns & for no other purpose whatever, and I hereby further Covenant and agree to and with the said Tho[ma]^s MARTIN his heirs and assigns, for myself & heirs the one half of the said negro Wench with

---

[895] Worcester County Court (Land Records). Bill of Sale from BAKER, Molly to GUNBY, Hannah. 20 July 1799. T, pp. 302-303, MSA CE 30-19. www.mdlandrec.net : accessed 14 June 2022.
[896] Worcester County Court (Land Records). Deed of Gift from MITCHELL, Elizabeth to MUMFORD, James. 12 August 1799. T, pp. 311-312, MSA CE 30-19. www.mdlandrec.net : accessed 14 June 2022.

her increase against the right title and claim of all manner of persons whatever for ever to warrant and defend, In Testimony whereof I have hereto set my hand and Seal affixed this Seventh day of June anno Do[mini] 1799

Witness W[illia]^m RUSSELL. ~   George Ker WISE   (Seal)"

*followed on folio 313 with the acknowledgement by Baltimore County Justice of the Peace William RUSSELL on 07 July 1799, the recordation by Baltimore County court clerk William GIBSON, and the recordation on 26 June 1799 by Worcester County court clerk John C. HANDY[897]

Liber T, folios 320-321; 10 August 1799

"Worcester County, State of Maryland Know all Men by these presents that I Annanias HUDSON of William) the the County and State above written for and in consideration of the Sum of One hundred and Sixty Dollars to me in hand paid by Richard SAMPSON of the County and State above written the Receipt whereof I do hereby acknowledge have bargained and Sold and by these presents do bargain and Sell unto the said Richard SAMPSON one Negro Boy named **Minea** aged Eleven years the Son of a Negro Woman named **Omey**, the said Boy now remaining and being in the County and State above written, and untill now in the possession of said HUDSON ~ To have and to hold the said negro Boy unto the said Richard SAMPSON his heirs Executors and Assigns, and I the said Annanias HUDSON of William for myself my Executors and Administrators the said negro Boy unto the said Richard SAMPSON his Executors Administrators and Assigns against me the said Annanias HUDSON of W[illia]^m my Executors Administrators and Assigns and against all and every other person or persons whatsoever, shall and will warrant and forever defend by these presents ~ I the said Annanias HUDSON (of W[illia]^m) have put the said Richard SAMPSON in full possession by delivering him said Negro Boy named **Minea** at the Sealing hereof. In Witness hereof I have set my hand and fixed my Seal 10th day of August, One thousand Seven hundred and ninety nine.

Sealed & delivered in   Annanias HUDSON   (Seal)
the presence of   John POSTLY"

*followed with the acknowledgment by Justice of the Peace John POSTLY and the recordation on folio 321 by court clerk John C. HANDY on 14 August 1799[898]

Liber T, folios 322-323; 10 August 1799

"Worcester County State of Maryland To all whom these presents shall come greeting, I Richard SAMPSON of the County and State af[oresai]^d for divers good causes and considerations me thereunto moved do hereby declare free manumit and enfranchise the Negro Boy named **Minnea** now aged Eleven years Old and to be free, when he comes to the age of twenty Eight years hereby acknowledging the said Negro discharged from all claim of Services and Right of property whatever from me my heirs Executors Administrators, as soon as said Boy is said Age of twenty Eight, As Witness my hand and Seal this tenth of August, in the Year of Our lord, one thousand seven hundred and ninety nine.

Sealed & delivered   Richard SAMPSON   (Seal)
in the presence of   John POSTLY."

*followed on folio 323 with the acknowledgment by Justice of the Peace John POSTLY and the recordation on 14 August 1799 by court clerk John C. HANDY[899]

---

[897] Worcester County Court (Land Records). Bill of Sale from WISE, George Ker to MARTIN, Thomas. 07 June 1799. T, pp. 312-313, MSA CE 30-19. www.mdlandrec.net : accessed 14 June 2022.

[898] Worcester County Court (Land Records). Bill of Sale from HUDSON, Annanias to SAMPSON, Richard. 10 August 1799. T, pp. 320-321, MSA CE 30-19. www.mdlandrec.net : accessed 14 June 2022.

[899] Worcester County Court (Land Records). Deed of Manumission from SAMPSON, Richard to **Minnea**. 10 August 1799. T, pp. 322-323, MSA CE 30-19. www.mdlandrec.net : accessed 14 June 2022.

Liber T, folios 341-342; 02 September 1799

"Worcester S^s. State of Maryland, To all to whom this writing shall come Be it known that I Benjamin HUDSON of the County and State aforesaid for and in Consideration of the faithful Service heretofore rendered unto me by my Negro Woman Slave **Comfort**, and also for and in Consideration of twenty five pounds to me formerly paid by Negro **Mingo** her Husband, do by these presents Manumate Emancipate Set at liberty & from the Service of me my heirs Executors Administrators & assigns forever discharge the aforesaid Negro Woman **Comfort**, and her sucking Child **Elisha** and do hereby Covenant and agree that said **Comfort & Elisha** as far as regards my claim or title in me to her, and her said child or their or either of their Services, shall enjoy and have all the previledges of free negroes ~ In Witness whereof I have hereunto set my hand & Seal in the presence of two witnesses this second day of September in the year of Our lord One thousand seven hundred and ninety nine ~

Sealed & delivered in   John POSTLY   Benjamin HUDSON (Seal)
the presence of   Anne POSTLY"

*followed on folio 342 with the acknowledgment by Justice of the Peace John POSTLY and the recordation on 03 September 1799 by court clerk John C. HANDY[900]

Liber T, folios 362-363; 07 October 1799

"Maryland Worcester County. Know all men by these presents that I Morgan BRADSHAW of the County and State af[ore]s[ai]^d for and in Consideration of the Sum of Six hundred Dollars Current Money of Maryland to me in hand paid by Hezekiah JOHNSON of the same place at and before the ensealing and delivery of these presents, the receipt whereof the said Morgan BRADSHAW doth hereby acknowledge and thereof forever acquit and discharge the said Hezekiah JOHNSON his heirs Executors & Administrators have Given granted bargained and Sold and by these presents doth give grant bargain and Sell unto him the af[ore]s[ai]^d Hezekiah JOHNSON and his heirs and assigns forever One Sloop called Sally together with all her Sales riggings amers and the Utensils thereunto belonging as he the said BRADSHAW purchased her of MARTIN & HOWARD, One Negro Woman called **Comfort**, One ditto called **Cyller** One Negro lad called **Peter** One ditto called **Jacob** One ditto called **Abram** and all the other negroes and all other kinds of personal Estate of whatsoever kind the same may be that he the said Morgan BRADSHAW now in anyway, possesses hath any right or title to ~ To have and to hold the af[ore]s[ai]^d Sloop and Rigan and all the other Utensils as above set forth and all the af[ore]s[ai]^d Negroes and other property as above described unto him the af[ore]s[ai]^d Hezekiah JOHNSON his heirs and Assigns forever and the said Morgan BRADSHAW for himself and his heirs doth hereby Covenant and agree to and with the aforesaid Hezekiah JOHNSON that he will warrant and forever hereafter defend the af[ore]s[ai]^d Sloop Negroes and other property as above described from himself and his heirs and every other person or persons that shall or may hereafter claim the same from by or under him or his heirs or any other person claiming the same from by or under him or his heirs them or any of them. In Testimony whereof the said Morgan BRADSHAW to these presents his hand hath set and Seal affixed this Seventh day of October Anno Dom[ini] One thousand seven hundred and ninety nine

Signed Sealed & delivered   Morgan BRADSHAW (Seal)
in presence of   Philip QUINTON"

*followed on folio 363 by Justice of the Peace Philip QUINTON and the recordation on 08 October 1799 by court clerk John C. HANDY[901]

---

[900] Worcester County Court (Land Records). Deed of Manumission from HUDSON, Benjamin to **Comfort & Elisha**. 02 September 1799. T, pp. 341-342, MSA CE 30-19. www.mdlandrec.net : accessed 14 June 2022.

[901] Worcester County Court (Land Records). Bill of Sale from BRADSHAW, Morgan to JOHNSON, Hezekiah. 07 October 1799. T, pp. 362-363, MSA CE 30-19. www.mdlandrec.net : accessed 14 June 2022.

Liber T, folio 366; 22 June 1799

"To all to whom these presents shall come Know ye that I Nancy NELMS of Worcester County and State of Maryland being desirous to set free and manumit my Negro **George** he being forty years Old for divers causes and considerations me thereunto moving, I the said Nancy NELMS do by these presents give grant set free and manumit Negro **George** immediately to have & to hold and freely enjoy his freedom as aforesaid without any lets hindrances or Authority of any person or persons whatsoever. In Testimony hereof I the said Nancy NELMS have hereunto set my hand and Seal this twenty second day of June One thousand seven hundred & ninety nine.

Witnessed Signed	W[illia]^m BRINTON	Nanncy NELMS (Seal)
Sealed & delivered in presence of us	Booz WALSTON"	

*followed with the acknowledgment by Justice of the Peace Booz WALSTON and the recordation on 09 October 1799 by court clerk John C. HANDY[902]

Liber T, folios 391-392; 05 November 1799

"Maryland Worcester County Ss^t. Know all men by these presents that I William CHAILLE of Worcester County in the State af[ore]s[ai]^d for and in Consideration of the Sum of fourty five pounds Current money of the State af[ore]s[ai]^d to me in hand well truly paid Ebenezard LEONARD of Worcester County af[ore]s[ai]^d before the Execution hereof the receipt whereof is hereby acknowledged, have bargained and Sold and by these presents do bargain and sell unto the said Ebenezard LEONARD his heirs and assigns One Negro Woman called and named **Bridget** with all her future increase To have and to hold the said Negro Woman called **Bridget** with all her future increase unto him the Ebenezard LEONARD his heirs & assigns to the only proper use benefit and behoof of him the said Ebenezar his heirs and assigns, and to or for no other use intent or purpose whatever. In Testimony whereof I have hereto set my hand and Seal this fifth day of November Anno Dom[ini] Seventeen hundred and ninety nine

Signed Sealed & delivered	Isaac HENRY	William CHAILLE (Seal)
in presence of	Booz WALSTON	
	Purnell JOHNSON"	

*followed with folio 392 with acknowledgment by Justices of the Peace Booz WALSTON and Purnell JOHNSON and the recordation on 11 November 1799 by court clerk John C. HANDY[903]

Liber T, folios 395-396; 01 November 1799

"State of Maryland Worcester County Ss^t. Know all Men by these presents that I James KING Jun[io]^r of the County and State af[ore]s[ai]^d for and in Consideration of the Sum of One hundred pound Specie to me in hand paid James KING Sen[io]^r of the same place the receipt whereof I the same James KING Jun[io]^r do by these presents acknowledge and myself therewith fully satisfied contented and paid and the receipt thereof acknowledge have Granted bargained and Sold and by these presents do give Grant bargain sell and deliver unto the said James KING Sen[io]^r and his heirs One Negro Man called **Ralph** originally the property of Presgrave KENNIT ~ To have and to hold the said bargained and Sold Negro **Ralph** unto the said James KING Sen[io]^r his heirs and assigns forever, and I the said James KING Jun[io]^r for myself and my heirs, and all and every person whatsoever claiming the said bargained & Sold Negro shall and will warrant and forever defend unto the said James KING Sen[io]^r and his heirs together with the delivery of the same In Witness whereof I the said James KING have to this my plail and open Sale set my hand and affixed my Seal this 1st day of November 1799

---

[902] Worcester County Court (Land Records). Deed of Manumission from NELMS, Nancy to **George**. 22 June 1799. T, p. 366, MSA CE 30-19. www.mdlandrec.net : accessed 14 June 2022.
[903] Worcester County Court (Land Records). Bill of Sale from CHAILLE, William to LEONARD, Ebenezard. 05 November 1799. T, pp. 391-392, MSA CE 30-19. www.mdlandrec.net : accessed 14 June 2022.

Signed Sealed & delivered   Jnº. P MITCHELL   James KING Jun[ior]   (Seal)
in presence of . . ."

*followed on folio 396 with the acknowledgment by Justice of the Peace John P. MITCHELL and the recordation on 15 November 1799 by court clerk John C. HANDY[904]

Liber T, folios 406-407; 25 November 1799

"Know all Men by these presents that I Azariah PURNELL of Worcester County & State of Maryland in Consideration of the Sum of thirty pounds current money of Maryland to me in hand paid by Negro **Stephen** of the County of Worcester have bargained sold released granted and confirmed and by these presents do bargain sell release grant and confirm unto the said negro **Stephen** a Negro Girl called **Ruth** ~ To have and to hold the said Negro Girl by these presents bargained sold released granted and confirmed unto the said Negro **Stephen** his Executors Administrators and assigns for every freely quietly peaceably and intirely without any Contradiction or disturbance of any person whatsoever so that neither I the said Azariah nor any other for me or in my name any right title Interest or demand of in to or for the said Negro ought to expect claim or demand at any time or times hereafter from all Actions right Estate title claim demand possession & Interest thereof shall be wholly bound and excluded by force of these presents and I the said Azariah for myself my Executors & Administrators the said Negro **Ruth** unto the said Negro **Stephen** father of the said Girl and against all and every other person or persons whatsoever shall & will warrant and forever defend by these presents of which negro I the said Azariah have put the said Negro **Stephen** in full possession by the delivery thereof at the signing and delivery hereof. In Witness whereof I have hereunto my hand set and Seal affixed this 25th day of November Anno Domini 1799

Sealed & delivered in   Jnº. P. MARSHALL, Ass.   Azariah PURNELL   (Seal)
presence of . ."

*followed on folio 407 with the acknowledgment by John P. MARSHALL and the recordation on 25 November 1799 by court clerk John C. HANDY[905]

Liber T, folios 425-426; 19 October 1799

"Worcester County State of Maryland To all to whom this writing shall come Be it known that I Levin MITCHELL of the County and State af[ore]s[ai]^d for and in Consideration of the faithful Service of my Negro Slave **Comfort** Wife of Negro **Sampson**, as also for the Consideration of forty five pounds paid to me by said **Sampson** her Husband, do by these presents Manumate Emancipate set at liberty and from the service of me, my heirs Executors Administrators and Assigns forever, discharge the aforesaid Negro **Comfort**, and do hereby Covenant and agree that she shall forever as far as regards any Claim or title in me to her or her services shall enjoy and have all the priviledges of a free negro In Witness whereof I have hereunto set my hand and Seal in the presence of two Witnesses this 19th day of October A[nno] domini Seventeen hundred and ninety nine.

Sealed & delivered in   Edward HENRY   Levin MITCHELL   (Seal)
the presence of.   John POSTLY"

*followed on folio 426 with the acknowledgment by Justice of the Peace John POSTLY and the recordation on 11 December 1799 by court clerk John C. HANDY[906]

---

[904] Worcester County Court (Land Records). Bill of Sale from KING, James Jr. to KING, James Sr. 01 November 1799. T, pp. 395-396, MSA CE 30-19. www.mdlandrec.net : accessed 14 June 2022.

[905] Worcester County Court (Land Records). Bill of Sale from PURNELL, Azariah to **Stephen**. 25 November 1799. T, pp. 406-407, MSA CE 30-19. www.mdlandrec.net : accessed 14 June 2022.

[906] Worcester County Court (Land Records). Deed of Manumission from MITCHELL, Levin to **Comfort**. 19 October 1799. T, pp. 425-426, MSA CE 30-19. www.mdlandrec.net : accessed 14 June 2022.

Liber T, folios 430-431; 12 December 1799

"Know all Men by these presents that I John BOANAN & Esther BOANAN his Wife of Worcester County, for and in Consideration of the Sum of One hundred & Eighty Eight pounds Current money of Maryland to us in hand paid by Samuel HANDY Sen[io]^r of the same County af[ore]s[ai]^d at and before the Sealing and delivery of these presents the receipt whereof I do hereby acknowledge, have bargained and sold released Granted and Confirmed and by these presents do bargain and Sell release Grant and Confirm unto the said Samuel HANDY Sen[io]^r his heirs and Assigns forever, One Negro Man Slave called **David**, five Cows and Calves two Yearlings two Yoke Stears, Six head Sheep three head of Horses, three hundred Bushels Corn four Beds and furniture Seventeen head of hogs ~ To have and to hold the said negro Man Slave named **David**, four Cows and Calves, two yoke Steers Six head Sheep, three head Horses, three hundred Bushels Corn, four Beds & furniture Seventeen head Sheep by these presents bargained Sold released Granted and Confirmed unto the said Samuel HANDY Sen[io]^r his heirs and assigns forever, to the only proper use benefit and behoof of the said Samuel HANDY and his heirs and assigns forever, and for no other use purpose whatsoever, and I the said John BOANAN and Esther BOANAN his Wife for Ourselves Our heirs Executors, and Administrators, the said Negro Man **David** Slave and the other property above mentioned, unto the said Samuel HANDY sen[io]^r his and Assigns against the said John BOANAN and Esther BOANAN his Wife their Executors and Administrators, and against all and every other person or persons whatsoever shall and will warrant and defend by these presents ~ In Witness whereof we have hereunto set Our hands & Affixed Our Seals this 12th day of December Anno Dom[ini] 1799

Signed Sealed & delivered   Tho[ma]^s DIXON.   John BOWHANAN (Seal)
in presence of . . .

                                                    her
                                         Easter X BOWHANAN (Seal)
                                                 Mark"

*followed with the acknowledgment by Justice of the Peace Thomas DIXON and the recordation on folio 431 by court clerk John C. HANDY on 28 December 1799[907]

Liber T, folios 432-433; 24 December 1799

"Maryland Ss^t. Know all men by these presents that I Walton COLLINS of Worcester County in State af[ore]s[ai]^d for and in Consideration of the Sum of thirty One pounds to me in hand by Joseph MILLER of the same place, the receipt whereof I do Acknowledge and am therewith fully satisfied have bargained and Sold and delivered unto the af[ore]s[ai]^d Joseph MILLER his heirs & Assigns One Negro Girl named **Beck** aged ten years old, which Negro **Beck** I do hereby Sell to said MILLER and I do hereby and will Warrant defend unto him the af[ore]s[ai]^d Joseph MILLER the af[ore]s[ai]^d bargained Negro Girl **Beck** against the right title of and claim all and every person or persons whatsoever claims. In Witness whereof I have hereunto set my hand and seal affixed this 24th day of December Anno Domini 1799.

Sealed & delivered   John POSTLY   Walton COLLINS (Seal)
in presence of"

*followed on folio 433 with the acknowledgment by Justice of the Peace John POSTLY and the recordation on 01 January 1800 by court clerk John C. HANDY[908]

Liber T, folio 436; 13 January 1800

"This Deed of Manumission dated this thirteenth day of January in the year of Our lord Eighteen hundred bears Testimony that I George MERICA do hereby Manumit release and by these

---

[907] Worcester County Court (Land Records). Bill of Sale from BOWHANAN, John and Easter to HANDY, Samuel Sr. 12 December 1799. T, pp. 430-431, MSA CE 30-19. www.mdlandrec.net : accessed 14 June 2022.

[908] Worcester County Court (Land Records). Bill of Sale from COLLINS, Walton to MILLER, Joseph. 24 December 1799. T, pp. 432-433, MSA CE 30-19. www.mdlandrec.net : accessed 14 June 2022.

presents set free a certain Negro Woman called **Jeb**, and do hereby authorise, and impower the said negro Woman called **Jib**, to Act do and in all things perform the part of a free Woman as fully & amply to all intents and purposes as if the said Negro Woman **Jeb** had been born free, any law Statute or Act to the contrary notwithstanding ~ To have and to hold her said freedom for and during the term of her natural life without the least hinderence or molestation of any person or persons whatsoever ~ In Testimony whereof I do to these presents set my hand and Seal affix the day and year above written ~

Signed Sealed & delivered   J[oh]n GUNBY.
in presence of …   George X AMERICA (Seal)

*followed with the acknowledgment by Justice of the Peace John GUNBY and the recordation on 14 January 1800 by court clerk John C. HANDY[909]

Liber T, folios 436-437; 01 January 1800

"State of Maryland Know all Men by these presents that I Abigail PARKER of Worcester County and State af[ore]s[ai]ᵈ for and in Consideration of the Sum of the value of ten pounds Current money of Maryland to me in hand paid by William PARSONS and Priscilla PARSONS of the same County and State af[ore]s[ai]ᵈ have bargained Sold set over and delivered by these presents in plain and open market according to the just and due form of law in that case made and provided do bargain set over and deliver unto the said William PARSONS and Prissella PARSONS One Negro Woman named **Venis** and also One Negro Girl named **Leah** ~ To have and to hold the said bargained premises to the said William PARSONS and Prissilla PARSONS their heirs Executors Administrators or Assigns forever and I the said Abigail PARKER for myself my heirs Executors & Administrators the said bargained premises unto the said William PARSONS and Prissilla PARSONS their heirs Executors Administrators or Assigns against all manner of persons shall and will warrant and forever defend the by these presents. In Witness whereof unto the said bargained premises I have my hand set and Seal affixed this first day of January One thousand Eight hundred

Signed Sealed & delivered   Booz WALSTON
in presence off.   Isaiah SMITH.   Abigail X PARKER (Seal)

*followed on folio 437 with the acknowledgment by Justice of the Peace Booz WALSTON and the recordation on 17 January 1800 by court clerk John C. HANDY[910]

Liber T, folios 445-447; 20 January 1800

"This Indenture made this twentieth day of January Eighteen hundred between Elisha PURNELL of Worcester County and State of Maryland of the One part and Dolly PURNELL of the first part, and Sally CHAILLEA of the second part, and Margaret CHAIELLA of the third part Comfort CHAILLEA of the fourth, John P. CHAILLEA of the fifth part and Moses CHAILLEA Ju[nio]ʳ of the Sixth part Witnesseth, that the said Elisha PURNELL for and in Consideration of love and Affection, and divers other good causes and Considerations him thereunto, moveing, and also for the Consideration of five Shillings, in hand paid, by each of the above maned Granters unto him the said Elisha PURNELL, the Receipt whereof is hereby acknowledged, and each of them, their Executors and Administrators therefrom discharged by these presents, hath given Granted and Confirmed and by these presents doth Give Grant and Confirm, unto the said Dolly PURNELL one Negro Woman **Tab**, One Negro **Leah**, One Bead and furniture, One looking Glass and Yoke of Steers and One Desk, unto her the said Dolly her Executors and Assigns forever, and this Indenture further Witnesseth, that the said Elisha hath

---

[909] Worcester County Court (Land Records). Deed of Manumission from AMERICA, George to **Jeb**. 13 January 1800. T, p. 436, MSA CE 30-19. www.mdlandrec.net : accessed 14 June 2022.
[910] Worcester County Court (Land Records). Bill of Sale from PARKER, Abigail to PARSONS, William and Priscilla. 01 January 1800. T, pp. 436-437, MSA CE 30-19. www.mdlandrec.net : accessed 14 June 2022.

Given Granted and Confirmed unto Sally CHAILLEA, One Negro Boy called **Peter**, One Bead and furniture, One Cow and Square Walnut Table, unto her the said Sally CHAILLEA, her Executors and Assigns forever. And this Indenture further Witnesseth, that the said Elisha PURNELL hath Given Granted & confirmed unto Margaret CHAILLEA One Negro Girl called **Candice**, one Bead and furniture One table, One Cow and Calf, and three head of Sheep, unto her the said Margaret CHAILLEA, her Executors and Assigns forever ~ And this Indenture further Witnesseth that the said Elisha PURNELL, hath Given Granted and Confirmed unto the aforesaid Comfort CHAILLEA, One Negro Girl, called **Silvia**, One bead and furniture, One Desk, One Cow and three Sheep, unto the said Comfort CHAILLEA her Executors and Assigns forever, And this Indenture further Witnesseth that the said Elisha PURNELL, hath Given Granted and Confirmed unto the above named John P. CHAILLEA and Moses CHAILLEA Jun[io]^r, One Negro called **Jack**, One Girl called **Rachel**, One Bead and furniture, One Desk One looking Glass and two heifers, to them the aforesaid John and Moses equally their Executors and Assigns forever ~ To have and to hold the above named Negroes, Goods and Chattles unto the several named Grantees Viz: Doll, Sally, Margret, Comfort, John and Moses CHAILLEA Jun[io]^r, their and each of their Executors and assigns forever, And to the only proper use and behoof of them the said Dolly, Sally, Margret, Comfort John and Moses CHAILLEA Jun[io]^r (except as herein after excepted) And to no other use intent or purpose watever, And the said Elisha further Covenants Grants and agrees to and with the said Dolly, Sally, Margret, Comfort, John and Moses CHAILLEA Junior, the within mentioned Negroes, Goods and Chattles, from himself, his Executors and Assigns and all persons claiming under him or them Except the above Negroes Goods and Chattles hereby Given unto Margret, Comfort, John & Moses during their several minorities, which are hereby committed to the care & possession of Esme PURNELL and Dolly his Wife in trust for the use of them the said Margret, Comfort, John and Moses CHAILLEA Jun[io]^r, by these presents shall and will warrant and defend. In Witness whereof the said Elisha hath hereunto set his hand and affixed his Seal the day and year first within written

Signed Sealed & delivered   Jno P MARSHALL (Ass. Jus[tice])   Elisha PURNELL   (Seal)
in presence of . . ."

*followed on folio 447 with the acknowledgment by John P. MARSHALL and the recordation on 24 January 1800 by court clerk John C. HANDY[911]

Liber T, folios 447-448; 10 January 1800

"Know all Men by these presents that I Thomas E NUTTER of Somerset County and State of Maryland for and in the consideration of the sum of fifteen pounds Current Money of Maryland to me in hand paid by Maj[or] DORMIN, whereof I do hereby acknowledge the Re[ceip]^t and myself therewith fully satisfied, and have bargained and Sold Set over & delivered, according to the true and just form of the law in that case made and do bargain set over and sell unto the af[ore]s[ai]^d Major DORMIN One Negro Woman called **Lare** hear younges Chile to him the said Maj[or] DORMAN his heirs and assigns forever, and by these presents I warrant and defend the said negro wench and Child unto the said Major DORMAN his heirs and assigns forever ~ In Testimony whereof I have set my hand and Seal this 10 day of January 1800

Tho[ma]^s E NUTTER   (Seal)

Testes   John CRASAFORD, Levin ABBETT"

*followed on folio 448 with the recordation on 24 January 1800 by court clerk John C. HANDY[912]

---

[911] Worcester County Court (Land Records). Deed of Gift from PURNELL, Elisha to CHAILLEA, Sally, Margaret, Comfort, John P., and Moses Jr., and PURNELL, Dolly. 20 January 1800. T, pp. 445-447, MSA CE 30-19. www.mdlandrec.net : accessed 14 June 2022.

[912] Worcester County Court (Land Records). Bill of Sale from NUTTER, Thomas E. to DORMAN, Major. 10 January 1800. T, pp. 447-448, MSA CE 30-19. www.mdlandrec.net : accessed 14 June 2022.

Liber T, folio 448; 27 December 1799

"State of Maryland Know all Men by these presents, that we Ezekiel CLAIWEL and **Jacob ARMSTRONG**, both of Worcester County and State aforesaid am held and firmly bound unto the State of Maryland more especially Worcester County, in the full and just Sum of thirty pounds lawful money of said State, to be paid to the said State of Maryland, more especially Worcester County, which payment well and truly to be made and done we bind Ourselves, and Our heirs firmly by these presents, Sealed with Our Seals, and dated this twenty Seventh day of December 1799 ~

The Condition of the above obligation is such that if the above written bounden Ezekiel CLAWELL and **Jacob ARMSTRONG** and their heirs do and shall forever hereafter keep harmless and indemnify the State of Maryland more especially Worcester County from any and all Cost and Charges that may or shall hereafter arise in Consequence **Sarah PARKER**s having an Eligimate Child named **Sally** born about the 4th of August 1798, then the above obligation to be void and of no effect or else to stand and remain in full force and virtue in law

Signed Sealed & delivered   Benjamin DENNIS
in the presents of   Ezekiel + CLAWELL (Seal)
                                                                          his mark
                                                                 Jacob + **ARMSTRONG** (Seal)
                                                                          mark"

*followed with the recordation on 24 January 1800 by court clerk John C. HANDY[913]

Liber T, folio 449; 27 December 1799

"State of Maryland, Know all Men by these presents that we Ezekiel CLAWELL and **Jacob ARMSTRONG** both of Worcester County and State aforesaid am held and firmly bound unto the State of Maryland, more especially to Worcester County in the full and just Sum of thirty pounds lawful money of Said State to be paid to the State of Maryland more especially Worcester County, which payment well and truly to be made and done we bind Ourselves Our heirs and each of us and each of Our heirs jointly and severally and firmly by these presents, Sealed with Our Seals and dated this twenty Seventh day of December 1799 ~

The Condition of the above Obligation is such that if the above bounden Ezekiel CLAWELL or **Jacob ARMSTRONG** or either of them or their heirs do and shall forever hereafter keep and save harmless and indemnifie the State of Maryland more especially Worcester County from all and any Cost or Charges that may arise in Consequence of **Sarah PARKER** having an Eligimate Child **Milby**, born about the twenty first day of July 1796, then the above Obligation to be void, or else to stand and remain in full force and virtue in law ~

Signed Sealed & delivered   Benjamin DENNIS
in the presence of . .   Ezekiel + CLAWELL (Seal)
                                                                          his mark
                                                                 Jacob + **ARMSTRONG** (Seal)
                                                                          mark"

*followed with the recordation on 24 January 1800 by court clerk John C. HANDY[914]

---

[913] Worcester County Court (Land Records). Bastardy bond from CLAWELL, Ezekiel and **ARMSTRONG, Jacob** to the State of Maryland. 27 December 1799. T, p. 448, MSA CE 30-19. www.mdlandrec.net : accessed 14 June 2022.

[914] Worcester County Court (Land Records). Bastardy bond from CLAWELL, Ezekiel and **ARMSTRONG, Jacob** to the State of Maryland. 27 December 1799. T, p. 449, MSA CE 30-19. www.mdlandrec.net : accessed 14 June 2022.

Liber T, folio 453; 27 January 1800

"Worcester Ss^t. State of Maryland To all to whom this writing shall come Be it known that I Edward HENRY Executor of William PURNELL late of Worcester County deceased for and in Consideration of the faithful Services heretofore rendered unto the af[ore]s[ai]^d William PURNELL deceased by a certain Negro Man Slave named **Amos** and his Wife **Sopha** together with their two Children **Josiah** and **Joshua**, do by these presents Manumate Emancipate set at liberty, and from the Service of me my heirs Executors Administrators and Assigns forever discharge the aforesaid negroes **Amos**, **Sopha**, **Josiah** and **Joshua**, and do hereby Covenant and agree that they shall forever as far as regards any claim or title in me to them or their Services shall enjoy and have all the previledges of free negroes In Witness whereof I have hereunto set my hand and Seal in the presence of two Witnesses this 27th day of January Anno Dom[ini] 1800

Testes Isaac EVANS, W[illia]^m COVINGTON   Edw[ar]^d HENRY   (Seal)"

*followed with the acknowledgment by Justice of the Peace Josiah MITCHELL and the recordation on 31 January 1800 by court clerk John C. HANDY[915]

Liber T, folio 454; 07 January 1800

"Know all Men by these presents that I Nathaniel BRATTEN Sen[ior] of Worcester County State of Maryland, in Consideration of the Natural love and Affection which I have and bear unto my beloved Grandson Nath[aniel] BRATTEN Jun[io]^r and also for divers other good causes and Consideration me that the said Nath[aniel] BRATTEN Sen[io]^r hereunto moving, have given granted and Confirmed, and by these presents do Give Grant and Confirm unto the said Nathaniel BRATTEN Jun[io]^r One Negro Boy called **Bob** ~ To have and to hold anjoy the said Nath[anie]^l BRATTEN Jun[io]^r his heirs Executors Administrators and Assigns forever, And I the said Nath[anie]^l BRATTEN Sen[io]^r do forever defend the above mentioned Gift unto the said Nath[anie]^l BRATTEN Jun[io]^r his heirs Ex[ecuto]^{rs} Adm[inistrato]^{rs} and Assigns against me the said Nath[aniel] BRATTEN Sen[io]^r my Ex[ecuto]^{rs} Adm[inistrato]^{rs} and all every other person and persons whatsoever shall and will Warrant and forever defend by these presents, As Witness my hand and Seal this 7th day of Jan[uar]^y Eighteen hundred

Testes Levi BISHOP   Nath[aniel] BRATTEN (Seal)"

*followed with the recordation on 04 February 1800 by court clerk John C. HANDY[916]

Liber T, folios 476-477; 28 January 1800

"State of Maryland Worcester County Ss^t. Be it Remembered that on this twenty Eight day of January A.D. One thousand Eight hundred for Sundry good Causes and in Consideration of Sixty pound to me James LANE in hand paid by **George LANE** (Negro) lately my property devised by my Father, and at this time for and in Consideration of the above Sum of Sixty pound to me the said James LANE in hand paid by the said **George**, the Receipt whereof I the said James LANE do hereby Acknowledge and myself therewith fully satisfied and and paid for the full amount and term of his the said **George**s Servitude in pursuance whereof I the said James LANE do by these presents Exonerate and forever quit Claim and at all times hereafter do by these presents disclaim and revoke all & every claim or demand that I the said James LANE or my heirs might or ever had to the said **George** or his heirs ~ In Testimony whereof I the said James LANE have to this my perpitual acquital and for ever discharge from this date set my hand and affixed my Seal this date first above written

---

[915] Worcester County Court (Land Records). Deed of Manumission from HENRY, Edward (Executor of William PURNELL) to **Amos**, **Sopha**, **Josiah**, and **Joshua**. 27 January 1800. T, p. 453, MSA CE 30-19. www.mdlandrec.net : accessed 14 June 2022.

[916] Worcester County Court (Land Records). Bill of Sale from BRATTEN, Nathaniel Sr. to BRATTEN, Nathaniel Jr. 07 January 1800. T, p. 454, MSA CE 30-19. www.mdlandrec.net : accessed 15 June 2022.

Signed Sealed & delivered   James LANE   (Seal)
in presence of . .   John P. MITCHELL"

*followed with the acknowledgment by Justice of the Peace John P. MITCHELL and the recordation on folio 477 on 13 February 1800 by court clerk John C. HANDY[917]

Liber T, folios 479-480; 01 January 1800

"State of Maryland, Know all Men by these presents that we William PARSONS and Prissilla PARSONS of Worcester County and State af[ore]s[ai]ᵈ for and in Consideration of the Sum of the value of Eighty five pounds two shillings and Six pence current money of Maryland to us in hand paid by Elisha PARKER of the same County and State af[ore]s[ai]ᵈ have bargained Sold set Over and delivered by these presents in plain and open market according to the just and due form of law in that Case made and provided, do bargain set Over and deliver unto the said Elisha PARKER, One Negro Woman named **Venis**, and also One Negro Girl named **Leah** ~ To have and to hold the said bargained premises unto the said Elisha PARKER his heirs Executors Administrators or Assigns forever and we William PARSONS and Prissilla PARSONS, for Ourselves and each of Our heirs Executors and Administrators the said bargained premises unto the said Elisha PARKER his heirs Executors Administrators or Assigns against all manner of persons, shall and will Warrant and for ever defend the same by these presents in Witness whereof unto the said bargained premises we have hereunto our hands set and Seal affixed this first day of January One thousand Eight hundred.

Signed Sealed & delivered   Booz WALSTON   William PARSON   (Seal)
in presents of us . .   Isaiah SMITH
                                                          her
                                               Prissilla X PARSONS   (Seal)
                                                         mark"

*followed on folio 480 with the acknowledgment by Justice of the Peace Booz WALSTON and the recordation on 17 January 1800 by court clerk John C. HANDY[918]

Liber T, folio 485; 15 February 1800

"To all to whom it may concern this Deed of Manumission dated the Fifteenth day of February 15ᵗʰ, in the year of Our lord, One thousand Eight hundred, witnesseth, that for and in Consideration of past services done for me by Negro Man **Isaac**, I James WILSON of Worcester County in the State of Maryland do hereby Manumit release, and set at full liberty from me and my heirs forever, the Negro Man **Isaac**, and I do hereby permit and empower the said Negro Man **Isaac** to labour and Act for his own Support and Maintenance to bargain and in all things to Act as a freeman ought to Act he behaveing himself as a free Man Ought to behave agreeable to the laws of Our Country ~ To have and to hold his said Freedom during the term of his Natural life without any let hindrance of any person or persons whatsoever. In Testimony whereof, I do to these presents set my hand and Seal affix the day and year first above written

Sealed & delivered in   James WILSON   (Seal)
the presence of   Jacob WHITE"

*followed with the recordation on 20 February 1800 by court clerk John C. HANDY[919]

---

[917] Worcester County Court (Land Records). Deed of Manumission from LANE, James to **LANE, George**. 28 January 1800. T, pp. 476-477, MSA CE 30-19. www.mdlandrec.net : accessed 14 June 2022.
[918] Worcester County Court (Land Records). Bill of Sale from PARSONS, William and Prissilla to PARKER, Elisha. 01 January 1800. T, pp. 479-480, MSA CE 30-19. www.mdlandrec.net : accessed 15 June 2022.
[919] Worcester County Court (Land Records). Deed of Manumission from WILSON, James to **Isaac**. 15 February 1800. T, p. 485, MSA CE 30-19. www.mdlandrec.net : accessed 15 June 2022.

Liber T, folio 493; 17 December 1799

"List of Nigroes {?} Imported to this State by me on 17th of December 1799 names & sexls as follows 1 Nigro named **Abel** 25 years old one woman named **Adah** 23 years old 1 Girl named **Betty** 5 years old 1 Boy named **Job** 3 years old 1 Boy named **George** 10 months old which Negroes I derived by my wife and my wife by her Father W[illia]m MARSHALL in his last will and Testment as was made a record of at accomack County and state of Virginia on January 30th Anno Domini 1787 . . . . .

John WARD"

*followed with the recordation on 22 February 1800 by court clerk John C. HANDY[920]

Liber T, folios 504-505; 15 March 1800

"Worcester Sst. Know all Men by these presents that I James DICKERSON of Worcester County in the State of Maryland for and in Consideration of the Sum of Sixteen pounds Seaven ten shillings to me in hand paid by the said John CHAILLER before the Ensealing and delivery hereof the Receipt whereof I do hereby acknowledge hath Granted bargained and Sold and by these presents do Grant bargain and Sell unto the said John CHAILLER his heirs and Assigns forever One Woman by the name **Floren**, and the said James DICKERSON doth for himself and his heirs Covenants and agree to and with the said John CHAILLER that she the said Negro **Floren** above mentioned will warrant and forever defend from all persons whatever claiming any right or title unto the said Negro **Floren**. In Witness whereof I have hereunto set my hand and Seal this 15th day March 1800.

Signed Sealed & delivered   James DICKERSON   (Seal)
in presents off . . .   Tho[ma]s DIXON"

*followed on folio 505 with the acknowledgment by Justice of the Peace Thomas DIXON and the recordation on 04 April 1800 by court clerk John C. HANDY[921]

Liber T, folio 521; 10 January 1800

"A List of Nigroes imported into the State of maryland from the State of Virginia the 10 Day of January Anno Dom[ini] 1800 by the Subscriber to wit one Negro Woman named **Leah** twenty one years of age the Title to which nigro I derived from my wife Elizabeth WHITTINGTON which Title She derived from her Father's last will and Testament Dated the 20th Day of may Anno Domini 1795 And recorded in the office of Accomack

John N WHITTINGTON"

*followed with the recordation on 14 April 1800 by court clerk John C. HANDY[922]

Liber T, folios 535-536; 22 April 1800

"Worcester Sst. Know all men by these presents that I John WATSON of Worcester County in the State of Maryland for and in consideration of the sum of seventy five pounds to me in hand paid by James COTTINGHAM before the Ensealing and delivery hereof the receipt whereof I do hereby acknowled hath given granted bargained and Sold and by these presents do grant bargain and Sell unto the said James COTTINGHAM his heirs and assigns for ever one nigro woman by the name **Effe** and the said John WATSON doth for himself and his heirs covenant and agree to and with the said James COTTINGHAM that he the said John WATSON the nigro woman by the name **Effe** and her increase will warrant and forever defend from all persons

---

[920] Worcester County Court (Land Records). Certificate of Importation into Maryland from WARD, John for **Abel, Adah, Betty, Job,** and **George**. 17 December 1799. T, p. 493, MSA CE 30-19. www.mdlandrec.net : accessed 15 June 2022.

[921] Worcester County Court (Land Records). Bill of Sale from DICKERSON, James to CHAILLER, John. 15 March 1800. T, pp. 504-505, MSA CE 30-19. www.mdlandrec.net : accessed 15 June 2022.

[922] Worcester County Court (Land Records). Certificate of Importation into Maryland from WHITTINGTON, John for **Leah**. 10 January 1800. T, p. 521, MSA CE 30-19. www.mdlandrec.net : accessed 15 June 2022.

whatsoever Claiming any Right title unto the Said nigro In Witness whereof I have hereunto Sell my hand and Seal this the twenty Second day of April 1800 . . . . .

Sealed and Deli[vere]^d
In the presents of.   Tho[ma]^s DIXON   John + WALSON (Seal)
                                                      his mark"

*followed on folio 536 with the acknowledgment by Justice of the Peace Thomas DIXON and the recordation on 25 April 1800 by court clerk John C. HANDY[923]

Liber T, folios 542-543; 28 March 1800

"Worcester Ss^t. Know all men by these presents that I Tabitha DALE widow of worcester County in the State of maryland, for and in consideration of the love and affection which I have for my Daughter Mary HOLLAND And for the further Consideration of the Sum of five Shillings Current Money of Maryland to me in hand paid by the said Mary of the same place at or before the Ensealing and Delivery of these presents the receipt whereof is hereby acknowledged and the said Mary HOLLAND his heirs Executors and Administrators thereform forever Discharge by these presents, Have bargained Sold and delivered and by these presents do fully Clearly and absolutely Bargain Sell and Deliver unto the Said Mary HOLLAND one Negro Girl named **Sall** about Elevin years of age To have and to hold the said negro Girl **Sall** unto the said Mary HOLLAND his Executors administrators or assigns to her & their proper uses and behoofs forever. And I the said Tabitha DALE my heirs Executors and administrators and Every of us the Said negro Girl **Sall** unto the Said Mary HOLLAND his heirs and assigns against all people Shall and will warrant acquit and forever Defend by these presents In Witness whereof the said Tabitha DALE to these presents her hand Set and Seal Affixed this twenty Eight Day of March in our Lord Eighteen hundred . . . . .

Sealed and Deliver[e]d   John POSTLY . .   her
In the presence of.   Elisha HOLLAND   Tabitha + DALE (Seal)
                                                         mark"

*followed on folio 543 with the acknowledgment by Justice of the Peace John POSTLY and the recordation on 11 April 1800 by court clerk John C. HANDY[924]

Liber T, folio 550; 08 May 1800

"Maryland Ss^t. Know all men by these presents that I Elizabeth TOWNSEND Executrix of the late Levin TOWNSEND dec[ease]^d of Worcester County, for and in Consideration of the Sum of forty five pounds Current money of Maryland to me in hand paid by Charles TOWNSEND of the same County and State af[oresai]^d at and before the Sealing and delivery these presents, the receipt whereof I do hereby acknowledge I have given granted bargained and Sold and by these presents do give grant bargain and sell and by these presents do give grant sell and confirm unto him the said Charles TOWNSEND his heirs and Assigns forever three Negros to wit, One Negro Woman named **Milly**, One Boy Named **Ned** One Girl named **Nanny** ~ To have and to hold the said Negro Slaves **Milly Ned** and **Nanny** unto him the said Charles TOWNSEND his heirs and Assigns forever. In Testimony whereof the said Elizabeth TOWNSEND have hereunto set my hand and affixed my Seal this Eighth of May 1800

Signed Sealed & delivered   Elizabeth TOWNSEND (Seal)
in presence of . . .   John COTTINGHAM"

---

[923] Worcester County Court (Land Records). Bill of Sale from WATSON, John to COTTINGHAM, James. 22 April 1800. T, pp. 535-536, MSA CE 30-19. www.mdlandrec.net : accessed 15 June 2022.
[924] Worcester County Court (Land Records). Bill of Sale from DALE, Tabitha to HOLLAND, Mary. 28 March 1800. T, pp. 542-543, MSA CE 30-19. www.mdlandrec.net : accessed 15 June 2022.

*followed with the acknowledgment by Justice of the Peace John COTTINGHAM and the recordation on 09 May 1800 by court clerk John C. HANDY[925]

Liber T, folios 555-556; 19 May 1800

"Know all Men by these presents that I Edward STEVENSON of Worcester County for and in Consideration of the Sum of One hundred pounds to me in hand paid by John ROCK at and before the Sealing and delivery of these presents the Receipt whereof is hereby acknowledged, hath granted bargained and Sold, and by these presents do grant bargain Sell and confirm, and will warrant and forever defend said Negro **Jack** unto John ROCK of the same County Negro Man named **Jack** to him and his heirs forever, to be his right title, interest and claim, according to the true intent and purport of this Bill of Sale. In Testimony whereof I have hereunto set my hand and affixed my Seal this nineteenth day of May Anno Dom[ini] Eighteen hundred

Signed Sealed & delivered　　　　　　　　　　　　　　　　　Edward STEVENSON　(Seal)
in the presence of　　　　Philip QUINTON"

*followed on folio 556 with an additional note and the acknowledgment by Justice of the Peace Philip QUINTON and the recordation by court clerk John C. HANDY[926]

Liber T, folios 556-557; 19 May 1800

"Know all Men by these presents that I John ROCK of Worcester County and State of Maryland for and in Consideration of the Sum of Thirty Eight pounds Current Money of Mary[l][and] to me in hand paid by Edward STEVENSON of the same place at and before the Sealing and delivery of these presents, the receipt whereof I do hereby acknowledge have bargained and Sold and by presents do bargain and Sell unto the said STEVENSON his heirs and Assigns One Negro Girl named **Jane**. To have and to hold the said Negro Girl above mentioned unto the said Edward STEVENSON his heirs and Assigns forever, and for no other use or purpose whatsoever, and he the said John ROCK for himself and his heirs doth Covenant and agree to and with the said Edw[ar]d STEVENSON that he the said John ROCK hath a good and sufficient title to sell and dispose of the said Negro named **Jane** so as to Convey unto the said Edward STEVENSON a good Sure and firm title to the said Negro named **Jane** and that to no person but he the said John ROCK hath any right or title to the same ~ In Testimony whereof the said John ROCK hath affixed his hand and Seal this 19th day of May in the year of Our lord One thousand Eight hundred

Signed Sealed & delivered　　　　　　　　　　　　　　　　　John ROCK　(Seal)
in presence of　　　　Philip QUINTON"

*followed on folio 557 with the acknowledgment by Justice of the Peace Philip QUINTON and the recordation on 20 May 1800 by court clerk John C. HANDY[927]

Liber T, folios 566-567; 29 May 1800

"Know all Men by these presents that I Elizabeth HANDY of Worcester County for and in Consideration of the Sum of twenty five pounds Current Money of Maryland to me in hand paid before the Sealing hereof, the Receipt whereof I do hereby Acknowledge, have bargained Sold and delivered unto my Nephew James BACON all my right title Interest and Estate of and to my Negro Man named **Jesse** ~ To have and to hold the said bargained and Sold Negro Man **Jesse** unto the said James BACON his heirs Executors Adm[inistrato]rs and Assigns forever ~ And I the said Elizabeth HANDY and each of my heirs Executors Adm[inistrato]rs and Assigns doth by virtue of these presents hereby Covenant to and with the said James BACON to forever

---

[925] Worcester County Court (Land Records). Bill of Sale from TOWNSEND, Elizabeth (Executrix) to TOWNSEND, Charles. 08 May 1800. T, p. 550, MSA CE 30-19. www.mdlandrec.net : accessed 15 June 2022.

[926] Worcester County Court (Land Records). Bill of Sale from STEVENSON, Edward to ROCK, John. 19 May 1800. T, pp. 555-556, MSA CE 30-19. www.mdlandrec.net : accessed 15 June 2022.

[927] Worcester County Court (Land Records). Bill of Sale from ROCK, John to STEVENSON, Edward. 19 May 1800. T, pp. 556-557, MSA CE 30-19. www.mdlandrec.net : accessed 15 June 2022.

warrant and defend the right and property of said Negro Man from all persons unto the said James BACON and his heirs & Assigns forever ~ In Testimony whereof the said Elizabeth HANDY hath hereto set her hand and affixed her Seal the 29th day of May Anno Domini 1800

Signed Sealed & delivered Elizabeth HANDY   (Seal)
in the presence of   John COTTINGHAM"

*followed on folio 567 with the acknowledgment by Justice of the Peace John COTTINGHAM and the recordation on 09 June 1800 by court clerk John C. HANDY[928]

Liber T, folios 596-597; 08 July 1800

"Know all Men by these present I Barzillia PARKER of Worcester County and State of Maryland for and in consideration of the Sum of seventy Six pounds lawful Money of the State af[oresai]^d in hand paid by Samuel PARKER of the same place the rec[eip]^t whereof I do har by acknowledge, I have bargained and sold and by these presents do bargain and sell unto the said PARKER his heirs or assigns for One Negro Girl by the name of **Chany** One Bade and furniture and One Wanut Table One half dozen Chairs One Cow One horse Colt One Desk and Brakfast Table One Saft. To have and to hold the said prop[er]ty above mentioned unto the said S. PARKER his heirs and Assigns forever and for no other use or purpose whatsoever, and the said B. PARKER for himself and his heirs doth Covenant and agree to and with the said Samuel PARKER, that he the said B. PARKER hath a good an sufficient title to Sell and dispose of the said property so as to Convey unto the said S. PARKER a good sure and firm title to the same In Witness whereof I have hereunto set my hand and Seal affixed this Eighth day of July Anno Dom[ini] 1800.

Signed Sealed & delivered   Barzillia PARKER   (Seal)
in the presence of   John COTTINGHAM"

*followed on folio 597 with the acknowledgment and an additional note by Justice of the Peace John COTTINGHAM and the recordation on 13 July 1800[929]

*The acknowledgment clarifies the girl's name as "**China**".

Liber T, folios 602-603; 03 July 1800

"State of Maryland Know all Men by these presents that I Samuel GILLITT of Worcester County in the State of Maryland for and in Consideration of the Sum of fifty five pounds lawful Money of Maryland to me in hand paid by John BLADES of the af[oresai]^d State and County at or before the Sealing and delivery of these presents the receipt whereof I the said Samuel GILLITT do hereby acknowledge have bargained and sold and by these presents do grant bargain and Sell unto the said John BLADES his heirs Executors Administrators and Assigns all the property herein after mentioned that is to say One Negro Woman called **Violett** aged about twenty five years also One Negro Girl named **Hannah** aged three years, which said property is now in the possession of the said GILLITT. To have and to hold all and singular the s[ai]^d Negroes above bargained and sold or intended so to be to the s[ai]^d John BLADES his heirs or assigns untill such time, not exceeding Six Months from the date hereof, the s[ai]^d Samuel GILLITT shall repay the s[ai]^d Sum of fifty five pounds with legal Interest to the s[ai]^d John BLADES his heirs or assigns and the said Samuel GILLITT for myself my heirs Executors Administrators and Assigns all and singular the said property unto the said John BLADES his heirs or assigns, against me the said Samuel GILLITT my heirs or assigns & against all and every person or persons whatsoever shall and will warrant and forever defend by these presents agreeable to the true intent & meaning hereof. In Witness whereof, I the said Samuel GILLITT have hereunto my hand set and Seal affixed this third day of July 1800

---

[928] Worcester County Court (Land Records). Bill of Sale from HANDY, Elizabeth to BACON, James. 29 May 1800. T, pp. 566-567, MSA CE 30-19. www.mdlandrec.net : accessed 15 June 2022.
[929] Worcester County Court (Land Records). Bill of Sale from PARKER, Barzillia to PARKER, Samuel. 08 July 1800. T, pp. 596-597, MSA CE 30-19. www.mdlandrec.net : accessed 15 June 2022.

Signed Sealed & delivered   Samuel GILLITT (Seal)
in the presence of . .   John HOLLAND"

*followed with an additional note and the acknowledgment by Justice of the Peace John HOLLAND and the recordation on folio 603 on 25 July 1800 by court clerk John C. HANDY[930]

Liber T, folios 641-643; 03 June 1800

"This Indenture made this third day of June in the year of Our lord One thousand Eight hundred between Belitha OWENS of Worcester County in the State of Maryland of the One part and Negro **Ebenezar FOOKS** of the same County and State of the other part Witnesseth that the said Belitha OWENS for and in Consideration of the Sum of forty pounds Current money of Maryland, to him in hand paid by the aforesaid **Ebenezar FOOKES** before the Sealing and delivery of these presents the Receipt whereof is hereby acknowledged and confessed, and the said **Ebenezar FOOKES** his heirs Executors and Administrators therefrom forever acquitted and discharged, and he the said Belitha OWENS hath granted bargained and Sold and by these presents doth absolutely grant bargain Sell Convey and Confirm unto him the said **Ebenezar FOOKES** his heirs and assigns forever part of a Tract of land called Lingos purchase setuate lying and being in Worcester County bounded as followeth," … "containing and now laid Out for forty Acres of land, more or less, together with all previledges & appurtenances whatsoever thereto belonging. To have and to hold the aforesaid forty Acres of land af[oresai]^d limited and described together with all and singular the appurtenances thereto belonging unto af[ore]s[ai]^d **Ebenezar FOOKES** his heirs and assigns forever, and the said Belitha OWENS for himself his heirs Executors and Administrators will forever hereafter warrant and defend the above mentioned lands and premises with all its Appurtenances against the lawful claim of him the said Belitha OWENS and his heirs or any person by or under his athority unto him the said **Ebenezar FOOKES** his heirs and Assigns forever. In Testimony whereof the said Belitha OWENS to these presents his hand hath set and Seal affixed the day and year above written.

Signed Sealed & delivered   Booz WALSTON   Belitha OWENS (Seal)
in the presence of . .   John CATHELL . ."

*followed on folio 642 with the acknowledgment by Justices of the Peace Booz WALSTON and John CATHELL and the recordation on 13 August 1800 by court clerk John C. HANDY[931]

*The acknowledgment identifies the wife of the grantor as Mary OWENS.

*This transcription was abbreviated to its most relevant portions. The full court record entry can be viewed at the citation provided.

Liber T, folio 663; 02 September 1800

"I Samuel H. ROUND on removal from the State of Delaware into this State on the thirteenth day of June in the year of our lord Eighteen hundred brought with me a Negro Girl named **Harriet**, the daughter of Negro **Lydia**, who had been my Slave about twenty years in the State of Maryland and Delaware.

Sam[ue]^l H. ROUND"

*followed with the recordation on 02 September 1800 by court clerk John C. HANDY[932]

---

[930] Worcester County Court (Land Records). Bill of Sale from GILLITT, Samuel to BLADES, John. 03 July 1800. T, pp. 602-603, MSA CE 30-19. www.mdlandrec.net : accessed 15 June 2022.
[931] Worcester County Court (Land Records). Deed from OWENS, Belitha to **FOOKES, Ebenezar**. 03 June 1800. T, pp. 641-643, MSA CE 30-19. www.mdlandrec.net : accessed 15 June 2022.
[932] Worcester County Court (Land Records). Certificate of Importation into Maryland from ROUND, Samuel H. for **Harriet**. 02 September 1800. T, p. 663, MSA CE 30-19. www.mdlandrec.net : accessed 15 June 2022.

Liber T, folio 668; 18 September 1800

"Know all Men by these presents that I Peter CHAILLE Sen[io]ʳ of Worcester County Maryland, for and in Consideration of the Sum of fifty pounds to me in hand paid, the receipt whereof is hereby acknowledged, I have Granted bargained and Sold, and by these presents do grant bargain and Sell unto Peggy LONG, Littleton LONG and Henny LONG, the Children of my Daughter Comfort LONG, the following Negroes to wit, a Negro Woman called **Minta** and the following Negros to wit, **Grace   Levin   George** and **Linda**, children of the said Negro Woman called **Minta** ~ To have and to hold the said negros unto the only proper use and behoof of the said Peggy, Littleton & Henny LONG their Executors Administrators and Assigns, and I do covenant to warrant and defend the same unto them and their Executors Adm[inistrato]ʳˢ & Assigns ag[ain]ˢᵗ myself and all persons claiming by from or under me ~ As Witness my hand and Seal this 18ᵗʰ September 1800 ~

Signed Sealed & delivered   Peter CHAILLE   (Seal)
in presence of . . . .   W[illia]ᵐ WHITTINGTON"

*followed with the acknowledgment by 4ᵗʰ District Chief Justice William WHITTINGTON and the recordation by court clerk John C. HANDY[933]

---

[933] Worcester County Court (Land Records). Bill of Sale from CHAILLE, Peter Sr. to LONG, Peggy, Littleton, and Henny. 18 September 1800. T, p. 668, MSA CE 30-19. www.mdlandrec.net : accessed 15 June 2022.

Every Name Index

_____, **Abb** 355, 399; **Abbow** 18, 28; **Abel** 22, 66, 134, 146, 231, 255, 280, 294, 313, 375, 432, 446; **Abigail** 108, 109; **Able** 167, 188, 189, 337, 338; **Abner** 1, 98, 130, 131, 138, 173, 204, 208, 209, 210, 243, 244, 256, 313, 355; **Abraham** 34, 93, 180, 227, 248, 300, 321, 322; **Abram** 190, 237, 437; **Adah** 446; **Adam** 4, 12, 17, 19, 29, 36, 53, 137, 152, 160, 179, 180, 260, 309, 343, 354, 391, 396; **Addam** 396; **Agur** 165, 166; **Alce** 386; **Alic** 10; **Alse** 299; **Ame** 101; **Amelia** 72, 275, 406, 417; **Amey** 30, 56, 105, 250; **Amos** 83, 242, 276, 294, 319, 323, 444; **Amy** 152, 160, 184, 240, 249, 400, 403; **Anas** 153; **Andrew** 16, 21; **Aneas** 97; **Ann** 11, 269, 283, 313, 425; **Anna** 367, 368; **Anne** 379; **App** 310; **Appleby** 37; **Aproba** 72; **Arcy** 303; **Argile** 190; **Argill** 180; **Armwell** 293; **Arnold** 37; **Ary** 303; **Athaliah** 141; **Auther** 351; **Azariah** 330; **Barbary** 343; **Barshaba** 93, 96, 97; **Barsheba** 18, 28, 279; **Bartlett** 76; **Beck** 70, 118, 138, 242, 257, 325, 440; **Belender** 263; **Belinda** 220; **Belitha** 266; **Bella** 133; **Ben** 14, 38, 123, 133, 142, 160, 161, 175, 181, 196, 205, 220, 227, 230, 248, 250, 256, 283, 284, 294, 333, 343, 380, 386, 388; **Benjamin** 81, 196, 264, 390; **Benn** 10, 86, 387; **Bersheba** 262, 282; **Bess** 10, 55, 59, 82, 307; **Bet** 294, 317; **Bets** 97; **Bett** 37, 68, 149, 150, 228, 249, 308, 319, 323, 327, 328, 368; **Bette** 161; **Betts** 152; **Betty** 4, 5, 7, 8, 11, 22, 47, 68, 72, 142, 145, 166, 256, 262, 291, 317, 446; **Bill** 389; **Boatswain** 31; **Boatswan** 210; **Bob** 1, 53, 102, 138, 210, 213, 221, 377, 378, 382, 400, 444; **Bobb** 1, 103, 228, 229, 276, 387; **Bradis** 294; **Bridget** 44, 45, 54, 286, 438; **Bristor** 42; **Cable** 219; **Caesar** 59, 77; **Cage** 329; **Caleb** 22, 47, 206, 229, 235, 290, 298, 342, 358; **Calop** 342; **Candice** 442; **Candis** 167, 244, 245, 247, 299, 339, 420; **Candiss** 235; **Capel** 59; **Caprell** 180; **Capril** 196, 420; **Cary** 346; **Casandra** 350; **Casesa** 270; **Casesay** 270; **Cassandra** 350; **Cate** 228, 303; **Cato** 210, 313, 360; **Ceaser** 49, 395; **Ceasor** 73; **Celar** 343; **Cesar** 246; **Chany** 449; **Charity** 78, 79, 159, 161, 250, 360; **Charles** 80, 105, 206, 215, 216, 318, 348; **China** 449; **Chloe** 154, 245, 316; **Ciller** 294; **Cloah** 435; **Cloe** 42, 68, 133;

Cobbo 112; **Coffe** 59; **Coffee** 184; **Comfort** 11, 181, 184, 193, 198, 199, 203, 210, 223, 262, 294, 303, 313, 315, 322, 339, 344, 346, 350, 351, 354, 380, 402, 403, 411, 437, 439; **Conselo** 68; **Cuff** 121; **Cuggo** 358; **Cupet** 113; **Cupit** 59; **Cyller** 437; **Cynta** 133; **Daniel** 10, 24, 68, 90, 215, 245, 246, 296, 313, 326, 354, 359; **Danniel** 396; **Daul** 30; **David** 65, 134, 156, 272, 310, 311, 318, 440; **Davy** 261; **Deborah** 108; **Dennis** 262; **Derrah** 212; **Derrum** 117; **Derry** 268, 390; **Dianna** 389; **Diannah** 425; **Dick** 4, 22, 37, 65, 68, 72, 77, 119, 285; **Dider** 170; **Dina** 107; **Dinah** 8, 11, 27, 33, 61, 79, 93, 137, 265, 266, 286, 304, 321, 322, 413, 420; **Diner** 8; **Dinniah** 158; **Doary** 168; **Doctor** 424; **Dolby** 363; **Dolby Job** 238; **Dol** 343; **Doll** 87; **Dorcas** 104; **Dorcos** 393; **Dorkus** 11; **Dorset** 80; **Dover** 338; **Easter** 262, 265, 303, 370, 427; **Easther** 95, 308; **Eazer** 315; **Eben** 80, 207, 208, 231, 264, 378, 384; **Eby** 137; **Edea** 240; **Edith** 70, 92, 95; **Edmond** 262; **Effe** 446; **Elezebeth** 316; **Eli** 144; **Elijah** 243, 249, 250, 256, 266, 315, 325; **Elinor** 368; **Elisha** 119, 437; **Elizabeth** 316; **Elizebeth** 316; **Elon** 409; **Epheram** 157; **Ephraim** 392; **Esau** 362; **Esaw** 362; **Esler** 11; **Estar** 410; **Ester** 189, 292, 410; **Esther** 13, 41, 59, 94, 95, 111, 120, 129, 135, 136, 164, 167, 229, 235, 245, 256, 273, 286, 292, 313, 339, 340, 358, 370, 374, 413, 414; **Eunice** 98; **Eve** 18, 28; **Ezekiel** 240; **Fan** 183; **Fanny** 360; **Feaby** 341; **Fella** 86; **Fender** 109; **Filer** 69, 287; **Fillis** 99; **Fisher** 142; **Flora** 87, 260, 313, 339, 384; **Floren** 446; **Florow** 69; **Florrow** 36, 37; **Flowra** 33; **Fortune** 316, 398; **Fosida** 80; **Frank** 68, 71, 74, 109, 114, 142, 360, 405; **Frederic** 309; **Friday** 182; **Fryday** 86; **Gelica** 298; **Genny** 157; **Georg** 308; **George** 38, 43, 48, 50, 65, 76, 77, 134, 146, 149, 154, 155, 159, 161, 167, 172, 177, 180, 190, 193, 196, 214, 215, 216, 218, 232, 241, 243, 251, 257, 259, 269, 271, 273, 283, 288, 289, 312, 313, 332, 340, 360, 364, 395, 399, 406, 418, 438, 444, 446, 451; **George Dulany** 376; **George Shadrach** 238; **Gib** 152; **Gilbert** 161; **Gin** 365; **Ginne** 220; **Glasgow** 39, 294; **Gone** 85; **Grace** 173, 203, 262, 275, 277, 318, 356, 370, 451;

Green 133; Guy 238; Hagar 141, 268; Hager 141, 230, 253, 264, 283, 295; Hanah 59, 81, 105, 140, 142, 213, 377; Handy 16, 239, 300; Hannah 10, 49, 81, 95, 104, 115, 119, 134, 137, 146, 158, 159, 167, 184, 186, 203, 229, 242, 247, 249, 262, 267, 269, 286, 294, 309, 314, 322, 323, 342, 343, 369, 413, 414, 415, 425, 449; Hannah Jr. 95; Harrah 154; Harriet 450; Harry 4, 5, 18, 28, 35, 37, 39, 74, 104, 110, 119, 136, 195, 220, 228, 253, 286, 305, 306, 354, 375, 384, 393, 412, 413, 414, 416, 427, 428; Hatter 169; Heaster 203; Hector 21, 412; Henna 301; Henney 257; Henny 191; Henry 356 ; Hesse 421, 422; Hette 318; Hetty 249; Hinna 301; Hope 44, 45, 47, 53, 108, 109, 251, 317; Hornton 196; Hulda 155, 216, 411; Huldy 411; Ibbey 103; Iby 115; Isaac 93, 96, 122, 129, 146, 152, 160, 161, 165, 171, 173, 184, 202, 218, 242, 245, 252, 256, 260, 262, 267, 271, 319, 321, 322, 323, 344, 345, 353, 355, 360, 363, 366, 419, 421, 427, 432, 434, 445; Isabella 103; Ishmael 233; Izabel 247; Jabe 135; Jack 10, 69, 72, 75, 77, 78, 82, 97, 106, 118, 165, 210, 235, 252, 268, 271, 295, 296, 304, 345, 353, 388, 389, 429, 442, 448; Jacob 39, 49, 88, 93, 101, 115, 121, 133, 152, 153, 164, 178, 196, 204, 210, 226, 268, 274, 278, 281, 286, 303, 310, 312, 313, 321, 330, 332, 344, 346, 366, 376, 402, 403, 420, 430, 437; Jacob Freeborn 303; Jake 355; Jame 269; James 24, 134, 142, 158, 177, 197, 234, 235, 246, 292, 297, 309, 313, 324, 345, 368, 370, 417, 432; James Handy 399, 404; James Townsend 399; Jamey 6, 15; Jane 105, 131, 155, 203, 448; Jean 313, 405; Jeb 441; Jebb 200; Jeffrey 4; Jemima ; Jemimah 341; Jemmey 17; Jen 279, 282; Jenna 225; Jenny 10, 68, 137, 170, 216, 219, 231, 256, 348, 374, 426; Jer 49; Jeremiah 93, 96; Jerom 432; Jerum 288; Jesper 48, 316; Jess 216; Jesse 62, 108, 109, 113, 155, 359, 360, 448; Jethro 46, 50; Jib 441; Jibb 163; Jid 403; Jim 69, 158, 370; Jioe 10; Jo 112, 113; Joab 65; Joabe 65; Joan 17, 256; Job 108, 424, 446; Jobe 303; Joe 105, 183, 256, 294; John 48, 68, 161, 262, 294, 313, 349, 376, 389, 394, 407, 408; Jone 143; Joseph 303; Joshua 40, 86, 131, 147, 161, 208, 292, 293, 444; Josiah 444; Juda 2, 383, 403, 416; Judah 116, 286, 377; Jude 149, 150; Judy 10, 356; Ju{?} 22; Kent James 142; Kesiah 281; Kiah 256, 293; Laney 159; Lanta 340; Lare 442; Larry 202; Leah 31, 48, 60, 66, 81, 128, 133, 137, 143, 149, 150, 160, 161, 165, 168, 173, 194, 224, 229, 240, 260, 262, 264, 267, 269, 286, 289, 294, 308, 313, 324, 329, 342, 356, 370, 426, 432, 433, 434, 441, 445, 446; Leak 87, 88; Lear 124; Leash 399; Leb 262; Leeds 197; Let 37, 294; Leveanah Jenkins 105; Leven 173, 303; Leven the elder 303; Levi 260, 261, 387; Levin 119, 132, 176, 194, 206, 210, 218, 219, 224, 229, 289, 318, 327, 361, 362, 375, 378, 385, 451; Levinah 131, 147; Leviner 153, 154, 163; Libb 142; Lid 69; Lidde 274, 298; Liddia 161; Liddy 220; Lidey 383; Lidia 40; Lige 181; Limas 154; Limus 189; Linda 235, 451; Lish 279, 282, 311, 401; Lisha 88, 313, 355; Lishe 394, 395; Littleton 303, 328; Liz 211; Liza 211, 401; Lizey 210; London 49; Lonnon 84; Lott 320, 332; Lotte 332, 336; Loviey 101; Lowhill 110; Luca 303; Lucey 37, 369; Lucre 303; Lucretia 321, 322; Lucy 235; Lue 257; Luke 150, 184, 315, 427; Lura 256; Luse 396; Lusey 300; Lycia 223; Lyd 169; Lyda 370; Lydda 161, 162, 308; Lydia 235, 256, 288, 312, 450; Lymus 189; Magor 339; Majar 341; Major 110, 309, 380, 381; March 82, 107, 108; Mareor 274; Margarit 156; Margery 198, 360; Margo 158; Marina 41; Martha 44, 45, 47, 242, 313, 343; Mary 12, 170, 172, 220, 267, 313, 396, 419; Matthias 407, 408; May 22; Melby 217; Mellah 116; Mellea 116; Mereum 214; Merica 313; Merier 396; Mertin 251; Micajah 329; Middlesex 256; Milby 196, 325, 328, 335, 372, 373, 404; Mill 240; Milla 181, 256, 367; Mille 300, 429; Milley 37, 270; Milly 203, 447; Minea 436; Mingo 10, 33, 192, 336, 437; Minna 315; Minnea 435; Minta 220, 221, 222, 226, 227, 247, 344, 451; Mintay 203; Minte 422; Minty 255, 409, 410; Mirom 187, 200; Missyrow 121; Moll 6, 42, 247; Monday 68, 74; Moses 46, 121, 185, 307, 313, 339; Murreah 89; Murrur 83; Nabb 160; Name 138; Nan 31, 37, 102, 128, 136; Nance 201, 290, 295, 296, 333, 387, 416; Nancey 201; Nancy 61, 128, 148, 254, 262, 290, 303, 348, 373, 375, 400, 417; Nann 339; Nanncy 328; Nanne 111; Nanney 161; Nanny 123, 328, 381, 401, 411, 447; Nany 83, 348; Nathan 174, 266; Nathaniel 257, 266; Nead 161; Nebo 310;

Ned 9, 11, 142, 190, 212, 243, 249, 251, 255, 260, 302, 368, 417, 447; **Nell** 69, 77, 157, 212, 253, 280, 282, 289, 327, 377; **Nelle** 367; **Nelli** 367; **Neomi** 333; **Neomy** 400; **Nice** 124, 126, 127, 228, 401; **Nimrod** 5; **Niomi** 333; **Norah** 97; **Oaford** 37; **Obed** 401; **Omey** 436; **Orris** 286, 413, 414; **Orson** 50; **Oxford** 72; **Parker Able** 338; **Pashents** 232; **Pat** 318, 323; **Patience** 22, 48, 49, 99, 133, 176, 177, 196, 214, 295, 296, 303, 375, 431; **Patrick** 381, 385; **Patty** 363; **Paul** 44, 45; **Peet** 258; **Peg** 327, 347; **Pegg** 156; **Peggey** 319; **Peggy** 142; **Pelinah** 78, 79; **Perrey** 161; **Peter** 26, 60, 61, 100, 106, 110, 169, 180, 181, 186, 197, 209, 222, 228, 229, 234, 256, 276, 308, 397, 407, 416, 431, 437, 442; **Peter Guy** 238; **Phebe** 49, 133; **Pheby** 303; **Philis** 303, 336; **Phillace** 125; **Phillis** 38, 89, 90, 98, 106, 124, 126, 133, 146, 153, 204, 301, 302, 322, 330, 335, 339; **Pink** 257; **Pleasant** 1, 4, 6, 15, 18, 21, 28, 61, 76, 102, 138, 144, 160, 180, 190, 294; **Pleasent** 152, 410; **Plymoth** 105; **Poll** 147; **Pomp** 67, 83, 90, 94, 106, 107; **Pompey** 82, 286; **Pompy** 58, 134, 302, 314; **Preseler** 111; **Price** 262; **Pricilla** 183; **Prim** 72; **Prince** 396; **Priscilla** 262, 266, 313; **Prisciller** 357; **Priss** 138, 143, 269, 435; **Prissella** 313; **Prissey** 331; **Racel** 134; **Rach** 93; **Rachal** 149, 187; **Rachael** 260; **Rachel** 10, 25, 37, 97, 161, 178, 187, 249, 252, 286, 313, 331, 333, 370, 400, 413, 414, 429, 442; **Rachell** 93, 178, 191, 207, 235, 310, 387, 410; **Rafe** 190; **Ralph** 210, 438; **Rebecca** 268, 313; **Rebeckah** 2; **Rhoda** 42, 97, 100, 114, 142, 158, 159, 161, 184, 262, 266, 274, 288, 313, 326, 344; **Rhodah** 330; **Rhodey** 406; **Rhody** 184, 286, 328; **Richard** 256; **Rielman** 346; **Robbin** 297, 434, 435; **Robert** 192, 268, 282, 341, 342; **Robin** 49, 130, 133, 209, 236, 242, 304, 360, 362, 365, 425; **Rodah** 278, 413, 414; **Roday** 75, 143; **Rodger** 95, 101; **Rohoda** 262; **Rose** 4, 5, 10, 35, 42, 44, 45, 64, 86, 91, 94, 141, 153, 154, 166, 175, 206, 207, 235, 237, 249, 344, 346, 395; **Ruiksom** 217; **Ruth** 11, 423, 424, 439; **Sabary** 76; **Sabra** 149; **Sabray** 303; **Sabroe** 370; **Sabrough** 313, 321, 322; **Sal** 161, 185, 187, 200, 233, 240, 258, 422, 423, 429; **Sall** 104, 157, 159, 160, 185, 210, 233, 258, 295, 296, 334, 335, 447; **Sam** 37, 55, 122, 161, 170, 179, 268, 272, 295, 296, 305, 322, 367, 393; **Sambo** 59, 310; **Sampson** 15, 20, 23, 59, 69, 77, 85, 94, 191, 261, 294, 307, 319, 332, 435, 439; **Sampton** 239; **Samson** 398; **Samuel** 78, 79, 116, 372; **Sandey** 346; **Sandy** 82; **Santa** 343; **Santee** 326; **Santy** 106; **Sarah** 13, 14, 22, 32, 47, 48, 94, 97, 145, 149, 152, 155, 167, 168, 172, 180, 190, 193, 198, 206, 220, 229, 236, 240, 244, 245, 249, 254, 260, 264, 274, 288, 294, 302, 315, 339, 341, 347, 355, 377, 381, 393, 407, 408, 411, 429, 435; **Sarah Nan** 310; **Sary** 227; **Saul** 223, 375, 397; **Savannah Isaac** 360; **Scott** 377; **Sear** 126, 127; **Sebb** 265; **Shadrach** 165; **Shadrack** 22, 256, 277, 354; **Shadrick** 47; **Sharp** 212, 279; **Shederik** 211; **Shepard** 263; **Sib** 407, 408; **Signer** 240; **Silbey** 124, 126; **Silby** 277; **Sillar** 296; **Siller** 296; **Silva** 26, 125, 187, 226, 227; **Silvia** 11, 442; **Silvy** 220; **Sinah** 343; **Siner** 113; **Sino** 278; **Sinor** 194; **Sipeo** 65; **Siss** 142; **Soloman** 266; **Solomon** 59, 93, 96, 97, 266, 432; **Somerset** 134; **Sopha** 444; **Sophia** 142, 165, 166, 268; **Sothey** 259; **Sothy** 232; **Southey** 321; **Southy** 26, 28, 256, 322; **Standbridge** 26, 28; **Stephan** 316; **Stephen** 81, 96, 107, 108, 109, 131, 147, 187, 200, 230, 239, 265, 333, 352, 357, 358, 381, 387, 394, 427, 439; **Steven** 134; **Su** 206; **Sub** 422, 423; **Sue** 145, 163, 216, 219, 222, 260, 347, 372, 400; **Suffiah** 314; **Susannah** 59, 341; **Susey** 161; **Sussey** 399; **Sylby** 98; **Sylva** 90; **Sylvia** 145; **Tab** 49, 209, 221, 222, 295, 441; **Tabb** 235; **Tabitha** 256, 262, 313, 418, 419; **Tamar** 180, 274; **Tamer** 77, 135, 190, 197, 260, 288, 433; **Tamery** 433; **Tamour** 220; **Taymor** 258, 259; **Tempy** 270; **Terrey** 37; **Thamer** 161; **Thanah** 84; **Thomas** 133, 270; **Tib** 349; **Tillan** 182; **Tinna** 261; **Tite** 343; **Titus** 278; **Tom** 10, 183, 201, 206, 225, 241, 326, 379; **Tonney** 409; **Tony** 32; **Trip** 251; **Tylus** 84; **Ufamey** 351; **Unice** 90; **Venis** 65, 441, 445; **Venus** 120, 407, 416; **Vilett** 291; **Violet** 21; **Violett** 310, 449; **Watt** 48, 59; **Will** 27, 33, 44, 77, 120, 132, 138, 141, 150, 151, 156, 188, 199, 204, 250, 260, 319, 320, 323, 334, 335, 370, 389, 411; **William** 120, 303, 418, 432; **Yeany** 20; **Zadock** 49, 174, 201; **Zebulon** 294; **Zed** 412; **Zedegial** 291; **Zedegiel** 291; **Zepheniah** 141;

ABBETT, **Levin** 442;

ACKWORTH, **Handy** 300; **Henry** 300;

ADAMS, Andrew 123; **App** 310; **Ben** 123; **David** 65, 310; **Easter** 370; George 65, 66, 123; Jacob 370; **Jacob** 310; James 310; **Jim** 370; **Joab** 65; **Joabe** 65; John 65, 66; **Nanny** 123; **Nebo** 310; **Pomp** 94; **Rachel** 370; **Rachell** 310; **Sambo** 310; **Sarah Nan** 310; **Sipeo** 65; Stephen 123; **Violett** 310; **Will** 370; William 66, 94;

ADDAMS, **Isaac** 105, 271, 345; **Jack** 271, 345; Jacob 105, 271, 345; **Leveanah Jenkins** 105; **Peter** 105; **Pleasant** 105;

ADKINS, **Belender** 263; John 263; Joseph 270; Sarah 270; **Shepard** 263; Stanton 263, 264; **Tempy** 270;

ADKINSON, Angaler 221; Angello 221; **Bob** 221;

ALEXANDER, **Bridget** 54; John 54; Mary 54;

ALLAN, Robert 12;

ALLEN, **Alce** 386; **Alic** 10; **Anas** 153; **Aproba** 72; **Ara** 1; **Benn** 10; **Bess** 10; **Betty** 72; **Daniel** 10; **Dianna** 389; **Dick** 72; Elianor 10; Elizabeth 10; **Francis** 428, 431, 432; **Frank** 142; **Hannah** 10, 425; **Hope** 47; **Jack** 72; **James** 345; **Jenny** 10; **Jioe** 10; John 142, 375, 385; **Joseph** 10; **Judy** 10; **Levin** 375; **Martha** 47; Mary 1, 9, 10; **Mingo** 10, 192; Moses 10; **Oxford** 72; **Patrick** 385; **Phillis** 153; **Prim** 72; **Rachel** 10; **Robert** 341; **Rose** 10, 153; Stephen 389; **Tom** 10; **Will** 10; William 10, 22, 47, 54, 59, 71, 72, 127, 137, 138, 153, 192, 341, 345, 386, 425;

AMBLER, Richard 72;

AMERICA, George 441; **Jeb** 441; **Jib** 441;

AMMON, Lemuel 67;

ANDERSON, **Dorset** 80; **Fosida** 80; Hezekiah 80;

ANDRSON, Stephn 404;

ARBUCKLE, Amos 83; **Murreah** 89; **Murrur** 83; **Nany** 83; William 83, 89;

ARMSTRONG, Bayham 423; **Comfort** 223; **Jacob** 211, 223, 305, 306, 373, 374, 443; John 423; **Liz** 211; **Liza** 211; **Lycia** 223; **Milby** 443; **Sally** 443;

ARMWOOD, Daniell 298; **Gelica** 298;

ATKINS, **Bett** 327, 328; Hannah 328; Hannah J. 328; Priscelly 327; Priscielly 328; Priscilly 327; Priselley 327;

ATKINSON, **Adam** 17, 209; **Agur** 165, 166; Angello 222, 413, 414; Angelo 86, 209, 285, 418; Angelo Jr. 86; Angelow 222; Ann 285; Anna 414; Benjamin 285, 414; Betsey 285, 413; Betsy 413, 414, 415; **Betty** 145; **Bridget** 286; **Chloe** 154; Comfort 285, 286, 287; **Dinah** 286, 413, 414; **Esther** 286, 413, 414; **Fella** 86; **Fryday** 86; George 285, 414; **George** 154; **Hannah** 286, 413, 414, 415; **Harry** 286, 413, 414; **Hector** 21; Henry 164, 165; **Hope** 251; Isaac 41, 415; **Isaac** 165; **Jack** 165; **Jacob** 286; James 127, 140, 164, 165, 209, 251; John 86, 383; Joshua 21, 22, 86, 415; **Juda** 383; **Judah** 286; **Leah** 286; **Limas** 154; **Littleton** 328; **Marina** 41; Mary 154; Milby 89; **Minta** 222; **Murreah** 89; **Nanncy** 328; **Nanny** 328; **Nice** 127; **Orris** 286, 413, 414; **Peter** 26, 209, 222; **Pleasant** 21; **Pompey** 286; **Rachel** 286, 413, 414; **Rhody** 286, 328; **Robin** 209; **Rodah** 413, 414; **Rose** 86, 154; Samuel 17, 26, 27; **Shadrach** 165; **Sophia** 165, 166; **Sylvia** 145; **Tab** 209, 222; Thomas 328; **Violet** 21; William 145, 165, 166, 209, 210;

AYDELOTT, Benjamin 74; **Cage** 329; **Esau** 362; **Esaw** 362; **Esther** 358; **George** 418; **Harry** 74; John 329; Joshua 418; Levinia 329; Mary 418; **Micajah** 329; William 358, 361, 362;

AYRES, **Abel** 294; **Abraham** 227; **Amos** 294; **Ben** 227, 294; **Bet** 294; **Betty** 166; **Bradis** 294; **Bridget** 44, 45; **Ciller** 294; **Comfort** 193, 294; **Derrah** 212; **George** 193; **Glasgow** 294; **Hannah** 294; Henry 16, 44, 45, 154; **Hope** 44, 45; **Isaac** 294; Isaac 171; James 166; **Joe** 294; John 191, 193, 194, 212, 227, 243, 244, 372, 383, 384, 423; **John** 294; **Leah** 171; **Leah** 294; **Let** 294; **Lidey** 383; **Martha** 44, 45; **Paul** 44, 45; **Pleasant** 294; **Rose** 44, 45; **Sampson** 294; Sarah 193, 294; **Zebulon** 294;

BACON, **Beck** 118; Hannah 233; **Ishmael** 233; Jacob 118; James 448, 449; **Jesse** 448; William 136, 280;

BAKER, **Estar** 410; **Ester** 410; **Isaac** 434; **Leah** 434; **Molley** 434; Molly 433, 434,

455

435; **Robbin** 434, 435; Selathel 410; Selathil 410; **Tamer** 433; **Tamery** 433;

BALDING, Caleb 72;

BALL, **Bob** 378; **Cato** 360; David 360, 361, 362; **Fanny** 360; **Frank** 360; **Jesse** 360; John 85, 129, 156, 159, 261, 378, 397; **Leah** 143; Luya 159; **Margery** 360; **Priss** 143; **Robin** 360, 362; **Roday** 143; **Sampson** 85, 261; William 143, 161;

BALLARD, Charles Jr. 28; Daniel 372; **Lydda** 161, 162; **Sue** 372; William 161, 162;

BANDS, **Peter** 407; Rody 407; **Venus** 407;

BANESTER, Charles 203, 204; **Comfort** 203; **Grace** 203; **Hannah** 203; **Jane** 203; **Milly** 203; **Mintay** 203;

BANISTER, Charles 203, 204; **Comfort** 203; **Grace** 203; **Hannah** 203; **Jane** 203; **Milly** 203; **Mintay** 203;

BANKS, John 67, 68;

BANTEN, **Bob** 382; William 382;

BANUM, **Bett** 308; **Leah** 308; William 308;

BAPTIST, James 65;

BARCOMEN, Edward 294;

BARNS, Thomas 102;

BAUDES, **Peter** 407; Rody 407; **Venus** 407;

BAUDS, **Peter** 407; Rody 407; **Venus** 407;

BAYLY, Elizabeth 60; Esme 81, 121, 192, 300; Henry 60; Lisha 60; Whittington 60;

BEACHBOARD, **Isaac** 252, 353; **Jack** 252; Joshua 432; **Jerom** 432; Levi 252; Levin 252; Sarah 353;

BEACHBORD, **Jack** 304; Sarah 304;

BEAVENS, Charles 86; **Leah** 60; Thomas 60; William 4, 60; William Jr. 60;

BELL, **Abb** 399; **Abner** 131; **Bett** 149, 150; Elijah 399; George 276, 399, 404; **George** 149; Henry 131, 132, 206, 427; **Hope** 294; Isaac 427; James 399; **James** 234; **James Handy** 399, 404; **James Townsend** 399; John 75; Joshua 399; **Jude** 149, 150; Katrine 106; **Leah** 149, 150; Levin 149, 150; **Luke** 294, 427; Mary 234; Nancy 399, 404; Polly 399; **Sabra** 149; **Sussey** 399; **Tom** 206; William 294, 426, 427;

BENNET, **Abner** 208; **Abram** 237; Charles 237; James 208;

BENNETT, **Abner** 208; **Abram** 237; Charles 112, 152, 164, 165, 237, 384; **Eben** 384; **Henny** 191; **Isaac** 165, 353; **Jack** 165; James 187, 191, 195, 208, 285, 353; Jesse 362, 368, 371, 393, 395, 402, 406, 408, 410, 411, 423; John 8; Nancy 402; **Rachell** 191; **Shadrach** 165;

BENNITT, Charles 379, 384, 385; **Dianna** 389; **Eben** 384; Jesse 355, 364, 366, 372, 374, 376, 379, 385, 389, 413, 414, 426; Nancy 385; William 389, 390;

BENSON, **Able** 167; **Ben** 196; **Benjamin** 196; **Candis** 167; **Esther** 167; **George** 167; **Hannah** 167; John 167; Joseph 195, 196; **Rose** 64; Thomas 139, 140; William 64, 65;

BENSTON, Thomas 205;

BETHARDS, Richard 380, 381;

BETTIT, Edward 125; **Rose** 124;

BETTS, Nancy 168;

BEVANS, James 334; Mills 334; **Philis** 336; **Phillis** 335; Rowland 334, 335, 336; **Sall** 334, 335; **Will** 334, 335; William 334;

BEVENS, **Phillis** 335; Rowland 335; **Sall** 335; **Will** 335;

BIRD, Empson 88; **Jacob** 88;

BISHOP, **Abner** 210; Abraham 248; **Ben** 248; **Bill** 389; Charles 196, 210, 211; Comfort 401; **Comfort** 210; **Doary** 168; Edward 401; **Esther** 229; Hannah 196, 197; **Jacob** 196, 210; James 229; John 163, 248, 317, 401; John Sr. 401; Joseph 229; **Leeds** 197; Levi 444; **Levin** 210; **Leviner** 163; **Lish** 401; **Liza** 401; **Nanny** 401; **Nice** 401; **Obed** 401; Samuel 389; Smith 70; **Will** 389; William 168;

BLADES, **Hannah** 449; John 449; **Violett** 449;

BLAICK, **George** 52;

BLAKE, **Betty** 142; **Comfort** 142; **Doary** 168; Easter 56, 58; Ester 57; Esther 51; **Friday** 182; **George** 50, 51, 55, 56, 57, 58, 62, 63, 117, 387, 388; **George Sr.** 392; **Hannah** 142; **John** 142; Levin 158, 164, 168, 182; **Levin** 285; **Limus** 189; **Lymus** 189; **Mary** 117, 142, 285, 319, 423; **Molly** 423; **Peggey** 319; **Samuel** 56, 57, 116, 117; Slocomb 69; **Susey** 142; **Tillan** 182;

BLEAK, **George** 51, 52;

BLUETT, Eleanor 202; **Isaac** 202;

BOANAN, **David** 440; Esther 440; John 440;

BONNEWELL, **Abel** 375; John 375, 376;

BOSER, Joseph 366; **Milla** 367;

BOSTON, **Adam** 354; **Comfort** 354; **Daniel** 354; Isaac 354; **Shadrack** 354;

BOUD, **Peter** 416; Rhoday 416; **Venus** 416;

BOUDS, **Peter** 416; Rhoday 416; **Venus** 416;

BOUNDS, **Amey** 105; Ann 105; **Charles** 105; **Hanah** 105; Jacob 104, 105; Jacob Jr. 105, **Jane** 105; **Jesse** 105; **Joe** 105; **Plymoth** 105;

BOUSSEY, **Hope** 251; Joseph 251, 252; **Rachel** 252;

BOUSSY, Joseph 254; **Nancy** 254;

BOWEN, **Charles** 341, 411; **Comfort** 411; Eli 336, 337; **George** 288, 312; **Hulda** 411; **Huldy** 411; Joshua 274, 288, 289, 312; **Lidde** 274; **Lotte** 336; **Lydia** 288, 312; **Rhoda** 274, 288; **Sarah** 274, 288, 341, 411; **Tamar** 274; **Tamer** 288;

BOWHANAN, **David** 440; Easter 440; John 440;

BOWIE, John 143;

BOWIN, **Capril** 196; **Charles** 206; **Comfort** 203; **George** 196; **Grace** 203; **Hannah** 203; **Hornton** 196; **Jane** 203; Jethro 196, 206; John 196; **Milby** 196; **Milly** 203; **Mintay** 203; **Patience** 196; **Rose** 206; **Sarah** 206; William 203, 204;

BOWSER, Joseph 366, 367; **Milla** 367;

BOYKINS & CHALMERS 418;

BRADFORD, **Jack** 429; John 428, 429; Samuel 258, 259; **Taymor** 258, 259;

BRADSHAW, **Abram** 437; **Comfort** 437; **Cyller** 437; **Jacob** 437; **Lish** 311; Morgan 311, 437; Morgin 312, 359; **Peter** 437; Sarah 311;

BRATTEN, **Amy** 184; Ann 184, 185, 198, 199; Anne 173, 198; **Ben** 388; **Bob** 444; **Coffee** 184; **Comfort** 184; **Grace** 173; **Hannah** 184; **Isaac** 173, 184; Joseph 122, 184, 185; Josiah 388; **Leven** 173; Nathaniel Jr. 444; Nathaniel Sr. 444; **Rhoda** 184; **Sam** 122; Samuel 388;

BRAVARD, Adam 336;

BREINGTON, Elizabeth 214; **George** 214;

BREUSTON, **Samson** 398; William 398, 399;

BREUTON, **Charles** 348; Frances 348; Francis 348; Francs 348; George 348; Nany 348; **Nancy** 348; **Nany** 348; Polley Adkins 348; Polly 348; Polly A. 348; Polly Adkins 348; William 348;

BREWERTON, **Leash** 399; William 399;

BREWINGTON, Elizabeth 214; **George** 214, 412; **Harry** 412; William 214, 412;

BRINGHAM, James 284;

BRINTON, William 438;

BRITTINGHAM, Belitha 154, 229, 230, 363; **Betty** 5, 8, 47; **Caleb** 47, 229; **Daniel** 215; **Derrum** 117; **Dolby** 363; Elijah 254, 349; **Esther** 229; **Florrow** 36, 37; **Hannah** 229; **Harry** 5; Isaac 5, 6, 8, 36, 37, 47, 48, 119, 349; John 119; Joshua 215, 232; Lavina 5; Leah 119; **Leah** 165, 229; **Melby** 217; **Nimrod** 5; Poynter 35; Purnell 318; Rachell 5; Rebecca 5; Rhodia 5, 8; **Rose** 5, 35; Samuel 53; Sarah 117, 118; **Sarah** 47, 229; **Shadrick** 47; **Silva** 26; Suffiah 5; Thomas 217; William 5, 26, 165; William Sr. 165;

BRODWATTE, James 250; **Will** 250;

BRODWATTER, James 418; **William** 418;

BROWN, **Benn** 86; Charles 86; John 11; Wilson 139, 140;

BROWNSON, **Handy** 239; Reubin 239; Rubin 239;

BRUENTON, **Casesa** 270; **Casesay** 270; **Milley** 270; **Thomas** 270; William 270;

BRUFF, **Hector** 412; John 412;

BRUMBLY, **Levin** 375; Tabitha 375;

BRUSTON, **Leash** 399; William 399;

BRUTON, **George** 412; **Harry** 412; William 412;

BUCHANAN, James 85;

BUNCLE, Alexander 21, 26;

BUNTING, Ismay 254;

BURBBAGE, Hampton 328;

BURETON, **Harry** 416; **Nance** 416; William 416;

BURINGTON, **Harry** 416; **Nance** 416; William 416;

BURROUGHS, Asher 329, 349, 350; **Leah** 329;

BURTON, **Harry** 416; **Nance** 416; Robert 122; William 416;

BUSSELLS, James 220, 221, 226, 227; **Minta** 220, 226, 227; Sarah 220, 221; **Silva** 226, 227; **Silvy** 220;

BYRD, **Doctor** 424; Thomas 424;

CABELS, Isaac 89;

CAIREY, Thomas 157;

CALDWELL, John 3; Tim 188; William 128;

CALLAHAN, Griffith 428; **Harry** 428;

CALLAWAY, **Abner** 138; **Bob** 138; **Bobb** 103; **Ibbey** 103; **Iby** 115; **Isabella** 103; **Name** 138; **Patience** 99; Peter 99, 103, 115, 138, 139; **Pleasant** 138; **Will** 138;

CALLOWAY, **Caesar** 77; **Dick** 77; **George** 77; **Jack** 75; **Nell** 77; Peter 75, 77; **Sampson** 77; **Tamer** 77; **Will** 77;

CAMBREDG, Esther 364;

CAMBRIDGE, Elizabeth 379; Esther 405, 406; George 319; **Leaven** 371, 379; **Leavin** 319, 337; **Levin** 319, 337, 352, 364, 371, 378, 379, 404, 405; **Peggey** 319; William 337, 405;

CAMPBELL, **Cloe** 42; **Comfort** 315; Ebenezer 83, 88, 95, 101; **Hannah** 115; **Jacob** 115; John 42, 185; John Simpson 315; **Luke** 315; Margaret 315; **Rodger** 95, 101; **Sal** 185; **Sall** 185; Samuel 115; **Sarah** 315;

CANNON, **Caesar** 77; **Dick** 77; Elijah 77, 78; **Esther** 111; **George** 77; Hughit 107; **Nell** 77; **Sampson** 77; **Tamer** 77; Thomas 111; **Will** 77;

CAREY, **Comfort** 322; **Epheram** 157; **Genny** 157; Hezekiah 207, 219; **Jenny** 219; Jonathan 322; **Nell** 157; **Rose** 207; **Sall** 157; **Sam** 322; Thomas 157, 219;

CARPENTER, **Caleb** 342; **Calop** 342; **Hannah** 342; Isaac 342; **Leah** 342;

CARREY, **David** 156; Levin 156; Thomas 156;

CARY, James 73; Solomon 51;

CATHEAL, **James** 235; Levi 235;

CATHELL, **Eunice** 98; James 85, 90, 91, 98, 123, 124, 125, 126; **James** 235; James Jr. 91; John 123, 124, 126, 450; Joshua 111, 125; **Lear** 124; Levi 235; **Ned** 123, 124; **Nice** 124, 126; **Phillis** 90, 98, 124, 126; **Sear** 126; **Silbey** 124, 126; **Silva** 125; **Sylby** 98; **Sylva** 90; **Unice** 90;

CAUDRY, **Ben** 196; **Benjamin** 196; John 196;

CHAIELLEA, **Leah** 433; Moses 433;

CHAILLA, **Leah** 433; Moses 433;

CHAILLE, **Abel** 255, 280; **Abner** 173; **Abraham** 227, 248; Amelia 427; **Amey** 30; **Ben** 227, 248; **Bridget** 438; **Caleb** 235; **Candiss** 235; Comfort 30, 451; **Daul** 30; **Easter** 427; **Eben** 378; **Esther** 235; **Filer** 69; **Florow** 69; George 451; **Ginne** 220;

Grace 451; **Harry** 427; **Jack** 69, 235; **Jim** 69; John 173, 304; **Leah** 173, 426; **Levin** 451; **Lid** 69; **Lidde** 274; **Liddy** 220; **Linda** 451; **Lydia** 235; **Mereum** 214; **Minta** 221, 222, 451; Moses 151, 152, 221, 222, 227, 234, 235, 248, 255, 280, 295, 425, 426; **Nell** 69; **Patience** 214; Peter 69, 164, 176, 178, 190, 206, 208, 210, 211, 213, 214, 219, 220, 240, 274, 381, 393, 427; **Peter** 222; Peter Jr. 202; Peter Sr. 451; **Rachell** 235; **Rhoda** 274; **Sampson** 69; **Sarah** 220, 274; **Stephen** 427; **Tab** 221, 222, 295; **Tabb** 235; **Tamar** 274; **Tamour** 220; **Will** 151; William 377, 378, 438;

CHAILLEA, **Candice** 442; Comfort 441, 442; **Jack** 442; John P. 441, 442; **Leah** 433; Margaret 441, 442; Margret 442; Moses 433; Moses Jr. 441, 442; **Peter** 442; **Rachel** 442; Sally 441, 442; **Silvia** 442;

CHAILLER, **Floren** 446; John 446;

CHAMBERS, John 94, 95; **Edith** 95;

CHAPMAN, **Hager** 253; Joshua 19, 29; **Nell** 253; Peirce 253; Pierce 253, 254;

CHIPMAN, **Ben** 38; Paris 38; Peris 38; **Phillis** 38; Sarah 38;

CHRISTOPHER, Stephen 207, 209; **Rose** 207;

CLARKSON, Bennah 65; **Dick** 65; **George** 65; Thomas 65; **Venis** 65;

CLAWELL, Ezekiel 443;

CLAIWEL, Ezekiel 443;

CLAYWELL, **Abel** 66; **Ame** 101; Comfort 66; **Leah** 66, 128; Lucrecia 66; Lucrecy 128; Lucresey 128; Lucresy 66; Peggy 100, 101; Shadrick 8, 9; Solomon 66, 128;

CLERK, Benjamin 285;

CLIFTON, Jonathan 2; **Rebeckah** 2;

COCHRAN, **Esther** 52; George 52;

COFFAN, Abner 285;

COFFEN, **Dick** 285; Leven 285; Levin 285;

COFFIN, Comfort 285; Cornelius 285;

COLBARN, John 149; **Sarah** 149;

COLBOARN, John 149; **Sarah** 149;

COLBORN, John 149; **Sarah** 149;

COLEBURN, **Amy** 240; **Ezekiel** 240; John 240; **Sarah** 240;

COLINS, **Auther** 351; Elizabeth 351; **Ufamey Steavens** 351;

COLLECT, **Mary** 290; **Nancy** 290; **Samuel 3**, 290; **Samuel Jr.** 290;

COLLICK, Easter 371, 372; **Samuel 4**, 371, 372, 417, 418;

COLLINGS, **Bess** 59; **Coffe** 59; **Dinah** 79; Elijah 79; Joseph 58, 59; **Sambo** 59; **Sampson** 59; **Watt** 59;

COLLINS, Andrew 1; **Auther** 351; **Beck** 440; **Bess** 59; **Coffe** 59; **Dinah** 79; Elisha 80; Elizabeth 349, 351; **Frank** 71; John 2; **John** 349; Joseph 71; **Rebeckah** 2; **Sambo** 59; **Sampson** 59; Thomas 2; **Ufamey Steavens** 351; Walton 440; **Watt** 59; William 2;

COLWELL, Samuel 67;

CONNER, **Abner** 204, 243, 355; Frederic 156; Frederick 155, 156, 204, 243, 355; Fredreck 402; Fredrick 402; Morris 86; **Will** 156;

CORBIN, **Abner** 98; **Aneas** 97; Betty 97, 98; **Hannah** 309; **Norah** 97; Peter 54; Peter S. 309, 428, 431; Peter Spencer 97, 428; **Will** 250; William 98, 250;

CORD, Ann 270; **Jame** 269; John Robins 229; Nancy 269; Rachel 183, 184; Rachell 184; **Tom** 183; William 269;

CORDARY, **Ben** 196; **Benjamin** 196; John 196;

CORDRAY, Abraham 148; Jonathan 148; **Nancy** 148; William 148;

CORDURY, John 195;

CORMACK, Benjamin W. 228;

CORNFEET, **Gin** 365; James 365;

CORNISH, **Amos** 204, 205;

COSTON, **Abel** 231; **Agur** 165, 166; **Derry** 268; Ezekiel 165, 166, 267, 268; **Hagar** 268; **Jacob** 268; Rebecca 268;

Rhoda 231; **Robert** 268; **Sam** 268; **Sophia** 165, 166, 268;

COTTINGHAM, **Ben** 14, 333; Daniel 14; David 192; **Edea** 240; **Effe** 446; Elisha 403; Isaac 240; **Jack** 268; **Jacob** 403; James 351, 446; John 14, 312, 316, 317, 328, 333, 334, 336, 364, 367, 370, 376, 385, 406, 408, 417, 447, 449; Joshua 298, 403; **Nance** 333; **Rachel** 333; **Robert** 192; **Sal** 240; **Stephen** 333; Thomas 174, 176, 192, 268; William 14;

COTTMAN, **Mingo** 192; William 192;

COULBOURN, **Beck** 138; Rachel Handy 138 ;

COULEBURN, **Amy** 240; **Ezekiel** 240; John 240; **Sarah** 240;

COVENTON, **Ned** 212; **Nell** 212; **Sharp** 212; William 212, 213;

COVINGTON, **Ned** 212; **Nell** 212; **Sharp** 212, 279; William 212, 213, 279, 280, 444;

COX, **Adam** 137; **Barsheba** 279; **Bersheba** 282; **Beck** 138; **Eby** 137; **Jen** 279, 282; **Jenny** 137; **John** 279, 282; **Leah** 137; **Lish** 279, 282; Mary 137, 138, 279, 282; **Priss** 138; William 279, 282;

CRASAFORD, John 442;

CRIPPS, **Ben** 333; **Benn** 387; **Bobb** 387; Francis 333, 334, 387; **Levi** 387; **Nance** 333, 387; **Nell** 387; **Rachel** 333; **Rachell** 387; **Stephen** 333, 387;

CROPPER, **Amy** 400; John 251; Joseph 240, 241; **Leah** 240; **Mill** 240; **Nancy** 400; **Neomy** 400; **Rachel** 400; **Signer** 240; Sophia 400; Soppiah 400; **Sue** 400; William 400; William Sr. 400; Zadok 240, 241;

CULVER, **Heaster** 203; John 207; **Levin** 224; Nathan 203, 224; **Rachell** 207;

CUTLER, **Bob** 378; **Comfort** 402, 403; John 378, 381, 388, 402, 403, 409, 410, 413; **Minty** 409, 410;

DAGWORTHY, John 32, 112; **Sarah** 32; **Tony** 32;

DALE, **Armwell** 293; Ebenezer 294; Elizabeth 409; **Elon** 409; **Isaac** 344, 363; **Jack** 353; Jacob 353; Jacob 344; Josiah 293; Joshua 365; Mathew 325; Matthew 325; **Minta** 344; **Patty** 363; **Rhoda** 344; **Rose** 344; **Sall** 447; **Sam** 294; Tabitha 447; Thomas 173, 241, 344, 363, 409; William 336, 430;

DART, William 2;

DASHIELD, **Hope** 47; **Martha** 47; Thomas 47;

DASHIEL, Clement 24, 25; **Daniel** 24;

DASHIELL, **App** 310; Benjamin F.A.C. 233; Benjamin Frederick Augustus Ceazer 233; Benjamin Frederick Augustus Ceesar 202; Benjamin Frederick Augustus Cezar 233; **David** 310; George 182, 183, 310, 311; **Isaac** 202; **Ishmael** 233; **Jacob** 310; **James** 134; **Joe** 183; Joseph 78, 99, 121, 131, 133, 134, 136, 183, 207, 233; Joshua 84, 210; Josiah 134; Levin 72; **Nebo** 310; **Pompy** 134; **Rachell** 310; **Sambo** 310; **Sarah Nan** 310; **Somerset** 134; **Steven** 134; **Thanah** 84; **Tylus** 84; **Violett** 310; William Rit 210;

DAUGHERTY, James 141; **Will** 141;

DAVIS, **Abel** 22; Abijah 263; Abisha 285, 315; **Betty** 22; **Caleb** 22; **Dick** 22; **Eazer** 315; **Frank** 74; **George** 43, 232, 259; **Hannah** 267; James 219, 421, 422; **Jenny** 219; John 66, 71, 73, 74; Joseph 428; **Ju{?}** 22; Margaret 22; Matthew Purnell 267; **Mary** 267; Mathew Purnell 267; Matthias 233; **May** 22; **Minna** 315; **Monday** 74; **Moses** 284; Nathaniel 232, 256, 259; Nehemiah 250; Nixson 429; **Patience** 22; **Peter** 100; Samuel 43, 88; **Sarah** 22; **Shadrack** 22; **Shepard** 263; **Sothey** 259; **Sothy** 232; **Southy** 256; Turner 100;

DECKESON, **Harry** 35; Isaac 35; Levin 35;

DELANEY, **George** 397, 398;

DELANY, **George** 397; 398;

DELASTATIUS, Betsey 354; Betsy 354; **Harry** 354; Joseph 351, 387;

DENNIS, **Abel** 134; **Adam** 396; **Addam** 396; **Ann** 269; **Appleby** 37; **Aproba** 72; **Arnold** 37; Benjamin 301, 302, 306, 311, 315, 317, 334, 337, 347, 350, 353, 358, 371, 377, 379, 391, 393, 395, 398, 405, 423, 443; **Bett** 37; **Betty** 72; **Cable** 219;

Caleb 235; **Candiss** 235; **David** 134; **Dick** 37, 72; **Esther** 235; **Flowra** 33; **George** 134; **Gin** 365; **Hannah** 134, 269; **Harry** 37, 119, 136; **Jack** 72, 118, 235; James 347; John 37, 72, 136, 143, 365, 366; John Jr. 71, 72; **Leah** 143, 269; **Let** 37; **Levin** 219; Littleton 54, 59, 69, 72, 92, 93, 105, 118, 119, 124, 125, 279, 282, 425; **Lucey** 37; **Lydia** 235; **Milley** 37; **Nan** 37; **Oaford** 37; **Oxford** 72; **Peg** 347; **Prim** 72; **Priss** 143, 269; **Racel** 134; **Rach** 93; **Rachel** 37; **Rachell** 93, 235; Robert 114, 118, 219, 235; **Roday** 143; **Rose** 124; **Sam** 37; Sampson 15; **Sue** 219; Susanna 134; **Tabb** 235; **Terrey** 37; Valentine 269, 378, 379, 417; Wheatly 33, 396; Wheaty 33; Wheetley 15; Wheetly 15, 16, 311, 315;

DENWOOD, Leah 91;

DICKENSON, **Judah** 116; **Mellah** 116; **Mellea** 116; Rebeckah 116;

DICKERSON, **Floren** 446; James 446; Joshua 137; Josiah 102; **Pleasant** 102;

DICKESON, **Bartlett** 76; Cornelius 298; **George** 76; **Harry** 35; Isaac 35; Josiah 76, 77, 102; **Pleasant** 76, 102;

DIKES, Daniel 103;

DIKS, Daniel 157;

DINGLE, Edward 135; **Jabe** 135;

DIRICKSON, Joseph 38, 42, 64, 74, 81, 149; Levin 76, 149;

DISHAROON, **Amelia** 275; **Dick** 119; **Elisha** 119; George 119; **Hannah** 119; John 119, 274, 275; **Levin** 119; **Nance** 290; **Nancy** 290; Polly 290; Salley 119; Stephen 119;

DISHEROON, **Amelia** 275; **Dick** 119; **Elisha** 119; George 85, 119; **Gone** 85; **Hannah** 119; John 119, 275; **Levin** 119; Salley 119; Stephen 119;

DISHROON, Stephen 291; **Vilett** 291;

DIXON, **Arcy** 303; **Ary** 303; **Cate** 303; **Comfort** 303; **Genny** 157; **Jacob** 303; **Jacob Freeborn** 303; **Jenny** 219; **Jobe** 303; **Joseph** 303; **Leven** 303; **Leven the elder** 303; **Littleton** 303; **Luca** 303; **Lucre** 303; **Nancy** 303; Nathaniel 303; **Nell** 157; Outerbridge 157, 219; **Patience** 303; **Pheby** 303; **Philis** 303; Thomas 316, 370, 382, 390, 394, 400, 406, 407, 440, 446, 447; **William** 303; William Quinton 396;

DONAM, Asher 68;

DONAMA, Asher 68;

DONE, **Betty** 145; **Bridget** 45; **Hope** 45; John 45, 46, 63, 64, 114, 147, 233, 276, 284, 285; **Martha** 45; **Moses** 46; **Paul** 45; Robert 136, 145, 147, 182; **Rose** 45, 64; **Sylvia** 145;

DONHAM, Asher 68;

DONOHO, Daniel 14; Joshua 147; **Poll** 147;

DONOHOE, Joshua 147; **Poll** 147;

DORMAN, Hannah 275; **Grace** 275; John 275; **Lare** 442; **Leviner** 153, 154; Major 442; Nehemiah 153, 154, 201, 220;

DORMIN, **Lare** 442; Major 442;

DOUGLAS, George 4;

DOWNES, **Adam** 179, 180; **Levin** 132; **Linda** 235; **Lucy** 235; Mitchell 179, 180; **Rose** 235; Sarah 132, 235;

DOWNS, George 132; **Levin** 132; Sarah 132;

DREADEN, **Dinah** 304; Moses 304;

DRUMMOND, George 34;

DRYDEN, William 205;

DUER, **Ben** 333; **Benn** 387; **Bobb** 387; **Dolby** 363; **Jacob** 274; James 274, 285, 333, 334, 363, 387; Joshua Sr. 238; **Levi** 387; **Mareor** 274; **Nance** 333, 387; **Nell** 387; **Rachel** 333; **Rachell** 387; **Stephen** 333, 387;

DULANY, **George** 376;

DUNBAR, James 278; John 278, 435; **Rodah** 278; **Sino** 278; **Titus** 278;

DUNBARE, James 278; John 278; **Rodah** 278; **Sino** 278; **Titus** 278;

DUNCAN, Henry 433, 434; **Isaac** 434; **Jack** 429; **Leah** 434; Milby 433; **Nancy** 434; **Rachel** 429; Sarah 429; **Tamer** 433; **Tamery** 433; Thomas 428, 429;

DUNKIN, Thomas 48;

DUNLAP, **Esther** 41, 52; William 41, 52;

DYMOCK, **Bob** 213; **Hanah** 213; William 213;

ELLEGOOD, William 56, 57, 58, 64, 139;

EMORY, John 212;

ENNELLS, Coll. 176; Leah 176;

ENNIS, **Amos** 319, 323; **Benjamin** 264 ; **Bett** 319, 323; Boaz 122; Cornelius 320; **Easter** 303; **Isaac** 122, 319, 323; Jesse 64, 129, 332; John 289; Joseph 126; **Lott** 320; **Lotte** 332; Luke 145, 229; Mary 204; Nathaniel 122, 319, 323; **Pat** 323; Rachel 303; Rebecca 122, 123; **Sabray** 303; Sarah 303; **Sarah** 145, 264; **Will** 319, 323; Zadoc 264; Zadok 264;

ENNISS, Cornelius 232; Cornelius Jr. 232; Joseph 126, 232; **Pashents** 232 ;

ESHOM, **Filer** 287; Solomon 287;

ESHUM, **Filer** 287; Solomon 287;

ESHUN, **Grace** 277; Jonathan 188, 277; **Will** 188;

EVANS, **Eben** 207, 208, 231; Ebenezer 33, 44; Elisa 340; Elizabeth 409; **Elon** 409; **Esther** 340; **George** 155, 215, 340; **Hulda** 155, 216; Isaac 155, 215, 216, 444; **Isaac** 363; **Jane** 155; **Jenny** 216; **Jess** 216; Jesse 155; John 35, 40, 42, 44, 50, 71, 207, 208, 230, 231, 340, 363, 412; John Sr. 409; Joshua 82, 107, 108, 369; **Lanta** 340; **March** 82, 107, 108; **Patty** 363; Polly 340; Sally 340; **Sarah** 155; **Stephen** 107, 108; **Sue** 347; **Will** 44; Zeno 347;

EVENS, Ephraim 53, 54; William 53, 54;

FALCONER, James 146;

FARLOW, Elisabeth 236; Elizabeth 235; **James** 235;

FARRINGTON, George 84; **Thanah** 84; **Tylus** 84;

FARSETT, Daniel 129;

FASSETT, **Abel** 294; **Amos** 294; **Ben** 294; **Bet** 294; **Bradis** 294; **Ciller** 294; **Comfort** 262, 294; **Edmond** 262; **Glasgow** 294; **Hannah** 294; **Joe** 294; John 185; **John** 294; **Leah** 294; **Leb** 262; **Let** 294; Margaret 272, 294; Marget 272; Margit 272; Margraet 262; **Pleasant** 294; Rouse 185; **Sal** 185; **Sall** 185; **Sam** 272; **Sampson** 294; **Sarah** 294; **Zebulon** 294;

FASSITT, **Abel** 294; **Amos** 294; **Ben** 294; **Bet** 294; **Bradis** 294; **Ciller** 294; **Comfort** 262, 294, 315; David 115; **Edmond** 262; **Glasgow** 294; **Hannah** 115, 294; **Jacob** 115; James 305; **Joe** 294; **John** 294; **Leah** 294; **Leb** 262; **Let** 294; **Luke** 315; Margaret 294; Margaret Simpson 315; Margraet 262; **Pleasant** 294; **Sam** 305; **Sampson** 294; **Sarah** 294, 315; William 315; **Zebulon** 294;

FEAGUS, John 78;

FEDDEMAN, Joseph 4; Joseph Jr. 4;

FENICY, John 66;

FERGUSON, Elizabeth 97;

FINCH, **Fillis** 99; John 90, 94, 99; **Pomp** 90, 94;

FISHER, Jabez 141; **Will** 141;

FITZ, John 11;

FLEMING, **Adam** 137; **Eby** 137; **Jenny** 137; John 137; **Leah** 137; Sarah 137; William 20;

FLEMMING, **Adam** 396; **Addam** 396; **Comfort** 402, 403; **Doctor** 424; Eleanor 403, 424; Elennor 396; Elenor 396, 402, 403; John 396, 424;

FLOYD, William 340;

FOOKES, Benjamin 339; **Dover** 338; **Ebenezar** 450;

FOOKS, **Ann** 425; **Ben** 133; Benjamin 338; **Diannah** 425; **Dover** 338; **Eben** 264; **Ebenezar** 450; **Hager** 264; Jesse 425; Mary 133; William 246, 264;

FORMAN, Joseph 64, 65; **Rose** 64;

FOUNTAIN, **James** 24; Nicholas 23, 24; Samuel 338, 348; Wise 337, 338;

FRANKLIN, **Ben** 284; Ebenezer 216, 280; Henrey 167; Henry 167, 168; **Hulda** 216; Isaac 280; **Jenny** 216; **Jess** 216; John 167, 168; **Leah** 167, 168; Lemuel 211, 284; **Nell** 280; **Sarah** 167, 168; **Shederik** 211; **Sue** 145; William 145, 146, 211, 284; William (of William) 211;

FRANKLYN, **Dinah** 27; Edward 27; **Will** 27;

FREEMAN, Moses 435;

FURNESS, Thomas 254;

FURNIS, Ephraim 412; **Hager** 253; **Hector** 412; Littleton 412; **Nell** 253; Thomas 253;

FURNISS, **Charles** 318; **Grace** 318; **Hager** 253; **Hette** 318; **Levin** 318; **Nell** 253; **Pat** 318; Thomas 254, 317, 318; William 317, 318;

GAULTE, Rhoda 102;

GEDDES, **Amelia** 72; Robert 23; William 72, 73;

GEMMILL, Hugh 327; **Levin** 327; **Nell** 327;

GEORGE, **Southey** 310; **Southy** 309;

GIBBINS, **Amey** 105; Ann 105; Anne ; **Hanah** 105; Joshua 105;

GIBBS, **Dinniah** 158; Elizabeth 158; Hannah 158; **Hannah** 158; John 158; **Margo** 158; Polley 158;

GILLET, **Adam** 19, 29; **Harry** 74; Samuel 29; William 19, 29, 30, 74;

GILLETT, **Harry** 74; **James** 246; Joseph 246; William 19, 30, 74, 75;

GILLITT, **Hannah** 449; **James** 246; Joseph 246; Samuel 449, 450; **Violett** 449;

GIVAN, **Caleb** 358; Isaac 429; Robert 358;

GIVANS, Brittingham 250; James 199; **Will** 199;

GLASGOW, **Abigail** 108, 109; Betty 108; **Deborah** 108; **Fender** 109; **Frank** 109; **Hope** 108, 109; **Jesse** 108, 109; **Job** 108; **Lowhill** 110; **Major** 110; Martha 108, 109, 110; Nancy 109; Patrick 109, 110; **Stephen** 109;

GLASS, Christopher 12;

GODFREY, **Abner** 130, 131; Belitha 122; Charles 88, 285, 337, 352, 353; **Comfort** 322; Elizabeth 195; Jemima 184, 194, 195, 322; Jemomy 184; Joseph 130, 131, 132; Leah 194; **Lisha** 88; **Luke** 184; Nancy 194, 195; **Rhody** 184; **Sam** 322;

GODWIN, Nahor 106, 107; **Pomp** 107;

GOOTRY, Moses 75; **Rhoda** 75; **Roday** 75;

GORDEY, Jacob 88; **Jacob** 88;

GORDY, **Cuggo** 358; **Kesiah** 281; Peter 85; William 281, 358, 359;

GORE, **Harry** 375; **Nancy** 375; **Patience** 375; **Saul** 375; Thomas T. 375; Thomas Teakle 375;

GOTHERY, **March** 82, 108; Moses 75, 82, 83, 108, 126; **Rhoda** 75; **Roday** 75; **Stephen** 108;

GRAY, **Abner** 130; **Amelia** 275; Anna 113; Benjamin 130, 142; **Bett** 68, 368; **Betty** 68; **Bobb** 228, 229, 276; **Cloe** 68; **Conselo** 68; **Daniel** 68; David 350; Eleanor 140; **Esther** 52; **Frank** 68; **Hanah** 140; **Harrah** 154; **Jacob** 420; James 68, 69; Jedediah 140; Jedidiah 130; **Jenny** 68; Jesse 154, 155, 420; **John** 68; Johnson 228, 229, 274, 275, 276, 368; Joseph 130, 272; **Juda** 416; Mary 113; **Milby** 404; **Monday** 68; **Ned** 368 ; **Peter** 228, 229, 276; **Robin** 130; Rouse 404, 416; **Sam** 272; Thomas 52, 229, 276, 368; Thomas Jr. 114, 130; Thomas Sr. 228, 276, 368; William 31, 33;

GREEN, **George** 241; Hillary 150; Joseph 150, 241, 258; **Luke** 150; Mary 241; **Peet** 258; **Sall** 258;

GRIFFEN, Belitha 315, 316; **Chloe** 316;

GRIFFITH, Joseph 67;

GRUMBLE, George 139;

GUM, Samuel 174; **Zadock** 174;

GUN, John 168, 169; **Lyd** 169;

GUNBY, Ann 343, 351; **Barbary** 343; **Comfort** 351; Hannah 434, 435; **Hannah** 343; James 39; John 310, 341, 343, 344, 356, 363, 381, 383, 384, 392, 394, 407, 427, 441; Nancy 343, 351; **Robbin** 434, 435;

GUNN, Betty 412, 413; Henry 319, 320; **Isaac** 419; John 285; Leah 419; **Mary** 419; Nancy 419; **Ned** 302; **Sampson** 191, 319;

Sarah 302; Samuel 191, 302, 304, 319, 412; **Zed** 412, 413;

GURBY, Levin 187;

GUTHERY, **Caleb** 290; Ellinor 264; James 283, 289, 290; **Leah** 264;

GUTTERY, **March** 107, 108; Moses 107, 108; Philip 17; **Stephen** 107, 108;

GUY, **Ann** 313; **Cato** 313; **Comfort** 313; **Daniel** 313; David 329; **Esther** 313; **Esther (old)** 313; **Flora** 313; **George** 313; **Jacob** 313; **James** 313; **John** 313; **Joshua** 131, 147; **Leah** 313; **Levinah** 131, 147; **Lisha** 313; **Major** 130, 131, 147, 313; **Martha** 313; **Mary** 313; **Merica** 313; **Moses** 313; **Peter** 238; **Priscilla** 313; **Prissella** 313; **Rachel** 313; **Rebecca** 313; **Rhoda** 313; **Sabrough** 313; **Stephen** 131, 147; **Tabitha** 313;

HALE, Matthew 294;

HALL, Adam 106; **Andrew** 21; **Bob** 102; **Caesar** 77; **Dick** 77; Dixon 425; Elizabeth 226, 231; **Esther** 13; Ezekiel 359; **George** 77, 218, 273, 288, 312; **Ginne** 220; **Jacob** 226; **Jenny** 231; **Jesse** 359; John 13, 16, 20, 21; John Jr. 16, 20; Jordan 102; Joshua 60; **Lidde** 274; **Liddy** 220; **Lydia** 288, 312; **Nan** 102; **Nell** 77; **Peter** 106; **Rhoda** 274, 288; Richard 218, 219, 220, 274; **Sampson** 77; Samuel 77; **Sarah** 220, 274, 288; Stephen 173; **Tamar** 274; **Tamer** 77, 288; **Tamour** 220; Thomas 273, 274, 288, 289, 312; **Will** 77; William Jordan 149; **Yeany** 20;

HAMILTON, John 24;

HAMMON, **David** 318; William 318;

HAMMOND, Charles 103, 104; **Dorcas** 104; Edward 104, 152, 177, 258, 397; Edward Sr. 103, 104; Edward Jr. 103, 104, 397; **Hannah** 104; **Harry** 104; John 103, 104; Leah 258; Martha 103, 104; Mary 103, 104; **Peter** 397; Rachel 258; **Sal** 258; **Sall** 104; Zadekiah 201; **Zadock** 201; Zedekiah 201;

HANCOCK, Elizabeth 50, 51; William 50, 57;

HANDBY, **Jenny** 426;

HANDCOCK, Elizabeth 51;

HANDY, **Abel** 255, 280; **Amey** 30; Benjamin 27, 30, 38, 39, 42, 44, 47, 55, 56, 58, 95, 124; **Bridget** 286; **Bristor** 42; Comfort 286, 413, 414; **Daul** 30; **David** 440; **Dinah** 286; Ebenezer 133, 134, 183, 203, 207, 214, 219, 223, 228, 269, 277, 278; Elizabeth 42, 114, 448, 449; **Esther** 94, 286, 413, 414; George 90, 235; **George** 38, 269; **Hannah** 286, 425; **Harry** 286, 413, 414; Henry 90; **Hope** 317; Jacob 425; **Jacob** 286; James 55, 286, 317; **James** 399; **Jesse** 448; John 30, 38, 39; **John** 407; John C. 240, 408; John Jr. 85; Joseph 90; Joyce 286; **Judah** 286; **Leah** 286; **Linda** 235; **Lonnon** 84; **Lucy** 235; Matt 202; **Matthias** 407; **Moll** 42; **Nell** 377; **Orris** 286, 413, 414; **Phillis** 38; **Pomp** 90; **Pompey** 286; **Pompy** 313; **Rachel** 286, 413, 414; **Rhoda** 42, 114; **Rhody** 286; **Rodah** 413, 414; **Rose** 42, 91, 94, 235; **Sampson** 94; Samue 406; Samuel 84, 87, 91, 94, 123, 280, 364, 377, 404, 405, 406, 407, 408, 440; Samuel Sr. 404, 405, 440; **Sarah** 94, 407; **Sib** 407; **Silby** 277; **Suffiah** 314; Thomas 30, 43, 45; Thomas R. 415; Thomas Robins 286, 414; William 222, 223, 231, 235, 236, 239, 244, 245, 247, 249, 252, 254, 255, 285, 286, 287, 314, 336, 413, 414, 415;

HARDY, Isaac 75; **Jack** 75;

HARGRAVE, Elizabeth 282;

HARMANSON, **Amos** 242; **Beck** 242; Edward 242; **Hannah** 242; **Isaac** 242; **Robin** 242;

HARMON, Abel 426;

HARRIS, Benton 70, 77, 102, 108, 109, 110, 114, 119, 131, 132, 136;

HARRISON, Rouse 130; Thomas 412;

HAYNIE, Ezekiel 289; **Leah** 289;

HAYWARD, **Aproba** 72; Benjamin 169, 170, 174, 176, 177, 178; **Betty** 72; **Dick** 72; **Dider** 170; George 69, 71, 72, 74, 87, 91, 94, 97, 98, 104; Harriet 178; Harriot 176; Henry 178; **Jack** 72; Leah 176, 177; **Mary** 170; **Nathan** 174; **Oxford** 72; **Patience** 176, 177; Polly 178; **Prim** 72; **Rachel** 178; **Rachell** 178; **Rose** 91; Sally 178; **Sam** 170; William 17, 23, 32, 72; **Zadock** 174;

HAZARD, **Cloe** 42; Jonathan 42, 43;

HAZZARD, Elihu 142, 184, 194, 195, 329, 349; Elihue 329; **Leah** 194, 329; **Libb** 142; **Luke** 184; **Rhody** 184; Sarah 142; **Siss** 142;

HEARN, Betty 107; **Dina** 107; John 107; Prissa 107;

HELLAM, Joshua 25;

HENDERSON, **Abbow** 18, 28; **Adam** 4, 12, 36; Ailce 43; Alice 13, 14, 43; **Amey** 56; **Barsheba** 18, 28; **Beck** 138; **Betty** 5, 8; Betty Barnaby 12; Benjamin 12, 18, 28, 29, 310, 320; Charles 12; Comfort 43; **Dinah** 8; **Diner** 8; Elizabeth 12, 13, 14, 138; **Eve** 18, 28; **Florrow** 36; **George** 43; **Harry** 18, 28, 110; Henry Jenckins 310; James 13, 14, 170; Jemima 56, 110, 111, 185; Jemimah 56; Jenckins 309, 310; Jenkins 370; **Jenny** 170; John 5, 8, 9, 36, 407; John Laws 416; Levi 170; Mary 36, 37; **Mary** 12; **Moses** 185; **Peter** 110, 407, 416; Peter Holland 310; **Pleasant** 18, 28; **Priss** 138; Rhodia 5, 8; Sarah 4, 8, 9, 36, 37, 170; **Sarah** 13, 14; Sarah Cox 138; **Stephen** 230; **Venus** 407, 416; William 12; William B. 230; William Bivens 416;

HENREY, **Alse** 299; Francis Jnkens 299;

HENRY, **Alse** 299; Edward 234, 439, 444; Francis J. 299; Francis Jenkins 294, 300; Isaac 438; **Jemmey** 17; **Joan** 17; John 6, 16, 17, 21, 27; **Peter** 234; Robert Jenkins 7, 16, 17, 21;

HESON, John 285;

HEYWARD, Benjamin 175; **Rose** 175;

HICKMAN, Rachel 329;

HICKMON, Rachel 350;

HILCH, Joseph 65;

HILL, **Beck** 257; **Ben** 380; **Betty** 166; Christian 359; **Comfort** 380; Elizabeth 380; Frederick 257; **Harry** 384; **Henney** 257; **Jacob** 226; **Jenny** 231; John 380; Johnson 384; Joshua 102, 113, 380; Laban 380; Labin 232, 380; Labin Jr. 380; Labin Sr. 380; Levin 66, 91, 132, 257; **Lue** 257; **Nathaniel** 257; **Pashents** 232; **Pink** 257; Releck 185; Sarah 380; William S. 166; William Stephen 226, 231; William Steven 166;

HILLOM, **Benjamin** 81; **Hanah** 81; Isaac 81; **Leah** 81; **Stephen** 81;

HILMON, **Pompy** 314; Samuel 314; **Suffiah** 314;

HINDMAN, Edward 137, 138; Jacob 9, 10;

HINNAN, James 393;

HOLLAND, **Abraham** 180; **Abram** 190; **Ann** 283; **Argile** 190; **Argill** 180; **Ben** 248, 283; Betty 9, 89; Bridgett 9; **Candis** 245; **Caprell** 180; **Daniel** 326; **Dorcos** 393; Elisha 447; **George** 180, 190; **Hager** 283; **Harry** 393; John 171, 351, 375, 385, 390, 391, 393, 426, 432, 450; Levi 282, 283, 431; Mary 283, 447; **Ned** 9; Nehemiah 9, 181, 331, 393; Peter 393; **Pleasant** 180, 190; **Rafe** 190; **Rhoda** 326; **Sall** 447; **Sam** 393; Samuel 248; Sarah 9; **Sarah** 180, 190, 245; Scarboroug 393; Scarborough 393; Scarbrough 393; Tabitha 9; **Tamar** 180; **Tamer** 190; Thomas 9, 248, 393; William 9, 80, 125, 180, 190, 191, 244, 245, 326, 331, 393;

HOLLAWAY, Aaron Sr. 228; **Cate** 228; **Harry** 228; Joseph 228; Moses 228; Thomas 228;

HOLTE, Sarah 99;

HOPKINS, **Daniel** 245, 246; **Edith** 70, 92, 95; Hampton 281, 282; Levi 87; Levin 126, 245, 246; Mathew 83; Matthew Jr. 50; **Nell** 282; **Orson** 50; Robert 83, 86; **Robert** 282; Samuel 21, 26, 27, 50, 70, 92, 94, 95; **Silva** 26; William 10, 245, 246;

HORSEY, Edward 312, 313; **Heaster** 203; Isaac 203; **Jacob** 312, 313; Stephen 157; William 157;

HOSIER, **Lott** 320; **Ruiksom** 217; Samuel 217, 320;

HOSIERR, Samuel 218;

HOUGH, Nathaniel 33;

HOUR, Hannah 25;

HOUSTON, **Abel** 134, 146; **Amey** 30; **Athaliah** 141; **Beck** 70; Betsey Wise 146; **Betty** 4; **Comfort** 411; **Daul** 30; **David** 134; **Dick** 4; **George** 134, 146; **Hagar** 141; **Hannah** 134, 146; **Harry** 4, 5; **Hulda** 411; **Huldy** 411; Isaac 132, 141; **Isaac** 146;

Jack 118; James 84, 85, 111, 134, 135, 214, 372, 373, 430; **Jeffrey** 4; Jehu 95; John 4, 5, 118; Joseph 4; Joseph Sr. 30; Levi 416; **Lonnon** 84; **Mereum** 214; **Milby** 372, 373; **Nimrod** 5; **Patience** 214; **Pleasant** 4; **Racel** 134; Rachell 5; Robert 37, 70, 71; **Rose** 4, 5, 141; Sally Minors 70; Sally Simmons Minors 70; Sarah 146; **Sarah** 411; William 411; William J. 411; William Jarman 411; **Zepheniah** 141;

HOVENTON, **Sarah** 149; William 149;

HOWARTH, **George** 154; Laurence 154; **Limas** 154; Sarah 154;

HUDSON, Ananias 102, 222, 223; Annanias 200, 436; Annanias (of William) 436; Benjamin 437; **Betty** 47; **Caleb** 47; **Comfort** 437; Dennis 232, 233; **Elisha** 437; Esther 364, 365; **George** 271, 273, 288, 364; Isaac 365; Jesse 327; John 411; Jonathan Jr. 418; Joshua 271; **Lydia** 288; Mary 47, 48; McKimmey 285; **Minea** 436; **Mirom** 200; **Omey** 436; **Peg** 327; **Rhoda** 288; Robert 47, 48, 273, 288; **Robin** 365; **Sal** 200, 233; **Sall** 233; **Sarah** 47, 288; **Shadrick** 47; **Stephen** 200; **Sue** 222; **Tamer** 288; **Will** 411;

HUNT, Esther 371; **Leavin** 337; **Levin** 337, 352, 371; William Cambridge 371;

HUTCHERSON, **Fan** 183; **Handy** 300; Jonathan 174, 300; **Pricilla** 183;

HUTCHESON, **Fan** 183; Jonathan 183; **Pricilla** 183;

HUTSON, Ananias 216; Annanias 216; Jonathan 116; **Sue** 216;

HUTSOND, Annanias 217;

IRONS, **Lucey** 369; Thomas 369;

IRONSHIRE, **George** 155; **Hulda** 155; **Jane** 155; **Jesse** 155; Joseph 155; **Sarah** 155;

JACOBS, **Nimrod** 357; **Prisciller** 357;

JAMERSON, David 44;

JAMES, **Ben** 142; **Betty** 142; **Fisher** 142; **Hanah** 142; **Kent** 142; **Ned** 142; **Peggy** 142; **Rhoda** 142; **Sophia** 142;

JARMAN, **George** 48; **Jesper** 48; John 48; **Leah** 48; **Sampson** 85; **Sarah** 48; **Watt** 48; William 85;

JEATER, **Frank** 114; William 114; William Jr. 114;

JENKINS, **Juda** 2; Rebecca 2; Rebeka 2;

JENKINSON, **Abner** 1; Jesse 1, 5; John 1; **Pleasant** 1;

JOHNSON, Alce 311, 314, 315, 316; **Abram** 437; **Ben** 175; Benjamin 157; Burnett 289; **Chloe** 316; Christian 127; **Comfort** 437; **Cyller** 437; **Daniel** 90; **David** 311; **Dinah** 265; Eleazar 311; Elles 315, 316; **Eli** 144; **Elijah** 315; **Elzey** 316; Ezekiah 305; Fanna 298; **Hannah** 159, 323; **Harry** 305; **Henny** 191; Henry 127, 144; Hezekiah 186, 305, 437; **Isaac** 171; **Jacob** 437; John 239, 261, 298, 315, 369, 370; John (of Leonard) 239; **Leah** 324; Lemuel 89, 90, 129, 159, 171, 175; Leonard 324; Levina 191, 192; **Lidde** 298; **Lyda** 370; Mary 159, 186; Nancy 186; **Ned** 190; **Nice** 127; **Peter** 186, 437; **Pleasant** 144; Purnell 264, 265, 270, 278, 281, 291, 438; **Rachell** 191; **Sampton** 239; Samuel 155, 156; **Sarah** 341; **Sear** 127; Severn 155, 156, 187, 190, 304; **Stephen** 239; **Tinna** 261; **Will** 156; William 323; **William** 140; Zebulon 156, 341;

JONES, **Abraham** 321, 322; Ameala 368; Aimla 368; **Anne** 379; **Bartlett** 76; **Dinah** 321, 322; George 3, 123; **George** 43, 76; **Hannah** 309, 314; **Isaac** 321, 322; James 282; Jesse 238, 379; **James** 368; **Jo** 112, 113; John 309, 314, 321, 322, 331; John Sr. 331; **Lucretia** 321, 322; Macclama 112; Macclammy 112, 113, 120; Macclemmy 112; Morgan 251, 280; **Pleasant** 76; **Rachel** 331; **Sabrough** 321, 322; Sampson 20, 23; **Southey** 321; Southy 28, 322; **Standbridge** 28; Sterling 404; Thomas 20, 23, 28, 43, 47, 76; **Will** 120; William 67, 68, 319; **William** 120;

JORDAN, John 61; **Mary** 172; Patrick 172, 192; **Sarah** 172;

JORDON, **Mary** 172; Patrick 172; **Sarah** 172;

KELLAM, **Abel** 313; **Abner** 313; **Handy** 162; Isaac 96, 126; James 162; **Jean** 313; Joseph 313, 338; **Stephen** 96;

KELLY, Henry 88, 100; **Lisha** 88; **Peter** 100;

KENDALL, **Charles** 80; **Eben** 80; John 80, 81;

KENDEL, **Esau** 362; **Esaw** 362; **Esther** 361, 362;

KENNET, **Esther** 41; **Pasgrave** 41; Turville 41;

KENNETT, **Esther** 41; **Pasgrave** 41; Presgrave 42; Turville 41, 42;

KENNIT, Presgrave 438;

KERBY, **Bett** 308; **Leah** 308; Nancey 308; Nancy 308;

KILBEE, John 11; **Silvia** 11;

KILBIE, John 11; **Silvia** 11;

KILLAIM, **Ben** 388; Nancy 388;

KILLAM, **Ben** 196, 388; **Benjamin** 196; **Bill** 389; **Easther** 95; **Esther** 95; **Handy** 239; **Hannah** 95; **Hannah Jr.** 95; Isaac 95, 96, 196; Jemima 196; **Jenny** 348; John 239; Joseph 338, 348, 389; Nancy 388; **Sampton** 239; **Stephen** 96, 239; **Will** 389;

KILLEAM, **Handy** 239; John 239;

KILLIAM, **Ben** 388; Nancy 388;

KILLIM, Joseph 180;

KILLIOM, **Handy** 239; John 239;

KILLY, Henry 224; **Leah** 224;

KING, **Abbow** 18, 28; **Adam** 19, 29; **Barsheba** 18, 28; Ephraim 84; **Harry** 18, 28; **Eve** 18, 28; James 184, 206, 279, 410, 411; James Jr. 438, 439; James Sr. 438; **Jamey** 6, 15; Jediah 113; **Pleasant** 6, 15, 18, 28; **Pleasant** 410; **Rachell** 410; **Ralph** 438; Robert 6, 7, 15, 18, 19, 28, 29, 30; Robert Jr. 7; **Sharp** 279; **Tom** 206;

KINGSLOW, John 67;

KINSLOW, John 68;

KIRBY, John 336; **Mingo** 336;

KITCHEN, **Betty** 7; William 2, 7;

KNOX, Ezekiel 169;

KOLLOCK, Simon 105;

LAMBDEN, **Betty** 7; **Hector** 21; **Jamey** 6, 15; **Jemmey** 17; **Joan** 17; **Pleasant** 6, 15, 21; **Rach** 93; **Rachell** 93; Sarah 16, 17; Thomas 6, 7, 15, 16, 17, 21, 22, 23, 93; Thomas Jr. 92, 93; **Violet** 21;

LAMBERSON, Robert 51, 52;

LANE, **Abner** 256; **Ben** 256; **Betty** 256; **Elijah** 256; Elizabeth 140; **Esther** 256; Ezekiel 57, 58; Francis 332; **George** 332, 444; **Hanah** 140; **Isaac** 256; Israel 300; **Jacob** 332; James 444, 445; **Jenny** 256; **Joan** 256; **Joe** 256; **Kiah** 256; Leah 191; **Lott** 332; **Lura** 256; **Lusey** 300; **Lydia** 256; **Middlesex** 256; **Milla** 256; **Mille** 300; **Nice** 126; **Peter** 256; **Phillis** 126; **Richard** 256; **Sampson** 191, 332; **Sear** 126, 127; **Shadrack** 256; **Silbey** 126; **Tabitha** 256; William 5, 14, 18, 19, 126, 127, 256; **Zilpah** 300;

LANKFORD, Benjamin 39;

LARRAMORE, **Bess** 59; **Coffe** 59; Levin 58, 59; **Sambo** 59; **Sampson** 59; **Watt** 59;

LARRAMUR, **Bess** 59; **Coffe** 59; Levin 59; **Sambo** 59; **Sampson** 59; **Watt** 59;

LAW, **Amy** 403; **Jid** 403; **Juda** 403; William 403;

LAWES, **Danniel** 396; John 366, 367, 396; **Luse** 396; **Mary** 396; **Merier** 396; **Milla** 367; **Prince** 396; Thomas 396;

LAWRENCE, Mary 285; Molly 285;

LAWS, Elijah 221; Elijah Jr. 220, 221, 227; James 285; **Jesse** 359; John 359, 367; **Milla** 367; **Minta** 220, 227; **Silva** 227; **Silvy** 220;

LAYFIELD, Caty 428; Esther 428; George 158, 254; Isaac 196;

LECOUNT, **Caleb** 229; **Esther** 229; **Hannah** 229; **Henna** 301; **Hinna** 301; James 229, 230, 301; **Leah** 229; **Sarah** 229;

LEEDS, John 164;

LEONARD, **Bridget** 438; Ebenezar 438; Ebenezard 438;

LEVENSTON, James 236; Sarah 236;

LEVINGTON, **Casandra** 350; **Cassandra** 350; James 350;

LINCH, David 285;

LINDSEY, **Harry** 306; James 306;

LINDZEY, **Harry** 306; James 306;

LINGO, **Ben** 133; John 133;

LINGOE, **Ben** 133; John 133;

LISTER, **Betty** 291; William 291; **Zedegial** 291; **Zedegiel** 291;

LIVINGSTON, **Amelia** 72; Benjamin 246; **Cesar** 246; George 72, 73, 246; Ted 246;

LONG, **Abner** 208, 209; **Ben** 250; **Charity** 250; Colborn 370; Coleborn 371; Colevern 315, 320; Comfort 451; Coulborn 320; Elisha 105; **Esther** 370; George 48, 451; **Grace** 370, 451; **Hannah** 425; Henny 451; **Jacob** 420; **James** 370; **Jesper** 48; John 48, 49; **Leah** 48, 370; Leavin 252; Levin 175, 208, 209, 252, 425; **Levin** 451; **Linda** 451; Littleton 451; **Lott** 320; Lucresla 151; Lucresta 151; **Minta** 451; **Patience** 48; Peggy 451; **Rachel** 252; **Rose** 175; **Sabroe** 370; Samuel 250, 251; **Sarah** 48; Solomon 420; **Watt** 48; **Will** 151;

LOWE, Thomas 99;

LOWES, **App** 310; **David** 310; **Hope** 47; **Jacob** 310; **Martha** 47; **Nebo** 310; **Rachell** 310; **Sambo** 310; **Sarah Nan** 310; Tubman 47, 310; **Violett** 310;

MACKALLAN, **Adam** 12; Arthur 2, 12;

MADDUX, **Bobb** 103; Daniel 335; Marey 335; Zachariah 103;

MARCH, **Amy** 184; **Coffee** 184; **Comfort** 184, 198, 199; **Hannah** 184; **Isaac** 184; Martha 184, 185, 198, 199; **Rhoda** 184;

MARSH, **Abel** 432; **Isaac** 432; **James** 432; **Leah** 432; Philip 432, 433; Polly 432; **Solomon** 432; **William** 432;

MARSHALL, **Abel** 446; **Adah** 446; **Betty** 446; Fanna 298; George 318, 373; **George** 446; Isaac 214, 217, 234, 242 262, 266, 267, 284, 295, 310, 316, 319, 321, 323, 322, 346; **Job** 446; John P. 234, 439, 442; Levin 298; **Lidde** 298; **Nancy** 373; Rebecca 373; **Ruiksom** 217; William 446;

MARTIN, **Adam** 179, 180; **Belitha** 266; **Bersheba** 262; **Betty** 262; **Bridget** 44, 45; **Bristor** 42; **Candis** 299; **Ceaser** 49; **Dennis** 262; **Dinah** 266; **Easter** 262, 265; **Ephraim** 392; **Frank** 114; George 50, 114, 266, 379; **Grace** 262; **Hannah** 49, 262; **Hope** 44, 45; **Isaac** 218, 262; **Jacob** 49; James 6, 46, 84, 204, 218, 265, 285, 299, 367, 421, 422, 430, 431; **James** 324; James Sr. 299; **Jer** 49; **Jethro** 46, 50; John 43, 44, 45, 46, 179, 180, 233, 331, 332; **John** 262; **Larry** 468; **Leah** 262; **Levi** 299; Levin 242, 381, 382, 392; **Levin** 218; **Martha** 44, 45, 242; Mary 42, 46, 50, 379, 431; **Moll** 6, 42; **Moses** 46; **Nancy** 262; **Nathaniel** 266; **Patience** 49; **Paul** 44, 45; **Phebe** 49; **Price** 262; **Priscilla** 262; **Priss** 435; **Rhoda** 42, 262; Robert 244; **Robin** 49; **Rohoda** 262; **Rose** 42, 44, 45; **Sam** 367; Sarah 49; **Sebb** 265; **Stephen** 265, 381; **Tab** 49; **Tabitha** 262; **Thanah** 84; Thomas 44, 45, 49, 50, 202, 262, 265, 266, 305, 306, 324, 326, 372, 373, 374, 383, 435; Thomas (of James) 202, 324; Thomas Sr. 262, 266, 371; **Tom** 379; **Tylus** 84; William 46; **Zadock** 49;

MARTIN & HOWARD 437;

MASON, **Jabe** 135; William 135;

MASSEY, **Esther** 374; **Jenny** 374; John 374; William 37; Zeporah 250;

MAXFIELD, Easten 31; **Leah** 31; **Nan** 31; Sarah 30, 31; Stephen 30, 31; Steven 30; Susanah 30; Susannah 30, 31;

McALLEN, Alexander 166, 169, 331; Allexander 169; **Hatter** 169; Margaret 166, 169; **Peter** 169; Rachel 166, 167, 169; Rachell 166; **Rose** 166; Sarah 166, 167, 169;

McBRYDE, **Abner** 138; **Bob** 138; **Name** 138; **Pleasant** 138; Sarah 357; **Stephen** 357; **Will** 138; William 138, 139, 310, 311; William & Co. 327;

McCALL, Mark 188;

McCAY, Abel 52;

McCLEMMEY, William 15;

McCORMACK, Benjamin 185, 241, 248, 282, 328; Comfort 416, 417; **Juda** 416;

McFADDEN, James 386;

McGEE, Barckley 287; Barkley 287; David 131; **Filer** 287; **Jane** 131;

McGREGOR, **Tonney** 409; William 409;

McGREGGOR, **George** 215; William 215;

McILVAINE, David 32; **Sarah** 32; **Tony** 32; William 32;

McIVER, **Daniel** 326; John 326; **Rhoda** 326;

McKALLEN, Alexander 205, 223; **Saul** 223;

McLURE, **Davy** 261; John 247, 261; **Minta** 247;

McNEAL, Thomas 199; **Tib** 349; Robert 349;

McNEALL, John 125; **Phillace** 125;

McNEIL, John 125; **Phillace** 125; Robert 349; **Tib** 349;

MEARE, **Dinah** 265; Sarah 265;

MEARS, **Dinah** 265; Sarah 265, 266;

MELBOURN, **Isaac** 353; William 353;

MELSON, Daniel 270, 275, 281; Daniel Sr. 270; **Grace** 275; John 339; **Kesiah** 281; **Magor** 339; **Tempy** 270; William 275;

MERICA, George 440;

MERRILL, **Amey** 56; **Caleb** 298; **Candis** 420; Comfort 43, 56, 185, 186, 187, 305; **Easter** 370; **Easther** 308; Elijah 185, 305, 306, 307; **Esme** 370; **Georg** 308; **George** 43; Gertrude 370; **Hannah** 186; **Harry** 110, 305, 306; **Jim** 370; John 43, 56, 110; Levi 298, 308, 327; Levin 297; **Lucey** 369; **Lydda** 308; **Moses** 185, 307; **Peg** 327; Peter 110, 186, 308; **Rachel** 370; Robert M. 369; **Robbin** 297; Tabitha 420; Thomas 420; **Will** 370;

MIDDLETON, Betsey 210; **Boatswan** 210; **Bob** 210; **Cato** 210; Ignatious 210; **Jack** 210; **Levin** 210; **Lizey** 210; **Ralph** 210; **Sally** 210;

MIDZLEY, Thomas 44; **Will** 44;

MIFFLIN, **Ben** 142, 161; **Bette** 161; **Betty** 142; **Charity** 161; Daniel 116, 117, 161; Daniel Jr. 142; Daniel Sr 142; **Fisher** 142; **Frank** 142; **George** 161; **Gilbert** 161; **Hanah** 142; **Isaac** 161; **James** 142, 345; **Kent James** 142; **John** 161; **Joshua** 161; **Leah** 161; **Liddia** 161; **Nanney** 161; **Nead** 161; **Ned** 142; **Peggy** 142; **Perrey** 161; **Perry** 431; **Rachel** 161; **Rhoda** 142, 161; **Robert** 341, 342; **Sal** 161; **Sam** 161; **Sophia** 142; **Susey** 161; **Thamer** 161; Warner 341, 342, 345;

MILBOURN, Caleb 35; **Easter** 370; **Isaac** 105, 252, 271, 345, 353; **Jack** 252, 271, 304, 345; **Jim** 370; **Leveanah Jenkins** 105; **Peter** 105, 397; **Pleasant** 105; **Rachel** 370; Sarah 105; Solomon 105; Thomas 35, 252, 271, 370; **Will** 370; William 252, 271, 304, 345, 353, 397;

MILBURN, **Isaac** 271; **Jack** 271; Thomas 271; William 271;

MILES, Mathias 367; **Sam** 367;

MILLER, **Abraham** 300; Barsheba 330; Basheba 300; Bathsheba 295; **Beck** 118, 440; **George** 271; **Hager** 295; John 271; Joseph 11, 349, 440; Levin 271; **Nance** 295; **Phillis** 330; Sarah 118; **Tib** 349;

MILLS, **Abner** 173; Benjamin 135; **Ceasor** 73; John 60, 73; **Leah** 173; Levi 304, 320; Rachel 140; Robert 173; **Robin** 304; Samuel 73; **Will** 320;

MINORS, **Beck** 70; Charles 76; Sally 70; Sally Simmons 70;

MITCHELL, **Abel** 294; **Amos** 294; **Ben** 294; **Benn** 86; **Bet** 294, 317; **Betty** 317; **Bradis** 294; **Ciller** 294; **Cloah** 435; **Comfort** 262, 294, 439; Cyrus 101; **Edmond** 262; Elizabeth 435; **Glasgow** 294; **Hannah** 294; **Harrah** 154; **Hope** 47; Isaac 263, 431; **Jacob** 101; James 135; **Joe** 294; John 66, 67, 77, 83, 106, 107; **John** 294; John P. 184, 228, 248, 266, 275, 294, 295, 296, 325, 326, 335, 342, 345, 353, 368, 420, 431, 433, 434, 435, 439, 445; John Pope 80, 154, 324; Joshua 25, 38, 47, 52, 80, 83, 84, 89, 104, 142, 262, 305; Josiah 168, 180, 199, 204, 206, 215, 218, 219, 221, 223, 224, 233, 240, 243, 260, 262, 263, 272, 278, 284, 294, 296, 300, 305, 313, 320, 365, 366, 427, 430; **Leah** 294; **Leb** 262; **Let** 294; Levin 317, 439; **Loviey** 101; **Martha** 47; **Pleasant** 294; **Pomp** 67, 83, 107; **Rachal** 187; **Rachel**

187; Robert 67, 83, 86, 101, 294; **Sampson** 294, 435; **Sarah** 294, 435; **Silva** 187; Stephen 187; **Zebulon** 294;

MOLLERTON, William 188;

MOORE, Augustine 37;

MORAS, Amela 187; **Rachal** 187; **Rachel** 187; **Silva** 187;

MORGAN, Avery 59, 258; Avery Jr. 59; **Caesar** 59; **Capel** 59; **Cupet** 113; **Cupit** 59; **Esther** 59; **Hanah** 59; John 59, 113; Mary 59; **Peet** 258; **Sall** 258; Sarah 59; **Solomon** 59; **Susanah** 59;

MORGUN, Avery 258; **Peet** 258; **Sall** 258;

MORRIS, Amela 187; Amelay 187; **Ann** 283; **Ben** 230, 283; **Bess** 307; **Capril** 420; **Charity** 360; **Chloe** 245; **Dinah** 420; **Esther** 245; **George** 289, 360; **Hager** 230, 283; **Harry** 136; **Hesse** 421, 422; **Isaac** 245, 330, 360, 421; **Jack** 295, 296; James R. 245; James Round 245; Joshua 307; **Levin** 289, 327; **Milby** 404; **Minte** 422; **Nance** 295, 296; **Nell** 289, 327; **Patience** 295, 296; **Rachal** 187; Rachel 283; **Rachel** 187, 230; Rachell 283; **Sal** 422, 423; **Sall** 295, 296; **Sam** 295, 296; **Sampson** 307; **Saul** 397; **Savannah Isaac** 360; **Silva** 187; **Sub** 422, 423; Thomas 289; William 136, 216, 226, 245, 285, 289, 295, 296, 307, 308, 327, 330, 360, 397, 404, 420, 421, 422; William (of Thomas) 289;

MORRISS, **Ann** 283; **Ben** 283; **Hager** 283; **Levin** 327; **Milby** 404; **Nell** 327; Rachel 283; Rachell 282, 283; William 327, 404;

MORSS, **Dinah** 27, 33; Joshua 27, 31, 32, 33; **Mingo** 33; **Will** 27, 33;

MUMFORD, James 435; Major 342, 343; **Martha** 343; Mary 402; Methias 151; Sacker 122; **Sam** 122; **Sampson** 435; **Santa** 343; **Sarah** 435; **Tite** 343;

MUMFORT, James 435; **Sampson** 435; **Sarah** 435;

MURAY, **Abel** 294; **Amos** 294; **Ben** 294; **Bet** 294; **Bradis** 294; **Ciller** 294; **Comfort** 294; **Glasgow** 294; **Hannah** 294; **Joe** 294; **John** 294; **Leah** 294; **Let** 294; Mary 294; **Pleasant** 294; **Sampson** 294; **Sarah** 294; **Zebulon** 294;

MURRAY, **Bridget** 54; David 49, 285; **Doll** 87; Duncan 143, 211, 212, 213, 279, 280; Dunkin 280; **Flora** 87; Isaac 49, 95; James 54, 87; John 3; **London** 49; Mary 262; **Ned** 212; **Nell** 212, 280; **Sharp** 212, 279; **Shederik** 211;

MURREY, Duncan 212, 213; **Ned** 212; **Nell** 212; **Sharp** 212;

MURRY, **Abel** 294; **Amos** 294; **Ben** 294; **Bet** 294; **Bradis** 294; **Ciller** 294; **Comfort** 294; **Glasgow** 294; **Hannah** 294; **Joe** 294; **John** 294; **Leah** 294; **Let** 294; **Mary** 294; **Pleasant** 294; **Sarah** 294; **Sampson** 294; **Zebulon** 294;

NAIRNE, **Glasgow** 39; **Harry** 39; **Jacob** 39; James 177; John 39; Robert 39;

NEILLE, John 176; **Patience** 176;

NELMS, **Bett** 228; Edmond Northen 270; Edmund Northen 99; **Fillis** 99; Frankey 270; **George** 438; Nancy 227, 228, 438; Nanncy 438; **Nice** 228;

NELSON, **Appleby** 37; **Arnold** 37; **Bett** 37; **Dick** 37; **Harry** 37; **Let** 37; **Lucey** 37; **Milley** 37; **Nan** 37; **Oaford** 37; **Rachel** 37; **Sam** 37; **Terrey** 37; William 37;

NEVAN, **Esther** 111; James 111;

NEWLAND, **Daniel** 24; **Rachel** 25; **Southy** 26, 28; **Standbridge** 26, 28; William 24, 25, 26, 28; William Sr. 25;

NEWTON, Daniel 67; **George** 172; **James** 197; **Joshua** 208; Selby 172, 176, 197, 208; **Tamer** 197;

NICHOLSON, **Candis** 247; **Fortune** 316; **Hannah** 247; Isaac 361; **Izabel** 247; **Jacob** 274; **Jesper** 316; John 247; **Levin** 361; **Mareor** 274; Matthias 274, 316, 317; **Moll** 247;

NILSON, Samuel 27, 40; William 13, 16, 17, 21, 27, 40, 350;

NOBLE, James 40; **Joshua** 40;

NUTTER, **Lare** 442; Thomas E. 442;

ONEAL, **Dick** 65; **George** 65; Thomas 65; **Venis** 65;

OSBORN, Joseph 212;

OUTTEN, Abraham 3, 94; **Dick** 65; **Esther** 94; **Filer** 69; **Florow** 69; **Flowra** 33; **George** 65; **Jack** 69; **James** 177; **Jim** 69; Levi 177, 209, 411; Levin ; **Lid** 69; Matthew 33, 69, 100; **Nanny** 411; **Nell** 69; Obadiah 65; Rhoda 3; **Rose** 94; **Sampson** 69, 94; **Sarah** 94; **Venis** 65;

OWENS, Belitha 450; Elisabeth 101; Elizabeth 101; **Jacob** 101; **Loviey** 101; Mary 450;

PAIN, Isaac 62;

PAINE, **Ben** 196; **Benjamin** 196; Levin 196;

PANK, Betty 350; Bety 350; **Casandra** 350; **Cassandra** 350; Elizabeth 395; Moses 350, 395;

PANKS, Betty 350; **Casandra** 350; **Cassandra** 350; Moses 350;

PARKER, Abigail 441; **Adam** 309; B. 449; Barzillia 449; **Candis** 244, 245; **Chany** 449; Charles 35, 87, 88, 158, 177; **Charles** 215, 216; **China** 449; **Cuggo** 358; **Eben** 378; Elisha 339, 377, 378, 445; **Daniel** 359; **Fortune** 398; **Frederic** 309; **George** 215, 216, 218, 257, 273; George A. 309; George Anderson 309; Henry 201, 244, 245, 254, 296, 380, 381; Henry Jr. 201, 224, 236, 254, 256, 296; **Isaac** 171; **Jack** 296; **Jacob** 204; **James** 158, 177, 309; **Jim** 158; John 277, 278, 359; **Leah** 441, 445; **Leak** 87, 88; **Magor** 339; **Major** 309, 380, 381; **Margery** 198; **Milby** 443; **Nance** 201; **Nancey** 201; Nancy 241; **Phillis** 204; Rebecca 215, 216, 406, 407; **Rhoda** 158; **Rhodey** 406; **Rose** 35; S. 449; **Sally** 443; **Sampson** 261; Samuel 261, 359, 398, 449; Samuel (of Samuel) 261; **Sarah** 198, 236, 244, 245, 254, 443; Schoolfiel 273; Schoolfield 218, 273, 309, 380, 381; Selby 171, 175, 198; **Silby** 277; **Sillar** 296; **Siller** 296; **Sothey** 259; **Southy** 256; Thomas 177, 201, 256, 259; **Tom** 241; **Venis** 441, 445; **Will** 204; William 257, 309, 337, 341, 342, 372; William A. 204, 216, 241; William Anderson 215, 216, 241; **Zadock** 201;

PARRAMORE, **Ann** 313; **Daniel** 326; **Esther (old)** 313; **James** 324; John 161, 172, 181, 191, 324; Mary 324, 326; **Priscilla** 313; **Rhoda** 326; Thomas 313;

PARRET, John 114; **Rhoda** 114;

PARSON, **Leah** 445; Prissilla 445; **Venis** 445; William 445;

PARSONS, **Harry** 416; Jonathan 103, 124; Jonathan Jr. 68; **Leah** 441, 445; **Leash** 399; Margaret 398, 399, 416; **Nance** 416; Porter 339; Priscilla 441; Prissella 441; Prissilla 441, 445; **Samson** 398; **Venis** 441, 445; William 441, 445;

PAYNE, **Ben** 196; **Benjamin** 196; **Feaby** 341; **Jemimah** 341; Jeptha 287, 288; Jepthah 288; **Jerum** 288; Levin 195, 196; **Majar** 341; Moses 287, 288, 341; Moses Sr. 287; **Susannah** 341;

PAYNTER, John 335;

PEAL, **Sampson** 20; Thomas 16, 19, 20;

PEALE, Thomas 20, 23; **Sampson** 23;

PEEL, **Sampson** 15; Thomas 15;

PEELE, **Sampson** 23; Thomas 23;

PEPPER, **Jack** 391; John 87, 88, 376; **Leak** 87, 88; Saccar 391; Solomon 376, 391;

PERDUE, James 207;

PERKINS, **Abraham** 300; James 331; John 300, 330, 331; Mary 300, **Philis** 330; **Phillis** 330; **Prissey** 331; Solomon 331;

PETERSON, **Daniel** 359; Peter 359;

PETTETT, Easter 402; Edward 401; **Lish** 401; **Liza** 401; **Nanny** 401; **Obed** 401;

PETTIT, Bartholomew 41; Edward 124, 401; Esther 401; **Lish** 401; **Liza** 401; **Marina** 41; **Nanny** 401; **Obed** 401; Rose 124;

PHILLIPS, Isaac 223; **Saul** 223;

PHILLIPSHILL, Charles 200, 201; **Tom** 201;

PITT, **Grace** 173; Hillary 150, 173; **Isaac** 173; **Leven** 173; **Luke** 150;

PITTS, **Boatswain** 31; **Grace** 173; Hillary 173, 255; **Isaac** 173; **Leven** 173; Mary 253; **Minty** 255; **Ned** 255; Peter 26; **Rachel** 331; Robert 26, 27, 31; **Southey** 331; **Southy** 331; William 150, 255;

POAHEN, **Estar** 410; **Ester** 410; Selathal 410;

POAHER, **Estar** 410; **Ester** 410; Selathal 410

POINTER, John 21; **Jone** 143; **Leah** 143; Thomas 143;

POLIT, Mary 135;

POLK, Gilliss 195; James 83; Josiah 59, 69; **Milby** 325; William 325;

POLLARD, **Poll** 147; William 147;

POLLITT, **Athaliah** 141; **Hagar** 141; **Jacob** 321; John 141; Levin 321, 399, 408; **Rose** 141; **Zepheniah** 141;

POPE, Andrew 21; Comfort 21; **Dinah** 27; **Jesse** 62; John 16, 27; John Jr. 16, 21; Thomas 62; **Will** 27;

PORTER, **Abb** 355; **Abel** 231; **Amelia** 406; Betty 355, 356; **Comfort** 193, 350; Elizabeth 192, 193, 194, 229, 362; **Ester** 189; Ezekiel 128; **George** 193, 269, 406; **Hannah** 369; **Hesse** 421; **Isaac** 355, 421; **Jake** 355; John 406; **Leah** 128; **Levin** 194, 229, 362; Mary 49; McKemmey 407; McKimey 407; McKimmey 269, 406; McKimmy 189, 190, 231, 350, 352, 355, 406; McKinney 174; McKinny 162, 163; **Nan** 128; **Nancy** 128; **Nathan** 174; Purnell 421; **Rhodey** 406; Samuel 422; **Sarah** 193, 355; **Stephen** 352; **Sue** 162; William 369;

POSTLY, Anne 155, 184, 230, 308, 345, 437; **Job** 424; John 106, 155, 167, 173, 179, 184, 199, 206, 209, 213, 215, 216, 224, 229, 230, 241, 242, 255, 270, 272, 276, 280, 283, 286, 287, 291, 292, 293, 304, 308, 313, 322, 323, 345, 349, 399, 401, 404, 409, 411, 417, 424, 436, 437, 439, 440, 447;

POWELL, **Alse** 299; Ananias 429; Annanias 283, 299, 429; Annanies 283; Belitha 365; **Comfort** 322; George 283, 364, 418; Jacob 418; Jesse 155, 364, 410; John 232, 233; **Joshua** 292, 293; **Kiah** 293; **Mille** 429; **Pleasent** 410; **Rachell** 410; **Robin** 365; **Sal** 233, 429; **Sall** 233; **Sam** 322; Zadok 292, 293, 322;

PREDEAUX, Joshua 347;

PRICE, Arthur 186; **Hannah** 186;

PRIDEAUX, Joshua 320; **Will** 320;

PRUITT, Charles 376; **John** 376;

PURKINS, Ann 429, 430; John 331, 332, 429, 430; **Jone** 143; **Leah** 143; Mary 332; Mic{?} 401; Michael 143; **Mille** 429; **Nice** 401; **Sal** 429; Solomon 401; William 429, 430;

PURNALL, **Jack** 78; Walton 78;

PURNELL, Abel 22; **Amos** 83, 319, 323, 444; Ann 89, 276; **Ann** 11; Azarariah 145; Azariah 145, 146, 330, 423, 424, 439; **Azariah** 330; Benjamin 179, 197, 198, 199, 318; Benjamin (of W) 318; Benjamin (of Walton) 197, 199; Benjamin Jr. 143, 153; **Bett** 319, 323; **Betty** 22; **Caleb** 298; **Candice** 442; **Charity** 78, 79; Chesed 10, 11; **Cloe** 42; **Comfort** 11; **David** 318; **Dick** 22; **Dinah** 11; **Dolby Job** 238; Dolly 441, 442; **Dorkus** 11; Elenar 238; Eleoner 238; Elisha 10, 11, 22, 23, 348, 418, 431, 441, 442; **Esler** 11; Esme 397, 401, 411, 420, 424, 426, 433, 442; Euphamia 83; G.W. 384; George 276, 294, 343; **George Shadrach** 238; Hezekiah 78, 79; Isaac 200, 285; **Isaac** 319, 323, 427; **Jack** 442; **Jacob** 330, 430; John 100, 259, 260, 329, 330, 384, 425, 426, 430, 433; John L. 286; John S. 287, 288, 307, 326; John Selby 348, 349; **Jone** 143; **Joshua** 208, 444; **Josiah** 444; **Ju{?}** 22; Lamuel 10; **Leah** 143, 426, 433, 441; Lemuel 11; Littleton R. 421, 422; Lurana 11; Luranah 10, 11; Mary 100; **May** 22; **Melby** 217; Milby 319, 323; **Milby** 325; **Minte** 422; **Murreah** 89; **Murrur** 83; Nancy 238; **Nany** 83; **Ned** 11; **Pat** 323; **Patience** 22; **Pelinah** 78, 79; **Peter** 106, 197, 442; **Rachel** 442; **Rhoda** 100; **Rhodah** 330; Robert 208; **Ruth** 11, 423, 424, 439; **Sal** 422, 423; **Sam** 272; **Samuel** 78, 79; Sarah 10, 11; **Sarah** 22; **Shadrack** 22; **Silvia** 442; **Sopha** 444; **Sub** 422, 423; **Sue** 145, 347; **Tab** 441; Thomas 115, 298, 299, 347; Thomas (of William) 346, 347; Thomas M. 427; **Will** 199, 319, 323; William 10, 11, 106, 204, 217, 218, 232, 235, 259, 260, 267, 272, 281, 290, 294, 303, 330, 360, 380, 444; **Young Betty** 11; Z. 325; Zadock 42, 325; Zadok 43, 355;

PURNIEL, Sarah 150, 151; **Will** 150, 151;

QUINTON, Daniel 62; Dixon 105, 119; James 211; Philip 170, 191, 192, 200, 206, 220, 227, 230, 231, 237, 255, 256, 257,

264, 265, 266, 268, 271, 273, 274, 280, 287, 297, 303, 304, 313, 315, 318, 319, 321, 322, 324, 326, 330, 332, 334, 337, 338, 340, 341, 345, 346, 348, 352, 353, 356, 357, 368, 369, 371, 372, 374, 376, 377, 378, 379, 382, 383, 386, 387, 392, 396, 397, 403, 405, 407, 413, 418, 424, 430, 433, 437, 448; **Sam** 170;

RACKLIFFE, **Amey** 250; **Amy** 249; **Bett** 249; Charles 274; **Elijah** 249; **Hannah** 249; James 249, 250; **Ned** 249; **Rachel** 249; **Rose** 249; **Sarah** 249;

RAMSEY, **Dinah** 33; **Mingo** 33; Nathaniel 32, 33, 106; **Will** 33;

RAMSON, **Amelia** 275; Jacob 274, 275, 290, 291; **Nance** 290; **Nancy** 290; **Vilett** 291;

RANDALL, **Esther** 164; Francis 164; Frederick 415;

READ, James 429;

READY, **Ibbey** 103; **Isabella** 103; John 103;

REDDEN, **Grace** 356; **Henry** 356; **Judy** 356; Shadrack 356; Susanna 356;

REDDISH, **Epheram** 157; John 157; **Sall** 157;

REED, Coventon 332, 336, 337; **Lotte** 332, 336; Pearce 82 ;

RENCH, Walter 39;

RICE, Abraham 333; Nancy 333; **Neomi** 333; **Niomi** 333;

RICHARDS, **Abel** 294; **Amos** 294; Barshaba 335; **Ben** 294; **Bet** 294; **Bradis** 294; **Ciller** 294; **Comfort** 294; **Glasgow** 294; **Hager** 295; **Hannah** 294; Jacob 332, 335; Jane 334; Jean 334, 335, 336; Jenny 295; **Joe** 294; John 217, 294, 336; **John** 294; Joseph 132, 295, 335; **Leah** 294; **Let** 294; **Nance** 295; Nathaniel 336; **Philis** 336; **Phillis** 335; **Pleasant** 294; **Sall** 334, 335; **Sampson** 294; **Sarah** 294; **Will** 132, 334, 335; **Zebulon** 294;

RICHARDSON, **Benjamin** 81; Charles 81, 82, 95, 96, 111, 112; **Comfort** 346; **Easther** 95; Esther 86, 87; **Esther** 95; George 236; **Hanah** 81; **Hannah** 95; **Hannah Jr.** 95; John 163; **Joshua** 86;

Leah 81; **Leviner** 163; Mary 192; **Nanne** 111; **Preseler** 111; **Robert** 192; Robert M. 346, 357; **Robin** 236; Shadrack 81, 95, 96, 111; **Stephen** 81, 96; Thomas 163; William 407, 408; William Marshall 118;

RICKARDS, William 10;

RIDLEY, Leah 400; **Neomy** 400; **Sue** 400;

RIDLY, Leah 400; **Neomy** 400; **Sue** 400;

RIEN, John 148; **Nancy** 148;

RIGGAN, Isaac 394, 395; Isaack 394; **Lishe** 394, 395;

RIGGEN, Darby 137, 175; **Dinah** 137; **Hannah** 137; John 54; **Levin** ;

RIGGON, Darby 175, 176; Isaac 395; Levin 286; **Levin** 176; **Lishe** 395;

RIGGS, John 6; **Moll** 6;

RILEY, Benjamin 210; Betsey 210; **Boatswan** 210; **Bob** 210; **Cato** 210; **Jack** 210; **Levin** 210; **Lizey** 210; **Mary** 172; Michael 172; **Ralph** 210; **Sall** 210; **Sarah** 172;

RINE, John 148; **Nancy** 148;

RITCHIE, James 327, 357; **Levin** 327; **Nell** 327;

ROACH, Anne 195; Betsey 195; **Harry** 195; James 195; Leavin 195; Levin 195; Mary Bozman 195; Matty 195; Nelly 195; Sarah 113, 195; William 195;

ROAN, William 200;

ROBARDS, **Bess** 55; Ransher 55; **Sam** 55;

ROBBINS, Bowden 57; Bowdoin 43;

ROBENSON, **Cobbo** 112; William 112;

ROBERTS, **Benjamin** 390; **Bess** 55; **Derry** 390; Rencher 54, 55; **Sam** 55; Silvanus U. 390; Silvanus Uriah 390; Sylvanus U. 390;

ROBERTSON, **Elezebeth** 316; **Elizabeth** 316; George 377; La{?} 66; **Nell** 377; **Stephan** 316; **Stephen** 316; Thomas 316;

ROBINS, **Abel** 22; **Adam** 260; Anna 215, 232, 259, 260, 267; Anne 267; **Betty** 22; **Bob** 221; Bowdoin 51, 55, 62, 63, 93, 415; **Caleb** 22; **Daniel** 215; **Dick** 22; **Esther**

370; **Flora** 260; **George** 232, 259; **Grace** 356; **Hannah** 267; **Henry** 356; **Isaac** 260; J.P. 343; **James** 370; **James** 370; James B. 330, 355, 370, 405; James Bowdin 404; James Bowdoin 371, 404; John Purnell 89, 96, 106, 115, 123, 149; **Ju{?}** 22; **Judy** 356; **Leah** 260, 370; **Levi** 260; **Lisha** 355; Littleton 89, 165, 215, 221, 260, 348, 349; **Mary** 267; **May** 22; Michael 356; **Patience** 22; **Phillis** 89; **Rachael** 260; **Rodger** 95, 101; **Sabroe** 370; **Sarah** 22, 260; **Shadrack** 22; **Sothey** 259; **Sothy** 232; **Stephen** 96; **Sue** 260; Susanna 356; **Tamer** 260; Thomas 22, 89, 95, 101, 102; Thomas Jr. 75; **Will** 260;

ROBINSON, Annanias 331; Cornelius 112; Edea 219; **Jack** 10; Mary 10; **Prissey** 331; Thomas 10;

ROCK, **Bob** 400; **Jack** 448; **Jane** 448; John 372, 373, 392, 400, 448; **Milby** 372, 373;

ROCKE, **Bob** 400; John 399;

RODNEY, Caleb 424;

ROLEY, Arthur 366, 385, 393; Bettey 385; **Levin** 385; **Sarah** 393;

ROSS, **Hope** 47; John 47; **Martha** 47;

ROSSE, **Alce** 386; Elizabeth 342, 386; Frances 407, 408; Francis 407, 408; George 342, 386; **Hope** 47; John 47; **John** 407, 408; **Martha** 47; **Matthias** 407, 408; **Sarah** 407, 408; **Sib** 407, 408;

ROUND, **Armwell** 293; **Elijah** 243; **George** 243; H. 312; Hampton 243, 320; **Harriet** 450; James 50; **Lott** 320; **Lydia** 450; **Ned** 243; **Orson** 50; **Rachel** 429; Samuel H. 243, 293, 450; Samuel Hopkins 293; **Sarah** 429; William 429;

ROWLEY, Arthur 385, 393; Bettey 376, 377, 385; Betty 377; **Jacob** 376; **Levin** 385; **Sarah** 393; Scott 377;

ROWND, **Amey** 250; **Amy** 249; Ann 118; **Armwell** 293; **Bett** 249; Edward 118; **Elijah** 243, 249, 251; **George** 243, 251; Hampton 243, 249, 250, 251; **Hannah** 249; Mary 360; **Mertin** 251; **Ned** 243, 249, 251; **Patience** 431; **Peter** 431; **Rachel** 249; **Rose** 249; **Ruth** 423; Samuel H. 251, 293; Samuel Hopkins 243, 251; **Sarah** 249; **Stephen** 360, 423; **Trip** 251; William 431;

ROWNDS, **Ruth** 423; **Stephen** 423;

RUSSELL, Alexander Thomas 133; **Bella** 133; **Cloe** 133; **Cynta** 133; **Green** 133; **Jacob** 133; **Leah** 133; **Patience** 99, 133; **Phebe** 133; **Phillis** 133; Price 133; **Robin** 133; Solomon 99; **Thomas** 133; William 436;

SAMPSON, **Minea** 436; **Minnea** 436; **Omey** 436; Richard 436;

SATCHELL, Henry 40; John 86, 87, 130, 131, 147; **Joshua** 40, 86, 131, 147; **Levinah** 131, 147; **Stephen** 131, 147;

SAVAG, **Milby** 335; Zadok 335;

SAVAGE, Isaac 328; **Milby** 328;

SAVEG, **Milby** 335; Zadok 335;

SAWYER, Charles 163; **Leviner** 163;

SCARBOROUG, **Bob** 400; **Frank** 405; **Jean** 405; John Sr. 405; McKimey 400; McKimmy 400, 405;

SCARBOROUGH, **Abb** 355; Bettey ; **Bob** 377, 400; **Comfort** 193; Edward 369, 370, 383, 384, 394, 395, 426; **Ester** 189; **Frank** 405; **Hanah** 377; **Harry** 384; **Isaac** 355, 366; **Jacob** 366, 376; **Jake** 355; **Jean** 405; **Jo** 113; **John** 1, 3, 8, 9, 25, 35, 41, 42, 43, 45, 46, 48, 62, 70, 77, 78, 113, 119, 128, 140, 356, 377, 385, 393; John Jr. 25, 62, 63, 112, 113; John Sr. 376, 377, 385, 393, 395, 405; Jon 393; **Juda** 383; **Judah** 377; Kendall 193, 194, 338; **Levin** 194, 385; **Lidey** 383; **Lishe** 394, 395; **Lyda** 370; McKimey 399, 400; McKimmy 377, 383, 400, 405; Molly 366; **Nabb** 160; **Rachel** 25; Sally 193, 194; Samuel 113, 120, 160, 189, 190, 193, 355, 356, 362, 366; **Sarah** 355, 377, 393; **Scott** 377; **Sinor** 194;

SCARBOUGH, Kendall 338;

SCHOOLFEILD, John 285; **Rachal** 149; Robert 148, 149;

SCHOOLFIELD, **Adam** 179, 180, 343; **Belinda** 220; **Ben** 220, 343; Benjamin 154; **Celar** 343; **Dol** 343; **Esther** 129; **Harry** 220; J.B. 137; **Jack** 296; John 130; **Mary** 220; **Rachal** 149; Robert 149, 179, 180, 296, 297, 342, 343; **Sillar** 296; **Siller** 296; **Sinah** 343; Thomas Givan 129; William 220;

SCOTT, Ann 154; Benjamin 61; **Chloe** 154; **Dinah** 61; Elisabeth 6; **Gelica** 298; **Handy** 162; **Hannah** 322; James 322, 323; John 1, 6, 8, 10, 11, 26, 298; John Ennal 162; John Ennals 158, 162, 189; **Limus** 189; **Lymus** 189; Mary 154; **Nancy** 61; **Pleasant** 61; **Rose** 154; William 28;

SCROGIN, John 224; **Levin** 224; Philip 224; Robert 224;

SEALS, Joseph 418;

SELBY, **Abel** 313, 432; **Able** 188, 189, 337, 338; **Abner** 313; **Abraham** 34, 93, 180; **Abram** 190; **Adam** 152, 160, 391; **Amy** 152, 160; Ann 344; **Argile** 190; **Argill** 180; **Barbary** 343; **Barshaba** 93, 96, 97; **Ben** 160, 181; **Bets** 97; **Betts** 152; **Caprell** 180; **Ceaser** 49; **Charity** 78, 79; **Comfort** 181, 223, 344, 350, 351; Daniel 152, 160, 161, 163, 164, 178, 351; David 212; **Derrah** 212; **Dinah** 93; **Eben** 207, 208, 231, 384; Eleanor 302; Elizabeth 129; **Fortune** 316; George 383; **George** 172, 180, 190; **Gib** 152; **Grace** 277; Hanah 189, 338; Hannah 188, 189, 313, 337; **Hannah** 49; **Isaac** 93, 96, 129, 152, 160, 171, 267, 321, 432; **Jacob** 49, 93, 152, 164, 178; **Jack** 97, 388, 389; James 150, 171, 201, 217, 236, 264, 297, 302, 350, 351, 399, 404; **James** 158, 432; **James Handy** 404; **Jean** 313; **Jebb** 200; **Jer** 49; **Jeremiah** 93, 96; **Jesse** 62; **Jesper** 316; **Jibb** 163; **Jim** 158; John 34, 43, 49, 50, 51, 52, 56, 57, 58, 59, 62, 63, 71, 72, 75, 79, 81, 87, 92, 93, 94, 96, 97, 98, 108, 113, 117, 118, 127, 129, 141, 149, 152, 153, 160, 161, 164, 166, 169, 170, 174, 180, 185, 186, 189, 197, 198, 201, 202, 220, 225, 226, 230, 231, 237, 248, 249, 251, 252, 257, 259, 261, 267, 338, 432, 433; John (of John) 230; **John** 140, 389, 394; Kendall ; **Leah** 96, 97; **Leah** 160, 165, 264, 267, 432; Lemuel 316, 327, 384, 391; Levin 96, 97; **Levin** 176; **Lidia** 40; **Lige** 181; **Lusey** 300; **Lyd** 169; **Lydda** 161, 162; Margaret 158, 178, 302; Margarett 158; **Margarit** 156; Martha 78, 79, 100; Mary 34, 40, 96, 97, 129, 302, 321; Mathew 77; Matthew 93, 120, 277; Micaijah 96, 97; Micajah 40, 129, 171, 301, 302, 321; **Milla** 181; **Mille** 300; **Nance** 201; **Nancey** 201; Parker 34, 93, 115, 116, 152, 164, 188, 189, 277, 337, 338, 432; Parker Jr. 116; Parker (of M) 277; Parker (of Matthew) 432; **Parker Able** 338; **Patience** 49; **Pegg** 156; **Pelinah** 78, 79; **Peter** 180, 181, 197; **Phebe** 49; Philip 164, 165, 168, 169, 172, 175, 176, 180, 181, 190, 191, 197, 200; **Phillis** 301, 302; **Pleasant** 160, 180, 190; **Pleasent** 152; Polly 432; **Pompy** 302; **Rachel** 97; **Rafe** 190; **Rhoda** 97, 100, 158; **Robbin** 297; **Robin** 49, 425; **Rose** 344; **Sall** 160; **Sam** 305; **Samuel** 78, 79; Sarah 49, 150, 267; **Sarah** 97, 152, 180, 190; **Shadrack** 277; **Solomon** 93, 96, 97, 432; **Tab** 49; Tabitha 394; **Tamar** 180; **Tamer** 190, 197; Thom 156; Thomas 92, 146, 305; **Will** 120, 188; William 49, 96, 97, 129, 152, 156, 158, 161, 162, 171, 180, 185, 186, 188, 189, 192, 205, 223, 227, 267, 301, 302, 329, 330, 331, 332, 333, 339, 344, 354, 356, 357, 361, 362, 363, 369, 370, 373, 374, 375, 381, 388, 389, 425; **William** 120, 432; William A. 181, 202, 208; William Atkinson 181, 201, 207, 208; William Jr. 125, 158, 162, 267; William Sr. 301, 302, 303; Zadock 96, 97, 156, 180; **Zadock** 49; Zadok 180, 188, 197, 198, 301, 302, 321, 344, 351, 388; Zadok Sr. 301; Zilpah 300;

SEROGIS, Philip 348;

SHEALY, Moses 227; **Sary** 227;

SHELDON, John 8, 22, 26;

SHINGLE, **Doll** 87; **Flora** 87; Frederick 87;

SHOCKLEY, **Eli** 144; Elijah 131, 144; Elizabeth 307; **George** 177; **Jane** 131; Jonathan 357; **Minta** 226, 227; **Pleasant** 144; Richard 177, 226, 307; Richard Sr. 226; **Sampson** 307; **Silva** 226, 227; Solomon 177, 226, 227; **Stephen** 357;

SHOWELL, **Comfort** 198, 199; Eli 289; **George** 289; Lemuel 185, 198, 199; **Levin** 289; **Nell** 289;

SIMPLER, Andrew 102; **Bob** 102; **Nan** 102;

SLATERY, Elizabeth 400; **Rachel** 400;

SLAUTERY, Elizabeth 400; **Rachel** 400;

SLOAN, Samuel 82;

SLOCOMB, **Jerom** 432; **Moses** 307; William 307, 432;

SLOCUM, **Casesa** 270; **Casesay** 270; Gabriel 270; Gabril 270; George 182, 183; **Joe** 183; **Milley** 270; **Thomas** 270;

475

SLOSS, Thomas 32;

SMACK, Henry 394; **John** 394;

SMITH, **Abel** 66; Anna Gray 113; **Anne** 379; **Benjamin** 390; Benjamin Dingley 113; **Bet** 317; Betty 107, 128; **Betty** 317; **Bob** 382; **Cary** 346; Comfort 66; David 390; **Dina** 107; **Dinah** 79; Elijah 107; George 66; **George** 257; George Sr. 66; **Hannah** 81, 314; Isaiah 441, 445; **Jacob** 278, 346; James 81; **Jesse** 113; John 278, 279, 345, 346; Joseph 79; **Leah** 66, 128; **Martha** 242; Milby 295; Moses 66, 128; Purnell 278, 279, 379, 380; **Rielman** 346; Robert 378; **Robin** 236; **Rose** 346; Samuel 268; **Sandey** 346; **Siner** 113; Thomas 257; Thomas Jr. 257; Thompson 114; Tommison 113; Walter 236, 242, 314, 317, 382, 383;

SMOCK, **Derrah** 212; Henry 388, 394; **Jack** 388, 389; **John** 389, 394; Kendall 198, 212; Leah 198; **Margery** 198; McKemmy 187; McKimmey 187; McKimmy 187, 188; **Mirom** 187; **Sal** 187; Samuel 20, 21; **Sarah** 198; **Stephen** 187; **Yeany** 20;

SMYLY, **Rachell** 207; Robert 207; Samuel 182, 202;

SNEAD, Henry 143, 155;

SOMMERS, Horsey 333; Nancy 333; **Neomi** 333; **Niomi** 333;

SOROGIN, John 78;

SPENCE, Adam 33, 36, 37, 41, 43, 44, 48, 49, 51, 52, 70, 71, 72, 81, 82, 85, 93, 95, 97, 98, 100, 103, 108, 109, 110, 112, 117, 118, 281; **Ame** 101; Betty 75; **Easther** 95; **Esther** 95; George 75, 108, 281, 376, 397, 398; **George Dulany** 376; **Hannah** 95; **Hannah Jr.** 95; Jacob 281; John 107, 108, 112; **March** 107, 108; Margaret 36, 37, 101; Mary 101; **Rhoda** 75; **Roday** 75; Sally 215; Sarah 112; **Stephen** 107, 108;

SPICER, Elsey 153, 154; **Leviner** 153, 154;

SPIERS, **Fan** 183; **Pricilla** 183; William 183;

STATON, William 107;

STEAVENS, **Auther** 351; **Ufamey** 351;

STEEL, Jesse 320;

STERLING, **Barsheba** 279; **Bersheba** 282; **Jen** 279, 282; Joseph 279, 282; **Lish** 279, 282;

STEUART, George 147; **Joshua** 147; **Levinah** 147; **Stephen** 147;

STEVENS, **Anna** 367, 368; **Ben** 248; **Elinor** 368; **James** 24; Joshua 248; Littleton 368; **Nelle** 367; **Nelli** 367; William 23, 24, 367;

STEVENSON, **Amos** 276; **Bob** 221; **Ceasor** 73; **Derrum** 117; **Dinah** 61; Edward 448; Hannah 101; **Jack** 448; James 106, 209, 221, 222; **Jane** 448; Jonathan 117; **Minta** 221; **Nancy** 61; Peter 60, 61, 209; **Pleasant** 61; Robert 60, 61; **Robin** 209; Samuel 60, 61, 73; **Tab** 209, 221; William 271, 276, 280;

STEWART, **Able** 167; **Candis** 167; **Esther** 167; George 130, 131, 147, 182; **George** 167; **Hannah** 167; John 167; **Joshua** 131, 147; **Levinah** 131, 147; **Stephen** 131, 147;

STONE, William 269, 314;

STOY, Stephen 12, 13;

STUART, Levin 69;

STURGES, Joshua 395;

STURGESS, **Milby** 328; Zadok 328;

STURGIS, Abraham Outten 141; **Boatswan** 210; **Bob** 210; **Candis** 244; **Cato** 210; Esther 238; **Jack** 210, 268; **James** 292, 368; Jesse 291; John 385; Joshua 200, 201, 210, 431; Joshua Jr. 16; Joshua Sr. 210; **Levin** 210; **Lizey** 210; Martha 292; **Milby** 335; Outten 90, 206, 253, 292, 303, 323, 393; **Patrick** 385; **Ralph** 210; **Sall** 210; **Sarah** 244; Thomas 127, 128, 141; **Tom** 201; William 253; Zadok 244, 268, 291, 292, 335, 368;

SUMMERS, Horsey 333; Nancy 333; **Neomi** 333; **Niomi** 333;

SYMPLER, Andrew 102; **Bob** 102; **Nan** 102;

TALBOTT, Moor 207;

TARR, **Ester** 292; **Esther** 292; **Guy** 238; John 160; John (of M) 426; John (of Michael) 426; Michael 96; **Peter Guy** 238; Samuel 238, 292, 298; Samuel Jr. 238;

TAYLOR, **Adam** 160; Alexander 160; **Amy** 160; **Ben** 160; **Bob** 3; **Bobb** 1; **Cary** 346; Elias 289; Elisha 322, 323; **Hannah** 322, 323; Honou{?} 322; Hope 416; **Isaac** 160; **Jacob** 346; **Jebb** 200; **Jibb** 163; Joseph Gray 254; Joshua 323; **Leah** 160, 289; Nancy 289; **Nell** 282; Patience 323; Peter 1, 3; **Phillis** 322; **Pleasant** 160; **Rielman** 346; **Robert** 282; **Rose** 346; **Sall** 160; Samuel 33, 281, 282; **Sandey** 346; Sarah 1; **Sarah** 254; **Sary** 227; Stephen 217; **Stephen** 230; Thomas 163, 200, 227, 230; William 289, 345, 346;

TEACKLE, John 135;

TEAGE, Jacob 363;

TEAGUE, Jacob 352, 363; **Stephen** 352;

TENESSY, John 60;

TENNENT, Ann 106; **Bess** 82; Charles 82, 106; **Jack** 82, 106; Katrine 106; Martha 106; **Phillis** 106; **Pomp** 106; **Pompey** 82; **Sandy** 82; **Santy** 106; William 106; William Macky 82;

THARPE, **Candis** 299; **Levi** 299; William 299;

THOMAS, Elizabeth 65;

TIER, Jacob 431; **Patience** 431; **Peter** 431; Thomas 431;

TILGHMAN, **Ben** 230; **Edea** 240; **Hager** 230; **Iby** 115; Joseph 230, 240; Nehemiah 115; **Sal** 240;

TILNEY, **Charles** 80; **Eben** 80; Jonathan 80, 81;

TINDAL, Ann 121; **Cuff** 121; **Esther** 120; Hannah 120; Holland 121; **Jacob** 121; Levinah 120; **Missyrow** 121; **Moses** 121; Purnel 121; Purnell 121; Sarah 121; Samuel 120, 121; **Venus** 120;

TINDALL, Ann 121; **Cuff** 121; **Esther** 120; Hannah 120; Holland 121; **Jacob** 121; Levinah 120; **Missyrow** 121; **Moses** 121; Purnel 121; Purnell 121; Sarah 121; Samuel 120, 121; **Venus** 120;

TINGLE, **Bob** 213; Caleb 213; Caleb Sr. 278; **Hanah** 213;

TOADVINE, **Ben** 205; **Bess** 55; Henry 277; Isaac 205; James 205; Nancy 205; Outten 225; **Sam** 55; **Shadrack** 277; **Tom** 225; William 55;

TOMSON, **Gone** 85; William 85;

TONE, Mary 79;

TOWNSEND, **Adam** 12, 17, 391; **Amelia** 417; Barkley 112, 205, 249; Bartley 205, 225, 260, 272; Bartly 205; **Ben** 14, 205, 386; **Bett** 228; Brickus 44; **Cable** 219; **Caleb** 206, 235, 290; **Candiss** 235; **Charity** 159; Charles 447; **Comfort** 346; Daniel Jr. 81; **David** 272; **Dider** 170; **Easther** 308; Elizabeth 447; **Esther** 13, 129, 235; **Georg** 308; George 159, 283; **Hannah** 81; **Hetty** 249; **Hope** 294; **Isaac** 427; Israel 285; Isreal 285; **Jack** 235; **Jacob** 204, 321; James 159, 228; James (of Littleton) 159; **James** 234, 292, 399, 417; **Jenna** 225; Jeremiah 179; **Jo** 112; John 150, 151, 177, 205; Joshua 146, 147, 151, 152, 153, 156, 159, 162, 163, 164, 165, 166, 167, 168, 169, 170, 172, 175, 177, 182, 183, 190, 196, 197, 200, 204, 205, 206, 216, 219, 221, 234, 235, 277, 279, 285, 290, 297, 299, 301, 305, 306, 307, 308, 309, 312, 314, 321, 325, 361; **Joshua** 160, 292, 293; **Juda** 2; **Kiah** 293; **Laney** 159; **Leah** 128; **Leeds** 197; Lemuel 146; Levi 249, 417; Levin 91, 92, 206, 372, 386, 391, 417, 447; Levin (of John) 381; **Levin** 219, 361; Littleton 2, 361; Luke 234, 418, 419; **Luke** 294; **Lydda** 308; **Lydia** 235; Major 129, 160, 177, 308; Martha 225; **Mary** 170; **Milly** 447; **Nabb** 160; **Nan** 128; Nancy 146; **Nancy** 128, 417, 419; **Nanny** 447; **Ned** 260, 417, 447; Nehemiah 139, 140; **Nice** 228; **Patrick** 381; Peter 258, 259, 272, 427; **Peter** 285, 308; **Phillis** 146, 204; **Rachell** 235; Rhoda 260; **Rhoda** 159; Rives R. 290, 291, 292, 346; Rives Rackliffe 283, 289, 290, 292; **Rose** 91; **Sall** 159; **Sam** 179; Saul 12, 13, 14, 17; Solomon 316; Solomon (of Marshel) 250; **Su** 206; **Sue** 219, 372; **Tabb** 235; **Tabitha** 418, 419; **Taymor** 258, 259; **Tom** 225; **Will** 150, 151, 204; William 179, 292, 293, 294; William Barkley 128, 249; William Bartholomew 12; Zadock 146;

TRACEY, **Dinah** 304; James 304;

TRAHERN, **Elijah** 266; James 266; **Nathan** 266; **Priscilla** 266; **Rhoda** 266; **Soloman** 266; **Solomon** 266;

TRAYDER, Henary 224;

TREHERN, **Elijah** 266; James 266; **Nathan** 266; **Priscilla** 266; **Rhoda** 266; **Soloman** 266; **Solomon** 266;

TREHORN, **Elijah** 266; James 266; **Nathan** 266; **Priscilla** 266; **Rhoda** 266; **Soloman** 266; **Solomon** 266;

TRUIT, Elizabeth 40, 129; **Isaac** 129; **Lidia** 40; Mary 40; Samel 217; Samuel 216, 217, 222; Samuel Sr. 216; **Sue** 216, 222; Tabitha 40;

TRUITT, **Ben** 250; Benjamin 356; **Cable** 219; **Caleb** 206; **Charity** 250; Elizabeth 77, 129; **Esther** 273; George Jr. 164; George Sr. 149; **Isaac** 129, 218; **Jack** 77, 78; John K. 356; **Leah** 356; **Levin** 206, 218, 219; Outten 77, 78; **Rachal** 149; Samel 217; Samuel 205, 206, 217, 218, 219, 223, 273, 356; Samuel Sr. 216; Samuell 273; **Su** 206; **Sue** 216, 219; William 250, 251; William Jr. 250, 251;

TUBB, Samuel 285;

TULL, **Daniel** 90, 296; **James** 297; John 90, 91, 296, 297; John Jr. 89, 90;

TULLY, John 285;

TUNNELL, **Frank** 71; William 71;

TURNER, **Ben** 386; **Esther** 273; George 224, 386; Henry 26, 88, 273; Jackson 386; **Leah** 224;

TURPIN, **Bob** 3; **Bobb** 1; **Easter** 265; John 1; William 1, 3, 265;

TWIFIRD, John O. 367;

UNDERHILL, **Peter** 234; William 234;

UNDRILL, **Flora** 384; **Minty** 409, 410; **Peter** 234; William 234, 384, 409, 410;

VALLANU, Nicolas 343;

VANDOME, **Adam** 260; Edward 260; **Flora** 260; **Isaac** 260; **Leah** 260; **Levi** 260; **Rachael** 260; **Sarah** 260; **Sue** 260; **Tamer** 260; **Will** 260;

VERNETSON, **James** 297; William 297;

VICTERY, **Jack** 353; Thomas 353;

VICTOR, **Ben** 196, 388; **Benjamin** 196; **Ceaser** 395; Elizabeth 395; **George** 395; Hanah 347; Hannah 347, 348; **Jack** 353; James 395; John 237; **Peg** 347; **Rose** 237, 395; **Sarah** 347; Thomas 189, 196, 237, 353, 380, 395; Thomas Jr. 191, 195, 196; Thomas Sr. 237;

VINSON, **Fortune** 398; Isaac 398;

WAGGAMAN, **Bett** 68; **Betty** 68; **Cloe** 68; **Conselo** 68; **Daniel** 68; Ephraim 17, 18, 19, 31; **Frank** 68, 74; Henry 20; **Jenny** 68; **John** 68; Mary 66; **Monday** 68, 74; William 68; William E. 69, 74; William Elliot 73, 74;

WALLER, Samuel 10; Ebenezer 65;

WALLIS, **Adam** 152; **Amy** 152; **Betts** 152; **Gib** 152; **Hannah** 159; **Isaac** 152; Mary 152, 159, 160; **Pleasent** 152; **Sarah** 152; **Sarrah** 152;

WALLOP, Anne 393; **Candis** 339; **Comfort** 339; **Dorcos** 393; **Esther** 339; **Flora** 339; **Harry** 393; John 339; **Moses** 339; **Nann** 339; **Phillis** 339; **Sam** 393; **Sarah** 339;

WALSON, John 447;

WALSTON, Booz 311, 327, 339, 359, 378, 396, 398, 399, 410, 412, 416, 438, 441, 445, 450;

WALTER, **Cupet** 113; John 195; Peleg 113;

WALTERS, Patrick Sr. 394; **Stephen** 394;

WALTON, **Charity** 159; Fisher 159; **George** 159; Job 34; **Laney** 159; Mary 93; **Rhoda** 159; **Sall** 159; William 158, 159;

WAPLES, Nathaniel 145; **Sarah** 145;

WARD, **Abel** 446; **Adah** 446; **Betty** 446; **George** 446; **Job** 446; John 446;

WARRAN, John 187, 200; **Mirom** 187, 200; **Sal** 187, 200; **Stephen** 187, 200;

WARREN, Isaac 326, 344, 345; **Isaac** 344; **Jacob** 344; John 187, 188; **Minta** 344; **Mirom** 187; **Rhoda** 344; **Rose** 344; **Sal** 187; **Santee** 326; Stephen 187;

WARWICK, **Doctor** 424; Eleanor 424; William 424;

WATERS, **Abraham** 248; **Ben** 248; John 15; **Ned** 190; Patrick 190, 193, 194, 248; Peter 73; **Sinor** 194;

WATSON, **Anna** 367; Comfort 137; **Dinah** 137; **Effe** 446; **Elinor Stevens** 368; **Esther** 135; **Hannah** 137; John 349, 367, 368, 446; **John** 349; Mary 135, 136; **Nanny** 381; **Nelle** 367; **Nelli Stevens** 367; Rebecca 381; **Sarah** 381; **Tamer** 135;

WATTS, **Amos** 242; **Beck** 242; Charles 115, 116; **Hannah** 242; **Isaac** 242; **Judah** 116; Mary 115, 116; **Mellea** 116; **Mellah** 116; **Nancy** 373; **Nanny** 381; Rebecca 373; **Robin** 242; **Sarah** 381; William 242, 381;

WEBB, **Leah** 324; **Mille** 429; **Nancy** 254; **Sal** 429; Solomon 254; Thomas 285, 324, 429, 430;

WEBBER, Rachel 419;

WEIR, **Hannah** 322; James 322;

WELLS, **Abel** 22; **Betty** 22; **Caleb** 22; Daniel 22, 23, 25, 26; **Dick** 22; **Ju{?}** 22; Margaret 22, 23; **May** 22; **Patience** 22; **Sarah** 22; **Shadrack** 22; **Southy** 26; **Standbridge** 26;

WELSH, **Mary** 172; Richard 172; **Sarah** 172;

WEST, Elijah 107; **Pomp** 107;

WHARTON, **Adam** 53; **Bob** 53; Charles 53, 54; Custis 41; **Hope** 53; John 53; William 53, 54;

WHEELER, **Amelia** 406; **George** 406; Zadock 406;

WHITAKER, **Boatswain** 31; Nathaniel 25, 26, 31; Nathaniell 17;

WHITE, **Abel** 294; **Amos** 294; Archibald 29, 30; Barkey 211; Barkley 181, 182, 189; Barkly 181; Bartlet 211; Bartley 211; **Ben** 181, 294; **Bet** 294; **Bradis** 294; **Cage** 329; Catty 241; **Ciller** 294; **Comfort** 181, 294; **Esther** 340; **George** 241, 340; **Glasgow** 294; **Hannah** 294; **Henna** 301; **Hinna** 301; Jacob 445; **Joe** 294; **John** 294; Joshua 301; **Lanta** 340; **Leah** 294; **Let** 294; Levinia 329; **Lige** 181; **Limus** 189; **Liz** 211; **Liza** 211; **Lymus** 189; Major 340, 341; **Micajah** 329; **Milla** 181; **Peter** 181; Philip 329; **Pleasant** 294; **Sampson** 294; **Sarah** 294; Stephen 294; **Zebulon** 294;

WHITTINGTON, **Benjamin** 390; **Candis** 247; **Derry** 390; **Edith** 70, 92; Elizabeth 446; **Esther** 136; George 247; **Hannah** 247; **Izabel** 247; John 390; **John** 408; John N. 446; **Leah** 446; Mary King 92, 136; **Matthias** 408; **Moll** 247; **Nan** 136; **Sarah** 408; **Sib** 408; William 70, 92, 136, 388, 408, 421, 422, 451;

WILEY, Jarrard 11; Jerrard 11; **Sylvia** 11;

WILLETT, **Abram** 237; **Davy** 261 ; **Esther** 164; Henry 163, 164; Henry J. 227, 237, 247, 262; Henry Johnson 237, 247, 261; **Minta** 247; **Sary** 227; **Sue** 163;

WILLEY, Jerrard 11; **Sylvia** 11;

WILLIAMS, **Bett** 327, 328; Esau 294, 295; **Estar** 410; **Ester** 410; **Esther** 135; Ezekiel 419; Henry 66, 67; Isaac 327, 328, 415; James 115, 132, 135; John 12, 13, 107, 275, 328, 408, 409, 410; Joseph 83; Littleton 328; Mary 107; Nancy 331, 332; **Nanncy** 328; **Nanny** 328; **Pomp** 67, 83, 107; **Rhody** 328; **Rose** 64; **Sam** 294; **Tamer** 135; Thomas 83, 107; **Tonney** 409; **Will** 132; William 63, 64;

WILLISS, Jabez 182;

WILLIT, Henry J. 236; Henry Johnson 236; **Minta** 247; **Sarah** 236;

WILLITT, **Abram** 237; **Esther** 164; Henry 162, 163, 164; Henry Johnson 237; **Sue** 162, 163;

WILMAN, Ellis 67;

WILSON, **Abigail** 108, 109; David 326; **Hope** 108, 109; **Isaac** 445; James 108, 109, 355, 445; James P. 424; **Jesse** 108, 109; Levin 29, 30; Martha 108, 109; Samuel 73; **Tom** 326;

WINDER, **Eunice** 98; **Phillis** 90, 98; **Sylby** 98; **Sylva** 90; **Unice** 90; William 91, 124; William Jr. 90, 98;

WINGATE, **Dorset** 80; **Fosida** 80; **Frank** 71; John 80; Love 76; Luranah 75, 76; **Nan** 76; **Sabary** 76; Sarah 75, 76; Thomas 71;

WIRE, **Hannah** 323; James 323;

WISE, Betsey 392; Betsy 435; Betty M. 392; Elizabeth 392; **Ephraim** 392; George 381; George C. 394; George K. 392, 394; George Ker 392, 435, 436; Hampton Hopkins 92, 95; **Jacob** 152; John 152, 197, 204, 213, 242, 244; **Martha** 242; **Ned** 302; Nicl. 389; **Priss** 435; Samuel 435; **Sarah** 302; **Stephen** 381, 394; Tabitha

WOODEN, Benjamin 102; Edward 58; John 58; **Pleasant** 102; **Pompy** 58;

WOOTEN, John 58; **Pompy** 58;

WOOTTEN, Benjamin 115; Edward 58; **Hannah** 115; **Jacob** 115; John 58; **Pompy** 58;

WRIGHT, **Belinda** 220; **Ben** 175, 220; Elizabeth 128; **Harry** 220; Hezekiah 141; John 220, 241; **Mary** 220; Purnell 141; **Will** 141; Zadock 141; Zadok 175;

YOUNG, Bayley 253; Daniel 253; Dannel 253; Ezekiel 254; **Harry** 253; Mary 253; Nancy 253;

Notes

Notes